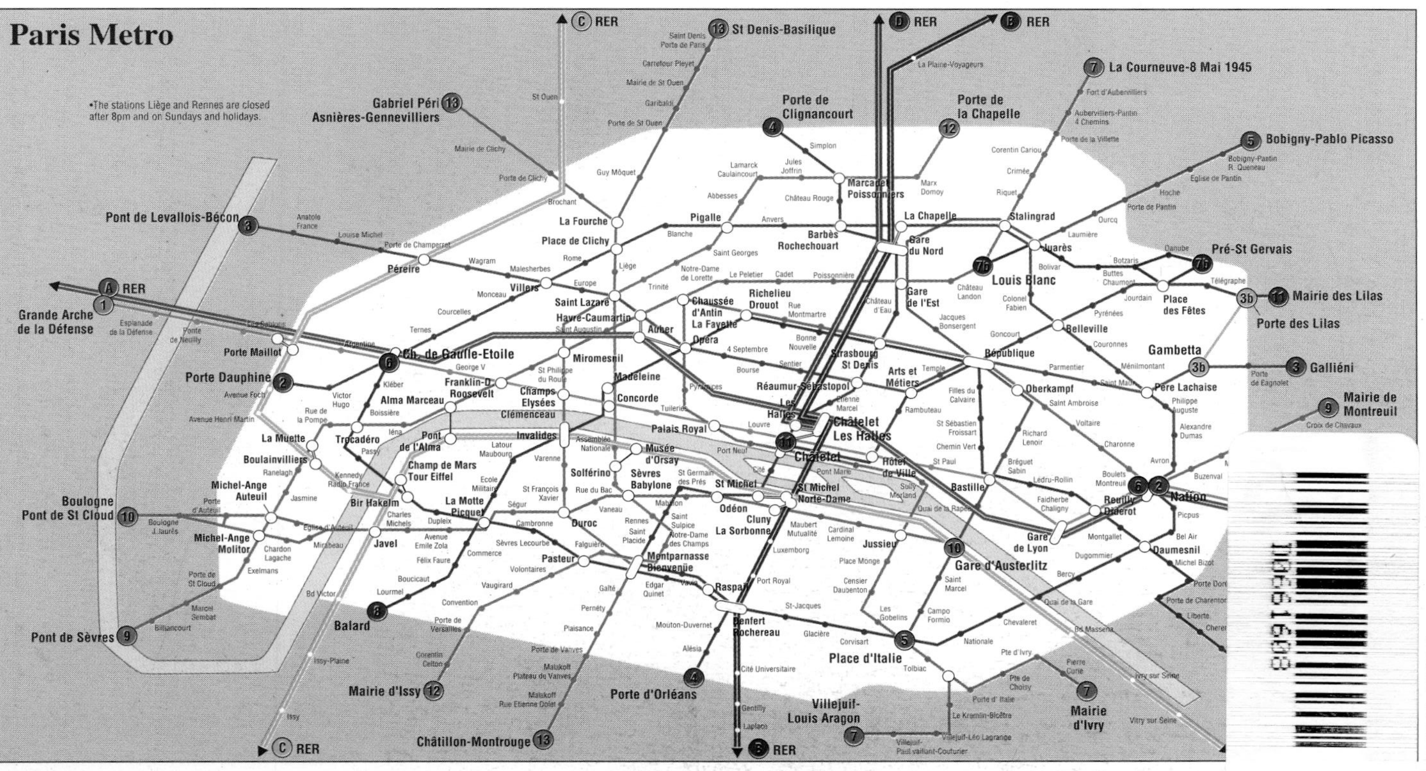
Paris Metro
•The stations Liège and Rennes are closed after 8pm and on Sundays and holidays.
Grande Arche de la Défense
Pont de Levallois-Bécon
Gabriel Péri Asnières-Gennevilliers
St Denis-Basilique
Porte de Clignancourt
Porte de la Chapelle
La Courneuve-8 Mai 1945
Bobigny-Pablo Picasso
Pré-St Gervais
Mairie des Lilas
Porte des Lilas
Galliéni
Mairie de Montreuil
Mairie d'Ivry
Villejuif-Louis Aragon
Porte d'Orléans
Châtillon-Montrouge
Mairie d'Issy
Balard
Pont de Sèvres
Boulogne Pont de St Cloud
Porte Dauphine
Porte Maillot
Ch. de Gaulle-Etoile
Châtelet Les Halles
Gare du Nord
Gare de l'Est
République
Bastille
Gare de Lyon
Gare d'Austerlitz
Place d'Italie
Denfert Rochereau
Montparnasse Bienvenüe
Invalides
Concorde
Madeleine
Opéra
Saint Lazare
Nation
RER

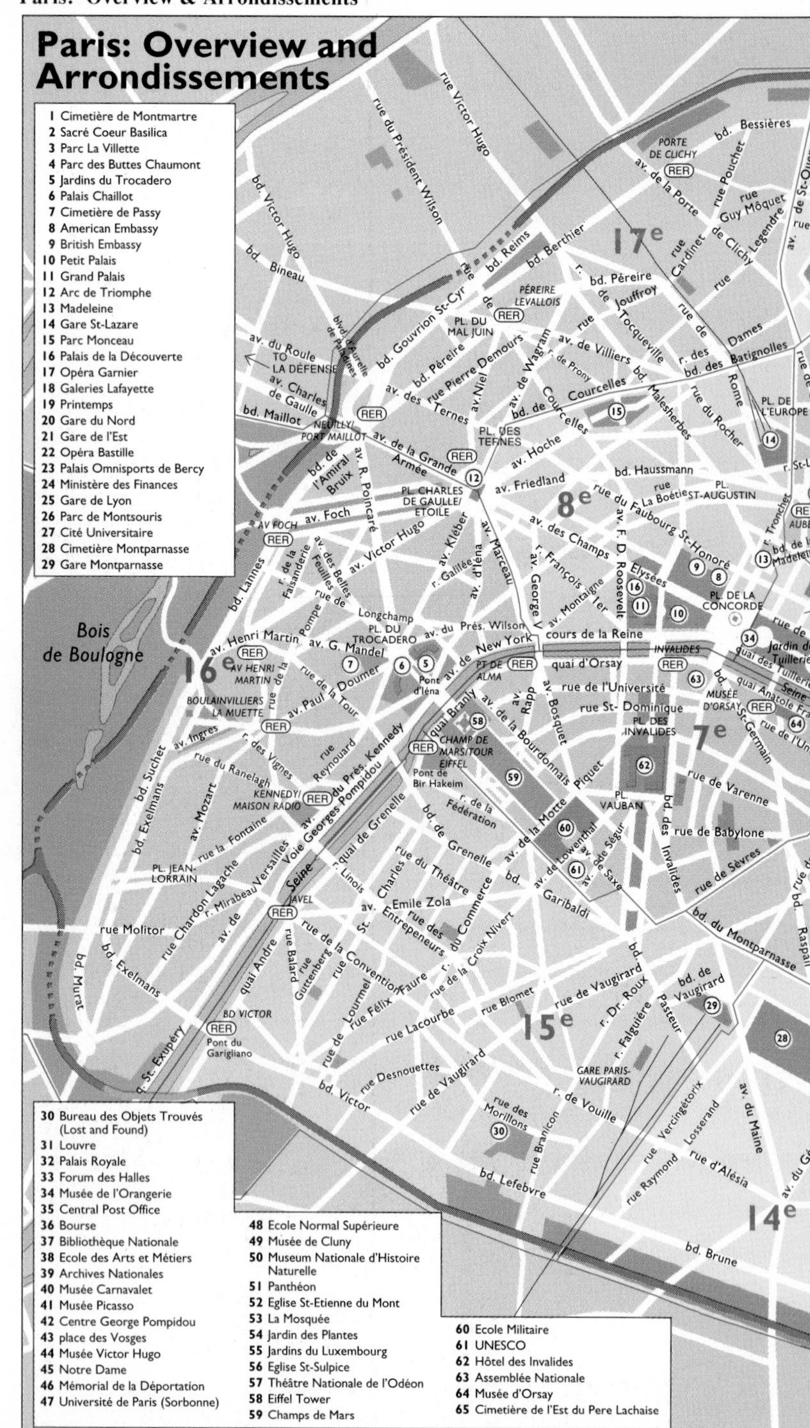
Paris: Overview and Arrondissements
1 Cimetière de Montmartre
2 Sacré Coeur Basilica
3 Parc La Villette
4 Parc des Buttes Chaumont
5 Jardins du Trocadero
6 Palais Chaillot
7 Cimetière de Passy
8 American Embassy
9 British Embassy
10 Petit Palais
11 Grand Palais
12 Arc de Triomphe
13 Madeleine
14 Gare St-Lazare
15 Parc Monceau
16 Palais de la Découverte
17 Opéra Garnier
18 Galeries Lafayette
19 Printemps
20 Gare du Nord
21 Gare de l'Est
22 Opéra Bastille
23 Palais Omnisports de Bercy
24 Ministère des Finances
25 Gare de Lyon
26 Parc de Montsouris
27 Cité Universitaire
28 Cimetière Montparnasse
29 Gare Montparnasse
30 Bureau des Objets Trouvés (Lost and Found)
31 Louvre
32 Palais Royale
33 Forum des Halles
34 Musée de l'Orangerie
35 Central Post Office
36 Bourse
37 Bibliothèque Nationale
38 Ecole des Arts et Métiers
39 Archives Nationales
40 Musée Carnavalet
41 Musée Picasso
42 Centre George Pompidou
43 place des Vosges
44 Musée Victor Hugo
45 Notre Dame
46 Mémorial de la Déportation
47 Université de Paris (Sorbonne)
48 Ecole Normal Supérieure
49 Musée de Cluny
50 Museum Nationale d'Histoire Naturelle
51 Panthéon
52 Eglise St-Etienne du Mont
53 La Mosquée
54 Jardin des Plantes
55 Jardins du Luxembourg
56 Eglise St-Sulpice
57 Théâtre Nationale de l'Odéon
58 Eiffel Tower
59 Champs de Mars
60 Ecole Militaire
61 UNESCO
62 Hôtel des Invalides
63 Assemblée Nationale
64 Musée d'Orsay
65 Cimetière de l'Est du Pere Lachaise
17e
8e
16e
7e
15e
14e
Bois de Boulogne
Seine
TO LA DÉFENSE
PORTE DE CLICHY
PÉREIRE LEVALLOIS
PL. DU MAL JUIN
NEUILLY/PORT MAILLOT
PL. DES TERNES
PL. CHARLES DE GAULLE/ETOILE
AV FOCH
PL. DE L'EUROPE
PL. ST-AUGUSTIN
AUBER
PL. DE LA CONCORDE
PL. DU TROCADERO
AV HENRI MARTIN
PT DE ALMA
INVALIDES
MUSÉE D'ORSAY
BOULAINVILLIERS LA MUETTE
CHAMP DE MARS/TOUR EIFFEL
KENNEDY/MAISON RADIO
PL. DES INVALIDES
PL. VAUBAN
PL. JEAN-LORRAIN
JAVEL
BD VICTOR
Pont du Garigliano
Pont d'Iéna
Pont de Bir Hakeim
GARE PARIS-VAUGIRARD
Jardin des Tuilleries
av. des Champs Elysées
cours de la Reine
quai d'Orsay
bd. Haussmann
rue du Faubourg St-Honoré
bd. Malesherbes
bd. de Courcelles
av. de la Grande Armée
av. Foch
av. Victor Hugo
av. Kléber
av. Marceau
av. d'Iéna
av. F. D. Roosevelt
av. Montaigne
av. George V
av. de New York
av. du Prés. Wilson
av. Henri Martin
av. Paul Doumer
av. de Wagram
av. Niel
av. Hoche
av. Friedland
bd. Péreire
bd. Berthier
bd. des Batignolles
rue de Rome
rue de l'Université
rue St- Dominique
rue de Varenne
rue de Babylone
rue de Sèvres
bd. St-Germain
bd. des Invalides
bd. du Montparnasse
bd. Raspail
bd. de Grenelle
bd. Garibaldi
av. de la Motte Piquet
av. de Ségur
av. de Saxe
av. de Lowenthal
av. Emile Zola
rue de la Convention
rue de Vaugirard
rue Lecourbe
bd. de Vaugirard
bd. Pasteur
bd. Victor
bd. Lefebvre
bd. Brune
av. du Maine
rue d'Alésia
bd. Murat
bd. Exelmans
rue Molitor
bd. Suchet
av. Mozart
rue du Ranelagh
bd. Lannes
av. Georges Pompidou
quai Branly
quai de Grenelle
quai André Citroën
av. de Versailles
av. du Prés. Kennedy

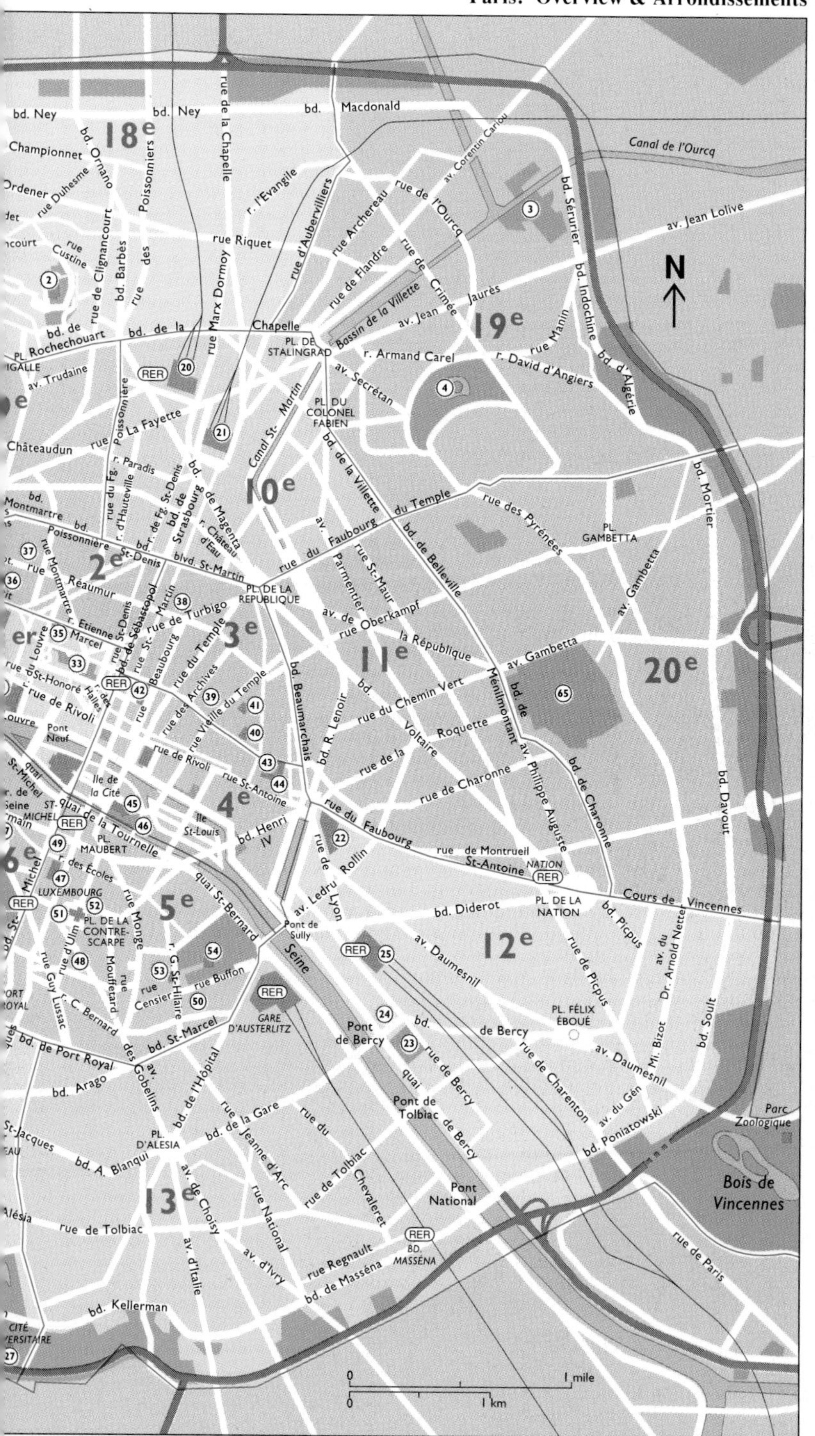
18e
19e
10e
2e
3e
11e
20e
4e
5e
12e
13e
bd. Ney
bd. Macdonald
Canal de l'Ourcq
Championnet
bd. Ornano
rue de la Chapelle
rue Riquet
rue Marx Dormoy
rue d'Aubervilliers
rue de Flandre
rue de Crimée
rue de l'Ourcq
av. Corentin Cariou
av. Jean Lolive
bd. Sérurier
bd. Indochine
bd. d'Algérie
av. Jean Jaurès
Bassin de la Villette
PL. DE STALINGRAD
r. Armand Carel
r. David d'Angiers
rue Manin
av. Secrétan
PL. DU COLONEL FABIEN
Canal St-Martin
bd. de la Villette
rue du Faubourg du Temple
rue des Pyrénées
PL. GAMBETTA
bd. Mortier
av. Gambetta
bd. de Belleville
PL. DE LA REPUBLIQUE
av. Parmentier
rue St-Maur
rue Oberkampf
av. de la République
rue du Chemin Vert
bd. Ménilmontant
bd. de Charonne
bd. Davout
bd. Beaumarchais
bd. R. Lenoir
rue de la Roquette
bd. Voltaire
rue de Charonne
av. Philippe Auguste
rue du Faubourg St-Antoine
rue de Montreuil
NATION
PL. DE LA NATION
Cours de Vincennes
bd. Diderot
av. Daumesnil
rue de Picpus
bd. Picpus
av. du Dr. Arnold Netter
PL. FÉLIX ÉBOUÉ
bd. de Bercy
rue de Charenton
av. du Gén Mi. Bizot
bd. Soult
bd. Poniatowski
Parc Zoologique
Bois de Vincennes
rue de Paris
bd. Henri IV
rue de Lyon
av. Ledru Rollin
Pont de Sully
Seine
GARE D'AUSTERLITZ
Pont de Bercy
rue de Bercy
quai de Bercy
Pont de Tolbiac
Pont National
rue de Tolbiac
rue du Chevaleret
rue Jeanne d'Arc
rue Nationale
bd. de la Gare
bd. de l'Hôpital
av. d'Ivry
rue Regnault
bd. de Masséna
BD. MASSÉNA
av. d'Italie
av. de Choisy
PL. D'ALESIA
bd. A. Blanqui
bd. Kellerman
CITÉ UNIVERSITAIRE
bd. Arago
av. des Gobelins
bd. St-Marcel
bd. de Port Royal
rue Monge
rue Mouffetard
rue d'Ulm
rue Gay Lussac
r. C. Bernard
r. G. St-Hilaire
rue Censier
rue Buffon
PL. DE LA CONTRESCARPE
LUXEMBOURG
PL. MAUBERT
r. des Écoles
quai de la Tournelle
quai St-Bernard
Ile de la Cité
Ile St-Louis
rue St-Antoine
rue de Rivoli
Pont Neuf
rue Vieille du Temple
rue des Archives
rue du Temple
rue Beaubourg
rue St-Martin
bd. de Sébastopol
rue de Turbigo
rue Étienne Marcel
rue Réaumur
rue Montmartre
rue du Louvre
rue St-Honoré
Halles
bd. Poissonnière
bd. St-Denis
blvd. St-Martin
bd. de Magenta
bd. de Strasbourg
r. Château d'Eau
r. de Fg. St-Denis
r. d'Hauteville
rue du Fg. Poissonnière
r. Paradis
rue La Fayette
rue de Châteaudun
av. Trudaine
bd. de Rochechouart
bd. de la Chapelle
PL. PIGALLE
rue de Clignancourt
bd. Barbès
rue des Poissonniers
rue Custine
rue Duhesme
r. l'Evangile
RER
N
0
1 mile
1 km

Paris: 1er and 2e

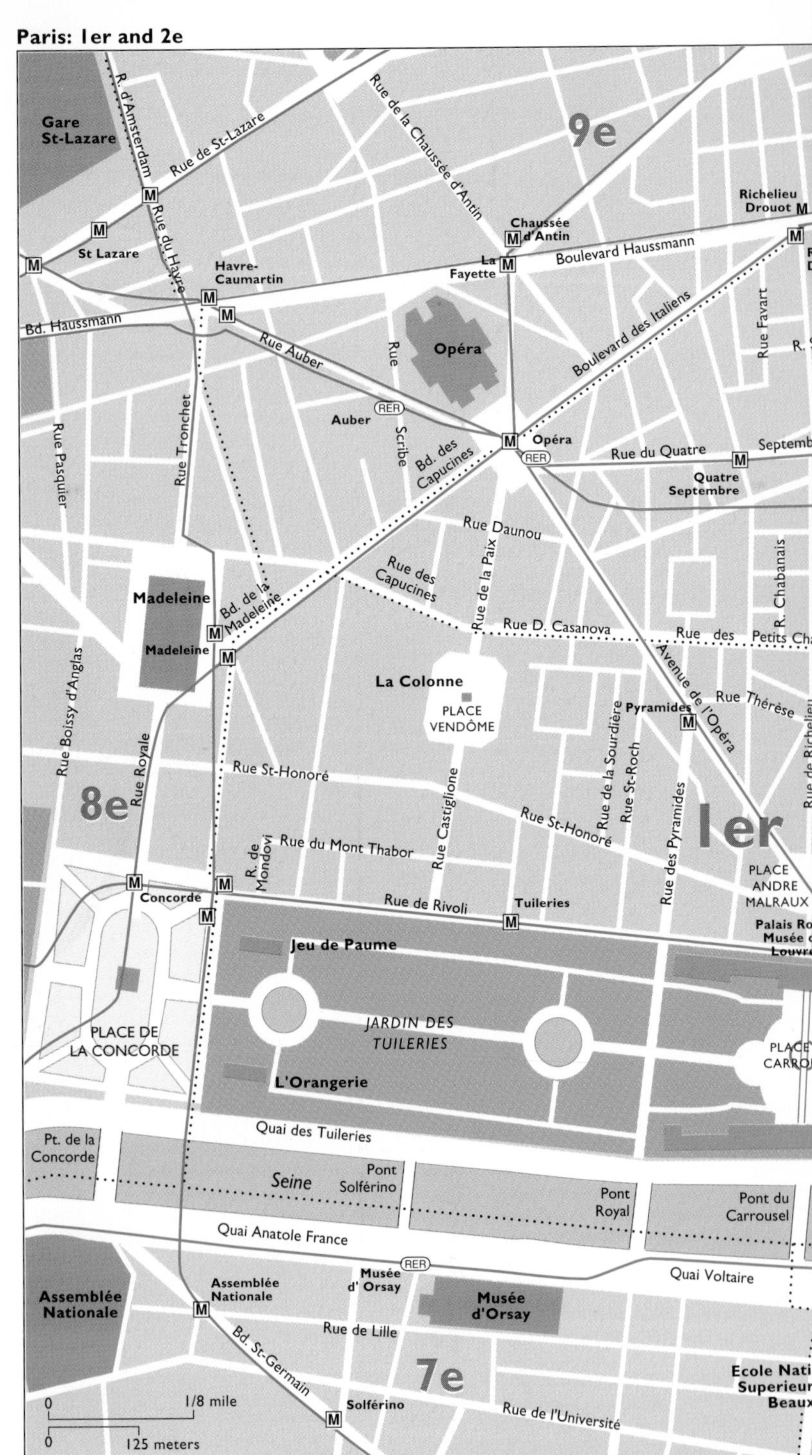

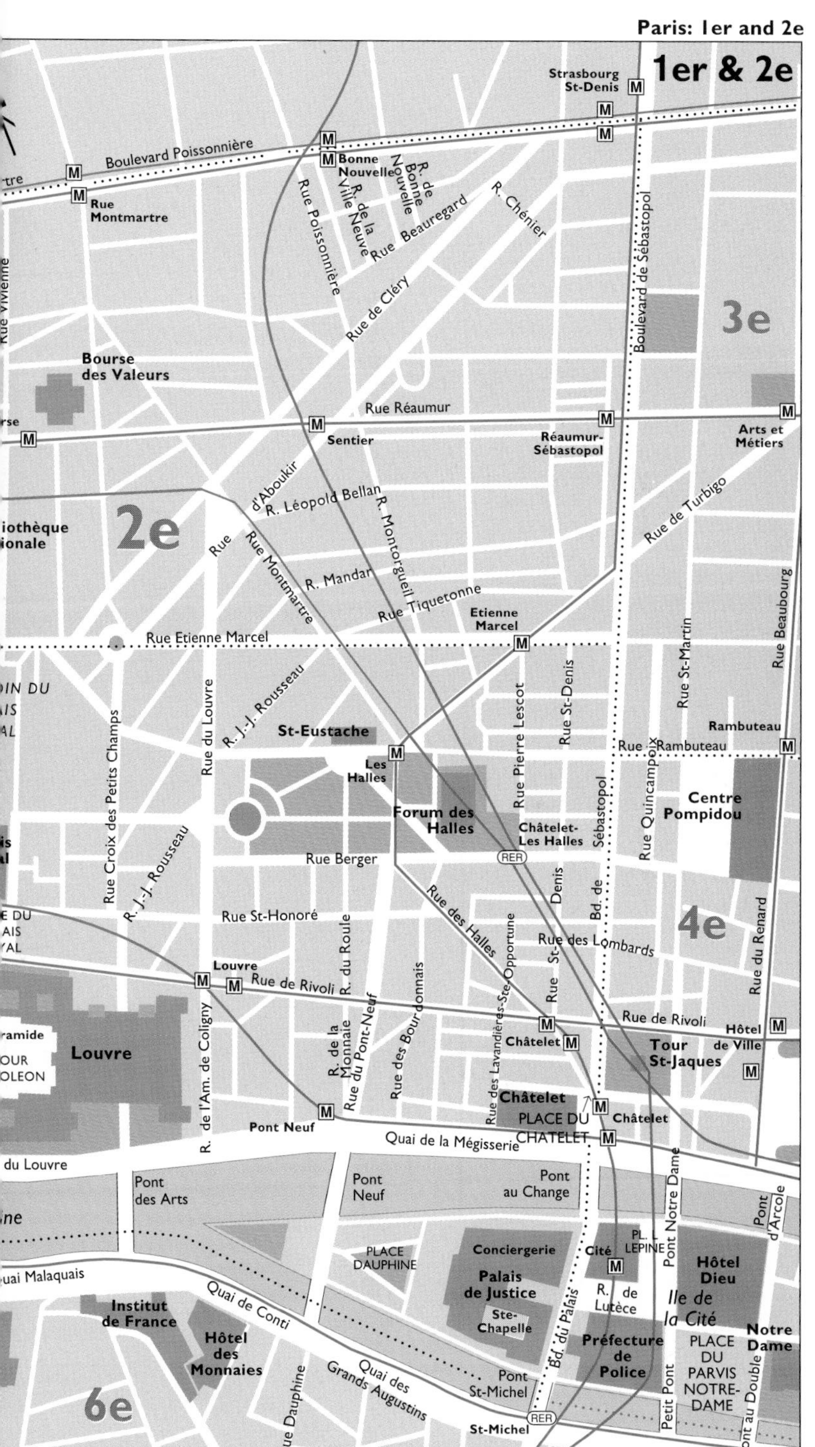
1er & 2e
Strasbourg St-Denis
Boulevard Poissonnière
Bonne Nouvelle
Rue Montmartre
R. de Bonne Nouvelle
R. de la Ville Neuve
Rue Poissonnière
Rue Beauregard
R. Chénier
Rue de Cléry
Boulevard de Sébastopol
3e
Bourse des Valeurs
Rue Réaumur
Sentier
Réaumur-Sébastopol
Arts et Métiers
R. d'Aboukir
R. Léopold Bellan
R. Montorgueil
Rue de Turbigo
2e
Rue Montmartre
R. Mandar
Rue Tiquetonne
Etienne Marcel
Rue Etienne Marcel
Rue Beaubourg
Rue St-Martin
R. J.-J. Rousseau
St-Eustache
Rue du Louvre
Rue Pierre Lescot
Rue St-Denis
Rambuteau
Rue Rambuteau
Rue Croix des Petits Champs
Les Halles
Forum des Halles
Châtelet-Les Halles
Bd. de Sébastopol
Rue Quincampoix
Centre Pompidou
Rue Berger
RER
Rue des Halles
Rue St-Honoré
R. du Roule
Rue des Lombards
4e
Rue du Renard
Louvre
Rue de Rivoli
Rue des Bourdonnais
Rue des Lavandières-Ste-Opportune
Rue St-Denis
R. de la Monnaie
Rue du Pont-Neuf
R. de l'Am. de Coligny
Châtelet
Hôtel de Ville
Tour St-Jaques
Louvre
Pont Neuf
Châtelet
PLACE DU CHATELET
Quai de la Mégisserie
Pont des Arts
Pont Neuf
Pont au Change
Pont Notre Dame
Pont d'Arcole
PLACE DAUPHINE
Conciergerie
Cité
PL. L LEPINE
Hôtel Dieu
Palais de Justice
R. de Lutèce
Ile de la Cité
Ste-Chapelle
Préfecture de Police
Notre Dame
PLACE DU PARVIS NOTRE-DAME
Bd. du Palais
Quai de Conti
Institut de France
Hôtel des Monnaies
Quai des Grands Augustins
Pont St-Michel
Petit Pont
Pont au Double
6e
Rue Dauphine
St-Michel
Quai Malaquais

Paris: 5e and 6e

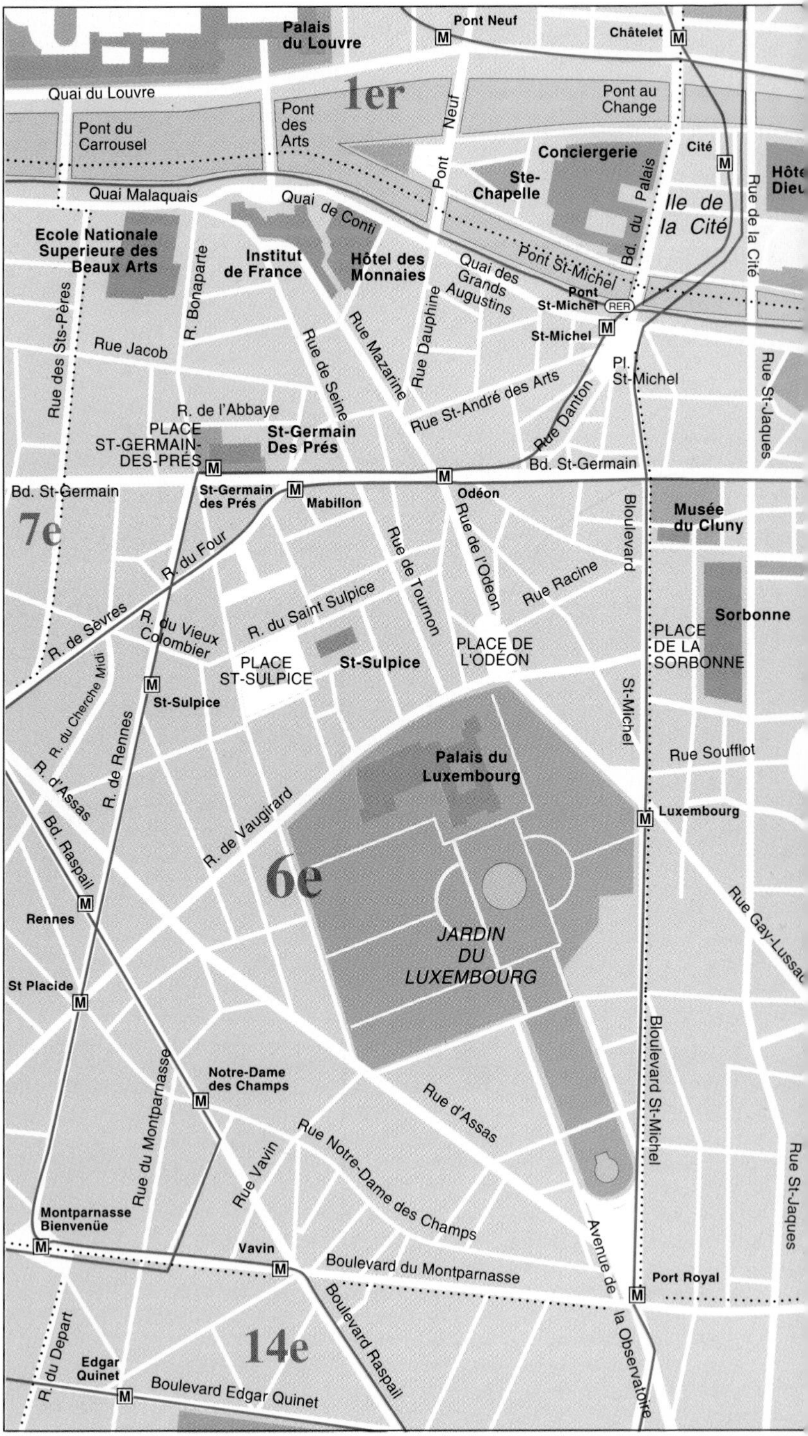

Palais du Louvre
Pont Neuf
Châtelet
1er
Quai du Louvre
Pont du Carrousel
Pont des Arts
Pont Neuf
Pont au Change
Conciergerie
Cité
Hôtel Dieu
Ste-Chapelle
Quai Malaquais
Quai de Conti
Bd. du Palais
Ile de la Cité
Rue de la Cité
Ecole Nationale Superieure des Beaux Arts
R. Bonaparte
Institut de France
Hôtel des Monnaies
Quai des Grands Augustins
Pont St-Michel
Pont St-Michel
RER
Rue des Sts-Pères
Rue Jacob
Rue de Seine
Rue Mazarine
Rue Dauphine
St-Michel
Pl. St-Michel
Rue St-Jaques
Rue St-André des Arts
Rue Danton
R. de l'Abbaye
PLACE ST-GERMAIN-DES-PRÉS
St-Germain Des Prés
Bd. St-Germain
Bd. St-Germain
St-Germain des Prés
Mabillon
Odéon
7e
Rue de l'Odeon
Boulevard St-Michel
Musée du Cluny
R. du Four
Rue de Tournon
Rue Racine
R. du Saint Sulpice
Sorbonne
R. de Sèvres
R. du Vieux Colombier
PLACE ST-SULPICE
St-Sulpice
PLACE DE L'ODÉON
PLACE DE LA SORBONNE
St-Sulpice
R. du Cherche Midi
R. de Rennes
Palais du Luxembourg
Rue Soufflot
R. d'Assas
Luxembourg
Bd. Raspail
R. de Vaugirard
6e
Rue Gay-Lussac
Rennes
JARDIN DU LUXEMBOURG
St Placide
Notre-Dame des Champs
Rue d'Assas
Rue du Montparnasse
Rue Notre-Dame des Champs
Rue Vavin
Boulevard St-Michel
Rue St-Jaques
Montparnasse Bienvenüe
Vavin
Boulevard du Montparnasse
Avenue de la Observatoire
Port Royal
Boulevard Raspail
14e
R. du Depart
Edgar Quinet
Boulevard Edgar Quinet

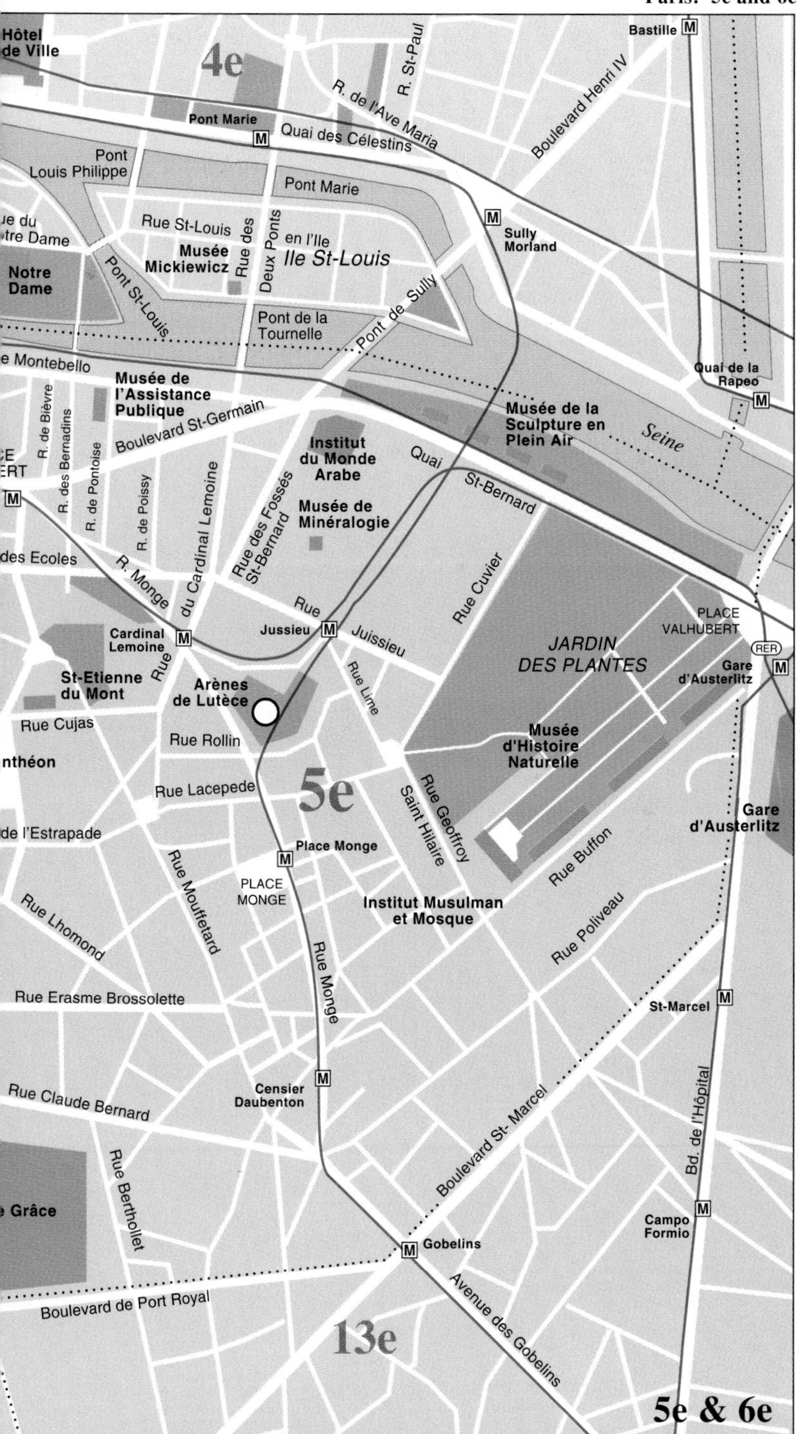
Hôtel de Ville
4e
Pont Marie
Quai des Célestins
R. St-Paul
R. de l'Ave Maria
Boulevard Henri IV
Bastille
Pont Louis Philippe
Pont Marie
Rue St-Louis
en l'Ile
Ile St-Louis
Musée Mickiewicz
Rue des Deux Ponts
Notre Dame
Pont St-Louis
Pont de la Tournelle
Pont de Sully
Sully Morland
Montebello
Musée de l'Assistance Publique
Boulevard St-Germain
R. de Bièvre
R. des Bernadins
R. de Pontoise
R. de Poissy
Rue du Cardinal Lemoine
Rue des Fossés St-Bernard
Institut du Monde Arabe
Musée de Minéralogie
Quai St-Bernard
Musée de la Sculpture en Plein Air
Seine
Quai de la Rapeo
des Ecoles
R. Monge
Rue Cuvier
Rue Juissieu
Jussieu
Cardinal Lemoine
PLACE VALHUBERT
JARDIN DES PLANTES
RER
Gare d'Austerlitz
St-Etienne du Mont
Arènes de Lutèce
Rue Lime
Rue Cujas
Rue Rollin
nthéon
Musée d'Histoire Naturelle
Rue Lacepede
5e
Rue Geoffroy Saint Hilaire
Gare d'Austerlitz
de l'Estrapade
Place Monge
PLACE MONGE
Rue Mouffetard
Rue Buffon
Institut Musulman et Mosque
Rue Lhomond
Rue Poliveau
Rue Monge
Rue Erasme Brossolette
St-Marcel
Censier Daubenton
Rue Claude Bernard
Boulevard St- Marcel
Bd. de l'Hôpital
Rue Berthollet
Grâce
Campo Formio
Gobelins
Boulevard de Port Royal
Avenue des Gobelins
13e
5e & 6e

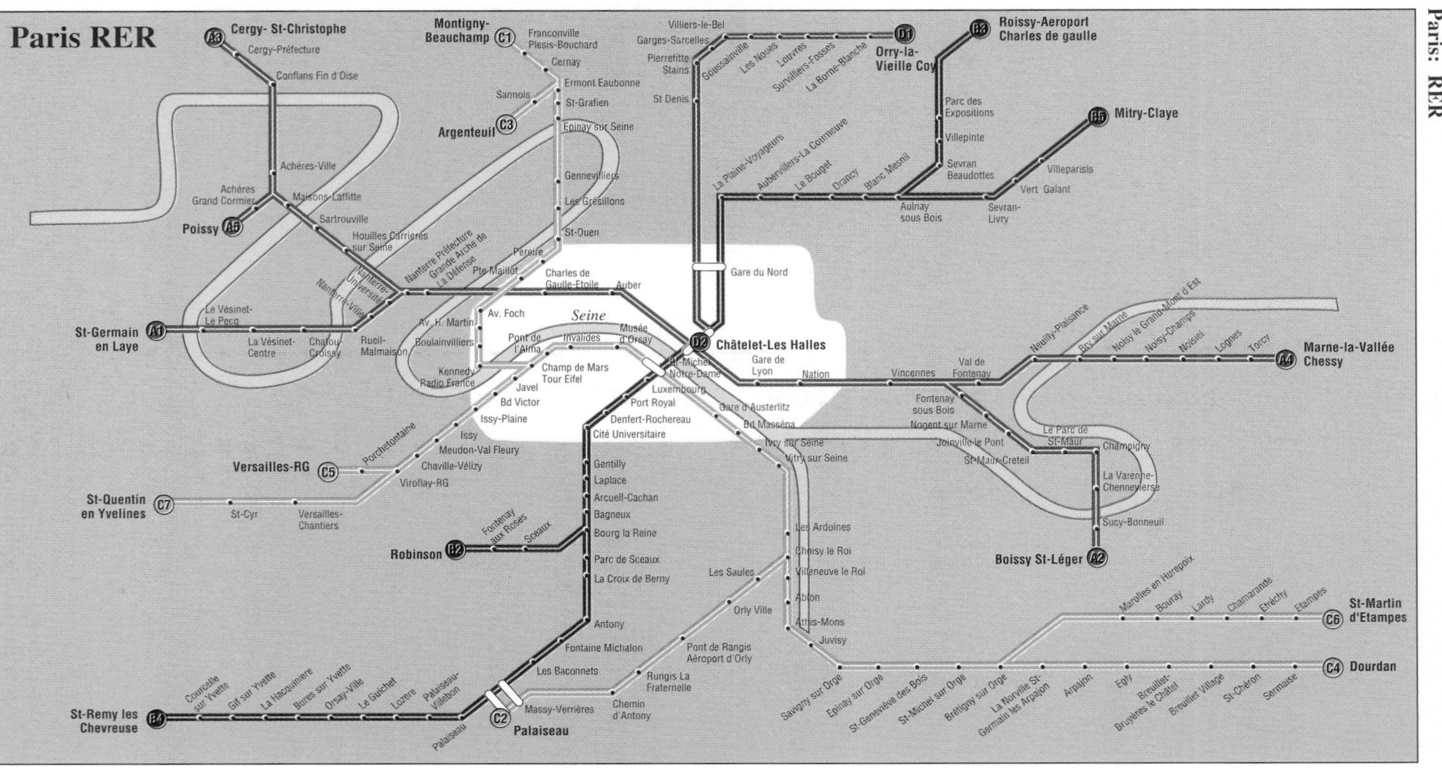
Paris RER
Cergy- St-Christophe
Cergy-Préfecture
Conflans Fin d'Oise
Achères-Ville
Achères Grand Cormier
Poissy
Maisons-Laffitte
Sartrouville
Houilles Carrières sur Seine
Nanterre Préfecture Grande Arche de La Défense
Nanterre-Université
Nanterre-Ville
Rueil-Malmaison
Chatou Croissy
La Vésinet-Centre
Le Vésinet-Le Pecq
St-Germain en Laye
Montigny-Beauchamp
Franconville Plesis-Bouchard
Cernay
Ermont Eaubonne
St-Grafien
Sannois
Argenteuil
Epinay sur Seine
Gennevilliers
Les Grésillons
St-Ouen
Pereire
Pte Maillot
Av. Foch
Av. H. Martin
Boulainvilliers
Kennedy Radio France
Pont de l'Alma
Invalides
Musée d'Orsay
Seine
Champ de Mars Tour Eifel
Javel
Bd Victor
Issy-Plaine
Issy
Meudon-Val Fleury
Chaville-Vélizy
Viroflay-RG
Porchetontaine
Versailles-RG
Versailles-Chantiers
St-Cyr
St-Quentin en Yvelines
Charles de Gaulle-Etoile
Auber
St-Michel Notre-Dame
Luxembourg
Port Royal
Denfert-Rochereau
Cité Universitaire
Gentilly
Laplace
Arcueil-Cachan
Bagneux
Bourg la Reine
Sceaux
Fontenay aux Roses
Robinson
Parc de Sceaux
La Croix de Berny
Antony
Fontaine Michalon
Les Baconnets
Massy-Verrières
Palaiseau
Palaiseau-Villebon
Lozere
Le Guichet
Orsay-Ville
Bures sur Yvette
La Hacquinière
Gif sur Yvette
Courcelle sur Yvette
St-Remy les Chevreuse
Villiers-le-Bel
Garges-Sarcelles
Pierrefitte Stains
St Denis
Goussainville
Les Noues
Louvres
Survilliers-Fosses
La Borne-Blanche
Orry-la-Vieille Coy
Gare du Nord
Châtelet-Les Halles
Gare de Lyon
Nation
Vincennes
Val de Fontenay
Fontenay sous Bois
Nogent sur Marne
Joinville-le Pont
St-Maur-Creteil
Le Parc de St-Maur
Champigny
La Varenne-Chennevierse
Sucy-Bonneuil
Boissy St-Léger
Neuilly-Plaisance
Bry sur Marne
Noisy le Grand-Mont d'Est
Noisy-Champs
Noisiel
Lognes
Torcy
Marne-la-Vallée Chessy
La Plaine-Voyageurs
Aubervilliers-La Courneuve
Le Bouget
Drancy
Blanc Mesnil
Aulnay sous Bois
Sevran Beaudottes
Villepinte
Parc des Expositions
Roissy-Aeroport Charles de gaulle
Sevran-Livry
Vert Galant
Villeparisis
Mitry-Claye
Gare d'Austerlitz
Bd Masséna
Ivry sur Seine
Vitry sur Seine
Les Ardoines
Choisy le Roi
Villeneuve le Roi
Ablon
Athis-Mons
Juvisy
Les Saules
Orly Ville
Pont de Rangis Aéroport d'Orly
Rungis La Fraternelle
Chemin d'Antony
Savigny sur Orge
Epinay sur Orge
St-Geneviève des Bois
St-Michel sur Orge
Brétigny sur Orge
La Norville St-Germain les Arpajon
Arpajon
Egly
Breuillet-Bruyères le Châtel
Breuillet Village
St-Chéron
Sermaise
Dourdan
Marolles en Hurepoix
Bouray
Lardy
Chamarande
Etréchy
Etampes
St-Martin d'Etampes

Let's Go:

France

"Its yearly revision by a new crop of Harvard students makes it as valuable as ever." **—*The New York Times***

"Value-packed, unbeatable, accurate, and comprehensive." **—*The Los Angeles Times***

"A world-wise traveling companion—always ready with friendly advice and helpful hints, all sprinkled with a bit of wit." **—*The Philadelphia Inquirer***

"Lighthearted and sophisticated, informative and fun to read. [Let's Go] helps the novice traveler navigate like a knowledgeable old hand." **—*Atlanta Journal-Constitution***

"All the essential information you need, from making a phone call to exchanging money to contacting your embassy. [Let's Go] provides maps to help you find your way from every train station to a full range of youth hostels and hotels." **—*Minneapolis Star Tribune***

"Unbeatable: good sight-seeing advice; up-to-date info on restaurants, hotels, and inns; a commitment to money-saving travel; and a wry style that brightens nearly every page." **—*The Washington Post***

■ Let's Go researchers have to make it on their own.

"The writers seem to have experienced every rooster-packed bus and lunar-surfaced mattress about which they write." **—*The New York Times***

"Retains the spirit of the student-written publication it is: candid, opinionated, resourceful, amusing info for the traveler of limited means but broad curiosity." **—*Mademoiselle***

■ No other guidebook is as comprehensive.

"Whether you're touring the United States, Europe, Southeast Asia, or Central America, a Let's Go guide will clue you in to the cheapest, yet safe, hotels and hostels, food and transportation. Going beyond the call of duty, the guides reveal a country's latest news, cultural hints, and off-beat information that any tourist is likely to miss." **—*Tulsa World***

■ Let's Go is completely revised each year.

"Up-to-date travel tips for touring four continents on skimpy budgets." **—*Time***

"Inimitable.... Let's Go's 24 guides are updated yearly (as opposed to the general guidebook standard of every two to three years), and in a marvelously spunky way." **—*The New York Times***

Let's Go Publications

Let's Go: Alaska & The Pacific Northwest
Let's Go: Britain & Ireland
Let's Go: California
Let's Go: Central America
Let's Go: Eastern Europe
Let's Go: Ecuador & The Galápagos Islands
Let's Go: Europe
Let's Go: France
Let's Go: Germany
Let's Go: Greece & Turkey
Let's Go: India & Nepal
Let's Go: Ireland
Let's Go: Israel & Egypt
Let's Go: Italy
Let's Go: London
Let's Go: Mexico
Let's Go: New York City
Let's Go: Paris
Let's Go: Rome
Let's Go: Southeast Asia
Let's Go: Spain & Portugal
Let's Go: Switzerland & Austria
Let's Go: USA
Let's Go: Washington, D.C.

*Let's Go **Map Guide:** Boston*
*Let's Go **Map Guide:** London*
*Let's Go **Map Guide:** New York City*
*Let's Go **Map Guide:** Paris*
*Let's Go **Map Guide:** San Francisco*
*Let's Go **Map Guide:** Washington, D.C.*

LET'S GO

The Budget Guide to
France
1997

Thomas F. Moore
Editor

Julie R. Cooper
Associate Editor

Lisa M. Nosal
Assistant Editor

St. Martin's Press New York

HELPING LET'S GO

If you want to share your discoveries, suggestions, or corrections, please drop us a line. We read every piece of correspondence, whether a postcard, a 10-page e-mail, or a coconut. All suggestions are passed along to our researcher-writers. Please note that mail received after May 1997 may be too late for the 1998 book, but will be retained for the following edition. **Address mail to:**

Let's Go: France
67 Mt. Auburn Street
Cambridge, MA 02138
USA

Visit Let's Go at **http://www.letsgo.com,** or send e-mail to:

Fanmail@letsgo.com
Subject: "Let's Go: France"

In addition to the invaluable travel advice our readers share with us, many are kind enough to offer their services as researchers or editors. Unfortunately, the charter of Let's Go, Inc. enables us to employ only currently enrolled Harvard-Radcliffe students.

Map revisions pp. 2-3, 4-5, 6-7, 155, 165, 241, 265, 323, 391, 437, 443, 461, 471, 511, 531, 533, 556-557, 591, 629, 631, 657 by Let's Go, Inc.

Distributed outside the USA and Canada by Macmillan.

ISBN: 0-312-14652-3

First edition
10 9 8 7 6 5 4 3 2 1

Let's Go: France is written by Let's Go Publications, 67 Mt. Auburn Street, Cambridge, MA 02138, USA.

Printed in the USA on recycled paper with biodegradable soy ink.

About Let's Go

THIRTY-SIX YEARS OF WISDOM

Back in 1960, a few students at Harvard University banded together to produce a 20-page pamphlet offering a collection of tips on budget travel in Europe. This modest, mimeographed packet, offered as an extra to passengers on student charter flights to Europe, met with instant popularity. The following year, students traveling to Europe researched the first, full-fledged edition of *Let's Go: Europe*, a pocket-sized book featuring honest, irreverent writing and a decidedly youthful outlook on the world. Throughout the 60s, our guides reflected the times; the 1969 guide to America led off by inviting travelers to "dig the scene" at San Francisco's Haight-Ashbury. During the 70s and 80s, we gradually added regional guides and expanded coverage into the Middle East and Central America. With the addition of our in-depth city guides, handy map guides, and extensive coverage of Asia, the 90s are also proving to be a time of explosive growth for Let's Go, and there's certainly no end in sight. The first editions of *Let's Go: India & Nepal* and *Let's Go: Ecuador & The Galápagos Islands* hit the shelves this year, and research for next year's series has already begun.

We've seen a lot in 37 years. *Let's Go: Europe* is now the world's bestselling international guide, translated into seven languages. And our new guides bring Let's Go's total number of titles, with their spirit of adventure and their reputation for honesty, accuracy, and editorial integrity, to 30. But some things never change: our guides are still researched, written, and produced entirely by students who know first-hand how to see the world on the cheap.

HOW WE DO IT

Each guide is completely revised and thoroughly updated every year by a well-traveled set of 200 students. Every winter, we recruit over 120 researchers and 60 editors to write the books anew. After several months of training, Researcher-Writers hit the road for seven weeks of exploration, from Anchorage to Ankara, Estonia to El Salvador, Iceland to Indonesia. Hired for their rare combination of budget travel sense, writing ability, stamina, and courage, these adventurous travelers know that train strikes, stolen luggage, food poisoning, and marriage proposals are all part of a day's work. Back at our offices, editors work from spring to fall, massaging copy written on Himalayan bus rides into witty yet informative prose. A student staff of typesetters, cartographers, publicists, and managers keeps our lively team together. In September, the collected efforts of the summer are delivered to our printer, who turns them into books in record time, so that you have the most up-to-date information available for *your* vacation. And even as you read this, work on next year's editions is well underway.

WHY WE DO IT

At Let's Go, our goal is to give you a great vacation. We don't think of budget travel as the last recourse of the destitute; we believe that it's the only way to travel. Living cheaply and simply brings you closer to the people and places you've been saving up to visit. Our books will ease your anxieties and answer your questions about the basics—so you can get off the beaten track and explore. Once you learn the ropes, we encourage you to put Let's Go away now and then to strike out on your own. As any seasoned traveler will tell you, the best discoveries are often those you make yourself. When you find something worth sharing, drop us a line. We're Let's Go Publications, 67 Mt. Auburn St., Cambridge, MA 02138, USA (e-mail: fanmail@letsgo.com).

HAPPY TRAVELS!

Contents

Maps

Color Maps

Acknowledgments

France thanks: Amanda, bringer of good things; Lauren, for a Paris we could never forget; the rest of the oh-so-swanky Romance Room—Alexa, Amy, Bill, Corey, and Greg; the super-duper Production Team; Michelle, PD goddess; Jen; Anne, looking out for us; everyone who typed, proofed, or otherwise saved our butts; the fab MEs; all the boys 'n' girls of *Let's Go;* and the R-Ws, especially Corinna, Emily, and Jefferson, who were nothing short of *vachement chouette.*

Tom thanks: Julie, the best thing to come out of Harvard's English Department since 1636; Lisa, by whom the passive voice was eradicated right and left; Amanda and Mike, my dream roommates; Andrew, Kate, and Rebecca, whom I thoughtlessly dissed last year; the Beans, who inspired me to Lumpy heights; Joel, the host with the most; Caroline, Covie, Marg, David, and Dave; G&S; Mrs. Katsaros; and Mom, Dad, Corinna, and Grandpa, who constantly show me how lucky I am to have them.

Julie thanks: Tom for tea and sympathy, a liberal lending policy, and out-of-this-world *tapenade;* Lisa for editorial *éclat* that awed the room of Romance; Amanda, gentle reader and ferry friend; Henns and Coopers everywhere; Jesse, for making me apply; Margaret, for enduring my French and never licking a gift horse in the mouth; and Drew, eart'sha arlingda, superchef, and magnet of hiccup mercy.

Lisa thanks: Tom, woo-hoo! it's done—aw yeah; Julie, the Gypsy Queen; Corey & Amy, who are definitely the tits; Steve, for constant encouragement; Caitlin, the *über*-babe; Miranda, wayward wanderer; Dave, my fellow Dunsterite; Allison, who knows about Thomas Nast; Kath, Lynn, & Jan, for gossip and goodies; Mom, the creative genius; Dad, the passive-voice terminator; and Derek, the depth in the pool.

The R-Ws thank: Ed Hillis, Grais and Bill Brown, Jennifer Loucks, Sarah Jones; Gilbert, Lucy, and Olivia Harman; Frederic, Fabian, Flash, and Charly; Turner Deckert, les Lagueux, Wedge, Mem, and Pep; Corinna and the Moores, Glen, Christina, Tyler, Natalie Reti and the Alizès crew; the Stollers, les Deboves, les Caillards, and Twingo!

Editor	Thomas F. Moore
Associate Editor	Julie R. Cooper
Assistant Editor	Lisa M. Nosal
Managing Editor	Amanda K. Bean
Publishing Director	Michelle C. Sullivan
Production Manager	Daniel O. Williams
Associate Production Manager	Michael S. Campbell
Cartography Manager	Amanda K. Bean
Editorial Manager	John R. Brooks
Editorial Manager	Allison Crapo
Financial Manager	Stephen P. Janiak
Personnel Manager	Alexander H. Travelli
Publicity Manager	SoRelle B. Braun
Associate Publicity Manager	David Fagundes
Associate Publicity Manager	Elisabeth Mayer
Assistant Cartographer	Jonathan D. Kibera
Assistant Cartographer	Mark C. Staloff
Office Coordinator	Jennifer L. Schuberth
Director of Advertising and Sales	Amit Tiwari
Senior Sales Executives	Andrew T. Rourke
	Nicholas A. Valtz, Charles E. Varner
General Manager	Richard Olken
Assistant General Manager	Anne E. Chisholm

Researcher-Writers

Amy K. Brown *Loire Valley, Poitou-Charentes, Aquitaine*
Château-hopping was no obstacle for our lithe Loire breadwinner, who dashed over moats and gardeners at *très grande vitesse.* Leaving no fortress unplundered and no door unopened, Amy reveled in mushrooms and wine cellars and wowed French teenyboppers with her *suaveté.* The lustrous prose, veggie havens, and personal camera crew of our super-sleuth have made us salivate for two years running.

Elizabeth Harman *Bordeaux, Basque Country, Gascony, Languedoc, Marseille*
Liz took a leave of absence from theater and philosophy and hoofed it through medieval cities, towering green mountains, and surfboard meccas. Her neat-as-a-pin copy (with color illustrations) kept us on our toes, and her voice on the telephone kept our days sunny and bright. She braved illness, the elements, and a thousand and one other perils to bring us research that was savvy, sassy, and on the mark.

Jesse Hawkes *The Alps, Lyon and the Auvergne, Burgundy, Franche-Comté*
If the world ends, we will take Jesse Hawkes with us. Our very own MacGyver snaked his way through the Alps, eluded frostbite and SNCF conductors at every turn, and rescued wildlife critters. Scaling peaks with a carabiner welded to his sternum, this self-proclaimed "Let's Go Boy" beautified the "green thumb" of Besançon with his marginalia and kept the *gendarme* at bay. Boy Scouts of America, beware!

Robert C. Lagueux *Normandy, Brittany*
Rob is as good as they come. He peppered his stellar copy with anagrams, haikus, and cryptic rebuses that kept us in stitches. He showered us with treats to fatten us up and keep us safe. With his guardian angels—Fréd and Wedge—looking over his shoulder, Rob survived indoctrination by Enya, chilled with j-j-j-jammin' monks, fed at the teat of Brest, and showed that if anyone has *le droit,* it's him.

Sasha S. Mervyn *Corsica, The Côte d'Azur, The Rhône Valley*
As a Vancouverite in exile, Sasha was earnest and energetic, always pushing herself to discover and describe more than the day before. She showed the Corsicans what-for, dazzled the Riviera, and out-Provenced the *Provenceaux,* showering us with jealousy-inducing postcards. Indulging her love of swimming and *panini* from Ajaccio to Avignon, Sasha gave us copy that would make Alphonse Daudet proud.

Nicholas Stoller *Burgundy, Alsace-Lorraine, Champagne, The North*
Chasing down Twingos was no trouble for our comedian—er—researcher, Nick, who finished all of his copy with a bottle of Gewürztraminer firmly in hand. Recreating Champagne and the towns of the north in medal-winning prose was as easy for him as teaching a troupe of clowns in Semur-en-Auxois how to sing, and he captured the nuances of Alsace-Lorraine (and its vineyards) with perfect aplomb.

Lauren Feldman *Paris Editor*
Lisa Abend *Andorra*
Willow Crystal *Paris, Giverny*
Raphael Folsom *Paris*
Jennifer Lefcourt *Paris*
Jefferson Packer *The Côte d'Azur*
Emily M. Tucker *The Côte d'Azur*

How to Use This Book

Our researchers travel on a shoestring, so their worries are the same as yours: how to fulfill all their dreams of seeing France in the most economical way possible. Of course, they're also looking for the cheapest laundromats, cleanest $17 hotel rooms, and quickest bus transfers so you won't have to. We go everywhere, and we're concerned about the value you get for your money; if a place isn't worth it, we'll say so.

Let's Go: France divides the country into regions roughly corresponding to the historical provinces to which the French themselves feel allegiance. Geographically, the chapters are arranged in a spiral centered in Paris and radiating outward counterclockwise. Each chapter tries to capture the flavor of its region with an introduction that tells you enough about its history, culture, food, and wine to whet your appetite. These introductions can be quick signposts to regions you might want to explore in more detail. Will you venture towards the Loire châteaux, the prehistoric etchings of the Dordogne, the unparalleled Corsican coast, or other Gallic delights?

Once you've begun daydreaming about the perfumes of Provence, delve into the city descriptions. In each town's **Practical Information** section, we give you the nitty-gritty of how to get around in town and of services you might need while you're there—bike rentals, the best rates on currency exchange, or how to find grape-harvesting jobs, for example. Next come listings of **accommodations,** including hostels, hotels, and campgrounds, ranked according to our estimate of their value and quality. Once you've found that mountainside chalet, check the **Food** section. We'll list markets where the cheese is so fresh it practically moos and excellent deals on local cuisine, vegetarian options, and "foreign" foods for days when you've stared down the barrel of one too many baguettes. We forge onwards to the **sights** a town has to offer—from the Matisse chapel or the table salt museum to dayhikes past cascades and castles. The city ends on a rollicking note with nighttime **entertainment,** and—if concerts in Roman arenas or Franco-techno isn't your cup of tea—popular annual festivals. In smaller towns, the order remains the same, but sections may be combined.

The book's opening, **Essentials,** guides you through a maze of red tape, whispering traveling hints along the way. Look there for info about applying for passports, studying abroad, packing tips, tickets to and through France, and crucial things you'll need to know to make it past customs or out of the Paris metro. **France: An Introduction** is a 20-page tour of France's history, culture, and cuisine.

As invaluable as we try to make this book, we hope that sometime you will tuck it into your pack and explore on your own. To this end, we offer suggestions for investigation—be they urban neighborhoods or rural pockets of paradise. *Let's Go* has always been written and read by people who love to go just a little farther down the trail. We hope you will follow in their footsteps and break a path of your own.

A NOTE TO OUR READERS

The information for this book is gathered by *Let's Go*'s researchers during the late spring and summer months. Each listing is derived from the assigned researcher's opinion based upon his or her visit at a particular time. The opinions are expressed in a candid and forthright manner. Other travelers might disagree. Those traveling at a different time may have different experiences since prices, dates, hours, and conditions are always subject to change. You are urged to check beforehand to avoid inconvenience and surprises. Travel always involves a certain degree of risk, especially in low-cost areas. When traveling, especially on a budget, always take particular care to ensure your safety.

ESSENTIALS

PLANNING YOUR TRIP

A note: The workings of the French telephone network recently changed dramatically. Even if you are familiar with French phones, you may want to turn to page 57 for an explanation of the new system.

Useful Information

FRENCH GOVERNMENT SERVICES

Cultural Services of the French Embassy: U.S., 972 Fifth Ave., New York, NY 10021 (tel. (212) 439-1400). **U.K.,** 23 Cromwell Rd., London SW7 2EL (tel. (0171) 838 2055). Offers general information about France, including culture, student employment, and educational possibilities.

French Government Tourist Office: Write for info on regions of France, festival dates, tips for travelers with disabilities, and a youth travel guide. They also provide a travel planner called *The France Discovery Guide* and the paper *France Insider's News.* **U.S.,** (tel. (900) 990-0040, costs 50¢ per minute); 444 Madison Ave., 16th floor, New York, NY 10022; 676 N. Michigan Ave., #3360, Chicago, IL 60611; 9454 Wilshire Bd. #715, Beverly Hills, CA 90212. **Canada,** 1981 Ave. McGill College, #490, Montréal, Québec H3A 2W9 (tel. (514) 288-4264); 30 St-Patrick St., Suite #700, Toronto, Ontario M5T 3A3 (tel. (416) 593-4723; fax (416) 979-7587). **U.K.,** 178 Piccadilly, London W1V OAL (tel. (0171) 629 1272). **Ireland,** 35 Lower Abbey St., Dublin 1 (tel. (01) 703 4046). **Australia,** BNP building, 12th fl., 12 Castlereagh St., Sydney, NSW 2000 (tel. (02) 231 52 44). **New Zealanders** should contact this branch or the Consular Section within the French Embassy for info at 1 Willeston St., Wellington (tel. (64) 4 4720 200).

USEFUL RESOURCES

Council on International Educational Exchange (Council), 205 East 42nd St., New York, NY 10017-5706 (tel. (888) COUNCIL (268-6245); fax (212) 822-2699; e-mail info@ciee.org; http://www.ciee.org). A private, nonprofit organization, Council administers work, volunteer, and academic programs around the world. They also offer identity cards, including the ISIC and the GO25, and a range of publications, including the magazine *Student Travels* (free). Call or write for more information.

The College Connection, Inc., 1295 Prospect St., Suite A, La Jolla, CA 92037 (tel. (619) 551-9770; fax 551-9987; e-mail eurailnow@aol.com; http://www.eurailpass.com). Publishes *The Passport*, a booklet that covers all aspects of travel abroad and is free to *Let's Go* users; send requests by e-mail or fax.

Federation of International Youth Travel Organizations (FIYTO), Bredgade 25H, DK-1260 Copenhagen K, Denmark (tel. 33 33 96 00; fax 33 93 96 76; e-mail mailbox@fiyto.org), is an international organization promoting educational, cultural and social travel for young people. Member organizations include language schools, educational travel companies, national tourist boards, accommodation centers and other suppliers of travel services to youth and students.

Forsyth Travel Library, P.O. Box 480800, Kansas City, MO 64148 (tel. (800) 367-7984; fax (816) 942-6969; http://www.forsyth.com). Mail-order service that stocks a wide range of maps, as well as guides for rail and ferry travel in Europe; also sells rail tickets and passes. Sells the *Thomas Cook European Timetable* for trains, a complete guide to European train departures and arrivals (US$28, or $39 with full map of European train routes; postage $4.50 for priority shipping).

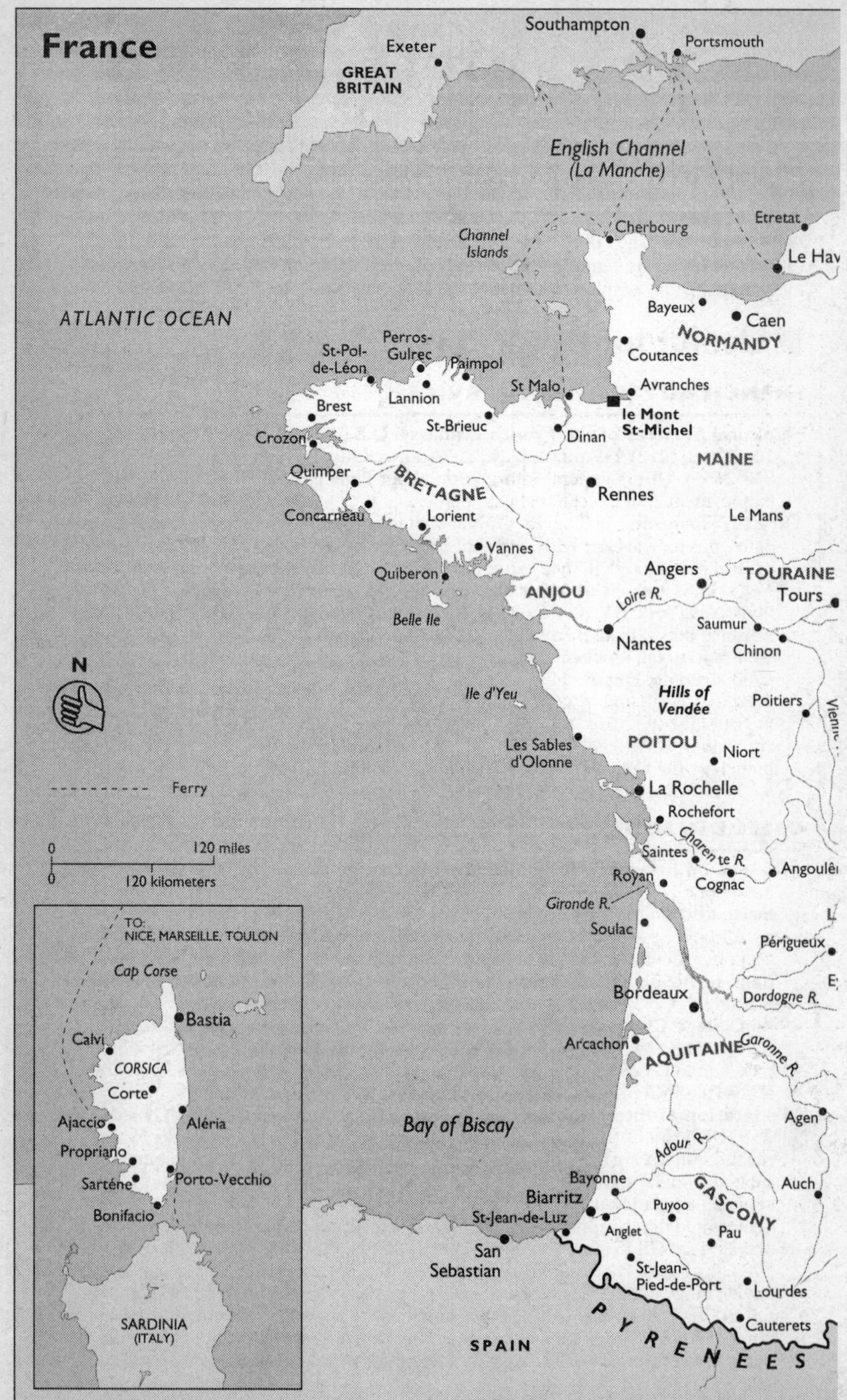
France
Southampton
Portsmouth
Exeter
GREAT BRITAIN
English Channel
(La Manche)
Channel Islands
Cherbourg
Etretat
Le Hav
ATLANTIC OCEAN
Bayeux
Caen
NORMANDY
Coutances
Perros-Gulrec
St-Pol-de-Léon
Paimpol
Lannion
St Malo
Avranches
Brest
le Mont St-Michel
St-Brieuc
Dinan
Crozon
MAINE
Quimper
BRETAGNE
Rennes
Concarneau
Lorient
Le Mans
Vannes
Quiberon
Angers
TOURAINE
ANJOU
Loire R.
Tours
Belle Ile
Saumur
Nantes
Chinon
N
Ile d'Yeu
Hills of Vendée
Poitiers
Vienne
Les Sables d'Olonne
POITOU
Niort
Ferry
La Rochelle
Rochefort
Charente R.
0
120 miles
Saintes
Angoulê
0
120 kilometers
Royan
Cognac
Gironde R.
TO: NICE, MARSEILLE, TOULON
Soulac
Périgueux
Cap Corse
Bordeaux
Dordogne R.
Bastia
Calvi
Arcachon
AQUITAINE
Garonne R.
CORSICA
Corte
Ajaccio
Aléria
Bay of Biscay
Agen
Propriano
Adour R.
Sartène
Porto-Vecchio
Bayonne
GASCONY
Auch
Bonifacio
Biarritz
Puyoo
St-Jean-de-Luz
Anglet
Pau
San Sebastian
St-Jean-Pied-de-Port
Lourdes
SARDINIA (ITALY)
SPAIN
Cauterets
PYRENEES

BELGIUM
GERMANY
LUX.
SWITZ.
ITALY
ANDORRA
MONACO
FLANDERS
PICARDIE
ILE-DE-FRANCE
LORRAINE
ALSACE
CHAMPAGNE
ORLEANAIS
FRANCHE COMTE
BURGUNDY
MARCHE
AUVERGNE
MASSIF CENTRAL
SAVOIE
THE ALPS
DAUPHINÉ
CEVENNES MTS.
PROVENCE
LANGUEDOC
CAMARGUE
ROUSSILLON
COTE D'AZUR
Calais
Dunkerque
Lille
Brussels
Cologne
Boulogne
Arras
Douai
Amiens
Dieppe
St-Quentin
Noyon
Laon
Rouen
Beauvais
Compiègne
Reims
Metz
Épernay
Châlons-sur-Marne
Paris
Meaux
Bar-le-Duc
Nancy
Strasbourg
Chartres
Troyes
Sens
Epinal
Colmar
Fontainebleau
Orléans
Mulhouse
Auxerre
Semur-en-Auxois
Belfort
Blois
Amboise
Avallon
Vézelay
Dijon
Dole
Besançon
Bourges
Nevers
Autun
Beaune
Arbois
Bern
Chalon-sur-Saône
Lons-le-Saunier
Tournus
Cluny
Lake Geneva
Montluçon
Vichy
Geneva
Annecy
Mont Blanc
Chamonix
Limoges
Riom
Clermont-Ferrand
Lyon
Aix-les-Bains
Chambéry
Grenoble
Turin
Brive
Les Eyzies
Souillac
Aurillac
le Puy
Sarlat
Rocamadour
Cahors
Vaison-la-Romaine
Orange
Montauban
Albi
Avignon
Nîmes
Menton
Nice
Cannes
Castres
Montpellier
Arles
Aix-en-Provence
Toulouse
Pézenas
Béziers
Marseille
Toulon
St Tropez
Carcassonne
Narbonne
Perpignan
Golfe du Lion
Mediterranean Sea
TO CORSICA
Somme R.
Seine R.
Marne R.
Loire R.
Indre R.
Saône R.
Rhône R.
Isère R.
Lot R.
Tarn R.
Durance R.
Aude R.
Rhine River

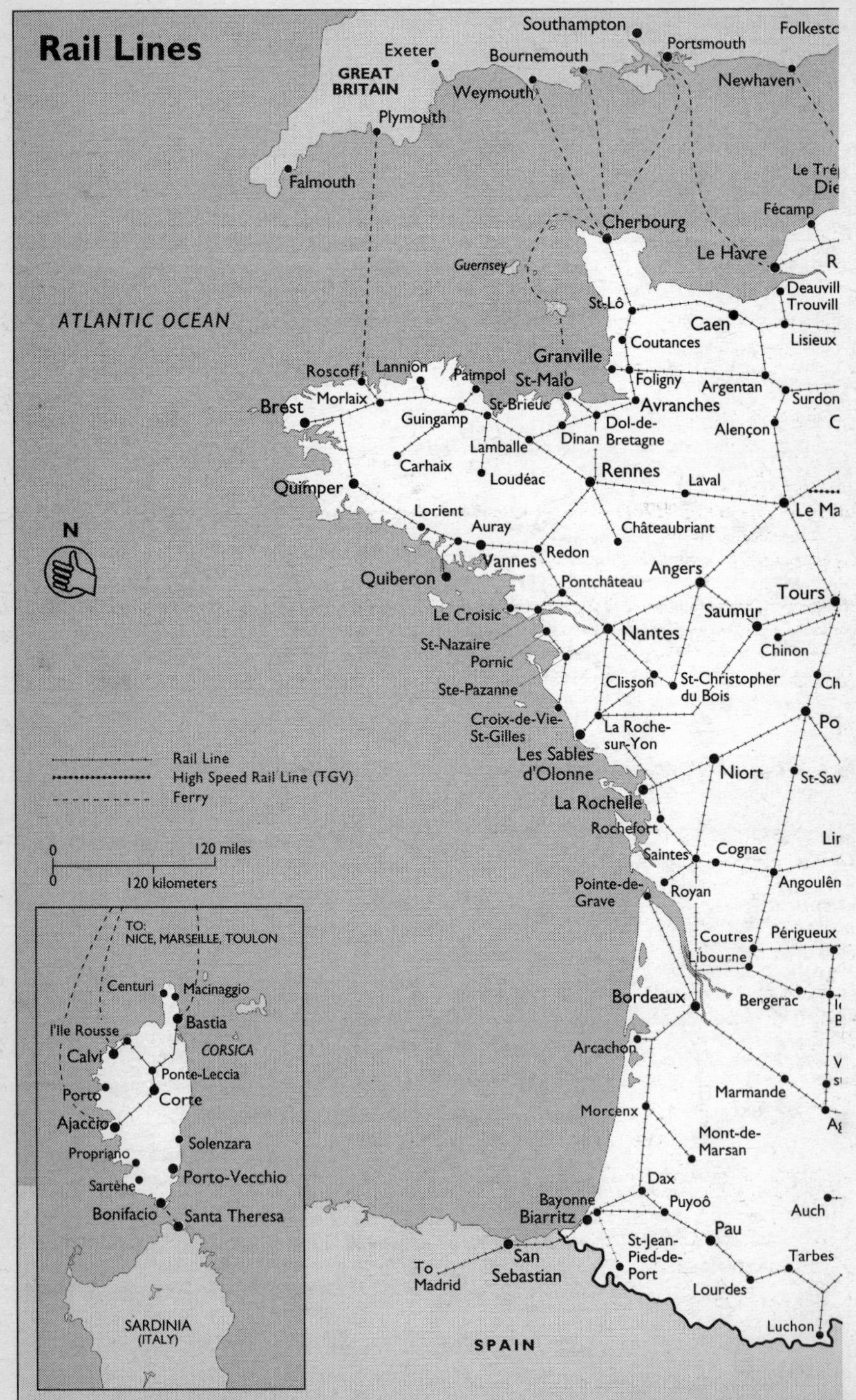
Rail Lines
GREAT BRITAIN
Southampton
Exeter
Bournemouth
Portsmouth
Newhaven
Weymouth
Plymouth
Falmouth
Fécamp
Cherbourg
Le Havre
Guernsey
St-Lô
Caen
Lisieux
ATLANTIC OCEAN
Coutances
Granville
Roscoff
Lannion
Paimpol
St-Malo
Foligny
Argentan
Brest
Morlaix
St-Brieuc
Avranches
Surdon
Guingamp
Dol-de-Bretagne
Dinan
Alençon
Lamballe
Carhaix
Loudéac
Rennes
Laval
Quimper
Lorient
Auray
Châteaubriant
N
Redon
Vannes
Quiberon
Pontchâteau
Angers
Tours
Le Croisic
Saumur
St-Nazaire
Nantes
Chinon
Pornic
Ste-Pazanne
Clisson
St-Christopher du Bois
Croix-de-Vie-St-Gilles
La Roche-sur-Yon
Les Sables d'Olonne
Niort
Rail Line
High Speed Rail Line (TGV)
Ferry
La Rochelle
Rochefort
0
120 miles
0
120 kilometers
Saintes
Cognac
Royan
Pointe-de-Grave
TO: NICE, MARSEILLE, TOULON
Coutres
Périgueux
Libourne
Centuri
Macinaggio
Bastia
Bordeaux
Bergerac
l'Ile Rousse
CORSICA
Calvi
Ponte-Leccia
Arcachon
Porto
Corte
Marmande
Ajaccio
Morcenx
Solenzara
Propriano
Mont-de-Marsan
Porto-Vecchio
Sartène
Dax
Bonifacio
Santa Theresa
Bayonne
Puyoô
Auch
Biarritz
Pau
San Sebastian
St-Jean-Pied-de-Port
Tarbes
To Madrid
Lourdes
SARDINIA (ITALY)
Luchon
SPAIN

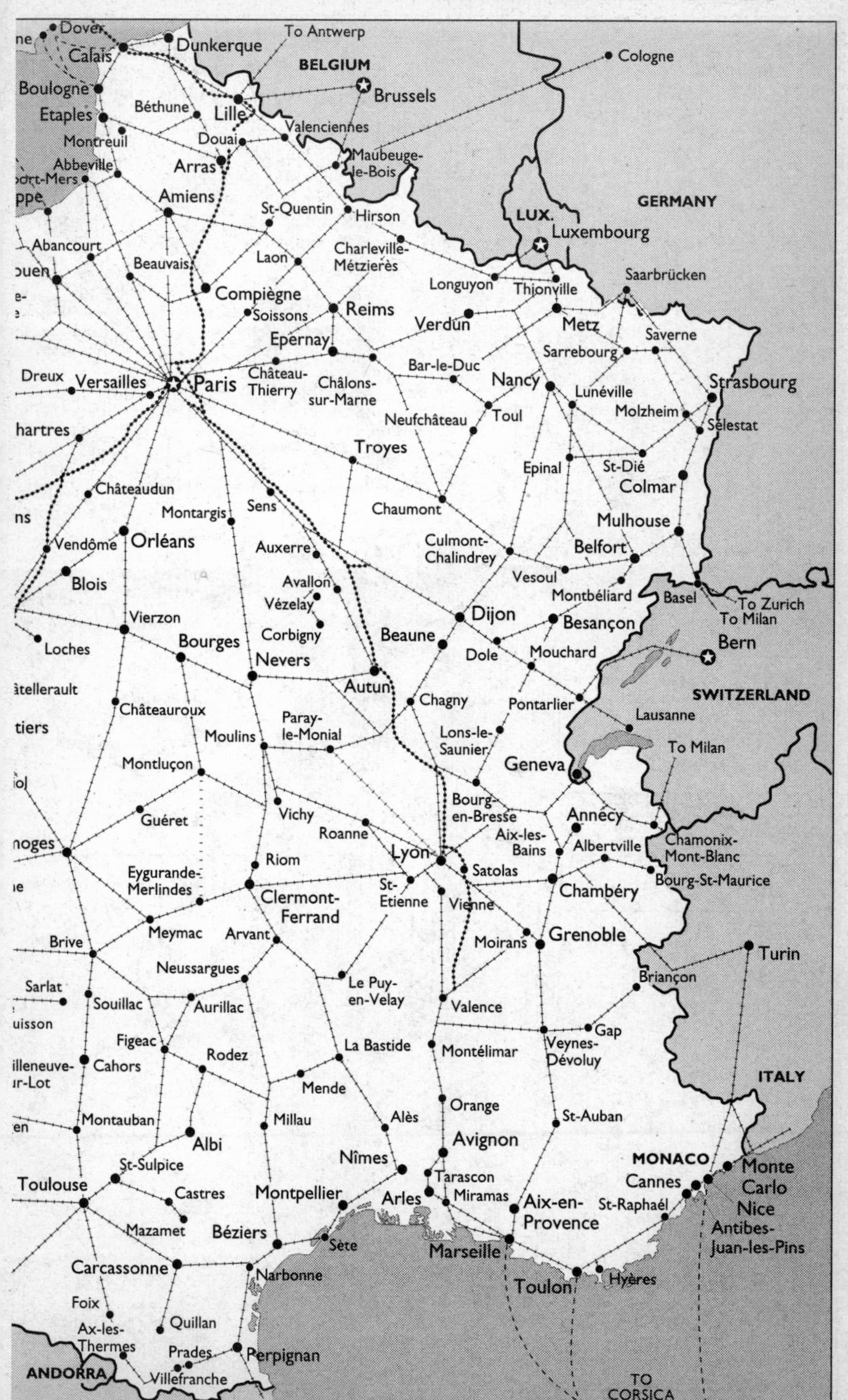

BELGIUM
GERMANY
LUX.
SWITZERLAND
ITALY
MONACO
ANDORRA
Dover
Calais
Dunkerque
To Antwerp
Brussels
Cologne
Boulogne
Etaples
Béthune
Lille
Valenciennes
Montreuil
Douai
Arras
Abbeville
Maubeuge-le-Bois
Amiens
St-Quentin
Hirson
Luxembourg
Abancourt
Laon
Charleville-Métzierès
Beauvais
Compiègne
Longuyon
Thionville
Saarbrücken
Soissons
Reims
Verdun
Metz
Epernay
Saverne
Sarrebourg
Dreux
Versailles
Paris
Château-Thierry
Châlons-sur-Marne
Bar-le-Duc
Nancy
Strasbourg
Lunéville
Molzheim
Sélestat
Toul
Neufchâteau
Troyes
Epinal
St-Dié
Colmar
Châteaudun
Montargis
Sens
Chaumont
Mulhouse
Vendôme
Orléans
Auxerre
Culmont-Chalindrey
Belfort
Blois
Avallon
Vesoul
Vézelay
Montbéliard
Basel
To Zurich
To Milan
Vierzon
Corbigny
Dijon
Besançon
Bern
Loches
Bourges
Nevers
Beaune
Dole
Mouchard
Autun
Chagny
Pontarlier
Châteauroux
Paray-le-Monial
Lausanne
Moulins
Lons-le-Saunier
To Milan
Montluçon
Geneva
Bourg-en-Bresse
Annecy
Guéret
Vichy
Roanne
Aix-les-Bains
Albertville
Chamonix-Mont-Blanc
Lyon
Riom
Satolas
Bourg-St-Maurice
Eygurande-Merlindes
Clermont-Ferrand
St-Etienne
Vienne
Chambéry
Meymac
Arvant
Moirans
Grenoble
Brive
Turin
Neussargues
Le Puy-en-Velay
Briançon
Sarlat
Souillac
Aurillac
Valence
Figeac
Gap
Rodez
La Bastide
Montélimar
Veynes-Dévoluy
Cahors
Mende
Orange
Montauban
Millau
Alès
St-Auban
Albi
Avignon
Nîmes
St-Sulpice
Tarascon
Monte Carlo
Toulouse
Cannes
Castres
Montpellier
Arles
Miramas
Aix-en-Provence
St-Raphaël
Nice
Mazamet
Béziers
Antibes-Juan-les-Pins
Sète
Marseille
Carcassonne
Narbonne
Toulon
Hyères
Foix
Quillan
Ax-les-Thermes
Prades
Perpignan
Villefranche
TO CORSICA

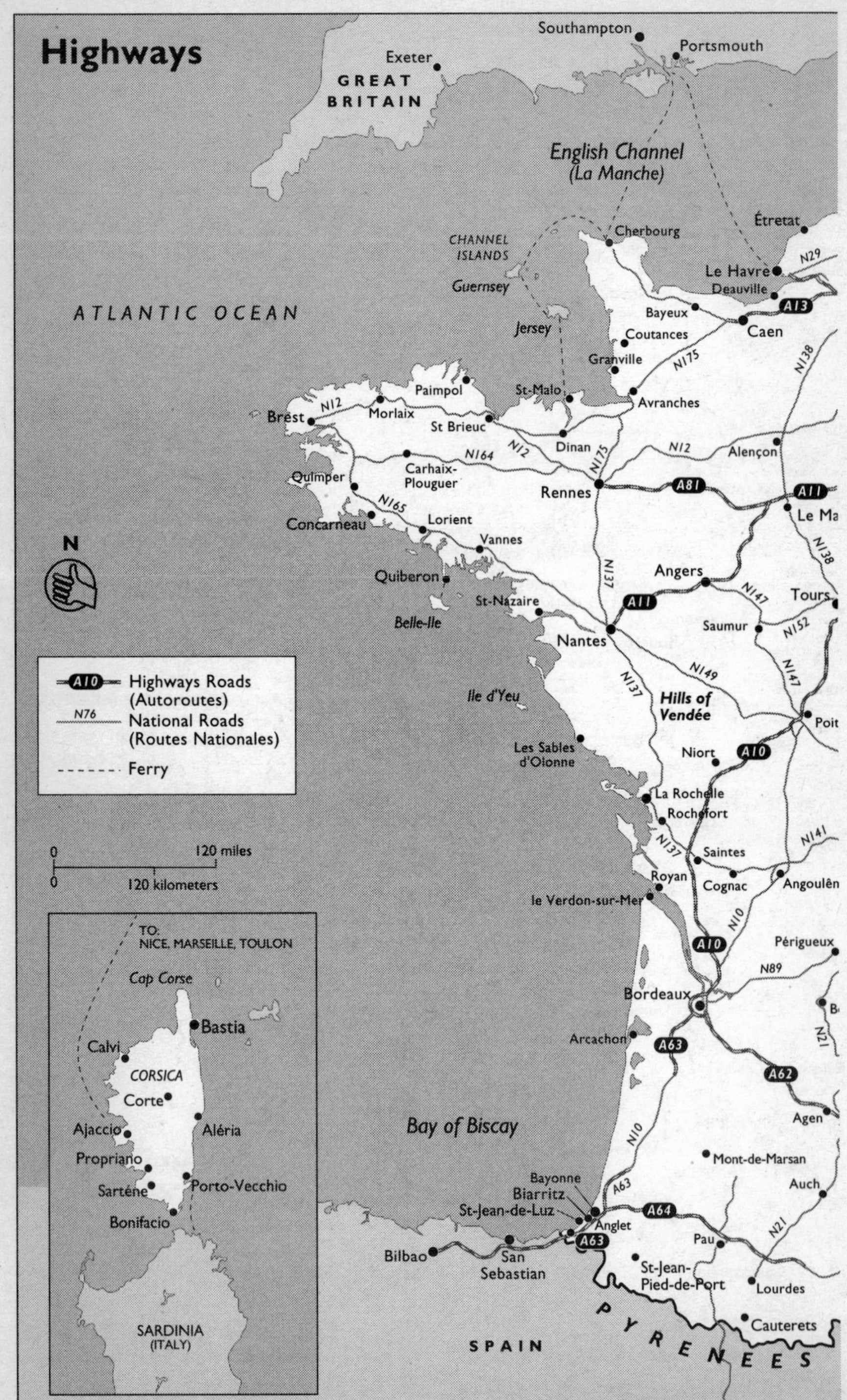
Highways
Southampton
Portsmouth
Exeter
GREAT BRITAIN
English Channel (La Manche)
CHANNEL ISLANDS
Guernsey
Jersey
Cherbourg
Étretat
Le Havre
Deauville
Bayeux
Caen
Coutances
Granville
St-Malo
Avranches
ATLANTIC OCEAN
Brest
Morlaix
Paimpol
St Brieuc
Dinan
Alençon
Quimper
Carhaix-Plouguer
Rennes
Le Ma
Concarneau
Lorient
Vannes
Quiberon
Belle-Ile
St-Nazaire
Angers
Tours
Saumur
Nantes
Ile d'Yeu
Hills of Vendée
Poit
Les Sables d'Olonne
Niort
La Rochelle
Rochefort
Saintes
Royan
Cognac
Angoulên
le Verdon-sur-Mer
Périgueux
Bordeaux
Arcachon
Agen
Bay of Biscay
Mont-de-Marsan
Bayonne
Biarritz
St-Jean-de-Luz
Anglet
Auch
Pau
Bilbao
San Sebastian
St-Jean-Pied-de-Port
Lourdes
Cauterets
SPAIN
PYRENEES
N
A10 Highways Roads (Autoroutes)
N76 National Roads (Routes Nationales)
Ferry
0 120 miles
0 120 kilometers
TO: NICE, MARSEILLE, TOULON
Cap Corse
Bastia
Calvi
CORSICA
Corte
Ajaccio
Aléria
Propriano
Sarténe
Porto-Vecchio
Bonifacio
SARDINIA (ITALY)

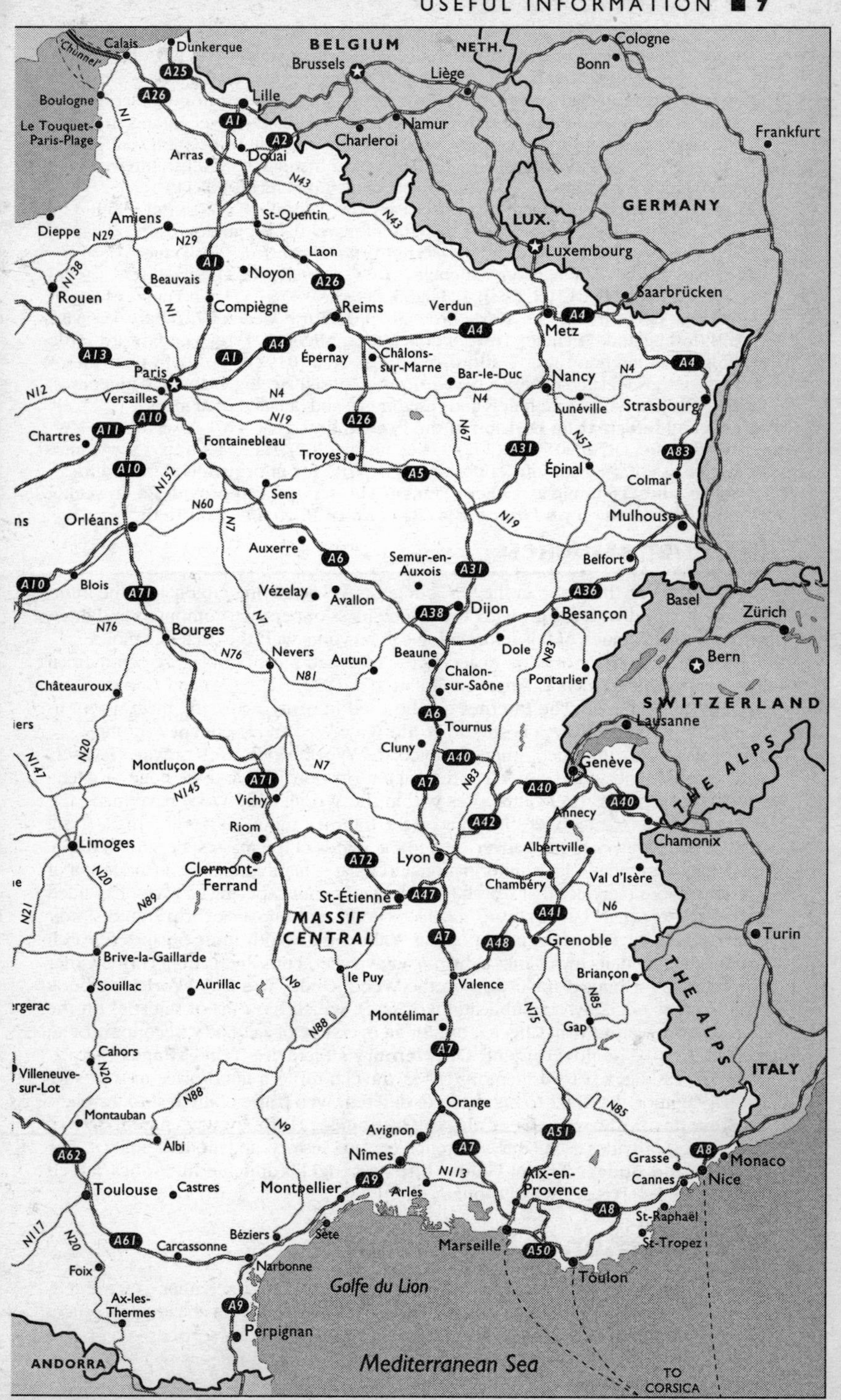

'Chunnel'
Calais
Dunkerque
BELGIUM
NETH.
Cologne
Brussels
Bonn
Liège
Lille
Boulogne
Le Touquet-Paris-Plage
Namur
Charleroi
Frankfurt
Arras
Douai
N43
GERMANY
LUX.
St-Quentin
Amiens
Dieppe
N29
Laon
Luxembourg
N138
Noyon
Beauvais
Rouen
Compiègne
Reims
Saarbrücken
Verdun
Metz
Épernay
Châlons-sur-Marne
Paris
Bar-le-Duc
Nancy
N12
Versailles
N4
Lunéville
Strasbourg
Chartres
N19
Fontainebleau
N67
N57
Troyes
Épinal
Colmar
N152
Sens
N60
Orléans
N7
Mulhouse
Auxerre
Semur-en-Auxois
Belfort
Blois
Vézelay
Avallon
Basel
Zürich
N76
Dijon
Besançon
Bourges
Nevers
Dole
Bern
Autun
Beaune
N83
N81
Chalon-sur-Saône
Pontarlier
Châteauroux
SWITZERLAND
Tournus
Lausanne
Cluny
N20
N147
Montluçon
Genève
THE ALPS
N145
Vichy
Annecy
Riom
Limoges
Chamonix
Lyon
Albertville
Clermont-Ferrand
Val d'Isère
Chambéry
St-Étienne
N6
N89
N21
MASSIF CENTRAL
Grenoble
Turin
Brive-la-Gaillarde
le Puy
Briançon
Souillac
Aurillac
Valence
N9
N85
N75
N88
Montélimar
Gap
Cahors
ITALY
Villeneuve-sur-Lot
Orange
Montauban
Avignon
Albi
N113
Nîmes
Grasse
Monaco
Aix-en-Provence
Cannes
Nice
Toulouse
Castres
Montpellier
Arles
N117
Béziers
Sète
St-Raphaël
Marseille
St-Tropez
Carcassonne
Narbonne
Foix
Toulon
Golfe du Lion
Ax-les-Thermes
Perpignan
ANDORRA
Mediterranean Sea
TO CORSICA
A1
A2
A4
A5
A6
A7
A8
A9
A10
A11
A13
A25
A26
A31
A36
A38
A40
A41
A42
A47
A48
A50
A51
A61
A62
A71
A72
A83

International Student Travel Confederation, Herengracht 479, 1017 BS Amsterdam, The Netherlands (tel. 31 20 421 2800; fax 31 20 421 2810; http://www.istc.org; e-mail istcinfo@istc.org) The ISTC is a nonprofit confederation of student travel organizations that promotes and facilitates travel among students. Member organizations include International Student Rail Association (ISRA), Student Air Travel Association (SATA), ISIS Travel Insurance, and the International Association for Educational and Work Exchange Programs (IAEWEP).

Hunter Publishing, 300 Raritan Center Parkway, Edison, NJ 08818 (tel. (908) 225-1900; fax 417-0482). Extensive catalogue of travel books, guides, language tapes, and quality maps, among them *Charming Small Hotel Guide* for France (US$13).

Michelin Travel Publications, Michelin Tire Corporation, P.O. Box 19001, Greenville, SC 29602-9001 (tel. (800) 423-0485; fax (800) 378-7471); in France Michelin Services de Tourisme, 46, av. de Breteuil 75324 Paris, Cedex 07 (tel. 01 45 66 12 39); in England, Michelin Travel Publications, Michelin Tyre, The Edward Hyde Bldg., 38 Clarendon Rd., Watford, WD1 1SX (tel. (0192) 341 5000) publishes 3 lines of travel-related material: *Green Guides,* for sightseeing, maps, and itineraries; *Red Guides,* which rate hotels and restaurants; and detailed road maps.

Press and Information Division of the French Embassy, 4101 Reservoir Rd. NW, Washington, DC 20007 (tel. (202) 944-6060; fax (202) 944-6040; http:// www.info-france-usa.org; e-mail info@amb-wash.fr). Write for information about political, social, and economic aspects of France. The service also provides a bi-weekly newsletter, *News from France,* as well as *France Magazine,* a quarterly.

INTERNET RESOURCES

Along with everything else in the 90s, budget travel is moving rapidly into the information age. And with the growing user-friendliness of personal computers and internet technology, much of this information can be yours with the click of a mouse.

There are a number of ways to access the **Internet.** Most popular are commercial Internet providers, such as **America Online** (tel. (800) 827-6394) and **Compuserve** (tel. (800) 433-0389). The Internet can be used in many ways; the most useful to "'net-surfing" budget travelers are the World Wide Web and Usenet newsgroups.

Increasingly the Internet forum of choice, the **World Wide Web** provides its users with graphics and sound, as well as textual information. This and the huge proliferation of "web pages" (individual sites within the World Wide Web) have made the Web the most exciting of destinations on the Internet, though it has also made it the newest path from corporate advertisers to the minds of the masses; be sure to distinguish between what is good information and what is marketing. The introduction of **search engines** (services that search for web pages under specific subjects) has aided the search process. **Lycos** (http://a2z.lycos.com) and **Infoseek** (http://guide.infoseek.com) are the two of the most popular. **Yahoo!** is a slightly more organized search engine; check out its travel links at http://www.yahoo.com/Recreation/Travel. Other helpful sites for budget travel info on the Web include: **The CIA World Factbook** (http://www.odci.gov/cia/publications/95fact), which has tons of statistics on the country you want to visit. Check it out for an overview of a country's economy or an explanation of its government. **Dr. Memory's Favorite Travel Pages** (http://www.access.digex.net/~drmemory/cyber_travel.html) is a good place to start surfing. Dr. Memory has links to hundreds of different web pages of interest to travelers. **Le Coin des Francophones et autres Grenouilles** (http://www.cnam.fr/fr/welcome.html) provides useful info on French culture, history, and modern politics. **The Student and Budget Travel Guide** (http://asa.ugl.lib.umich.edu/chdocs/travel/travel-guide.html) is just what it sounds like.

Documents & Formalities

File all applications well in advance of your departure date; remember, you are relying on government agencies to complete these transactions. Plan ahead; most offices suggest that you apply in the off-season (Aug.-Dec.) for speedier service.

When you travel, always carry on your person two or more forms of identification, including at least one photo ID. A passport combined with a driver's license or birth certificate usually serves as adequate proof of your identity and citizenship. If you plan a longer stay, register your passport with the nearest embassy or consulate.

U.S. citizens seeking information about documents, formalities and travel abroad should request the booklet *Your Trip Abroad* (US$1.25) from the **Superintendent of Documents,** U.S. Government Printing Office, P.O. Box 371954, Pittsburgh, PA 15250-7954 (tel. (202) 512-1800; fax 512-2250).

FRENCH EMBASSIES AND CONSULATES

The French consulate in your home country can supply you with important legal information concerning your trip, arrange for visas, and direct you to a wealth of other information about tourism, education, and employment in France.

U.S.: Consulate General, 31 St. James Ave., Park Square Building, Suite #750, Boston, MA 02116 (tel. (617) 542-7374; fax 542-8054); **Visa Section,** (tel. (617) 542-7374; open 8am-noon). There are 12 branch offices across the U.S.; contact the Consulate General to locate the branch nearest you.

Canada: 1, Place Ville Mairie, 02601 Montréal, Québec 83B 4S3 (tel. (514) 878-4385); other consulates in Moncton, Québec City, Toronto, Edmonton and Vancouver. The French Embassy is in Ottawa.

U.K.: 21 Cromwell Rd., London SW7 2DQ (tel. (0171) 838 2000). **Visa Section,** 6A Cromwell Pl., London SW7 2EW (tel. (0891) 887 733).

Ireland: Consult the Consular Section within the French Embassy at 36 Ailesbury Road, Ballsbridge, Dublin 4 (tel. (01) 260 1666; fax (01) 283 0178).

Australia: 31 Market St., 26th fl., Sydney, NSW 2000 (tel. (02) 261 57 79; (02) 261 57 99 or (02) 261 40 66 for visa info). **New Zealanders** should address inquiries to this consulate or the Consular Section within the French Embassy (see above).

ENTRANCE REQUIREMENTS

Citizens of the U.S., Canada, the U.K., Ireland, Australia, New Zealand, and South Africa all need valid **passports** to enter France and to re-enter their own country. Travelers from most European countries, the U.S., Canada, and New Zealand do not require visas. All others, including Australians and those planning to stay more than three months, must obtain a visa from the French consulate in their home country. When you enter France, dress neatly and carry **proof of your financial independence,** such as a visa to the next country on your itinerary, an airplane ticket to depart, enough money to cover the cost of your living expenses, etc. Admission as a visitor does not include the right to work, which is authorized only by a work permit. Entering France to study requires a special visa, and immigration officers may want to see proof of acceptance from a school, proof that the course of study will take up most of your time in the country, and proof that you can support yourself.

PASSPORTS

Before you leave, photocopy the page of your passport that contains your photograph and identifying information, especially your passport number. Carry this photocopy in a safe place apart from your passport, and leave another copy at home. These measures will help prove your citizenship and facilitate the issuing of a new passport if you lose the original document. Carry an expired passport or an official copy of your birth certificate in your baggage separate from other documents.

If you do lose your passport, it may take weeks to process a replacement, and your new one may only be valid for a limited time. In addition, any visas stamped in your old passport will be irretrievably lost. If this happens, notify the local police and the nearest embassy or consulate of your home government. To expedite its replacement, you will need to know all information previously recorded and show identification and proof of citizenship. Some consulates can issue new passports within two days if you provide proof of citizenship. In an emergency, ask for immediate temporary traveling papers that will permit you to reenter your home country.

Your passport is a public document belonging to your nation's government. You may have to surrender it to a foreign government official, but if you don't get it back in a reasonable amount of time, inform the nearest mission of your home country.

United States US citizens may apply for a passport, valid for 10 years (five years if under 18) at any federal or state **courthouse** or **post office** authorized to accept passport applications, or at a **U.S. Passport Agency,** located in Boston, Chicago, Honolulu, Houston, Los Angeles, Miami, New Orleans, New York, Philadelphia, San Francisco, Seattle, Stamford, or Washington D.C. Refer to the "U.S. Government, State Department" section of the telephone directory, or call your local post office for addresses. Parents must apply in person for children under age 13. You must apply in person if this is your first passport, if you're under age 18, or if your current passport is more than 12 years old or was issued before your 18th birthday. You must submit the following: 1) proof of U.S. citizenship (a certified birth certificate, certification of naturalization or of citizenship, or a previous passport); 2) identification bearing your signature and either your photograph or physical description (e.g. an unexpired driver's license or passport, student ID card, or government ID card); and 3) two identical (2in. by 2in.) photographs with a white or off-white background taken within the last six months. It will cost US$65 (under 18 US$40). **Renew** your passport by mail or in person for US$55. Processing takes two to four weeks. Passport agencies offer **rush service** for a surcharge of US$30 if you have proof that you're departing within ten working days (e.g., an airplane ticket or itinerary). Abroad, a U.S. embassy or consulate can usually issue a new passport, given proof of citizenship. If your passport is lost or stolen in the U.S., report it in writing to Passport Services, U.S. Department of State, 111 19th St. NW, Washington DC, 20522-1705 or to the nearest passport agency. For more info, contact the U.S. Passport Information's **24-hour recorded message** (tel. (202) 647-0518).

Canada Application forms in English and French are available at all **passport offices, post offices,** and most **travel agencies.** Citizens may apply in person at any one of 28 regional Passport Offices across Canada. Travel agents can direct the applicant to the nearest location. Canadian citizens residing abroad should contact the nearest Canadian embassy or consulate. Along with the application form, a citizen must provide: 1) citizenship documentation (an original Canadian birth certificate, or a certificate of Canadian citizenship); 2) two identical passport photos taken within the last year; 3) any previous Canadian passport; and 4) a CDN$60 fee (paid in cash, money order, or certified check) to Passport Office, Ottawa, Ont. K1A OG3. The application and one of the photographs must be signed by an eligible guarantor (someone who has known the applicant for two years and whose profession falls into one of the categories listed on the application). Processing takes approximately five business days for in-person applications and three weeks for mailed ones. Children under 16 may be included on a parent's passport, though some countries require children to carry their own passports. A passport is valid for five years and is not renewable. If a passport is lost abroad, Canadians must be able to prove citizenship with another document. For additional info, call (800) 567-6868 (24hr.; from Canada only) or call the Passport Office at (819) 994-3500. In Metro Toronto, call (416) 973-3251. Montréalers should dial (514) 283-2152. Refer to the booklet *Bon Voyage, But...* for further help and a list of Canadian embassies and consulates abroad. It is available free of charge from any passport office.

Britain British citizens, British Dependent Territories citizens, British Nationals (overseas), and British Overseas citizens may apply for a **full passport.** For a full passport, valid for 10 years (five years if under 16), apply in person or by mail to a passport office, located in London, Liverpool, Newport, Peterborough, Glasgow, or

Belfast. The fee is UK£18. Children under 16 may be included on a parent's passport. Processing by mail usually takes four to six weeks. The London office offers same-day, walk-in rush service.

Ireland Citizens can apply for a passport by mail to either the Department of Foreign Affairs, Passport Office, Setanta Centre, Molesworth St., Dublin 2 (tel. (01) 671 16 33), or the Passport Office, 1A South Mall, Cork (tel. (021) 627 25 25). Obtain an application at a local Garda station or request one from a passport office. The new Passport Express Service offers a two week turn-around and is available through post offices for an extra IR£3. Passports cost IR£45 and are valid for 10 years. Citizens under 18 or over 65 can request a three-year passport that costs IR£10.

Australia Citizens must apply for a passport in person at a post office, a passport office, or an Australian diplomatic mission overseas. An appointment may be necessary. Passport offices are located in Adelaide, Brisbane, Canberra, Darwin, Hobart, Melbourne, Newcastle, Perth, and Sydney. A parent may file an application for a child who is under 18 and unmarried. Application fees are adjusted frequently. For more info, call toll-free (in Australia) 13 12 32.

New Zealand Application forms for passports are available in New Zealand from travel agents and Department of Internal Affairs Link Centres, and overseas from New Zealand embassies, high commissions, and consulates. Completed applications may be lodged at Link Centres and at overseas posts, or forwarded to the Passport Office, PO Box 10-526, Wellington, New Zealand. Processing time is 10 working days from receipt of a correctly completed application. An urgent passport service is also available. The application fee for an adult passport is NZ$80 in New Zealand, and NZ$130 overseas for applications lodged under the standard service.

South Africa Citizens can apply for a passport at any Home Affairs Office. Two photos, either a birth certificate or an identity book, and a $12 fee must accompany a completed application. South African passports remain valid for 10 years. For further information, contact the nearest Department of Home Affairs Office.

VISAS

A visa is an endorsement that a foreign government stamps into a passport; it allows the bearer to stay in that country for a specified purpose and period of time. Most visas cost US$10-70 and allow you to spend about a month in a country, within six months to a year from the date of issue. Visas are required of all visitors to France except those from EU member countries, the U.S., Canada, New Zealand, Andorra, Austria, the Czech Republic, Cyprus, Finland, Hungary, Iceland, Japan, the Republic of Korea, Liechtenstein, Malta, Monaco, Norway, Poland, San Marino, Sweden, and Switzerland. Note that Australia is absent from this list. A visa is required for anyone planning to stay more than three months. It must be obtained from the French consulate *in your home country.* In the U.S., for more information send for *Foreign Visa Requirements* (50¢) from the **Consumer Information Center,** Pueblo, CO 81009 (tel. (719) 948-3334), or contact the **Center for International Business and Travel (CIBT),** 25 West 43rd St. #1420, New York, NY 10036 (tel. (800) 925-2428 or (212) 575-2811). CIBT secures visas for travel to and from all countries. The service charge varies; the average cost for a U.S. citizen is US$50 per visa.

Requirements for a long-stay visa vary with the nature of the stay: work, study, or *au pair.* Apply to the nearest French consulate at least three months in advance. For a **student visa,** you must present a passport valid until at least 60 days after the date you plan to leave France, an application with references, a passport photo, a letter of admission from a French university or a study abroad program, a notarized guarantee of financial support for US$ 600 per month, and a fee which fluctuates according to the exchange rate (about US$ 60). To obtain a **work visa,** you must first obtain a work permit. After securing a job and a work contract, your French employer will obtain this permit for you and will forward it with a copy of your work contract to the consulate nearest you. After a medical checkup and completion of the application, the visa will be issued on your valid passport. Note, however, that it is illegal for foreign students to work during the school year, although they can receive permission from a *Direction départementale du travail et de la main-d'oeuvre étrangère* to work in summer (see below). For an *au pair* stay of more than three months, an **au pair's visa** is required and can be obtained by submission of a valid passport, two completed application forms, two passport photos, a fee (varies between US$15-25), a medical certificate of good health completed by a consulate-approved doctor, two copies of the *au pair's* work contract signed by the *au pair,* and proof of admission to a language school or university program.

In addition to securing a visa, if you are staying longer than 90 days in France for any reason, you must obtain a **carte de séjour** (residency permit) once in France. Report to the local *préfecture* of the *département..* You must present a valid passport stamped with a long-stay visa, a medical certificate, six (yes, six) application forms completed in French, six passport photos, a letter of financial guarantee, and, if you're under 18, proof of parental authorization. Be prepared to jump through hoops, bark like a dog, and stand in line, perhaps repeatedly. Bring your Proust.

CUSTOMS: ARRIVING IN FRANCE

Unless you plan to import a BMW or a barnyard beast, you will probably pass right through the customs barrier with minimal ado. Visitors have an allowance of what they can bring into France. Anything exceeding the allowance is charged a duty. All travelers must declare articles acquired abroad, but only the truly profligate budget traveler will have to pay. Record the serial numbers of expensive (especially foreign-made) items that will accompany you abroad. Have this list stamped by a customs office before you go; this will prevent your being taxed on items you already own. To avoid problems when you transport prescription drugs, mark bottles clearly and carry a copy of the prescription to show the customs officer.

CUSTOMS: GOING HOME

Upon returning home, you must declare certain items from abroad and pay a duty on the value of those articles that exceed the allowance established by that country's **customs** service. Holding onto receipts for purchases made abroad will help establish values when you return. It is wise to make a list, including serial numbers, of any valuables that you carry with you from home; if you register this list with customs before your departure and have an official stamp it, you will avoid import duty charges and ensure an easy passage upon your return. Be careful to document items manufactured abroad. Keep in mind that gifts purchased at duty-free shops abroad are not exempt from duty or sales tax at your point of return; "duty-free" merely means that you need not pay a tax in the country of purchase.

United States Citizens returning home may bring US$400 worth of accompanying goods duty-free and must pay a 10% tax on the next US$1000. You must declare all purchases, so have sales slips ready. Goods are considered duty-free if they are for personal or household use (this includes gifts) and cannot include more than 100 cigars, 200 cigarettes (1 carton), and 1L of wine or liquor. You must be over 21 to bring liquor into the U.S. If you mail home personal goods of U.S. origin, you can avoid duty charges by marking the package "American goods returned." For more information, consult the brochure *Know Before You Go,* available from the U.S. Customs Service, Box 7407, Washington DC 20044 (tel. (202) 927-6724).

Canada Citizens who remain abroad for at least one week may bring back up to CDN$500 worth of goods duty-free once per calendar year. Canadian citizens or residents who travel for a period between 48 hours and six days can bring back up to CDN$200 with the exception of tobacco and alcohol. You are permitted to ship goods except tobacco and alcohol home under this exemption as long as you declare them when you arrive. Citizens of legal age (which varies by province) may import in person up to 200 cigarettes, 50 cigars, 400g loose tobacco, 400 tobacco sticks, 1.14L wine or alcohol, and 24 355mL cans/bottles of beer; the value of these products is included in the CDN$500. For more information, write to Canadian Customs, 2265 St. Laurent Blvd., Ottawa, Ontario K1G 4K3 (tel. (613) 993-0534).

Britain Citizens or visitors arriving in the U.K. from outside the EU must declare any goods in excess of the following allowances: 200 cigarettes, 100 cigarillos, 50 cigars, or 250g tobacco; still table wine (2L); strong liqueurs over 22% volume (1L), or fortified or sparkling wine, other liqueurs (2L); perfume (60 cc/mL); toilet water (250 cc/mL); and UK£136 worth of all other goods including gifts and souvenirs. You must be over 17 to import liquor or tobacco. These allowances also apply to duty-free purchases within the EU, except for the last category, other goods, which then has an allowance of UK£71. Goods obtained duty and tax paid for personal use (regulated according to set guide levels) within the EU do not require any further customs duty. For more info about U.K. customs, contact Her Majesty's Customs and Excise, Custom House, Nettleton Road, Heathrow Airport, Hounslow, Middlesex TW6 2LA (tel. (018) 19 10 37 44; fax 19 10 37 65).

Ireland Citizens must declare everything in excess of IR£34 (IR£17 per traveler under 15 years of age) obtained outside the EU or duty- and tax-free in the EU above the following allowances: 200 cigarettes; 100 cigarillos; 50 cigars; or 250g tobacco; 1L liquor or 2L wine; 2L still wine; 50g perfume; and 250mL toilet water. Goods obtained duty and tax paid in another EU country up to a value of IR£460 (IR£115 per traveler under 15) will not be subject to additional customs duties. Travelers under 17 are not entitled to any allowance for tobacco or alcoholic products. For more information, contact The Revenue Commissioners, Dublin Castle (tel. (01) 679 27 77; fax 671 20 21; e-mail taxes@ior.ie; http://www.revenue.ie) or The Collector of Customs and Excise, The Custom House, Dublin 1.

Australia Citizens may import AUS$400 (under 18 AUS$200) of goods duty-free, in addition to the allowance of 1.125L alcohol and 250 cigarettes or 250g tobacco. You must be over 18 to import either of these. There is no limit to the amount of Australian and/or foreign cash that may be brought into or taken out of the country. However, amounts of AUS$5000 or more, or the equivalent in foreign currency, must be reported. All foodstuffs and animal products must be declared on arrival. For information, contact the Regional Director, Australian Customs Service, GPO Box 8, Sydney NSW 2001(tel. (02) 213 20 00; fax 213 40 00).

New Zealand Citizens may bring home up to NZ$700 worth of goods duty-free if they are intended for personal use or are unsolicited gifts. The concession is 200 cigarettes (1 carton) or 250g tobacco or 50 cigars or a combination of all three not to exceed 250g. You may also bring in 4.5L of beer or wine and 1.125L of liquor. Only travelers over 17 may bring tobacco or alcoholic beverages into the country. For more information, consult the *New Zealand Customs Guide for Travelers,* available from customs offices, or contact New Zealand Customs, 50 Anzac Ave., Box 29, Auckland (tel. (09) 377 35 20; fax 309 29 78).

South Africa Citizens may import duty-free: 400 cigarettes; 50 cigars; 250g tobacco; 2L wine; 1L of spirits; 250mL toilet water; and 50mL perfume; and other items up to a value of SAR500. Amounts exceeding this limit but under SAR10,000 are taxed at 20%. Items such as golf clubs and firearms require a duty higher than the

ESSENTIALS

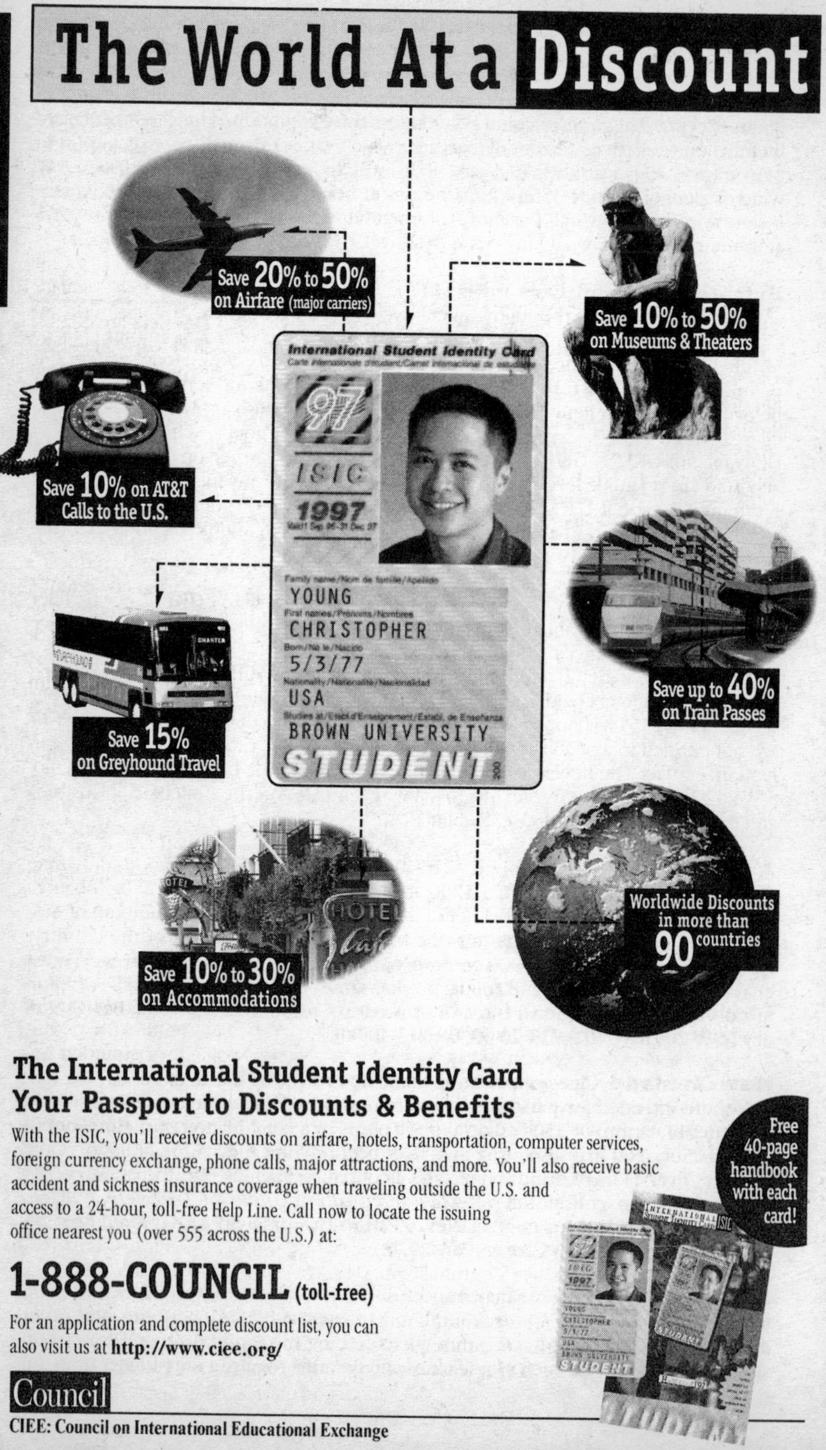
The World At a Discount
Save 20% to 50% on Airfare (major carriers)
Save 10% to 50% on Museums & Theaters
International Student Identity Card
97
ISIC
1997
YOUNG
CHRISTOPHER
5/3/77
USA
BROWN UNIVERSITY
STUDENT
Save 10% on AT&T Calls to the U.S.
Save up to 40% on Train Passes
Save 15% on Greyhound Travel
Save 10% to 30% on Accommodations
Worldwide Discounts in more than 90 countries
The International Student Identity Card
Your Passport to Discounts & Benefits
With the ISIC, you'll receive discounts on airfare, hotels, transportation, computer services, foreign currency exchange, phone calls, major attractions, and more. You'll also receive basic accident and sickness insurance coverage when traveling outside the U.S. and access to a 24-hour, toll-free Help Line. Call now to locate the issuing office nearest you (over 555 across the U.S.) at:
1-888-COUNCIL (toll-free)
For an application and complete discount list, you can also visit us at http://www.ciee.org/
Free 40-page handbook with each card!
Council
CIEE: Council on International Educational Exchange

standard 20%. Goods acquired abroad and sent to the Republic as unaccompanied baggage do not qualify for any allowances. You may not export or import South African bank notes in excess of SAR500. Persons who require specific information can address their inquiries to the Commissioner for Customs and Excise, Private Bag X47, Pretoria 0001. This agency distributes the pamphlet *South African Customs Information,* for visitors and residents who travel abroad. South Africans residing in the U.S. should contact the Embassy of South Africa, 3051 Massachusetts Ave., NW, Washington, D.C. 20008 (tel. (202) 232-4400; fax 244-9417) or the South African Home Annex, 3201 New Mexico Ave. #380 NW, Washington, D.C. 20016 (tel. (202) 966-1650).

YOUTH, STUDENT, & TEACHER IDENTIFICATION

In the world of budget travel, youth has its privileges. Younger travelers are eligible for discounts that make trips to far-flung destinations practical. Before you can get the discounts, you have to prove that you deserve them. The **International Student Identity Card (ISIC)** (US$19) is the most widely accepted form of student identification. Flashing this card can procure you discounts for sights, theaters, museums, accommodations, train, ferry, and airplane travel, and other services. Present the card wherever you go, and ask about discounts even when none are advertised. It also provides accident insurance of up to US$3000 with no daily limit. In addition, cardholders have access to a toll-free Traveler's Assistance hotline whose multilingual staff can provide help in medical, legal, and financial emergencies overseas.

Many student travel offices issue ISICs. When you apply for the card, request a copy of the *International Student Identity Card Handbook,* which lists by country some of the available discounts. You can also write to Council (p. 1) for a copy. The card is valid from September to December of the following year. Applicants must be at least 12 years old and degree-seeking students of a secondary or post-secondary school. The US$20 **International Teacher Identity Card (ITIC)** offers similar but limited discounts, as well as medical insurance coverage. For more info on these handy cards consult the organization's new web site (http://www.istc.org).

Federation of International Youth Travel Organizations (FIYTO) issues a discount card to travelers who are under 26 but not students. Known as the **GO25 Card,** this one-year card offers many of the same benefits as the ISIC, and most organizations that sell the ISIC also sell the GO25 Card. To apply, you will need a passport, valid driver's license, or copy of a birth certificate, and a passport-sized photo with your name printed on the back. The fee is US$16, CDN$15, or UK£5. For information, contact Council in the U.S. or FIYTO in Denmark.

DRIVING PERMITS AND INSURANCE

An **International Driving Permit** (IDP, a translation of your driver's license into nine languages) is required to drive in France. A valid driver's license from your home country must accompany the IDP. Most car rental agencies do not require the permit. It is a good idea to get one anyway, in case you're in an accident or stranded in a smaller town where the police may not read or speak English.

Your IDP must be issued in your own country before you depart. U.S. license holders can obtain an IDP (US$10), valid for one year, at any **American Automobile Association (AAA)** office or by writing to the main office, AAA Florida, Travel Agency Services Department, 1000 AAA Drive (mail stop 28), Heathrow, FL 32746-5080 (tel. (407) 444-4245; fax 444-4247).

Canadians can obtain an IDP (CDN$10) through any **Canadian Automobile Association (CAA)** branch office in Canada, or by writing to CAA Central Ontario, 60 Commerce Valley Drive East, Thornhill, Ontario L3T 7P9 (tel. (416) 221-4300).

Most credit cards cover standard insurance. If you rent, lease, or borrow a car, you will need a **green card,** or **International Insurance Certificate,** to prove that you have liability insurance. Obtain it through the car rental agency; most of them include coverage in their prices. If you lease a car, you can obtain a green card from the dealer. Some travel agents offer the card, and it may be available at the border. Verify whether your auto insurance applies abroad; even if it does, you will still need a green card to certify this to foreign officials. If you have a collision while in France, the accident will show up on your domestic records if you report it to your company. Rental agencies may require you to purchase theft insurance in some countries that they consider to have a high risk of auto theft. Ask your rental agency about each of your destination countries.

Money Matters

The old adage warns us that a love of money is at the root of all evil. For travelers, money—and its plastic and paper permutations—is often at the root of travel woes. Research as thoroughly as possible how your credit cards, ATM cards, and traveler's checks will work in France before your departure.

CURRENCY AND EXCHANGE

US$1 = 5.008F	**1F = US$0.200**
CDN$1 = 3.646F	**1F = CDN$0.274**
UK£1 = 7.776F	**1F = UK£0.129**
IR£1 = 8.076F	**1F = IR£.124**
AUS$1 = 3.729F	**1F = AUS$0.258**
NZ$1 = 3.317F	**1F = NZ$0.292**
SAR1 = 1.383F	**1F = SAR0.723**

A Note on Prices and Exchange Rates

The information in this book was researched in the summer of 1996. Since then, inflation will have raised most prices at least 10%. The exchange rates listed were compiled on August 2, 1996. Since rates fluctuate, confirm current rates before you go. The rate listed in the finance section of major newspapers is the bulk trading rate for currency. This is better than the rate you will find at banks and exchange offices, but is the rate you usually receive from ATM withdrawals.

CURRENCY AND EXCHANGE

If you stay in hostels and prepare your own food, expect to spend anywhere from 100-250F per person per day, depending on the local cost of living and your needs; transportation can increase these figures.

The basic unit of currency in France is the franc, divided into 100 centimes and issued in both coins and paper notes. It is more expensive to buy francs at home than in France, but converting some money before you go will allow you to zip through the airport while others languish in exchange lines. It's a good idea to bring enough French currency to last for the first 24-72 hours of a trip, depending on the day of the week you will be arriving. Check newspapers to get some idea of the standard rate of exchange.

Banks often offer good rates but usually charge commission. Large local or national banks such as the **Banque de France** have good rates and charge low commissions; however, individual banks determine their own exchange rates. A good rule of thumb is to go to banks or *bureaux de change* that have only a 5% margin between their buy and sell prices. Anything more, and they are making too much profit. Be sure that both prices are listed. Some post offices offer currency exchange for no commission and great rates. Avoid exchanging money at airports, train stations, hotels, or restaurants; their convenient hours and locations allow them to offer less-favorable exchange rates. Banks are often open only on weekdays; be sure to procure enough cash to carry you through weekends, holidays, and side trips in isolated areas. To minimize losses on commission, exchange large sums at one time, though never more than is safe to carry around. If you are using traveler's checks or bills, carry some in small denominations (US$50 or less), especially for times when you are forced to exchange money at less-than-stellar rates. Most banks will not exchange large bills (US$100 or equivalent) due to the proliferation of counterfeits.

TRAVELER'S CHECKS

Traveler's checks are one of the safest and least troublesome means of carrying funds. Several agencies and many banks sell them, usually at face value plus a 1% commission. (Members of the American Automobile Association can get American Express checks commission-free through AAA.) American Express and Visa are the most widely recognized, though other major checks work with almost equal ease. Keep in mind that in small towns traveler's checks are less readily accepted than in cities with large tourist industries. Nonetheless, there will probably be at least one place in every town where you can exchange them for francs. If you're ordering your checks, do so well in advance, especially if large sums are being requested.

Each agency provides refunds if your checks are lost or stolen, and many provide additional services. (Note that you may need a police report verifying their loss or theft.) To expedite the refund process in the event of check theft or loss, keep your check receipts separate from your checks and store them in a safe place or with a traveling companion; record check numbers when you cash them and leave a list of check numbers with someone at home; ask for a list of refund centers when you buy your checks. Keep a separate supply of cash or traveler's checks for emergencies. Be sure never to countersign your checks until you're prepared to cash them. Always bring your passport with you when you plan to use the checks.

While British and U.S. citizens can easily exchange their respective currencies for francs in France, Australians and Canadians may have more difficulty. Buying **French franc traveler's checks** eliminates the need for expensive multiple transactions (such as Canadian to U.S. dollars and then U.S. dollars to francs). Most banks will cash French franc traveler's checks commission-free (but be sure to ask *before* you give them your money). Depending on the changing value of the franc, you may gain or lose money by buying checks in francs in advance.

American Express: Call (800) 221-7282 in the U.S. and Canada; in the U.K. (0800) 52 13 13; in New Zealand (0800) 44 10 68; in Australia (008) 25 19 02. Elsewhere, call U.S. collect (801) 964-6665. American Express traveler's checks are available in francs. Checks can be purchased for a fee at American Express Travel Service Offices, banks, and American Automobile Association offices (AAA members can buy the checks commission-free). Cardmembers can also purchase checks at American Express Dispensers at Travel Service Offices at airports and by phone (tel. (800) ORDER-TC (673-3782)). You can also buy *Cheques for Two* which can be signed by either of two people traveling together. Request American Express booklet "Traveler's Companion," listing travel office addresses and stolen check hotlines. American Express offices **cash their checks** commission-free, although they generally offer worse rates than banks. Once you're in France, for refund of **stolen checks,** call toll-free 05 90 86 00 24hr.

Thomas Cook MasterCard: Call (800) 223-9920 in the U.S. and Canada; elsewhere call U.S. collect (609) 987-7300; from the U.K. call (0800) 62 21 01 free or (1733) 50 29 95 collect or (1733) 31 89 50 collect. Offers checks in francs. Try buying the checks at a Thomas Cook office for potentially lower commissions.

Visa: Call (800) 227-6811 in the U.S.; in the U.K. (0800) 89 54 92; from anywhere else call the U.K. collect (1733) 31 89 49. Call the above numbers and give them your zip code to be directed to the nearest office to purchase traveler's checks. Any Visa traveler's checks can be reported lost at the Visa number.

CREDIT CARDS

Although they can be sources of frustration, credit cards are exceptionally useful. Major credit cards—**Visa** and **MasterCard** are the most welcomed—instantly extract cash advances from associated banks and teller machines throughout France in local currency. This can be a great bargain, since credit card companies get the wholesale exchange rate, which is generally 5% better than the retail rate used by banks. However, you will be charged hefty interest rates if you don't pay off the bill quickly, so be careful when using this service. Sundry banks in France, indicated by the sticker *CB/ VISA ou EC*, will allow you to withdraw money at a teller with a Visa or MasterCard (the equivalents of the British Access and Barclay cards). Additionally, Visa and MasterCard cash machines proliferate in France. **American Express** cards also work in ATMs at **Crédit Lyonnais** banks, as well as at AmEx offices and major airports. All such machines require a four-digit **Personal Identification Number (PIN),** which credit cards in the United States do not always carry. You must ask American Express, MasterCard, or Visa to assign you one before you leave; without this PIN, you will be unable to withdraw cash with your credit card abroad. Keep in mind that MasterCard and Visa have different names elsewhere ("EuroCard" or "Access" for MasterCard and "Carte Bleue" or "Barclaycard" for Visa); some cashiers may not know this until they check their manuals.

Credit cards are also invaluable in an emergency—an unexpected hospital bill or ticket home or the loss of traveler's checks—which may leave you temporarily without other resources. Furthermore, credit cards offer an array of other services, from insurance to emergency assistance—these depend completely, however, on the issuer. Some even cover car rental collision insurance.

American Express (tel. (800) CASH-NOW (528-4800)) has a hefty annual fee (US$55) but offers a number of services. AmEx cardholders can cash personal checks at AmEx offices abroad. U.S. Assist, a 24-hr. hotline offering medical and legal assistance in emergencies, is also available (tel. (800) 554-2639 in U.S. and Canada; from abroad call U.S. collect (301) 214-8228). Cardholders can also take advantage of the American Express Travel Service; benefits include assistance in changing airline, hotel, and car rental reservations, sending mailgrams and international cables, and holding your mail at one of the more than 1700 AmEx offices around the world.

MasterCard (tel. (800) 999-0454) and **Visa** (tel. (800) 336-8472) are issued in cooperation with individual banks and some other organizations.

If you **lose your credit card**, call your company immediately. The Paris numbers are: **MasterCard,** 01 45 67 84 84 (customer service at 01 43 23 41 52); **Visa,** 01 42 77 11 90; **American Express,** 01 47 77 72 00.

CASH CARDS

Cash cards—popularly called **ATM** (Automated Teller Machine) cards—are widespread in Europe. Depending on the system that your home bank uses, you will probably be able to access your own personal bank account whenever you're in need of funds. ATMs get the same wholesale exchange rate as credit cards. Despite these perks, do some research before relying too heavily on automation. There is often a limit on the amount of money you can withdraw per day, and computer network failures are not uncommon. Be sure to memorize your PIN code in numeral form since machines abroad often don't have letters on the keys. Also, if your PIN is longer than four digits, ask your bank whether the first four digits will work, or whether you need a new number.

The two international money networks you should know about are **Cirrus** (U.S. tel. (800) 4-CIRRUS (424-7787)) and **PLUS** (U.S. tel. (800) 843-7587)). Throughout France, **Crédit Mutuel** and **Crédit Agricole** teller machines are on the Cirrus network. PLUS, while not quite so extensive, works in most Visa ATMs. Institutions that support PLUS are: **Crédit Commercial de France, Banque Populaire, Union de Banque à Paris, Point Argent, Banque Nationale de Paris, Crédit du Nord, Gie Osiris,** and the national post office ATM system, **La Poste.** In the U.S. call (800) 847-2399 for the nearest bank selling them; elsewhere call U.S. collect (410) 581-9091. It may be a good idea to carry two cards, one linked to each network. That way you're covered regardless of which system covers your particular area.

A new option for getting money from ATMs is **Visa TravelMoney,** a system whereby you pay the sum of your choice to a bank and receive in return a cash card with that amount coded onto it. You choose a PIN when you buy the card and can call a 24-hr. assistance line if it is lost, making the "money" more easily replaced than traveler's checks. You'll pay about 2% commission, but your card will work in any Visa ATM, you'll get a good exchange rate. and you'll avoid a transaction fee.

GETTING MONEY FROM HOME

One of the easiest ways to get money from home is to bring an **American Express** card. AmEx allows cardholders to draw cash from their checking accounts at any of its major offices and many of its representatives' offices, up to US$1000 every 21 days (no service charge, no interest). AmEx also offers Express Cash, with over 100,000 ATMs located in airports, hotels, banks, and shopping areas around the world. Express Cash withdrawals are automatically debited from the cardmember's specified bank account or line of credit. Cardholders may withdraw up to US$1000 in a seven day period. There is a 2% transaction fee for each cash withdrawal with a US $2.50 minimum. To enroll in Express Cash, cardmembers may call (800) CASH-NOW (227-4669). Outside the U.S. call collect (904) 565-7875.

Money can be wired abroad through international money transfer services operated by **Western Union** (tel (800) 325-6000). Credit card transfers do not work overseas; you must send cash. The rates for sending cash are generally US$10 cheaper than with a credit card. The money is usually available in the country you're sending it to within an hour, although in some cases this may vary.

Another way to send money abroad is in cash via **Federal Express;** this has both advantages and disadvantages. On the minus side, it is illegal and also involves an element of risk. Because Federal Express will not deliver *poste restante,* you must remain at an address for a day or two to wait for the money's arrival. It is reasonably reliable, avoids transmission fees and taxes, and is doable with a minimum of fuss.

In emergencies, U.S. citizens can have money sent via the State Department's **Overseas Citizens Service, American Citizens Services**, Consular Affairs, Public Affairs Staff, Room 4831, U.S. Department of States, Washington, DC 20520 (tel. (202) 647-5225; at night and on Sundays and holidays (tel. (202) 647-4000; fax 647-3000 ; http://www.travel.state.gov). For US$15, the State Department will forward money within hours to the nearest consular office, which will then disburse it according to instructions. The office serves only Americans in the direst of straits.

VALUE-ADDED TAX

The Value-Added Tax (abbreviated TVA, in France) is a varying sales tax levied especially in the European Union. The French rate is 18.6% on all goods except books, food, and medicine. Luxury items such as video cassettes, watches, jewelry, and cameras are taxed 33%. If you spend more than 2000F (4200F for EU members) in a particular store, you can participate in a complex, over-the-counter export program for foreign shoppers that exempts you from paying TVA. Ask the store for an official *formulaire de détaxe pour l'exportation* (detax invoice) and a stamped envelope. At the border, show the invoices and your purchases to the French customs officials, who will stamp the invoices. If you're at an airport, look for the window labeled *douane de détaxe,* and be sure to budget at least an hour for the intricacies of the French bureaucracy. On a train, find an official (they won't find you) or get off at a station close to the border. Then send a copy back to the vendor. With this official TVA-exempt proof, they will refund the agreed amount. The refunds are sent to your bank account, a process which may take as long as six months.

TIPPING AND BARGAINING

Service is almost always included at meals in restaurant and cafés; look for the phrase *service compris* on the menu. If service is not included, then tip 15-20%. Even when service is included, it is polite to leave extra *monnaie* (change) at a café, bistro, restaurant, or bar—one franc for a glass of wine, several francs for a meal. You should tip hairdressers, cabbies, and others 15%. Ushers in theaters are not shy about letting you know how much to tip; signs are often posted instructing patrons to leave a 2F tip.

Museum and tour guides may expect 5-10F after a tour. If you stay in a hotel for some time, you should tip the chambermaid, bellhop, and anyone else who has assisted you, usually a minimum of 10F each.

Safety and Security

Safety should be every traveler's first priority. Self-preservation, as the safety-conscious Frenchman Jean-Jacques Rousseau once argued, is essential to life; it is particularly crucial to travel. Protect yourself and your belongings with vigilance.

PERSONAL SAFETY

While France is a relatively safe and stable country, tourists are particularly vulnerable to crime for two reasons: they often carry large amounts of cash and they are not as street savvy as locals. To avoid such unwanted attention, try to **blend in** as much as possible. Respecting local customs (in many cases, this means dressing more conservatively) can often discourage would-be hecklers. Walking directly into a cafe to check your map beats checking it on a street corner. Look over your map before leaving the hotel so that you know where you are going.

When you get to a place where you'll be spending some time, find out about unsafe areas from tourist information or from the manager of your hotel or hostel. If you are traveling alone, be sure that someone at home knows your itinerary. Never say that you're traveling alone. Carry a small **whistle** to scare off attackers or attract attention. Jot down the number of the police if you'll be in town for a couple days.

When walking at night, you should turn day-time precautions into mandates. Stick to busy, well-lit streets and avoid dark alleyways. Do not attempt to cross through parks, parking lots or any other large, deserted areas. Whenever possible, *Let's Go* warns of unsafe neighborhoods and areas, but only your eyes can tell you for sure if you've wandered into one; buildings in disrepair, vacant lots, and general desertedness are all bad signs. A district can change character drastically in the course of a single block. Many notoriously dangerous districts have safe sections; look for children playing, women walking in the open, and other signs of an active community. If you feel uncomfortable, leave as quickly as you can.

Making **photocopies** of important documents will allow you to replace them if they are stolen or lost. Carry one copy separate from the documents and leave another at home. If you are using a **car,** learn local driving signals. Park your vehicle in a well-traveled area. Learn your route before you hit the road; some roads have poor shoulders, few gas stations, and (depending on where you go) loose animals.

Sleeping in your car is a dangerous way to get your rest. If your car breaks down, wait for the police to assist you. If you must sleep in your car, do so as close to a police station or a 24-hour service station as possible. Sleeping out in the open can be more dangerous—camping is recommended only in official, supervised campsites or in wilderness backcountry. *Let's Go* does not recommend **hitchhiking,** particularly for women—see **By Thumb** on page 47.

There is no sure-fire set of precautions that will protect you from all of the situations you might encounter when you travel. A good self-defense course will give you concrete ways to react to different types of aggression, but it might cost you more money than your trip. **Model Mugging,** a national organization, offers a comprehensive course on self-defense. Contact Lynn S. Auerbach on the East Coast (617) 232-7900); Alice Tibits in the Midwest (612) 645-6189); and Cori Couture on the West Coast (415) 592-7300). Course prices vary from US$400-500. Community colleges frequently offer self-defense courses at more affordable prices.

FINANCIAL SECURITY

Among the more colorful aspects of cities like Paris or Marseille are **con artists.** Con artists and hustlers often work in groups, and children, unfortunately, are among the most effective at the game. Be watchful for groups of children who might distract you while others seize your belongings. A firm "no," or *"laissez-moi tranquille"* (LAY-say mwah trahn-KEEL) should communicate that you are no dupe. Do not respond or make eye contact, walk quickly away, and keep a tight grip on your belongings. Contact the police if a hustler seems particularly insistent or aggressive.

Don't put money in a wallet in your back pocket. Never count your money in public and carry as little as possible. If you carry a purse, buy a sturdy one with a secure clasp and carry it crosswise on the side, away from the street with the clasp against you. As far as packs are concerned, buy some small combination padlocks which slip through the two zippers, securing the pack shut. A **money belt** is the best way to carry cash; you can buy one at most camping supply stores. The best combination of convenience and invulnerability is the nylon, zippered pouch with belt that should sit inside the waist of your pants or skirt. A **neck pouch** is equally safe, although far less accessible. Refrain from pulling out your neck pouch in public; if you must, be very discreet. Avoid keeping anything precious in a fanny-pack (even if it's worn on your stomach); your valuables will be highly visible and easy to steal. Making **photocopies** of important documents will allow you to recover them in case they are lost or filched. Carry one copy separate from the documents and leave another copy at home. Keep some money separate from the rest to use in an emergency or in case of theft. Label every piece of luggage both inside and out.

Be particularly watchful of your belongings on **buses**. Don't check baggage on trains—especially if you're switching lines—and don't trust anyone to "watch your bag." **Trains** are easy spots for thieving. Professionals wait for tourists to fall asleep and then carry off everything they can. When traveling in pairs, sleep in shifts; when alone, never stay in an empty car. Keep important documents on your person and try to sleep on top bunks with your bags stored above you (if not in bed with you).

Let's Go lists **locker** availability in hostels and train stations, but you'll often need your own padlock. Lockers are useful if you plan on sleeping outdoors or don't want to lug everything with you, but don't store valuables in them. Never leave your belongings unattended; even the most demure-looking hostel (convents included) may be a den of thieves. If you feel unsafe, look for places with either a curfew or a night attendant. When possible, keep expensive jewelry, valuables, and anything you couldn't bear to part with at home. Keep valuables on your person if you're staying in low-budget hotels where someone else may have a key. If you take your **car** on your travels, conceal any valuables or luggage in the trunk.

Travel Assistance International by Worldwide Assistance Services, Inc. provides its members with a 24-hr. hotline for emergencies and referrals. Their year-long frequent traveler package (US $226) includes medical and travel insurance, financial assistance, and help in replacing lost documents. Call (800) 821-2828 or (202) 828-5894); fax (202) 828-5896), or write them at 1133 15th St. NW, Suite 400, Washington, D.C. 20005-2710. More complete information on safety while traveling may be found in *Americans Traveling Abroad: What You Should Know Before You Go,* available at Barnes and Noble booksellers across the country.

DRUGS AND ALCOHOL

Possession of drugs in France can end your vacation abruptly; convicted offenders can expect a jail sentence and fines. Never bring any illegal drugs across a border. Prescription drugs, particularly insulin, syringes, or narcotics, should be accompanied by a statement from a doctor and left in original labeled containers. In France, police may stop and search anyone on the street—no reason is required. It is not unknown for a pusher to increase profits by first selling drugs to a tourist and then turning that person in to the authorities for a reward. If you are arrested, your home country's consulate can visit you, provide a list of attorneys, and inform family and friends, but it cannot get you out of jail. Write the Bureau of Consular Affairs, Public Affairs #5807, Department of State, Washington, DC 20520 (tel. (202) 647-1488) for more information and the pamphlet *Travel Warning on Drugs Abroad.*

Health

Common sense is the simplest prescription for good health while you travel: eat well, drink and sleep enough, and don't overexert yourself. Drinking lots of fluids can often prevent dehydration and constipation, and wearing sturdy shoes and socks and using talcum powder can help keep your feet dry. To minimize the effects of jet lag, "reset" your body's clock by adopting the time of your destination upon arrival. Most travelers feel used to a new time zone after two or three days.

BEFORE YOU GO

For minor health problems, bring a compact **first-aid kit,** including bandages, ibuprofen or pain-killers, antibiotic cream, a thermometer, a Swiss Army knife with tweezers, moleskin, a decongestant for colds, motion sickness remedy, medicine for diarrhea or stomach problems, sunscreen, insect repellent, and burn ointment.

In your passport, write the names of any people you wish to have contacted in case of a medical emergency and list any allergies or medical conditions that might affect treatment. If you wear glasses or contact lenses, carry an extra prescription and pair of glasses. Bring extra solution, enzyme tablets, and eyedrops—the price for lens solution can be exorbitant in France, and French brands with familiar names may have different formulations. For heat disinfection, you'll need outlet and low-watt voltage adapters. Allergy sufferers should find out if their conditions are likely to be aggravated in the regions they plan to visit and obtain a full supply of any necessary medication before the trip, since matching a prescription to a foreign equivalent is not always easy, safe, or possible. Carry up-to-date, legible prescriptions or a statement from your doctor, especially if you use insulin, a syringe, or a narcotic. While traveling, be sure to keep all medication with you in carry-on luggage.

Take a look at your **immunization** records before you go; some countries require visitors to carry vaccination certificates. For up-to-date information about which vaccinations are recommended for France, try these resources: The **United States Centers for Disease Control and Prevention,** Traveler's Health, 1600 Clifton Rd. NE, Atlanta, GA 30333, a good source of information for travelers around the world, maintains an international travelers' hotline (tel. (404) 332-4559; fax 332-4565; http://www.cdc.gov). The CDC publishes the booklet "Health Information for International Travelers" (US$14), a global rundown of disease, immunization, and general health advice. The **United States State Department** compiles Consular Information Sheets on health, entry requirements, and other issues for all countries of the world. For quick information on travel warnings, call the **Overseas Citizens' Services** (tel. (202) 647-5225). To receive the same Consular Information sheets by fax, dial (202) 647-3000 directly from a fax machine and follow the recorded instructions. For written info, send a self-addressed, stamped envelope to the Overseas Citizens' Services, Bureau of Consular Affairs, Room 4811, U.S. Department of State, Washington, DC 20520. If you are HIV-positive, call (202) 647-1488 for country-specific entry requirements or write to the Bureau of Consular Affairs, CA/P/PA, Department of State, Washington, DC 20520.

Those with medical conditions (e.g. diabetes, allergies to antibiotics, epilepsy) may want to obtain a stainless steel **Medic Alert** identification tag (US$35 the first year, and $15 annually thereafter), which identifies the disease and gives a 24-hour collect-call information number. Contact Medic Alert at (800) 825-3785, or write to Medic Alert Foundation, 2323 Colorado Avenue, Turlock, CA 95382.

If you are concerned about being able to access medical support while traveling, contact one of these two services: **Global Emergency Medical Services (GEMS)** provides 24-hour international medical assistance and support coordinated through registered nurses who have on-line access to your medical information, your primary physician, and a worldwide network of screened, credentialed English-speaking doctors and hospitals. Subscribers also receive a pocket-sized, personal medical record that contains vital information in case of emergencies. For more information call

(800) 860-1111; fax (770) 475-0058, or write: 2001 Westside Drive, Suite 120, Alpharetta, GA 30201. The **International Association for Medical Assistance to Travelers (IAMAT)** offers a membership ID card, a directory of English-speaking doctors around the world who treat members for a set fee schedule (US$55 for office visits, US$75 house calls, US$95 night/holiday house calls), and detailed charts on immunization requirements, climate, and sanitation. Membership is free, though donations are appreciated and used for further research. Contact chapters in the **U.S.,** 417 Center St., Lewiston, NY 14092 (tel. (716) 754-4883; fax (519) 836-3412; e-mail iamat@sentex.net; http://www.sentex.net/iamat), **Canada,** 40 Regal Road, Guelph, Ontario, N1K 1B5 (tel. (519) 836-0102) or 1287 St. Clair Avenue West, Toronto, M6E 1B8 (tel. (416) 652-0137; fax (519) 836-3412), **New Zealand,** P.O. Box 5049, Christchurch 5.

ON-THE-ROAD AILMENTS

For medical emergencies in France, dial 15. At night and on Sundays, the local *commissariat de police* (tel. 17) will supply the address of the nearest open *pharmacie de garde* (late-night drugstore) and that of a doctor on duty. The *pharmacie de garde* is also noted in newspapers and on the doors of pharmacies in town. French pharmacies almost invariably sport a distinctive bright green cross in the shape of the Red Cross logo. For an ambulance, call the medical emergency number (15) or look in the phone book under *ambulances municipales*. *Let's Go* lists emergency numbers at the end of most Practical Information listings.

French pharmacies are good places to turn for mild problems; they offer medical advice and suggest over-the-counter medication. Keep in mind, however, that they can be very expensive. Look for items such as sunscreen, tampons, and common medicines in supermarkets, which tend to offer more reasonable prices.

When traveling, protect yourself against the dangers of the sun and heat—France can get unbearably hot in the summer. Common sense helps in preventing **heat exhaustion:** relax in hot weather, drink lots of non-alcoholic fluids, and lie down indoors. Continuous heat stress can eventually lead to **heatstroke,** characterized by a rising body temperature, severe headache, and cessation of sweating. Wear a hat, sunglasses, and a longsleeve shirt to avoid heatstroke. Victims must be cooled off with wet towels and taken to a doctor as soon as possible.

Always drink enough liquids to keep your urine clear. Alcoholic beverages are dehydrating, as are coffee, strong tea, and caffeinated sodas. If you'll be sweating a lot, be sure to eat enough salty food to prevent electrolyte depletion, which causes severe headaches. Less debilitating, but still dangerous, is **sunburn.** If you're prone to sunburn, bring sunscreen with you, and apply it liberally and often to avoid burns and risk of skin cancer. If you get sunburned, drink more fluids than usual.

Overexposure to cold brings the risk of **hypothermia.** Warning signs are easy to detect: body temperature drops rapidly, resulting in an inability to produce body heat. You may shiver, have poor coordination, feel exhausted, have slurred speech, feel sleepy, hallucinate, or suffer amnesia. *Do not let hypothermia victims fall asleep* if they are in the advanced stages—their body temperature will drop more, and if they lose consciousness they may die. To avoid hypothermia, keep dry and stay out of the wind. In wet weather, wool and most synthetics will keep you warm but most other fabric, especially cotton, will make you colder. Dress in layers, and watch for **frostbite** when the temperature is below freezing. Look for skin that has turned white and cold, and if you find frostbite do not rub the skin. Drink warm beverages, get dry, and slowly warm the area with dry fabric or steady body contact.

Before exerting themselves, those traveling at **high altitudes** must allow their bodies a couple of days to adjust to lower oxygen levels in the air. Also be careful about alcohol—many foreign brews and liquors pack more punch, and at high altitudes where the air has less oxygen, any alcohol will do you in quickly.

Food poisoning can spoil any trip. Watch out for perishable food carried for hours in a hot backpack. All food, including seafood, dairy products, and fresh produce, is normally safe in France. Tap water is safe (though your body may need to take time to adjust to it), but water from train faucets is normally not for consumption; if a sign reads *eau non potable,* do not drink the water or use it to brush your teeth.

CRISIS LINES

When disaster strikes, helplines can be a happy and welcome recourse. Certain helplines, such as **SOS Amitié,** a friendship line, **SOS Suicide,** a suicide prevention line, and **SOS Racisme,** a hotline which addresses racial issues, have bases throughout the country. *Let's Go* lists them in the Practical Information section of many cities. The following lines are toll-free and national.

Drug Information: Drogue Info Service, tel. 0 800 23 13 13. Provides counseling on issues relating to drug abuse.

Rape Crisis SOS Viol, tel. 0 800 05 95 95. Provides counseling, medical and legal advice, and referrals. Open Mon.-Fri. 10 am-6pm.

AIDS Information: SIDA Info Service, tel. 0 800 36 66 36. Provides information on AIDS in French and English. Open 24hr.

BIRTH CONTROL AND ABORTION

Reliable **contraceptive devices** may be difficult to find while traveling. To obtain **condoms** in France, visit a pharmacy and say, "*Je voudrais une boîte de préservatifs*" (zhuh-voo-DRAY oon BWAHT duh pray-ZEHR-va-TEEF) A box of condoms costs about 10F. The French branch of the International Planned Parenthood Federation, the **Mouvement Français pour le Planning Familial (MFPF)** in Paris (tel. 02 48 07 29 10), can provide more information.

Women on the **pill** should bring enough to allow for possible loss or extended stays and should bring a prescription, since forms of the pill vary a good deal. If you use a **diaphragm**, be sure that you have enough contraceptive jelly on hand.

Abortion is legal in France, where the abortion pill, **RU-486,** was pioneered. If you are in France and want information on **abortion,** contact your embassy; they can provide you with a list of ob/gyn doctors who perform abortions. For general information on contraception, condoms, and abortion worldwide, contact the **International Planned Parenthood Federation,** European Regional Office, Regent's College Inner Circle, Regent's Park, London NW1 4NS (tel. (0171) 486-0741, fax (0171) 487-7950).

AIDS, HIV, STDS

Acquired Immune Deficiency Syndrome (AIDS, SIDA in French) is a global problem. The World Health Organization estimates that 13 million people are infected with the HIV virus. Over 90% of adults newly infected with HIV acquired their infection through heterosexual sex; women represent 50% of all new HIV infections.

The easiest mode of HIV transmission is through direct blood to blood contact with an HIV-positive person; *never* share intravenous drug, tattooing, or other needles. The most common mode of transmission is sexual intercourse. Health professionals recommend the use of latex condoms. For more information on AIDS, call the **U.S. Center for Disease Control's** 24-hour hotline at (800) 342-2437 (Spanish tel. (800) 344-7332, daily 8am-2am). In Europe, write to the **World Health Organization,** attn: Global Program on AIDS, 20 Avenue Appia, 1211 Geneva 27, Switzerland (tel. (22) 791-2111), for statistical material on AIDS.

Sexually transmitted diseases (STDs) such as gonorrhea, chlamydia, genital warts, syphilis, and herpes are far more prevalent than HIV. It's a wise idea to *look* at your partner's genitals before you have sex. If anything seems amiss, that should be a warning signal. When having sex, condoms may protect you from certain STDs, but oral or even tactile contact can lead to transmission.

Insurance

Beware of buying unnecessary travel coverage—your regular policies may well extend to many travel-related accidents. **Medical insurance** (especially university policies) often cover costs incurred abroad; check with your provider. Canadians are protected by their home province's health insurance plan for up to 90 days after leaving the country; check with the provincial Ministry of Health or Health Plan Headquarters for details. Australia has Reciprocal Health Care Agreements (RHCAs) with several countries; when traveling in these nations Australians are entitled to many of the services that they would receive at home. The Commonwealth Department of Human Services and Health can provide more information. Your **homeowners' insurance** (or your family's coverage) often covers theft during travel. Homeowners are generally covered against loss of travel documents (passport, plane ticket, railpass, etc.) up to $500.

The **ISIC** and **ITIC** provide US$3000 worth of accident and illness insurance and US$100 per day up to 60 days of hospitalization. They also offer up to US$1000 for accidental death or dismemberment, up to US$25,000 if injured due to an airline, and up to US$25,000 for emergency evacuation due to an illness. The cards also give access to a toll-free Traveler's Assistance hotline (in the U.S. and Canada tel. (800) 626-2427; elsewhere call the U.S. collect (713) 267-2525) whose multilingual staff can provide help in emergencies overseas. **Council** offers the inexpensive Trip-Safe plan with options covering medical treatment and hospitalization, accidents, baggage loss, and even charter flights missed due to illness; **STA** offers a more expensive, more comprehensive plan. **American Express** cardholders receive automatic car rental and travel accident insurance (excluding collision coverage) on flight purchases made with the card. Call customer service at (800) 528-4800.

Remember that insurance companies usually require a copy of the police report for thefts, or evidence of having paid medical expenses (doctor's statements, receipts) before they will honor a claim, and they may have time limits on filing for reimbursement. Always carry policy numbers and proof of insurance. Check with each insurance carrier for specific restrictions and policies.

Access America, 6600 West Broad St., PO Box 11188, Richmond, VA 23230 (tel. (800) 284-8300; fax (804) 673-1491). 24-hr. hotline.

Globalcare Travel Insurance, 220 Broadway Lynnfield, MA 01940 (tel. (800) 821-2488; fax (617) 592-7720); e-mail global@nebc.mv.com; http://www.nebc.mv.com/globalcare). Complete medical, legal, emergency, and travel-related services. Benefits for trip cancellation and interruption.

Travel Guard International, 1145 Clark St., Stevens Point, WI 54481 (tel. (800) 826-1300 or (715) 345-0505; fax (715) 345-0525). Comprehensive insurance programs starting at US$44. Programs cover trip cancellation and interruption, bankruptcy and financial default, lost luggage, medical coverage abroad, emergency assistance, accidental death. 24-hr. hotline.

Alternatives to Tourism

STUDY

Foreign study programs vary tremendously in expense, academic quality, living conditions, degree of contact with local students, and exposure to the local culture and language. Most American undergraduates enroll in programs sponsored by U.S. universities, and many colleges give academic information about study abroad programs. Local libraries and bookstores are also helpful sources for current information on study abroad, and the Internet has a study abroad website at **www.studyabroad.com/liteimage.html**.

If you choose your program well, study in France could be one of the most exciting experiences you'll ever have. For free pamphlets on various fields of study in France,

contact the **Cultural Services of the French Embassy.** Many American undergraduates enroll in programs sponsored by domestic universities, and many colleges give info on study abroad. Your university may also allow you to enroll in programs sponsored by other colleges. Consider enrolling directly in the French universities—by far the cheapest and most authentic (if least organized) way to go. Decide whether you want a homestay program or the greater independence (but less individual attention) afforded by life in a dormitory or your own apartment. For additional information regarding study abroad, contact any of the following:

American Field Service (AFS), 220 E. 42nd St., 3rd floor, New York, NY 10017 (tel. (800) 237-4636, (800) 876-2376; fax (212) 949-9379; http//www.afs.org/usa). AFS offers summer, semester, and year-long homestay international exchange programs for high school students and graduating high school seniors and short-term service projects for adults. Financial aid available.

American Institute for Foreign Study, College Division, 102 Greenwich Ave., Greenwich, CT 06830 (tel. (800) 727-2437; http://www.aifs.org) for high school students, (800) 888-2247). Organizes year, semester, quarter, and summer programs for study in foreign universities. Open to adults. Scholarships available. Also offers *au pair* for those aged 18-26.

Central College Abroad, Office of International Education, 812 University, Pella, IA 50219 (tel. (800) 831-3629; fax (515) 628-5316; e-mail admissions@central.edu). Offers semester- and year-long study abroad programs in Paris. US$20 application fee. Scholarships available. Applicants must be at least 18 years old, have completed their freshman year of college, and have a minimum 2.5 GPA.

Council sponsors over 40 study abroad programs throughout the world. Contact them for more information (see **Travel Organizations,** above).

Institute of International Education (IIE), 809 United Nations Plaza, New York, NY 10017-3580 (tel. (212) 984-5413 for recorded information; fax 984-5358). For book orders: IIE Books, Institute of International Education, PO Box 371, Annapolis Junction, MD 20701 (tel. (800) 445-0443; fax (301) 953-2838; e-mail iiebooks@iie.org.). A nonprofit, international and cultural exchange agency. IIE's library of study abroad resources is open to the public Tues.-Thurs. 11am-3:45pm. Publishes *Academic Year Abroad* (US$43 plus US$4 shipping) detailing over 2300 semester- and year-long programs worldwide and *Vacation Study Abroad* (US$37 plus US$4 shipping) which lists over 1800 short-term, summer, and language school programs. Write for a list of publications.

Language Partners International, White Birch Rd., Putnam Valley, NY 10579 (tel. (800) 444-3924 or (914) 526-2299; fax 528-9187) is a language exchange program for those age 21 years and over. One-to 4-week homestay programs are offered (up to 14 days, US$950; 15-28 days, US$1350). Includes room and board, teaching materials, processing fees and organizational assistance. Opportunities to host visitors from same countries in USA.

Open Door Student Exchange, 839 Stewart Ave., Suite D, Garden City, NY 11530 (tel. (800) 454-6736 or (516) 745-6232; fax 745-6233). High school exchange program in over 35 countries. Provides homestay and educational experiences in summer, semester and academic-year programs.

World Learning, Inc., Summer Abroad, P.O. Box 676, Brattleboro, VT 05302 (tel. (800) 345-2929 or (802) 257-7751; http://www.worldlearning.org). Founded in 1932 as The Experiment in International Living, it offers high school programs in France as well as language-training programs with elective homestays. Programs are 3-5 weeks long. Positions as group leaders are also available.

LANGUAGE SCHOOLS

Language instruction is a booming business in France; programs are run by foreign universities, independent international or local organizations, and divisions of French universities. The **tourist office** in Paris has a list of language schools. Make sure the program you choose matches your age and commitment to study; some cater to businesspeople, others to preteens. Ask to speak to former participants.

Alliance Française, Ecole Internationale de Langue et de Civilisation Françaises, 101, bd. Raspail, 75006 Paris or 75270 Paris Cedex 06 (tel. 01 45 44 38 28; fax 01 45 44 89 42; e-mail info@paris.alliancefrancaise.fr; http://www.paris.alliancefrancaise.fr; M.Notre-Dame-des-Champs). French courses at all levels starting from US$250.

Cours de Civilisation Française de la Sorbonne, 47, rue des Ecoles, 75005 Paris (tel. 01 40 46 22 11; fax 01 40 46 32 29). Academic-year course can be taken by the semester; four-, six-, eight-, and eleven-week summer programs with civilization lectures and language classes offered at all levels. You can take the Cours de Civilisation through the **American Institute for Foreign Study (AIFS),** 102 Greenwich Ave., Greenwich, CT 06830 (tel. (800) 727-2437), which arranges accommodations and meals in Paris.

Eurocentres, 101 N. Union St. #300, Alexandria, VA 22314 (tel. (800) 648-4809; fax (703) 684-1495); http://www.clark.net/pub/eurocent/home.html) or Eurocentres, Head Office, Seestrasse 247, CH-8038 Zurich, Switzerland (tel. (01) 485 50 40; fax 481 61 24). Coordinates language programs and homestays for college students (Paris, La Rochelle, Amboise, Lausanne, Neuchâtel). In Paris at 13, passage Dauphine, F-75006 (tel. 01 43 25 81 40; fax 46 34 65 34). Programs cost about US$500-5000 and last from 2 weeks to 3 months. Financial aid is available.

FRENCH UNIVERSITIES

If your French is already extremely competent, direct enrollment in a French university can be more rewarding than a language or civilization class filled with Americans and Australians. It can also be up to three or four times cheaper than an American university program, though it can be harder to receive academic credit at your home university. After 1968, the **Université de Paris** split into ten isolated universities, each occupying a different site and offering a different range of fields. The centuries-old Sorbonne, now the Université de Paris IV, devotes itself to the humanities. For a more experimental approach, try one of the more modern universities. Each of them requires at least a *baccalauréat* degree or its equivalent (British A-levels or two years of college in the United States) for admission. Contact the cultural services office at the nearest French consulate. Start this well ahead of time and expect confusion—the bureaucracy of the French educational system is notorious.

As a student at a French university, you will receive a student card *(carte d'étudiant)* from your school upon presentation of your residency permit and a receipt for your university fees. In addition to standard student benefits, many additional benefits available to students in France are administered by the **Centre Régional des Oeuvres Universitaires et Scolaires (CROUS).** Founded in 1955 to improve the living and working conditions of students of each academy, this division of the Oeuvres Universitaires welcomes foreign students and can be of great help in answering your questions. The regional center for Paris is at 39, av. Georges-Bernanos, 75005 Paris or 75231 Paris Cedex 05 (tel. 01 40 51 36 00; RER Port-Royal; fax 01 40 51 36 99). CROUS also publishes the brochure *Le CROUS et Moi,* which lists addresses and information on every aspect of student life in Paris. Pick up the helpful guidebook *Je vais en France,* in French or English, free from any French embassy.

WORK

There's no better way to submerge yourself in a foreign culture than to become part of its economy. To work in France, you need both a **work permit** and a **work visa**. With the exception of *au pair* jobs, it is illegal for foreign students to hold full-time jobs during the school year. Students registered at French universities can get work permits for the summer with a valid visa, a student card from a French university, and proof of a job. After spending one academic year in France, Americans with a valid student *carte de séjour* can find part-time work if they will be enrolled at a French university again in the fall. Check the fact sheet *Employment in France for Students,* put out by the Cultural Services of the French Embassy (see page 1).

If you are a full-time student at a U.S. university, one easy way to get a job abroad is through work permit programs run by the **Council on International Educations Exchange (Council)** and its member organizations (see Travel Organizations, above). For a US$225 application fee, Council can procure three- to six-month work permits (and a handbook to help you find work and housing) for France. French positions require evidence of language skill.

Many books list work-abroad opportunities. In order to avoid scams from fraudulent employment agencies that demand large fees and provide no results, educate yourself using publications from the following sources:

Addison-Wesley, Jacob Way, Reading, MA 01867 (tel. (800) 822-6339). Published *International Jobs: Where They Are, How to Get Them* in 1993-1994 (US$16).

Surrey Books, 230 E. Ohio St., Chicago, IL 60611(tel. (800) 326-4430; fax (312) 751-7330) publishes *How to Get a Job in Europe: The Insider's Guide.* Includes info on the Baltics, Turkey, and France, among others.

Check help-wanted columns in French newspapers, especially *Le Monde, Le Figaro,* and the English-language *International Herald Tribune.* The best tips on jobs for foreigners come from other travelers, so be alert and inquisitive. Ask at cafés, restaurants, and hotels. Be aware of your rights as an employee; should a crafty national try to refuse to pay you at the end of the season, it'll help if you have a written confirmation of your agreement. Youth hostels frequently provide room and board to travelers willing to help run the place.

You may want to stop by the **American Church in Paris,** 65, quai d'Orsay, 7ème (tel. 01 47 05 07 99), which posts a bulletin board full of job and housing opportunities targeting Americans abroad. It also holds *France-USA Contacts,* a weekly circular filled with classifieds. Those with ambition and an up-to-date resume in both French and English should stop by the **American Chamber of Commerce in France,** 21, av. George V, 1st floor, 8ème 75008 Paris (tel. 01 40 73 89 90; M. George V or Alma Marceau), an association of American businesses in France. Your resume will be kept on file for two months and placed at the disposal of French and American companies. Chamber of Commerce membership directories may be purchased at the Paris office for about US$110. Otherwise, browse through the office's copy (library open Tues. and Thurs. 10am-12:30pm; admission 50F). The **Agence Nationale Pour l'Emploi (ANPE),** 4, impasse d'Antin, 8ème Paris (tel. 01 43 59 62 63; M. Franklin D. Roosevelt), has specific information on employment. You can also visit the **Centre d'Information et de Documentation Jeunesse (CIDJ),** 101, quai Branly, 15ème Paris (tel. 01 44 49 12 00; fax 01 40 65 02 61; e-mail charbo@worldnet.net), a government-run information clearinghouse on every imaginable practical concern for young people, including education, resumes, employment, careers, long-term accommodations, camping, touring, and sports (open Mon.-Sat. 10am-6pm). Part-time job listings are posted at 9am on the bulletin boards outside. Of particular interest are pamphlets on university enrollment for foreign students (ref. 1.63212 and 1.633); courses, jobs, and *au pair* positions for foreigners (ref. 5.5701-5.577); concerns and associations related to handicapped visitors and general tourism in France (ref. 7.51-7.53). Consult these pamphlets for free in the reading room or buy a copy of the pertinent ones for 10F. First pick up a free brochure entitled *Les publications du CIDJ,* which lists the holdings and their reference numbers.

Several programs offer practical experience to people with technical and business skills. The **International Association for the Exchange of Students for Technical Experience (IAESTE)** program, a division of the Association for International Practical Training (AIPT), is an internship exchange program for science, architecture, engineering, and math students who have completed at least two years at an accredited four-year institution. There is a non-refundable US$50 fee. Apply to 10400 Little Patuxent Parkway, #250, Columbia, MD 21044-3510 (tel. (410) 997-3068 or 3069). Applications are due December 10 for summer placement. If none of the above suggestions appeals to you, you may want to enlist in the French Foreign Legion *(La Légion étrangère);* the number in Paris is 01 45 51 48 50.

Au pair

Au pair positions are reserved primarily for single women aged 18 to 30 with some knowledge of French; a few men are also employed. The *au pair* cares for children and does light housework five or six hours each day for a French family while taking courses at a school for foreign students or at a French university. Talking with children can be a great way to improve your French, but looking after them may be extremely strenuous. Make sure you know in advance what the family expects of you. *Au pair* positions usually last six to 18 months; during the summer the contract can be as short as one to three months, but you may not be able to take courses. You'll receive room, board, and a small monthly stipend. In addition, the following *au pair* agencies can help you find work as a nanny in a foreign country.

InterExchange, 161 Sixth Avenue, New York, NY 10013 (tel. (212) 924-0446; fax 924-0575). Provides information in pamphlet form on international work programs and *au pair* positions.

Childcare International, Ltd., Trafalgar House, Grenville Place, London NW7 3SA (tel. (0181) 959 36 11 or 906 31 16; fax 906 34 61; e-mail office@childint.demon.co.uk; http://www.ipi.co.uk/childint). Member of the International *Au Pair* Association. UK£60 application fee.

L'Accueil Familial des Jeunes Etrangers, 23, rue du Cherche-Midi, 75006 Paris (tel. 01 42 22 50 34; fax 01 45 44 60 48; M. Sèvres-Babylone), which arranges 10-month *au pair* jobs beginning in September. They have a placement fee of 700F and will help you switch families if you are not happy at the initial location.

Teaching English

Securing a position will require patience and legwork; teaching English abroad has become exceedingly popular. Professional English-teaching positions are harder to get; most European schools require at least a bachelor's degree and training in teaching English as a foreign language.

Office of Overseas Schools, A/OS Room 245, SA-29, Department of State, Washington, DC 20522-2902 (tel. (703) 875-7800). Keeps a list of schools abroad and agencies that arrange placement for Americans to teach abroad.

International Schools Services, PO Box 5910, Princeton, NJ 08543 (tel. (609) 452-0990) publishes a free newsletter, *NewsLinks;* call or write to get on the mailing list. Its Educational Staffing Department, that coordinates placement of teachers, publishes *Your Passport to Teaching and Administrative Opportunities Abroad.* The *ISS Directory of Overseas Schools* (US$34.95) is also helpful.

VOLUNTEERING

The Archaeological Institute of America, 656 Beacon Street, Boston, MA 02215-2010 (tel. (617) 353-9361; fax (617) 353-6550), puts out the *Archaeological Fieldwork Opportunities Bulletin* (US$11 non-members) which lists over 250 field sites throughout the world. This can be purchased from Kendall/Hunt Publishing, 4050 Westmark Drive, Dubuque, Iowa 52002 (tel. (800) 228-0810).

Club du Vieux Manoir, 10, rue de la Cossonnerie, 75001 Paris (tel.45 08 80 40; fax 42 21 38 79), works to protect the environment and restore churches, castles, fortresses, and other historical French monuments. The club offers summer- and year-long programs. Anyone 15 or over is eligible, and the application fee is 90F.

Compagnons Bâtisseurs, Secrétariat International, Sud-Ouest Résidence, 2 rue Claude-Bertholet, 81100 Castres (tel. 63 72 59 64; fax 63 72 59 81), an international volunteer association, renovates and converts local buildings into facilities for the economically underprivileged and those with mental and physical disabilities. Terms run two to three weeks, June to Oct.; apply two months early.

Council (see **Travel Organizations,** above) offers 2- to 4-week environmental or community service projects in over 30 countries around the globe through its Voluntary Services Department (US$250-750 placement fee). Participants must be at least 18 years old.

REMPART, 1 rue des Guillemites, 75004 Paris (tel. 42 71 96 55; fax 42 71 73 00) works to protect the environment and restore churches, castles, and historical monuments. The association offers summer- and year-long programs. Anyone 15 or over is eligible. Programs cost about 40F per day (plus a 220F insurance fee).

Volunteers for Peace, 43 Tiffany Rd., Belmont, VT 05730 (tel. (802) 259-2759; fax 259-2922; e-mail vfp@vermontel.com; http://www.vermontel.com/~vfp/home.html). A non-profit organization that arranges for speedy placement in workcamps in Europe. Most complete and up-to-date listings provided in the annual *International Workcamp Directory* (US$12). Registration fee US$175. Some workcamps are open to 16 and 17 year olds for US$200. Free newsletter.

Willing Workers on Organic Farms (WWOOF) releases the names of organic farmers who offer room and board in exchange for help on the farm. Include an international postal reply coupon with your request. Contact: WWOOF, Postfach 615, CH-9001 St. Gallen, Switzerland (e-mail fairtours@gn.apc.org) Wwith a wwittle wwillingness, wwone can wwork wwonders.

Specific Concerns

WOMEN TRAVELERS

Women exploring on their own face additional safety concerns. Consider staying in hostels offering single rooms that lock from the inside or in religious organizations that offer rooms for women only; avoid any hostel with "communal" showers. Stick to centrally located accommodations and avoid late-night treks or metro rides. Hitching is never safe for lone women, or even for two women traveling together. Choose train compartments occupied by other women or couples; ask the conductor to put together a women-only compartment if she doesn't offer to do so first.

When in a foreign country, look as if you know where you're going (even when you don't) and consider approaching women or couples for directions if you're lost or feel uncomfortable. In general, dress conservatively. If you spend time in cities, you may be harassed no matter how you're dressed. Women in France may feel beset by tenacious followers, especially in the south. Exercise reasonable caution without feeling that you must avoid all local men. Your best answer to verbal harassment is no answer at all. Memorize emergency numbers and always carry a télécarte for the phone. *Let's Go* lists emergency numbers (including rape crisis lines) in the Practical Information listings of most cities. Carry a whistle and don't hesitate to use it. Seek out a police officer if you are being harassed. In crowds, you may be pinched or squeezed by oversexed slimeballs; wearing a wedding band may help prevent such incidents. Feigning deafness, sitting motionless and staring at the ground will do a world of good that no reaction will ever achieve.

For general information, contact the **National Organization for Women (NOW),** which boasts branches across the country that can refer women travelers to rape crisis centers and counseling services, and provide lists of feminist events. Main offices include 22 W. 21st St., 7th Fl., **New York,** NY 10010 (tel. (212) 260-4422); 1000 16th St. NW, 7th Fl., **Washington, DC** 20004 (tel. (202) 331-0066); and 3543 18th St., **San Francisco,** CA 94110 (tel. (415) 861-8960).

Directory of Women's Media is available from the National Council for Research on Women, 530 Broadway, 10th Floor, New York, NY 10012 (tel. (212) 274-0730; fax 274-0821. The publication lists women's publishers, bookstores, theaters, and news organizations (mail orders, $30).

A Journey of One's Own, by Thalia Zepatos, (Eighth Mountain Press US$17). The latest thing on the market includes a specific and manageable bibliography of books and resources and metes out excellent advice.

Women Travel: Adventures, Advice & Experience by Miranda Davies and Natania Jansz (Penguin, US$13). Info on specific foreign countries plus a decent bibliography and resource index. The sequel, *More Women Travel,* is $15.

OLDER TRAVELERS

Senior citizens are eligible for a wide range of discounts on transportation, museums, movies, theaters, concerts, restaurants, and accommodations. If you don't see a senior citizen price listed, ask and you may be delightfully surprised.

AARP (American Association of Retired Persons), 601 E St., NW, Washington, DC 20049 (202) 434-2277). Members 50 and over receive benefits and services including discounts on lodging, car rental, and sight-seeing. Annual fee US$8 per couple; lifetime membership US$75.

Elderhostel, 75 Federal St., 3rd Fl., Boston, MA 02110-1941 (tel. (617) 426-7788, fax 426-8351; www at http://www.elderhostel.org). For those 55 or over (spouse of any age). Programs at colleges, universities, and other learning centers in over 50 countries on varied subjects lasting one to four weeks.

Gateway Books, 2023 Clemens Road, Oakland, CA 94602 (tel. (510) 530-0299, credit card orders (800) 669-0773; fax (510) 530-0497; e-mail donmerwin@aol.com; http://www.hway.com/gateway/). Publishes *Europe the European Way: A Traveler's Guide to Living Affordably in the World's Great Cities* (US $14) and *Adventures Abroad* (US$13), which offer general hints for the budget-conscious senior considering a long stay or retiring abroad.

National Council of Senior Citizens, 1331 F St. NW, Washington, DC 20004 (202-347-8800). Memberships are US$12 a year, US$30 for three years, or US$150 for a lifetime. Individual or couple can receive hotel and auto rental discounts, a senior citizen newspaper, use of a discount travel agency, supplemental Medicare insurance (if you're over 65), and a mail-order prescription drug service.

BISEXUAL, GAY, AND LESBIAN TRAVELERS

Gay life continues to be rather discreet outside Paris, with more openness in Nice, Lyon, Marseille, Toulouse, and Nantes. Indispensable to the bisexual, gay, or lesbian traveler in France is the encyclopedic *Guide Gai 1997,* that lists hotels, clubs, restaurants, and support groups across the country (look for it at newsstands and bookstores). **Les Mots à la Bouche,** 6, rue Ste-Croix de la Bretonnerie, 75004 Paris (tel. 01 42 78 88 30) carries the city's most extensive collection of gay and lesbian literature including novels, essays, books on art, and magazines in French, English, German, and Italian. This book lists gay centers in the Practical Information section of many cities. For more general travel information, consult the following guides:

Are You Two...Together? A Gay and Lesbian Travel Guide to Europe. A travel guide with anecdotes and tips for gays and lesbians traveling in Europe. Includes overviews of regional laws relating to gays and lesbians, lists of gay/lesbian organizations, and establishments catering to, friendly to, or indifferent to gays and lesbians. Available in bookstores. Random House, $18.

Ferrari Guides, PO Box 37887, Phoenix, AZ 85069 (tel. (602) 863-2408; fax 439-3952; e-mail ferrari@q-net.com). Gay and lesbian travel guides: *Ferrari Guides' Gay Travel A to Z* (US$16), *Ferrari Guides' Men's Travel in Your Pocket* (US$14), *Ferrari Guides' Women's Travel in Your Pocket* (US$14), *Ferrari Guides' Inn Places* (US$16), *Ferrari Guides' Paris for Gays & Lesbians* (Fall 1996). Available in bookstores or by mail order (postage/handling US$4.50 for the first item, US$1 for each additional item mailed within the US).

Gay Europe (Perigee Books, US$14). A gay guide providing a quick look at gay life in countries throughout Europe, including restaurants, clubs, and beaches. Intros to each country cover laws and gay-friendliness. Available in bookstores.

Spartacus International Gay Guides (US$32.95), published by Bruno Gmunder, Postfach 110729, D-10837 Berlin, Germany (tel. (615) 00 30; fax (615) 91 34). Lists bars, restaurants, hotels, and bookstores around the world catering to gays. Lists homosexuality laws and international hotlines for gays.

Women Going Places (Inland Book Company, US$14). An international women's guide emphasizing women-owned enterprises, geared toward lesbians.

DISABLED TRAVELERS

Countries vary in their general accessibility to travelers with disabilities. Those with disabilities should inform airlines and hotels of their disabilities when making arrangements for travel; some time may be needed to prepare special accommodations. Call ahead to restaurants, hotels, parks, and other facilities to find out about the existence of ramps, the widths of doors, the dimensions of elevators, etc.

Arrange transportation well in advance to ensure a smooth trip. If you give sufficient notice, some major car rental agencies offer hand-controlled vehicles at select locations. Rail is probably the most convenient form of travel in Europe. The French national railroad offers wheelchair compartments on all TGV (high speed) and Corail trains. Guide dog owners should inquire as to the specific quarantine policies of each destination country. At the very least, they will need to provide a certificate of immunization against rabies. The following organizations provide info or publications that might be of assistance:

American Foundation for the Blind, 11 Penn Plaza, New York, NY 10011 (tel. (212) 502-7600), open Mon.-Fri. 8:30am-4:30pm. Provides information and services for the visually impaired.

L'Association des Paralysées de France, Délégation de Paris, 22 rue de Père Guérin, 75013 Paris (tel. 01 44 16 83 37). Publishes Où ferons-nous étape? (70F), which lists French hotels and motels accessible to persons with disabilities.

Directions Unlimited, 720 N. Bedford Rd., Bedford Hills, NY 10507 (tel. (800) 533-5343; in NY (914) 241-1700; fax 241-0243). Specializes in arranging individual and group vacations, tours, and cruises for the physically disabled.

The Guided Tour Inc., Elkins Park House, Suite 114B, 7900 Old York Road, Elkins Park, PA 19027-2339 (tel. (800) 783-5841 or (215) 782-1370; fax 635-2637). Organizes travel programs for persons with developmental and physical challenges.

Mobility International, USA (MIUSA), P.O. Box 10767, Eugene, OR 97440 (tel. (514) 343-1284 voice and TDD; fax 343-6812). International Headquarters in Brussels, rue de Manchester 25 Brussels, Belgium, B-1070 (tel. (322) 410 6297; fax 410 6874). Info on travel programs, work camps, accommodations, access guides, and organized tours for those with physical disabilities. Membership US$25 per year, newsletter US$15. Sells the expanded *A World of Options: A Guide to International Educational Exchange, Community Service, and Travel for Persons with Disabilities* (US$14, nonmembers US$16). In addition, MIUSA offers courses that teach strategies helpful for travelers with disabilities.

Twin Peaks Press, PO Box 129, Vancouver, WA 98666-0129 (tel. (360) 694-2462, orders (800) 637-2256; fax (360) 696-3210). Publishers of *Travel for the Disabled,* which provides travel tips, lists of tourist attractions, and advice on other resources for disabled travelers ($20). Also publishes *Directory for Travel Agencies of the Disabled* ($20), *Wheelchair Vagabond* ($15), and *Directory of Accessible Van Rentals* ($10). Postage $3 for first book, $1.50 for each additional book.

VEGETARIAN AND KOSHER TRAVELERS

Vegetarians will have trouble eating cheaply in restaurants, since *menus à prix fixe* almost always feature meat or fish. Ordering a salad may prove cheaper (if you don't eat eggs, beware of green salads with eggs in them). *Viande* means red meat. If you don't eat other animal products like pork, chicken, fish, eggs, or dairy products, you should clearly state this to the server. Try eating at Tunisian, Moroccan, Indian, Vietnamese, and Chinese restaurants; such establishments often offer couscous or rice and hearty vegetable platters. Although the natural foods movement began in Europe, American-style health food merchandising has not caught on outside of cities, and you may have to search long and hard for tofu and tahini. Health food stores, called *diététiques* or *maisons de régime,* are expensive. Health food products are referred to as *produits diététiques* and can be found in large supermarkets.

Let's Go often notes restaurants with good vegetarian selections in city listings. For more, contact the **North American Vegetarian Society,** P.O. Box 72, Dolgeville, NY 13329 (518) 568-7970 for info about travel-related publications, such as *Transformative Adventures,* a guide to vacations and retreats (US$15). Membership in the society is US$20; family membership is US$26, and members receive a ten percent discount on all publications.

Kosher food certainly exists in France, which has one of Western Europe's largest Jewish populations, but tracking it down may prove difficult. It can be hard to find a kosher restaurant or deli in rural regions, but they are present in larger cities. In Paris, kosher delis and restaurants abound in the *3ème* and *4ème* *arrondissements,* particularly on *rue des Rosiers* and *rue des Ecouffes*. Travelers who keep kosher should contact synagogues in larger cities for information on kosher restaurants. If you are strict in your observance, consider preparing your own food on the road.

The European Vegetarian Guide to Restaurants and Hotels ($13.95, plus $1.75 shipping) at Vegetarian Times Bookshelf (tel. (800) 435-9610, orders only).

The International Vegetarian Travel Guide (UK£2) was last published in 1991. Order copies from the Vegetarian Society of the UK (VSUK), Parkdale, Dunham Rd., Altringham, Cheshire WA14 4QG (tel. (0161) 928 07 93). VSUK also publishes *The European Vegetarian Guide to Hotels and Restaurants.* US$12.

The Jewish Travel Guide (US$12, postage US$1.75) lists synagogues, kosher restaurants, and Jewish institutions in over 80 countries. Available from Ballantine-Mitchell Publishers, Newbury House 890-900, Eastern Ave., Newbury Park, Ilford, Essex, U.K. IG2 7HH (tel. (0181) 599 88 66; fax 599 09 84). It is available in the U.S. from Sepher-Hermon Press, 1265 46th St., Brooklyn, NY 11219 (tel. (718) 972-9010; $13.95 plus $2.50 shipping).

Packing

Plan according to the type of travel (multi-city backpacking tour, week-long stay in one place, etc.) and the high and low temperatures in the area you will be visiting. If you don't pack lightly, your back and wallet will suffer. The larger your pack, the more cumbersome it is to store. Before you go, pack your bag, strap it on, and imagine yourself walking on hot asphalt for the next two hours. A general rule is to lay out only what you absolutely need, then take half the clothes and twice the money.

LUGGAGE

Backpack: If you plan to cover most of your itinerary by foot, the unbeatable baggage is a sturdy backpack. Some convert into more normal-looking suitcases. In general, **internal-frame** packs are easier to carry and more efficient for general traveling purposes. If you'll be doing extensive hiking, you may want to consider an **external-frame** pack, which offers added support and distributes weight better. In any case, get a pack with a strong, padded hip belt to transfer weight from your shoulders to your hips. Quality packs cost anywhere from US$150 to US$420.

Suitcase/trunk/other large or heavy luggage: Fine if you plan to live in one or two cities and explore from there, but a bad idea if you're going to be moving around a lot. If you do decide that it best suits your needs, make sure it has wheels and consider how much it weighs even when empty.

Daypack, rucksack, or courier bag: Bringing a smaller bag in addition to your pack or suitcase allows you to leave your big bag in the hotel while you go sight-seeing. More importantly, it can be used as an airplane carry-on: keep the absolute bare essentials with you to avoid the lost-luggage blues.

Moneybelt or neck pouch: Guard your money, passport, railpass, and other important articles in either one of these, and keep it with you *at all times.* Money belts and neck pouches are available at any good camping store. (See Safety and Security, page 20) for more information on protecting you and your valuables.

CLOTHING AND FOOTWEAR

Clothing: Packing lightly does not mean dressing badly. When choosing your travel wardrobe, aim for versatility and comfort, and avoid fabrics that wrinkle easily (to test a fabric, hold it tightly in your fist for twenty seconds).

Walking shoes: Not a place to cut corners. Well-cushioned **sneakers** are good for walking, though you may want to consider a good water-proofed pair of **hiking boots.** A double pair of socks—light silk or polypropylene inside and thick wool outside—will cushion feet, keep them dry, and help prevent blisters. Bring a pair of flip-flops for protection against the foliage and fungi that inhabit some hostel showers. Talcum powder in your shoes and on your feet can prevent sores, and moleskin is great for blisters. Whatever kind of shoes you choose, break them in before you leave.

Rain gear: Essential in France. A waterproof jacket and a backpack cover will take care of you and your stuff at a moment's notice. Gore-Tex® is a miracle fabric that's both waterproof and breathable. Avoid cotton as outer-wear, especially if you will be in the outdoors a lot, because it is useless if wet.

MISCELLANEOUS

Only Noah had a complete list. However, you will find the following items valuable: resealable plastic bags (for food, shampoo and other spillables); alarm clock; water-proof matches; sun hat; moleskin (for blisters); needle and thread; safety pins; sunglasses; a personal stereo with headphones; pocketknife; string (makeshift clothesline and lashing material); towel; padlock; whistle; rubber bands; flashlight; cold-water soap; earplugs; insect repellant; electrical tape (for patching tears); clothespins; maps and phrasebooks; tweezers; garbage bags; sunscreen; vitamins. It is always a good idea to bring along a **first-aid kit.**

Sleepsacks: If planning to stay in **youth hostels,** make the requisite sleepsack yourself (instead of paying the linen charge). Fold a full size sheet in half the long way, then sew it closed along the open long side and one of the short sides.

Washing clothes: *Let's Go* attempts to provide information on laundromats in the Practical Information listings for each city, but sometimes it may be in your best interest just to use a sink. Bring a small bar or tube of detergent soap, a soft squash ball to stop up the sink, and a travel clothes line.

Electric current: In most European countries, electricity is 220 volts AC, enough to fry any 110V North American appliance. Visit a hardware store for an adapter (which changes the shape of the plug) and a converter (which changes the voltage). Don't make the mistake of using only an adapter (unless appliance instructions explicitly state otherwise), or you'll melt your radio.

GETTING THERE

Budget Travel Agencies

The organizations below offer youth fares on air and train travel, sell student ID cards, railpasses, and hosteling cards, and provide useful information. *Let's Go* also lists budget travel services in the Practical Information section of many cities.

Campus Travel, 52 Grosvenor Gardens, London SW1W 0AG (http://www.campus-travel.co.uk.) Student and youth fares on plane, train, boat, and bus travel. Discount and ID cards for youths, travel insurance for students and those under 35. Telephone booking service: in Europe call (0171) 730 3402; in North America call (0171) 730 2101; worldwide call (0171) 730 8111; in Manchester call (0161) 273 1721; in Scotland (0131) 668 3303.

Council Travel (http://www.ciee.org/cts/ctshome.htm), the travel division of Council, is a full-service travel agency specializing in youth and budget travel. They offer railpasses, discount airfares, hosteling cards, guidebooks, budget tours, travel gear, and student (ISIC), youth (GO25), and teacher (ITIC) identity cards. U.S. offices include: Emory Village, 1561 N. Decatur Rd., **Atlanta,** GA 30307 (tel. (404) 377-9997); 2000 Guadalupe, **Austin,** TX 78705 (tel. (512) 472-4931); 273 Newbury St., **Boston,** MA 02116 (tel. (617) 266-1926); 1138 13th St., **Boulder,** CO 80302 (tel. (303) 447-8101); 1153 N. Dearborn, **Chicago,** IL 60610 (tel. (312) 951-0585); 10904 Lindbrook Dr., **Los Angeles,** CA 90024 (tel. (310) 208-3551); 1501 University Ave. SE, **Minneapolis,** MN 55414 (tel. (612) 379-2323); 205 E. 42nd St., **New York,** NY 10017 (tel. (212) 822-2700); 953 Garnet Ave., **San Diego,** CA 92109 (tel. (619) 270-6401); 530 Bush St., **San Francisco,** CA 94108 (tel. (415) 421-3473); 4311½ University Way, **Seattle,** WA 98105 (tel. (206) 632-2448); 3300 M St. NW, **Washington, D.C.** 20007 (tel. (202) 337-6464). **For U.S. cities not listed,** call (800) 2-COUNCIL (226-8624). Also 28A Poland St. (Oxford Circus), **London,** W1V 3DB (tel. (0171) 437 7767).

Council Charter: 205 E. 42nd St., New York, NY 10017 (tel. (212) 661-0311; fax (212) 972-0194). Offers a combination of inexpensive charter and scheduled airfares from a variety of U.S. gateways to most major European destinations. One-way fares and open jaws (fly into one city and out of another) are available.

Let's Go Travel, Harvard Student Agencies, 67 Mt. Auburn St., Cambridge, MA 02138 (tel. (800)-5-LETS GO/553-8746) or (617) 495-9649). Railpasses, HI-AYH memberships, ISICs, ITICs, FIYTO cards, guidebooks, maps, bargain flights, and a complete line of budget travel gear. See catalog insert.

Rail Europe Inc., 226 Westchester Ave., White Plains, NY 10604 (tel. (800) 438-7245; fax 432-1329; http://www.raileurope.com). Sells all Eurail products and passes, national railpasses, and point-to-point tickets. Up-to-date information on all rail travel in Europe, including Eurostar, the English Channel train.

STA Travel, 6560 Scottsdale Rd. #F100, Scottsdale, AZ 85253 (tel. (800) 777-0112 nationwide; fax (602) 922-0793). A student and youth travel organization offering discount airfares for young travelers, railpasses, accommodations, tours, insurance, and ISICs. 16 offices in the U.S. including: 297 Newbury Street, **Boston,** MA 02115 (tel. (617) 266-6014); 429 S. Dearborn St., **Chicago,** IL 60605 (tel. (312) 786-9050; 7202 Melrose Ave., **Los Angeles,** CA 90046 (tel. (213) 934-8722); 10 Downing St., Suite G, **New York,** NY 10003 (tel. (212) 627-3111); 4341 University Way NE, **Seattle,** WA 98105 (tel. (206) 633-5000); 2401 Pennsylvania Ave., **Washington, DC** 20037 (tel. (202) 887-0912); 51 Grant Ave., **San Francisco,** CA 94108 (tel. (415) 391-8407), **Miami,** FL 33133 (tel. (305) 461-3444). In the U.K., 6 Wrights Ln., **London** W8 6TA (tel. (0171) 938 47 11 for North American travel). In New Zealand, 10 High St., **Auckland** (tel. (09) 309 97 23). In Australia, 222 Faraday St., **Melbourne** VIC 3050 (tel. (03) 349 69 11).

Travel CUTS (Canadian Universities Travel Services Limited): 187 College St., Toronto, Ont. M5T 1P7 (tel. (416) 979-2406; fax 979-8167; e-mail mail@travelcuts). Canada's national student travel bureau and equivalent of Council. Also in the U.K., 295-A Regent St., **London** W1R 7YA (tel. (0171) 637 3161). Discounted airfares open to all; special student fares to all destinations with valid ISIC.

Usit Youth and Student Travel, 19-21 Aston Quay, O'Connell Bridge, Dublin 2 (tel. (01) 677 8117; fax 679 8833). In the USA: New York Student Center, 895 Amsterdam Ave., New York, NY, 10025 (tel. (212) 663 5435). Additional offices in Ireland. Specializes in youth and student travel. Offers low cost tickets and flexible travel arrangements all over the world.

Wasteels, 7041 Grand National Drive #207, Orlando, FL 32819 (tel. (407) 351-2537; in **London** (0171) 834 7066). A huge chain in Europe. Sells the Wasteels BIJ tickets, which are discounted (30-45% off regular fare) 2nd class international point-to-point train tickets with unlimited stopovers (must be under 26 on the first day of travel); sold *only* in Europe.

By Plane

The first challenge to the budget traveler is getting there. The **airline industry** attempts to squeeze every dollar from customers; finding a cheap airfare in their deliberately confusing jungle will be easier if you understand the airlines' systems better than most people do. Call every toll-free number and ask about discounts. Have several knowledgeable **travel agents** guide you; better yet, find an agent who specializes in the region(s) where you will be traveling.

Students and "youth" (people under 26) should never need to pay full price for a ticket. Seniors can also get great deals; many airlines offer senior traveler clubs or airline passes and discounts for their companions as well. Sunday newspapers often have travel sections that list bargain fares from the local airport. Outsmart airline reps with the phone-book-sized *Official Airline Guide* (check your local library; at US$397, the tome costs as much as some flights), a monthly guide listing nearly every scheduled flight in the world (with prices) and toll-free phone numbers for all the airlines which allow you to call in reservations directly. *The Airline Passenger's Guerrilla Handbook* (US$15; last published in 1990) is a renegade's resource. On the web, try the **Air Traveler's Handbook** (http://www.cis.ohio-state.edu/hypertext/faq/usenet/travel/air/handbook/top.html).

Most airfares peak between mid-June and early September. Midweek (Mon.-Thurs. morning) round-trip flights run about US$40-50 cheaper than on weekends. Traveling from hubs will win a more competitive fare than from smaller cities. Flying to London is usually the cheapest way across the Atlantic, though special fares to other cities such as Amsterdam, Luxembourg, or Brussels can be even lower. Traveling with an "open return" ticket can be pricier than fixing a return date and paying to change it. Whenever flying internationally, pick up your ticket well in advance of the departure date, have the flight confirmed within 72 hours of departure, and arrive at the airport at least two hours before your flight.

COMMERCIAL AIRLINES

The commercial airlines' lowest regular offer is the **APEX** (Advance Purchase Excursion Fare); specials advertised in newspapers may be cheaper, but they often have more restrictions and fewer available seats. APEX fares provide you with confirmed reservations and allow "open-jaw" tickets (landing in and returning from different cities). Generally, reservations must be made seven to 21 days in advance, with seven- to 14-day minimum and up to 90-day maximum stay limits, and hefty cancellation and change penalties (fees rise in summer). Book APEX fares early. For the adventurous, there are other, perhaps more inconvenient or time-consuming options, but before shopping around it is a good idea to find out the average commercial price in order to measure just how great a "bargain" you are being offered.

TICKET CONSOLIDATORS

Ticket consolidators resell unsold tickets on commercial and charter airlines at unpublished fares. Consolidator flights are the best deals if you are travelling on short notice; on a high-priced trip; to an offbeat destination; or in the peak season, when published fares are jacked way up. There is rarely a maximum age or stay limit, but unlike tickets bought through an airline, you won't be able to use your tickets on another flight if you miss yours, and you will have to go back to the consolidator to get a refund. Keep in mind that these tickets are often for coach seats on connecting (not direct) flights on foreign airlines, and that frequent-flyer miles may not be credited. Decide what you can and can't live with(out) before shopping.

Consolidators come in three varieties: wholesale only, who sell only to travel agencies; specialty agencies (both wholesale and retail), and **"bucket shops"** or discount retail agencies. Look for bucket shops' tiny ads in weekend papers (in the U.S., the *Sunday New York Times* is best). In London, the bucket shop center, the Air Travel Advisory Bureau (tel. (0171) 636 5000) provides a list of consolidators.

Ask to receive your tickets as quickly as possible so you can fix any problems. Get the company's policy in writing: insist on a **receipt** that gives full details about tickets, refunds, and restrictions, and record who you talked to and when. It may be worth paying with a credit card (despite the 2-5% fee) so you can stop payment if you never receive your tickets. Beware the "bait and switch" gag: shyster firms will advertise a super-low fare and then tell a caller that it has been sold. Although this is a viable excuse, if they can't offer you a price near the advertised fare on *any* date, it is a scam to lure in customers—report them to the Better Business Bureau.

For destinations worldwide, try **Airfare Busters,** (offices in Washington, DC (tel. (800) 776-0481, Boca Raton, FL (tel. (800) 881-3273). For a processing fee, **Travel Avenue,** Chicago, IL (tel. (800) 333-3335) will search for the lowest international airfare available and even give you a rebate on fares over US$300.

To Europe, try **Rebel,** Valencia, CA (tel. (800) 227-3235) or Orlando, FL (tel. (800) 732-3588); or **Discount Travel International,** New York, NY (tel. (212) 362-3636; fax 362-3236). Kelly Monaghan's *Consolidators: Air Travel's Bargain Basement* (US$7 plus US$2 shipping) from the Intrepid Traveler, P.O. Box 438, New York, NY 10034 (e-mail intreptrav@aol.com), is a valuable source for more information and lists of consolidators by location and destination. Cyber-resources include **World Wide** (http://www.tmn.com/wwwanderer/WWWa) and Edward Hasbrouck's incredibly informative website: **Airline ticket consolidators and bucket shops** (http://www.gnn.com/gnn/wic/wics/trav.97.html).

STAND-BY FLIGHTS

If budget travel inspires your utmost bravery and patience, **Airhitch,** 2641 Broadway, Third Floor, New York, NY 10025 (tel. (800) 326-2009 or (212) 864-2000) and Los Angeles, CA (tel. (310) 726-5000), will add a thrill to the prospects of when you will leave and where exactly you will end up. Be warned that otherwise tangible savings on flights (tickets US$169-269 one-way from the U.S.) may go up in smoke once you've paid for transport to your departure city (or to your chosen destination city from where they've sent you) and lodgings while you wait for a flight, sometimes over a week. **Air-Tech, Ltd.,** 584 Broadway #1007, New York, NY 10012 (tel. (212) 219-7000, fax 219-0066) offers a very similar service. *Let's Go* readers have complained about both Airhitch and Air-Tech; the Better Business Bureau of New York has received complaints about Airhitch. Be sure to read all the fine print in your agreements with either company. It is difficult to receive refunds, and clients' vouchers will not be honored when an airline fails to receive payment in time.

CHARTER FLIGHTS

The theory behind a **charter** is that a tour operator contracts with an airline (usually one specializing in charters) to fly extra loads of passengers to peak-season destinations. Charter flights fly less frequently than major airlines and have more restrictions, particularly on refunds. They are also almost always fully booked, and schedules and itineraries may change or be cancelled at the last moment (as late as 48 hours before the trip, and without a full refund); you'll be much better off purchasing a ticket on a regularly scheduled airline. As always, pay with a credit card if you can; consider traveler's insurance against trip interruption.

Try **Interworld** (tel. (305) 443-4929); **Travac** (tel. (800) 872-8800) or **Rebel** in Valencia, CA (tel. (800) 227-3235) or Orlando, FL (tel. (800) 732-3588).

Eleventh-hour **discount clubs** and **fare brokers** offer members savings on European travel, including charter flights and tour packages. Research your options carefully. **Last Minute Travel Club,** 1249 Boylston St., Boston, MA 02215 (tel. (800) 527-8646 or (617) 267-9800), and **Discount Travel International** New York, NY (tel. (212) 362-3636; fax 362-3236) are among the few travel clubs that don't charge a membership fee. Others include **Moment's Notice** New York, NY (tel. (718) 234-6295; fax (718) 234 6450), air tickets, tours, and hotels; US$25 annual fee, and **Travelers Advantage**, Stanford, CT, (tel. (800) 835-8747; US$49 annual fee); and **Travel Avenue** (tel. (800) 333-3335; see **Ticket Consolidators**, above). Study these organizations' contracts closely; you don't want to end up with an unwanted layover.

COURIER COMPANIES AND FREIGHTERS

Those who travel light should consider flying to Europe as **couriers.** The company hiring you will use your checked luggage space for freight; you're only allowed to bring carry-ons. You are responsible for the safe delivery of the baggage claim slips (given to you by a courier company representative) to the representative waiting for you when you arrive—don't screw up or you will be blacklisted as a courier. Restrictions to watch for: you must be over 18, have a valid passport, and procure your own visa (if necessary); most flights are round-trip only with short fixed-length stays (usually one week); only single tickets are issued (but a companion may be able to get a next-day flight); and most flights are from New York. Round-trip fares to Western Europe from the U.S. range from US$250-400 (during the off-season) to US$400-550 (during the summer). **NOW Voyager,** 74 Varick St. #307, New York, NY 10013 (tel. (212) 431-1616), acts as an agent for many courier flights worldwide, primarily from New York. They offer special last-minute deals to such cities as London, Paris, and Rome for as little as US$200 round-trip plus a US$50 registration fee. Other agents to try are **Halbart Express,** 147-05 176th St., Jamaica, NY 11434 (tel. (718) 656-5000), and **Discount Travel International**, (tel. (212) 362-3636).

You can also go directly through courier companies in New York, or check your bookstore or library for handbooks such as *Air Courier Bargains* (US$15 plus$3.50 shipping from the Intrepid Traveler, P.O. Box 438, New York, NY 10034. *The Courier Air Travel Handbook* (US$10 plus US$3.50 shipping) explains how to travel as an air courier and contains names, phone numbers, and contact points of courier companies. It can be ordered directly from Bookmasters, Inc., P.O. Box 2039, Mansfield, OH 44905 (tel. (800) 507-2665). **Travel Unlimited**, P.O. Box 1058, Allston, MA 02134-1058, publishes a comprehensive, monthly newsletter detailing all possible options for courier travel (often 50% off discount commercial fares). A one-year subscription is US$25 (outside of the U.S. US$35).

By Train

In May 1994, the **Channel Tunnel** (Chunnel) was completed, physically connecting England and France. This union is symbolized by the attendants on the new *Eurostar* trains who speak fluent English and sport uniforms created by the French designer Balmain. *Eurostar* operates as an airline with similar discounts, reservations, and restrictions. France, Brit, BritFrance, Eurail, and Europasses may help secure discounts, as will being a youth. Call (800) EUROSTAR, 387-6782 to purchase your ticket. In the U.K., call (0123) 361 7575 for more information.

By Ferry

To get to the Continent from Ireland or Britain, cross the English Channel by **ferry** (Stena Sealink Line, Head Office, Charter House, Park St., Ashford, Kent TN24 8EX, England (tel. (0123)364 7047)

By Bus

Take an **express bus** from London to over 270 destinations in Europe with Eurolines (UK) Ltd., 4 Cardiff Rd. Luton, Bedfordshire LU1 1PP (1582) 404 511. (London to Paris: UK£44, youth UK£33; return UK£49; youth UK£39.) The Air Travel Advisory Bureau, 28 Charles Square, London N16ST, England (tel. (0171) 636 50 00) will put you in touch with the cheapest carriers out of London for free.

ONCE THERE

Helpful People

TOURIST OFFICES

Most cities in France have an **Office de Tourisme.** Smaller French towns that attract a significant number of visitors have a tax-supported office called the **Syndicat d'Initiative** to provide information on the town and the surrounding area. In the smallest of towns the **Mairie,** or mayor's office, deals with tourist enquiries. Don't hesitate to use them; they can be invaluable sources of up-to-the-minute information.

CONSULATES

If anything goes wrong—arrest, theft, death of a companion, etc.—make your first inquiry at your country's consulate in France. The distinction between an embassy and a consulate is significant. An embassy houses the offices of the ambassador and his or her staff; you won't gain access unless you know someone inside. All facilities for dealing with nationals are in the consulate. If your passport gets lost or stolen, your status in France is immediately rendered illegal—go to the consulate of your country *as soon as possible* to get a replacement. A consulate is also able to lend up to 100F per day (interest free), provide lists of local lawyers and doctors, and notify family members of accidents, but its functions end there. Do not ask the consulate to pay for your hotel or medical bills, investigate crimes, obtain work permits, post bail, or interfere with standard French legal proceedings. Consulates are generally found only in the very largest cities; *Let's Go* lists consulates in the Practical Information sections of relevant cities and in the index ("consulates"). Consulates other than those of your home country will often help you in emergencies.

Getting Around

BY TRAIN

France is connected by rail to nearly every other destination on the continent, and the national rail company, the **Société Nationale de Chemins de Fer (SNCF),** is generally efficient. They have a information line at (tel. 08 36 35 35 35; open 7am-10pm), although at 2F a minute it's more than a little pricey. The SNCF line may seem perpetually busy—visiting a local travel agency will let you buy your tickets or make your reservations with more personal attention and little to no fee. If you want to get info from outside France, your best bet is to telephone the Paris office (tel. 01 45 82 50 50; daily 8am-8pm). Locate the ticket counters *(guichets),* the platforms *(quais)* and the tracks *(voies)*, and you're ready to roll. In France, second-class travel is pleasant and an excellent venue to meet folks of all ages and nationalities. Bring some food and bottles of water on all train trips; the train café is always expensive, and train water is undrinkable. Trains are in no way theft-proof; lock the door of your compartment if you can and keep your valuables on your person at all times. Trains are seldom late—get to the station on time. If you don't smoke, don't think that you'll be able to stand the smoking car, even for a bit.

Point-to-point tickets can be purchased in France or from a travel agent in North America. They are "open" tickets, specifying only points of departure and arrival, not specific dates or seat assignments. Remember to validate your ticket in one of the orange ticket punches (with signs marked *"compostez votre billet"*) at the entrance to the platforms. This stamps the date on the ticket, making it valid for that day of travel. If you break your journey with a stop along the way, you must validate your ticket again after the stopover. The SNCF will slap you with a fine if you fail to *composte.* Always keep your ticket with you, as you may have to present it during your trip and when you finally leave the train. When you buy a ticket, check it to see whether you will need to transfer; the ticket seller will not automatically tell you.

Many train stations have different counters for domestic tickets, international tickets, and seat reservations; check before lining up. Europe has several special high-speed trains, including the international EuroCity (EC) and InterCity (IC) trains as well as the French TGV *(train à grande vitesse)*. All three require you to purchase a ticket, a ticket supplement (US$3–18), and a seat reservation (US$2-3). If you have a railpass, you do not need to pay the supplement, but you will still need to pay for a reservation. Make the reservation as far ahead of time as you possibly can, at least several hours in advance; many places stop selling reservations a few hours before the train's departure. On the train, don't settle down in a seat marked "reservée," for you will almost certainly be bumped by the assigned occupant.

Opinion is divided as to whether it is worthwhile to save money on accommodations by taking night trains. Some consider a sleeping berth in a six-person, bunkbedded *couchette* car, with linen provided, an affordable and even necessary luxury (about US$20; reserve at the station several days in advance). Others are happy to curl up on a regular coach seat. Use your own judgment, but be aware that thieves regard with glee a sleeping, unaccompanied traveler.

Every major railroad station in France carries schedules and provides train information at computer tellers, via various representatives at the station or most commonly on poster timetables. You can purchase the complete **SNCF timetable** at newsstands in the stations. The timetables are divided into blue and white periods; during white periods (the busier times) tickets cost more. Friday nights, Saturday mornings, Sunday nights, Monday mornings, and public holidays are white periods.

Discount Tickets

For those under 26, BIJ tickets (*Billets Internationals de Jeunesse,* sold under the **Wasteels, Eurotrain,** and **Route 26** names) are good alternatives to railpasses. Available only for international trips within Europe and Morocco, they save an average of 30-45% off regular second-class fares. Tickets are sold from point to point with free and unlimited stopovers along the way. However, you cannot take longer than 60 days to complete your trip, and you can stop only at points along the direct route of your ticket. In Paris, **Eurotrain** is located at the **Student Travel Center (STC)** 20, rue des Carmes, 75005 (tel. 01 43 25 00 76). Most major cities have Eurotrain or Wasteels offices. Check at STC's Travel Services Desk or at any office in Europe for addresses and information. In the U.S. contact Wasteels Travel (see page 39).

A number of special discounts can be applied to point-to-point tickets purchased in France. The **Carrissimo,** available for travelers 12-25 years old traveling alone or with up to three friends all under the age of 26, offers discounts of 50% on blue period trips, or 20% discounts during the white period (valid for 1 year, 200F for 4 trips, 350F for 8). The **Carte Vermeille** entitles travelers over 60 to a 50% discount on first- or second-class tickets in blue periods. Cardholders get a 20% discount on white period travel. The pass can be obtained at large rail stations (valid for 1 year, 255F for unlimited trips). A second option entitles senior travelers to identical discounts on 4 trips (valid for 1 year, 135F for 4 trips). Another reduction, **place Joker,** is for tickets reserved 30-60 days in advance. These tickets are sold only in Europe.

Railpasses

Buying a railpass is a popular and sensible option under many circumstances. A variety of different railpasses exist, allowing unlimited train travel during a fixed period or travel over a given number of days in a fixed period. To figure out whether a railpass is worth its cost, find a travel agent with a copy of the *Eurailtariff* manual (or call Rail Europe in the U.S. at (800) 4-EURAIL (438-7245) and ask for the latest edition of the *Europe on Track* booklet), add up the second-class fares for the major routes you plan to cover, deduct 5% (the listed price includes a commission) deduct about 35% if you're under 26 and eligible for BIJ on the international portions of the trip, and compare. If the total cost of all your trips comes close to the price of the pass, the convenience of avoiding ticket lines and the added flexibility of the pass may well be worth the difference. You need to have the teller at the train station **validate** your pass the first time you use it. *Do not validate it yourself.* If you start an overnight trip after 7pm, you can write down the next day's date on your pass.

Eurailpass is often the best option among European rail passes for North Americans. Eurailpasses are valid in most of Western Europe (including France, but not the U.K.); contact **Rail Europe** for information (see Budget Travel Services on page 37). There is a bewildering array of options: **Eurailpasses** (unlimited first-class travel; US$522 for a 15-day pass, US$678 for a 21-day pass, US$838 for a one-month pass, US$1148 for two months, US$1468 for a three-month pass); **Eurail Flexipasses** (first-class travel within a 2-month period; ten days for US$616, 15 days for $812); **Eurail Saverpasses** (unlimited first-class travel for two or more people traveling together for most of the year, 3 or more people traveling together from April-Sept.) A 15-day pass costs US$452 per person, a 21-day pass is US$578 per person, and a 1 month pass is US$712 per person); **Eurail Youthpasses** (unlimited second-class travel for those under 26 for 15 days—US$418, one month—US$598, or two months—US$768; **Youth Flexipasses** (second-class travel for those under 26 within a 2-month period; 5 days US$255, 10 days $438, and 15 days for US$588). The **Europass,** also valid for two months, allows travelers to combine only the most popular European countries: France, Germany, Italy, Spain, and Switzerland. Tourists buying the minimum 5-days-of-travel plan can select three of the above countries to travel in; selecting 8-10 days of travel allows you to choose four countries; and an 11-15 day travel plan allows unlimited travel in all five countries. The Europass begins at US$316 (first-class) and US$210 (second-class youth).

Eurail passes can technically only be bought by non-Europeans from non-European distributors. A few major train stations in Europe sell them (though American agents usually deny this). If you're stuck in Europe and unable to find someone to sell you a Eurailpass, make a transatlantic call to an American railpass agent, who should be able to send a pass to you by express mail. Eurailpasses are not refundable once validated; you will be able to get a replacement if you lose one *only* if you have purchased insurance on the pass from Eurail—something that cannot be done through a travel agent. Ask a travel agent for specifics.

With a **France Railpass,** travelers can ride for three days within a one-month period (1st class US$185, 2nd class US$145). The days of use need not be consecutive. Up to six additional days can be purchased (US$30 each). Included is a pass for the Paris metro, good for travel from Orly or Roissy-Charles de Gaulle Airports to downtown Paris and back. You can buy the railpasses in North America at offices of Rail Europe or from travel agents. France passes cannot be purchased or used by residents of France. If your itinerary includes Britain as well, you might consider purchasing a **BritFrance Railpass.** The pass is good for rail travel in France and Great Britain for 5 days within a one-month period for US$375 first class or US$280 second class. A second option allows for 10 days of travel within a one-month period for US$545 first class or US$410 second class.

Look for Lenore Baken's *Camp Europe by Train*, which covers all aspects of train travel. Houghton Mifflin recently took over the publishing of the two annual **Eurail Guides:** the *Eurail Guide to Train Travel in the New Europe* (US$15) and the *Eurail Guide to World Train Travel* (US$19), available in bookstores. The *New Europe* guide gives timetables, instructions, and prices for international train trips, day trips, and excursions in Europe. For information write to **Houghton Mifflin Co.,** 222 Berkeley St., Boston, MA 02116. Rick Steves' free *Europe Through the Back Door* travel newsletter and catalog, 120 Fourth Ave. N., P.O. Box 2009, Edmonds, WA 98020 (tel. (206) 771-8303; fax 771-0833; e-mail ricksteves@aol.com; http://www.halcyon.com) provides comprehensive information on railpasses. The ultimate reference is the **Thomas Cook European Timetable** (US$25.95, US$35.95 includes a map of Europe highlighting all train and ferry routes, US$4 for postage). This timetable covers most major and minor train routes in Europe. In the U.S., order it from **Forsyth Travel Library** (see page 1).

BY BUS

In France, buses usually serve tour groups or fill in gaps in train service. In some regions, buses (as opposed to trains) are the primary method of transportation. When buses and trains cover the same routes, the bus is usually slightly cheaper and slower. For routes and fares, check at the local tourist office or bus station (*gare routière,* often next to the railway station). *Let's Go* lists important bus connections and fares to most cities and towns in Practical Information listings.

BY CAR

Cars offer great speed, great freedom, and access to the countryside. Although a single traveler won't save by renting a car, four usually will; groups of two or three may find renting cheaper than a railpass (although gas in France is expensive; about US$4 per gallon). Rail Europe (see page 38) offers economical "Euraildrive" passes.

You can **rent** a car from either a U.S.-based multinational with its own European offices, from a Europe-based company with local representatives, or from a tour operator which will arrange a rental for you from a European company. The multinationals offer greater flexibility, but tour operators often strike good deals and may have lower rates. Rentals vary considerably; expect to pay at least US$150 a week plus tax for a tiny car. Reserve well before leaving for Europe and pay in advance if you can; rates within Europe are harsh. Always check if prices quoted include tax and collision insurance. Some credit card companies (American Express is one) cover this automatically. Ask about discounts and be flexible in your itinerary; picking up your car in Brussels or Luxembourg is cheaper than renting in Paris. Ask your airline about special packages; sometimes you can get up to a week of free rental. Age restrictions vary; most companies require renters to be over age 20 and have a credit card. Many require that you have held your driver's license for over one year. Ask if the car is standard or automatic; most European cars are stick shifts.

Try **Auto Europe**, 39 Commercial St., Portland, ME (tel. (800) 223-5555); **Avis Rent a Car** (tel. (800) 331-1084), which offers a special discount in many SNCF stations (advertisements tell you that you need a train ticket to get it, but in fact it's available to anyone); **Budget Rent a Car** (tel. (800) 472-3325); **Europe by Car,** Rockefeller Plaza, New York, NY 10021 (tel. (800) 223-1516); **France Auto Vacances** (tel. (800) 846-0846); **Hertz Rent a Car** (tel. (800) 654-3001); **The Kemwel Group** (tel. (800) 678-0678); or **Payless Car Rental** (tel. (800) PAYLESS (729-5377)). **Europcar** is at 145, av. Malakoff, 75016 Paris (tel. 01 45 00 08 06).

For longer than three weeks, **leasing** can be cheaper than renting; it may be the only option for 18- to 20-year-olds. The cheapest leases are actually agreements where you buy the car, drive it, and then sell it back to the manufacturer at a pre-agreed price. As far as you're concerned, though, it's a simple lease and doesn't entail financial transactions. Leases include insurance coverage and are not taxed. The most affordable leases start around US$500 for 23 days and US$1000 for 60 days. Contact Foremost, Europe by Car, and Auto Europe. Arrange in advance.

If you know what you're doing, **buying** a used car or van in Europe and selling it before you leave can provide the cheapest wheels. David Shore and Patty Campbell's *Europe By Van and Motorhome* (US$14, US$2 postage in the USA and Canada, US$6 overseas) guides you through the process. To order, write to 1842 Santa Margarita Dr., Fallbrook, CA 92028 (tel. and fax (619) 723-6184 or (800) 659-5222). *How to Buy and Sell a Used Car in Europe* (US$6 plus US$1 postage) contains useful tips; write to Gil Friedman, 1735 J Street, Arcata, CA 95521 (tel. (707) 822-5001).

Caravaning gives the advantages of car rental without the hassle of finding lodgings or cramming six friends into a Renault. Most of these vehicles are diesel-powered and deliver roughly 30 miles per gallon of fuel, which is cheaper than gas. *Moto-Europa*, by Eric Bredesen (US$16 plus US$3 shipping to North America, US$7 overseas), from Seren Publishing, P.O. Box 1212, Dubuque, IA 52004 (tel. (800) EUROPA-8 (387-6728)) is a complete guide to these options.

Once you have wheels, you'll have to adjust to the French road system. The speed limit on *autoroutes* is 130kph, or 80mph. Somewhat slower (about 100kph) are the *routes nationales* and *routes départmentales.* For info on **French driving regulations,** write to the French Government Tourist Office (see page 1). Cars drive on the right side of the road in France. Be especially aware of the *priorité à droite:* cars approaching from the right always have right of way. An international driving permit is technically required to drive in France (see page 15). Accidents in France will appear on your domestic record. Michelin makes good **road maps;** the large map #989 is especially useful. Suggested roads, drawn in yellow, bypass congested areas.

BY BOAT AND PLANE

France has more than 11,000km of navigable rivers, canals, lakes, and sea coast. To float through the country or take advantage of your time at the seaside, contact the **Syndicat National des Loueurs de Bateaux de Plaisance,** Port de la Bourdonnais, 75007 Paris (tel. 01 45 55 10 49), who can find you any boat you could desire. For information on canoeing, contact the **Fédération Française de Canoe-Kayak,** 87 BP 58-94340 Joinville Le Pont (tel. 01 45 11 08 50; fax 01 48 86 13 25).

BY BICYCLE

Imagine gliding down a deserted country road in the cool morning air. Imagine sitting on something really small for five hours at a time. Biking is one of the key elements of the classic budget Eurovoyage. *France by Bike,* by Karen and Terry Whitehill (US$15), is a great source of ideas for tours, as is their broader-focused *Europe by Bike.* Also try *Cycling Europe: Budget Bike Touring in the Old World*, by N. Slavinski (US$13). Cyclists should avoid major *autoroutes* and heed the round road sign bordered in red with a diagram of a bike—this means bikes are forbidden. Bikers (and hikers) may also want larger-scale maps (25-53F) from the **Institut Géographique National (IGN),** at Espace IGN, 107, rue la Boétie, 75008 Paris (tel. 01 42 56 06 68).

These excellent maps cover France's regions in super-detail and include trails and *gîtes d'étapes*.

Mountain biking is growing more popular in France every year. The French call a mountain bike a *vélo tout terrain* **(VTT),** or sometimes a *vélo tout chemin* **(VTC)** Trails marked "VTT" on maps welcome bikers. Bikes are not permitted on trails reserved for hikers; local tourist offices can show you legal bicycle routes. Helmets are not required by law in France but are always a good idea. Remember that a *vélo* refers to a city or touring bike; you must ask for a *VTT* to get a mountain bike.

If you are nervous about striking out on your own, you might want to consider an organized **bicycle tour.** College Bicycle Tours offers bicycle tours through Europe that are exclusively for the college-aged and arranges discounted airfares for its participants; contact them at (800) 736-BIKE (736-2453) in U.S. and Canada for details.

For touring info, consult the tourist bureau annexed to most French embassies. The **Fédération Française de Cyclotourisme,** 8, rue Jean-Marie Jégo, 75013 Paris (tel. 01 44 16 88 88), is a nonprofit liaison between 3000 cycle-touring clubs. Although they are not a travel agency or tourist information bureau, they will advise foreign cyclists on a limited basis. (Include three reply coupons for a response.)

Within Europe, most ferries let you take your bike for free. Once in France, you can combine biking with **train** travel. For information in advance, write to SNCF for the brochure *Guide du train et du vélo.* Regardless of how far you go, it will cost about 45F to register a bicycle as baggage for transport. The SNCF provides cartons (about 15F) to protect the bike in transit. Look for the SNCF advertisements that say *"Dans certains trains votre vélo peut voyager avec vous, gratuitement"* (on certain trains your bike can travel with you for free). On trains thus advertised (sometimes called *trains omnibus),* your bike travels with you and you save the registration fee. On other trains, your bike may arrive up to 48 hours after you.

For those who opt to **rent,** bike rental shops require a deposit of some sort, generally from 100-2000F in cash or the deposit of your passport or a credit card imprint. *Let's Go* lists rental shops in most cities and towns. Some youth hostels rent bicycles. In addition, many train stations rent bikes and often allow you to drop them off elsewhere in the country without a charge.

BY MOPED AND MOTORCYCLE

Motorized bikes offer an enjoyable, inexpensive way to tour coastal areas and countryside. They don't use much gas, can be put on trains and ferries, and are a compromise between the high cost of car travel and the limited range of bicycles. Mopeds are slow (40km per hr.), dangerous in the rain, and unpredictable on rough roads. Always wear a helmet, and never ride wearing a backpack. In general expect to pay US$20-40 per day; try auto repair shops and remember to bargain. Motorcycles are faster and more expensive, and they normally require a special license. Before renting, ask if the quoted price includes tax and insurance or you may be hit for an extra fee. Avoid handing your passport over as a deposit; if you have an accident you may not get it back until you cover all repairs. Pay ahead of time instead.

BY THUMB

> *Let's Go* strongly urges you to consider seriously the risks before you choose to hitch. We do not recommend hitching as a safe means of transportation, and none of the information presented here is intended to do so.

Anyone can drive a car, and hitching means trusting a random person who happens to stop. Risks include theft, sexual harassment or even rape, physical assault, or death. Women traveling alone should *never hitch.* It is incredibly dangerous. A man and a woman are a safer combination; two men will have a hard time finding a ride, and three will go nowhere.

ESSENTIALS

Experienced hitchers pick a spot outside of built-up areas where drivers can stop, return to the road without causing an accident, and have time to look over potential passengers as they approach. Hitching—*"faire le stop"* in French—on hills or curves is hazardous. Hitching (or even standing) on *autoroutes* is generally illegal. One may thumb at rest stops, or at the entrance ramps to highways—*in front* of the blue and white superhighway pictograph (a bridge over a road). Hitchers travel light and stack their belongings in a compact, visible cluster. Many Europeans write their destination on a sign in large, bold letters and draw a smiley face under it. Drivers like hitchers who are neat. No one stops for anyone wearing sunglasses.

Avoid getting in the back of a two-door car, and never let go of your backpack—certainly don't put it in the trunk. Hitchhiking at night can be particularly dangerous; stand in a well-lit place and expect drivers to be leery of nocturnal thumbers. Always know how to get out of the car in a hurry. Couples may avoid hassles with male drivers if the woman sits in the back or next to the door. If you ever feel threatened, insist on being let off, regardless of where you are. If the driver refuses to stop, act as if you're going to open the car door or vomit on the upholstery, or actually open the car door; this may be enough of a surprise to slow the driver down.

You may be able to find rides by checking message boards in student travel offices or in student gathering places. **Allostop Provoya,** 84, passage Brady, 75010 Paris (tel. within Paris 01 42 46 00 66, outside Paris 01 47 70 02 01; Minitel: 3615 Code Provoya), with offices in many cities, brings together drivers and riders to share expenses. Call or write a few days in advance if you can. For passengers, the service costs 250F for eight trips within a two-year period. Single trip rates depend on the distance traveled, but fall between 30 and 70F. In either case, gas and tolls are extra.

Safety and Security

Emergency Police: tel. 17
Emergency Ambulance *(Service d'Aide Médicale d'Urgence,* or SAMU): tel. 15
Fire: tel. 18
Poison Control in Paris: tel. 01 40 37 04 04

Accommodations

Just one night in an overpriced, undercleaned hotel will put a damper on the most spirited vacation. Plan ahead when it comes to accommodations, and be flexible. If you arrive in a town without an advance reservation, stop at the nearest phone booth or the local tourist office. Tourist offices across France distribute extensive accommodations listings free of charge and many reserve rooms for a small fee.

HOTELS

The French government publishes a comprehensive guide that classifies hotels with a star system: 4L (luxury), 4, 3, 2, and 1. Most hotels in *Let's Go* are one-star or unclassified establishments, though two-star hotels offering inexpensive rooms are sometimes included. As a general rule, two traveling together can sleep less expensively than one. Expect to pay at least 105F for singles and 130F for doubles. "Double" in France usually implies a room with one large bed; be sure to confirm that your double will have the desired number of beds, or else you and your companion may sleep closer together—or further apart—than you'd like. If your room has no *douche,* or shower, you may have to pay for use of one (10-25F) or, especially in small hotels, go without. Many North Americans are surprised to discover a strange toilet-like apparatus located in bathrooms. This is called a *bidet;* it is intended for the cleansing of private body parts. No matter how desperate you are, do not use your *bidet* as a toilet. You will cause yourself much embarrassment and force your unfortunate host to bleach the bowl and clean out the pipes. When looking at hotels, also keep in mind

that the French call the ground floor the *rez-de-chaussée;* the floor *above* the ground floor is called the first floor *(premier étage).*

Many hotels serve a *petit déjeuner obligatoire* (obligatory breakfast), which costs 15-25F. Be aware of hotels, usually in heavily touristed areas, that require *demi-pension* (one obligatory meal with each night's stay).

French **hotel chains** cater exclusively to the budget traveler. Chains such as **Hôtels Formule I** and **Villages** charge about 140F for rooms for one, two, or three people. Only consistently practical for those with a car, the hotels are usually on the outskirts of towns. All rooms have a sink and TV, with hall showers, toilets, and telephones. When reception is closed, you can rent a room automatically with your credit card (V, MC, AmEx). For further details, call the Formule 1 (tel. 08 36 68 56 85) or Villages (tel. 03 80 71 50 60) national information numbers.

If you plan to visit a popular tourist area, especially during a festival, it is advisable to write or fax ahead for reservations. Send a deposit in the form of a traveler's check in francs. *Do not* reserve for more nights than you need. If you decide to leave early or switch hotels, don't expect to get all your money back. When in doubt, reserve for just one night; you can usually extend your stay once you arrive.

HOSTELS

Especially in the summer, Europe is overrun by young, budget-conscious travelers. Hostels are the hub of this gigantic student subculture, providing innumerable opportunities to meet people from across the globe, find new traveling buddies, trade stories, and learn about places to visit. A night in an *auberge de jeunesse* averages 45 to 80F, with breakfast (usually not obligatory and often included) averaging an additional 15F. Only camping is cheaper. Accommodations usually consist of bunk beds in single-sex dormitories, and most hostels either serve evening meals or have kitchen facilities you can use. Be aware that while some hostels are extremely well kept and situated, others are rundown and far from town.

Hostel life has its drawbacks: many stays might include an early curfew (usually 10-11pm, in Paris midnight-2am), lack of privacy, prohibitions against smoking and drinking, a 10am-5pm lockout during which you may not enter your room, a three-day limit to your stay, and hordes of vacationing school-children. But the prices compensate for these inconveniences, and many hostels fill quickly in July and August. Lockout and curfew times are often flexible—many hostels leave a back door open most of the night or will give you a key for a deposit. Some hostels accept reservations—it's worth calling ahead—but always arrive early if you can.

For sanitary reasons, hostels often prohibit sleeping bags and instead require **sheet sleeping sacks,** which they rent or sell. Make your own by folding a sheet lengthwise and sewing the long side and one end. You can also get a sleeping sack before you go from many travel organizations for US$14-16.

Prospective hostelers should become members of the official youth hostel association in their country; all national associations are part of **Hostelling International (HI).** You needn't be a member to stay in an HI hostel, but when hostels get crowded, members are given priority for beds. For a small fee, HI hostels will call or fax ahead to reserve space for you at other HI hostels along your route. While it is better to secure membership in your home country, you don't have to become a member in advance; if you show up at an HI hostel but have not joined a national youth hostel association, the hostel should issue you a blank membership card with space for six validation stamps. Each night you'll pay a non-member supplement (equal to one-sixth of the membership fee; about 20F) and earn a "Welcome Stamp"; get six stamps and you're a member. Most student travel agencies sell HI cards, or you can contact one of the national hostel organizations listed below.

Hostelling Membership

Hostelling International-American Youth Hostels (HI-AYH), 733 15th St. NW, Suite #840, Washington, D.C. 20005 (202) 783-6161; fax 783-6171; http://

www.taponline.com/tap/travel/hostels/pages/hosthp.html).12-month memberships: adults US$25, under 18 US$10, over 54 US$15, US$35 for family cards.

Hostelling International-Canada (HI-C), 400-205 Catherine St., Ottawa, Ontario K2P 1C3, Canada (tel. (613) 237-7884; fax 237-7868). Canada-wide membership/customer service line (800) 663-5777. Membership fees: 1-yr., under 18 CDN$12; 1-yr., over 18 CDN$25; 2-yr., over 18 CDN$35; lifetime CDN$175.

Youth Hostels Association of England and Wales (YHA), Trevelyan House, 8 St. Stephen's Hill, St. Albans, Hertfordshire AL1 2DY, England (tel. (0172) 785 5215; fax 784 4126). Enrollment fees are: UK£9.30, under 18 UK£3.20, UK£18.60 for both parents with children under 18 enrolled free, UK£9.30 for one parent with children under 18 enrolled free, UK£125.00 for lifetime membership.

An Óige (Irish Youth Hostel Association), 61 Mountjoy St., Dublin 7 (tel. (01) 830 4555; fax 830 5808; http://www.touchtel.ie). One-year membership is IR£7.50, under 18 IR£4, family IR£7.50 for each adult with children under 16 free.

Youth Hostels Association of Northern Ireland (YHANI), 22 Donegall Rd., Belfast BT12 5JN, Northern Ireland (tel. (01232) 315435; fax 439699). Annual memberships UK£7, under 18 UK£3, family UK£14 for up to 6 children.

Scottish Youth Hostels Association (SYHA), 7 Glebe Crescent, Stirling FK8 2JA (tel. (01786) 45 11 81; fax 45 01 98). Membership UK£6, under 18 UK£2.50.

Australian Youth Hostels Association (AYHA), Level 3, 10 Mallett St., Camperdown NSW 2050 (tel. (02) 565 1699; fax 565 1325; e-mail YHA@zeta.org.au). Membership: AUS$42, renewal AUS$26; under 18 AUS$12.

Youth Hostels Association of New Zealand (YHANZ), P.O. Box 436, 173 Gloucester St., Christchurch 1 (tel. (643) 379 9970; fax 365 4476; e-mail hostel.operations@yha.org.nz; http://yha.org.nz/yha). Annual membership fee NZ$24.

Hostel Association of South Africa, P.O. Box 4402, Cape Town 8000 (tel. (21) 419 1853). Membership SAR45; Students SAR 30; Group SAR120; Family SAR90; Lifetime SAR225.

Independent, non-HI-affiliated hostels vary greatly in quality. To avoid unpleasant surprises, ask to see rooms and bathrooms before paying.

In many cities and towns, rooms are available in **Foyers de Jeunes Travailleurs et de Jeunes Travailleuses,** residence halls founded for young workers with jobs in cities far from home. They are usually single-sex dorms with single rooms and a bathroom in the hall; kitchen facilities are sometimes offered. They accept foreign travelers if there's space available and offer the advantages of hostels without a lockout or curfew. The *foyers* offer a fairly good deal to the single traveler (about 80F per night), and they almost always have room—especially in the summer—because tourists don't know about them. As with hostels, however, quality varies widely.

ALTERNATIVE ACCOMMODATIONS

Short-term student housing is available in summer in the dormitories of most French universities. Contact the **Centre Régional des Oeuvres Universitaires et Scolaires (CROUS)** (see page 25). Those interested in summer housing and students looking for year-long lodgings can contact the **Cité Internationale Universitaire de Paris,** 19, bd. Jourdan, 75690 Paris Cedex 14 (tel. 01 44 16 64 48 or 01 44 16 64 46).

For a more pastoral experience, look for **logis** and **auberges de France,** hotels and restaurants roughly comparable to country inns. They serve excellent food and charge reasonable prices for comfortable rooms. A list of them is available by writing to **La Fédération Nationale des Logis de France,** 83, av. d'Italie, 75013 Paris (tel. 01 45 84 70 00; fax 01 45 83 59 66).

Gîtes d'étape are rural accommodations designed for cyclists, hikers, and other ramblers. They tend to be in tiny villages, located in areas where one might hike, sail, or ski, and may consist of furnished lodgings in farmhouses, cottages, and even campgrounds. Though they vary in quality, you can expect *gîtes* to provide beds, a kitchen facility, and a resident caretaker. Some will have sheets; others require that you bring your own sleeping bag. Some have hot showers; others have Turkish toilets. Most are communal sleep-over style where you simply leave your belongings on your bunk while you are out. During the popular vacation months, *gîtes* in resort towns fill up fast with travelers, yet many honor phone reservations. Averaging 60F a night and spaced in towns along hiking trails, *gîtes* allow you to pass through for a night or stay several days, and sometimes to take advantage of guided hikes led by caretakers. For further information, contact the **Fédération Nationale des Gîtes de France,** 35, rue Godot-de-Mauroy, 75439 Paris Cedex 09 (tel. 01 49 70 75 75).

Two other types of French lodgings are mostly used by hikers on extended treks. A **refuge** is a rustic shelter generally guarded by a caretaker moonlighting as a chief, fix-it person, and sage. *Refuges* dot the wilderness and range in price from 45-80F. Expect to pay another 80F for a hot, home-cooked meal. *Refuges* are not guarded year-round, though the doors remain open throughout the seasons to accommodate hikers and skiers on the road. Operating on a purely drop-in basis, **cabanes** are unguarded shelters open to hikers shunning all amenities on their trek. Simple and primitive, *cabanes* provide only one of the basic human needs—shelter—and, as is almost never the case, for free. Not all *cabanes* are open year-round; ask at local tourist and national park offices or along the trail before heading off to one.

Also try the **Accueil France Famille,** a nonprofit organization that offers placements to visitors as paying guests in French families everywhere in France. Write them at 5, rue François Coppée, F-75015 Paris (tel. 01 45 54 22 39). **Monasteries** are ideal for those seeking a few days of peaceful contemplation. Reservations must be made well in advance. For a list of monasteries, *Guide des Monastères* (about 100F), write to **La Procure,** 3, rue de Mézières, 75006 Paris (tel. 01 45 48 20 25).

Camping & the Outdoors

Camping liberates you from hostel regulations and drab hotels. Campgrounds dot the French countryside—many by peaceful lakes, rivers, or even the ocean. In August, you might have to arrive in the morning to ensure yourself a spot.

French campgrounds, like hotels and restaurants, are classified by a star system. Three- and four-star sites are usually large, grassy campgrounds with hot showers, bathrooms, a restaurant or store, and often a lake or pool nearby. You may also choose to camp unofficially in fields or forests at your own risk; be discreet, polite, and ask permission. Respect the environment and don't ever light a fire.

If you plan to camp extensively, you should buy the *Guide Officiel Camping/Caravaning,* which provides good maps and lists ordinary campsites, and *terrains à la ferme* (farm sites). It is available from the **Fédération Française de Camping et de Caravaning,** 78, rue de Rivoli, 75004 Paris (tel. 01 42 72 84 08). **REI,** P.O. Box 1700, Sumner, WA 98352–0001 (tel. (800) 426-4840), publishes *Europa Camping and Caravanning* (US$20), a good source for an annually updated catalog of European campsites. Michelin publishes a similar but less comprehensive guide, *Camping Caravaning,* geared to car-camping and designed to accompany the Michelin scale maps. Another useful publication is *Camping and Caravanning in Europe* (UK£8), available from the **Automobile Association,** Norfolk House, Basingstoke, Hampshire RG24 9NY, England (tel. (01256) 491 651, (01256) 491 524 for orders).

An International Camping Carnet (membership card) is required by some European campgrounds but can usually be bought on the spot. The card entitles you to a discount at some campgrounds, and may be substituted for your passport as a security deposit. In the U.S., it's available for US$30 through the **Family Campers and RVers/National Campers and Hikers Association, Inc.,** 4804 Transit Rd., Bldg. #2, Depew, NY 14043 (tel. and fax (716) 668-6242). Their magazine *Camping Today* is distributed to all members (*carnet* price includes a membership fee). Consult a good camping goods store for advice on what you will need.

If you are camping, you will need a **sleeping bag.** Better sleeping bags—down (lightweight and warm) or synthetic (cheaper, heavier, more durable, lower maintenance, and warmer when wet)—have ratings for specific minimum temperatures; check these carefully. Prices for good bags range from US$65-80 for a three-season synthetic to US$270-550 for a down bag you can use in the winter. **Sleeping bag pads** range from US$15-30, while **air mattresses** go for about US$25-50.

The best **tents** are free-standing, with their own frames and suspension systems. Good two-person tents start at about US$135; US$200 fetches a four-person. If you intend to do a lot of hiking, you should have a **frame backpack.** See "Packing" on page 35. A canteen, a pocket knife, insect repellent, a lighter, waterproof matches, and a lantern are other camping basics. For more information about camping equipment and other camping concerns, contact **Wilderness Press,** 2440 Bancroft Way, Berkeley, CA 94704-1676 (tel. (800) 443-7227 or (510) 843-8080; fax 548-1355), which publishes over 100 hiking guides including *Backpacking Basics* (US$11), and *Backpacking with Babies and Small Children* (US$11). The mail-order firms listed below offer lower prices than those you're likely to find in stores, and they can also help you determine which item you need:

Campmor, P.O. Box 700, Saddle River, NJ 07458-0700 (tel. (800) 526-4784; http://www.campmor.com). Has a wide selection of name brand equipment at low prices. One-year guarantee for unused or defective merchandise.

Eastern Mountain Sports (EMS), One Vose Farm Rd., Peterborough, NH 03458 (tel. (603) 924-7231). EMS has stores from Colorado to Maine. Though slightly higher priced, they provide great service and guaranteed customer satisfaction.

Recreational Equipment, Inc. (REI), 1700 45th St. E, Sumner, WA 98390 (tel. (800) 426-4840; http://www.rei.com). Stocks a range of camping gear and holds great seasonal sales. Items guaranteed for life (excluding normal wear and tear).

L.L. Bean, Casco St., Freeport, ME 04033-0001 (U.S. and Canada tel. (800) 221-4221, International, tel. (207) 865-3111; U.S. fax (207) 797-8867, Canada and International (207) 878-2104). High-quality equipment and outdoor clothing. The customer is guaranteed 100% satisfaction on all purchases; if it doesn't meet your expectations, they'll replace or refund it. Open 24hr. per day, 365 days per year.

Sierra Trading Post, 5025 Campstool Rd., Cheyenne WY 82007-1802 (307) 775-8000; fax 775-8088). Savings on name brand outdoor clothing and equipment. Mail order and two locations in Cheyenne and Reno, NV.

WILDERNESS AND SAFETY CONCERNS

The three most important things to remember when hiking or camping: stay warm, stay dry, and stay hydrated. The vast majority of life-threatening wilderness problems stem from a failure to follow this advice. If you are going on any hike that will take you more than one mile from civilization, you should pack enough equipment to keep you alive should disaster befall. This includes raingear, warm layers (not cotton!), especially hat and mittens, a first-aid kit, high energy food, and water. *There are no exceptions to this list.* Always check weather forecasts and pay attention to the skies when hiking. Always let someone know that you are going hiking. Above all, do not attempt a hike beyond your ability—you will endanger your life. For general hiking information, consult **The Mountaineers Books,** 1001 SW Klickitat Way, Ste. 201, Seattle, WA 98134 (tel. (800) 553-4453 or (206) 223-6303; fax 223-6306; http://www.mbooks@mountaineers.org) and its many titles on hiking (the *100 Hikes* series), biking, mountaineering, natural history, and conservation.

If you prefer countryside to cityscape, try hiking France's extensive network of long-distance footpaths, the *Grandes Randonnées.* The **Fédération Française de Randonnée Pédestre (FFRP),** 64, rue de Gergovie, 75014 Paris (tel. 01 45 45 31 02; fax 01 43 95 68 07) M. Pernety, sells maps (*topo-guides,* around 54F) with itineraries for 120,000km of footpaths. Members of the federation organize trips in the countryside. FFRP will design free itineraries if you buy the corresponding *topo-guide.*

Mountainous regions have unpredictable weather; check reports before you set out. Dial 08 36 68 02 followed by the number of the *département* (the first two digits of the of the postal code) for a recorded **weather report** in French.

Proper **hiking gear** is essential. Lightweight, non-leather hiking boots are lighter, more comfortable, less expensive, and just as rugged as the old-fashioned thick leather ones. Wear hiking boots appropriate for the terrain you are hiking. Twisted or sprained ankles can be very serious, and could keep you from walking for hours or days. Your boots should be sized so that they fit snugly and comfortably over one or two wool socks and a thin liner sock. Be sure that the boots are broken in; a bad blister will ruin your hike. If you feel a "hot-spot" coming on, cover it with moleskin immediately. You will also need a sweater, water-proof poncho, long pants, shorts, and a comfortable pack with a hip belt. You may find a light butane or white gas stove and a mess kit useful. High altitudes and hot sun make mid-day trekking unsafe; bring sunscreen, a hat, and plenty of water. Make sure that you have a good map and compass and know how to use them.

For more information about hiking, contact the **Club Alpin Français,** 24, av. de Lumière, 75019 Paris (tel. 01 42 02 68 64; fax 01 42 03 55 60). A 40F fee gives you use of their library for a year (open Tues.-Wed. 1:30-6pm, Thurs. 1:30-8pm, Fri. 1:30-5:30pm, Sat. 8am-12:30pm). These books may also help you plan your journey: *Walking in the Alps* (Hunter); *Hiking and Walking Guide to Europe* (Passport Books); and *Walking in France* (Oxford Illustrated Press).

The first thing to preserve in the wilderness is you—health, safety, and food should be your primary concerns. (For information about basic medical concerns and first aid, see Health, p. 22.) Water can be contaminated with bacteria such as *giardia,* which causes gas, cramps, loss of appetite, and violent diarrhea. To protect yourself from the effects of this invisible trip-wrecker, always boil your water for at least ten minutes before drinking it, or use an iodine solution made for purification. Camping or hiking alone is unwise over all but the shortest distances; if something happens to you, there is no one to go for help. If you're going into an area that is not well-traveled or well-marked, bring along flares or a radio. Cultivate a respect for the environment while remembering that the environment will not always return the favor. Weather patterns can change instantly. A bright blue sky can turn to rain—or even snow—before you can say "hypothermia."

Whether in a densely populated campground ten minutes from a major city, or alone in the middle of the wilderness, there are several things that you need to remember about camping safety. The most important thing is to protect yourself from the environment. This means having a proper tent with rain-fly, warm sleeping bag, and proper clothing. A good guide to outdoor survival is *How to Stay Alive in the Woods,* by Bradford Angier (Macmillan, US$8).

Be concerned with the safety of the environment. Don't unneccesarily trample vegetation by walking off established paths. Because firewood is scarce in popular areas, campers are asked to make small fires using only dead branches or brush; using a campstove is the more cautious (and efficient) way to cook. Don't cut vegetation, and don't clear new campsites. Make sure your campsite is at least 150 feet from water supplies or bodies of water. If there are no toilet facilities, bury human waste at least four inches deep and 150 feet or more from any water supplies and campsites. Always pack your trash in a plastic bag and carry it away with you.

SKIING

France's **ski slopes** rank among the world's finest. If you plan on skiing in France, consider bringing skis from home. You'll get good prices and better service; season-long rentals at home are often comparable to a few days' rental at a ski resort. Although it means that you'll have to lug your skis around France, the inconvenience may be worth it if skiing is the main reason for your trip. If you rent skis in France, the closer you get to the mountain, the more you'll pay; try to rent in a large base town before you ascend into the mountains. Be warned that the French color-coding system denotes levels of difficulty differently from those in the U.S. and Canada. Green still means easy, and blue still stands for intermediate, but red is the color for expert; black is reserved for ultra-expert trails ("double diamonds").

Miles of empty fields of powder may seem enticing, but they can be very dangerous. Before hitting the slopes, find out the weather conditions from the ski patrol. Fresh snow, warm temperatures, and wind are ingredients for an avalanche. When skiing off-*piste,* always ski with a **BIP,** a small radio locator device that can save your life if you get caught in an avalanche. BIPs are issued at park or resort offices to off-*piste* skiers. Glaciers are always the most dangerous places to ski, with hidden crevasses that can swallow the unsuspecting skier. If you've never skied on glaciers before, don't go without a guide. (For ski areas, see Skiing in the index.)

Keeping in Touch

MAIL

Post offices are marked on some maps in France by their abstract flying-letter insignia; in towns and cities, look for the yellow and blue **PTT** signs. Streets with post offices are often marked by a sign at the corner. Most post offices have **telephones;** many have **ATMs, faxes,** and **photocopiers.** Avoid lines by buying **stamps** at *tabacs* or from the yellow coin-operated vending machines outside major post offices.

Air mail between Paris and North America takes five to 10 days and is fairly dependable. Send mail from the largest post office in the area. Surface (*par eau* or *par terre*) mail is by far the cheapest way to send mail but takes one to three months to cross the Atlantic. It's adequate for getting rid of books you no longer need; a special book rate makes this option more economical. It is vital to distinguish your airmail from surface mail by labeling it clearly **par avion.** To airmail a 20g (about 1 oz.) letter or postcard from France to the U.S. or Canada costs 5F; to Australia or New Zealand,

5F10. The **aerogramme,** a sheet of fold-up, pre-paid airmail paper, requires no envelope and costs 5F. To airmail a package, you must complete a green customs slip. Registered mail is called **avec recommandation** and costs 25F. To be notified of a registered letter's receipt, ask for an **avis de récéption** and pay an additional 7F70. In France there are two grades of express mail: letters mailed **exprès** costs an extra 30F and arrive within 5 days to North America; letters mailed **chronopost** arrive in 3 days at a soaring cost of 280F for a letter-sized package. Chronopost is only available until 6pm.

Postcards and letters sent from the U.S. cost 50¢ and 60¢. The post office also sells aerograms for 50¢. Many U.S. post offices offer Express Mail service, which sends packages under 8 oz. to major overseas cities in 40 to 72 hours (US$11.50-14). Private mail services provide the fastest, most reliable overseas delivery. **DHL** (US$30), **Federal Express** (US$32), and **Airborne Express** (US$34, max. 8 oz.) can get mail from North America to Paris in 2 days. You must complete a customs form to send any package over 1kg (2kg for letter-post rate) via air mail.

Mail can be sent internationally through **poste restante** (the international phrase for General Delivery). In Paris, poste restante is handled by the 24-hour post office at 52, rue du Louvre, 1er (tel. 01 40 28 20 00 for urgent telegrams and calls; 01 42 80 67 89 for postal information; M. Châtelet-les-Halles) and available in any city or town in France. Ask correspondents to address your mail to: LAST NAME (in capitals), first name; Poste Restante; R.P. *(Recette Principale);* poste restante code/ city name. A town's poste restante code is often different from its postal code; in this book, assume that the codes are the same unless a separate poste restante code is listed. You must show your passport as identification and pay 3F for each letter received. Poste restante will refuse express mail service and balks at accepting boxes.

When picking up your mail, bring your passport or other ID. If the clerks insist that there is nothing for you, have them check under your first name as well. In a few countries you may have to pay a minimal fee per item received. *Let's Go* lists post offices in the Practical Information section for each city and most towns.
Most post offices will charge exorbitant fees or simply refuse to send Aerogrammes with enclosures. Airmail between Europe and the U.S. averages one to two weeks. Allow *at least* two weeks for Australia, New Zealand, and most of Africa. Much depends on the national post office involved.

Surface mail is by far the cheapest and slowest way to send mail. It takes one to three months to cross the Atlantic, appropriate for sending large quantities of items you won't need to see for a while. It is vital, therefore, to distinguish your airmail from surface mail by explicitly labeling "airmail" in the appropriate language. When ordering materials from abroad or making hotel reservations, always include one or two **International Reply Coupons (IRCs)**—a way of providing the postage to cover delivery. IRCs should be available from your local post office (US$1.05).

American Express offices throughout the world will act as a mail service for cardholders if you contact them in advance. Under this free **"Client Letter Service,"** they will hold mail for 30 days, forward upon request, and accept telegrams. Just like poste restante, the last name of the person to whom the mail is addressed should be capitalized and underlined. Some offices will offer these services to non-cardholders , but you must call ahead to make sure. *Let's Go* lists AmEx office locations for most large cities. A complete list is available free from AmEx (tel. (800) 528-4800) in the booklet *Traveler's Companion.*

TELEPHONES

Almost all French pay phones accept only **télécartes;** in outlying districts and cafés and bars, some phones are still coin-operated. You may purchase the card in two denominations: 41F for 50 *unités* and 98F for 120 *unités,* each worth between 6 to 18 minutes of conversation, depending on the rate schedule. Local calls cost one *unité* each. The *télécarte* is available at post offices, metro stations, and *tabacs.* The best places to call from are phone booths and post offices. If you phone from a café, hotel, or restaurant, you risk paying up to 30% more. Emergency calls and numbers beginning with **0 800** are free. Numbers beginning with **08** are much more expensive than others (the equivalent of 900 numbers in the USA; about 2F per minute).

A brief **glossary:** A call is *un coup de téléphone* or *un appel;* to dial is *composer;* a collect call is made *en PCV* (pay-say-vay); a person-to-person call is *avec préavis.* A small digital screen on the phone will issue a series of simple commands: *décrochez* means pick up, *racrochez* hang up. On some *télécarte* phones, you need to *fermer le volet;* pull down the lever directly above the card slot and wait for a dial tone.

On October 18, 1996, all the phone numbers in France changed from eight digits to 10. Any eight-digit number you see listed is **wrong.** Telephone numbers in Paris and the Ile-de-France acquired 01 in front of them, in the northwest of France 02, in the northeast 03, in the southeast and Corsica 04, and in the southwest 05.

You can make **international calls** from any phone booth, but it will cost less to have your correspondent call you back. Most French pay phones receive incoming calls. The number is posted on a sticker inside the booth, prefaced by *ici le.* For all international calls, simply dial France's international access code (00), the country code for the country you're calling, the area code or city code, and the local number you want to reach. Country codes are posted inside most telephone booths.

To call France, dial the **international access code** (011 from the U.S. and Canada, 00 from the U.K., 0011 from Australia, 00 from New Zealand, 09 from South Africa), 33 (France's country code), and the phone number *minus the zero.* So to dial the French number 01 23 45 67 89 from the U.S. you would dial 011 33 1 23 45 67 89.

AT&T's **USA Direct** service allows you to be connected instantly to an operator in the U.S. from France. Simply dial 00, wait for the tone, then dial 0011. USA-France rates vary according to the day and time of calls but average US$1-2 per minute. Another AT&T service is **World Connect,** which is for calling between two countries other than the United States. Calls must be made either collect (US$2.75 surcharge) or billed to an AT&T calling card (US$2.50); the people you are calling need not subscribe to AT&T service. For more information call AT&T at (800) 331-1140 or (800) 545-3117. To call **Canada Direct** from France, dial 00, wait for the tone, then dial 0016 and the number. It will be billed as a person-to-person call. **Australia Direct** and **New Zealand Direct** are similar, though not so extensive. For information in Canada, call (800) 561-8868; in Australia, dial 0102; and in New Zealand, dial 018. **MCI** provides a service called **World Phone.** It lets you call the U.S. using your MCI calling card and an access code, which you receive before leaving for France. For more information, call MCI at (800) 444-3333. **Telephone rates** from America to France are cheapest from 6pm-7am. Remember **time differences**—France is one hour ahead of Greenwich Mean Time and six hours ahead of New York.

Telephone rates from France are reduced Monday through Friday 9:30pm-8am, Saturday 2pm-8am, and Sunday all day for calls to the EU and Switzerland; Monday through Friday noon-2pm and 8pm-2am, and Sunday afternoon to the U.S. and Canada; Monday through Saturday 9:30pm-8am and Sunday all day to Israel.

AT&T operator: tel. 00 00 11. **MCI operator:** tel. 00 00 19.
Directory information *(Renseignements téléphoniques):* tel. 12.
International information: 00 33 12 + country code (Australia 61; Ireland 353; New Zealand 64; U.K. 44; U.S. and Canada 1).
International Operator: tel. 00 33 11. **Operator** *(Opérateur):* tel. 10.

English-speaking operators are often available for both local and international assistance. Operators in most countries will place **collect calls** for you. It's cheaper to find a pay phone and deposit just enough money to be able to say "call me" and give your number (though some pay phones can't receive calls).

Some companies, seizing upon this "call-me-back" concept, have created callback phone services. Under these plans, you call a specified number, ring once, and hang up. The company's computer calls back and gives you a dial tone. You can then make as many calls as you want, at rates about 20-60% lower than you'd pay using credit cards or pay phones. This option is most economical for loquacious travellers, as services may include a US$10-25 minimum billing per month. For information, call America Tele-Fone (tel. (800) 321-5817), Globaltel (tel. (770) 449-1295), International Telephone (tel. (800) 638-5558), and Telegroup (tel. (800) 338-0225).

A **calling card** is another, cheaper alternative; your local long-distance phone company will have a number for you to dial while travelling (either toll-free or charged as a local call) to connect instantly to an operator in your home country. The calls (plus a small surcharge) are then billed either collect or to a calling card. For more information, call **AT&T** about its **USADirect** and **World Connect** services (tel. (800) 331-1140, from abroad (412) 553-7458), **Sprint** (tel. (800) 877-4646), or **MCI WorldPhone** and **World Reach** (tel. (800) 996-7535). MCI's WorldPhone also provides access to MCI's Traveler's Assist, which gives legal and medical advice, exchange rate information, and translation services. For similar services for countries outside the U.S., contact your local phone company. In Canada, contact Bell Canada **Canada Direct** (tel. (800) 565 4708); in the U.K., British Telecom **BT Direct** (tel. (800) 34 51 44); in Ireland, Telecom Éireann **Ireland Direct** (tel. (800) 250 250); in Australia, Telstra **Australia Direct** (tel. 13 22 00); in New Zealand, **Telecom New Zealand** (tel. 123); and in South Africa, **Telkom South Africa** (tel. 09 03).

OTHER COMMUNICATION

To send a telegram to France from the U.S., Western Union (tel. (800) 325-6000) charges 76¢ per word plus a US$9 international fee. There is a US $14.32 minimum and delivery is same-day. Major cities in Europe also have bureaus where you can pay to send and receive **faxes.**

Between May 2 and October, EurAide (P.O. Box 2375, Naperville, IL 60567; tel. (708) 420-2343; fax (708) 420-2369) offers **Overseas Access,** a service most useful to travelers in Europe without a set itinerary. It costs US$15 per week or US$40 per month for an electronic message box (plus a US$15 registration fee). To reach you, people call, fax, or use the internet to leave a message; you receive it by calling Munich whenever you wish, which is cheaper than calling overseas. You may also leave messages for callers to pick up by phone. For an additional US$20 per month, EurAide will forward mail sent to Munich to any addresses you specify.

Domestic and international **telegrams** offer an option slower than phone but faster than post. Fill out a form at any post or telephone office; cables to North America arrive in one or two days. Telegrams can be quite expensive, so you may wish to consider **faxes,** for more immediate, personal, and cheaper communication. Major cities across Europe have bureaus where you can pay to send and receive faxes.

If you're spending a year abroad and want to keep in touch with friends or colleagues in a college or research institution, or simply are addicted to the blinking cursor of the cyber-world, **electronic mail (e-mail)** is an attractive option. With a minimum of computer knowledge and a little planning, you can beam messages anywhere for no per-message charges. Befriend college students as you go and ask if you can use their e-mail accounts. If you're not the finagling type, look for bureaus that offer access to e-mail for sending individual messages. Search through http://www.easynet.co.uk/pages/cafe/ccafe.htm to find a list of cybercafes around the world from which you can drink a cup of joe and e-mail him too.

MINITEL

Minitel is a computer system which provides telephone numbers, addresses, and professions of French telephone subscribers, as well as on-screen newspapers (including the *International Herald Tribune*), the weather, train schedules, and lots of other information. If you have a listed telephone number, you can lease your own from the phone company. But at 2F a minute, Minitel could break your budget before you're even aware of it. Minitel has a free cousin found in post offices. Use the little yellow machines as phone books to find numbers and services. They can be used with the most rudimentary knowledge of French.

Let's Go Picks

When our researchers departed for France, we asked them to send back their recommendations for the *crème de la crème* of mountains, beaches, museums, and restaurants that they'd uncovered in their months of travel. Six lists—and about 50 postcards later—we compiled this hit parade of what Amy, Jesse, Liz, Nick, Rob, and Sasha consider must-sees for any trip to France (plus one or two of our own).

Best Museums and Churches:

The Louvre in **Paris** (well, what did you expect?); the Hôtel d'Orléans in **Orléans;** the Fondation Vasarely in **Aix-en-Provence;** the Musée de l'Art du Sucre in **Cordes-sur-Ciel;** the Musée Fabre in **Montpellier;** the ruins of the Abbaye de Beauport in **Paimpol;** the Matisse Chapel in **Vence;** and the Château d'Eau in **Toulouse.**

Best Views or Scenery:

The parking lot in Mittelsbergheim on the **Route du Vin;** anywhere in **Chamonix;** La Petite France in **Strasbourg;** the **Ile d'Ouessant** near Brest; and the top of the Eiffel Tower in **Paris.**

Best Food:

La Parenthèse in **Blois;** La Paninotoca in **Troyes;** La Romana in **Saintes;** Le Café in Tours; anywhere in **Grenoble** or **Lyon;** La Pizzeria in **La-Roche-sur-Yon;** Le Soleil Brille Pour Tout Le Monde in **La Rochelle;** La Capri in **St-Malo;** Woolloomoolloo in **Avignon;** Chez les Fondues in the 18*ème* in **Paris;** and the Family Home in **Bayeux.**

Best Picnic Spots:

Anywhere on the **Côte d'Or** and the Jardin d'Eté (while eavesdropping on a summer concert) in **Arles.**

Researcher City Picks:

Collioure in Languedoc-Roussillon; **Strasbourg** in Alsace-Lorraine; **Grenoble** in the Alps; **Ile d'Ouessant** in Brittany; **Toulouse** in Languedoc-Roussillon; **Tours** in the Loire Valley; and **St-Jean-Cap-Ferrat** on the Côte d'Azur.

Miscellaneous Bests:

Best Beach (Bathing): **St-Malo**
Best Beach (Ogling): **Quiberon**
Most Quintessentially French Town: **Beaune**
Best Port City: **Boulogne**
Funkiest Town: **Le Puy-en-Velay**
Most Condoms in One Place: The nightclub Latex Paradis in **Poitiers**
Best Glowing Rocks: The Maison des Minéraux in **Morgat**
Best Non-Glowing Rocks: **Carnac**
Best Place to See Fish (Live): The Musée Océanographique in **Monaco**
Best Place to See Fish (Dead): The anchovy exhibit at the Château Royal in **Collioure**
Best Place to Eat Fish: **Camaret**
Best Movie None of Us Has Ever Seen: **Chacun Cherche Son Chat**
Best Line in the Guide: "An arch to the right of the house leads to the **Canal des Tanneurs,** where Pasteur's father cured hides."

France: An Introduction

History and Politics

You write to me that it's impossible; the word is not French.
— Napoleon Bonaparte

The diminutive emperor aptly captured the defiant spirit of France's history. With its enlightened empires and bloody republics, flamboyant bourgeois and humble monarchs, French history chronicles the impossible as it becomes the very likely and soon thereafter, the *fait accompli.*

EARLY HISTORY: CELTS, FRANKS, AND ROMANS

France's productive countryside has supported rich cultures for tens of thousands of years. In 1940, children playing in the caves near the village of **Lascaux** in southwest France discovered a set of paintings produced by an advanced and creative people some 15-17,000 years ago. A similar cave in the Ardèche was dated as at least 30,000 years old in 1995; this is the oldest large-scale artistic creation in the world to date. Neolithic peoples left megaliths strewn over southern and western France in the 4th millennium BC. They saved the most impressive remains for Brittany; stone alleys of menhirs at **Carnac** reach lengths of 1,500m, and the megalithic tombs at **Locmariaquer** are equally stunning examples of the dedication of the people who built these monuments.

By 1000 BC, **Celtic** tribes had swept into western France, establishing permanent settlements and building hill forts in the lush valleys of the Rhône. Many examples of Celtic art in metal and pottery have been found in eastern and northern France. Between 750 and 550 BC, Aegean Greeks settled France's south coast, building cities such as Massilia (Marseilles) and influencing the Rhône Celts. Centuries later these close-knit clans and cities were strong enough to pose a significant challenge to **Rome,** which was turning its eye (and its armies) toward the region. In 121 BC, the Romans established a colony in southern France which guarded precious trade routes connecting Spain and Italy. Many of the baths, amphitheaters, temples, and homes the Romans built there are still standing. Rome gradually recognized the region's merits and sought to wrest it from the people they called "Gauls." Julius Caesar led the struggle and chronicled it dramatically in his famous work, the *Gallic Wars*. Caesar's final victory in 52 BC over king Vercingetorix at Alesia, in addition to giving the Romans control over a new colony, catapulted him to fame, power, and, eventually, the leadership of the soon-to-be-Empire. For the next two centuries, France appreciated the peace, trade, and civilization of the Pax Romana.

By the 3rd century AD, however, the collapse of that Empire was imminent. Its economic base began to erode as long-distance trade declined. Spread too thin over the enormous Empire, the army could not prevent invasions of barbarian tribes from the east such as the Vandals, Visigoths, and Franks (who ultimately gave their name to the region and people of Gaul). In the countryside, inhabitants clustered around powerful lords, swapped agricultural services for protection, and gradually became bound to the land.

Storming out of the low countries, the Franks conquered the Roman Duchy of Syagrius (northern France) in 486. Ten years later, the Frankish chieftain **Clovis** (c. 466-511), of the **Merovingian** family, converted to Catholicism and, with the support of the Church of Rome, was able to consolidate his power over much of Gaul. From this day, religion and politics became bedfellows in France. The Merovingians had difficulty asserting their claims to sovereignty over stubborn nobles, but they did manage to establish some order amid the surrounding chaos.

A Great Lady in an Age of Great Men

Eleanor of Aquitaine (1122-1204), and her duchy, were hastily married off to King Louis VII at her parents' death in 1137. Louis, who often wore a scratchy hairshirt, was a poor match for his beautiful, spirited bride. After two disappointingly female children and a disastrous crusade to the Holy Land, the marriage was dissolved at Eleanor's request. Two months later, Eleanor married Henry Plantagenêt, eleven years her junior, Louis' most detested rival, and imminent King of England. A year later, Eleanor gave birth to a son, the first of eight children. Though the marriage started out well for everyone but Louis, things deteriorated quickly. In 1162, Henry implemented the murder of archbishop Thomas à Becket. The royal couple separated in 1168. Eleanor returned to her beloved Aquitaine where troubadours entertained her famous "Courts of Love" and Eleanor plotted a devilish scheme against Henry. At her incitement, her three sons attacked their father's lands in 1172; the bewildered king was forced to hire a mercenary army to defend himself. He quickly squashed the rebellion and imprisoned his wife. In 1188, King Richard's first act was to release his mother; his second was to make her regent. Eleanor set about reducing corruption by creating a standard set of weights and measures and new coinage. Richard left her in charge of his lands for three years while he went on the Third Crusade. When he was kidnapped by the Holy Roman Emperor, Eleanor negotiated Richard's release and oversaw the collection of 35 tons of pure silver for his ransom. In 1199, John succeeded Richard, to bloody challenges. Eleanor, then 77, canvassed the French countryside like the politician she was, promoting John's reign to her adoring subjects and defending Mirebeau castle from her usurping grandson. King Philippe Auguste captured Eleanor and Henry II's French possessions by 1203, to the massive indifference of King John. Broken-hearted by the loss, Eleanor retired to the abbey at Fontevraud, where in 1204 she was buried with Richard, her daughter Joanna, and, whether she liked it or not, Henry.

CHARLEMAGNE: RECONSOLIDATION & CONQUEST

As the reign of the Merovingian dynasty continued, the actual power of government fell increasingly to the "mayor of the palace," the king's steward. Starting with **Pepin I** (d. 639), this office was controlled by the **Carolingian** family. **Charles Martel (the Hammer)** stopped the Muslim advance from Spain at **Poitiers** in 732, leaving an enormous kingdom to his son **Pepin III (the Short).** Pepin, with the approval of **Pope Zacharias,** shut the last Merovingian king, **Childeric III,** up in a monastery and set himself on the throne in 751. By the year 800, the Carolingians controlled an area stretching from the Pyrénées to the Elbe and from the Atlantic to Austria. On Christmas Day in that year their most famous son, **Charlemagne** (742-814), was crowned **Holy Roman Emperor** by **Pope Leo III.** Charlemagne conquered much of Aragón, Italy, and Germany, loosely reuniting a large part of the former Roman Empire. His rule renewed interest in the art and literature of the ancients, initiating what is now known as the **Carolingian Renaissance.** Though illiterate, Charlemagne insisted that St. Jerome's Latin Bible be read aloud to him as he dined and sponsored attempts to preserve the decaying texts of Classical Greece.

Charlemagne's empire did not remain in one piece for long. His son, **Louis the Pious,** could not prevent his son's division of the empire into France, Germany, and Italy. When a new wave of invaders—this time consisting of **Normans** (or Vikings), **Magyars** (Hungarians), and Muslim **Saracens**—pounced on Europe in the 9th and 10th centuries, France crumbled into feudal fragments.

THE MEDIEVAL PERIOD: THE BIRTH OF FRANCE

As the turn of the millennium approached, France consisted of scores of independent feudal lordships. Lords controlled huge tracts of land which they distributed among lesser nobles, who were free in turn to grant land to other nobles or peasants. Vassals, as the dependent nobles and peasants were called, owed allegiance to their superior lords as demonstrated by military service or monetary tribute. This hierarchy of social, economic, military, and political relationships was more fluid than it might seem; while peasants were tied to the land, they were not slaves, and lords were not absolute rulers. Bonds of allegiance were often confused and contorted, and both the lords and the king had great difficulty in gaining absolute control over anything. In 987, the lords elected **Hugh Capet** to the throne of France, establishing the **Capetian** dynasty that would rule France for centuries. Capet's power was very limited; he personally controlled no more than the swath of land cradling Paris known as the Ile de France. However, his 12th-century descendants embarked on a program of centralization, pulling together the lordships one by one, continually struggling against the centripetal pull of the feudal system.

Meanwhile, the many lords and ladies of the land were off pursuing their own, often very independent, goals. In 1066, for example, **William, Duke of Normandy** invaded England. The Bayeux Tapestry (see page 183) was begun soon after to commemorate the conquest. The Norman rule of Britain created a cultural link between England and France, leaving a permanent French stamp on the English language. The Anglo-Norman-French conflicts continued into the 12th century, when **Eleanor of Aquitaine,** the independent-minded ruler of vast territories around Bordeaux in southwestern France, had her marriage to the French King Louis VII annulled in order to marry Henry II of England, thereby yielding her autonomy and much of western France to the British ruler.

The Capetians continued to corral lordships into their fold as the feudal system began ever so slowly to weaken. New technology increased farming yields, long-distance commerce revived with the advent of the **Crusades** (1095-1291), and new towns sprang up. The Capetians convinced the territorial lords, who sensed their power waning as the economic base of feudalism slipped, that central authority would give the country greater economic and political stability. Perhaps more importantly, a series of astute marriages multiplied the land under the direct control of Paris. During his 43-year reign, from 1180 to 1223, **Philippe II Auguste** singlehandedly married into the Artois, Valois, and Vermandois families and took Normandy and Anjou from England. The unification of France neared completion.

By Philippe II's death, France was the most powerful country in Europe. French language and culture dominated Western Europe; even popes were not immune to French dominance. When **Pope Boniface VIII** forbade **Philippe IV (the Fair)** to tax the French clergy, Philippe publicly insulted the Pope and assaulted him in his home. Boniface died of shock, and his successors—under pressure from the French king—moved the papal court to **Avignon,** France, which became the center of the Church for most of the 14th century.

Noise from across the Channel soon disrupted France's glory, however. When the last Capetian, **Charles IV,** passed away in 1328, **Edward III** of England staked his claim to the French throne, based partly on the land Eleanor of Aquitaine had ceded to England and partly on his relation to the Duke of Normandy. Edward and his son, the Black Prince, invaded France, initiating the **Hundred Years War.** The English experienced victory after victory, the most notable at **Agincourt** in 1415 (Shakespeare's *Henry V* gives an entertaining account of the events surrounding that battle). **Joan of Arc,** a French peasant girl convinced that she heard voices telling her to save France, rallied the disheartened French troops and brought about the coronation of the Valois French King **Charles VII** in 1429. Unfortunately for France (and for her), she was captured by the English and burned at the stake as a heretic in **Rouen** in 1431. Still, even without Joan, France emerged victorious in 1453, driving the English back to Calais.

In the meantime, the Renaissance was fast approaching. **Johannes Gutenberg** invented movable type in Alsace around 1450. In the 16th century, shortly after the end of a series of destructive but unprofitable Italian wars, **François I** imported **Leonardo da Vinci** (many of whose works are on display at the Louvre in Paris) and other Italian artists and artisans.

Despite the humanist strain of thought introduced by the Renaissance, religion remained a central part of daily life in medieval and Renaissance times. The monarch derived his political legitimacy from "divine right"—the idea that his powers were God-given. The importance of religion in this time was evident, too, in the **Wars of Religion** waged by the **Huguenots** (French Calvinists) against the Catholics between 1562 and 1598. François' son, **Henri II,** continued his father's poor treatment of Protestants; he revelled in watching them burn. Henri died a messy death in a jousting accident in 1559, and his widow, **Catherine de Médicis,** effectively became France's ruler. Deciding that killing the leaders of the Huguenots would solve the problem, she had over 2000 people massacred on St. Bartholomew's Day in 1572. Unfortunately, her plan did not work as she had expected; in 1589, **Henri de Navarre,** a target of the massacre, acceded to the throne as **Henri IV** of **Bourbon.** Keenly aware of the relationship between the state and the Church, he converted to Catholicism, waving off the magnitude of the decision with a nonchalant, *"Paris vaut bien une Messe"* (Paris is well worth a mass). He did not fully abandon his Protestant kin, however; in 1598 Henri enacted the **Edict of Nantes,** which guaranteed the Huguenots religious and political rights and ended the Wars of Religion

THE OLD REGIME: ABSOLUTE EXCESS

The 17th century was the crowning achievement of the French monarchy, a period of burgeoning absolutism when the kings nearly drowned in their own splendor and ceremony. Henri IV was succeeded in 1610 by **Louis XIII,** whose reign is perhaps better remembered for his first minister—**Cardinal Richelieu** (1585-1642). Richelieu began to fashion the greatest centralized state Europe had ever seen, a nation where sovereignty rested entirely with the monarch. This absolutist state strained the already taut social fabric of France as Richelieu manipulated nobles into submission and teased the bourgeoisie with promises of social advancement.

The power and glamor of the Old Regime culminated under the Sun King, **Louis XIV,** who rose to the throne as a five-year-old in 1643 and reigned for 72 years. Moving the court from Paris to **Versailles,** he made his capital into a magnificent showcase for regal opulence and noble privilege. Indeed, the king himself was on display; favored subjects could come to watch the complex and public rituals surrounding his getting up in the morning, dining with his family, and going to bed at night. Louis worked hard to put down any form of dissent within France; operating on the principle of *"un roi, une loi, une foi"* (one king, one law, one faith), he revoked the Edict of Nantes in 1685. He waged many wars but also negotiated a delicate series of alliances. He ensured that French culture should come to dominate Europe, with the works of Molière, Descartes, and Racine circulating almost as widely outside of France as within its borders.

However, the light emanating from the French throne could not eclipse serious domestic problems. The lavish expenditures of Louis XIV and his successors left France with an enormous debt (the improvements to Versailles consumed over half of his annual revenues for many years), and Louis' manipulation of the nobility led to simmering resentment. The middle class demanded political rights more in keeping with their share of the tax burden. While a strong king could hold these clamoring factions in check, a weak one could do little to hold back the rising tide.

THE REVOLUTION: TO RAZE AND BUILD ANEW

By 1787, a financial crisis beset Versailles and **Louis XVI** called an Assembly of Notables to seek solutions. They suggested that an **Estates General,** an archaic French parliament including clergy, nobility, and bourgeoisie, be called for the first time since Louis XIII had dismissed it in 1614. Debate ensued over the proper balance of power between the estates. In frustration, the bourgeoisie broke away and declared itself to be a **National Assembly.** When locked out of their usual chamber, the delegates moved to the Versailles tennis courts (of all places). There they swore the Oath of the Tennis Court on June 20, 1789, promising to draft a new constitution.

The Paris mob soon joined in, angered by high prices for bread and worried by the disarray of the government. On July 14, the mob stormed the old fortress of the **Bastille** looking for arms and political prisoners to liberate (they only found a few petty debtors), and the Revolution acquired the violent character that would haunt it until its end. On August 4, 1789, the Revolution succeeded in its goal of eradicating feudal privilege. In the Assembly on that hot summer night, preordained nobles rose one by one and renounced their hereditary feudal rights. Three weeks later, with the enactment of the **Declaration of the Rights of Man,** the revolutionaries began to build society anew on the ashes of the old order. The Declaration embodied the principles of *liberté, égalité,* and *fraternité*. The history of the tumultuous decade following the Revolution of 1789, and of the entire 19th century, represents France's attempt to institutionalize these ideals in the form of a stable government. In many ways, this was not achieved until well into the 20th century.

In the years between 1789 and 1799, France saw a flip-flopping of regimes and the execution of Louis XVI, who continued to side with the disenfranchised nobles. Dr. Guillotine's invention, originally designed as a humane method of killing sheep, was put to good use by **Maximilien Robespierre** and his Committee of Public Safety. The bloody nature of the Terror and the surrounding confusion unsettled the French people and cleared the way for **Napoleon Bonaparte's** rise to power. An accomplished general and unquestionable genius, Napoleon wielded the scepter of power selfishly but judiciously. He established a strong central bureaucracy and a code of law that lies at the foundation of legal systems around the world. But he was not satisfied with his control of France and extended France's expansion (already underway) through a series of military campaigns that nearly gave him control over the entire European continent. Only the harsh Russian winter of 1812 prevented French domination. In the wake of Napoleon's wars, European leaders took a step backward in time at the Congress of Vienna, resetting the French borders to those of 1792 and installing **Louis XVIII,** the late king's brother, on the throne.

THE 19TH CENTURY: SEARCH FOR STABILITY

The 19th century continued the Revolution's quest for a stable regime. Caught in a cycle of revolution and reaction, the country swapped monarchy for republic, for dictatorship, for monarchy, for republic, for empire, and for republic once again in the course of 80 years. Finally, with the founding of the Third Republic (the First created by the Revolution and the Second a mere parenthesis between 1848 and 1851), a relatively stable regime was created that would endure until World War II.

In 1830, Frenchmen revolted against the conservative king, **Charles X.** While the Revolution of 1830 could hardly be called a change of regime, the new "citizen king" **Louis-Philippe**—the former Duke of Orléans—extended suffrage and adopted a self-consciously bourgeois life-style. Yet, through a series of underhanded politics, he managed to rule France almost single-handedly. In 1848, Louis-Philippe was overthrown by a moderate Republic, which crushed a more radical workers' uprising a few months later. The first president of the **Second Republic,** elected by an overwhelming majority, was **Louis Napoleon,** nephew of the former emperor. Louis Napoleon out-maneuvered parliament, won over the army, found financial backing, and seized the government before the election of 1851. A year later he was proclaimed Emperor Napoleon III by national plebiscite.

The nation brimmed with optimism. Science had unlocked many of nature's deepest secrets, and new technology had improved the quality of life and the capacity for production across the continent. A belief in the notion of progress—that civilization was moving forward toward a state of Utopian bliss unblemished by the poverty, hunger, and war that had plagued life in the 18th century—pervaded France. Bolstered by this spirit of improvement, French society was overhauled from within. Napoleon III commissioned **Baron Haussmann** to redesign Paris; he replaced its narrow and twisting streets with broad avenues in an effort both to beautify the city and prevent the populace from throwing up barricades as it had in the Revolution of

1848. **Gustave Flaubert** reinvented the French novel. **Edouard Manet, Claude Monet** and other Impressionists transformed painting.

Industrialization sped ahead under Napoleon III. In foreign affairs, however, he was bested by the wilier and more cynical chief minister of Prussia, **Otto von Bismarck.** The growing power of Prussia threatened France. In 1870, Bismarck, who was succeeding in his goal of uniting Germany, shifted his sights to the west. Paris fell to the Germans in the **Franco-Prussian War,** and France was forced to cede Alsace-Lorraine in the peace treaty, a concession that would remain a source of conflict until the beginning of World War II. Napoleon III was exiled, and the **Third Republic** was born. The Republican regime received its first challenge from the **Paris Commune** of 1871. Angry at the government for neglecting the lower classes and for signing a humiliating peace with Germany, Parisians rioted and established a communal government. National forces regained control by pitilessly exterminating the *communards.* But while the Franco-Prussian war was a great embarrassment, it did little to slow France's industrial and cultural expansion. Early modern art and writing flourished in the late 19th century, and the **Eiffel Tower** was built for the Paris Exposition in 1889 to celebrate the centennial of the French Revolution.

Still, industrialization and urbanization had introduced many new social problems that challenged the Third Republic. Although the regime reluctantly reformed, laying the foundation for the contemporary welfare state, social tensions continued to grow. **Emile Zola** chronicled the crises of the late 19th century in a string of novels and articles that exposed the wretched condition of the poor and the extreme corruption of the government. The hypocrisy of French society was laid bare in 1894 with the **Dreyfus Affair,** in which Captain Alfred Dreyfus, a Jewish army officer, was found guilty of treason and sent to Devil's Island. While evidence pointing to his innocence mounted up, the army refused to reopen the case. In a dramatic diatribe, *J'accuse,* Zola condemned the army, the government, and all of society for the anti-Semitic prejudice that had allowed the corruption to persist. Dreyfus was finally vindicated in 1906, but he returned to France broken in spirit and body by his long penal servitude. The ethnic tensions Zola identified did not disappear, but rather became a strong undercurrent in the stream of events of the 20th century.

THE 20TH CENTURY: STABILITY LOST & FOUND

The coming of **World War I** eroded Europe's faith in progress. In the 19th century, European diplomats had managed to skirt international conflict by maintaining a balance of power among nations, preventing any one country from dominating the others. The system broke down in the early years of the 20th century, as the actions and negotiations of the Germans split Europe into two tripartite alliances: the Triple Entente (England, France, and Russia) versus the Triple Alliance (Germany, Italy, and Austria-Hungary). The continent was a delicately balanced see-saw, and a crisis in the Balkans provided just the disturbance needed to up-end all of Europe. War erupted and northeast France and Belgium were transformed into a maze of trenches and rubble. The entrance of the Americans in 1917 tilted the balance in favor of the French and British, and on November 11, 1918, the fighting stopped. Although France was technically a victor, the devastation to its countryside and populace left it exhausted. The enormous reparations demanded of Germany by the Allies bred resentment and sowed the seeds of the Second World War.

The world-wide economic downturn of the **Great Depression** struck at the very foundations of the Third Republic, and government after government rose and fell as coalitions formed and dissolved. Overrun by factions, France was unprepared for the blow delivered by a newly militarized and antagonistic Germany. After taking over Czechoslovakia, conquering Poland in less than a month, and invading Norway and Denmark, Hitler's armies swept into Paris on June 13, 1940. The French signed an armistice with the Germans whereby the northern third of the country was ceded to the Nazis and the lower portion was controlled by a French government set up in Vichy (see page 581). The collaborationist Vichy government under **Marshal Pétain** cooperated with the Nazis in various ways, including the deportation of 76,000

French and foreign Jews to Germany between 1942 and 1944. Recently the French government has acknowledged some degree of responsibility for the deportations, but the issue remains controversial.

The French are more proud of the women and men of the Resistance, who fought in secret against the Nazis throughout the occupation. At the same time, the *Forces Françaises Libres* (Free French Forces) were established by **General Charles de Gaulle** who declared his *Comité National Français* to be the government-in-exile, first in London in 1941, and later in Algiers. After Churchill and Roosevelt grudgingly recognized the irascible de Gaulle's legitimacy, the Allied effort to drive the Nazis out of France gained a focus. On June 6, 1944, British, American, and Canadian troops launched a major invasion on Normandy's coast (see **Near Bayeux: The D-Day Beaches,** page 186); by September Paris was free. As the Germans were pushed east, the provisional government sent delegates to the newly liberated areas, maintaining the bureaucracy that had been preserved intact since before the war. In October of 1946, the Fourth Republic was proclaimed. French women were given the vote after the war, 25 years after English and American suffragettes prompted their governments to take the same action.

Similar institutionally to the Third Republic, the Fourth Republic suffered from the same shortcomings, particularly the lack of a strong executive to keep the country running when the legislature stalemated. In 1946, de Gaulle resigned during the wrangling over the form of the constitution. Problems with the colonial empire (left over from the 17th and 18th centuries) plagued the regime, which saw the turnover of 22 governments and 17 prime ministers in the space of 12 years. Defeat in 1954 at Dien Bien Phu in **French Indochina** (also known as Vietnam) and the horrors of war in **Algeria** culminated in an attempted revolution in the latter country staged by right-wing settlers, or **Pied-Noirs.** The Fourth Republic came to an end in the midst of chaos overseas. De Gaulle, off-stage but not forgotten, was voted into power by the National Assembly in 1958, and he began an effort to solve the enormous problems in North Africa. Despite fierce resistance to the proposal by French nationalists, a 1962 referendum granted Algeria independence.

The form of the **Fifth Republic** was very much shaped by de Gaulle. Enormous executive power is held by the president, who is elected by popular vote for a seven-year term. He appoints a Council of Ministers and prime minister, whom he can dismiss if he so chooses. He can also, in extreme cases, dissolve the National Assembly. The Council of Ministers is responsible to the parliament, which consists of the 317-member Senate and the 491-member National Assembly, both elected by universal suffrage of citizens 18 and older.

MODERN POLITICS

Though France under de Gaulle remained a member of NATO, de Gaulle's foreign policy displayed a certain distrust of the United States. France created an independent nuclear force and withdrew from NATO's integrated military command in an effort to increase French independence and international prestige. Presiding over an era of domestic stability and economic growth, de Gaulle's firm and attentive leadership faltered during the revolts of May 1968. The regime almost collapsed in 1968, when demonstrations by students and workers virtually paralyzed the country. For two weeks, students fought to alter the authoritarian French university system. Demonstrations gave way to riots and students took over the Sorbonne. Soon 10 million workers joined the hundreds of thousands of students, decrying low wages and slow social reform. The National Assembly was dissolved, but a new election returned the ruling Gaullists to power. When de Gaulle's referendum proposing further decentralization was defeated in 1969, he resigned and the presidency passed to his former prime minister, **Georges Pompidou.** Both Pompidou and his successor, **Valéry Giscard d'Estaing,** carried on de Gaulle's legacy in attempting to concentrate on economic development and increase *le rang de la France* (the rank of France) in international affairs. The oil shocks of the 1970s, which threw France into repeated recessions, did not help matters.

Finally in 1981, the Socialists got a chance to test their ideas with the election of **François Mitterrand.** Within two weeks of taking office, Mitterrand had raised the minimum wage and instituted a mandatory fifth week of annual vacation. He continued to enact traditional socialist legislation, but recession in 1983 forced him to advance a number of unpopular deflationary policies. Soon after, socialists suffered serious setbacks in local and European parliamentary elections. The 1986 legislative elections saw the emergence of a new racist, ultra-rightist, ultra-nationalist party—the *Front National* (FN), headed by **Jean-Marie Le Pen.** Le Pen ran under the slogan, *"La France pour les français,"* ("France for the French"—with a very narrow view of French identity). He gained 10% of the vote that year.

Le Pen's emergence is symptomatic of the great difficulty France has had adjusting to the influx of immigrants which has accompanied the dissolution of its colonial empire. Traditional French culture and religious ideas have not always proved compatible with the customs newcomers have brought with them. And with unemployment running high, many blame new arrivals from Africa and the Middle East for the work shortage. At some point in your travels you may see racist graffiti or hear derogatory comments about *"les bruns."* Widely accepted terms are *"noires"* or *"africains"* when referring to blacks, *"maghrebains"* or *"orientals"* when speaking of those of Middle-Eastern descent, and *"asiatiques"* when referring to Asians.

In 1988, Mitterrand was re-elected president and was joined by France's first female prime minister, **Edith Cresson,** who stepped down in March 1992 due to her immense unpopularity. She was replaced by **Pierre Bérégovoy** whose mission, when he took office, was to "lance the abscess of corruption." However, in the parliamentary elections of March 1993, the Socialists suffered their worst defeat in 25 years. The outgoing Prime Minister Bérégovoy, himself accused of improper behavior, committed suicide weeks later.

The government's corruption and the public's boredom combined to undermine the party, and the more conservative **Edouard Balladur** (from the RPR, or *Rassemblement Pour la République* party) assumed office as prime minister after the Socialist defeat. Balladur blamed the Socialists for France's deepening economic problems and asked the French to sacrifice by taxing gasoline and alcohol, cutting government spending on health care, and extending eligibility for pensions from 37½ to 40 years. The public seemed to accept these austere measures; Balladur's approval ratings remained at 70% even after he introduced the plan.

In European politics, the French have been a major force in the development of the **European Community.** In January of 1992, France, along with 12 other EU member-nations, began a program of tariff reduction that will eventually allow goods and workers to pass freely from nation to nation. A recent agreement has also set Europe in motion towards monetary union, whereby all member countries would use a common currency, controlled by a single central bank. You will sometimes see references in the media to this coin without a country, the *Ecu.* Some historians believe this "shared sovereignty" marks but the first step toward an ultimate political union. Yet in the wake of the Maastricht treaty, which pulled the 12-nation European Community into the even more tightly-knit **European Union,** the French people have manifested a profound unease about further integration. Many fear a loss of French national character and autonomy to the overarching authority of the EU. Conservatives, in fact, have labeled the Socialists (who support the treaty) as unthinking Europhiles.

France's investments in Francophone Africa once again became problematic with the eruption of violence in **Rwanda.** Since 1975, France has been in military cooperation with the Rwandan government, despite its atrocious human rights record. In the summer of 1994, 2500 French peace-keeping troops attempted to quell the tribal warfare between the Hutus and Tutsis that threatened to decimate Rwanda. The French succeeded in creating a "safety zone" for the fleeing Hutus through "Operation Turquoise;" they also helped to draw international attention to the crisis. However, these successes have been balanced by a striking failure to provide any lasting solution to the conflict.

THIS YEAR'S NEWS

1996 got off to a slow start, beginning in early January with the death of the former president of France, **François Mitterrand.** Mitterrand, the Socialist party leader and president for 14 years, succumbed to prostate cancer after a year of fending off party financial scandals and controversial media coverage of his collaboration with the Vichy government. Shortly after Mitterrand's death, President **Jacques Chirac,** his conservative successor, was denounced around the globe for conducting underground nuclear weapons tests in the South Pacific. **Greenpeace** and international governments responded to the indignation of South Pacific island countries opposing these tests by collectively condemning the French government. Despite rioting in **Tahiti** and demonstrations worldwide, Chirac insisted that the tests were necessary to assure that France would have at its disposal "a viable and modern defense." After a series of tests beneath Pacific atolls—the last test six times more powerful than the atomic bomb dropped on Hiroshima—Chirac announced a definitive end to nuclear testing.

Following France's termination of controversial nuclear underground testing and subsequent rescinding of nuclear warhead production, Chirac introduced his plan to downsize the French military. His plan to abolish **conscription** and to reduce the uniformed military from 500,000 to 350,000 in a volunteer-only force by 2002 has been met with mixed reactions in France and beyond. Since the end of the Cold War, the U.S., the U.K. and Germany have all cut military spending by about a third; Chirac's proposed reduction in military spending may reflect his goal of cutting the $59.3 billion budget deficit by 1997, in order to conform with requirements to join the common **European currency** by the end of the century.

Chirac acknowledges: "You can't change France without the French." Still, he and Prime Minister **Alain Juppé** have been widely criticized for sweeping changes in the national health care system that are intended to help cut spending and trim the budget deficit. The new French system resembles the changes proposed in American health care, including a centralized tracking of individual doctors and identity cards for all French health care users.

Art and Architecture

ANCIENT AND MEDIEVAL

France's Classical forbearers—the ancient Greeks and Romans—left an impressive artistic legacy. In many ways, much of French art and architecture has developed either in sympathy with, or in reaction to, the Greek quest for artistic perfection of the human figure. As for Rome, the remains of some of the city's most ambitious architectural undertakings still dot the countryside of southern France, like the majestic triple-arched aqueduct completed in 19 BC that carried water to Nîmes (see **Pont du Gard,** page 433). Still, while classical civilization left many themes and ideals for French art, the birth and death of Jesus provided centuries' worth of subject matter. No scene has been depicted more often in French art than the Crucifixion. No village or town, however tiny, lacks a grand cathedral or simple church.

With the rise of Charlemagne in the 9th century, art and architecture flourished across Western Europe. Under his generous patronage, artists combined elements of the classical legacy with elements of the northern Barbarian tradition to achieve the first distinctively "Western" style. Almost exclusively religious, this was very much a symbolic art, focused on conveying feeling rather than representing reality.

Powerful symbols of religious omnipresence, the French churches of the 11th and 12th century were direct descendants of secular Roman basilicas. Dubbed **Romanesque** and characterized by round arches and barrel-vaulting, their beauty is one of simple grandeur rather than the complexity of the Gothic style. Romanesque churches, like the **Basilique St-Sernin** in Toulouse and the church of the Madeleine at **Vézelay,** were designed to accommodate large crowds of worshipers. The great pilgrimages of the period provided both reason and inspiration for many of the cathedrals built; the great structures grew along the pilgrimage routes, their designs influenced by ideas brought by the pilgrims themselves. The simple beauty of the Romanesque was gradually replaced with another style, one which called for soaring structures with thin walls filled with jewel-like stained glass.

This architecture evolved into the **Gothic** style that has come to symbolize the late Middle Ages. One of its first proponents was Abbot Suger of St-Denis, whose rebuilding of the **Basilique St-Denis** in the late 12th century set the stage for later Gothic structures. While the barrel-vaulted roofs in Romanesque buildings rest on fortified pillars, Gothic architecture utilizes a system of arches that distribute weight outward rather than straight down. Flying buttresses (the stone supports jutting out from the sides of the cathedral) counterbalance the pressure of the ribbed vaulting, relieving the walls of the roof's weight. As a result, the walls of Gothic churches seem to soar effortlessly, and light streams in through enormous stained glass windows. The cathedrals at **Noyon** and **Laon** in northern France embody the early Gothic style, characterized by simplicity in decoration. The high Gothic style of the later Middle Ages, though similar, embodied the extreme ornamentation as seen in the cathedrals of **Amiens, Chartres,** and **Reims.**

Less immediately accessible are the other arts of the Middle Ages—manuscript illumination, tapestry weaving, and decorative arts—on view in various museum collections, notably the **Musée de Cluny** in Paris and the seminary in **Bayeux.** As the medieval period wore on, Christian themes continued to inform the day's art, but works of art slowly began to creep out of the cathedrals into more secular venues. Even in religious art, individual human beings, realistically portrayed, began to figure more prominently than before—witness the impressive biblical figures poised tirelessly on the portals of the Chartres cathedral.

RENAISSANCE AND EARLY MODERN

A new focus on the human realm, coupled with a nostalgia for the classical past, strongly colored the art of the 16th-century **Renaissance. François I,** who ruled France from 1515 to 1547, was quick to recognize the importance of the new artistic achievements in Italy, but it was Italian artists, not French, who benefitted from his patronage. François brought the aging **Leonardo da Vinci** to his court, and in 1528 he hired Italian artists to improve his lodge at **Fontainebleau;** Il Rosso's fabulous paintings remain one of the château's greatest attractions. François also commissioned the remarkable **Château de Chambord** (see page 259 and the cover of this book) and additions to the **Louvre,** combining flamboyant French Gothic motifs with aspects of Italian design.

Kings were not the only ones building palaces during the Renaissance. As French aristocrats moved away from Paris to the surrounding countryside, they demanded suitably lavish living quarters. Great châteaux sprung up in the Loire Valley, providing escapes from the poverty of Paris as well as convenient access to the nobility's hunting grounds. **Fouquet,** Louis XIV's finance minister, commissioned **Le Vau, Le Brun,** and **Le Nôtre** to build him the splendid **Château de Vaux-le-Vicomte.** Louis used the same team of architect, artist, and landscaper to expand his mansion at **Versailles.** He moved there in 1672, shifting the seat of the French government away from the ancient capital. Here Louis commissioned the world's largest royal residence, an exorbitantly beautiful palace full of crystal, mirrors, and gold, surrounded by formal gardens dotted with marble statues and intricate fountains.

Under Louis, an indigenous French art flourished and, indeed, rose to European dominance. Secular themes became more prevalent than religious symbolism. **Georges de la Tour** and the **Le Nain** brothers chose simple subjects for their paintings and made striking use of light and shadow. **Nicolas Poussin** elaborated the theory of the "grand manner," with its huge canvases and panoramic subjects taken from mythology and history. The **French Royal Academy,** founded in 1648, came to value this style above all others and subsequent French painters had to contend with its weighty "academic" conventions. Drawing on the academic style, two 18th-century artists, **Watteau** and **Boucher,** developed an art to please the aristocracy, a fluffy and extravagant genre since dubbed **Rococo.** The sugary creations of **Fragonard,** such as *The Bathers* in the Louvre, are still more elaborate, depicting French nobles at play. **Elisabeth Vigée-Lebrun,** one of only two women artists in the Academy, also painted Europe's rich and famous; her appealing portrait of Marie Antoinette and her children draped in crimson robes is on display at Versailles.

Yet already painters espousing middle class, bourgeois values began to break with tradition. **Chardin,** for one, painted the everyday with realistic, unembellished strokes. His *Back from the Market* (also at the Louvre) shows a Parisian woman returning from the market place, bathed in soft, beautiful light without gaudiness. This nascent style soon triumphed, as the austerity of the Revolution of 1789 threw the flamboyant art of the aristocracy into disfavor. The chief painter of the Republic, **Jacques-Louis David,** looked to Rome for subjects that would convey contemporary Republican values. His *Oath of Horatii* (1784) depicts three sons swearing to their father that they will defend the Republic of Rome. David also depicted contemporary subjects, like the death of Marat (a Revolutionary who was stabbed in his bath) and the coronation of Napoleon. All of David's works are distinguishable by the clarity of the forms, devoid of Rococo ornamentation, by the absence of visible brushstrokes, and by the frieze-like way the figures are positioned across the canvas. The Napoleonic period adopted this **Neoclassicism** as its official style.

In reaction to David's staid compositions, the **Romantics** of the first half of the 19th century relied on vivid color and expressive brush strokes to create an emotional and subjective visual experience. Artists like **Théodore Gericault** and **Eugène Delacroix** took as their subject the exotic, the violent, the grotesque—anything to provoke spontaneous emotion while shunning classical harmony. Consider two of Géricault's titles: *Decapitated Heads* (c. 1818) and *Portrait of a Child Murderer* (1822-23). His gifted contemporary, Delacroix, shared Géricault's interest in great drama; his *Liberty Leading the People* (1830) is a triumphant scene of the bare-breasted Lady Liberty ushering in the new republic. Delacroix's passionate and swirling brushstrokes, as well as his bold use of color (look for his trademark red swatches), influenced the later Impressionists.

Tradition did survive the powerful influence of the Romantics, however, transmitted in part by the work of **Jean-Auguste Dominique Ingres,** a student of David. Like his master, he chose historical subjects and refused to let the surface of his canvases be marred by his brushstrokes. Yet Ingres was less concerned with conveying a political message; his interest lay instead in opulent materials and delicate colors. Ingres' talent for evoking sensual surfaces is apparent in such works as *Odalisque,* in which a woman peers coyly over her shoulder from a luxurious harem couch.

THE MODERN

If the Revolution of 1789 ushered in an art with a political conscience, the Revolution of 1848 introduced an art with a social conscience. **Realists** like **Gustave Courbet** looked closely at, and indeed glorified, the "humble" aspects of peasant life. His *Burial at Ornans* (1850), at the Musée d'Orsay, caused a scandal when first exhibited because it used the grand scale of history painting to depict a simple village scene—also perhaps because the gaping grave in the bottom center of the painting makes the viewer feel on the verge of falling into it. Fellow Realist **Jean Millet** showed the dignity of peasants, the value of their work, and the idyllic simplicity of their lives. **Honoré Daumier,** best known for his lithographed caricatures, also painted vivid social commentaries. His cartoons were always biting; one depicts a befuddled Parisian in a nightcap staring as the walls of his apartment are knocked down to accommodate Haussmann's newer, wider avenues. Perhaps best known is his *Third Class Carriage,* in which working women and men sit together in a train, yet somehow remain in complete isolation. Another group of mid-19th-century painters, particularly **Camille Corot** and **Théodore Rousseau,** transformed landscape painting, depicting rural subjects from direct observation and paying close attention to light and atmosphere.

The 1850s and 60s in Paris saw **Baron Georges-Eugène Haussmann** commissioned to modernize the city, to give it light, circulation, and safety. Haussmann's solution was to flatten many of Paris's hills and tear long, straight boulevards through the tangled clutter of the city's old alleys. These overhauls of Paris served to increase circulation of goods and people, to modernize the water, sewer, and gas lines, and to make it impossible for Paris' citizens to rebel by barricading the streets. Most importantly, Haussmann's work made Paris a work of art, a splendid capital worthy of France, transformed from an intimate medieval city to a bustling metropolis. Wide sidewalks (demolished in the next century to make room for automobiles) encouraged the proliferation of sidewalk cafés, kiosks, peddlers, crowds, and *flâneurs* (people strolling conspicuously).

At about this time, an artistic movement developed which displayed an interest in the new visual language afforded by modern Paris and its suburbs. **Impressionism** changed art forever through its revolutionary approach to visual experience; its painters tried to capture the effects of color and light during a particular moment of vision. Nature and landscape proved excellent subjects through which to explore this vision, but so did the changing faces of urban middle-class society. From Monet's paintings of train stations to Renoir's depictions of cafés and balls to Degas' scenes of horse races and cabarets, Impressionism trumpeted the emergence of the modern and explored the implications of the new social milieu.

Indeed, the critics and the public saw in this exploration an implicit critique, an attack on staid values and tastes. Perhaps the most shocking of the group was **Edouard Manet,** whose paintings did away with much of the fine shading and modeling of academic art. Manet's *Olympia* (1863), now at the Musée d'Orsay, symbolized the end of bourgeois societal dominance by presenting a nude prostitute who did not submit to the subjugating stare of the observer, in contrast with more traditional paintings such as Ingres' *Odalisque*. His *Le Déjeuner sur l'Herbe (Luncheon on the Grass;* 1863), depicting a picnic party composed of a nude woman and two men in contemporary clothing, revolutionized the possibilities of subject matter and perturbed his contemporaries.

Lighter and airier than Manet, **Claude Monet** is perhaps the most famous of the Impressionists. His repeated renderings of haystacks and of Rouen's cathedral dramatically showed that the same subject could be completely transformed by light and atmosphere. Towards the end of his life, plagued by cataracts, Monet painted a monumental series of waterlilies *(nymphéas),* notable for their rich colorings and abstract quality. Monet was generally acknowledged by his peers as head of the group, so it is fitting that his painting *Impression: Soleil Levant (Impression: Sunrise)* of 1872 gave the movement its name (although the name was originally assigned by a mocking critic who hated the style). The Impressionists, once relegated to a *"Salon des Réfusés,"* became a huge success and paved the way for 20th-century Western art.

Although Monet's soft style has become synonymous with Impressionism, the group was far from monolithic. **Camille Pissarro,** who became a teacher to many of the Post-Impressionists (see below), worked with fragmented brushstrokes. **Gustave Caillebotte** is recognizable for his dramatic use of traditional perspective; looking at his paintings, you feel as if you're being pulled into a vortex. **Pierre Auguste Renoir,** by contrast, painted in a sugary, shimmering manner. **Bèrthe Morisot,** the group's only woman, **Alfred Sisley,** a landscape painter, and **Frédéric Bazille,** who died in the Franco-Prussian War before he could fulfill his incredible artistic promise, developed their own individual styles.

Edgar Degas' many paintings, sculptures, and innovative pastels of racehorses and dancers demonstrate his continuing interest in line and movement. The influence of photography and of Japanese prints is evident in Degas' unusual perspectives and cropped frames. **Mary Cassatt,** an American expatriate and a great friend of Degas, was known for her technically stupendous prints and for scenes of women and children remarkably lacking in sentimentality. Impressionism's influence extended to sculpture as well. **Auguste Rodin** and **Camille Claudel** tried to capture growth instead of light; the visible signs of Rodin's hands are analogous to Monet's visible brushstrokes. The **Musée Rodin** and the surrounding gardens in Paris offer ample examples of their affecting and emotional work.

The inheritors of the Impressionist tradition share the label of **Post-Impressionism,** though they largely went their separate ways. **Paul Cézanne** worked in Aix-en-Provence and created still lifes, portraits, and geometric landscapes (among them his many versions of the prominent *Mont Ste-Victoire,* 1885-87), using planes of orange, gold and green. His style, with its bold geometric blocks of color, anticipated cubism. **Georges Seurat** took this fragmentation of shape a step further with his **Pointilism,** a style in which thousands of tiny dots of paint merge into a coherent picture in the viewer's eye. **Paul Gauguin,** on the other hand, used large, bold, flat blocks of color with heavily drawn outlines to paint "primitive" scenes from Brittany, Arles, Tahiti, and Martinique. Gauguin went to Arles to join his friend **Vincent Van Gogh,** a Dutch painter who had moved to Paris and then to the south of France in search of new light, color, and imagery. Van Gogh, in his own words, "tried to express the terrible passions of humanity by means of red and green." His wavy, tumultuous strokes of color and thick impasto often seem to express the emotional turmoil of the artist, who was plagued throughout his short life by poverty and mental illness. Similarly tortured in his art and life was **Henri de Toulouse-Lautrec,** a man of noble lineage who was disabled by a bone disease and a childhood accident. Toulouse-Lautrec's well-known posters capture the dynamic nightlife of 19th-century Paris. **Henri Matisse** and the other **Fauves** ("wild beasts") exchanged the pale Impressionist palette for intensely bright colors.

Former Fauve artist **Georges Braque** and Spanish-born **Pablo Picasso,** working so closely together that even experts cannot always identify who painted what picture, used lessons learned from Cézanne in developing **Cubism.** Matisse baptized the movement when he exclaimed that the paintings looked like they were made up of "little cubes". Cubist canvases are composed of Cézanne-inspired shaded planes, not cubes. By converting everyday objects—fruits, glasses, vases, newspapers—into these cross-cutting planes, Braque and Picasso sought to analyze pictorial space in a new way. Though they often painted still lifes, portraits, and landscapes, many find it difficult to identify what objects are being depicted in Cubist paintings. It was this basic idea—that a painting could be something other than an "objective" rendering of visual experience—that paved the way for much of modern art.

After developing Cubism in the mid-1910s, Braque and Picasso's careers diverged. Picasso became possibly the greatest artist of the 20th century, constantly innovating and breaking new artistic ground. Picasso's career, spanning many decades and movements, is chronicled at the **Musée Picasso** in Paris and at the older Musée Picasso in Antibes. In the 1920s and 30s, Picasso was the brightest star in a group of amazingly talented artists that came to Paris from all over the world to practice their craft in the exciting, avant-garde atmosphere of inter-war Paris.

This **School of Paris** was made up of members such as **Marc Chagall** and **Giorgio de Chirico,** who immigrated to Paris from Russia and Italy with culturally influenced visions. Chagall created his Cubist-fairytale pictures of Russian villages and Jewish legends, while de Chirico painted his strange, often sinister images that became the darlings of the later Surrealist movement. **Marcel Duchamp** lead the **Dadaists,** a group of artists who focused on utter nonsense and non-art—drawing a mustache on a picture of the Mona Lisa, exhibiting a urinal turned upside down, sticking nails onto an iron or a bicycle wheel onto a stool and calling it sculpture. In 1924, **André Breton** published his **Surrealist Manifesto** and launched the Surrealist movement among a group of former Dadaists. The Surrealists claimed to create an art of the subconscious, seeking out the dream world that was more real than the rational world around them. **René Magritte, Salvador Dalí, Yves Tanguy,** and **Max Ernst** painted and etched their now-playful, now-disturbing images of top hats, castles, angels, misplaced nude bodies, and melting clocks.

The art of the **late 20th century** cannot be easily labeled; it revels instead in a chaotic mix of revolution and reaction, torn between further abstraction and a return to more concrete representation. For information on contemporary art in France, check out the numerous art magazines such as *Gazettes des Beaux-Arts* and *L'Oeil*, newspapers such as *Le Monde* and *Le Figaro,* or the galleries around Les Halles, the Bastille, or the bd. St-Germain in Paris.

Similarly revolutionary trends in architecture have resulted in a number of controversial building projects in Paris. The **Centre Pompidou,** hated by some and adored by others, was built in 1970 by **Richard Rogers** and **Renzo Piano.** With its innards (heating and plumbing pipes, electrical wires, and escalators) on the outside, the building houses a cultural center and modern art museum in its vast interior space. **I.M. Pei's** postmodern glass pyramid, planted smack in the middle of the Louvre courtyard, was blocked for months while the conservative Finance Ministry took its time moving out of the offices in the Richelieu branch of the ancient palace. Conservatives have succeeded, however, in keeping towering urban architecture (except for the Montparnasse tower) out of Paris proper. Skyscrapers are exiled to the business and industrial suburb of **La Défense,** home to the **Grande Arche,** a giant, hollowed-out cube of an office building aligned with the Arc de Triomphe, the smaller arch in the Tuileries, the place de la Concorde, and the Louvre.

Literature

Before the 10th century, when the colloquial Latin spoken in Gaul evolved into a form of French, French literature did not really exist. One of the first texts composed in the nascent French language—closer to Latin than to modern French—was the *Serment de Strasbourg,* a contractual oath written on February 14, 842. As the language continued to develop in the 11th century, many literary forms emerged, such as the *chansons de geste,* epic poems celebrating heroic deeds in the age of Charlemagne, and the *fabliaux,* simple, amusing, and often very bawdy tales of peasant life in verse. Indeed, writings in verse far outnumbered prose writings in this period and displayed remarkable complexity, variety, and subtlety.

The 15th-century **Renaissance** brought not so much a shift in form and style as a transformation of subject matter. The Italian **humanist** movement that had restored secular life as the focus of art and literature quickly swept into France. With the invention of the printing press around 1450, literature addressing the very foundations of human nature was in mass circulation. Meanwhile, the still-unstandardized and somewhat unstable French language accorded prosaists a great deal of stylistic freedom. The greatest literary figures of the 16th century all wrote in prose: **Rabelais,** the moralist, **Calvin,** the reformer, and **Montaigne,** the essayist. While each profoundly affected the literary discipline, Montaigne in particular left to posterity the personal essay, a form of self-exploration he more or less invented.

While the 16th century's liberating approach to subject matter persisted into the 17th century, its freedom of style and language did not. The **Académie Française,** founded in 1635, gathered some 40 men to regulate and codify French literature, grammar, spelling, and rhetoric. The standards they set loosely at this time would soon solidify into rigid regulations. Hence was born the **Classical** age of French literature. Heralded by the moralizing animal fables of **La Fontaine,** as well as the crystal clear poetry of **Malherbe,** the age yielded the three most influential **dramatists** in the nation's history: **Corneille, Molière,** and **Racine.** All three focused generally, and often quite sarcastically, on the elite of French society. Corneille penned *Le Cid,* a story of love, honor, and family set in Spain, criticized by the Académie for not conforming to increasingly dogmatic standards. Racine's most important work, *Phèdre* (considered by some to be the greatest work in the French literary canon), recounts the tale of the incestuous love of Phèdre for her step-son Hippolyte. Finally, Molière, perhaps the most talented of the three, sacrificed a stable career in the family business—upholstery—for a try at the stage. In a country since overrun with furniture and always craving good theater, it cannot be denied that his decision was auspicious. His comedies of manners, including *Le Misanthrope, Le Bourgeois Gentilhomme (The Bourgeois Gentleman), Les Femmes Savantes (The Learned Ladies),* and *Tartuffe,* satirize the habits and speech of his time with a deadly wit matched by a faultless sense of comedy. In the realm of philosophy, French thinkers reacted to the philosophy of skepticism that had arisen in the wake of humanism by establishing the foundations of **Rationalism**—logical thought based on first principles. *"Cogito, ergo sum"* ("I think, therefore I am") is the motto by which **René Descartes** forced Western thought into the modern age. **Blaise Pascal** was another of the new breed of thinkers. Mathematician, scientist, and Christian philosopher, Pascal wrote a series of *Pensées (Thoughts),* in which he pondered man's place in an infinite universe.

The trend toward Rationalism—inherent, some say, in the French mentality—crescendoed in the 18th century, when thinkers came to believe that they could uncover a rational set of laws to explain human nature and human institutions, not unlike the laws Newton had found for the cosmos. No work captures the century's literary mood better than the *Encyclopédie,* compiled by **Denis Diderot,** a multi-volume work that sought to catalog, systematize, and rationalize the whole of human knowledge. Some of the period's greatest minds participated in the project: Voltaire, d'Alembert, Rousseau. Born amid this questioning, the century's creative literature bore a distinctly philosophical tone. **Voltaire's** *Candide* relates the story of a young man who travels the world over, convinced that "all is the best in the best of all possible worlds," only to meet misfortune at every turn. In the end, the reluctant hero realizes that he must focus not on the world but on cultivating his own individual possibilities; the Voltairean philosophy is nicely encapsulated in the work's final line, *"Il faut cultiver notre jardin"* (We must tend our own garden).

Taking the cynicism of the age to its logical extreme, many thinkers began to question and criticize the French state itself, albeit quietly in most cases. One of the more vocal critics, **Jean-Jacques Rousseau,** introduced the concept of the "social contract," an implicit bond between the individual and society, whereby individuals sacrifice a measure of personal freedom in return for the protection of their interests by the state. Unfortunately, he felt, the inhabitants of Old Regime France had "negotiated" a very poor contract; some historians believe that his attacks on the state helped to launch the French Revolution. Nonetheless, while Enlightenment philosophers maintained an attitude of cynicism toward the world as it was, they had faith in the power of reason to sort everything out. The violent and chaotic Revolution struck a blow to this faith, and the 19th century opened with uncertainty.

Deeply influenced by German Romantics like Goethe, the 19th century in France began with a new literary movement in reaction to restrictive literary precepts of the 17th century and the omnipresence of "reason" in the 18th. Initiated by **Mme. de Staël, François-René de Chateaubriand,** and **Benjamin Constant** and crystallized by **Victor Hugo,** the **Romantic** movement was colored by a preoccupation with the self and the emotions, often conveyed through lyric poetry. For the first time, the novel flourished as a primary mode of literary expression, with the penning of masterpieces like Hugo's *Les Misérables,* which traces the fortunes and complex social interactions of Paris and the provinces in the 1830s. Still, 19th-century literature saw as many changes as the political sphere. Romanticism soon fell out of vogue, when writers grew tired of its sugary emotionalism and flowery lyrics. They preferred to focus on the common, the everyday, the ordinary citizen. **Gustave Flaubert's** *Madame Bovary* relates the life of the dreamy wife of a bourgeois doctor, detailing her hopes and wishes, both simple and extravagant. As a whole, **Realists** like Flaubert crafted exacting, almost scientific descriptions of scenes and characters. **Honoré de Balzac** was another who rejected the ideals of the Romantics; his *Comédie Humaine*—a series of novels examining virtually every facet of French society—dealt unflinchingly with the often harsh realities of life under Louis-Philippe. At the same time, in 1861, **Charles Baudelaire** published his infamous *Les Fleurs du Mal (The Flowers of Evil),* ushering in a new age of poetry that focused on the sordid world of contemporary Paris—the crowd, the wanderers, the prostitutes, the meaninglessness, or *ennui.* As the century closed, a new movement known as **Symbolism** emerged, grounded in the experiments of Baudelaire, heralded by **Paul Verlaine** and **Arthur Rimbaud,** and brought to fruition by **Stéphane Mallarmé** and later **Paul Valéry.** Symbolists decried the concern of their predecessors for the world of appearances and of the senses.

Through symbols and carefully crafted language, they felt they could probe a more profound reality, reaching into the subjective natural world and into the human psyche.

The psychological explorations of the Symbolists anticipated the subconscious and existential literature of the 20th century. As in art, 20th-century literature moved toward abstraction. **Surrealist** poets, like **André Breton** and **Paul Eluard,** attempted to escape the mundane world of bourgeois life by looking to a more exciting, albeit ephemeral, world of dreams. At the turn of the century, the philosopher **Henri Bergson** introduced stunning and abstract notions of time, duration and memory, strikingly similar to those encoded mathematically in Einstein's 1905 Theory of Relativity. Inspired by Bergson, novelist **Marcel Proust** infused many of his own works with the philosopher's ideas. His monumental *A la Recherche du Temps Perdu* (*The Remembrance of Things Past,* or more accurately, *In Search of Lost Time*) explores upper-class life during the Belle Epoque, investigating the experience of time and memory as well as the narrative means of rendering them.

Continuing the trend of profound psychological and ontological questioning, author/philosophers **Jean-Paul Sartre** and **Albert Camus** explored the very foundations of human nature in treatises and works of fiction. Sartre's philosophy of **Existentialism,** introduced in his tome *L'Etre et le Néant (Being and Nothingness),* holds that existence has no inherent meaning or value. At each moment of existence, Sartre claimed, a human must reforge a personal set of values and meanings. Thus it is not being which matters, but becoming. Camus, weaving with Sartre's existential threads, initiated a literature of the absurd. In works such as *L'Etranger (The Stranger)* and *La Peste (The Plague),* he confronted the fundamentally disorienting experience of being human. **Simone de Beauvoir** applied Existentialism more specifically to women in such masterpieces as *The Second Sex.*

While Sartre and Camus preserved somewhat traditional literary styles, experimental writing in the 1950s and '60s produced the **Nouveau Roman** (the New Novel), which challenged the reader by abandoning conventional narrative techniques and embracing subject matter previously considered too trivial and mundane. Among its best known exponents are **Alain Robbe-Grillet** and **Nathalie Sarraute.** The latter presents character dialogue with an emphasis on *sous conversation* (what people think as they converse), as opposed to actual dialogue. Accompanying this new writing came new criticism: **Roland Barthes, Jacques Derrida,** and **Claude Lévi-Strauss** revolutionized literary and cultural criticism. For the latest in French writing (in French), check the lists of best sellers in the weekly magazine *Livre* or look for reviews in the literary sections of national newspapers.

Print Media

French newspapers' political leanings do not necessarily determine who reads them. *Libération* (7F), a socialist newspaper, is carried everywhere by students in search of amusingly written but comprehensive news coverage of world events. Heavy on culture, including theater and concert listings, "*Libé*" (as it is known in France) has excellent controversial interviews and thought-provoking full-page editorials. Readers with a penchant for politics will disappear behind a copy of *Le Monde* (7F), decidedly centrist in outlook with a tendency to wax socialist. The equally respectable, solid *Le Figaro* (6F) leans to the right, with an entire section of financial news. *Le Parisien* (4F50), *François* (5F), *France-Soir* (5F), and *Quotidien* (7F) also write from the right, though their efforts tend toward the more-style-than-substance end of the journalistic spectrum. *La Tribune* (7F) is France's *Wall Street Journal.* The Communist Party puts out *L'Humanité* (6F). Militants and revolutionaries will want to buy *Lutte Ouvrière,* carried at few newsstands; look for it in the streets and metro. Those homesick for the *Washington Post* and the *New York Times* will find little solace in their wire stories in the *International Herald Tribune* (8F50). *L'Equipe* (6F), the sports and automobile daily, offers coverage and stats on most sports you can think of and some that you cannot.

Many local publications list events taking place in the towns you are visiting. Though most booklets are in French, *concert* and *film* are self-evident terms. Pick one up and head for events most tourists miss: local culinary festivals, theme nights at dance clubs, theater, and even concerts by your favorite anglophone rock and jazz artists—their relative obscurity in France makes tickets cheap and available. Local events are a great way to learn about French culture and meet people. *Let's Go* gives info about these publications in the tourist office listing of most towns.

Film

Many of the cinematic experiments of the early French *metteurs en scène* reveal the surrealist influences of Salvador Dali and Luis Buñuel. The 1928 debut of *Un Chien Andalou* and its provocative slicing of an eye opened French directors' eyes to the rich possibilities of the symbol. Bringing sex to the fore of their *avant garde* productions, French directors acknowledged human passion and its foibles long before anyone in Hollywood dared. As a result, pre-war French films gleam with a modernist realism that is entirely foreign to saccharine American classics. In *cinéma vérité,* characters swear, heroes die, lovers part, and their lives are full of unresolved complications and extenuating circumstances. *La règle du jeu* (1939), directed by **Jean Renoir,** has no fewer than nine main characters, all of whom are connected by a series of infidelities. Fascinated by the evolution and organization of social classes, Renoir chose to represent these historical changes in his complex, theatrical models of life in 1930s France.

World War II, the Nazi occupation and the Resistance dramatically affected both the composition and content of French film. The late-1940s development of *film noir* mirrored a bleak, gritty postwar world with neither humor nor light to relieve the tension. **Jean Cocteau's** *La belle et la bête* (Beauty and the Beast; 1946) is a tragic poetic rendition of the famous fairy tale, dramatically enhanced by the Beast's eerie castle. Cocteau dedicated himself to *dévoilement,* or "unveiling" in his films; his search for privileged moments in the everyday has yielded rare cinematic revelations in films such as *Le Sang d'un Poète* and *Le Testament d'Orphée.* In the 1950s, **François Truffaut** moved away from ecstatic moments and pioneered the *nouvelle vague* (New Wave), exploring the absurdist sensibility of Sartrean Existentialism in *Les quatre cents coups* (1959-60) and *La mariée était en noir.* Truffaut paired documentary footage from World War II with bucolic scenery to recreate *la Belle Epoque* in his controversial portrayal of a friendship between two men and the woman they love in *Jules et Jim* (1961). **Jean-Luc Godard** followed suit with the futuristic *Alphaville* and *A bout de souffle,* in which **Jean-Paul Belmondo** steals cars, imitates Humphrey Bogart, and does (not) fall in love with **Jean Seaburg.**

More recent films retain their unique Frenchness, but many have blended with Hollywood, such as *Nikita,* a spy shoot-em-up sex film. Other recent greats include *Jean de Florette,* starring the ubiquitous **Gérard Depardieu.** The re-release of Jacques Demy's *The Umbrellas of Cherbourg* is testimony to the ongoing popularity of its heroine, **Catherine Deneuve,** a veteran actress still considered by many to be the most beautiful woman in France. The late **Louis Malle,** one of France's most daring and artistically innovative directors, entertained both a native French and largely English-speaking foreign audience; his critical triumphs explored provocative, often sexual, subject matter and include *My Dinner with André, Atlantic City, Pretty Baby, Les fous de mai,* a serio-comic work about bourgeois shock paranoia during May 1968, and *Au revoir, les enfants,* an autobiographical film based on the experiences of school children in Vichy France.

Though cinema has advanced significantly from the era of silent film, **Jean-Jacques Anaud** is doing his best to make us forget it. His film *L'ours* (*The Bear*) featured live bears in a drama that rivals *Bambi* as a tear-jerker. The memorable film, which includes a baby bear's hallucinogenic frog dream sequence, achieved tremendous success in France but went barely noticed elsewhere. Similarly, **Luc Besson's** *Le grand bleu,* starring Rosanna Arquette, has become a cult movie in France, yet it hardly caused a ripple in the rest of the world. While France churns out a tremendous number of movies that catch the eyes of Hollywood producers—*Point of No Return, Three Men and a Baby, The Bird Cage,* and others are remakes of French originals—it also maintains a specifically French genre impermeable to cultural homogenization. Recent hits, including *Olivier, Olivier, Les Visateurs* and *La Haine*—an unflinching look at the cultural tensions facing modern urban France—seem to point to a rebirth of creative and realist French cinema.

Films in France are sometimes shown in their original language with French subtitles. Look for listings marked *version original (v.o.)* to see English-language films in France. Ever since the New Wave crested in the early 70s, French interest in American movies has been phenomenal; in fact, many American films play in France that have not been shown in U.S. cinemas for years.

Food

The French will only be united under the threat of danger. No one can simply bring together a country that has 265 kinds of cheese.

—Charles de Gaulle

De Gaulle, in fact, underestimated France's culinary diversity; it produces over 400 kinds of cheese. The aristocratic tradition of extreme richness and elaborate presentation known as *la haute cuisine* originated in the 12-hour feasts of Louis XIV at Versailles but is preserved today only in traditional homes and restaurants. In their works and writings, great 19th-century chefs made food an essential art of civilized life. To learn about the skills involved, leaf through the *Larousse Gastronomique,* first compiled in the 19th century. The style made famous in the U.S. by Julia Child is *la cuisine bourgeoise,* high-quality home-cooking. A glance through her *Mastering the Art of French Cooking I & II* will give you ideas for dishes to try in France.

Both *haute cuisine* and *cuisine bourgeoise* rely heavily on the *cuisine des provinces* (provincial cooking, also called *la cuisine campagnarde,* or country cooking), which creates traditional country dishes using refined methods. The trendy *nouvelle cuisine,* consisting of tiny portions of delicately cooked, artfully arranged ingredients with light sauces, became popular in the 1970s; since then, its techniques have been integrated with heartier provincial fare. Though *le fast-food* and *le self-service* have hit France with a vengeance, a great many French people still shop daily, make the effort to create fine meals, and take the time to enjoy them. Read the Regional Introductions to find out more about each area's unique food and wine.

The French breakfast *(le petit déjeuner)* is usually light, consisting of bread *(le pain)* or sometimes *croissants* or *brioches* (buttery breads almost like pastries), and an espresso with hot milk or a hot chocolate (*le chocolat,* often served in a bowl, or *bol*). This is the breakfast you will receive in most hotels for 20-30F. Many people still eat the largest meal of the day *(le déjeuner)* between noon and 2pm. Most shops, businesses, and government agencies close during this time, even in big cities. Visitors trying to pack in activities are often initially frustrated by this sacred tradition—but linger over a two-hour lunch once or twice and you'll be hooked.

Dinner *(le dîner)* begins quite late; revelers sometimes extend their meals into the early morning. Restaurants may not serve you if you want to dine at 6:00 or 6:30pm; eating at 8:00pm is more acceptable. A complete French dinner includes an *apéritif,* an *entrée* (appetizer), *plat* (main course), salad, cheese, dessert, fruit, coffee, and a *digestif* (after-dinner drink, typically a cognac or other local brandy, such as *calvados* in Normandy). There are five major *apéritifs: kir,* white wine with *cassis,* a black currant liqueur (*kir royale* substitutes champagne for the wine); *pastis,* a licorice liqueur diluted with water; *suze,* fermented *gentiane,* a sweet-smelling mountain flower that yields a wickedly bitter brew; *picon-bière,* beer mixed with a sweet liqueur; and *martini.* The French virtually always take wine with their meals. You might hear the story of the famous director who dared to order a coke with his 1500F meal; he was promptly kicked out of the restaurant by the head chef. Of him, it was said, *"Il manque de savoir vivre"*—he doesn't know how to live.

Most restaurants offer *un menu à prix fixe* (fixed-price meal) that costs less than ordering *à la carte.* The *menu* may include an *entrée* (appetizer), a main course *(plat),* cheese *(fromage),* and dessert (see **Menu Reader,** page 695 for translations of common dishes). Some also include wine or coffee. For lighter fare, try a *brasserie,* which has a fuller menu than a café but is more casual than a restaurant.

Bread is served with every meal. It is perfectly polite to use a piece of bread to wipe your plate (in extraordinarily refined circles, French diners may push their bread around their plates with a fork). French etiquette dictates keeping one's hands above the table, not in one's lap. Elbows must not rest on the table. If you want to eat in true French manner, hold your fork in your left hand, your knife in the right, and scoop food onto your fork with the sharp edge of the knife (not with the dull edge—that's British). It is also acceptable in France to eat as soon as your food is served rather than waiting for all at the table to receive their food; the French would not do a disservice to the chef (or to themselves) by letting food get cold. The exception to this rule is dessert; wait until everyone is served before starting yours.

Mineral water is ubiquitous; order sparkling water *(eau pétillante* or *gazeuse)* or flat mineral water *(eau plate).* Ice cubes *(glaçons)* are rare. To order a pitcher of tap water, ask for *une carafe d'eau.* Finish the meal with espresso, which comes in lethal little cups with blocks of sugar. When *boisson comprise* is written on the menu, you are entitled to a free drink (usually wine) with the meal. You will usually see the words *service compris* (service included), which means the tip is automatically added to the check *(l'addition).* Otherwise you should tip 15%.

For an occasional 90F spree you can have a marvelous meal, but it's easy to find satisfying dinners for under 60F or to assemble inexpensive meals yourself with staples such as cheese, pâtés, wine, bread, and chocolate. Having learned its lesson in the Revolution, the government controls the prices of bread, so you can afford to indulge with every meal. Do as the French do: go from one specialty shop to another to assemble a picnic, or find an outdoor market *(un marché).* A *charcuterie,* the French version of the delicatessen, offers cooked meats, pâtés, *quiches* and sausages. *Crémeries* sell dairy products, and the corner *fromagerie* may stock over 100 kinds of cheese. A *boulangerie* sells breads, including the *baguette* (the long, crisp, archetypal French loaf). Be sure to try the many other types of bread the bakeries carry—*pain de campagne* or *pain complet* (wheat bread), *pain au levain* (sourdough), *pain de seigle* (rye)—as well as different shapes—*une batarde* (a thicker loaf), or *une boule* (round loaf). A *pâtisserie* offers pastry and candy, and a *confiserie* stocks candy and ice cream (though the distinction between these two kinds of stores is lusciously unclear). You can buy fruits and vegetables at a *primeur.* For the adventurous carnivore, a *boucherie chevaline* sells horse-meat (look for the gilded horse-head over the door); the more timid can stick to steaks and roasts from a regular *boucherie.* A *traiteur* is a combination of a *charcuterie* and a *boulangerie.*

The *supermarché* (supermarket) has invaded France. Look for chains such as Carrefour, Casino, Monoprix, Prisunic, Stoc, and Rallye. *Epiceries* (grocery stores) also carry staples, wine, produce, and a bit of everything else. The open-air markets, held at least once a week in every town and village, remain the best places to buy fresh fruit, vegetables, fish, and meat. Competition is fierce, and prices are low.

Cafés in France figure pleasantly in the daily routine. When choosing a café, remember that you pay for its location. Those on a major boulevard can be much more expensive than smaller establishments a few steps down a sidestreet. Prices in cafés are two-tiered, cheaper at the counter *(comptoir)* than in the seating area *(salle).* Both these prices should be posted. Coffee, beer, and (in the south) the anise-flavored *pastis* are the staple café drinks, but there are other refreshing options. Consider the cool *perrier menthe,* a bottle of Perrier mineral water with mint syrup. *Citron pressé* (lemonade)—*limonade* is a soda—and *diabolo menthe* (peppermint soda) are popular non-alcoholic choices. If you order *café,* you'll get espresso; for coffee with milk, ask for a *café crème* or a *café au lait* (although the latter is considered *passé* in Paris). If you order a *demi* or a *pression* of beer, you'll get a pale lager on tap. A glass of red is the cheapest wine in a café (starting at 4-6F), with white costing about twice as much; southerners often prefer rosé to white. Tips are not expected in cafés, except for *trop* chic ones in the big cities. Cafés are not suited to cheap meals, but snacks are usually quite economical.

Wine

Wine is an institution in France and is served at almost every occasion. The character and quality of a wine depend upon the climate, soil, and variety of grape from which it is made. Long, hot, and fairly dry summers with cool, humid nights create the ideal climate. Soil is so much a determining factor that identical grapes planted in different regions yield remarkably different wines. White wines are produced by the fermentation of grapes carefully crushed to keep the skins from coloring the wine. The fermentation of rosés allows a brief period during which the skins are in contact with the juice; this period is much longer with red wines.

Wine-producing regions are distributed throughout the country. The Loire Valley produces a number of whites, with the major vineyards at Angers, Chinon, Saumur, Anjou, Tours, and Sancerre. Cognac, farther south on the Atlantic coast, is famous for the double-distilled spirit of the same name. Centered on the Dordogne and Garonne Rivers, the classic Bordeaux region produces red and white Pomerol, Graves, and sweet Sauternes. *Armagnac*, similar to *cognac*, comes from Gascony, while Jurançon wines come from vineyards higher up the slopes of the Pyrénées. Southern wines include those of Languedoc and Roussillon on the coast and Limoux and Gaillac inland. The vineyards of Provence on the coast near Toulon are recognized for their rosés. The Côtes du Rhône from Valence to Lyon in the Rhône Valley are home to some of the most celebrated wines of France, including Beaujolais. Burgundy is especially famous for its reds, from the wines of Chablis and the Côte d'Or in the north, to the Mâconnais in the south. Alsatian whites tend to be spicier and more pungent. Many areas produce sparkling wines; however, the only one which can legally be called "Champagne" is distilled in the area surrounding Reims.

France passed the first comprehensive wine legislation in 1935, and since then the *Appellation d'Origine Controlée* regulations (*AOC* or "controlled place of origin" laws) have ensured the quality and fine reputation of French wines. All wines are categorized according to place of origin, alcohol content, and wine-making practices; only about 16% of French wines are deemed worthy of the top classification. Categories include *Vins Délimités de Qualité Supérieure* (VDQS or "restricted wines of superior quality") and *Vins de Pays* (country wines). Still, a budget traveler in France will be pleasantly surprised by even the least expensive of *vins de tables* (table wines), which are what most folk drink.

When confused about which wine to choose, simply ask. Most waiters in good restaurants and employees in wine shops will be more than happy to recommend their favorites to you. A combination of politeness and curiosity will get you far. Another option, and a very attractive one at that, is trying before you buy; many distributors (both small producers and the great châteaux) offer tastings, or *dégustations.* However, bear in mind that these are not free drink services; producers will not take kindly to excessive sampling of their wares with no intention of buying. Discretion (the most basic element of which is not arriving already tipsy) and an honest interest will go much further than greed.

Paris

France is often described as *Paris et la Province*—Paris and the provinces, Paris and everything else. Thousands worldwide (d'Artagnan and de Beauvoir, Wilde and Joyce, Stein and Baldwin) have left their native lands to seek in Paris the happiness they couldn't find at home. Wandering its tortuous medieval alleys and expansive *grands boulevards,* they felt alternately like the prodigal son and the cash-strapped stranger, the Henry Miller and the Albert Camus.

Like New York or London, Paris is an island in its own land, regarded with suspicion in the countryside. Apart from its reputation for cosmopolitanism and loose living, Paris monopolizes a quarter of France's manufacturing and the bulk of the country's luxury and service trades—fashion, higher education, banking, law, and government. Seductive, arch, and sassy, Paris exudes a *joie de vivre* that seems to gush from the Seine into the city's famous sewers and infect everything it passes. Let yourself be carried away; with attitude, anything is acceptable in the City of Lights.

Originally home to the Parisii on the Seine, the city was named Lutetia (Lutèce) by the conquering Romans in 52 BC. In AD 987, when Hugh Capet, count of Paris, became King of France, he brought prestige to the tiny medieval town by naming it his capital. King Philippe Auguste (1180-1223) consolidated the crown's possessions and established the basic geography that still characterizes the city: political and ecclesiastical institutions on the Ile de la Cité, academic on the Left Bank, and commercial on the Right Bank. Over the centuries, the city expanded outward in concentric ovals, swallowing up whole villages, now called *arrondissements.* Baron Haussmann's redesign of Paris in the mid-19th century created broad avenues intended to facilitate the movement of troops through the city in the event of foreign invasion or domestic insurgency. The construction of the *grands boulevards* through ancient residential neighborhoods ripped apart the social fabric of the city; only the bourgeoisie and the aristocracy could afford homes in the new Paris, and lower income groups were pushed out into the suburbs. Nonetheless, small pockets—Montmartre, the Marais, and parts of the 5ème and 6ème—still flicker with the remains of a medieval, even Gallo-Roman, village.

As the nation's capital and the seat of the French government, Paris once presided over an empire embracing Algiers, Hanoi, and Port-au-Prince. With its colonial empire dismantled, the city has become the foster home of many of its former subjects. These cultures are quite visible, especially in the 10ème, 19ème, and 20ème *arrondissements,* which have sizeable North African and Caribbean communities. The last generation has seen an influx of Vietnamese and Chinese immigrants. Despite underlying ethnic tension, these new groups add spice to the flavor of Paris.

If Paris did not exist, we would have to invent it. If we did not exist, Paris would not care. Sample the delights of Hemingway's moveable feast: the regal architecture, the delicious finery displayed in the shop windows and market baskets, the smoky riffs of the jazz clubs, and the population of exuberant citizens. Paris is there for you to taste now and savor for the rest of your life. For more detailed coverage of Paris and its surroundings than we can provide here, consult *Let's Go: Paris 1997.*

Orientation

Flowing languidly from east to west, the Seine River forms the heart of modern Paris. The Ile de la Cité and neighboring Ile St-Louis sit at the geographical center of the city, while the Seine splits Paris into two large expanses—the renowned Rive Gauche (Left Bank) to its south and the Rive Droite (Right Bank) to its north. In the time of Louis XIV, the city had grown to 20 *quartiers;* Haussmann's 19th-century reconstructions shifted the *quartiers'* boundaries but kept the same number. Modern Paris is divided into 20 *arrondissements* (districts) which spiral clockwise around the Lou-

Paris: Overview and Arrondissements
1 Cimetière de Montmartre
2 Sacré Coeur Basilica
3 Parc La Villette
4 Parc des Buttes Chaumont
5 Jardins du Trocadero
6 Palais Chaillot
7 Cimetière de Passy
8 American Embassy
9 British Embassy
10 Petit Palais
11 Grand Palais
12 Arc de Triomphe
13 Madeleine
14 Gare St-Lazare
15 Parc Monceau
16 Palais de la Découverte
17 Opéra Garnier
18 Galeries Lafayette
19 Printemps
20 Gare du Nord
21 Gare de l'Est
22 Opéra Bastille
23 Palais Omnisports de Bercy
24 Ministère des Finances
25 Gare de Lyon
26 Parc de Montsouris
27 Cité Universitaire
28 Cimetière Montparnasse
29 Gare Montparnasse
17e
8e
16e
7e
15e
14e
Bois de Boulogne
30 Bureau des Objets Trouvés (Lost and Found)
31 Louvre
32 Palais Royale
33 Forum des Halles
34 Musée de l'Orangerie
35 Central Post Office
36 Bourse
37 Bibliothèque Nationale
38 Ecole des Arts et Métiers
39 Archives Nationales
40 Musée Carnavalet
41 Musée Picasso
42 Centre George Pompidou
43 place des Vosges
44 Musée Victor Hugo
45 Notre Dame
46 Mémorial de la Déportation
47 Université de Paris (Sorbonne)
48 Ecole Normal Supérieure
49 Musée de Cluny
50 Museum Nationale d'Histoire Naturelle
51 Panthéon
52 Eglise St-Etienne du Mont
53 La Mosquée
54 Jardin des Plantes
55 Jardins du Luxembourg
56 Eglise St-Sulpice
57 Théâtre Nationale de l'Odéon
58 Eiffel Tower
59 Champs de Mars
60 Ecole Militaire
61 UNESCO
62 Hôtel des Invalides
63 Assemblée Nationale
64 Musée d'Orsay
65 Cimetière de l'Est du Pere Lachaise

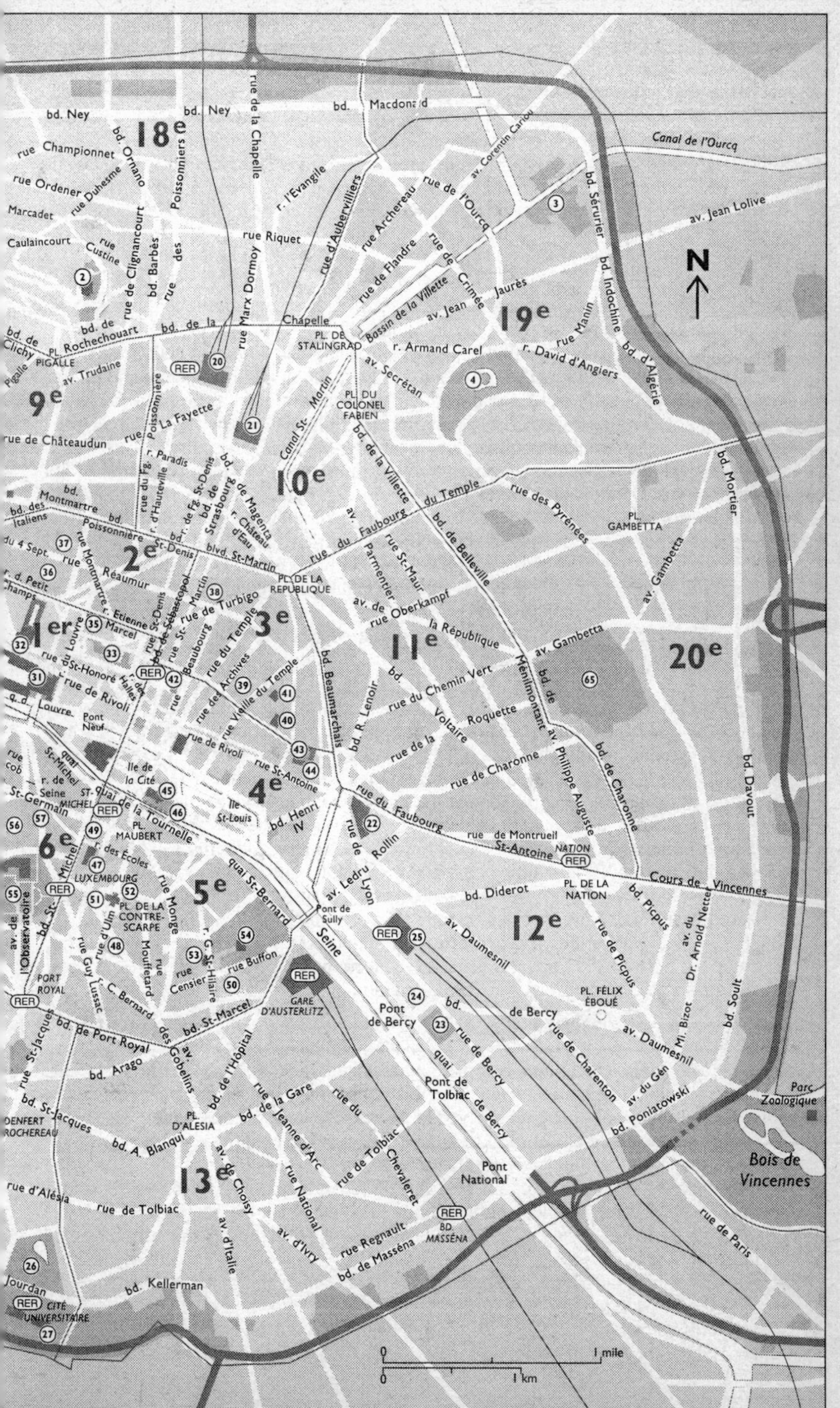
18e
19e
20e
10e
11e
12e
13e
9e
2e
3e
4e
5e
6e
1er
N
bd. Ney
bd. Macdonald
rue de la Chapelle
Canal de l'Ourcq
av. Jean Lolive
bd. Sérurier
bd. Indochine
bd. d'Algérie
bd. Mortier
bd. Davout
bd. Soult
rue Championnet
rue Ordener
bd. Ornano
rue Riquet
rue Marx Dormoy
rue d'Aubervilliers
rue de Flandre
rue de Crimée
av. Jean Jaurès
Bassin de la Villette
PL. DE STALINGRAD
r. Armand Carel
r. David d'Angiers
av. Secrétan
PL. DU COLONEL FABIEN
bd. de la Villette
bd. de Belleville
rue des Pyrénées
PL. GAMBETTA
av. Gambetta
PL. DE LA RÉPUBLIQUE
rue Oberkampf
rue du Chemin Vert
rue de la Roquette
rue de Charonne
bd. de Charonne
bd. de Ménilmontant
bd. Beaumarchais
rue du Faubourg St-Antoine
NATION
PL. DE LA NATION
Cours de Vincennes
bd. Diderot
av. Daumesnil
rue de Picpus
PL. FÉLIX ÉBOUÉ
rue de Charenton
bd. Poniatowski
Parc Zoologique
Bois de Vincennes
rue de Paris
GARE D'AUSTERLITZ
Seine
Pont de Bercy
Pont de Tolbiac
Pont National
quai de Bercy
bd. de l'Hôpital
PL. D'ALESIA
bd. A. Blanqui
rue de Tolbiac
av. d'Italie
av. d'Ivry
bd. de Masséna
bd. Kellerman
CITÉ UNIVERSITAIRE
DENFERT ROCHEREAU
bd. Arago
bd. de Port Royal
bd. St-Michel
LUXEMBOURG
PL. DE LA CONTRE-SCARPE
rue Mouffetard
rue Monge
quai St-Bernard
quai de la Tournelle
Ile de la Cité
Ile St-Louis
rue de Rivoli
rue St-Antoine
rue du Temple
rue de Turbigo
bd. de Sébastopol
bd. St-Martin
bd. de Magenta
bd. de Strasbourg
rue La Fayette
rue de Châteaudun
bd. Montmartre
bd. Poissonnière
rue Réaumur
PIGALLE
bd. de Rochechouart
bd. de Clichy
av. Trudaine
RER
0 1 mile
0 1 km

vre. The orientation that follows is an overview of neighborhoods; for specific listings, see the respective sections below.

RIVE GAUCHE (LEFT BANK)

The *"gauche"* in Rive Gauche once signified a secondary, lower-class lifestyle, the kind flaunted by the penny-pinching, perennially impoverished students that stayed there. Today, the Left Bank is the traveler's first choice for accommodations because of the cachet of its alternative, bookish crowd; the allure of its inexpensive restaurants and fashionable cafés and bars; and the remoteness from the frantic tourists of the Louvre and the Centre Pompidou.

The **Latin Quarter,** spiritually focused on the **Sorbonne** and actually encompassing the **5ème arrondissement** and parts of the **6ème,** has been home to students for centuries. The boundary between the 5*ème* and the 6*ème*, **bd. St-Michel,** overflows with cafés, movie theaters, boutiques, and bookstores. As you head southeast from this strip, hotel prices gradually shrink. Farther east, the neighborhood around **pl. de la Contrescarpe,** at the center of the 5*ème*, is less commercial, more intimate, and even cheaper. A rainbow of ethnic restaurants compete for customers along **rue Mouffetard,** the indisputable culinary heart of the 5*ème arrondissement.*

Crossing bd. St-Michel and running east-west, **boulevard St-Germain** in the **6ème arrondissement** practically defines **St-Germain-des-Prés,** a neighborhood that has turned the sidewalk café into an art form, amusing everyone from Rimbaud to Sartre. Budget hotels are sparse in this gallery-filled *quartier* that stretches from the Seine to the bd. Montparnasse. Tiny restaurants with super-cheap *menus* snuggle around rue de Buci, rue Dauphine, rue du Seine, and especially **rue Grégoire de Tours,** as do daily street markets with loads of fresh produce.

Don't stay in the **7ème** for the view or for the party atmosphere. A civil servant heaven filled with traveling businesspeople, the 7*ème* proffers pricey, spatially challenged rooms, many promising, but not necessarily providing, views of the Eiffel Tower. The military and ministerial 7*ème* houses serious date restaurants but little in the way of affordable food, other than in markets like the one on **rue Cler.**

Montparnasse, where the chic 6*ème* meets the commercial **14ème arrondissement** just south of the Latin Quarter, attracted expatriates in the 1920s. Picasso, Hemingway, and Stein bunkered down and kicked up their heels in the cafés and *crêperies* of this locale. Today, areas closest to the fashionable **boulevard du Montparnasse** maintain their glamor while adjoining blocks have become residential. Be prepared for sex-shops and sleazy nightlife at the northern end of av. du Maine. On the other side of the 14*ème*, the **13ème,** Paris's "Chinatown," deluges visitors with post-colonial cuisine from Vietnam, Laos, Thailand, and Cambodia.

The expansive **Parc des Expositions,** just outside the Porte de Versailles at the southern tip of the **15ème,** attracts executives in the winter. In summer hotels scramble for guests, and tourists can sometimes haggle with the district's hotel owners.

RIVE DROITE (RIGHT BANK)

The first four *arrondissements* comprise what has historically been central Paris and contain the oldest streets and residences in the city. Still, because of the Left Bank's appeal, hotels here may have unexpected vacancies. In general, hotel prices rise with proximity to the Louvre and the Opéra, and supermarkets and inexpensive restaurants are fewer and farther between than elsewhere.

In the shadow of the Louvre, much of the **1er** remains true to its royal past: expensive and posh. Cartier, Chanel, and the Banque de France set the scene; the few budget hotels lurking here are rarely accompanied by budget accoutrements (laundromats, grocery stores, etc.). Although the 1*er* is one of the safest areas in Paris, it is best to shun M. Châtelet or Les Halles at night, when their labyrinthine tunnels are claimed by muggers and drug dealers.

Devoid of its own sights, the **2ème arrondissement** is within easy walking distance of the Marais, the Centre Pompidou, the Louvre, the Palais Royal, Notre-Dame, and more. Many little restaurants and hotels, often quite cheap, stand in this mostly working-class area, making it an excellent place to stay. Although the rue St-Denis, at the eastern end, is a center of prostitution and pornography, its seediness does not spill over very far into neighboring streets.

Absolutely *the* place to live in the 17th century, the **Marais** has regained its swish, thanks to 30 years of extensive renovations. Once-palatial mansions have become exquisite museums, as interesting for their collections as for their aristocratic elegance, and the tiny twisting streets have been adopted by fashionable boutiques and galleries. Fascinating and lively quarters, the **3ème** and **4ème arrondissements** shelter some terrific accommodations at reasonable rates. Prices drop as you head north through the 4ème into the 3ème. **Rue des Rosiers,** running through the heart of the 4ème, is the focal point of the city's Jewish population. Here you'll find superb kosher delicatessens and excellent Middle Eastern and Eastern European food. The area stays lively on Sunday, when other districts shut down.

The **8ème arrondissement** is home to the world-famous and much-visited **av. des Champs-Elysées.** You should know better than to expect oodles of inexpensive restaurants amid the embassies and *haute couture* salons of the 8ème, where many of Paris's finest and most famous restaurants assemble. For the most part, travelers with thin wallets will want to visit the 8ème's *grands boulevards,* and then head elsewhere for supper.

The **9ème arrondissement** links some of Paris's wealthiest and most heavily touristed quarters—the 2ème and the 8ème —with the less affluent 10ème and 18ème. There are plenty of hotels here, but many in the northern half of the area are used for the local flesh trade. Avoid the Anvers, Pigalle, and Barbès-Rochechouart metro stops at night; use the Abbesses stop instead. A few nicer but not-so-cheap hotels are available near the more respectable and central bd. des Italiens and bd. Montmartre.

In response to the voluminous traffic that pours through the Gare de l'Est and the Gare du Nord, a flock of inexpensive hotels has come to roost in the **10ème.** These hotels are far from sights and nightlife, so you'll be forced to use taxis or feet once the metro stops running; however, they often have space when others are full. Lone travelers should look elsewhere; areas near the train stations are often far from safe. Exercise special caution in the area stretching west from pl. de la République along rue du Château d'Eau.

A working-class and immigrant population means that wondrous delicacies from Senegal, Pakistan, India, and elsewhere dovetail along the side streets of the 10ème. The best bargains are north of the (overpriced) Opéra area.

Five metro lines converge at "République," three at "Bastille," making the **11ème arrondissement** a transportation hub and mammoth center of action, the hangout of the young and electric. Budget accommodations line these streets and are likely to have space. The Bastille area hums with nightlife; it's rough, but mostly safe. At night, be wary in the pickpocket-strewn pl. de la République.

The **12ème arrondissement** is generally safe (though be careful around the Gare de Lyon train station); the streets around the Bois de Vincennes offer some of the city's cleanest and most pleasant places to stay, making up a bit for their distance from the city center. Budget hotels cluster near the Gare de Lyon, southeast of the Bastille, and near pl. de la Nation. Many have space during the summer.

Wealthy and residential, the **16ème arrondissement** is a short walk from the Eiffel Tower but a 20-minute metro ride to the big museums and real nightlife. Hotels here are relatively luxurious and apt to have vacancies in high season. Restaurants are scarce and upscale; stop by one of the markets—at av. Président Wilson or rue St-Didier—between visits to the area's myriad tiny museums. The **17ème** combines the elegance of its western neighbor with the sordidness of its eastern neighbor pl. Pigalle; some of its hotels cater to prostitutes, others to visiting businesspeople. Safety is an issue where it borders the 18ème, especially near pl. de Clichy.

The area known as **Montmartre** owes its reputation to the fame of artists who lived there. By day the **18ème** crawls with tourists; by night it can be dangerous, especially for newcomers. Hotel rates rise as you climb the hill to the Basilique Sacré-

Coeur. Near the church, the touristed cafés and restaurants of the pl. du Tertre are pricey for dinner but reasonable for snacks and coffee breaks. Downhill and south at seedy pl. Pigalle, hotels tend to rent by the hour. Avoid M. Anvers, M. Pigalle, and M. Barbès-Rochechouart; use the Abbesses metro stop instead, where you can wait for the huge elevator to take you to street level or walk up 564 steps.

The **19ème** and **20ème arrondissements** are by no means central; apart from the Parc de la Villette in the 19*ème* and Père LaChaise in the 20*ème*, expect at least a half-hour metro ride to the city's sights. On the bright side, the 19*ème*'s Parc des Buttes-Chaumont is a worthy picnic area and good place for a jog. Although cheap high-rises dot the hillsides, so do charming streets and open-air markets. Hotels offer two-star accommodations at reasonable rates in summer and are a good bet if you're stuck without a bed. Rue de Belleville can be dangerous at night.

Practical Information

Getting There

BY PLANE

Roissy-Charles de Gaulle

Most transatlantic flights land at **Aéroport Roissy-Charles de Gaulle,** 23km northeast of Paris. As a general rule, Terminal 2 serves Air France and its affiliates (tel. 08 36 68 10 48 for arrivals and departures; 01 44 08 24 24 for a real-live operator, 9am-9pm). Most other carriers operate from Terminal 1; for info call the 24-hour English-speaking passenger information center at 01 48 62 22 80.

The two cheapest and fastest ways to get into the city from Roissy-Charles de Gaulle and vice versa make use of the RATP local transit system (tel. 08 36 68 77 14). The **Roissy Rail** bus-train combination begins with a free shuttle bus from Aérogare 1 arrival level gate 28, Aérogare 2A gate 5, Aérogare 2B gate 6, or Aérogare 2D gate 6 to the Roissy train station. From there, the **RER B3** (one of the commuter rail lines) will transport you to central Paris. To transfer to the metro, get off at **Gare du Nord, Châtelet-Les Halles,** or **St-Michel,** all of which double as RER and metro stops. To go to Roissy-Charles de Gaulle from Paris, take the RER B3—any train with a name starting with the letter "E"—to "Roissy," which is the end of the line. Change to the free shuttle bus (RER daily 5am-12:30am, every 15min., train 30–35min., bus 10min., 45F). For more direct service to the airport, the **Roissybus** (tel. 01 48 04 18 24) runs from in front of the American Express office on rue Scribe, near M. Opéra, to gate 10 of Terminal 2A (which also serves terminal 2C), to gate 12 of Terminal 2D (which also serves Terminal 2B), and to gate 30 of Terminal 1, arrivals level (every 15min., to airport 5:45am-11pm, from airport 6am-11pm, 45min., 40F).

Alternatively, daily **Air France Buses** (tel. 01 44 08 24 24) run to and from: the **Arc de Triomphe** (M. Charles de Gaulle-Etoile) at 1, av. Carnot (every 12min. 5:40am-11pm, 35min., 55F); to and from the **pl. de la Porte de Maillot/Palais des Congrès** (M. Porte de Maillot), near the Air France booking agency (same schedule and prices); and to and from 13, bd. du Vaugirard near the **Gare Montparnasse** (M. Montparnasse-Bienvenue; to the airport every hr. 7am-9pm; from the airport every hr. 6:30am-7:30pm, 45min., 65F). At Roissy, the shuttle stops between terminals 2A and 2C; between 2B and 2D; and at terminal 1 on the arrivals level, outside exit 34. Call 01 41 56 89 00 for information, available in English, on all Air France shuttles.

Taxis take at least 50 minutes to central Paris and cost about 250F during the day, 280F at night. A new **TGV station** serves Roissy; call the SNCF for scheduling info.

Orly

Aéroport d'Orly (tel. 01 49 75 15 15 for passenger info, available in English daily 6am-11:45pm), 12km south of the city, is used by charters and many continental flights. From Orly Sud gate H or Orly Ouest arrival level gate F, take the shuttle bus (every 15min. 5:40am-11:15pm) to the **Pont de Rungis/Aéroport d'Orly** train stop where you can board the **RER C2** for a number of destinations in Paris (daily every 15min. 5:30am-11pm, 25min., 30F; call RATP at 08 36 68 77 14 for info).

Another option is the **RATP Orlyval** combination of metro, RER, and Val rail shuttle. To get to Orly, buy a combined Orlyval ticket (52F), take the metro to Gare du Nord, Châtelet-les-Halles, St-Michel, or Denfert-Rochereau, and change to the RER B. Make sure that the station Antony-Orly is lit up on the changing schedule panel next to the track (see **RER** on page 89). Get off at Antony-Orly and transfer to the Val train. Remember that with the combined ticket, your subsequent transfers in the Paris metro are included. From the airport, buy a ticket at an RATP office (Ouest gate W level 1 or J level O; sud gate E or F, baggage area; tel. 01 43 46 14 14). Note that weekly or monthly yellow or orange cards are not valid for Orlyval. (Val trains run from Antony to Orly Mon.-Sat. 6:30am-9:15pm, Sun. 7am-10:55pm; trains arrive at Orly Ouest 2min. after reaching Orly Sud. They run from Orly to Antony every 7min. Mon.-Sat. 6:30am-9:15pm, Sun. 7am-10:57pm, 30min. from Châtelet.)

Air France Buses run between Orly Montparnasse, 36, rue de Maine, 6*ème* (M. Montparnasse-Bienvenue), and the Invalides Air France agency (every 12min., 30min., 32F). Air France shuttles stop at Orly Sud, gates C or D and Orly Ouest, Gate E, arrivals level. Also, the RATP runs **Orlybus** to and from metro and RER stop Denfert-Rochereau, 14*ème*. Board at Orly Sud gate H, platform 4 or Orly Ouest level O, door D (Mon.-Fri. every 13min., Sat.-Sun. every 16-20min., 6am-11pm, 30min., 30F).

Taxis from Orly to town cost at least 120F during the day, 160F at night. Allow at least 45 minutes for the trip.

PARIS

BY TRAIN AND BUS

Each of the city's six train stations has two divisions: the *banlieue* and the *grandes lignes.* **Grandes lignes** serve distant destinations, whereas trains to the **banlieue** serve the suburbs of Paris. Within a given station, each of these divisions has its own ticket counters, information booths, and timetables; distinguishing between them before you get in line will save you hours of frustration. All train stations connect to at least two metro lines; the metro stop bears the same name as the train station. There is a free telephone with direct access to the stations on the right-hand side of the Champs-Elysées tourist office. In addition, there are yellow **automatic guichets** at every train station; you can use a MasterCard or Visa to buy your tickets.

A word on safety: though full of atmosphere, each terminal also shelters its share of thieves and other undesirables. Gare du Nord, for example, becomes rough at night, when drugs and prostitution take over; Gare d'Austerlitz can be similarly unfriendly. Be cautious in and around stations. Naïve tourists are prime targets for thieves and con-artists. In each train station metro stop, you will encounter friendly looking people who will try to sell you a metro ticket at exorbitant prices. It is not advisable to buy anything in the stations except at public counters.

Gare du Nord: Trains to northern France, Britain, Belgium, the Netherlands, Scandinavia, Eastern Europe, and northern Germany. To: Brussels (19 per day, 2hr., 220F); Amsterdam (6 per day, 5hr., 366F); Cologne (6 per day, 5-6hr., 332F); Boulogne (18 per day, 2½hr., 163F); Copenhagen (1 direct and 2 indirect per day, 16hr., 1343F); London (by the Chunnel, 7-9 per day, 2hr., 410-645F).

Gare de l'Est: To eastern France (Champagne, Alsace, Lorraine), Luxembourg, parts of Switzerland (Basel, Zürich, Lucerne), southern Germany (Frankfurt, Munich), Austria, and Hungary. To: Zürich (7 per day, 6hr., 412F); Munich (4 per day, 13hr., 613F); Vienna (2 per day, 13hr., 923F).

Gare de Lyon: To southern and southeastern France (Lyon, Provence, Riviera), parts of Switzerland (Geneva, Lausanne, Berne), Italy, and Greece. To: Geneva (5 per day, 3½hr., 498F); Florence (1 per day, 12hr., 650F); Rome (3-4 per day, 14-16hr., 632F); Lyon (20 per day, 2hr., 286-381F); Nice (4 per day, 7hr., 300-432F); Marseille (10-15 per day, 4-5hr., 180-357F).

Gare d'Austerlitz: To the Loire Valley, southwestern France (Bordeaux, Pyrénées), Spain, and Portugal. To Barcelona (3 per day, 12-14hr., 600F) and Madrid (4 per day, 12-16hr., 600F).
Gare St-Lazare: To Normandy. To Caen (10-15 per day, 2½hr., 153F) and Rouen (20 per day, 1½hr., 102F).
Gare Montparnasse: To Brittany, and the TGV to southwestern France. To Rennes (15 per day, 2-2½hr., 258F plus 32-80F TGV reservation).

Most international **buses** to Paris arrive at **Gare Routière Internationale du Paris-Gallieni,** 28, av. du Général de Gaulle, Bagnolet 93170 (tel. 01 49 72 51 51; M. Gallieni). Call ahead. For reservations on buses to England, contact **Hoverspeed Voyages** (tel. 03 21 46 14 14 for reservations). The Paris office of **Hoverspeed Voyages** is at 75, av des Champs-Elysées, 8ème. Buses arrive and leave from its Paris terminal, located at 165, av. de Clichy, 17ème (tel. 01 40 25 22 00; M. Porte du Clichy).

■ Getting Around

MAPS

A map of Paris is essential if you plan to do any serious strolling. By far the best guide to Paris is the **Plan de Paris par Arrondissement,** which includes a detailed map of each *arrondissement,* all the bus lines, a wealth of miscellany, and an essential index of streets and their nearest metro stops. You can pick up a copy of the red- or black-covered *plan* at almost any bookstore or newsstand for 56F. Unfortunately, the metro map in these guides is sometimes out of date. Pick up a free, updated one at any metro station; it also includes bus lines and the RER suburban system. If you're lost, keep your eyes out for a metro station; every station has a map of the neighborhood, with a street index. **L'Astrolabe,** 46, rue de Provence, 9ème (tel. 01 42 85 42 95; M. Chaussée d'Antin), and 14, rue Serpente, 6ème (tel. 01 46 33 80 06; M. Odéon), stocks more maps than you can imagine. Both locations sell guidebooks and travel literature in almost every language. At the 9ème *arrondissement* location, an entire floor is dedicated just to France (both open Mon.-Sat. 9:30am-7pm).

PUBLIC TRANSPORTATION

The **RATP (Régie Autonome des Transports Parisiens)** coordinates a network of subways, buses, and commuter trains in and around Paris. For info on RATP services, contact their office at the **Bureau de Tourisme RATP,** pl. de la Madeleine, 8ème (tel. 01 40 06 71 44; M. Madeleine; open Mon.-Sat. 8:30am-6:45pm). You can call the RATP at 08 36 68 77 14 (English sometimes spoken; open daily 6am-9pm).

If you're only staying in Paris for one day but expect to do a lot of traveling, consider buying a **metro pass.** At 70F for two days, 105F for three days, and 165F for five, you probably won't get your money's worth with the **Paris Visite** tourist tickets, which are valid for unlimited travel on bus, metro, and RER, and which give discounts on sightseeing trips, bicycle rentals, and more. A more practical saver-pass is the **Formule 1:** for 30F per day, you get unlimited travel on buses, metro, and RER within Paris. If you're staying in Paris for more than a few days, get a weekly *(hebdomadaire)* **coupon vert** or a monthly *(mensuel)* **coupon orange,** which allow unlimited travel (starting on the first day of the week or month) on the metro and buses in Paris. Both of these must be accompanied by the ID-style **carte orange**. To get your carte orange, bring an ID photo (taken by machines in most major stations) to the ticket counter, ask for a carte orange with a plastic case, and then purchase your handsome coupon vert (63F) or equally chic coupon orange (219F). No matter which *coupon* you have, write the number of your carte on your coupon before you use it. Remember that these cards have specific start and end dates and may not be worthwhile if bought in the middle or at the end of the month or week. All prices quoted here are for passes in zones 1 and 2 (the metro and RER in Paris and the immediate suburbs). If you intend to travel to the distant 'burbs, you'll need to buy RER passes for more zones (up to 5). Ask at the ticket windows for details.

Metro

Inaugurated in 1898, the *Paris Métropolitain* (metro) is one of the world's oldest and most efficient subway systems, able to whisk you within walking distance of nearly any spot in the city. Stations are marked with an "M" or with the *"Métropolitain"* lettering designed by Art Nouveau pioneer Hector Guimard. Trains run frequently and connections are easy. The first trains start running around 5:30am; the last leave the end-of-the-line stations (the *"portes de Paris"*) for the center of the city at about 12:15am. For the exact departure times of the last trains, check the poster marked **Principes de Tarification** (fare guidelines) in the center of each station.

Transport maps are posted on train platforms and near turnstiles; all have a *plan du quartier* (map of the neighborhood). Connections to other lines are indicated by orange *"correspondance"* signs, and the exits by blue *"sortie"* signs. Metro lines are numbered (1 is the oldest), but referred to by their final destination. Transfers to other lines are free if made in the same station, but it's not always possible to reverse direction on the same line without exiting the station and using another ticket.

Each trip on the metro requires one ticket. Tickets can be bought individually (8F), but a *carnet* of 10 (46F) is more practical. Don't buy tickets from anyone except the people in the ticket booths. To pass through the turnstiles, insert the ticket into the small slit in the metal divider just next to you as you approach the turnstile. It disappears for a moment, then pops out about a foot farther along, and a little green or white circle lights, reminding you to retrieve the ticket. If an electric whine sounds and a little red circle lights up, your ticket is not valid; take your ticket back and try another. **Hold onto your ticket** until you exit the metro, pass the point marked **Limite de Validité des Billets;** a uniformed RATP *contrôleur* (inspector) may request to see it on any train. If caught without one, you must pay a fine. Also, any *correspondances* to the RER require you to put your validated (and uncrumpled) ticket into a turnstile. Otherwise, you might need to buy a new ticket in order to exit. A word on being helpful to people who have "lost" their ticket and need to get through an entrance or exit; while it may seem a small matter to allow someone to follow you through the gate, be warned that **thieves** often use this strategy to insinuate their way into your bag or pocket. A metro ticket is valid only within Paris.

Most train lines are well traveled at night, and Parisian women often travel alone, although their familiarity with the city affords them a confidence you may lack. Violent crime in the metro is on the increase, so use common sense. Avoid empty cars and corridors. At night, many people ride in the first car, where the conductor is only a door away. Do not count on buying a metro ticket home late at night. Some ticket windows close as early as 10pm, and many close before the last train is due to arrive. Always have one ticket more than you need.

Stay away from the most dangerous stations at night (Barbès-Rochechouart, Pigalle, Anvers, Châtelet-Les-Halles, Gare du Nord, Gare de l'Est). Despite the good neighborhoods in which some of these stops are located, they are often frequented by thieves and other troublemakers looking to prey on the tourist or the wealthy. When in doubt, take a taxi. Should you choose to walk home, stay on well-lit streets.

RER

The **RER** (Réseau Express Régional) is the RATP's suburban train system, which passes through central Paris in deeper tunnels at higher speeds than the metro. Within the city, the RER is for all intents a quicker, more confusing set of metro lines. There are four RER lines, marked A-D, with different branches designated by a number, such as the C5 line to Versailles-Rive-Gauche. The principal stops within the city, which link the RER to the metro, are Gare du Nord, Nation, Charles de Gaulle-Etoile and Châtelet-les-Halles on the Right Bank, and St-Michel and Denfert-Rochereau on the Left Bank. To check your train, watch the electric signboards next to the track, which list all possible stops for trains running on that track. Be sure the little square next to your destination is lit up. There are two transit classes on RER trains. Unless you ask otherwise, you'll be sold a second-class ticket. Every RER car is marked "1" or "2"; second-class ticket holders will be fined if they use first-class cars. Second-class tickets cost 8F within the city; first-class tickets cost 12F. To get to the suburbs, you'll need to buy special tickets (10-38F one-way). Classier and more confusing, the RER differs from the metro on yet another count; **you'll need your ticket to exit the RER.** Insert your ticket just as you did to enter, and pass through.

Bus

Because the metro is so efficient and convenient, the Parisian bus system is often neglected by both locals and visitors, though bus rides can be cheap sight-seeing tours and handy introductions to the city's layout. The free bus map *Autobus Paris-Plan du Réseau* is available at the tourist office and at some metro info booths. The routes of each line are also posted at each stop. Bus tickets are the same as those used in the metro and are available in metro stations or on the bus. Most trips within the city and nearest suburbs cost one ticket. If your journey takes you out of the city you may need more—ask the driver. Enter the bus at the front door and punch your ticket by pushing it into the machine by the driver's seat. If you have a *coupon orange,* flash it at the driver, but **do not** insert the ticket into the machine. Inspectors may ask to see your ticket, so hold onto it until the end of the ride.

Most buses run from 7am to 8:30pm; those marked **Autobus du Soir** go until 12:30am. Still others, called **Noctambus,** run all night. Night buses (3 tickets) start their runs to the *portes* of the city from the "Châtelet" stop and leave every hour on the half hour from 1:30 to 5:30am. Buses from the suburbs to Châtelet run every hour on the hour 1 to 6am. Buses with three-digit numbers come from or are bound for the suburbs, while buses with two-digit numbers travel within Paris. Buses with numbers in the 20s come from or are bound for Gare St-Lazare; in the 30s Gare de l'Est; in the 40s Gare du Nord; in the 70s Châtelet/Hôtel de Ville (with exceptions); in the 80s Luxembourg (with exceptions); and in the 90s Gare Montparnasse.

For more detailed diagrams of all bus routes, consult the *Plan de Paris par Arrondissement* (see page 88). The RATP prints a number of useful brochures, including the *Grand Plan de Paris.* Buses worth riding from start to finish include:

Bus 20: From Gare St-Lazare to the Opéra, Montmartre-Poissonière, République, Bastille (35min.). A trip down the *grands boulevards.* Open platform in back.

Bus 21: From Gare St-Lazare to the Opéra, Palais Royal, the Louvre, the Pont Neuf, St-Michel, Gare du Luxembourg, Porte de Gentilly (40min.).

Bus 29: From Gare St-Lazare to Porte de Montempoivre (30-40min.). Intrepid ride through narrow streets of the Marais. Open platform in back.

Bus 83: From pl. d'Italie, along bd. Raspail, Gare des Invalides, pl. des Ternes (50min.). Paris's finest real estate and views of the *quais.* Open platform in back.

Bus 95: From the Tour Montparnasse, past St-Germain-des-Prés, the Louvre, Palais Royal, the Opéra, and to Montmartre, near the Sacré-Coeur (50min.).

TAXI

Taxi trips within Paris represent the height of decadence for the budget traveler. Rates vary according to time of day and geographical area, but they're never cheap. **Tarif A,** the basic rate, is in effect in Paris proper from 7am to 7pm (3F23/km). **Tarif B** is in effect in Paris proper Monday to Saturday 7pm to 7am, all day Sunday, and during the day from the airports (5F10/km). **Tarif C,** the highest, is in effect from the airports from 7pm to 7am (6F88/km). In addition, there is a *prix en charge* (base fee) of about 11F. Should you call a taxi, rather than getting one at a taxi stand, the base fee will increase according to how long it takes the driver to get to you. For all cabs, stationary time (at lights and in traffic jams) costs 120F per hour. Additional charges (5-10F) are added for luggage weighing over 5kg, a pet in the backseat, a fourth adult in the cab, or for taxis leaving from train stations and marked taxi stops. Make sure the meter is on when you start the ride. A 15% tip is customary (round up to the nearest

5F). If you must take a taxi, try picking one up at a train station or a stand, called *arrêt taxis,* usually found near bus stops. Calling a radio-cab (**Alpha Taxis,** tel. 01 45 85 85 85; **Taxis Radio Etoile,** tel. 01 41 27 27 27; **Taxis G7,** tel. 01 47 39 47 39; **Taxis Bleus,** tel. 01 49 36 10 10; or **Taxis 7000,** tel. 01 42 70 00 42) is far more expensive. Taxis cannot refuse to take a fare if their roof light is on but can refuse to take more than three people. Illegal overcrowding can bring heavy fines upon the driver. If you have a complaint, write to **Service des Taxis de la Préfecture de Police,** 36, rue des Morillons, 75015 (tel. 01 55 70 20 00; M. Convention).

BICYCLE

During the metro strike of December 1995, bike stores sold out to car-less Parisians, and the community of cyclists dreaming of an autoless Paris became more vocal. The government has promised that 1997 will bring 50km of Parisian streets reserved for motorless wheels. Nonetheless, if you have never ridden a bike in heavy traffic, don't use central Paris as a testing ground—the Bois de Boulogne and the Bois de Vincennes should be more your speed. The metro cannot accommodate bikes, but local trains list times when they allow bicycles on board for free. When renting from the following agencies, ask for a helmet. **Paris Bike,** 83, rue Daguerre, 14*ème* (tel. 01 45 38 58 58; M. Denfert-Rochereau), leads three-hour tours that focus on the west side of Paris; commentary is in French, but the guide is bilingual (tours Sun. at 10am and 2pm; 195F per person). **La Maison du Vélo,** 11, rue Fénelon, 10*ème* (tel. 01 42 81 24 72; M. Poissonière), has been "the English-speaking bike store in Paris" since 1979. Follow rue Lafayette in the direction of traffic. Rue Fénelon is the street running along the left side of the St. Vincent de Paul church. (Sells new and used bikes and repairs all models. Mountain bikes 150F per day, 260F for two days, 300F for three days, and 575F per week. Deposit 200F per bike.) For **motorcycles** or **scooters,** stop by **Agence Contact Location,** 24, rue Arc de Triomphe, 17*ème* (tel. 01 47 66 19 19; M. Etoile). (Scooters 235F per day, 870F per week. 7000F credit card deposit required. Motorcycles 660-815F per day, 2850-3350F per week. 20,000-30,000F credit card deposit required.)

CAR

"Somewhere you have heard a dark apocryphal statistic—that one driver out of every twelve in Paris has killed his man. On foot, the Parisian is as courteous as the citizen of any other city. But mounted, he is merciless." So wrote Irwin Shaw, and he *liked* Parisians. The infamous rotary at the Arc de Triomphe has trapped many an unwary tourist; at rush hour, cars move in any direction they want. Drivers may not honk their horns within city limits unless they are about to hit a pedestrian, but this rule is often broken. The legal way to show discontent is to flash the headlights; keep an eye peeled in case a law-abiding driver refrains from honking until just before impact. Parking is hard to locate, and garages are expensive. Foreigners need a passport, a license of at least one year's standing, and a credit card to rent in Paris. None of the agencies in Paris will rent to drivers under 21; all of them take MasterCard and Visa. **Inter Touring Service,** 117, bd. Auguste Blanqui, 13*ème* (tel. 01 45 88 52 37; fax 01 45 80 89 30; M. Glacière) rents Fiat Pandas (267F per day) with 200km and insurance. They also provide vehicles equipped for **drivers with disabilities** (open Mon.-Sat. 8:30am-6:15pm). **Autorent,** 98, rue de la Convention, 15*ème* (tel. 01 45 54 22 45; fax 01 45 54 39 69; M. Boucicaut), rents Fiats for 280F per day with 250km included; unlimited mileage for rentals of three days or more. Some cars have **automatic transmission** (open Mon.-Fri. 8:30am-7pm, Sat. 8:30am-midnight).

■ Tourist Offices

Though packed in the summer, these offices are usually able to keep the wait down to an hour at most; lines are worst in the afternoon. Tourist offices will help you find a room in a one-star hotel for 20F, two-star for 25F, three-star for 40F, and hostels for

PARIS

8F. The Champs-Elysées tourist office will also help you reserve rooms in other parts of the country, though no more than a month in advance, for a 30F charge and first night's deposit. The central branch also **exchanges currency** at decent rates with no commission and always has an English-speaking representative. Expect a wait at the **Bureau d'Accueil Central** (central office), 127, av. des Champs-Elysées, 8ème (tel. 01 49 52 53 54; M. Charles-de-Gaulle-Etoile; open daily 9am-8pm). There are six smaller Bureaux d'Accueil located at: the **Gare du Nord,** 10ème (tel. 01 45 26 94 82; M. Gare du Nord; open Easter-Oct. Mon.-Sat. 8am-9pm; Nov.-Easter Mon.-Sat. 8am-8pm); the **Gare de L'Est,** 10ème (tel. 01 46 07 17 73; M. Gare de l'Est; open May-Oct. Mon.-Sat. 8am-9pm; Nov.-April Mon.-Sat. 8am-8pm); the **Gare de Lyon,** 12ème (tel. 01 43 43 33 24; M. Gare de Lyon; open May-Oct. Mon.-Sat. 8am-9pm; Nov.-April Mon.-Sat. 8am-8pm); the **Gare d'Austerlitz,** 13ème (tel. 01 45 84 91 70; M. Gare d'Austerlitz; open Mon.-Sat. 8am-3pm); the **Eiffel Tower,** Champs de Mars, 7ème (tel. 01 45 51 22 15; M. Champs de Mars; open May-Sept. daily 11am-6pm); and the **Gare Montparnasse,** 15ème (tel. 01 43 22 19 19; M. Montparnasse-Bienvenue; open Easter-Oct. Mon.-Sat. 8am-9pm; Nov.-Easter Mon.-Sat. 8am-8pm). In addition, both **Orly and Charles de Gaulle airports** run tourist offices where you can make same-day hotel reservations (with deposit equal to 12% of room rate). The two offices at Orly (**Orly, Sud:** near gate H, tel. 01 49 75 00 90; **Orly, Ouest:** near gate F, tel. 01 49 75 01 39) are both open daily 6am-11:45pm. The office at **Roissy-Charles de Gaulle** is located near gate 36 arrival level (tel. 01 48 62 27 29; open daily 7:30am-9pm). Also call **Tourist Information** (tel. 01 49 52 53 56) where a recorded message in English (updated weekly) gives the major events in Paris—call 01 49 52 53 55 for info in French.

PARIS

■ Budget Travel Offices

Accueil des Jeunes en France (AJF): 119, rue St-Martin, 4ème (tel. 01 42 77 87 80; M. Rambuteau). Across the pedestrian mall facing the Centre Pompidou. Open Mon.-Sat. 10am-6:45pm. Also 139, bd. St-Michel, 5ème (tel. 01 43 54 95 86; M. Port-Royal) in the *quartier latin.* Open Mon.-Thurs. 10am-12:30pm and 1:45-6pm, Fri. 10:30am-12:30pm and 1:45-6pm. Another in Gare du Nord arrival hall next to Agence de Voyages SNCF (tel. 01 42 85 86 19). Open Mon.-Fri. 8am-5pm. The small Gare du Nord office only books accommodations. The other offices give out free maps, sell ISICs (60F, cash), and reserve rooms in Parisian hotels and hostels (10F fee; rooms around 115F per night). Reduced-price student plane, train, and bus tickets, budget weekend trips, and meal vouchers for hostels. Branches are well located, English-speaking, and ridiculously crowded. V, MC.

Centre Régional des Oeuvres Universitaires (CROUS): 39, av. Georges Bernanos, 5ème (tel. 01 40 51 37 10; M. Port-Royal). Next door to the OTU, this helpful university organization has information on student dormitory housing in Paris (2-day min. stay, 1-month max.) and on the many university restaurants that offer simple but filling meals for rock-bottom prices (see page 111 for listings).

Council on International Educational Exchange (Council): Main office at 1, pl. de l'Odéon, 6ème (tel. 01 44 41 74 74; fax 01 43 26 97 45). M. Odéon. Answers questions about work abroad. Has a complete library with useful info about jobs, travel, and housing opportunities (library open 3-6pm). Open Mon.-Fri. 9am-6pm.

Council Travel, 16, rue de Vaugirard, 6ème (tel. 01 44 41 89 89; fax 01 40 51 89 12; M. Odéon), or 22, rue des Pyramides, 1er (tel. 01 44 55 55 65; M. Pyramides). English-speaking budget travel service. Books international flights. Sells student train tickets, guidebooks, and ISICs (60F). BIJ/Eurotrain tickets. If you lose your Council Travel flight ticket, one of the offices will telex the U.S. for a substitute; penalty fee varies by flight. Vaugirard branch open Mon.-Fri. 9:30am-6:30pm, Sat. 10am-5pm. Pyramides branch open Mon.-Fri. 9am-7pm, Sat. 10am-6:30pm. V, MC.

Office de Tourisme Universitaire (OTU): 39, av. Georges Bernanos, 5ème (tel. 01 43 36 80 27; M. Port-Royal). A French student travel agency. English spoken. The same reduced train and plane tickets for students under 26, but more crowded. Bring an official form of ID. Also sells ISICs (60F) and BIJ tickets. Open Mon.-Fri. 10am-12:45pm and 2-6:45pm, Sat. 11am-12:45pm and 2-5:45pm.

■ Embassies and Consulates

U.S.: 2, av. Gabriel, 8ème (tel. 01 43 12 22 22; fax 01 42 66 97 83; M. Concorde). Open Mon.-Fri. 9am-6pm. **Consulate** at 2, rue St-Florentin (tel. 01 43 12 48 45; 01 40 39 82 91 for automated info), 3 blocks away. Passports replaced for $55 (under 18 $30). Open Mon.-Fri. 9am-3pm. Closed on both American and French holidays.

Canada: 35, av. Montaigne, 8ème (tel. 01 44 43 29 00; M. Franklin-Roosevelt or Alma-Marceau). Open Mon.-Fri. 9am-noon and 2-5pm. **Consulate** at same phone number and address. Ask for "consular services"; you will need to make an appointment. New passport 380F. Open Mon.-Fri. 9:30-10:30am and 2-3pm.

U.K.: 35, rue du Faubourg-St-Honoré, 8ème (tel. 01 42 66 91 42; M. Concorde). New passport 144F. **Consulate** at 16, rue d'Anjou (same tel. and M.) open Mon.-Fri. 9:30am-noon and 2:30-5pm. Visa bureau open Mon.-Fri. 9am-noon.

Australia: 4, rue Jean-Rey, 15ème (tel. 01 40 59 33 00; fax 01 40 59 33 10; M. Bir-Hakeim). **Consular services:** new passport 360F. Open Mon.-Fri. 9:30am-noon and 2-4pm.

New Zealand: 7ter, rue Léonard de Vinci, 16ème (tel. 01 45 00 24 11; fax 01 45 01 26 39; M. Victor-Hugo). New passport 880F, children 660F. Open Mon.-Fri. 9am-1pm and 2-5:30pm.

Ireland: 12, av. Foch, 16ème (tel. 01 45 00 20 87; fax 01 45 00 81 50 for passport services; M. Charles de Gaulle-Etoile). Open 9:15am-noon. **Consular services** at same phone and address. New passport 380F. Open 9:15am-noon.

South Africa: 59, quai d'Orsay, 7ème (tel. 01 45 55 92 37; fax 01 47 53 99 70; M. Invalides). New passport 100F. Open Mon.-Fri. 9am-noon.

■ Money

You have to approach **currency exchange** in Paris with a spirit of competition. Not every *bureau de change* offers the same rates, and most do not charge commission. Don't be fooled by what seem like fantastic rates. Make sure that no strings (having to exchange at least 15,000F worth of currency, for example) apply. The best rates in town are found at the **Banque de France,** on bd. de Clichy near place Pigalle (9ème); around the Opéra, on rue Scribe, rue Auber, and rue de la Paix (8ème); and near av. de Choisy around the rue du Javelot (13ème). Many post offices change cash and traveler's checks commission-free at competitive rates, and many have **ATMs.** Bureaus at train stations and airports offer less favorable rates; exchange only enough to get you into the center city, and change the rest there. There are **ATMs** everywhere—if you can't find one, you're not looking hard enough.

Most banks are open from 9am to noon and 2 to 4:30pm, but not all exchange money. Check before you queue. **American Express,** 11, rue Scribe, 9ème (tel. 01 47 77 77 07; M. Opéra or Auber), is across from the back of the Opéra. They have long lines in summer, especially Monday, Friday, and Saturday. They also hold mail for cardholders or those with AmEx traveler's checks; it's 5F per inquiry if you don't have a card or checks (open Mon.-Fri. 9am-6:30pm, Sat. 9am-5:30pm).

■ Communications

Post Office: 52, rue du Louvre, 75001 Paris, 1er (tel. 01 40 28 20 00; M. Châtelet-Les-Halles). Open 24hr. All **poste restante** mail is held at this office. Only urgent telegrams and calls. No bulk mailings or packages over 2kg outside of normal business hours. Complete telephone book collection. Long lines Sat. and Sun. Fax service on 3rd floor. The only other **branch office** with extended hours is at 71, av. des Champs-Elysées, 8ème (tel. 01 44 13 66 00; M. George V). Open Mon.-Sat. 8am-10pm, Sun. 10am-noon and 2-8pm. Many more branches throughout the city. Inquire at your hotel or hostel for the nearest one, or look for PTT signs. Generally open Mon.-Fri. 8am-7pm, Sat. 8am-noon. Lines longest noon-2pm. Avoid lines by purchasing stamps at local *tabacs* or from the yellow coin-operated vending machines outside major post offices.

Telephones: *Télécartes* are available at ticket windows in most metro stations, post offices, or at *tabacs.* 50-unit card 41F, 120-unit card 98F. Local calls cost 1 unit; long distance more. See page 57 for details on placing international calls.

■ Emergency, Health, and Help

Fire: tel. 18.

Emergency Medical Assistance: tel. 15. Outside of Paris, call 01 45 67 50 50.

Poison Control: tel. 01 40 37 04 04 or 01 42 05 63 29.

Police Emergency: tel. 17.

Police: Each *arrondissement* of Paris has its own *gendarmerie* (police force) to which you should take all your non-emergency concerns. Call the operator (tel. 12) and ask where your local branch is.

Rape Crisis: SOS Viol (tel. 0 800 05 95 95). Call from anywhere in France for counseling, medical and legal advice, and referrals. Open Mon.-Fri. 10am-6pm.

Hospitals: Hospitals in Paris are numerous and efficient. They will generally treat you whether or not you can pay in advance. Settle with them afterwards and don't let your financial concerns interfere with your health care. Unless your French is exceptionally good, you'll have the best luck at one of the anglophone hospitals. **Hôpital Franco-Britannique de Paris:** 3, rue Barbès, in the Parisian suburb of Levallois-Perret (tel. 01 46 39 22 22; M. Anatole-France). Considered a French hospital and bills like one. Has some English-speakers and a good reputation. **Hôpital Américain de Paris:** 63, bd. Victor Hugo, Neuilly (tel. 01 46 41 25 25; M. Port Maillot, then bus 82 to the end of the line). In a suburb of Paris. Employs English-speaking personnel, but much more expensive than French hospitals. You can pay in U.S. dollars. If you have Blue Cross, your hospitalization is covered so long as you fill out the appropriate forms first. Provides referrals.

Late Night Pharmacies: Pharmacie Dhéry, in the Galerie des Champs, 84, av. des Champs-Elysées, 8ème (tel. 01 45 62 02 41; M. George V). Open 24hr. **Grande Pharmacie Daumesnil,** 6, pl. Félix-Eboué, 12ème (tel. 01 43 43 19 03; M. Daumesnil). Open 24hr. **Drugstore St-Germain,** 149, bd. St-Germain, 6ème (tel. 01 42 22 80 00; M. St-Germain-des-Prés or Mabillon). Open Mon.-Sat. 8:30am-2am, Sun. 10am-2am. **Pharmacie Opéra Capucines,** 6, bd. des Capucines, 9ème (tel. 01 42 65 88 29; M. Opéra). Open Mon.-Sat. 8am-12:30am, Sun. 5pm-12:30am. V, MC, AmEx. Every *arrondissement* has a *pharmacie de garde* which will open in case of emergencies. Your local pharmacy can give the name of the nearest one; after hours, the info will be posted on each pharmacy's door.

AIDS information: AIDES, Fédération Nationale, 247, rue de Belleville, 19ème (tel. 01 44 52 00 00). AIDES is one of the oldest and most prolific AIDS public service organizations in France, roughly equivalent to the AIDS Action Committees found in most major American cities. AIDES runs a hotline that provides information in French and English (tel. 0 800 36 66 36; 24hr.).

Alcoholics Anonymous: 3, rue Frédéric Sauton, 5ème (tel. 01 46 34 59 65; M. Maubert-Mutualité). A recorded message in English will refer you to several numbers you can call to talk to telephone counselors. Daily meetings. Open 24hr.

Birth Control: Mouvement Français pour le Planning Familial, 10, rue Vivienne, 2ème (tel. 01 42 60 93 20; M. Bourse). Open Mon. noon-4pm, Tues. 5-7pm, Thurs. noon-3pm. Answers questions and provides information on birth control, pregnancy, and STD prevention.

Drug Problems: Hôpital Marmottan, 17-19, rue d'Armaillé, 17ème (tel. 01 45 74 00 04; M. Charles de Gaulle-Etoile). No guarantee of English speakers. For consultations or treatments, open Sept.-July Mon.-Wed. and Fri. 9:30am-7pm, Thurs. and Sat. 12:30-7pm; Aug. Mon.-Fri. only.

Emotional Health: Try calling **SOS Crisis Help Line: Friendship** (tel. 01 47 23 80 80). English-speaking. Support and information for the depressed and lonely. Open daily 3-11pm. For personalized crisis-control and counseling, the **American Church,** 65, quai d'Orsay, 7ème (M. Invalides or Alma-Marceau), offers the **International Counseling Service (ICS),** and the adjunct **American Student and Family Service (ASFS)** provides access to psychologists, psychiatrists, social workers, and a clerical counselor. Payment is nominal and negotiable. Open Mon.-Sat.

9:30am-1pm. The office is staffed irregularly July-Aug. but will respond to messages left on its answering machine. Call for an appointment (tel. 01 45 50 26 49 for both). The Church also offers **Free Anglo-American Counseling Treatment and Support** (FAACTS) for people with or affected by HIV.

STD Clinic: 43, rue de Valois, 1er (tel. 01 42 61 30 04; M. Palais-Royal). Testing and treatment for sexually transmitted diseases. Free consultations, blood tests, and injection treatments. Tests for HIV are free, anonymous, and include mandatory counseling. Some English spoken. Open Mon.-Fri. 9am-7pm.

■ Other Services

RELIGIOUS ORGANIZATIONS AND COMMUNITY CENTERS

The **American Church in Paris,** 65, quai d'Orsay, 7ème (tel. 01 47 05 07 99; M. Invalides or Alma-Marceau), is as much a community center as a church. *Free Voice,* a free English-language monthly specializing in cultural events and classifieds, is published here. Bulletin boards list jobs, apartments, and more. Inter-denominational services are held Sunday at 11am, followed by a coffee break and, during the school year, a 50F luncheon. The church also hosts meetings for AA, AL-ANON, ACOA, and FAACTS (also see page 30). The **Catholic Information Center,** 8, rue Massillon, 1er (tel. 01 46 33 01 01), provides information about religious activities, prayer, and pilgrimages (open Mon.-Fri. 9am-noon and 2-6pm). The **Society of Friends (Quakers),** hold meetings at 114bis, rue de Vaugirard, 6ème (tel. 01 45 48 74 23; M. St-Placide or Montparnasse-Bienvenüe). Messages are delivered in French, but nearly everyone is fluent in English. (Meeting Sun. 11am, preceded by a 10am discussion hour.) **St. Michael's Church,** 5, rue d'Aguesseau, 8ème (tel. 01 47 42 70 88; M. Concorde), holds **Anglican and Episcopalian** services in English Sundays at 10:30am and 6:30pm. Inside, bulletin boards list jobs, accommodations, and so on. (Office open Mon.-Tues. and Thurs.-Fri. 9:30am-12:30pm and 2-5:30pm.) The **Union Libéral Israélite de France,** 24, rue Copernic, 16ème (tel. 01 47 04 37 27; M. Victor-Hugo), holds services Friday at 6pm and Saturday at 10:30am, mostly in Hebrew with some French. Services are also held evenings and mornings of the High Holy Days (office open Mon.-Thurs. 9am-noon and 2-6pm, Fri. 9am-noon).

MISCELLANEOUS

Laundromats: Ask your hotel or hostel for the location of the closest one. Averages 30F per wash, 2F per 6min. to dry. Most open 8am-8pm; last wash earlier.

Lost Property: Bureau des Objets Trouvés, 36, rue des Morillons, 15ème (tel. 01 55 76 20 20; M. Convention). Visit or write and describe the object and when and where you lost it. No info given by phone. Open July-Aug. Mon.-Thurs. 8:30am-5pm; Sept.-June Mon. and Wed. 8:30am-5pm, Tues. and Thurs. 8:30am-8pm.

Public Baths: 8, rue des Deux Ponts, 4ème (tel. 01 43 54 47 40; M. Pont-Marie). Shower 7F, with soap and towel 15F. Scrub for the same price at 42, rue du Rocher, 8ème (tel. 01 45 22 15 19; M. St-Lazare), and at 40, rue Oberkampf, 11ème (tel. 01 47 00 57 35; M. Oberkampf). Clean, respectable, and popular in summer. All open Thurs. noon-7pm, Fri. 8am-7pm, Sat. 7am-7pm, and Sun. 8am-noon.

Weather: Allo Météo, 5-day recorded forecasts. Best to call from touch-tone phones. **Paris** tel. 08 36 68 02 75; **Ile de France** tel. 08 36 68 00 00; **France** tel. 08 36 68 01 01. You can also check out a map of the day's weather at the corner of Rapp and Université in the 7ème, posted by **Météorologie Nationale.**

■ Publications About Paris

Your most important printed resource will invariably be a map (see page 88). The tourist office distributes a free monthly booklet, *Paris Sélection,* that highlights exhibits, concerts, suggested walking tours, and other info. Similarly, the mayor's office publishes the monthly *Paris le Journal* (free) with articles and listings about what's on, touristically and culturally. It is available at the *mairie's* Salon d'Accueil, 29, rue de Rivoli, 4ème (tel. 01 42 76 42 42; M. Hôtel-de-Ville).

The weekly *Pariscope* (3F) and *Officiel des Spectacles* (2F; both published Wed.) list current movies, plays, exhibits, festivals, clubs, and bars. *Pariscope* is more comprehensive—buy one as soon as you arrive to get the scoop on Parisian life. *Pariscope* includes an English-language section *Time Out Paris,* a joint venture with British entertainment magazine *Time Out.* Wednesday's *Le Figaro* includes *Figaroscope,* a supplement about events in Paris. *Free Voice,* a monthly newspaper published at the American Church, is available there and at many student centers for free. *France-USA Contacts (FUSAC),* printed twice monthly and available free at English-friendly establishments (bookstores, restaurants, travel agencies) throughout Paris, lists job, housing, and service info for English speakers.

Accommodations

Three basic types of Parisian accommodations are suitable for the budget traveler: hotels, hostels, and *foyers*. While hotels are comfortable and give you complete privacy and independence, hostels and *foyers* are less expensive, especially for people traveling alone. According to the tourist office, high season in Paris falls around Easter, May to June, and September to October (when trade shows—*salons*—take over the city). Indeed, many hotels in the outer (numerically higher) *arrondissements* consider July and August to be off-season. But for hostels and other truly budget accommodations, the high season runs from June through August, and most places are perpetually full. Be aware that the city of Paris has a *Taxe de Séjour* of 1-5F per person per day within the city. Most hostels and *foyers* include this tax in their listed prices, but hotels may tack it on separately. Unless otherwise noted, we list hostel prices per person; prices elsewhere are per room. It is advisable to check the locks at the establishment where you choose to stay.

Every night, swarms of sleeping bags carpet the Gare du Nord and the Gare de l'Est. *Be extremely careful.* Many of these "campers" are homeless people who may resent fresh-faced backpackers' ample supplies. Police regularly rouse sleepers from these make-shift beds and send them onto the streets. If you decide, against the strongest recommendations to the contrary, to risk these dangers, store your bags in a locker and make sure that you never stretch out alone.

Try to make a reservation in advance, but don't panic if you arrive in Paris without one. The **Office du Tourisme** on the Champs-Elysées or one of its other bureaus should be able to find you a room, although the lines may be long and the selections not necessarily the cheapest (see page 91). Or stop by one of the following booking offices, located near train stations and major metro lines. Their English-speaking staffs can arrange for inexpensive stays throughout the city.

La Centrale de Réservations (FUAJ-HI), 4, bd. Jules Ferry, 11ème (tel. 01 43 57 02 60; fax 01 40 21 79 92; M. République). The best way to secure a bed in a hostel or to book any other Parisian budget accommodation (90-125F per night per person). Two buildings from the Jules Ferry hostel. Same-day reservations at affiliated hostels or budget hotels—a total of 10,000 beds in and around Paris. The earlier you show up the better, but they can usually help anyone any time. Books beds throughout France and Europe and arranges trips. Open Mon.-Sat. 9am-6pm.

Accueil des Jeunes en France (AJF), 119, rue St-Martin, 4ème (tel. 01 42 77 87 80; M. Rambuteau), across from the Pompidou Center. AJF guarantees "decent and low-cost lodging" for same-day reservation and immediate use. You must pay the full price of the *foyer* room when making your reservation, before seeing the room. AJF can also help find a hotel room for stays of up to 2 weeks. 10F service charge. Open Mon.-Sat. 10am-6:45pm. See page 92 for more information.

■ Hostels and Foyers

Paris's big-city hostels don't bother with many of the restrictions—sleep sheets, curfews, and the like—that characterize most hostels in the world, but they do have maximum stays (although even these rules are often flexible). Accommodations usually consist of bunkbeds in single-sex dormitories. There are only two HI hostels in Paris. Most dorm-like accommodations in Paris are either private hostels or *foyers.* Check for availability of rooms by calling ahead or arriving early in the morning.

C.IP/Paris Louvre, 20, rue J.-J. Rousseau, 1er (tel. 01 42 36 88 18; fax 01 42 33 40 53; M. Louvre). 200 beds. High-ceilinged, bright, dorm-style rooms. Courtyard hung with brass lanterns and strewn with *brasserie* chairs. 2-10 beds per room, 120F per person per room. Lunch or dinner 55F. Weekend reservations up to 1 week in advance; reserve 1 day ahead for weekday bookings. Rooms normally held 1hr. after your expected check-in time; call if you'll be late.

Maisons des Jeunes Rufz de l'Avison, 18, rue J.-J. Rousseau, 1er (tel. 01 45 08 02 10; M. Louvre—not "Musée du Louvre"—or Palais-Royal). From M. Louvre take rue du Louvre away from river, turn left on rue St.-Honoré and right on rue J.-J. Rousseau. During the academic year, it's a private residence for male college students. In summer it's a co-ed *foyer.* Flower-filled open-air courtyard—hay fever sufferers beware. 3-day min. stay. Reception open 9am-7pm. No curfew. Singles 200F. Doubles 140F per person. Beds in quads are close together, so it's better to come in a group or book long in advance. Shower and breakfast included. Reserve by mail with 1 night's payment or arrive early.

Hôtel des Jeunes (MIJE) (tel. 01 42 74 23 45; fax 01 42 74 08 93 or 01 42 71 61 02) books stays in "Le Fourcy," "Le Fauconnier," and "Maubuisson." All 3 are first-rate hostels located in former aristocratic residences of the Marais, close to sights and to one another. All give priority to groups of 10 or more and help organize tours; call well ahead. No smoking. English spoken. For groups, no age specifications or limits on length of stay. Individuals must be 18-30. 7-day max. stay. Reception open 7am-10pm. Check-out by noon. Lockout noon-4pm. Curfew 1am. Singles 168F. Doubles 148F per person. Larger rooms (3-8 beds) 120F per person. Shower in room, toilet down the hall, breakfast served 7:30-10am—all included. The budget **Restaurant la Table d'Hôtes,** entered through le Fourcy, offers a 1-course meal with Coke (32F) and 3-course "hosteler special" with Coke (52F). Open Mon.-Fri. 11:30am-1:30pm and 6:30-8:30pm. Lockers 2F deposit in each hostel. No towels. Individuals may reserve rooms only in person and by paying in full in advance. Rebooking must be requested before 10pm the day before. Groups may reserve 1 year in advance.

Le Fourcy, 6, rue de Fourcy, 4ème (M. St-Paul or Pont Marie). From M. St-Paul, walk opposite traffic down rue François-Miron and turn left on rue de Fourcy. Hostel surrounds a large courtyard ideal for meeting travelers or for open-air picnics. In summer, school groups raise Cain under evening skies; light sleepers shun rooms on the courtyard. Elevator. Call ahead for wheelchairs.

Le Fauconnier, 11, rue du Fauconnier, 4ème (M. St-Paul or Pont Marie). From M. St-Paul take rue du Prevôt, turn left on rue Charlemagne and then right on rue du Fauconnier. A luxury in modern hostelry. Airy, mostly 4- or 8-bed rooms.

Maubuisson, 12, rue des Barres, 4ème (M. Hôtel-de-Ville or Pont Marie). From M. Pont Marie, walk opposite traffic on rue de l'Hôtel de Ville and turn right on rue des Barres. A former girls' convent, lively Maubuisson offers smaller rooms of 2-7 beds. Faces St-Gervais monastery. Elevator. Call ahead for wheelchairs.

Young and Happy (Y&H) Hostel, 80, rue Mouffetard, 5ème (tel. 01 45 35 09 53; fax 01 47 07 22 24; M. Monge). Cross rue Gracieuse and take rue Ortolan to rue Mouffetard. Clean, cramped rooms. Serpentine staircase and incredibly tight halls. Management might switch your room during your stay. Rooms have phones and 2-4 beds (mostly bunks). Lockout 11am-5pm. Curfew 2am. 107F per night for doubles, 97F per night for quads, 670F per week. Breakfast 'n' shower included. Sheets 15F. Towels 5F. Reserve with 1 night's deposit, or show up at 8am.

Foyer International des Etudiantes, 93, bd. St-Michel, 6ème (tel. 01 43 54 49 63; M. Luxembourg). Across from Jardin du Luxembourg. Marbled reception, library,

TV lounge, kitchenettes, and laundry facilities are fitted with elegant wood paneling. Spacious and comfortable. Some rooms have balconies. Oct.-June women only: singles 133F, doubles 82F per person, breakfast and shower included; *foyer* open Sun.-Fri. 6am-1:30am, Sat. all night. July-Sept. co-ed: singles 165F, doubles 115F per person, breakfast and shower included; *foyer* open 24hr. Reserve in writing 2 months early, 200F deposit required. Call ahead or show up at 9:30am.

UCJF (Union Chrétienne de Jeunes Filles) or **YWCA,** 22, rue Naples, 8ème (tel. 01 45 22 23 49; M. Europe). Take rue de Constantinople and go left on rue de Naples. Organized, well-kept, homey, and for women only. Spacious, airy rooms, hardwood floors, large beds. Large oak-paneled common room with fireplace, TV, VCR, books, and family-style dining room. Congenial staff. 3-day min. stay June-Aug; longer stays for women 18-24 in Sept.-May. All guests must pay 30F for a YWCA membership, as well as a 50F (for week-long stays) or 100F (for stays 1 month or more) processing fee. Reception open Mon.-Fri. 8am-12:30am, Sat.-Sun. 8am-12:30pm and 1:30pm-12:30am. Visitors until 10pm; no men in bedrooms. No curfew. June-Aug. singles 120F per day; doubles or triples 100F per person per day; breakfast included. Sept.-May weekly: singles 800F, doubles 650F; monthly: doubles or triples 2195-2700F; breakfast and dinner included. 200F key deposit. Reserve if you can (200F deposit for stays under 2 weeks, else 500F). Also at 65 rue Orfila, 20ème (tel. 01 46 36 82 80; M. Gambetta), and 168, rue Blomet, 15ème (tel. 01 45 33 48 21; M. Convention). Men call the YMCA **Union Chrétienne de Jeunes Gens,** 14 rue de Trévise, 9ème (tel. 01 47 70 90 94).

Auberge de Jeunesse "Jules Ferry" (HI), 8, bd. Jules Ferry, 11ème (tel. 01 43 57 55 60; M. République). Walk east on rue du Faubourg du Temple and turn right on the far side of bd. Jules Ferry. 100 beds. Wonderfully located. Clean, large rooms. Teeming, friendly, party aura. Jovial, multilingual staff. Usually full by 10am, but they work with the Centrale de Réservations (above) to help find you other lodgings. 3-night max. stay. 24-hr. reception. Lockout noon-2pm, but receptionist can always answer questions or accept reservations. No curfew. Single-sex lodging, but they can accommodate male/female couples; entire room is consulted before going co-ed. 4- to 6-bed rooms 110F per person. Doubles 118F per person. Breakfast and shower included. Lockers 5F. Sheets 5F. Bike storage.

Résidence Bastille (AJF), 151, av. Ledru-Rollin, 11ème (tel. 01 43 79 53 86; M.Voltaire). Cross pl. Léon Blum and head south on av. Ledru-Rollin. Slowly renovating, with 2-4 bunks per room. 170 beds. Redone triples and quads have bathrooms in the room; else, use hall bathrooms. Less crowded than most hostels, with attractive rooms and a friendly, multilingual staff. Ages 18-35 (flexible). Male/female couples can be accommodated in doubles. Reception open 7am-1am. Curfew 1am. Lockout noon-4pm. March-Oct. dorms 120F, singles 171F; Nov.-Feb. dorms 110F, doubles 160F. Showers, breakfast, and sheets included. No reservations, so arrive early. A welcoming station at the Gare du Nord, in the *banlieue* station (tel. 01 42 85 86 19) makes same-day reservations.

Auberge Internationale des Jeunes, 10, rue Trousseau (tel. 01 47 00 62 00; fax 01 47 00 33 16; M. Ledru-Rollin). Walk east on rue du Faubourg St-Antoine and turn left on rue Trousseau. Lively atmosphere with lots of backpackers in the sunny breakfast room. Most of the cramped rooms have 4 beds, though a few have 2 or 6. Rooms on ground floor are off a quiet, outdoor passage in the back. Rooms on high floors look out over the roofs of Paris or onto the street. Safebox for valuables. Luggage storage closes at 10pm. Lockout 10am-3pm. Common rooms downstairs. March-Oct. 91F per person; Nov.-Feb. 81F per person. Breakfast and shower included. Sheets 5F. Show up at 8am to get a room. V, MC.

Centre International du Séjour de Paris: CISP "Ravel," 6, av. Maurice Ravel, 12ème (tel. 01 44 75 60 00; fax 01 43 44 45 30; M. Porte de Vincennes). Walk east on cours de Vincennes, turn right on bd. Soult, left on rue Jules Lemaître, and right on av. Maurice Ravel. Large, institutional-looking, efficient hostel on the edge of the city caters mostly to groups. Large rooms (most with 4 or fewer beds), bar, restaurant, and access to municipal pool next door (15F). Flexible 3-day max. stay. Reception open daily 6:30am-1:30am. Dorms 135F per person, singles 165F. Breakfast included. Restaurant open 7:30-9:30am, noon-1:30pm, and 7-8:30pm.

Association des Foyers de Jeunes: Foyer des Jeunes Filles, 234, rue de Tolbiac, 13ème (tel. 01 44 16 22 22; fax 01 45 65 46 20; M. Glacière). Walk 100m east on bd. Auguste Blanqui, turn right on rue de Glacière, then left on rue de Tolbiac. Large, modern foyer for young women (ages 18-30) with excellent facilities—kitchens on all floors, cable TV, washers, dryers, piano, exercise room, library, cafeteria, and garden. Friendly, helpful staff. Elevator. Sunny singles with sink, desk, chairs, and closet space. Excellent security. 24-hr. reception. July-Aug. 120F per night. Showers and breakfast (6:30-8:30am, no breakfast Sun.) included. Dinner 47F. 3135F per month; breakfast and dinner included. 30F registration fee (good for a year) required of first-time visitors. Usually vacancies in summer. Reserve by fax or call when in Paris. V, MC.

CISP "Kellerman," 17, bd. Kellerman, 13ème (tel. 01 44 16 37 38; fax 01 44 16 37 39; M. Porte d'Italie). Turn right on bd. Kellerman. Institutional complex affiliated with CISP Ravel. 248 beds. 2- to 4-bed rooms 118F per person, 8-beds 93F. Singles with shower and toilet 135F. Doubles with shower and toilet 143F. Breakfast (7-9:30am) included. Restaurant open 6:30-9:30pm. Call for wheelchairs.

Maison des Clubs UNESCO, 43, rue de Glacière, 13ème (tel. 01 43 36 00 63; fax 01 45 35 05 96; M. Glacière). Walk 100m east on bd. Auguste Blanqui and turn left on rue de la Glacière. Enter through garden on right. Small, no-frills rooms. Multilingual management. Caters to tour groups. Reception open 7am-2am. Curfew 1:30am. Singles 160F. Doubles 140F per person. Triples 120F per person. Showers and breakfast (7:45-9am) included. No individual reservations.

FIAP Jean-Monet, 30, rue Cabanis, 14ème (tel. 01 45 89 89 15; fax 01 45 81 63 91; M. Glacière). From bd. St-Jacques, take 1st left (rue Ferrus), then right on rue Cabanis. International student center has 500 beds, mostly full of tour groups in summer. Comfortable rooms are spiffily maintained and equipped with bathrooms. The lobby has a café with kiosks posting upcoming Parisian attractions and offering stacks of tourist info. The hostel has disco and jazz concerts at night (free), French language classes, 12 conference rooms, game room, laundry room, and cheap cafeteria. Some wheelchair accessibility. Curfew 2am. 8-bed dorms 125F. Singles 260F. 2-bed doubles 170F. 3- or 4-bed rooms 150F. V, MC.

Auberge de Jeunesse "Le d'Artagnan" (HI), 80, rue Vitruve, 20ème (tel. 01 40 32 34 56; fax 01 40 32 34 55; M. Porte de Bagnolet or Porte de Montreuil). From M. Porte de Bagnolet, walk south on Boulevard Davout and turn right on rue Vitruve. 411 beds. 7-floor compound with restaurant, bar, and movie theater. Free microwave access. Most rooms have 3 beds, but a few have 2 or 8. English spoken. Flexible 3-day max. stay. Open 24hr. Lockout 10am-2pm. 110F per person, 129F per person in a double. Breakfast and sheets included. Lockers 10F. Wash 15F, dry 5F, soap 3F. Hostel packed Feb.-Oct.

■ Hotels

Of the three classes of Parisian budget accommodations, hotels may be the most practical for many travelers. You'll find privacy, no curfew, and (usually) concerned managers. Most important, hotels accept reservations. Budget hotels in Paris are not significantly more expensive than their hostel/*foyer* counterparts. Groups of two, three, and four may find it cheaper to stay in a hotel since, unlike *foyers,* hotels rent by the room and not by the body. Expect to pay at least 150F for a single.

Paris has a number of very good hotels in the 150-200F range. They are often small and simple and do not offer the amenities of a Sheraton or Hilton. The hotels listed have clean, well-furnished rooms and adequate toilet and shower facilities. Most newly renovated hotels have double-paned glass windows that insulate against cold and noise. Many hotels serve breakfast for 15-25F. Because local cafés often serve croissants and coffee for less, you may want to eat out. Parisian law forbids hanging laundry from windows or over balconies to dry.

FIRST ARRONDISSEMENT

Henri IV, 25, pl. Dauphine (tel. 01 43 54 44 53; M. Cité). Walk toward the Conciergerie, turn right on bd. du Palais, and left on quai de l'Horloge; turn left at the front of the Conciergerie onto pl. Dauphine. The last outpost of cheap accommodations on Ile de la Cité, and one of the best-located hotels in the city, overlooking a quiet park. Somewhat run-down, average-sized rooms with squishy beds. To reach the quirky first floor toilet, follow the staircase that curls around the building. All other toilets located (inside) on each floor. Collection of guidebooks for guests' use. Singles 115-140F. Doubles 145-200F, with shower 225-255F. Triples 200-225F. Quads 260F. Reserve 2 months in advance; send a check for 1 night.

Hôtel Montpensier, 12, rue de Richelieu (tel. 01 42 96 28 50; fax 01 42 86 02 70; M. Palais-Royal). Walk left around the Palais Royal to rue de Richelieu. Fresh scents, lofty ceilings, and friendly staff welcome the clientele. Its spaciousness, good taste, and elevator distinguish it from most hotels in this area and price range. Bright lounge with stained-glass ceiling. 43 rooms, 36 with bath. TVs in rooms with shower or bath. Singles 250F. Doubles 260F. Singles or doubles with toilet 295F, with shower, toilet, and sink 385F, with bath, toilet, and sink 450F. Extra bed 70F. Shower 25F. Breakfast 35F. Reserve 2 weeks ahead. V, MC, AmEx.

Hôtel du Palais, 2, quai de la Mégisserie (tel. 01 42 36 98 25; fax 01 42 21 41 67; M. Châtelet). Location by the Seine at the corner of pl. du Châtelet and quai de la Mégisserie gives all rooms (except on the top floor) splendid views—though the sounds of traffic waft through open windows. 18 rooms have sound-dampening windows. High ceilings on first floor; funky eaves and tiny rooms on top floor. Singles with shower 280F, with shower and toilet 320F, with bath and toilet 350F. Doubles with shower 320F, with shower and toilet 350F, with bath and toilet 380F. Triples 420F. Large quad (480F) and quint (550F) with bathroom. On garret-like top floor, singles 180F, doubles 230F. Extra bed 70F. Hall shower for top-floor rooms. Breakfast 30F. Reserve 3 weeks ahead. V, MC.

Hôtel Lion d'Or, 5, rue de la Sourdière (tel. 01 42 60 79 04; fax 01 42 60 09 14; M. Tuileries or Pyramides). From M. Tuileries walk down rue du 29 Juillet away from the park, turn right on rue St-Honoré; turn left on rue de la Sourdière. Carpeted, sparsely decorated rooms with colorful bedspreads and double-paned glass; you'll hear the bells toll from nearby Eglise St-Roch, but little else. English-speaking staff. Prices change seasonally. In general, singles 195F, with shower 260F. Doubles 270F, with shower 320-340F, with bath and toilet 390-395F. Extra bed 60F. Showers 20F. Breakfast 35F. 5% discount for stays over 3 nights. V, MC, AmEx.

SECOND ARRONDISSEMENT

Hôtel Bonne Nouvelle, 17, rue Beauregard (tel. 01 45 08 42 42; fax 01 40 26 05 81; M. Strasbourg-St-Denis or Bonne Nouvelle). From M. Bonne Nouvelle follow traffic down rue Poissonnière and turn left on rue Beauregard. A bright, calico-trimmed lobby and somber men's-club hallways lead to sizeable rooms with TVs and antique-style furnishings. Spotless bathrooms come equipped with hairdryers. Singles 250F, with shower and toilet 310F. Doubles with toilet and shower or bath 310-370F. Triples with toilet and bath 450-580F. 1 quad with toilet and bath 540-580F. Breakfast 30F, in room 35F. Reserve with 1 night's deposit. V, MC.

Hôtel Vivienne, 40, rue Vivienne (tel. 01 42 33 13 26; fax 01 40 41 98 19; M. rue Montmartre). Walk down bd. Montmartre past the Théâtre des Variétés and turn left on rue Vivienne. From its tiled hall to its spacious rooms outfitted with armoires, TVs, and full-length mirrors, this hotel successfully reconciles gracious living with tight budgets. Singles and doubles with shower 350F, with shower and toilet 420F, with bath and toilet 440F. 2-bed doubles with bath and toilet 460F. 3rd person under 10 yrs. free, over 10 yrs. 30% extra. Breakfast 40F. Elevator. V, MC.

Hôtel La Marmotte, 6, rue Léopold Bellan (tel. 01 40 26 26 51; M. Sentier). Follow traffic on rue Réaumur, turn right onto rue Montorgueil, and then right again at rue Léopold Bellan. Reception in ground-floor bar. Relatively modern building. Clean, quiet rooms come with fairly good mattresses, classy patterned bedspreads, and TVs. Some English spoken. Singles and doubles with shower and toilet 270-300F. 2-bed doubles with shower and toilet 320F. Extra bed 80F. Breakfast 25F. Shower 15F. Reserve 2-3 weeks in advance. V, MC, AmEx.

Hôtel Ste-Marie, 6, rue de la Ville Neuve (tel. 01 42 33 21 61; fax 01 42 33 29 24; M. Bonne Nouvelle). From the rue Poissonnière metro exit, turn right on rue Poissonnière, then left on rue de la Lune and right onto rue de la Ville Neuve. This route avoids the blue movie theater on rue de la Ville Neuve, the one blemish in an otherwise good area. This bright hotel has recently been renovated with candy-striped walls, new mattresses, and clean bathrooms. Some English spoken. Singles 173F, with shower and toilet 243F. Doubles 206F, with shower and toilet 281F. Triples with shower and toilet 392F. Shower 10F. Breakfast 20F.

THIRD ARRONDISSEMENT: NORTHERN MARAIS

Hôtel du Séjour, 36, rue du Grenier St.-Lazare (tel. 01 48 87 40 36; M. Etienne Marcel or Rambuteau). From M. Rambuteau, walk opposite traffic on rue Beaubourg and turn left on rue du Grenier St.-Lazare. One block from Les Halles and the Centre Pompidou, this inexpensive hotel is being redone 1 room at a time. Ask for a renovated room. The hotel isn't oozing with charm, but the Portuguese couple who run it love to chat and will gladly watch your bags. Reception 7am-9:30pm, call ahead if you'll arrive later. Singles 130F. Doubles 180F, with shower 250F, with shower and toilet 270-280F. Shower 20F.

Hôtel de Roubaix, 6, rue Greneta (tel. 01 42 72 89 91; fax 01 42 72 58 79; M. Réaumur-Sébastopol or Arts-et-Métiers). From M. Réaumur-Sébastopol, walk opposite traffic on bd. de Sébastopol and turn left on rue Greneta. A wonderful older couple who enjoy giving advice to travelers run the hotel, which is upscale for the price. Very clean rooms with flowered wallpaper and brand new bathrooms. Breakfast room, 2 other lounges. All rooms have shower, toilet, and cable TV. Rooms on the street are noisy if the windows are open, rooms on the courtyard are quiet. Singles 300-330F. 2-bed doubles 390-410F. Triples 415-435F; 3-bed triple 480F. Quad 500F; 5 people 525F. Breakfast included. Elevator. V, MC.

Hôtel Picard, 26, rue de Picardie (tel. 01 48 87 53 82; fax 01 48 87 02 56; M. République or Filles-du-Calvaire). From M. République walk down rue du Temple, make the first left on rue Béranger, turn right on rue de Franche-Comté, then turn left on rue de Picardie. Quiet, clean hotel a 5-min. walk from the Centre Pompidou or the Musée Picasso. Twin doubles are bunk-bed style. Mention *Let's Go* for a 10% discount. English spoken. Elevator. Singles 200F, with shower and toilet 250F, with bath and toilet 320F. Doubles 240-260F, with shower and toilet 320F, with bath and toilet 390F. Extra bed 120F. Shower 20F. Breakfast 30F. V, MC.

FOURTH ARRONDISSEMENT: SOUTHERN MARAIS

Hôtel Practic, 9, rue d'Ormesson (tel. 01 48 87 80 47; fax 01 48 87 40 04; M. St-Paul). From the metro, walk opposite traffic on rue de Rivoli, turn left on rue de Sévigné and right on rue d'Ormesson. No elevator or fresh flowers, but nevertheless, this low-budget hotel is the kind one always hopes for: clean, quiet, and right on a cobblestone square in the heart of the Marais (ask for a room with a view of the square). Reserve 2 weeks in advance (longer for singles). TV in all rooms. English spoken. Singles 150F. Doubles 230F, with shower 275F, with toilet and shower 340F. Hall shower free. Breakfast 25F.

Castex Hôtel, 5, rue Castex (tel. 01 42 72 31 52; fax 01 42 72 57 91; M. Bastille or Sully-Morland). Exit M. Bastille on bd. Henri IV and take the third right on rue Castex. Rooms in this family-run hotel are spotless and quiet (they look onto either a side street or a courtyard with a slanting metal roof and plants). TV room on main floor. English spoken. Check-in 1pm. Reception open 7am-midnight. All rooms with telephone, sink, and shower or bath. Singles 220F, with toilet 240-270F. Doubles 300F, with toilet 320-340F. 2-bed doubles with toilet 320F, with bath and toilet 340F. Triple with bath and toilet 440F. Extra bed 70F, for baby 30F. Breakfast 25F. Reserve with 1 night's deposit 7-8 weeks in advance. V, MC.

Hôtel Sansonnet, 48, rue de la Verrerie (tel. 01 48 87 96 14; fax 01 48 87 30 46; M. Hôtel-de-Ville). Walk down rue du Temple with your back to the Hôtel de Ville and turn left on rue de la Verrerie. A long, white staircase with a Persian rug leads up to the reception area. Clean, tasteful rooms look out on a rather quiet street or courtyard. All rooms have cable TV, and most have hair dryers. English spoken. Singles 245-255F, with shower 285F, with shower and toilet 340F, with bath and toilet 365F. Doubles with shower and toilet 355F, with bath and toilet 380F. Showers 20F. Breakfast 32F. Reserve 3 weeks in advance. V, MC.

Hôtel Andréa, 3, rue St-Bon (tel. 01 42 78 43 93; M. Hôtel-de-Ville). Follow traffic on rue de Rivoli and turn right on rue St-Bon. On a quiet side street 5min. from Châtelet. Clean rooms with varied color schemes. Some have non-functioning fireplaces. To avoid noise, reserve a room on a high floor. Travelers in cheaper rooms must descend to use the 1st-floor shower. Rooms with shower or bath also have TV. Singles 210F, with toilet and shower or bath 300F. Doubles 210F, with toilet and shower or bath 330-350F. Extra bed 60F. Showers 15F. Breakfast 30F. Reserve 2 weeks in advance with 1 night's deposit. Elevator. V, MC, AmEx.

FIFTH ARRONDISSEMENT: LE QUARTIER LATIN

Hôtel d'Esmeralda, 4, rue St-Julien-le-Pauvre (tel. 01 43 54 19 20; fax 01 40 51 00 68; M. St-Michel). Walk along the Seine on quai St-Michel toward Notre-Dame and turn right at the park. Friendly staff, perfect location, and homey rooms make this a diamond in the rough. Beautiful views of the parc Vivani, the Seine, and Notre Dame. Nit-pickers might notice that the halls are a little tight, the ceilings a little low, and the stairs a bit steep. English spoken. Singles 160F, with shower and toilet 320F. Doubles with shower and toilet 420-490F. Triples with shower and toilet 550F. Quads with shower and toilet 600F. Breakfast 40F. Shower 10F.

Hôtel des Argonauts, 12, rue de la Huchette (tel. 01 43 54 09 82; fax 01 44 07 18 84; M. St-Michel). Rue de la Huchette is off bd. St-Michel, near the Seine. Located above a Greek restaurant of the same name. A pleasant surprise that may have vacancies when other hotels in the 5*ème* do not. Beautiful lobby decorated entirely in flower patterns. The clean, spacious rooms are surprisingly quiet given the bustling (and sometimes noisy) street. Singles 200F. Doubles with shower 250-350F, with toilet and shower 300-350F. Breakfast 25F. V, MC, AmEx.

Hôtel des Grandes Ecoles, 75, rue Cardinal Lemoine (tel. 01 43 26 79 23; fax 01 43 25 28 15; M. Cardinal Lemoine). From the metro take a left on rue Cardinal Lemoine in the direction of the Panthéon. The place to go all-out on a hotel in Paris. Built around a flower garden where guests breakfast in warm weather, this ivy-covered establishment maintains impeccably clean, tasteful rooms to the great pleasure of its faithful guests. Singles and doubles from 510F. Triples 610F. Several smaller, less well-equipped rooms available as singles or doubles 320-350F. Extra bed 100F. Breakfast 40F. Reserve well ahead. V, MC.

Hôtel St-Jacques, 35, rue des Ecoles (tel. 01 43 26 82 53; fax 01 43 25 65 50; M. Maubert-Mutualité). Walk up rue des Carmes and turn right on rue des Ecoles. Clean, quiet hotel, with big, well-maintained rooms. Impressive lobby with a glass chandelier and red carpet. English spoken. Singles 190F, with shower or bath and toilet 420F. Doubles with shower 320F, with shower and toilet 480F. Triples with shower and toilet 560F. Shower 25F. Breakfast 30F. Elevator. V, MC, AmEx.

Hôtel des Alliés, 20, rue Berthollet (tel. 01 43 31 47 52; fax 01 45 35 13 92; M. Censier-Daubenton). Walk down rue Monge in the direction of bd. Port-Royal, turn right on rue Claude Bernard and left on rue Berthollet. Less scenic than other hotels in the 5*ème* but offers very cheap, clean, comfortable rooms close to the markets of rue Mouffetard. Singles 145-160F. Doubles 200-300F, with shower and toilet 295F. Showers 15F. Breakfast 28F. V, MC.

Hôtel Marignan, 13, rue du Sommerard (tel. 01 43 54 63 81; M. Maubert-Mutualité). Turn left on rue des Carmes and right on rue du Sommerard. Quiet, spacious rooms, many with new handmade cabinets and paint jobs. Has a boardinghouse feel, with clientele of students, families, and everyone in between. Laundry room and breakfast room (with microwave) where residents can fix daytime meals. Singles with shower and toilet 190F. Doubles 290-310F. Triples 380-420F, with shower 440-490. Quads 440-480F, with shower 550-650F. Free hall shower and washing machine. Breakfast included. Reserve far in advance. Rates fall in winter.

SIXTH ARRONDISSEMENT: ST-GERMAIN-DES-PRÉS

Hôtel Nesle, 7, rue du Nesle (tel. 01 43 54 62 41; M. Odéon). From the metro walk up rue de l'Ancienne Comédie and onto rue Dauphine; take a left on rue du Nesle. One of the best hotels on the Left Bank. The Egyptianesque frescoes, ducks in the rose garden, warm management, and outrageously low prices make for a whimsical departure from the monotony of Paris's like-seeming budget hotels. Laundry. Singles with breakfast and shower 220F. Doubles with breakfast and shower 270-400F. No reservations; arrive between 10am and noon.

Hôtel Stella, 41, rue Monsieur-le-Prince (tel. 01 43 26 43 49; fax 01 43 54 97 28; M. Odéon or Luxembourg). From M. Odéon walk down rue Dupuytren and take a left on rue Monsieur-le-Prince. The hotel may be older than the hills, the hallways may seem to be under construction, and the office may be a steam bath in summer, but the wood-trimmed rooms are modern, comfortable, pleasant, and breezy—fantastic, in fact. Singles with toilet and shower 218F. Doubles with toilet and shower 298F. Triples 447F. Quads 516F. Reserve by fax or telephone.

Hôtel St-André des Arts, 66, rue St-André-des-Arts (tel. 01 43 26 96 16; fax 01 43 29 73 34; M. Odéon). From the metro take rue de l'Ancienne Comédie, walk 1 block, and take the first right on rue St-André-des-Arts. Unique fabric covers the walls, curtains, and bedding. Central location near restaurants and bars. All rooms have toilet. Singles 235F, with shower 310-350F. Doubles with shower 450F, with 2 beds and shower 480F. Triples with double bed, single bed, and shower 550F. Quads with 2 double beds and shower 600F. Breakfast included. V, MC.

Hôtel St-Michel, 17, rue Git-le-Coeur (tel. 01 43 26 98 70; M. St-Michel). From pl. St-Michel walk 1 block on rue St-André-des-Arts and turn right on rue Git-le-Coeur. Comfortable (if bland) rooms on a quiet street close to the Seine. Friendly staff. Singles 215F, with shower 310F, with shower and toilet 350F. Doubles 240F, with shower 335F, with shower and toilet 375F. 2-bed doubles with shower 390F, with shower and toilet 420F. Shower 12F. Breakfast 25F. Reserve with 1 night's deposit at least 2 weeks in advance.

SEVENTH ARRONDISSEMENT: THE EIFFEL TOWER

Hôtel de la Paix, 19, rue du Gros Caillou (tel. 01 45 51 86 17; M. Ecole Militaire). Walk up av. de la Bourdonnais, turn right on rue de Grenelle, then left on rue du Gros Caillou. The only true budget hotel in the 7ème, and it shows. Worn carpets, soft mattresses, peeling paint, but fairly quiet. English spoken. Reception open 9am-9pm. Ask for a key if you'll be returning after 9pm. Check-out at noon. Singles 160F, with shower 230F. Doubles with shower 295F, with shower and toilet 295-370F. Shower 15F. Breakfast 32F. Deposit required if you plan to arrive after 3pm, payable by traveler's checks. Call ahead.

Hôtel Malar, 29, rue Malar (tel. 01 45 51 38 46; fax 01 45 55 20 19; M. Latour Maubourg). Turn left on rue St-Dominique off bd. de la Tour Maubourg, then right on rue Malar. Provincial hotel with inner courtyard, on a quiet side street near the restaurants and shops of rue St-Dominique. All rooms have TV and direct telephone service. Singles with shower 280F, with shower and toilet 340-350F, with bath and toilet 350F. Doubles with shower 320F, with shower and toilet 380-400F, with bath and toilet 400F. Triples with shower 380F, with shower and toilet 440-460F, with bath and toilet 460F. Breakfast 28F. V, MC.

EIGHTH ARRONDISSEMENT

Hôtel d'Artois, 94, rue La Boétie (tel. 01 43 59 84 12 or 01 42 25 76 65; fax 01 43 59 50 70; M. St-Philippe de Roule), a stone's throw from the Champs-Elysées. From the metro take a left on rue la Boétie. Worn rug, has-been mattresses, but impeccable, spacious bathrooms and large bedrooms. Plant-filled lobby and incense-scented breakfast room. English spoken. Singles 240F, with shower 345F, with bath 390F, with bath and toilet 390F. Doubles 270F, with shower 375F, with bath 420F, with bath and toilet 420F. 2-bed doubles with bath and toilet 440F. Extra bed 100-125F. Showers 20F. Breakfast 25F. Elevator. V, MC, AmEx.

Hôtel Wilson, 10, rue de Stockholm (tel. 01 45 22 10 85; M. St-Lazare). Walk up rue de Rome; turn left on rue de Stockholm. No-frills hotel near Gare St-Lazare. Soft mattresses, aged carpet—but at this price, what did you expect? Bathrooms in rooms are newer than those off the halls. The occasional velvet chair offsets drabness. Clean, relatively spacious rooms. Singles 165-200F, with shower and toilet 220-240F. Doubles 225-230F, with toilet 245-260F. Triples 340F, with shower 360F. Quads 365F, with shower 395F. Shower 10F. Breakfast included.

NINTH ARRONDISSEMENT

Hôtel des Trois Poussins, 15, rue Clauzel (tel. 01 48 74 38 20; M. St-Georges). Uphill on rue Notre-Dame-de-Lorette, right on rue H. Monnier, and right on rue Clauzel. Renovations of this quiet, family-run hotel with courtyard and comfy rooms will be finished in Jan. '97. Singles 150F. Doubles 190F, with shower 220-240F, with shower, toilet, and stove 260F. Breakfast 30F. Reserve a month ahead.

Hôtel Beauharnais, 51, rue de la Victoire (tel. 01 48 74 71 13; M. le Peletier). Follow traffic on rue de la Victoire. Elegant array of beds, armoires, and mirrors span the centuries and showcase the owner's passion for antiques. No two rooms are alike. Lots of calm, sun, and fresh flowers. Singles and doubles with shower 300F, with shower and toilet 350F. Triples with shower and toilet 465F. Breakfast 25F.

TENTH ARRONDISSEMENT

Hôtel Palace, 9, rue Bouchardon (tel. 01 40 40 09 46 or 01 42 06 59 32; fax 01 42 06 16 90; M. Strasbourg St-Denis). Walk opposite traffic on bd. St-Denis until the small arch; turn left on rue René Boulanger and left on rue Bouchardon. The privacy of a hotel with the atmosphere of a hostel: friendly, young, and cheap. A dark hallway leads to small, cheerful, sunny doubles and triples, many of which face a plant-filled courtyard. Near a laundromat and a supermarket. English spoken. Singles 103F. Doubles 136-146F, with shower and toilet 236F, with bath and toilet 256F. Triples with shower and toilet 289F. Quad with shower and toilet 362F. Shower 20F. Breakfast 20F. Reserve 2 weeks ahead in summer. V, MC.

Cambrai Hôtel, 129bis, bd. de Magenta (tel. 01 48 78 32 13; fax 01 48 78 43 55; M. Gare du Nord). Follow traffic on rue de Dunkerque to pl. de Roubaix and turn right on bd. de Magenta. The hotel is almost directly on your left. A homey, family-owned, safe hotel near the *gare*. Clean, airy rooms with high ceilings and lots of natural light, plus an intimate breakfast room. Singles 125-150F, with shower 202F. Doubles 200F, with shower 250F, with shower and toilet 274F. 2-bed double with shower and toilet 313F. Triples with shower 376F. 2-room suite for 4 with shower 400F. Showers 20F. Breakfast included.

ELEVENTH ARRONDISSEMENT: THE BASTILLE

Hôtel de Nevers, 53, rue de Malte (tel. 01 47 00 56 18; fax 01 43 57 77 39; M. Oberkampf or République). From M. République, walk down av. de la République and take a right on rue de Malte. Spacious, bright, clean rooms with matching wallpaper and curtains. Ask for one on a high floor, away from the noise of the street. Owners love Americans and speak some English. Guests have access to refrigerator. Singles and doubles 170F, with shower 220F, with shower and toilet 245F. 2-bed doubles with shower and toilet 260F. Triples 310F. Quads 380F. Showers 20F. Breakfast 25F, served in the rooms. Reserve 2 weeks in advance with 1 night's deposit by check or credit card. 24-hr. reception. Elevator. V, MC.

Hôtel de Belfort, 37, rue Servan (tel. 01 47 00 67 33; fax 01 43 57 97 98; M. Père-Lachaise, St-Maur, or Voltaire). From M. Père-Lachaise, take rue du Chemin Vert and turn left on rue Servan. 15-min. walk from pl. de la Bastille (just keep walking on rue de la Roquette, past metro Voltaire and turn left on rue Servan when you hit a grassy square). Leather couches for lounging in the lobby. Not particularly memorable or attractive rooms except for the *Let's Go* backpacker special: just 100F per person per night in doubles, triples, and quads. All rooms with shower, toilet, phone, and TV. English spoken. Breakfast served in downstairs salon. Breakfast 15F with *Let's Go* special, served 7:30-9:30am. V, MC.

Hôtel Rhetia, 3, rue du Général Blaise (tel. 01 47 00 47 18; fax 01 42 61 23 17; M. St-Ambroise, St-Maur, or Voltaire). From M. Voltaire, take av. Parmentier, turn right on rue Rochebrune and take the next left onto rue du Général Blaise. Some rooms overlook a peaceful park. The hotel is calm and the neighborhood quiet, despite proximity to the Opéra Bastille. No elevator, dimly lit stairwell, and single beds are a bit narrow. Reception open Mon.-Fri. 7:30am-10pm, Sat.-Sun. and holidays 8am-10pm. Singles 170F, with toilet and shower or bath 210F. Doubles 190F, with toilet and shower or bath 230F. Triples 240F, with toilet and shower or bath 280F. Showers 10F. Breakfast 10F. TV 10F.

Plessis Hôtel, 25, rue du Grand Prieuré (tel. 01 47 00 13 38; fax 01 43 57 97 87; M. Oberkampf). From the metro, walk north on rue du Grand Prieuré. 5 floors of clean, pastel-hued rooms, with hairdryers and fans if you ask. The cheaper rooms are not so well equipped. Piano, TV, vending machines, and leather chairs in lounge. 10% discount for stays over 3 nights. Singles 195F, with shower, toilet, and TV 270F. Doubles 215F, with shower, toilet, and TV 295-315F. Triples with shower, toilet, and TV 360F. Shower 10F. Continental breakfast 32F, students 20F. Heartier, "American-style" breakfast 36F. In July singles 150F, doubles 170F; free shower. Ask about the 300F triple. Open Sept.-July. Elevator. V, MC, AmEx.

FOURTEENTH ARRONDISSEMENT: MONTPARNASSE

Hôtel de Blois, 5, rue des Plantes (tel. 01 45 40 99 48; fax 01 45 40 45 62; M. Mouton-Duvernet). From the metro, take a left onto rue Mouton Duvernet; at the end, go left onto rue des Plantes. Unquestionably one of the best deals in Paris, with rooms decked out with cable TV, telephones, and pseudo-Laura Ashley decor. Laundromat across the street. Singles or doubles with toilet 220-260F, with shower 250F, with shower and toilet 270F, with bath and toilet 320-350F. Triples with bath and toilet 360F. Shower 15F. Breakfast 25F. V, MC, AmEx.

Central Hôtel, 1bis, rue du Maine (tel. 01 43 20 69 15; fax 01 43 20 50 09; M. Edgar-Quinet). Facing the Tour Montparnasse, turn left on rue de la Gaîté, then right on rue du Maine. The exterior might not catch your eye, but the interior flashes with its bronze-mirrored lobby ceiling. Simple decor is predominantly peach, and all rooms have toilets, hairdryers, and showers or baths. Singles 345F. Doubles 375F. 2-bed doubles 415F. Triples 445F. Breakfast 35F. V, MC, AmEx.

Hôtel du Midi, 4, av. René-Coty (tel. 01 43 27 23 25; fax 01 43 21 24 58; M. Denfert-Rochereau). From metro, turn off av. Général Leclerc and into the sq. de l'Abbé Migne, then turn right onto av. René-Coty. Catering mostly to business travelers, this large, professionally run hotel has a stylish decor that extends to—yes—marbled bathrooms. Every room has hairdryer and satellite TV; some have A/C. Singles with shower 288F, with shower and toilet 298-398F, with bath and toilet 368-488F. Suite with all the extras 490F. Breakfast 38F. V, MC.

FIFTEENTH ARRONDISSEMENT

Hôtel Printemps, 31, rue du Commerce (tel. 01 45 79 83 36; fax 01 45 79 84 88; M. La Motte-Picquet). Smack in the middle of a lively section of the 15*ème*, surrounded by stores (including a Monoprix), this hotel offers a warm welcome and clean, bright, quiet rooms, all at hostel prices. Singles or doubles 140F, with shower 170F, with shower and toilet 200F. 2-bed doubles with shower and toilet 220F. Extra bed 30F. Shower 15F. Breakfast 20F. Reserve 3 weeks ahead. V, MC.

Mondial Hôtel, 136, bd. de Grenelle (tel. 01 45 79 73 57 or 01 45 79 08 09; fax 01 45 79 58 65; M. La Motte-Picquet). Near cafés, shops, and the metro. The moustached owner will welcome you to bright, clean, flowery rooms with saggy beds, modern showers, and a view of bd. de Grenelle. Singles 183F, with shower 223F, with shower and toilet 293F. Doubles 206F, with shower 246F, with shower and toilet 316F. Extra bed 73F. Shower 10F. Breakfast 20F. TV 20F per day. V, MC.

Food

"Paris is just like any other city, only people eat better..." Thus intones Maurice Chevalier in the film *Love in the Afternoon.* Parisians do not simply eat—they eat well, often, and at length. Fortunately, they do not necessarily eat expensively. You can eat satisfactorily for 50F, enjoyably for 65F, superbly for 90F, and unforgettably for 130F. The restaurants of Paris are a diverse lot. Don't hesitate to try one of the many inexpensive Vietnamese, North African, or Middle Eastern eateries that dot the city. Wander open-air markets, crunch a *croque monsieur* in the Latin Quarter, or relax with a slice of quiche at a sidewalk café. Tea rooms are popular lunch spots as well. For a meal with fantastic wine, hit one of Paris's many wine bars, cozy places that sidestep the tourist onslaught. Above all, be bold, be adventurous, and splurge at least once: this may be your only chance to slurp snails by the Seine.

■ Restaurants

Some say that the world's first restaurant was born in Paris not for the purpose of indulging in delicious foods, but rather to restore (from the French verb *restaurer*) over-fed party-goers to a state of physical health. Restaurants were a respite from the world of soirées, balls, and dinner parties; they served only a ghastly liquid made from meat and vegetables thought capable of reviving the appetite.

Happily, the only similarity between Parisian restaurants today and their primordial ancestors is that they remain highly social milieus. Should you tire of French food, there are scads of other options, from the Marais's Mexican and kosher scene to the many Thai and Chinese delights of the 13*ème* to the vast selection of Japanese, Moroccan, and West African restaurants sprinkled throughout the city.

When exploring restaurants on your own, avoid the telltale signs of an unsatisfying meal, such as an advertised "tourist special," a menu in any language but French, or any place that offers you raw vegetables, *crudités*—often just a mound of carrot shreds—as an *entrée* on a *prix-fixe* menu. Fast food has its allures, of course: it's cheap, and cheap food is good food. But why go to Paris to eat at McDonald's?

FIRST AND SECOND ARRONDISSEMENTS: THE LOUVRE AND LES HALLES

Pizza Sicilia, 26, rue de Beaujolais (tel. 01 42 96 93 55; M. Palais-Royal). On the corner of Montpensier and Beaujolais north of the Palais. Budget travel guides exist to publicize gastronomic gems like Pizza Sicilia. Friendly service, low prices and great food. Try the phenomenal *tortellini aux champignons* (tortellini with mushrooms)—at 42F, it's their most expensive pasta. 56F *menu* includes a salad, main course, and dessert or cheese. Open Mon.-Sat. noon-2:15pm and 5-11pm.

L'Epi d'Or, 25, rue J.-J. Rousseau (tel. 01 42 36 38 12; M. Les Halles). A small restaurant open to the street in summer, with high ceilings and antiques, copper pots, and fresh flowers. Frequented by journalists from the nearby *Figaro* offices. The staff is charming and the food ranges from excellent to rapturous. 2-course *menu* served until 9pm (105F). Main courses 90F and up. Try the *entrecôte bordelaise* (105F). Open Mon.-Fri. noon-2:15pm and 7:30pm-2am, Sat. 7:30pm-2am. Last orders at midnight. Closed Aug. and 1 week in Feb. Reserve ahead. V, MC.

Aux Lyonnais, 32, rue St-Marc (tel. 01 42 96 65 04; M. Bourse). Walk against the traffic on rue Vivienne and turn left on rue St-Marc. Copious, traditional French food set with floral tile and Victorian lamps. The ideal semi-fancy French restaurant for a romantic dinner. Dine upstairs or downstairs on *caille rôtie* (roast quail, 75F) or *lapin aux échalotes* (rabbit with shallots, 75F). 2-course *menu* 87F. Glass of wine 25F. Open Mon.-Fri. noon-2:30pm and 7pm-midnight, Sat. 7pm-midnight. Reserve a table for dinner. V, MC, AmEx.

Au Clair de Lune, 27, rue Tiquetonne (tel. 01 42 33 59 10; M. Etienne-Marcel). Walk against traffic on rue de Turbigo and turn left on rue Tiquetonne. Faithful regulars flock to this simple neighborhood restaurant for its huge plates of North African and French food. Couscous (54-70F) for ravenous (though discriminating) eaters. *Entrecôte* 62-65F. Sample such Algerian wines as *Gris de Medea* or *Sidi Brahim* (53F per bottle). Open daily noon-2:30pm and 7:30-11pm. V, MC.

THIRD AND FOURTH ARRONDISSEMENT: LE MARAIS

Vue du Parc, 4, rue du Parc Royal (tel. 01 48 04 90 50; M. Chemin-Vert). Take rue St-Gilles, which becomes rue du Parc Royal. Salads, tarts, and Brazilian cuisine in a sunny restaurant overlooking sq. Léopold Achille. Tasty salads like the *exotique* (with avocado and *roquefort)* are affordable (40-50F, or 20-25F as appetizer). Brazilian fare includes *boulettes* (rolled and grilled balls of cheese, corn, or ground meat, around 40F). Appetizers 25-27F. Main dishes 55-80F (most 55-60F). Desserts 23-28F. Open Mon.-Sat. 11:30am-3:30pm and 7:30-11pm. V, MC.

Le Hangar, 12, impasse Berthaud (tel. 01 42 74 55 44; M. Rambuteau). Take the impasse Berthaud exit from the metro. Tucked in an alley near the Centre Pompidou, Le Hangar is a quiet restaurant removed from the tourist-madness of the neighborhood. Tablecloths, fresh flowers, and a newspaper rack for those who come for tea on Sat. (3:30-7pm). Appetizers (28-58F) and many French specialties, including *ravioles de Romans* (cheese ravioli with an eggplant cream sauce, 48F), *foie gras de canard poêlé* (85F), and to-die-for chocolate cake (44F). Open Mon. 7pm-midnight, Tues.-Sat. noon-4pm and 6pm-midnight.

Chez Marianne, 2, rue des Hospitalières-St-Gervais (tel. 01 42 72 18 86; M. St-Paul). Follow rue de Rivoli a few steps and turn right on rue Pavée; turn left on rue des Rosiers and right on rue des Hospitalières-St-Gervais. Sample Middle Eastern and Eastern European specialties in this folksy canteen and specialty store. Wine bottles and bins of pickled delicacies stacked floor to ceiling provide a cheerfully cluttered backdrop for locals to converge *en famille* or with friends. Eat outdoors if weather permits. Sample 4, 5, or 6 specialties (55F, 65F, or 75F), including *zaziki,* tabouli, falafel, hummus, and *tarama.* Arrive before 7:45pm to avoid the dinner crowd. Take-out available. Open daily 11am-1am. V, MC.

L'Ebouillanté, 6, rue des Barres (tel. 01 42 71 09 69; M. St-Paul or Pont Marie). From M. St-Paul walk opposite traffic down rue François-Miron and turn left on rue des Barres. A casual restaurant and tearoom offering light snacks and meals in ambient calm, just steps from the bustle of cars and *bouquinistes* along the Seine. Open Tues.-Sun. noon-10pm.

FIFTH ARRONDISSEMENT: LE QUARTIER LATIN

Le Jardin des Pâtes, 4, rue Lacépède (tel. 01 43 31 50 71; M. Jussieu). From the metro walk up rue Linné and turn right on rue Lacépède. 8 tables unassumingly set with woven placemats are the meeting place for organic, gourmet pasta and a host of farm-fresh sauces—from sesame butter to duck and *crème fraîche.* Locals dig into the *pâtes de seigle,* with ham, white wine, and sharp *comté* cheese (56F). Many vegetarian offerings. Appetizers 19-25F, main courses 38-73F. Reservations recommended at night. Open Tues.-Sun. noon-2:30pm and 7-11pm.

Restaurant Perraudin, 157, rue St-Jacques (tel. 01 46 33 15 75; M. Luxembourg). From the metro take rue Royer Collard to rue St-Jacques. At this family-style bistro, locals gather to relax in the dark-wood interior. Try old favorites like *sautée d'agneau aux flageolets* (sautéed lamb with white beans, 58F). Come early to avoid crowds. 3-course lunch *menu* 63F. Appetizers 32F. Main dishes 56F. Desserts 28F. Glass of wine 9F. Open daily noon-2:15pm and 7:30-10:15pm.

Café Le Volcan, 10, rue Thouin (tel. 01 46 33 38 33; M. Cardinal Lemoine). Turn left on rue Cardinal Lemoine and take a right on rue Thouin. Boisterous restaurant heats up at night with a youthful crowd of regulars. Specializes in *moussaka* and other Greek dishes, with some North African food thrown in for good measure. The 3-course 57F *menu* is served until 9pm; at lunch it includes a glass of wine. Dinner *menus* 80-100F. Open Tues.-Sun. noon-2:15pm and 6:30-11:30pm. V, MC.

Simbad, 7, rue Lagrange (tel. 01 43 26 19 05; M. Maubert-Mutualité). Take your pick of tabouli, hummus, stuffed grape leaves—the works—either in sandwich form or as *plats* (sandwiches 18-20F, *plats* 20-45F). The small terrace outside is often full, but you can bring your food to the parc de St-Julien le Pauvre across the street and simultaneously absorb good food and a great view of Notre Dame. Delivery available in the 1ème-7ème *arrondissements* with a 75F minimum order (20F for orders 75-150F, free for orders above 150F). Open daily 11am-11pm.

SIXTH ARRONDISSEMENT: ST-GERMAIN-DES-PRÉS

Le Petit Vatel, 5, rue Lobineau (tel. 01 43 54 28 49; M. Odéon or Mabillon). From M. Mabillon, follow traffic on bd. St-Germain, turn right on rue de Seine, and then take your second right onto rue Lobineau. This *tiny* restaurant—3 tables fill the room—provides delicious, inexpensive meals. At lunch and on weekdays, choose a main dish and an appetizer or dessert from the 61F *menu* scribbled on the chalkboard, including such daily specialties as *poivrons farcis* (stuffed peppers), *gratin de courgettes au jambon* (zucchini casserole with ham), or *moussaka.* A vegetarian plate is always offered. Take-out available. Open Mon.-Sat. noon-3pm and 7pm-midnight, Sun. 7pm-midnight. Closed Dec. 25-Jan. 1. V, MC, AmEx.

Orestias, 4, rue Grégoire-de-Tours (tel. 01 43 54 62 01; M. Odéon). Walk against traffic on bd. St-Germain and turn left onto rue Grégoire-de-Tours. Stuffed heads line the walls of what is nonetheless an airy restaurant. The food here is French with a heavy Greek influence—*dolmata, baklava,* and Greek wine are offered alongside French foods. Fries and green beans accompany each meal. The 44F *menu* is an inspired bargain with copious 1st and 2nd courses and a choice of cheese or dessert. Open Mon.-Sat. noon-2:30pm and 5:30-11:30pm. V, MC.

Kiotori, 61, rue Monsieur-le-Prince (tel. 01 43 54 48 44; M. Odéon). From the metro walk to the end of rue Dupuytren, where it intersects rue Monsieur-le-Prince. A youthful international crowd packs this Japanese restaurant for succulent skewers of grilled beef, chicken, and shrimp and picture-perfect plates of sushi and maki. A large variety of *menus* (40-91F) all include soup, *salade de crudités,* a main course, and a saki *digestif.* Unbelievably fast service. Open Mon.-Sat. noon-3pm and 7pm-midnight. V, MC.

Crémerie Restaurant Polidor, 41, rue Monsieur-le-Prince (tel. 01 43 26 95 34; M. Cluny-Sorbonne or Luxembourg). From M. Cluny-Sorbonne walk down bd. St-Michel away from the river, take a right on rue Racine and your first left on rue Monsieur-le-Prince. The Polidor gleams with the mirrors, brass, and polished wood of over a century's worth of history. When Rimbaud lived on rue Monsieur-le-Prince, he ate here with Verlaine, and it's been a neighborhood joint ever since. The Polidor offers traditional French cuisine cooked perfectly; the *escargots* are an excellent introduction to snails for nervous first-timers and the *bavarois au cassis* (a cake soaked in blackberry liqueur) is famous. 2-course lunch *menu* 55F; 3-course dinner *menu* 100F. 3-course dining *à la carte* 120-130F. Open Mon.-Sat. noon-2:30pm and 7pm-12:30am, Sun. noon-2:30pm and 7-11pm.

SEVENTH ARRONDISSEMENT: LES INVALIDES

La Varangue, 27, rue Angereau (tel. 01 45 05 51 22; M. Ecole Militaire). Turn right on rue de Grenelle from av. de la Bourdonnais, then take a left onto rue Angereau. Two sisters make and serve family-style dishes and homemade desserts in this bright, intimate restaurant with a plant on every table. 74F *formule* for lunch and dinner includes an appetizer or dessert, main course, salad, and drink. *Grandes salades* with fresh vegetables (56-64F) and other vegetarian meals are always available. Wine 8F a glass. Desserts 10-32F. Open Sept.-July Mon. and Sat. noon-2:30pm, Tues.-Fri. 7-10pm; Aug. Mon-Sat. noon-2:30pm. V, MC.

Fontaine de Mars, 129, rue St-Dominique (tel. 01 47 05 46 44; M. Ecole Militaire). Walk north on av. Bosquet and turn left on rue St-Dominique. One of the best places in the 7*ème* for a dainty helping of sumptuous French fare. Picture-perfect restaurant with lace curtains, pine interior, and red-checkered tablecloths features food from southwestern France. Terrace overlooks the fountain after which the restaurant is named. House specialties include tomatoes and basil with fresh *chèvre* (45F) and duckling filet with mushrooms and sauteed potatoes (100F). Ample 85F lunch *menu* includes *steak tartare, pommes de terre* (potatoes), green salad, and dessert. Open Mon.-Sat. noon-2:30pm and 7:30-11pm. V, MC.

EIGHTH ARRONDISSEMENT: CHAMPS-ELYSÉES

Elliott Restaurant, 166, bd. Haussmann (tel. 01 42 89 30 50; M. Miromesnil). Walk up av. Percier and turn left on bd. Haussmann. A taste of home in the *arrondissement* that makes you feel like a stranger. Bistro-style restaurant with slick decor and food that's all-American. Buffalo wings (43F), hamburgers (62F), and selected American beers (23F). Huge American brunch Sat.-Sun. includes eggs Benedict (98F). Open Mon.-Sat. noon-3pm and 8pm-midnight, Sun. noon-4pm. V, AmEx.

Antoine's: Les Sandwichs des 5 Continents, 31, rue de Ponthieu (tel. 01 42 89 44 20; M. Franklin D. Roosevelt). Walk towards the Arc de Triomphe on the Champs-Elysées, turn right on av. Franklin D. Roosevelt and left onto rue de Ponthieu. Don't give into the temptation to grab fast-food on the Champs-Elysées; hop around the corner to this hip sandwich shop. Specialities include the Buffalo sandwich with barbecued chicken and melted cheese on hearty bread (23F). American desserts and ice-cream bars fill out the menu for a cheap, appetizing meal (12-18F). Beer 12-18F. Take-out available. Open Mon.-Fri. 8am-6pm.

Barry's, 9, rue de Duras (tel. 01 40 06 02 27; M. Champs Elysées-Clemenceau). From the metro, cross the Champs-Elysées, head straight up av. Marigny to pl. Beauvau, hang a right onto rue du Faubourg St-Honoré, and take the first left onto rue de Duras. A clean, quiet, low-budget sandwich emporium with *panini* (24-29F), sandwiches (20-25F), and desserts (15-17F). Surprisingly simple and good in this area of bright lights and rip-off tourist traps. Open Mon.-Fri. 11am-3pm.

Le Singe d'Eau, 28, rue de Moscou (tel. 01 43 87 72 73; M. Europe). Opened in 1992, the year of the water monkey *(singe d'eau),* this restaurant serves authentic Tibetan cuisine in a room outfitted in understated reds, yellows, and blues. Appetizers 10-40F, main courses 45-55F. A vegetarian menu is available. The "Full Moon Momos" and "Drhe," a kind of chicken curry, both get rave reviews from customers. English spoken. Open Mon.-Sat. noon-3pm and 7-11pm.

NINTH AND TENTH ARRONDISSEMENTS

Anarkali, 4, pl. Gustave Toudouze (tel. 01 48 78 39 84; M. St-Georges). Walk uphill on rue Notre-Dame-de-Lorette and branch right onto rue H. Monnier. On a secluded cobblestone square. Serves up a standard assortment of spicy South Indian fare. Relax on the terrace under wide, colorful umbrellas and revel in the lack of traffic. Meat dishes 55-60F, veggie dishes 30-40F. Chutneys cost an extra 6-8F. 3-course lunch *menu* 69F, 2-course *menu* 55F. Open Tues.-Sat. noon-2:30pm and 7pm-12:30am; also Sun.-Mon. 7pm-12:30am in summer. V, MC, AmEx.

Pizzéria King Salomon, 46, rue Richer (tel. 01 42 46 31 22; M. Cadet or Bonne Nouvelle). From M. Cadet descend rue Saulner and turn left on rue Richer. A popular kosher pizzeria in the heart of the 9ème's Jewish community. The *King Salomon* (58F) is topped with tomato, cheese, artichoke hearts, egg, basil, mushrooms, and olives. Delicious individual pizzas 42-58F. Slices 12-15F. Take-out, too. Open Sun.-Thurs. 11:30am-3pm and 4:30pm-midnight, Sat. 4:30pm-midnight.

Paris-Dakar, 95, rue du Faubourg St-Martin (tel. 01 42 08 16 64; M. Gare de l'Est). African masks and batiks decorate this popular, family-run restaurant. Try *Yassa* (chicken with lime and onions, 71F), *Maffé* (chicken or beef sauteed in peanut sauce, 69F), or *Tiep Bou Dieone,* the "national dish of Senegal" (fish with rice and veggies, 98F). Feast freely but carefully; the red-chili and oil concoction will cauterize your stomach. 3-course lunch *menu* with drinks 59F; 3-course dinner *menu* 99F. Open Tues.-Sun. noon-3pm and 7pm-2am. V, MC.

Brasserie Flo, 7, cour des Petites-Ecuries (tel. 01 47 70 13 59; M. Château d'Eau). Walk against the traffic on rue du Château d'Eau, turn left on rue du Faubourg St-Denis; the entrance to the *cour* is on the right. Elegant dining room with dark wood paneling and tuxedoed waiters, specializing in seafood. Every imaginable type of oyster is on the menu; 6 of the cheapest go for 60-84F. Dinner *à la carte* is exorbitant, but the 2-course *menu* provides a superb meal (119F lunch, 189F dinner). Reservations recommended. Open noon-3pm and 7pm-1:30am. V, MC.

ELEVENTH ARRONDISSEMENT: LA BASTILLE

Occitanie, 96, rue Oberkampf (tel. 01 48 06 46 98; M. St-Maur). Go northwest on av. de la République, take your first right onto rue St-Maur, and then turn right on rue Oberkampf. Burlap-covered refectory tables provide a rustic setting for southwestern French cuisine. 3-course midday *formule* at 52F includes a wine or coffee and a wide selection of salads and meats. Dinner *menus* are bargains at 62F (for 3 courses) and 89F (for 4 courses). Appetizers 30-50F, main courses 48-98F. Open Sept.-July Mon.-Fri. noon-2pm and 7-11pm, Sat. 7-11pm. V, MC, AmEx.

Au Petit Keller, 13, rue Keller (tel. 01 47 00 12 97; M. Ledru-Rollin). Walk north on av. Ledru Rollin and turn left on rue Keller. Traditional bistro in the heart of the vibrant Bastille district. The filling, wholesome food has a bit of a neighborhood fan club. At noon, the 70F *menu* includes main dish (veal, for example) and an appetizer (endive salad with *roquefort* cheese) or a dessert *(crème caramel),* and beer, wine, or mineral water. *Gâteau de riz* (rice cake) is a house specialty. Open Mon.-Sat. 8am-2:30pm and 7pm-midnight. V, MC.

A la Banane Ivoirienne, 10, rue de la Forge-Royale (tel. 01 43 70 49 90; M. Faidherbe-Chaligny). Walk west on rue du Faubourg St-Antoine and turn right on rue de la Forge-Royale. Run by a gregarious Ivoirian emigré who wrote his doctoral thesis on his country's banana industry. Come for such delicious West African specialties as *attieke,* made from cassava, and *aloko,* from bananas. Appetizers 25-35F. Main courses 50-80F. On Thurs., try the *Foutou National* (a dish with plantains) for 80F. Open Tues.-Sat. 7pm-midnight. V, MC (100F minimum).

Le Bistro St-Ambroise, 5, rue Guillaume Bertrand (tel. 01 47 00 43 50; M. St-Maur). Walk against traffic on rue St-Maur and turn left on rue Guillaume Bertrand. Old ads from French magazines cover the yellow walls of this cute bistro hidden away from tourists. Delicious food, a gourmet's wine *carte,* and an unrivaled repertoire of desserts (20-40F). Try the *travers de porc au miel* (honeyed pork, 54F) or the *confit de canard* (59F). 3-course lunch *menu* 68F. V, MC.

FOURTEENTH ARRONDISSEMENT: MONTPARNASSE

Aquarius Café, 40, rue de Gergovie (tel. 01 45 41 36 88; M. Pernety). Walk against traffic on rue Raymond Losserand and turn right onto rue de Gergovie. Wooden tables, an exceptionally friendly staff, and serene decorations enhance the mouthwatering meals in this inventive vegetarian restaurant. The famous "mixed grill" includes tofu sausages, cereal sausages, wheat pancakes, wheat germ, brown rice, and vegetables in a mushroom sauce (65F). Homemade desserts are well worth the 25-30F. Open Mon.-Sat. noon-2:15pm and 7-10:30pm. V, MC, AmEx.

Le Château Poivre, 145, rue du Château (tel. 01 43 22 03 68; M. Pernety). Walk with the traffic on rue Raymond Losserand and turn right onto rue du Château. The owner takes his food seriously, and the generous portions, enhanced by over 60 varieties of wine, will encourage you to do the same. With *à la carte* prices a little steep (the exquisite *crème caramel* will melt in your mouth as it slips 35F out of your wallet), the 89F *menu,* with such dishes as *escargots, andouillette au sauvignon,* and *mousse au chocolat,* is a steal. "Not just good, it's great!" says the modest owner. Open Mon.-Sat. noon-2:30pm and 7-10:30pm. V, MC, AmEx.

SIXTEENTH ARRONDISSEMENT

Casa Tina, 18, rue Lauriston (tel. 01 40 67 19 24; M. Charles-de-Gaulle-Etoile). Walk up av. Victor Hugo 1 block and take a left on rue Lauriston. This tiny Spanish restaurant provides excellent, light meals and a large dose of native charm. Terra cotta tiles, hanging peppers, and a guitar furnish an ambient setting for *tapas* (light Spanish delicacies 15-69F, or 98F for a meal of seven hot and cold dishes). The Andalusian chef also turns out a range of traditional dishes including *paella* (98-150F). Appetizers 18-28F, main dishes 68-124F. 100F *menu* includes a plate of *tapas*, the daily special, a glass of wine, and coffee. Open Mon.-Fri. 11:30am-3:30pm and 6pm-1am, Sat.-Sun. 7pm-2am. Reserve on weekends. V, MC, AmEx.

EIGHTEENTH ARRONDISSEMENT: MONTMARTRE

Chez les Fondues, 17, rue des Trois Frères (tel. 01 42 55 22 65; M. Abbesses). From the metro, walk down rue Yvonne le Tac and take a left on rue des Trois Frères. A small restaurant with only two main dishes: *fondue bourguignonne* (meat fondue) and *fondue savoyarde* (cheese fondue). Wine served in baby bottles; Freudian revulsion drives many to remove the nipples. Enjoyable and crowded. The 87F *menu* includes an *apéritif,* wine, appetizer, fondue, and dessert. Reserve or show up early. Open daily 5pm-2am, dinner served after 7pm.

Au Grain de Folie, 24, rue la Vieuville (tel. 01 42 58 15 57; M. Abbesses). This intimate restaurant on a quiet street serves a vast array of vegetarian dishes, from couscous and hummus to salads and cheese, in portions so huge that eating *à la carte* may be more economical than the 100F *menu* (main dish, dessert, and wine). Appetizers, including avocado in *roquefort* sauce, cost 18-30F; main dishes 45-65F;

desserts like frozen bananas in hot chocolate, 25-40F. Glass of wine 15-25F. Open Mon.-Fri. noon-2:30pm and 6-10:30pm, Sat.-Sun. noon-10:30pm.

Suzon-Grisou, 96, rue des Martyrs (tel. 01 46 06 10 34; M. Abbesses). Follow rue Yvonne le Tac away from the metro and turn left on rue des Martyrs. Enticing main dishes (70-80F) include *Mafe* chicken cooked in ground-nut purée and *Colombo* lamb cooked in curry with eggplant, zucchini, and green pepper. 2-course *menu* available before 9pm (79F); 3-course *menu* available all night (130F). Frequent live African music. Open daily 7pm-2am. V, MC.

UNIVERSITY RESTAURANTS

For travelers or long-term visitors truly strapped for cash, university restaurants provide cheap and dependable meals. Students can purchase meal tickets at each location when food is being served (12F70). The following university restaurants are most convenient, but the list is not nearly exhaustive. The restaurants are open on a rotating schedule during the summer, and it is extremely important to get a schedule before showing up. For more information—summer and weekend schedules, a list of other restaurant locations—visit **CROUS,** 30, av. Georges Bernanos, 5ème (tel. 01 40 51 36 00; M. Port-Royal; open Tues.-Sat. 11:30am-1:30pm and 6-8pm). All of the following except Citeaux, Grand Palais, and C.H.U. Necker are usually open between lunch and dinner for sandwiches and drinks: **Bullier,** 39, av. Georges Bernanos, 5ème (M. Port-Royal); **Cuvier-Jussieu,** 8bis, rue Cuvier, 5ème (M. Cuvier-Jussieu); **Censier,** 31, rue Geoffroy St-Hilaire, 5ème (M. Censier-Daubenton; closed for dinner); **Châtelet,** 10, rue Jean Calvin, 5ème (M. Censier-Daubenton); **Mazet,** 5, rue Mazet, 6ème (M. Odéon); **Assas,** 92, rue d'Assas, 6ème (M. Port-Royal or Notre-Dame-des-Champs); **Mabillon,** 3, rue Mabillon, 6ème (M. Mabillon); **Grand Palais,** cours la Reine, 8ème (M. Champs-Elysées Clemenceau); **Citeaux,** 45, bd. Diderot, 12ème (M. Gare de Lyon); **C.H.U. Pitie-Salpetrière,** 105, bd. de l'Hôpital, 13ème (M. St-Marcel); **Dareau,** 13-17, rue Dareau, 14ème (M. St-Jacques); **C.H.U. Necker,** 156, rue de Vaugirard, 15ème (M. Pasteur); **Dauphine,** av. de Pologne, 16ème (M. Porte Dauphine).

■ Sweets

Paris's pastries and chocolates, fail-safe cure-alls for the weary traveler, are generally made in the store where you buy them. Recently, American desserts—like *brownies* and *cookies* (pronounced kookeys)—have gained a strong following among Parisians young and old. You'll probably find French *glaces* (ice creams) to be lighter, wetter, and less creamy than their American counterparts. **Berthillon,** 31, rue St-Louis-en-l'Ile, 4ème (on Ile St-Louis; M. Cité or Pont Marie), serves the best ice cream and sorbet in Paris (open Sept.-July Wed.-Sun. 10am-8pm). Lines are quite long in summer; look for stores nearby that sell Berthillon products, where the wait is shorter and which are open in August, when the main Berthillon is closed. The **Maison du Chocolat,** 8, bd. de la Madeleine, 9ème (M. Madeleine), serves every imaginable kind of chocolate, as well as delicious ice cream and sorbets. Chocolates go for 3-4F each (open Mon.-Sat. 9:30am-7pm). The fabulous chocolatier **Peltier,** 66, rue de Sèvres, 7ème (M. Vaneau or Duroc), and at 6, rue St-Dominique, 7ème (M. Solférino), showcases portable edible art. The house specialty, a *tarte au chocolat,* is more gooey than rich (16F). (Open Mon.-Sat. 8:15am-7:45pm, Sun. 8:15am-7pm.)

■ Cafés

The French café has long been suffused with a glamor absent from its rough American counterpart, the coffee-shop. We suspect it has something to do with the leisurely waitstaff; since the café's invention in the 17th century, a few customers have written whole novels while sitting. Visitors to Paris who don't drink coffee should still regard cafés as worthwhile haunts. Take inspiration from the example of the Surrealists, themselves partially responsible for the café's global prestige—at Les Deux Magots, where André Breton held court, the Communist poet Pierre de Massot drank his morning bottle of Coke.

Order *café* in Paris and you'll get a demitasse of espresso for 10-15F; a *café crème* will cost about 25-30F. To get an approximation of an American cuppa joe, order a *grande crème*. You'll pay for it, but you may attain nirvana. Cafés also serve Coke, but it's awfully expensive. (See page 79 for a further introduction to cafés.) Contrary to popular belief, it is *not* appropriate to call a waiter *garçon*. Café waiters in Paris, unlike some part-time teenage waiters and waitresses back home, are in professional, career positions and take their jobs very seriously. They should be addressed politely as Madame or Monsieur.

Listed here are some of the most historically important cafés. These are definitely *not* budget establishments. Think of these cafés as museums—the price of coffee or soda here is comparable to the average admission fee, and, as in a museum, you will be given all the time you want to enjoy the surroundings.

La Closerie des Lilas, 171, bd. du Montparnasse, 6ème (tel. 01 43 26 70 50; M. Port-Royal). Exit the metro and walk one block up bd. du Montparnasse. This lovely, flower-ridden café was a favorite of Ernest Hemingway (a scene in *The Sun Also Rises* takes place here) and of the Dadaists and Surrealists before him. Picasso came here to hear Paul Fort recite poetry. If the gorgeous interior (see the baby grand?) suggests a culinary opulence that you can't afford, drink but don't eat. In summer, soak up the sun among the plants on the terrace. Coffee 15F, house wine 26F, *marquise au chocolat* 65F. Open daily 11am-1am. V, MC, AmEx.

La Coupole, 102, bd. du Montparnasse, 14ème (tel. 01 43 20 14 20; M. Vavin). Black-and-white-clad waiters get their aerobic exercise navigating this enormous Art Deco café, with its mirrors, modern sculpture, wooden chairs, and elegantly tiled floor. Part café and part restaurant, La Coupole has hosted the likes of Lenin, Stravinsky, Hemingway, and Einstein. The *menus* are expensive, but you can probably still afford coffee (10F). Desserts 29-49F. Open daily 7:30am-2am. Dancing on the weekends: Fri. 9:30pm-4am, Sat. 3-7pm and 9:30pm-4am. V, MC.

Les Deux Magots, 6, pl. St-Germain-des-Prés, 6ème (tel. 01 45 48 55 25; M. St-Germain-des-Prés). Sartre's second choice café and Simone de Beauvoir's first, it was here that the couple first spotted each other. Home to Parisian literati since it opened in 1875, Les Deux Magots is now a favorite among Left Bank youth and tourists. Named after two Chinese porcelain figures (*magots*), this café has beautiful high ceilings, gilt mirrors, and 1930s Art Deco decor. *Café des Deux Magots* 22F, *café crème* 25F, *chocolat des Deux Magots* (a house specialty) 30F, beer 28-38F. Desserts such as *gâteau au chocolat amer* (bittersweet chocolate cake) 40F, pastries 38F. Café open daily 7am-1:30am. V, MC. AmEx (100F minimum).

Le Dôme, 108, bd. du Montparnasse, 14ème (tel. 01 43 35 25 81; M. Vavin). This illustrious café shares all the literary history and fame of its neighbors, but its smaller interior and elegant 1920s décor make it one of the best cafés in town—and one of the most expensive, with menu items as high as 400F. The interior boasts marble tables, gilded mirrors with engravings of flappers, and Victorian stained-glass windows. Coffee 15F, beer 20-30F, sandwich of the day 20F. Open Tues.-Sun. noon-3pm and 7pm-12:30am. Closed Sun. in Aug. V, MC, AmEx.

Le Flore, 172, bd. St-Germain, 6ème (tel. 01 45 48 55 26). It was here, in his favorite hangout, that Jean-Paul Sartre composed *L'être et le néant (Being and Nothingness)*. Apollinaire, Picasso, André Breton, and even James Thurber also sipped their brew in this friendly atmosphere. *Café espresso spécial Flore* 23F, *café crème* 28F, beer 28-38F, sandwiches 34-62F. Open daily 7am-2am. AmEx.

Le Fouquet's, 99, av. des Champs-Elysées (tel. 01 47 23 70 60; M. George V). "Created" in 1899 in the shadow of the Arc de Triomphe, this spot is the premier gathering place for Parisian *vedettes* (stars) of radio, television, and cinema. Tourists, oblivious to the celebrities inside, bask on the terrace. James Joyce dined here with relish. Bank-breaking coffee and a chance to be seen 25F. Dishes from 85F. Open daily 8am-1am; food served noon-3pm and 7pm-midnight. V, MC, AmEx.

Café de la Paix, 12, bd. des Capucines, 9ème (tel. 01 40 07 32 32; M. Opéra). On the left as you face the Opéra. This institution just off rue de la Paix (the most expensive property on French Monopoly) has drawn a classy crowd ever since it opened in 1862. The café is located on the terrace only. The 2 restaurants inside are pricey, with *menus* around 300F; the people there spend their time fussing over where to go next (shopping at Armani or at St-Laurent?). Coffee 26F, *café crème* 31F, ice cream desserts 40-59F. Open daily 10am-1am.

■ Salons de Thé

Long a preferred afternoon meeting spot for women of all ages, Paris's *salons de thé* (tea rooms) now draw alterno-youth for low-key refinement, light meals, and Sunday brunch. Relax and regroup over an *infusion* (herbal tea), or try an invigorating *menthe* (mint) or *verveine* (vervain). At **Angelina's,** 226, rue de Rivoli, 1er (tel. 01 42 60 88 00; M. Concorde or Tuileries), a thick atmosphere of propriety dampens all sounds but the click of teacups, as mature ladies and sedate tourists enjoy the pleasures of afternoon tea (32F) and pastries (25-35F). Angelina's is also a tasty, but not exactly budget, restaurant. (Open Mon.-Fri. 9:00am-7pm, Sat.-Sun. 9:30am-7:30pm. V, MC.) **Ladurée,** 16, rue Royale, 8ème (tel. 01 42 60 21 79; M. Concorde), is the perfect spot to show your style. Sit suavely under the painted ceiling and order one of its famed macaroons (20F), flavored with chocolate, pistachio, coffee, vanilla, or lemon. Ladurée endures as *the* chic tea room near La Madeleine. Pastries go for 10-20F, although you pay less if you carry your goodies away with you. Lunch served daily 11:30am-3pm. (Open Mon.-Sat. 8:30am-7pm, Sun. 10am-7pm. V, MC, AmEx.)

■ Groceries and Markets

When cooking or assembling a picnic, buy supplies at the specialty shops found in most neighborhoods. Grocery stores are open in the morning until noon and then again from about 2 to 7pm. Most are very good, and their owners are endless sources of information about their respective food specialties. Remember that French shop owners are incredibly touchy about people touching their fruits and vegetables; unless there's a sign outside the corner store that says "*libre service,*" ask inside before you start grabbing produce outside. **Supermarkets** *(supermarchés)* are almost everywhere. Avoid the evening scramble, lest you be trampled by homemakers trying to get the last loaf of bread. Also take note that in many *supermarchés* it is up to you to weigh your produce, bag it, and label it. If you're in the mood for a five-and-dime complete with a supermarket, go to any of the **Monoprix, Prisunics, Franprix,** or **Uniprix** that litter the city. Also look for the small foodstore chains such as **Casino** and **Félix Potin.** Starving students and travelers-in-the-know swear by the ubiquitous **Ed l'Epicier.** Buy in bulk and watch the pile of francs you save grow; it's possible to end up paying 30-50% less than you would at other stores. Two of Ed's drawbacks are that you can't find non-Ed brands (alas, no Nutella) and some stores do not carry produce. **Picard Surgelés,** with 50 locations throughout the city, stocks every imaginable frozen food—from crêpes to calamari.

La Grande Epicerie, the gourmet food annex of the **Bon Marché** department store (38, rue de Sèvres, 7ème; tel. 01 44 39 81 00; M. Sèvres-Babylone), sells high-priced, hard-to-find ingredients for fancy French food and lots of "gourmet" American fare (open Mon.-Sat. 8:30am-9pm; V, MC, AmEx). Snack on *latkes* or *kishke* from **Finkelsztajn's,** 27, rue des Rosiers, 4ème (tel. 01 42 72 78 91), and 24, rue des Ecouffes, 4ème (tel. 01 48 87 92 85; both M. St-Paul), on your gambol through the Marais. Serving Eastern European Jewish delicacies since 1946, this is the place to go for everything to-go from strudel to chopped liver. Whopping sandwiches are yours for a mere 30-40F. (Rue des Rosiers branch open Wed.-Sun. 10am-1:30pm and 3-7pm. Rue des Ecouffes branch open Thurs.-Mon. 10am-1:30pm and 3-7pm.) **Poilâne,** 8, rue Cherche-Midi, 6ème (tel. 01 45 48 42 59; M. Sévres Babylone), services the huge bakery responsible for Paris's most famous bread. Fragrant, crusty sourdough loaves are baked throughout the day in wood-fired ovens. The bread is priced according to weight (about 38-40F per loaf); for just a taste, ask for a *quart* (¼-loaf, 10F). (Open Mon.-Sat. 7:15am-8:15pm.) **Tang Frères,** 48, av. d'Ivry, 13ème (tel. 01 45 70 80 00; M. Porte d'Ivry), is a tremendous grocery selling rices, spices, soups and oodles of noodles in bulk, canned goods, and high-quality, often hard-to-find Eastern and Western produce (open Tues.-Fri. 9am-7:30pm, Sat.-Sun. 8:30am-7:30pm). **Thanksgiving,** 20, rue St-Paul, 4ème (tel. 01 42 77 68 29; M. St-Paul or Pont Marie), hawks homemade American junk food (peanut butter), snacks (chili, BBQ ribs), and desserts (brownies, cookies). The restaurant upstairs serves brunch on weekends for about 85F (store open Mon.-Sat. 11am-8pm, Sun. 11am-6pm).

In the 5th century, the ancient Roman settlement of Lutèce held the first **market** on what is now Ile de la Cité. More than a millennium later, markets are now an integral part of daily life. Open-air markets, held at least once a week in most *arrondissements,* remain the best places to buy fresh fruit, vegetables, fish, and meat. Keep in mind that quality and price can vary significantly from one stall to the next, and that the freshest and best produce is usually gone by noon.

Marché Montorgeuil, 2ème (M. Etienne Marcel). Market extending from rue Réaumur to rue Etienne Marcel, along rue des Petits-Carreaux and rue Montorgeuil. Super-abundance of fishmongers, butchers, bakers, and greengrocers in this mall of food which dates back to the 13th century.

Rue Mouffetard, towards the intersection of bd. du Port-Royal, 5ème (M. Censier-Daubenton). Colorful, busy, and—yes—quaint. Find your favorite fresh produce, meat, fish, and cheese here; other tables are loaded with shoes, cheap chic, and housewares. Open Mon.-Sat. 9am-1pm and 4-7pm, Sun. 9am-1pm.

Marché Biologique, on bd. Raspail between rue Cherche-Midi and rue de Rennes, 6ème (M. Rennes). French hippies peddle everything from organic produce to 7-grain bread and tofu patties. A great place to buy natural beauty supplies, to stock up on homeopathic drugs, or just to people-watch. Prices are higher than at other markets but reflect the quality of the products. Open Sun. 7am-1:30pm.

Marché Raspail, on bd. Raspail between rue Cherche-Midi and rue de Rennes, 6ème (M. Rennes). A small open-air market with fresh fruits and vegetables, meats and cheeses, nuts and dried fruits, and a few household appliances (lampshades and the like). Open Tues. and Fri. 7am-1:30pm.

Marché St-Germain, at 3ter, rue Mabillon, 6ème (M. Mabillon). Walk down rue du Four to rue Mabillon. In an upscale building that will soon include sports facilities and a parking lot, the market is home to a wide variety of equally chi-chi foods. Ranges from the banal to the imported; may be the only *marché* in Paris to sell Corona beer. Open Tues.-Sat. 8am-1pm and 4-8pm, Sun. 8am-1:30pm.

Rue Cler, between rue de Grenelle and av. de la Motte-Picquet, 7ème (M. Ecole Militaire). A bustling market filled with produce, meat, cheese, and bread, on one of the most picturesque streets in Paris. Open Tues.-Sun. 8am-1pm and 4-7:30pm.

Marché Europe, 1, rue Corvetto, 8ème. Covered food-market. Open Mon.-Sat. 8am-1:30pm and 4-7pm, Sun. 8am-1pm.

Marché St-Quentin, 85bis, bd. de Magenta, 10ème (M. Gare de l'Est). Outside, this is a massive construction of iron and glass, built in 1866 and covered by a glorious glass ceiling. Inside, you'll find stalls of fresh fruits and vegetables, meats, cheese, seafood, and wines. Open Tues.-Sat. 8am-1pm and 3:30-7:30pm, Sun. 8am-1pm.

Marché Bastille, on bd. Richard-Lenoir from pl. de la Bastille north to rue St-Sabin, 11ème (M. Bastille). Fruit, cheese, veggies, exotic mushrooms, bread, meat, and cheap housewares stretch from M. Richard Lenoir to M. Bastille. Expect to spend at least an hr. here. Popular as a Sunday morning family outing for area residents. Open Thurs. and Sun. 7am-1:30pm.

Sights

For all its pizzazz and sight-laden glitz, Paris is a small city. In just a few hours, you can walk from the heart of the Marais in the east to the Eiffel Tower in the west and pass almost every monument in the city. Try to reserve one day for nothing but wandering: you don't have a true sense of Paris until you know how close medieval Notre Dame is to the modern Centre Pompidou, and the *quartier latin* of students to the Louvre of kings. After dark the glamour only increases. From dusk until midnight, Paris's monuments transform into glittering chandeliers as spotlights go up over everything from the Panthéon to the Eiffel Tower, Notre Dame, and Obélisque.

For a tour of Paris from the water, take a boat down the Seine. **Bateaux-mouches** (tel. 01 42 25 96 10) provide a classic, if goofy, tour of Seine-side Paris. Be prepared for one-and-a-half hours of nonstop sight-commentary in five languages and dozens of tourists straining their necks to peer over the next person. The ride is most bearable if taken at night. (Departures every 30min. 10am-11pm from the Right Bank pier near Pont d'Alma. M. Alma-Marceau. 40F, under 14 20F.) **Vert Galant** boats (tel. 01 46 33 98 38) are another option, with commentaries in French and English. (Departures every 30min. 10am-noon, 1:30-6:30pm, and 9-10:30pm from the Pont Neuf landing. M. Pont-Neuf or Louvre. 45F daytime, 50F at night. Ages 4-10 20F.) The **Canauxrama** (tel. 01 42 39 15 00) boat tours of Paris get excellent reviews for their three-hour trip down the Canal St-Martin. The tour leaves at 9:30am and 2:45pm from Bassin de la Villette, 5bis, quai de la Loire, 19ème (M. Jaurès), and at 9:45am and 2:30pm from Port de l'Arsenal facing 50, quai de la Bastille, 12ème (M. Bastille). (75F, students 60F, under 12 45F, under 6 free.)

SEINE ISLANDS

PARIS

Ile de la Cité

Once home of the *Parisii*—a Gallic tribe of hunters, sailors, and fisherfolk—and then center of the Roman colony of Lutèce, the Ile de la Cité is the heart of Paris. In the early 6th century, Clovis crowned himself king of the Franks and adopted the island as the center of his domain, making it also the heart of France. During the Middle Ages, the island started to collect the features for which it is best known and loved today: Notre-Dame and the Ste-Chapelle.

Construction of the **Cathédrale de Notre-Dame de Paris** (tel. 01 42 34 56 10; M. Cité) began in 1163 and ended in 1361. Dedicated to Reason during the Revolution, the building later fell into disrepair and even sheltered livestock. Victor Hugo's 1831 novel, *Notre-Dame de Paris (The Hunchback of Notre Dame),* inspired a push for restoration. Architect Eugène Viollet-le-Duc's modifications (including the spire, the gargoyles, and a statue of himself admiring his work) remain highly controversial: is it a medieval masterpiece or a 19th-century mock-up? The **façade** features magnificently carved wooden portals called the **Porte du Jugement** (door of Judgment). On the right, sinners—a chain gang of cardinals, kings, and peasants—are snatched off to hell by gleeful demons; on the left, happy, virtuous souls await entry into heaven. In the fervor of the moment, Revolutionaries attacked and decapitated the stone statues of the kings of Judea and Israel above the doors, mistaking them for French royalty. Found in a Parisian back garden in 1977, the original heads are now in the Musée de Cluny (see page 135), and replicas are on the church. Chips of paint on the heads lead to a surprising discovery: as with all medieval cathedrals, Notre-Dame's façade was once painted in bright and garish colors.

Spidery flying buttresses, which support the weight of the ceiling from outside, allow the walls to be used for decorative purposes (i.e., stained glass). Subtle optical illusions make the cathedral seem even more roomy; for example, smaller pillars surround the bigger ones, diminishing their apparent size. The most spectacular features of the interior are the enormous stained-glass **rose windows** that dominate the north and south ends of the transept. Free **guided tours** of the cathedral give a deeper understanding of its history and architecture; ask at the info booth to the right as you enter. (Tours in English Wed. at noon. Tours in French Mon.-Fri. at noon, Sat.-Sun. at 2pm. Free.) The cathedral's **treasury** (south of the choir) contains a rather humdrum assortment of robes and sacramental cutlery (open Mon.-Sat. 9:30am-6pm, last ticket 5:30pm; admission 15F, students 10F, under 17 5F).

Outside again, visit the haunt of the cathedral's most famous fictional resident, the Hunchback, by climbing the two **towers.** The perilous and claustrophobic staircase emerges onto a spectacular perch, where weather-worn gargoyles survey a stunning view of the city's heart. The climb generally deters the busloads of tourists, and you may even have the towers (more or less) to yourself if you come early. If you can face the stairs again, continue to the south tower, where a door lets you in to see the 13-

ton bell. Even on a good night, Quasimodo could never ring it; it requires the strength of eight full-grown folk to budge. (Towers open daily April to mid-Sept. 9:30am-6pm; mid-Sept. to Oct. 9:30am-5:30pm; Nov. 10am-5pm; Dec.-Jan. 10am-4pm; Feb.-March 10am-5pm. Admission 28F, seniors and students 18F, ages 12-17 15F, under 12 free. Cathedral open daily 8am-6:45pm.)

Far below the cathedral towers, beneath the pavement of the *Parvis* (the square in front of the church), the **Archaeological Museum,** pl. du Parvis du Notre-Dame (tel. 01 43 29 83 51), lets you wander amid architectural fragments from Roman houses to 19th-century sewers. (Open daily April-Sept. 10am-6pm; Oct.-March 10am-5pm. Admission 28F, seniors and students 18F, ages 12-17 15F.)

The **Mémorial de la Déportation,** behind the cathedral at the tip of the island, across from pl. Jean XXIII and down a narrow flight of steps, is a haunting memorial erected for the French victims of Nazi concentration camps. 200,000 flickering lights represent the dead, and an eternal flame burns over the tomb of an unknown deportee. The names of all the concentration camps glow in gold triangles that recall the design of the patch French prisoners were forced to wear for identification purposes. A series of quotations is engraved into the stone walls—most striking is the motto *"Pardonne; N'Oublie Pas"* (Forgive; Do Not Forget), engraved over the exit. The old men who frequently visit the museum may act as voluntary guides. You may hear one of them chanting the chillingly beautiful *kaddish,* the Jewish prayer for the dead (open Mon.-Fri. 8:30am-9:45pm, Sat.-Sun. 9am-9:45pm; free).

The **Palais de Justice** (tel. 01 44 32 51 51), taking up the western half of the island, harbors the infamous **Conciergerie,** prison of the Revolution, and the Ste-Chapelle, St. Louis' private chapel. Since the 13th century, the structures here have contained the district courts for Paris. *Chambre 1* of the *Cour d'Appel* witnessed Pétain's convictions after WWII. All trials are open to the public. Even if your French is not up to legalese, the theatrical sobriety and black-robed lawyers inside make a quick visit worthwhile (trials usually Mon.-Fri. 9am-noon and 1:30-5pm; free). Criminal cases are the most interesting (criminal courtrooms open Mon.-Fri. 1:30-4pm).

At the heart of the *palais,* the exquisite **Ste-Chapelle** (tel. 01 43 54 30 09) is one of the world's foremost examples of flamboyant Gothic architecture. Because the church is crowded in an interior courtyard, the passerby sees only its 19th-century iron steeple. The church was begun in 1241 to house the most precious of Louis IX's possessions, the crown of thorns from Christ's Passion (later moved to Notre-Dame—minus a few thorns given away as political favors). The ground floor has 19th-century painted walls, but upstairs is where it's at: walls of the oldest stained glass in Paris, with scarcely a stone in sight. Ask at the info booth about concerts. (Open daily April-Sept. 9:30am-6:30pm; Oct.-March 10am-5pm. Admission 32F, students and seniors 21F, ages 12-17 15F, under 12 free.)

As you leave Ile de la Cité from its western tip, you'll walk over the oldest bridge in Paris, ironically named the **Pont Neuf** (New Bridge). Completed in 1607, the bridge lacked the domestic residences lining its sides that were usual for the day. Before the construction of the Champs-Elysées, the bridge was the city's most popular thoroughfare, attracting peddlers, performers, thieves, and even street physicians. Although not of particular architectural interest, the bridge does have gargoyle capitals on its supports; to see them, hang your head over the edge.

Ile St-Louis

A hop across Pont St-Louis will get you to the elegant neighborhood of the **Ile St-Louis.** Originally two small islands (the Ile aux Vâches and Ile de Notre-Dame), it was considered suitable for duels, cows, and little else throughout the Middle Ages. In 1267, St. Louis departed for the Tunisian Crusade from the Ile aux Vâches, never to return; the island was later named in memoriam. A contractual arrangement between Henri IV and the bridge entrepreneur Christophe Marie, after whom the Pont Marie is named, made the island habitable in the 17th century. Virtually all of the construction on the island happened in a few decades in the mid-1700s, giving the island an architectural unity missing in most of Paris. The roster of bigwigs that have lived here includes Voltaire, Daumier, Baudelaire, Claudel, Cézanne, and Curie. Look for plaques advertising famous residents on the sides of buildings.

The central **rue St-Louis-en-l'Ile** is the "main drag" of the Ile St-Louis, filled with an array of gift shops, art galleries, and pricey restaurants. The brooding, soot-covered exterior of **Eglise St-Louis-en-l'Ile,** at the corner of rue St-Louis-en-l'Ile and rue Poulletier, disguises the airiest of Rococo interiors, magnificently decorated with gold leaf, marble, and graceful statuettes. (Open to the public Mon.-Sat. 9am-noon and 3-7pm.) Before heading off for more sight-seeing, take a break at **Berthillon,** which serves the best ice cream in Paris (see page 111).

FIRST ARRONDISSEMENT: THE LOUVRE AND LES HALLES

The 1er *arrondissement* has one of the highest concentrations of sights-per-block in the world. Hugging the Seine, the Louvre occupies about a seventh of the district's surface area. The Jardin des Tuileries, the Palais Royal, the Place Vendôme, and Les Halles round out the all-star lineup.

The **Palais du Louvre** is Paris's single largest building, the largest palace in Europe, the largest museum in the western hemisphere, and the most recognized symbol of art and culture in all history (for more, see page 132). The elevated terrace and central path of the **Jardin des Tuileries,** at the western foot of the Louvre, gives fantastic views of the Seine, the Musée d'Orsay, the pl. de la Concorde, the Champs-Elysées, and the Arc de Triomphe. Catherine de Médicis, yearning for the public promenades of her native Italy, had the gardens built in 1564; since then, they have been one of Paris's most popular public spaces.

The **pl. Vendôme,** three blocks north along the rue de Castiglione from the Tuileries, was begun in 1687 according to plans by Jules Hardouin-Mansart, who convinced Louis XIV and a group of five financiers to invest in a proposed ensemble of private mansions and public institutions. The project ran out of funds almost instantly; for decades before its completion in 1720, the theatrical and ostentatious pl. Vendôme remained no more than a series of empty façades. Many of the buildings were gutted in the 1930s, but their uniformly dignified, 17th-century exteriors were protected once again. Today, the same shells mask stores that make the entire *place* shimmer with opulence. Well-known banks, perfumers, and jewelers rub shoulders with memorable addresses: Chopin died at no. 12; Hemingway drank at no. 15 (the **Ritz Hotel**); no. 11 and 13, flagged by the *tricolore,* make up the Ministry of Justice. The **column** in the center of the square has acted as a barometer of French regimes for some 200 years. Originally, the square held a 7m statue of Louis XIV in Roman costume, but it was destroyed by Revolutionaries in 1792. In 1805, Napoleon erected a central column modeled after Trajan's in Rome. Through various revolutions and restorations, it was replaced by the white flag of the ancient monarchy, by Napoleon in military garb, and by a classical Napoleon modeled after the original. During the Commune, a group led by the artist Gustave Courbet toppled the entire column, planning to replace it with a monument to the "Federation of Nations and the Universal Republic." Later, Napoleon enjoyed a posthumous last laugh when the original column was rebuilt, cast from its original (toga) mold.

Farther east, across rue de Rivoli from the Louvre, is the **Palais Royal.** Constructed in 1639 as Richelieu's *Palais Cardinal,* it became a *Palais Royal* when Anne of Austria, Louis XIV's mother and regent, set up house there. Louis-Philippe d'Orléans, whose son became King Louis-Philippe, inherited the palace in 1780. Strapped for cash, in 1784 he built and rented out the elegant buildings that enclose the palace's formal garden, turning the complex into an 18th-century mega-mall. It held boutiques, restaurants, prostitutes, and—in lieu of a multi-screen cinema—theaters, wax museums, and puppet shows. Today, the galleries of the venerable buildings contain small shops and a few cafés, all with great views of the palace fountain and flower beds. Government offices occupy the upper levels and older parts of the palace. The *colonnes de Buren*—a set of black and white striped pillars and stumps that completely fill the *cour d'honneur* (main courtyard)—are popular among couples with an inconvenient height disparity. Planted there in 1986, Daniel Buren's columns created a storm of controversy a bit like the one that greeted I.M. Pei's Louvre pyramid. On the southwest corner of the Palais-Royal, facing the Louvre, Victor Louis' 1770 **Comédie Française** theater is home to France's leading dramatic group. In a theater on this site in 1673, Molière was taken fatally ill on stage while performing his play—ahem—*Le Malade Imaginaire* (Imaginary Invalid). Fans waited days for permission to bury the irreverent (and decomposing) luminary on holy ground.

Construction of **St-Eustache** (M. Châtelet-Les-Halles), right next to the Turbigo exit of the Les Halles metro, began in 1532 and dragged on for over a century. In 1754, the unfinished façade was knocked down and replaced with the Romanesque one that stands today. St-Eustache's organ is one of Paris's best; classical music lovers shouldn't miss its thrilling baritone. Berlioz heard his *Te Deum* here for the first time, and Liszt conducted his *Messiah* here in 1886. For info on the church's organ festival, check *Pariscope* or read the posters at the church. (Church open Mon.-Sat. 8:30am-7pm, Sun. 8:15am-12:30pm and 3-7pm. Tours Sun. at 3pm; June-July daily at 2pm. Mass Mon.-Fri. 10am and 6pm, Sat. 6pm, Sun. 8:30, 9:45, 11am (with organ and choir), and 6pm (with organ).)

In the 19th century, Emile Zola called the huge food market of **Les Halles** (M. Châtelet-Les-Halles) *"le ventre de Paris"* (Paris's belly). In 1135, Louis VI built two wooden buildings here to house a bazaar, birthing what became the largest market in Paris. Les Halles received a much-needed facelift in the 1850s and 60s with the construction of large iron and glass pavilions that sheltered the vendors' stalls, but slipped into disrepair again over the next century. Demolition of the old market began in 1971, but architects Claude Vasconi and Georges Penreach have since replaced it with an underground shopping mall, the **Forum des Halles.** Some 200 boutiques (the most fashionable of which have floated to the upper levels) are crammed into the complex, along with a swimming pool and some museums (see page 138). Watch your wallet inside Les Halles, and stay above ground at night.

SECOND ARRONDISSEMENT

Galerie Colbert and **Galerie Vivienne,** near the Palais Royal, are the finest remaining examples of Parisian *galeries*—marbled, pedestrian walkways built within city blocks to house exclusive boutiques (such as antique cork-screw stores). Both restored arcades date from the early 19th century and, like others of their ilk, are the ur-past of modern malls. Enter Galerie Vivienne at 4, rue des Petits Champs, where you can ooh at *trompe l'oeil* marble columns (made of wood). Follow the passage and turn left into the rotunda of Galerie Colbert, a luxurious pastel *galerie* graced with small boutiques. This is where Madonna visits her favorite designer, **Jean-Paul Gaultier** (6, rue Vivienne); it's also home to branches of the Bibliothèque Nationale.

The **Bibliothèque Nationale,** 58, rue de Richelieu (tel. 01 47 03 81 26), is the largest library in Continental Europe, holding over 12 million volumes, including two Gutenberg Bibles and assorted other first editions from the 15th century to the present. Since 1642, a year before Richelieu founded the Académie Française, every book published in France has been legally required to enter a national archive. The current library evolved out of the **Bibliothèque du Roi,** the royal book depository, and further expanded with chunky donations from noted bibliophiles and authors such as Victor Hugo (1885) and Emile Zola (1904). In the late 1980s, the government decided on a more permanent solution and resolved to build the huge, glass **Bibliothèque de France** (in the 13ème), where the B. N.'s collection is now being relocated. A strict screening process allows only scholars into the reading room.

THIRD AND FOURTH ARRONDISSEMENTS: LE MARAIS

The 3ème and 4ème *arrondissements* are called the Marais ("the swamp") because of the area's distinctive dampness before 13th-century monks drained it. With Henri IV's construction of the pl. des Vosges in the early 17th century, the area became the center of fashionable living. Leading architects and sculptors of the period designed the *hôtels particuliers* that still dot the Marais—elegant mansions with large front courtyards and rear gardens. Under Louis XV, the center of Paris life moved from the Marais to *faubourgs* St-Honoré and St-Germain, and construction of *hôtels* here dropped off. The 19th and early 20th centuries were not kind to this old *quartier*, and many *hôtels* fell into disrepair. The tide turned in 1964, when part of the Marais was declared an historic site and protected from further destruction.

An alleyway at 38, rue des Francs-Bourgeois, gives a sense of what Henri IV's Paris was like: dark and claustrophobic. The oldest houses here date from the 1600s, and most of them have overhanging second floors that jut out over the street. The **rue Vielle-du-Temple** is lined with stately residences such as the Hôtel de la Tour du Pin (no. 75) and the Hôtel de Rohan (no. 87). The **Hôtel Salé,** built for a 16th-century salt merchant, is currently home to the **Musée Picasso** (see page 140). During the Revolution the hotel served as a warehouse for censored books, but by the 19th century it was a *pension* for artists and students, including up-and-coming Honoré de Balzac. Around the corner on **rue de Sévigné** (M. Chemin Vert), the **Hôtel Carnavalet** houses a spectacular museum of Parisian history (see page 138). Even if you don't visit the museum, peek in at the gate and courtyard of the building; the statue of Louis XIV in the courtyard used to be in front of the Hôtel de Ville.

The **Hôtel de Lamoignon,** 24, rue Pavée (M. St-Paul), is one of the finest *hôtels particuliers* in the Marais. Built in 1584 for Diane de France, Henri II's daughter, the original *hôtel* consisted only of the section directly in front as you enter the courtyard. The left wing was built a generation later; the small courtyard to the right dates from 1968. Through the courtyard, you can enter the **Bibliothèque Historique de la Ville de Paris** (tel. 01 42 74 44 44), a noncirculating library of Parisian history (open Mon.-Sat. 9:30am-6pm). To glimpse the *hôtel's* gardens (closed to the public), exit on rue Pavée, go right on rue des Francs Bourgeois, and peer through the fence.

The **pl. des Vosges** (M. Chemin Vert, St-Paul) is Paris's oldest surviving public square. Several kings lived in mansions on this block until Catherine de Médicis ordered the Palais de Tournelles destroyed after her husband Henri II died in a jousting tournament there. The area housed a horse market until 1605, when Henri IV planned a new square with buildings designed "according to the same symmetry." All 36 buildings have arcades on the street level, each topped by two stories of pink brick capped by a steep, slate-covered roof. Cardinal Richelieu (no. 21), Victor Hugo (no. 6), Molière, Racine, and Voltaire filled the grand parlors with their wit and philosophy. Mozart played here at the age of seven. On summer weekends these arcades echo the mostly classical music of musicians who play in the square. Come at dusk for a romantic stroll amid iron lamps and gracious townhouses.

Since the 13th century, when Phillipe-Auguste ordered the Jewish population living in front of Notre-Dame move to the Marais (then outside of city limits), this quarter has been the Jewish center of Paris. The area around rue des Rosiers and rue des Ecouffes still forms the spine of the Jewish community, with two synagogues, one oratory, and dozens of kosher restaurants and delis. At 17, rue Geoffroy de l'Asnier, the solemn 1956 **Mémorial du Martyr Juif Inconnu** (Memorial to the Unknown Jewish Martyr; M. St-Paul) commemorates Parisian Jews who died at the hands of the Nazis. The eternal flame in the crypt downstairs burns above human ashes brought from concentration camps and the Warsaw ghetto. (Open Sun.-Thurs. 10am-1pm and 2-6pm, Fri. 10am-1pm and 2-5pm. Admission 15F.) Upstairs, the **Centre de Documentation Juive Contemporaine** (tel. 01 42 72 44 72) has a small Holocaust museum, a library with 400,000 documents relating to the Nazi era, and frequent temporary exhibits (open Mon.-Thurs. 2-6pm; admission 30F).

The **Hôtel de Ville** (M. Hôtel de Ville), Paris's ornate city hall, dominates a large square with fountains and Victorian lampposts. The present edifice is little more than a century old, a 19th-century structure that re-created the medieval structure built as a meeting hall for the *hause,* the cartel that controlled traffic on the Seine. In 1533 François I ordered the old building destroyed; construction of a more spacious version, designed by Boccadoro and meant to house Paris's municipal government, began on the same spot in the Renaissance style of the châteaux along the Loire. On May 24, 1871, *communards* doused the building with petrol and set it afire. The blaze, which lasted eight days, spared nothing but the frame. The Third Republic built a virtually identical structure on the ruins. Two blocks west, the **Tour St-Jacques** (between 39 and 41, rue de Rivoli) stands strangely alone in its own park. The flamboyant Gothic tower is the only remnant of the 16th-century Eglise St-Jacques-la-Boucherie, destroyed in 1802.

In the western part of the fourth, the startling **Centre Pompidou** is impossible to miss with its famous inside-out architecture. Built in 1977, the roaringly idiosyncratic Palais Beaubourg (as it is also known) sits where a vacant lot stood for decades; some Parisians wish it were still empty (see page 134 for more). An electric sign behind it counts down the seconds until the year 2000. In afternoons and early evenings, the vast cobblestone *place* in front of the center fills with street performers and peddlers. Although the area is wild fun, watch out for pickpockets and be careful here at night. The **Fontaine Stravinsky,** behind the museum, complements the Beaubourg crowd of minstrels and eccentrics as it spurts and splashes from brightly colored shapes and mechanical contraptions. The fountain's dancing G-clef and spinning hats pay tribute to the polytonal compositions of Russian composer Igor Stravisnsky, who shook Paris 80 years ago with his *Sacre du Printemps*.

FIFTH ARRONDISSEMENT: LE QUARTIER LATIN

Although Romans built some of the area's ancient streets, the *latin* in the *quartier latin's* name refers to the language of scholarship heard here in daily speech until 1798. Home to the 13th-century Sorbonne, the *quartier* has changed greatly since the student riots of May 1968 (after which the state decentralized and fragmented the university). Except for used bookstores and art-house cinemas, much of the area now resembles any other Parisian neighborhood, crushed by a tsunami of tourists.

The **bd. St-Michel,** with its fashionable cafés, restaurants, bookstores, and movie theaters, is the pulsing center of the *quartier*. **Pl. St-Michel**, at the northern tip of this avenue, is a microcosm of the entire area, with tourists, students, and street people. The **Hôtel de Cluny**, 6, pl. Paul Painlevé, at the corner of bd. St-Germain and bd. St-Michel, is Paris's second oldest residential building. Built in 1330 and modified to its present Gothic style in 1510, the *hôtel* is now home to the **Musée de Cluny,** one of the world's finest collections of medieval art and architecture (see page 135). Farther south, the café-lined **pl. de la Sorbonne** (M. Cluny-La Sorbonne; RER Luxembourg) is the focus of student life in the Latin Quarter. At the eastern end of the square stands the **Sorbonne,** 45-7, rue des Ecoles, one of Europe's oldest universities. Founded in 1253 by Robert de Sorbon as a simple dormitory for theology students, the Sorbonne became the administrative quarters for the University of Paris by the end of the 13th century. All the original buildings have been destroyed and rebuilt except for the Ste-Ursule-de-la-Sorbonne (the main building), commissioned in 1642 by Cardinal Richelieu. The Cardinal, himself a *sorbonnard,* lies buried inside, his hat suspended above him by a few threads hanging from the ceiling. Legend has it that when he gets out of Purgatory, the strings will snap. The public is admitted only to the chapel, which occasionally hosts art exhibits (open Mon.-Fri. 9am-5pm). Behind the Sorbonne is the less exclusive **Collège de France,** an institution created by François I in 1530 to contest the university's supreme authority. Outstanding courses, given by such luminaries as Henri Bergson and Paul Valéry, are free and open to all. Check the schedules that appear by the door in September. (Courses run Sept.-May. For more info, call 01 43 29 12 11.)

The proud dome of the **Panthéon** (tel. 01 40 51 75 81; M. Cardinal Lemoine; RER Luxembourg), visible from anywhere in the Latin Quarter, is only the latest church to be built on this hill. (The first was built by Clovis in 508 to the saints Peter and Paul, in celebration of his victory over Alaric at the Battle of Vouillé.) Louis XV ordered the current structure in 1754 in gratitude to Ste-Geneviève for helping him recover from a grave illness. The Revolution converted the church into a mausoleum of heroes, designed to rival the royal crypt at St-Denis. In the **crypt,** you'll find the remains of Voltaire, Rousseau, Hugo, Zola, Jaurès, and Braille decaying peacefully in stone tombs, which can be viewed from behind locked iron gates at each of their niches.

From the crypt, a twisting staircase winds upward to the roof and dome, although the dome will be closed until the spring of 1997. (Open daily 9:30am-6:30pm; admission 32F, students 21F.)

However circuitous the streets, lively the outdoor markets, or atmospheric the cafés, much of the 5ème is a neighborhood-turned-tourist-attraction. Not so, however, for the **Jardin des Plantes,** where actual Parisians go for trysts or family outings (tel. 01 40 79 30 00 for information concerning the entire complex; M. Jussieu; main entrance at pl. Valhubert, off quai St-Bernard). The 45,000-square-meter park, opened in 1640 by Guy de la Brosse, personal doctor to Louis XIII, was originally intended for the sole purpose of growing medicinal plants to promote His Majesty's health. Later it became a general garden for botanical research. Thomas Jefferson, an avid naturalist, loved the place. The park currently houses a three-part natural history museum, an insect gallery across the street, a hedge maze, an arboretum, greenhouses, and a full-fledged zoo. The arboretum—a series of rare trees labeled with metal nameplates, scattered throughout the park—and the hedge maze, located at the northeastern end of the park, are both free. All of the museums have separate tickets and hours (see page 138). Ask at the entrance gate for a free park map. The Jardin des Plantes also has two botanical theme parks, the **Jardin Alpin** and the **Serres Tropicales;** the first is full of rare flowers and plants from the Alpine domain and the second full of those from tropical and desert regions. (Serres Tropicales temporarily closed for renovations. Usually open Wed.-Mon. 1-5:30pm; admission 15F, students 10F. Jardin Alpin open Mon.-Fri. 8-11am and 1:30-5pm; free.) A new addition to the complex is the **Grande Galerie de l'Evolution** which houses temporary exhibits, a cultural center, and a conference hall. (Open Mon.-Fri. 10am-5pm, Sat.-Sun. 10am-6pm. Admission 30F, students 20F.)

As you walk west along the Seine towards pl. St-Michel, stop to rest in the **Jardin des Sculptures en Plein Air,** quai St-Bernard, a lovely collection of modern sculpture on a long stretch of green along the Seine. Avoid this area at night; exhibitionists frequent this park to show tourists their own special parts of Paris. Across the street is the **Institut du Monde Arabe** (see page 139).

SIXTH ARRONDISSEMENT: ST-GERMAIN

Less frenzied and more sophisticated than its neighbors, the 6ème *arrondissement* combines the vibrancy of the Latin Quarter to the east with the fashionable cafés, restaurants, and movie theaters of Montparnasse to the south. This area has long been the focus of literary Paris, and it remains less ravaged by tourists than other, more monumental quarters. Join the locals at one of the famous cafés on **bd. St-Germain**—former haunts of Picasso, Sartre, de Beauvoir, Prévert, Hemingway, and Apollinaire—and watch hordes of well-dressed Parisians scope each other out.

The **Jardin du Luxembourg** is the place to spot Parisians sunbathing, contemplating, writing, romancing, strolling, or just gazing at the luscious rose gardens. Inside the park, the **Palais du Luxembourg** was commissioned in 1615 by Marie de Médicis, who wanted an Italianate palace to remind her of her native Tuscany. The palace first served its current purpose, the meeting-place for the largely powerless French Senate, in 1852. The president of the Senate lives in the **Petit Luxembourg,** a gift from Marie de Médicis to her nemesis, Cardinal Richelieu. The **Musée du Luxembourg** (tel. 01 42 34 25 95), next to the palace on rue de Vaugirard, often shows free exhibitions of contemporary art.

The nearby **Théâtre Odéon** (M. Odéon) has competed with its rival, the Comédie Française, for centuries. The state currently runs the theater, whose façade was designed by Jacques-Louis David in 1818 (see page 121). Two blocks to the west, the awe–inspiring **Eglise St-Sulpice** (M. St-Sulpice) contains Delacroix frescoes in the first chapel on the right, a stunning *Virgin and Child* by Jean-Baptiste Pigalle in one of the rear chapels, and an enormous Chalgrin organ, among the world's largest and most famous with 6588 pipes. (Open daily 7:30am-7:30pm.)

From St-Sulpice, move north to the cafés, restaurants, and boutiques of the noisy, exciting **bd. St-Germain.** The **Eglise St-Germain-des-Prés** (M. St-Germain-des-

PARIS

Prés) watches benevolently over all the commotion. Dating from 1163, St-Germain is officially the oldest standing church in modern-day Paris and shows the wear of many centuries. Parts of the church were repeatedly torn down and rebuilt, producing a mélange of Romanesque, Gothic, and Baroque features.

To see what local art students are up to, walk around the **Ecole Nationale Supérieure des Beaux Arts (ENSBA),** 14, rue Bonaparte (tel. 01 47 03 50 00; M. St-Germain-des-Prés), at quai Malaquais. France's most acclaimed art school, the *école* was founded by Napoleon in 1811 and soon became *the* stronghold of French academic painting and sculpture. The current building for ENSBA was finished in 1838 in a gracious style much like that of the nearby **Institut de France.** One of the institute's branches is the prestigious **Académie Française,** which, since its founding by Richelieu in 1635, has assumed the task of compiling the official French dictionary and serves as guardian of the French language. Having registered its disapproval of *le weekend, le parking,* and other Franglais, the Academy recently triumphed with the passing of a constitutional amendment affirming French as the country's official language. It is so difficult to be elected to this 40-member society that Molière, Balzac, and Proust never made it.

SEVENTH ARRONDISSEMENT

Since the 18th century, the 7ème has stood its ground as the city's most elegant residential neighborhood. Home to the National Assembly, countless foreign embassies, the Invalides, the Musée d'Orsay, and the Eiffel Tower, this section of the Left Bank is a medley of France's diplomatic, architectural, and military achievements.

On some streets in the 7ème you might be the only one without a uniform, a gun, or a cellular phone; many policemen and soldiers guard the area's consulates and ministries. Once owned by Talleyrand, the **Hôtel Matignon,** at 57, rue de Varenne, is the official residence of the French Prime Minister. It cannot be visited without a personal invitation. The nearby **Hôtel Biron,** at no. 77, was built by Gabriel in 1728. Under the state's aegis, it became an artists' *pension* in 1904. The sculptor Auguste Rodin rented a studio on its ground floor in 1908. When the Ministry of Education and Fine Arts evicted all tenants in 1910, Rodin offered to donate all of his works to make the *hôtel* an art museum—on the condition that he be permitted to spend his last years there. The Hôtel Biron therefore houses the **Musée Rodin** (see page 135). Across the street stands the **Musée d'Orsay,** known for its architectural elegance and large collection of Impressionist paintings. Its glass and steel roof recalls the building's former function as a train station (see page 133).

Its original occupants would probably not recognize the **Palais Bourbon,** across the Seine from the pl. de la Concorde. Built in 1722 for the Duchess of Bourbon, daughter of Louis XIV and Mme. de Montespan, the palace was remodeled after 1750 to align with the pl. de la Concorde. Sold to the Prince of Condé in 1764, the building grew larger and more ornate under its new ownership. Napoleon erected the present Greek revival façade in 1807 to harmonize with that of the Madeleine (see page 125). From 1940-44, the Germans occupied the palace. Parts of it were damaged in the Liberation, and many of the library's books were destroyed. The **Assemblée Nationale** currently occupies the palace. Machine-gun-toting police are ostensibly there to prevent a replay of an attempted coup in 1934, during which rioters stormed the building. French speakers and political science majors might want to observe the Assembly in session. Foreigners should expect a one-hour security check before entering the chamber and will be required to present their passports. Appropriate dress is required. Foreign nationals interested in attending a session of the National Assembly must write for permission in advance to 33, quai d'Orsay 75007 Paris. (Sessions Oct.-June, weekday afternoons.) Guided tours (tel. 01 40 63 63 08) are also available and don't require a security check. Show up on Saturday at 10am, 2, or 3pm for a free tour (in French, with English pamphlet).

The green, tree-lined **Esplanade des Invalides** runs from Pont Alexandre III to the gold-leaf dome of the **Hôtel des Invalides,** 2, av. de Tourville (M. Invalides). In 1670 Louis XIV decided to "construct a royal home, grand and spacious enough to receive all old or wounded officers and soldiers." Architect Libéral Bruand's building accepted its first wounded in 1674, and veterans still live in the Invalides today. Jules Hardouin-Mansart provided the design for the **Eglise St-Louis,** the chapel within the Invalides complex. This church received Napoleon's body for funeral services in 1840, 19 years after the former emperor died in exile. Napoleon's ornate sarcophagus, now on display in the *hôtel,* wasn't completed for 20 more years. **Napoleon's tomb** (along with the **Musée de l'Armée, Musée d'Histoire Contemporaine,** and **Musée de l'Ordre de Libération**) lies within the Invalides museum complex (see page 135). Enter from either pl. des Invalides to the north or pl. Vauban and av. de Tourville to the south. Around the "back," to the left of the Tourville entrance, the **Jardin de l'Intendant** provides a shady, almost elegant place to rest on a bench.

At the opening of his impressive iron monument in 1889, Gustave Eiffel scrawled on the fan of an adoring spectator, "France is the only country in the world with a 300m flagpole." Today, the tricolor still flies from the **Tour Eiffel** (M. Bir-Hakeim), the globally admired symbol of the City of Lights. Judges chose Eiffel's design for the centerpiece of the 1889 World's Fair, held to celebrate the French Revolution's centennial. Shock waves of dismay reverberated around the city even before construction on the site at the end of the Champ de Mars began. Guy de Maupassant, Alexandre Dumas, *fils,* Charles Garnier, and Sully Prudhomme joined countless other artists in condemning it as "useless and monstrous." Maupassant allegedly ate his lunch in the two-and-a-half-acre expanse beneath it because it was the only place in Paris where he could avoid seeing it. Such a reaction was not altogether surprising: with metal girders and a boldly modern look, the tower was a triumph of engineering, not aesthetics, and seemed to cement the split between science and art. Eiffel patiently responded to critics by saying that his engineer's sense of beauty was delighted by design that served a purpose, and that the grand curves of the tower possessed the beauty of wind resistance. Eiffel was right about the structure's practicality; slated to meet the wrecking ball in 1909, the tower was spared only after the French army discovered it would make an excellent communications station.

While at the Eiffel Tower, buy exorbitantly priced souvenirs in the stores, eat good food in pricey restaurants, or send mail with the "only-available-here" Eiffel Tower postmark. The cheapest way to ascend the tower is to walk up the first two floors (12F). The Cinemax, a relaxing stop midway through the climb on the first floor, shows documentaries about the tower. Visitors should—must—take the elevator to the third story. You can buy tickets from the *caisse* or from the coin-operated dispenser. Enjoy the view of the city from the top floor and consult posted, captioned aerial photographs to locate landmarks. Accompanying blurbs, in English, fill in the history. (Tower open daily July-Aug. 9am-midnight, including holidays; Sept.-June 9:30am-11pm. Elevator to 1st floor 20F, 2nd floor 40F, 3rd floor 56F. Under 12 and over 60: 1st floor 10F, 2nd floor 21F, 3rd floor 28F. Under 4 free.)

Though close to the military monuments and museums, the **Champ de Mars** (Field of Mars) celebrates the god of war in name alone. This flower-embroidered carpet stretching from the Ecole Militaire to the Eiffel Tower is above all a well-equipped playground, with jungle gyms, monkey bars, and wood trains along its southwestern edge. The park's name comes from its previous function as a drill ground for the adjacent Ecole Militaire. In 1780, Charles Montgolfier launched the first hydrogen balloon (with no basket attached) from here. During the Revolution the park witnessed an infamous civilian massacre and numerous political demonstrations. Here, at the 1793 Festival of the Supreme Being, Robespierre proclaimed the new Revolutionary religion. During the 19th and 20th centuries it served as fairgrounds for international expositions in 1889, 1900, and 1937. After the 1900 Exhibition, the municipal council considered parceling off the Champ de Mars for development but concluded that Paris needed all the open space it had.

Louis XV founded the **Ecole Militaire** at the urging of his mistress, Mme. de Pompadour, who wanted to transform "poor gentlemen" into educated officers. In 1784, a 15-year-old Corsican named Napoleon Bonaparte arrived and within weeks presented the school's administrators with a comprehensive plan for its reorganization.

Its architectural and spiritual antithesis, **UNESCO (United Nations Educational, Scientific, and Cultural Organization),** stands in the shape of a "Y" across the street at 7, pl. de Fontenoy (M. Ségur). Nine appropriately international pieces of art decorate the building and garden, including ceramics by Miró and Artigas, a painting by Picasso, a Japanese garden, and an angel from the façade of a Nagasaki church destroyed by the atom bomb. (Hours vary with the exhibit. Free.)

EIGHTH ARRONDISSEMENT: CHAMPS-ELYSÉES

The 8ème *arrondissement* is home to Haussmann's *grands boulevards,* including the grand **Faubourg St-Honoré** and the even grander **av. des Champs-Elysées.** Fashionable streets with world-famous names harbor salons and boutiques of *haute couture.* Embassies crowd around the **Palais de l'Elysée,** state residence of the French president. The whole area bustles, and justifiably so: within a very few blocks are all the resources necessary to dine exquisitely, dress impeccably, and accessorize magnificently. You can indulge your esoteric music tastes, satisfy your penchant for sweets, and tuck away a ticket for a winter flight to Rio, all with minimum effort—and maximum expenditure. Most importantly, the pleasantly pretentious 8th and its tree-lined streets provide you the opportunity to show it all off.

The **Arc de Triomphe** (tel. 01 43 80 31 31; M. Charles de Gaulle Etoile), looming gloriously above the Champs-Elysées, moves every heart not made of stone. The world's largest triumphal arch and an internationally recognized symbol of France, this behemoth was commissioned in 1806 by Napoleon in honor of his *Grande Armée* and completed in 1836, 21 years after the defeat of said army. The Arc has seen disappointments (victorious Prussians marched through its opening in 1871) as well as triumphs (in 1919 the Allies, headed by Maréchal Foch, paraded through). The most bitter image for Parisians, however, was the Nazis goose-stepping under the arch in 1940. Finally, in 1944, the Free French and the Yanks sidled majestically through to liberate the war-torn city. The Tomb of the Unknown Soldier has rested beneath the arch since November 11, 1920; a flame is rekindled every evening at 6:30pm, when veterans and children lay wreaths decorated with blue, white, and red. De Gaulle's famous plea for *Résistance* is inscribed on a plaque under the Arc. Rather than risk an early death by crossing the traffic of the Etoile to reach the Arc, use the underpasses on the even-numbered sides of both the Champs-Elysées and av. de la Grande-Armée. Climb 205 steps up a winding staircase to the *entresol* and then brace yourself for the 29 more that lead to the *musée* (or tackle the lines at the elevator). The real spectacle lies just 46 steps higher—the *terrasse* at the top of the Arc provides a terrific view of the gorgeous av. Foch and the sprawling city. (Observation deck open April-Sept. Sun.-Mon. 9:30am-11pm, Tues.-Sat. 10am-10:30pm; Oct.-March Sun.-Mon. 10am-6pm, Tues.-Sat. 10am-10:30pm. Last entry 30min. before closing. Admission 35F, students 18-25 and seniors 23F, ages 12-17 15F, under 12 free. Expect lines; buy your ticket before going up to the ground level.)

The **av. des Champs-Elysées** is perhaps the most famous street in the world. No one can deny that this 10-lane wonder, flanked by exquisite cafés and luxury shops and crowned by the world's most famous arch, deserves its reputation. Le Nôtre planted trees here in 1667 to extend the Tuileries vista, completing the work begun under Marie de Médicis in 1616. It was only during the Second Empire, after considerable repair, that the street became the den of luxury that it is today. Today, you'll probably see more foreigners than Parisians here, but tourists and French film stars alike share **Fouquet's,** an outrageously expensive café near the Arc de Triomphe. Paris's answer to Hollywood's Sunset Strip, this stretch of the Champs-Elysées bears golden plaques with names of favorite French entertainers. Street performers move in at night. Six big avenues radiate from the Rond Point des Champs-Elysées, including av. Montaigne, which shelters houses of *haute couture.*

At the foot of the Champs-Elysées, the **Grand Palais** and the **Petit Palais** face one another on av. Winston Churchill. Built for the 1900 World's Fair, both are prime examples of art nouveau architecture. The glass-over-steel composition of the roof of the Grand Palais makes it look like a giant greenhouse. Both palaces house seasonal exhibits on art, architecture, and French history; the Grand Palais also houses the Palais de la Découverte museum. The Tsar's son, Nicholas II, placed the first stone of the **Pont Alexandre III,** the palaces' contemporary.

The **pl. de la Concorde** (M. Concorde), Paris's largest and most infamous public square, forms the eastern terminus of the Champs-Elysées. Constructed between 1757 and 1777 to provide a home for a monument to Louis XV, the vast area soon became the pl. de la Revolution, site of the guillotine that severed 1,343 necks. Louis XVI, Marie Antoinette, Charlotte Corday (Marat's assassin), and other celebrated heads rolled into baskets and were held up to cheering crowds right here. In an ironic twist, Robespierre, leader of the Terror, lost his head here in 1794. After the Reign of Terror, the square was optimistically renamed—*concorde* means peace. The gargantuan, rose granite **Obélisque de Louxor** was a gift offered by Mehemet Ali, Viceroy of Egypt, to Charles X in 1829. Dating from the 13th century BC, the obelisk, which depicts the deeds of Ramses II, is effectively Paris's oldest monument. In 1944, the *place* witnessed a tank battle, as the French 2nd Armored Division closed in on German headquarters nearby. Directly north of the *place,* like sentries guarding the gate to the Madeleine, stand the **Hôtel Crillon** (on your left) and the **Hôtel de la Marine** (on your right). Architect Gabriel built the impressive colonnaded façades between 1757 and 1770. The businesses along rue Royale boast their own proud history. **Christofle** has been producing works in gold and crystal since 1830. Renowned **Maxim's** restaurant (no. 3) won't even let you peep in the windows of what was once Richelieu's home.

PARIS

The **Madeleine,** formally called Eglise Ste-Marie-Madeleine, is the commanding building at the end of rue Royale. This architectural orphan was begun in 1764 at the command of Louis XV and modeled after a Greek temple. Construction halted during the Revolution, when the Cult of Reason proposed making the edifice into a bank, a theater, or a courthouse. In 1806, at the height of his power, Napoleon consecrated the partially completed building as a Temple of Glory. Completed as a church in 1842, the structure is distinguished by its four ceiling domes, which light the interior in lieu of windows, as well as by its 52 exterior Corinthian columns and its noticeable lack of even one cross. (Open Mon.-Sat. 7:30am-7pm, Sun. 7:30am-1:30pm and 3:30-7pm. Occasional organ concerts.) Stretching out just below the Madeleine, roughly parallel to the Champs-Elysées, is the highbrow and high-priced **rue de Faubourg St-Honoré.** Head west from rue Royale to rue Boissy d'Anglais, where you can stare at the lavish, sparkly, refined, and outrageously decorated windows of **Hermès, Yves St-Laurent, Guy Laroche,** and others.

The **Parc Monceau** (M. Marceau) borders on the elegant bd. de Courcelles. Whereas the Jardin du Luxembourg emphasizes show over relaxation, the Parc Monceau serves as a bucolic setting for children to play in the sun and parents to unwind in the shade. The Rotonde de Monceau, at the north end of the park, is a remnant of the Farmers-General wall of the 1780s. Designed to enforce customs duties rather than to keep out invaders, the wall and its fortifications reflected their creator's tastes in ornament more than the latest advances in military engineering. An array of architectural follies—a pyramid, a covered bridge, a pagoda, and picturesque Roman ruins—make this one of Paris's most pleasant spots for a *déjeuner sur* bench. (Open daily April-Oct. 7am-10pm; Nov.-March 7am-8pm. M. Monceau.)

NINTH ARRONDISSEMENT: L'OPÉRA

Charles Garnier's grandiose **Opéra** (tel. 01 44 73 13 99) is the most extravagant creation of the Second Empire, an outpouring of opulence and meaningless allegory. It did not actually open until 1875, five years after the Empire's collapse. With its grand staircase, enormous golden foyer, vestibule, and five-tiered auditorium, the Opéra was designed so that audience members could watch each other as much as the action onstage. The interior is adorned by Gobelin tapestries, gilded mosaics, a 1964 Chagall ceiling, and the six-ton chandelier that fell on the audience in 1896. Since 1989, when the new Opéra de la Bastille opened, most operas have taken place there; Garnier's hall is used mainly for ballets and films on dance. (Open for visits daily 10am-6pm. Last entry 5:30pm. 30F, ages 10-16 20F, auditorium closed on performance days. 1½-hr. tours in English and French 60F, ages 10-16 45F, under 10 25F; meet at the Rameau statue in the main hall Mon.-Sat. at 10:15am or 2:15pm.)

Directly across from the Opéra is the **Café de la Paix,** dating from the 19th century, which caters to the after-theater crowd and anyone else who doesn't mind paying 30F for espresso. West from this area along bd. Haussmann, toward M. Chaussée d'Antin and Trinité, lies the largest clothes shopping area in town, with two of Paris's big department stores, **Printemps** and **Galeries Lafayette** (see page 153).

The area north of rue Châteaudun is quiet and mostly residential, with many students and small ethnic restaurants. Farther north at the border of the 18*ème* *arrondissement* is **Pigalle,** an area famous not only as home to the **Moulin Rouge** cabaret and many popular *discothèques* but also as the center of much of the city's prostitution and hub of its sex-shop industry. Tourists, especially women, should never walk around here alone at night and should always be wary of pickpockets.

TENTH ARRONDISSEMENT

The **Gare du Nord** (M. Gare du Nord) is generally encountered out of necessity rather than curiosity, but it is worth a look. Jacques-Ignace Hittorf created the enormous station in 1863. A vast umbrella of glass and steel covers the platforms. Across from the station, a fringe of *brasseries* and cafés caters to the thousands of travelers who pass through every day. Nearby is the **Marché St-Quentin,** 85, bd. Magenta, a massive, elegant construction of iron and glass built in 1866. Inside you can find an enormous variety of goods, flowers, and fresh produce. (Open Tues.-Sat. 8am-1pm and 3:30-7:30pm, Sun. 8am-1pm.) Cross bd. de Magenta and follow rue du 8 Mai 1945 until it arrives at the **Gare de l'Est.** The *gare* conforms to the same neoclassical style in which all six of Paris's stations were built. Across from the station, the pl. du 11 Novembre 1918 opens into the **bd. de Strasbourg,** a hopping thoroughfare crowded with cafés, shops, and fruit stands.

Close by, the small **rue de Paradis** offers a quaint and prosperous little area bordered by shops displaying fine china and crystal. The beautiful and expensive objects mark the road to the headquarters of **Baccarat** and the **Baccarat Museum,** housed in an 18th-century building at 30-32, rue de Paradis (see page 137).

Going south on the **rue du Faubourg St-Denis,** you will walk through crowds of Parisians buying dinner ingredients in a very active market area. Individual stores, many owned by African, Arab, and Indian vendors, specialize in seafood, cheese, bread, or produce, rebuking supermarkets everywhere with the quality and selection they offer. **Passage Brady,** which intersects with bd. de Strasbourg and rue du Faubourg St-Martin, is lined with Indian and Pakistani stores that are stocked with exotic foodstuffs and prepared delicacies that the budget traveler can afford.

At the end of the Faubourg St-Denis, the **Porte Saint-Denis** (M. Strasbourg/St-Denis) welcomes visitors into Paris's inner city. Built in 1672 to celebrate the victories of Louis XIV, it is an imitation of the Arch of Titus in Rome. In the Middle Ages, this was the site of a gate in the city walls, but the present arch, characterized by André Breton as *"très belle et très inutile"* (very beautiful and very useless), was only a ceremonial marker on the old road to St-Denis.

The **pl. de la République** (M. République), at the meeting point of the 10th, the 3rd, and the 11th *arrondissements,* is a place to avoid at night, when prostitutes and swindlers are ubiquitous. In the center, a monument to the Republic of France celebrates the victories of the 23 years of republican rule between 1789 and its erection in 1880. A bit farther east lies the **Canal Saint-Martin,** 4.5km long and connecting the Canal de l'Ourcq to the Seine. The canal has several locks, which can be traveled by boat on one of the **Canauxrama** trips (see page 115).

ELEVENTH ARRONDISSEMENT

Near the dressed-down, plexiglass opera house at **pl. de la Bastille** (M. Bastille) disgruntled shopkeepers stormed the Bastille prison on July 14, 1789. Long since demolished, the prison was originally commissioned by Charles V to safeguard the eastern entrance to Paris. A treasury vault under Henri IV, the fortress became a state prison under his successor Louis XIII; internment there, generally reserved for religious heretics and political undesirables, followed specific orders from the king. In the last years of the Old Regime, however, the prison turned from draconian nightmare to deluxe hotel. Its titled inmates furnished their suites, brought their servants, and received guests. The Cardinal de Rohan held a dinner party for 20 in his cell. The prison itself provided fresh linen. Notable prisoners included Mirabeau, Voltaire, and the Marquis de Sade, one of the last seven prisoners to be held there. He left July 7, 1789, just a week before the prison's liberation.

When Revolutionary militants stormed the Bastille, they came for the prison's supply of gunpowder. After sacking the Invalides for weapons, they needed munitions. Surrounded by an armed rabble, too short on food to entertain a siege, and unsure of the loyalty of the Swiss mercenaries who defended the prison, the Bastille's governor surrendered. Demolition of the prison began the morrow of its capture and concluded in October 1792. Some of its stones were incorporated into the Pont de la Concorde, and a commemorative pile stands in square Henri Galli, a few blocks down bd. Henri IV from pl. de la Bastille. A certain Citizen Palloy, the main demolition contractor, used the stones to construct 83 models of the prison, which he sent to the provinces as reminders of "the horror of despotism." Original stones also outline the prison's original location.

The **Opéra Bastille,** a space-age conversation piece, is regularly the butt of jokes by passersby. Designed by Canadian architect Carlos Ott, the building is second only to Disneyland Paris in the minds of Parisians as an example of North American barbarism. It has further been described as a huge *toilette,* a version no doubt of the coin-operated facilities in the streets of Paris. Many complain that the acoustics of the hall leave much to be desired. Tours (50F, students 30F; 1-2 per day at 1 or 5pm) are the only way to see the interior unless you attend a performance. The schedule changes frequently. Call 01 40 01 19 70 for performance information; stop in the box office for a free brochure describing the season's events.

FOURTEENTH ARRONDISSEMENT: MONTPARNASSE

One of the most heterogeneous areas of Paris, the 14ème draws immigrants from elsewhere in France, Europe, the United States, and even just the other side of the Seine. In the early 20th century, floods of Bretons fleeing failed crops poured out of the Gare Montparnasse. Picasso, Gauguin, and others set up studios here, and an equally august set of writers—Hemingway, Sartre, de Beauvoir—found themselves stuck in the cafés of the bd. de Montparnasse. The 14ème remains a pastiche of different styles: business and tourism around Montparnasse, residential toward M. Denfert-Rochereau, and poor-student-dorm in the Cité Universitaire. **Bd. Montparnasse** remains devoted to people-watching as well as to crêpes, the renowned Breton invention. Around this chic thoroughfare, the intersection of the 6ème, 14ème, and 15ème *arrondissements* has become one of the capital's most modern business centers, though dominated by the architecturally tragic **Tour de Montparnasse.**

The **Cimitière Montparnasse,** 3, bd. Edgar Quinet (M. Edgar Quinet), is less than romantic. Shrouded by the black pall of the Tour Montparnasse, bisected by a street, too crowded by tombstones to have grass, piled with beer and mineral water bottles, the cemetery is better left to the dead. Armed with a free *Index des Celebrités* (the map available just left of the main entrance), determined sightseers thread their way through the unimportant to pay their respects to writers Baudelaire, de Maupassant, Beckett, Julio Cortázar (whose slab sports a sculpted smiley face), Sartre and de Beauvoir (who share a grave), car manufacturer André Citroën, composer Saint-Saëns, artist Man Ray, and non-traitor Alfred Dreyfus. (Open Mon.-Fri. 7:30am-6pm, Sat. 8:30am-6pm, Sun. 9am-6pm; Nov. 6-March 15 closes 5:30pm. Free.)

Along similarly morbid lines, **Les Catacombs,** 1, pl. Denfert-Rochereau (M. Denfert-Rochereau), crowd in five or six million lesser Parisians. The tunnels were originally excavated for stone, but by the 1770s much of the Left Bank was in danger of caving in. The city killed two birds with one stone, so to speak, by converting the quarry to a mass grave to relieve the stench emanating from cemeteries around Paris. Near the entrance reads the ominous caution, "Stop! Beyond Here Is the Empire of Death." During World War II, the Resistance set up headquarters among the old bones. Bring a sweater, a flashlight, and a friend for support. (Open Tues.-Fri. 2-4pm, Sat.-Sun. 9-11am and 2-4pm. Admission 27F, ages 7-25 19F, under 7 free.)

Parc Montsouris offers a sunny, sublime return to the land of the living. Doubling as an arboretum, the park offers sanctuary to hundreds of rare trees, all well labeled and cared for, along with an amazing variety of ducks and geese who splash contentedly in the artificial lake (whose designer killed himself after the water mysteriously drained at the park's opening ceremony). Across the bd. Jourdan, hundreds of thousands of students rage the night away in the **Cité Universitaire,** a 40-hectare rumpus park containing no fewer than 44 different dormitories.

FIFTEENTH ARRONDISSEMENT: TOUR MONTPARNASSE

The **Tour Montparnasse** (tel. 01 45 38 52 56; M. Montparnasse-Bienvenue) dominates the *quartier's* northeast corner. Standing 56 stories tall, this controversial building looks somewhat out of place amid the older architecture of Montparnasse. Some argue that the *tour,* completed in 1973, is a slice of Manhattan inserted awkwardly in the middle of Paris, but the French architects who designed the tower believed that it would revolutionize the Paris skyline. It has, but not without the disapproval of many Parisians. Shortly after it was completed, the city of Paris passed an ordinance forbidding any further such structures to be built within Paris proper.

L'Institut Pasteur, 25, rue Dr. Roux (M. Pasteur), founded by Louis Pasteur in 1887, is now a center for biochemical research. It was here that Pasteur developed his famous technique for purifying milk products. The institute gained fame in 1983 for the isolation of the AIDS virus, and some of the most cutting-edge research on HIV continues to be conducted here. The museum offers an exhaustive run-down of Pasteur's medical and artistic accomplishments, a tour of his laboratory equipment and living quarters, and a visit to the crypt currently housing the scientist's corpse. (Open Sept.-July Mon.-Fri. 2-5:30pm; admission 15F, students 8F.)

SIXTEENTH ARRONDISSEMENT

In 1860, the wealthy villages of Auteuil, Passy, and Chaillot banded together and joined Paris, forming the 16ème *arrondissement.* Over a century later, the area's original aristocratic families have stood their ground, making the 16ème a stronghold of culture, fashion, and conservative politics. In this sumptuous residential neighborhood, rows of elegant houses retire graciously from wide, quiet roads. Private homes share the *arrondissement* with 64 embassies. And if it's neither a home nor an embassy, then it's a museum—about half of Paris's are located here.

The Modernist **Palais de Chaillot** (M. Trocadéro) is a museum and entertainment complex that contains the **Musée du Cinéma Henri-Langlois,** the **Musée de l'Homme,** the **Musée de la Marine,** and the **Musée National des Monuments Français,** as well as the **Théâtre National de Chaillot** and the **Cinémathèque Française**. Built for the 1937 World Expo, Jacques Carlu's design features two curved wings built around a paved courtyard. Surveyed by the 7.5m-tall bronze Apollo, another Bouchard sculpture, the building's open-air centerpiece attracts tourists, vendors, roller-skating dancers, and political demonstrators. It also offers the best view in all Paris of the Eiffel Tower and Champ de Mars. The Palais Chaillot is actually the last of a series of buildings built on this site. Catherine de Médicis had a château here, later transformed into a convent by Henrietta of England. Napoleon razed the old château and planned to build a more lavish one on the same site for his son; construction came to a halt after the Battle of Waterloo. In the 1820s, the duc d'Angoulême built a fortress-like memorial to his victory at Trocadéro in Spain—hence the present name. That in turn was replaced in 1878 by a supposed exemplar of "Islamic" architecture built for the World Expo, also soon demolished.

Passy, the area immediately south and southwest of Trocadéro, was known historically for its restorative waters. The **Cimitière de Passy** runs along its northern walls. The tiny necropolis, shaded by a chestnut bower, contains the tombs of Debussy, Fauré, and Manet. Ask the concierge at the cemetery entrance for directions to these or other grave sites. The spirits of its famous residents linger on in the **Maison de Balzac** and the **Musée Clemenceau** (see page 138). Jean-Jacques Rousseau lived on rue Raynouard, and Benjamin Franklin, remembered by street and statue, built France's first lightning rod nearby. Northwest of the La Muette metro lies the former site of the Château de la Muette, where the first peopled balloon lifted off in 1783. Kids will love the old-style carousel (5F) at the **Jardin de Ranelagh.** On the other side of the park, the **Musée Marmottan** has an exquisite collection of Impressionist paintings and medieval illuminations (see page 136).

BOIS DE BOULOGNE

An 846-hectare green canopy at the western edge of Paris, the Bois de Boulogne (M. Porte Maillot, Sablons, Pont de Neuilly, Porte Dauphine, or Porte d'Auteuil) is a popular place for walks, jogs, and picnics. Formerly a royal hunting ground, the Bois was given to the city of Paris by Napoleon III in 1852. The emperor had become a dilettante landscape-architect during his exile in England and wanted Paris to have something comparable to Hyde Park. Acting on these instructions, Baron Haussmann filled in sand-pits, dug artificial lakes, and cut winding paths through thickly wooded areas. This attempt to copy nature broke with the tradition of French formal gardens—rectilinear hedges and flowerbeds—established by Le Nôtre.

The **Jardin d'Acclimatation** (tel. 01 40 67 90 82), at the north end of the Bois (M. Sablons), offers the thrill of a zoo, mini-golf, a carousel, and kiddie motorcycle racetrack. Except for the bumper cars, you must be child-size to use the rides. (Open daily 10am-6:30pm; ticket office closes 5:45pm. Admission 10F, under 3 free.)

Within the park, the **Musée en Herbe** (tel. 01 40 67 97 66) is a modern art museum designed for children. Previous shows have featured Chagall and Picasso. (Museum open Sun.-Fri. 10am-6pm, Sat 2-6pm; 16F. Studio sessions during school term Wed. and Sun., during holidays daily. Participation 35F, 45-60min.) Also in the garden is a participatory theater company for children (shows Oct.-July Wed. and Sat.-Sun.) and a puppet show (Wed., Sat.-Sun., and school holidays 3:15pm and 4:15pm; free). The **Pré Catelan** is a neatly manicured park supposedly named for a troubadour who died in these woods. Inside the Pré, the **Jardin de Shakespeare** (created 1952-53) features plants mentioned by the writer, grouped by play—there is a collection of Scottish highland vegetation in the *Macbeth* area, a Mediterranean section for *The Tempest,* and so on. In the center, an open-air theater, the **Théâtre de Verdure du Jardin Shakespeare,** gives performances of Shakespeare's plays (in French) in the summer (see page 143). Take the metro to Porte Maillot, then bus 244 to Bagatelle-Pré-Catelan. (Pré Catelan open 8:30am-7:30pm. Jardin de Shakespeare open daily 3-3:30pm and 4:30-5pm; admission 5F, students 3F, under 10 2F.) To get to the park from M. Porte Maillot, go to the big house marked l'Orée du Bois and follow the brown signs that point to the right of the building. Or you can go to the left of the building and take a little train. (Trains Wed., Sat.-Sun., and public holidays, daily during school vacations, every 10min., 1:30-6:30pm. 5F, under 3 free.)

The manicured islands of the **Lac Inférieur** (M. Porte Dauphine) can be reached by rented rowboat only. (Boathouses open late Feb.-early Nov. daily 10am-7pm. Boats 45F per hour, 400F deposit.) Rent **bicycles** across the street from the boathouse at the northern end of the Lac Inférieur and in front of the entrance to the Jardin d'Acclimatation. (Open daily April 16-Oct. 15 10am-7pm; Oct. 16-April 15 Wed., Sat., and Sun. 10am-7pm. 30F per hr., 80F per day, ID deposit.)

EIGHTEENTH ARRONDISSEMENT: MONTMARTRE AND THE SACRÉ-COEUR

Soaring above Haussmann's flattened city, the hill of Montmartre has a long and bloody history. The Romans decapitated St. Denis here in AD 272. Legend has it that he and two other martyred bishops picked up their heads and carried them to their final resting point, 7km away, where the Eglise St-Denis now stands—hence *Montmartre* (Hill of the Martyrs). Until the 19th century, it remained a farming area, covered with vineyards and wheat fields. The last of these vineyards is still operational.

The Paris Commune began here in the wee hours of March 18, 1871, on the heels of a conflict between the French army and the Parisian National Guard. After the Commune, the narrow streets and sharp corners of Montmartre attracted notable bohemians such as Charpentier, Toulouse-Lautrec, and Satie and performers such as "La Goulue" and Aristide Bruant. A generation later, Montmartre welcomed Picasso, Modigliani, Utrillo, and Apollinaire into its artistic circle. Montmartre's heyday has since passed. Most of the places which were once so alive with art and conversation are merely tourist traps, but it's still worthwhile to come at dusk to watch the lights of Paris turn on below and the famous gas lamps trace the steps up the hillside.

For the classic approach to the Sacré-Coeur, climb the switchbacked stairs leading up from **sq. Willette.** At night, crowds of students and tourists mingle in the square to enjoy guitar music, sing, smoke, and drink wine. (If you do come at night, use M. Abbesses.) The climb is steep but not particularly taxing and offers a splendid view of the receding metropolis below. A funicular ride up costs one metro ticket (6F), but it may not be worth the wait or the price unless you're truly exhausted. The famous narrow cobblestone stairs of the rue Foyatier, just to the west (to your left as you look uphill), offer a more romantic climb, as well as an escape from the crowds and street peddlers on the white marble steps of the park.

The **Basilique du Sacré-Coeur (Basilica of the Sacred Heart),** 35, rue du Cheval de la Barre (tel. 01 42 51 17 02; M. Anvers, Abbesses, Château-Rouge), crowns the very top of the *butte* Montmartre like an enormous meringue. The style of the onion domes and arches is pseudo-Romanesque-Byzantine. Climb the 112m bell tower to the highest point in Paris (yes, you *can* go higher than the Eiffel Tower) and a view that stretches as far as 50km on clear days. (Basilica open daily 7am-11pm; free. Dome and crypt open daily 9am-7pm in summer; in winter 9am-6pm. Admission to dome 15F, reduced tariff 8F; to crypt 15F, reduced 8F.)

Behind the basilica is the **pl. du Tertre,** the central square of the hillock. Crowded with overpriced restaurants and souvenir shops, this area caters to the unwieldy masses of tourists that congregate here. Portrait and landscape painters offer generally tacky souvenir sketches. At 21, pl. du Tertre, the **tourist office** (tel. 01 42 62 21 21) gives annotated maps (5F) and info about the area (open daily May-Sept. 10am-10pm; Oct.-April 10am-7pm). Around the corner, the **Musée Salvador Dalí** has a wonderful collection of the mustachioed artist's work (see page 138).

EASTERN PARIS: TWENTIETH ARRONDISSEMENT

The **Cimetière Père-Lachaise,** on bd. de Ménilmontant (tel. 01 43 70 70 33; M. Père-Lachaise), holds the remains of Balzac, Colette, Corot, Danton, David, Delacroix, La Fontaine, Haussmann, Molière, and Proust within its winding paths and elaborate sarcophagi. Foreigners buried here include Chopin, Jim Morrison, Sarah Bernhardt, Gertrude Stein, and Oscar Wilde. Napoleon created the cemetery in 1803, but Parisians were reluctant to bury their dead in a site which, at the time, was far from the city. To increase the cemetery's popularity, Napoleon ordered that the remains of a few famous figures be dug up and reburied in Père-Lachaise. The most adored grave has to be that of **Jim Morrison.** Within a radius of at least 100m of the Lizard King, graffiti on all the tombs points in his direction. French Leftists pay homage to the **Mur des Fédérés** (Wall of the Federals), where 147 *communards* were executed and buried after the suppression of the Commune. (Open March 16-Oct. Mon.-Fri. 8am-

6pm, Sat. 8:30am-6pm, Sun. and holidays 9am-6pm; Nov.-March 15 Mon.-Fri. 8am-5:30pm, Sat., Sun., and holidays 9am-5:30pm.)

BOIS DE VINCENNES

The **Bois de Vincennes** has never been quite so fashionable or formal as its sister, the Bois de Boulogne, but it is commensurately more peaceful. The **Parc Zoologique de Paris,** 53, av. de Saint-Maurice (tel. 01 44 75 20 10; M. Porte Dorée), is considered the best zoo in France. The zoo was something of a novelty when it opened in 1934 because it was designed to give the animals space to roam outside. (Open in summer Mon.-Sat. 9am-6pm, Sun. 9am-6:30pm; in winter Mon.-Sat. 9am-5pm, Sun. 9am-5:30pm. Ticket office closes 30min. before zoo. 40F; ages 4-16, students 16-25, and over 60 20F; under 4 and disabled free. Wheelchair accessible.) The **Château de Vincennes** was home away from Louvre for every French monarch from Charles V to Henri IV. The 52m **donjon** grew up from 1360 to 1370. The **Ste-Chapelle** was founded as a church in 1379. (Open daily May-Sept. 10am-6pm; Oct.-April 10am-5pm. Tours of the Ste-Chapelle and *donjon* daily at 10:15, 11, and 11:45am, and 1:15, 2, 2:45, 3:30, 4:15, and 5:15pm are the only way inside, but the monuments may be more impressive from outside. Tours are in French, but English translations are available. 32F; students, under 26, and seniors 14F.)

LA DÉFENSE

Located just outside the city limits, La Défense is a techno theme park that exposes all that is ridiculous about the French yen for modernity. The area boasts the sleeker-than-thou headquarters of 14 of France's top 20 corporations. Clustered around the Grande Arche (a 35-story office block in the shape of a hollowed cube), shops, galleries, trees, and a sprinkling of sculptures make the pedestrian esplanade a nice stroll, but no great shakes. The artwork found here—by such notables as Miró, Calder, and César—consists for the most part of open-air sculptures. The whole visit probably won't take longer than a few hours, including lunch.

The proliferation of office towers in the area began in 1956 as part of a scheme to provide office space for Paris without altering the city center. Originally the planners intended to limit buildings to certain heights and styles to create a unified complex, but by the late 60s and early 70s companies were building distinctive *gratte-ciels* (skyscrapers) "Manhattan-style." This disorder rapidly threatened the grandeur of the *axe historique,* the line that stretches from the Louvre down the Champs-Elysées to the Arc de Triomphe, and so in 1969 I. M. Pei suggested the first plan for a monument to anchor the end of the axis. (Ultimately, Pei's plan was not used for this side of the *voie triomphale;* instead, he was asked to redesign the eastern terminus—the courtyard of the Louvre.) French Presidents Pompidou, Giscard d'Estaing, and Mitterrand all sponsored contests for such a monument, but only Mitterrand acted on the results. Of 424 projects entered, four were presented anonymously to the president, who chose the plan of previously unknown Dane Otto von Spreckelsen for its "purity and strength." Spreckelsen backed out of the project before its completion, disheartened by red tape and his own design, which he deemed a "monument without a soul." Others celebrated the arch as a "window to the world" whose slight asymmetry gives the empty cube a dash of humanity. Spreckelsen, who died of cancer in 1987, never saw the completion of his work.

The **Grande Arche de la Défense,** inaugurated on the French Republic's bicentennial, July 14, 1989, now towers over the metro/RER stop bearing its name. The building's roof covers 2.5 acres—Notre-Dame cathedral could fit in its hollow core. Its walls are covered with white marble that shines blindingly in sunlight. Most of all, its modern design blends into the centuries-old architectural context of the *axe historique;* unlike the smaller arches, this one is aligned six degrees off the axis. A great view waits at the top. Tickets for the roof are sold near the elevator. (Ticket office open daily 9am-6pm; roof closes 1hr. after ticket office; 40F, under 18 30F.)

Near to and left of the Grande Arche as you face Paris, the funny-looking building that looks as if it's had a piece cut out of it is the **Bull Tower.** Also on the left is the **CNIT building.** At 37 years old, it's the oldest building in the complex and a center for congresses, exhibitions, and conferences (open daily 7am-11pm). To the right sits the **Musée de l'Automobile,** where 110 vintage *voitures* idle (open Mon., Wed., and Fri. noon-7pm, Tues., Thurs., and Sun. noon-8pm, Sat. noon-10pm; admission 30F, students, seniors, and under 16 20F). By 1997, construction should have started on the **Eglise Nôtre Dame de la Pentecôte,** a church planned for a site on the Paris side of CNIT. However, the slump of recent years has caused several other much-touted additions to La Défense to be abandoned, including the *Tour sans fin* (endless tower), which was to have been the tallest building in Europe.

The brightly colored sculpture at pl. de la Défense that looks remarkably like one of **Joan Miró's** anthropomorphic paintings come to life is, in fact, just that. Across the *place,* **Alexander Calder's** spidery red steel sculpture is a fitting counterpart. Just past the lawn is the white tube of the **Info Défense** booth (tel. 01 47 74 84 24), which fittingly provides info about La Défense (open Mon.-Fri. 9am-6pm, Sat.-Sun. 10am-6pm). For French tours of La Défense, call Défense-venement at 01 46 92 17 50 (admission 35F, students 25F). To the right of the booth, on a pedestal, is the bronze after which La Défense was named. Louis-Ernest Barrias' statue beat 100 other proposals, including one by Rodin, in an 1871 contest to commemorate the defense of Paris against the Prussians. A tree-lined path, flanked on both sides by apartments, takes you the rest of the way to the Esplanade de la Défense metro.

If you want to eat or shop in La Défense, the best place to go is the huge **4 Temps shopping center.** Enter from the Grande Arche metro stop, from doors behind the Miró sculpture, or from next to the Musée de l'Automobile. The multilingual information desk, on the first floor near the escalator to the metro, has maps of the complex. (Shops open Mon.-Sat. 10am-8pm. Supermarkets open Mon.-Sat. 9am-10pm.)

To get to La Défense from Paris, take the metro or RER. Older maps might not show the Grande Arche de la Défense metro stop at the end of line 1. The RER is faster, but the metro is cheaper; La Défense is zone 2 for the metro but zone 3 for the RER. If you take the RER, buy the more expensive ticket before your trip. A normal ticket may get you into the RER in Paris but won't get you out at La Défense.

Museums

Paris's national museums are multi-purpose, user-friendly machines shaped by public interest and state funds. Serving as forums for lectures, art films, concerts, and the occasional play, the museums here—especially the Louvre, Orsay, and Pompidou—broadcast Paris, past and present. For listings of temporary exhibits, consult the bimonthly *Le Bulletin des Musées et Monuments Historiques,* available at the tourist office. *Paris Museums and Monuments,* also at the tourist office, provides all the info you need on the museums (including wheelchair accessibility). *Pariscope* and *L'Officiel des spectacles* list museum hours and temporary exhibits.

Students, children, teachers, and senior citizens are eligible for reduced admissions at almost all of Paris's museums. Frequent museum-goers ineligible for these discounts may want to invest in a **Carte Musée,** which grants entry *without waiting in line* to 65 museums in Paris, as well as others in the suburbs. The card is available at all major museums and metro stops (1 day 70F, 3 days 140F, 5 days 200F).

MUSÉE DU LOUVRE

The Building

Construction of the Louvre, 1er (tel. 01 40 20 51 51; M. Palais-Royal/Musée du Louvre), began in 1200, and still isn't finished. The original Louvre was a fortress built by King Philippe-Auguste. When Charles V extended the city walls, the fortress sat useless in the middle of the city, so Charles converted the austere structure into a residence. In 1725, the Academy of Painting inaugurated annual *Salons* in the halls to show its members' paintings. In 1793, the Revolution made the exhibit permanent, creating the first Louvre Museum. Napoleon, who vastly increased the museum's collection with art plundered from the nations he vanquished, added the **Arc de Triomphe du Carroussel** to commemorate his victories of 1805. As for the glass **pyramid** in the middle of the courtyard, it made its dazzling appearance in 1989. Previous entrances, ill equipped for handling large crowds, were further hobbled by an inefficient welcoming service. Architect I. M. Pei's remarkable proposal, which was at first met with intense disapproval, is now acknowledged to be a stroke of genius. He moved the main entrance to the central Cour Napoléon but left the great space unspoiled by putting most of the entrance underground. This **Hall Napoléon** is illuminated by sunlight streaming through the pyramid overhead. The Grand Louvre project is further renovating the Richelieu wing to increase the museum's exhibition space. The Louvre is the largest museum in the world.

The Museum

The Musée du Louvre is enormous; don't try to do it all in a day. If you can, take in a few galleries over the course of several days. The extra admission fees are a small price to pay for the satisfaction of being able to remember what you saw. If you come on a Monday or Wednesday evening, there will be more paintings than people. Be aware, however, that curators plan to rearrange 80% of the museum's art over the next four years, meaning that at any given time a few rooms will be closed.

Best known for its European paintings, the Louvre displays some 400,000 works, divided into seven categories: Oriental antiquities, Greek and Roman antiquities, Egyptian antiquities, objets d'art, painting, drawing, and sculpture. (East Asian works are in the Guimet, and works after the mid-19th century in the Orsay or Pompidou.) The Greco-Roman works include such treasures as the *Venus de Milo* and the *Winged Victory of Samothrace.* Michelangelo's anguished *Slaves* writhe in the sculpture section. But paintings are the real stars. Early Renaissance masterpieces like Mantegna's sharply classical *Crucifixion* contrast with da Vinci's atmospheric *Virgin of the Rocks.* Of course, the celebrity among the Italian works is *La Joconde* (the *Mona Lisa*), bought by François I to hang over his tub in Fontainebleau. The mysterious lady is lucky to be here at all; she was stolen in 1911 by a former Louvre employee (although at first police thought Picasso committed the dirty deed).

Among the French works, the huge canvases of Neoclassicist Jacques-Louis David steal the show. The Revolution's chief painter, David, did *The Oath of the Horatii* to inspire his peers to virtuous deeds like those of Horatius' sons, who vowed to die for their country. *Brutus* shows an anguished father who has ordered his own son's execution for treason. Also unmissable are Ingres' sensual *Odalisque,* Géricault's gruesome *Raft of the Medusa,* and Delacroix's patriotic *Liberty Leading the People.*

English-language **tours** leave Monday and Wednesday through Saturday at 10 and 11:30am, and 2 and 3:30pm (33F, ages 13-18 22F, under 13 free with museum ticket). Call 01 40 20 52 09 for more information. (Museum open Mon. and Wed. 9am-9:45pm, Thurs.-Sun. 9am-6pm. Last entry 45min. before closing. The Hall Napoléon is open 10am-10pm Wed.-Sun.; additional admission 30F.)

MUSÉE D'ORSAY

The **Musée d'Orsay,** 1, rue de Bellechasse, 7ème (tel. 01 40 49 48 14; recorded info 01 45 49 11 11; M. Solférino; RER Musée d'Orsay), showcases the works of modernism's most popular artists, the avant-garde iconoclasts of 19th-century France. The museum is more than a temple to Impressionism—chronological exhibits highlight the development of an array of artistic styles in painting, sculpture, and decorative arts from 1848 to 1914. Sheltered within the renovated Gare d'Orsay, once the train station serving southwestern France, the museum is an architectural wonder.

To the left of the central courtyard, Edouard Manet's *Olympia* (1863), arguably the first "modern" painting, caused a scandal when exhibited at the 1865 Salon. Manet had borrowed from Titian's *Venus of Urbino* (1538), *the* standard for female nudes in Western art, but twisted the passive image to fit his modern vision. This was pornography, cried the critics, not art. Moreover, they hated the painting for being ugly: Olympia's hands and feet were too big, and she was too thin and muscular. While you're on the ground floor, check out the rooms of Realism, especially Natural-Realist Courbet's monumental *Burial at Ornans* (1850).

Upstairs, on the top floor, the Impressionist celebration begins. The glass-topped arcade of the station provides the perfect setting for viewing the works; soft light, filtered through heavy metal grillwork, highlights the interplay of colors on paintings such as Monet's *Gare St-Lazare* (1877). Filled with train stations, cabarets, crowded boulevards, and whirling balls, the paintings convey the new rhythm of bourgeois life in Haussmann's Paris. Manet's *Déjeuner sur l'Herbe* also caused a brouhaha when it was exhibited in 1863. Based on Titian's *Fête Champêtre,* the painting possesses Manet's characteristic twist: two respectable bourgeois gentlemen happily picnic in the woods—with a completely nude woman at their side. The work of Edgar Degas is shocking in a more subtle way. Paintings like *l'Absinthe* and *The Ironers* highlight the loneliness and isolation of Paris's working class.

Pushing on through the museum and art history, you'll arrive at the "Post-Impressionists," a blanket title for a diverse group of artists who anticipated abstract art in their experiments with light, color, and geometric form. Join the crowd around Vincent Van Gogh's *Portrait of the Artist* (1889). Paul Cézanne's still-lifes and landscapes experiment with shaded planes to redefine the painting surface. Be sure to check out the wooden doors and statuettes that Paul Gauguin made in Tahiti.

PARIS

Tours leave regularly from the group reception. (English tours Tues., Wed., Fri.-Sun. 11am, Thurs. 11am and 7pm, 90min.; 35F.) The booklet *Nouvelles du Musée d'Orsay,* free at the desk, gives details about current tours, conferences, concerts, and exhibits. You can also call 01 40 49 49 66 for concert information. (Museum open June 20-Sept. 20 Tues.-Wed. and Fri.-Sun. 9am-6pm, Thurs. 9am-9:45pm; Sept. 21-June 19 museum opens at 10am. Last ticket sales at 9:15pm Thurs., 5:15pm other days. Admission 36F; ages 18-25, over 60, and everyone on Sun. 24F; under 18 free.)

CENTRE POMPIDOU

Often referred to as the Beaubourg, the Centre National d'Art et de Culture Georges-Pompidou, 4ème (tel. 01 44 78 14 63 for recorded info in French; M. Rambuteau), has generated architectural controversy since its inauguration in 1977. Chosen from 681 competing designs, Richard Rogers and Renzo Piano's shameless building-turned-inside-out bares its circulatory system to all passers-by. Piping and ventilation ducts in various colors run up, down, and sideways along the outside (blue for air, green for water, yellow for electricity, red for heating). Framing the structure like a cage are huge steel bars that carry the building's weight, allowing great flexibility in the design of the unencumbered interior. The views from the escalator (which is bolted to the building's façade) and from the fifth-floor terrace are as dizzying as those from the Arche de la Défense—but they're free.

The **Musée National d'Art Moderne,** the center's main attraction, houses a rich selection of 20th-century art, from Fauves and Cubists to Pop and conceptual art. The entrance to the museum is on the fourth floor, which is particularly strong on modernism: Matisse, Derain, Picasso, Magritte, Braque, Kandinsky, and Yves Klein. Three terraces display sculptures by Miró, Tinguely, Ernst, and Calder. The lower level of the museum (reachable by a small escalator from the floor above) houses work from the 1960s to the present. (Museum open Mon. and Wed.-Fri. noon-10pm; Sat.-Sun. 10am-10pm. Ticket office shuts 1hr. before closing time. Admission 35F, under 25 and Sun. 24F, under 16 free. Temporary exhibits cost extra. One-day pass gives access to all exhibitions and the museum: 70F, under 25 45F, under 16 free. Buy your tickets on the main floor, since they are not available at the museum entrance; tickets do not permit reentry. Wheelchair accessible.)

THE INVALIDES MUSEUMS

The Invalides complex (7ème; M. Invalides, Latour-Maubourg, Varennes) guards a series of museums that revolve around French history and France's martial glory. Pacifists beware: the **Musée de l'Armée** (tel. 01 44 42 37 72 or 01 44 42 37 64) celebrates centuries of French military history, examining heroes ranging from Napoleon to de Gaulle, with lesser generals sandwiched in between. (Open daily April-Sept. 10am-6pm; Oct.-March 10am-5pm.) Upstairs, the **Musée des Plans-Reliefs** gathers a collection of 100 models of fortified cities, some of them enormous. (Open daily April-Sept. 10am-noon and 1:30-6pm; Oct.-March 10am-noon and 1:30-5pm.) In the same building, **Napoleon's Tomb** is lovingly placed under Jules Hardouin-Mansart's royal dome. Finished in 1861, the tomb itself is actually six concentric coffins, made of materials ranging from mahogany to lead. This riot of bombast delighted Adolph Hitler on his visit to Paris in 1940. (Open daily June-Aug. 10am-7pm; Oct.-March 10am-5pm; April-May and Sept. 10am-6pm.) One of the least celebrated but most worthwhile parts of the Invalides is the **Musée de l'Ordre de la Libération,** 51bis, bd. de Latour-Maubourg (tel. 01 47 05 04 10). Charles de Gaulle founded the order on November 16, 1940, to recognize individuals, organizations, and cities that distinguished themselves in the liberation of France. (Same hours as Musée de l'Armée. Admission to museums 35F; students, seniors, and under 18 25F; under 7 free. Ticket valid for 2 consecutive days. 30F rents an audioguide in English, at the info desk in the west wing.)

MUSÉE RODIN

Occupying both the mansion and the grounds of the Hôtel Biron, the Musée Rodin, 77, rue de Varenne, 7ème (tel. 01 44 18 61 10; M. Varenne), ranks among the top attractions in Paris. During his lifetime (1840-1917), Auguste Rodin was among the country's most controversial artists, often thought of as a sculpting Impressionist.

If you're short on time or money, consider paying the admission fee for the grounds only. You won't miss the stars of the collection: just inside the gates sits Rodin's most famous sculpture, *Le Penseur (The Thinker,* 1880-1904). On the other side of the garden, *Les Bourgeois de Calais (Burghers of Calais),* captures a near-tragic moment in the Hundred Years' War (see page 674). As with *Le Penseur,* Rodin sculpts for peak tension, grossly exaggerating the size and contortions of the hands and feet for dramatic effect. Beyond the Burghers stands Rodin's largest and most intricate work, *La Porte d'Enfer (The Gates of Hell),* whose tormented souls are drawn directly from the pages of Dante's *Divine Comedy.*

Rodin's smaller pieces are displayed inside the *hôtel,* where the sculptor lived and worked. Notice the versions of *Balzac,* commissioned as a tribute to the famous author. Rodin had a terrible time finishing the sculpture; he finally captured Balzac's greatness by wrapping the hulking figure in a large cloak. Conceived as a model of Dante's Paolo and Francesca, *Le Baiser (The Kiss)* freezes two intertwined lovers in white marble. In this and in *La Main de Dieu (The Hand of God),* Rodin experiments with the contrast between rough and smooth sculpture. Only a heart of stone could resist feeling the somber elegance of suffering portrayed in *La Douleur (Suffering), Le Cri (The Shriek), La Pleureuse (The Weeper),* and *Le Désespoir (Despair).* Also included are several beautiful works by Camille Claudel, Rodin's muse, student, and lover. (Museum open April-Sept. Tues.-Sun. 9:30am-5:45pm; Oct.-March 9:30am-4:45pm. Last admission 30min. before closing. Admission 28F; students, seniors, and under 18 18F; admission to park alone 5F.)

MUSÉE DE CLUNY

The **Musée de Cluny,** 6, pl. Paul-Painlevé, 5ème (tel. 01 43 25 62 00; M. Cluny-Sorbonne), not only houses one of the world's finest collections of medieval art, jewelry, and tapestries, but is itself a perfectly preserved medieval manor, built on top of Roman ruins. One of the three Roman baths in the Paris area, the *thermae* and their surroundings were purchased by the Abbot of Cluny, who then built his own residence upon them. Excavations begun after World War II unearthed what remains of the baths, since reincorporated into the layout of the building. The masterpiece of the collection, a series of six panels entitled **La Dame et la Licorne** (The Lady and the Unicorn), is considered the best surviving medieval tapestry series in the world. The rich red base, intricate work, and symbolism are fascinating. Specialists agree that five of the tapestries represent the five senses but have long debated what the sixth *(A Mon Seul Désir),* in which the lady holds a necklace, means.

Also upstairs, you'll find an entire room (XVI) devoted to medieval royal jewelry and crowns. The gold rush continues down the corridor in Room XIX with the rare and valuable gold altarpiece, a finely worked ornament from Basel, Switzerland. Downstairs, the *Galerie des Rois,* Room VII, proudly displays 21 13th-century stone heads of Judean and Israelite kings. These heads (attached to statues) sat atop Notre-Dame's portals until the Revolutionaries of 1793 separated them from their bodies, mistaking them for statues of French kings. (Open Wed.-Mon. 9:15am-5:45pm. Admission 28F; students, under 25, over 60, and Sun. 18F; under 18 free.) The museum also sponsors concerts of Renaissance and Baroque instruments. (Concerts Fri. at 12:30pm and Sat. at 5pm—call to confirm times. 52F; students and seniors 33F, under 18 15F with admission to the museum.) There are sometimes evening concerts as well; call 01 53 73 78 00 or stop by the museum for a schedule.

LA VILLETTE

The **Parc de la Villette** (M. Porte de la Villette) is a highly successful urban renewal project in the northeastern corner of the 19ème *arrondissement,* 150 acres large and growing. Former president Mitterrand inaugurated the project in 1985; the principal architect is Philippe Starck, and among his collaborators is the avant-garde American architect Peter Eisenmann. Perched on La Villette's northern end, the **Cité des Sciences et de l'Industrie** (tel. 08 36 68 29 30) is the largest science museum in France, dedicated to bringing science to the little people. A series of interactive displays make learning unavoidable. While there, sit under the stars at the complex's **planetarium.** If you're traveling with children, inquire about the special programs and demonstrations for the younger set. **La Géode** (tel. 01 40 05 12 12), the enormous mirrored sphere mounted on a water basin in front of the Cité, shows Omnimax movies on a 1000-square-meter hemispheric screen inside. Consult *Pariscope* to learn what's playing. (Showings Tues.-Sun. hourly 10am-9pm. Also Mon. 10am-6pm during school holidays. Tickets can sell out as much as 2 months ahead of time, so reserve early. Buy tickets at the Géode entrance: 57F, reduced 44F. No reduced rates weekends or holidays 1-6pm.)

A one-day "Cité-Pass" gives entrance to all exhibits of the museum, including the planetarium (45F, reduced 35F, after 4pm 25F, under 7 free). Combined tickets for Géode and Cité go for 92F, with reductions 79F. Reduced tickets for seniors, teachers, and under 25. (Museum open Tues.-Sat. 10am-6pm, Sun. 10am-7pm. *Médiathèque* open Tues.-Sun. noon-8pm; free.)

TRY TO SEE

Musée Marmottan, 2, rue Louis-Boilly, 16ème (tel. 01 42 24 07 02; M. La Muette). Follow Chausée de la Muette, which becomes av. Ranelagh, through the Jardin du Ranelagh park. Having inherited from his father both a hunting lodge near the Bois de Boulogne and a love of art, Paul Marmottan indulged his passion for the Napoleonic era by transforming the lodge into a mansion and furnishing it with Empire furniture and art. At his death in 1932, he bequeathed the building, his own collection, and his father's group of primitive German, Flemish, and Italian paintings to the Académie des Beaux-Arts. Later, Michel Monet added 80 of *his* father's paintings, many from the later years at Giverny, to the museum's existing collection. The numerous Impressionist canvases by Monet, Renoir, and others are stunning, and the apotheosis is Monet's *Impression: soleil levant (Impression: Sunrise).* Displayed in 1874 with 8 other paintings, it led one critic to refer derisively to "those *impressionistes,"* an epithet Monet and his colleagues embraced. The painting was recently recovered in Corsica after being stolen in 1985. The Wildenstein room contains 228 marvelous medieval illuminations. Open Tues.-Sun. 10am-5:30pm. 35F, students and seniors 15F, under 8 free.

Musée National des Arts Asiatiques (Musée Guimet), 6, pl. d'Iéna, 16ème (tel. 01 47 23 61 65; M. Iéna). Closed until 1999 for renovations, this large collection of Asian art represents 17 different countries and in the past has been one of the best organized and most peaceful museums in the 16ème. Although much of the collection is in storage, some pieces have been moved to an annex, the **Musée du Panthéon Bouddhique,** 19, av. d'Iéna (tel. 01 47 23 61 65), just a few steps away in the Hôtel Heidelbach. Housed in a turn-of-the-century Neo-Baroque *hôtel,* the Panthéon traces the religious history of Japan and China through a collection of statues, paintings, and sacred figures dating from the 4th through the 19th centuries. The Japanese garden behind the *hôtel,* while not entirely authentic, is entirely restful and refreshing. Open Wed.-Mon. 9:45am-6pm. 15F, under 18 free.

Musée d'Art Moderne de la Ville de Paris, 11, av. du Président Wilson, 16ème (tel. 01 53 67 40 80; M. Iéna). Often overshadowed by its more publicized peer, the Centre Pompidou, this museum contains one of the world's foremost collections of 20th-century art. Important works by Matisse *(The Dance)* and Picasso *(The Jester)* are on permanent display while temporary exhibits vary dramatically in topic and scope. The museum offers little more than a brief map and a list of artists to guide you through the labyrinth-like exhibition space. What the collection lacks in coherence it makes up for in size. A visit will undoubtedly lead to rewarding discoveries, whether your tastes run to Modigliani or life-size sculptures of horses made from plastic toys. Open Wed.-Mon. 10am-5:30pm. Admission to permanent collection 27F, students and seniors 15F; to collection and temporary exhibits 40F, students and seniors 30F.

Musée de l'Orangerie, 1er (tel. 01 42 97 48 16; M. Concorde). A small collection of Impressionist paintings nestled in the southwest corner of the Tuileries. Smaller and less of a knockout than Orsay, this museum is also less crowded, so you can admire the Cézannes, Renoirs, Matisses, Picassos, and others in comfort. Claude Monet's *Les Nymphéas (Water Lilies)* occupy 2 rooms of the underground level, each of which is paneled with 4 curved murals that were created for these chambers. On the day of the Armistice, in lieu of a bouquet of flowers, Monet decided to give France these paintings of the lilies in his garden at Giverny. He spent the rest of his life working on them, finishing just before his death in 1926. Open Wed.-Mon. 9:45am-5:15pm. 28F; ages 18-25, over 60, and Sun. 18F.

IF YOU HAVE TIME

Musée des Arts Africains et Océaniens, 293, av. Daumesnil, 12ème (tel. 01 43 46 51 61; M. Porte Dorée), on the western edge of the Bois de Vincennes. A stunning collection of several millennia of African and Pacific art. Highlights include the immense, breathtaking display of African statues and masks, and jewelry and wedding dresses from the Maghreb (Morocco, Tunisia, and Algeria). Built for the 1931 Colonial Exposition, the museum building still contains its original Eurocentric murals and friezes. Open Mon. and Wed.-Fri. 10am-noon and 1:30-5:20pm, Sat.-Sun. 12:30-5:50pm. Last entry 30min. before closing. Admission to aquarium, permanent collection, and exhibits 27F, students and seniors 18F, under 18 free.

Musée d'Art Juif, 42, rue des Saules, 18ème (tel. 01 42 57 84 15; M. Lamarck-Caulaincourt). Housed on the 3rd floor of the Jewish Center, the museum celebrates Judaism through exhibits on Jewish rituals, pictures, and models of synagogues, as well as an enormous model of Jerusalem at the time of King Solomon. The library displays beautifully illustrated texts and works by popular artists from North Africa and Eastern Europe, including several Chagalls. Scholars can call to inquire about access to documents in the library. Closed on Jewish holidays. 30F, students and groups 20F, children 10F. Open Sept.-July Sun.-Thurs. 3-6pm.

Cristalleries Baccarat, 30-32, rue de Paradis, 10ème (tel. 01 47 70 64 30; M. Gare de l'Est). Walk against traffic on bd. Strasbourg and turn right on rue de la Fidelité, which becomes rue de Paradis. The impressive building, built under the Directory between 1798 and 1799, houses both the Baccarat crystal company headquarters and the Baccarat museum. Since its founding in 1764, Baccarat has become one of the most prestigious and expensive of crystal makers, patronized by kings, czars, and shahs. The museum houses an array of every imaginable crystal object, including a life-sized chandelier-woman at the entrance. Open Mon.-Fri. 9am-6:30pm, Sat. 10am-6pm. Museum admission 15F.

Musée Carnavalet, 23, rue de Sévigné, 3ème (tel. 01 42 72 21 13; M. Chemin-Vert). Housed in a 16th-century *hôtel,* this museum traces Paris's history from its origins to the present. There are rooms that reconstitute Parisian homes from the 16th to the 19th centuries, Gallo-Roman and medieval archaeological collections, paintings, and all kinds of objects from the Revolutionary period. The reconstructed Bijouterie Fouquet may be the star of the show for art nouveau junkies. Call ahead for partial wheelchair access. Open Tues.-Sun. 10am-5:40pm. 27F, students 15F, seniors and under 18 free. French guided tour 25F (Tues. and Sat. at 2:30pm).

Musée Clemenceau, 8, rue Benjamin Franklin, 16ème (tel. 01 45 20 53 41; M. Passy), through a small courtyard. Journalist and statesman Georges Clemenceau (1841-1929) has been both revered and vilified for nearly a century. The museum documents his life as a journalist, when he published Emile Zola's article *"J'accuse,"* thus pronouncing his anti-governmental stance during the Dreyfus Affair; as mayor of Montmartre; as prime minister of France; as Président du Conseil; as minister of war; and as the negotiator of the Versailles Treaty. On the ground floor, Clemenceau's apartment has been left as it was when he died. Open Tues., Thurs., Sat.-Sun., and holidays 2-5pm. 20F, students and seniors 15F.

Fondation Le Corbusier, 10, sq. du Docteur-Blanche, 16ème (tel. 01 42 88 41 53; M. Jasmin). Walk up rue de l'Yvette, take a left on rue du Docteur-Blanche and another left at no. 55 into sq. du Docteur-Blanche. The foundation is located in the Villas La Roche and Jeanneret, designed by Le Corbusier. The Villa La Roche, commissioned by the young banker La Roche to house his collection of Cubist art, contains the museum, or rather, is the museum. It offers an exceptional glimpse of some of Le Corbusier's architectural trademarks—his use of light, his attempt to harmonize with the natural world, and his preference for curved forms. Open Sept.-July Mon.-Thurs. 10am-12:30pm and 1:30-6pm, Fri. 10am-12:30pm and 1:30-5pm. Admission 15F, students 10F.

Musée Salvador Dalí (Espace Montmartre), 11, rue Poulbot, 18ème (tel. 01 42 64 40 10; M. Anvers or Abbesses). From pl. du Tertre follow rue du Calvaire toward the view, then turn right onto rue Poulbot. This museum dedicated to the "Phantasmic World of Salvador Dalí" is full of lithographs and sculptures by the Spanish Surrealist, with scads of incarnations of his famous droopy clocks. The museum is laid out in "Surrealist surroundings," which amount to wonderful spacing, interesting lighting, and slightly ridiculous space-music in the background. Open daily 10am-6pm; last ticket at 5:30pm. 35F, students 25F.

Musée des Egouts de Paris (Museum of the Sewers of Paris), actually inside the sewers, at the corner of the quai d'Orsay and pl. de la Résistance, 7ème (tel. 01 47 05 10 29; M. Pont de l'Alma). Enjoy a tour of the history of this city beneath the city, held whenever enough people are present. The smell can be overwhelming; hold your nose as you near the 2 sewage basins that are part of the tour. Open May-Sept. Sat.-Wed. 11am-6pm; Oct.-Dec. and Feb.-April Sat.-Wed. 11am-5pm. Last ticket sold 1hr. before closing. 25F, students and under 10 20F, under 5 free.

Musée Grévin, 10, bd. Montmartre, 9ème (tel. 01 42 46 13 26; M. Rue Montmartre). The halls of this wax museum are filled with illustrious personages, present and past. Open daily 1-7pm (during school holidays 10am-7pm), last entry 6pm. 50F, ages 6-14 35F. The smaller branch at level "-1" of the **Forum des Halles,** near the Porte Berger, 1er (tel. 01 40 26 28 50; M. Châtelet-Les Halles), presents a fascinating spectacle of Paris during the "Belle Epoque" (1885-1900). A terrific *son et lumière,* in French, recreates the turn of the century. The show can be put on in English; ask at the door and wait for more English-speaking tourists. Open Mon.-Sat. 10:30am-7pm, Sun. and holidays 1-7:15pm. Ticket office closes 45min. before museum. Admission 42F, ages 6-14 32F, under 6 free.

Musée d'Histoire Naturelle, in the Jardin des Plantes, 5ème (tel. 01 40 79 39 39; M. Gare d'Austerlitz). A 3-building museum that covers 3 fields within the natural sciences. The **Gallery of Comparative Anatomy and Paleontology** houses a dinosaur exhibit, whose triumph is the 7m skeleton of an iguanodon. In the Grande Galerie next door, the **Musée de Minéralogie,** surrounded by rose trellises, contains diamonds, rubies, and sapphires along with assorted *objets d'art* fashioned from them, including two marble Renaissance tables inlaid with lapis lazuli, amethyst, and other semi-precious stones. Downstairs, a collection of giant crystals gleams along with an exhibit addressing the practical uses of minerals. Both open Mon. and Tues.-Fri. 10am-5pm, Sat.-Sun. 10am-6pm. 30F, students 20F.

Musée de l'Homme (Museum of Man), pl. du Trocadéro, in the Palais de Chaillot, 16ème (tel. 01 44 05 72 00 or 01 44 05 72 72; M. Trocadéro). A painted cart from Sicily, a Turkish shop, and a 10m British Columbian totem pole are all elements of the museum's presentations, covering civilizations and cultures worldwide from prehistory to today. Perpetual renovations don't spoil the show. Labels in French accompany self-explanatory displays. Open Wed.-Mon. 9:45am-5:15pm. 30F, under 27 and seniors 20F, children under 4 and disabled persons free. Films Wed. and Sat. at 3 and 4pm; call 01 44 05 72 59 for info.

Galerie Nationale de Jeu de Paume, 1er (tel. 01 47 03 12 50; recorded info at 01 42 60 69 69; M. Concorde). Huge windows bathe this spectacular exhibition space in afternoon sunlight, accentuating its graceful curves and sharp angles. Languid connoisseurs and clueless tourists alike come to appreciate the world-class contemporary art exhibitions here. There is also a café with sandwiches (27F) and tarts. Open Tues. noon-9:30pm, Wed.-Fri. noon-7pm, Sat.-Sun. 10am-7pm. 35F, students 25F, under 13 free.

Centre de la Mer et des Eaux, 195, rue St-Jacques, 5ème (tel. 01 44 32 10 90; M. Luxembourg). More than just the requisite tanks of coral and tropical fish, this is a multimedia marine experience. A "hands-on" learning area lets you push buttons and pull handles to learn about fish disguises and algae life cycles. An entire room is devoted to "The Mysterious Voyage of Eels." Films and exhibitions change, but most come from the adventures of that sea-*czar,* Jacques Cousteau. All labels in French; all chairs for small-sized French students. Open Tues.-Fri. 10am-12:30pm and 1:15-5:30pm, Sat.-Sun. 10am-5:30pm. 30F, students 18F.

Institut du Monde Arabe (Institute of the Arab World), 23, quai St-Bernard, 5ème (tel. 01 40 51 38 38; M. Jussieu). Arguably the most architecturally innovative of Parisian museums, it opened in 1987 as a cooperative project among several Arab nations and the French government to promote education about Arab history, art, culture, and language. The museum assembles art from 3 Arab regions (Maghreb/Spain, the Near East, and the Middle East) from the 3rd through the 18th centuries. Level 4 is devoted entirely to contemporary Arab art. A library holds works of literature in Arabic, French, and English, as well as periodicals, all open to the public. At night, the auditorium hosts Arab movies (subtitled in English and French; 30F, students 20F) and plays (free). Call for a schedule. On Level 9, a delightful cafeteria cooks up 3-course lunches (79F), including many Arabic specialties. The rooftop terrace has a fabulous (free) view of Paris. Museum and library open Tues.-Sun 10am-6pm. Museum admission 25F, ages 12-18 20F, under 12 free. 90-min. guided tour of museum Tues.-Fri. at 3pm and Sat.-Sun. at 2 and 4pm, 40F. Admission to temporary exhibits and permanent collection 50F. Institute open Tues.-Sun. 10am-6pm. Cafeteria open Tues.-Sun. 11:30am-6pm.

Petit Palais (also called the **Palais des Beaux-Arts de la Ville de Paris**), av. Winston Churchill, 8ème (tel. 01 42 65 12 73; M. Champs-Elysées-Clemenceau). Built for the 1900 World Expo, this "palace" displays gems from ancient art through 19th- and 20th-century painting and sculpture. Each room in the permanent collection has a theme—17th-century Flemish and Dutch paintings or canvases depicting the French Revolution, for example. It houses Jean-Baptiste Carpeaux's *Young Fisher with the Shell;* Camille Claudel's bust of Rodin, Monet's *Sunset at Lavacourt,* as well as the odd Rubens, Rembrandt, Cézanne, Pissarro, and Renoir. Call ahead for wheelchair access. Open Tues.-Sun. 10am-5:40pm, last entry 5pm. Admission to permanent collection 27F, students 15F, seniors and under 18 free. Admission to temporary exhibits roughly 40F, under 25 and seniors 30F. Conference visits (1½hr. or so, Thurs. and Sat. at 2:30pm; in French and English) on special themes are held in the afternoon; call or visit for a schedule.

Musée Picasso, 5, rue de Thorigny, 3ème (tel. 01 42 71 25 21; M. Chemin Vert). When Pablo Picasso died in 1973, his family opted to pay the French inheritance tax in artwork, which is how the French government came to own this collection. (The 17th-century Hôtel Salé, which houses the museum, never belonged to Picasso; see page 119.) Many works are of minor significance, but the collection as a whole is great, thanks to the museum's well-paced and informative layout (with explanations translated into English). Light fixtures by Diego Giacometti (brother of sculptor Alberto) illuminate the first rooms of a circuit that traces the artist's development. Alongside Picasso's pieces are works by artists who influenced him, including Braque, Cézanne, Miró, and anonymous African sculptors. In addition, photos of Picasso's friends—Marie Laurencin, Braque, and Cocteau among others—provide a who's who of the early 20th-century avant-garde. Don't skip the sculpture and pottery on the lower level. A restriction on school groups after 1pm ensures more peaceful viewing. Museum open April-Sept. Wed.-Mon. 9:30am-6pm, last entrance 5:15pm; Oct.-March 9:30am-5:30pm, last entrance 4:45pm. 27F, ages 18-25, over 60, and Sun. 18F. A special exhibition is planned for Feb.-May '97 on photographic sources of Picasso's work, 1899-1930.

PARIS

Entertainment

Paris teems with cabarets, discos, and smoky jazz clubs; with U.S. and European cinema; with avant-garde and traditional theater; and with rock and classical concerts. Consult the two bibles of Paris entertainment: the magazine **Pariscope** (3F) and the **Officiel des Spectacles** (2F), both on sale weekly at any newsstand. Even if you don't understand French, you should be able to decipher the listings of times and locations. Or, contact **Info-Loisirs,** a recording that keeps tabs on what's happening in Paris (English tel. 01 49 52 53 56; French tel. 01 49 52 53 55).

Paris is one of the world's premier jazz capitals, and big-name American artists make frequent stops here. The city also offers a mixed diet of West African music, Caribbean calypso and reggae, Latin American salsa, North African raï, and rap. Classical concerts play both in expensive concert halls and more affordable churches, especially during the summer. To get more information and to buy tickets for rock, jazz, or classical concerts, check out **FNAC Musique,** 24, bd. des Italiens, 9ème (tel. 01 48 01 02 03), or 1, rue de Charenton, 12ème (tel. 01 43 42 04 04).

Parisians are inveterate film-goers and are particularly keen on American classics; frequent English-language film series and annual festivals make Parisian cinema a popular, accessible, and affordable entertainment option for visitors and locals alike.

The famous Montmartre cabarets still pack in American businessmen for all-girl, topless revues. Other cabarets, such as the comedy-oriented *café-théâtres* and the music-oriented *chansonniers,* perpetuate the ambience of 1930s Parisian cabarets, which helped launch the careers of Edith Piaf and Jacques Brel.

Keep in mind that the neighborhoods around popular night-spots are not always safe. The areas around Pigalle, Gare St-Lazare, and the Centre Pompidou fill nightly with prostitutes and drug dealers. Also remember to keep an eye on the time in order to avoid expensive, late-night taxis; although the metro runs until 1am, you should hop on a train at about 12:30am if you have to make a connection.

CINEMA

Ever since the Lumière brothers premiered cinema here (the first movie opened at the Grand Café, 14, bd. des Capucines, in 1895), Paris has had a movie scene of international proportions. Don't expect megaplexes and greasy popcorn; film-going in Paris is an evening on the town. Cafés, bars, and restaurants cohabit with projector rooms in some of the city's smaller theaters, whose intimate rooms may have as few as 20 seats (almost always plush, roomy, and comfy). The **Fête du Cinéma,** a three-day, all-day, city-wide celebration, transforms Paris and the rest of France into a community of film fans of all ages. The **Parc de la Villette,** 19ème, hosts annual genre film festivals in July and August (see page 150) . Call to see what's on for '97.

Proof of Paris's movie enthusiasm are the mile-long lines for anything from Robert Mitchum to Bambi. Beating the crowds requires some know-how. The two big theater chains—**Gaumont** and **UGC**—offer **cartes privilèges** for frequent customers. The *carte Gaumont,* at 165F for five entries, allows bearers to skip lines and reserve seats in advance. UGC offers a similar deal: 120F for four films, 180F for six. Cards are active for two months, at all shows and franchise locations.

Catering to the city's enormous student population, most cinemas offer tons of discounts. On Mondays and Wednesdays prices usually drop about 10F. Check *Pariscope* for details—days and reductions vary with the theater. The confederation of independent cinemas, a bulwark of little guys competing with Gaumont and UGC, offers reduced tickets for all on both days. In addition to students and seniors, *chômeurs* (the unemployed) get reduced rates—that last one only for the French.

The entertainment weeklies list show times and theaters. Film festivals are listed separately. The notation **v.o. (version originale)** after a movie listing means that the film is being shown in its original language with French subtitles; watching an English-language film with French subtitles is a great way to pick up new (and sometimes very interesting) vocabulary. When a film is marked **v.f. (version française)** it means that it has been dubbed—an entirely avoidable phenomenon in Paris. If you're braving summertime heat spells, make sure the movie theater is **climatisé** (air-conditioned).

PARIS

Action Christine, 4, rue Christine, 6ème (tel. 08 36 68 05 98; M. Odéon). Off rue Dauphine. Plays an eclectic, international selection of art and cult films. Always *v.o.* Admission 40F; reduced (for students on weekdays and for all on Mon.) 30F. Weekdays showing at 6 or 7pm only 25F. For 150F (plus a 30F fee at the first purchase), buy a pass good for 1 yr that admits you to 6 movies. One of the 2 rooms is wheelchair accessible; descend a steep staircase to reach the other.

L'Entrepôt, 7-9, rue Francis de Pressensé, 14ème (tel. 01 45 43 41 63; M. Pernety). Turn right off rue Raymond Losserand. A venue for independent films, this cinema organizes a variety of week-long festivals, some with director forums. 3 screens show films in *v.o.* Admission 39F, students and seniors 29F. The delightful restaurant/bar (tel. 01 45 40 60 70) at the same address serves meals on a secluded garden terrace. 2 branches show great independent, classic, and foreign films: **Les Trois Luxembourg,** 67, rue Monsieur-le-Prince, 6ème (tel. 01 46 33 97 77; M. Odéon). All films in *v.o.* Admission 40F, students 30F. **Le St-Germain-des-Prés,** 22, rue Guillaume Apollinaire, 6ème (tel. 01 42 22 87 23; M. St-Germain-des-Prés). Admission 40F, students, seniors, Mon., Wed., and noon show 30F.

La Pagode, 57bis, rue de Babylone, 7ème (tel. 01 36 68 75 07; M. St-François-Xavier). Turn right on rue de Babylone from bd. des Invalides. The intimate *salle japonaise,* with velvet seats and painted screens, helps make this Paris's most charming cinema. Specializing in contemporary films of the artsy ilk, the Pagode is a well-disguised outpost of Gaumont, and the *carte Gaumont* works here. Admission 44F, students and seniors Mon.-Fri. before 6pm, and everyone on Wed. 37F. 3-5 shows per day. Shows in the *salle japonaise* are a few francs more. Also visit the *salon de thé,* whose terrace spills into the Japanese garden. Tea or pastries 22F. *Salon de thé* open Mon.-Sat. 4-9:45pm, Sun. and holidays 2-8pm.

THEATER

Generally, Parisian theatergoers are either ushered into large, plush playhouses or crowded onto benches in the smallest of rooms. Intimate performance spaces like *café-théâtres* and *chansonniers* book anything from Vaudevillian comics to accordionists. National theaters, especially the Comédie Française, are stately venues with generally classical repertoires. The famed *grands guignols* (puppet shows) are intended for children but attract adults as well. Most theaters close during August. *Pariscope* and *l'Officiel des Spectacles* provide complete listings of current shows.

Theater tickets can run as high as 200F, but reduced student rates are nearly always available. In addition, a number of theaters sell rush tickets 30 to 45 minutes before performances. You can also try one of the following ticket box-offices.

Kiosque Info Jeune, 25, bd. Bourdon, 4ème (tel. 01 42 76 22 60; M. Bastille). Also at 4, rue Louis Armand (in Aquaboulevard), 15ème (tel. 01 40 60 64 06; M. Balard). A youth info service provided by the Paris *Mairie.* Sells theater tickets at half-price and distributes free passes to concerts and plays. You must be under 26 to be eligible for discounts. Bastille branch open Mon.-Fri. noon-7pm; Aquaboulevard branch open Tues. and Thurs. 2-7pm, Wed. noon-8pm, Fri.-Sat. 2-8pm.

Kiosque-Théâtre, 15, pl. de la Madeleine, 8ème. (M. Madeleine.) Far and away the best discount box office. Sells tickets at ½-price the day of the show (plus 16F per seat commission). No student discounts. Open Tues.-Sat. 12:30-8pm, Sun. 12:30-4pm. Also in metro stop Châtelet-les-Halles. Open Tues.-Sat. noon-5pm.

Alpha FNAC: Spectacles, 136, rue de Rennes, 6ème (tel. 01 49 54 30 00; M. Montparnasse-Bienvenue). Also at: Forum des Halles, 1-7, rue Pierre Lescot, 1er (tel. 01 40 41 40 00; M. Châtelet-Les Halles); 26-30, av. des Ternes, 17ème (tel. 01 44 09 18 00; M. Ternes); and 71, bd. St-Germain, 5ème (tel. 01 44 41 31 50). Tickets for theater, concerts, and festivals. Open Mon.-Sat. 10am-7:30pm. V, MC.

Virgin Megastore, 52, av. des Champs-Elysées, 8ème (tel. 01 49 53 50 50; box office tel. 01 44 68 44 08; M. Franklin D. Roosevelt). Like FNAC, easy pick-up but no discounts. Look for the office below the first floor. V, MC. (Also see page 154.)

PARIS

National Theaters

Four of France's five national theaters are located in Paris (the fifth is in Strasbourg). With the advantages of giant auditoriums, great acoustics, veteran acting troupes, and, in certain cases, centuries of prestige, they're stage polished, extremely popular productions. Although they occasionally put on modern works, Molière, Racine, Goethe, and Shakespeare (all in French) are more common. Unless you're banking on last-minute rush tickets, make reservations a fortnight in advance.

La Comédie Française: Salle Richelieu, 2, rue de Richelieu, 1er (tel. 01 44 58 15 15; M. Palais Royal). Founded by Molière, now the granddaddy of all French theaters. Much pomp and prestige, with red velvet and chandeliers. Expect wildly gesticulated slapstick farce in the much parodied *"style Comédie Française."* You don't need to speak French to understand the jokes. 892 seats. 1997 will feature works by Racine, Turgenev, and others. Open Sept. 15-July; usually no shows on Mon. Box office open daily 11am-6pm. Admission 60-185F, under 25 60-70F. Rush tickets (25F) available 45min. before show; line up 1hr in advance. The *comédiens français,* as actors here are known, also mount plays in the 330-seat **Théâtre du Vieux Colombier,** 21, rue du Vieux-Colombier, 6ème (tel. 01 44 39 87 00 or 01 44 39 87 01; recorded info 08 36 68 01 50; M. St-Sulpice). 1997 will feature works by Hugo and Gênet. Tickets 130F; rush tickets (60F) sold 45min. before performances, available to students under 27 and anyone under 25.

Odéon Théâtre de l'Europe, 1, pl. Odéon, 6ème (tel. 01 44 41 36 36; M. Odéon). Eclectic programs run the gamut from classics to avant-garde. 1042 seats. Also at the **Petit Odéon,** an affiliate with 82 seats. Open Sept.-July. Box office open Mon.-Sat. 11am-6:30pm. 50-165F for most shows; student rush tickets (60F) available 45min. before performance. Petit Odéon 70F, students 50F. V, MC.

Théâtre National de Chaillot, pl. du Trocadéro, in the Palais de Chaillot, 16ème (tel. 01 47 27 81 15; M. Trocadéro). Plays and occasional music and dance concerts take place in 2 rooms, 1 with 1000, and the other with 400, seats. Call to make arrangements for wheelchair access. 1997 season includes: *Béjart Ballet Lausanne,* Jan. 17-Feb. 9; *Macbeth,* some performances with English translation, Jan. 23-March 8; Guy Bedos, Feb. 18-23; *Dommage qu'elle soit une putain ('Tis a Pity She's a Whore),* some performances with English, March 20-June 1; *Adam et Eve,* April 24-June 28. Box office open Mon.-Sat. 11am-7pm, Sun. 11am-5pm. Admission 160F, under 25 and seniors 120F. Same-day student rush 80F. V, MC.

Private Theaters

Paris's private theaters, less celebrated than their state-run counterparts, often stage outstanding shows. Yet in this realm of the weird and wonderful, risky performances often misfire. Check reviews in newspapers and entertainment weeklies before investing in a seat. Find schedules on the green, cylindrical *spectacles* boards all over town, in *Pariscope* or *l'Officiel des Spectacles,* or at the theaters themselves.

Athénée-Louis Jouvet, 4, sq. de l'Opéra, 9ème (tel. 01 47 42 67 27; M. Opéra or Auber). 687 seats. Hard to find, with a bland exterior, but a magnificent 18th-century interior and outstanding classical productions in 2 *salles*. Open Oct.-April. Box office open Mon.-Sat. 11:30am-6pm. Admission 95-150F in the large theater (80-100F reduced), 120F in the small theater (90F reduced). 40F for lousy seats.

Jardin Shakespeare du Pré Catelan, in the center of the Bois de Boulogne, west of the Lac Inférieur (tel. 01 40 19 95 33). Take bus 244 from Porte Maillot. 450 seats. Summertime Shakespeare (and other classics) in French, set in a garden of plants mentioned by the bard. Tickets at the door or at FNAC. Shows usually Fri.-Sat. night, with Sat.-Sun. matinees. Buses stop running before late shows end, and walking in the large deserted Bois de Boulogne is dangerous even if you know your way out. Instead, take a taxi to Porte Maillot. Admission 100F, reduced 60F.

Théâtre de la Huchette, 23, rue de la Huchette, 5ème (tel. 01 43 26 38 99; M. St-Michel). 100 seats. Tiny theater whose productions of Ionesco's *La cantatrice chauve* (The Bald Soprano) and *La leçon* (The Lesson) are still popular after 39 years. A good choice for people with functional high school French. Shows Mon.-Sat. Box office open Mon.-Sat. 5-7pm. *La cantatrice chauve* starts at 7:30pm, *La leçon* at 8:30pm; no one admitted after curtain goes up. Admission 100F, students 70F; for both shows 160F, students 100F. No discounts Sat.

Théâtre Mogador, 25, rue de Mogador, 9ème (tel. 01 53 32 32 00; M. Trinité). With 1792 seats, one of the largest theaters in Paris. Grandiose comedies and musicals on a colossal stage. Frequent matinees Sat. 4pm. Open Sept.-May Tues.-Sat. Box office open Mon.-Fri. 11am-7pm. Admission 160-260F, matinees 140-230F.

Théâtre du Rond Point, Salle Renaud-Barrault, 2bis, av. Franklin D. Roosevelt, 8ème (tel. 01 44 95 98 00; M. Franklin D. Roosevelt). 920 seats. Also **Salle Jean Vautier** with 150 seats. Large stage hosts a wide range of theatrical spectacles from musical comedy to Beckett. The smaller stage is more experimental. Open Sept.-July. Box office open Tues.-Sat. 11am-6pm. Admission 110-140F, students and seniors 100F. *Petite salle* 120F, reduced 60-90F.

Théâtre de la Ville, 2, pl. du Châtelet, 4ème (tel. 01 42 74 22 77; M. Châtelet). 1000 seats. Excellent productions include classical music and ballet. Open Oct.-June. Box office open Mon.-Fri. 11am-7pm; telephone sales Mon. 9am-6pm, Tues.-Sat. 9am-8pm. Admission 90-190F, student rush tickets ½-price. V, MC.

Café-Théâtres

Visit one of Paris's *café-théâtres* for an evening of word play and social satire in mostly black-box theater settings. Expect low-budget, high-energy skits filled with political puns and double-entendres; in general, knowledge of French slang and politics is a must for audience members. One-(wo)man shows are a mainstay.

Au Bec Fin, 6, rue Thérèse, 1er (tel. 01 42 96 29 35; M. Palais Royal). A tiny, 60-seat theater, with 2 different shows per night. Dinner and 1 show from 178F, Sat. 210F. Dinner and 2 shows from 300F. Shows at 7, 8:30, and 10:15pm. Auditions sometimes open to the public, 50F. Admission 80F, students 65F; Mon.-Tues. 50F.

Café de la Gare, 41, rue du Temple, 4ème (tel. 01 42 78 52 51; M. Hôtel-de-Ville). Couched in the cobbled courtyard of the Centre de Danse du Marais, where it attracts an engaging, youthful crowd to bold performances ranging in comic flavor and cast size. Recent acts include solo comics and a look-alike Addams Family. Reservations daily 3-7pm. Otherwise, the box office opens 45min. before the show. Most shows start at around 8 or 10pm. Admission 50-100F. V, MC.

Petit Casino, 17, rue Chapon, 3ème (tel. 01 42 78 36 50; M. Arts-et-Métiers). Left off rue Beaubourg. Once a plumbing store, now a basement dinner-theater with a stage that's 4 paces wide. Self-serve smorgasbord of salads, charcuteries, desserts, and wine (as much as you want). Performances tend toward low comedy. Dinner starts at 7:30pm, 1st show at 9pm, 2nd show at 10:30pm. Call for reservations daily 9am-8pm. Dinner and 2 shows 130F. Shows without dinner 80F. V.

Le Point Virgule, 7, rue Ste-Croix-de-la-Bretonnerie, 4ème (tel. 01 42 78 67 03; M. Hôtel-de-Ville). An intimate and interactive theater. Capacity crowds of 140 sit shoulder-to-elbow on small benches. Shows generally feature 1 or 2 actors. Frequent slapstick acts are ideal for non-French speakers. Reservations accepted 'round the clock. 3 shows daily at 8, 9:15, and 10:15pm. Tickets to 1 show 80F, (students 65F); 2 shows 130F; 3 shows 150F. Open 5pm-midnight.

Cafés-Chansonniers

The *café-chansonnier* is the musical cousin of the *café-théâtre.* In the spirit of old Paris, audience members sing along to French folk songs. The better your French, the better a time you'll have. Come to belt out French classics you don't even know. Admission usually includes one drink.

Au Lapin Agile, 22, rue des Saules, 18ème (tel. 01 46 06 85 87; M. Lamarck-Coulaincourt). From the metro turn right on rue Lamark, then right again up rue des Saules. Picasso, Verlaine, Clemenceau, Renoir, Apollinaire, and Max Jacob hung out here in their day; now a mainly tourist audience crowds in for comical poems and songs. Arrive early for a good seat. Shows at 9:15pm. Admission and first drink 110F, students 80F. Subsequent drinks 25-30F. Open Tues.-Sun. 9pm-2am.

Caveau de la République, 1, bd. St-Martin, 3ème (tel. 01 42 78 44 45; M. République). A mostly Parisian crowd fills the 482 seats of this 90-year-old venue for political satire. Shows string together 6 or 7 separate acts; the sequence is known as the *tour de champs* (tour of the field). Tickets sold up to 6 days in advance, 11am-6pm. Shows Sept.-June Tues.-Sat. 9pm, Sun. 3:30pm. Admission 170F; students and over age 60 Tues.-Fri. 105F. V, MC.

Deux Anes, 100, bd. de Clichy, 18ème (tel. 01 46 06 10 26; M. Blanche). 300 seats. Shows Mon.-Sat. 9pm. Reservations by phone or in person 11am-7pm, 2 weeks in advance. Admission 120F, students 95F. Open Sept.-June.

Guignols

These renowned puppet shows are for adults and children alike. The puppets speak French, but you'll have no problem understanding their outrageous antics. Almost all parks have *guignols*—check *Pariscope* for exact schedules and locations.

Marionettes des Champs-Elysées, Rond-Point des Champs-Elysées, 8ème (tel. 01 42 57 43 34; M. Champs-Elysées-Clemenceau), at the intersection of av. Matignon and Gabriel. The classic adventures of the *guignol* character. Shows Sept. to mid-July Wed. and Sat.-Sun. 3, 4, and 5pm. Admission 13F.

Marionettes du Luxembourg, Jardin du Luxembourg, 6ème (tel. 01 43 26 46 47; M. Luxembourg or Notre-Dame-des-Champs). The best *guignol* in Paris. This roofed-in theater plays the same children's classics it has since it opened in 1933: *Little Red Riding Hood, The Three Little Pigs,* and so on. Running time is about 45min. Arrive 30min. early for good seats. 1-2 shows daily at around 3 and 4pm. Call ahead for precise time. Admission 21F.

Theatre Guignol du Parc des Buttes Chaumont, 19ème. (M. Laumière.) "If you aren't with your parents, stay in your seat until the end! There are lots of people in the park," warns the sage puppet. Young children love starting a discussion and puppets gladly respond. 7 different rotating shows. Wed. 3 and 4pm; Sat., Sun., and holidays 3, 4, and 5pm. Shows last 40min. Admission 12F.

MUSIC

Classical Music, Opera, and Dance

Paris toasts the classics under lamppost, spire, and chandelier. The city's squares, churches, and concert halls feature world-class performers from home and abroad, although visitors may find France's cultural capital to be a giant with a limp, favoring classical music and opera in lieu of dance. Acclaimed foreign and provincial dance companies swing into town to take up the slack; watch for posters and read *Pariscope.* Summer music and, to a lesser extent, dance festivals bring soloists from all over the world. Connoisseurs will find the thick, indexed *Programme des Festivals* indispensable (free at *mairies* and the tourist office). Paris offers cheap tickets to high culture in great quantities, thanks to a decade of socialism that peddled gentler arts to the masses. Beware, however, of rock-bottom prices. The Opéra Bastille suffers from poor acoustics, and while Balanchine may have said "see the music, hear the dance," you may not be able to do either from the back row of the Opéra Garnier. Check a theater floor plan whenever possible. See page 141 for booking agents, and page 150 for information about seasonal events.

IRCAM, Institut de Recherche et Coordination Acoustique/Musique, Centre Pompidou, 1, pl. Igor-Stravinsky, 4ème (tel. 01 44 78 48 16; M. Rambuteau). This institute, which invites scholars, composers, and interpreters to come together in the study of music, often holds concerts that are open to the public. Contemporary compositions sometimes accompanied by "film" or "theater." Stop by the office near the Stravinsky fountain or at the info desk in the Centre Pompidou for schedules. Two computers in the lobby allow you to "visit" IRCAM and play musical games. The institute also houses a music library.

Musée du Louvre, 1er (tel. 01 40 20 52 99 for information; 01 40 20 52 29 for reservations; M. Palais-Royal/Musée du Louvre). Classical music in a classy auditorium. Tickets for concerts 65-130F. Music-film combos 25F. Open Sept.-June.

Opéra de la Bastille, pl. de la Bastille, 11ème (tel. 01 43 43 96 96; M. Bastille). The Opéra de la Bastille staged its first performance on July 14, 1989, during the bicentennial jubilee. Hailed by some as the hall to bring opera to the masses, decried by others as offensive to every aesthetic sensibility, this huge theater features elaborate opera and ballet, often with a modern spin. Subtitles in English and French during hard-to-understand performances. Tickets 30-610F. Call, write, or stop by for a free brochure of the season's events. Tickets can be purchased: by writing and sending a traveler's check; by phone (tel. 01 44 73 13 00; open Mon.-Sat. 11am-6pm); by Minitel (3615 code THEA then Opéra Bastille); or in person (Mon.-Sat. 11am-6:30pm). Tickets go on sale 14 days in advance of each performance. Rush tickets for under 25, students, and over 65, often available 15min. before show; 110F for operas, 60F for ballets, and 50F for concerts. For wheelchair access, call 01 44 73 13 73 at least 15 days in advance. V, MC.

Opéra Comique, 5, rue Favart, 2ème (tel. 01 42 44 45 46; M. Richelieu-Drouot). Operas on a lighter scale. '97 season includes: *Les Contes d'Hoffman,* Dec. 3-11; *Le Comte Ory,* Jan. 20-Feb. 3; *Owen Wingrave,* Feb. 21-25; *La Dame blanche,* April 19-29; *La Cantatrice Chauve,* March 5-8; *Le Mariage Secret,* May 5-16. Buy tickets at the box office Mon.-Fri. 11am-6pm or by phone. Tickets 35-490F.

Opéra Garnier, pl. de l'Opéra, 9ème (tel. 01 44 73 13 99 for info; 01 44 73 13 00 for reservations; M. Opéra). Although the renovations of this historic opera house will not be finished until 2002, it will be open for the 1996-97 season. The Garnier also hosts the ballet de l'Opéra de Paris. Tickets available at the box office 2 weeks before each performance (Mon.-Sat. 11am-6pm). Ballet tickets 30-370F; Opera tickets up to 600F. Lowest-end tickets often have obstructed views. V, MC.

Orchestre de Paris, in the Salle Pleyel, 252, rue du Faubourg St-Honoré, 8ème (tel. 01 45 61 65 65; M. Ternes). The renowned orchestra delivers first-class performances under director Semyon Bychkov. 1997 season includes works by Stravinsky, Brahms, Mozart, and Mahler. Season runs Sept.-June; call or stop by for concert calendar. Box office open Mon.-Sat. 11am-6pm. Tickets 54-288F. V, MC.

Théâtre des Champs-Elysées, 15, av. Montaigne, 8ème (tel. 01 49 52 50 50; M. Alma Marceau). Top international dance companies and orchestras. To play here is to "arrive" on the highbrow music scene. Season runs Sept.-June. Buy tickets 3 weeks in advance. Reserve by telephone Mon.-Fri. 10am-noon and 2-6pm; box office open Mon.-Sat. 11am-7pm. Tickets 40-500F.

Théâtre Musical de Paris, pl. du Châtelet, 1er (tel. 01 42 33 00 00; M. Châtelet). A superb 2300-seat theater normally reserved for guest orchestras and ballet companies. Magnificent acoustics. Call for a schedule. Tickets run 70-300F. V, MC.

Free concerts are common in churches and parks, especially during summer festivals. These are super-popular: get there early if you want to breathe. Check the entertainment weeklies and the Alpha-FNAC offices for concert notices. **AlloConcerts'** 24-hour hotline provides info in French on free open-air concerts in the parks (tel. 01 42 76 50 00). The **American Church in Paris,** 65, quai d'Orsay, 7ème (tel. 01 47 05 07 89; M. Invalides or Alma-Marceau), sponsors free concerts (Oct.-June Sun. at 6pm). **Eglise St-Merri** is also known for its free concerts (Sat. at 9pm and Sun. at 4pm, except in Aug.); contact Accueil Musical St-Merri, 76, rue de la Verrerie, 4ème (tel. 01 42 71 93 93; M. Châtelet). Sunday concerts take place in the **Jardin du Luxembourg** band shell, 6ème (tel. 01 42 37 20 00); show up early for a seat or prepare to stand. Infrequent concerts in the **Musée d'Orsay** are free with a museum ticket. The **Maison de la Radio-France** hosts concerts, some of which are free.

Eglise St-Germain-des-Prés, 3, pl. St-Germain-des-Prés, 6ème (M. St-Germain-des-Prés), **Eglise St-Eustache,** rue du Jour, 1er (M. Les Halles), and **Eglise St-Louis-en-l'Ile,** 19, rue St-Louis-en-l'Ile, 4ème (M. Pont Marie), stage frequent concerts that are a bit pricey but have stellar acoustics and atmosphere. For info call 01 42 50 70 72. Arrive 30 to 45 minutes early for front-row seats. The **Ste-Chapelle** has summer concerts a few days per week. The box office is at 4, bd. du Palais, 1er (tel. 01 46 61 55 41; M. Cité; open daily 1:30-5:30pm; admission 120-150F, students 90-120F).

Jazz

Some critics mourn that Paris is not the jazz capital it once was. Even so, there are a healthy number of gigs to choose from nightly, ranging from French unknowns to big-name Americans. Frequent summer festivals sponsor free or almost-free jazz concerts (see page 150). The Fête du Marais often features big-band jazz, while Halle That Jazz has jazz orchestras with a Latin beat. In fall, the Jazz Festival of Paris comes to town. Venues high and low open up to celebrity and arriving artists (late Oct. to early Nov.). *Jazz Hot* (45F) and *Jazz Magazine* (35F)—France's *Downbeat* and *Metronome*—are both great sources of information, as is the hard-to-find, bimonthly *LYLO (Les Yeux, Les Oreilles).* If it isn't in bars or FNACS, try the main office, 55, rue des Vinaigriers, 10ème (tel. 01 42 09 62 05). Finally, read *Pariscope.*

Au Duc des Lombards, 42, rue des Lombards, 1er (tel. 01 42 33 22 88; M. Châtelet). Murals of Duke Ellington and Coltrane cover the exterior of this premier jazz joint. The best French jazz, with occasional American soloists. Dark, smoky, and packed with regulars. English spoken. 70-80F admission, 50F for music students. Beer 28F, cocktails 60F. Featured musicians play from 8:30-10pm. Thereafter, a jazz trio plays until all hours of the night. Open daily 7:30pm-4am. V, MC.

New Morning, 7-9, rue des Petites-Ecuries, 10ème (tel. 01 45 23 51 41; M. Château d'Eau). 400-seat former printing plant with the biggest American headliners in the city. Halfway between club and concert hall, it only feels cozy when it's packed; come for music, not ambience. Sit in the lower front section or in the near wings for best acoustics. Good sound system, a grand piano, and a large stage. Attracts big names like Wynton Marsalis, Bobby McFerrin, and Betty Carter. All the greats have played here—from Chet Baker to Stan Getz and Miles Davis; Archie Shepp is a regular. Open Sept.-July from 9:30pm; times vary. Admission 110-130F. Tickets available at box office, FNAC, or the Virgin Megastore. V, MC.

Le Petit Journal Montparnasse, 13, rue du Commandant-Mouchotte, 14ème (tel. 01 43 21 56 70; M. Gaîté). Look for the large, animated neon sign featuring a horn player. An elegant club, popular with a well-to-do, older clientele. Very good piano and sound system at the service of the best contemporary mainstream French jazz; 1996 saw Michel Legrand, Eddy Louis, and Joshua Redman. Obligatory first drink 120F. Open Mon.-Sat. 9pm-2am; music begins at 10pm.

Le Petit Journal St-Michel, 71, bd. St-Michel, 5ème (tel. 01 43 26 28 59; M. Luxembourg). A crowded but intimate establishment, where students mix with forty-somethings reminiscing about the riots of 1968. New Orleans bands and first-class performers play in this Parisian center of the "Old Style." Open Mon.-Sat. 9:30pm-1:30am. Obligatory first drink 100F.

Le Petit Opportun, 15, rue des Lavandières-Ste-Opportune, 1er (tel. 01 42 36 01 36; M. Châtelet). A relaxed and unpolished pub with some of the best modern jazz trios and quartets around, including a lot of American bands and soloists. The club is tiny (60 seats), but so popular it ought to seat 500. Come early. Open Sept.-July Tues.-Sat. from 11pm; bar open until 3am. Cover charge 50-80F depending on the performer. Drinks from 25F.

Slow Club, 130, rue de Rivoli, 1er (tel. 01 42 33 84 30; M. Châtelet). Miles Davis's favorite in Paris. Big bands, traditional jazz, and Dixieland in a great old-time setting. Expect dancing and a crowd in their 30s. Weekday cover 60F, women and students 55F. Weekend cover from 75F. Drinks from 19F. Open Tues.-Thurs. 10pm-3am, Fri.-Sat. 10pm-4am.

Discos and Rock Clubs

Paris, like New York, is a city that never sleeps. The streets are teeming with clubs, many of them inconspicuous. Some Parisian clubs are small and nearly impossible to find out about unless you're a native. Others are larger-than-life and outrageously flashy. The discos that are "in" (or even in business) change drastically from year to year; only a few have been popular since the 1960s. Many Parisian clubs are officially private, which means they have the right to pick and choose their clientele. The management evaluates prospective customers through peepholes in the front doors; be aware that people of Arab or African descent often find it difficult to win club owners' approval. Parisians tend to dress up more than North Americans for a night on the town; weary backpackers may want to try a bar instead.

In general, word of mouth is the best guide to the current scene. Some of the smaller places in the *quartier latin* admit almost anyone who is sufficiently decked out. To enter one of the more exclusive places, you may need to accompany a regular. Women often get a discount or get in free, but don't go alone unless you're looking for lots of amorous attention. Men will generally have an easier time getting into clubs with gay flair, such as Le Queen. Weekdays are cheaper and less crowded; you'll have a better chance of moving, but most action happens on weekends.

Les Bains, 7, rue du Bourg l'Abbé, 3ème (tel. 01 48 87 01 80; M. Réaumur-Sébastopol). Ultra-selective, ultra-expensive, ultra-popular club. The artists formerly known as Prince made the club's reputation with a surprise free concert here a few years back. It used to be a public bath, visited at least once by Marcel Proust. More recently, Madonna, Jack Nicholson, and Roman Polanski have stopped in. Lots of models and super-attractive people. They sometimes have "fashion shows" that may be considered offensive to women. Cover and 1st drink Sun.-Thurs. 100F, Fri.-Sat. 140F. Subsequent drinks 100F. Open daily midnight-6am.

Flash Back, 18, rue des Quatre-Vents, 6ème (tel. 01 43 25 56 10; M. Odéon). Two levels of secluded lounges and a small mirrored dance floor with disco ball. On Tues. retro-nights, DJ spins hits from the 70s and early 80s. Thurs. night floor show features anything from Lola the Showgirl to fly dancers. Comfortable, easy atmosphere among Paris's beautiful youth. Cover 70F, Tues.-Thurs. women free. Drinks 70F. Open Tues.-Sat. 11pm-dawn.

Le Palace, 8, rue du Faubourg Montmartre, 9ème (tel. 01 42 46 10 87; M. Rue Montmartre). A funky disco, although its days as the hottest club in Paris have gone by. If you hit a private party and still get in, the music and crowd can be killer. Otherwise, it's all too Top 40. A mix of happy high school students and some older people reliving their youth. The place is huge (up to 2000 people per night), with multi-level dance floors, each with separate bars and different music. Sun. features the Gay Tea Dance, a 15-year institution of the Parisian gay scene. Cover and 1 drink Wed.-Thurs. 50F, Fri. and Sat. 100F, Sun. before 4pm 40F, Sun. after 4pm 60F. Subsequent drinks 60F. Open Tues.-Sat. 11:30pm-6am, Sun. 2-11:30pm.

Le Queen, 102, av. des Champs-Elysées, 8ème (tel. 01 42 89 31 32). Come taste the fiercest funk in town where drag queens, superstars, models, moguls, and Herculean go-go demigods get down to the rhythms of a 10,000 gigawatt sound system. Her Majesty (a pretty nice girl) is open 7 days a week, midnight to dawn. Mon. is disco (50F cover plus 50F obligatory drink). Tues. is house music, mostly gay men, and gallons of soap suds (50F cover, 50F drink). Wed. is Latin house, (free entry). Thurs. is house, (free entry). Fri. and Sat. are house (80F entry, 50F obligatory drink), and Sun., with its hits from the 80s, is free. Le Queen is at once the cheapest and most fashionable club in town, and thus the toughest to get into. Dress your most (insert adjective) and pray to Madonna they'll let you inside.

Le Saint, 7, rue Saint-Séverin, 5ème (tel. 01 43 25 50 04; M. Saint-Michel). Plays a wide range of music, rap, soul, R&B, retro, reggae, and zouk. A small comfortable club set in 13th-century *caves* and filled with regulars who come to dance. Tues.-Thurs. cover 60F, Fri. 80F, Sat. 90F. Drinks 15-50F. Open 11pm-6am.

Also popular in Paris are clubs specializing in **Brazilian samba** and **African music:**

Le Tango, 13, rue au Maire, 3ème (tel. 01 42 72 17 78; M. Arts et Métiers). Crowd dances Thurs.-Sat. to Antillean, African, salsa, and zouk music. Regulars (ages 20-35) all know each other. Kind of square, red decor compensated for by nifty Art Deco lamps and good sound. One Sun. per month is Argentinian tango. Cover for special evenings 50F, regular evenings 60F, Sat. afternoon 25F, Sun. afternoon 35F. Open Thurs.-Fri. 11pm-5am, Sat. 2-7pm and 11pm-5am, Sun. 2-8pm.

Aux Trois Mailletz, 56, rue Galande, 5ème (tel. 01 43 54 00 79; M. St-Michel). The basement houses an exceptional jazz café featuring world music. Leans towards the Latin and Afro-Cuban scenes, but also has jazz, blues, and gospel musicians from Europe and the states. 70F admission to club, admission to bar is free. Beer 22-40F, cocktails 65F. Bar open 5pm-dawn every day, *cave* 8:30pm to dawn.

PARIS

BARS AND WINE BARS

Apart from booze and chairs, there is no common denominator to the Parisian bar scene. Bars tend to be more relaxed (and cheaper) than clubs; however, they also tend to close around 2am, when clubs are just beginning to get hot. To find the bar for you, let *arrondissement* reputations be your guide. Bars in the 5ème and 6ème often cater to anglophone students, while the Marais and Bastille—the chic quarters *du jour*—are always jumping with crowds of Paris's young, hip, and friendly, no matter what day or how late. Draft beer is *bière pression,* of which the most common incarnation is *un demi* (a half-pint). The bartender is the *bar-man.* As with cafés, expect two lists of prices for drinks; stand at the bar and pay less or sit and pay a few francs more for *ambience.* Rare, expensive wines, exorbitant by the bottle, have become somewhat affordable by the glass. Still, wine bars are not the place for pinching pennies. Expect to pay at least 15F for a glass of high-quality wine; you'll find it's easy to spend five times as much to develop a distinguishing palate for the stuff. Law dictates a price increase after 10pm, but few go out before this wee hour.

Le Bar du Caveau, 17, pl. Dauphine, 1er (tel. 01 43 26 81 84; M. Cité), facing the front steps of the Palais de Justice. Luscious cheeses and delectable wines attract fashionable Parisians to this traditional brass and wood saloon. The Caveau's cuisine is simple, rustic, and delicious. Wines by the glass (12-23F) and by the bottle (70-155F). Plate of cheese 47F. Open Mon.-Fri. 8:30am-8pm.

Le Franc Pinot, 1, quai de Bourbon, 4ème (tel. 01 43 29 46 98; M. Pont Marie). A fixture on the Ile St-Louis since the island became habitable; notorious in the 17th and 18th centuries as a meeting place for enemies of the state. The exterior's metal grillwork was installed in 1642 to prevent prisoners from escaping once trapped inside. The labyrinthine *caves* have been wonderfully preserved as the dining room of this restaurant/wine bar. The wine bar occupies only the main floor. Burgundy wines are a specialty, by the glass 15-36F and up. Check chalkboards for daily specials. Downstairs restaurant has a *menu* and music later in the evening. Open Tues.-Sat. 8am-2am, Sun. 2pm-2am. V, MC, AmEx.

Jacques Mélac, 42, rue Léon Frot, 11ème (tel. 01 43 70 59 27; M. Charonne). *The* Parisian family-owned wine bar and bistro. In Sept., Mélac and friends harvest, tread upon, and extract wine from grapes grown in his own vineyard. Wine at 16F a glass or 85F a bottle (38F to go). Daily special and omelettes (33F), plates of cold cuts (such as ham, 29F). You'll find no pretension here. Open Sept.-July Mon. 9am-7pm, Tues.-Fri. 9am-10:30pm. V, MC.

Caveau des Oubliettes, 11, rue St-Julien-le-Pauvre, 5ème (tel. 01 43 54 94 97; M. St-Michel). Located in what were once the bowels of the Petit-Châtelet Prison. Irish pub with French style and management. Happy hour 5pm-9pm, beer 18-35F. Open Mon.-Sat. 5pm-2am. V, MC.

La Chope des Artistes, 48, rue du Faubourg St-Martin, 10ème (tel. 01 42 02 86 76; M. Strasbourg-St-Denis). The tone is mellow, intimate elegance. You could almost be in a Belle Epoque Parisian café, with Apollinaire sinking into one of the spacious chairs next to you and leaning over the slightly-too-small table to whisper sweetly in your ear. The theater crowd shows up before the shows start. Coffee 10F. Beer 25F. Cocktails 28-50F. Open Mon.-Sat. 8:30am-2am.

Le Piano Vache, 8, rue Laplace, 5ème (tel. 01 46 33 75 03; M. Cardinal Lemoine or Maubert-Mutualité). A young crowd patronizes this poster-plastered alterna-grotto, hidden in the winding streets near the Panthéon. Popular with both French college students and tourists who stumble upon it. Beer on tap 20-34F. Open July-Aug. daily noon-2pm and 4pm-2am; Sept.-June Mon.-Sat. noon-2am.

BISEXUAL, GAY, AND LESBIAN ENTERTAINMENT

While the bisexual, gay, and lesbian communities of Paris may not be so politically active as those in New York or San Francisco, the scene is far from closeted. This is Gay Paree, where Eartha Kitt is Queen Camp, where Jean-Paul Gaultier fits Madonna's bullet bras, and where everybody's had a rough day at the gym.

The scene is much more happening for men than women; lesbians are not very visible in Paris, and what lesbian entertainment exists is scattered across the city. That said, the undisputed center of lesbian and gay life is still the Marais, known throughout Paris as the *chic*-est part of the city. There, in the 3ème and the 4ème *arrondissements,* you'll find gay and lesbian café/bars, bookstores, and restaurants, as well as window displays of Gay-Pride wear. As usual, it's helpful to dress well. Anyone seeking the hippest club scene in Paris might want to drop in at Le Queen, which is an unofficially gay club. Quieter gay spots line the rue Vieille-du-Temple.

For the most comprehensive listing of gay and lesbian restaurants, clubs, hotels, organizations, and services, consult Gai Pied's *Guide Gai 1997* (English and French, 69F at any kiosk or *papeterie*). *Lesbia's* ads are a good gauge of what's hot, or at least what's open (25F). *Pariscope* has an English-language section called *A Week of Gay Outings.* The magazines *3 Keller* and *Exit,* available at the Centre Gai et Lesbian and at many bars and clubs, can also help point you to the hot spots.

Le Bar du Palmier, 16, rue des Lombards, 4ème (tel. 01 42 78 53 53; M. Châtelet). From bd. Sébastopol turn right on rue des Lombards. Palm trees, piña coladas, and margaritas (50F) mean "exotic" in French. Fantastically mixed clientele come to this hot-spot and what may be the only terrace in a Marais bar. Music from soul and jazz to techno. Beer 20-33F. Drinks 45-50F. Happy hour (half price on draft beer) 6-8pm. Open daily 5pm-5am. V, MC.

Le Champmeslé, 4, rue Chabanais, 2ème (tel. 01 42 96 85 20; M. Pyramides or Bourse). This intimate (and she-she) lesbian bar has plush couches, dim lighting, and a yuppie clientele. Cabaret on Thurs. Starting at 10pm, come on the 15th of the month for the *soirée zodiaque;* if it's your birthday month, you get a free drink. No cover. Drinks 25-40F. Open Mon.-Sat. 5pm-dawn. V, MC, AmEx.

Le Club, 14, rue St-Denis, 1er (tel. 01 45 08 96 25; M. Châtelet-Les Halles). Found in a less chic, but *très* gay area of Beaubourg, next to the Marais. A dark, subterranean, intimate spot to dance. Women and straight men welcome. Wed. is garage-techno night. Le Club is known for its Thurs. theme parties. Cover (48F including 1st drink) Fri.-Sat. only. Drinks 32-50F. Daily 11:30pm-dawn. V, MC.

Open Bar, 17, rue des Archives, 4ème (tel. 01 42 74 62 60; M. Hôtel-de-Ville). As its name suggests, Open Bar is open to the street and to any and every sex, gender, and preference. A stylish young crowd relaxes to the sounds of disco and house. One of the most fashionable gay establishments in town. Beer 30F, Cocktails 45F. Open daily noon-2am. Monthly ladies night. V, MC, AmEx.

Le Palace Gay Tea Dance, 8, rue Faubourg Montmartre, 9ème (tel. 01 42 46 10 87; M. Rue Montmartre). A fabulous place to meet on Sun. afternoons. Here, the queer elite sip drinks and gossip about less swanky gay and lesbian establishments.

Mostly techno music. Occasional male strip shows. Cover and 1 drink 40F before 4pm, after 4pm 60F. Both sexes welcome. Open Sun. 2-11:30pm.

Le Piano Zinc, 49, rue des Blancs Manteaux, 4ème (tel. 01 42 74 32 42; M. Rambuteau). According to some, *the* seasoned gay hangout in the Marais. The piano downstairs sparks campy homage performances to Judy, Liza, Eartha, Madonna, Bette, Grace Jones, and Edith Piaf. Xeroxed lyric sheets allow all to join in the bar theme song: *"Moi je suis dingue dingue dingue du Piano Zinc."* Happy hour 6-8pm, beer 10F, cocktails 37F. After 8pm, beer 14F, cocktails 44F. Open Tues.-Sun. 6pm-2am; piano bar open Tues.-Sun. 10pm-2am. V, MC, AmEx.

FESTIVALS AND OTHER SEASONAL EVENTS

At the slightest provocation, Parisians rush to the streets, drink, dance, and generally lose themselves in the spirit of the *fête* (festival) or *foire* (fair). While the city-wide Fête de la Musique (see below) and the pomp and splendor of Bastille Day are difficult to miss—even if you want to—some of the smaller festivities must be ferreted out. The **Office de Tourisme** (see page 92), distributes the multilingual *Saisons de Paris 96/97,* a booklet listing all the celebrations. The English information number (tel. 01 47 20 88 98 or 01 49 52 53 56) gives a weekly summary of current festivals, as does *Pariscope.* You can also get a listing of festivals from the **French Government Tourist Office** (see page 1) before you leave home.

Bastille Day. *Vive la République* and pass the champagne. The day starts with the army parading down the Champs-Elysées and ends with fireworks. The fireworks can be seen from any bridge on the Seine or from the Champ de Mars. Groups also gather in the 19ème where the hilly topography allows a view to the Trocadéro. Traditional street dances are held on the eve at the tip of Ile St-Louis (the Communist Party always throws its gala there), the Hôtel de Ville, pl. de la Contrescarpe, and pl. de la Bastille, where it all began. The so-called *Bals de Pompiers* take place in front of every fire station in the city and are free of charge and crowded with jubilant people. Unfortunately, the city also becomes a nightmarish combat zone of leering men tossing firecrackers under the feet of unsuspecting bystanders; avoid the metro and deserted areas if possible. July 14.

Christmas Eve. At midnight Notre-Dame becomes what it only claims to be the rest of the year: the cathedral of the city of Paris. Dec. 24.

Concours International de Danse de Paris (tel. 01 45 22 28 74 for information and auditions). Classical and contemporary dance competition at the Opéra Comique, pl. Boïeldieu, 2ème. Late Nov. to early Dec.

Course des Serveuses et Garçons de Café, starts and finishes at the Hôtel de Ville, 4ème (tel. 01 42 96 60 75). If you thought service was slow by necessity, let this race change your mind. Tuxedoed waiters sprint through the streets carrying a full bottle and glass on a tray. One day in mid-June; look for posters.

End of the Tour de France. Expect a huge crowd along the banks of the Seine on the Right Bank, as well as along the av. des Champs-Elysées. Join the crowd in the cheering; you may never see calves this strong again in your life. 4th Sun. in July.

Festival d'Art Sacré (tel. 01 45 61 54 99). Festival of sacred music in churches and cultural centers throughout Paris. Easter and Dec.

Festival d'Automne (tel. 01 42 96 96 94). Drama, ballet, and music arranged around a different theme each year. Many events held at the Théâtre du Chatelet, 1er; the Thèâtre de la Ville, 4ème; the Odéon-Thèâtre de l'Europe, 6ème; and the Opéra National de Paris Bastille, 12ème. Mid-Sept. to Dec.

Festival Chopin (tel. 01 45 00 22 19 or 01 45 00 69 75). From M. Porte Maillot, take bus 244 to Pré Catelan stop. A dozen concerts and recitals held at the Orangerie du parc de Bagatelle in the Bois de Boulogne. Not all Chopin, but all piano music, arranged each year around a different aspect of the Polish Francophile's *oeuvre.* Times and prices vary annually. Mid-June to mid-July.

Festival du Cinéma en Plein Air, parc de la Villette, 19ème (tel. 01 40 03 76 92; M. Porte de la Villette or Porte de Pantin). A screen is set up, seats are arranged in the Prairie du Triangle, and Paris sits down for its version of a drive-in. Movies focus on 1 theme, although exceptions are made for cult classics defying notions of theme and category. 1996 was *les liaisons dangereuses.* Rent a chair (for 40F) or bring a blanket. All films shown in *v.o.* Mid-July to mid-Aug., Tues.-Sun. 10:30pm.

Festival Foire St-Germain, 6ème (tel. 01 40 46 75 12). Antique and book fair in pl. St-Sulpice, and concerts in the Auditorium St-Germain (4, rue Félibien; tel. 01 46 33 87 03). Both free. Early June to July.

Festival Internationale de la Guitare (tel. 01 45 23 18 25). Concerts in many Parisian churches. Mid-Nov. to mid-Dec.

Festival du Marais, 68, rue François Miron, 4ème (tel. 01 48 87 60 08; M. St-Paul). Open-air classical music, theater, and exhibits animate the splendid courtyards and backyards of many of the beautiful *hôtels* of the district. Concerts held in the pl. des Vosges, at the Musée Cognacq-Jay, and elsewhere. Mid-June to mid July.

Festival de Musique de St-Denis (tel. 01 48 13 12 10). A 4-week classical and contemporary concert series, both instrumental and choral. Early June to early July.

Festival Musiqueen l'Ile (tel. 01 44 62 70 90). Chamber and classical music in some of the most exquisite-sounding churches in Paris: Ste-Chapelle, Eglise St-Louis, and Eglise St-Germain-des-Près. Mid-July to mid-Sept.

Festival de l'Orangerie de Sceaux (tel. 01 46 60 07 79) is a weekend series of chamber music concerts from mid-July to mid-Sept. Call for information.

Festival d'Orgue à St-Eustache, 2, rue du Jour, 1er (tel. 01 42 94 82 57; M. Châtelet-Les Halles). Organ concerts in the St-Eustache church. Tickets 70-120F, on sale at ARGOS, 34, rue de Laborde, 8ème (M. St-Augustin). Mid-June to early July.

Fête du Cinéma. Purchase 1 ticket at full price and receive a passport that admits you to an unlimited number of movies for the duration of the 3-day festival at a cost of 10F each. Most cinemas in Paris participate, so choose your first film carefully; the maximum ticket price varies considerably from theater to theater. Expect long lines and get there at least 30min. early for popular movies. Look for posters or ask at cinemas for the specific dates (around June 28).

Fête de l'Humanité, parc de la Courneuve. Take the metro to Porte de la Villette and then 1 of the special buses. The fair of the Communist Party—like nothing you've ever seen. Recent entertainers have included Charles Mingus, Marcel Marceau, and the Bolshoi Ballet. A cross between the Illinois State Fair and Woodstock; you don't have to be a Communist to enjoy it. 2nd or 3rd week of Sept.

Fête de la Musique (tel. 01 40 03 94 70). Also called *"faîtes de la musique"* (make music!), this summer solstice celebration gives everyone in the city the chance to make as much of a racket as possible; noise laws don't apply on this day. Closet musicians fill the streets, strumming everything from banjos to Russian balalaikas. Major concerts at La Villette, pl. de la Bastille, and pl. de la République. Partying in all open spaces. Avoid the metro to evade asphyxiation. Free. June 21.

Fêtes du Pont Neuf (tel. 01 42 77 92 26; M. Pont Neuf). The bridge is opened for dancing, music, street artists, and minstrels. A weekend in late June.

Fête à Neu-Neu, Bois de Boulogne, Chemin du Lac Supérieur, 16ème (tel. 01 46 27 52 29). A big amusement park. Late Aug. to early Oct.

Fête des Vendanges à Montmartre, rue Saules, 18ème (tel. 01 42 62 21 21; M. Lamarck-Caulaincourt). A celebration of the wine-grape harvest from Montmartre's own vineyards. Features costumed picking and tromping of the last vineyard's grapes. First Sat. in Oct.

Feux de la St-Jean (tel. 01 45 08 55 61). Magnificent fireworks at 11pm on the quai St-Bernard, 5ème, in honor of the Feast of St. John the Baptist. For a spectacular bird's-eye view of the spectacle, stand in front of the Sacré-Coeur. Call for verification of the location. June 24.

Foire du Trône, Reuilly Lawn, Bois de Vincennes, 12ème (tel. 01 46 27 52 29; M. Porte Dorée). A gigantic amusement park. Open Sun.-Thurs. 2pm-midnight, Fri., Sat., and holidays 2pm-1am. End of March to early June.

Grandes Eaux Musicales de Versailles, Parc du Château de Versailles (tel. 01 39 50 36 22). Weekly outdoor concerts and fountain displays throughout the park. Every Sunday early May to mid-Oct. and Aug. 15.

La Grande Parade de Montmartre, 18ème (tel. 01 42 62 21 21). This newly inaugurated event is just what it sounds like—a big parade. Marching bands from across the world join with Montmartre locals and various costumed brigades (including green Santa Clauses) to parade across the *butte.* New Year's Day.

18h-18F is a newly inaugurated film festival sponsored by the *Mairie* of Paris. A seat for the 18h (6pm) showing of a film at any of the participating theaters throughout Paris will cost 18F. Look for posters or inquire at cinemas. Feb. 14-20.

Journées du Patrimoine (tel. 01 44 61 21 50) are the days each year when palaces, ministries, and some townhouses open to the public. Free. Sept.

Musique en Sorbonne, 47, rue des Ecoles, 5ème (tel. 01 42 62 71 71 for information and to audition; M. Maubert-Mutualité). Classical music. Admission 60-140F. Late June to early July.

New Year's Eve. Bd. St-Michel and the Champs-Elysées are transformed into pedestrian malls, much to the dismay of the cops, who still attempt to direct traffic. More of the brouhaha that you tried to avoid on the 14th of July.

Piscinéma, in the Piscine des Halles. Before the Fête du Cinéma, the **Vidéothèque de Paris** (2, Grande Galerie, at Porte St-Eustache in the Forum des Halles, 1er; tel. 01 44 76 62 00) hosts this 3-night event which turns movie-watching into a spectator sport. Literally. Don your bathing suit, tread water, and watch a specially selected classic projected on a big screen above the pool. Video clips and documentaries with water themes play in the changing rooms and at the entrance to the pool. Call for tickets and film info. In late June.

Rallye Paris-Deauville (tel. 01 46 24 37 38). 100 vintage cars assemble at the Trocadéro fountains to leave for Deauville (in Normandy). 7am on a Fri. in early Oct.

La Saison Musicale de L'Abbaye de Royaumont consists of weekend concerts in the hall of a 13th-century monastery. The *abbaye* arranges for free transportation from the train station in nearby Viarmes. Tickets 115F, students and seniors 90F. call 01 34 68 05 50 for info and reservations. From mid-June to late Sept.

Le Temps des Livres (tel. 01 49 54 68 64). Debates, open-houses, lectures, and celebrations with books throughout France. Mid- to late Oct.

Les Trois Heures de Paris (tel. 01 49 77 06 40). A day-long regatta on the Seine. Races between pont d'Austerlitz and Ile St-Louis. On a Sun. in May.

La Villette Jazz Festival, parc de la Villette (tel. 01 40 03 75 75 or 01 44 84 44 84; M. Porte de Pantin). A week-long celebration of jazz from big bands to new international talents, as well as seminars, films, and sculptural exhibits. 1996 saw Max Roach, Cecil Taylor, and B.B. King. Marching bands parade every day and an enormous picnic closes the festival. Some concerts are free; call for info and ticket prices. A *forfait-soirée* gives access to a number of events for 1 night of the festival for 170F, students and seniors, 135F. Late June to early July.

PARIS

Shopping

The most famous of Paris's clothing boutiques skirt the **rue du Faubourg St-Honoré,** which runs northwest through the 8ème. Gawk at the bags at **Hermès** (no. 24), the classically cut velour at **Sonia Rykiel** (no. 70), the untouchables of all types at **Yves Saint Laurent** (no. 38), and the austere design at the Japanese **Ashida** (no. 34). **Pierre Balmain, Karl Lagerfeld,** and **Versace** boutiques mingle nearby. (Pierre Cardin designs for Balmain; Karl Lagerfeld designs for Chanel.) The streets projecting from **pl. des Victoires** (1er and 2ème) harbor more *maisons de couture.* Running southwest from the Rond Point des Champs-Elysées, **av. de Montaigne** flaunts the houses of **Christian Dior** (no. 32), **Chanel** (no. 42), **Valentino** (no. 17-19), and **Nina Ricci** (no. 39). **Pierre Cardin** rests regally in pl. François 1er. The windows in **pl. Vendôme** and along **rue de la Paix** (north towards the Opéra) glitter with the designs of **Cartier, Van Cleef & Arpels,** and others of the city's jewelry overlords.

The sad truth is that Paris, though fashionable to a fault, is not a budget shopper's haven. Still, even some of the *plus haute* of the city's *haute couture* boutiques join in the twice-yearly *soldes* (sales) that sweep the city in January and late June or early July. Find what you like on bd. St-Germain, but hunt around for better bargains around rue de Seine and the top of bd. St-Michel. Boutiques in the Marais and the Bastille tend to be more trendy.

Magasins de troc are large shops that resell clothes bought and returned at more expensive stores. Given the prices at Chanel and Dior, the bargains can be astonishing. Try **Troc Mod,** 230, av. du Maine, 14ème (tel. 01 45 40 45 93; M. Alésia; open

June-Aug. Tues.-Sat. 11am-7pm; Sept.-May Tues.-Sat. 10am-7pm); **Troc'Eve,** 25, rue Violet, 15ème (tel. 01 45 79 38 36; M. Dupleix; open Tues.-Sat. 10am-7pm); **Mouton à Cinq Pattes,** 8-10-18, rue St-Placide, 6ème (tel. 01 45 48 86 26; M. Sèvres-Babylone), and at 19, rue Grégoire de Tours, 6ème (tel. 01 43 29 73 56; M. Odéon; both open Mon.-Fri. 10:30am-7:30pm, Sat. 10:30am-8pm; V, MC, AmEx); **Réciproque,** king of *trocs* with outlets at 92, 95, 101, and 123, rue de la Pompe, 16ème (tel. 01 47 04 30 28; M. Pompe; open Tues.-Sat. 10:30am-7pm).

You can check it all out at one of Paris's numerous **grands magasins** (department stores), many of which have snazzy turn-of-the-century architecture. **Galeries Lafayette,** 40, bd. Haussmann, 9ème (tel. 01 42 82 34 56; open Mon.-Sat. 9:30am-6:45pm; V, MC, AmEx), offers the ultimate in high-quality department store fare. Neighbor **Au Printemps,** 64, bd. Haussmann, 9ème (tel. 01 42 82 50 00; M. Chaussée d'Antin), also vies for the title of best *grand magasin.* As elegant as the Galeries Lafayette, it claims to be the "Most Parisian Department Store" (open Mon.-Sat. 9:30am-7pm; V, MC, AmEx). **Bon Marché,** 3, rue de Sèvres, 7ème (tel. 01 44 39 80 00; M. Sèvres-Babylone), is Paris's oldest department store and perhaps its best—as chic as Galeries Lafayette without the tourists and chaos (open Mon.-Sat. 9:30am-7pm; V, MC, AmEx). Along the Right Bank, **Samaritaine,** 19, rue de la Monnaie, 1er (tel. 01 40 41 20 20; M. Pont-Neuf), is strong on housewares but has less designer-wear than its more upscale counterparts (open Mon.-Wed. and Fri.-Sat. 9:30am-7pm, Thurs. 9:30am-10pm; V, MC, AmEx). The **Bazar de l'Hôtel de Ville (BHV),** 52, rue de Rivoli, 4ème (tel. 01 42 74 90 00; M. Hôtel de Ville), has huge bargains on housewares but less fashion (open Mon.-Tues. and Thurs.-Sat. 9:30am-7pm, Wed. 9:30am-10pm; V, MC, AmEx). **Tati,** 11, pl. de la République, 3ème (tel. 01 48 87 72 81; M. République); 106, rue Faubourg du Temple, 11ème (tel. 01 43 57 92 80; M. Belleville); 140, rue de Rennes, 6ème (tel. 01 45 48 68 31; M. Montparnasse); and 4, bd. de Rochechouart, 18ème (tel. 01 42 55 13 09; M. Barbès-Rochechouart), is the original bargain store (hours vary, but open roughly Mon.-Sat. 10am-7pm).

Books *(livres)* in France are much more expensive than in North America; scope the banks of the Seine, where *bouquinistes* sell their multilingual wares from little green boxes. The most famous English bookseller is **Shakespeare and Co.,** 37, rue de la Bûcherie, 5ème (M. St-Michel), across the Seine from Notre-Dame. Run by George Whitman (alleged great-grandson of Walt), this niche of bohemian pedantry tries to re-create the atmosphere of Sylvia Beach's original establishment at 8, rue Dupuytren and later at 12, rue de l'Odéon, extraordinary gathering spots for expatriate writers of the 20s like Joyce and Hemingway. Shakespeare and Co.'s current location and owner have absolutely no official link to Beach or any other Lost Generation notables (open daily noon-midnight). For an extensive selection of American literature and guidebooks, find **Brentano's,** 37, av. de l'Opéra, 2ème (tel. 01 42 61 52 50; M. Opéra; open Mon.-Sat. 10am-7pm; V, MC). The **Village Voice,** 6, rue Princesse, 6ème (tel. 01 46 33 36 47; M. Mabillon), has terrific sci-fi and a decent collection of feminist literature, plus the *Village Voice* (open Mon. 2-8pm, Tues.-Sat. 11am-8pm; V, MC, AmEx). **W.H. Smith,** 248, rue de Rivoli, 1er (tel. 01 44 77 88 99; M. Concorde), has magazines and British literature. The Sunday *New York Times* is available on Tuesday (open Mon.-Sat. 9:30am-7pm, Sun. 1pm-6pm; V, MC). **Gibert Jeune,** 5, pl. St-Michel (tel. 01 43 25 71 19; M. St-Michel), is the best bookstore in town, though mostly French. **Les Mots à la Bouche,** 6, rue Ste-Croix-de-la-Bretonnerie, 4ème (tel. 01 42 78 88 30; M. Hôtel-de-Ville), is a serene bookstore with French and English titles, magazines, and newsletters of interest to both gay men and lesbians (open Mon.-Sat. 11am-11pm, Sun. 2-8pm; V, MC). Take kids to **Chantelivre,** 13, rue de Sèvres, 6ème (tel. 01 45 48 87 90; M. Sèvres-Babylone), a children's literary playground with some English titles (open Mon. 1-6:50pm, Tues.-Sat. 10am-6:50pm; V, MC over 100F). At **Un Regard Moderne,** 10, rue Git-le-Coeur, 6ème (tel. 01 43 29 13 93; M. St-Michel), underground comic books (please, "graphic novels") rub shoulders with graphic maybe-not-art in a cramped room with books piled from floor to ceiling. This is the place to find that delightful piece of ultra-violence or arty porn you yearn for (open Mon.-Sat. 11am-8pm; V, MC).

CDs, records, and **cassettes** are luxury goods here (CDs 100F and up). Used LPs *(disques d'occasion)* can be found at *marchés aux puces* (flea markets, see below). In general, you'll find larger selections of certain musical types (French, African, and anything by Tom Waits) than in North America. **B.P.M.,** 1, rue Keller, 11*ème* (tel. 01 40 21 02 88; M. Bastille), caters to your rave needs; it serves as a clubhouse, info point, and music store for house and techno fans (open Mon.-Sat. noon-8pm). **Gibert Joseph,** 26, bd. St-Michel, 6*ème* (tel. 01 44 41 88 88; M. Cluny-Sorbonne) stocks new and used tapes, CDs, and LPs in the basement. (Open Mon.-Sat. 9:30am-7:30pm; V, MC.) Stop in at **FNAC (Fédération Nationale des Achats de Cadres),** with branches throughout the city: **Montparnasse,** 136, rue des Rennes, 6*ème* (tel. 01 49 54 30 00; M. Rennes); **Etoile**, 26-30, av. des Ternes, 17*ème* (tel. 01 44 09 18 00; M. Ternes); **Forum des Halles,** 1-7, rue Porte Lescot, 1*er* (tel. 01 40 41 40 00; M. Les Halles); and **Italiens,** 24, bd. des Italiens, 9*ème* (tel. 01 48 01 02 03; M. Opéra). All locations stock a ton of tapes, CDs, and stereo equipment. The Italiens branch screens videos all day in a public viewing room. (Montparnasse, Etoile, and Les Halles open Mon.-Sat. 10am-7:30pm; Italiens open Mon.-Sat. 10am-midnight. V, MC.) If it's been recorded, it's probably at **Virgin Megastore,** 52-60, av. des Champs-Elysées, 8*ème* (tel. 01 49 53 50 00; M. Franklin Roosevelt). This huge store, complete with a restaurant and listening stations, has recordings you've never heard of but can't do without (open Mon.-Sat. 10am-midnight, Sun. noon-midnight; V, MC).

PARIS

MARKETS

Although the days are long gone when the eagle-eyed might spot Rembrandt's smudged signature in the corner of a 5F painting, the wise shopper can still strike bargains in Paris's swarm of flea markets. Be aware that in any of these markets, pickpockets will be watching your wallet as well as the merchants.

A Paris flea market has everything: vendors sell food, antiques, second-hand clothing (plus pricier "vintage clothing"), and such random other desirables as books, records, and hair supplies. Arrive early and be prepared to bargain. The **Marché aux Puces de St-Ouen,** 17*ème* (M. Porte de Clignancourt; Sat.-Mon. 7am-7:30pm), is the largest flea market in Paris and one of the largest in Europe. It's huge. Huge. Almost scary, it's so huge. It sells everything from antiques to suede jackets (from 250F). (Huge.) The one at the **Porte de Vanves,** 14*ème* (M. Porte de Vanves; Sat.-Sun. 7:30am-noon), is less impressive and less crowded. The **Marché du Temple,** Carreau du Temple, 3*ème* (M. Temple), on the corner of rue Dupetit Thouars and rue de Picardie, has clothes (especially leathers and furs) at wholesale prices, subject to haggling (open Tues.-Fri. 9am-12:30pm, Sat.-Sun. 9am-1pm).

Pl. Louis Lépine, on the Ile de la Cité, 4*ème* (M. Cité), blooms with color as the **Marché aux Fleurs** carpets the small square (open Mon.-Sat. 9am-7pm). On Sunday, a bird and animal market appears in its stead, starring goldfish, rabbits, gerbils, and pet food stalls (open 9am-6pm). For antique books, prints, or posters, check out the *bouquinistes* stalls that line the Right Bank of the Seine from the Louvre past the Hôtel de Ville and the Left Bank, from quai de Conti to quai de Montebello.

Daytrips from Paris

VERSAILLES

A child during the aristocratic insurgency called the Fronde, Louis XIV is said to have entered his father's bedchamber one night to find (and frighten away) an assassin. Scared of conniving aristocrats for the rest of his life, Louis fled Paris for the suburbs. Settling in the town of Versailles, he turned his father's hunting lodge into a royal residence. The new court became the center of noble life; over a thousand of France's greatest aristocrats vied for the king's favor there. Busily attending to Louis XIV's wake-up *(levée)* and bed-going *(coucher)* rituals, they had little time for subversion.

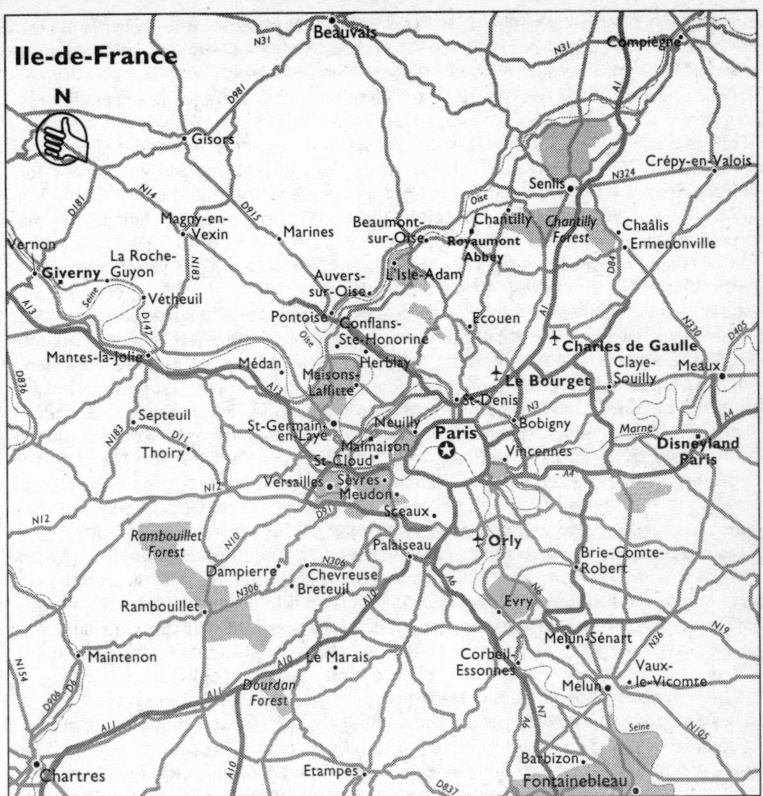

Louis had successfully drawn the high nobility away from their fiefs and under his watchful eye, but he outlawed duels at court, to be extra safe.

Entrance A, to the right as you enter the North Wing, is the main entry for individual visitors. Lines can be long, especially on Sundays and summer afternoons. This door leads to the *State Apartments of the King and Queen,* the War and Peace Drawing Rooms; the *Galerie des Glaces* (Hall of Mirrors); and the dauphin's and children's apartments. You need to take guided tours to see the rest. Most of these rooms are now a museum of French history, full of pictures of the French aristocracy. Get a guide of some kind, or the symbolic freight of the architecture and artwork will pass you by. Audioguides (28F) last about an hour and require an ID deposit; they also don't necessarily follow the sequence of the actual visit. The best written guide is by Daniel Meyer, a curator of the château (50F for 96 pages).

The general admission ticket starts you off in the **Musée de l'Histoire de France,** created in 1837 by Louis-Philippe to celebrate his country's glory. Along its textured walls hang portraits of men and women who shaped the course of French history. Each of the drawing rooms in the **State Apartments** is dedicated to a mythological god—Hercules, Mars, and the ever-present Apollo (the Sun King identified with the Sun God), etc. Maybe less brilliant than you'd expect, the gilt wood is still something else. Framed by the **War and Peace Drawing Rooms** is the **Hall of Mirrors,** a somewhat gloomy passageway until Mansart added a series of mirrored panels, joined together and set in wooden frames, to double the room's light. Each of these mirrors was the largest that 17th-century technology could produce; the ensemble was an unbelievable extravagance. Many of the mirrors are old and cloudy, yet visitors still get a thrill from looking down the Hall past the mirror-filled arches, gold figures, and chandeliers. This hall is where in 1871 Wilhelm of Prussia became Kaiser Wilhelm I of Germany; fifty years later, in 1919, a vengeful France forced Germany to sign the ruinous Treaty of Versailles in the very room of that country's birth.

Guided tours allow you to skip long lines and begin at Entrance D. Seven different tours are offered, though only three are in English, and the English of the tour guides varies in quality. A tour of the **Opera,** given a few times per day, is one of the best, as is the "best-of-Versailles" tour. Other tours are fairly uninspiring and will appeal only to French-aristocracy addicts. Expect empty rooms with limited decoration—Versailles was sacked during the Revolution and only a smidgen of its original glory has been restored. (1hr. tours 25F, under 7 free; 2hr. tours 45F, ages 7-17 34F, under 7 free. Château open May-Sept. Tues.-Sun. 9am-6:30pm; Oct.-April 9am-5:30pm. Last entry 30min. before closing. Admission to the palace 42F; ages 18-25, over 60, and Sun. 28F; the *carte musée* admits to Versailles. For more on the *carte,* see page 132.)

Versailles' gardens are breathtaking and enormous, the palace's perfect match. Numerous artists—Le Brun, Mansart, Coysevox—erected statues and fountains here, with master gardener André Le Nôtre providing the master plan. Just behind the château, the **Latone Parterre** holds the **Bassin de Latone,** where Latona, mother of Diana and Apollo, shields her children from the attack of people whom Jupiter is turning into frogs. Past the Latona group lies the **Tapis Vert (Green Carpet),** the central strip of grass linking the château to the much-photographed **Fountain of Apollo.** Pulled by four prancing horses, the Sun King as Sun God rises out of dark water to enlighten the world. On the north side of the garden is Marsy's incredible **Bassin d'Encelade.** One of the giants who tried to unseat Jupiter from Mount Olympus, Enceladus cries in agony under the weight of rocks that Jupiter has used to bury him. When the fountains are turned on, a 25m jet bursts from Enceladus's mouth. The culmination of any visit to the gardens is the **Fountain of Neptune,** the largest of all the fountains, with 99 water jets and a menacing Neptune rising from the deep. (Gardens open sunrise-sundown. Free, except May-Sept. Sun. 20F.)

The **Trianons,** cozy palaces designed to give the royal family some privacy, prove that even kings and queens need a break. Built by Mansart, the single-story, marble-decorated **Grand Trianon** was intended to be a meeker château in which the king could reside alone with his family if need be. All but four rooms of the **Petit Trianon,** built for Louis XV and Mme. de Pompadour, are being restored; don't bother going in. (Trianons open May-Sept. Tues.-Sat. 10am-6:30pm; Oct.-April Tues.-Sun. 10am-12:30pm and 2-5:30pm. Admission to the Grand Trianon 25F, reduced 15F; to the Petit Trianon 15F, reduced 10F; to both 30F, reduced 20F. Trams leave from behind the main palace to the Trianons; roundtrip 31F, ages 3-12 19F.) Closed to the public, **Le Hameau** (the Queen's Hamlet) is a group of Norman cottages built so that Marie-Antoinette could play peasant, to the great disgust of the real thing.

Sundays from 3:30 to 5pm from May through September, come to see (and hear) the **Grandes Eaux Musicales,** when the 24 fountains are in full operation and musically accompanied. Aglitter with geysers, the park becomes the sensuous feast it was designed to be. A smaller version, the *grande perspective,* runs from11:15 to 11:35am. A free pamphlet suggests a walking path. The same info is in the Meyer guide. (Admission to gardens during *Grandes Eaux* 20F.)

The **Grande Fête de Nuit,** a musical and fireworks extravaganza, imitates the huge *fêtes* of Louis XIV. The garden at Versailles had to be finished in 1664 in time for one such party, the Fête of the Enchanted Isle, for which Molière wrote an up-to-the-minute *masque* (theatrical vignette). (*Fêtes* held at the Neptune Fountain 4 Sat. each summer, 10pm. 80min. 60-185F, reduced rates for children. Call 01 39 59 36 22 for dates and ticket info.) Tickets go on sale at the tourist office and box offices within Paris. Doors open one hour before the show; enter at 2, bd. de la Reine.

Take the **RER** C5 from Paris's M. Invalides to the Versailles Rive Gauche station (every 15min., 35-40min., 26F roundtrip). Any train whose label begins in "V" will do. Buy your RER ticket *before* getting to the platform; though your metro ticket will get you onto the train, it will not get you through the RER turnstiles at Versailles.

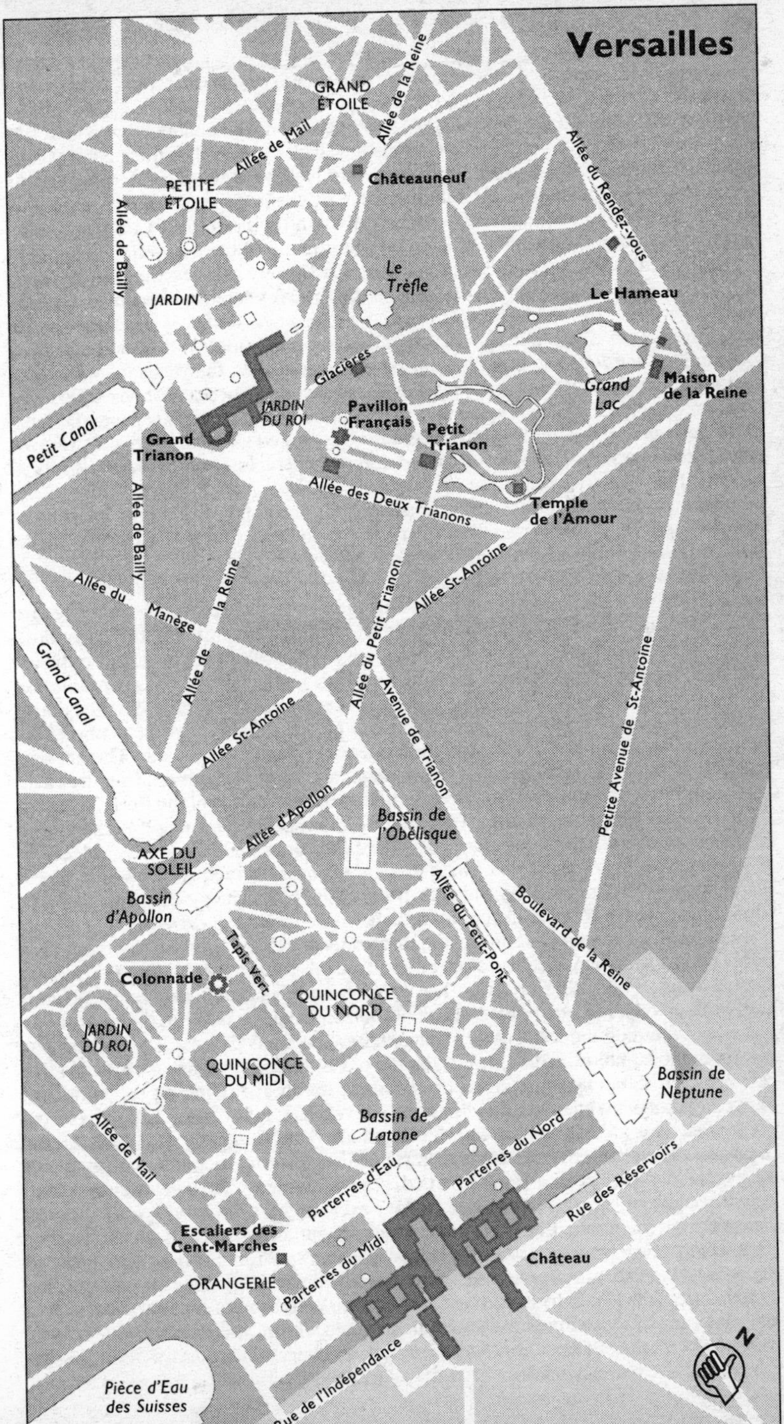

Versailles

GRAND ÉTOILE
Allée de la Reine
Allée de Mail
Châteauneuf
Allée du Rendez-vous
PETITE ÉTOILE
Allée de Bailly
Le Trèfle
JARDIN
Le Hameau
Glacières
Grand Lac
Maison de la Reine
JARDIN DU ROI
Pavillon Français
Petit Trianon
Petit Canal
Grand Trianon
Allée des Deux Trianons
Temple de l'Amour
Allée de Bailly
Allée St-Antoine
Allée du Manège
Allée de la Reine
Allée du Petit Trianon
Grand Canal
Avenue de Trianon
Allée St-Antoine
Petite Avenue de St-Antoine
Allée d'Apollon
Bassin de l'Obélisque
AXE DU SOLEIL
Bassin d'Apollon
Allée du Petit-Pont
Boulevard de la Reine
Tapis Vert
Colonnade
QUINCONCE DU NORD
JARDIN DU ROI
QUINCONCE DU MIDI
Bassin de Neptune
Allée de Mail
Bassin de Latone
Parterres du Nord
Parterres d'Eau
Rue des Réservoirs
Escaliers des Cent-Marches
Château
ORANGERIE
Parterres du Midi
Rue de l'Indépendance
Pièce d'Eau des Suisses
N

PARIS

CHARTRES

The Cathedral

The stunning **Cathédrale de Chartres** is one of the most sublime creations of the Middle Ages. In 876, Charlemagne's grandson, Charles the Bald, made a gift to Chartres of the *Sancta Camisia,* the cloth believed to have been worn by Mary when she gave birth to Christ ever since. Pilgrims have flocked to the cathedral to see the sacred relic. In 911 its magic was confirmed when the citizens of Chartres, under attack from Vikings, placed the relic on view at the top of the city wall. The infidels ran away, and their leader Rollin converted to Christianity and became the first duke of Normandy. Disaster struck in 1194 when the third fire in 200 years burned all but the enormous crypts, the new west tower, and the Royal Portal. When they discovered that Mary's relic (hidden in the crypt by three loyal priests who stayed with it, sweating out the fire) had emerged unsinged by the flames, the villagers took it as a sign not only of Mary's love but her desire for a better cathedral. Clerics seized the moment by soliciting funds on a grand scale and building at a furious pace: the bulk of the cathedral was completed by 1223 and consecrated in 1260. Spared by bureaucratic inefficiency after being condemned during the Revolution, Chartres is now perhaps the finest surviving example of Gothic architecture, sculpture, and stained glass in the world. The record-breaking speed of its construction means that it preserves, uncorrupted, one shining moment of the early Gothic era, with an extraordinary fusion of Romanesque and Gothic architectural motifs.

The exterior of the church is marked by three entrances. The famous 12th-century statues of the Royal Portal present an assembly of Old Testament figures at the height of late Romanesque sculpture. Those in the central bay, attributed to the "Master of Chartres," are especially beautiful: their elongated, simple figures have an unparalleled stillness and elegance. The 13th-century North and South Porch represent the life of Mary and Christ triumphant, respectively. On the North Porch, John the Baptist sadly examines the disc he holds; decorated with a lamb and cross, it symbolically predicts the coming of Christ and the imminence of John's own death. The left bay tells the story of the Visitation and shows Mary and Elizabeth turning to greet each other, like two nuns chatting privately in their convent's cloister.

Most of the glass dates from the 13th century and was saved from both World Wars by authorities, who dismantled over 3000 square meters and stored them piece by piece until the end of hostilities. The merchant sponsors of each window are shown in the lower panels, giving a record of daily life in the 13th century. The famous "Blue Virgin" window, an object of pilgrimage and one of the few pieces of 12th-century glass to survive the fire, is visible at the first window of the choir, on the right. The window has four panels with a large picture of the Virgin Mary dressed in blue (hence its name), holding Christ on her lap; the other panes of glass were 13th-century additions. The façade holds the rest of the 12th-century glass: on the right is the tree of Jesse and on the left is the Passion and Resurrection of Christ. The center window is the Incarnation, which shows the life of Christ from the Annunciation to the ride into Jerusalem. Mary is given the place of honor at the top of the window, flanked by kneeling angels. Bring binoculars if you can; many of the stories told by the stained glass are barely visible with the naked eye. Also remember to look down: the mosaic labyrinth provided a path for the penitent pilgrim to follow on hands and knees, and the floor's slope permitted the cathedral to be washed—particularly necessary because of pilgrims billeted on its floor every night.

World-renowned tour guide Malcolm Miller, an authority on Gothic architecture, has brought the cathedral to life for English-speaking visitors for the past 38 years. Miller is the greatest thing since sliced bread. He knows everything, presents it brilliantly, and makes each tour different. If you can, take both of his tours when you visit. You may want to invest in a 40F guide as well. (1¼hr. tours April-Jan. Mon.-Sat. noon and 2:45pm. 30F, students 20F. Avoid Sat. and Tues.—busy days in the high season. Private tours on request: tel. 01 37 28 15 58; fax 01 37 28 33 03. Tours also offered in German and French; check inside the cathedral for more info.)

The *Sancta Camisia* is on display with other memorabilia in the cathedral's east end, in the **treasury** (open Mon.-Sat. 10am-noon and 2-6pm, Sun. and holidays 2-6pm; Oct. 16-March 15 Mon.-Sat. 10am-noon and 2:30-4:30pm, Sun. and holidays 2-5pm; free). Climb the south tower and cross over to the north tower, **Tour Jehan-de-Beauce,** named after its architect and completed in 1513, for a magnificent look at the cathedral roof, its flying buttresses, and the city below. A snazzy example of flamboyant Gothic, it's also a neat contrast to its more sedate neighbor (and predecessor by 300 years), the octagonal steeple built before the 1194 fire. (Towers open April-Sept. Mon.-Sat. 9:30–5:30pm, Sun. 2-5:30pm. Call for winter hours. Admission 14F, ages 12-17 10F, under 12 free.)

The cathedral is open daily in summer from 7:30am to 7:30pm and in winter from 7:30am to 7pm. No casual visits are allowed Saturdays from 5:45 to 7pm or Sundays from 9:15 to 11am because of religious services. If you want the true Chartres experience, however, try attending one of these services. Call the tourist office (see below) for information on concerts in the cathedral, as well as the annual student pilgrimage in late May and other festivals throughout the year.

The Town

Rightly called a *ville d'art* (city of art), Chartres celebrates the medieval crafts showcased in its cathedral. In addition to the workshops and galleries, the downtown area is a vision to behold (a sight unto itself, one might say). The charming *vieille ville* has the cobblestone staircases, gabled roofs, half-timbered houses, and iron lamps of a village almost forgotten by time. Old streets are named for the trades once practiced there; rue de la Poissonerie, for example, was home to the fishmonger. Charming stone bridges and iron-trimmed walkways cross the Eure River. Although the town is surrounded by flat wheat fields, Chartres is built on a hill, and some of the best views of the cathedral can be found by walking down the well-marked tourist circuit. Free maps are available from the tourist office.

The **tourist office** (tel. 01 37 21 50 00), opposite the cathedral's main entrance, helps find accommodations in and near Chartres (10F fee), suggests restaurants, has brochures, and gives a map marked with a walking tour. For 35F, you can use an audioguide to see the old city. (40F for 2 people, 1½hr. tour; English available; must be returned while the office is open: May-Sept. Mon.-Fri. 9:30am-6:45pm, Sat. 9:30am-6pm, Sun. 10:30am-12:30pm and 2:30-5:30pm; Oct.-April Mon.-Fri. 9:30am-6pm, Sat. 9:30am-5pm, Sun. 10:30am-1pm.)

Le Musée des Beaux-Arts, 29, Cloître Notre-Dame (tel. 01 37 36 41 39), next to the cathedral in the 17th- and 18th-century former Episcopal palace, includes works by Zurbarán, Holbein, and Vlaminck, plus local scenes and polychrome statues from the 13th century on (open Wed.-Mon. 10am-6pm; Nov.-March 10am-noon and 2-5pm; admission 10F, students and seniors 5F). **La Galerie du Vitrail,** 17, rue du Cloître Notre-Dame (tel. 01 37 36 10 03), is an expensive and impressive stained glass store. Prices range from 200 to 2000F, but you don't have to buy to enjoy (open April-Oct. Tues.-Sat. 9:45am-7pm; Nov.-March 9:45am-1pm and 2-6:30pm).

Chartres is accessible by **trains** from Paris's Gare Montparnasse (1 per hr., 1hr., roundtrip 138F; in Paris call 08 36 35 35 35 for info; in Chartres call 01 47 20 50 50). To reach the cathedral from the station, walk straight to the pl. de Châtelet, turn left onto the *place,* turn right onto rue Ste-Même, then left onto rue Jean Moulin.

ST-DENIS

The home of the famed **Basilique St-Denis,** the burial place of France's kings and queens, this town is named after the missionary bishop Denis. According to legend, Denis was beheaded by the Romans in Montmartre in AD 250 and walked north carrying his head until he reached this village and was buried here in a plowed field. Today, St-Denis (M. St-Denis-Basilique) is a working-class town with a large, vibrant population of West and North African immigrants, and a most amazing church.

Originally, St-Denis was a little church dedicated to the saint and the repository of French royal tombs. In 1136, Abbot Suger began rebuilding in a revolutionary style. Dissatisfied with dark, heavy Romanesque interiors, with their small windows and forests of thick columns, he brought together already-known architectural elements to create the first Gothic church. The vaulted arches of the nave funneled the weight of the roof into a few points, supported with a few long, narrow columns inside and flying buttresses outside. Freed from the burden of supporting the roof, the walls could be pierced with huge stained-glass windows and could even disappear completely in some places. The chapels around the first ambulatory have no walls between them, creating a second ambulatory that encircles the first.

Suger himself died in 1151, well before most of his basilica was finished. His successors altered his plans slightly, creating an unusually wide transept with magnificent rose windows that gave much-needed space to bury the ever-growing number of dead monarchs. In 1593, Henri IV converted to Catholicism here with his famous statement: "Paris is well worth a mass." He was buried here in 1610 with the rest of France's Catholic kings. St-Denis' royal ties incurred the wrath of the Revolution, and most of its tombs were desecrated or destroyed. With the restoration of the monarchy in 1815, Louis XVIII ordered that the necropolis be reestablished, beginning with the burial (in great pomp) of Louis XVI and Marie-Antoinette.

Virtually all of St-Denis' original windows were destroyed by Revolutionaries. In the front of the ambulatory you can still find some of the 12th-century glass. Look at the bottom panes and you'll see something other than biblical tales—Abbot Suger put little pictures of himself in the windows (he had his name written above to make sure everyone recognized him). The room on the left of the church (outside the necropolis) contains the royal family's funerary garments. (Church open daily May-Sept. 10am-7pm; Oct.-April 10am-5pm. Admission 25F, seniors and students 20F, under 18 10F. Ticket booth closes 30min. before church. Tours in French daily at 10:30 and 11:30am, and 3, 3:45, and 4:30pm. Free organ concerts Sun. 11:15am.)

VAUX-LE-VICOMTE

Some might consider **Vaux-le-Vicomte** a hut compared to Versailles in terms of size and opulence. But as Le Vau, Le Brun, and Le Nôtre's first masterpiece, it is in many ways the more coherent creation and the place you'd more likely call home. Nicolas Fouquet, Louis XIV's Minister of Finance, assembled the team of architect, artist, and landscaper to build Vaux for him between 1656 and 1661. The château itself (tel. 01 64 14 41 90) recalls both the grandeur of a Roman past, with its rusticated columns, and a French fort, complete with squat walls and moat. Notice the ornate scripted Fs around the château, and keep an eye out for the ever-present squirrel, Fouquet's industrious symbol, and the tower with three battlements, his second wife's crest. The **Minister's Bedchamber** sports an opulent red and gold bed under an allegorical ceiling in which Apollo bears the lights of the world. **Mme. Fouquet's Closet** once had walls lined with small mirrors, the forerunner of Versailles's Hall of Mirrors. In the **Square Room,** Le Brun's portrait of Fouquet hangs over the fireplace, and exquisite beams decorate the Louis XIII-style ceiling.

Vaux-le-Vicomte presented André Le Nôtre with his first chance to create an entire formal garden. Three villages, a small château, and many trees were destroyed to open up space, though countless trees were later replanted to stress the contrast between order and wilderness. Even a river was rerouted to provide the desired effect. The **Pool of the Crown,** named for the gold crown at its center, is the most ornate of the garden pools. The **Water Mirror,** farther down the central walkway, was designed to reflect the château perfectly. Climb to the **Farnese Hercules** (the vanishing point when you look from the castle), and survey the scene before going.

Vaux is 60km out of Paris. By **car,** take route A4 or A6 from Paris and exit at Val-Maubué or Melun, respectively. Head toward Meaux on N36 and follow the signs. Or take the **train** to Melun on the SNCF *banlieue* line (every 15-30min. from Gare du Nord or Les Halles, 45min., 80F roundtrip). To carry you the last 6km, a **taxi** will cost around 75F each way (Sun. 100F; pick one up at the *gare;* call 01 64 52 51 50 from

Vaux). Fit troopers might not mind the 70- to 90-minute hike for at least one part of the trip, but should be prepared to jump off the shoulder-less highway and into the grass at any minute. To **walk,** follow av. de Thiers through its many name-changes to highway 36 (direction: "Meaux") and follow signs to Vaux-Le-Vicomte.

On Saturday evenings from May to mid-October (8:30-11pm), the candlelit château reminds one of a wedding cake. The fountains in the gardens are turned on from 3 to 6pm every second and last Saturday of the month from April to October. (Château open April-Oct. Mon.-Sat. 10am-1pm and 2-6pm, Sun. and holidays 10am-6pm; last entry 5:30pm daily. Visits by appointment in winter; call for info. Gardens open daily 10am-6pm. Admission to château and gardens 56F; students, seniors, and ages 6-16 46F; under 6 free. Admission to gardens 30F, students, seniors, and ages 6-16 24F, under 6 free. Estate open May to mid-Oct. Sat. 8:30-11pm for candle-lit evenings. Admission 75F, students, seniors, and under 16 65F.)

FONTAINEBLEAU

When you think "hunting lodge," do you see a log cabin with a stuffed deer head, tucked away in the thick of the woods, maybe with a gun rack and a stone hearth? Not the men who commissioned and designed the Château de Fontainebleau...they thought big; and their efforts converged in this sprawling structure and its splendiferous interior extravagance. Fixed up by François I in 1528, it was the first home for much Italian Renaissance art, including the *Mona Lisa* and the *Virgin in the Rocks.* It was also just the place to welcome the pope, who came to crown Napoleon in 1804, and then to imprison His Holiness from 1812 to 1814.

The **Grands Appartements,** the standard visitors' tour, gives a lesson in the history of French architecture and decoration; guides available in English (15-25F) give the visit a shred of sense. In the **Gallery of François I,** muscular figures by Mannerist artist Il Rosso tell mythological tales of heroism and bravado, brilliantly illuminated by light flooding in from windows overlooking the Fountain Courtyard. The **Ball Room's** magnificent octagonal ceiling reminds the visitor that much of Fontainebleau should be observed with a craned neck. Every Queen of France since the 17th century has slept in the gold, green, and leafy **Queen's** (later Empress's) **Bed Chamber;** the gilded wood bed was built for Marie-Antoinette, but she never used it. In the **Emperor's Private Room** (also called the **Abdication Chamber**), Napoleon signed his 1814 abdication, and the **Cour des Adieux** was the site of his farewell. (Open Nov.-May Wed.-Mon. 9:30am-12:30pm and 2-5pm; June and Sept.-Oct. 9:30am-5pm; July-Aug. 9:30am-6pm. Last entry 45min. before closing. Admission 31F, students, seniors, and Sun. 20F, under 18 free. 1½hr. tours in French—and maybe English—Wed. and Sat.-Sun. at 11am and 3pm, daily in summer; 34F, students, seniors, and Sun. 20F. Call 01 60 71 50 70 for info.)

The same ticket admits you to the **Musée Napoléon,** a collection of imperial kitsch, like his tiny shoes, his toothbrush, and his son's toys (same hours as Grands Appartements, but closed 11am-2:30pm). Also included is the **Musée Chinois de l'Impératrice Eugénie,** a welcome respite from the crowds upstairs. These four rooms were remodeled in 1863 by the Empress to house the collection which she called her *"Musée chinois,"* a gathering of Far Eastern porcelain, jade, and crystal. (Open same hours as château, but closed 11:15am-2:30pm.)

The gardens in the main courtyard of Fontainebleau are unimpressive but make for a pleasant enough stroll. Quieter and more refined are the **Jardin Anglais,** complete with rustic grotto and the famous Fontaine-belle-eau, and the **Jardin de Diane,** guarded by a statue of the huntress. (Courtyard and gardens open daily sunrise-sunset.) You can also tool around the **Etang des Carpes** in a rented boat and throw bread at the fish. (4-person max. per boat. Boat rental May 23-Aug. daily 10am-12:30pm and 2-7pm; Sept. Sat.-Sun. 2-6pm. 40F per 30min., 60F per hr.)

Hourly **trains** run from the Gare de Lyon (45min., 92F roundtrip); when you get there, take the **bus** Car Vert A (direction: Château-Lilas; 8F70) to the Château stop.

DISNEYLAND PARIS

It's a small world after all, and Disney seems hell-bent on making it even smaller. When Disneyland Paris (EuroDisney) opened, it was met with the jeers of French intelligentsia and the press. Resistance seems to have subsided since Walt & Co. renamed it Disneyland Paris; a touch of class goes a long way. Whether you're there to celebrate or to mock, the park is a great place for a day, even for budget travelers; each show, attraction, and ride is included in the admission, as is the chance to see Europeans get off their high horses and sway to Michael Jackson's "Captain Eo."

For the wildest rides, look for those with the greatest warnings. While "may frighten certain young children" might sound promising, it only means that the ride is dark and things pop out at you. Warnings directed at pregnant women and people with chronic heart problems are the hallmarks of the real thing. The park is divided into five areas. **Main Street,** the first area you'll pass through after the gate, is home to City Hall and a whole bunch of stores. The **Château de la Belle au Bois Dormant (Sleeping Beauty's Castle)** contains one stupendously high-tech smoke-breathing dragon in the dungeon, and a shop where you can buy the crown jewels for 3200F. It makes one heck of a landmark. Out the back is **Fantasyland,** whose tame rides include **Alice's Curious Labyrinth,** a hedge maze replete with squirting fountains and a hookah-smoking caterpillar. Drift through a world of laughter, a world of tears, a world of hopes, and a world of fears on **It's a Small World,** where tiny automated dolls from around the world sing you into submission.

Off to the left, **Adventureland** has a mix of themes from "adventurous regions"—the Middle East, West Africa, and the Caribbean. **Pirates of the Cambeau** stages 15 minutes of frighteningly lifelike corsairs and a fantastic water-dungeon set. Be warned: the line outside is only a fraction of the total wait. **Indiana Jones and the Temple of Doom** features what was the first 360° loop ever on a Disney ride; unfortunately, it's only a three-minute ride. Next, mosey over to **Frontierland,** where **Thunder Mesa,** a towering sunset-colored reproduction of a New Mexican desert mesa, hosts the park's most breathtaking ride: **Big Thunder Mountain,** with a line at high noon that is almost as deadly as the ride. Off on a scraggly hill, the creaky **Phantom Manor** is the park's classic haunted house. While the Haunted Mansion at Disneyland in Florida is a huge scary fortress, the architecture had to be changed in Europe, where fortresses and châteaux are common; this haunted Manor is based instead on the Victorian mansion in the film *Psycho.* The newest ride at Disneyland Paris, **Space Mountain** puts the Florida and California versions of this ride to shame: travel at speeds of up to 70km per hour through three loops in pitch blackness—a 360° loop, a corkscrew, and a 180° horseshoe—while a synchronized eight-speaker soundtrack almost makes you think you're on your way to the moon.

In addition to the rides, Disney also puts on three daily special events: a **Disney Character Parade** with myriad elaborate floats; the **Main Street Electrical Parade** (for the best view of the parades stand to the left at the top of Main Street near the pseudo-rotary—that's where the special effects on the floats are timed to go off); and a fantastic **fireworks** show, set against the background of the château.

To reach Disneyland Paris from Paris, take **RER** A4 (direction: Marne-la-Vallée) to the last stop, "Marne-la-Vallée/Chessy" (every 30min., 45min., 74F roundtrip). The last train to Paris leaves Disney at 12:22am, but won't reach Paris before the metro closes. By **car,** take the A4 highway from Paris for about 30 minutes until exit 14, marked "Parc Disneyland Paris." Park for 40F in any of the 11,000 spaces in the parking lot. **Disneyland Paris Buses** make the rounds between the terminals of both Orly and Roissy/Charles de Gaulle airports and the bus station near the Marne-la-Vallée RER (every 45-60min. 8:30am-7:45pm, 40min., 85F). **Eurail** holders take heed: the TGV runs from Roissy/Charles de Gaulle to the park in a mere 15 minutes.

Buy tickets at the 50 windows on the ground floor of the Disneyland Hotel, or at the Paris Champs-Elysées tourist office; buy ahead if you plan to visit on a weekend. (Admission 195F, ages 3-11, 150F. Open daily 9am-11pm. Hours can change in winter. Reduced prices Oct.-Dec. 22 and Jan. 8-March 31.)

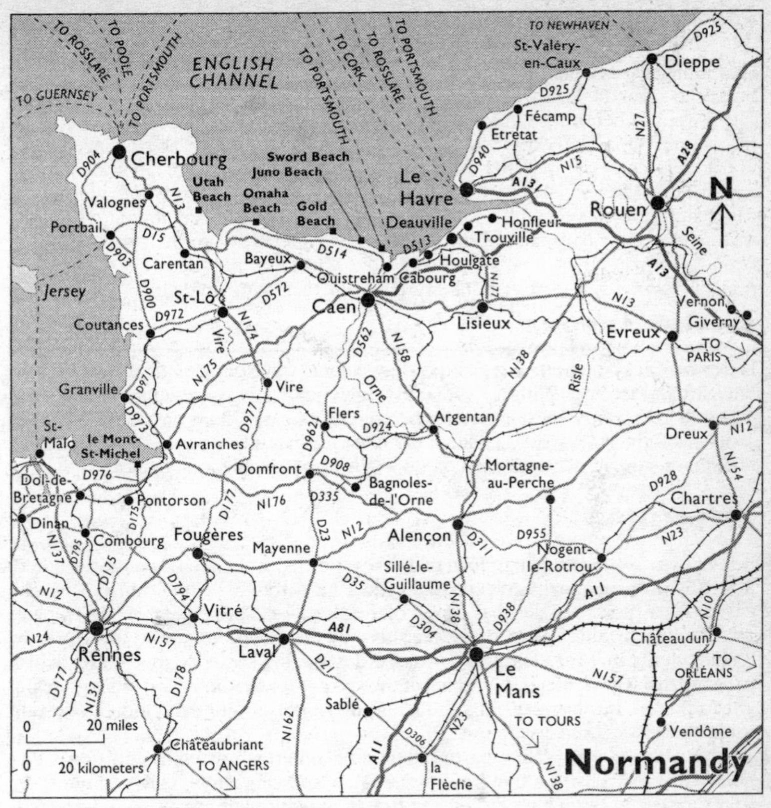

Normandie (Normandy)

Normandy, whose jagged coastline, sloping valleys, and elaborate cathedrals inspired the Impressionists, remained largely separate from the rest of France until the 15th century. Seized by Vikings in the 9th century, Normandy was officially recognized as independent in 911, when the pragmatic and acquiescent king Charles the Simple ceded Rouen and its surroundings to the invading Norsemen (later corrupted to "Normans"). The great age of Norman independence and territorial expansion lasted from the 10th to 13th centuries. During this period, the Normans created their greatest Romanesque monuments, a string of mammoth cathedrals. Their most impressive achievement, however, was the invasion in 1066 of the island just across the Channel. William the Conqueror's victory in England was celebrated by a magnificent tapestry that still hangs in Bayeux.

During the Hundred Years' War, the English had their revenge: they invaded and overpowered fierce Norman resistance. English troops, led by the Duke of Bedford and aided by French traitors, succeeded in capturing Joan of Arc after a great victory on September 8, 1430. Charged with heresy and sorcery, Joan was imprisoned in a tower in Rouen that stands today; on May 30, 1431, at the age of 19, she was burned at the stake. The British did not relinquish their last French possession until the Duke of Guise and his army of 30,000 pushed them into the sea at Calais in 1558. When the English finally attempted another invasion, on June 6, 1944, they returned with American and Canadian allies to wrest Normandy from German occupation in history's largest military assault. The beaches near Bayeux, where the Allies came ashore, still bear scars from the D-Day attack.

Gustave Flaubert once wrote, "All of us Normans have a drop of cider in our veins. It's a bitter, fermented drink which sometimes bursts the gut." The province's traditional *cidre* comes both hard *(brut)* and sweet *(doux). Calvados,* an apple brandy aged 12 to 15 years, ranks with the finest cognacs. *Galettes* (thin whole wheat pancakes stuffed with vegetables, cheese, or meats) and crêpes are ubiquitous, filling, and inexpensive. Norman cuisine also borrows liberally from the produce of the famous Norman cows, who supply all France with dairy products. Try the creamy, pungent *camembert* cheese, but be sure it's ripe (soft in the middle).

GETTING AROUND

Le Havre, Dieppe, Caen, and Cherbourg welcome travelers arriving by water from England and Ireland. Within Normandy, only major towns are connected by rail; buses fill in the gaps. SNCF buses are covered by railpass; others are not. Since many spots lie off the main roads, a bike or car helps for extended touring. Cyclists should note that roads are hilly and that coastal winds blow roughly west to east.

Rouen

Best known as the city where Joan of Arc was burned and Emma Bovary was bored, Rouen is no provincial hayseed. From the 10th through 12th centuries, the city enjoyed prosperity and status as capital of the extensive Norman empire. After Joan's great campaign, she was held prisoner here by the English and tried for heresy by French clergy in 1431. The clerics passed down a life sentence, but under British pressure this was changed to burning at the stake. No fear, though—Joan is gone but not forgotten; her name adorns the main thoroughfare and every hotel, souvenir shop, and *tabac* for miles around.

In the 19th century, Victor Hugo dubbed Flaubert's birthplace and Corneille's hometown the "city of a hundred spires." Monet's many attempts to capture those spires made the cathedral's façade a fixture in museums around the world. Unfortunately, this century hasn't been so kind. American and German troops bombed away much of Rouen's history during the World Wars, and pollution has taken its toll on the city's appearance. Once-imposing edifices have only recently begun to regain their former glory through ongoing conservation efforts.

ORIENTATION AND PRACTICAL INFORMATION

To get to the *centre ville* from the station, take rue Jeanne d'Arc for several blocks. A left onto the cobblestone **rue du Gros Horloge** leads to **pl. de la Cathédrale** and the tourist office; a right leads to **pl. du Vieux Marché** and its restaurants.

Tourist Office: 25, pl. de la Cathédrale (tel. 02 32 08 32 40; fax 02 32 08 32 44). Free map. **Le P'tit Normand,** covering Rouen (49F), is sold here and at *tabacs.* Open April 15-Sept. Mon.-Sat. 9am-7pm, Sun. 9:30am-12:30pm and 2:30-6pm; Oct.-April 14 Mon.-Sat. 9am-12:30pm and 2-6:30pm, Sun. 10am-1pm. For 24-hr. **accommodations service** call **Club Hôtelier Rouennais** (tel. 02 35 71 76 77).

Budget Travel: Wasteels, 111bis, rue Jeanne d'Arc (tel. 02 35 71 92 56; fax 02 35 07 48 75). Open Mon.-Fri. 9am-12:30pm and 1:30-7pm, Sat. 9am-12:30pm and 1:30-6pm. **Forum Voyages,** 72, rue Jeanne d'Arc (tel. 02 35 98 32 59; fax 02 35 70 24 43). Open Mon.-Fri. 9:30am-7pm, Sat. 10am-12:30pm and 2-6pm.

Money: ATMs git down at **Crédit Agricole,** 37, rue Jeanne d'Arc, and **Crédit Mutuel,** 44, rue Jeanne d'Arc (open 7am-11pm), near the *gare routière.* **BRED,** 27, rue Jeanne d'Arc and 137, rue St-Sever, also dispenses moolah from its **ATMs.**

American Express: 1-3, pl. Jacques-Lelieur (tel. 02 32 08 19 20 or 02 32 08 19 30; fax 02 35 98 19 18). Open Mon.-Fri. 8:45am-noon and 1:30-6pm.

Trains: rue Jeanne d'Arc (tel. 02 35 98 50 50), at the head of the street. To: Paris (every hr., 1¼hr., 122F); Lille (3 per day, 3hr., 160F); Caen (every 2hr., 2hr., 117F);

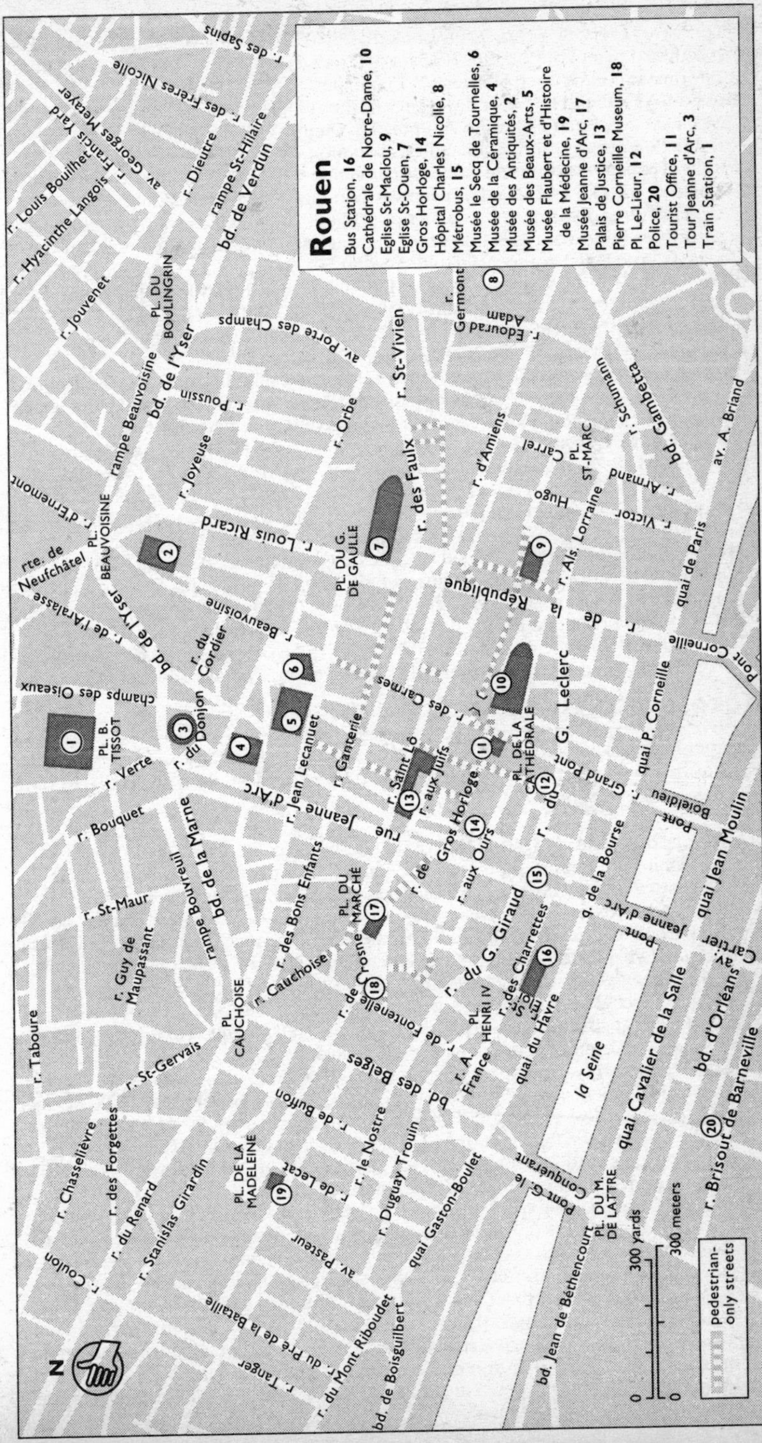

Rouen
Bus Station, 16
Cathédrale de Notre-Dame, 10
Eglise St-Maclou, 9
Eglise St-Ouen, 7
Gros Horloge, 14
Hôpital Charles Nicolle, 8
Métrobus, 15
Musée le Secq de Tournelles, 6
Musée de la Céramique, 4
Musée des Antiquités, 2
Musée des Beaux-Arts, 5
Musée Flaubert et d'Histoire de la Médecine, 19
Musée Jeanne d'Arc, 17
Palais de Justice, 13
Pierre Corneille Museum, 18
Pl. Le-Lieur, 12
Police, 20
Tourist Office, 11
Tour Jeanne d'Arc, 3
Train Station, 1
N
300 yards
300 meters
0
pedestrian-only streets
la Seine
PL. DU BOULINGRIN
PL. BEAUVOISINE
PL. B. TISSOT
PL. DU G. DE GAULLE
PL. DE LA CATHÉDRALE
PL. ST-MARC
PL. DU MARCHÉ
PL. CAUCHOISE
PL. HENRI IV
PL. DE LA MADELEINE
PL. DU M. DE LATTRE
bd. de Verdun
bd. de l'Yser
bd. de la Marne
bd. des Belges
bd. d'Orléans
bd. de Boisguilbert
bd. Jean de Béthencourt
bd. Gambetta
rue Jeanne d'Arc
r. de la République
r. du G. Leclerc
r. des Carmes
r. Louis Ricard
r. des Faulx
r. St-Vivien
r. d'Amiens
r. Beauvoisine
r. Jean Lecanuet
r. du Gros Horloge
r. Cauchoise
r. du G. Giraud
quai du Havre
quai de Paris
quai Jean Moulin
quai Cavalier de la Salle
quai Gaston-Boulet
quai de la Bourse
quai P. Corneille
Pont Corneille
Pont Boïeldieu
Pont Jeanne d'Arc
Pont G. le Conquérant
av. Jean Moulin
av. A. Briand
av. Porte des Champs
av. Pasteur
rte. de Neufchâtel
rampe Beauvoisine
rampe St-Hilaire
rampe Bouvreuil
champs des Oiseaux

NORMANDY

Le Havre (every hr., 1hr., 71F). **Lockers** 15-30F. Leave bicycles for 35F per day; consignment open Mon.-Fri. 8:15am-7:45pm, Sat. 9:15am-12:30pm and 2-6pm. Information office open Mon.-Sat. 7:15am-7pm.

Buses: SATAR and **CNA,** at the corner of rue St-Eloi and rue des Charrettes (tel. 02 35 71 23 29), open daily 6am-7:30pm. To: Dieppe (1-2 per day, 2hr., 63F) and Le Havre (2-3 per day, 3hr., 80F). Office open Mon.-Fri. 8am-6pm, Sat. 8-11am.

Public Transportation: Métrobus, rue Jeanne d'Arc, in front of the Théâtre des Arts (tel. 02 35 52 52 52). Both subway and bus systems run Mon.-Sat. 7am-7pm. *Carte* 7F50 (good for 1hr.), *carnet* of 10 56F. Unlimited 1-day *carte* 20F, 2-day *carte* 30F, 3-day *carte* 40F. Info office at train station open Mon.-Sat. 6:30am-7pm.

Taxis: 67, rue Jean Lecanuet (tel. 02 35 88 50 50). 24hr.

Bike Rental: Rouen Cycles, 45, rue St-Eloi (tel. 02 35 71 34 30). 120F per day. Passport deposit. Open Tues.-Sat. 9am-12:30 pm and 2-7:30pm. V, MC.

Laundromat: 73, rue Beauvoisine (tel. 02 35 70 80 10). 21F for 8kg of dirty duds. 3F for 4min. of drying, 10F for 20min. Open daily 8am-8:30pm.

English Bookstore: ABC Bookshop, 11, rue des Faulx, in front of Eglise St-Ouen (tel. 02 35 71 08 67). Windows display ads for *au pairs* and tutors for hire. Open Tues.-Sat. 10am-6pm; closes earlier in July. Usually closed around Aug.1-15.

Youth Center: Centre Rouen Information Jeunesse (CRIJ), 84, rue Beauvoisine (tel. 35 98 38 75), helps find accommodations and work and has info on activities. Also makes hostel reservations. Open Mon.-Fri. 10:30am-6:30pm.

Help Lines: SOS Amitié (tel. 02 35 60 52 52) when you need to talk; 24hr. **ACT-UP Rouen** (tel. 02 35 70 32 71) has info on gay and lesbian concerns.

Hospital: Hôpital Charles Nicolle, 1, rue de Germont (tel. 02 35 08 81 81).

Medical Assistance: SOS Médecins (tel. 02 35 03 03 30). 24-hr. doctors on call.

Ambulance: 1, rue de Germont (tel. 02 35 88 44 22). **Medical emergency** tel. 15.

Police: 9, rue Brisout de Barneville (tel. 02 35 63 81 17). **Emergency** tel. 17.

Post Office: 45bis, rue Jeanne d'Arc (tel. 02 35 15 66 66). Poste restante. **Currency exchange.** Open Mon.-Fri. 8am-7pm, Sat. 8am-noon. **Postal code:** 76000.

ACCOMMODATIONS AND CAMPING

Cheaper lodgings lie on the side streets between the train station and Hôtel de Ville. For information on **CROUS** lodgings, call 02 35 15 74 40 (usually available only weekends June to Sept.).

Auberge de Jeunesse (HI), 118, bd. de l'Europe (tel. 02 35 72 06 45), across the river 5km from train station. From the station, take the metro (direction: Hôtel de Ville-Sotteville) to "Europe." Walking, go straight across the river on rue Jeanne d'Arc and its extensions, av. Jacques Cartier and av. de Bretagne. Turn left on bd. de l'Europe; the hostel is 50m down on the left. In the more industrial Rive Gauche and somewhat distant from historic Rouen, but worth the walk. Clean, well-kept 4- and 6-person rooms and hot showers. Minimal kitchen facilities. 59F per person, breakfast included. 100F deposit gets you sheets and a locker. Reception 5-10pm; lockout 10am-5pm. Curfew 11pm, 10pm in winter. If you need to leave early in the morning, make sure the doors will be open. Reserve in advance.

Hôtel Normandya, 32, rue du Cordier (tel. 02 35 71 46 15), near the train station off rue du Donjon. Owned by a friendly, *Let's Go*-loving couple who could be your grandparents. Most rooms are well-lit and have excellent views of the city. In others the only natural light is supplied by a skylight (in other words, no views). Tiny toilets. Singles 100F, with shower 140F. Doubles 110F, with shower 150F. Triple with shower 190F. Shower 10F. Breakfast 20F.

Hôtel St-Ouen, 43, rue des Faulx (tel. 02 35 71 46 44), across from Eglise St-Ouen. Cheerful, motherly owner and her amiable dogs maintain equally cheerful and amiable rooms, many with breathtaking views of the city, and one with a private terrace. Singles 100F, with toilet 120F, with shower 130F, with both 150F. Doubles 10F more. Triples with toilet and shower 200F. Shower 16F. Breakfast 20F.

Hostellerie du Vieux Logis, 5, rue de Joyeuse (tel. 02 35 71 55 30), off rue Louis-Ricard. A 150-year old mansion as beautiful as it is somber. Rooms are clean and neat, each with its own distinctive feel. Some offer views of the Seine and beyond, others of the Dominican convent across the street. Elderly *propriétaire* is very willing to engage you in conversation. 1-bed rooms (for 1 or 2people) 100F; 2-bed rooms 150F. Breakfast 17F, dinner 65F.

Hôtel du Palais, 12, rue Tambour (tel. 02 37 71 41 40), off rue du Gros Horloge. Clean, large rooms can be dim and noisy. Singles and doubles 120F, with toilet 150F, with shower 140F, with toilet and shower 200F. Triples with toilet 150F, with toilet and shower 200F. *Petit déjeuner* 20F, ham and eggs 35F.

Camping: Camping Municipal de Déville, rue Jules Ferry in Déville-les-Rouen (tel. 02 35 74 07 59), 4km from Rouen. Take bus 2 from station to "Mairie." Attractive sites with squeaky-clean bathrooms. Hot showers. 22F per person, 7F per tent or car, 14F per caravan. Open May-Sept. for tents; year-round for caravans.

FOOD

Many munch lunch in the streets north of **pl. du Vieux Marché.** An **open-air market** is in the *place* itself (Tues.-Sun. 7am-12:30pm). There are plenty of eateries near the **Gros Horloge,** too; prices seem to increase based on the proximity to anything with "Jeanne d'Arc" in its name. Packaged foods crinkle at **Monoprix,** 73-83, rue du Gros Horloge (tel. 02 35 70 25 39; open Mon.-Sat. 8:30am-9pm), and **Marché U,** pl. du Vieux-Marché (tel. 02 35 71 83 04; open Mon.-Sun. 9am-12:45pm and 2:30; V, MC).

Le Queen Mary, 1, rue du Cercle (tel. 02 35 71 52 09), off pl. du Vieux-Marché. If you have a craving for *moules* (mussels), this is the place for you. Prepared in any of about 12 ways, a kg of mussels with fries runs 48-75F. Super salads 38-45F. Open Tues.-Sun. 11:30am-2pm and 7:30-11pm (also Mon. July-Aug.). V, MC.

Natural Gourmand'grain, 3, rue du Petit Salut (tel. 02 35 98 15 74), off pl. de la Cathédrale. Delicious, organic vegetarian food in a small, informal setting. 62F *menu* offers plate of grains and vegetables, choice of drink (try carrot-orange juice), dessert, coffee; 40F *menu* has the plate and dessert. Also a small health-food store and a *salon du thé* after 3pm. Open Tues.-Sat. noon-6pm. V, MC.

Pizzeria du Drugstore, 2, rue Beauvoisine (tel. 02 35 98 43 18). 3-tiered restaurant located in an enchanting old building under a drugstore. 56F lunch *menu* includes pizza, dessert, drink, and coffee. The 70F *menu* offers an *apéritif,* pizza, dessert, and coffee. Open Mon.-Sat. 11:45am-2pm and 7-11pm. V, MC.

La P'tite Flambée, 24, rue Cauchoise (tel. 02 35 70 02 38), off pl. du Vieux-Marché. Watch as—right before your eyes—they make your crêpes in the open kitchen. Outdoor seating available. *Galettes* (10-47F) 'n' crêpes galore (10-35F). Open Tues.-Sat. 11:30am-2:30pm and 6:30-11:30pm. V, MC.

Les Flandres, 5, rue des Bons-Enfants (tel. 02 35 98 45 16). Traditional French food. A 65F *menu* gives you 3 courses; the *plats du jour* run 30-45F; the wonderful salads are 36-40F. Open Mon.-Fri. noon-2pm and 7:30-9pm, Sat. noon-2pm.

SIGHTS AND ENTERTAINMENT

A good start to your Rouen tour might be the **Tour Jeanne d'Arc,** near the station on rue du Donjon. This is the last remaining tower of the château that confined Joan before she was burned to death on May 30, 1431 in the pl. du Vieux Marché. Admission grants you the dubious privilege of walking up a narrow, winding staircase to view two cursory exhibits on the history of Philippe-Auguste's château, of which the tower was a part. Don't look for "Joan was here '31" scrawled on the wall; there isn't that much here unless you're a real buff (open Wed.-Mon. 10am-noon and 2-5:30pm; admission 10F, large groups, senior citizens, students 5F).

A block up rue Jeanne d'Arc is the **Musée des Beaux-Arts,** square Verdrel (tel. 02 35 71 28 40); wheelchair access is at 26bis rue Jean-Lecanuet, to the right of the main entrance. This excellent museum holds works by European masters from the 16th through 20th centuries—Monet, Sisley, Renoir, Modigliani, and Marcel Duchamp—as well as works by Rouen natives Jacques Emile Blanche and Géricault. (Open Wed.-Sun. 10am-6pm; admission 30F for exposition only, 20F permanent collection only, 35F both collections. Reduced admission (20F, 13F, 25F) for groups and those 18-25. Handicapped, under 18, and art history students free.) A step away, at 2 rue Jacques-Villon, is the **Musée Le Secq des Tournelles de Ferronnerie** (tel. 02 35 88 42 92). For those who are interested, it demonstrates the historical development of the iron-wrought key and door handle, as well as presenting a complete array of signs, tools, and coffee grinders, all unified by their common iron *mentalité*. The "therapeutic" iron corsets, 16th-century cleavers, and 18th-century surgical saws are worth a peek (open Wed.-Mon. 10am-1pm and 2-6pm; admission 13F, students 9F). Located in the Hôtel d'Horqueville, behind the Musée des Beaux-Arts, up the stairs off rue du Baillage, the **Musée de la Céramique,** 1, rue Faucon (tel. 02 35 07 31 74 or 02 35 71 28 40), displays a varied collection. Normandy's distinctive *faïence* is the center of attention, though there's a parenthetical nod to Wedgewood porcelain. The exhibit on the influence of "Orientalism" on French ceramics is interesting, but unless you have a particular craving for earthenware it may all begin to look the same after a while (open Wed.-Mon. 10am-1pm and 2-6pm; admission 13F, students 9F, under 18 free). Nearby, at 198, rue Beauvoisine, the **Musée des Antiquités,** in Cloître Ste-Marie (tel. 02 35 98 55 10), houses a substantial collection of Gallo-Roman, medieval, and Renaissance objects, from crosses and croziers to tapestries and cathedral columns (open Mon. and Wed.-Sat. 10am-12:30pm and 1:30-5:30pm, Sun. 2-6pm; admission 20F, seniors 10F, students free).

NORMANDY

The **Eglise St-Ouen,** pl. du Général de Gaulle, once belonged to a Benedictine monastery. Begun in 1318, construction of the church was interrupted by the Hundred Years' War and not completed until the 16th century. Inquire about concerts. (Open March 15-Oct. Wed.-Mon. 10am-12:30pm and 2:30-6pm; Nov.-Dec. 14 and Jan. 16-March 14 Wed. and Sat.-Sun. 10am-12:30pm and 2-4:30pm.)

Continue your tour of Rouen's ecclesiastical treasures with the **Cathédrale de Notre-Dame,** up rue de la République on your right. The cathedral is among the most important in France and incorporates nearly every intermediate style of Gothic architecture. Parts of the façade—familiar from dozens of Monet canvases—are disappointingly dingy. Moreover, many of what were once beautiful *vitraux* have been replaced with frosted glass, giving the impression of a very holy bathroom. Renovations are in progress, though, and the church is becoming brighter and more beautiful as the effects of aging are reversed. Don't miss the Chapelle St. Jean de la Nef, with its stained-glass depiction of the beheading of St. John the Baptist. The 12th-century **Tour St-Romanus** rises to your left as you face Notre-Dame. To the right lies the 17th-century **Tour de Beurre,** which was financed through dispensations granted to those who wanted to eat butter during Lent. The cathedral, whose central tower is the tallest in France (151m), is illuminated nightly in summer (open Mon.-Sat. 8am-7pm, Sun. 7:30am-6pm).

Just behind, on pl. Barthélémy, the 15th-century **Eglise St-Maclou** presents a striking contrast to its neighbor. Built in 80 years, St-Maclou displays an extraordinary Gothic uniformity. The organ, with its elaborately carved friezes of saints and musicians, is its most striking feature. Ask about concerts. (Open March-Oct. Mon.-Sat. 10am-noon and 2-6pm, Sun. 3-5:30pm; Nov.-Feb. Mon.-Sat. 10am-noon and 2-5:30pm, Sun. 3-5:30pm.) Beyond the church, a small, poorly marked passageway at 186, rue de Martainville leads to the **Aitre St-Maclou.** This cloister served as the church's charnel house and cemetery through the later Middle Ages—including the years of the devastating plagues. Evidence of this sad legacy can be found in the gory 15th-century frieze that decorates the beams of the inner courtyard. The *Rouennais* entombed a live cat within the walls to exorcise spirits; a glass panel to the right of the entrance lets visitors gawk at the unlucky feline (open daily 8am-8pm; free).

From the cathedral, turn onto the pedestrian **rue du Gros Horloge.** Built into a bridge across the street, the **Gros Horloge** (Big Clock) is charmingly inaccurate. When the belfry is eventually repaired, visitors will be able to ascend for a view of the 14th-century clockwork and the rooftops of Rouen. Until then, though, the trip is worth neither the time nor the money; seek your rooftops elsewhere (open April-Sept. Wed.-Mon. 10am-1pm and 2-6pm; admission 10F, students and under 18 free).

A half-block from the rue du Gros Horloge and next to the pockmarked (from heavy bombardment) **Palais de Justice,** stands an 11th-century building known as the **Monument Juif** (Jewish Monument). Uncovered during the 1980s, the structure may

Quel Scandale!

Flaubert's book about a provincial doctor's wife, *Madame Bovary,* may have changed the realistic novel, but it also caused quite a stir in his hometown. Struggling with a subject for his first great work, Flaubert took inspiration from an anecdote told to him by a school friend and from his own dissatisfaction with bourgeois family life. When word got around that the tale was based on a real incident, every woman in Normandy fancied herself the model for Emma Bovary, and infuriated local pharmacists took Flaubert's corrupt chemist as a personal attack. Unfortunately they were not his only readers; the regime of Napoleon III read between the lines and brought the author and his publisher up on immorality charges. Neither the crime nor the ill-fated genuine Mme. Bovary was ever pinned down. At the tourist office, Flaubert fanatics can get info about visiting the estate in nearby **Croisset,** where he retired to write as a young man.

have been a synagogue, a Talmudic school, or a private house; regardless, it is one of the few remaining traces of the Jewish presence in medieval Europe. You must call the tourist office two days in advance to take a guided tour in French (given Sat. 2pm, also May-Sept. Sun. 11am; 30F, under 25 and over 60 25F). On the other side of rue Jeanne d'Arc and pl. du Vieux Marché is the **Eglise Ste-Jeanne d'Arc,** a massive structure designed in 1979 to resemble an overturned boat. Its unconventional, sprawling shape hides the fact that the interior "church in the round" is actually quite tiny. The wall of luminous stained glass was recovered from the Eglise St-Vincent, destroyed during World War II. A 6.5m cross outside marks the spot where the Maid of Orléans met her fiery end on May 30, 1431 (open Mon.-Fri. 10am-12:30pm and 2-6pm, Sat.-Sun. 2-6pm).

Novelist **Gustave Flaubert** grew up several blocks to the west of the church at 51, rue de Lecat, next door to the Hôtel-Dieu hospital (which bears the same address). Now the fascinating **Musée Flaubert et d'Histoire de la Médecine** (tel. 02 35 15 59 95), the building houses a few of Flaubert's possessions. The museum's prize is its collection of gruesome pre-anesthesia-age medical instruments (including a battlefield amputation kit and gallstone crushers-and-removers) used by Flaubert's father, a physician (open Tues.-Sat. 10am-noon and 2-6pm; free English brochure). Dramatist **Pierre Corneille's** former home is at 4, rue de la Pie (tel. 02 35 71 63 92), off pl. du Vieux Marché (open Thurs.-Mon. 10am-noon and 2-6pm, Wed. 2-6pm; admission 5F, under 18 free).

The yuppie watering hole, **Café Leffe,** 36, pl. des Carmes (tel. 02 35 71 93 30; open 7pm-2am; V, MC), is named for the Belgian beer French students adore. For a younger crowd, try **Le Scottish,** 21, rue Verte (tel. 02 35 71 46 22), with weekend jazz concerts on its terrace (cocktails 48-52F, beer 18-65F; open Mon.-Sat. 12:30pm-2am). Jazz and blues concerts seize the night at **Carpe Diem,** 11, rue des Boucheries St-Ouen (tel. 02 35 07 00 15), near the Eglise St-Ouen, a mellow 14th-century building with an older clientele. Choose from the impressive list of alcoholic and non-alcoholic drinks (43-60F) or the not-so-impressive beer list (20-45F; open Mon.-Sat. 6pm-2am; V, MC). The **Underground Pub,** 26, rue des Champs Maillets (tel. 02 35 98 44 84), offers billiards and darts (drafts 15-20F; open Mon.-Sat. 5pm-2am; V, MC). One of the few gay bars in town, **Le Kox,** 138, rue Beauvoisine (tel. 02 35 07 71 97), offers yet another way to miss hostel curfews (open daily 6pm-2am; V, MC). **Big Ben Pub,** 95bis, rue du Gros Horloge (tel. 02 35 88 44 50), has an outdoor terrace for crowd-watching (beer 13-48F; open Mon.-Sat. noon-2am; V, MC).

■ Near Rouen: Giverny and Vernon

As you travel between Rouen and Paris, take the opportunity to visit painter Claude Monet's house and gardens in the village of Giverny. The master Impressionist bought the property in 1883 and lived here until his death in 1926. The **Musée Claude Monet** (tel. 02 32 51 28 21) consists of the renovated house and gardens. Inside its walls of crushed pink brick, the small rooms are lined with Monet's collection of Japanese prints. The kitchen is stocked with the china he designed for his home. The painter's garden was one of his greatest passions; the air is filled with the scent of lavender and iris. Stroll by the pond, whose Japanese bridge and *nymphéas* (waterlilies) featured in Monet's canvases. Arrive early in the day or visit in May; the line can stretch into a Disneyesque wait. (House and garden open April-Oct. Tues.-Sun. 10am-6pm. Admission 35F, students and ages 12-18 25F, ages 7-12 20F; garden only 25F.) About 100m down rue Claude Monet, the **Musée d'Art Américain** (tel. 02 32 51 94 65) is a recent addition to Giverny that purports to show American art in comparison with European works. Though mostly a collection of paintings by little-known Monet hangers-on, it has a room of Whistlers, a few Singer-Sargent sketches, and some poignant Mary Cassatts. (Open April-Oct. Tues.-Sun. 10am-6pm. Admission 35F, students, seniors, and ages 12-18 20F, under 12 15F.)

Giverny is easily accessible by public transport. The train station of **Vernon,** across the river and 6km from the museum, lies along the Rouen-Paris-St-Lazare line. Trains leave from Rouen (every 2hr., 40min., 52F) and Paris (every 2hr., 45min., 65F). To get to Giverny, rent a **bike** (55F per day, 1000F deposit) or take a **bus** (Mon.-Sat. 6 per day, 3 on Sun., 10min., 11F or 17F roundtrip), both at the station.

Consider climbing up the valley into the **Forêt de Vernon,** alongside Giverny, to see the beautiful poppy-covered countryside. The Vernon **tourist office,** 36, rue Carnot (tel. 02 32 51 39 60), distributes maps of the best hiking trails. From the station, take rue Emile Loubet, turn left on rue d'Albuféra and right on rue Carnot. (Open April-Oct. Tues.-Sat. 9:30am-noon and 2:30-6:30pm, Sun. 10am-noon; Nov.-March Tues.-Sat. 10am-noon and 2:30-5:30pm.) Frequent signs lead the way from the Vernon station to the tourist office and Giverny.

Dieppe

The first boats to come to this town were those of the Vikings, who creatively named the harbor "Dieppe," from the Norse word meaning "deep." Since the 19th century, Dieppe's pebble-strewn beach has been a favorite spot for British and Parisian vacationers. On August 19, 1942, the beaches were home to less leisurely activity as thousands of Allied (mostly Canadian) troops fought in vain to wrest the port from Nazi control. The *Dieppois* have been expressing their gratitude ever since, with plaques, two monuments, and even a rue de 19 août 1942. Though the town is now a tourist haven, Dieppe's *pêcheurs* still support the city's economy with boatloads of *fruits de mer.* The bounteous seafood, imposing château, and gorgeous beach certainly merit a weekend away from Normandy's larger cities.

ORIENTATION AND PRACTICAL INFORMATION

The **Stena ferry terminal** is at Dieppe's outer port; take the courtesy bus from the terminal to the **centre ville,** defined roughly by the intersection of **Grande Rue, quai Duquesne,** and **quai Henri IV;** the tourist office is on **pont Jehan Ango,** 100m down quai Dugesne. From the train station, turn right and walk along quai Duquesne for about ten minutes to reach the *centre ville.*

Tourist Information: pont Jehan Ango (tel. 02 35 84 11 77; fax 02 35 06 27 66), right on the water in the *centre ville;* follow the fishy smell. Friendly, multilingual staff books rooms (20F) and provides maps and info about the town. Open July-Aug. Mon.-Sun. 9am-1pm and 2-8pm; May, June, and Sept. Mon-Sat 9am-1pm and 2-7pm, Sun. 10am-1pm and 3-6pm; Oct.-April Mon.-Sat. 9am-noon and 2-6pm. Check out **Les Informations Dieppoises,** which lists local happenings and hotspots. Published each Tues. and Fri., available at any *tabac* (5F50).

Money: Banks cluster around pl. St-Jacques, on **rue d'Ecosse,** and on the aptly named **Grande Rue. Crédit Agricole,** 200, Grande Rue, has a 24-hr. **ATM. Banque Maritime du Nord,** quai Duquesne, exchanges currency on Sun.

Trains: bd. G. Clemenceau (tel. 02 35 98 50 50 for information, 02 35 06 69 33 for reservations). To: Paris St-Lazare via Rouen (8-10 per day, Sat. and Sun. 6 per day,

2½hr., 114F); Rouen (7-9 per day, 2½hr., 54F); Caen (change at Rouen, 143F); Le Havre (change at Rouen, 104F). Ticket office open daily 5:45am-6:45pm. **Lockers** 5-30F. Information office open Mon.-Sat. 9am-12:30pm and 1:30-6:30pm. Free buses from the train station to the ferry terminal for those with ferry tickets.

Buses: Compagnie Normande d'Autobus (tel. 02 35 84 21 97), next to the train station. To: Rouen (4 per day, 2hr., 66F) and Fécamp (2 per day, 2hr., 70F). Buy tickets on board. Information office open Mon.-Sat. 8am-12:15pm and 2-6:15pm.

Ferries: Stena, *gare maritime* across the canal at the outer port. Take the courtesy bus from the tourist office (tel. 02 35 06 39 00 for info and foot passenger reservations, 02 35 06 39 04 for car reservations). To Newhaven (4 per day, Jan.-Feb. 3 per day, 3hr., 220F, students 200F, bikes free). Office open Mon.-Fri. 9am-6pm.

Public Transportation: Société des Transports Urbains Dieppois (yes, **STUD**), 1, pl. Ventabren (tel. 02 35 84 49 49), runs buses throughout Dieppe and to the hostel and campgrounds. 6F for one ticket, 38F for 10 tickets *bleus*.

Taxis: Radio-Taxis, pont Jehan Ango (tel. 02 35 84 20 05). 24hr.

Bike Rental: MJC, 8, rue du 19 Août 1942 (tel. 02 35 84 16 92). 55F per ½-day, 90F per day. Also rents kayaks and windsurfing equipment (45F per ½-day, 65F per day). In the summer, MJC relocates to the beach, near the thassalotherapy center.

Laundromat: 48, rue de l'Ecosse. Open daily 7:15am-10pm.

AIDS Hotline: SIDA tel. 0 800 36 66 36.

Hospital: av. Pasteur (tel. 02 35 06 76 76). **Ambulance:** tel. 15 or 02 35 06 75 75.

Police: bd. Clemenceau, next to station (tel. 02 35 84 87 32). **Emergency** tel. 17.

Post Office: 2, bd. Maréchal Joffre (tel. 02 35 06 99 20). Poste restante. **Currency exchange.** Open Mon.-Fri. 8-11am and 2-6pm, Sat. 8am-noon. **Postal code:** 76200.

ACCOMMODATIONS AND CAMPING

Dieppe's hotels are small and expensive. Call ahead to reserve a room.

Auberge de Jeunesse (HI), 48, rue Louis Fromager (tel. 02 35 84 85 73). Take bus 2 (direction: Val Druel) from the station; get off at "Château Michel" stop. If walking, turn left outside the station onto bd. Clemenceau, which later becomes rue de Blainville. At the end of the street, turn right on rue de la République and make a sharp left on rue Gambetta. Climb the hill and keep on truckin'. Turn right at the rotary onto D295, and take the left 200m up the hill (rue Louis Fromager). The hostel is on your right (30min.). Rooms and bathrooms are clean, spacious, and modern, if somewhat oddly arranged. Single-sex rooms with bunk beds. Kitchen facilities. 45F. Sheets 16F. Reception open 8-9am and 5-10pm. No curfew.

Hôtel de l'Entracte, 39, rue du Commandant Fayolle (tel. 02 35 84 26 45). From tourist office follow quai Duquesne as it becomes rue Duquesne and turn left onto bd. de Verdun. The hotel is behind Les Tourelles, at the end of the boulevard. The mattresses are worn and it's a bit noisy, but the location is fantastic—mere steps from the beach. Singles 85F. Doubles with shower 142F. Extra bed 25F. Tax 1F per person. No hall showers. Restaurant and bar below.

Hôtel de la Jetée, 5, rue de l'Asile Thomas (tel. 02 35 84 89 98), near the beach. Large, sunny rooms; firm mattresses. Doubles 135F, with bath 195F. Triple with shower 295F. Five-person room 250F. Extra bed 35F. Breakfast 25-30F.

Chez Fanfan, chemin de la Falaise (tel. 02 35 84 16 84), behind Notre-Dame de Bonsecours. From station, take bus 1 (direction: 4 Poteaux) or 8 (direction: Puys) to cliff top. If walking, take a deep breath and cross two bridges from the tourist office. Follow rue de Pollet and then ascend rue Cité de Limes. Turn left onto chemin des Semaphones, and left again at the end of it. The hotel is on your left, next to the chapel. Beautiful location has a striking view of the harbor but is rather removed from the *centre ville.* Plain singles and doubles with shower 170F. Extra bed 50F. Breakfast 30F. Reception closed Tues.

Camping: Camping Vitamin (tel. 02 35 82 11 11) lies on the coast a few km from downtown Dieppe on chemin des Vertus. Take bus 2 (direction: Val Druel) or bus 10 (direction: St-Aubin-sur-Scie) from station to "Vasarely." Bar, café, pool. 20F per person. 24F per small tent (2-3 people). 40F per large tent (3-5 people).

FOOD

Inexpensive *brasseries, boulangeries,* and *crêperies* abound on Grande Rue, quai Henri IV, and around the Eglise St-Jacques. The *centre ville's* side streets hold small restaurants that proudly serve up the local fish specialties: *sole dieppoise, harengs marinés* (marinated herring), *soupe de poisson* (fish soup), and *marmite dieppoise* (a fish and shellfish chowder). Head to **Les Tourelles,** 43, rue Commandant Fayolles (tel. 02 35 84 15 88), for a delicious and inexpensive meal. Three-course *menus* start at 60F; seafood dishes run 32-45F (open Thurs.-Mon. noon-2:30pm and 7-10:30pm, Tues. noon-2:30pm). Just as tempting is the **Resto-Crêpe,** 22, rue de la Morinière, off Grande Rue, which flips a mouth-watering 47F *menu express,* including a steaming *galette* or crunchy *salade,* a sweet crêpe or *glace,* and a beverage (open Wed.-Mon. 11:30am-2pm and 6-10pm). At **Restaurant au Grand Duquesne,** 15, pl. St-Jacques (tel. 02 35 84 21 51), slightly more expensive regional *menus* start at 70F. The seaside picnicker should try **Shopi,** with two locations, on rue Gambetta near the hostel (open Mon.-Sat. 8:30am-12:30pm and 3-7:30pm, Sun. 9:30am-noon) and on rue de la Barne (open 9am-7:30pm). If canned tuna gets you down, you'll find livelier fish at the **marché de poissons** in front of the tourist office when the weather is good enough for local fishing boats to go out (starts at 8am, Mon.-Sat.).

SIGHTS AND ENTERTAINMENT

Most of Dieppe's summer visitors come to roast on the long pebbly **beach,** bordered by cliffs to the west and the port to the east. Atop these cliffs rises the imposing 15th-century **château** (tel. 02 35 84 19 76), now an interesting civic museum with an ivory collection, a collection of 18th- to 20th-century paintings, and temporary exhibits ranging from a study of *les sirènes* to showings of cubist Georges Braque's prints (open daily 10am-noon and 2-6pm; Oct.-May closed Tues.; admission 13F).

In town, **Eglise St-Jacques** offers a cool stone refuge from the sun (or, since this *is* Normandy, from the rain). The structure was begun in 1182 and ravaged so often that it wasn't completed until 1543. Ongoing restoration projects seek to repair damage done more recently by German bombardment during World War II. A somber reminder of this is the **Canadian Cemetery** in nearby **Hautot-sur-Mer,** where each identified gravestone bears a poem or inscription in English (some better than others). To get there, turn right from the hostel, walk 15 minutes, and turn right at the cross and sign. Or take the #2 bus, every 20 minutes from the tourist office.

In the eastern part of town, atop the cliffs, the **Chapelle de Notre-Dame-de-Bon-Secours** commands a stunning view of the harbor. It's a long way, but you'll get triffic pics of the city and cliffs. Take bus 1 (direction: 4 Poteaux) or 8 (direction: Puys).

Dieppe's newest attraction is the **Cité de la Mer** (tel. 02 35 06 93 20), at 37, rue de l'Asile Thomas. This sea museum contains aquariums as well as exhibits detailing fishing technology and demonstrating how a maritime economy has influenced the development of the city. Meet the mollusks you'll be having for dinner. (Open daily April-Sept. 10am-12:30pm and 2-7pm; Oct.-Mar. 10am-noon and 2-6pm; closed Mon. mornings, and Dec. 24-Jan. 3; admission 25F, 4-16 years 15F.)

For a boisterous night, try **Le Brunswick,** rue St-Rémy, where hipster Bertrand attracts a young crowd with loud music, a friendly atmosphere, and occasional free concerts. Ninety-six more beer choices can be had at **Le Scottish** on the rue St-Jacques. If you've been bitten by the boogie bug, try **Djin's Club** (tel. 02 35 82 33 60), at the **Casino,** 3, bd. de Verdun (admission 50F Tues.-Fri., 80F Sat., free for women Fri. before midnight; cover includes first drink).

Music comes to Dieppe on June 21 with the **Fête de la Musique.** In July and August, Dieppe's **Centre Jean Renoir** (tel. 02 35 82 04 43) at 1, quai Bérigny, hosts **L'été au Cinéma,** a film festival with screenings ranging from Tim Burton to François Truffaut. In late August and early September, look for the **Festival de Musique Ancienne de Dieppe** (tickets 100F per concert, students 70F). In even-numbered years (alas, not until '98) Dieppe soars for two weeks in September with the **International Kite Festival.** Write to Dieppe Capitale du Cerf-Volant, Les Tourelles, bd. de Verdun,

76200, Dieppe (tel. 02 32 90 04 95; fax 02 32 90 07 72). Dieppe also hosts its **Herring and Scallop Fair** during the second week of November with tastings and street performers on the *quai.*

Fécamp

Legend surrounds the history of **Fécamp** (pop. 22,000), located between Dieppe and Le Havre. According to the story, a few drops of Christ's blood, preserved by Joseph of Arimathea and his uncle Nicodemus in a hollow fig-tree trunk, washed up here in the 6th century, causing a spring to gush forth. Fécamp became an important destination for religious pilgrims seeking to view the *précieux-sang* (precious blood). A thousand years later, Benedictine monks stumbled upon a more financially lucrative liquid while seeking a healing draught, and today Fécamp is known for its potent native after-dinner *liqueur.* The monks are long gone, but their *Bénédictine* and its palatial former distillery remain Fécamp's prime draws.

ORIENTATION AND PRACTICAL INFORMATION

The *centre ville* is behind the Eglise St-Etienne, across the street from the station, up the stairs. To reach the **tourist office,** 113, rue Alexandre Le Grand (tel. 02 35 28 51 01; fax 02 35 27 07 77), follow rue St-Etienne (off pl. St-Etienne) as it becomes rue de Mer. Turn left at the Palais Bénédictine. The office is across from the distillery; it dispenses maps, books rooms (10F), and more. (Open July-Aug. Mon.-Sat. 10am-6pm; Sept.-March Mon.-Fri. 9am-12:15pm and 1:45-6pm, Sat. 10am-12:15pm and 2-6pm; March-June Mon.-Fri. 9am-12:15pm and 1:45-6pm, Sat.-Sun. 10am-12:15pm and 2-6pm.) A **branch office** (tel. 02 35 29 16 34) is at the corner of quai de la Vicomté and bd. Albert 1er (open July-Aug. 11am-1pm and 3-8pm). **ATMs** eat their young at **Crédit Agricole,** 15, rue Jacques Huet (tel. 02 35 10 33 00), **Société Générale,** 23, pl. de Gaulle (tel. 02 35 10 31 30), and around pl. St-Etienne. The **train station** is at bd. de la République (tel. 02 35 28 24 82, for info 02 35 43 50 50). Trains boogey on down to: Le Havre (5 per day, 45min., 43F); Paris (7 per day, 2½hr., 141F); Rouen (7 per day, 1¼hr., 69F); Dieppe via Rouen (7 per day, Sun. 2 per day, 104F). Station open Mon.-Sat. 5:15-6:15am, 9:15am-11:45pm, and 1:20-6pm, Sun. 7:45am-12:45pm and 1:30-9:10pm. **Buses** from the **Compagnie Normande d'Autobus** (tel. 02 35 70 06 06) stop at the train station and run to Rouen via Yvetot (1 per day, 3hr., 65F) and to Dieppe via St-Valéry-en-Caux (3 per day, 2½hr., 68F). **Auto-Car Gris** buses stop outside their office at 8, rue Gambetta (tel. 02 35 27 04 25), on their way to Le Havre via Etretat (8 per day, 1½hr., 41F). **Bike rental** is at **Cycles Folio,** 2, av. Gambetta (tel. 02 35 28 45 09; 45-50F per day, 200F per week; passport deposit). Open Tues.-Sat. 9am-12:15pm and 2-7pm; July-Aug. 15 also open Mon. 2-7pm. In a **medical emergency,** dial 15. **Police** (tel. 02 35 28 06 68; **emergency** tel. 17) are on the corner of rue de l'Inondation and bd. de la République. **Post office,** 1, rue de Jacques Huet, behind Eglise St-Etienne (open Mon.-Fri. 8:30am-noon and 1:30-6:30pm, Sat. 8:30am-noon; **postal code:** 76400).

ACCOMMODATIONS AND FOOD

Fécamp's most affordable rooms are located around the Eglise St-Etienne, where you can be awakened in the morning by the frantic clanging of church bells. **Hotel Martin,** 18, pl. St-Etienne (tel. 02 35 28 23 82), offers clean, bright rooms, all of which have TVs (singles 130F, with shower 150-180F, with bath 170-200F; breakfast 28F; V, MC). The **Restaurant Martin** below lures guests down with the aroma of local specialties (*menus* 65-140F). The owner's favorites include *morue fraîche au cidre* (fresh cod in cider sauce) and *soufflé normand au calvados* (soufflé in Norman apple brandy). The cheery owner of the **Hôtel Moderne,** 3, av. Gambetta (tel. 35 28 04 04), offers clean, well-decorated rooms (singles or doubles 130-160F, with shower 180-190F; bath down the hall 15F). **Hôtel de l'Univers,** 5, pl. St-Etienne (tel. 35 28 05 88), is clean and modern. Each room features a space-saver shower that swivels into its own nook. (Singles or doubles with shower 170F, with shower and TV or bath 190F, with all 3 210F. Breakfast 28F. V, MC.) Across town from pl. St-Etienne, the **Camping de Reneville** (tel. 35 28 20 97) roosts over the beach (2 people, tent, and car 45F). The baker drives through at 8:30am with croissants.

Most of Fécamp's waterfront restaurants are a bit pricey, especially those on *quai Bérigny.* Nestled among more expensive eateries, **Le Norois,** 63, bd. Albert 1er (tel. 02 35 29 22 92), is just as swanky without producing that great sucking sound in your wallet (68-88F *menus;* open noon-2:15pm and 7-9:30pm; V, MC). Locals flock to **Le Vicomté,** 4, rue de Coty (tel. 02 35 28 47 63), where the sumptuous 76F *menu* includes *ravioli de saumon, côte de veau normande* with cream and mushrooms, and a simply sinful *tarte aux pêches* (open Thurs.-Tues. noon-2:30pm and 7-9pm, Wed. noon-2:30pm; V, MC). To satisfy your Nutella craving, there's a **Marché-Plus supermarket** at 83, quai Berigny (open Mon.-Sat. 7am-9pm, Sun. 9am-1pm; V, MC). There is also a **public market** every Saturday at pl. St-Etienne.

SIGHTS AND ENTERTAINMENT

Fécamp's rocky **beach** and picture-perfect **port** are pleasant areas for strolling and staring dreamily off to sea. For hard-core tourists, a kitschy **chapel** flanks the spring that allegedly sprang up from Christ's blood, located at 12, rue de l'Aumône.

But the crowds don't go to Fécamp to find inner calm; they go for the magnificent, Renaissance-inspired **Palais Bénédictine,** 110, rue Alexandre Le Grand (tel. 02 35 10 26 10). From the 16th century through the 18th, Fécamp's Benedictine monks mixed a mysterious elixir of 27 regional plants and oriental spices (including the myrrh featured on the tour) as a healing agent. Local wine merchant Alexandre Le Grand rediscovered the recipe, lost during the French Revolution, and built the *palais* in 1888 to distill the spirit, christened in homage to the monks who invented it. Today, the palace houses neither monks nor the distillery but a glorious collection of medieval and Renaissance religious artifacts gathered by Le Grand, and hundreds of counterfeit "interpretations" of the sacred *liqueur.* As you wander through the stately *palais,* the carved and painted ceilings and incredible stained-glass tributes to Le Grand and the inventive monks astound your eyes, the fragrant scent of spices caresses your nose, and ultimately the tour's modest sample of *Bénédictine* tantalizes your tastebuds (be sure to ask for it). The palace also houses contemporary art exhibitions that change every two months. (Open May 16-Aug. 1 9:30am-6pm; Aug. 2-Nov.11 10am-noon and 2-5:30pm; Nov. 12-Dec. 31 2-5pm; March 16-May 15 10am-noon and 2-5:30pm. 27F, ages 10-18 13F50.)

Admission to the Palais Bénédictine is half-price if you buy a ticket to both of Fécamp's lesser museums. **Le Musée Centre-des-Arts,** near the Abbey at 21, rue Alexandre-Legros (tel. 02 35 28 31 99), displays regional art and objects such as furniture, paintings, and architectural relics (open Wed.-Mon. 10am-noon and 2-5:30pm; admission 20F, students 10F). Behind the museum is a small but pleasant garden that is home to a number of rare trees (open daily from 8am-8pm). Across town on the beach, the **Musée des Terre-Neuves et de la Pêche,** 27, bd. Albert 1er (tel. 02 35 28 31 99) uses model ships, paintings, exhibits, and recreated storefronts to recount the adventures of local cod fishers who crossed the ocean to Newfoundland's Grand Banks. (Open July-Aug. Mon.-Sun. 10am-noon and 2-6:30pm; Sept.-June Wed.-Mon. 10am-noon and 2-5:30pm. Admission 20F, students 10F.)

Back at the foot of the pedestrian **rue Jacques Huet** is Fécamp's massive 11th-century **Abbatiale de la Trinité** (tel. 02 35 28 53 88), with its 127m nave (as long as that of Notre-Dame de Paris) and its tower, 70m tall at the transept. At the eastern end of the nave, near the chapel to the Virgin, sits a gold box containing the relic of the *précieux-sang,* the fig trunk that carried the legendary blood (open daily 9am-7pm).

In late June, Fécamp hosts a **Festival des Majorettes**—bring your baton and twirl into the fun. On July 1, the **Fête de la Mer** features a parade and street performers.

Le Havre

Everybody comes to Le Havre (pop. 197,000), but no one stays. Founded in 1517 by King Francis I as a replacement for the ports of Honfleur and Harfleur, France's largest transatlantic port has unfortunately committed itself entirely to that calling. World War II took its toll on Le Havre; the city responded by enlisting the aid of architect Auguste Perret, whose apparent belief that reinforced concrete was the building material of the future is evident from even a cursory look at the results. Le Havre's harbor is its most important feature, since most North American cruise ships stop here, as well as ferries from the British Isles. *Malheureusement,* the sheer quantity of aquatic traffic robs the port of any picturesque qualities it may have once had. Ultimately, Le Havre's value is solely as a stopover en route to more enticing places. Get in, get out, and no one gets hurt.

ORIENTATION AND PRACTICAL INFORMATION

To get to the tourist office from the train station, walk down bd. de Strasbourg which runs right into **pl. de l'Hôtel de Ville.** From the P&O terminal, turn left onto rue G. Faidherbe, left again onto quai de Lamblardie and then right onto rue de Paris which will take you to the town hall (25min.). From the Irish ferry terminal, take bus 3 from Perry or walk down rue de Paris (10min.). The *centre ville* is behind the Hôtel de Ville, on and around **av. René Coty** and **pl. Thiers.**

Tourist Information: Maison du Tourisme (tel. 02 35 21 22 88; fax 02 35 42 38 39), inside the Hôtel de Ville. Free maps, lists of hotels and restaurants, room booking. Walk or take bus 1, 3, 4, 5, 6, or 12 from station. Open May-Sept. Mon.-Sat. 9am-7pm, Sun. 10am-12:30pm and 2:30-6pm; Oct.-April open Mon.-Sat. 8:45am-12:15pm and 1:30-6:30pm, Sun. 10am-1pm. The monthly **Cité Le Havre** (3F50) and weekly **Le Petit Futé,** 5F, available at *tabacs,* list doings and clubs.

Money: Banks with **ATMs** swarm on bd. de Strasbourg near the Hôtel de Ville.

American Express: 57, quai Georges V (tel. 02 35 42 59 11). Open Mon.-Fri. 8:45am-noon and 1:30-6pm.

Trains: cours de la République (tel. 02 35 98 50 50). Information office open Mon.-Sat. 9am-6:30pm. To: Paris St-Lazare (Mon.-Sat. 9 per day, 7 on Sun., 1hr., 144F); Rouen (Mon.-Sat. 13 per day, 7 on Sun., 1hr., 72F); Fécamp (5 per day, 1hr., 44F). **Lockers** 5-20F. Ticket office open Mon.-Sat. 5:25am-12:30pm and 1-8:20pm, Sun. 7am-1:30pm and 2-9:25pm.

Buses: bd. de Strasbourg (tel. 02 35 26 67 23), across from *gare.* **CNA** to: Rouen (Mon.-Sat. 6 per day, 2 on Sun., 3hr., 80F) via St-Romain, Bolbec, Lillebonne, Caudebec, and Duclair. **Bus Verts** (tel. 02 31 44 77 44) to Caen (4 per day, 3½hr., 119F) and Honfleur (3 per day, ½hr., 42F) via Pont Audemer. **Car Gris** to Fécamp via Etretat (4 per day, 1½hr., 42F). Office open Mon.-Fri. 8am-noon and 2-5pm.

Public Transportation: Bus Océan, 115, rue Jules Lecesne (tel. 02 35 19 75 75); also at kiosk next to tourist office. 7F50 per trip; *carnet* of 10 48F. *Ticket Ville* (18F) allows a day's unlimited travel. Most service stops after 9pm. Buy tickets on the bus or at the office, open Mon.-Fri. 8am-noon and 1:45-5pm.

Ferries: P&O European Ferries, av. Lucien Corbeaux (tel. 02 35 19 78 50). To Portsmouth, England (3 per day, 5½hr., 7½-8hr. at night; April 1-Oct. 19 395F, age 4-14 205F; Oct. 20-Dec. 31 350F, age 4-14 180F; Jan. 1-March 31 270F, age 4-14 140F; car 850-2250F; from April-Dec. the 8:30am ferry is cheaper). Ticket and info office open daily 6:45am-11pm. **Irish Ferries,** quai de Southampton (tel. 02 35 22 50 28). Take bus 3 from Hôtel de Ville or train station to stop "Marceau." To: Rosslare (8-13 per month, 20hr. overnight, May-June and Sept. 530F, students 450F; July 1-5 and Aug. 11-31 580F, students 500F; July 6-Aug. 10 635F, students 555F; Oct.-April 415F, students 335F); and Cork (June-Aug. 1 per week, 20½hr. overnight, same prices as Rosslare). An excursion fare allows a maximum of 10 nights in Ireland for 720F round-trip (740F from July 6-Aug. 10; there's also a 5-night option for 710F for these dates). Eurailpass holders may board free after paying a tax (30F). In summer, travelers should call a couple of days ahead to reserve.

Taxis: Radio-Taxis (tel. 02 35 25 81 81), at the train station.

Laundromat: 23, rue Jean de la Fontaine. Open daily 7am-9pm.

Youth Center: Centre Information Jeunesse, 2, rue Léon Gautier (tel. 02 35 19 49 84), off rue Jules Lecesne. Brochures for the young and hip (or just young). Info on area concerts and other events as well as on job and housing opportunities. Open Mon.-Sat. 8:45am-12:15pm and 1:30-6:30pm.

Women's Center: Foyer des Jeunes Femmes, 29, rue du Mont Joly (tel. 02 35 24 59 00). 2-3km out of town. Counseling services for women. Occasionally takes female travelers, but they generally only have room for long-term residents.

Hospital: Centre Hospitalier du Havre, 29, av. Pierre Mendès France, Montivilliers (tel. 02 35 55 25 25). **Medical emergency** tel. 15 or 02 35 21 33 33.

Police: rue de la Victoire (tel. 02 35 21 77 00). **Emergency** tel. 17.

Post Office: rue Jules-Siegfried (tel. 02 32 92 59 00). Poste restante. **Currency exchange.** Open Mon.-Fri. 8am-7pm, Sat. 8am-noon. **Postal code:** 76600.

ACCOMMODATIONS AND CAMPING

One-star hotels, offering mostly singles, line cours de la République. Two-star establishments glitter along bd. de Strasbourg. Avoid walking alone at night, especially among the sinister characters populating the seedy areas near the station and port.

Hôtel Le Commerce, 12, rue Dupleix (tel. 02 35 42 64 60), on the street behind the AmEx office on quai George V. Small, clean rooms at great prices. Singles and doubles 91F, with shower 110F. Shower 10F. Breakfast 24-28F. V, MC.

Hôtel Jeanne d'Arc, 91, rue Emile Zola (tel. 02 35 21 67 27; fax 02 35 41 26 83). Delightful hostess lets beautiful, clean, and bright rooms. Singles 132F, with shower 147-157F. Doubles 149F, with shower 164-174F. Extra bed 55F. Free showers. Breakfast 19F. Telephone and TV in every room. V, MC.

Hôtel Séjour Fleuri, 71, rue Emile Zola (tel. 02 35 41 33 81; fax 02 35 42 26 44), off rue de Paris. Comfortable rooms. Singles and doubles 105F, with TV 120-130F, with shower 145F, with shower and TV 160F. Free showers. Breakfast 22F.

Hôtel le Relax, 97, rue de la République (tel. 02 35 26 53 07). Close to the station in a mildly unsavory part of town. Singles 90F, with shower 125F. Extra bed 35F. Shower 10F. Breakfast 21F. V, MC.

Camping Municipal du Havre (tel. 02 35 46 52 39). From the station, take bus 1, 8, or 11 (last buses around 9pm) to pl. Jenner and walk cautiously about 20min. to the northeast corner of the park. Driving, follow bd. de la République from the station and to the Forêt de Montgeon. The site is near the other end of the *forêt.* 1-2 people, tent, and car 73F. Gates closed 11pm-6:30am. Open April 15-Sept.

FOOD

Restaurants crowd rue Victor Hugo near the Hôtel de Ville; the streets between rue de Paris and quai Lamblardie frame a plethora of neighborhood restaurants. **Le Tilbury,** 39, rue Jean de la Fontaine, serves an elegant 80F *menu* and a delicious three-course 60F lunch (open Tues.-Fri. noon-1:30pm and 7-10pm, Sat. 7-10pm, Sun. noon-1:30pm; V, MC). At **Le P'tit Comptoir,** rue Jean de la Fontaine at av. Faidherbe by the port, workers, execs, and tourists rub elbows over the 63F and 88F *menus,* wine *compris* (open daily 9am-2pm and 6-9:30pm; V, MC). Nearby, **Restaurant La Salamandre,** 33, rue Jean de la Fontaine (tel. 02 35 43 63 01), serves salads, crêpes, and *galettes* (8-45F; open Mon.-Fri. noon-1:30pm and 7-9:15pm). Stock up for the ferry voyage in the **Nouvelles Galeries,** quai George V (open daily 9am-7pm; V, MC) or at the **Monoprix,** 38-40, av. René Coty (open Mon.-Sat. 8:30am-8:30pm; V, MC).

SIGHTS AND ENTERTAINMENT

Jean-Paul Sartre named Le Havre "Bouville" (Mudville) in his novel *La Nausée,* even before it was bombed to rubble during WWII. Seizing the opportunity to recreate the city, architect Auguste Perret (1874-1954) embarked on an odyssey of urban design that dumped endless tons of concrete into the city between 1946 and 1964. The city's one skyscraper is Perret's interpretation of a church, the **Eglise St-Joseph.**

Movie-theater-style seating surrounds the altar, which lies below the gargantuan 107m steeple. Filled with a multitude of bite-sized *vitraux*, the church gives the visitor the sense of being at the center of a cosmic Lite Brite. If modern geometry oppresses your soul, take a stroll among **pl. de l'Hôtel de Ville's** fountains or enjoy the quiet shade of **Jardin Sarraute's** weeping willows (av. Foch). The **Musée des Beaux-Arts-André Malraux,** on bd. Kennedy (tel. 02 35 42 33 97), houses a collection of canvases by Eugène Boudin and Norman Impressionists, as well as works by Dufy, Pissarro, Monet, and others (open Wed.-Mon. 10am-noon and 2-6pm; admission 10F, students 5F). The huge white structure vaguely resembling an overturned toilet in l'Espace Oscar Niemeyer, pl. Gambetta, is actually the **Maison de la Culture du Havre** (tel. 02 35 21 21 10). It holds a state-of-the-art theater and cinema, which admits students to classic and new films for only 26F (closed July 20-Sept.). The gossamer pedestrian suspension bridge arching above the Maison's basin offers a decent view of the *centre ville,* should you *want* a good view of it.

There's actually quite a bit to do if you work up the nerve to venture into Le Havre at night. Shake your booty over to **Le Grillon,** 15, rue Edouard Herriot (tel. 02 35 21 46 89), where locals cavort merrily to techno and, *bien sûr, les hits américains*. **Café Leffe,** 77, rue Louis Brindeau (tel. 02 35 41 24 42), attracts the 20-something to 40-something crowd, while **McDaid's Irish Pub,** 97, rue Paul Doumer (tel. 02 35 41 30 40), is the place to find your pint of Guinness and soccer hooligans. They also offer a nice 40F buffet. If you just got off a ferry and can't bear to lose your sea legs, mosey on over to **Le Cap** (tel. 02 35 42 71 94), in the Bassin du Commerce, along Quai George V. That's right, it's a nightclub in a boat.

The Côte Fleurie

In contrast to Normandy's working port cities, the smaller villages along the coast of Lower Normandy, known as the Côte Fleurie, are decidedly playful. Casinos and beach umbrellas dot the wide sandy stretches between Honfleur and Cabourg, fighting for space with hastily built summer homes. Doubling as resort towns and thalassotherapy centers, where the affluent come to be slathered in mud or massaged with healing oils, these coastal towns have served as weekend destinations for Paris's elite since the mid-19th century. Today they cater to a more international crowd, which means the tourist office won't turn up its nose at your French. Of course, such hospitality has its price. You'll find no such thing as a budget hotel, although the beach is *compris,* and some get away with sleeping on it.

Consider basing yourself in the hostel or a hotel in **Caen. Bus Verts du Calvados** (tel. 02 31 44 77 44, in Caen) connects the towns scattered along the coast (see **Buses,** page 180). Ask about youth reductions, and consider a *Carte Liberté* if you plan on traveling in the region; it allows unlimited travel on Bus Verts' lines, and at 90F for one day, 140F for three days, and 245F for 7 days, you will quickly recoup your loss. The *Carte* also includes the use of Caen's near-luxurious bus system. It is not valid, however, on the InterNormandie buses between Le Havre and Honfleur.

HONFLEUR

Like many coastal towns, Honfleur (pop. 10,000) stresses its historical and maritime heritage to tourists; unlike other villages, Honfleur has something to boast about. The town has been a defensive bastion against English invaders during the Hundred Years' War, the port from which Champlain sailed on his trip to found Québec, and the birthplace of composer Erik Satie. The town escaped unscathed from World War I and looks with pride to the marvelously intact 15th- and 16th-century buildings that line the cobblestone streets of the *centre ville.* Shops, restaurants, and artists surround the sailboat-filled **Vieux Bassin,** one of the oldest remnants of the town's earlier maritime glory. A block away from the Bassin's waters is the 15th-century **Eglise Ste-Catherine,** pl. Ste-Catherine. Its all-wood construction lends the church a warmth that many monstrous Gothic masterpieces lack; the ceiling looks awfully similar to a pair of overturned ship hulls (open daily 9am-noon and 2-6pm).

Paintings of Honfleur by Eugène Boudin and the Ferme St-Siméon became popular in the 19th century. Some critics consider their works precursors of Impressionism; visitors can decide for themselves at the **Musée Eugène Boudin** (tel. 02 31 89 54 00), at pl. Erik Satie off rue de l'Homme de Bois. The lower level contains an informative and interesting display of Norman ethnography, and the upper levels hold the vast collection of Boudin, Dubourg, and their contemporaries. (Open March 16-Sept. Wed.-Mon. 10am-noon and 2-6pm; Oct.-March 15 Mon. and Wed.-Fri. 2:30-5pm, Sat.-Sun. 10am-noon and 2:30-5pm. Closed Jan. 2-Feb. 20. Admission 19F, students 5F.) For the full maritime treatment, check out the **Musée de la Marine** in the former Eglise St-Etienne, quai St-Etienne on the Vieux Bassin. The tiny museum holds a sizeable collection telling the tale of Honfleur's affair with the sea. (Open April-Sept. daily 10am-noon and 2-6pm; Oct.-Dec. and Feb. 15-Mar. Mon.-Fri. 2-6pm, Sat.-Sun. 10am-noon and 2-6pm. Admission 15F, students 10F.) A spectacular view and photo-op of the looming **Pont de Normandie** wait at the peak of **Mont-Joli.** To get there, fill your water bottle and follow rue du Puits from pl. Ste-Catherine until you come to a steep, unassuming asphalt ramp sloping up to the right.

NORMANDY

The **bus station** (tel. 02 31 44 77 44) is located at the end of quai Lepaulmier near the Bassin de l'Est. **Bus Verts** connect Honfleur to Caen (3 per day, 2hr., 82F) and Le Havre (3 per day, 30min., 40F). To get to the **tourist office,** 33, pl. Arthur Boudin (tel. 02 31 89 23 30; fax 02 31 89 31 82), follow quai Lepaulmier to the right from the bus station and turn right on shop-lined rue de la Ville. The office, at the end of the street, has info on hotels, restaurants, and more. (Open Easter-July 14 and Sept. Mon.-Sat. 9am-12:30pm and 2-6:30pm, Sun. 10am-4pm; Oct.-Easter Mon.-Sat. 9am-noon and 2-5:30pm.) A **Crédit Agricole,** complete with **ATM,** awaits you on quai Ste-Catherine, right on the Vieux Bassin. Free spirits can **rent bikes** at **Town and Country Location de Cycles,** 12 quai Lapaulmier (tel. 02 31 89 46 04; 1hr. 30F, 5hr. 75F, 1 day 90F, weekend 150F; passport deposit; open daily 10am-10pm).

Budgeteers should make Honfleur a daytrip—hotels here have more stars than most small galaxies. If you're in a jam, try the **Hotel Le Hamelin,** 16, pl. Hamelin (tel. 02 31 89 16 25), which offers 160F singles by the port. The seaside **Le Phare Campsite** (tel. 02 31 89 10 26) is at a quiet location about 300m from the *centre ville* at the end of rue Haute. (Reception 9am-noon and 2-7pm. 25F per person, 35F per tent and car. Campsite traffic "lockout" 10pm-7am. Open April-Sept.) Honfleur's other campsite, **La Briquerie** (tel. 02 31 89 28 32), is 3km from town. Take bus 50 (direction: Lisieux) for 10F or the local HO (4F50) bus from the bus station to "Equemauville" (24F per adult, 12F per child, 26F per tent or car; open April-Sept.).

Restaurant prices provide no relief for your wallet's sun-stroke. **Le Goéland,** 21, rue de la Ville, in a central location near the bus station, serves *galettes* and a tasty 78F *menu* including such specialties as almond trout and escalloped duck (open daily Feb.-Dec. noon-10pm). **Les Flots,** pl. Hamelin, offers traditional *menus* (78F for 3 courses, 90-145F for 4 courses). **La Maison du Governeur,** 15 rue Haute (tel. 02 31 89 42 42) offers a lunch *menu* with a choice of many seafood specialities for a mouthwatering 55F. For picnic provisions, drop by the **Champion,** pl. Sorel. The town **market** takes place in front of the tourist office (Sat. 9am-1:30pm).

HOULGATE AND CABOURG

The beach-blessed resort towns to the west of Honfleur are quieter and more affordable than their neighbor. **Houlgate's** 1½km of sandy beach is strewn with seashells and teased by the waves of the Channel. Farther east, the sea swells crash into the **Vache Noir cliffs,** so named because the fossil deposits of ancient crustaceans lend a dark hue to the cliffs' exposed limestone. A tide table is available at Houlgate's **tourist office** (tel. 02 31 24 34 79; fax 02 31 24 42 27), to the right of the town hall on bd. des Belges next to (we're serious) the Bus Verts stop "Stop" (open in summer Mon.-Sat. 10am-7pm, Sun. 2-6pm; in winter Mon.-Sat. 9am-noon and 2-7pm). The **post office,** at the corner of bd. des Belges and bd. de St-Philbert, does the **currency exchange** thang (open Mon.-Fri. 8:30am-noon and 2-5pm, Sat. 8:30am-noon).

Room prices rise with the temperature in July and August. Ask for a list of *chambres d'hôtes* at the tourist office. For those who reserve in advance, it's hard to beat the multilingual **Maison Evangélique,** 4, passage Evangélique (tel. 02 31 28 70 80; fax 02 31 24 60 46; from the Bus Verts "Imbert" stop follow the paved path paralleling the train tracks that starts at the corner of rue des Bains and rue Sebastian). Its clean but small rooms (1-6 people) feature narrow beds. (Nov.-March 63-132F; July 4-Sept. 3 168-284F; April-July 4 and Sept. 4-Oct. 96-194F. Free breakfast. Housekeeping fee of 17F per person per day. Annual membership fee of 25F per person, 40F per couple required.) **Hôtel 1900,** 17, rue des Bains (tel. 02 31 28 77 77; fax 02 31 28 08 07), is pricier but pleasant, with spacious rooms above a luxurious restaurant. (Singles, doubles, triples, and quads 160F, with toilet 180-195F, with shower 220-230F, with bath and shower 230-290F. Extra bed 72F. Breakfast buffet 38F. V, MC.) **Camping de la Plage,** at the end of rue Henri Dobert (tel. 02 31 28 73 07), is in a wonderful location near the beach. (20F per person, 23F per car, 10F per extra car, 17F electricity. Showers free. Open April-Sept. Gates closed 10pm-7:30am.)

Sick of seafood? **La Fromentine,** 36, rue du Général-Leclerc (tel. 02 31 24 53 25) serves tasty crêpes and *galettes* for a song. The *galette normande* with cream, mushrooms, chicken, and a salad is a mere 48F. (Open daily for lunch and dinner. V, MC.) **Le Globe Bar,** 44, rue des Bains (tel. 02 31 28 74 50) is a laid-back and unassuming establishment where you can find both *moules* and pizza from 32-36F (V, MC). A **8 à huit supermarket** is just a block up on the same street. (Open Tues.-Sat. 8:30am-1pm and 3-7:30pm, Sun. 4-8pm; Sept.-June Tues.-Sat. 8am-12:30pm and 3-7:30pm, Sun. 8am-12:30pm.) There's another at 39, rue des Bains, near the beach.

NORMANDY

A little farther down the coast, **Cabourg** enchants visitors with its chic beachfront. Marcel Proust (see page 76) spent many summers looking for himself only to find that he was losing time while penning his *A la Recherche du Temps Perdu* at Cabourg's **Grand Hôtel.** The **tourist office,** Jardins du Casino (tel. 02 31 91 01 09; fax 02 31 24 14 49), lies immediately in front of the posh hotel at the edge of its small, formal gardens. (Open daily July-Aug. 9am-7pm; Sept.-June Mon.-Fri. 9:30am-12:30pm and 2-6:30pm, Sat. 9:30am-7:30pm, Sun. 10am-12:30pm and 2:30-6pm.) Rent **bikes** and windsurfing gear at **Le Menhir** surf shop, av. de la Brèche Buhot (tel. 02 31 91 11 11), 50m from the beach. (80F per hr, 160F per ½-day, 260F per day, 900F per week, 1900F per month. Passport or 1000F deposit. Open Mon.-Sun. 10:15am-12:30pm and 2:30-6:30pm.) Across the Dives River, the Dives-Cabourg **train station** (tel. 02 31 91 00 74) serves Paris St-Lazare (2 per day, 2hr., 150F), although from October to mid-June trains run only on weekends. **Bus Verts** run from any of five in-town stops ("pl. du 8 Mai" is closest to the beach and tourist office) to Caen, Houlgate, Honfleur, and Le Havre. Buy your ticket from the driver.

For those looking for the time to write their own masterpieces, tranquil **Hôtel Rally,** 5, av. Général Leclerc (tel. 02 31 91 27 35), offers small, pink rooms 10m from bus stop "Pasteur." (Singles, doubles, and triples 160F, with shower and toilet 210F. Quads 350F. Extra bed 50F. Breakfast 27F. Telephone and TV in all rooms.) The *brasserie* downstairs has a 50F *menu* including a buffet, and *moules marinière* for 35F. The pretty and spacious rooms of **L'Oie qui Fume,** 18, av. de la Brèche-Buhot (tel. 02 31 91 27 79), 300m from the beach at the opposite end of av. Georges Clemenceau from the tourist office, come with quiet gardens but no cigar-toting geese. (Singles and doubles 240F, with bath 255F, with shower 270F, with bath and shower 280F. Extra bed 40F. Showers free. Breakfast 28F. V, MC.) To camp in Cabourg, take the bus to "Oasis" and follow chemin Cailloué to either **Camping Joli** (tel. 02 31 91 68 43; 24F per person, 20F per tent and car, showers 5F) or **Camping de la Pommeraie** (tel. 02 31 91 54 58), with more extensive grounds (adults 24F, tent 30F; open April-Sept.). There is a **Champion supermarket** between the campsites and the *centre ville,* where route de Caen (D513) becomes av. Guillaume le Conquérant (open Mon.-Sat. 9am-7:15pm; daily in July-Aug.).

For a satisfying meal after a day in the sun, try **Le Champagne,** pl. du Marché (tel. 02 31 91 02 29), with three-course *menus* starting at 75F and four-course *menus* from 85F (open daily mid-June to Aug. noon-2pm and 7-9pm; Sept. to mid-June Tues.-Sat. noon-2pm and 7-9pm; V, MC). Many pizzerias and *crêperies* flank the hopping av. de la Mer; for more sea-faring fare, head two blocks away to 8, av. Piat, where lobsters (200F for 500g), oysters (78F for 12), and tortoises (75F) lurk at local favorite **L'Escailler du Romantique** (tel. 02 31 24 10 92; open 10am-10pm; V, MC). Or head to pl. du Marché and revel in freshness at the open **market** (Mon.-Fri. in summer; Wed. only off-season). A short walk from the beach leads you away from the wind and the higher prices. **Le St-Michel,** 1, rue Neuve de l'Eglise (tel. 02 31 24 08 09), offers seafood *menus* from 49F (V, MC).

Caen

"One moment it was there; the next, the whole town—parks, churches, shops—dissolved into a pile of dust." So gasped an American soldier to reporters after he witnessed Caen's destruction in 1944. Today, Caen avoids the oppressive architecture and sluggish temperament characteristic of many cities pounded to pieces during the war. A chic student population and international travelers have made this city of 116,000 a major rail, ferry, and party center. Less scholarly than stylish and arrogant, the students lingering in cafés, bookstores, and squares lend the town a cosmopolitan air and keep the city pumping at night. Summer vacationers elbow out this cultural elite-in-training to cultivate well-defined tan lines at nearby beaches or, occasionally, to explore the city's famous Romanesque edifices.

ORIENTATION AND PRACTICAL INFORMATION

Caen's train station and youth hostel are on the south side of the Orne River, far enough from the *centre ville* that you may want to take the bus (6F). The life-saving Bus Verts *Carte Liberté* grants liberal access to Caen's convenient and luxurious city buses (see page 177). All of the buses leaving from the front of the train station stop in the vicinity of **Eglise St-Pierre** and the *centre ville*. Get a map at the CTAC kiosk before heading into the city. From the station, av. du 6 Juin and rue St-Jean parallel each other northwest to the *centre ville*. The liveliest commercial districts are located between **rue St-Pierre** and **rue de l'Oratoir.**

Tourist Information: pl. St-Pierre (tel. 02 31 27 14 14; fax 02 31 27 14 18), by Eglise St-Pierre. Free accommodations service if you're staying in town. Super-organized office proffers itineraries of biking and "cider routes." Free vague map (detailed one 25F) and events calendar. Tours of city in French by day or night (July-Aug. 2 per day, 45F). **Currency exchange** with decent rates. Open May-Sept. Mon.-Sat. 9am-7pm, Sun. and holidays 10am-12:30pm and 3-6pm; Oct.-April Mon. 10am-12:30pm and 2-6:30pm, Tues.-Sat. 9am-12:30pm and 2-6:30pm. **Le Mois à Caen** lists local concerts and miscellaneous happenings (at *tabacs*). **Caen Université** is a magazine about life at the U. of Caen, available at CIJ (see below).

Money: Currency exchange and 24-hr. **ATMs** are both on offer at **Crédit Agricole,** on the corner of rue St-Jean and bd. Maréchal Leclerc (1 block from the tourist office). Other banks cluster near pl. de la République.

Trains: pl. de la Gare (tel. 08 36 35 35 35). To: Paris (5-7 per day, 2½hr., 150F); Rouen (4 per day, 2hr., 115F); Cherbourg (7-10 per day, 5 on Sun., 1½hr., 95F); Rennes (2 per day, 3hr., 165F); Tours (6 per day, 3½hr., 257F). **Lockers** 15-30F, 3-day max. Information office open Mon.-Sat. 7:30am-7pm.

Buses: To the left of the train station (tel. 02 31 44 77 44). **Bus Verts** blanket the region. To Bayeux (3 per day, 1hr., 36F) and Le Havre (4 per day, 2½hr., 115F). Office open Mon.-Fri. 7:30am-7pm, Sat. 8:15am-7pm, Sun. 9am-6pm.

Ferries: Brittany Ferries, BP 109 (tel. 02 31 36 36 00), in Ouistreham, 13km north of Caen. To Portsmouth (3 per day, 6-7hr.; Jan.-March and Nov.-Dec. 140F, students 120F; April-June and Sept.-Oct. 180F, students 160F; July-Aug. 225F, students 210F;

with a car, 445F, 635F, and 950F respectively; price includes 1 traveler). Bus Verts links Ouistreham to Caen's *centre ville* and *gare* (30min.).

Public Transportation: CTAC (tel. 02 31 15 55 55). Information booth outside station. One ticket 6F, unlimited 1-day travel 15F50, *carnet* of 10 50F. Booth open Mon.-Fri. 7am-7:30pm, Sat. 9am-1:45pm and 2:15-5:20pm. Closed Sun.

Taxis: Abbeilles Taxis Caen, 19, pl. de la Gare (tel. 02 31 52 17 89). 24-hr.

English Books: Stephen King lurks in a corner of **FNAC,** Centre Paul Doumer on rue Doumer. Open Mon. 2-7pm, Tues.-Fri. 10am-7pm, Sat. 9:30am-7pm.

Youth Center: Centre Information Jeunesse, 16, rue Neuve-St-Jean (tel. 02 31 85 73 60), off av. du 6 Juin next to the Hôtel de la Paix. Sells BIJ tickets. Brochures on events, jobs, and lodging. Open Mon. 1-6pm, Tues.-Fri. 10am-6pm.

Laundromat: 15, rue des Equipes d'Urgence, near Eglise St-Jean. Wash 18F. Dry 3F per 5min. Open Mon.-Sat. 7am-8pm, Sun. 8am-noon.

Crisis Lines: SOS Amitié (tel. 02 31 44 89 89). **AIDS Info** (tel. 0 800 36 66 36).

Hospital: Centre Hospitalier Universitaire (CHU), av. Côte de Nacre (tel. 02 31 27 27 27). **Medical emergency** tel. 15.

Police: rue Jean Romain (tel. 02 31 30 45 50). **Emergency** tel. 17.

Post Office: pl. Gambetta (tel. 02 31 39 35 78). From pl. St-Pierre, take rue St-Pierre and turn left on rue St-Laurent. **Currency exchange.** Poste restante—designate "Gambetta." Open Mon.-Fri. 8am-7pm, Sat. 8am-noon. **Postal code:** 14000.

ACCOMMODATIONS AND CAMPING

There are many hotels in Caen's *centre ville,* but few go for under 150F a night. Student accommodations are also plentiful, but they fill up quickly; reserve in advance. If all else fails, there's a **Centre International de Séjour** (tel. 02 31 95 41 00) 5km north of town in Hérouville-St-Clair off the road to Ouistreham (singles 105F).

Auberge de Jeunesse (HI), Foyer Robert Reme, 68bis, rue Eustache-Restout (tel. 02 31 52 19 96; fax 02 31 84 29 49). From the station walk right, take a left up the hill at the end of the street, and catch bus 5 or 17 (direction: Fleury or Grâce de Dieu) to "Lycée Fresnel." On foot, walk to the right out of the train station and turn left onto rue de Falaises. Turn right onto bd. Foucauld; the Lycée Fiesnel is on your right, and the foyer is right behind it. Clean 4-person, single-sex rooms with showers and kitchen facilities in a building that doubles as a *foyer* for young workers. Happening place. Ping-pong, TV, and billiards. 58 beds. 59F. Sheets 15F. Breakfast 10F. Reception open June to mid-Sept. 5-10pm. No curfew. No lockout.

University Housing: CROUS, 23, av. de Bruxelles (tel. 02 31 94 54 50), north of the château at "Bruxelles" bus stop. Reception in *loge centrale* (a blue-white building 100m down the lawn) open Mon.-Fri. 9am-noon and 2-4pm; if you have a reservation, the guard can give you the key daily 8am-8pm. Reservations by mail only. No curfew. Adequate singles 43F. Open to tourists mid-June to mid-Sept.

Hôtel Auto-Bar, 40, rue de Bras (tel. 02 31 86 12 48), off rue de Strasbourg 1 block from rue St-Pierre. Central location in a lively but somewhat noisy district. Large rooms. Singles 90-110F. Doubles 115-125F. Extra bed 43F. Showers free. Breakfast 22F. V, MC.

Hôtel du Havre, 11, rue du Havre (tel. 02 31 86 19 80), close to Eglise St-Jean. Small but clean rooms. Singles 95-120F, with shower 135F. Doubles 100-130F, with shower 170F. Extra bed 40F. Shower 15F. Breakfast 21F. Pets 20F. V, MC.

Hôtel de la Paix, 14, rue Neuve-St-Jean (tel. 02 31 86 18 99), off av. du 6 Juin. Well-located with comfortable, plain rooms and helpful proprietor. Singles 120F, with shower 175F. Doubles 130F, with shower 195F. Shower 20F. Breakfast 23F. All rooms with telephone, almost all with TV. V, MC.

Hôtel St-Pierre, 40, bd. des Alliés (tel. 02 31 86 28 20; fax 02 31 85 17 21) near the **Tour Leroy.** Small, comfortable rooms, all with phone and TV and many with a great view of the *Tour.* Singles 120F, with shower 150F, with shower and toilet 160F. Doubles 130F, 170F, and 180F respectively. Triples 160F, 200F, and 210F respectively. Showers 10F. Breakfast 25F. V, MC.

Camping: Terrain Municipal, route de Louvigny (tel. 02 31 73 60 92). Take bus 13 (direction: Louvigny) to "Camping." Near the river. Reception open 8-11:45am and 6-9:30pm. 16F per person, 10F per tent, 10F per car. Open May-Sept.

FOOD

Crêperies, brasseries, and ethnic restaurants *(ethnisseries?)* all line the aged streets of the **Quartier Vaugueux** near the château and gather between Eglise St-Pierre and Eglise St-Jean. Nearby, pl. Courtonne stages a colorful morning **market** Tuesday through Saturday. Culinary daredevils should seek out *tripes à la mode de Caen*—ox stomachs cooked in an earthenware pot with vegetables, herbs, and *calvados.* The fastest of all fast food (and beer!) can be found under a pair of golden arches, around the corner from the tourist office and across from a *cinéma* that shows American movies—why not get it all out of your system at once? Nearby at 45, bd. du Maréchal Leclerc is a **Monoprix supermarket** (open Mon.-Sat. 8am-8:30pm).

La Petite Auberge, 17, rue des Equipes-d'Urgence (tel. 02 31 86 43 30), next to Eglise St-Jean. Excellent Norman-style *menus.* 3-course 68F and 4-course 85F *menu* both offer warm goat cheese salad and that succulent Caen tripe. A special 60F *menu minceur* helpfully offers those on a diet a dozen oysters and chocolate mousse. Open Tues.-Sat. noon-2pm and 7-9pm, Sun. noon-2pm.

Chez Michel, 24, Jean Romain (tel. 02 31 86 16 59), off rue St. Jean. 5-course 48F *menu. Mais si, c'est vrai!* There is a take-out option (but not for the 48F *menu*). Open Mon.-Fri. 11:30am-1:30pm and 6:30-8:30pm, Sat. 11:30am-1:30pm. V, MC.

Couscous Le Kouba, 12, rue du Vaugueux (tel. 02 31 93 68 47). An extensive wine list accompanies a selection of meats and couscous (55-69F). Traditional lunch *menu* of regional specialties 55F. Refined atmosphere in a picturesque old house. Open Tues.-Sun. 8pm-midnight. V, MC.

Au Petit Chef, 40, rue de l'Oratoire (tel. 02 31 85 47 68). An inexpensive, popular, family-run *crêperie* with wide-ranging selections. Crêpes from 10F50, *galettes* from 23F, omelettes from 23F. Open Mon.-Sat. 11am-2pm and 6:30-10pm. V, MC.

Chantegrill, 17, place de la République (tel. 02 31 85 23 64). Creative interpretations of French classics, with *menus* from 60F. Show the French how it's done by pile-driving the all-you-can-eat salad and dessert buffet (59F). Open daily 11:45am-2:30pm and 6:45-11pm. V, MC.

SIGHTS

Caen got its start as the seat of William the Conqueror's duchy from 1035 to 1087, and the city's legacy of first-class Romanesque architecture is due chiefly to William himself, who married his distant cousin Matilda despite the pope's interdiction. As penance, the duke and his wife built several ecclesiastical structures, most notably Caen's twin abbeys. In 1064 William began the **Abbaye-aux-Hommes,** off rue Guillaume le Conquérant, to hold his tomb (not to mention his place in heaven). Rebuilt in the 18th century, the abbey served as a high school and now functions as Caen's Hôtel de Ville (admission 10F; guided tours in French daily 9:30am, 11am, 2:30pm, and 4pm). The adjacent **Abbatiale Ste-Etienne,** which sheltered citizens during the Battle of Caen in 1944, features a cavernous 11th-century façade and nave and a brilliant rose window (open 8:15am-noon and 2-7:30pm). The smaller and more intimate **Eglise de la Trinité** of Matilda's **Abbaye-aux-Dames,** off rue des Chanoines (her resting place and the penance for her marriage), has two 16th-century towers and a Romanesque interior with sparkling, Lite-Brite-esque *vitraux.* To visit the crypt, enter through the low doorway in the south transept (open daily 8am-6pm; free entry; guided tours in French daily at 2:30 and 4pm). The abbey houses art expositions throughout the year (expositions open daily 2-6pm; free).

Across from the tourist office sprawl the ruins of William's **château;** a walk here provides some relief from the *centre ville* bustle, though the modern café not-so-unobtrusively hidden within mars the serenity somewhat. (Open daily May-Sept. 6am-9:30pm; Oct.-April 6am-7:30pm.) The château's walls hide the amazing **Musée des Beaux-Arts** (tel. 02 31 85 28 63), which contains an especially fine selection of 16th- and 17th-century Flemish works (by Rubens and van Dyck, among others) and 19th-century Impressionist paintings of Normandy by Monet, Braque, Courbet, and Boudin. Noteworthy is Perugino's *Le Mariage de la Vierge* of 1504, which depicts

Mary and Joseph's wedding in brilliant color (open Wed.-Mon. 10am-6pm; admission 25F, students 15F). Much less interesting is the ethnographic collection in the neighboring **Musée de Normandie** (tel. 02 31 86 06 24), which traces Norman peasant life through the years. (Open April-July Wed.-Mon. 10am-12:30pm and 1:30-6pm; Oct.-March Sat.-Mon. 9:30am-12:30pm and 2-6pm. Admission 10F, students free. Wed. free.) Just outside, the **Jardin des Simples** holds a collection of plants (some poisonous, some medicinal) worth a glance as you wander the château's walls (open daily May- Sept. 6am-9:30pm; Oct.-April 6am-7:30pm).

Commemorating an era of turbulence, the powerful **Mémorial: Un Musée pour la Paix** (tel. 02 31 06 06 44) presides over manicured lawns in the northwest corner of the city. A must for any visit to Caen, it incorporates a unique array of footage from World War II, high-tech audio-visual aids, and displays on pre-war Europe and the Battle of Normandy. The short and haunting testimonial to the victims of the Holocaust is particularly heartwrenching. A spectacularly futuristic tunnel dramatically details the accomplishments of Nobel Peace Prize laureates, while the Canadian and American memorial gardens outside offer a touching tribute by each nation to the war dead. From the *centre ville,* take bus 17 to "Mémorial." (Open daily June-Aug. 9am-7pm; Sept.-May 9am-6pm. Admission 67F, students 57F, veterans free.)

Caen boasts ten noteworthy churches scattered throughout the city. In the shadow of the château stands **Eglise St-Pierre,** on pl. St-Pierre, whose famous bell tower and detailed exterior illustrate the evolution of the Gothic style from the 13th through the 16th centuries (open daily 9am-noon and 2-6pm). Down rue St.-Jean, on pl. de la Resistance, teeters the **Eglise St-Jean.** Erected on marshlands, the church boasts a tower that leans *à la* Pisa and is illuminated at night.

For a break from the bustle of Caen's *centre ville,* take a walk around the castle walls on rue de Geôle, turning left on rue Bosnières, to reach the **Jardin des Plantes** on pl. Blot. Winding paths lead past plants and flowers in a sheltered, romantic, herbaceous environment (open daily June-Aug. 8am-sunset; Sept.-May 8am-5:30pm).

ENTERTAINMENT

Caen's streets pulsate by night, especially around **rue de Bras** and **rue St.-Pierre.** Locals head to **Joy's/Le Paradis,** 10, rue Strasbourg (tel. 02 31 85 40 40), to flail to techno (open daily 10pm-5am; cover 60F, includes first drink). The same owner runs the popular karaoke bar **Bus Stop Café** at 7, rue de Bras (tel. 02 31 85 72 72), where a beer runs 15-30F (open 3pm-2:30am, Sun. 3-8pm). The wood interior and billiards draw locals to **Le Dakota,** 54, rue de Bernières (tel. 02 31 50 05 25); beer starts at 15F (open Mon.-Sat. 4pm-1am, Sun. 8:30pm-1am). At the **Pub Concorde,** 7, rue Montoir Poissonnerie (tel. 02 31 93 61 29), the "century-and-a-half-club" samples 150 beers from around the globe (open Mon.-Sat. 8pm-3am). Those in need of an e-mail fix double-click on over to the student-infested **Berlin West** (tel. 02 31 85 10 10), rue de Croissiers, where alcohol-inhabited cyber-dreams become reality.

Bayeux

If it were possible, Bayeux would roll out the red carpet for you; as it is, they've already rolled out the embroidered tapestry. More than just a town with a fancy rug, Bayeux (pop. 17,000) has been important from medieval times to the present. Bayeux opens its arms to those who want to see the town's treasures (a glorious cathedral and museums, not to mention the *tapisserie*), as well as to those who use the town as a convenient place from which to explore the D-Day beaches and cemeteries a few km to the north. But Bayeux's cozy, shop-lined streets eschew the postcards and other paraphernalia which are symptomatic of other tourism-driven locales; its small size and multi-faceted offerings make it required visiting.

ORIENTATION AND PRACTICAL INFORMATION

Bayeux's train station is about 10 minutes from the town center. Turn left onto the highway (bd. Sadi-Carnot); bear right at the rotary, still on bd. Sadi-Carnot, following the signs to the *centre ville.* Once there, continue up rue Larcher until it hits **rue St-Martin,** Bayeux's commercial avenue. On your right, at **rue St-Jean,** the tourist office lies at the edge of the pedestrian zone.

Tourist Office: pont St-Jean (tel. 02 31 92 16 26; fax 02 31 92 01 79), corner of rue St-Jean and rue Larcher. Books rooms. **Currency exchange.** Open Mon.-Sat. 9am-noon and 2-6pm, Sun. 9:30am-noon and 2:30-6pm; Sept. 15-July 1 closed Sun.
Money: Banks with **ATMs** are easily found on rue St-Malo and at pl. St-Patrice.
Trains: pl. de la Gare (tel. 02 31 92 80 50), 10min. from the center of town. To Paris (5 per day, 2½hr., 164F) and Caen (12 per day, 20min., 33F). Ticket counters open Mon.-Fri. 6am-9pm, Sat.-Sun. 7am-9pm.
Buses: Bus Verts, pl. de la Gare (tel. 02 31 92 02 92), serves points west as well as Le Havre and other towns to the east, via Caen (4 per day, 1hr., 38F). Buy tickets at the office (open Mon.-Fri. 9:15am-12:15pm and 1:45-6pm) or from the driver.
Taxis: Taxi du Bessin (tel.02 31 92 92 40). From the station, 20F to the cathedral.
Bike Rental: Family Home, 39, rue Général de Dais (tel. 02 31 92 15 22), in the Auberge de Jeunesse. 3-speeds 60F per day. 100F deposit. A map of cycling itineraries comes with the bike. Open daily 7am-7pm.
Laundromat: 10, rue Maréchal Foch. Wash 20F. Open daily 8am-8pm.
English Books: Maison de la Presse, 53, rue St-Martin (tel. 02 31 92 05 36), 1 block from tourist office. Recent best-sellers, newspapers, and magazines.
Hospital: rue de Nesmond (tel. 02 31 51 51 51), next to the tapestry center.
Ambulance: rue St-Jean (tel. 02 31 92 15 38). **Medical emergency** tel. 15.
Police: av. Conseil (tel. 02 31 92 02 42). **Emergency** tel. 17.
Post Office: rue Larcher (tel. 02 31 92 01 00). Poste restante. **Currency exchange.** Open Mon.-Fri. 8am-6:30pm, Sat. 8am-noon. **Postal code:** 14400.

ACCOMMODATIONS, CAMPING, AND FOOD

Inexpensive lodging exists in Bayeux, but plenty of tourists compete for limited spaces (especially July-Aug.); try to arrive early or reserve in advance. Getting a room around June 6, the anniversary of D-Day, will require all your charm and skill.

Auberge de Jeunesse (HI)—Family Home, 39, rue Général de Dais (tel. 02 31 92 15 22). Follow the signs to "Family Home" and "Auberge de Jeunesse" from the train station. Turn left from the station onto bd. Sadi-Carnot, bearing right at the rotary. Bd. Sadi-Carnot turns into rue Larcher. Take a left onto rue Leforestien right before the cathedral; this becomes rue de la Maitrise and intersects rue Général de Dais. Take a right; the hostel is on your right, 100m ahead. Centrally located 17th-century residence converted into a labyrinth of rooms. June often brings writhing hordes of school children. Lukewarm showers, but 150 comfortable beds. 90F; non-members 100F. Breakfast included. Copious dinner served nightly at 7:30pm (65F, includes wine). Reception open daily 7:30am-11pm. Reservations accepted and often necessary. Bike rentals 60F per day, 100F deposit.
Centre d'Accueil Municipal, 21, rue des Marettes (tel. 02 31 92 08 19). From station, follow bd. Sadi-Carnot left as it becomes bd. Maréchal Leclerc and bd. Fabien Ware. Big, modern *centre* across from Musée de la Bataille de Normandie. Small, somewhat antiseptic singles 89F. Small breakfast included. Reception 7am-10pm.
Hôtel Notre-Dame, 44, rue des Cuisiniers (tel. 02 31 92 87 24; fax 02 31 92 67 11), across from cathedral. Great location with cathedral views above a classy restaurant. Comfortable rooms with TV and phone. Singles and doubles 150F, with shower 240F, with toilet 290F. Extra bed 90F. Shower 20F. Breakfast 30F. V, MC.
Hôtel de la Gare, pl. de la Gare (tel. 02 31 92 10 70; fax 02 31 51 95 99). A plain, busy hotel across from station. Locals stop in at bar below after work for *café* and *calvados.* Singles 85F. Doubles 100F. Quads 160F. Showers free. Breakfast 27F.

Camping: Camping Municipal, bd. d'Eindhoven (tel. 02 31 92 08 43), within easy reach of town center and N13. Follow rue Genas Duhomme; continue straight on av. de la Vallée des Prés. Swimming pool. Great showers. 14F per person, 17F per tent and car. Gates closed 10pm-7am. Open March 15-Nov. 15.

The **Family Home** hostel serves a bountiful feast for 65F (see above). They choose the menu; you eat until you're stuffed. Call to reserve if you're not staying there. Dine with those in the know at **Le Petit Normand,** 35, rue Larcher (tel. 02 31 22 88 66), where you can eat fantastic native fare in a 16th-century building overlooking the cathedral. *Menus* 58-125F (open daily noon-2:30pm and 7-10pm; Oct.-March closed Sun. night; V, MC). After a long day in the mist, venture to **Pizza Milano,** 18, rue St-Martin (tel. 02 31 92 15 10), for stomach-warming pastas (30-45F) and creative pizzas (30-53F; open Mon.-Sat. 11am-2:30pm and 6:30-10:30pm). *Boulangeries* and *charcuteries* congregate around the intersection of rue Larcher with rue St-Jean and rue St-Martin. A Saturday morning **market** is held on pl. St-Patrice, about three blocks behind the church, while a Wednesday morning one is found on rue St-Jean near the tourist office. For processed goodies, try the **Proxi** at pl. St-Patrice. (Open Tues.-Sat. 7:30am-12:30pm and 2:30-7:30pm, Sun. 9am-12:30pm. V, MC.)

SIGHTS

The celebrated **Tapisserie de Bayeux** illustrates in vibrant detail the events that led up to and culminated in the Battle of Hastings on October 14, 1066. On that date, William the Conqueror (*né* "the Bastard") earned himself a more suave-sounding nickname by crossing the Channel to conquer his cousin Harold, who according to the Norman version of the tale held a title rightfully belonging to William—King of England. His victory, the last successful foreign invasion of England, united that island and the Duchy of Normandy under one rule. The tapestry, which details the story in comic-strip style with Latin explication, was probably woven at the request of Odo, Bishop of Bayeux and William's half-brother, to hang around the nave of Bayeux's cathedral on the Feast of the Holy Relics. A mere 50cm wide but a gargantuan 70m long, the surviving tapestry hangs in all its glory at the **Centre Guillaume le Conquérant,** a renovated 18th-century seminary on rue de Nesmond (tel. 02 31 92 05 48). Though lengthy introductory exhibits clearly detail the tapestry's contents, you may choose to cut to the chase by viewing a short film that will refresh your memory of 11th-century history. This film and the audio guided tour headsets (in French, English, German, Dutch, Italian, or Japanese; 5F) make an informed viewing of the tapestry easy and painless. (Open daily March 16-Sept. 15 9am-7pm; Sept. 16-Oct. 15 and March 15-April 30 9am-12:30pm and 2-6:30pm; Oct. 16-March 15 9:30am-12:30pm and 2-6pm. Admission 33F, students 14F. **Museum pass** to the tapestry and Bayeux's other museums 65F, students 30F.)

Bayeux's impressive **Cathédrale Notre-Dame** stands nearby. A Gothic edifice begun with Romanesque intentions, the church is a marvelous compendium of styles. The Roman crypt, below the choir, is a delightfully eerie place to investigate. Above ground, the distinctive *vitraux* of each chapel bathe the arcade in multi-hued light. The soothing blue of St. Exupère's chapel and the mellow yellow of Ste. Marguerite's merit a pause and reflection. (Open Mon.-Sat. 8am-7pm, Sun. 9am-7pm; Sept.-June Mon.-Sat. 8:30am-noon and 2:30-7pm, Sun. 9am-12:15pm and 2:30-7pm.)

The **Musée de la Bataille de Normandie,** bd. Fabian Ware (tel. 02 31 92 93 41), recounts the events of June-August of 1944 through American, English, French, and German newspapers of the era. The museum has all the powerful immediacy of a scrapbook; each of the countless clippings captures a moment in a time capsule. Multitudinous photographs, weapons, and uniform-wearing mannequins complement this vivid and anxiety-ridden picture of the beginning of the end of WWII. A 30-minute film, "Images of the Battle of Normandy," available in English and French, shows Allied and German footage of the battlefront from land, air, and sea (open daily May-Sept. 15 9:30am-6:30pm; Sept. 16-April 10am-12:30pm and 2-6pm; admission

30F, students 14F). The **British Cemetery** depicted in the final scenes of the film is located across the street from the museum.

The **Musée Baron Gerard,** pl. de la Liberté (tel. 02 31 92 14 21), just below the cathedral, has a solid permanent collection of tapestries, 16th- and 17th-century paintings (including Boucher, David, and Corot), and local porcelain and lace (open 9am-7pm; Sept. 16-May 31 10am-12:30pm and 2-6pm; admission 19F, students 10F). Across from the cathedral, the **Musée Diocésain d'Art Religieux** brings together 18th- and 19th-century reliquaries, icons, vestments, and religious paintings in the former bishop's residence (open daily July-Aug. 10am-12:30pm and 2-7pm; Sept.-June 10am-12:30pm and 2-6pm; admission 15F, students 6F).

■ Near Bayeux: The D-Day Beaches

Normandy's shores have been gnawed and sculpted by tireless waves for thousands of years, but one tragic and glorious month five decades ago left a mark like none before. In June of 1944, over a million Allied soldiers emerged from the English Channel onto the beaches of Normandy. The invasion was the first step in an incredible battle over the Nazi-occupied Continent. Today, the record of the battle can be clearly read in sobering gravestones and the pockmarked landscape; remnants of German bunkers dot the coastline, and craters left by bombs are still unfilled. The invasion's horrible price was not paid for nothing, however; less than a year later, Allied forces rolled into Berlin and Germany surrendered.

Preparations for the attack began at the Québec conference of 1943, when the Allied leaders decided to attempt a landing on the European continent. While using false intelligence reports to feed German suspicion that the attack would fall farther north at Calais or Le Havre, the British, American, and Canadian masterminds of "Operation Overlord" planned a landing on the Normandy coast between the Cotentin Peninsula and the Orne River. In the pre-dawn hours of June 6, 1944, the invasion began. Sixteen thousand American and British paratroopers tumbled from a moonlit sky. The American 82nd (All-American) and 101st Airborne (Screaming Eagles) divisions were to sever road and rail links between Paris and Cherbourg and to cover the beach landings in the west. The British 6th Parachute Brigade was to capture bridges over the Orne River and protect the eastern flank of the invasion. Reeling in confusion, the scattered troops searched for their rendezvous points on dark, unfamiliar terrain. After regrouping, they were able to execute their missions with surprising success.

A few hours later, 135,000 troops and 20,000 vehicles landed in fog and rain on the beaches code-named Utah, Omaha, Gold, Juno, and Sword. The most difficult landing was that of the 1st U.S. Infantry Division at Omaha Beach, where a rough sea and well-fortified enemy compounded the challenge of ascending a steep cliff face. In one of the day's most dramatic moments, 225 specially trained U.S. Rangers scaled the sheer 30m cliffs at **Pointe du Hoc.** Having neutralized the key German position, the Rangers were left to defend it against enemy counterattack for two days and nights until Allied help arrived for the 90 survivors. By month's end over a million soldiers had come ashore, and the Battle of Normandy raged on until August 21. On August 24, 1944, the Allied forces entered and liberated Paris.

Museums and cemeteries scattered from Cherbourg to Caen commemorate the battle. At **Omaha Beach,** next to **Colleville-sur-Mer** and just east of the Pointe du Hoc, almost 10,000 American graves stretch over a 172½-acre coastal reserve. The grounds of this **American Cemetery,** which officially belong to the United States, contain a simple marble chapel and an impressive memorial amongst the rows of immaculate white crosses. A 22-ft. bronze statue, *The Spirit of American Youth Rising from the Waves,* stands in the semicircular monument, facing the soldiers' graves, while the Garden of the Missing, behind the memorial, lists those whose remains were never recovered (open April-November 8am-6pm; Dec.-March 9am-5pm; the office can help locate the graves of specific soldiers or divisions).

At Ste-Mère-Eglise, near **Utah Beach** and west of the Pointe du Hoc, the parachute-shaped **Musée des Troupes Aéroporteés,** pl. du 6 Juin (tel. 02 33 41 41 35), houses the plane that spilled paratroopers over the district—one of whom was left dangling from the steeple of Ste-Mère's church when his parachute snagged. (Open daily May-Sept. 15 9am-6:45pm; April and Sept. 16-30 9am-noon and 2-6:45pm; Feb.-March and Oct.-Nov. 15 10am-noon and 2-6pm; Nov.16-Dec.15 Sat.-Sun. 10am-noon and 2-6pm. Admission 25F, students 20F.) The **Voie de la Libération** (Liberty Highway) begins at km "0" in front of the town hall; similar markers designate each km of the U.S. Army's advance to Bastogne in Belgium. On Utah Beach, near **Ste-Marie-du-Mont,** the **Musée du Débarquement** (tel. 02 33 71 53 35) occupies a blockhouse near the American Commemorative Monument. Films and models show how 836,000 soldiers, 220,000 vehicles, and 725,000 tons of equipment came ashore. (Open daily July-Aug. 9:30am-7:30pm; April-May 9:30am-6:30pm; June 9:30am-7pm; Dec.-March Sat.-Sun. 9:30am-6:30pm. Admission 27F, students 22F.)

Ten km north of Bayeux on D514 is **Arromanches,** a small town at the center of **Gold Beach.** Here the British built Port Winston in a day, on June 6, 1944, using retired ships and 600,000 tons of concrete towed across the Channel and sunk in a wide semi-circle a mile out to sea. The enormous artificial harbor provided shelter while the Allies unloaded their supplies. The hulking ruins of a port designed to last 18 months remain 50 years later within view of the beach. The **Musée du Débarquement** on the beach (tel. 02 31 22 34 31) houses relics and photos of the Allied landings and explains the logistics of the attack. One model moves to stimulate waves, demonstrating the flexibility of the bridge spans used in the temporary port. A diorama uses lights, slides, and other effects to recount the attack, and a fascinating film details the creation of the port. Both are available in English and are free with admission. (Open daily Sept. 4-March 9-11:30am and 2-5:30pm; April-May 5 9-11:30am and 2-6pm; May 6-Sept. 3 9am-6:30pm; Sept.-May opens at 10am on Sun. Admission 32F, students 27F.) The **Arromanches 360° Cinéma** (tel. 02 31 22 30 30) shows an 18-minute film, *Le Prix de la Liberté (The Price of Freedom),* on its circular screen. The film combines images of modern Normandy with those of D-Day landings. To reach the cinema from the museum, turn left onto rue de la Batterie and follow the steps to the top of the cliff (open daily Oct.-March 10am-5pm; April-Sept. 9am-7pm; admission 20F, students 17F).

Juno Beach, the landing site of the Canadian forces, lies east of Arromanches. Every June 6, two veterans of the battle place poppy-laden crosses on the stone monument. The **Canadian Cemetery** is located at **Bény-sur-Mer-Reviers,** and there are commemorative monuments at Bernières, Courseulles, and St-Aubin. The second British beach, **Sword Beach,** continues east from Juno Beach. There are **British cemeteries** at **Hermanville-sur-Mer** and **Ranville.** War museums at **Benouville** and **Merville** recall the battles fought at twilight. The **Musée à Pegasus Bridge** (tel. 02 31 44 62 54) in Benouville tells the story of the British Parachute Brigades' operations on the Dives River. (Open March 19-May and Sept. 5-Oct. 9:30am-12:30pm and 2-6pm; June-July 2 9:30am-12:30pm and 2-7pm; July 3-Sept. 4 9am-7pm. Admission 20F, students 15F.) In Ouistreham, the **N°4 Commando Museum,** pl. Alfred Thomas (tel. 02 31 96 63 10) retells the story of British and French troops who participated in the D-Day attack on Sword Beach.

Four km west of Arromanches in tiny **Longues-sur-Mer, Les Batteries de Longues** (tel. 02 31 06 06 45) serve as an ominous reminder of the German presence. These *batteries* are bunkers constructed in 1944 that once held artillery with a range of 12km. Today, rusted shells mar the otherwise picturesque coastal landscape. One is the only cannon in the region that still contains its original artillery.

Whichever of the many sites you see, be sure to include Arromanches and its comprehensive museum as well as the American and Canadian cemeteries in your visit. The road that follows the coast, D514, is narrow and tortuous; cycling is dangerous (and hitchhiking always is). Even those with cars might consider taking one of the excellent **bus tours** in order to get an overall impression of the beaches. Several tour guides based in Bayeux arrange inexpensive visits to the sites. **Bus Fly** (tel. 02 31 22

00 08; fax 02 31 92 35 10) has knowledgeable local guides, and their tours include Pointe du Hoc, Omaha Beach, the American cemetery, and the Musée du Débarquement entrance fee. The bus can pick you up at the tourism office, train station, or from Family Home, 39, rue Général de Dais, in Bayeux (daily 8:30am and 1:30pm, 160F, students 140F). **Normandy Tours,** 26, pl. de la Gare (tel. 02 31 92 10 70; fax 02 31 51 95 99) runs flexible tours in both English and French for one to eight people. Prices vary depending on the itinerary (100F for a 3-4hr. tour). Make reservations a day or two in advance for both tours. If you prefer the silent treatment, **Bus Verts** (tel. 02 31 92 02 92 in Bayeux) offers a Mon.-Sat. bus trip that leaves from the Bayeux train station and the *centre ville* shortly after noon and drops visitors off at various spots for a short time, then moves on to the next. The bus returns around 6pm (85F). **Camping Reine Mathilde,** at Etreham, near Port-en-Bessin (tel. 02 31 21 76 55) is 2.5km from the sea, 7km from Omaha Beach, 9km from Bayeux, and always densely packed (24F per person, 24F per tent and car; electricity 19F; open April-Sept.). Bayeux's tourist office can help you find accommodations in *chambres d'hôte* along the coast.

Cherbourg

With its strategic location at the tip of the Cotentin Peninsula, Cherbourg (pop. 28,000) was the "Gateway to France," the major supply port following the D-Day offensive of 1944. It is a still gateway today as the destination of a plethora of trains and ferries. Though Cherbourg is not so scenically interesting as other cities on the northern French coast, it has been fairly successful in resisting the encroachment of the "port city" atmosphere that plagues Le Havre and other cities. Nevertheless, be aware that late night *sorties* to Cherbourg's active nightlife are not always safe, especially around the dimly lit canal and north of the train station.

PRACTICAL INFORMATION

The helpful **tourist office** (tel. 02 33 93 52 02), at the northern end of the Bassin du Commerce, near the bridge Pont Tournant, has plenty of brochures on the Cotentin and accommodations, leads guided hikes in the summer, and books rooms for free (open Mon.-Sat. 9am-6:30pm in summer; Mon.-Fri. 9am-noon and 2-6pm off-season). The **annex** at the *gare maritime* is open during arrivals and departures of ferries—approximately Sun.-Fri. 5-8:30am and 2-10:30pm, Sat. 11:30am-10:30pm. There's **currency exchange** at the ferry terminal or banks around pl. Gréville. Major **banks** such as **BNP** are located near the tourist office on rue Gambetta, west of the Bassin du Commerce. The **post office,** rue de l'Ancien Quai, has a 24-hour **ATM** and poste restante (**postal code:** 50100; open Mon.-Fri. 8am-7pm, Sat. 8am-noon).

All **ferries** to Britain and Ireland leave from the **gare maritime** northeast of the *centre ville*, along bd. Maritime (open daily 5:30am-11:30pm). **Irish Ferries** (tel. 02 33 23 44 44) sends ferries to Rosslare (June-Aug. 2 per week, Sept.-May 1 per week, 16hr. overnight; July 1-5 and Aug. 11-31 580F, students 500F; July 6-Aug. 10 635F, students 555F; May-June and Sept. 530F, students 450F; Oct.-April 415F, students 335F). Reserve 21 days in advance for the special roundtrip fare (max. 5 nights in Ireland; May 1-July 5 and Aug. 11-Sept. 31 650F, students 490F; July 6-Aug. 10 710F, students 550F). The roundtrip excursion fare allows up to 10 nights in Ireland for 720F, students 560F; July 6-Aug. 10 740F, students 580F. Eurailpass holders may board free after paying a tax (30F). Interail passholders are entitled to significant reductions (one-way 225F, July-Aug. 260F). HI members get student rates. **P&O European Ferries** (tel. 02 33 88 65 70) serves Portsmouth, England. Be sure to consult the very complicated ferry schedule. Some trips are made only on certain days of the week (4 per day, 5hr., 9hr. overnight; Jan.-March 24 and Nov.-Dec. 170F; March 25-July 22 and Sept. 5-Oct. 190F; July 23-Sept. 4 280F). Interail passholders get 30% off all prices. **Brittany Ferries** (tel. 02 33 88 44 88) sails to Poole, England. (1-2 per day, 2½hr., overnight 5hr.; one-way trip or roundtrip with 5 nights in U.K. Nov.-March 270-330F, students 220-290F; April-Oct. 390-430F, students 350-380F.) **STENA** (tel. 02 33 88 57 01) goes to Southampton (2-3 per day, 6 hr. One-way or roundtrip with max. 5 nights in England April-Dec. 24 180F, students 170F; Jan.-March 31 110F, students 90F. Roundtrip with min. 5 nights in England April-Dec. 24 370F, students 320F; Jan.-March 31 200F, students 180F). **Lockers** are in the same building as the ferry office (5F). A **shuttle bus** runs between the *gare maritime* and the train station. Tickets are 5F and can be purchased from the driver.

The **train station** (tel. 02 33 57 50 50) lies at the base of the Bassin du Commerce, a 20-minute walk from the ferry terminal. Follow bd. Félix Amiot to av. A. Briand, which becomes av. Carnot. The *gare* will be across the intersection of av. Carnot and av. Millet, to the right (open daily 5:30am-8:20pm). Trains to: Paris (6 per day, 3½hr., 210F); Rouen (2 per day, 3hr., 179F); Caen (9 per day, 1½hr., 97F); Bayeux (6 per day, 1hr., 78F); Rennes (change at Caen, 2 per day, 4hr., 168F). Across from the station, **Autocars STN** (tel. 02 33 44 32 22), makes **bus** runs to Barfleur, Carenton, Valognes, St-Lô, Ste-Mère-Eglise, and elsewhere (open Mon.-Fri. 8:15am-noon and 2-6:30pm). **SCETA buses** leave from behind the train station and go to Coutances (3 per day, 2 on weekends, 1½hr., 65F). **Lockers** in the train station (15-30F). **Baggage** open Mon.-Fri. 8:45am-noon and 1:30-5:45pm, Sat.-Sun. 12:45-8:15pm.

ACCOMMODATIONS AND FOOD

Cherbourg's few budget accommodations are often available, since most tourists leave town as soon as they step off the ferry. Opposite the train station, the **Hôtel de la Gare,** 10, pl. Jean Jaurès (tel. 02 33 43 06 81; fax 02 33 43 12 20), sparkles with pretty, bright, clean rooms, all with telephone, many with TV. (Singles and doubles 125F, with shower 160-180F, with shower and toilet 205-210F. Shower 20F. Breakfast 25F. V, MC.) **Hôtel Divette,** 15, rue Louis XVI (tel. 02 33 43 21 04), is five minutes from the station. From pl. Jaurès, follow quai Alexandre III, turn left onto av. Delaville, and take a right before the square. Rooms are spacious but old. (Singles, doubles, and triples 95-120F, with shower 160F. Shower 15F. Breakfast 20F.) Near the *avant port,* **Le Grand Hôtel,** 42, rue de la Marine (tel. 02 33 43 04 02; fax 02 33 43 32 22), offers two-star quality at one-star prices. (Singles 100F, with shower 140F, shower and toilet 200F. Doubles 170F, with shower 180F, with shower and toilet 240F. TV and phone in most rooms. Free showers. Breakfast 27F.) Your best deal, though, may be one of Cherbourg's inexpensive **bed and breakfasts,** where rooms start at 100-120F. The tourist office maintains a list of local B&Bs.

Popular restaurants line quai de Caligny. Close to the *basilique* (see below), **Le Petit Grilladin,** 31, rue de la Paix (tel. 02 33 53 50 33), offers snazzy *menus* from 85F, as well as a tantalizing *fondue bourguignonne* for 90F (open daily June-Aug. 11:30am-4:30pm and 6:30-11pm; Sept.-May closed Wed.). There is a huge **market** on Tuesday, Thursday, and Saturday mornings in the pl. du Théâtre. For simpler provisions, stock up at the **Continent supermarket,** quai de l'Entrepôt, next to the station (open Mon.-Sat. 8:30am-9:30pm).

SIGHTS AND ENTERTAINMENT

If you're stuck in Cherbourg between connections, visit the stunning **Eglise de Notre-Dame-de-Voeu,** a block north from bd. Pierre Mendès France. The 12th-century church was built as Empress Mathilde's "thank-you" to St. Mary for helping her escape a tempestuous death in the Channel. Light seeps into the sanctuary through brilliant *vitraux* depicting the life of the Virgin Mary from birth to her coronation in heaven. The windows sparkle in a rainbow of deep colors, and the carved capitals are subtle but gorgeous. Off quai de Coligny, the stately **Basilique de la Trinité** spans centuries of architectural styles. Its foundations were laid in the mid-11th century, the transept dates from the 15th, the massive altar-ornament has a rococo twist, and the red and blue stained glass windows are modern. The nave's columns are notable for their elaborate "just-been-tattooed" appearance.

Should you long for a panoramic view of a working harbor, or yearn for an uphill climb, head to the **Musée de la Libération** (tel. 02 33 20 14 12), perched high up on the **Fort du Roule,** in the old citadel. The museum recounts life in Cherbourg during the Nazi occupation, the town's liberation, and its reconstruction. Vichy propaganda posters, films, and photographs breathe life into the events of the 1940s despite the museum's overall sterility (open April-Sept. daily 10am-6pm; Oct.-March Tues.-Sun. 9:30am-noon and 2-5:30pm; admission 20F).

At night the streets around the Hôtel de Ville perk up, especially the pedestrian **rue de la Paix.** Numerous bars and *brasseries* lounge in the pedestrian district around rue du Commerce and rue du Château. **Fifty's Diner,** 2, rue des Tribunaux (tel. 02 33 43 58 20), offers a taste of yesteryear, while **Le Commerce,** 42, rue François la Vieille (tel. 02 33 53 18 20), and **L'Eldorado,** 52, rue François la Vieille (tel. 02 33 53 08 68), have more traditional atmospheres. Students populate **L'Ataverne,** 10, pl. République (tel. 02 33 93 00 81), giving it a lively, youthful flavor.

Coutances

Walls embrace Coutances as if to guard the rapturous views of the countryside that surrounds the town. No fewer than three churches preside over Coutances, but it is the largest that is the jewel in its crown. Miraculously unscathed by World War II, this 13th-century cathedral was described by Victor Hugo as second only to Chartres in beauty. Time spent in Coutances is curiously satisfying, despite the lack of typical tourist attractions. Its steep cobblestone streets, at once quiet and lively, are a complement and a contrast to the serenity reposing beyond its walls.

PRACTICAL INFORMATION

Coutance's *centre ville* is essentially everything within a few hundred meters of the cathedral. Look up, find the tall spires, and walk toward them. From the train station, walk down the street and cross at the rotary. Climb the ramp across the street, and proceed (against traffic) up rue St-Pierre, through pl. de la Poissonerie, and bearing left, along rue Puils Notre-Dame. The **tourist office** (tel. 02 33 45 17 79) is a block away from the front door of the cathedral, behind the Hôtel de Ville. **Currency exchange** and 24-hour **ATM** services are offered by the **Crédit Agricole** (open Mon.-Fri. 8:30am-noon and 2-5:30pm, Sat. 8:30-11:30am) at pl. de la Poste, a block to the right as you leave the cathedral. Other banks lounge on rue du Geoffroy de Montbray, between the cathedral and Eglise St-Pierre. The **train station** (tel. 02 33 07 50 77) is a 15-minute walk downhill from the cathedral. Trains run to: Rennes (3 per day, 2hr., 105F); Caen (6 per day, 1½hr., 80F); Paris (2 per day, 4hr., 195F); Granville (3 per day, 30min., 40F); and Avranches (3 per day, 40min., 42F). **SCETA buses** (tel. 02 35 98 13 38 or 02 35 52 15 59) leave from the train station and connect Coutances with Cherbourg (3 per day, 2 on weekends, 1½hr., 61F), while **STN buses** (tel. 02 33 05 65 25) run to Granville and St-Lô. The **post office** (open Mon.-Fri. 8am-6:30pm, Sat. 8am-noon; poste restante; **postal code:** 50200), on pl. de la Poste, is a block to the right as you leave the cathedral.

ACCOMMODATIONS, CAMPING, AND FOOD

The **Hôtel de Normandie,** pl. du Général de Gaulle (tel. 02 33 45 01 40), has clean, comfortable rooms, some with views of the cathedral. (Singles 95F, with shower 160F, with shower and toilet 190F, with bath and toilet 220F. Doubles 145F, with shower 190F, with shower and toilet 230F, with bath and toilet 250F. All with TV, most with phones. Extra bed 50F. Showers free. Breakfast 28F. V, MC.) Downstairs, a sea of blue tablecloths ripples under wood-beamed ceilings, poised to uphold the restaurant's reputation for good Norman fare. *Menus* 50 and 72F (open Tues.-Sat. noon-2pm and 6-11pm, Sun. noon-2pm). The **Hôtel des Trois Pilliers,** 11, rue des Halles (tel. 02 33 45 01 31), run by a pleasant couple, has small, modern rooms near the cathedral. The hoppin' bar downstairs often overflows with *coutanceian* teens. (Singles or doubles 125-155F, with shower 155-165F. Breakfast 26F. Free hall showers. V, MC.) The **Hôtel le Champ'Bord,** 8, rue du Lycée, is one block down the street, above a bar popular with local workers (singles and doubles 120F; extra bed 80F; showers free; breakfast 20F). **Camping Les Vignettes,** 27, route de St-Malo (tel. 02 33 45 43 13), is within walking distance of the *centre ville,* off the D44 to Agon and Coutainville (13F50 per person, 14F for tent and car; electricity 9F50-28F). The centrally located **Crêperie La Morinière,** 1, rue Quesnel-Morinière (tel. 02 33 07 52 20), serves creative *galettes* and crêpes (9-48F) in a quiet, homey atmosphere (open Thurs.-Mon. 11:45am-2pm and 7-9:30pm, Tues. 11:45am-2pm; V, MC). Behind the Eglise St-Pierre at 55, rue du Geoffroy du Montbray, **Le Vieux Coutances** (tel. 02 33 47 94 78) serves a more traditional *menu* for 80 or 95F (open Tues.-Sun. noon-2pm and 7-9pm; V, MC). The **supermarket Stoc,** rue de la Verjustière, is at the bottom of the hill behind Eglise St-Nicolas (open Mon.-Fri. 9am-12:45pm and 2:30-7:30pm, Sat. 9am-1pm and 2-7:30pm), but you can find grocery stores nearer the cathedral. On Thursday mornings, a **market** fills pl. de la Cathédrale (9am-1pm).

SIGHTS AND ENTERTAINMENT

Coutances' grand **cathedral,** completed in 1274, stretches its spires some 78m into the sky. Inside, the 13th-century stained-glass windows and ornate pillars of the axial chapel contrast with the spartan decor of the side chapels and nave. Renovation of the façade and stained glass triptych of the Last Judgment should be completed in 1997. Until then, have a look at the reliquary chapel in the right of the transept. It contains a morsel of the True Cross and various bits of sundry saints (open 8am-7pm). On the opposite side of the town hall from the cathedral is the **Musée Quesnel Morinière** (tel. 02 33 45 11 92) in the **Jardin des Plantes.** The museum houses an interesting collection of 18th- and 19th-century paintings, pottery, period costumes, and hip temporary exhibits of modern art. (Open daily July-Sept. 14 10am-noon and 2-6pm; Sept. 15-Dec. and Jan.-June Mon.-Sat. 10am-noon and 2-5pm, Sun. 2-5pm. Admission 10F, Sun. free.) The garden is worth a stroll for its flora and the view of the surrounding fields (open daily July-Sept. 9am-11:30pm; Oct.-March 9am-5pm; April-June 9am-8pm). The 15th- and 16th-century **Eglise St-Pierre,** south of the cathedral, will be closed until renovations are complete in '97.

Coutances hosts a **Jazz Festival** every May (May 3-10 in 1997) and sponsors performances in the Jardin des Plantes and squares around town. On weekends in July and August, organ and classical concerts resound in the cathedral. Many are free or charge reduced rates for students. Contact the tourist office for info and schedules.

Coutances doesn't exactly light up with nightlife, but it isn't quite dead, either. **Le Triskell,** 10, rue Louis Beuve (tel. 02 33 45 01 01), has a faithful local following, as does **Le Monaco,** 16, pl. de la Poissonerie (tel. 02 33 45 28 52). For a U.K. feel with a touch of *français,* schlep over to **La Taverne** at pl. du Pavis (tel. 02 33 45 13 55).

Granville

Sprawling over a rocky peninsula on the western coast of Normandy, Granville does not show up in history books until the 15th century, when the English used "le Roc" as a base for battling the French at Mont-St-Michel. The victorious French decided to develop the city, now a resort that boasts rugged cliffs outlined by ribbons of white sand and a seemingly infinite horizon. Granville's distance from Paris keeps it less crowded and less expensive than other Norman resorts. Though it sells itself as a convenient base for exploring Mont-St-Michel and Britain's Channel Islands, Granville itself holds enough to keep the most jaded of budget travelers content.

PRACTICAL INFORMATION

To get to the *centre ville,* bear left as you leave the *gare* and follow av. Maréchal Leclerc as it becomes rue Couraye (10min. downhill). At the *place,* turn right onto cours Joinville (follow the rails); the **tourist office,** 4, cours Joinville (tel. 02 33 91 30

03; fax 02 33 91 30 19), lies ahead to the right, with info and free reservations. (Open July-Aug. Mon.-Sat. 9:15am-1:15pm and 2-7pm, Sun. 10:30am-12:30pm; Sept.-June Mon.-Sat. 9:15am-12:30pm and 2-7pm, Sun. 10:30am-12:30pm.) **ATMs** plot the overthrow of the government at **Crédit Agricole,** 14, rue Couraye, and **Crédit Mutuel,** 46, rue Couraye. The **train station** (tel. 02 33 50 05 45) is on av. de la Gare, off av. Maréchal Leclerc (open Mon.-Fri. 5:15am-12:30pm and 1:15-8:30pm, Sat. 6am-12:30pm and 1:30-8:30pm, Sun. and holidays 1:30-8:30pm). Trains run to: Paris (3-4 per day, 4hr., 189F); Cherbourg (change at Coutances, 2 per day, 3hr., 113F); and Bayeux (change at Folligny, 2-3 per day, 1½hr., 86F). **STN buses** (tel. 02 33 50 77 89) leave from the *gare* or their office, opposite the tourist office, to Coutances (1 per day, 45min., 31F) and Avranches (3 per day, 1hr., 31F; office open Mon.-Fri. 8am-noon and 1:30-6:30pm, Sat. 8:45am-12:15pm and 2-6pm). **Emeraude Lines** (tel. 02 33 50 16 36; fax 02 33 50 87 80), at the *gare maritime,* sails to the Chausey Islands (July 11-Aug. 31, 1-2 per day; April 18-July 10 and Sept. 1-15, 1 per day; 43F one way), Jersey, and Guernsey (call for prices and times). Next to the tourist office, the **post office** (tel. 02 33 91 12 30) has **currency exchange,** a 24-hr. **ATM,** and poste restante (open Mon.-Sat. 8am-6:30pm, Sun. 8am-noon; **postal code:** 50400).

ACCOMMODATIONS AND FOOD

Granville welcomes its share of tourists in the summer, so don't expect solitude or a surplus of hotel rooms. The **Auberge de Jeunesse,** bd. des Amiraux Granvillais (tel. 02 33 50 18 95; fax 02 33 50 51 99), is no exception; reserve ahead. Five minutes from the *centre ville,* this resort-style hostel features spacious rooms with 1-4 beds, clean showers, balconies looking out to sea, a restaurant, bar, patio, ping-pong, billiards table, and beach. To get there, follow the signs to the **Centre Régional de Nautisme,** also on the premises. The sailing center also hosts summer camps, so you may have to share your space with temperamental teeny-boppers. (Singles 97F. Doubles and triples 76F. Quads 56F. Sheets 22F. Breakfast 17F; other meals 56F. No curfew. 24-hr. reception.) Rent **windsurfing gear** here (85F per hr.). You'll find more privacy at **Hôtel Ambre Gris,** pl. Alsace Lorraine (tel. 02 33 90 16 06). Turn left on av. Leclerc as you leave the station. Though some of the 30 clean, wood-finished rooms face a busy rotary, sound-proof windows eliminate the noise. (Singles 100F, with shower and toilet 140F. Doubles 130-150F, with shower 150-170F, with shower and toilet 170-190F. Triples with shower 190F, with shower and toilet 210F. Quads 250F. TV 20F. Breakfast 25F. V, MC.) Closer to the station, the **Hôtel Terminus,** 5, pl. de la Gare (tel. 02 33 50 02 05), has some of the least tacky of all French hotel wallpaper in its spacious, comfortable rooms with firm beds, TV, and sparkling bathrooms. (Singles 115F, with shower 150F. Doubles 155F, with shower 185F, with bath 205F. Triples 195F, with shower 230F, with bath 255F. Quads 225F, with shower 270F. Breakfast 22F.) Hidden from *granvillais* traffic, **Hôtel Michelet,** 5, rue Jules Michelet (tel. 02 33 50 06 55; fax 02 33 50 12 25), welcomes visitors to its spacious rooms in a fantastic location near the beach promenade. (Singles 120F. Doubles 130-140F. Extra bed 50F. Shower 15F. Breakfast 28F. V, MC.)

Finding good eats isn't difficult, but restaurants in town tend to be a bit pricey. Near the hostel, **Monte Pego,** 13, rue St-Sauveur (tel. 02 33 90 74 44), serves pastas (42-52F), pizzas (38-50F), salads (30-45F), and huge calzones (45F; open Tues.-Sat. noon-1:30pm and 7-9:30pm, Sun. noon-1:30pm; V, MC). **Crêperie St-Sauveur,** a few doors down at 4, rue St-Sauveur (tel. 02 33 90 20 77), proffers up *galettes* and crêpes (9-38F). Save room for a *crêpe flambée* with rum, Calvados, Cointreau, or Grand Marnier (open Tues.-Sun. noon-2pm and 7-9:30pm; V, MC). A **market** takes place Saturday mornings on cours Joinville and Wednesday mornings near the stadium on D924, just outside town. For processed goodies, check **Monoprix,** on the corner of rue Lecampion and rue Poirier (open July-Aug. Mon.-Sat. 9am-7:30pm, Sun. 10am-1pm; Sept.-June Mon.-Fri. 9am-12:30pm and 2-7pm, Sat. 9am-7pm).

SIGHTS

Granville offers plenty of options for vacationers looking to get out of the sun for an hour or two. The **Musées Aquarium-Coquillage-Minéraux-Papillons,** bd. Vaufleury (tel. 02 33 50 19 83), are no mere piles of rocks and shells. Clever artists have used shells and minerals to create works of startling detail and color. The seashell *vitraux* rival those of any cathedral, and the *Birth of Venus* is reborn in its mussel-bound medium. Replicas of famous diamonds await you in the Minerals museum, while the Butterfly museum will feed many months' worth of nightmares (open daily mid-March to mid-Nov. 9:30am-noon and 2-6pm; 40F). Nearby sits the massive 15th-century **Eglise de Notre-Dame,** where classical concerts are held on weekend evenings in summer. Walking back through the twisting streets of the *haute ville* towards Granville's **casino** will lead you to the **Musée Richard Anacréon,** perched on a cliff high above the beach. It's the only modern art museum in the region, and it's a dandy. The museum focuses on Fauvism and its offshoots; bright and colorful works by Dufy, Dérain, and Friesz, along with several Rodins, make this a wonderful diversion for any bored beachcomber (open Wed.-Mon. 2-6pm; admission 15F, students 8F). On the other side of the casino, off av. de la Libération, lies the calm **Jardin Public Christian Dior,** a piece of oceanfront property donated a century ago by Granville's famous son and now brimming with rosebushes. A trip here is well worth it for the walk alone. Take the promenade du Plat Gousset along the oceanfront and climb the many stairs to the garden (garden open daily 9am-9pm; free).

Granville's main attraction is its silky-smooth **beach.** Still, should you get bored with this *plage* there are plenty of others nearby. From May to September, boats leave daily for the **Chausey Islands,** an archipelago of anything from 52 to 365 islets (depending on the tide), with few inhabitants and lovely sands. **Vedette "Jolie France"** (April-June 15 and Sept. 1 per day; June 15-Aug. 1-3 per day, roundtrip 86F; for off-season departure times call 02 33 50 31 81 or fax 02 33 50 39 90) and **Emeraude Lines** both serve the islands and operate offices in the *gare maritime.* Make reservations in July and August. A lovely road leads south of Granville to Mont-St-Michel, offering excursion possibilities for drivers and bikers. If you're planning to pedal all the way to the Mont, think twice—it's 100km away.

Mont-St-Michel

Rising from the sea like something from another world, the fortified island of Mont-St-Michel is visible for kilometers in every direction. The Mont, a work in progress since its founding in 708, is a dazzling labyrinth of stone arches, spires, and stairways that climb (and keep climbing) to the abbey itself. Just as overwhelming as the Mont's beauty, though, are the crowds that fill its streets. The island has been a popular spot for pilgrims both religious and secular almost since day one. Each August sees as many as 200,000 enraptured visitors daily. Brave the crowds, absorb the spirituality, and remind yourself that you're part of a long and glorious tradition.

ORIENTATION AND PRACTICAL INFORMATION

Because the Mont is isolated from the mainland and the town proper is a tiny village, you should plan your visit to avoid being stranded in a place where "budget hotel" is an oxymoron. Make Mont-St-Michel a daytrip—it is easily accessible from Pontorson, St-Malo, and Avranches. Trains go to Pontorson via Caen, Bayeux, and Rennes, where STN buses go to the Mont. The walk from Pontorson to the Mont takes about two hours. The only break in the outer wall is the **Porte de l'Avancée.** Inside, the tourist office lies immediately to the left; to the right, the **Porte du Boulevard** and **Porte du Roy** open onto the town's major thoroughfare, **Grande Rue.** All hotels, restaurants, and sights are on this spiraling street, but so are the crowds—sneak off via stairwells and archways to explore Mont-St-Michel's less-visited corners.

Tourist Office: BP 4 (tel. 02 33 60 14 30; fax 02 33 60 06 75), behind the wall to your left after you enter the city. Busy, busy, busy! Ask about organized 2-hr. hiking expeditions over the sand to the **Ile de Tombelaine** (April-Sept. at low tide) or for the useful and free tide table *Horaire des Marées.* Avoid the **currency exchange** here. Open July-Aug. Mon.-Sat. 9am-7pm; Sept.-June 9am-12:30pm and 2-6:30pm. Off-season the staff take irregular weeks off; call if you need their help.

Money: Société Générale, next to the tourist office before you enter Grande Rue.

Trains: The nearest train station is in Pontorson (tel. 02 33 60 00 35). Open Mon.-Fri. 8:30am-noon and 1:30-7:30pm, Sat. 8:30am-noon and 2-6:15pm, Sun. 2:30-9:45pm. To Paris (1 per day, 4hr., 235F plus 36-90F TGV supplement) and Dinan (6 per day, 1¼hr., 38F). **Lockers** 3F.

Buses: Buses leave from Porte du Roy; buy tickets on board. **STN Buses** (tel. 02 33 60 00 35 in Pontorson; 02 33 50 08 99 in Granville) link the Mont to Pontorson and elsewhere in the region (last bus leaves the Mont at 5:45pm). To Pontorson (4 per day, 15min., 14F, roundtrip 21F). STN Buses also link the Mont directly with Avranches (1 per day, 45min.) and Granville (1 per day, 2hr.), while **SCETA** (tel. 02 33 50 77 89 in Granville) goes to Folligny (1 per day, 1hr.) and Avranches (1 per day, 30min.). **Courriers Bretons** (tel. 02 33 60 11 43) runs from Pontorson to St-Malo (1-3 per day, 1hr., 44F), Avranches (1-2 per day, 30min., 24F), and Rennes (3 per day, 1 Sun., 54F). Office open Mon.-Sat. 10am-noon and 4-6:30pm.

Bike Rental: At the Pontorson **train station.** Mountain bikes 44F per ½-day, 55F per day. Deposit 1000F or passport.

Medical emergency tel. 15. **Police emergency** tel. 17.

Post Office: Grand Rue (tel. 02 33 60 14 26), near Porte du Roy. **Currency exchange** at tolerable rates. Open Mon.-Fri. 9am-6pm, Sat. 9am-5pm; mid-Sept. to June Mon.-Fri. 9am-noon and 2-5pm, Sat. 9am-noon. **Postal code:** 50116.

ACCOMMODATIONS, CAMPING, AND FOOD

Plan ahead to reserve a room you can afford; prices climb faster than the bay's famous tides. Pontorson, St-Malo, and Avranches offer accommodations at more reasonable prices. Most of the listings below are in Pontorson (**postal code:** 50170), a small Norman town with a terrific hostel.

Centre Duguesclin (HI), rue Général Patton (tel. 02 33 60 18 65), in Pontorson. From the train station, turn right onto rue du Tizon, take your first left (rue du Couesnon) and then a right onto rue St-Michel, until you come to the inconspicuous post office on the right. Turn left, and behind the cathedral lies rue Hédou. Follow it to its end and take a right on rue Général Patton. The hostel is on your left, 1 block down (10min.). Dorm-style 4- to 7-person rooms (51 beds) are bright and conducive to communal gathering, as is the kitchen and dining area. Clean, hot showers. No sheets or blankets provided. 41F. Reception daily 8-10am and 6-10pm. Lockout 10am-6pm. Open June to mid-Sept.

Pleine Fougères (HI, FIYTO), 19, rue de Normandie (tel. 02 99 48 75 69), 5km (1hr. on foot) from Pontorson. Buses only during the school year (1 per day, departs Pontorson at 6:30am, returns to Pontorson at 6:30pm). Clean 2- to 6-person rooms in a pretty stone house. 63 beds, TV room with fireplace, volleyball, ping-pong, and tennis. HI, FIYTO members only. (FIYTO cardholders 5F off). 45F. Breakfast 15F. Sheets 15F. Groups should reserve. Reception 24hr. No curfew.

Hôtel de l'Arrivée, 14, rue du Docteur Tizon (tel. 02 33 60 01 57), across from the Pontorson train station. Comfortable, quiet rooms. Singles and doubles 87-110F, with shower 155F. Triples 160F, with shower 200F. Quads 180F. Shower 15F. Breakfast 27F. Reception closes at 8pm. Bar and restaurant downstairs. V, MC.

Hôtel de la Poste, 92, rue Couesnon (tel. 02 33 60 00 45; fax 02 33 70 98 88), left of the station on Pontorson's main street. Bright, hospital-white rooms separated from traffic by a restaurant. Singles 100F. Doubles 130-180F, with shower 180-220F. Triples 180F, with shower 260F. Quads 290F. Shower 35F. Breakfast 35F.

Camping: Camping Municipal de Pontorson, chemin des Soupirs (tel. 02 33 68 11 59), off rue Général Patton near the hostel, 10min. from the station. Tranquil, bright, unforested sites with sound sanitary equipment. 13F per person. 13F per tent. 6F50 per car. Electricity 13F. Open June-Sept. **Camping du Mont-St-Michel,**

BP 8 (tel. 02 33 60 09 33), a mere 1.8km from the Mont at the junction of D275 and N776. Clean, pleasantly shaded sites fill fast. Great free showers. **Supermarket** next door. 14F per person, 13F per car or tent. Open Feb. 15-Nov. 15. **Camping St-Michel,** route du Mont-St-Michel (tel. 02 33 70 96 90), by the bay in Courtils. A bit far from the Mont (9km), but the Granville bus stops 200m from entrance. Buses go to the Mont at 10:30am and 5pm. Sites are quiet and near a swimming pool, common room, and telephone. 13F per person. 16F per car and tent. 3F more in high season. Open April-Oct. 15.

If you dare invest in more than a postcard and sandwich on the Mont, look for local specialties such as *agneau du pré salé* (lamb raised on surrounding salt marshes) and *omelette poulard,* a fluffy soufflé-like dish (about 45F). The cozy **Chapeau Rouge,** Grande Rue (tel. 02 33 60 14 24), offers these delicacies along with *jambon au porto* (ham in port) and seafood treats (3-course *menus* 65-75F). To eat in a room with a view, walk along the ramparts and take your pick of the restaurants; all sport terraces or glass walls. **Les Terrasses Poulard,** Grande Rue (tel. 02 33 60 14 09), has a beauty of a terrace and an 80F *menu* that includes their own *omelette poulard* (open daily April-Sept. 11am-midnight; Oct.-March noon-2pm and 7-9pm). Duck into **La Sirène,** Grande Rue (tel. 02 33 60 08 60), past the post office on the left, for a crêpe experience you won't soon forget. Conservative types will enjoy the 55F *formule* (a *galette,* a crêpe with butter and sugar, and *cidre*)—or go wild and cut straight to the chocolate-banana crêpe (29F), stuffed to bursting and topped with a dash of sugar and a *mont* of chocolate sauce (open daily noon-9:30pm). Or pack a picnic and eat in the abbey gardens near the top of the hill (a few flights below the entrance). A **Champion supermarket** is on the way to Mont-St-Michel from Pontorson, conveniently located across the street from the rue St-Michel STN bus stop (open Mon.-Fri. 9am-12:30pm and 2:30-7:15pm, Sat. 9am-7:30pm).

SIGHTS

A gigantic wave created the island in the 7th century when it swamped the forest of Sissy and isolated the Mont from the mainland. In 708, the Archangel Michel appeared twice in the dreams of the Bishop of Avranches, instructing him to build a place of worship on the barren and rocky island north of Pontorson. The doubting bishop ignored the first two appearances. It was only after the frustrated angel insisted a third time that plans were laid out for several crypts around the rock itself to provide a foundation for the church. Keeping track of the changes the Mont has undergone since then is dizzying, though tour guides will try to summarize them anyway. Only a few stones remain from the original oratory. Additions began in 966, when a group of monks made a pilgrimage to the Mont and were so inspired by its beauty and power that they began an even larger church on the site.

Its construction mostly complete by the 14th and 15th centuries, the Mont was used by French kings as a fortress during the Hundred Years' War. While its outer walls repelled English attacks, its inner walls still cloistered the Benedictines, who spent their time copying and illuminating the famous *manuscrits du Mont-St-Michel,* now on display in nearby Avranches (see page 198). They received religious pilgrims (including St. Louis) until 1789, when the Revolutionary government turned the island into a state prison. Sinners traveled to the rock no longer to confess their misdeeds, but to pay for them. The monastery was home to only 60 monks during this era but held over 600 prisoners, including that most revolting of revolters, Robespierre. Mont-St-Michel remained under government control from then on, continuing to serve as a prison until Emperor Napoleon III recognized its historical significance; his patronage set in motion renovations that began after his fall from power. In 1874, Mont-St-Michel was classified as a national monument and topped by the crowning bronze statue of St. Michel. In 1987, a helicopter removed the salt-saturated statue for polishing; now he looks as good as new.

Exploring Mont-St-Michel on your own can be very rewarding. New surprises wait in every nook and cranny, and it's pretty much impossible to get lost. If you'd prefer a more structured visit, pick up one of the guides available at the booths on Grande Rue for 25-80F. Enter through the **Porte de l'Avancée** and **Porte du Roy** onto **Grande Rue,** a winding pedestrian street full of souvenir stands and restaurants. A climb up several flights of stairs places you at the **abbey** entrance (tel. 02 33 89 80 00), the departure point for one-hour tours. (Open daily May-Sept. 9:30am-5:30pm, Oct.-April 10am-4pm. Tour times vary, though English tours leave roughly every 2hr. and French tours about every 45min., starting at 10am. Admission 36F, ages 18-25 22F, under 18 15F.) For a special treat, take a **visite conférence.** These two-hour tours (in French) allow you to walk atop a flying buttress and crawl inside the pre-Roman crypts. (Tours daily at 10:15am and 2:30pm. No reservations necessary. Admission 56F, ages 18-25 and over 60 42F, under 18 35F.) Mass is still held daily at 12:15pm, though you need to be at the doors of the abbey church by noon.

Beneath the church lie the Mont's frigid crypts. Descent to the crypts passes through the refectory and leads into the dark, chilly church foundations where the walls are two meters thick at some points. **La Merveille,** an intricate 13th-century cloister, encloses a seemingly endless web of passageways and chambers. If you're not impressed with its architectural complexities, the mechanical simplicity of the Mont's treadmill will surely catch your attention. Prisoners held in the Mont during the French Revolution would walk here for hours, their foot labor powering the elaborate pulley system that carried heavy stones up the side of the Mont. To escape the sweaty masses trying to climb the narrow street, take a short-cut through the **Logis Tiphaine.** Bertrand Duguesclin, born so fat and ugly that his mother rejected him, went on to become governor of Pontorson and marry a beautiful young woman named Tiphaine. He built this four-story villa in 1365 to protect his wife from the English while he was fighting in Spain. Today, the *logis* houses an interesting museum above the Grande Rue which displays well-preserved 15th- to 17th-century furniture, fireplaces, and objects of everyday use, including a chastity belt. Each floor has its own garden, and the top story leads to the abbey. (Open Feb. 16-Nov. 14 daily 9am-6pm. Admission 25F, students 20F, under 18 5F.)

After the tour, escape down the ramparts and into the abbey garden, where you can reflect upon the soaring stone buttresses that wrap around the entire island and the coastline of Normandy and Brittany. To avoid the crowds on the main street, descend to the **Porte du Bavole** via the ramparts.

There are a few museums in Mont-St-Michel that are moderately interesting summaries of the Mont's history and a hodge-podge of historical "artifacts." The fact that each museum exits into a gift shop should be the first clue that the prices may be prohibitively expensive. The **Musée Historique** contains exhibits on medieval torture devices and the Mont's most rapscallious prisoners, while the **Musée Maritime** has a collection of 300 antique scale model boats. The **Archéoscope** is most worth visiting. Its 20-minute presentation discusses the legends and history of the Mont with film, slides, music, and an intricate model that rises from the water amid angelic smoke. Admission to each museum runs at 40F or more, but you can buy a ticket to all three for 75F (students 60F). On the other hand, you might be better off buying a good Mont-related book for about half that price.

Do not wander off too far on the sand. The broad expanses are riddled with **quicksand,** and the bay's **tides** are the highest in Europe, shifting every six hours or so. During high-tide days, twice a month (3 days after the new moon and 3 days after the full moon), the *mascaret* (initial tidal wave) rushes in at 2m per second, flooding the beaches along the causeway. While the tides no longer rush in "faster than a horse at full gallop," they can be dangerous. To see this spectacle, you must be within the abbey fortifications two hours ahead of time.

When darkness falls, illumination transforms the Mont into a glowing jewel, best seen from either the causeway entrance or across the bay in Avranches (June-Aug. Mon.-Sat. 10pm-1am; Sept. 9pm-midnight). Dusk is also the time to revisit the crypts of the Abbey. **Les Imaginaires** immerse the sanctuary's corridors in a flood of light and music for the benefit of nocturnal visitors, projecting carpets and tapestries on the floors and walls in a brilliant spectacle of light. (Mid-May to Aug. 10pm-1am; Sept.

9pm-midnight; admission 60F, students 35F, under 12 free; last entry 1hr. before closing). In May, the Mont celebrates **St-Michel de Printemps,** when costumed men and women parading throughout the Mont recapture the local Breton traditions and dance to medieval and Renaissance music. The fall event, **St-Michel d'Automne,** held on the Sunday before the feast of St-Michel (late Sept.-early Oct.), is similar but more religious and more authentic. Call the tourist office for '97 dates.

■ Near Mont-St-Michel: Avranches

Balanced on a hill in a northern corner of the bay of Mont-St-Michel, Avranches (pop. 10,000) offers another base from which to explore the fortified island. But before rushing off to Normandy's *über*-attraction, give Avranches itself some time. After all, it was St. Aubert, the 8th-century Bishop of Avranches, who gave in to angelic pressure and built the Mont. As a result, the two are inextricably linked, both in place and time, and Avranches serves as a good primer for later trips island-ward. To get to the *centre ville* from the train station, cross the highway via the footbridge to the right of the station and lean into the heart-pounding hike uphill. The **tourist office,** 2, rue Général-de-Gaulle (tel. 02 33 58 00 22; fax 02 33 68 13 29), adjacent to the town hall, reserves rooms (10F) and gives out free town maps and brochures (open daily July-Aug. 9am-8pm; Sept.-June 9am-noon and 2-6pm). An **annex** (tel. 02 33 58 59 11) squats next to the entrance to the Jardin des Plantes (open July-Aug. 9am-noon). 24-hr **ATMs** can be found at **Société Générale,** across from the tourist office; **Crédit Agricole,** two blocks to the left of the tourist office on rue du Pot d'Etain; and **Crédit Mutuel,** two blocks from the tourist office at the corner of rue de la Constitution and rue St-Symphorien. The tourist office shares its building with **STN** (tel. 02 33 58 03 07), which sends buses to Mont-St-Michel (1 per day July-Aug., 23F50, roundtrip 45F; Sept.-June 1 per week) and to Granville (31F). (Station open Mon., Tues., and Thurs. 10:30am-noon and 3:30-6pm; Wed. and Fri. 10:30am-noon and 3:30-5pm.) The Caen-Rennes train line passes through Avranches' **BF station** at the bottom of the hill. Destinations include Granville (2 per day, 15min., 32F) and Paris via Foligny (2 per day, 5hr., 187F; station open Mon.-Sat. 8:30am-7pm, Sun. 1:45-10pm). The **post office** on rue St-Gervais offers **currency exchange** and poste restante (open Mon.-Fri. 8am-6:30pm, Sat. 8am-noon; **postal code:** 50300).

The popular **Hôtel de Normandie,** bd. L. Jozeau-Marigné (tel. 02 33 58 01 33), sits at the end of the steep footpath you'll encounter after crossing the footbridge to the right of the station. Run by an exceptionally friendly staff, the ivy-covered building offers cozy rooms with views of the patchwork countryside. A flash of your *Let's Go* makes the owners friends for life. (Singles 150F, with bath 170F. Doubles 180F, with bath or shower 230F. Shower 25F. TV 30F. Breakfast 30F. V, MC.) Opposite the tourist office, **Hôtel Record,** 7, rue Général de Gaulle (tel. 02 33 58 03 28), rents large rooms above a popular bar. (Singles and doubles 130F, with shower or bath 180F, with shower and toilet 200F. Extra bed 30F. Breakfast 22F.) Your cheapest bet might be a **chambre d'hôte.** The tourist office has a list of rooms that start at 100F per night. Avranches' **campground** (tel. 02 33 58 05 45), on rue de Verdun, should be open in 1997 after closing for renovations in '96. Call or ask at the tourist office.

Numerous cheap *brasseries* and restaurants surround the tourist office. **Le Commerce,** just across, offers three-course *menus* (60-74F) with specialties from all over Normandy—tripe and mussels alike (open Mon.-Sat. noon-2:30pm and 6:45-9:30pm; V, MC). At pl. St-Gervais, **Pizzeria l'Anticario** (tel. 02 33 58 32 10) serves up a great lunchtime menu for 45F that includes a *plat* and *dessert du jour,* all in a cozy, intimate, elegant, expressionist, non-toxic environment. (Open Tues.-Fri. noon-2pm and 7-11pm, Sat. noon-2pm and 7pm-midnight, Sun. 7pm-midnight.) Each Saturday from 9am to 3pm, a **market** fills pl. du Marché, off rue des Chapeliers. On another side of the square, the **supermarket Stoc** stocks picnic provisions (open Mon.-Fri. 9am-12:30pm and 2:30-7:30pm, Sat. 9am-7:30pm, Sun. 9:30-11:45am). A *baguette* bought at Stoc will taste even better in the shaded alleys of the **Jardin des Plantes,** pl. Carnot. Dotted with Romanesque arches, the garden's sprawling grounds provide a good view of the distant Mont-St-Michel. The garden is illuminated nightly from 8:30 to 11:30pm.

When Henry II, King of England and Duke of Normandy, in a fit of frustration over his tense relations with Archbishop of Canterbury Thomas à Becket, cried out, "Will no one rid me of this turbulent priest?" he didn't intend for it to be an order. At least that's what he told the pope after four of his knights galloped off to Canterbury and slew Becket. Nonetheless, Henry was excommunicated. A year and a half later, on May 22, 1172, Henry made penance on the steps outside Avranches' cathedral (no longer standing, *grâce à* the Revolution). A stone still marks the spot where he stood; it's near the **Terrace,** a pleasant hillside stroll behind the town hall.

A short distance away is Avranches' **museum.** It houses exhibits of regional garb and crafts, as well as a replica of a medieval scriptorium, which explains the materials and techniques used by Avranches' most famous residents. Most impressive, however, is the collection of Mont-St-Michel's manuscripts, which, in their multi-colored, calligraphic way, detail the finer points of theology, astronomy, and music. The summer finds many of the manuscripts in the *mairie* (June-Aug. daily 10am-noon and 2-6pm; 10F). Your preparation for Mont-St-Michel continues in pl. St-Gervais. The **Eglise St-Gervais** is an impressive, granite church whose 74-m tower contains a 32-bell chime, but the real treasure is inside. When the Archangel Michael appeared to Bishop Aubert and commanded him to build Mont-St-Michel, Aubert ignored the order. When Michael appeared again, Aubert continued to delay. The angel, realizing that he and an infinite number of friends could dance on this pinhead, decided that Aubert needed more forceful persuasion. Michael scolded Aubert by tapping him on the forehead, but he pressed his finger into the unwitting bishop's brow so enthusiastically that a dent resulted. You can see Aubert's skull (and the divot) in the **treasury,** right inside the door of the church.

Down rue de la Constitution, the **Patton Memorial** is officially American soil. The huge stone obelisk commemorates Operation COBRA's successful break through the German front between St-Lô and Périers in July of 1944. Patton's victory here resulted in the liberation of Avranches, a drive west into Brittany, and an advance east into the Loire Valley and on to Paris.

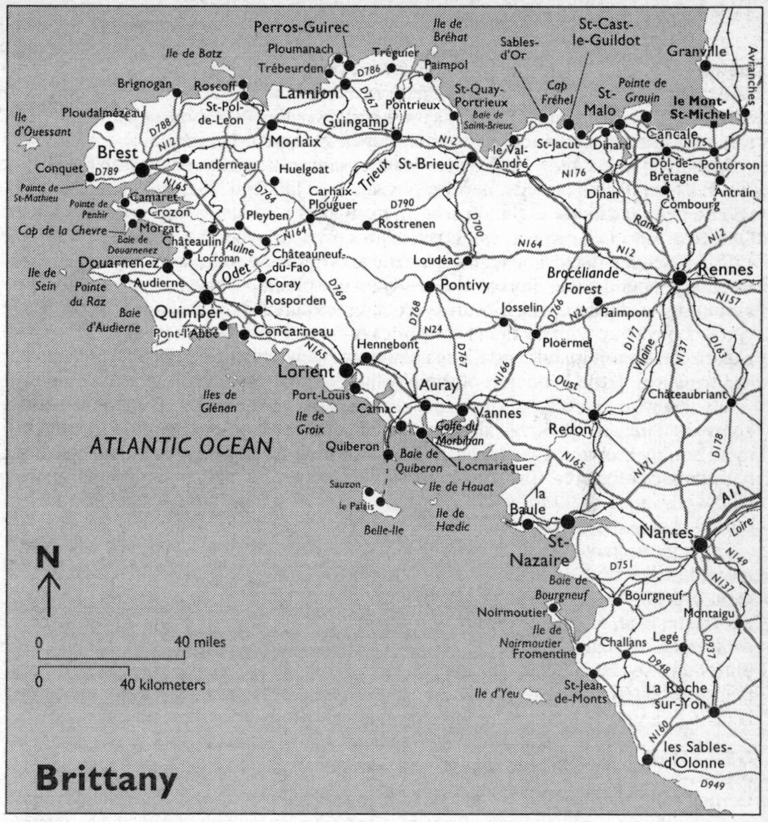

Bretagne (Brittany)

This peninsula, its cliffs gnawed by the sea into long crags and inlets, tugs away from mainland France, intent on its own direction. Unlike most of their compatriots, Bretons are a Celtic people whose ancestors crossed over from Britain to escape Anglo-Saxon invaders in the 5th and 6th centuries. They settled in the ancient Kingdom of Armor, converting its inhabitants to Christianity and renaming it "Little Britain," or Brittany. Many of Brittany's customs date back to its centuries as an independent duchy. The traditional costume of Breton women, the black dress and lace coiffe (an elaborate headdress), appears in museums, folk festivals, and even some markets. Lilting Brezhoneg (Breton) is spoken energetically at pubs and ports in the western part of the province, and some children learn the old Celtic tongue in school.

Modernization has come only in the postwar period to this relatively poor province, but it has come with a vengeance. Traditional vocations like farming and fishing have become increasingly difficult to pursue, and many young Bretons emigrate to large cities elsewhere in France or abroad. In the past, economic difficulties have fueled an active separatist movement, but recently the French government has granted more autonomy to the local leadership and has begun to support the preservation of Breton culture. In 1979, under Giscard d'Estaing's administration, students were allowed to replace one language section of the *baccalauréat* exam with Breton. François Mitterrand made Brittany more accessible with extensive road-building projects and the construction of TGV lines to Brest and Quimper. Today, separatist graffiti is not so conspicuous as it was fifteen years ago, when it adorned walls from Brest to Paris. Still, the Bretons remain proud of their distinct cultural heritage. Astérix and Obélix, two of Brittany's most famous natives, symbolize the Bretons' history of resistance to outsiders, whether they be Roman or French.

Brittany is lined with spectacular beaches and misted, almost apocalyptic headlands. If you dislike crowds, beware of visiting in July and August—French tourists will be here in droves. In the off season, many of the coastal resorts such as St-Malo, Quiberon, and Concarneau essentially shut down, but the churches, beaches, and cliffs still seduce the visitor with their eerie and romantic solitude. Whatever the season, try to spend some time on the crowded but pristine islands off the mainland or in the Argoat interior, where tourists are rarer and Breton traditions less disturbed—you'll come away with far richer memories of the people and the land.

Both the Breton islands and the mainland lay claim to some inscrutable archaeological treasures. Little is known of the Neolithic people who settled here before the Gauls and who erected the thousands of megaliths visible today. The Romans, who conquered the area in 56 BC, decorated some of these monuments and incorporated them into their own rituals. Later, the Christian Bretons capped some standing stones with crosses or carved Christian symbols into them. Menhirs are large single stones that weigh up to 100 tons and point skyward. Dolmens, stones stacked to form roofed passages that were once covered with earth, served as burial mounds.

The region's *crêperies* offer more than just the famed regional specialty. *Galettes* of ground buckwheat flour *(sarrasin)* wrapped around eggs, mushrooms, seafood, or ham, precede dessert crêpes made of ground wheat flour *(froment)* and filled with chocolate, fruit, or jam. These are accompanied by the dry *cidre brut* or the sweeter *cidre doux*. Brittany's *pâtisseries* display *kouign amann* (flaky sheets saturated with butter and sugar) and the custard-like *far breton*. Whatever the meal, rest assured that seafood *(fruits de mer)* will be a part of it; Brittany's coastal location ensures that aquatic fare will be fresh, plentiful, and creatively prepared.

GETTING AROUND

Getting to Brittany is hardly a problem; high-speed trains leave Paris' Gare Montparnasse and arrive in Rennes and Brest two and four hours later, respectively. Getting around Brittany is a different matter. The main train lines run between Rennes and Brest; between Rennes and Quimper; and between Nantes and Quimper. Smaller, less frequent trains and SNCF buses connect other cities to the main lines but not necessarily to each other. Private bus lines connect towns that the train lines miss, but they are often infrequent and inconvenient. **Cycling** is the best way to travel, especially since the most beautiful sights are also the least accessible by public transport. The terrain is relatively flat but gets a bit hillier in the interior. **Hikers** can choose from a number of routes, including the long-distance footpaths **GR341, GR37, GR38, GR380,** and the spectacular **GR34** along the northern coast.

Rennes

In 1720, a drunken carpenter knocked over his lamp and set most of Rennes ablaze. Despite this destructive conflagration, which consumed all but the heart of the wood-heavy city, Rennes (pop. 204,000) survived to become the administrative center of Brittany. Unlike other local towns, Rennes is most active during the school year, when 60,000 students move in and rouse the city from its summer slumber. Rennes is a popular stopover between Paris and Mont-St-Michel and a good base from which to explore the **Brocéliande forest** (see page 203). The small, charming *vieille ville* warrants a wander in any season, but those looking for deep insight into traditional Breton culture may find themselves itching to skip town.

ORIENTATION AND PRACTICAL INFORMATION

The **Vilaine river** cuts the city in two, with the station to the south and most sights and shopping to the north (20min. away). From the northern exit of the *gare,* **av. Jean Janvier** (straight ahead) goes to the river. The tourist office annex upstairs in the station can start you off. The main office is near the river, off pl. de la Liberté.

Tourist Information: Tourist Office Annex (tel. 02 99 53 23 23; fax 02 99 53 82 22), opposite the tix window at the *gare.* Free map, lists of hotels and restaurants. Open Mon.-Fri. 8am-7pm, Sat.-Sun. 10am-1pm and 3-6pm. **Main office,** pont de Nemours (tel. 02 99 79 01 98; fax 02 99 79 31 38), also provides schedules of seasonal events. Tours in French (July-Sept. daily at 3pm; Oct.-June weekly; 35F). Open Mon. 1-6pm, Tues.-Sat. 9am-6pm. **Le Rennais** is a bimonthly magazine that keeps you up to date on all that's happening in Rennes. Free at the tourist office.

Money: Banks with 24-hr. **ATMs** lurk in the *vieille ville,* the *gare,* and rue d'Isly.

Trains: pl. de la Gare (tel. 02 99 65 50 50, reservations 02 99 65 18 65), at the end of av. Jean Janvier. To: St-Malo (11 per day, 1hr., 67F); Nantes (8 per day, 2hr., 112F); Tours (8 per day, 3½hr., 179F plus 36-90F TGV reservation) via Le Mans (2hr., 116F); Caen (3 per day, 3½hr., 164F); St-Brieuc (10 per day, 1¼hr., 81F); Brest (3 per day, 4 TGV per day, 2½hr., 2hr. by TGV, 159F plus TGV reservation); Paris (3 per day, 9 TGV per day, 3½hr., 2hr. by TGV, 216F plus 36-90F TGV reservation). **Lockers.** Office open Mon.-Sat. 8am-7:30pm, Sun. 10am-7:30pm.

Buses: 16, pl. de la Gare (tel. 02 99 30 87 80). **TIV** (tel. 02 99 31 34 31) serves St-Malo (5 per day, Sat.-Sun. 1-2 per day, 1½hr., 55F) and Paimpont (Mon.-Sat. 5-7 per day, 1hr., 16F). **Cariane Atlantique** (tel. 02 40 20 46 99, in Nantes) goes to Nantes (Mon.-Sat. 2 per day, 2hr., 90F). **TAE** (tel. 02 99 50 64 17) travels to Dinard (4-5 per day, 3 on Sun., 1¾hr., 65F) and Dinan (6-7 per day, 4 on Sun., 1hr., 50F). **Anjou Bus** (tel. 02 41 69 10 00, in Angers) goes to Angers (2 per day, 3hr., 92F). **Les Courriers Bretons** (tel. 02 99 56 79 09) run to Mont-St-Michel (4 per day, 1 on Sun., 2½hr., 60F). Ticket window open Mon.-Fri. 9am-6:30pm.

Public Transportation: Star, office at 12, rue du Pré Botté (tel. 02 99 79 37 37). Buses run daily until about 6:30-7:30pm. Ticket 6F, *carnet* of 10 tickets 42F50. Office open Mon.-Fri. 7am-7pm, Sat. 9:30am-noon and 2-6:30pm.

Taxis: At the train station (tel. 02 99 30 79 79). 24hr.

Bike Rental: Kiosk in pl. de la République (tel. 02 99 79 63 72). 3-speeds free first hr., 2hr. 5F, 5hr. 15F, 10hr 25F. Deposit 1000F or passport. Open daily 9am-7pm.

Laundromat: Fluff and fold at 59, rue Duhamel. Open daily 8am-10pm.

English Books: Forum du Livre, on quai Lamartine (tel. 02 99 79 38 93). Open Mon.-Sat. 9:30am-7pm.

Hiking and Biking Information: Association Bretonne des Relais et Itinéraires (ABRI), also known as **Maison de la Randonnée,** 9, rue des Portes-Mordelaises (tel. 02 99 31 59 44; fax 02 99 30 02 96). ABRI offers piles of info on GR trails and lists of *gîtes d'étape.* Open Mon.-Sat. 9am-6pm.

French-American Center, 7, quai Chateaubriand (tel. 02 99 78 22 66), arranges joint French-American activities and exchange programs. Office on 2nd floor can help with visas, work permits, and French formalities in general. Open Mon.-Thurs. 9am-12:30pm and 1:30-6pm, Fri. 9am-12:30pm and 1:30-5pm.

Youth Center: Centre d'Information Jeunesse Bretagne, 6, cours des Alliés (tel. 02 99 31 47 48; fax 02 99 30 39 51), on 2nd floor. List of budget hotels. Info on cycling, cultural events, work opportunities, and more. Open Mon.-Fri. 10am-6pm, Sat. 10am-noon and 2-6pm; mid-July to mid-Aug. Mon.-Fri. 2-6pm.

Gay and Lesbian Organizations: Femmes entre elles, 9, rue de la Paillette (tel. 02 99 59 50 32), organizes events for lesbians and has a library. Open first and third Wed. of each month from 7-8pm. **AD-HOC (Association des Homosexuels de Condate),** 39B, rue Motte Brûlon (tel. 02 99 30 59 25), is a gay center.

Crisis Lines: Aides Bretagne, 2, quai Richemont (tel. 02 99 30 01 30), for AIDS info. **Intersecteur en Toxicomane,** 4, rue Edith Cawell (tel. 02 99 79 41 00), is for drug problems. **SOS Amitié** (tel. 02 99 59 71 71), for friendship. **SOS Racisme** (tel. 02 99 38 59 77).

Hospital: Hôpital de Pontchaillou, rue Henri Le Guilloux (tel. 02 99 28 43 21).

Medical emergency (SAMU) tel. 15 or 02 99 59 16 16.

Police: rue d'Echange (tel. 02 99 65 00 22), off pl. Ste-Anne. **Emergency** tel. 17.

Post Office: 27, bd. du Colombier (tel. 02 99 01 22 11), 1 block left of *gare* exit. **Branch office,** pl. de la République (tel. 02 99 79 50 71). **Currency exchange.** Poste restante. Open Mon.-Fri. 8am-7pm, Sat. 8am-noon. **Postal code:** 35000.

ACCOMMODATIONS AND CAMPING

You should reserve in the first week of July during the annual Tombées de la Nuit festival. In July and August, a university dorm remains open to student travelers for short stays (singles 92F per night). To check availability, call **CROUS,** 7, pl. Hoche (tel. 07 99 36 46 11; open Mon.-Fri. 8:30-4pm). A number of moderately priced hotels lie to the east of av. Jean Janvier between quai Richemont and the *gare.*

Auberge de Jeunesse (HI), 10-12, Canal St-Martin (tel. 02 99 33 22 33; fax 02 99 59 06 21). From the *gare,* follow av. Jean Janvier straight to the canal, where it becomes rue Gambetta. Go 5 blocks; take a left onto rue des Fossés. Follow rue de la Visitation, which ends across the street from pl. Ste-Anne. On the northern side of the *place,* rue St-Malo leads to the hostel (30min.). Or, take bus 20 on weekdays, 1 or 18 on weekends (direction: Centre Commercial Nord) to "Hôtel Dieu." From the bus stop, continue down the road, turn right onto rue St-Malo, and follow the street over a mini-canal to the intersection. The hostel is on the right. 1- to 4-person rooms. Laundry, kitchen, cafeteria. Discounts on train, ferry, and bus tickets. 80F. Singles 130F. Doubles 90F per person. Breakfast included. Reception 8-10am and 6-11pm. Lockout Sat.-Sun. 10am-6pm.

Hôtel Venezia, 27, rue Dupont des Loges (tel. 02 99 30 36 56; fax 02 99 30 78 78), off quai Richemont. Take av. Jean-Jaurès from the station. Turn right onto rue Dupont des Lopes, a block before the canal. *Let's Go*-loving couple lets spacious, well-decorated rooms in a great location. Singles 110F, with shower and TV 150F, with shower, toilet, and TV 170F. Doubles 125F, 170F, and 190F respectively. A flash of your *Let's Go* gets you a welcome and a good rate. All-you-can-eat breakfast with juice 25F. Call ahead for weekends in summer. V, MC.

Hôtel Riaval, 9, rue Riaval (tel. 02 99 50 65 58; fax 02 99 41 85 30). Exit the *gare* through the southern "Cour d'Appel" doors, and turn left. Clean and cozy hotel in a quiet neighborhood. Top-floor views of the city. Singles and doubles 115F, with shower 140F, with shower and toilet 165F. Triples 140F, with shower 180F. Quads with shower and toilet 200F. Shower 15F. Breakfast 26F. V, MC.

Hôtel Richemont, 8, rue Dupont des Loges (tel. 02 99 30 38 21; fax 02 99 31 73 20). Down the street from Hôtel Venezia. Bright rooms with showers. Singles 185-205F, with toilet 208-215F. Doubles 205-255F, with bath 240-270F. Breakfast 27F. V, MC.

Camping: Municipal des Gayeulles, near Parc des Bois (tel. 02 99 36 91 22). Take bus 3 from rue de Paris, the southern border of the Jardin de Thabor, to "Parc les Gayeulles." Grassy, scenic, isolated site. Adults 13F, child 6F, dog 6F, car 5F, motorcycle 3F, 4-person tent or trailer 15F, small tent 11F, electricity 17F, kitchen sink free. Hot shower 6F, cold shower free.

FOOD

Rennes is a *gourmand* traveler's dream. Be it Greek, Indian, Lebanese, Pakistani, or even French cuisine you're looking for, you'll find it on **rue St-Malo, pl. St-Michel,** or **rue St-Georges.** Party-poopers will find a **supermarket** in the **Nouvelles Galeries** on quai Duguay-Trouin (open Mon.-Sat. 9am-8pm). A **covered market** is held Monday through Saturday from 7am-6:30pm in Les Halles, behind the post office. There's an **open market** in a different place daily; ask the tourist office for locations.

Crêperie au Boulingrain, 25, rue St-Melaine (tel. 02 99 38 75 11). Formerly a prison, this place now serves *galettes* worth some jail time. The *boulingrain,* the restaurant's namesake, is a crêpe stuffed with apples, caramel, and almonds (37F). Open Mon.-Fri. 11:30am-2pm and 6:30-11pm, Sat.-Sun. 6:30-11pm.

L'Escale, 178, rue St-Malo (tel. 02 99 59 19 55), near the hostel. Smoky and cozy with a local clientele. Bounteous and inexpensive red wine. *Galettes* 10-38F, crêpes 6-22F, main dishes 20-50F. Open Wed.-Sun. 7:30pm-midnight. V, MC.

SIGHTS AND ENTERTAINMENT

The **Musée de Bretagne** (tel. 02 99 28 55 84) and the **Musée des Beaux-Arts** (tel. 02 99 28 55 85) occupy the same building by the canal at 20, quai Emile Zola. The Musée de Bretagne provides an introduction to the region's history and traditions with tools, costumes, and jewelry from prehistory to today. The Musée des Beaux-Arts displays an interesting collection of art from the 14th century to the present, including some decent Picassos (both open Wed.-Mon. 10am-noon and 2-6pm; tours Wed. and Fri. July-Aug. at 2:30pm; admission to Bretagne 15F, Beaux-Arts 20F, both 25F). Full ethnological indoctrination occurs at the **Ecomusée du pays de Rennes,** route de Châtillon-sur-Seiche (tel. 02 99 51 38 15), located on a former farm at the city's edge. Learn about Rennes' daily farm life since the early 1600s and picnic in the apple orchards. From pl. de la République, take bus 14 (#1 on Sun.) to "Le Gacet" (open Wed.-Fri. 9am-noon and 2-6pm, Sat. 2-6pm, Sun. 2-7pm; admission 26F, students 14F; admission to Musée de Bretagne plus Ecomusée 34F).

Those at the limits of museum tolerance can catch their breath in the startlingly green **Jardin du Thabor** behind the Renaissance **Eglise Notre-Dame** and **Cloître Ste-Melanie.** To reach the garden, follow rue Jean Janvier across the river as it turns into rue Gambetta and rue du Général Guillaudot until you see the church on the right. Concerts and art shows are often held in the garden (open June-Sept. daily 7am-9:30pm). On your way, step inside the church to gaze at the magnificent chapel altar and the blazing colors of the *vitraux* in the choir. Church-lovers will revel in the rust-colored columns and chandeliers of the magnificent **Cathédrale St-Pierre,** in the *vieille ville.* If its 16th- and 17th-century towers don't impress you, take in the amazing ceiling (open daily 9am-noon and 2-5pm).

In early July, Rennes holds the **Tombées de la Nuit,** nine days of non-stop music, dance, partying, theater, and mime by international performers who prowl the streets from noon to midnight. For info, write the Office de Tourisme, Festival de TN, 8, pl. du Maréchal Juin, 35000 Rennes (tel. 02 99 79 01 98 or 02 99 30 38 01).

Rennais nightlife grooves even during the summer, when the university empties out. **Rue St-Michel** is packed with hopping theme bars, while **rue St-Malo** bops with jazz clubs and boisterous Irish pubs. If you want to shake your boo-tay, boogie on down to the popular **Le Pyms,** 27, pl. du Colombier (tel. 02 99 67 30 00; cover 80F, Sun.-Tues. and Thurs. 60F; open daily 11pm-6am). Pink-pillared **L'Espace Loisirs,** 43, bd. de la Tour d'Auvergne (tel. 02 99 30 21 95), is worth a try (cover Fri.-Sat. 80F, Sun.-Wed. 50F, Thurs. 60F; open daily 11pm-5am). Talk and drink 'til 1am at **La Bernique Hurlante,** 40, rue St-Malo (tel. 02 99 36 21 12). The inconspicuous **Le Batchi,** 34, rue Vasselot (tel. 02 99 79 62 27; open until 5am), is Rennes' gay scene.

■ Near Rennes

BROCÉLIANDE FOREST

Brocéliande, rumored to have been the haunt of Merlyn and Arthur, is the largest remnant of the ancient forest that once covered Brittany and is well worth a daytrip. Be prepared to rent a bike, as the woods are vast. The village of **Paimpont,** nestled in the middle of a grove by a lake, is the best base for exploring the network of roads and paths leading to the **Fontaine de Jouvence** (Fountain of Youth), **Tombeau de Merlyn** (Merlyn's tomb), and the **Val Sans Retour** (Valley of No Return).

The forest is 45km from Rennes. **TIV buses** leave from Rennes (Mon.-Sat. 5-7 per day, 1hr., 16F) and stop near the tourist office in Paimpont. The **tourist office** (tel. 02 99 07 84 23; fax the *mairie* at 02 99 07 88 18) has a free map of suggested bike and car routes and lists of local accommodations; it also sells a useful cycling guide (*VTT en Brocéliande,* 35F) and a booklet of local legends (28F) full of dragons and fairies.

Time in a Bottle

While the "Fountain of Youth" conjures up images of Ponce de León traipsing around Florida in a fruitless search for longevity, the Brocéliande Forest's *Fontaine de Jouvence* takes its name from a different ritual, one that is more pragmatic but equally mystical. When druids still ran amok in Brittany's wooded area, the summer solstice (June 21 or June 22) was one of the most important dates on the calendar. On this day, all newborn infants were brought to the fountain; their names were then entered into the official register as the newest members of the community. The most recently born were often too weak to be presented at the fountain, so their entry into the census was delayed until the next year. As a result, year-old babies could be entered into the register, declaring them newborn and reducing their age by a year, granting them youth anew.

If you have a car, you can hire a guide at the office to show you the sights. (July-Aug. Thurs. and Sat. only; morning visit of the lower forest 15F, afternoon visit of the upper forest 25F, day-long tour 35F. Open daily July-Aug. 9:30am-12:30pm and 1:30-6:30pm; Sept.-June 10am-noon and 2-6pm.)

A wonderful **gîte d'étape** (tel. 02 99 07 81 40) is just 3km to the southeast in **Trudeau.** Follow directions to Plélan-le-Grand, then turn left toward St-Péran at the intersection; Trudeau is the first village on the road. Reception is in the ivy-colored house, 200m into the village on your left (30 beds in 2 dorm-style rooms, 44F). The owners also keep **chambres d'hôtes** (doubles with shower 210F, with toilet and shower 230F; triples with shower 270F, with toilet and shower 290F), a **table d'hôtes** for the *gîte* guests (90F 3-course meal includes drink), and a superb local inn (120F *menu* is a gargantuan feast; reservations only). This Jack-of-all-trades family business also **rents bikes** (40F per ½-day, 50F per day) and runs the **campground** across the street (15F per person, 15F per site; electricity 10F; free hot showers).

BRITTANY

Brocéliande's **Auberge de Jeunesse (HI)** (tel. 02 97 22 76 75) lies in Choucan, 12km from Paimpont on the GR37. From Paimpont take the road towards Concoret; turn at the sign to La Ville Danet and follow directions to Choucan. The hostel is a simple affair with 22 beds (40F; open June-Sept. 15). **Mountain bikes** are available in the bar **Le Brécilien,** next to the tourist office (20F per hr., 60F per ½-day, 90F per day; passport deposit). The **Camping Municipal de Paimpont** (tel. 02 99 07 89 16) is a basic site across the narrow arm of the lake from the intersection (14F per person, 12F per place and tent, 4F per car; electricity 15F; reception across the street, May 15-Sept. 30 daily 8am-8pm).

JOSSELIN

The word "château" is most often associated with the Loire Valley, but the town of Josselin (pop. 3000) nestled comfortably in the Oust Valley gently asserts Brittany's modest claim to these magnificent structures. A mere 80km from the bustle of Rennes, Josselin maintains the look and feel of a medieval hamlet. **Le Bellier Buses** (tel. 02 99 31 33 62 in Rennes) run to Josselin from Rennes and Pontivy (Mon.-Sat. 3-4 per day, Sun. 2 per day, 1¼hr., 44F from Rennes, 50min., 25F from Pontivy), and **Cariane Atlantique** (tel. 02 97 47 29 64 in Vannes) sends buses from Vannes (Mon.-Fri. 2 per day, 50min., 42F). All buses stop at pl. de la Résistance (on Sun., at the STOC supermarket, 1.5km up rue St-Jacques from the *place*). Walk into town on rue Olivier de Clisson and follow the signs to the **tourist office,** pl. de la Congrégation (tel. 02 97 22 36 43; fax 02 97 22 20 44). They offer a useful (and free) map of the town, as well as information on all of the surrounding communities (open July-Aug. daily 10am-6pm; Sept.-Oct. and April-June 10am-noon and 2-6pm; Nov.-March Mon. 2-6pm, Tues.-Fri. 10am-noon and 2-6pm, Sat. 10am-noon). If it's cash you're after, there's a 24-hour **Crédit Agricole ATM** behind the basilica on rue Monseigneur Joubier and a **Crédit Mutuel** money machine in pl. des Remparts. The **police** await your calls at 02 97 22 00 07; in an **emergency** dial 17 before screaming. The **hospital** (tel. 02 97 73 13 13) is on rue St-Jacques. The **post office** is on rue Olivier de Clisson and loves to **exchange currency.** There's an **ATM** inside, along with poste restante (**postal code:** 56120; open Mon.-Fri. 9am-noon and 2-5pm, Sat. 9am-noon).

If you decide to while away more than one day in Josselin, bunk out at the **gîte d'étape** (tel. 02 97 22 21 69 or 02 97 22 24 17 at the *mairie*) at the base of the castle. If you descend to the water from the tourist office, turn left on rue de Canal and walk about 500m. They offer many dorm-style beds and two doubles (44F, 3-night max. stay). You can rough it at **Camping du Bas de la Lande** (tel. 02 97 22 22 20), between Josselin and Guégon. Situated on the Oust with beautiful views, mini-golf, and fishing (12F per person, 9F per car, 9F per tent, 13-16F for electricity).

The stately **château** (tel. 02 97 22 36 45) on the banks of the river is, quite justifiably, Josselin's pride and joy. Constructed in the 11th century, it has been the subject of dispute since its inception, beginning with the decision of the English King Henry II Plantagenêt (the same fellow who "ordered" Thomas à Beckett's death) to raze the structure as punishment to the Bretons who opposed his attempted takeover of the duchy. In 1370, Olivier de Clisson assumed control of the rebuilt château and expanded it to its present form, adding four towers, a 26m-diameter keep, and a castle (entrance building). Later work added the flamboyant Gothic and Renaissance longhouse as well as the granite lacework. Note the repeated "A+" decorative motifs; it's the Rohan family motto. The library bears an "A" formed by three salamanders—the "A" is the symbol of Duchess Anne de Bretagne, and the salamanders are emblems of the Visconti family, allies of the Rohans. Since the castle is still a private home, you can only see it by taking a 45-minute tour (in French or English). The château's former stables are now home to the **Musée de Poupées,** 3, rue des Trent (tel. 02 97 22 36 45). Glass cases full of dolls stare back at visitors in all their eerie lifelessness; "Benetton Barbie" (1991) stands next to a hand-carved wooden doll of the 18th century. Each summer, a temporary exhibit features international dolls. 1997's subject is set to be Africa. (Château and museum open daily 10am-6pm; April-May and Oct. Tues. and Sat.-Sun. 2-6pm; June and Sept. daily 2-6pm. Admission to château 30F, to museum 29F, to both 56F.)

In the town center sits the **Basilique Notre-Dame du Roncier**—its placement here is a bit of a minor miracle. In 808 a farmer discovered a statue of the Virgin resting in a pile of brambles. He took it home, only to discover later that the plant-loving statue had migrated back to the brambles. This event was repeated until the farmer realized that the Virgin wanted a glorious basilica built on the site of the thorny bushes. Revolutionaries, as is their wont, burned the wooden statue in 1793, but a fragment was salvaged. The toothpick-like remnant can be seen in a reliquary to the right of the Lady Chapel. On the right of the main altar is Olivier de Clisson and Marguerite de Rohan's tomb. The mourning figures around the base of the tomb were beheaded by generous Revolutionaries, who apparently could not bring themselves to disfigure the tomb itself. (Free guided tours of the church Mon.-Sat. 10:30am-12:30pm and 2:30-5:30pm.) To raise yourself to new heights, and to bring your legs to new heights of lactic acid production, climb the 138 steps to the top of the church tower. It's a great view, if you can handle the vertigo on the way down (open daily 10:30am-12:30pm and 2-6pm; free).

Crêperies and *brasseries* guard the church in pl. Notre-Dame. In this medieval square sits the **Hôtel Restaurant de France,** 6, pl. Notre Dame (tel. 02 97 22 23 06). They serve up a 79F *menu* with a multitude of options—lamb, veal, duck, and salmon (open daily 12:15-2pm and 7:15-9pm; closed Sun. night and all day Mon. in the off season; V, MC). Dine with Josselin's glory in full view at the **Hôtel-Restaurant du Château,** just across the canal at 1, rue Général de Gaulle (tel. 02 97 22 20 11). In an elegant dining room that lends itself to château-watching, indulge in the 82F *menu* featuring fish and goose (open daily noon-2pm and 7:30-9:30pm; V, MC).

Fougères

Fougères (pop. 25,000), situated prominently in the Nançon Valley on the border of Brittany and France, has long been at the confluence of conflicting ideas. The object of feuding land-hungry barons in the Middle Ages, the city is today watching its traditional shoe-making industry wither under encroaching modern industries. The *vieille ville* clings tenaciously to its medieval heritage, however, and a stroll through its streets and fantastic château is as close to time travel as one can get.

ORIENTATION AND PRACTICAL INFORMATION

Fougères is 50km from Rennes. No trains run here; the *gare* only serves buses. **TIV buses** (tel. 02 99 99 08 77 in Fougères, 02 99 30 87 80 in Rennes) run from Rennes (Mon.-Fri. 9 per day, Sat. 5 per day, Sun. 2 per day, 1hr., 47F). **Courriers Bretons** (tel. 02 99 99 08 77) sends 'em here from St-Malo (2 per day, 2¼hr., 75F) via Pontorson (2 per day, 1hr., 42F) and Vitré (Mon., Wed., and Fri. 2 per day, 1½hr., 61F). The SNCF (tel. 08 36 35 35 35) runs to Laval (2 per day, 1hr., 60F). The bus station is at pl. de la République (open Mon.-Sat. 9:30am-noon and 2-7pm). Walk up bd. Jean-Jaurès as it curves right into pl. Aristide Briand to find the **tourist office** (tel. 02 99 94 12 20; fax 02 99 99 46 21). They have loads o' free maps and goodies (open July-Sept. Mon.-Sat. 9am-7pm, Sun. 9am-2pm; Oct.-June Mon.-Sat. 9:30am-12:30pm and 2-6pm, Sun. 10am-noon and 2-4pm). Fill your wallet at the **Crédit Mutuel ATM,** 15, rue du Tribunal, or its comrade **Crédit Agricole,** 8, bd. Leclerc. The **hospital** is at 133, rue Forêt (tel. 02 99 99 31 34). The **police** kick back at 02 99 94 25 25. In an **emergency,** dial 17. Get your philatelistic kicks at the **post office,** av. Général de Gaulle. There's a 24-hour **ATM,** currency exchange, poste restante (**postal code:** 35300), and candy (open Mon.-Fri. 8:30am-6:30pm, Sat. 8:30am-noon).

ACCOMMODATIONS AND CAMPING

Hôtel Le Flaubert, 1, rue Gustave Flaubert (tel. 02 99 99 00 43), offers pretty, spacious rooms in a not-so-pretty neighborhood. From the *gare,* walk down the street directly across from the police station, through the rotary, onto rue Canrobert. Take the second left (rue Victor Hugo); the hotel is on the right, one block up (singles and doubles 100F, with shower 135F, with shower and toilet 170-240F; extra bed 36F; breakfast 22F; V, MC). Right across from the bus station is the adequate **Hôtel de Bretagne,** 7, pl. de la République (tel. 02 99 99 31 68). A quirky couple lets drab rooms with firm mattresses. (Singles 90-100F. Doubles 100-110F, with shower 125F, with shower and toilet 140F. Triples 135F, with shower 160F, with shower and toilet 185F. Quads 160F, 200F, and 220F respectively. Breakfast 20F. V, MC.) The stars shine brightly on **Camping Municipal Paron,** route de la Chapelle-Janson (tel. 02 99 99 40 81), and its pleasant, shady sites. (12F per person, 14F per tent, 8F per vehicle, 15-19F for electricity. Open mid-June to Sept. Office open 9-11am and 5-8pm.)

The *vieille ville* is chock-full o' *crêperies,* but rumor has it that you can't beat **La Maison des Loriers,** 1, rue de la Pinterie (tel. 02 99 94 34 44). High-quality *galettes* (13-38F) and crêpes (14-37F), including concoctions like the *exotique,* piled with pineapple, coconut, and ice cream (37F). There's also a 45F crêpe-*galette* lunchtime *menu* (open daily noon-2:30pm and 7-11pm; Sept.-May closed Mon. night and Tues.; V, MC). The spicier side of life is at the bottom of the hill: **Le Samsara,** 80, rue de la Pinterie (tel. 02 99 99 68 62), serves up curry and other Indian treats. Try the three-course 52F lunch *menu* (open daily noon-2pm and 6-9pm; V, MC).

SIGHTS

Fougères' magnificent **château** (tel. 02 99 99 79 69) rests comfortably on a promontory flanked by rock walls and the Nançon River. A paradigm of military architecture, its construction began around AD 1000 and continued well into the 16th century. Despite the wonderful defensive position afforded by its swampy, valley location, the château was unfortunately in the more offensive position of Fougères itself, the one medieval stronghold between Brittany and France. As a result, the château was conquered no fewer than five times, continually razed and rebuilt. Each cycle of capture and reconstruction led to progressively stronger fortifications; one of the many destructive forays of the English King Henry II resulted in the replacement of wood

Snake Woman

One of the stained-glass windows in Fougères' Eglise St-Sulpice bears the image of a beautiful woman with long blond hair, a mirror in her hand, and the lower body of a snake: Mélusine, daughter of the King of Albania, killed her father when she discovered him abusing her mother. As punishment, she was turned into a serpent-woman every Saturday. On these days, she would hide herself in the château's underground passages. One day, however, her husband became suspicious of his wife's frequent absences and peered through the keyhole of her hiding place. There he beheld his bride in her bath, brushing her long hair, while her scaly extremities flailed about. Understandably upset, he burst into the room, only to have Mélusine scream in terror and slither into the Fougères castle's subterranea, never to be seen again. Legend has it that her screams can be heard on the eve of any tragedy and have foretold not only plagues but also the beginning of the World War II bombardments in 1944.

with stone. Nowadays, the château is in ruins, not only through warfare but also because Fougères' resourceful citizens made off with much of the stone for their own dwellings; after all, a man's home is his castle. Thirteen towers remain, including the behemoth Mélusine tower; this giant is 13m in diameter with 3½m thick walls and rises 31m into the air. (Open daily 9am-7pm. 45-min. tours (in French) hourly from 9-11am and 2-6pm; tours (in English) leave 5min. after the French tours 10-11am and 2-5pm. Admission 22F, students 16F50. Combined ticket château and clocher St-Leonard 27F, students 22F.)

Right outside the castle walls is Fougères' oldest church, the 15th- to 18th-century **Eglise St-Sulpice.** The flamboyant Gothic nave is altogether unassuming, featuring *vitraux* that illustrate martyrdom in exquisite detail. The nave's simplicity contrasts with the magnificent choir and elaborate Baroque altar. Note St-Sulpice's flabbergasted expression to the right of the altar, as well as the rare image of Mary breastfeeding Christ (in the Chapel Notre-Dame des Marais, on the left of the nave).

BRITTANY

Outside the church's doors is the *über*-mediæval **pl. du Marchix.** Enjoy the leaning house fronts and narrow streets as you wander uptown. A stop in the well-kept **Jardin Public** will let you catch your breath and enjoy the panoramic view of the château, church, and surrounding countryside. An even more glorious lookout awaits at the top of the tower of **Eglise St-Leonard.** The 15th- to 16th-century church is not all that striking, save for its elegantly carved façade and primary-colored *vitraux.* What will strike you is the effort it takes to reach the top of the tower; the view is almost worth it (open Mon.-Sat. 11am-12:30pm and 2-6pm, Sun. 2-7pm; admission 11F, less if seen in conjunction with château, see above). A short walk down rue Nationale leads to the **Musée Emmanuel de la Villéon** (tel. 02 99 99 19 98). It houses a collection of Impressionist works by de la Villéon, who was born in Fougères and skipped town as soon as he could walk (open mid-June to Sept. daily 11am-12:30pm and 2:30-6pm; free).

St-Malo

St-Malo is the ultimate getaway spot—and everybody knows it. To a 6th-century Welshman, St. Malo, the island was a refuge from marauding Angles and Saxons. To privateers and pirates, the growing city offered protection from aggressors of all stripes. To the writer Chateaubriand, St-Malo's ever-changing shore provided Romantic inspiration. Now a bustling city of 49,000, St-Malo is a wonderful place to visit; walk on the walls, explore the tiny streets, and duck into the restaurants and shops scattered throughout its *vieille ville.* Although 80% of the city was destroyed in World War II, St-Malo did not rush to rebuild by burdening itself with tons of concrete; taking its time, it has been reconstructed so well that it's nearly impossible to distinguish the old from the new. Within its towering stone walls, a web of cobblestone streets winds among 15th- to 17th-century-style buildings. Almost as impressive as the city's miles of ramparts are its miles of beaches—warm brown sands that dismiss the multitudes of sun-worshippers as the engulfing tide rolls in.

ORIENTATION AND PRACTICAL INFORMATION

The walled city *(intra muros)* is the northernmost point of St-Malo. The train station is in the town center; cross bd. de la République and follow av. Louis-Martin straight to the tourist office (10min.). Take bus 2, 3, or 4 (7F, every 20min.) from the stop on bd. de la République to "St-Vincent." To get to the tourist office from the ferry terminals, turn left onto quai St-Louis as you leave the *gare maritime.*

Tourist Information: Tourist Office, esplanade St-Vincent (tel. 02 99 56 64 48), near the entrance to the old city. Very busy staff offers free map and list of accommodations and restaurants. Open daily July-Aug. 8:30am-8pm; Sept.-June Mon.-Sat. 9am-12:30pm and 1:30-6pm. **Le Pays Malouin** lists local happenings and hotspots. It comes out on Fridays and is available at any *tabac* (5F).

Money: ATMs can be found in the *vieille ville* at **Crédit Agricole,** rue Gouin de Beauchesue and at **Banque Populaire,** rue Rorcon de la Barbinais.

Trains: pl. de l'Hermine (tel. 02 99 40 70 20). To: Paris-Montparnasse (3 per day, 5hr., 291F); Rennes (8-12 per day, 1hr., 67F); Caen via Dol (8 per day, 3½hr., 141F); Dinan via Dol (8 per day, 1hr., 44F). Open Mon.-Fri. 5:30am-8:05pm, Sat. 6am-7:45pm, Sun. 7:30am-8:20pm. **Lockers** 15-30F; **luggage storage** 30F per day per item. **Bike rental** July-Aug. (10-speed 44F per day, *VTTs* 55F per day).

Buses: Offices in the pavilion opposite the tourist office. **Tourisme Verney** (tel. 02 99 40 82 67) jogs to: Rennes (Mon.-Fri. 6 per day, Sat. 2 per day, Sun. 1 per day, 2¼hr., 54F); Dinan (Mon.-Sat. 6 per day, 1hr., 33F); Cancale (Mon.-Sat. 3-4 per day, 50min., 20F). Buses leave from the esplanade St-Vincent and stop briefly at the train station. Office open Mon.-Sat. 8:30am-7pm; Sept.-June Mon.-Fri. 8:30am-noon and 2-6:30pm, Sat. 8:30am-noon. **Courriers Bretons** (tel. 02 99 56 20 44) run to Mont-St-Michel (1-2 per day, 1½hr., 98F roundtrip) and Cancale (3 per day, Sun. 1 per day, 30min., 20F, 40% senior discount). Office open Mon.-Fri. 8:30am-7pm, Sat. 8:30am-6pm; Sept.-June Mon.-Fri. 8:30am-noon and 2-6:15pm, Sat. 8:30am-noon. **Les Courriers Bretons** (tel. 02 99 56 74 73) offer trips to Cap Fréhel (June and Sept. Wed., 5hr., 80F), Mont-St-Michel (April-Oct. Tues., Wed., and Fri., 9hr., 115F), Brocéliande (mid-June-mid-Sept. Fri., 6hr., 165F), and the D-Day beaches (July-Aug. Thurs., 11hr.). Office open July-Aug. Mon.-Sat. 8am-7pm, Sun. 8:30am-noon and 3-6pm; Sept.-June Mon.-Fri. 8:30am-noon and 2-6:30pm.

Ferries: Brittany Ferries, Gare Maritime de la Bourse (tel. 02 99 40 64 41; fax 02 99 82 55 01). To Portsmouth (1 per day March 12-Nov. 15, irregular service Nov. 16-March 11; April-Oct. 19, 210F, students 180F. Oct. 20-March 31 180F, students 150F; 7hr., same prices for roundtrip with 5 nights in Britain); Plymouth (same fares as Portsmouth; 7½hr.); Poole (May-Sept. only; 4 per week; 8½hr.; May-June and Sept. 200-240F, students 180-210F; July-Aug. 240-250F, students 210-230F; same prices for roundtrip with 5 nights in Britain); Cork (March-Sept. only; 1-3 per week; 18hr.; July-Aug. 430-530F, students 380-470F; Sept.-June 340-370F, students 310-340F; roundtrip with 10-night max. stay in Ireland July-Aug. 520-670F, students 460-600F; Sept.-June 420-450F, students 380-410F). **Condor Ferries** (tel. 02 99 20 03 00; fax 02 99 56 39 27) run ferries from the Gare Maritime de la Bourse to Jersey (275F roundtrip, students 195F), Guernsey (315F roundtrip, students 270F), and Sark (rates same as Guernsey). **Emeraude Lines** (tel. 02 99 40 48 40; fax 02 99 40 04 43) run to the same islands (all 275F roundtrip). **Courriers Bretons** organizes trips to Ile de Bréhat (June-Sept. Wed., 13½hr., 145F).

Public Transportation: St-Malo bus (tel. 02 99 56 06 06), in the bus office pavilion. Tickets 7F (valid 1hr.); *carnet* of 10 tickets 49F. 24-hr. pass 20F.

Taxis: Allô Taxis Malouins (tel. 02 99 81 30 30) leave from St-Vincent and station.

Bike Rental: Diazo, 47, quai du Duguay-Trouin (tel. 02 99 40 31 63; fax 02 99 56 35 72). 3-speeds 40F per ½-day, 50F per day, 250F per week. Mountain bikes 60F per ½-day, 80F per day, 480F per week. 500F or passport deposit. Open Mon.-Fri. 9am-noon and 2-6pm, Sun. 10am-noon, 2-3pm, and 5-6pm.

Windsurfer Rental: Surf School St-Malo, 2, av. de la Hoguette (tel. 02 99 40 07 47; fax 02 99 56 44 96). Walk along the Grande Plage until you see the signs. First rental 150F per hr., 250F per ½-day; subsequent rentals 100F per hr., 200F per ½-day. Four 2-hr. lessons 800F. Open daily 9am-noon and 2-6pm.

Laundromat: 27, bd. de la Tour d'Auvergne. Open daily 7am-9pm.

Help Center: Planning Familial, 10, rue Ernest Renan (tel. 02 99 56 20 75). HIV tests, medical counseling. Open Mon.-Fri. 9am-noon and 2-7pm; Aug. 2-7pm.

Hospital: Centre Hospitalier Broussais, 1, rue de la Marne (tel. 02 99 21 21 21).

Ambulance: 87, bd. Gambetta (tel. 02 99 40 02 02 or 02 99 56 30 64). 24hr.

Police: pl. des Frères Lamennais (tel. 02 99 40 85 80). **Emergency** tel. 17.

Post Office: 1, bd. de la Tour d'Auvergne (tel. 02 99 20 51 70), at the intersection with bd. de la République. Poste restante (postal code: 35401). **ATM.** Open Mon.-Fri. 8am-7pm, Sat. 8am-noon. **Branch office,** pl. des Frères Lamennais in the *vieille ville* (tel. 02 99 40 89 90). **Currency exchange. Postal code:** 35400.

ACCOMMODATIONS AND CAMPING

Reserve up to six months in advance to repose in the *vieille ville* in July and August. Don't sleep on beaches—St-Malo's sands disappear each night under the tides.

Auberge de Jeunesse/Centre de Rencontres Internationales (HI), 37, av. du Révérend Père Umbricht (tel. 02 99 40 29 80). From the station, take bus 5 (direction: Paramé) to "Auberge de Jeunesse" (last bus at 7:30pm). On foot, from the front of the station follow bd. de la République to the right. After 2 blocks, turn right onto av. Ernest Renan. Follow it for 3 blocks, then turn left onto rue Guen, which becomes av. de Moka after the rotary. Turn right on av. Pasteur, which becomes av. du Révérend Père Umbricht (keep right; 30min.). Plantation-like building fronted by tennis court, 3 blocks from the beach. Kitchen. Laundry in the Foyer (25F). 250 beds. 4- to 8-person rooms 69F per person. Singles 75F, with shower 110F. Doubles 75F per person. Sheets 16F. Breakfast included. Lunch or dinner 37F. Reception all day, except noon-2pm. Lockout (only for people in collective rooms) 10am-5pm. No curfew. After 9:30pm the guard in the **Foyer des Jeunes Travailleurs,** next door, can let you in. Reservations vital July-Aug.

Hôtel Gambetta, 40, bd. Gambetta (tel. 02 99 56 54 70). Close to the hostel. Pretty, clean rooms in a calm area. Singles 110F, with shower and toilet 150F. Doubles 140F, with shower and toilet 220F. Quads and quints with shower and toilet 300F. Showers 16F. Breakfast 30F. V, MC.

Hôtel le Neptune, 21, rue de l'Industrie (tel. 02 99 56 82 15). Good, quiet location 5min. from beach, *gare,* and *vieille ville.* Pleasant, beige rooms with pitched ceilings on the top floor. Slow-paced bar downstairs. Singles and doubles 120F, with shower 150F, with shower and toilet 170F, with bath and toilet 190F. Triples and quads with shower 210F. Quint 245F. Extra bed 45F. Shower 15F. Breakfast 28F.

Les Chiens du Guet, 4, pl. du Guet (tel. 02 99 40 46 77). Marvelous location *intra muros,* right next to the ramparts and promenade and 1min. from the beach. Energetic owner loves to practice her English. Attractive singles 150-190F, with shower 180-230F. Triples with shower and toilet 280-350F. Off-season, prices drop to 140-150F, 150F, and 180F respectively. Shower 15F, but the fee is often waived off-season. Breakfast 28F. Popular restaurant downstairs caters to tourists, with 60-180F *menus* of those ever-groovy regional specialties. V, MC.

Camping: Camping Municipal de la Cité d'Aleth, (tel. 02 99 81 60 91) near promenade de la Corniche at the western tip of St-Servan. Buses 1 and 6 run to "Aleth." Simple sites in a beautiful location. Decent sanitary facilities. 20F per adult, car and tent 27F.

FOOD

If you aren't a fan of crêpes or *fruits de mer,* you might as well go home. You'll have to poke around in the *vieille ville* to find places that serve more exotic fare. **Outdoor markets** sprout from 8am-12:30pm behind Eglise Notre-Dame-des-Grèves (Mon., Thurs., and Sat.); on **pl. Bouvet** in St-Servan and at the **Marché aux Légumes** (both Tues. and Fri.); and on **pl. du Prieuré** in Paramé (Wed. and Sat.). **Stoc supermarket,** on av. Pasteur, near the youth hostel, sells food in cans and boxes (open Mon.-Fri. 8:30am-12:30pm and 2:30-7:30pm, Sat. 8:30am-7:30pm, Sun. 9:30am-noon; V, MC). Before you head out onto the sands to picnic, a **Proxi Mart** in the *vieille ville* can set you up with the grub you need (at the Marché aux Légumes; open Mon.-Sat. 8am-1pm and 3:30-8pm; Sun. 9am-1pm and 3:30-8pm).

La Capri, 10, rue de Boyer (tel. 02 99 40 40 03), serves traditional crêpes at non-traditional prices. The 49F *menu Breton* or 70F *menu* offers a variety of *galettes,* crêpes, *moules,* pizzas, and desserts. Friendly owner offers *moule*-eating lessons. Open daily 11:30am-3pm and 6:30-midnight. V, MC.

Chez Ferhat, 4, rue de la Vieille Boucherie (tel. 02 99 40 54 40). Welcome relief from the crêpe onslaught. Big ol' servings of chicken and lamb couscous (65F) with pitchers of sangria. Check out the 55F lunch *menu.* Open daily 10:30am-3pm and 6-11pm; Sept.-June open Tues.-Sun. V, MC.

Le Robert Surcouf, 16, rue Toulouse (tel. 02 99 40 47 65), near the Musée de Poupées. English-speaking owner serves 68F and 98F *menus* of regional specialties in a quiet, elegant setting. Open Tues.-Sat. 11:15am-1pm and 6-10pm, Sun. 11:15am-1pm. V, MC.

El Patio, 4, av. du Révérend Père Umbricht (tel. 02 99 40 15 01). Sit down or take away huge pizzas (30-50F). They deliver, too, if you don't want to make the 20min. walk from the hostel. Try the immense Pizza El Patio (54F). Open Tues.-Sun. noon-2pm and 7pm-midnight. V, MC.

SIGHTS AND ENTERTAINMENT

The best view of St-Malo is from its ramparts—the old town on one side and a long stretch of sea on the other. The reconstruction of the 15th- to 17th-century slate and stone buildings is evident from this vantage point. The top of the Porte St-Vincent opposite the tourist office overlooks pl. Chateaubriand, where street performers serenade café- and restaurant-goers. On the other side of the Hôtel de Ville, Porte St-Thomas looks out to the **Fort National,** accessible only at low tide. Farther along, the **Tour Bidouane** marks the end of the old city. Climb down to the beach and stroll along the stone walkway to **Le Grand Bé.** This small island holds the grave of the writer Chateaubriand (1768-1848), who asked to be buried near the roaring of the waves and wind. Don't set out if the sea is within 10m of the submersible walkway; you may get stranded in the surf. The **Piscine de Bon-Secours,** down the beach from Tour Bidouane, is a swimming pool whose stone walls hold the water that enters them at high tide. At low tide, they become a favorite teen hang-out. Though the map from the tourist office helps navigation, it's easier (and more fun) to stash the map and follow your nose. The *vieille ville* is too small for you to lose your way, so trust your senses and explore the streets independently.

St-Malo's museums can't compare to the beauty of the city itself. Still, if it should rain, while away the wetness at the **Musée de la Ville** (tel. 02 99 40 71 11), at the Hôtel de Ville near Porte St-Vincent, which explores the city's history through maps, models, and pirate paraphernalia. You can also climb the watchtowers for a panoramic view of the city and sea. The **Musée du Pays Malouin** covers everything from boat-building to Breton headgear, including a section on St-Malo's reconstruction (open Wed.-Mon. 10am-noon and 2-6pm; admission to both 25F, students 12F50). At the **Tour Solidor** on the other side of the *vieille ville* is the **Musée du Long-Cours.** It houses objects connected to sea voyages, from models to sailors' artwork (open daily May-Oct. 10am-noon and 2-6pm; Nov.-April closed Tues.; admission 25F, students 12F50). Admission to all three museums is 37F50, students 19F.

Perhaps the liveliest "museum" in town is at pl. du Québec, near the Tour Bidouane, where **La Maison du Québec** welcomes crazy *Québécois* and anyone who has interest in their brotherhood with the *Malouins.* The most famous of them all was adventurer Jacques Cartier who, *à la* Columbus, thought he had found Asia when he landed on the shores of a forested land in 1534. He named it "Canada," which he thought was the natives' name for their country. It still bears the name,

Photo: R. Olken

Greetings from LET'S GO

With pen and notebook in hand, a change of clothes in our backpack, and the tightest of budgets, we've spent our summer roaming the globe in search of travel bargains.

We've put the best of our research into the book that you're now holding. Our intrepid researcher-writers went on the road for months of exploration, from Anchorage to Angkor, Estonia to Ecuador, Iceland to India. Editors worked from spring to fall, massaging copy into witty and informative prose. A brand-new edition of each guide hits the shelves every fall, just months after it is researched, so you know you're getting the most reliable, up-to-date, and comprehensive information available.

We try to make this book an indispensable companion, but sometimes the best discoveries are the ones you make on your own. If you've got something to share, please drop us a line. We're Let's Go Publications, 67 Mount Auburn Street, Cambridge, MA 02138 USA (e-mail: fanmail@letsgo.com). Good luck and happy travels!

though further investigation revealed that natives were just pointing out their "small collection of huts" nearby. Free expositions and great concerts by *québécois* artists liven up the Maison in summer. Call 02 99 56 34 32 for info or just stop by.

Meet your daily Gothic church quota with a visit to the **Cathédrale St-Vincent.** The 12th-century nave and its traditional stained-glass windows contrast beautifully with the geometric shards of pastel-colored glass in the *vitraux* behind the altar. The entire sanctuary is a work of modern art, constructed of bronze (some of which has a green tinge from oxidation). The four corners of the altar merit pause; they're abstract renderings of the symbols of the four evangelists. *Québécois* (and others) can pay a visit to Cartier's tomb in one of the small chapels on the left of the sanctuary (open daily June-Aug. 8am-7pm; Sept.-May 8am-noon and 2-7pm).

Doll fetish got you down? Over 300 dolls and furnished doll houses fill the displays of the **Musée de la Poupée et de Jouets,** 13, rue de Toulouse (tel. 02 99 40 15 51; open July-Sept. 15 daily 10am-1pm and 2-7pm; admission 20F, children 15F).

For karaoke head to the **Cutty Sark,** 20, rue de la Herse (tel. 02 99 40 85 70). Sangria 20F. Jazz on Friday and Saturday (open daily July-Sept. 5pm-3am, Oct.-June. Mon.-Sat. only). The **Angelus Bis,** 3, rue des Cordiers, is a popular bar featuring red couches and Greek statues (open nightly 10pm-5am). Dress snazzily. Beer from (ouch!) 30F. A smaller crowd crowds **O'Flaherty's Irish Bar,** rue des Cordiers, where you can practice ordering your Guinness (40F) in French (open daily 6pm-midnight; off-season hours change weekly). The **Casino,** chausée du Sillon, outside the Porte St-Vincent, is a hot spot holding a *discothèque* (open daily 11pm-5am, 18 and over) and the roulette-like *la broule* (open 8:30pm-3am, 18 and over). Sneakers and shorts are frowned upon.

Dinan

Like much of Brittany, Dinan was caught in the medieval tug-of-war between England and France. In fact, in 1364 its fate turned on the outcome of a duel—the Frenchman du Guesclin won, Sir Thomas of Canterbury yielded, and the English forces withdrew across the Channel. Today, Dinan boasts proudly of its reputation as the best-preserved medieval town in Brittany. In the *vieille ville,* 66m above the Rance river, 15th-century houses line cobblestone streets, and artisans ply their trades as they did centuries ago along precipitous paths that descend to the port. Tranquil Dinan (pop. 12,400) is not for those seeking riotous fun, but it provides a welcome respite from its more popular neighbor to the north, St-Malo.

ORIENTATION AND PRACTICAL INFORMATION

To reach the tourist office in the *vieille ville* from the station, bear left across pl. du 11 Novembre 1918 onto rue Carnot, then right onto rue Thiers, which brings you to a large rotary intersection, pl. Duclos. Enter the *vieille ville* through the Porte de Brest on the left (rue du Marchix, which becomes rue de la Ferronnerie). Turn left at pl. du Champ onto rue Ste-Claire; the office is up a block and around the corner to the left on rue de l'Horloge.

Tourist Office: 6, rue de l'Horloge (tel. 02 96 39 75 40; fax 02 96 39 01 64). A granite-pillared 16th-century mansion. Helpful staff. Walking tours July-Aug. daily at 10am and 3pm (25F, children 15F), off-season by reservation. Map and excellent guide 15F. Open daily 9am-7pm; Oct.-May Mon.-Sat. 8:30am-12:30pm and 2-6pm.

Money: Banks with **ATMs** are scattered near the post office and pl. du Champ, including a Crédit Mutuel on rue de la Ferronnerie.

Trains: pl. du 11 Novembre 1918 (tel. 02 96 39 22 39). To: St-Brieuc (2-3 per day, 1hr., 54F); Morlaix (2-3 per day, change at St-Brieuc, 3hr., 108F); St-Malo (5 per day, change at Dol, 1¼hr., 44F); Rennes (6 per day, 1¼hr., 70F); Paris (6 per day, 5hr., 244F). Office open Mon.-Sat. 6am-7pm, Sun. 8:35am-7pm. **Lockers** 3F.

Buses: CAT/TV (tel. 02 96 39 21 05), at the train station. Buses leave pl. Duclos for St-Malo year-round (Mon.-Sat, 3-5 per day, 30min., 33F). July-Aug. excursions to

Mont-St-Michel (1-2 per week, roundtrip 100F). Office open Mon.-Fri. 8am-noon and 2-6pm, Sat. 8am-noon. **TAE** (Rennes tel. 02 99 50 64 17). Buses leave the *gare* for Rennes (2-6 per day, 1hr., 48F) and Dinard (1-4 per day, 30min., 20F).

Bike Rental: Cycles Scardin, 30, rue Carnot (tel. 02 96 39 21 94). 50F per day, 300F per week; 500F deposit. Mountain bikes 100F per day, 500F per week; 1800F or passport deposit. Open Tues.-Sat. 9am-12:30pm and 2-7pm. V, MC.

Canoe and Kayak Rental: Club de Canoë, port de Dinan (tel. 02 96 39 01 50), across from rue du Quai. Kayaks 70F per ½-day, 100F per day. Canoes 100F per ½-day, 150F per day; passport deposit. Open July-Aug. 10am-noon and 2-4pm. Knowledgeable staff can suggest good routes.

Hospital: rue Chateaubriand (tel. 02 96 85 72 85), in Léhon.

Police: pl. Du Guesclin (tel. 02 96 39 03 02). **Emergency** tel. 17.

Post Office: pl. Duclos (tel. 02 96 85 83 50). **Currency exchange.** Open Mon.-Fri. 8:30am-6:30pm, Sat. 8am-noon. **Postal code:** 22100.

ACCOMMODATIONS AND CAMPING

Auberge de Jeunesse (HI) (tel. 02 96 39 10 83; fax 02 96 39 10 62), Moulin du Méen in Vallée de la Fontaine-des-Eaux. During the summer, the laid-back owner may pick you up at the station if you call and ask nicely. Turn left from the station's main exit, turn left across the tracks, and follow the signs (30min.). From the *vieille ville,* exit the walls through the Porte de Jerzual (at the end of rue du Jerzual). Descend the very steep rue Petit Fort, turn left onto rue du Quai, and walk 15min. Follow the signs and look left. Wonderful, friendly place by a babbling brook and weeping willows. Kitchen. 70 beds in small, clean 2- to 8-bed rooms. 47F. Sheets 16F. Breakfast 18F. Hearty dinner 47F. Lockers 5F. Reception daily 9-11am and 3-11pm. No lockout. Flexible curfew 11pm.

Hôtel du Théâtre, 2, rue Ste-Claire (tel. 02 96 39 06 91), across the street from the tourist office. Small, dimly lit but pleasant rooms above a bar in a beautiful building in the center of town. Singles 80-120F. Doubles 110F, with shower 150F. Triples with shower and toilet 200F. Showers free. Breakfast 22F.

Hôtel-Restaurant de l'Océan, pl. du 11 Novembre 1918 (tel. 02 96 39 21 51), across from the station. Spacious, bright, clean rooms let by a pleasant couple. Singles and doubles 115F, with shower 145F, with shower and toilet 175F. Triples with shower 175F. Quads with shower and toilet 205F. Extra bed 30F. Showers free. Breakfast 23F. V, MC.

Hôtel le Sporting, 20, rue Carnot (tel. 02 96 39 03 67). All rooms with TV and phone. Singles and doubles 120F, with shower 140F. Triples with shower and toilet 200F. Quad with shower and toilet 250F. Breakfast 26F. V, MC.

Camping: 1 campground at the **youth hostel** (26F). The tourist office lists others; closest is the **Camping Municipal,** 103, rue Chateaubriand (tel. 02 96 39 11 96). As you face the post office in pl. Duclos, rue Chateaubriand is on the right. Simple grounds next to a busy road 300m from *centre ville.* 13F per adult, 12F per tent, 9F per car. Electricity 12F. Reception 8am-1pm and 2-8pm. Open March-Nov.

FOOD

Simple bars and *brasseries* line the streets linking rue de la Ferronnerie with pl. des Merciers. The **Monoprix supermarket,** on rue de la Ferronnerie next door, offers a packaged alternative (open Mon.-Fri. 9am-12:30pm and 2:30-7:30pm, Sat. 9am-7pm). Pl. du Champ and pl. du Guesclin in the *vieille ville* host the town's **outdoor market** (Thurs. 8am-noon), where you can buy a picnic of fruit and crêpes to dine *al fresco* in the Jardin Anglais behind the church. Quiet places serve specialty meals in the *ruelles* just outside the ramparts, between the old town and the quai.

Le Cantorbery, 6, rue Ste-Claire (tel. 02 96 39 02 52), near the tourist office. Classy, cozy spot caters to a loyal clientele. 67F *menu* includes the filling *gratin aux poissons,* a steaming pot-pie stuffed with *fruits de mer*—and that's only the first course. Open daily noon-2pm and 7-10pm; Sept.-May closed Mon.

Crêperie des Artisans, 6, rue du Petit Fort (tel. 02 96 39 44 10). Featured in the *New York Times.* Terrific owner serves feasts under warm wooden rafters or on the terrace. Crêpes 6-23F, *galettes* 7-25F. Two crêpes and 2 *galettes menus* 47-64F, plus a deliciously steaming 39F lunch *formule express.* Open daily July-Aug. noon-2:30pm and 7-10:30pm; Sept.-June closed Mon.

La Kabylie, 48, rue du Petit Fort (tel. 02 96 39 62 76), close to the river, tucked into the steepest hill in Dinan. If you're cuckoo for couscous, try it with your choice of meat for 52-82F, or as part of the 60F *menu.* Open daily noon-3pm and 6:30-10:30pm; Sept. open Wed.-Mon.; Oct.-June open Wed.-Sun.

Le Connétable, 1, rue de l'Apport (tel. 02 96 39 06 74), in the *vieille ville.* Reputedly the oldest *crêperie* in Dinan and a great people-watching spot. Wonderful crêpes (10-25F) and *galettes* (10-38F) in a dark-timbered 15th-century house. *Crêpes flambées* (with Grand Marnier and kirsch) 23-25F. Open daily July-Aug. 10am-10:30pm; Sept.-Nov. and April-June Tues.-Sun. 10am-10:30pm. V, MC.

SIGHTS AND ENTERTAINMENT

The **Promenade des Petits-Fossés** follows the looming ramparts to the 13th-century **Porte du Guichet,** the entrance to the **Château de la Duchesse Anne.** Inside the oval tower, the decent **Musée de Dinan** (tel. 02 96 39 45 20) displays a selection of *dinannais* art including 17th-century furniture, 18th-century statuettes, and landscape paintings. Cooler than the museum is the château itself; climb the 150 steps to the terrace and you'll be rewarded with a panorama of the town. The **Tour de Coëtquen** holds galleries with temporary exhibits and a spooky subterranean room chock-full of tomb sculptures. (Open daily June-Oct. 15 10am-6:30pm; Oct. 16-Nov. 15 and March 16-May Wed.-Mon. 10am-noon and 2-6pm; Nov. 16-Dec. and Feb. 7-March 15 Wed.-Mon. 1:30-5:30pm. Admission 25F, students 10F.)

As you re-enter the *vieille ville* through port St-Louis, take a right onto rue Général de Gaulle and follow the signs for the *jardin* to get to the **Promenade de la Duchesse Anne,** at the end of which stands the beautiful **Jardin Anglais.** In the garden, the 12th-century **Basilique St-Sauveur** boasts a façade carved in pale sandstone and *vitraux* that eerily portray the lives of the saints by depicting the most interesting feature of most saints' lives—the ways in which they died. The northern arch of the transept houses a 14th-century tombstone containing the heart of Bertrand Du Guesclin, High Constable of France. The garden looks out over the river, viaduct, and port below. At the far end, a path and tiny staircase lead down to the river.

From the port, infiltrate the walled city by **rue du Petit Fort,** which becomes **rue du Jerzval,** one of Dinan's prettiest (and steepest) roads. Interrupt your hike with visits to artisans who blow glass, carve wooden statuettes, and weave cloth in their shops just as they (or their predecessors, anyway) have for centuries.

Back in the center of town, on Grande Rue, **Eglise St-Malo** contains a remarkable polychrome organ (built by Englishman Alfred Oldknow in 1889) and a massive Baroque altar. For a schedule of organ concerts, contact the tourist office. The day-glo colors of the 1920s stained-glass windows illuminate the church's interior and illustrate memorable events from Dinan's history; the second window from the rear on the right commemorates *dinannais* soldiers killed in World War I. The font next to the 15th-century baptismal font depicts the devil grudgingly bearing the vat on his back. If you're willing to pay for the exercise, the 15th-century **Tour de l'Horloge** on rue de l'Horloge commands a brilliant view of Dinan's jumbled medieval streets and the surrounding countryside (open daily June-Sept. 10am-7pm; April-May 2-6pm; admission 13F; call the tourist office to climb the tower off-season).

Dinan isn't exactly a happening joint, but you already knew that. The closest it gets is at **Le Chapeau Rouge,** 4-6, rue du Port (tel. 96 39 47 47), which hosts jazz concerts every two weeks and has a piano bar Thursdays (beer 10-30F; open Tues.-Sun. 5pm-2am, Fri.-Sat. 5pm-3am). For a more laid-back time, **Le P'tit Marcel,** 20, rue Haute Voie (tel. 02 96 39 06 95), is a cozy place where the local twentysomething crowd gathers over darts (beer 10-28F; open daily 11am-1am, Fri.-Sat. 'til 2am). The first weekend in September brings the biennial **Fête des Remparts,** complete with medieval costumes, chivalric combat, and the chance to explore the town's otherwise forbidden ramparts. Unfortunately, the next one's not until 1998.

Near Dinan: Combourg

About 20km from *über*-mediævel Dinan lies **Combourg.** You must be determined to come here—public transport isn't plentiful. **Trains** come in from Dinan (3-4 per day via Dol, 40F) and Rennes (3-4 per day, 55F). **Buses** arrive at the *gare* as well; **Autocars d'Ile-et-Vilane** runs from Dinan (1-3 per day, 30min.-1hr., 27F). The Combourg office is at 12, av. du Général-de-Gaulle (tel. 02 99 39 12 30); in Dinan it's 7, Grande Rue (tel. 02 96 39 12 30). To get to town, exit the station to the right, turn left onto av. de la Libération, and march until you see the château's walls. For info on the town, stop at the **Syndicat d'Initiative** (tel. 02 99 73 13 93), pl. Albert-Parent, on the right of av. de la Libération as you encounter civilization. (Open June-Sept. 15, Mon.-Sat. 10am-12:30pm and 2:30-6:30pm, Sun. 10am-12:30pm.)

Combourg's accommodations are neither abundant nor inexpensive. A *chambre d'hôte* may be a good choice; ask the Syndicat for a list. Or try **Hôtel Le Romantic,** 12, pl. des Déportés (tel. 02 99 73 05 52). The rooms are classy, clean, bright, and right next to Combourg's big attraction. (Singles 150-160F. Doubles 180-250F. Quads 220F. Breakfast 28F. Shower 12F. V, MC.) Get in touch with your dark side at the **Hôtel de France et de Chateaubriand,** 18, rue des Princes (tel. 02 99 73 07 58). Its rooms overlook cows grazing on the château's lush lawn and are as somber as Chateaubriand himself. (Singles 100F. Doubles 160F. Triples and quads 200F. Breakfast 25F. V, MC.) A cheaper option is Combourg's municipal **campground,** on Route de Lanrigan behind the Lac Tranquille (tel. 02 99 73 07 03; fax the town hall at 02 99 73 00 18). Sites are hedged in for privacy, next to tennis courts. (Open 8am-9pm. 14F per person, 9F for tent or car. Electricity 10F.) For eats, just walk through town; *brasseries* and bars gossip together on and around rue des Princes and pl. A. Parent.

BRITTANY

If you're not a fan of French literature or musty castles, Combourg may not be for you. Indeed, the one tourist attraction is the looming **château** (tel. 02 99 73 22 95) which was home to **François-René de Chateaubriand,** that towering pillar of Romanticism. The author spent only two formative years here, but they influenced him so much that he once declared, *"C'est dans les bois de Combourg que je suis devenu ce que je suis."* ("It was in the woods of Combourg that I became what I am.") Indeed, one glance at the château makes it easy to understand why Chateaubriand was such a melancholy word-monger. Begun in the 11th century by the Bishop of Del-de-Bretagne as a defensive structure, it was looted during the Revolution (surprise, surprise) and remained uninhabited for almost a century. Chateaubriand was among the first in a series of residents present to this today. Guided tours allow you to see the castle in all its morose glory, as well as a mötley collection of paraphernalia. The archive room has Chateaubriand's passport (proof of ambassadorship), lineage (proof of nobility), and an IOU he wrote (proof of poverty). It is his room that provides the best insight into the author himself, however. Located at the top of what has been dubbed the "Cat Tower," Chateaubriand's bedroom is completely isolated from the rest of the castle, illuminated only by two miniscule windows. It was here that he was "visited" by ghosts and roaring wind as he lay in bed, petrified (he later wrote that he could have slept with a corpse after so many lengthy encounters with fear in that room). In fact, a corpse is available for those who want to have a go at it—the mummified remains of a live cat interred in the walls to exorcise malevolent spirits now lie in a glass case (hence, Cat Tower), its mouth agape, its lips pulled back in a sneer. (Château open April-Oct. Wed.-Mon. 2-5:30pm. Park open 9am-noon and 2-6pm. Enter through the inconspicuous gate off rue des Princes. Admission to château and park 25F, students 21F. Park only 8F.)

St-Brieuc

St-Brieuc (pop. 100,000) isn't a particularly bad town—there just isn't a whole heck of a lot to see here. Though the *vieille ville* retains a certain Breton charm, the rest of the city seems to have given itself over entirely to its role as the economic and administrative center of the Côtes d'Armor. Outside the *centre ville,* a web of similarly paved streets lined with mediocre restaurants and hotels weaves its way to either the *vieille ville* or the train station. St-Brieuc's location between the Côte d'Emeraude and the Côte de Granite Rose makes it a perfect launch pad for daytrips to the countryside. A self-described *"carrefour touristique"* ("tourist crossroads"), St-Brieuc is just that: a place from which to escape to more appealing surroundings.

ORIENTATION AND PRACTICAL INFORMATION

From the train station, walk straight ahead onto rue de la Gare, which leads into the *centre ville.* Stay right when the road forks and you'll reach pl. de la Résistance, where the post office is located. The tourist office and pedestrian streets are nearby.

Tourist Information: Tourist Office, 7, rue St-Gouéno (tel. 02 96 33 32 50; fax 02 96 61 42 16), directly to the right across the *place* as you stand in the parking lot, facing the post office. Free map; more detailed one 10F; whole lotta brochures. Open Mon.-Sat. 9am-7pm, Sun. 10am-1pm; Sept.-June Mon.-Sat. 9am-noon and 2-6:30pm. **Le Griffon,** a bimonthly free at the tourist office, lists regional events.

Money: Banks with 24-hr. **ATMs** and **currency exchange** at decent rates worship Mammon at pl. Champ de Mars, off rue du 71ème Régiment d'Infanterie.

Trains: bd. Charner (tel. 02 96 01 61 64). To: Rennes (15 per day, 1hr., 81F); Morlaix (8-11 per day, 1hr., 72F); Dinan (2-3 per day, 1hr., 54F). **Lockers** 15-30F. Info and reservations Mon.-Sat. 8am-7pm, Sun. 9:30am-7pm. Ticket office open Mon.-Thurs. 5:30am-9pm, Fri. 5:30am-10pm, Sat. 5:30am-8:30pm, Sun. 5:30am-1pm.

Buses: Bus station at rue du Combat des Trente (tel. 02 96 33 49 49). Turn right onto rue du 71ème Régiment d'Infanterie from rue de la Gare. Also at train station. **CAT** buses serve St-Cast (1 per day, 2¼hr., 45F); Paimpol (7 per day, 1½hr., 39F); and, July-Sept., Cap Fréhel (4 per day, 1½hr., 40F). Ticket window open July-Aug. Mon.-Sat. 9am-12:15pm and 1-7pm; Sept.-June Mon.-Fri. 10:15am-noon and 1:15-6:30pm, Sat. 10:15am-noon and 3:30-6:30pm.

Public Transportation: TUB (tel. 02 96 33 47 42). Buses leave from Champ-de-Mars/pl. du Guesclin. Look for the bus shelters. Ticket 6F, 10 for 48F. Office open Mon.-Fri. 8am-6:30pm, Sat. 8am-noon.

English Books: Librarie Person, pl. de la Résistance. A small selection including the great masters, Shakespeare and Mary Higgins Clark. Open Tues.-Fri. 9:15am-noon and 2-7pm, Mon. 2-7pm, Sat. 9:15am-12:15pm and 2-7pm.

Bike Rental: At the **youth hostel** (tel. 02 96 78 70 70). Mountain bikes 65F. Deposit 500F or passport.

Laundromat: 4, pl. du Martray (tel. 02 96 01 99 81), behind the cathedral. Wash 20F. Dry 2F per 5min. Detergent 2F. Open 7am-10pm.

Hospital: rue Marcel Proust (tel. 02 96 01 71 23). **Medical emergency** tel. 15.

Police: 17, rue Joullan (tel. 02 96 33 36 66). **Emergency** tel. 17.

Post Office: pl. de la Résistance (tel. 02 96 61 10 60). Poste restante. Open Mon.-Fri. 8am-7pm, Sat. 8am-noon. 24-hr. **ATM** is right outside. **Postal code:** 22000.

ACCOMMODATIONS, CAMPING, AND FOOD

Several cheap hotels crowd around the train station on bd. Charner and rue de la Gare. Only a few have a lot of rooms, so reserve ahead in high season.

Manoir de la Ville Guyomard (HI) (tel. 02 96 78 70 70; fax 02 96 78 27 47). Take bus 3 (direction: Les Villages) to "Van Meno" or "Jean Moulin" (last bus around 8:15pm, 6F). It's a long walk, but if you do hoof it, head straight out of the station down rue de la Gare (ignore the "Auberge de Jeunesse" signs for now). At the first major intersection, turn left onto rue du 71ème Régiment, continuing as it becomes rue de Brest and rue de la Corderie, and follow signs for Ville Guyomard toward the hostel (50min.). Modernized 15th-century manor with 70 beds, its own patio, and a mini-golf course. Spacious 3- to 4-person rooms with low beds. No lockout or curfew. Under 26 55F, over 26 60F. Breakfast 20F. Sheets 20F. Meals 55F. Kitchen facilities, laundromat (20F wash or dry), and bike rental (65F).

Hôtel de la Paix, 30, bd. Charner (tel. 02 96 94 04 80), across from the station. Old-style, slightly dim but spacious rooms, all with telephone. Frequent serenades from arriving trains. Singles 98-110F, with shower 120F, with shower and toilet 140F. Doubles 115-125F, with shower 135-155F, with shower and toilet 155-165F. Triples 165F. Breakfast 30F. V, MC. Restaurant downstairs serves a good 3-course 55F *menu* of seafood and other goodies.

Hôtel Le Welcome, 34, bd. Charner (tel. 02 96 94 00 87). Fab rooms and friendly young owner. Hip bar below. Singles and doubles 120F, with shower 130-150F. Triple with shower and toilet 170F. Reception 6pm-3am.

Bar-Hôtel de la Banque, 14, rue de la Gare (tel. 02 96 33 12 83), near the train station. Ideal for a Valentine's Day getaway—all the rooms are a mélange of red and pink. Singles 110F, doubles 149-190F. Shower 10F.

Camping: At the youth hostel. Simple grounds atop a hill. Plenty of space. 24F per person. Free access to hostel facilities.

There are boatloads of *brasseries* and restaurants lining rue de la Gare and all of the *centre ville.* One of the best *crêperies* in town is **Crêperie Le Charner,** 12, bd. Charner (tel. 02 96 94 16 89), with a cozy ambience and extensive selection, including crêpes (8-22F), *galettes* (8-43F), and salads (33-37F; open Tues.-Sat. 11:30am-3pm and 7-10:30pm, Sun. 7-10:30pm; take-out Thurs.-Fri. from 8am; V, MC). **La Bocca,** 22, rue de la Gare (tel. 02 96 33 67 71), offers big, hot pizzas (32-55F) and big, cold beers (12-20F)—a tasty combination at a nice price. Scenic **Monoprix supermarket** does its thing in pl. de la Résistance (open Mon.-Sat. 8:30am-7:15pm). The public **market** is around the cathedral on Wednesday and Saturday mornings.

SIGHTS

BRITTANY

St-Brieuc may be a commercial center, but it doesn't offer much in the way of sights. It is worth taking the time to visit the **Cathédrale St-Etienne,** pl. de Gaulle. Construction began at the end of the 12th century and was more or less complete by the 14th, but additions continued for the next five hundred years. While almost every cathedral in France is a mixture of Romanesque and Gothic, St-Brieuc's mixes the unassuming with the elaborate better than most. The austerity of the nave's monolithic columns sets off the flamboyance of the Baroque Chapel of the Holy Sacrament in the south transept. Soak in the church from the nave; the space of the side and apsidal chapels is sensed rather than seen and lends the stone a warmth absent from similar edifices (free guided visit in French Mon.-Fri. 10:30am and 3pm).

The mildly interesting but well-assembled **Museum of St-Brieuc,** rue des License Martyrs (tel. 02 96 62 55 20), in the *centre ville,* offers an imaginative look at Breton life and the transition from traditional to modern, as well as an explanation of fishing and navigation tools and techniques (open Tues.-Sat. 9:30-11:45am and 1:30-5:45pm, closed Sun. afternoon; admission 20F). St-Brieuc's *vieille ville* may well be its most charming attraction. Wander through its streets for a while, and you may forgive the town its limited cultural resources.

In July and August, St-Brieuc celebrates **l'Eté en Fête.** On Fridays (and some Thursdays) during the festival, entertainment ranging from clowns to opera explodes onto the city. Ask for a schedule of events at the tourist office.

■ Near St-Brieuc: Cap Fréhel

When landscape artists go to sleep at night, they dream of Cap Fréhel. Visions of the Cap's surf float through the minds of fisherfolk in their quiet moments. Romantics searching for a place to propose marriage pine for its drama-engorged *falaises* (cliffs). Acrophobes in their most frantic fits of panic feel their pulses race at the thought of the Cap. Few words can describe the awesome majesty of this northernmost point of the Côte d'Emeraude. The lush fecundity of the vegetation, dark green dotted by wildflowers with points of red, yellow, and regal purple, would be artwork enough. But paint these wonders on a canvas of rust-hued cliffs that plummet a dizzying 70m to inlets caressed by an azure sea, decorated with the white lace of cresting waves, and you begin to understand why this windswept peninsula is such a popular loca-

Giving 'Em the Finger

While geologists may claim to know what gives the cliffs of Cap Fréhel their vibrant red color, locals know the real reason. In the fifth century, Irish monks evangelizing along the Côte d'Emeraude ran into opposition from powerful druids. One of the monks, after assembling a group of Fréhel's residents, decided to demonstrate the power of his faith by cutting off one of his own fingers. As soon as the first drop of blood hit the earth, the entire coast turned red. To this day, the cliffs retain the color as a vestige and reminder of the monk's sacrifice.

tion for hiking, self-discovery, and postcard photography. The Cap does not appear to offer much solitude in the summer, as hundreds flock here to follow the well marked **GR34** trail. Wander off the trail, though, and you're bound to find a less crowded (if not private) nook for rainy-day *randonnées* or sun-soaked naps. **CAT buses** go to the Cap in July and August (3 per day from St-Brieuc, 40F).

Red-and-white-striped **GR34** markers painted on the rocks guide ramblers along the edge of the peninsula. An easy walk southwest from the Cap leads to a breathtaking and secluded little beach. Feast your eyes on the scenic buffet that awaits on the 1½hr. walk to **Fort La Latte** (tel. 02 96 41 40 31), a 13th-century castle complete with drawbridges and a hair-raising view of the Cap and St-Cast (open daily 10am-12:30pm and 2:30-6:30pm; Oct.-May Mon.-Fri. 2:30-5:30pm; admission 17F).

If you're making the Cap more than just a daytrip—and why not?—check out the **Auberge de Jeunesse Cap Fréhel (HI),** la Ville Hadrieux, Kerivet, near Plévenon (tel. 02 96 41 48 98; Sept. 16-April 02 98 78 70 70). Take a bus to the Cap and walk toward Plévenon on D16, then follow the inconspicuous little signs bearing the fir-tree hostel symbol (30-40min.). If you're going to the Cap off-season, the kind owner may be able to pick you up at Sables d'Or if you call and sound charming. Small kitchen, dining room. Many of those vacationing here turn up their noses at the luxury of a solid roof and barracks-style beds, opting for the two tents beyond the bonfire pit outside (44F inside and out; lockout 11am-4pm; camping 24F; breakfast 20F; sheets 20F; dinner 49F; open May-Sept.). The hostel also rents **bikes** (25F per ½-day) and has maps of the GR34. If you ask at St-Brieuc's hostel, they will allow you to leave a rented bike at Cap Fréhel and vice-versa.

Paimpol

The *pampolais* coat of arms, a silver boat against an azure background, aptly portrays this small town's close tie to the sea. Anchored on the border of the Côte de Granite Rose and the Côte de Goëlo, Paimpol (pop. 8000) once fueled its economy with fishing expeditions to Newfoundland and Iceland. Fishing is still important, but the port is also chock-full of postcard vendors. This is no hollow tourist town, though; the surrounding islands, cliffs, beaches, and multitudinous hiking trails make Paimpol an ideal place to relax while exploring the region's charms.

ORIENTATION AND PRACTICAL INFORMATION

To reach the port and *centre ville,* turn right from the station, then left at the rotary.

Tourist Information: Tourist Office, pl. de la République (tel. 02 96 20 83 16; fax 02 96 55 11 12). As you exit the train station, go straight onto the rue du 18 Juin. take the first right onto rue de l'Oise, which becomes rue St-Vincent, into the *place;* the office is on the right (5min.). Comprehensive info on the area, including guides to the region's hiking trails. Open July-Aug. Mon.-Sat. 9am-7:30pm, Sun. 10am-1pm; Sept.-June open daily 10am-12:30pm and 2:30-6pm. **La Presse d'Armor** has a schedule of events, available at the tourist office (5F).

Trains: av. du Général de Gaulle (tel. 02 96 20 81 22). To: St-Brieuc (4-5 per day, 1hr., 58F) via Guingamp (45min., 35F); Pontrieux (5 per day, 15min., 16F). Office open Mon.-Sat. 6:40-7:10am and 8am-7pm, Sun. and holidays 9am-7pm.

Buses: Buses leave from the train station. **CAT** (tel. 02 96 33 36 60) links Paimpol with Pointe de l'Arcouest (5 per day, 15min., 11F) and St-Brieuc (3-7 per day, 1¼hr., 40F). **Cars Guégan** (tel. 02 96 20 59 50; info at the Tourisme Evasion office, 6, av. du Général de Gaulle; open Mon.-Fri. 9:30am-noon and 1:30-6:30pm) runs to Lannion (Mon.-Sat. 2-4 per day, 1hr., 32F50) via Tréguier (30min., 20F).

Money: A 24-hr. **ATM** is at Banque Populaire on quai Duguay-Trouin. There's **currency exchange** at comparable rates at both **Banque de Bretagne,** pl. du Martray (open Tues.-Fri. 8:20am-12:15pm and 1:30-5:15pm, Sat. 8:20am-12:15pm and 1:30-5pm), and **Crédit Maritime,** 37, quai Morand (open Tues.-Fri. 8:30am-12:15pm and 1:30-5:30pm, Sat. 8:30am-12:15pm and 1:30-4:30pm).

Bike Rental: Cycles du Vieux Clocher, pl. de Verdun (tel. 02 96 20 83 58). 50F per day. Mountain bikes 80F per day. Open Mon.-Sat. 8:30am-noon and 2-5pm, Sun. 8am-noon. V, MC.

Laundromat: 23, rue du 18 Juin (tel. 02 96 20 96 41). Wash 22F. Dry 8F for 15min. Detergent 2F. Open daily 8am-10pm.

Hospital: Centre Hospitalier, Chemin de Malabry (tel. 02 96 55 60 00). **Medical emergency** tel. 02 96 55 15 15 or 15.

Police: rue R. Pellier (tel. 02 96 20 80 17). **Emergency** tel. 17.

Post Office: av. du Général de Gaulle (tel. 02 96 20 82 40). **Currency exchange.** Poste restante. 24-hr. **ATM.** Open Mon.-Fri. 8am-noon and 1:30-5:30pm, Sat. 8am-noon. **Postal code:** 22500.

ACCOMMODATIONS, CAMPING, AND FOOD

There are few budget hotels in Paimpol, but the hostel usually has room. Call ahead to be sure. Most hotels are located in the small but lively port area.

Auberge de Jeunesse and Gîte d'Etape (HI), at Château de Kéraoul (tel. 02 96 20 83 60). Turn left onto av. Général de Gaulle, right at the first light, left at the next light, and follow rue Bécot, staying to the right when the road forks and becomes rue de Pen Ar Run. Take a left when the street ends. The hostel is at the second driveway on the right (20min.). An old manor house on top of a hill with a beautiful view. 80 beds in 2- to 6-person rooms. Great showers. Comfortable and convenient—no lockout, no curfew (new guests not admitted after 9pm). Clean, well-equipped kitchen. 44F. Huge breakfast with crêpes and honey (18F). Camping 25F. Lunch or dinner 47F. Sheets 16F.

Hôtel R. Raoult, 50, rue Jean Renaud (tel. 02 96 20 80 56), 10min. from the *centre ville* on an extension of rue du Général Leclerc. Slightly worn but well-furnished rooms at unbeatable prices near the abbey. Hall bathrooms. Singles and doubles 120F, with shower 130F. Triples 160F. Free showers. Breakfast 25F.

Hôtel Berthelot, 1, rue du Port (tel. 02 96 20 88 66). Outrageously orange hallways connect twelve clean, airy rooms in a great location. Friendly, chic owner. Singles and doubles 150F, with toilet 170F, with bath 220F, with shower, toilet, and TV 240F. Triples and quads 200F. Showers free. Breakfast 27F. V, MC.

Hôtel-Restaurant Le Terre-Neuvas, quai Duguay-Trouin (tel. 02 96 20 80 76). Ten simple, well-kept rooms next to the port. Singles and doubles with or without shower 160F, with shower and toilet 190F. Quad 200F. Showers free. Breakfast 28F. Popular restaurant downstairs has a 50F *menu* featuring local catches.

Camping: at the youth hostel or **Camping Municipal de Cruckin,** near the plage de Cruckin (tel. 02 96 20 78 47). From the tourist office, turn left onto rue de la Marne, left onto av. du Général de Gaulle, then veer right and follow schizophrenic rue du Général Leclerc as it twists through four name changes. Rue de Cruckin branches off to your left from rue du Commandant le Conniat. Comfortable, flat site. Gates closed 11pm-6am, off-season 10pm-7am. Tent and 3 people 60F, extra person 15F. Showers 7F50. Electricity 12-16F. Open April-Sept. Reception Mon.-Sat. 8am-noon and 5-9pm, Sun. 8-10am and 6-8:30pm.

Picnickers can find supplies either at Paimpol's Tuesday morning **market,** which invades the whole town, or at the **Intermarché supermarket** on av. du Général de Gaulle to the left of the *gare* (open Mon.-Fri. 8:30am-12:15pm and 2:30-7:15pm, Sat.

8:30am-7:15pm). Bars and *brasseries* surround the park. Locals say you can't beat the **Hôtel-Restaurant Le Terre-Neuvas** (see above) for elegant food at backpacker prices. *Crêperies* are as numerous as the boats in the port, but the **Crêperie du Moulin à Mer,** on route de Lanmodez (tel. 02 96 20 19 49), in nearby Lézardrieux was recently judged the region's crêpe champion (crêpes 9-25F, *galettes* 9-56F). Head east on D786 for about 10km to hit this cozy, way-out-of-the-way joint (open daily noon-10pm; V, MC). For something completely different (and within walking distance), **Restaurant Long-Van,** 9, rue Général Leclerc (tel. 02 96 20 55 79), specializes in Vietnamese and Chinese dishes and offers a 3-course 50F *menu* that may include crab-and-asparagus soup (open daily noon-2pm and 7-11pm).

SIGHTS

Hidden from the road by vegetation, the ruins of **l'Abbaye de Beauport,** chemin de l'Abbaye (tel. 02 96 20 97 69), look dreamily out to sea. Dating from 1202, the abbey (east of Paimpol, near the campground) was once an important stop on the pilgrimage route to Santiago de Compostela. Nowadays the roofless church and beflowered refectory flow seamlessly into the gardens proper. (Open daily June 15-Sept. 15 10am-1pm and 2-7pm; March-June 14 and Sept. 16-Nov. 30 Wed.-Mon. 10am-noon and 2-5pm. Dec.-Feb. call for an appointment. Admission 25F, students 20F.) From the abbey you can embark on the **GR34** along the coast to the port (2hr.).

Back in town, the **Musée de la Mer** on rue Labenne (tel. 02 96 55 31 70), tucked away on a side street near the port, displays models of sea craft from fishing boats to battle ships, as well as other things nautical. Temporary sea-related exhibits complete your education. Listen for your favorite French sea chanty. (Open April-Sept. daily 10am-noon and 3-7pm. Admission 18F50, students 10F.) Those who need a tequila shot of Breton Culture—quick but effective—should mosey on over to the miniscule **Musée du Costume,** rue R. Pelletier. (Open daily July-Aug. 11am-12:30pm and 2-6pm. Admission 12F, students 7F; ticket to this museum and the Musée de la Mer 26F50.) One km south of town, a 10m menhir looms over the Field of Grief. According to local legend, the rock fell to earth and is slowly sinking, its complete disappearance timed to coincide with the end of the world.

Nightlife in Paimpol is limited to the port. Locals favor **La Falaise,** quai de Kernoa, and **Le Pub,** 3, rue des Islandais, which swings as a piano bar from 7-11pm; from 11pm to closing, it turns up the techno as a *discothèque*.

Every summer, Paimpol dedicates a Sunday to the **Fête des Islandais,** a religious festival during which the port is blessed by a local priest; mass frolicking ensues. Call the tourist office for the exact date in 1997.

■ Near Paimpol

Six km north of Paimpol at the terminus of D789, the peninsula ends with a dramatic flourish in the tumbling pink granite of the **Pointe de l'Arcouest.** Those in the know say that the blue-green waters flowing around this archipelago provide some of France's best sea-kayaking. To reach the Pointe, take a **CAT bus** from Paimpol (8 per day, 7 on Sundays; 12min., 11F50). **Les Vedettes de Bréhat** (tel. 02 96 55 86 99) send boats from the Pointe to the main isle of the archipelago, the idyllic **Ile de Bréhat** (10-15 per day in season, 10min., roundtrip 38F, passenger and bike 88F; bring your windsurfing gear for 45F; your lap dog is *gratuit*). They also offer tours for 65-110F. Three km in length, the island (pop. 300) is small enough that it's impossible to get lost. You can rent a bike for 70 to 90F a day, but you really don't need one. Strut off the boat past all the tourist kitsch and find an "undiscovered" beach on which to while away a sunny afternoon. But be sure to bring a mat—most of Bréhat's beaches are rocky. Also make sure to get to the **Chapelle St-Michel** on the west side of the island—the view is unparalleled. For more info, call the island's **tourist office** (tel. 02 96 20 04 15; open Mon.-Sat. 9am-6pm).

Back on the mainland, inland from Paimpol at the point of the Trieux River estuary, the little port town of **Pontrieux** nestles snugly in a green valley. Pontrieux is the best place from which to reach an even more elusive destination, the **Château de la Roche-Jagu** (tel. 02 96 95 62 35). High above the estuary, the 15th-century château offers tours of its interior and also hosts annual expositions ranging from artistic *tableaux* to historical musical instruments (open July-Aug. 10am-7pm; April-June and Sept. to mid-Nov. 10:30am-12:30pm and 2-6pm; admission 35F, students and seniors 25F). The **syndicat d'initiative,** in the "Tour Eiffel" in the *centre ville* (tel. 02 96 65 14 03; fax the town hall at 02 96 95 36 09), has info on the château as well as on kayak/canoe rentals and hiking trails (open Mon.-Fri. 10:30am-12:30pm and 2:30-6:30pm; Sat.-Sun. 10:30am-12:30pm and 3-6pm). Like most places worth visiting in Brittany, it's a little out of the way, which makes the **gîte d'étape** (tel. 02 96 95 62 35; call after 6pm) all the more convenient. In a stone building adjacent to the château, the *gîte* has 19 beds in its two-level attic, a kitchen, and a warm-hearted caretaker (44F; showers included; reception 6-8pm). Unfortunately, there's no bus service. The 5km walk from Pontrieux takes 45 minutes. From the Pontrieux train station go left along the river, cross the little bridge to the other side and turn right. This road (D787) leads up hills and across fields to the château; you'll know it by the wide, tree-lined boulevard leading off to the right, the Côte d'Armor flags, and the sign that says "Château Roche-Jagu." The trip to the town by **train** on the Guingamp-Paimpol line (4 per day, 1hr., 17F) is an adventure in itself; from Paimpol, the train chugs alongside the Trieux river valley, passes the château, and then crosses the river on a 21m-high viaduct. It's the only way to go.

Morlaix

Morlaix was founded in Gallo-Roman times, when Armorican Celts built a fort here called "Mons Relaxus" (Mount of Rest). Situated at the intersection of the rivers Jarlot and Queffleuth, the town was plagued during the Middle Ages by continuous invasions by the Duchy of Brittany, the French Crown, and the British, all of whom wanted control of Morlaix's enviably located port. In 1522, British invaders ransacked the town but made the mistake of celebrating their victory to drunken excess. When Morlaix's avenging citizens returned to reverse the earlier battle's outcome, the British were caught unawares. From this confrontation came Morlaix's motto: *"S'ils te mordent, mords-les!"* (If they bite you, bite them back). Clinging to the hillside, modern Morlaix (pop. 17,600) is a town of steeply winding streets and staircases that stand under the protective shadow of a towering, two-tiered viaduct.

ORIENTATION AND PRACTICAL INFORMATION

From the train station, walk straight onto rue Gambetta, then turn left onto a steep path that leads down to the *centre ville.* From there, walk left beyond the Hôtel de Ville through pl. des Otages to find the tourist office, a rustic hut below the viaduct.

Tourist Information: Tourist Office, pl. des Otages (tel. 02 98 62 14 94; fax 02 98 63 84 87). The usual info given out by an unusually friendly staff. Guided tours July-Aug., Thurs. 2:30pm (30F). Info on nocturnal tours led by a theatrical troupe. Open Mon.-Sat. 9am-7pm, Sun. 10am-12:30pm; Sept.-July 9 Mon.-Sat. 9am-noon and 2-6pm. Grab **Le Telegramme,** a daily that lists events (4F20), at any *tabac.*

Money: Banks with 24-hr. **ATMs** twiddle their thumbs around pl. des Otages and pl. Traoulen, near the hostel. **Banque de France exchanges currency** at pl. Cornic, as does **Crédit Maritime,** on the corner of rue du Mur and rue Carnot.

Trains: rue Armand Rousseau (tel. 02 98 80 50 50, reservations 02 98 63 56 24). On the Paris-Brest line. To: St-Brieuc (6-10 per day, ¾hr., 74F); Brest (8-10 per day, ¾hr., 52F); Quimper (change at Landerneau, 5-7 per day, 2hr., 93F); and Roscoff (4-5 per day, ½hr., 28F). Info office open daily 9:10am-7:30pm. **Lockers** 5F.

Buses: CAT (tel. 02 98 62 16 72) runs to Lannion from the train station (Mon.-Sat. 2-3 per day, 1½hr., 39F). **SCETA buses** (tel. 02 98 93 06 98) serve Carhaix (1-3 per day, 1½hr., 47F) via Huelgoat (1hr., 34F). Travelers under 26 get 50% off regular roundtrip tickets during holidays. **Tourisme Verney,** at 25, pl. Cornic, has more bus info (open Mon. and Thurs. 8:30am-noon), as does the tourist office.

Public Transportation: TIM (Transports Intercommunaux Morlaisiens), kiosk on pl. Cornic (tel. 02 98 88 82 82). Ticket 6F, 10 for 50F. Buses run 'til 7pm.

Taxis: Radio Taxis (tel. 02 98 88 36 42), at pl. des Otages and the train station.

Bike Rental: Cycles Le Gall, 1, rue de Callac (tel. 02 98 88 60 47), at the bottom of the hill near the hostel. 3-speeders 50F per day, 25F each extra day, 150F per week; mountain bikes 60F per ½-day, 90F per day, 300F per week. Deposit 200F. Open Mon.-Sat. 8:30am-noon and 2-7pm.

Hospital: Hôpital Général, rue Kersaint Gilly (tel. 02 98 62 61 60). **Ambulance** tel. 02 98 88 31 32.

Police: 17, pl. Charles de Gaulle (tel. 02 98 88 17 17). **Emergency** tel. 17.

Post Office: 15, rue de Brest (tel. 02 98 88 23 03). **Currency exchange,** poste restante, 24-hr. **ATM.** Open Mon.-Fri. 8:30am-6:30pm, Sat. 8:30am-noon. **Postal code:** 29600.

ACCOMMODATIONS, CAMPING, AND FOOD

Morlaix has some cheap hotels, but you should call ahead in July and August. Ask the tourist office about **gîtes d'étape** or **chambres d'hôte** in the area, which cost 100-200F per night. The **Auberge de Jeunesse (HI),** 3, route de Paris (tel. 02 98 88 13 63; fax 02 98 88 81 82), has a cavernous eating area and 52 beds in 2- to 9-person rooms, as well as a so-so kitchen. From the train station head straight down rue Gambetta. When it curves, go left down the steps, then farther down the endless steps of rue Courte. Cross pl. Emile Souvestre and continue straight ahead on rue Carnot. Take a right onto rue d'Aiguillon as it becomes rue de Paris, and then a left at the roundabout onto route de Paris. The hostel is ½km up the hill around the curve to the right (20min.). (45F. Sheets 15F. Breakfast 18F. Reception 8-11am and 6-9pm, but you can leave your bags any time. Lockout 10am-6pm. Curfew midnight; off-season 11pm.) **Hôtel Le St-Melaine,** 75-77, rue Ange de Guernisac (tel. 02 98 88 08 79), has a good location and 14 rooms varying widely in quality from luxurious and recently refurbished to dim and stuffy. (Singles 90-130F, with shower 140F. Doubles 130, with shower 160F. Extra bed 35F. Breakfast 25F. V, MC.) The elegant and popular restaurant downstairs serves *menus* for 55 and 80F. **Hôtel Les Halles,** 23, rue du Mur (tel. 02 98 88 03 86; fax 02 98 63 47 96), offers clean and utterly characterless rooms; they do have telephone and TV, though. (Singles 115F, with shower 145F. Doubles 125F, with shower 160F. Breakfast 25F. V, MC.) The restaurant downstairs offers *menus* at 53 and 71F. Close to town, next to the hamlet of Garlan, lies **Camping Croas-Men** (tel. 02 98 79 11 50). Buses don't run there, so if you don't have a car you'll have to walk the 5km. From the *centre ville,* follow signs first to Plouigneau and then to Garlan (14F per person, car plus tent 15F, under age 7 10F; open all year; gates open 24hr., pay the following day if reception is closed).

The **quartier St-Mathieu** and **rue Ange de Guernisac** offer plenty of eateries. For an elegant night out, try **Le Bains-Douches,** 45, allée du Poan-Ben (tel. 02 98 63 83 83), across from the Palais de Justice. The waterside restaurant offers a solid 55F lunch *menu* and a scrumptious 75F dinner *menu*—you can't beat the *tarte aux fraises* (open noon-2pm and 7-11pm; V, MC). If it's pizza night, you can't go wrong with **Le Pizzaiolo,** 31, rue Ange de Guernisac (tel. 02 98 88 46 42), which serves up filling pizzas for 33-50F, 28-34F salads, and *paella* (specialty of the house) for 48F (open daily 11:30am-2:30pm and 7-10:30pm; V, MC). **Crêperie Ar Bilig,** 6, rue au Fil (tel. 02 98 88 50 01), between pl. de Viarmes and pl. des Jacobins, feeds that insatiable hunger for crêpes with a three-course 46F *menu* (open Mon.-Sat. 11:45am-2pm and 6:30-9pm, Sun. 11:45am-6:30pm; Sept.-Jun. closed Sun.-Mon.; V, MC). The **market,** on pl. Cornic (behind town hall), is open all day Saturday. **Marché Plus,** rue de Paris, hawks food every day of the week (open Mon.-Sat. 7am-9pm, Sun. 9am-noon).

SIGHTS AND ENTERTAINMENT

Morlaix's collection of sights, though small, is eclectic and borders on fascinating. Even those sick of Breton museums may relish the **Musée des Jacobins,** pl. des Jacobins (tel. 02 98 88 68 88), which is located in the Church of the Jacobins, built from 1238-1250. A fabulous mélange of old and new, the museum combines traditional displays of Breton life with modernist paintings of the region; also features fantastic temporary exhibits (open daily July- Aug. 10am-12:30pm and 2-6:30pm; Sept.-June Wed.-Mon. 10am-noon and 1:30-6:30pm; admission 25F, students 12F). Across pl. Allende on rue du Mur is **La Maison de la Reine Anne** (tel. 02 98 88 23 26), which commemorates Queen Anne's 1505 visit to the city. One of many "lantern houses" in Brittany, the vast space was intended to allow one lantern suspended from the ceiling 17m above to light the entire building. (Open Mon.-Sat. 10:30am-12:15pm and 1:30-6:30pm. Free.) Nearby, the **quartier St-Mathieu** is a lively district of restaurants and old residences. If you want to get away from (or above) it all, climb the stairs up to the **viaduct** and stroll across, taking in the view of the *mairie* and port. Continue on to the network of paths known as the **Circuit des Venelles** and discover Morlaix for yourself.

For the ale-addicted, **La Brasserie des Deux Rivières,** 1, pl. de la Madeleine (tel. 02 98 63 41 92), gives free tours with a complimentary *dégustation* of its all-natural Coreff beer (Mon.-Wed. at 10:30am, 2pm, and 3:30pm). There aren't any free tastings at **Café de l'Aurore,** pl. Allende (tel. 02 98 88 03 05), but there are a desperately hip crowd and free concerts most Saturdays and Wednesdays in July and August. **Fado,** 5, rue Gambetta (tel. 02 98 88 60 75), is an oh-so-trendy-overstuffed-chair-coffee-music-house extravaganza that attracts all kinds.

In July and August, there's dancin' in the streets as Morlaix's **Les Arts dans la Rue** takes over each Wednesday night with clowns, dancers, and novelty acts.

Huelgoat

Although **Argoat** (AR-gwah) still means "wooded country" to Breton ears, centuries of clearing have made the Argoat (a term which encompasses the whole interior of Brittany) one of the least forested regions in France. Only a few scattered plots remain of the great oak and beech forest that Obélix and other menhir-carvers once trod. Paimpont, Merlyn's legendary stronghold, is one; Huelgoat (OO-el-gwah), or "high forest" in Breton, is another. As part of the **Parc Régional d'Armorique,** which stretches from the coast 70km eastward, the rocky, ravine-like Huelgoat forest enjoys significant governmental protection. On the edge of a sparkling lake, the tiny village of Huelgoat (pop. 2000) is a perfect launching-pad for forays into the forest's curious grottoes and rocks. Breton megaliths, natural rock formations, and superb hiking trails await those who leave the coastline behind and head for the refreshingly untouristed Argoat interior.

ORIENTATION AND PRACTICAL INFORMATION

Huelgoat's tiny center is on the eastern bank of the lake. All buses stop on pl. Aristide Briand, less than a minute's walk from both the lake and the **tourist office** (tel. 02 98 99 72 32), behind the church on pl. de la Mairie. The staff offers information on the grove grottoes and a confusing 5F map (open June-Aug. Mon.-Sat. 10am-noon and 2-6pm; Sept.-May Mon.-Fri. 2-5pm). When the office is closed, the *mairie* (tel. 02 98 99 71 55) next door provides much the same info (open Sept.-June Mon.-Thurs. 8:30am-12:15pm and 1:15-5:30pm, Fri. 8:30am-12:15pm and 1:15-4:30pm, Sat. 8:30am-noon; July-Aug. closed Sat.). An **ATM** does its thing at the **Crédit Agricole** on rue des Cendres, right off pl. Aristide Briand. **SCETA buses** (tel. 02 98 93 06 98) connect Huelgoat to Morlaix in the north (2 per day, 1hr., 33F). **CAT buses** (tel. 02 98 62 16 72) link Morlaix and Huelgoat at the same rates. During holidays those under 26 get 50% off for any roundtrips on this line. Buses stop by the church on pl. Aristide Briand; schedules are posted on the bus stop pole. From Morlaix, hitchers and cyclers often take D769 to Berrien and D14 to Huelgoat (30km). The **post office,** rue des Creux (tel. 02 98 99 73 90), offers poste restante (open Mon.-Fri. 9am-noon and 2-5pm, Sat. 9am-noon; **postal code:** 29690).

ACCOMMODATIONS, CAMPING, AND FOOD

Huelgoat's accommodations are limited to one solid hotel and a campground, so reserve in summer. The tourist office has a list of *gîtes d'étape,* which cost 100-200F per night and are within 15km of town. The **Hôtel de l'Armorique,** 1, pl. Aristide Briand (tel. 02 98 99 71 24), has spacious and dim but otherwise unremarkable rooms. (Singles and doubles 110F. Triples 180F. Quads 200-215F. Quints 230F. Shower 20F. Breakfast 32F. V, MC.) The **Camping Municipal du Lac,** rue du Général de Gaulle (tel. 02 98 99 78 80), five minutes from the bus stop, fills a sunny lakeside location (16F per person, 18F per tent; reception Mon.-Sat. 7:30am-8pm, Sun. 8am-noon and 4-8pm; open June 15-Sept. 15). Less convenient but more pleasant, the **Camping de la Rivière d'Argent** (tel. 02 98 99 72 50) is 3km from town on the way to Carhaix (15F per person, 19F per tent; open May-Sept.).

Huelgoat's **market** takes place on the first and third Thursday of the month from 8am to 1pm on pl. Aristide Briand and along rue du Lac, while a fish-only market graces the same area every Thursday. A small **Shopi supermarket** (open Mon.-Sat. 8am-12:30pm and 2:30-7:15pm, Sun. 9am-12:30pm) and a few bakeries and *crêperies* are on pl. Aristide Briand. The most happenin' joint in town is **La Chouette Bleue,** 1, rue du Lac, a bar, *crêperie,* snack bar, and restaurant by the lake. Let a dozen *escargots* slide down your gullet for 42F. (Main dishes 28-52F, crêpes 9-42F. Open April-Sept. Bar open daily 10:30am-1am. *Crêperie* and restaurant open daily noon-10pm; Sept.-June closed Mon. Snack bar open July-Aug. noon-10pm. V, MC.)

SIGHTS

The hilly terrain of the Argoat is much better suited to walking than cycling. The **Fédération Française de la Randonnée Pédestre** has excellent maps that include hiking tours. The organization **ABRI** has designed routes that follow scrupulously marked trails from one *gîte d'étape* to the next (about 40F per night). These maps are available for 20-45F at area tourist offices, including Morlaix and Huelgoat's.

The network of footpaths begins at the end of rue du Lac, where the lake empties into the Argent river. The labyrinthine path is strewn with signs, making the tourist office map superfluous. The forest is studded with such natural wonders as the **Grotte du Diable** (Devil's Grotto), **Mare aux Sangliers** (Pond of Boars), and the **Roche Tremblante,** a 100-ton monster mineral balanced more-or-less precariously on the hillside. Legend has it that applying pressure in *just* the right place will set the whole thing a-trembling. On your way to the rocks, stop at the **Miellerie de Huelgoat,** 5, rue de La Roche Tremblante (tel. 02 98 99 94 36), for a guided tour of the honey world (or *monde du miel,* as the case might be; free). Watch the bees in action, then taste the fruit of their labors—honey in such flavors as blackberry and oak. Take home a jar, or ask them to ship it (30-60F; open daily 9am-8pm; V, MC).

The town of **Pleyben,** 26km southwest of Huelgoat, is the site of **Eglise St-Germain l'Auxerrois.** With its domed Renaissance bell tower and magnificently ornate *calvaire* (calvary), this is one church in Brittany worth a detour. On the first Sunday of August, a *pardon* takes place here. To reach Pleyben, leave Huelgoat via the road to Quimper, which becomes D14. After 20km, turn left on D785.

Roscoff

Although ferries stream into Roscoff's port, the town has avoided the all-too-common "harbor blight" consequences by moving to the other extreme—Roscoff aims to be positively *chic.* Its beautiful location and famous thalassotherapy center attract thousands of health-seekers who swarm to the town in summer, seeking its healing, bubbly mud; the elite beat the heat and meet to eat in ocean-front restaurants that alter their prices as one would expect—straight up. Luckily, the Ile de Batz is a mere 15 minutes away and offers better sights and better prices.

ORIENTATION AND PRACTICAL INFORMATION

Roscoff's **port** is where the action is. Turn right out of the train station and make an immediate right onto rue Ropartz. Follow the signs and the tantalizing scent of the salty sea-air. The **tourist office,** 46, rue Gambetta (tel. 02 98 61 12 13; fax 02 98 69 75 75), has lots of goodies for you and yours (open Mon.-Sat. 9am-12:30pm and 1:30-7pm, Sun. 9:30am-12:30pm; Sept.-June Mon.-Sat. 9am-noon and 2-6pm). **Currency exchange** and **ATMs** await on rue Pasteur and rue Amiral Réveillère, near the church. **Trains** go to Morlaix (5-7 per day, 45min., 28F) and Brest (3 per day, 2hr., 67F). **CAT buses** connect Roscoff to Morlaix (3 per day, 30min., 40F) and Quimper (2 per day, 1 on Sun., 2¼hr., 110F). Buses leave from the *centre ville* and **gare maritime,** port de Bloscon, a 10-minute walk away. Follow quai d'Auxerre away from the tourist office and continue straight on rue de Plymouth at the roundabout. From the port, **Brittany Ferries** (tel. 02 98 29 28 29; fax 02 98 29 28 91) sends boats to Plymouth (5hr.; March 16-Nov. 15 1-2 per day, 190-230F, students 170-200F; Jan.-March 15 1 per week, 160F, students 140F; same prices for roundtrip with 5 nights in U.K.) and Cork (14hr.; May 20-June and Sept. 3 per week, 340-370F, students 310-340F; July-Aug. 3 per week, 430-530F, students 380-470F; March 15-May 19 1 per week 340F, students 310F). **Irish Ferries** (tel. 02 98 61 17 17; fax 02 98 61 17 46) sends boats to Rosslare (15hr.; May 25-July 10 and Sept. 2 per week, 530-635F, students 450-555F) and Cork (15hr.; June-Aug. 1 per week, same prices as Rosslare). The **post office,** 17, rue Gambetta (tel. 02 98 69 72 19), offers poste restante (open Mon.-Fri. 9am-12:30pm and 1:45-5:15pm, Sat. 9am-noon; **postal code:** 29681).

ACCOMMODATIONS, CAMPING, AND FOOD

Roscoff's hotels cater to the rich—ignore them and head for the **chambre d'hôte** at 4, rue Brizeux (tel. 02 98 69 70 33), the best (indeed, only) deal in town. Mme. Guivarch, the proprietor, offers three spacious, classy, and flawlessly decorated rooms five minutes from the port in a quiet, residential area. Call a week or two in advance. Your own private paradise and a scrumptious breakfast with homemade *confiture* runs 190-240F for two people (call ahead for rates if you're alone). Be sure to mention *Let's Go.* If slumbering under the stars is your thing, check out **Camping de Kérestat,** south of town on rue de Pontigou (tel. and fax 02 98 69 71 92; 1 person, tent, and car 62F; 2 people, tent, and car 80F). The Ile de Batz's proximity and wonder-hostel, as well as the fact that ferries run more often than most city buses, make it a convenient, affordable, and tranquil accommodations option.

Restaurants serving 80-100F *menus* of *fruits de mer* line the port, but for a real deal try the **Hôtel des Arcades,** 15, rue Amiral Réveillère (tel. 02 98 69 70 45). The elegant 58 and 75F meat and seafood *menus* are filling (open daily noon-2:30pm and 6-9:30pm; V, MC). Locals vote for **Ti Saozon,** 30, rue Gambetta (tel. 98 69 70 89). Crêpes, crêpes, and crêpes 11-44F (open Tues.-Sun. 6-9:30pm; V, MC).

SIGHTS AND ENTERTAINMENT

There isn't too much in Roscoff for the budget-conscious. Still, the 16th-century **Eglise Notre-Dame de Kroaz-Batz** merits a gander. Its massive, gold Baroque choir contrasts sharply with the simple white altar before it. Outside you can marvel at the Renaissance belfry. Next to the church is the vaguely interesting **Aquarium et Exposition-Musée,** pl. Georges Tessier (open daily 10am-noon and 1-7pm; admission 25F, students 22F). The **Jardin Exotique** (tel. 02 98 69 70 45) is on the coast about 1km past the *gare maritime.* More a botanical museum than a garden, the Jardin carefully labels and arranges its plants in a businesslike rather than artistic manner—it's not really a place to picnic. The view from the "largest flowered rock" in France is pretty impressive (open Mon.-Fri. 10am-7pm, Sat.-Sun. 10am-1pm and 2-7pm; Sept.-June Mon.-Sat. 10am-noon and 2-6pm; admission 20F, students 10F).

■ Near Roscoff: Ile de Batz

Roscoff's sights may be a bit thin on the ground, but who needs 'em when you've got the **Ile de Batz** right there? This tiny treasure of an island is so small that the streets have no names. Quiet and rugged, it can easily be explored in a day—though you may never want to leave. Two competing **ferry** companies, **CFTM** (tel. 02 98 61 79 66) and **Armein** (tel. 02 98 61 77 75), send boats every 30min. from 7:45am-8pm (15min., 38F roundtrip). Once on the island, you can stop at the small **tourist office** (tel. 02 98 61 75 70) at the port (open daily 10:30am-12:30pm and 2:30-4:30pm), but you don't really need a map—there are signs all over the Lilliputian island pointing the way to stores, restaurants, and so on.

Walk straight up the hill from the port, bearing left at the fork and following the signs for "Centre Nautique—AJ" for five minutes to reach the idyllic **Auberge de Jeunesse (HI),** Créach ar Bolloc'h (tel. 02 98 61 77 69), at an amazing location with a view of the ocean through the trees, two minutes from a great beach. Ask for info about kayak and canoe trips. (44F. Annex rooms with outdoor plumbing 40F. Bunk-cots in a big tent 36F. Camping 30F. Meals 47F. Sheets 16F. Breakfast 18F. Good kitchen. No lockout, no curfew. Reception 6:30-8:30pm, but you can leave your bags any time.) The **Hôtel Roch Ar Mor** (tel. 02 98 61 78 28; fax 02 98 61 78 12), facing the port, lets singles and doubles with a view (170F; free showers; extra bed 60F; breakfast 26F). There's **camping** near the lighthouse on the other side of the island. You pick a spot, and someone comes by every day to collect the fee (6F per adult, 6F per site; cold showers). The **Hôtel-Restaurant Ker-Noel** (tel. 02 98 61 79 98) serves up huge and deelish pizzas cooked before your eyes (32-57F; open daily 9am-2pm and 6-10pm; V, MC). **La Crêpe d'Or** (tel. 02 98 61 77 49) has a golden selection of you-know-whats for 10-32F (open daily noon-9pm). A **8 à huit supermarket** lies a couple of "blocks" away (open daily 9am-12:30pm and 1:30-7:30pm).

A great tour of Brittany's little piece o' paradise can be had by following the GR34 ("Tour de l'Ile") either east or west from the port. The 14km circuit should keep your feet busy for four hours or so. While strolling round the island, stop by the **Jardin Exotique Georges Delaselle** (tel. 98 61 75 65), past the hostel on the southeast tip of the island. Revel in the verdure as you savor the spectacular view of the sea (open daily 2-5:30pm; May 1-June 15 closed Tues. and Fri., April and Sept. 15-Oct. weekends only; admission 20F). Nearby stand the ruins of the 6th-century **Chapelle Ste-Anne.** Only two walls remain of this chapel dedicated to the patron saint of sailors. Locals tell of a time when, having returned safely home after finishing their service, sailors would hang their caps in the chapel's courtyard as a sign of thanks.

Brest

Situated on the southern side of Finistère's northern peninsula, Brest (pop. 220,000) has a natural harbor so ideal that in 1631, Cardinal Richelieu designated it as France's major naval base. The city grew and prospered, known to sailors around the world. Used by Americans to enter Europe during the First World War, Brest was carefully watched and controlled by the Germans in World War II. Consequently, Allied bombing pulverized most of the city's sites in 1944. Reconstructed in a spartan architectural style similar to that of Le Havre, Brest has overcome this adversity to maintain a happy, youthful atmosphere. As home to Brittany's second-largest university and a large naval base, it's a bustling city.

ORIENTATION AND PRACTICAL INFORMATION

From the *gare*, av. Georges Clemenceau leads to the tourist office and the central **pl. de la Liberté,** the intersection of Brest's two main streets, rue de Siam and rue Jean Jaurès. **Rue de Siam** holds the title of liveliest street in the city, where bookshops, clothing stores, and restaurants cling to the pavement like barnacles to a ship's hull.

Tourist Office: pl. de la Liberté (tel. 02 98 44 24 96; fax 02 98 44 53 73), near the Hôtel de Ville. Free map and info on food, hotels, and tours. Open July-Sept. Mon.-Sat. 9:30am-12:30pm and 1:30-6:30pm, Sun. 2-6pm; Oct.-June closed Sun.

Budget Travel: Bureau Information Jeunesse, pl. de la Liberté (tel. 02 98 43 01 08). Open July-Aug. Mon.-Fri. noon-6pm; Sept.-June Mon.-Sat. noon-6pm.

Money: ATMs relinquish their loot around pl. de la Liberté.

Flights: Aéroport International de Brest-Guipavas, just outside the town (tel. 02 98 32 01 00). By car, follow directions to Morlaix and take the Guipavas exit off the expressway. No buses run there. Daily flights by **Air Inter** (tel. 02 98 8473 33) to Paris and by **Brit' Air** (tel. 02 98 62 10 22) to London-Gatwick and Lyon. Airport open daily 5:15am-midnight.

Trains: Gare SNCF, pl. du 19ème Régiment d'Infanterie (tel. 02 98 80 50 50). To: Paris (7 TGVs per day, 4½hr., 305F plus 36-90F TGV reservation); Morlaix (10 per day, 45min., 51F); Nantes (6 per day, 4hr., 208F); Rennes (5-6 per day, 1½hr., 159F). Information and reservations office open Mon.-Fri. 8:30am-8pm, Sat. 8:30am-7pm, Sun. 9:45am-7pm. **Lockers** 15-30F.

Buses: *Gare routière* in front of the train station (tel. 02 98 44 46 73). Buses traipse to: Quimper (4 per day, 1¼hr., 81F); Camaret (4 per day, 1½hr., 57F); Roscoff (3 per day, 2hr., 38F). Office open Mon.-Fri. 7am-12:30pm and 1-7pm, Sat. 7:15-11am and 1-6:30pm, Sun. 8:45-10:15am, 1-2pm, and 5:15-8pm. *Quels horaires!*

Public Transportation: Bibus, pl. de la Liberté (tel. 02 98 80 30 30). Kiosk open Mon.-Fri. 8:15am-12:15pm and 1-6:30pm, Sat. 9am-noon and 1-5:45pm. Ticket 6F, *carnet* of 10 48F, students 34F, full-day ticket 18F. Service until about 8pm.

Ferries: Penn Ar Bed sends boats at 8:30am to Ouessant (1 per day, 2½hr., round-trip 170F, students 128F) and Molène (1 per day, 1¾hr., 150F). Buy tickets at the Brest tourist office or at **Société Maritime Azenor,** port de Plaisance du Moulin Blanc (tel. 02 98 41 46 23). Boats return from Ouessant at 5pm.

Taxis: Allô Taxis Brestois, 234, rue Jean Jaurès (tel. 02 98 42 11 11).

Bike rental: ACB Cycles, 7, rue Siam (tel. 02 98 43 24 10), near Pont de Recouvrance. 60F per day, 1000F deposit. Open Tues.-Sat. 10am-noon and 2:15-7pm.

English Books: Dialogues, Forum Roull (tel. 02 98 44 32 01), rue de Siam. Open Tues.-Sat. 9:30am-7:30pm, Mon. 9:30am-12:30pm and 1:30-7:30pm.

Crisis Lines: SOS Amitié (tel. 02 98 46 46 46), anonymous friendship in French.

Hospital: Centre Hospitalier Régional et Universitaire de Bretagne, av. Foch (tel. 02 98 22 33 33). **Medical emergency** tel. 18 or 02 98 46 11 33.

Police: rue Colbert (tel. 02 98 80 08 50). **Emergency** tel. 17.

Post Office: rue de Siam, across from tourist office at pl. Général Leclerc (tel. 02 98 51 87 76). **Currency exchange** *and* a 24-hr. **ATM.** Poste restante (postal code: 29279). Open Mon.-Fri. 8am-7pm, Sat. 8am-noon. **Postal code:** 29200.

ACCOMMODATIONS, CAMPING, AND FOOD

Brest has many inexpensive hotels and one of the swankiest hostels in France. Be sure to call ahead in July or August, or you may find yourself sleeping outside.

Auberge de Jeunesse (HI), rue de Kerbriant (tel. 02 98 41 90 41; fax 02 98 41 82 66), about 4km from the train station and right near Océanopolis, next to the artificial beach in le Moulin Blanc. Exit the station, walk through the *gare routière,* cross the street, and look left for the bus stop. Take bus 7 (6F) to its final stop at "Port de Plaisance." Once there, facing down the street towards the port take your first right, another right, and the hostel will be on your right; look for the sign in Breton *"ostaleri ar yaouankiz."* 4-tree hostel with carpeted rooms, 70s architectural subtleties, great bathrooms, a kitchen, and laundry. Ping pong, foosball, and TV room, all in a lush setting. 67F. Small breakfast included. Dinner 47F. Lockers 5F. Reception Mon.-Fri. 7-9am and 5-8pm, Sat.-Sun. 7-10am and 5-8pm. Lockout 10am-6pm. Curfew July-Aug. midnight, Sept.-June 11pm.

Hôtel Vauban, 17, av. Clemenceau (tel. 02 98 46 06 88; fax 02 98 44 87 54). Prim and proper Victorian comfort. Singles and doubles 110-130F, with toilet 140-170F, with shower and toilet 200F, with bath and toilet 230F. Triples 280F, with bath, toilet, and TV 300F. The restaurant/bar downstairs has 60 and 80F *menus.*

Hôtel Astoria, 9, rue Traverse (tel. 02 98 80 19 10; fax 02 98 80 52 41), off rue de Siam. Classy place with clean, modern bathrooms and TV and phone in all rooms. *Let's Go*-loving proprietor. Singles and doubles 130F, with shower and toilet 210-230F, with bath and toilet 240F. Triples 260-265F. Breakfast 29F.

Hôtel St-Louis, 6, rue Algésiras (tel. 02 98 44 23 91; fax 02 98 46 07 94), near pl. de la Liberté. English-speaking owner. Large rooms with TV and phone. Singles and doubles 130F, with shower 150F, with shower and toilet 160F. Breakfast 25F.

Camping: Camping du Goulet (tel. 02 98 45 86 84) lies 6km from Brest and 1km from the sea in Ste-Anne du Portzic; take bus 14 to "Le Cosquer" or bus 7, 11, 12, or 26 to "Route de Conquet." (17F per person, 9F per child, 20F per tent. Free hot showers.) **Camping St-Jean,** in Plougastel Daoules (tel. 02 98 40 32 90), is farther away but located on a small beach. By car, head to Quimper, then to Plougastel. Or take bus 25, which runs to Plougastel from pl. de la Liberté, and walk the remaining 2km. (16F per person, 8F per child, 14F per tent. Free showers.)

Markets take place every day in various locations; the tourist office has a complete list. *Boulangeries, pâtisseries,* and vegetable stores can be found on rue de Siam, as can a **Monoprix supermarket** (open Mon.-Sat. 8:30am-7:30pm). **Chez Marie-Françoise,** 27, rue Navarin (tel. 02 98 80 46 30), off rue Jean Jaurès, is a typical Breton eatery in the middle of the not-quite-pretty *quartier St-Martin.* Crêpes go for 12-35F; more elaborate dishes up to 88F. (Open Mon.-Sat. noon-2pm and 7-10pm. V, MC.) The **Bel-Canto,** 6, rue Louis Pasteur (tel. 02 98 44 44 37), plays music from the operas after which its pastas and pizzas (25-70F) are named. Try the magical *"Flute Enchantée"* calzone, with ham, mushrooms, tomatoes, cream, and egg (50F; open Tues.-Sun. 7pm-2am). **Ma Petite Folie,** port de Plaisance du Moulin Blanc (tel. 02 98 42 44 42), near the hostel, has wonderful seafood and a pricey wine list (open Mon.-Sat. 12:45-2:45pm and 7:15-9:45pm; V, MC). Also near the hostel is the satisfying *crêperie* **Blé Noir** (tel. 02 98 41 84 66; open daily noon-9:30pm).

SIGHTS AND ENTERTAINMENT

Brest's **château** was the only building to survive the bombings in World War II. Now the world's oldest active military institution (it dates from the 3rd century), the sprawling fortress houses the **Musée de la Marine** (tel. 02 98 22 12 39), detailing the history of the town and its maritime tradition (open Wed.-Mon. 9:15-noon and 2-6pm; admission 24F, students 12F). Across the waterway stands the **Musée de la Motte Tanguy,** pl. Pierre Péron (tel. 02 98 45 05 31). The 14th-century tower shelters dioramas of historic *brestois* architecture and culture, as well as 100% of your recommended daily *coiffe*-viewing allowance. (Open daily July-Aug. 10am-noon and 2-7pm; June and Sept. 2-7pm; Oct.-May Wed.-Thurs. 2-7pm, Sat.-Sun. 2-6pm. Free.) On rue de Denver, the **Monument Américain** towers over the Port du Commerce. This red-brick structure commemorates the landing of American troops in 1917.

Back up off rue de Siam, the **Musée des Beaux-Arts** on rue Traverse (tel. 02 98 44 66 27), off rue de Siam, has a large but not altogether inspiring collection ranging from the 16th century to the 20th focusing on works from the Pont-Aven school (open Mon. and Wed.-Sat. 10-11:45am and 2-6:45pm, Sun. 2-6:45pm; free).

A little farther from the *centre ville* is the impressive **Océanopolis Brest,** port de Plaisance (tel. 02 98 34 40 40). Not just a fish museum, the Océanopolis holds space-age exhibits and games meant to emphasize biodiversity and the need for conservation, as well as big-eyed seals and a marine-life petting tank. From the stop across from and to the left of the train station, take bus 7 (every 30min. until 7:40pm, 6F) to "Océanopolis" (open daily June 15-Sept. 14 9:30am-6pm; Sept. 15-June 14 closed Mon. and at 5pm on weekdays; admission 50F, ages 18-24 40F).

The first place to look for evening entertainment is the port, which, unusually, is a relatively safe place to hang out. **Les Jeudis du Port** rock the dock on Thursdays in July and August with popular concerts. **Les Fauvettes,** 24, quai de la Douane, offers 150 kinds of beer while its "headquarters" at 27, rue Conseil St-Martin (tel. 02 98 44 46 67) vends a whopping 600 different varieties (open daily 10am-1am). **Les Quatres**

Vents is also on quai de la Douane, with a boat for a bar and a mellower crowd (open daily 11am-1am). Slurp down the milkshake you've been craving at **Jimmy's Diner,** 95, rue de Siam (tel. 02 98 80 24 58), one of France's only sources of Buffalo wings (35F) and cheese fries (14F). (Open daily 11am-3am.)

■ Near Brest: Ile d'Ouessant

Windswept Ile d'Ouessant (*Enez Eussa* in Breton), off Finistère's western coast, is a 2½-hour boat ride from Brest. The island's sheep-dotted meadows, stone crosses, and strong sense of tradition enchant despite summertime flocks of noisy tourists on rented bikes. Legend has it that mermaids once inhabited the island; perhaps this explains why *ouessantine* women have always had the upper hand. Traditionally, in fact, *ouessantine* maidens propose marriage. After the ceremony, the indefatigable women do the farming while their men voyage with the navy or in lobster boats.

ORIENTATION AND PRACTICAL INFORMATION

From May to September, **Penn Ar Bed** (tel. 02 98 80 24 68, in Brest) ferries ply between Brest and Ouessant, stopping at **Le Conquet,** on the western end of the peninsula. (1hr. between Brest and Le Conquet, 1½hr. between Le Conquet and Ouessant; ferries leave Brest at 8:30am, Ouessant at 5pm; from Brest roundtrip 174F, students 132F; from le Conquet roundtrip 146F, students 111F). **Cars de St-Mathieu** (tel. 02 98 89 12 02) buses landlubbers west along D789 from Brest to Le Conquet (daily at 7:30am from Brest's *gare routière,* 40min., 22F50). **Finist'mer** ferries (tel. 02 98 89 16 61) also connect Le Conquet and Ouessant (135F, students 105F) and offer 40F one-way tickets. Tickets are available at both ports and at the tourist office in Brest; reserve in summer. Once on the island, bikes or your own two feet can take you to the main town of **Lampaul,** 3.5km from Port du Stiff. **Riou** and **Jean Avril** buses also run there (10F). **Malgorn** (tel. 02 98 48 83 44), **Savina** (tel. 02 98 48 80 44), and **OuessanCycles** (tel. 02 98 48 83 44) **rent bikes** from the port (all 55F per day, mountain bikes 75F per day, no deposit); you can rent by the hour (15-25F) from the companies' **annexes** in town. The boats from Brest and Le Conquet charge for bikes (30F each way), so it may not be worth lugging your own. On foot, it's a pleasant 45-minute stroll along the main road. Lampaul's **tourist office** (tel. 02 98 48 85 83; fax 02 98 48 87 09), near the church in the center of town, provides maps (open Mon.-Sat. 10am-12:30pm and 2:30-5pm; Sun. 10am-12:30pm).

ACCOMMODATIONS, CAMPING, AND FOOD

There are four hotels on the isle, three of which do not require *pensions.* The **Duchesse Anne** (tel. and fax 02 98 48 80 25), 200m from the town center, lets large, comfortable rooms in a great location near the beach and away from the noise of the *centre ville.* (Singles and doubles 130-150F, with shower 150-170F. Triples and quads 160-190F, with shower 190F. Extra bed 30F. Shower free. Breakfast 30F. V, MC.) **L'Océan** (tel. and fax 02 98 48 80 03) has airy rooms and a mellow TV lounge on the second floor. (Singles and doubles 160F, with shower 220F. Triples 220F, with shower 280F. Breakfast 32F. V, MC.) **Roc'h Ar Mor** (tel. 02 98 48 80 19; fax 02 98 48 87 51) has small singles (135-155F), doubles (145-165F), and triples (140-195F). Baths are free, and breakfast goes for 33F. You can **camp** at **Pen-ar-Bed** (tel. 02 98 48 84 65), 2km from the port (12F per person, 12F per tent).

The **Duchesse Anne** cooks up tasty *plats* (28-76F) and pastas and pizzas (40-55F), along with 82-98F *menus* (V, MC). **L'Océan** serves up 85-120F seafood *menus.* A half-pint of Guinness goes for 18F at the adjacent bar. (Bar and restaurant open daily noon-2:30pm and 7:30-10:30pm. V, MC.) A **SPAR supermarket** squats next to the tourist office (open Mon.-Sat. 8:30am-8:30pm, Sun. 9am-1pm).

SIGHTS

At the **Ecomusée du Niou-Uhella** (tel. 02 98 48 86 37), about 1km northwest of Lampaul, you can take a look inside a traditional *ouessantine* home. The museum features Breton costumes, religious statues, and more. Take D81 uphill out of town and watch for the turnoff sign (open May-Sept. and school holidays daily 10:30am-6:30pm; April Tues.-Sun. 2-6:30pm; Oct.-March Tues.-Sun. 2-4pm; admission 25F). The **Musée des Phares et Balises** (tel. 02 98 48 80 70) is devoted to the history of lighthouses and maritime signaling. Don't look directly into the demonstration light's vortex unless you want to see spots for the rest of your stay (same hours and prices as eco-museum; admission to both museums 40F). The real sight, though, is the island itself. The cliffs by the lighthouse, beaten by the salty surf and wind for centuries, are a wonder to behold. At every turn, you'll be confronted with some of the most beautiful scenery you've ever seen.

Crozon Peninsula

To the north and south, Finistère's two larger peninsulas overshadow Crozon, a tiny point of land jutting out between the profiles of Léon and La Cornouaille. From jagged clifftops lined with hiking paths, you can gaze across the surrounding bays—azure pools marred only by the occasional dark swell of a protruding rock formation. Cycling opportunities abound, but the hilly terrain can be challenging.

From Brest, a boat is the way to go. **Vedettes Armoricaines** (tel. 02 98 44 44 04, in Le Fret) runs from Brest's *gare maritime* to Le Fret on the peninsula, then shuttles people from Le Fret to Crozon, Morgat, and Camaret (3 per day, 52F, with shuttle bus 56F). **Douget buses** (tel. 02 98 27 02 02, in Crozon) connect Brest to Crozon or Camaret (1-2 per day, 1½hr., 50F). From Quimper, the peninsula is best reached by bus. **SCETA** buses (tel. 02 99 29 11 15) run to Crozon, Morgat, and Camaret (3 per day, 1 Sun. in winter, 57F). Getting around between Camaret, Crozon, and Morgat is another story. While buses run between Camaret and Crozon (2-3 per day, 10min., 10F), to get to Morgat itself, you either need to go to Crozon and walk or bike the 3km (easier) or wait for the Vedettes Armoricanes shuttle bus (inconvenient, 10F). The **post office** is open Monday to Friday 9am-noon and 2-5pm, Saturday 9am-noon (**currency exchange,** poste restante; **postal code:** 29570).

Budget hotels are nonexistent on the peninsula. Its four **gîtes d'étape,** however, offer beds for 40F. The *gîte* at St-Hernot (call Mme. Le Guillou at 02 98 27 15 00) sits on a cliff a few km south of Crozon. Only feet, wheels, or thumbs can get you there. Another *gîte* is in Landennec (call the town hall at 02 98 27 72 65). North of Crozon, the Larrial *gîte* can be reached from the route de Camaret (call M. or Mme. Le Bretton at 02 98 27 62 30). The fourth *gîte* is at Telgruc sur Mer (tel. 02 98 27 33 83). **ULAMIR,** route de Camaret in Crozon (tel. 02 98 27 01 68), has more info.

Camaret's tourist office, quai Toudouze (tel. 02 98 27 93 60; fax 02 98 27 87 22), is next to pl. de Gaulle (open Mon.-Sat. 9:15am-7pm, Sun. 10am-12:30pm and 2:30-5pm). **Buses** stop outside Café de la Paix, 30, quai Toudouze (tel. 02 98 27 93 05).

There are plenty of bars and *brasseries* along the port in Camaret from which to enjoy the view and an inexpensive meal. To really savor the flavor, though, head down the street to **Belle Etoile,** quai du Styvel (tel. 02 98 27 85 85). The phenomenal 59F *menu* offers a salad of *fruits de mer,* a big ol' bowl of *moules marnières,* and a chocolate crêpe to help it all down. The 49F and 80F *menus* offer similar fare in different orders of magnitude. (Open daily noon-3pm and 7-11pm. V, MC.)

Camaret's port is a beautiful area for wandering, but the really spectacular sights are in the town's outskirts. While there is no place to rent bikes in Camaret, the tourist office can call Crozon and have them bring some wheels to Camaret for you. Whether on bike or hoofin' it, head out of town on the D8. A few minutes' travel brings you to the **Alignements de Lagatjar,** some 50 rocky monoliths arranged in an open-box formation. The stones are believed to have been erected around 2500 BC for sun-worshipping rites. Right behind the menhirs are the ruins of the **Château de**

St-Pol Roux. The scenic but breezy path through the mortar shell-pocked cliff-side leads to the **Pointe de Penhir,** one of the most splendid capes in Brittany. A memorial to the Bretons of the Free French forces stands out in sharp contrast to the sky. Beyond the memorial is a spine-tingling 76-m drop to the sea. Those who climb out onto the rocks will be rewarded with a blood-curdling view of the isolated rock clusters of the **Tas de Rois,** which point accusingly at the clouds like monstrous fingers. On the other side of town, the D355 leads to **Pointe des Espagnols,** another dramatic promontory with a view over Brest and Plougastel Peninsula.

Mondays in July and August, Camaret plays host to **Les Lundis Musicaux,** with concerts ranging from classical recitals to gospel jams. Call 02 98 27 90 49 for info.

Morgat, several km south of Camaret, is noteworthy for its enormous beach, cliff scenery, and marine grottoes carved out by the sea. Surfing fanatics flock to Morgat's sands, along with a camera-toter or two. From May through September, **Vedettes Tertu** (tel. 02 98 26 26 90), **Vedettes Rosmeur** (tel. 02 98 27 10 71), and **Vedettes Serenes** (tel. 02 98 26 20 10) offer English tours of the caves (45min., 20-35F). Crozon and Morgat, because of their proximity, share resources. Thus, the **tourist offices** in both towns are open Monday to Saturday 10am-7:30pm. Crozon's office (tel. 02 98 27 07 92; fax 02 98 27 24 89), next to the *gare* on bd. de Pralognan, is also open Sun. 10:30am-12:30pm, while Morgat's bureau (tel. 02 98 27 29 49), across from the beach on bd. de la Plage, is the place for summer Sunday afternoons 4-7:30pm. **Renting a bike** is the best way to explore the town and its environs. If you find yourself in Crozon, **Presqu'Ile Loisirs** (tel. 02 98 27 00 09), across from the *gare* and tourist office, can set you up with a mountain bike for 60F per day. (Open Mon.-Sat. 9am-noon and 2-7pm, Sun. 10am-noon. 1000F or passport deposit. V, MC.) If you walk the short distance downhill to Morgat, Denis and his cohorts at **Crapato Bicyclo,** in the *centre ville* at pl. de l'Eglise, will gladly lend you a **mountain bike** (60F per afternoon, 80F per day, 390F per week), **boogie board** (50F per ½-day, 80F per day), or fully equipped **kayak** (40F per hour, 100F per ½-day, 140F per day for a 1-person craft; for 2-person craft, 60F, 150F, 250F; open daily 9am-7pm). Send postcards of Morgat's luxurious *plage* to jealous friends from the **post office,** across from the beach. (Open Mon.-Sat. 9am-noon; mid-July to Aug. also 2-4:45pm.)

Take a break from tanning and head up the hill to the **Maison des Minéraux,** route du Cap de la Chèvre (tel. 02 98 27 19 73), about 3.5km outside town on D155. The museum displays the geological history of the region, then turns out the lights to show off its impressive collection of fluorescent minerals. (Open daily July-Sept. 10:30am-7pm; June 10:30am-12:30pm and 2-7pm; Oct.-Dec. Sun.-Fri. 2-5:30pm; Jan.-May daily 10am-noon. Admission 25F, students 18F.) Keep on truckin' to the **Cap de la Chèvre,** where the Crozon sidewalk ends. The Cap itself is positively anticlimactic after the view you get from your bike on the way there. Backtrack down the road a bit, lock your wheels to a post, and descend one of the steep *sentiers* from the road for a better perspective. To make Morgat more than a daytrip, check out one of the *gîtes d'étape* (see above) or stop at **Camping du Bouis** (tel. 02 98 26 12 53), 1.5km outside town on the way to the Cap (adults 35F, 2 adults 62F, each additional person 15F; showers 5F; gates closed 11pm-8am; open Easter-Sept.).

Quimper

Although staunch half-timbered houses with crooked façades share the *vieille ville*'s cobblestone streets with legions of tourists, Quimper (Kem-PAIR; pop. 62,000), capital of La Cornouaille, has managed to retain its Breton flavor. Some women wear *coiffes* to market and to church on Sunday, stores display Celtic books and records prominently, one local high school conducts its classes in Breton, and for over 300 years, delicate hand-painted *faïencerie* (stoneware) has been crafted here. Each year between the third and fourth Sundays of July, Quimper recalls its heritage with the *Festival de Cornouaille,* a cavalcade of mirth and music in Breton costume and one of Brittany's largest celebrations.

ORIENTATION AND PRACTICAL INFORMATION

Quimper is at the *kemper* ("confluence" in Breton) of the Steir and Odet rivers in the heart of La Cornouaille. From the *gare,* go right onto av. de Fare and follow it to rue Aristide Briand. To reach the tourist office, stay on the left side of the river Odet and walk along bd. Dupleix until it ends at pl. de la Résistance. For the *vieille ville,* cross the river along rue Aristide Briand, turn left onto bd. de Kerguélen, and turn right onto rue de Roi Gradlon, leading to the cathedral at pl. St-Corentin (10min.).

Tourist Information: Tourist Office, 7, rue de la Déesse (tel. 02 98 53 04 05; fax 02 98 53 31 33), off pl. de la Résistance. Accommodations service (2F). Free, detailed map. Tours 30F, students 15F; May-June and Sept. Mon.-Sat. 2pm, Tues. in English; July-Aug. Mon.-Sat. 11am-5pm, Tues. 2pm in English. Excursion tickets to nearby sights such as Pointe du Raz (95F, students 90F) and Pont-Aven (100F, students 95F). Open Mon.-Sat. 8:30am-8pm, Sun. 9:30am-12:30pm and 3-6pm; Sept.-June Mon.-Sat. 9am-noon and 1:30-6pm. An **annex** (same hours) is in front of the cathedral. **Quimper Magazine** lists events.

Money: 24-hr. **ATMs** lurk near the cathedral and throughout town.

Budget Travel: Tourisme Verney, 7, rue Elie Fréron, up from pl. St-Corentin (tel. 02 98 95 88 40). Sells BIJ and Wasteels tickets and offers 25% student discounts.

Trains: av. de la Gare (tel. 02 98 90 26 21 or 02 98 90 50 50). To: Paris (2-3 per day, 5 per day TGV, 7½hr., 5hr. TGV, 311F plus 36-90F reservation for TGV); Rennes (8 per day, 3hr., 162F); Nantes (6 per day, 3hr., 166F); Brest (6 per day, 1½hr., 80F). Info office open daily 9:30am-7pm. **Lockers** 15-30F.

Buses: The *gare routière* (tel. 02 98 90 88 89) is next to the train station. Buses leave from there or across the street. **CAT** (tel. 02 98 40 68 40) runs to Brest (4 per day, 1 on Sun., 1hr., 80F); Roscoff (1 per day, 2hr., 110F) via Huelgoat and Morlaix; Pointe du Raz (6 per day Mon.-Sat., 1½hr., 45F) via Audierne; and Bénodet (8 per day, 30min., 24F). **SCETA** (tel. 02 98 93 06 98) serves Camaret (3-5 per day, 1½hr., 55F) via Châteaulin, Le Fret, and Crozon; Douarnenez (5-7 per day, 45min., 29F). **Transports Caoudal** (tel. 02 98 56 96 72) goes to Quimperlé (4-6 per day, 1¾hr., 42F) via Concarneau (½hr., 22F). **Tourisme Verney** (tel. 02 98 95 02 36) guides tours of the region (Pointe du Raz 95F, students 90F; Crozon Peninsula 100F, students 95F; the Argoat 130F, students 125F; Pont-Aven 100F, students 95F; difficult-to-reach inland churches 130F, students 125F). Office open Mon.-Sat. 7am-12:30pm and 12:45-7:15pm.

Public Transportation: QUB (tel. 02 98 95 26 27). Buses (tickets 6F; *carnet* of 10 45F, students 34F) run 6am-7:30pm. Bus 1 serves the hostel and campground.

Taxis: in front of the station (tel. 02 98 90 16 45 or 02 98 90 21 21).

Bike Rental: MBK s.a. Lennez, 13, rue Aristide Briand (tel. 02 98 90 14 81), off av. de la Gare. Bikes (60F per day, 200F per week); *VTTs* (90F per day, 360F per week). Passport deposit. Open Tues.-Sat. 9am-noon and 1:45-7pm.

Laundromat: Laverie de la Gare, 4, rue Jacques Cartier. Open daily 8am-9:30pm.

Hospital: Centre Hospitalier Laënnec, 14bis, av. Y.-Thépot (tel. 02 98 52 60 60).

Police: rue Théodore Le Hars (tel. 02 98 90 15 41). **Emergency** tel. 17.

Post Office: 37, bd. Amiral de Kerguélen (tel. 02 98 95 88 40). 24-hr. **ATM** outside. **Currency exchange.** Poste restante (postal code: 29109). Open Mon.-Fri. 8am-6:30pm, Sat. 8am-noon. **Postal code:** 29000.

ACCOMMODATIONS AND CAMPING

It's a good idea to reserve in writing as far ahead as possible from July 15 to August 15. As an alternative to hotels, ask the tourist office about private homes offering bed and breakfast (from 150F for 2 people).

Centre Hebergement de Quimper, 6, av. des Oiseaux (tel. 02 98 64 97 97; fax 02 98 55 38 37). A prodigal hostel, it seceded from HI but may soon be returning to the mother ship. 2km out of town in the Bois de l'Ancien Séminaire. Take bus 1 (direction: Penhars) from the *gare* or the stop by the tourist office, to stop "Chaptal." The *centre* is across, 50m up the street, on your left (20min.). On foot, cross the river from pl. de la Résistance and go left on quai de l'Odet. Turn right onto pont l'Abbé and go straight to the hostel (on your left, just before the wood). 60 beds in 8- to 10-person co-ed rooms. 45F. Sheets 15F. Breakfast 18F. Kitchen. Reception daily 9-10am and 4:30-9:30pm; call if arriving late. Lock-out (except from kitchen and bathrooms) 9:30am-5pm. Open April-Oct.

Hôtel de l'Ouest, 63, rue le Déan (tel. 02 98 90 28 35), near the station in a quiet neighborhood. Take rue Jean-Pierre Calloch (across from station), turn left onto rue le Déan. Friendly owner and her small dog love *Let's Go*-toters. Clean rooms, firm mattresses. Singles 100-130F, with shower and toilet 170F. Doubles with toilet 150F, with shower 190F. Triples with shower 210F. Quads with toilet 220F. Extra bed 30F. Shower 15F. Breakfast 27F.

Hôtel Celtic, 13, rue de Douarnenez (tel. 02 98 55 59 35), in a great location 1 block up from Eglise St-Mathieu. Friendly ex-Marine owner speaks English and 4 other languages. 38 rooms. Singles and doubles 120F, with shower 160F, with shower and toilet 210F. Triples and quads 145F. Extra bed 95F. Shower free. Breakfast 25F. Restaurant downstairs has 2 58F seafood *menus*.

Hôtel Le Transvaal, 57, rue Jean Jaurès (tel. 02 98 90 09 91). Turn right onto av. de la Gare. Continue along Odet river as it becomes bd. Dupleix. Take a left onto rue Ste-Catherine, across the river from the Cathedral, and go to rue Jaurès (10min.). Closed for renovations in '96, but will be open "soon." Singles and doubles were 120-200F, but prices may rise with increased spiffiness.

Camping: Camping Municipal, av. des Oiseaux in the Bois du Séminaire (tel. 02 98 55 61 09), next to the hostel. Take bus 1 to "Chaptal." Crowded, clean facilities. 16F50 per person, children 8F30, car 6F20, tent 3F60, electricity 14F40. Hot shower free; ask receptionist for tokens. Reception Mon.-Tues., Thurs., Sat. 8-11am and 3-8pm; Wed., Sun. 9am-noon; Fri. 9-11am and 3-8pm.

FOOD

The lively **covered market (Les Halles),** off rue Kéréon on rue St-François, is the perfect place to satisfy your craving for bargains—produce, seafood, meats, and cheeses all abound here (open Mon.-Sat. 7am-8pm, Sun. 9am-1pm). It's also a great spot for inhaling bargain crêpes (20F for a ham, egg, and cheese crêpe). An open market takes place twice a week (Wed. at pl. St-Corentin and Sat. outside Les Halles, both 9am-6pm; Sept.-May 9am-2pm or later). Merchants come from all over the region for the larger Saturday market; Wednesday draws a local crowd. An **Unico supermarket** is on av. de la Gare (open Mon.-Sat. 8am-8pm, Sun. 8:30am-8pm).

Le Saint Co., 20, rue Frout, just off pl. St-Corentin. Small restaurant specializing in meat dishes such as steak tartare (71F, includes salad). 67F and 88F *menus*. Open daily July-Aug. noon-11:30pm; Sept.-June 11am-2pm and 6pm-midnight. V, MC.

Le Café des Arts, 4, rue Ste-Catherine, across the river from the cathedral. Black-and-white photos of contemporary *artistes* cover the pastel walls of this relaxed people-watching place. The atmosphere is stirred, not shaken. Salads 13-44F. *Entrecôte* 56F. Beer 17-31F. Open Mon.-Sat. 11am-1am, Sun. 3pm-1am. V, MC.

Les Cariatides, 4, rue du Guéodet (tel. 02 98 95 15 14), on a busy street near Les Halles. Above a rollicking bar in a 16th-century house, the management serves up tasty family fare (10-45F). Open Mon.-Sat. noon-2:30pm and 7-9:30pm. V, MC.

Le St-Mathieu, 18, rue St-Mathieu (tel. 02 98 53 74 04). Try the *Salade St-Mathieu* (*langoustines*, melon, and ham 34F). 58 and 69F *menus*. Open July-Aug. Mon.-Sat. 8am-midnight; Sept.-June Mon.-Fri. 8am-8pm, Sat. 8am-1am. V, MC.

SIGHTS AND ENTERTAINMENT

At the entrance to the old quarter towers the **Cathédrale St-Corentin.** It's a hodgepodge of a church dedicated to Quimper's patron, one of dozens of Breton saints not recognized by the Church in Rome. The spiritual advisor of King Gradlon, the 6th-century bishop is said to have lived off a single fish. After lunch, he threw half of it back into the river, only to have his scaly friend return regenerated the next day. A statue of Gradlon, erected in 1856, stands between the cathedral's spires.

From the small cathedral garden, climb to the **old city ramparts** for views of the cathedral and the Odet river (open daily 8am-6pm). From the garden, you can enter the **Musée Départemental Breton,** 1, rue du Roi Gradlon (tel. 02 98 95 21 60), housed in the former episcopal manor. Finistère's history, archaeology, and ethnography are represented in cleverly designed exhibits of pottery, artifacts, and costumes. A strange quirk of the museum's construction allows you to play count-the-phalluses in the Greco-Roman room then move through the door into the medieval room and play count-the-Virgins. (Open daily June-Sept. 9am-6pm; Oct.-May Tues.-Sat. 9am-noon and 2-5pm, Sun. 2-5pm. Admission 25F, students 12F.)

From the cathedral, cross the street onto charming rue Kéréon ("shoemaker" in Breton). In the Middle Ages, each street in this quarter was devoted to a single trade. Rue des Boucheries (butchers), on the right of rue Kéréon, leads to rue Sallé (salted meat), and right again to pl. Beurre (butter).

Across the Odet River is an area of Quimper dedicated to the town's distinctive pottery. The **Musée de la Faïence Jules Verlingue,** 14, rue Jean-Baptiste Bousquet (tel. 02 98 90 12 72), along the quai past the allées de Locmaria, traces Quimper's 300-year history as a center of art. The museum houses hundreds of pieces of pottery—icons, pitchers, glorified chips-and-salsa plates—and sells it next door (open April 15-Oct. 26 Mon.-Sat. 10am-6pm; admission 26F, students 21F). More plates lurk at the **Faïenceries de Quimper H. B. Henriot,** rue Haute (tel. 02 98 90 09 36), a studio where you can watch potters design Quimper's finest. Tours in French and English (open Mon.-Fri. 9-11:15am and 1-4:15pm; admission 15F, students 8F). One km out of town *en route* de Bénodet, the **Faïenceries Keraluc** (tel. 02 98 53 04 50) leads free tours (must reserve; open Mon.-Fri. 9am-noon and 2-6pm).

The **Musée des Beaux-Arts,** 40, pl. Saint Corentin (tel. 02 98 95 45 20), holds a collection of 14th- to 20th-century paintings including Breton works and paintings from the school of Pont-Aven by Sérusier, Moret, Slewinsky, Maufra, and Meyer de Haan (open July-Aug. daily 10am-7pm; Sept.-June Wed.-Mon. 10am-noon and 2-6pm; admission 25F, students 15F). Modern art aficionados will enjoy the small, eclectic collection of the trippy **Centre d'Art Contemporain,** 10, Parc du 137ème Régiment d'Infanterie (tel. 02 98 55 55 77), but traditionalists may want to save their francs for a rainy day. To reach the museum, take a left off rue Douarnenez, across from the St-Mathieu church (open Tues.-Sat. 10am-6pm, Sun. 2-5pm; guided tours Sat. 2:30pm; admission 20F, students 15F). For discounts on the museums, consider the **Passeport Culturel** (includes Musée Départemental, Musée de la Faïence, Centre d'Art Contemporain, Musée des Beaux-Arts, Faïencerie H.B. Henriot, and tour of city; 50F for 3 of these visits, 100F for all 6).

Those who missed the *Festival de Cornouaille* (see introduction above) can still catch other celebrations of Breton culture. Every Thursday from late June to early September, the cathedral gardens fill with **Breton dancers** in costume, accompanied by lively *biniou* and *bombarde* players (9pm, 20F). The first three weeks in August, Quimper holds its **Semaines Musicales.** Orchestras and choirs perform nightly in the Théâtre Municipal and cathedral; call the tourist office for more info.

By night, **Céili Pub,** 4, rue Aristide Briand (tel. 02 98 95 17 61), gathers a hip young crowd of *Quimpérois* (open Mon.-Sat. 10:30am-1am, Sun. 5pm-1am), while Anglophiles migrate to **St. Andrew's Pub,** 11, pl. Styvel (tel. 02 98 53 34 49), for their Guinness fix (open daily 11am-1am). The **Coffee Shop,** 26, rue du Frout (tel. 02 98 95 43 30), survives as a gay and lesbian enclave in bourgeois Quimper. Draft beer 11-20F (open daily 5pm-1am; from 7-8pm, 2 drinks for the price of 1).

■ Near Quimper

LOCRONAN

About 20km northwest of Quimper on D39, beautiful Locronan (pop. 800) sits high on a hill above the countryside. Its perfectly preserved 15th- to 17th- century stone houses are more than just tourist draws; one of the more than 20 films shot here was

Roman Polanski's *Tess.* Locronan once thrived on a successful sail-making industry and now snoozes away in peace, thriving on a successful sale-making industry.

The **tourist office** at pl. de la Mairie (tel. 02 98 91 70 14) has a free guide to the town and **changes money** at decent rates (open daily July to mid-Sept. 10am-7pm). **Crédit Agricole** has a 24-hour **ATM** in its magic money wall on rue du Prieurié. Rent **bikes** at **Roue Libre** (tel. 02 98 91 71 71), a few hundred meters up rue St-Mathieu to the left of the church. (Mountain bikes 30F per hr., 60F per ½-day, 100F per day; passport deposit. Open June 15-Sept. 15 daily 9am-7pm.) **SCETA buses** (tel. 02 98 93 06 98 in Carhaix) drop in on Locronan from Quimper (5-8 per day, 20min., 21F). In **medical emergencies** call 15. **Police** at 02 98 91 70 01. Next door to the tourist office, the **post office** offers **currency exchange** and satisfies your postal needs (open Mon.-Fri. 9am-noon and 2-5pm, Sat. 9am-noon; **postal code:** 29180).

In the heart of town, **La Grande Place** is surrounded by impeccably preserved 17th- and 18th-century houses that once belonged to the town's rich merchants and officials. The **Eglise Priorale,** a 15th-century church built with the help of the dukes of Brittany, towers over all else in town. The smaller, more spartan **Chapelle Notre-Dame de Bonne Nouvelle** sits in a tranquil spot down the hill, guarded by a small calvary. Poster buffs will get a kick out of the **Musée de l'Affiche** (tel. 02 98 51 80 59), on the venelle des Templiers off rue St-Maurice, at the top of the hill above the church. From early July to early October, the museum showcases a different aspect of Breton life (open daily Oct. 14-Aug. 10am-7pm; Sept.-Oct. 13 10am-1pm and 2-6pm; admission 20F). Two km east of town, capped by a chapel, the **Montagne de Locronan** offers a stunning view of the countryside and the deep blue sea beyond.

On the second Sunday in July, Locronan celebrates its Celtic roots with **La Troménie,** a ritual march around the town's outskirts. Wearing traditional Breton costume, the participants follow the path druids used in their rites of consecration but bear crosses and banners rather than unlucky virgins. This small-town tradition is a wonderful (and mercifully untouristed) spectacle. Try to be one of the throng if you're in the area. Every six years, on the second and third Sundays in July (sorry, come back in 2001), **La Grande Troménie** draws crowds from all over the region, who follow a longer path and act out a play about their Irish patron, St. Ronan.

PONT-AVEN

Between Quimper and Quimperlé, tiny Pont-Aven is a jewel whose beauty has been immortalized on countless canvases. The first to paint the town was Paul Gauguin (1848-1903), who, having grown tired of mainstream Parisian Impressionism, discovered his personal stroke and style here. Inspired by Gauguin, the Pont-Aven school developed as a movement emphasizing pure color, absence of perspective, and simplification of figures. The town's other claims to fame are its spectacular art galleries—some of the finest in Brittany—and its Traou Mad cookie factory.

Pont-Aven is connected by **Transports Caoudal** (tel. 02 98 56 96 72) to Quimper (4-6 per day, 1hr., 30F) and other towns nearby. **Buses** stop at pl. Gauguin, close to the **tourist office,** pl. de l'Hôtel de Ville (tel. 02 98 06 04 70; fax 02 98 06 17 25). The office sells a nifty walking tour guide for 2F (open July-Aug. daily 9:30am-7:30pm; Sept.-June 9:15am-12:30pm and 2-7pm; Dec.-March closed Sun.). Your deepest stamp-licking desires can be satisfied at the **post office,** rue des Abbés Tanguy, which exchanges currency at mouthwatering rates with no commission. (Open Mon.-Fri. 9am-noon and 1:45-4:45pm, Sat. 9am-noon. **Postal code:** 29930.) There's nothing in Pont-Aven that resembles budget accommodations. If you need two days to visit the galleries, your best best is the **Auberge de Jeunesse (HI)** on quai de la Croix (tel. 02 98 97 03 47) in Concarneau, 30 minutes away by bus. (45F. Breakfast 18F. Reception daily 9am-noon and 6-8pm. No lockout, no curfew.)

Before heading straight for the canvases, use the tourist office's maps to explore the area around Pont-Aven and see the source of the painters' inspiration. Wander through the tranquil **Bois d'Amour** (Lovers' Wood) to the **Chapelle de Trémalo,** whose 17th-century polychrome-wood crucifix provided the subject for Gauguin's *Yellow Christ.* The calvary next to the 15th-century church at **Nizon,** about 1.5km northwest of Pont-Aven, inspired his *Green Christ.* Your return to nature fully prepares you for a visit to the **Musée de L'Ecole de Pont-Aven,** up the street from the tourist office (tel. 02 98 06 14 43). It houses both permanent and temporary exhibitions and shows superb slides on the school. The permanent section may disappoint Gauguin devotees with its limited collection of drawings, letters, and sculptures, but it does contain a beautiful display of works by artists from Gauguin's school, as well as paintings by local masters. Those familiar with Finistère may experience a pleasant sense of *déjà vu*—canvases depicting the cliffs of Ile d'Ouessant, the caves of Camaret, and other regional attractions are prominently displayed on the museum's walls. (Open daily Sept.-June 10am-12:30pm and 2-6:30pm; July-Aug. 10am-7pm; Nov.-March closes at 6pm. Admission 25F, off-season 20F, students 12F). For a more structured format, take one of the guided tours of Pont-Aven and its museum, organized by the tourist office. (June-Sept. at 10:30, 11:30am, 4:30, and 5:30pm. Tour 22F. Museum 30F. Tour and museum 35F, under age 21 20F.)

After staring at canvases all day, refuel yourself by gorging on *Les Galettes de Pont-Aven* at the **Biscuiterie Traou Mad** (tel. 02 98 06 01 03; fax 02 98 06 17 50), near the tourist office in the *centre ville.* Since 1920, these light, flaky, crispy cookies have been made using only fresh butter, sugar, eggs, milk, and flour. The company can send a box home to the ones you love [mmm—thanks, Rob]. (Open Mon.-Sat. 9:15am-12:15pm and 2-7pm, Sun. 10am-12:30pm and 2:30-7pm. V, MC.)

Quiberon

All roads in Quiberon lead to the smooth, sandy, and wonderfully clean Grande Plage in the heart of town. Connected to the mainland by only a narrow strip of land, this *presqu'île* (literally, "almost island") is a colorful popsicle stand of a place that draws hordes of tourists in the summer and is almost overwhelmed with resort souvenirdom. Beyond its convenience as a base to explore nearby Belle-Ile, Quiberon offers ample opportunities to escape "traditional Breton culture" and nurture the more hedonistic side of the your soul. Walk the beach, eat ice cream, and check out your neighbor's tan—everyone needs some mindless fun once in a while.

ORIENTATION AND PRACTICAL INFORMATION

To find the **tourist office,** 14, rue de Verdun (tel. 02 97 50 07 84; fax 02 97 30 58 22), from the train station, turn left and walk down rue de la Gare. Veer to the right of the church and down rue de Verdun; the office is on the left. It distributes a flashy guide to the town and info on campsites, hotels, restaurants, local B&Bs (150-250F per night), and house rentals (open July-Aug. Mon.-Sat. 9am-8pm, Sun. 10:30am-noon and 5-8pm; Sept.-June Mon.-Sat. 9am-12:30pm and 2-6:30pm). **Trains** (tel. 02 97 50 07 07) run only in July and August and only to Auray. Take either a normal train (8 per day, 40min., 27F) or a scenic but slow *tire-bouchon* choo-choo (12F). There are **lockers** (5-20F) at the station (ticket windows open 6:30am-7:40pm). **TIM** buses also run to Auray (10 per day, 5 on Sun., 1 hr., 35F) via Carnac (30min., 22F). For info, call **Cariane Atlantique** in Vannes (tel. 02 97 47 29 64). **Quiberon Voyages,** 21, pl. Hoche (tel. 02 97 50 15 30), runs trips all over the province (including an excursion to Carnac and Vannes for 110F), while **Compagnie Morbihanaise et Nantaise de Navigation** (tel. 02 97 31 80 01, in Le Palais) serves Belle-Ile from the *gare maritime* on quai de Houat (5-13 per day, roundtrip 85F—58F if you leave at certain (inconvenient) times—bikes 38F, cars 358-682F). **Banks** with 24-hour **ATMs** frolic across from the train station on rue de la Gare.

Cruise the boardwalk or explore the **Côte Sauvage** on bikes, tandems, 3-seaters, pedal carts, or mopeds from **Cyclomar,** 47, pl. Hoche (tel. 02 97 50 26 00; fax 02 97 50 36 40; 5-speeds 36F per ½-day, 49F per day, deposit 800F or passport; mountain bikes 49F per ½-day, 71F per day, deposit 1000F or passport; 10% off with ISIC card; open daily July-Aug. 8am-midnight; Oct.-Jan. 5 and Feb. 7-June 8:30am-12:30pm and 2-7:30pm; **annex** at the train station open July-Aug. daily 8:30am-8pm). The **Centre**

Hospitalier du Pratel in Auray is the nearest hospital. For an **ambulance,** call Le Dortz, 66, rue du Point du Jour (tel. 02 97 50 34 65). The **police** are at 147, rue du Port de Pêche (tel. 02 97 50 07 39). In an **emergency,** dial 17. The **post office** is on pl. de la Duchesse Anne (tel. 02 97 50 11 92) and has **currency exchange** and poste restante (open Mon.-Fri. 9am-6pm, Sat. 9am-noon; Sept.-June Mon.-Fri. 9am-noon and 2-5pm, Sat. 9am-noon; **postal code:** 56170).

ACCOMMODATIONS AND CAMPING

Quiberon's thrills don't come cheap; luckily there's a small but comfy **Auberge de Jeunesse (HI),** 45, rue du Roch-Priol (tel. 02 97 50 15 54), just 10 minutes from the station and five minutes from the beach. From the station turn left, take rue de la Gare through pl. du Repos to the right of the church, take rue de Lille, and turn left on rue Roch-Priol. Truck on for a few blocks until you reach the *auberge.* 30 beds in clean eight-person rooms. (46F. Sheets 16F. Breakfast 18F. Kitchen facilities. Lockout 10am-6pm. No curfew. Open May-Sept.) The hep manager also rents tents for two (35F per person) and camping space (25F per person). **Hôtel de l'Océan,** 7, quai de l'Océan (tel. 02 97 50 07 58; fax 02 97 50 27 81), lets clean, color-coordinated rooms on the boardwalk facing the harbor. There's a TV room, too. (Singles and doubles 160-190F, with shower 210-240F, with shower and toilet 250-280F. Extra bed 80F. Shower 10F. Breakfast 31F. V, MC.) **Au Bon Accueil,** 6, quai de L'Houat (tel. 02 97 50 07 92), has plain, inexpensive rooms above a busy restaurant. (Singles and doubles 155F, with shower 185F. Triples 215F, with shower 245F. Breakfast 32F. V, MC.) The campsite nearest the city is **Camping du Goviro** (tel. 02 97 50 13 54), adjacent to the lovely beach of the same name. It's almost always full in-season; reserve. (9F50 per person, 5F50 per tent, 5F per car. 11F50 electricity, cold showers free, hot showers 6F70. Reception Mon.-Sat. 8:30am-6pm, Sun. 9:30am-noon and 3-6pm; Sept. 16-May Mon.-Sat. 8:30am-noon and 2-5:30pm, Sun. 10am-noon. Gates closed between 10:30pm and 6am.) Right behind is the slightly more spacious **Camping Bois d'Amour** (tel. 02 97 50 13 52; off-season 02 97 30 24 00), which boasts a heated swimming pool. Reserve in summer (open April-Sept.; 15-30F per person, 2-person tents 32F, car and caravan 58F, electricity 18F).

FOOD

Given its peninsular location, seafood *(fruits de mer)* is Quiberon's main specialty. The Quiberon bonbon of choice is the *niniche,* a caramel-like hard candy. At **La Criée,** 11, quai de l'Océan (tel. 02 97 30 53 09), an outgoing, good-humored man serves superb seafood. Grab a friend or two and belly up to the *plateau gargantua,* an orgasmic array of oysters, crab, *langoustines,* and other tasty aquatic critters (295F). If you stay inside you can try a more subdued collection o' swimmers for 95F or the daily catch, served fresh on an 89F *menu* (open July-Aug. daily noon-2pm and 7-10:30pm; Sept.-June closed Sun. night and Mon; V, MC). For light Italian fare, try **Bella Vita,** 3, pl. Hoche, which offers salads (25-48F) and pizzas (36-70F) and a terrace with a great view of the beach (open daily in season noon-midnight; off-season Thurs.-Tues. noon-3pm and 7-11pm; closed Jan.). Three blocks from the hostel at 54, rue de Port Haliguen, the mega-*crêperie* **Aux Armes de Bretagne** (tel. 02 97 50 01 20) graciously serves 240 (yes, 240) different kinds of crêpes (15-69F) in a classy, rose-colored decor. Try the *pêcheur,* which features *quiberonnais* smoked tuna, fresh cream, and lemon (51F). Crazy dessert crêpes go for 14-51F. (Open daily noon-2:30pm and 7-11pm. V, MC.) A **Stoc supermarket** on rue de Verdun can fulfill your every nutritional need and dietary desire (open Mon.-Sat. 8:45am-12:30pm and 3-7:15pm), while closer to the hostel on rue de Port Haliguen, a **Casino supermarket** does well nigh the same thing (open Mon.-Fri. 9am-8pm, Sat. 9am-noon).

SIGHTS AND ENTERTAINMENT

Spectacular Belle-Ile is just a ferry ride away, and the craggy **Côte Sauvage** stretches a wild and windy 10km along the western edge of the Quiberon peninsula. Heed the signs marked *Baignades Interdites* (swimming forbidden); many have drowned in these tempting but treacherous waters.

The beach is the place to be, but if the smell of coconut oil drives you nutty, head for the small, rocky **Plage du Goviro** near the campgrounds. From the port, follow bd. Chanard east along the water as it becomes bd. de la Mer then bd. du Goviro.

An Australian diver who has traveled around the world and somehow landed in Quiberon runs **L'Hemisphère Sud,** 4, rue du Phare (tel. 02 97 30 51 76), off pl. Hoche. The pub is filled with a young crowd of tanned *Quiberonnais* (open daily 8pm-3am). For live music, head to **Le Carnaby Street,** pl. Hoche (tel. 02 97 30 40 52; open July-Aug. Mon., Wed., and Fri.10pm-4am). The groove reigns supreme at **Le Suroit,** 29, rue de Port-Maria (tel. 02 97 50 10 67), a disco with a boat for a bar and a striking view (open 10pm-4am; cover 50F, first drink 25F; V, MC).

Strings and swing serenade the musically minded during the two weeks of Quiberon's **Passions Presqu'Ile.** A week of classical concerts in July (admission 100F per concert) and a week of jazz in August (admission 80F per concert) comprise this tuneful festival. Call the tourist office for more info.

■ Near Quiberon: Belle-Ile

At least five boats depart daily from Quiberon's Port-Maria for Belle-Ile, an island whose name is as well known as it is appropriate. Belle-Ile's magnificent coast merges high cliffs, narrow creeks, and crashing seas. Farther inland, patches of heather and ferns color the fields. At 20km in length, Belle-Ile necessitates some kind of transportation more efficient than the most dedicated pair of feet. Bring your bike or rent one on the island. The crossing takes about 45 minutes; you can take your wheels with you (roundtrip 85F per person, 40F per bike).

ORIENTATION AND PRACTICAL INFORMATION

Boats dock at Le Palais, the island's largest town, located on the northern coast. The other main towns—Sauzon, Bangor, and Rocmaria—lie respectively at the northwest tip, the center, and the east coast of the island. The most spectacular area, the Côte Sauvage, is in the south and accessible only by bike, foot, or thumb.

Join the rest of your fellow ferry passengers in parading *en masse* to the **tourist office** (tel. 02 97 31 81 93; fax 02 97 31 56 17); walk to the left end of the quai as you leave the boat. The office distributes a free guide to the island (in English), a comprehensive French brochure with hiking and biking plans, and a detailed 45F walking map (open July-Aug. Mon.-Sat. 8:30am-8pm, Sun. 9am-12:30pm; Sept.-June Mon.-Sat. 9am-noon and 2-6pm, Sun. 10am-noon). You'll find an **ATM** next to the **Crédit Agricole,** pl. de la Résistance. **Buses** link Le Palais (from the port on quai de Bonnelle) with Sauzon only (3 per day, 30min., 12F). To reach other parts of the island, rent a bike at **Cyclotour,** quai de Bonnelle (tel. 02 97 31 80 68), near the tourist office on the port (bikes 40-60F per ½-day, 50-80F per day, depending on model; passport deposit; open July-Aug. daily 8:15am-7pm; Sept.-June Mon.-Sat. 9am-noon and 2-7pm). You can also rent bikes at **Location 2 Roues** (tel. 02 97 31 84 74), also at the port on quai de l'Acache (50-60F per ½-day, 60-80F per day; 1000F or passport deposit; open daily June-Sept. 9am-7pm). The **hospital** (tel. 02 97 31 48 48) is in Le Palais. The **police** are at Les Glacis (tel. 02 97 31 80 22; **emergency** tel. 17). The **post office** (tel. 02 97 31 80 40), on quai Nicolas Foucquet in Le Palais, across from quai Gambetta, has poste restante, an **ATM,** and **currency exchange** (open Mon.-Fri. 9am-12:30pm and 2-5pm, Sat. 9am-noon; **postal code:** 56360).

ACCOMMODATIONS AND FOOD

Inexpensive accommodations on the island include campgrounds, two *gîtes d'étape*, and an **HI youth hostel.** The tourist office in Le Palais can help you find cheap rooms. The campground and the hostel are near the citadel, a 10-minute hike from Le Palais' port. Turn right from the port and follow the quai to the footbridge leading to the citadel; cross the bridge, walk diagonally left through the parking lot. follow the street to the left until you reach the municipal showers, and enter **Camping Les Glacis** (tel. 02 97 31 41 76; 15F per person, 28F per tent, 10F per car, 3F per bike, 11F per hot shower; reception Mon.-Sat. 9-11:30am and 4:30-6:30pm, Sun. 9-11:30am). To reach the hostel, continue on, climb another hill, follow the road through a small residential neighborhood, and look for the sign to the *auberge* on the right. A former juvenile prison, the hostel (tel. 02 97 31 81 33) has comfortable two- or three-bed rooms, a kitchen, and bathroom facilities with wheelchair access. To camp on the lawn you must rent a tent (48F; sheets 16F; tent 25F per person; breakfast 18F; lunch or dinner 48F; no lockout or curfew; reception open 8-10am and 6-8pm). Le Palais' **La Frégate,** quai de l'Acadie (tel. 02 97 31 54 16), in front of where the ships dock, has cheap rooms above a friendly bar and restaurant (singles and doubles 112-152F, with shower and toilet 212F; triples with shower and toilet 252F; shower free; breakfast 24F; open April-Oct. V, MC). The tourist office also has information about the island's *gîtes d'étape* and *centres d'accueil.*

For a tasty meal among the locals, head to **Traou-Mod,** 9, rue Willaumez (tel. 02 97 31 84 84), off pl. de la Résistance in Le Palais. Choose from a wide selection of *galettes* (7-74F) and dessert crêpes (7-43F) as well as huge salads (18-53F; open April-Nov. 11:30am-12:30am. V, MC). **La Chaloupe,** 8, av. Carnot in Le Palais (tel. 02 97 31 88 27), purveys an enormous variety of crêpes (12-85F) and is open 'til midnight in July and August (V, MC). **Café de la Cale,** quai Guerveur in Sauzon (tel. 02 97 31 65 74), prepares delicious salads (45-90F). Seafood lovers might consider the *grande assiette dégustation* (92F), with a bit of everything. A small **market** is held every morning in Le Palais at pl. de la République; on Saturday it takes over the *place.* A **supermarket** is behind the church on rue Le Brix (open Mon.-Fri.9am-12:30pm and 2-7pm, Sat. 9am-7:30pm, Sun. 9am-noon).

SIGHTS

The massive 16th- to 17th-century **Citadelle Vauban** (tel. 02 97 31 84 17) catches your eye the second you glimpse the island from the boat. Built in 1549 by Henri II to protect *bellilois* monks from marauding pirates, the fort now harbors a grass-roofed museum that presents the citadel's history and gossip about Sarah Bernhardt, Claude Monet, and other celebrities who have lived on the island. Lizards slither over the walls of the courtyard, and numerous musty nooks and crannies beckon to the curious. How can you resist? The citadel also affords access to the ramparts (open daily May-Oct. 9am-7pm; Nov.-April 9:30am-noon and 2-6pm; admission 28F).

Bike 6km to **Sauzon,** a tiny fishing port with picture-book façades and crystal-clear waters. From Sauzon, continue another 4km to the storm-battered **Pointe des Poulains,** at the northernmost tip of the island. The nearby deserted fort was home for many years to actress Sarah Bernhardt (1844-1923). Four km southwest on the Côte Sauvage, the impressive **Apothecairerie** towers over the raging sea. The grotto took its name from the cormorant nests that once lined the rocks like bottles in an apothecary's shop. Travelers report that a 5-minute walk down the rocks beyond signs that specifically prohibit such activity affords an awesome view of the electric blue waters. You'll shoot your eye out. From the grotto, follow D25 south first to the **Plage de Port-Donnant,** where waves crash onto the sandy beach between high stone cliffs, then onward to the rough **Aiguilles de Port-Coton,** which Claude Monet captured in an 1886 painting.

Carnac

Stretches of countryside with great pine forests and open heaths lie northeast of the Quiberon Peninsula. Mesolithic people roamed this area of Brittany as much as 10,000 years ago. Three thousand years later, their older and wiser Neolithic heirs settled down and called the place home, leaving thousands of menhirs and dolmens as proof. Carnac, a 30-minute bus ride north of Quiberon, has the world's most impressive series of these ancient monuments. If monster rocks aren't your style, small pulverized ones may fit the bill—the luxurious stretch of beach is a great place to unwind after a day of ogling stones.

ORIENTATION AND PRACTICAL INFORMATION

To get to Carnac, take the **TIM bus** (tel. 02 97 47 29 64, in Vannes) from Quiberon (at least 7 per day, 30min., 21F) or Auray (7 per day, 30min., 22F). You can also take the **train** to Plouharnel and catch a bus from there (7 per day, 5min., 3F). There are two bus stops. The first, "Carnac-Ville," is convenient for the town and its sights; the second is close to the beach in front of the main **tourist office** at 74, av. des Druides (tel. 02 97 52 13 52; fax 02 97 52 86 10; open July-Aug. Mon.-Sat. 9am-7pm, Sun. 3-7pm; Sept.-June Mon-Sat. 9am-noon and 2-6pm). To walk back to the *centre ville,* take av. des Druides and walk up towards the church. Av. des Druides becomes av. de la Poste, which leads into the square where the **tourist office annex** squats at pl. de l'Eglise (same tel. as main office; open July-Aug. Mon.-Sat. 9:30am-12:30pm and 2:30-7pm, Sun. 10am-12:30pm; Sept.-June Tues.-Sat. 9:30am-12:30pm and 2-6pm).

Ensure your financial solvency with a trip to the 24-hour **ATM** at **Crédit Mutuel,** 27, rue Cornély, between the church and "Carnac-Ville" stop. Rent **bikes** at **Cycles Lorcy,** 6, Rue de Courdriec (tel. 02 97 52 09 73; 30F per ½-day, 45F per day and 200F per week; 1000F or passport deposit; open July-Aug. Mon.-Sat. 8:30am-12:15pm and 2-7pm, Sun. 8:30am-12:15pm; Sept.-June open Tues.-Sat.). You can also rent at **Le Randonneur,** 20, av. des Druides (tel. 02 97 52 02 55; 25-50F per ½-day, 35-65F per day, 150-300F per week; deposit 1300F (800F or passport for 3-speeds); open daily 8:30am-7pm). In a **medical emergency,** dial 15. The **police station** is at 40, rue St-Cornély (tel. 02 97 52 06 24). In an **un-medical emergency,** dial 17. The **post office,** av. de la Poste (tel. 02 97 52 03 90), just outside the *centre ville,* has **currency exchange** and poste restante (open July-Aug. Mon.-Fri. 9am-6pm, Sat. 9am-noon; Sept.-June Mon.-Fri. 9am-noon and 2-5pm, Sat. 9am-noon; **postal code:** 56430).

BRITTANY

ACCOMMODATIONS, CAMPING, AND FOOD

Carnac is best as a daytrip. Its handsome beach attracts many visitors—and as the summer tides rise, so too do hotel prices. B&Bs are the cheapest housing option; ask the tourist office for a list (doubles run 100-150F). A kind, amiable woman runs the **Hôtel Chez Nous,** 5, pl. de la Chapelle (tel. 02 97 52 07 28). This two-star hotel has a B&B atmosphere; each room is tastefully decorated, and the bathrooms are big. (Singles or doubles 210-330F, off-season 190-270F. Breakfast 33F. V, MC.) A plethora of campgrounds dots the area around Carnac. The **Alignements de Kermario** (tel. 02 97 52 16 57) is across the road from the megaliths in a lush, private setting. (16F per person, 30F per tent, 10F per car. Free showers in luxurious facilities. Electricity 10-12F. Prices fall off-season to 12F, 20F, and 7F respectively. Open May-Sept.) **Camping Kerabus** (tel. 02 97 52 24 90) is about three minutes away from the big old rocks on allée des Alouettes, off route d'Auray (15F per person, 18F per tent plus car; cold showers free, hot shower 4F50; electricity 11F50-14F; open May-Sept. 15).

Crêperies surround the St-Cornély church. You might try **Chez Marie,** 8, pl. de l'Eglise (tel. 02 97 52 07 93). Crêpes run 9-50F, and salads go for 17-55F; try the *galette* with *moules marinières* (50F). (Open daily noon-3pm and 7-11pm. V, MC.) **Supermarkets** strut their stuff in both parts of Carnac. **Marché U** is next to the beach and tourist office (open Mon.-Sat. 8:30am-8pm, Sun. 8:30am-12:30pm). **Casino** is on av. des Salines, close to the *ville* (same hours). At the awesome **market** in the parking lot behind the church at pl. du Marché (Wed. and Sun.), you'll see more underwear than during your entire trip. You can also sample everything from homemade honey and tasty Breton pastries to horse meat and spring rolls.

SIGHTS

The "Carnac-Ville" stop drops you close to the **Musée de Préhistoire,** 10, pl. de la Chapelle (tel. 02 97 52 22 04), your first opportunity to encounter Carnac's numerous collections o' rocks. It contains an impressive collection of burial chambers, engraved stones, jewelry, metal, pottery, and other artifacts that shed light on Brittany's history from 450,000 BC to the early Middle Ages. (Open July-Aug. Mon.-Fri. 10am-6:30pm, Sat.-Sun. 10am-noon and 2-6:30pm; June and Sept. Wed.-Mon. 10am-noon and 2-6pm; Oct.-May 10am-noon and 2-5pm. Admission 30F, students 12F.)

A five-minute walk up rue du Tumulus leads to the **Tumulus de St-Michel** (c. 4500 BC), where the ashes of a tribal chief were buried with those of his compatriots. The chief's followers were eager to perish on the pyre to secure themselves a comfy eternity. The passageways have been stripped of most of their original decorations. (Open daily July-Aug. 9:30am-7:30pm; Sept.-Oct. and Easter-June 10am-noon and 3-6pm. Tours in French every 15min. Admission 7F, students 4F.) The mysterious **Alignements du Ménec** are 10 minutes from both the museum and the Tumulus. Head north on rue de Courdriec, rue de Paul Person, or rue des Korrigans until you see the menhirs on route des Alignements. More than 1000 menhirs, some over 3m tall, stretch over 2km in a line toward the horizon. Nearby on route de Kerlescan, it's more of the same with the **Alignement de Kermario,** adjacent to which stand the anticlimactic **Géant du Manio** (a big rock) and the **Quadrilatère** (rocks in a square). Concern for the trampled greenery, coupled with the nagging fear that a menhir could topple and crush a megalith-ignorant tourist, have led to the erection of fences around the stones. Join tourists on the observation boardwalk who stand, menhir-like, sucking on popsicles and observing the array before them. For a real thrill, trip on over to the psychedelic **Archéoscope** (tel. 02 97 52 07 49), across from the Alignements du Ménec, a sound and light spectacle that uses lasers, films, and moving scenery to plumb the mystery of the megaliths' origin. (Open daily July-Aug. 10am-5:30pm; Sept.-Nov. 12 and Feb.11-June closed Sun. Admission 45F, students under 19 30F.) Work off that well-stoned brain at the **Whiskey Club,** 8, av. des Druides (tel. 02 97 52 10 52). It's one of Carnac's few night-spots, if you can handle 30F fruit juice and 50F cocktails (open daily 10:30pm-4am).

Nantes

Administratively, Nantes is part of the Pays de la Loire. Culturally, most *Nantais* feel an allegiance to Brittany. High-tech industries, 27,000 college students, stately rue Crébillon and pl. Graslin, and bountiful greenery invigorate modern Nantes, while its 15th-century cathedral and many museums chronicle past glories and extraordinary horrors. From the city's 15th-century château, Henri IV proclaimed the 1598 Edict of Nantes, establishing religious freedom for Protestants. The château later housed the infamous Bluebeard, the Maréchal de Retz, before the *Nantais* burned him at the stake. Between the 16th and 18th centuries, Nantes further demonstrated its malevolent streak by establishing itself as an apex of the "triangle trade." This slave trade bolstered Nantes' economy, making it France's largest port. During the Terror of 1793, hundreds of people, stripped and bound in pairs, were drowned in the Loire when Revolutionaries decided the guillotine was inefficient. The Revolution did have reforming effects, however—slavery was abolished, and Nantes turned its economy to innocuous canneries and cookie factories. While there aren't many must-see sights in Nantes (pop. 500,000), its ideal location, year-round festivals, and vibrant nightlife make it a smart stop between Brittany and points south.

ORIENTATION AND PRACTICAL INFORMATION

50km from the Atlantic, Nantes is a tangled conglomeration of *quartiers,* hills, and pedestrian streets spread out along the north bank of the Loire and shadowed by its four-story skyscraper, the **Tour Bretagne.** The city's major axes are **cours John Kennedy,** which becomes **cours Franklin Roosevelt** and later **Quai Fosse,** running east to west; and **cours des 50 Otages,** running north to south. To get to the *centre ville* and the tourist office, turn left out of the north exit *(accès nord)* of the train station onto **allée du Charcot** which transmutes itself into cours John Kennedy in a mat-

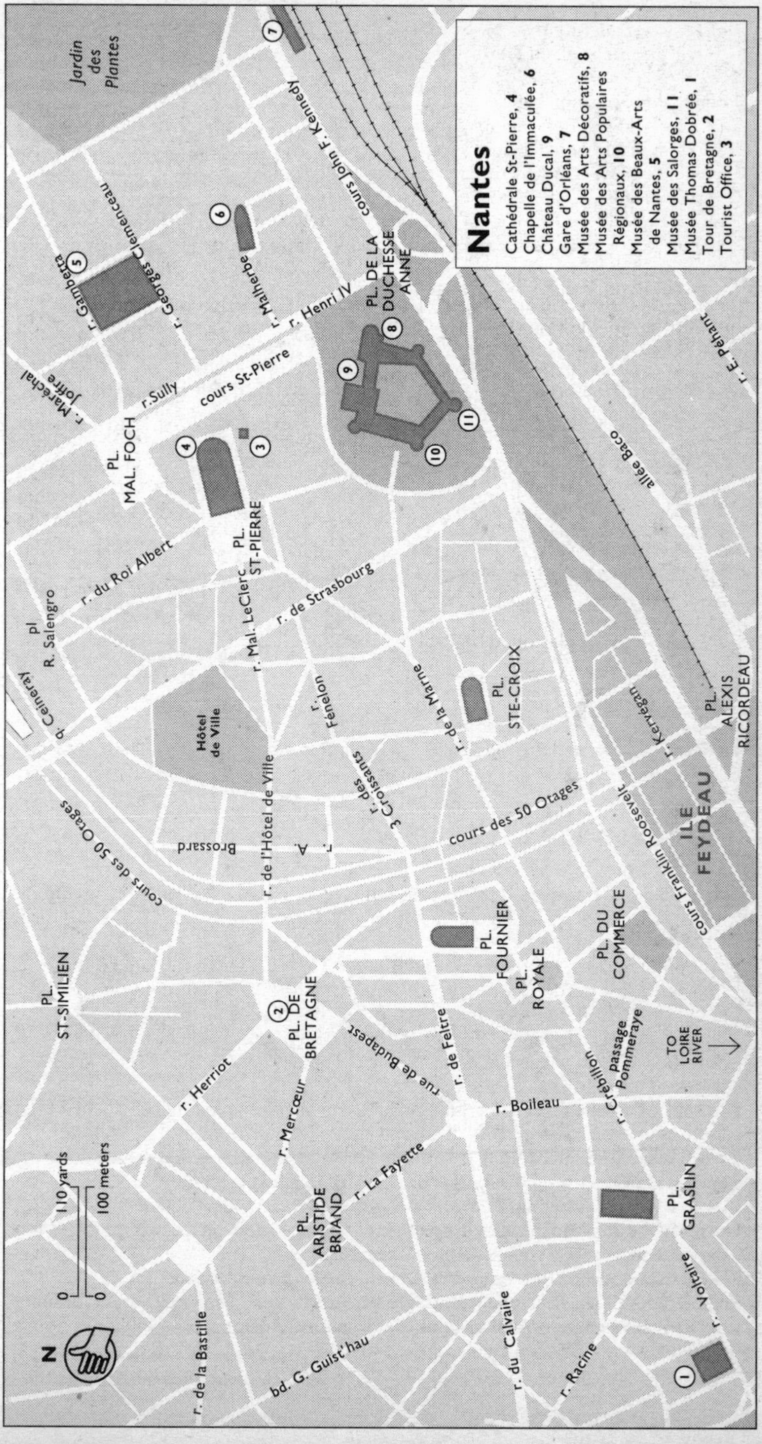
Nantes
Cathédrale St-Pierre, 4
Chapelle de l'Immaculée, 6
Château Ducal, 9
Gare d'Orléans, 7
Musée des Arts Décoratifs, 8
Musée des Arts Populaires Régionaux, 10
Musée des Beaux-Arts de Nantes, 5
Musée des Salorges, 11
Musée Thomas Dobrée, 1
Tour de Bretagne, 2
Tourist Office, 3
Jardin des Plantes
PL. MAL. FOCH
PL. ST-PIERRE
PL. DE LA DUCHESSE ANNE
PL. STE-CROIX
PL. ALEXIS RICORDEAU
ILE FEYDEAU
PL. DU COMMERCE
PL. ROYALE
PL. FOURNIER
PL. DE BRETAGNE
PL. ST-SIMILIEN
PL. ARISTIDE BRIAND
PL. GRASLIN
Hôtel de Ville
pl R. Salengro
r. Gambetta
r. Georges Clemenceau
r. Malherbe
r. Henri IV
cours John F. Kennedy
r. Sully
cours St-Pierre
r. Maréchal Joffre
r. du Roi Albert
r. Mal. LeClerc
r. de Strasbourg
r. Fénelon
r. de la Marne
r. des 3 Croissants
r. A. Brossard
r. de l'Hôtel de Ville
cours des 50 Otages
allee Baco
r. E. Pehant
r. Kervégan
cours Franklin Roosevelt
r. Crébillon
passage Pommeraye
TO LOIRE RIVER
r. de Feltre
rue de Budapest
r. Boileau
r. Herriot
r. Mercœur
r. La Fayette
r. de la Bastille
bd. G. Guist'hau
r. du Calvaire
r. Racine
r. Voltaire
N
0 110 yards
0 100 meters

BRITTANY

ter of blocks. Patiently pass **pl. Bouffay,** cross cours des 50 Otages, and the tourist office will appear at **pl. du Commerce** (20min.).

Tourist Information: Tourist Office, pl. du Commerce (tel. 02 40 47 04 51; fax 02 40 89 11 99), in the 19th-century commerce building. Stingy **currency exchange** rates. Good maps and info. Organizes tours (1 per day, 35F, students 25F, reservations recommended). Open Mon.-Fri. 9am-7pm, Sat. 10am-6pm.

Consulate: U.K., 5, rue des Cadeniers (tel. 02 40 63 43 02).

Money: Banque de France, 14, rue Lafayette (tel. 02 40 12 53 53). Open Mon.-Fri. 8:45am-12:30pm and 1:45pm-3:30pm. **Banque Nationale de Paris,** is on cours des 50 Otages, near pl. du Commerce (tel. 02 51 25 06 30; open Tues.-Fri. 8:25am-12:35pm and 1:50-5:30pm, Sat. 8:40am-12:40pm and 1:45-3:30pm).

Flights: The airport is 10km south of Nantes (tel. 02 40 84 80 00). A **Tan Air** shuttle (tel. 02 40 29 39 39) runs from the pl. du Commerce and the SNCF station *(accès sud)*. Mon.-Fri. 13 shuttles per day, Sat. 8 per day, Sun. 3 per day; 25min.; 36F. **Air Inter** (tel. 02 51 88 31 08) flies daily to Marseille, Lyon, Nice, and Paris. **Air France** (tel. 02 40 47 12 33) sends 6 flights per week to London.

Trains: (tel. 02 40 08 50 50). The station has two entrances: north (27, bd. de Stalingrad and cours John Kennedy) and south (bus connections at rue de Loumel) across the tracks. To: Paris (4-5 per day, 3-4hr., 220-265F; by TGV 13-15 per day, 2hr., add 36-90F TGV reservation); Bordeaux (6-8 per day, 4hr., 218F); La Rochelle (8-11 per day, 2hr., 122F); Rennes (10 per day, 3 on Sun., 2hr., 111F). **Lockers** 15-30F.

Buses: Cariane Atlantique, 5, allée Duquesne (tel. 02 40 20 46 99), sends buses to Rennes (Mon.-Sat. 2 per day, 2hr., 90F) and Vannes (Mon.-Sat. 1 per day, 2½hr., 104F). Buses leave from the train station's south entrance and from the **gare routière** (tel. 02 40 47 62 70) on allée Baco. Office open Mon.-Fri. 6:30am-7pm.

Public Transportation: TAN (tel. 02 40 29 39 39) runs a network of buses and two tram lines until about 8pm. Info booth at 3, rue Bellier, across the street from pl. du Commerce (open Mon.-Fri. 7:15am-7pm, Sat. 9am-7pm). Ticket 7F, valid 1hr. Mini-*carnet* of 5 tickets 29F, *carnet* of 10 tickets 52F, daypass 18F.

Taxis: At the train station, or call **Allô Taxis Nantes Atlantique** (tel. 02 40 69 22 22).

Bike Rental: Les Vélos de l'Eté, pl. du Commerce (tel. 02 40 12 02 07). 50F per day. Passport deposit (open daily June-Sept. 9am-7pm). Or **Bernard Seguin** (tel. 02 40 46 56 32), 38 rue des Alouettes, near the Musée Jules Verne.

Laundromat: allée Duguay Trouin. Wash 20F, dry 2F per 5min. Open daily 7am-9pm. Also at 7, Hôtel de Ville. Same rates. Open daily 7am-8:30pm.

English Books: Librairie Beaufreton, 3rd level of passage Pommeraye, behind the tourist office. Classics and lighter fare from 42F. Open Mon. 2-7pm, Tues.-Sat. 9:15am-12:30pm and 1:30-7pm. V, MC.

Youth Information, Hitchhiking, and Budget Travel: Centre Régional d'Information Jeunesse (CRIJ) 28, rue du Calvaire (tel. 02 51 72 94 50). Info on youth and employment opportunities open Mon. noon-7pm, Tues.-Fri. 10am-7pm, Sat. 10am-noon and 2-5pm. **Voyage au Fil** (tel. 02 40 89 04 85), at the CRIJ, matches riders with drivers for a fee. Open Mon. noon-1pm and 2-6pm, Tues.-Fri. 10am-7pm, Sat. 10am-noon and 2-5pm. V, MC, AmEx.

Women's Center: Legal and crisis help at 5, rue Maurice Duval (tel. 02 40 48 13 83). Open Mon. 9:30am-noon, Tues.-Wed. and Fri. 2-5:30pm, Thurs. 9:30am-5:30pm.

Crisis Lines: AIDS information at **Amitiés SIDA,** 21, rue Dufour (tel. 02 40 47 14 14). Friends at **SOS Amitié** (tel. 02 40 04 04 04). **SOS Alcool,** 17, rue Arsène Leloup (tel. 02 40 73 49 25). **Viol Info Femmes** (tel. 0 800 05 95 95). Rape hotline.

Hospital: Centre Hospitalier Régional, pl. Alexis Ricordeau (tel. 02 40 08 33 33). **Medical emergency** tel. 02 40 08 37 37 or 15.

Police: tel. 02 40 37 21 21, on pl. Waldeck-Rousseau. **Emergency** tel. 17.

Post Office: pl. de Bretagne (tel. 02 40 92 62 53), near Tour Bretagne. **Currency exchange.** Open Mon.-Fri. 8am-7pm, Sat. 8am-noon. **Postal code:** 44000.

ACCOMMODATIONS AND CAMPING

Nantes has plenty of good hotels and lots of student dormitory space in the summer. Most budget places are within a 10-minute walk or bus ride of the pl. du Commerce.

Cité Internationale/Auberge de Jeunesse (HI), 2, pl. de la Manufacture (Jun.-Aug. tel. 02 40 29 29 20, Sept.-May tel. 02 40 20 57 25; fax 02 40 20 08 94). Turn right onto bd. de Stalingrad from the station, left onto rue Manille, and then left onto pl. de la Manufacture (10min.). Or take the tram from the train station to "Manufacture" (7F). Multilingual staff. 66 beds in 1- to 4-person rooms, kitchen (bring your own pots), bar, and TV room. 60F. Sheets 16F. Breakfast 18F. Lunch or dinner 47F. Reception 7am-10pm. Reserve ahead for July 15-Aug. 15. From Sept. 15-June 30, the Cité Internationale runs the site as a **foyer des jeunes travailleurs,** but travelers with a hostel card are welcome. 64F. Reception 5-10pm.

Foyer des Jeunes Travailleurs, Beaulieu (HI), 9, bd. Vincent Gâche (tel. 02 40 12 24 00; fax 02 51 82 00 05). From the station, take tram to pl. du Commerce and take bus 24 (direction: Beaulieu) to "Albert" (7F). 200 beds in 1- to 4-person rooms with showers and toilets. Kitchen. 50F. Singles 100F (95F per night for 2 or more nights; breakfast included). Sheets 11F. Breakfast 12F. Lunch or dinner 38F. Reception 8am-midnight. Curfew midnight. No lockout.

Foyer des Jeunes Travailleurs, L'Edit de Nantes, 1, rue du Gigant (tel. 02 40 73 41 46; fax 02 40 69 11 55). From the station, take tram to pl. du Commerce, walk up cours des 50 Otages to "St-Nicolas," catch bus 21 or 23 to "Edit de Nantes." Or from pl. du Commerce, catch bus 24 or 56 to "Edit de Nantes." The foyer is across the street. 60 beds in 1- to 2-person rooms with shower and toilet. 60F. Lunch and dinner 37F. Reception Mon.-Fri. 9am-9pm. In winter, call 2-4 days in advance.

Hôtel d'Orléans, 12, rue du Marais (tel. 02 40 47 69 32), off cours des 50 Otages. Run by a congenial young family. 15 well-kept rooms. One tiny, clean single at 70F. Singles and doubles 105-120F, with shower 130-145F, with bath and toilet 175F. Triples with shower or bath 175-220F. Quads 220F. Breakfast 23F. Carry *Let's Go* and the 10F shower's free. Make reservations *en été.* V, MC, AmEx.

Hôtel Roosevelt, 28, rue des Petites Ecuries (tel. 02 40 47 17 00), off cours Franklin Roosevelt. A dream location and only 15min. from the station. Small rooms and firm beds. Singles and doubles 90-120F, with shower 120-140F. Triples 140F, with shower 160-170F. Shower 12F. Breakfast 18F. V, MC.

Hôtel St-Daniel, 4, rue du Bouffay (tel. 02 40 47 41 25; fax 02 51 72 03 99), just off pl. du Bouffay, next to cours Franklin Roosevelt. 19 big, clean rooms with phones, some overlooking the Ste-Croix church garden. Most with showers. Singles 110-130F, doubles 130-150F. Triple or quad 180-190F. Breakfast 20F. V, MC.

Hotel Sainte Reine, 3 rue Anatole le Braz (tel. 02 40 74 35 61), just off rue Bellamy. Comfy beds, friendly owners, pristine rooms, and new everything else make up for some unfortunate decorating decisions. Worth the walk. Singles and doubles 109F, with the works 165F.

Camping: Camping du Val de Cens, 21, bd. du Petit Port (tel. 02 40 74 47 94), a 10-min. tram ride (take line 2 north to "Marhonnière") from pl. du Commerce. Superb site with hot water and showers. 15F per person, 20F per tent, 30F per tent and car, 40F per caravan plus car. Electricity 12F. No reservations by phone; arrive early in summer. Reception open 5:30-11pm.

FOOD

Nantes is a good place to eat your fill of Chinese, Italian, Turkish, Indian, and Vietnamese cuisine before facing their absence around Brittany or the Loire Valley châteaux. Restaurants on **rue Kervégan** and **rue de la Juiverie,** in the St-Croix quarter, will sautée, boil, skewer, toss, marinade, and grill just about anything edible. Local specialties include seafood *au beurre blanc* (with butter sauce) and *canard nantais* (duck) prepared with grapes, as well as the white wines, Muscadet and Gros Plant. Nantes' dessert offerings are *frillandises*—candies, chocolates, and cakes. Mass-marketed favorites, Le Petit Beurre cookies, are a local invention, as are the lesser-known *muscadines* (little chocolates filled with grapes and Muscadet wine). **Open-air mar-**

kets take place Tuesday, Friday, and Sunday 9am to 1pm on **pl. du Bouffay** and at the **Marché de Talensac,** along rue de Bel-Air near pl. St-Similien, behind the post office. The ubiquitous **Monoprix** supermarket appears off cours de 50 Otages on 2, rue de Calvaire (open Mon.-Sat. 9am-9pm; V, MC).

Crêperie Jaune, 1, rue des Echevins (tel. 02 40 47 15 71), off pl. du Bouffay. A Nantes institution, students line up for the house specialty, an immense, meaty, double-decker *galette* called *pavé nantais* (45-54F). Vegetarian version available (54F); *plat du jour* 42F. Open Mon.-Sat. noon-3pm and 7pm-2am. V, MC.

La Paëlla, 4, rue de la Juiverie (tel. 02 40 89 13 40), rustles up classic tapas or a 3-course menu of, of course, homemade paella and gazpacho. Open Thurs.-Mon. noon-2pm and 7-11pm, Tues.-Wed.7-11pm. V, AmEx.

Mangeoire, 16, rue des Petite Ecuries (tel. 02 40 48 70 83), around the corner from pl. du Bouffay and the Crêperie Jaune. Quiet and elegant, excellent local cuisine. *Grosses salades* at 33-46F. 58F lunch *menu* with duck, fish, and wonderful desserts. Open Tues.-Sat. noon-2pm and 7-10pm, Sun. noon-2pm. V, MC.

L'Arbre de Vie, 8, allée des Tanneurs (tel. 02 40 08 06 10), on cours des 50 Otages, past the Tour Bretagne. Small vegetarian restaurant. Salads 35-62F. *L'Alpage* salad is a meal in itself (62F). *Plat du jour* 48F, *menus* from 60-80F. Open Tues.-Wed. noon-1:45pm, Thurs.-Sat. noon-1:45pm and 7:30-10pm. V, MC.

Chez Suyen, 1bis, rue Kervégan (tel. 02 40 20 09 10). Good Vietnamese across cours Roosevelt from pl. du Bouffay. Try the *salade vietnamienne* (25F) or the *brochettes de boeuf* (beef kebab, 45F). Dinner menus 55F, 70F, and 90F. Open Tues.-Sat. noon-2pm and 7-10:30pm, Mon. 7-10:30pm. V, MC.

SIGHTS

Many of Nantes' sights appeal to narrow interests. If you don't have much time, choose the places that sound genuinely interesting before delving into an endless walking tour of the city. Ask the tourist office about the **global pass** to the château museums, the Musée des Beaux-Arts, the Musée d'Histoire Naturelle, and the Musée Jules Verne. Except for the planetarium, Nantes' museums are free on Sundays.

Built in the 15th century by François II, Nantes' heavily fortified **château** (tel. 02 40 41 56 56) has seen as much history as any on the Loire. Its imposing walls once held Gilles de Retz (the original Bluebeard), who was convicted of sorcery in 1440 for sacrificing hundreds of children in grotesque rituals. In 1598, Henri IV composed the Edict of Nantes here in an effort to soothe national tensions (see page 64). The better of the château's two museums, the **Musée des Arts Populaires Régionaux,** displays traditional Breton costumes and furniture. The **Musée des Salorges** explores Nantes' colonial and commercial influence since the 18th century. (Open July-Aug. daily 10am-noon and 2-6pm; Sept.-June Wed.-Mon. 10am-noon and 2-6pm. Courtyard and ramparts open daily 10am-7pm; Sept.-June 10am-noon and 2-6pm. Château and museums 30F, students 15F.)

Thanks to lightweight Vendée stone, the Gothic vaults of **Cathédrale St-Pierre,** pl. St-Pierre, soar 37.5m into the heavens—higher than the arches of Notre-Dame in Paris. Since 1434, the church has endured a 450-year construction odyssey. Following the 1944 Allied bombing and a 1972 fire that nearly gutted the church, the city undertook a 13-year restoration project; St-Pierre is now the only cathedral in France with a completely restored interior. Anne of Brittany commissioned the elaborate tomb in the south transept for her parents, who built Nantes' château. Their figures are guarded by the Virtues (note two-faced Prudence, a young girl who consults the past to see the future). During the Revolution, a tribunal ordered the tomb destroyed, but a local architect squirreled it away until a royalist government was reinstalled. The cathedral boasts the largest stained-glass window in the country, a 25m-tall representation of native saints (cathedral open daily 8:45am-7pm; crypts open Mon.-Sat. 10:30am-12:30pm and 2-6pm, Sun. 2-6:30pm).

Two blocks from the cathedral at 10, rue Georges Clemenceau, is Nantes' **Musée des Beaux-Arts** (tel. 02 40 41 65 65), that prompted Henry James to reflect on his peculiar fondness for provincial museums: "The pictures may be bad, but...from bad pictures, in certain moods of the mind, there is a degree of entertainment to be derived." James' assessment notwithstanding, the collection includes fine canvases from the 13th century on, including works by Delacroix, Ingres, Courbet, and Kandinsky. Derive entertainment from Comerre's *Le Déluge,* a haunting portrait of men, women, and animals fearfully clinging to a mountaintop as the world enters its 40-day flood (open Mon., Wed.-Thurs., and Sat. 10am-6pm, Fri. 10am-9pm, Sun. 11am-6pm; admission 20F, students 10F; take bus 11 or 12 to "Trébuchet").

The **Musée Thomas Dobrée,** pl. Jean V (tel. 02 40 71 03 50), contains rare books and manuscripts, including two rooms chronicling Nantes' rapport with China in the early 1800s. Dobrée's furniture, paintings, and porcelain, as well as archaeological displays and temporary exhibits, complete the collection (open Tues.-Sun. 10am-noon and 1:30-5:30pm; 20F). A block away, the **Musée d'Histoire Naturelle,** 12, rue Voltaire (tel. 02 40 41 67 67), showcases a mind-boggling array of stuffed and live mammals, birds, and reptiles, including a puff adder who really can puff (open Tues.-Sat. 10-11:45am and 2-5:45pm, Sun. 2-5:45pm; admission 30F, students 15F. For either museum, take bus 11 to "Jean V" or tram 1 to "Médiathèque.")

Captain Nemo and Phileas Fogg fans will especially enjoy the innovative **Musée Jules Verne,** 3, rue de l'Hermitage (tel. 02 40 69 72 52), near the river in pl. M. Schwob, which recreates Verne's wonderful world through a collection of the author's novels, letters, and photographs. The 11-year-old Verne made an ill-fated attempt to stow away on a sailing ship before resigning himself to imaginary voyages (open Mon. and Wed.-Sat. 10am-noon and 2-5pm, Sun. 2-5pm; admission 8F, students 4F). The nearby **planetarium** at 8, rue des Acadiens (tel. 02 40 73 99 23), off pl. Moysan, takes you to the same places Verne did, with a few more visual effects. Relax to galactic vistas and an exploration of our rotating solar system (showings and 1-hr. rides Tues.-Sat. 10:30am, 2:15pm, and 3:45pm, Sun. 2:15pm and 3:45pm; admission 24F, students and seniors 12F). Take bus 21 to "Garennes."

ENTERTAINMENT

Nantes does not lack nightlife, and a good deal of it is listed in the weekly **Nantes Poche** (6F at any tabac). **The Katorza,** 3 rue Corneille (tel. 08 36 68 06 60), rolls nightly films—many of them independent film festival winners—in *v.o.* Afterwards, the nearby **rue Scribe** is chock-full of late-night bars and cafés (try **Le Duo, Le Scribe,** or **Le Corneille**). **Pickwick's Tavern,** at the corner of rue Rameau and rue Suffren, has a judiciously selected array of bottled beers (25-38F) as well as the ubiquitous half-pint of Heineken (16F). Live music on Thursdays 10pm-2am. (Open Mon.-Tues. 6pm-2am, Wed. and Fri. 6pm-4am, Sat. 4pm-4am.) The bastion of the young and funky, quartier St-Croix averages three bars per block and just as many cafés and ice cream cone pit stops, making it a nighttime crowd-pleasing destination. Rue Kerrégan yields pleasant surprises including **Le Dugueselin,** 13 rue Kerrégan (tel. 02 40 89 14 89), a friendly gay bar with the foresight to hand out condoms with drinks and free copies of *West and Boys,* a guide to gay male entertainment and resources in northwestern France. (Open Mon.-Sat. 3pm-2am, Sun. 5pm-2pm.) The **Second Soufflé,** 1 rue Kerrégan (tel 02 40 20 14 20), is primarily a lesbian bar, but often *"mixte."* (Open daily 5pm-midnight.) Anything can happen in Nantes' notorious gay disco, **Le Temps d'Aimer,** 14, rue Alexandre Fourny (tel. 02 40 89 48 60); from pl. de la République on Ile Beaulieu follow rue Victor Hugo until rue Fourny appears on the left.

Eastern Orthodox chanters, blues rockers from Mali, and masqueraders from Trinidad and Tobago perform at the international **Festival d'Été,** which takes place each year in early July. The **Festival des Allumées** lights up the town in mid-October, honoring the theater, dance, and music of a different city each year (call 02 40 69 50 50 for info). Up-and-coming Asian, African, and South American filmmakers are honored in the **Festival des Trois Continents,** in late November (tel. 02 40 69 74 14). *Nantais* boast their **Carnaval** is one of the biggest in France, with parades and an all-night party on a phat Tuesday 41 days before Easter (tel. 02 40 35 75 49).

Pays de la Loire (Loire Valley)

The Loire, France's longest and most celebrated river, shares this fertile valley between Paris and Brittany—its vineyards, history, and famous châteaux—with a web of smaller rivers, including the Indre, the Cher, the Vienne, and the Maine. Châteaux in the region can be anything from grim, dilapidated medieval fortresses to elegant Renaissance homes, entrancingly reflected in pools surrounded by spectacular gardens. The surprisingly sordid history of many of these dignified mansions presents a mixed bag of mischief, genius, promiscuity, and dirty-dealing—fodder for the imagination when tours grow tiresome. Though each seems to eclipse the next, don't overlook other Loire pleasures: extraordinary museums, a graceful landscape ideal for long bike tours, lively big cities, and the small towns that have quietly blossomed for centuries in the shadows of their more vainglorious castles.

Most châteaux were built in the 16th and 17th centuries, when French monarchs left Paris to rule from the countryside around Tours so they could enjoy hunting excursions while attending to their state duties. Some castles, however, endure from the days before the region belonged to a unified French crown. In the 12th century, Henry II and Richard the Lionheart, who ruled England, Ireland, and half of modern France, mobilized two of their oldest communities, Chinon and Beaugency, to defend the region from the Paris-based Capetian monarchs. The English and the French played catch with the Loire region until Joan of Arc rallied the French to claim it in the Hundred Years' War (1337-1453). Under the Valois kings, the 15th-century French monarchy overran the region with a flux of martial and marital activity. Formerly considered to be primarily defensive holdings, the châteaux were heaped with masterworks of fine arts and design during the Renaissance, fostering one-upmanship and opulence never imagined before or since. With this unprecedented luxury came some extraordinary examples of debauchery; listen closely in tours of Blois and Chambord, among others, for sizzling 400-year-old gossip.

The valley was scarred by the wars of religion (1562-1598), whose terror culminated in the Duke of Guise's murder of Protestants at Amboise. The Loire settled into a political nap in the 17th century when Louis XIV summoned the nobles to court at Versailles, but awoke once again during the Revolution when rural peasants violently protested Republican policies, provoking a guerilla war against the new regime that ended only when Napoleon took power. The region's rivers served as handy boundaries for warring sides in the Franco-Prussian War and during World War II, when Hitler and Pétain met at Montoire-sur-le-Loir to decide that the Cher would separate annexed France from Vichy France.

Besides anchoring the foundations of the valley's architectural wonders, the rich soil of the Loire region nurtures such gastronomic delights as *asperges* (asparagus), *fraises* (strawberries), *champignons* (mushrooms), and of course the *raisins* (grapes) that go into the Loire's famous wines, white (Touraine, Montlouis, and Vouvray) and red (Chinon, St-Nicolas-de-Bourgeuil, and Saumur). Modern *cuisiniers loirois* would have done justice to the châteaux's ornate dining rooms. Their specialties include *rillettes* (a cold minced pork pâté), *fromage de chèvre* (goat cheese), and the sweet, creamy *camembert* and *port salut* cheeses. The Loire has lent its veal *escalope* and *coq au vin* to the international palate.

GETTING AROUND

Faced with such ubiquitous glamour and grandeur, many travelers plan over-ambitious itineraries which result in hazy memories of highways and big stone houses. Don't try to see more than two châteaux a day or you'll go numb. After a week of castle-gazing, you may secretly come to consider the challenges of getting to isolated

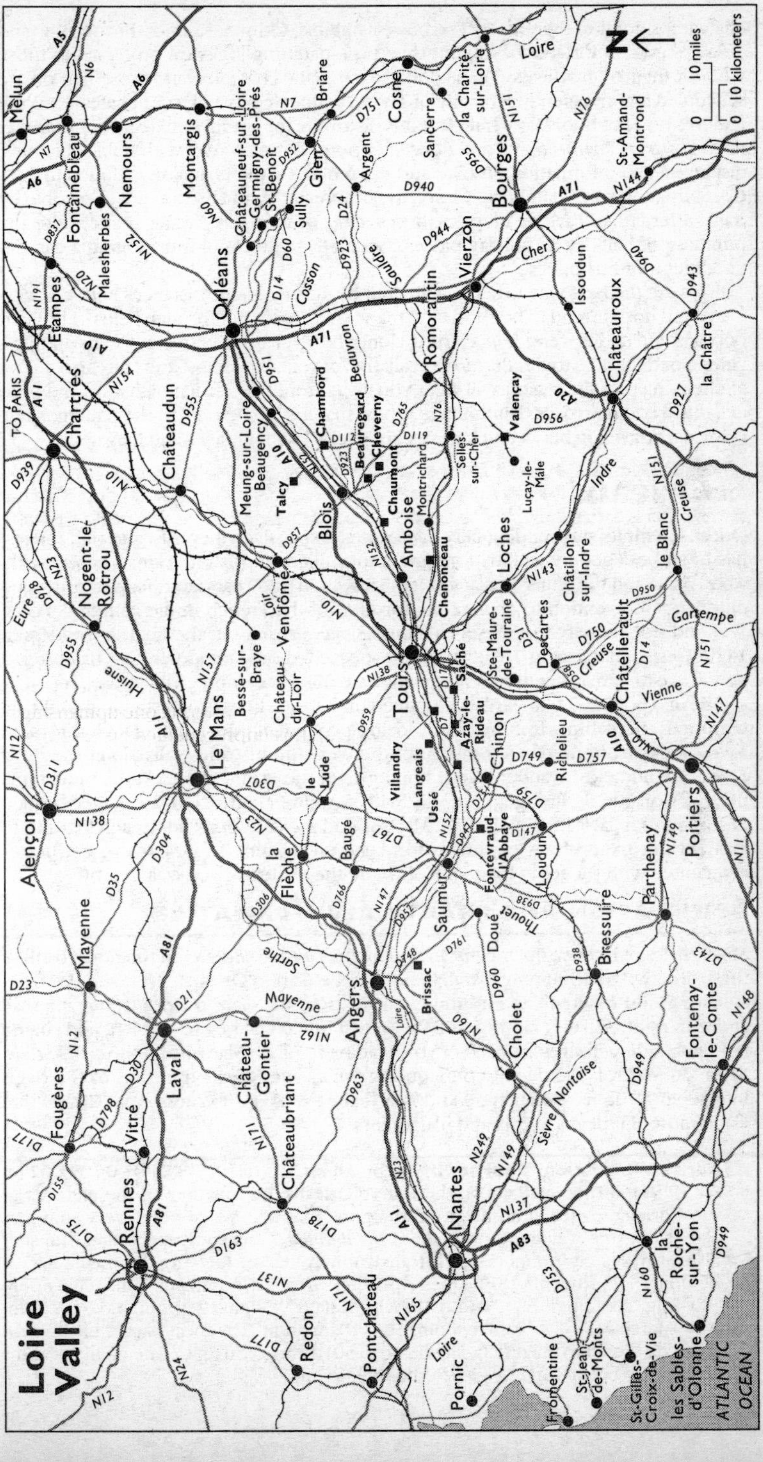

Loire Valley

châteaux a point in their favor. The hostels in Blois, Chinon, Saumur, Beaugency, and Orléans are comfortable bases, but they pose daunting logistical problems to those without their own wheels. Trains don't reach many châteaux, and those that do are scheduled inconveniently. The city of Tours (connected by rail to 12 châteaux) is the region's best rail hub. Many train stations distribute the useful booklets *Les Châteaux de la Loire en Train Été '97* and *Châteaux pour Train et Vélo,* with train schedules, distances, and information on bike and car rental. Of the châteaux included in *Let's Go,* Sully-sur-Loire, Chambord, Cheverny, Beauregard, and Ussé are not accessible by train. Alternatives include bicycles, buses, cars, or tour bus circuits that require the purchase of half-day or full-day passes. Generally, a group of four renting a car can undercut tour bus prices.

Bikes are the best way to see this flat but beautiful region. Distances between châteaux and hostels tend to be short, and many small roads cut through fields of brilliant poppies and sunflowers. A *levée* runs along the river bank between towns and provides a perfect bike route. Bikes are available for rental in almost any Loire town. The Michelin map of the region will steer you away from truck-laden highways and onto delightful country roads. Hitchhikers report that lifts come only to the patient, since many cars traveling between châteaux are packed with families and luggage.

Orléans

Orléans, with its surrounding fairy-tale castles, expansive vineyards, and rich forests, has been besieged by jealous foreigners for millennia. Bishop Aignan barely withstood Atilla and the Huns' onslaught in 451. A thousand years later, Joan of Arc relied on divine intervention to change the fortunes of the French in the Hundred Years' War and free the city from a seven-month siege, driving out the English invaders in 1429. German attacks in 1870 and 1940 succeeded only temporarily; it has taken a new wave of Parisian commuters to penetrate this once impregnable town.

Orléans (pop. 200,000) strikes an uncertain balance between past glories and contemporary hardships, fretting about losing prominence to Tours, down the river. Two blocks from Aignan's tomb, graffiti covers the historic walls along rue de la Folie. The homeless wander by the boutiques of rue Jeanne d'Arc. At the same time, the cafés on rue de Bourgogne bustle with youthful chatter, old ladies meet underneath Joan's regal statue in place du Martroi, and the *Orléanais* unite each May 8th to reenact her triumphant parade around the city. Come to Orléans to get better acquainted with the feisty Joan, or to explore the châteaux that wait nearby.

ORIENTATION AND PRACTICAL INFORMATION

Most places of interest in Orléans, including the *centre ville,* are on the north bank of the Loire, five to 10 minutes' walk south of the Gare d'Orléans. To reach the main square, **pl. du Martroi,** ascend the escalator from the Gare d'Orléans into the mall and turn right. As you exit the mall, the tourist office will be on your left, and **rue de la République** will stretch ahead of you, leading to pl. du Martroi and the *centre ville.* At pl. du Martroi, rue de la République becomes **rue Royale** and runs to the river, intersecting **rue de Bourgogne** and **rue Jeanne d' Arc**—two essential streets that claim most of Orléans' sights and restaurants.

Tourist Information: Tourist Office, pl. Albert 1er (tel. 02 38 24 05 05; fax 02 38 54 49 84), off the mall above the Gare d'Orléans. Information on the plethora of local drama, dance, and music productions that take place here every summer. Hands out free walking tour guide of *vieille ville.* **Currency exchange.** The staff also provides city tours (English translation available) July-Aug. Wed. and Sat. at 2:30pm (35F, students 18F). Open April-Oct. Mon.-Sat. 9am-7pm, Sun. 10am-noon; July-Aug. also open Sun. and national holidays 9:30am-12:30pm and 3-6:30pm; Nov.-March Mon.-Sat. 9am-6:30pm, Sun. 10am-noon. The local paper, **La République du Centre** (in French, Mon.-Sat., 4F50), brings you up to date on news, movies, theater events, and Orléans' other goings-on.

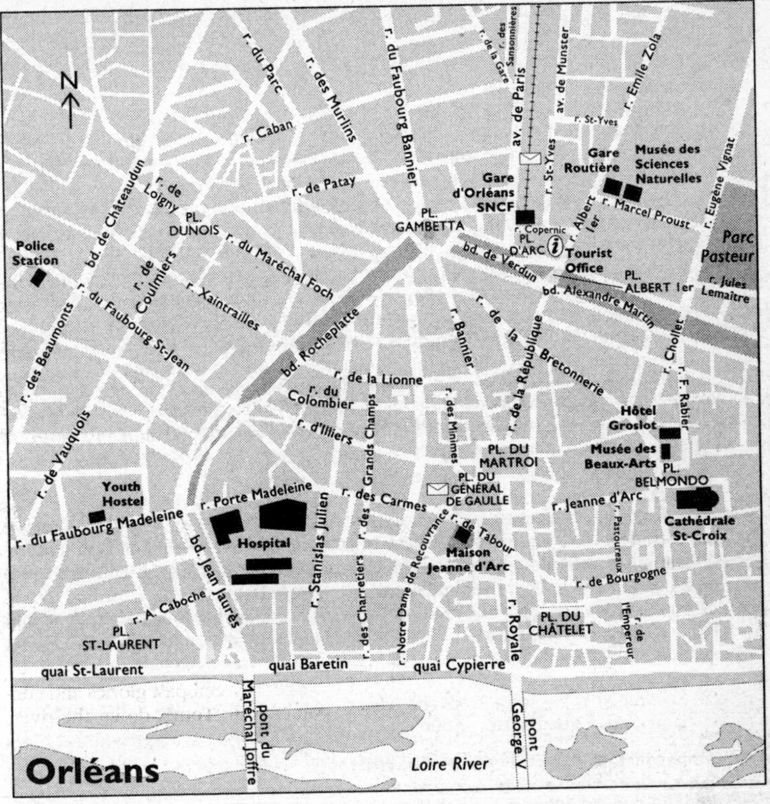

American Express: 12, pl. du Martroi (tel. 02 38 78 96 96, or 0 800 90 86 00 for 24-hr. service). Open Mon.-Fri. 9am-12:30pm and 2-6pm.

Money: Most banks are located on rue de la République and pl. du Martroi. **ATMs** are everywhere, and most are open 24hr.

Trains: Orléans has two stations, **Gare d'Orléans** and **Gare Les-Aubrais.** Most trains stop at both, but several longer routes only stop at Les-Aubrais. Gare d'Orléans, pl. Albert 1er (tel. 02 38 53 50 50), is more useful to most travelers and is centrally located. Info office open Mon.-Sat. 9am-7pm. Ticket booths open daily 5:30am-9pm. Lockers 10-30F. To: Paris-Austerlitz (about 3 per hr., 1¼hr., 89F); Blois (19 per day, 40min., 50F); Tours (15 per day, 1¼hr., 88F); Amboise (12 per day, 1hr., 73F); Nantes (2 nonstop per day, 2hr., 186F). Gare Les-Aubrais, rue Pierre Semard (tel. 02 38 79 91 00), is a 30-min. walk north from the *centre ville.* If a train isn't stopping at Gare d'Orléans, a free train (usually from platform 2) shuttles there within 5min. of arrivals at Les-Aubrais.

Buses: Les Rapides du Val de Loire, 2, rue Marcel Proust (tel. 02 38 53 94 75), near the Gare d'Orléans, connected to pl. d'Arc by an overpass. Buses depart from the *gare routière* downstairs from the ticket office. Schedules change often. Buses travel to Chartres, and near Germigny, Sully, and Beaugency at prices comparable to the trains'. Open Mon. 8am-1pm and 4-7pm, Tues. and Thurs. 10am-1pm and 4-7pm, Wed. and Fri. 10am-1pm and 2-7pm, Sat. 10am-1pm.

Public Transportation: SEMTAO (tel. 02 38 71 98 38) runs local buses in and around town. The main booth is directly across the alley to the left of the Gare d'Orléans. Line "S" goes from pl. Albert 1er to the university and Parc Floral, until 12:30am. Tickets 7F50 (good for 1hr.), *carnet* of 10 57F, 1-week pass 60F.

Taxis: Taxi Radio d'Orléans, rue St-Yves (tel. 02 38 53 11 11). 24-hr. service.

Car Rental: Hertz, 47, av. Paris (tel. 02 38 62 60 60), 5 min. from the Gare d'Orléans. **Avis,** 13, rue Sansonnières (tel. 02 38 62 27 04), 2 blocks past Hertz on the left. **Budget,** 5, rue des Sansonnieres (tel. 02 38 54 54 30). **Breakdowns (of cars, that is):** tel. 02 38 78 28 92, 24hr.

Bike Rental: CAD, 95, Fbg. Bannier (tel. 02 38 81 23 00), rents bikes for 70F per day, 170F per day for scooters. Open Mon.-Sat. 9am-noon and 2-7pm. **Kit Loisirs,** 1720, rue Marcel Belot (tel. 02 38 63 44 34), 7km south of Orléans. Take the "A" bus to Olivet. Bikes around 100F per day. Open daily 9am-9pm.

Laundromat: Lavarie Libre Service de la Madeleine, 4, rue de Fbg. Madeleine, near hostel. Open daily 7am-9pm. Also 26, rue du Poirier. Open daily 7am-10pm.

English Books: Librairie Loddé, 41, rue Jeanne d'Arc (tel. 02 38 65 43 43), left of rue Royale. Look in the basement. Open Tues.-Sat. 9am-noon and 1:45-7pm, Mon. 2-7pm. Smaller selection at **Coopérative du Livre,** 4, rue Hallebarde (tel. 38 53 37 74). Open Mon. 2-7pm, Tues.-Sat. 9am-12:30pm and 1:30-7pm.

Youth Information: Centre Régional d'Information Jeunesse (CRIJ), 5, bd. de Verdun (tel. 02 38 78 91 78), facing tourist office. Info on jobs, sports, vacations; tickets sales for local events, student bus tickets, and BIJ tickets. Open Mon. and Thurs. 1-6pm, Tues., Wed., and Fri. 10am-6pm, Sat. 2-6pm. **ANPE,** 1, pl. du Matroi (tel. 02 38 79 85 00), provides info on jobs in the region. Open Mon.-Fri. 8:30am-12:30pm and 1:30pm-3pm, Tues.-Thurs. closes at 5pm, Fri. closes at 4pm.

Crisis Lines: Alcooliques Anonymes (tel. 02 38 62 51 48). **SOS Amitié** (tel. 02 38 62 22 22), for froggy friendship.

Hospital: Centre Hospitalier Régional, 1, rue Porte Madeleine (tel. 02 38 51 44 44). From the pl. d'Arc mall, turn right onto bd. Verdun. Continue straight across pl. Gambetta onto bd. Rocheplatte, which becomes bd. Jean Jaurés. Turn left onto rue Porte Madeleine. In a **medical emergency,** dial 15.

Police: 63, rue du Fbg. St-Jean (tel. 02 38 81 63 00). Follow bd. Rocheplatte from pl. Gambetta and turn right onto rue du Fbg. St-Jean. **Emergency** tel. 17.

Post Office: pl. du Général de Gaulle (tel. 02 38 77 35 14). Poste restante. **Currency exchange.** Photocopies 1F. Open Mon.-Fri. 8am-7pm, Sat. 8am-noon. Branch office on rue St-Yves, 3min. from the Gare d'Orléans. Open Mon.-Fri. 8am-6:30pm, Sat. 8am-noon. **Postal code:** 45000.

ACCOMMODATIONS AND CAMPING

Although inexpensive hotels dot the town, inexpensive hotels with a pleasant atmosphere and safe location are harder to come by. Most hotels fill up by early evening in July and August. In these months, try to arrive early or call ahead.

Auberge de Jeunesse (HI), 14, rue du Fbg. Madeleine (tel. 02 38 62 45 75), on the west side of town. Walking from pl. d'Arc, turn onto bd. Alexandre Martin. Cross pl. Gambetta to bd. Rocheplatte, which becomes bd. Jean-Jaurès. Turn right onto rue du Fbg. Madeleine (20min.) or take bus "B" (direction: Paul-Bert) in front of the Gare d'Orléans (7F50, until 8:20pm). 2 clean single-sex dorms, excellent kitchen facilities, and bike storage. Strict curfew and management, but the hostel retains a homey atmosphere nonetheless. Lockout 9:30am-5:30pm. Curfew 10:30pm (Feb.-May 10pm). Members only. 40F. Breakfast 18F. Sheets 16F. Reception daily 7-9:30am and 5:30-10pm. Closed Sat. in Feb. and March.

Hôtel de Paris, 29, bd. du Fbg. Bannier (tel. 02 38 53 39 58). Leaving the Gare d'Orléans, turn right onto bd. Verdun. At pl. Gambetta, turn right on rue du Fbg. Bannier in front of the space-ageish Médiathèque. The hotel is on the left corner, 1 block away. 5-min. walk from the train station in pleasant residential area. Gregarious proprietor lived in New York for 17 years and teaches his staff English. Clean, pastel rooms. *Brasserie* on the first floor. Storage for bicycles. Singles 108-140F. Doubles 123-200F. Triples 240F. Shower 20F. Breakfast 25F. V, MC, AmEx.

Hôtel de Sonis, 46bis, bd. de Châteaudun (tel. 02 38 53 72 36). At pl. Gambetta, continue down bd. Rocheplatte. Take the third right onto rue du Maréchal Foch. Continue straight past pl. Dunois. At the tree-lined bd. de Châteaudun, turn right. The hotel will be on the next corner on the right. A bit farther from the *centre ville* than Hôtel de Paris, the de Sonis offers pleasant rooms and a charming breakfast area. Amiable proprietors; the husband speaks English. Plenty of room for bikes in the garden behind the hotel. Singles 102-112F. Doubles 118-140F. Triples 138-150F. Breakfast 19F. Extra bed 25F. Bathrooms 8-10F extra. V, MC.

Hôtel Coligny, 80, rue de la Gare (tel. 02 38 53 61 60). From Gare d'Orléans, turn right onto av. de Paris, left on rue de la Gare. At first traffic light, turn left; hotel is on the right (20min.). Clean, white rooms with phones and firm beds. Singles 85-115F. Doubles 95-150F. All rooms come with shower. Breakfast 17F. V, MC.

Camping: St-Jean-de-la-Ruelle, chemin de la Roche (tel. 02 38 88 39 39). A wooded site along the Loire, 5km from Orléans. Take bus "D" from pl. Albert 1er to "La Roche Aux Fées." 3 people and car 38F. Extra person 10F. Showers. Wheelchair accessible. Reception 7am-noon and 4-9pm. Open daily 6am-10pm April-Sept. **Camping Municipal Olivet,** rue du Pont Bouchet, (tel. 02 38 63 53 94). Take bus "S" (direction: Concyr) to "Aumône." 2-star site by the Loire, 5km from Orléans. Free hot showers. Wheelchair accessible. 2 people, tent, and car 46F. May have laundry facilities this year. Open daily 7am-10pm April-Oct. 15.

FOOD

The gastronomic customs of the kings live on in Orléans. In late summer and autumn, locals feast on *le gibier* (game), freshly procured in the nearby forests. **La Chancellerie,** 27, pl. du Matroi, (tel. 02 38 53 57 54), specializes in game stew (120-130F; open Mon.-Sat. 7am-midnight). If visiting the rest of the year, be satisfied with the old standbys: *pâté d'alouettes* (lark pâté), *saumon à l'oseille* (salmon in sorrel), and *le sandre* (a river fish). Orléans' cheese is *frinault cendré,* a savory relation of *camembert.* Wash it all down with the local Gris Meunier or Auvergnat wines (about 20F in the supermarket). To gorge yourself but not your wallet, wander **rue de Bourgogne** and its myriad *brasseries,* pizzerias, exotic restaurants, and bars.

For produce, **Les Halles Châtelet,** pl. du Châtelet, left off the rue Royale, is an indoor, all-you-can-imagine market. On Sunday mornings, it expands outdoors to pl. Châtelet (open Tues.-Sun. 7am-7pm). **Carrefour's** battalions of aisles besiege shoppers at pl. d'Arc (open Mon.-Sat. 8:30am-9pm; V, MC). **Monoprix,** 46, rue de Fbg. Bannier, counters with some of the cheapest baguettes in town (open Mon.-Thurs. 8:30am-12:45pm and 2:30-7:30pm, Fri. 8:30am-8pm, Sat. 8:30am-7pm; V, MC).

Ste-Catherine, 64, rue Ste-Catherine (tel. 02 38 53 40 87), just off pl. du Martroi. An all-you-can-eat restaurant…in France!?!? Gorge yourself on plate after plate of mussels and fries (55F) or carpaccio of beef (60F), all while watching the world go by from the terrace. Open 11:45am-3pm and 6:45-10:30pm. V, MC, AmEx.

Brasserie Alsacienne, 1, rue de Gourville, right off rue de la République (tel. 02 38 62 51 42). The salads (44-51F) are a meal unto themselves; the seafood or vegetarian *tartes flambées* (49-56F) go even further. A young crowd livens things up at night. Open Tues.-Sat. noon-3pm and 7pm-midnight. V, MC, AmEx.

Restaurant Tex-Mex, 21, rue Bannier (tel. 02 38 53 19 80). Burgers, tacos, and enchiladas at spicy prices (60-75F). Lively local hangout and bar at night. Open Mon.-Sat. 11:30am-1am, till 2am on weekends. V, MC, AmEx.

L'Arlequin, at the corner of rue des Minimis and rue d'Illiers, off pl. du Martroi (tel. 02 38 62 38 62), offers belly-satisfying pizza in a convivial atmosphere (38-51F). Becomes a popular bar later at night. Open Mon.-Sat. 9pm-midnight. V, MC.

Impérial d'Arc, 81, bd. Alexandre Martin (tel. 02 38 81 17 26). Joan's favorite Asian place? Yummy *nem* (dumplings, 25F) and saucy *canard laqué* (duck, 49F). A bit upscale. Open Mon.-Sat. noon-2pm and 7-10:30pm. V, MC.

SIGHTS

Most of Orléans' historic and architectural features are near pl. Ste-Croix. In 1429, having liberated the *Orléanais* from a seven-month siege by the bellicose Brits, Joan of Arc triumphantly marched down nearby **rue de Bourgogne,** the city's oldest street. The scene is vividly captured in *Jeanne d'Arc,* at the Musée des Beaux-Arts.

With its towering Gothic buttresses and intricate façade, the **Cathédrale Ste-Croix** pays glorious tribute to everyone's favorite liberator. Stained glass windows depict Joan's dramatic story, down to the flames that consumed her. Flags bearing the emblems of her companions—including Charles of Orléans and the Maréchal de Boussac—line the cathedral's main aisle. King Henri IV commanded the church's reconstruction after its damage in 1568 at the hands of the Huguenots during the wars of religion (open daily June-Sept. 9:15am-7pm; Oct.-May 10am-noon and 2:15-6:45pm). Tours of the upper parts of the cathedral are also available (May-June Sat. 3:30pm and 4:30pm; July-Sept. daily 3pm, 4pm, 5pm; admission 30F, students 15F).

The **Musée des Beaux-Arts** at 1, rue Paul Belmondo (tel. 02 38 79 21 83), to the right as you exit the cathedral, displays French and Dutch works from the 17th to 20th centuries. (Open Wed.-Mon. 10am-noon and 2-6pm. Admission 18F, students 9F.) Around the corner at pl. de l'Etape sits the 16th-century **Hôtel Groslot d'Orléans** (tel. 02 38 79 22 30). Now an annex to the town hall, the *hôtel* opens its sumptuously decorated rooms and romantic garden to the public and an occasional wedding. A long line of kings tarried in this Renaissance mansion, including François II, Charles IX, Henri III, and Henri IV. In 1559, François II died here amidst scandal at the age of 17. (Open July-Sept. Sun.-Fri. 9am-7pm, Sat. 5-9pm; Oct.-June Sun.-Fri. 10am-noon and 2-6pm, Sat. 4:30-6pm. Free tours in English or French.)

The **Maison de Jeanne d'Arc,** 3, pl. de Gaulle, off pl. du Martroi (tel. 02 38 52 99 89), explains Orléans' obsession with the formidable female fighting machine. This reconstruction of the original house where Joan of Arc stayed—profoundly modified after a 1940 bombing raid—consists of fragments of other 15th-century houses. Using period costumes and suits of armor, the museum details the life of Joan and the history of her times. Don't miss the 10-minute audio-visual presentation of the Battle of Orléans upstairs. (Open May-Oct. Tues.-Sun. 10am-noon and 2-6pm; Nov.-April Tues.-Sun. 2-6pm. Admission 12F, students 6F50, under 16 free.)

Two museums free your mind from Joan this, Joan that. The **Musée Archéologique et Historique de l'Orléannais,** housed in the **Hôtel Cabu,** at pl. Abbé Desnoyers, off rue Ste-Catherine (tel. 02 38 79 25 60), displays a beautiful collection ranging from 2nd-century bronze *sangliers* (wild boars) on the first floor to 18th-century royal porcelains on the third. In the Cabu's collection of ancient newspapers, one headline trumpets an attack by a *bête sauvage et horrible,* a wolf which devoured three *Orléanais* (open Wed.-Mon. 10am-noon and 2-6pm; admission 12F, students 6F). The new **Musée des Sciences Naturelles,** 2, rue Marcel-Proust (tel. 02 38 54 61 05), may liven up with the opening of a rain forest *biodôme* this year. Call the museum or the tourist office for details (open Sun.-Fri. 2-6pm).

Next to the university and the high-rise city of Orléans-la-Source, the **Parc Floral** (tel. 02 38 49 30 00) cultivates fields of luscious seasonal flowers. The immense park surrounds the source of the Loiret, a Loire tributary, flowing past haughty pink flamingos to the village of **Olivet,** a few km to the west. It is ideal for strolling, picnicking, and playing. (Open April-Nov. 11 daily 9am-6pm; admission 19F, students 10F. Nov. 13-March open daily 2-5pm, admission 10F. Bus "S" to "Université.")

ENTERTAINMENT

In the first weekend of July, Orléans sponsors a **jazz festival.** All formal performances are in the Campo Santo, near the cathedral (tickets 130F, reserve at the tourist office). On weekends in November and December, the **Semaines Musicales Internationales d'Orléans (S.M.I.O.)** brings the Orchestre National de France.

Many *Orléanais* head to Paris for nighttime action, but the city still buzzes after dark, especially in the bars along **rue Bannier** and **rue de Bourgogne.** Those destined to dance descend to the **George V,** Les Halles Châtelet (tel. 02 38 53 08 79), on the corner of rue Ducereau and pl. du Châtelet (50F cover includes 1 drink; open daily 10:30pm-5am; V, MC, AmEx). Take your mates to **Paxton's Head,** 264, rue de Bourgogne (tel. 02 38 81 23 29), for live jazz in a jolly British pub. For an expatriate thrill, order your drinks (15-80F) in English (open daily 3pm-3am; V, MC). By contrast, billiards is the only thing vaguely British about the laid-back **Bar Darlington,** 3, rue du Colombier (tel. 02 38 54 67 98), off rue Bannier. Games of anything on felt 35-50F (open daily 3pm-3am; V, MC). For more fun in the dark, **UGC,** pl. d'Arc (tel. 08 36 68 70 14), shows first-run French and dubbed foreign movies. **Select-Studios,** 45, rue

Jeanne d'Arc (tel. 08 36 68 69 25), shows first-run English films, as well as the occasional arthouse flick (tickets 25F).

■ Near Orléans

MEUNG-SUR-LOIRE

Most châteaux of the Loire Valley were built as peaceful getaways for the rich. After you've had enough of tranquility head to Meung-sur-Loire, whose 1500-year history is steeped in blood. The earliest records of the castle date back to the 4th century, when St. Liphard quit his job as governor of Orléans to devote himself to God and build a monastery. After being torched by the Vandals in AD 406, Meung was rebuilt, only to be plundered in 869 by invading Normans. At the end of the 11th century, the newly renovated château-cum-fortress-cum-monastery was occupied by bishops who stayed until the French Revolution. English forces captured Meung in the Hundred Years' War but were defeated by (drum roll, please) Joan of Arc.

After its seizure from the bishops in the Revolution, the well-worn château fell into the hands of Baron Lecoulteux, who himself had narrowly escaped the Republic's wrath through some well-placed bribes. Ironically, Lecoulteux was later named Treasurer of the Republic and became famous for founding the Banque de France.

The **château** itself is a strange mix of country home serenity and medieval evils. In the course of their 700-year stay, Meung's bishops were put in charge of dispensing justice in the area. Although they were forbidden to shed blood or perform executions, the prelates discovered some creative loopholes in their own edicts that allowed them to torture prisoners with Bible-sanctioned glee. Meung-sur-Loire is the only château in the area to boast a torture chamber as part of the tour. Most impressive is the **oubliette,** a pit where the bishops left prisoners to die so they didn't have to kill them. Convicts were lowered down and thrown bread and water once a day. Its most famous resident and only escapee, the 15th-century French poet François Villon, was jailed for stealing gold chalices from a church and was released when Louis XI mistook his insulting poetry for flattery and ordered his liberation. You'll also visit the cells and torture chamber which later were used as wine *caves.* If you're still thirsty, take a sip from the bishops' interrogation apparatus. Because they couldn't shed blood, they devised a system called **la question par l'eau,** whereby a prisoner was pumped with 50 pints of water and left in the cell to "leak off." When he came to, his captors would interrogate him about his wrongdoings.

The castle's present owner has beautifully furnished the interior with everything from a 9th-century statue of St. George slaying the dragon to a 19th-century Ingres painting. Keep an eye out for the trap door in the stairwell—it sits over a 15m well. (Open daily June-Sept. 9:30am-12:30pm and 2-6:30pm; Oct.-May 10am-noon and 2-5pm. Admission 30F, students 20F, children 15F. Tours in French every 30min.)

The **town** of Meung-sur-Loire is criss-crossed by canals and streams. The remarkably harmonious gray stone buildings are flanked by greenery and many a cute footbridge. Though the château grounds are not open to picnickers, any spot in town should do. For info, contact the **tourist office** at 42, rue Jehan de Meung (tel. 02 38 44 32 28; fax 02 38 45 30 88). From the train station, follow the signs to the *centre ville.* Meung is easily accessible by **train** from Orléans (21 per day, 11min., 20F). By car, Meung is off the N152 (direction: Orléans-Tours) and A10.

BEAUGENCY

The cobblestone streets of Beaugency, 35km southwest of Orléans, and the town's strategically important Loire bridge survived the Hundred Years' War, the wars of religion, and World War II, but now play host to a new invasion—tourists who flock here on their way to château country. Never fear, Beaugency (pop. 3500) has survived many trials and endures this latest with grace, offering its treasures to all.

In spite of his unfortunate name, the Bastard of Orléans became Joan of Arc's valued companion in arms. In 1440 he rebuilt the Château Dunois, which now houses the impressive **Musée Régional de l'Orléannais** (tel. 02 38 44 55 23). The museum displays artifacts, clothing and colorful prints from 15th-century Orléans, regional archaeological remains, and the neo-cubist sculpture of an adopted *Beaugençois*, Bostonian John Storrs. (Open April-Sept. Wed.-Mon. 10am-noon and 2-6:30pm; Oct.-March Wed.-Mon. 10am-noon and 2-5pm. Admission 20F, students 15.) Next to the château, the imposing 11th-century **Tour de César** stands 36m tall, although funds have never been raised to restore the interior, ravaged by fire in 1567.

In 1152, the **Eglise Notre-Dame,** across from the château, hosted the Church Council that ended the marriage of Louis VII and Eleanor of Aquitaine on grounds of consanguinity. The Council unwittingly freed her to marry an equally close cousin, Henry Plantagenêt, six weeks later. The church's small windows and massive columns exemplify the Romanesque style of the 12th century. The characteristic darkness is challenged by small, dazzling *vitraux* that sprinkle heavenly yellow and blue light onto the nave. A memorial to victims of the town's 1944 bombing brings the outside world into this quiet sanctuary. Uphill from the church rises the 16th-century **St-Firmin Steeple and Porch.** Turning right before the steeple will lead you to the central pl. du Martroi, bustling with activity. On Saturdays, vendors at its **outdoor market** hawk fresh fish, *fromage de chèvre* (goat cheese), and regional wines.

If Beaugency is more than a daytrip for you, head for the **Auberge de Jeunesse (HI),** 2km out of town at 152, route de Châteaudun (tel. 02 38 44 61 31; fax 02 38 44 14 73). From the Château Dunois, follow rue de Pont away from the river and turn right at the first light (av. d'Orléans). Go down two blocks and turn left on rue de Châteaudun. The hostel is about 1.5km down the road, on your right (30min.). Jacques Thomas, the proprietor, organizes outdoor excursions and is a helpful resource for planning itineraries in the region. Even though the hostel accommodates 100 people on firm mattresses, reservations are a good idea. Excellent kitchen facilities and living rooms with fireplaces. (48F per night. Sheets 16F. Breakfast 18F. Dinner 48F. **Bike rental** 50F per day.) Campers can pitch their tents on lovely Loire-side sites at the **Camping Municipal Le Val de Flux** (tel. 02 38 44 50 39; 10F70 per adult, 14F80 per site; open March-Sept.; reception 9am-noon and 4-8pm).

Beaugency has a number of relatively cheap regional restaurants. At **Les Quatres Saisons,** 17, rue de la Maille d'Or (tel. 02 38 46 41 21), the traditional *menu du jour* (68F) or *plat du jour* (38F) could be anything from fowl to seafood (open Wed.-Mon. 11:30am-11:30pm; V, MC). **Le Grain du Sel,** two blocks down at 13, rue de la Bretonnerie (tel. 02 38 46 44 73), also offers such traditional fare as *brochettes d'agneau* (lamb, 52F; open daily noon-11pm; V, MC). In the 10th century, King Raoul minted a coin with his name on one side and the Beaugency citadel on the other. What else was there for the town to do but coin a bonbon for the occasion? **La Pâtisserie P. LeRoux,** 12, pl. du Martroi, still sells the candy coins, *les deniers du roi Raoul,* at 32F per 100g, and well worth a taste (V, MC, AmEx).

The friendly **tourist office,** 3, pl. de l'Hôtel de Ville (tel. 02 38 44 54 42; fax 02 38 46 45 31), has info on the area (open daily June-Sept. 9:30am7pm; Oct.-May 9:30am-12:30pm and 2:30-6:30pm). From the station, walk down rue de la Gare. Just past the traffic lights, turn right onto rue Maille d'Or. At pl. du Martroi, pass the **banks** and 24-hour **ATMs** to turn left onto rue de l'Ours (in front of the SAP). At Le Balto Tabac, turn left. The tourist office is on the right. The **train station,** rue de la Gare (tel. 02 38 44 50 28), is 5 minutes from the *centre ville* (open daily 6am-10pm). Trains run to Blois (20 per day, 20 min., 20F) and Orléans (20 per day, 20 min., 27F). The **post office** is at 11, rue des Chevaliers (tel. 02 38 44 52 00; open Mon.-Fri. 8:30am-12:30pm and 1:30-5:30pm, Sat. 8:30am-noon; **postal code:** 45190).

GERMIGNY, ST-BENOÎT, AND SULLY

An excellent daytrip for drivers from Orléans east along the Loire takes in these three towns, each possessing a château or cathedral from a different era. About 30km southeast of Orléans, the 9th-century Carolingian church of **Germigny-des-Près** (tel. 02 38 58 27 97) is one of the oldest in France. Once a private oratory of the villa belonging to Théodulfe, the energetic Spanish Bishop of Orléans and friend of Charlemagne, the east nave is all that remains of the original Greek cross plan. The half-dome 5th-century **Byzantine mosaic,** unique in France, depicts archangels and the Ark of the Covenant in dazzling glass and gold-leafed cubes thought to have been brought from Italy. The mosaic, concealed during the wars of religion, was rediscovered in 1840 when local children came across tiny glass cubes in the church. The curator gives guided tours in French (open daily 9:30am-5:30pm).

In **St-Benoît-sur-Loire,** about 35km southeast of Orléans, the intricately carved columns on the Romanesque basilica porches have interpreted the Book of Revelations for commoners since the 11th century. Inside, the stunning 5th century Roman floor mosaic has been trampled by pilgrims since it was imported from Italy in 1531. Their goal is another Italian import, the relics of St. Benedict, exhumed from Monte Casino in 655 and venerated on this site ever since. Resting in the crypt, the founder of the Benedictine order has blessed the church with wealth, scholarship, and prosperity, broken only during the wars of religion, when his original urn was melted down for gold. Also in the basilica, a plaque honors the surrealist poet Max Jacob (1876-1944), who retired here before his internment and death in a concentration camp; his grave is in the village cemetery. (Open daily 6:30am-10pm. Tours only for groups, but you can connect with one if it's already happening. Monks sing services in Gregorian chant Mon.-Fri. at noon, and Sun. at 11am.)

The 14th-century fortress of **Sully-sur-Loire** (tel. 02 38 36 36 86), 8km farther downstream, dominates the surrounding countryside. Guarding the intersection of four major roads, this château required three drawbridges to protect the main residence. Though it has played host to a somnolent Charles VII, a frustrated Joan of Arc, a hunted Louis XIV, and an exiled Voltaire, the château's most enduring personality is that of the industrious and eccentric Duc de Sully, friend and war minister to France's first Protestant king, Henri IV. Awarded the château in the early 17th century, the newly minted duke was so fearful of the Catholic townsfolk that he forbade them to come near his property and destroyed the bridge to town. Rising daily at 3am, he kept four secretaries occupied with his memoirs. Ever cautious, he imported a printing press to publish them. The duke's bedroom contains a wall-spanning Flemish landscape tapestry. Sully's sprawling, grassy grounds and wooded pathways are perfect for picnics, walks, and its June concerts; past performers include Ray Charles and B.B. King. (Open daily June 16-Sept. 15 10am-6pm; May 1-June 15 and Sept. 16-Oct. 10am-noon and 2-6pm; March-April and Nov. 10am-noon and 2-5pm; closed Dec. and Jan. Admission 15F, students 10F.) **Camping Sully-sur-Loire,** chemin de la Salle Verte (tel. 02 38 36 23 93), surveys the château from the riverbank (10F per person, 7F per tent, 5F per vehicle).

Germigny, St-Benoît, and Sully are all accessible by **bus** from the *gare routière* in Orléans, but the times (leaving Orléans at 6:45am, 12:10 and 5:30pm; returning from Sully at 7:37am, 12:40pm, and 6:26pm) are not meant for travelers. (To: Sully, 1hr., 40F; Germigny, 45min., 30F.) **Driving,** take the N60-E60 east to the D60, 24km east of Orléans, for Sully. To return from Sully to Orléans, follow the D948 north to the D952 west. Bikers may choose to make the challenging 90km roundtrip from Orléans. The *levée* on the south bank of the Loire is a scenic **bike route** that winds along the Loire, passing tiny villages and sunflower fields along the way.

Blois

Blois (pop. 55,000) relishes its position as gateway to the Loire Valley and welcomes over half a million visitors who find themselves drawn to the town's bucolic charms and the nearby châteaux. Recent restoration projects have made the town's brilliant past seem even more luminous. Blois' creamy façades, blue slate roofs, red brick chimneys, and narrow cobblestone lanes evoke the simple beauty of villages painted by Vermeer. Just as alluring as the aesthetic delights of Blois are the culinary pleasures to be found in local *pâtisseries* that preserve the flavor of lost centuries with rich *blésian* chocolate. When you've had your fill of its chocolates, Chambord and Cheverny are an hour's bike trip or a 20-minute bus ride away.

ORIENTATION AND PRACTICAL INFORMATION

The train station is five-10 minutes north of the château and the town center. Exiting the station, go straight ahead down **av. Jean Laigret.** The tourist office is on the left near the bottom of the hill before **square Augustin-Thierry.** The *centre ville* is three minutes farther in this direction. The **rue Porte-Côte** leads to the bustling café-lined pedestrian quarter. When in doubt, descend; all roads go down to the *centre ville.*

Tourist Office: 3, av. Jean Laigret (tel. 02 54 74 06 49; fax 02 54 56 04 59), in Anne of Brittany's lovely Renaissance pavilion. Complete info on châteaux, including tickets for bus circuits and shows at the Blois châteaux. **Currency exchange** with 32F commission. Open April-Sept. Mon.-Sat. 9am-12:30pm and 2-7pm, Sun. 10am-1pm and 4-7pm; Oct.-March Mon.-Sat. 9:15am-noon and 2-6pm. A branch office (tel. 02 54 78 06 34) with info and bike rental, is located on rue de la Voûte du Château to the immediate right and down the hill from the Château (open July and Aug. 9:30am-7:30pm). **Maison du Loir-et-Cher,** 5 rue de la Voute du Château (tel. 02 54 78 55 50), has a wealth of artfully displayed brochures on regional lodging, camping, activities, and events (open 10am-7pm).

Money: In July and Aug., stores displaying the *No Francs, No Problem* sign offer souvenir-hunters the chance to purchase goods with currencies ranging from dollars to yen at no commission. Banks and **ATMs** are scattered throughout the *centre ville:* near the Loire, along rue Denis Papin, and around pl. de la Résistance. **Banque de France,** 4, av. Jean Laigret (tel. 02 54 55 44 00), on the right as you walk down the hill to the tourist office, defies a hefty commission (open Tues.-Sat. 8:45am-12:15pm and 1:45-3:45pm; currency exchange in the morning only).

Trains: pl. de la Gare (tel. 02 47 20 50 50). To: Orléans (14 per day, ½hr., 49F); Paris-Austerlitz via Orléans (8 per day, 1¾hr., 120F); Tours (10 per day, 1hr., 49F); Amboise (10 per day, 20min., 32F); Angers via Tours (10 per day, 3hr., 109F). Info office open 6am-10pm. **Lockers** 5F and 10F.

Buses: Point Bus, 2, pl. Victor Hugo (tel. 02 54 78 15 66), 2min. from the tourist office. Buses depart from train station June 10-Sept. 10. Two circuits visit the châteaux with the **Transports Loir-et-Cher** line (**TLC;** tel. 02 54 78 15 66). Circuit 1 to Chambord and Cheverny 65F, students 50F. Leaves 9:10am and 1:20pm, returns 1 and 6:10pm. Circuit 2 to Chaumont, Chenonceaux, and Amboise leaves 9:10am, returns 6pm. Passes include reduced admission to châteaux. Buy tickets at the station, tourist office, or on bus. Ask about special tours. Open Mon. 1:30-6pm, Tues.-Fri. 8am-12:15pm and 1:30-6pm, Sat. 9am-12:15pm and 1:30-4:30pm.

Taxis: Taxis Radio, pl. de la Gare (tel. 02 54 78 07 65), in front of the *gare.* 24hr.

Bike Rental: Atelier Cycles, 44, levée des Tuileries (tel. 02 54 74 30 13), across the river from the La Boire campground. Near the "Verdun" bus stop on line 4. 10-speeds 25-50F per day. Mountain bikes 35-100F per day. Passport deposit. Open 9am-9pm. **Intersport,** 2-4, rue Porte Côté (tel. 02 54 78 06 57), just below pl. Victor Hugo. Bikes 50F per day, 1000F deposit. Open Mon. 2-7pm, Tues.-Sat. 9am-noon and 2-7pm. V, MC. Tourist office branch, rue de la Voute du Château (tel. 02 54 78 06 34) rents mountain bikes (80F per day, 60F per ½-day, 600F deposit; open July and Aug. 9:30am-7:30pm).

LOIRE VALLEY

Laundromat: pl. Louis XII. Wash 15F per 5kg. Dry 2F per 5min. Open 7am-10pm.

Youth Center: Bureau Information Jeunesse de Loir-et-Cher, 7, av. Wilson (tel. 02 54 78 54 87), across the bridge and on the right. Distributes free brochures, gives employment advice, and sells train tickets at reduced prices.

Emergency Hotline: Centre de Secours, 11, rue Gutenberg (tel. 02 54 51 54 00). Offers support in legal and emotional crises such as rape and abuse.

Hospital: Centre Hospitalier de Blois, Mail Pierre Charlot (tel. 02 54 55 66 33). **Emergency** tel. 15.

Police: 42, quai St-Jean (tel. 02 54 55 17 99). **Emergency** tel. 17.

Post Office: 5, rue Gallois (tel. 02 54 44 68 58), near pl. Victor Hugo, to the left of the château with your back to the *gare.* **Currency exchange. ATM.** Telephones. Poste restante. Open Mon.-Fri. 8am-7pm, Sat. 8am-noon. **Postal code:** 41000.

ACCOMMODATIONS

Each summer, tourists from all parts of the globe descend on Blois en route to the châteaux and points west. To be sure that you are one of those who will spend the night in a bed, call at least a day in advance to reserve. By the same token, if you do not need your reservation, it is *de rigueur* to call and inform your expectant hosts. Note that sleeping on the banks of the Loire is illegal, not to mention unpleasant.

Auberge de Jeunesse (HI), 18, rue de l'Hôtel Pasquier (tel. 02 54 78 27 21), 5km outside Blois in Les Grouets (1hr. walking). From tourist office, follow rue Porte Côté, bear right onto rue Denis Papin down to the river, and take bus 4 (direction: Les Grouets). Get off at "Eglise des Grouets" (10min., 6F). Mon.-Sat. last bus at 7:30pm. Sun. *only* bus leaves hostel at 9am, returns from *gare* at 5:50pm. Excellent kitchen facilities, but no supermarkets nearby. Jovial, countryside atmosphere in the evenings. 48 bunks in 2 single-sex dorms. Hot showers. 41F. Sheets 16F. Breakfast 19F. Bag storage during 10am-6pm lockout. Summer reservations highly recommended. Office open 7-10am and 6-10:30pm. Open March-Nov. 15.

Foyer des Jeunes Travailleurs, 37, rue Pierre et Marie Curie (tel. 02 54 43 56 01). Take bus 3 (direction: Sauvageau) from front of train station to "Pierre et Marie Curie." 3-night minimum stay. Priority for French workers, but singles can be rented to anyone ages 16-25. 60F, with shower 75F. Passport deposit. Breakfast included. Monthly rates available. In summer, call a week in advance.

Hôtel du Bellay, 12, rue des Minimes (tel. 02 54 78 23 62; fax 02 54 78 52 04), at top of porte Chartraine 2min. above the *centre ville*. Renovated and in excellent condition, the Bellay offers telephones in every room and spotless bathrooms. Singles and doubles 130-185F. Breakfast 22F. Call in advance. V, MC, AmEx.

Le Pavillon, 2, av. Wilson (tel. 02 54 74 23 27; fax 02 54 74 03 36), just across the bridge and overlooking the Loire. Bustling neighborhood surrounds clean, bright rooms. Singles 100F. Doubles 110F, with toilet 130F, with toilet and shower 160F. Triples 200F. Showers 15F. Breakfast 30F. V.

Hôtel St. Jacques, 7, rue Ducoux (tel. 02 54 78 04 15; fax 02 54 78 33 05), to the right as you exit the *gare*. Large, immaculate rooms with big beds and high ceilings. Singles and doubles 120-205F, breakfast 25F, showers 15F. V, AmEx.

Camping: La Boire (tel. 02 54 74 22 78) is 2km out of town on route 951. One person and tent, 33F, each extra person 10F. Showers included. Electricity 19F. Open March-Nov. **Lac de Loire** (tel. 02 54 78 82 05; fax 02 54 78 62 03) has two-and four-star sites. 40F per person plus tent at the two-star site, 12F per extra person; 60F per person plus tent at the four-star site, 15F per extra person, 7F per child. Showers included. Open April-Oct. 15. Check at tourist office for info on shuttle bus to campgrounds.

FOOD

Blois melts, molds, sculpts, smothers, and indulges its citizens in chocolate. Locals have been perfecting *le chocolat blésois* ever since Catherine de Médicis introduced *pâtissiers* from Italy. Sumptuous *pavé du roi* (chocolate-almond cookies) and *malices du loup* (orange peels in chocolate) peer invitingly from *pâtisseries* along **rue Denis Papin.** For those who cling to the dinner-before-dessert convention, tourist traps jostle more homespun restaurants along **rue St. Lubin** and around **pl. Poids du Roi,** near the cathedral. Flee to the *boulangeries* and fruit stands on **rue des Jacobins,** right below the château, or to the **Intermarché supermarket** at 16, av. Gambetta (tel. 02 54 42 42 00), five minutes from the station (open Mon.-Fri. 9am-12:30pm and 3-7:15pm, Sat. 9am-12:30pm and 2:30-7:15pm; V, MC).

La Parenthese, 2 pl. du Château (tel. 02 54 74 52 75). Insert this relaxing *salon de thé* into your afternoon. Salmon and *chèvre* quiche (58F), vegetable flan (50F), gooey chocolate cake (28F), and an irresistible rooftop terrace. Open Tues.-Wed. 11:30am-7pm, Thurs.-Sat. 11:30am-11pm, Sun. 9:30am-7pm. V.

La Forge, 18, rue du Bourg Neuf (tel. 02 54 74 43 45). All-you-can-eat buffet of cold vegetables and pâtés with dessert or cheese (65F) in a rustic setting. They're especially proud of their meats, cooked over an open fire. Peppersteak with buffet and dessert 90F. Open Mon. noon-2pm, Tues.-Sat. noon-2pm and 7:30-11pm.

Le Maidi, 42, rue St. Lubin (tel. 02 54 74 38 58). Generous 3-course dinner (55F) includes a hearty beef, chicken, liver, or lamb stew, couscous salad, and dessert. Vegetarians won't go hungry, either. A photo montage on the wall chronicles Blois' history. Open Mon.-Sun. 11am-2pm and 6-11pm. V, MC.

Le Bistrot, 12, Henri Drussy, just off pl. de la Résistance (tel. 02 54 78 47 74). Husband and wife whip up a large and delicious *jambon de Paris* (ham) or pâté sandwich (12F). Delightful outdoor patio. Open Mon.-Sun. 8am-11pm.

SIGHTS AND ENTERTAINMENT

Home to French monarchs Louis XII and François I, Blois' **château** (tel. 02 54 78 06 62 for recorded info, 02 54 74 16 06 for a live operator) was as influential in the late 15th and early 16th centuries as Versailles was in subsequent ages. The ornate octagonal **spiral staircase,** built under François I, juts out into the courtyard whose once-crumbling façades now glisten as the result of a massive restoration project. François (1494-1547), the "Cavalier King," invited artists and scientists to his court and enforced unprecedented respect for court women. Stone salamanders wriggle on the staircase as symbols of his power, articulated by the Latin motto, *"Nutrisco et extingo"* (I nourish and extinguish). On the first floor, don't miss the craftily crafted chamber of Catherine de Médicis. Ascend the staircase to the **Aile François I,** where the murderous deeds of King Henri III can be followed with the aid of an invaluable pamphlet (in French and English, 4F at front desk). In 1588, the king cowered in a small antechamber while his eight hired assassins fatally stabbed the Duke of Guise, a Catholic rival supported for the French throne by most nobles and the powerful king of Spain. According to contemporary accounts, Henri emerged from his hiding place, surveyed the lacerated Duke, who measured almost seven feet tall, and quipped coolly, "He looks even bigger dead than alive." The next day, Henri dispatched the Duke's brother, the Cardinal of Guise, in similar fashion, but his luck ran out quickly. His mother, Catherine de Médicis, died at the château less than two weeks later and, within eight months, Henri received his just desserts from the deadly blade of Jacques Clément. The basement of this wing houses medieval tapestries and a bust of Denis Papin, Blois' native son who invented the steam engine. (Château open daily June 15-Aug. 9am-8pm; March 15-June14 and Sept.-Oct.14 9am-6:30pm; Oct. 15-March 14 9am-12:30pm and 2-7:30pm. Tours in French and English leave frequently in the summer; other seasons, call ahead. Admission 33F, students under 25 17F. The château presents a spectacular *son et lumière* every evening May-Sept. at 10:30pm, in French, 60F.)

Houdini lovers should keep their eyes out for the appearance of the **National Center for the Art of Magic and Illusion** scheduled to open in 1997 across the *place* from the château. Not cutting-edge in its presentation, the **Musée de la Résistance de la Déportation et de la Liberation,** 1 pl. de la Gréve (tel. 02 54 56 07 02) will nevertheless tug at both your head and your heart in the 14 minutes it takes to saunter through. (Open Tues.-Sun. 2:30-5:30pm, free tours.) Visit the **Musée d'Histoire Naturelle** (tel. 02 54 74 13 89), past the château off rue Anne de Bretagne, which features minerals, flora, and fauna from the Loire region, and tropical specimens (open Jan.-May and Sept.-Dec. Tues.-Sun. 2-6pm; June-Aug. Tues.-Sun. 10am-noon and 2-6pm). Next door in the Couvent des Jacobins, budding and confirmed theologians can contemplate nirvana at the **Musée Diocésain des Arts Religieux** (tel. 02 54 78 17 14), which displays religious objects dating back to the 15th century (open Tues.-Sat. 2-6pm; admission to both museums 25F, students 15F).

Though Blois does hold its own in a land of monuments and cathedrals, what you are most likely to enjoy and remember are the labyrinthine cobblestone streets and ancient staircases. Rue St-Lubin and rue des Trois Marchands are invitingly lined with bars and *boulangeries* en route to the 12th-century Abbaye St-Laumer, now the **St-Nicolas cathedral,** a towering master-stroke of medieval architecture (open 9am-dusk). At sunset, cross the Loire and turn right onto the quai Villebois Mareuil for a shimmering view of the kingly château rising above the commonfolk's abodes.

Nightlife is quiet in Blois; most tourists rest up for early-morning château-stalking. However, around the pl. Poids du Roi, several pubs attract a wide clientele. A beer will run you around 15F in these British-styled pubs: **Loch Ness Pub,** 7, rue Juifs (tel. 02 54 56 08 67; open Mon.-Sat. 6pm-4am), **Pub Mancini,** rue Fontaine des Elus (open Mon.-Sat. 6pm-4am), and the **River Side,** 3, rue Henry Drussy (tel. 02 54 78 33 79; open Mon.-Sat. 5:30pm-4am).

■ Châteaux Near Blois

Ensconced deep in the heart of the Loire Valley, lovely Blois would be the perfect base from which to explore the surrounding châteaux—were it not for the problem of *les transports.* All châteaux except Chaumont are inaccessible by train from Blois. Eurorail pass holders may want to consider switching their mode of transportation to bus or bike, as both prove to be easier, cheaper, and more successful ways of getting anywhere near the châteaux. On the bright side, the cheapest bus trips leave from Blois; from June 10-Sept. 10, **Point Bus** in Blois sends buses on the TLC line to the châteaux (see **Buses** in Blois, page 256). Those on two wheels should have less of a problem, as the châteaux are within easy biking range. From Blois, the 15km trip to Chambord takes about an hour, the 10km ride to Cheverny takes around 45 minutes, and the 6km ride to Beauregard is only 30 minutes long. Bikers should start by crossing the Loire in central Blois and riding to the roundabout 1km down av. Wilson. The châteaux and towns are well-marked along the roads. Bicyclists are advised to stay off of the major —and narrow—French highways. The tourist office branch at the Châteaux de Blois has small maps of routes which will lead you safely and efficiently to the châteaux of your choice. Pay attention to route numbers on road maps, as the roads are marked by the name of their destination. The Regional Committee of Tourism (tel. 02 54 78 62 52) offers week-long cycling packages, which include bike rental, transportation of luggage, meals, accommodations, and admission to châteaux. Those who hitch report some success near the roundabout to Cheverny; Chambord is supposedly more difficult.

CHAMBORD

From 1519 through 1545, François I fulfilled his most egotistical fantasies by constructing **Chambord** (tel. 02 54 79 96 29), a cozy hunting retreat 128m long, with 440 rooms and a fireplace for every day of the year. The king nearly bankrupted himself creating this intricate palace, letting his sons rot without ransom in Spain, commandeering his subjects' silver, and "borrowing" treasures from churches rather than letting Chambord go without one of its 83 staircases. Now the largest and most extravagant of the Loire châteaux, massive Chambord (see front cover photo) holds 700 of François' trademark stone salamanders, 14 4m-tall tapestries depicting his hunting conquests, and his initials splayed across its forest of stone chimneys on the rooftop terrace, which was ideal for court intrigues. At the heart of the château coils a spectacular double-helix staircase, attributed to François I's protégé, Leonardo da Vinci, and constructed so that one person can ascend and another descend, keeping constant sight of one another without ever meeting. The château was a favorite *auberge* of Louis XIV, whose icy reception of Molière's *Pourceaugnac* and *Le Bourgeois Gentilhomme* performed here nearly made their first performances their last.

To improve the forest setting, François I wanted to divert the Loire but had to be satisfied with rerouting the more manageable river Cosson. Louis XIV planted the magnificent kilometer-long, tree-lined avenue approaching the château. Like a great white elephant, Chambord was alternately adored and abandoned by French monarchs until they were no more; their heirs sold it to the state for 11 million francs in 1932. Today, the sprawling grounds cover over 5350 hectares—1200 of which are open to the public—forming a game preserve surrounded by the longest wall in

France, 2.5m high and 33km long. If you're lucky you might even see a *sanglier* (wild boar) roaming the enormous forest.

Rooms in the château are adequately labeled in English, but the 3F English pamphlet with a map and guide greatly clarifies the château's complex layout. (Open July-Aug. daily 9:30am-7:15pm; April-June and Sept. daily 9:30am-6:15pm; Feb.-March and Oct.-Dec. daily 9:30am-12:15pm and 2-5:15pm. Closed Jan. Admission 35F, students 22F.) 45min.-1hr. by bike from Blois—take route D956 south 2-3km then turn left onto D33.

Avoid the **currency exchange** (32F commission) at Chambord's **tourist office** (tel. 02 54 20 34 86), but make use of their accommodations service, tickets for the *son et lumière* at Chambord and Cheverny, and **bike rentals** (30F per hr., 45F per 2hr., 60F per 3-4hr., 80F per day; office open April-Oct. 15 10am-7pm). Campers may trek to **Camping Huisseau-sur-Cosson,** 6, rue de Châtillon (tel. 02 54 20 35 26), about 5km southwest of Chambord on D33 (35F for 2 people and tent, showers free; open April-Sept.). Two-star **Camping des Châteaux,** on route de Chambord in **Bracieux** (tel. 02 54 46 41 84), has a pool, tennis court, and free showers (15F per person, 10F per tent; parking 9F; open daily April-Oct. 15 8am-noon and 2-8pm).

CHEVERNY

Privately owned by the Hurault family since its completion in 1634, **Cheverny** (tel. 02 54 79 96 02; fax 02 54 79 25 38) and its impeccably manicured grounds radiate a personal touch unique among the major châteaux. It may lack the royal historical intrigues of other châteaux in the region, but its modest lifestyle has enabled Cheverny to retain magnificent furnishings. Admire Spanish leather-upholstered walls, delicate Delft vases, stunning French armor, the elaborate royal bedchamber (still awaiting the visit of its first French king), and a richly hued, action-packed Gobelin tapestry, *The Abduction of Helen.* Don't sneak up to the 3rd floor to see how the current count lives—just admire his family photo on the ground floor.

Outside, fans of Hergé's Tintin books may recognize Cheverny's stately Renaissance façade as the inspiration for the design of Marlinspike, Captain Haddock's mansion. In the **Orangerie** behind the château (closed to the public) the *Mona Lisa* smiled bravely while German artillery shelled Paris during World War II. The castle's **kennels** still host 70 more lively guests, mixed English-Poitevin foxhounds who live and love to stalk stags. Cheverny's *soupe des chiens* is not a dubious regional dish but an opportunity to see them gulp down bins of ground meat in less than 60 seconds. (Feedings Mon.-Sat. 5pm; Sept.-March Mon. and Wed.-Fri. 3pm. On Tues. and Thurs. in the fall, they're in the woods.) Next to the kennels, thousands of antlers poke out of the ceilings of the **trophy room** around a striking *vitrail* (stained glass window) of the hunt made in Chartres. (Château open daily June-Sept. 15 9:15am-6:45pm; Sept. 16-Sept. 30 9:30am-noon and 2:15-6pm; Oct. and March 9:30am-noon and 2:15-5:30pm; Nov.-Feb. 9:30am-noon and 2:15-5pm. Admission 31F, students 20F. To bike to Cheverny from Blois, take D956 south for 45min.) Cheverny is home to the "biggest hot air balloon in the world." A breathtaking (even for non-acrophobes) view of the countryside, château admission included, costs 79F, students 69F. Cheverny's *son et lumière,* with 300 actors playing 1000 roles, tells the history of the château, with fireworks and lasers on weekends in July and August (shows at 10:15pm, 1½hr., 80F; call the Blois tourist office for reservations).

Two km away on the road to Contres is **Camping Les Saules** (tel. 02 54 79 90 01). 80F covers two people, their tent, and hot showers (open June-Sept.).

BEAUREGARD

Before François I unleashed his fancy on Chambord, he designed **Beauregard** (tel. 02 47 47 05 41; fax 02 54 70 36 74) as a hunting lodge for his uncle. You'll be hard-pressed to spot any similarities between the two châteaux. Located 8km south of Blois, lovely Beauregard presents its treasures in a cozier setting. Paul Ardier, treasurer to king Louis XIII, commissioned Jean Mosnier to paint what was to become the world's largest **portrait gallery.** The awe-inspiring collection of 327 17th-century paintings is a *Who's Who* of European powers from 1378 through Louis XIII, including all of the Valois royal families, Elizabeth I, Thomas More, and Columbus. The floor's 5616 tiles, undergoing a 20-year restoration project, portray Louis XIII's army—cavalry, artillery, and infantry—solemnly marching to war. Outside the château, ruins of a 14th-century chapel invite a walk in the woods. (Open Oct.-Mar. Thurs.-Tues. 9:30am-noon and 2-5pm; April-June and Sept. daily 9:30am-noon and 2-6:30pm.; July-Aug. daily 9:30am-6:30pm. Admission 25F, students 18F. Extremely enthusiastic staff offers frequent tours in French and English.)

Beauregard is pleasantly devoid of crowds, in part because it is inaccessible by public transportation (the only bus runs infrequently and stops several km away). However, it is a simple half-hour bike ride from Blois. Beauregard lies *en route* to Cheverny, off route 956 (direction: Collettes) and is an easy detour from the main road. The direct route takes you along D765, a busy two-lane highway; ask at a bike rental shop for the touring route, which weaves through the forest to the right of the highway. Hitchhikers heading south on D956 report that rides are relatively easy to come by.

CHAUMONT-SUR-LOIRE

Perched high above the Loire river and surrounded by dense vegetation, **Chaumont-sur-Loire** (tel. 02 54 20 98 03; fax 02 54 20 91 16) could be described as a château in the rough—not a pleasure palace, but a castle built to defend a kingdom. A long, steep road leads to this compact feudal fortress whose tower, turrets, moat, and fully functional drawbridge (one of only three in France) predate the more lavish Renaissance châteaux. Fiery volcanoes—*chauds monts,* in fact—decorate the exterior. Catherine de Médicis lived here until the death of her husband, Henri II. She then forced Henri's mistress, Diane de Poitiers, to vacate the more desirable Chenonceau in exchange for Chaumont. The château is best known for its luxurious *écuries* (stables), where the horses ate from porcelain troughs in richly upholstered stalls with elegant overhanging lamps. A collection of clay medallions features the smiling face of Voltaire and the more sober mien of Louis XV. The view down the Loire from the château's terrace is nothing short of stunning. Throughout the summer, Chaumont hosts the **International Festival of Gardens** (tel. 02 54 20 99 24) and various music ensembles (château open daily March 15 -Sept. 9:30am-6pm; Oct.-March 14 10am-4:30pm; admission 26F, students 17F). Those looking for a place to rest can head to the sheltered **Camping Grosse Grève,** just off the bridge on the southern bank of the Loire (tel. 02 54 20 95 22; 2 people and tent 38F; electricity 7F; open May 15-Sept. 30). Trains run to Chaumont from Blois (17 per day, 15min., 15F) and Tours (17 per day, 25min., 11F). The **train station** (tel. 02 47 20 50 50) lies in **Onzain,** 3km north of Chaumont. By bike, follow signs from the roundabout 1km down av. Wilson in Blois to the D751 (direction: Amboise).

Amboise

Amboise's postcard-perfect location has enticed royalty for the past 500 years. Partly destroyed after the Revolution, the château is neither as ornate as Chambord nor as charming as Chenonceau, but it retains its medieval and fortress-like character. Charles VIII, Louis XI, Louis XII, and the bacchanalian François I all ruled France from the hillside château and enjoyed the extraordinary panorama of the river valley below. The high priest of inventors, Leonardo da Vinci, spent his last years in Amboise. Today, granddaddy of rock Mick Jagger gets his satisfaction in a modest castle nearby. Similar to Blois in small-*ville*-meets-big-château charm, Amboise (pop. 12,000) is worth an afternoon of exploration in spite of its summer crowds.

ORIENTATION AND PRACTICAL INFORMATION

To reach the château and the tourist office, follow rue Jules-Ferry from the station, and cross the bridge onto the residential **Ile d'Or.** The *centre ville* is just across the next bridge; the château is ahead; and the tourist office, shaped like a B-movie flying saucer, is 30m to the right, on the quai Charles de Gaulle along the river (15min.).

Tourist Office: quai du Général de Gaulle (tel. 02 47 57 09 28; fax 02 47 57 14 35). Friendly, quatralingual staff distributes brochures, bus, and château information. Books rooms for a 2F phone call. What more could your touristic little heart desire? Open July-Aug. Mon.-Sat. 9am-8:30pm, Sun. 10am-noon and 4-7pm; Sept.-June Mon.-Sat. 9am-12:30pm and 3-6pm, Sun. 10am-noon. Next door in the same building a **change office** (tel. 02 47 57 69 15) will convert your money for a 20F commission daily 9:15am-6:30pm.

Trains: bd. Gambetta (tel. 02 47 23 18 23). On the main Paris-Blois-Tours line. To: Tours (14 per day, 20min., 27F); Blois (15 per day, 15min., 32F); Orléans (14 per day, 1hr., 72F); Paris (5 per day, 2¼hr., 136F). **Lockers** 5F. Station open Mon.-Sat. 6:45am-9:40pm, Sun. 7:30am-9:40pm.

Buses: Tourisme Verney (in Tours, tel. 02 47 37 81 81), runs to Tours at odd hours (5 per day, 25min., 28F) and to Chenonceaux (2 per day, 30min., roundtrip 40F). Buses leave from the parking lot next to the tourist office.

Bus Tours: Touraine Voyages, 1, rue Voltaire (tel. 02 47 57 00 44). Offers full-day tours of châteaux, including Blois, Cheverny, Chambord, Chaumont, and Villandry. Tours (180-400F) leave from various locations in Amboise (check schedule). Office open Mon.-Sat. 9am-12:30pm and 1:30-6:30pm, or ask at the tourist office.

Taxis: Bordier Taxi, 10, rue Descartes (tel. 02 47 57 30 39).

Bike Rental: V.T.T. Cycles Richard, 2, rue de Nazelles (tel. 02 47 57 01 79), on the north bank by the first bridge as you walk away from the station. 10-speeds 50F per day, mountain bikes 100F per day. Deposit 800F or passport. Open Tues.-Sat. 9am-noon and 2:30-7pm. **Cycles Leduc,** 5, rue Joyeuse (tel. 02 47 57 00 17), across from the Post Office Museum. All bikes 50F per ½-day, 90F per day. Passport deposit. Open Tues.-Sat. 9am-noon and 2-7pm, Sun. 9am-noon.

Youth Center: Point Information Jeunesse d'Amboise, 16, pl. Richelieu (tel. 02 47 30 41 64). Turn left onto rue Orange from rue Nationale and follow it 2 blocks to pl. Richelieu. Brochures about jobs and study abroad. Open Mon. and Thurs. 2-6pm, Tues. 9am-noon and 2-6pm, Wed. and Fri. 9am-noon and 2-5pm.

Laundromat: LavCentre, 5 allée du Sergent Turpin, across from tourist office and behind the fountain. 2F per 5-min. wash. Open 7am-9pm.

Hospital: Centre Hospitalier Robert-Debré, rue des Ursulines (tel. 02 47 23 33 33). Turn left from rue Nationale at pl. St-Denis onto rue Bretonneau; the hospital is about 1km down on the left. **Medical emergency** tel. 15.

Police: Gendarmerie Nationale, rue de Blois (tel. 02 47 57 26 19), at the bridge across the river from the château. **Emergency** tel. 17.

Post Office: 20, quai Général de Gaulle (tel. 02 47 57 08 80), 3 blocks down the street to the left as you face the tourist office. **Currency exchange** with 24-hr. **ATM.** Poste restante. Photocopies 1F. Open Mon.-Fri. 8:30am-noon and 1:30-6:15pm, Sat. 8:30am-noon. **Postal code:** 37400.

ACCOMMODATIONS AND CAMPING

Amboise's few inexpensive hotel rooms tend to be full during the summer. You may have better luck finding a place to hang your hat in nearby Blois or Tours.

Maison des Jeunes—Centre Charles Péguy/Auberge de Jeunesse (HI), Ile d'Or (tel. 02 47 57 06 36). Follow rue Jules-Ferry from the station and turn right downhill after the first bridge (10min.). Join dance classes, ping-pong, and billiard games in the youth center downstairs. A beautiful, quiet setting; ask for a room with a view of the Loire and the château. 74 beds in 3-8 berth rooms. Reception open Tues.-Sun. 3-9pm. No lockout or curfew; room key provided. 48F; Nov.-Feb. 34F. Sheets 16F. Breakfast 15F. In summer, arrive early or call ahead.

La Brèche, 26, rue Jules-Ferry (tel. 02 47 57 00 79). On the left from the station, walking toward the *centre ville.* 12 well-kept rooms without the *centre ville* prices, some with a balcony overlooking the fountain in the lush garden below. Singles 160-260F. Doubles 200-280F. Most rooms have a shower. Enjoy breakfast in the garden or inside, 35F. Garage facilities. Closed Oct. 20-Jan. V, MC, AmEx.

Hôtel à la Tour, 32, rue Victor Hugo (tel. 02 47 57 25 04), across from the château. Small, clean rooms with the essentials. 4 singles 100F. 3 doubles 155F. Breakfast 27F. Closed Thurs. Call ahead July-Aug. V, MC.

Hôtel Les Platanes, bd. des Platanes (tel. 02 47 57 08 60). Turn right from the front of the train station, walk 300m on bd. Gambetta, cross to the right under the tracks, and walk straight for 100m; the hotel is on the left. Quiet, countryside atmosphere in a residential neighborhood. Large, immaculate, modern bedrooms and a pleasant dining room. Singles 130-150F, with shower 180F. Doubles 130-150F, with shower 200F. Breakfast 25F. V, MC.

Camping: Ile d'Or (tel. 02 47 57 23 37), offers a spectacular view of the Loire and the château. Clean facilities in excellent condition. 12F per person, 22F per site. Electricity 10F. Showers included. Crowded swimming pool (10F, children 7F). The mini-golf course is fairly challenging (15F per adult, 10F per child).

FOOD

Camera-toters have overrun the restaurants and *brasseries* along quai Charles de Gaulle and rue Victor Hugo. Go instead to the inexpensive *boulangeries* and fruit stands on rue Nationale to picnic along the Loire, where the view is better anyway. For picnic materials, climb up the hill to **ATAC supermarket,** at the intersection of rue Grégoire de Tours and the allée de Mazère just south of the *centre ville* (open Mon.-Fri. 8:30am-1pm and 2:30-8pm, Sat. 9am-8pm, Sun. 9:30am-12:30pm). Equidistant, but on flatter terrain, **Intermarché,** on av. de Tours, soothes every hunger pang (open Mon.-Thurs. 9am-12:30pm and 2:30-7:30pm, Fri.-Sat. 9am-7:30pm, Sun. 9am-noon). **La Trattoria,** 4, rue Jean-Jacques Rousseau (tel. 02 47 57 67 57), right off the quai, dishes up extra-large pizzas for 22-45F (open Mon.-Tues. and Thurs.-Sat. 10am-2pm and 7-11pm, Sun. 7-11pm; V, MC). On Ile d'Or, **La Salamandre,** 1, quai Maréchal Foch (tel. 02 47 57 69 95), serves salads, *galettes,* and pizzas. 15F for an egg *galette,* up to 50F for a "mega roma" pizza. **Salon de Thé-Le Fournil,** pl. du Château (tel. 02 47 57 04 46), between the quai and the château, has been meeting the townspeople's daily chocolate quotas since 1913.

SIGHTS

The battlements of the 15th-century **Château d'Amboise** (tel. 02 47 57 00 98) stretch out above the town like protective arms, an unsettling sight to those who thought of attacking the castle that four French kings called home. Ghastly events have haunted the château over the years. In 1498, as the four-foot-tall Charles VIII rushed out with his queen to watch a suspenseful tennis match, he bumped his head on a low door and died a few hours later. In 1560, Charles V tripped over a torch-bearer who was leading him into the castle and burned himself alive. Finally, during the wars of religion, François II ordered some treasonous Huguenots thrown into the Loire in sacks and others killed on the château balcony, now described by smiling tour guides as the "Balcony of the Hanging People."

Sadly, only 20% of the once-sprawling structure remains. The ailing government sold its treasures during the Revolution, and Napoleon awarded the château to a colleague who demolished two wings rather than pay for their upkeep. Today, the jewel of the grounds is the late 15th-century **Chapelle St-Hubert,** where a superb relief above the door depicts the legends of St. Christophe and St. Hubert. A plaque inside marks Leonardo da Vinci's supposed resting place.

The interior of the main part of the château, the **Logis de Roi,** contains extraordinary original furniture. The 16th-century Gothic chairs with intricately carved webbing stand over six feet high to prevent surprise attacks from behind. A beautiful 1832 rosewood pianoforte was a gift from the king of Brazil, whose daughter married into King Louis Phillipe's family. Throughout the castle, side-by-side depictions of the *fleur-de-lis* and the ermine symbolize the union between Charles VII and Anne of Brittany that united France and Brittany in the 15th century. You can climb the **Tour des Minimes,** also known as the **Tour des Chevaliers** because of the horse-drawn carriages that were once pulled up this spiralling, five-story ramp. Perched high above the Loire, the château commands an amazing view of the countryside. (Open daily July-Aug. 9am-8pm; April-June and Sept.-Oct. 9am-6pm; Nov.-March 9am-noon and 2-5pm. Admission 34F, students 24F, children 15F. 40-min. guided tour in French; English brochure. *Son et lumière* Wed. and Sat. June 21-Sept. Call 02 47 57 14 47 for reservations.) Just beneath the château, the **Caveau,** rue Victor Hugo (tel. 02 47 57 23 69), offers free *dégustations* of the region's white, red, and rosé wines. The bubbling demi-sec wines are prepared in the same manner as champagne (*dégustations* April-Sept. 10am-7pm).

From the château, follow the cliffs along rue Victor Hugo beside centuries-old **maisons troglodytiques,** houses hollowed out of the cliffs and still inhabited today. Up the road about 400m is the **Clos Lucé** (tel. 02 47 57 62 88), the manor where Leonardo da Vinci, invited by François I, spent the last four years of his life. Inside, a museum contains his furnished bedroom, library, drawing room, and chapel. It also features several fascinating models that IBM constructed from Leonardo's 15th-century sketches, demonstrating that he intuited the principles on which modern hydraulic lifts, cannons, automobiles, and helicopters are built (open daily Nov.-Dec. and Feb. 9am-7pm; March-Sept. 9am-6pm; admission 35F, students 26F). The gardens and a reasonably priced tea room are pleasant places to relax.

Just down the street from the exit of the château at 7, rue du Général Foy, **La Maison Enchantée** (tel. 02 47 23 24 50) is a kinetic toy museum. Over 200 foot-high automated figures strut in 20 different scenes accompanied by music. Relive Cocteau's *Beauty and the Beast* or witness the transformation of Dr. Jekyll into Mr. Hyde in his laboratory. (Open April-Oct. Tues.-Sat. 10am-7pm; Nov.-March Tues.-Sat. 10am-noon and 2-5pm; admission 25F, children 15F.)

Housed in a delightful 16th-century house with a Renaissance garden, the **Musée de la Poste,** 6, rue Joyeuse (tel. 02 47 57 00 11), off rue Nationale, re-creates the history of mail carriers in France. Especially interesting for stamp collectors, this museum contains some of the first French stamps ever printed. (Open April-Sept. Tues.-Sun. 9:30am-noon and 2-6:30pm; Oct.-March Tues.-Sun. 10am-noon and 2-5pm. Admission 20F, students 10F, free for art students.)

Tours

Tours is located in the heart of the Loire Valley, but visitors expecting another thatched-roof, cobblestone-lined medieval town may be disoriented when they step off the train. A modern city teeming with traffic, youth, restaurants, and nightlife, Tours is too large to be charming and too impersonal to be endearing. Kings from Charles VII to François I held court here during the 15th and 16th centuries; their châteaux, 60km away, and a *vieille ville* are all that remain of past glories. The writer Balzac was born here, but a multiplex cinema flickers where his crib once stood. Having outgrown its Gallo-Roman roots, Tours is finding that even its identity as a tourist hub is a little bit too confining. Low-rise gray buildings seem to stretch on forever, and a mix of tourists and foreign exchange students makes Tours more of a melting pot than a bastion of French culture. Yet thanks to this young crowd, it's the hotspot of the Loire. They inject the otherwise soulless city with a day-and-night vibe, most evident along the cafés and bars of **pl. Plum'** (Plumereau). If you're willing to give up historical majesty for fabulous nightlife and a world of cheap food, Tours (pop. 300,000) will suit you fine.

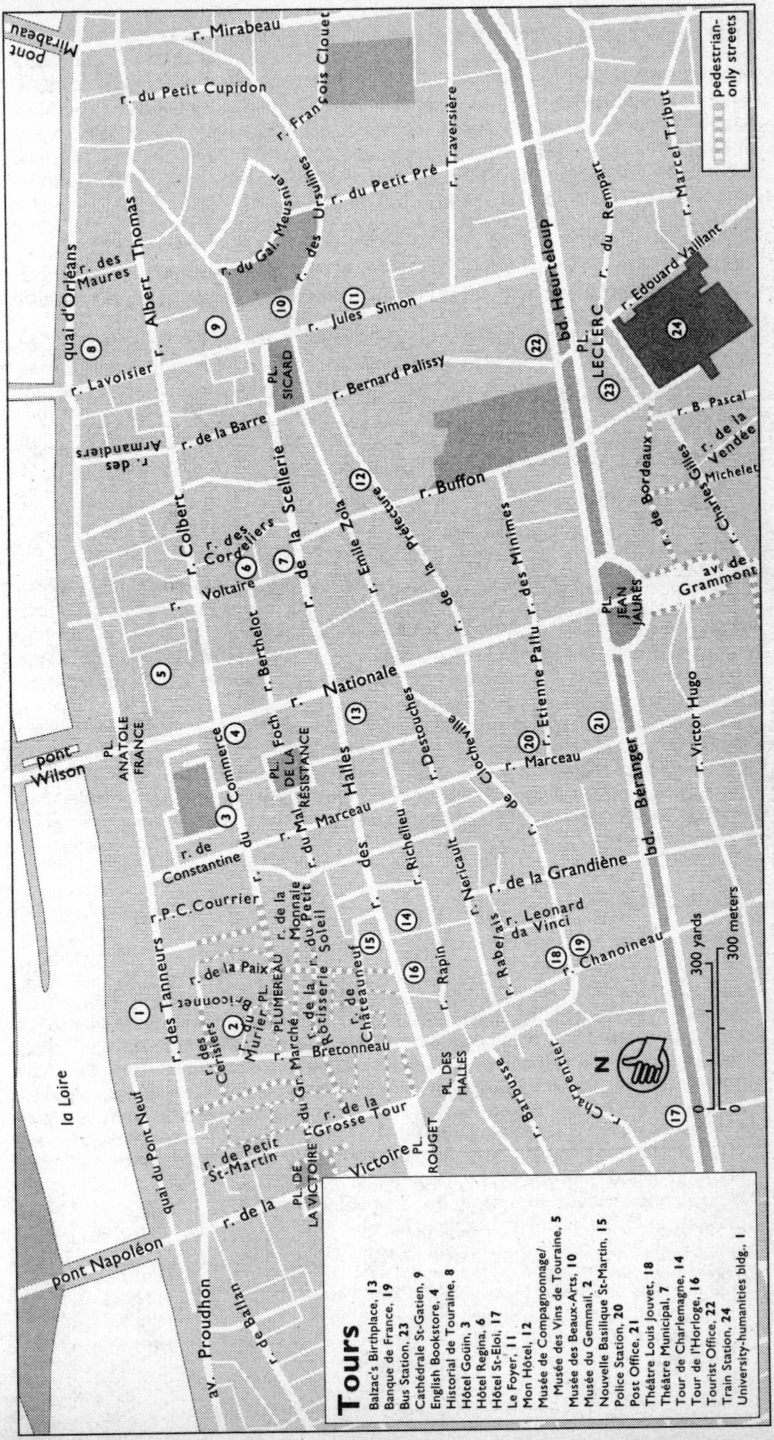

Tours
Balzac's Birthplace, 13
Banque de France, 19
Bus Station, 23
Cathédrale St-Gatien, 9
English Bookstore, 4
Historial de Touraine, 8
Hôtel Goüin, 3
Hôtel Regina, 6
Hôtel St-Eloi, 17
Le Foyer, 11
Mon Hôtel, 12
Musée de Compagnonnage/
Musée des Vins de Touraine, 5
Musée des Beaux-Arts, 10
Musée du Gemmail, 2
Nouvelle Basilique St-Martin, 15
Police Station, 20
Post Office, 21
Théâtre Louis Jouvet, 18
Théâtre Municipal, 7
Tour de Charlemagne, 14
Tour de l'Horloge, 16
Tourist Office, 22
Train Station, 24
University-humanities bldg., 1
pedestrian-only streets
300 yards
300 meters
N
la Loire
pont Mirabeau
pont Wilson
pont Napoléon
quai d'Orléans
quai du Pont Neuf
r. Mirabeau
r. du Petit Cupidon
r. François Clouet
r. du Petit Pré
r. Traversière
r. des Maures
r. Albert Thomas
r. du Gal. Meusnier
r. des Ursulines
r. Jules Simon
r. Lavoisier
PL. SICARD
r. Bernard Palissy
bd. Heurteloup
r. du Rempart
r. Marcel Tribut
r. Edouard Vaillant
PL. LECLERC
r. des Armandiers
r. de la Barre
r. Colbert
r. Scellerie
r. Emile Zola
r. de la Préfecture
r. Buffon
r. B. Pascal
r. de la Vendée
r. Michelet
r. de Bordeaux
r. Charles Gilles
r. des Cordeliers
r. Voltaire
r. des Minimes
PL. JEAN JAURÈS
av. de Grammont
PL. ANATOLE FRANCE
r. Berthelot
r. Nationale
r. Etienne Pallu
r. Foch
PL. DE LA RÉSISTANCE
r. du Commerce
r. des Halles
r. Destouches
r. de Clocheville
r. Marceau
r. Victor Hugo
bd. Béranger
r. de Constantine
r. du Mal
r. Richelieu
r. Néricault
r. de la Grandière
r. P.C. Courrier
r. de la Monnaie
r. du Petit Soleil
r. Leonard da Vinci
r. Rabelais
r. Chanoineau
r. des Tanneurs
r. de la Paix
r. Briçonnet
r. du Murier
PL. PLUMEREAU
r. de la Rotisserie
r. de Châteauneuf
r. Rapin
r. des Cerisiers
r. du Gr. Marché
r. Bretonneau
PL. DES HALLES
r. Barbusse
r. Charpentier
r. de la Grosse Tour
r. de Petit St-Martin
PL. DE LA VICTOIRE
r. Victoire
PL. ROUGET
r. de la
av. Proudhon
r. de Ballan

ORIENTATION AND PRACTICAL INFORMATION

The **pl. Jean-Jaurès** forms the core of Tours, with four major boulevards radiating from it. The **rue Nationale** runs north to the Loire, while **av. de Gramont** runs into the Cher to the south. **Bds. Béranger** and **Heurteloup** run west and east respectively from the *place*. The mostly pedestrian *vieille ville*, lively pl. Plum', and tourist draws are northwest of pl. Jean-Jaurès towards the Loire. To reach the tourist office from the station, cross the park and turn right at bd. Heurteloup. The office is the glass building on the left past the futuristic Centre de Congrès.

Tourist Office: 78/82, rue Bernard Palissy (tel. 02 47 70 37 37; fax 02 47 61 14 22). Multilingual staff distributes maps, books accommodations, and arranges bus tours to the châteaux. A general **bus tour** covering only the exteriors of sites (May-Oct. 10am, 2½hr., 30F) and a detailed historical tour on foot (June-Sept. 2:30pm, 2hr., 25F) both depart daily from the glass-box office. Open Oct.-April Mon.-Sat. 9am-12:30pm and 1:30-6pm; May and Sept. 8:30am-6:30pm; June-Aug. 8:30am-7pm. Sundays and holidays 10am-12:30pm and 3-6pm. **Tours Spectacle** is a free monthly events magazine available at the tourist office.

Money: The office in the circular structure in the **train station** (tel. 02 47 20 00 26) has okay rates and no cash commission. 15F per traveler's check. (Open 7:30am-7:30pm.) As usual, the best deal is at **Banque de France,** 2, rue Chanoineau, off bd. Heurteloup. 1% commission on traveler's checks. (Open Tues.-Sat. 8:45am-noon and 1:20-3:30pm.) A 24-hr. **ATM** can be found at **Crédit Agricole** in pl. Jean-Jaurès and at the **Centre de Congress** facing the tourist office.

Trains: 3, rue Edouard Vaillant, pl. du Maréchal Leclerc (tel. 02 47 20 50 50). Many long-distance trains require you to change at St-Pierre-des-Corps, an industrial stop 5min. outside Tours; check schedules. To: Amboise (14 per day, 20min., 27F); Chenonceau (3 per day, 1 on Sun., 45min., 32F); Chinon (3 per day, 1hr., 44F); Azay-le-Rideau (1 per day, 30min., 26F); Paris-Austerlitz (22 per day, 2¼hr., 151F); Poitiers (17 per day, ½-1hr., 81F); Bordeaux (13 per day, 2½hr., 230F); TGV to Paris-Montparnasse via St-Pierre-des-Corps (16 per day, 1hr., 190-245F with reservation). Ticket windows open Mon.-Sat. 8am-7pm, Sun. 8am-noon.

Buses: Fil Bleu (tel. 02 47 66 70 70) will get you to the Auberge de Jeunesse, but that's about all for tourists. Ticket 6F50, *carnet* of 5 28F, of 10 54F. Day pass 20F.

Taxis: Artaxi (tel. 02 47 20 30 40). 24hr.

Buses: Eurolines, 76, rue Bernard Palissy (tel. 02 47 66 45 56). Trips to cities in Europe, North Africa, and the UK. Open Mon.-Sat. 9am-noon and 2-6:30pm.

Châteaux Bus/Van Tours: Drivers for the tours below speak English and French. Energetic **Touraine Evasion** (tel. 02 47 60 30 00; fax. 02 47 64 88 54) leads small, personal minivan tours from the tourist office, a different one each day. Tours begin at 9:30am. To: Chenonceau, Clos-Lucé, and Amboise (Mon., ½-day, 130F); Blois, Chambord, and Cheverny (Tues., full day, 195F); Azay-le-Rideau, Ussé, and Villandry (Sun., ½-day, 130F). Groups of 5-7 can create their own itineraries. Entrance fees not included, but groups receive a discount. Reserve 1-2 days ahead. Call daily from 8am-7pm for info and reservations, or contact tourist office. This excellent service is also offered during the winter Mon.-Sat. (except Jan.). **Service Touristique de la Touraine** (tel. 02 47 05 46 09) sits in a large office at the train station next to the *bureau de change*. Half-day tours of Chenonceau, Amboise, and Vouvray; Saché, Azay-le-Rideau, and Villandry; Langeais and Ussé. Tours depart at 1:15pm from pl. Leclerc, return at 6:30pm, and cost 100F. Full-day tours to Blois, Chambord, and Cheverny (160F, depart 9am from pl. de la Gare). Summer *son et lumière* trips include admission. To: Azay-le-Rideau (115F), Le Lude (145F), and Amboise (125F). Daily departures late March to early Oct. Office open Mon.-Sat. 8-11am and 3:30-7pm, Sun. 8-11am. Reserve there or at tourist office a day in advance. **Touraine Decouverte** (tel. 02 47 60 30 77) leaves from the tourist office and gives full and ½-day tours. Full day tours leave at 10am (190F), ½-day tours at 1:30pm (130F), and both return by 6:45pm. Reservations recommended. March-Oct. **Silonne Val** (tel. 02 47 92 18 34) offers ½-day (120-160F) or full-day (160-200F) tours of châteaux and other local sights.

Bike Rental: Grammont Cycles, 93, av. de Grammont (tel. 02 47 66 62 89). VTTs 80F per day, 150F per weekend (Sat.-Mon.), deposit 700F. Open Tues.-Sat. 9am-noon and 2-7pm.

Car Rental: Avis (tel. 02 47 20 53 27) in the train station. 575F per day includes 300km, insurance, and fees. Passport, driver's license, and credit card required. Mon.-Fri. 8am-noon, 1:15-7pm, Sat. 8am-noon, 2-6pm. V, MC, AmEx.

Laundromat: 20, rue Bernard Palissy, near the station. Wash 10F per 5 kg. Dry 2F per 5min. Soap 2F. Open daily 7am-8:30pm. Also at 149, rue Colbert. Wash 18F, dry 2F per 5min. Soap 4F. Open daily 8am-7:45pm.

English Books: La Boîte à Livres de l'Etranger, 2, rue du Commerce (tel. 02 47 05 67 29). Large selection of novels and *Let's Go.* Open Mon. 4:15-7pm, Tues.-Fri. 9:15am-12:30pm and 1:30-7pm, Sat. 9:30am-12:30pm and 1:30-7pm. V, MC.

Map Store: Géothèque, 6, rue Michelet (tel. 02 47 05 23 56; fax 02 47 20 01 31), supplies maps of the region for hikers, cyclists, and drivers.

Services for people with disabilities: tel. 02 47 37 60 00.

Crisis Lines: SOS Amitié (tel. 02 47 54 54 54), a general counseling line. **SIDA âllo j'ecoute** (tel. 02 47 20 16 56), for information on AIDS.

Hospital: Hôpital Bretonneau, 2, bd. Tonnelle (tel. 02 47 47 47 47). Walk left from the *gare* down bd. Béranger; the hospital is on right (10min.). Or from tourist office, take bus C-4 to "Hôpital." **Medical Emergency:** tel.15

Police: 70-72, rue de Marceau (tel. 02 47 60 70 69). Take rue Nationale from pl. Jean Jaurès; turn left on rue Etienne Pallu. Station is at end of the street on your right. **Emergency** tel. 17.

Post Office: 1, bd. Béranger (tel. 02 47 60 34 20). Poste restante. **Currency exchange.** Telephones. Photocopies 1F. Open Mon.-Fri. 8am-7pm, Sat. 8am-noon. **Postal code:** 37000.

ACCOMMODATIONS AND CAMPING

A number of good, reasonably priced hotels are scattered around the city, most within a 10-minute walk of the station. If you arrive in the morning and it's not a holiday, feel free to try your luck without reservations. At other times, call a day or two in advance. The hostel draws crowds in the summer. Call **CROUS** (tel. 02 47 05 17 55) for information about discount student meals and long-term housing.

Auberge de Jeunesse (HI), av. d'Arsonval, Parc de Grandmont (tel. 02 47 25 14 45; fax 02 47 48 26 59), 4km from station, across the river, in a park by the freeway. 45min. walking, or take bus 1 (direction: Jotie Blotterie, 7F) or bus 6 (direction: Chambray, 7F) from stop on right side of av. de Grammont, 30m down from pl. Jean Jaurès and bd. Heurteloup (last bus at 8:15pm). Get off at "Auberge de Jeunesse." 170 beds, kitchen facilities, and TV. Reception 5-11pm; off-season 5-10pm. Lockout 10am-4pm. Curfew 11pm, but you can get a key (50F deposit). 62F, breakfast included. Dinner 45F. Sheets 16F. Open Feb.-Dec. 14.

Le Foyer, 16, rue de Bernard Palissy (tel. 02 47 60 51 51), near tourist office. Lets pristine singles (including shower and toilet, 100F) in its newly renovated facility to French workers, students and travelers from all countries.

Hôtel St-Eloi, 79, bd. Béranger (tel. 02 47 37 67 34; fax. 02 47 39 34 67). From the station, take a left on bd. Béranger; the hotel is on your right past the hospital and Banque de France (10min.). Newlywed owners have created a pleasant, homey atmosphere. 10 rooms with phone and toilet; 9 have TV; 5 have showers. Singles and doubles 95-170F. Breakfast 25F. Showers 10F. Reservations recommended.

Mon Hôtel, 40, rue de la Préfecture (tel. 02 47 05 67 53), first left off rue Bernard Palissy. Floral wallpaper brightens newly decorated rooms with phones; some are a tight fit. Singles 100F, with shower 125-180F. Doubles 115F, with shower and toilet 140-200F. Showers 15F. Breakfast 25F. V, MC, AmEx.

Hôtel Regina, 2, rue Pimbert (tel. 02 47 05 25 36). From station, turn left on bd. Heurteloup, take first right on rue de Buffon, left in front of the theater, and first right (5min.). Airy rooms in an excellent, albeit noisy, location. Friendly dog. Singles start at 105F. Doubles 230-250F. Showers 15F. Breakfast 25F. V, MC.

Mr. Bed, 25, rue Etienne Cosson (tel. 02 47 28 24 25; fax 02 47 27 89 47). Just outside of Tours on the N10. 150F for 1-3 people. Includes Mr. Shower, Mr. Toilet, Mr. Phone, and Mr. TV. Breakfast 25F. Great for those who have wheels, but you can come from Tours by taking bus 6 (direction: Chambray-les-Tours). V, MC.

Le Lys d'Or, 23, rue de la Vendée (tel. 02 47 05 33 45; fax 02 47 64 19 00), 5min. from the station, follow the signs. The owner thinks *Let's Go*-ersare great; don't forget to remind him you're one. 15 newly renovated, clean, spacious rooms in a quaint though dimly lit neighborhood. Singles 85-135F. Doubles 110-155F. One quint 310F. Telephones. 20F special *"Let's Go*-discounted" breakfast. V, MC, AmEx.

Tours Hôtel, 10, rue Edouard Vaillant (tel. 02 47 05 59 35), immediately to the right of the station. The owner proudly notes this is "one of the oldest hotels in Tours—over a century old." Clean, with prices perhaps a bit more charming than the rooms. Singles 70-75F. Doubles 75-140F. Showers 10F.

Camping: The tourist office has a list of dozens of campgrounds within a 30km radius, most near châteaux and the Loire. The closest is **Camping Tours Edouard Peron** (tel. 02 47 54 11 11), a 2-star site on N152, 25min. away via bus 7 (direction: Ste.-Radégonde, 7F). 10F per tent, 14F per adult, 8F per child. Open May 11-Sep. 8. **Camping Municipal "Les Acacias,"** rue Berthe Morisot (tel. 02 47 44 08 16), is 6km east of Tours along D751. Site and 2 adults 40F. Electricity 15-30F. Open April-Sept.

FOOD

Tours is not a premier culinary hotspot of France, but *la cuisine tourangelle* still entices gourmands with *rillons* (morsels of hot or cold smoked pork), *andouilletes* (sausages), *fromage de chèvre* (goat cheese), melt-in-your-mouth macaroons, and anything *aux pruneaux* (with prunes). Connoisseurs praise the quality of the *touraine* wines; poets have praised the light whites of Montlouis and Vouvray.

The **market** at pl. des Halles has everything from exotic fruits to smoked *andouilletes* and bread—sounds like a picnic (open Mon.-Sat. 6am-7:30pm, Sun. 6am-1pm). **Supermarkets** are all over town; for greatest convenience charge to **ATAC,** 7, pl. Maréchal LeClerc (open Mon.-Sat. 8:30am-8pm, Sun. 9:30am-12:30pm), just to the left of the train station. **Monoprix** is in the Galeries Lafayette on the corner of rue Etienne and rue Nationale, just north of pl. Jean Jaurès. **Le Grandmont** (tel. 02 47 25 14 61), in the same park as the hostel, serves from 11:30am-1:15pm and 6:45-8pm. Follow the hordes of Tours' business people—they know their noontime economics well—for inexpensive sandwiches (10-25F) along rue Nationale, rue Grommeau, and rue Colbert; shops are nestled between cheap *boulangeries* and *pâtisseries.* Full course meals await your culinary whims on rue Grand Marché. To do as the students do, pass the afternoon with a couple of pals and a cup of coffee at one of the innumerable cafés on pl. Plumereau in the *vieille ville.* Scores of good, cheap restaurants serve the college crowd along rue Colbert and the pl. Plum'.

Au Lapin qui Fume, 90, rue Colbert (tel. 02 47 66 95 49). Try the 65F *menu* (Mon.-Fri.) or the 87F *menu* with *noissettes d'agneau* (lamb chops) or *civet de lapin* (rabbit stew) in this understated atmosphere. The rabbit here is *smokin!* Open Mon. and Wed.-Sat. noon-2pm and 7-11pm, Tues. noon-2pm. V, MC.

Le Patat' Chaud, 41, rue Lavoisier (tel. 02 47 66 96 45), on the corner of rue Colbert a block from the Cathédrale St-Gatien. This local favorite dishes up large potatoes in every imaginable form, from the vegetarian *Patat' Fermière* (36F) to the fishy *Patat' Nordique* (52F). Wonderful salads (30-42F). Open Mon.-Sun. 11:30am-2:30pm, 7-11pm. V, MC.

Il Vesuvio, 14, rue Charles-Gilles (tel. 02 47 66 51 08). This large, brightly lit, bustling pizza and pasta joint serves favorites to locals. A 67F *menu* includes dessert and wine. Two blocks from the train station. Open noon-2:30pm, 6:30-11pm.

Le Charolais, 123, rue Colbert (tel. 02 47 20 80 20), features new culinary creations each day. From basil cream sauce to peach soup, expect the unexpected at this intimate restaurant *gourmand.* 65F menu and a vast selection of regional wines. Open Tues.-Sat. noon-2pm, 7:30-10:30pm, Mon. 7:30-10:30pm. V, AmEx.

Le Café, 39, rue Bretonneau, (tel. 02 47 61 37 83). Located on a quiet terrace, this artsy café serves omelettes with salad (30-40F) and smoked salmon with lemon butter and toast (38F) and plays nightly host to dance troupes and bands. No cover. Beers 14-22F. Open Mon.-Fri. 9:30am-2am, Sat. 4pm-2am, Sun. 6pm-2am.

L'Escale des Iles, 23/25, rue de Chateauneuf (tel. 02 47 05 05 08), brings copious platters of island specialties direct from Réunion, in the Antilles. Try the curried rabbit with rice and your choice of vegetables (59F). Three-course lunch specials Tues.-Fri. Open Mon.-Sat. noon-11pm. V, MC.

SIGHTS

Take a break from châteaux-hopping and spend a day tooling around Tours and its many accessible, low-key sights. A trip to the tourist office will equip you with information about smaller museums. Ask for the 50F **Carte Multivisite,** which admits you to eight sites around Tours, including the Historial de Touraine and the Musée des Beaux-Arts and entitles you to the tourist office's 2:30pm tour of the city. Don't neglect the less tangible forms of tourism; thousands of students make the *vieille ville* an excellent place to stroll and join in the relaxed laughter of young café-goers.

The glowing **Musée du Gemmail,** 7, rue du Murier (tel. 02 47 61 01 19), right off rue Bretonneau near pl. Plumereau uses 20th-century *gemmail,* named after the *gemmes* (gems—or glass) and *émail* (enamel) that form it, to take stained glass to a higher level. Layers of illuminated, brightly colored glass shards blend to yield a "painting of light." The museum holds several *gemmaux* by Picasso; the 12th-century underground chapel houses Cocteau's *Orphée Attaquée,* a striking *gemmail* of a young man whose face glows intensely in blue and pale green as he angrily grits his teeth. (Open March-Nov. 15 Tues.-Sun. 10am-noon and 2-6:30pm; Nov. 16-Feb. Sat.-Sun. 10am-noon and 2-6:30pm, admission 30F, students 20F.)

Even if Romanesque columns and Gothic spires tire rather than inspire you, drag yourself to admire the **Cathédrale St-Gatien,** rue Jules Simon (tel. 02 47 05 05 54), left off bd. Heurteloup. From the colorful emblems of the French kings to the matching sunbursts, this may be the most dazzling collection of stained glass in the Loire. An intricate façade and multiple flying buttresses—one of which plants itself in the courtyard of the neighboring house and in Balzac's *Le Curé de Tours*—are worth the crick in your neck (open Easter-Sept. 8:30am-noon and 2-8pm; Oct.-Easter 8:30am-noon and 2-5:30pm). Practically next door to the cathedral, the **Musée des Beaux-Arts,** 18, pl. François Sicard (tel. 02 47 05 68 73), houses the work of Monet, Reubens, Rembrandt, Delacroix, and Degas. The museum also exhibits a significant collection of 19th- and 20th-century furniture and ceramics. Formerly the ancient Palais des Archevêques, it may be worth seeing solely for its gorgeous rooms and well-kept garden. The 40m Lebanese cedar outside was planted during Napoleon's reign. (Open Wed.-Mon. 9am-12:45pm and 2-6pm. Admission 30F, students 15F. Gardens open daily 7am-8:30pm in summer, 7am-6pm in winter.)

For an unsettling encounter with history, hit the **Historial de Touraine,** 25, quai d'Orléans, two blocks down rue Lavoisier in the Château Royale. In this Madame Tussaud's of regional history, wax figures recreate scenes, including the marriage of Charles VIII and Anne of Brittany and the hanging of the Huguenots. Kitschy sound effects enhance your viewing experience. (Open daily July-Aug. 9am-6:30pm; mid-March to June and Sept.-Oct. 9am-noon and 2-6pm; Nov. to mid-March 2-5:30pm. Admission 33F, students 23F. Guide booklets in many languages 3F.)

Pre-industrial artisans' tools might normally be dull as mud, but the **Musée de Compagnonnage,** 8, rue Nationale (tel. 02 47 61 07 93), five minutes along quai d'Orléans from the Historial de Touraine, is surprisingly interesting. The museum also houses artisanal masterpieces including miniature spiral staircases carved in wood and châteaux made from sugar. (Open daily mid-June to Sept. 9am-6:30pm; March to mid-June Wed.-Mon. 9am-noon and 2-6pm; Oct.-Feb. Wed.-Mon. 9am-noon and 2-5pm. Admission 20F, students 10F.) Downstairs, the **Musée des Vins de Touraine** (tel. 02 47 61 07 93) fills an ancient wine cellar. Regrettably, not even the genial

St. Martin's Dress

The 4th-century patron saint of Tours found his calling while a legionary in the decidedly unsaintly Roman army. Traveling near Amiens one cold night, legend says that Martin sliced his cloak in half to share it with a poor man. Imagine his surprise when he dreamt the next night of Jesus wearing the missing half of his cape. With a quick stop at a baptismal font, he went to Poitou and founded the first Gallois monastery. Invited to be bishop of Tours, Martin fought paganism with the same fervor that he built churches. At his death in 397, the *Tourangeaux,* not to be deprived of his soon-to-be relics, spirited his body up the Loire and away from their neighbors. Evidently someone approved, because the next day, Tours' November chill gave way to spring flowers and sunshine. St. Martin's shrine became a popular pilgrimage destination of beleaguered kings, including Hugh Capet, whose name, and that of his dynasty, is derived from the cape Martin so fortuitously donated to a stranger.

pitcher shaped like a beer-bellied (wine-bellied?) man sitting on a wine cask gives samples (same hours as Compagnonnage; admission 10F, students 5F).

At the **Hôtel Goüin,** 25, rue du Commerce (tel. 02 47 66 22 32), the finest Renaissance façade in Tours conceals a mildly interesting archaeological collection spanning Gallo-Roman utensils to Renaissance sculptures to 17th-century scientific instruments. (Open daily July-Aug. 10am-7pm; mid-March to June and Sept. 10am-12:30pm and 2-6:30pm; Oct.-Nov. and Feb. to mid-March 10am-12:30pm and 2-5:30pm: closed Jan. and Dec. Admission 18F, students 12F.)

Flanking rue des Halles, the **Tour de l'Horloge** and the **Tour de Charlemagne** are fragments of the 11th-century Basilique St-Martin, a gargantuan Romanesque masterpiece that collapsed in 1797, coincidentally a few years after Revolutionary looters removed its iron reinforcements. The **Nouvelle Basilique St-Martin,** a *fin-de-siècle* church in the popular Byzantine style, partially overlaps the foundation of the old structure. St. Martin himself, the city's first bishop, slumbers on undisturbed in his crypt, at least until September 21, 1996, when the Pope is scheduled to arrive for the opening festivities of *l'Année martinienne* (Nov. 11, 1996 to Nov. 11, 1997), marking the 1600th anniversary of the death of Tours' saintly third bishop.

ENTERTAINMENT

In late June, Tours hosts the **Fêtes Musicales en Touraine,** a 10-day celebration of voices and instruments. From Saint-Saëns to Gershwin, they've got it and they're playing it (80-280F per night; call 02 47 21 65 08 for info). Tours has active theater year-round in the **Théâtre Louis Jouvet,** 12, rue Leonardo da Vinci (tel. 02 47 64 50 50), and in the **Théâtre Municipal,** 34, rue de la Scellerie (tel. 02 47 05 37 87).

The large student population demands a swinging and varied **nightlife,** even if summers do quiet down considerably. **Pl. Plum'** is a peach of a place to find cheerful students sipping drinks and chattering at countless cafés and bars. **L'Alexandra,** 106, rue du Commerce (tel. 02 47 61 48 30), is often crammed with an international crowd sampling 10F tequila shots and 13F ½-pint beers. (Open Mon.-Thurs. noon-2am, Fri.-Sun. 3pm-2am.) Next door, **Le Pasadena Café** (tel. 02 47 64 07 84) features posters of American celebrities and an "All-American" cocktail (25F). **Le Morgan,** 25, rue de la Rôtisserie (tel. 02 47 47 02 20) is cocktail heaven. If you can't decide between the "Cadillac" and the "Chevrolet Sister," try your luck with the 15F *cocktail du jour* (open daily 11am-2am). Three clubs on the *place* are stacked one above the other. Downstairs at **Le Pharoan,** sweaty *jeunes* party to loud rock cover-free. Moving up to the 17th century, at **Louis XIV,** busts of Descartes and *le roi soleil* himself keep the café crowds in line. The pinnacle of human evolution brings you to jazzy **Duke Ellington** (all three open daily 'til 2am, tel. 02 47 05 77 17). For a taste of the future, **L'Atomic Café,** 5bis, pl. Plumereau (tel. 02 47 20 75 00), and its cool international staff bring you the best up-and-coming rock bands of Tours (no cover, open daily 4pm-2am). Jazz fanatics head a couple of blocks off the square to **Le Petit Faucheux,**

23, rue des Cerisiers (tel. 02 47 38 67 62), where bands kick loose every Tuesday and Thursday to Saturday until 2:30am (90F cover, students and military 50F). Blues and rock groups cover American favorites and play their own at **Les Trois Orfèvres,** 6, rue des Orfèvres (tel. 02 47 64 02 73), a good no-frills place to chill (open Tues.-Sat. 10pm-4am; 30-50F cover includes a drink).

You'll have no problem raising your own Saturday Night Fever in Tours' dance clubs. A lively, youthful crowd frequents the alternate technopop and jazz nights at **Rhythm and Blues,** 19, rue Petit Soleil (tel. 02 47 05 96 67; open daily 11pm-4am; 30F cover includes a drink, 50F Fri.-Sat., Sun. free). You must get by the well-muscled bouncers to enter **L'Excalibur,** 35 rue Briçonnet (tel. 02 47 64 76 78). Dress up if you want to be considered—or try pulling a sword out of a stone (open Mon.-Sat. 10:30-4am; 50F cover). The more democratic **Pym's,** 170, av. de Grammont (tel. 02 47 66 22 22), draws youth, and sometimes their parents, to its magic hall and ball of mirrors. Theme nights pack this local institution (open Tues.-Sun. until 2am; cover 20-70F includes a drink). **L'Inox,** 18, rue de la Longue-Echelle (tel. 02 47 05 13 14). As the tension rises so do the prices. Obligatory drinks. "Gay Sundays" are an excuse for locals to trot out their *cuir et chiffon* (leather and lace—you had to ask) and techno and disco nights bring just about any outfit out of the closet. V.

■ Châteaux Near Tours

Dozens of beautiful and historic châteaux lie within 60km of Tours. Biking along the Loire between châteaux is fantastic, even if bus tours are more efficient. On your way to château-land, don't neglect the wine cellars offering free *dégustations.* **Vouvray's** 30 cellars (tel. 02 47 52 75 03), 9km east of Tours on the N152, specialize in sweet white wine. By bus, take 61 from pl. Jean-Jaurès to "les Patis" (Mon.-Sat. 14 per day, 20min., 16F). In **Montlouis,** across the river to the south, and accessible by train from Tours (Mon.-Sat. 3 per day, 20min., 12F), the 10 *caves* pour forth wonderful dry white wine. See transportation info in Tours (page 266).

CHENONCEAU

Women are responsible for the graceful beauty and exquisite detail at **Chenonceau.** Sheltered by an ancient forest 35km east of Tours, the château (tel. 02 47 23 90 07) cultivates an intimacy with its natural surroundings that resists even the most ferocious of crowds. Royal tax-collector Thomas Bohier originally commissioned this château on the ruins of a medieval mill on a tiny island in the Cher river. While he fought in the Italian Wars (1513-21), his wife Catherine oversaw its practical design, which features four rooms radiating from a central chamber and innovative straight (rather than spiral) staircases. In 1547, Henri II gave the château to his mistress, Diane de Poitiers, who added sublime symmetrical gardens and constructed the arched bridge over the Cher so she could hunt in the nearby forest. When Henri II died in 1559, his wife Catherine de Médicis forced Diane to exchange her beloved castle for Chaumont (see page 261). Catherine designed her own set of gardens and the most spectacular wing of the castle, the two-story gallery spanning the Cher. A remarkable succession of women added to the château until the late 19th century. The notable Mme. Dupin contributed a more intellectual heritage in the 18th century by hiring Jean-Jacques Rousseau as her son's tutor, prompting him to write the monumental classic on children's education, *Emile.* Mme. Dupin was so loved by the villagers that they protected her château from the ravages of the Revolution, preserving its original furniture for future generations. The gallery over the Cher served as a military hospital during World War I and marked the division of annexed France and Vichy France during World War II. Chenonceau's flowering Renaissance gardens and medieval tower will move even the most jaded, crowd-jostled castle-goer. (Open daily March 16-Sept. 15 9am-7pm; call for off-season hours. 40F, students 25F. Late June-Sept., *son et lumière* at 10:15pm. 40F, students 25F.)

The village of Chenonceaux (the town has an "x" and the château doesn't) is 214km from Paris (2hr.) and 34km from Tours (25min.) by car on the A10. **Trains** go to Tours (3 per day, 45min., 34F). The station is 2km from the château. Don't follow the mob: cross the tracks and turn right, where the blue sign directs you to the château. Continue straight past the campground. **Tourisme Verney** (tel. 02 47 37 81 81, in Tours) runs buses from Tours via Amboise (3 per day, ½hr., 44F roundtrip) to Chenonceaux (1hr., 62F roundtrip), stopping at the castle gates.

Chenonceaux's tiny **campground** (tel. 02 47 23 90 13) is a few blocks left of the entrance to the château (9F per person, 6F per site, 8F per car, electricity 12F; open April 15-Sept.). **Civray** (tel. 02 47 23 92 13) is 1km away (15F per person, 10F per site, 6F per car; open June 15-early Sept.).

LOCHES

Fresh from her victory over the English in Orléans in 1429, Joan of Arc told the indifferent *dauphin* in the state room of Loches that she had cleared the way for him to travel to Reims to be crowned king. 40km southeast of Tours, the château consists of two distinct wings at opposite ends of its hill. To the south, the 11th-century **donjon** (keep) and watchtowers went from keeping enemies out to keeping them in when Charles VII turned it into a state prison, complete with suspended cages. His mistress, Agnes Sorèl, had a more civilizing influence on Charles and the château. From 1500-1508, the imprisoned and evidently *ennuyé* Duke of Milan, Ludovico Sforza, covered his cell walls with mystic messages and symbols, eagerly awaiting the day of his release, upon which the unfortunate duke died of excitement. The more conventional **castle** wing housed French kings, beginning with Phillipe-Auguste, who snatched it from Richard the Lionheart, until the 15th century. (*Donjon,* tel. 02 47 59 07 86, opens and closes 30min. after castle. Castle tel. 02 47 59 01 32; open daily July-Aug. 9am-7pm; mid-March to June and Sept. 9am-noon and 2-6pm; Feb. to mid-March and Oct.-Nov. 9am-noon and 2-5pm. Admission to both 26F.) The castle stages a *son et lumière* about Joan of Arc's adventures. (Shows the 2nd and 4th Fri. and Sat. in July 10:30pm; in Aug. every Fri. and Sat. at 10pm., 1½hr. Admission 60F, ages 5-12 40F. Call Loches tourist office for info and reservations.)

The medieval town of **Loches** surrounds its grand château. Four buses per day make the 50-minute trek from in front of the Tours train station to Loches (44F; pay on board). Nine trains also make the journey (1hr., 42F). The **tourist office** (tel. 02 47 59 07 98), in a pavilion near the station on *brasserie*-lined **pl. de la Marne,** can help you find a room for a 6F fee (open daily June-Aug. 9am-7pm; Sept.-May 9:30am-12:30pm and 2-6pm). **Crédit Agricole,** also on the *place,* will spin your dollars into gold at a fair rate (open Tues.-Sat. 8:30am-12:30pm and 2-5pm, closes at 4pm Sat.). Two blocks from the tourist office, a **Monoprix,** 21, rue Picois, holds a treasure-trove of picnic supplies (open Mon.-Sat. 9am-12:30pm and 2:30-7pm). **Camping Municipal de la Citadelle** (tel. 02 47 59 05 91), av. A. Briand, has a pool, fishing, and tennis next door. Take N143 south, and follow route de Châteauroux to Stade Général Leclerc (55F for 2 people and tent).

VILLANDRY

Completed in 1536, Villandry (tel. 02 47 50 02 09) was one of the last great Renaissance-style châteaux to be built on the banks of the Loire. There are no feudal remnants here; the château's tower and fortress-like layout serve a symbolic and decorative purpose. Jean le Breton, François I's Secretary of State, built Villandry and it remained in his family until the 19th century. In 1906, Dr. Joachim Carvallo, the present owner's grandfather, bought the château and gave up his scientific career to supervise the renovation of the decaying structure. He also planted the extensive, spectacular **gardens** that have become Villandry's main attraction. Today 60% of revenues go toward tending the gardens and maintaining the château, but 40% has been directed toward a massive renovation project, slated to last six years. The results, thus far, have been astounding, if somewhat hidden by scaffolding.

The three-storied garden is Eden for any green thumb. Start at the lowest level and make your way up; the view just gets better. At the highest level behind the château, you can see all 120,000 plants. The kitchen garden, designed like an Italian monastery garden, harvests so much fresh produce that it gets given away. The middle level ingeniously uses knee-high hedges and flowers to form patterns: a Maltese cross, a *fleur-de-lis,* and a reproduction of the *carte de tendre* with symbols of the four kinds of *amour* (adulterous, tragic, tender, passionate). This level also includes an exotic garden of medicinal plants and herbs. The upper level includes lime trees, swan pools, waterfalls, and vine-covered walkways. The château pales before its more regal cousins, but the gardens are unparalleled in the Loire valley and worth the visit. (Gardens open daily 8:30am-8pm; Sept.-May 9am-nightfall. Admission to gardens 30F, students 23F; to château and garden 40F. Château open daily June to mid-Sept. 9am-6:30pm; mid-Feb. to May and mid-Sept. to Nov.11 9:30am-5:30pm.)

Villandry is 15km from Tours, one of the closest châteaux but one of the hardest to get to via public transportation. Take one of the infrequent trains to Savonnières (4 per day, 10min., 14F) and walk or bike the remaining 4km along the Loire. Many minibus tour agencies include it in their full-day and ½-day tours (see page 266). From Tours, cyclists should follow tiny D16, a narrow marvel that winds along the bank of the Cher past Villandry to Ussé; drivers should stick to D7.

AZAY-LE-RIDEAU AND SACHÉ

Lounging on an island in the Indre River, **Azay-le-Rideau** gazes vainly at its reflection in a purely decorative moat, but its narcissism is well deserved. Though smaller than François I's **Chambord,** Azay-le-Rideau (tel. 02 47 45 42 04; fax 02 47 45 26 61) took shape between 1518 and 1523 and was intended to rival its contemporary in beauty and setting. The corrupt royal financier, Gilles Berthelot, and Azay's designer—his wife Philippa—succeeded so well that the jealous François I seized the château before its third wing was completed. On the exterior walls, salamanders without crowns mark the castle as a nonroyal residence built under François I. The crowned salamander over the fireplace is a 19th-century renovation blooper. Azay's flamboyant style is apparent in the furniture and the ornate second-floor staircase with the carved faces of 10 kings and queens, including Henri of Navarre and Anne of Brittany. Enter through the ultra-modern foyer and step back four centuries. (Open daily July-Aug. 9am-7pm; April-June and Sept. 9:30am-6pm; Oct.-March 9:30am-12:30pm and 2-5:30pm. Admission 31F, students 20F.) The all-new *son et lumière* features costumed actors in boats. (Shows daily May-July at 10:30pm; Aug.-Sept. at 10pm. Tickets 60F, children 35F.)

The château is a 2km walk from Azay-le-Rideau's **train station** (1 train per day from Tours, ½hr., 27F). Turn right from the front of the station and head left on the D57. The **tourist office,** 26, rue Gambetta (tel. 02 47 45 44 40; fax 02 47 45 31 46), 1km from the train station along av. de la Gare, can help with accommodations, few of which are cheap (open daily 9am-1pm and 1-7pm). **Buses** run from the Tours station to Azay-le-Rideau's tourist office three times daily (once on Sun., 45min, 50F, pay on bus). **Rent bikes** at **Le Provost,** 13, rue Carnot (tel. 02 47 45 40 94; 40F per ½-day, 55F per day, passport deposit; open Tues.-Sat. 9am-noon and 2:30-7pm). You can also rent bikes (50F per day, 40F per ½-day, 500F deposit) at the **Camping Parc de Sabot** (tel. 02 47 45 42 72), across from the château on the banks of the Indre. Plenty of room here with canoeing, kayaking, and tennis next door (45F per 2 people with tent, showers included; open Easter-Oct.).

Though unconnected by bus or train, **Saché** (tel. 02 47 26 86 50) is a gratifying step off the beaten track. Once Honoré de Balzac's vacation home, the19th-century château now houses the Musée Balzac, a modest collection of his original scribblings, letters, first editions, political cartoons, etchings, and a copy of Rodin's famous sculpture of the controversial writer. Saché is first and foremost a summer home, and its pastoral serenity has been preserved as well as its stones. (Open daily July-Aug. 9:30am-6:30pm; March 15 to June, and Sept. 9:30am-noon and 2-6pm; Oct.-Nov. and Feb. to March 15 Thurs.-Tues. 9:30am-noon and 2-5pm. Admission 21F, 7-18 years old 14F.) Saché is 6.5km east of Azay-le-Rideau on the D17.

USSÉ

In the 15th and 16th centuries, the builders of Ussé (tel. 02 47 95 54 05) prepared a royal suite, hoping that a king would visit. He never did. Another famous name roused Ussé from its tranquility: Charles Perrault, who was supposedly inspired by Ussé's pointed towers, white turrets, chimneys, and thick surrounding *forêt de Chinon* (now cleared away) to transcribe the old French folktale, *La Belle au Bois Dormant* (Sleeping Beauty). Inside, wax figures pose in scenes from the folktale. Ussé is like a modern Sleeping Beauty, lovely to view, but also expensive and rather vacuous—it might be best to let Sleeping Beauties lie. 60km west of Tours, Ussé is reached by bus. (Open Feb.-Nov. 9am-noon and 2-6:45pm; admission 54F.)

LANGEAIS

Between Villandry and Ussé, 23km west of Tours, lies the forbiddingly feudal Langeais (tel. 02 47 96 72 60), one of the last châteaux built strictly for defense. Constructed in 1465-1469 for Louis XI, Langeais guarded the route from Brittany through the Loire Valley. The château abandoned its defensive posture when it hosted the union of Charles VIII and Anne of Brittany, which incorporated independent Brittany into the French kingdom. Today, the château displays wax figures of the bride and groom at their actual diminutive heights (recall that the king died after somehow managing to hit his head on a door frame in Amboise, and that Anne was pregnant 16 times). Langeais is one of the few fully furnished châteaux; its authentic 15th- and 16th-century decor creates a vivid sense of its times. Gothic and Renaissance tapestries decorate the walls, including one which depicts a gutted stag being thrown to the hounds. Guided tours in French and English take you past a fabulous model of Cologne's Dom Cathedral, which doesn't miss a single cross, before continuing along the château's outer wall and its 171 **machicoulis** (holes through which defenders poured boiling oil on the enemy, and probably relished the great view of the town). After the tour, explore the gardens and the **donjon de Foulques Nerra.** In 994, the notorious count of Anjou, otherwise known as the "Black Falcon," inhabited this crumbling keep. (Open daily 9am-6:30pm; mid-July to Aug. 9am-9pm; Nov. to mid-March 9am-noon and 2-5pm. Admission 35F, students 20F.)

At least six trains daily stop in Langeais en route to Saumur or Tours. Allow a bit of time to enjoy this village and its Renaissance edifices. The **train station** (tel. 02 47 96 82 19) is 300m from the château; follow the signs. The 10km bike ride on the D16 from Villandry or Ussé is delightful. In summer, hitchers report traffic on the D57 from Azay-le-Rideau; at other times, the roads are empty. Let's Go doesn't recommend hitching. The **tourist office,** 9, rue Gambetta (tel. 02 47 96 58 22), is across from the château (open June 15-Sept. 15 Mon.-Sat. 9am-7pm, Sun. 10am-12:30pm and 2:30-5pm; Sept. 15-March Mon.-Sat. 2-5:30pm; April-June 14 Mon.-Sat. 9am-12:30pm and 2:30-5pm). There is a **Camping Municipal** (tel. 02 47 96 85 80), on N152, 1km from the château (10F per person, 10F per site; open June-Sept. 15).

To calm the emerging château cynic within, **Le Musée Cadillac** (tel. 02 47 96 81 52), in the Château de Planchour 4km away in **St-Michel-sur-Loire,** shows off the largest collection of Cadillacs outside the U.S., and they're beauties. From the midnight-blue 1926 roadster to the 1966 cherry-red Eldorado convertible, all 55 have been restored to gleaming mint condition. Go west of Langeais on N152. (Open daily Feb.-Dec. 10am-6pm; closed Tues. Oct.-April. Admission 39F, ages 6-18 22F.)

Chinon

Henry II, Richard the Lionheart, Philippe Auguste, St. Louis, Charles VII, Joan of Arc, and Cesare Borgia, among many others, were guests at Chinon's fortress. The château itself is in ruins, but this doesn't diminish its history or the view of the Vienne river from atop the noble pile of rocks. For those with active imaginations, the château comes alive in the tour or a walk along its decrepit walls and towers. Nearly overshadowed by its crumbling royal resident, tiny Chinon (pop. 9000) was the birthplace of the great 16th-century comic writer François Rabelais, who celebrated the virtues of *vin* in his tales of the giants *Gargantua* and *Pantagruel.* Today, Chinon's steep, narrow, and winding streets are dotted with artisans' studios, cafés, and regional specialty shops, making it a worthwhile day trip from Tours.

PRACTICAL INFORMATION

From the station, walk along the quai Jeanne d'Arc, and take a right at the Café de la Paix to get to Chinon's **pl. du Générale de Gaulle** and the **tourist office** at 12, rue Voltaire (tel. 02 47 93 17 85; fax 02 47 93 93 05). The office books rooms for 2F and changes money (open Mon.-Sat. 9am-7pm, Sun. and holidays 10am-12:30pm). The best rates are at **Crédit Agricole,** pl. de Gaulle (open Tues.-Fri. 8:45am-12:30pm and 2-5:15pm, Sat. 9am-12:30pm and 2-4pm), with a 24-hr. Cirrus **ATM. Trains** run to Tours (3 per day, 1hr., 44F) and SNCF **buses** make the trip three times daily (1½hr., 45F). **Les Bus du Chinonais** (tel. 02 47 46 06 60) also circulate in the area. Chinon is a stop on many of the bus tours of the region (page 266). The **post office** is a few blocks down rue du Commerce, across from quai Jeanne d'Arc (open Mon.-Fri. 8am-noon and 1:30-5:45pm, Sat. 8am-noon; **postal code:** 37500).

ACCOMMODATIONS, CAMPING, AND FOOD

The **Auberge de Jeunesse (HI),** rue Descartes (tel. 02 47 93 10 48; fax 02 47 98 44 98), is 20 minutes from town along the quai Jeanne d'Arc, around the corner from the train station. The large, modern building contains 52 beds and excellent kitchen facilities across the street from tennis courts and the Vienne (44F; sheets 16F; reception daily 5am-10pm). The hostel also hosts sports activities and **rents bikes** for exploring the area (30F per ½-day, 50F per day, 90F per weekend; passport deposit). The big, clean rooms at the **Hôtel du Point du Jour,** 102, quai Jeanne-d'Arc (tel. 02 47 93 07 20), are a good value, though one can hear the speeding traffic through the walls (singles and doubles with shower 135-160F; breakfast 22F; reservations often necessary). The pleasant but crowded 2-star **Camping de l'Ile Auger** (tel. 02 47 93 08 35) lies across the river at Ile Auger off N749. The campground offers free access to tennis courts, fishing, and a pool (12F per person, 7F children; 10F per tent; 12F per car). The supermarket **Galerie Corsaire,** 22, pl. Général de Gaulle (open Mon.-Sat. 8:30am-8:30pm, Sun. 8am-12:30pm) will make your picnic plentiful. There is also an open-air **produce market** on pl. de Gaulle on Thursdays. Good, inexpensive restaurants are difficult to find, but try the Italian **La Grappa,** 50, rue Voltaire (tel. 02 47 93 19 29), for the 68F three-course *menu* or its large 32-46F pizzas. Pictures of the homeland keep you company while the oven keeps you warm. (Open in July and Aug. Tues.-Sun. noon-2pm and 7-10:30pm, in Sept.-June Tues.-Sun. noon-2pm and 5-10pm; V, MC, AmEx.) If you hanker for something fiery and local, **Restaurant le Jeanne d'Arc,** pl. Général de Gaulle (tel. 02 47 93 02 85), whips up a 60F 3-course *menu* (open Tues.-Sun. noon-2:30 and 7-11pm; V, MC).

SIGHTS AND ENTERTAINMENT

The **Château de Chinon** (tel. 02 47 93 13 45) presides in august rubble above the Vienne river. In the great hall, Joan of Arc passed the court advisors' first major test of her divine mission when she ignored the man dressed in the *dauphin's* robes and addressed herself to the real prince, hidden among 300 nobles. First erected in the 10th century, the château crumbled not under attack but through neglect under Cardinal Richelieu and, later, Napoleon. (Open daily July-Aug. 9am-7pm; April-June and Sept. 9am-6pm; Oct. 9am-5pm; Nov.-March 9am-noon and 2-5pm. Closed Dec.-Jan. Admission 25F, students 17F.) If you have some extra time in Chinon, go to the **Cave Plouzeau,** 94, rue Voltaire (tel. 02 47 93 16 34) and the **Musée Animé du Vin et de la Tonnellerie,** 12, rue Voltaire (tel. 02 47 93 25 63), behind the tourist office, where M. Plouzeau and sons conduct free tours and pour out some of their superb red wines in their *cave* deep in the hillside beneath the château. After nipping from the 30 or so vintages, show your appreciation by purchasing a 25-30F bottle (open Tues.-

Sun. 10:30am-12:30pm and 2-5:30pm). The Musée Animé du Vin illustrates the wine-making process from grape-crushing to barrel-making. Costumed automatons in bad wigs demonstrate, lacing their speech with Rabelais quotes, including the classic, "Which came first: drinking or thirst?" The 15- to 20-minute tour in English and French, with a glass of Chinon wine and a nip of wine-based jam, ends with the exhortation "drink always and never die" (open April-Sept. Fri.-Wed. 10am-12:30pm and 2-7pm; admission 22F).

Chinon's **medieval fair** takes the city back a few centuries for one Sunday in mid-August with costumes, parades, and markets. The tourist office has more info. For a night of drinks, billiards, and more drinks, head to **Café Français,** 37, rue de la Lamproie (tel. 02 47 93 32 78) until 1am. To make your stay in Chinon unforgettable, or unrememberable, pop up at **Le Magic,** 27, pl. de Général de Gaulle (tel. 02 47 93 13 76), and dance to rave and techno until 4am (Tues.-Sat. 50F cover includes a drink).

Saumur

Saumur has always prided itself on the exceptional. Once famous for St. Louis's (1226-1270) feasts and parties—events so uniquely extravagant they were known as *Non Pareils* (nothing-like-its), Saumur now offers the visitor its unparalleled mushrooms and its wines. Silkworm farms, a thriving carnival mask industry, the resident elite *Cadre Noir* equestrian corps, a tank museum, and an unbelievable vista along the Loire have earned Saumur a spot on the French government's list of eight places in France you simply must see. Coco Chanel was born in the town's pedestrian district, whose chic boutiques and pleasant cafés now emulate her world-famous style. The quarter was also the setting for *Eugénie Grandet,* Balzac's classic characterization of the French bourgeoisie. Munch a mushroom and enjoy, as Balzac did, "the essential strangeness of the place."

ORIENTATION AND PRACTICAL INFORMATION

The tourist office and most sights are on the left bank of the Loire, a 10-to-15 minute walk from the train station, which is located on the right bank. The hostel is on an island between the two. Exit to the right of the train station onto av. David d'Angers, then turn right onto the bridge. Cross pont des Cadets and turn left immediately to get to the hostel, or continue straight on av. de Général de Gaulle to reach the *centre ville.* The tourist office will be to your left, at the corner of quai Lucien Gautier.

Tourist Information: Tourist Office, pl. Bilange (tel. 02 41 51 03 06; fax 02 41 67 89 51), next to pont Cessart. To bypass the walk, take local bus A from station. Upbeat, multilingual staff will book beds (5F), provide free maps, and suggest tours of châteaux, vineyards, and mushroom *caves* (underground farms). Open Mon.-Sat. 9:15am-7pm, Sun. 10:30am-12:30pm and 3:30-6:30pm; Sept. 16-June 14 Mon.-Sat. 9:15am-12:30pm and 2-6pm. **La Nouvelle République** (in French, 4F20) has more Saumur-based **events info** than other local papers.

Money: Banks and 24-hr. **ATMs** cluster around rue d'Orléans, 3 blocks past the tourist office. Best rate is at the **Banque de France,** 26, rue Beaurepaire (tel. 02 41 40 12 00), fourth right down rue Orléans after crossing the bridge. No commission (open Mon.-Fri. 8:45am-noon and 1:45-3:45pm). The **Banque de Paris,** 30, rue Dacier (tel. 02 41 83 34 34), is the fourth left from the bridge (open Mon.-Fri. 8:30am-noon and 1:30-5:15pm, Sat. 8:15am-12:15pm and 1:30-4:45pm).

Trains: av. David d'Angers (tel. 08 36 35 35 35). From pl. Bilange in the *centre ville,* take bus A (direction: St-Lambert or Chemin Vert, 7F). To: Tours (12 per day, ¾hr., 54F); Angers (10 per day, ½hr., 40F); Nantes (7 per day, 1hr., 95F). **Lockers** 3-5F. From Saumur, take the train to **Port-Boulet** (16F), then the bus to Chinon (14F). Call **Les Bus du Chinonais** (tel. 02 47 46 06 60) for more info.

Buses: pl. St-Nicolas (tel. 02 41 51 11 87). Facing the river, take a left at Jackson Burger; the station is in the 2nd square. To Angers only (7 per day, 1½hr., 44F).

Public Transportation: Buses Saumur (tel. 02 41 51 11 87) leave from pl. Roosevelt Mon.-Sat. 7am-7:30pm. 7F. Office to the right of pl. Roosevelt (facing the river). Open Mon.-Fri. 9am-noon and 1:45pm-6pm, Sat. 9am-noon and 2-5pm.

Bike Rental: Camping Municipal, on Ile d'Offard (tel. 02 41 67 45 00) rents 10-speeds for 40F per ½-day, 60F per day, and 280F per week; passport deposit. Or try **Cycles Carlos,** 57, quai Mayaud, (tel. 02 41 67 69 32), on the road to the mushroom *caves.* 10-speeds 65F, mountain bikes 85F per day. Passport deposit.

Laundromat: 12, rue Maréchal Leclerc. Wash 16F. Dry 2F per 6min. Takes 2F and 10F coins. Open daily 7am-9:30pm. Also at the campgrounds on the Ile d'Offard.

English Books: Librairie du Val de Loire, 46, rue d'Orléans (tel. 02 41 40 16 60), has a large selection of classics. Open Tues.-Fri. 9am-noon and 1:45-7pm, Sat. 9am-12:30pm and 2-7pm, Mon. 3-6:30pm. July-Aug. closed Mon. V, MC.

Medical Assistance: Centre Hospitalier, 7, rue Seigneur (tel. 02 41 53 25 00). **Emergency (SAMU)** tel. 15.

Police: rue Montesquieu (tel. 02 41 51 04 32). **Emergency** tel. 17.

Post Office: rue Volney (tel. 02 41 51 08 05). **Currency exchange.** Photocopies. Address poste restante to "Saumur Volney" (**postal code:** 49413), or it will go to the main office (tel. 02 41 50 13 00), ½hr. out of town. Volney branch open Mon.-Fri. 8am-6:30pm, Sat. 8am-noon. **Branch office** across from the *gare.*

ACCOMMODATIONS AND CAMPING

You could easily see Saumur in a day, but why not loiter in wine and mushroom heaven? The fungi and fermented grape juice will leave you lusting for more but, before running off to the *caves,* reserve your room; in summer, tourists pop up like toadstools. The town's magic seems to have rubbed off on the hostel prices and inexpensive hotels are scarce. If there's no room in the inn, try Angers or Tours.

Auberge de Jeunesse (HI)/Centre International de Séjour, rue de Verden (tel. 02 41 67 45 00; fax 02 41 67 37 81), on Ile d'Offard, between station and tourist office. Large, modern hostel next to a 4-star campsite in a shady spot along the sluggish Loire. Incomparable view of the brightly lit château at night. Helpful multilingual staff and a swimming pool (15F). TV, pinball, laundry facilities. Reception open 8am-10pm. Lockout 10am-5pm (winter only). Key deposit 20F. Sheets and breakfast included. 8-berth rooms 82F, 2-berths 105F. V, MC, AmEx.

Le Canter, pl. de la Sénatorerie (tel. 02 41 50 37 88), in nearby St-Hilaire. Twenty-min. walk from town, or take bus "B" (direction: St-Hilaire, to "Sénatorerie"). Airy, bright rooms with gleaming white bed covers. Eight rooms without shower (110F), 12 with shower (130F). Breakfast 22F. Reservations are essential.

Hôtel de Londres, 48, rue d'Orléans (tel. 02 41 51 23 98; fax 02 41 51 12 63). Excellent location in the *centre ville,* near Monoprix. Statuesque 19th-century marble staircase leads to the reception desk—but the price isn't *too* bad. Bright, spacious rooms with cable TV and showers 160-330F. Breakfast 32-37F. V, MC.

Camping: Camping Municipal de l'Ile d'Offard (tel. 02 41 67 45 00), next to hostel on Ile d'Offard, at end of rue Verden. Free pool. Washing machines, tennis courts, and snack shop. 256 pitches, many with spectacular views. June-Aug. 26F50 per person; Sept.-May 21F50 per person. 45F50 per tent; 35F in off-season. Electricity 17-19F. Reception open 8am-10pm. Open Jan. 16-Dec. 14. **Camping Municipal Dampierre** (tel. 02 41 67 87 99), a 10-min. bus ride southeast along D947. Take bus 16 or D (direction: Dampierre, 7F) from Saumur's train station. 15F per person, 8F per tent, 8F per car. Open June-Sept. 15.

FOOD

At **Au Petit Duc,** 3-5, rue du Puits Neuf (tel. 02 41 51 26 20), the 49F *menu* tradition lives on in the form of mushroom *galette,* fruit crêpe, ice cream and *balée* (hard-edged cider) designed to tempt even the most persnickety stomach. One can dine *al fresco* on the terrace by the fountain (open 7am-11pm; V, MC). After a rough day sampling mushrooms and wine, make your way to **Le Relais,** 31, quai Mayaud (tel. 02 41 67 75 20), a bar that serves over 30 regional wines by the glass, accompanied by local specialties. Waiters will explain the unique features of each vintage. The wide terrace, with its stucco walls and red geraniums, is a delicious setting in which to relish the Loire Valley's delicate flavors. Try duck *terrine, rillettes* (shredded pork), *escargots* in mushrooms, and *foie gras,* all for under 100F (open Mon.-Fri. noon-2pm and 6-11pm, Sat. 6-11pm; reservations recommended). At **Le 30 Fevrier,** 9, pl. de la Républic (tel. 02 41 51 12 45), add a day to your life with healthy salads (32-50F), pizza (31-57F), and vegetarian casserole (40F). Bright, cheery, and filled with artwork. (Open Mon.-Sat. noon-2pm, 7-10:30pm, Sun. 7-10:30pm. V, MC.)

A small, fresh **produce market** fills pl. de la République and av. de Gaulle every Thursday morning. On Saturday mornings, a larger **outdoor market** flows between **pl. de la République** and **pl. St-Pierre.** The **Monoprix** supermarket is well-located, two blocks straight from the bridge on rue Franklin D. Roosevelt (tel. 02 41 83 54 54; open Mon.-Fri. 9am-7:30pm, Sat. 8:45am-7:40pm. V, MC). While the town sleeps Sunday away, head towards pl. St-Pierre and its offshoots for light fare and drinks.

Wine and Mushrooms

If a meal in Saumur whets your appetite for *les vins* and *les champignons,* you may want to head to the dark, damp sources of such delicacies. Prized since the 12th century, when Plantagenêt kings took their favorite casks with them to England, Saumur wines have tempted many a taster. The tourist office has extensive information about *dégustations* and *cave* visits. Bike, bus, foot or car are the only ways to reach the *caves*. Take Bus B to St-Hilaire, a roundabout located 10 to 15 minutes. (1hr. by foot) from the *centre ville,* but don't get stranded—the bus does not run on Sundays. Either way, the beautiful ride winds along the Loire. Signs and ads will direct you to impressive *caves* and free tastings. Follow them to the chic **Bouvet-Ladubey,** which charges 5F for an extensive tour of its facility, which includes an art gallery (wines by the bottle or case 25-300F). Watch vintners ferment a local sparkling red wine, the only one in the world. Founded in 1864, popular **Gratien et Meyer,** route de Chinon (tel. 02 41 51 01 54), stretches several km in limestone *caves* cut into the hills. Take bus D from pl. Bilange to "Beaulieu." Taste and tour for 15F, or sign up for a 50F 1-hr. wine-tasting course (open daily Sept.-July 9am-noon and 2-6pm; Aug. 9am-6pm; Nov.-Feb. only Sat.-Sun. 10-11:45am and 3-5:15pm).

Once you've drunk your fill, continue 4km down the road to the **Musée du Champignon** (tel. 02 41 50 31 55), where exotic fungi (and increasingly large rings of tourists) await deep inside their dank *cave* homes. Tours in French, English, and German trace the history of the mushroom, with emphasis on the growth of its industry in France, surpassed only in production by the U.S. and China (open daily Feb.-Nov. 10am-7pm; admission 38F, students 28F). The mushroom grill outside the museum serves gourmet *hors d'oeuvres* (28F cold, 36-46F warm) from noon-3pm. The **Champignonnière du Saut-aux-Loups** (tel. 02 41 51 70 30), one of the area's mushroom *caves,* is located in Montsoreau, 10km outside of Saumur on the way to Chinon. Take Anjou bus 16 from the train station to **Montsoreau.** You're not hallucinating—that really is a **2m-tall mushroom** on the hill to the right. The *caves* are at the town entrance (open daily March-mid Nov. 10am-6:30pm; admission 20F). Taste the delectable fungi on the terrace or in the *cave* itself, where cultivators serve a lunch composed entirely of mushrooms (July-Aug. Tues.-Sun. noon-2pm; June and Sept. Sun. noon-2pm; about 70-80F).

SIGHTS AND ENTERTAINMENT

The 14th-century **château** (tel. 02 41 51 30 46) stands aloof above Saumur's otherwise modest skyline. Charles V's brother, Louis I of Anjou, built this pre-Renaissance edifice as a country residence. For two centuries, Protestants studied and prospered at the château, with its large stairwells and crenelated walls. In 1685, however, the Edict of Nantes was revoked, the Protestants evicted, and the château converted to a prison. Inside, the **Musée des Arts Décoratifs** (tel. 02 41 51 30 46) has assembled an interesting collection of medieval and Renaissance painting and sculpture, 15th- and 16th-century tapestries, and brightly decorated *faïence* (stoneware). One small sculpture, a 16th-century rendition of St. Antoine, was meant to be particularly realistic;

the artist used mice teeth in the saint's mouth and glass eyes in his sculpted sockets to achieve the proper effect. The horse-crazy **Musée du Cheval** upstairs, with bridles, bits, horseshoes, saddles, and even horse skeletons, will appeal mostly to equestrians. (Château and museums open daily June-Sept. 9am-6pm; until 10pm Wed. and Sat. in July-Aug.; April-May 9:30am-noon and 2-5:30pm; Oct.-March Wed.-Mon. 9:30am-noon and 2-5:30pm. Admission 33F, students 25F.) On certain Mondays, Thursdays, and Fridays in July, the château organizes a **son et lumière** with a twist. Eighty actors appear in pl. St-Pierre at 9:30pm and, in a carnival atmosphere, lead the public up to the château where they reenact medieval festivities and mysteries with the help of the audience (10pm at the château). Also within the château is the **Musée de la Figurine-Jouet** (tel. 02 41 67 39 23), a collection of 20,000 toy soldiers. Here, Joan of Arc charges against the English; nearby, perfect brigades of French cavalry stand smartly at attention (open daily July 15-Sept. 15 9:30am-1pm and 3-6:30pm; April-June and Sept. 10:30am-noon and 2:30-6pm; admission 12F).

Saumur is famous for its equestrian associations. One of the most notable of these, the 18th-century military training facility **Ecole de Cavalerie,** rue d'Alsace (tel. 02 41 83 93 06), right off rue d'Orléans, houses a **museum** of riding uniforms and paraphernalia (open Sept.-July Tues.-Thurs. and Sun. 9am-noon and 2-5pm, Sat. 2-5pm; free). The spectacular **Cadre Noir** riding tradition is taught within the civilian **Ecole Nationale d'Equitation** (tel. 02 41 53 50 50; fax 02 41 67 63 08), on rue de Marson in nearby St-Hilaire-St-Florent. The Ecole's palatial 19th-century grounds are 15 minutes (by car or bus D to "Ecole d'Equitation") from the center of town. Tradition demands unwavering obedience from the horses and irreproachable decorum from the riders, who have followed the dictates of M. Cordier, the first master-in-chief, since 1825, donning "black dress decorated with gold, and 'lampion' hats worn ready for battle." April to September, the school offers guided visits. (Visits with a peek at equestrian drills begin from 9:30-10:30am Tues.-Sat. and last 1½hr.; visits without performances offered from 2:30-4pm Mon.-Sat. and last 1hr. Morning admission 30F, students 20F. Afternoon admission 20F, students 15F). In late July, the cavalry school and the local tank school join forces in the celebrated annual **Carrousel.** After two hours of graceful equestrian jumping and stunts, the spectacle degenerates into a three-hour motorcycle show and dusty tank parade (admission 50-150F). Saumur annually hosts dozens of (often free) international equestrian events. Call the tourist office to see if you can catch one while you're in town.

Near the Ecole d'Equitation on rue de l'Abbaye, the **Musée du Masque Jules César** (tel. 02 41 50 75 26) displays a fabulous collection of carnival masks in thematic scenes. (Open daily April-Oct. 15 10am-12:30pm and 2:30-6:30pm; Oct. 16-March Sat.-Sun. 9am-noon and 2-6pm. Admission 25F, children 15F.) On a different note, the **Musée des Blindés (tank museum)** on rue Beaurepaire near the Eglise St-Nicolas (tel. 02 41 53 06 99) gathers 500 tanks, 45 of which are on display. The tanks are accompanied by a documentary (in French) and a show with real French soldiers driving real French tanks like bumper cars (open daily 9am-noon and 2-6pm; admission 20F).

Eight km out of town in **Turquant,** in the direction of the wine and mushroom *caves,* the **Musée des Pommes Tapées** (tel. 02 41 51 48 30) gives demonstrations of the ancient tradition of dehydrating apples. The resulting fermented beverage was especially popular with the British Royal Navy in the 19th century. Nearby, visitors can marvel at the fantastic **troglodytic cliff homes,** where Frenchmen continue to live a *vie sauvage.* (Museum open daily July 10am-noon and 2:30-6:30pm; Aug.-June same hours, closed Mon.; admission 24F, children free.)

The **Théâtre de Saumur** (tel. 02 41 83 30 85), next to the tourist office, hosts everything from *galas de danse* to jazz and classical concerts in its 19th-century hall. The **International Festival of Military Music** bugles here in late June and early July. Call the theater or the tourist office for further insights. If you prefer your music a bit less regimented, **Le Blues Rock Magazine,** 7, rue de la Petite Bilange (tel. 02 41 50 41 69), might be your spot. Live concerts from mellow jazz to uproarious rock nightly 6:30-9:30pm, followed by dancing from 11pm-4am (cover 40-50F; drinks 25-30F;

open May-Sept. daily; Oct.-April Tues.-Sun; V, MC). **L'Ascot Bar-Club,** 15, rue Molière (tel. 02 41 67 77 55), behind the theater and tourist office, is open Mon.-Sat. until 4am (karaoke nights Tues. and Fri., piano bar Fri.-Sat.; V, MC).

■ Near Saumur: Fontevraud

The Abbaye de Fontevraud (tel. 02 41 51 71 41) has left nine centuries of visitors in awe of its beauty and power and the recent extensive renovation efforts assure its radiance well into the future. Founded on 35 acres of Loire Valley soil in 1101 by Robert d'Arbissel as a progressive holy community for both women and men, Fontevraud was ruled for many years by an abbess. It was known until the Revolution as a place of refuge for women of all classes in dire straits—reforming prostitutes, betrothal-escaping princesses, and abused wives—such as Eleanor of Aquitaine and her daughter Joanna. The spectacular **kitchen,** which once served 1000 members of this thriving community daily, gives an idea of the size of the abbey at its height. Sixteen of the 36 abbesses between 1115 and 1792 were of royal blood, many with egos to match. 16th-century Abbess Renée de Bourbon ordered her portrait painted onto an existing tableau under the arched ceilings of the **Salle Capitulaire.** Never mind that this tableau showed scenes from the life of Jesus, 1500 years earlier. Later abbesses demanded the same treatment and today Jesus holds counsel, not with Mary Magdalene, but with seven abbesses of Fontevraud (note the misplaced foot in the right-hand corner of the mural depicting the Judas kiss). The Abbey's function as a facility of reform took a different form as it became, from 1804 to 1963, one of the most important prisons in France.

The abbey holds the remains of the conquering Plantagenêts, including Eleanor, her beloved son Richard the Lionheart, and his father, King Henry II. Polychrome figures—colors faded and impact undiminished—depict each ruler in quiet repose in the abbey church. Their serene expressions seem to reveal a blissful ignorance of the controversy surrounding their tombs. The original figures were destroyed during the Revolution and the British government repeatedly sought the transfer of the royal remains to Westminster, but in vain. The Plantagenêts, the French maintain, were dukes of Anjou first, kings of England second. Gregorian chants on assorted summer evenings. Ask for details. (Abbey open daily June-3rd Sunday in Sept. 9am-7pm; Sept. 18-Oct. 31 9:30am-12:30pm and 2-6pm; Nov. 2-Mar. 31 9am-12:30pm and 2-5:30pm or dusk. Admission 28F, students 18F. 1hr. tours in French and English.) Four **buses** a day make the 14km jaunt east from Saumur to Fontevraud. Take bus 16 from the train station (40min., 12F).

Between Saumur and Fontevraud, in **Le Coudray-Macouard,** persists another ancient industry of the Loire region: **silkworm breeding.** Before the French Revolution, silks from the Loire Valley were world renowned and today the tradition continues at **La Magnanerie du Coudray** (tel. 02 41 67 91 24). From mid-May to mid-Oct., visitors can tour the mulberry plantation and investigate the activities of cocoons, moths, and delicate silkworms (open daily 10am-6pm; admission 22F).

■ Angers

From behind the massive, imposing walls of their château in Angers, the Dukes of Anjou ruled over the surrounding territory and an island across the Channel from France. The 13th-century château and its walls remain exceptionally well preserved, though the rest of the dukes' once-verdant valley has been supplanted by acres of cafés, shops, museums, and gardens—in short, a bustling city of 220,000. In the *centre ville,* café-lined streets proudly link a remarkable array of museums. With 25,000 college students, Angers offers inexpensive restaurants and a youthful atmosphere that keeps the town wide awake well into the night. Two extraordinary tapestries, crafted in the 14th and 20th centuries, provide more than an excuse to visit. If neither the ancient nor the contemporary arts stimulate you, the city that once ruled Western Europe is still a useful rail hub.

ORIENTATION AND PRACTICAL INFORMATION

To reach the château and tourist office, exit the train station onto rue de la Gare. Turn right at the second rotary, **pl. de la Visitation,** onto rue Talot. At the traffic light, a left onto bd. du Roi-René leads to the château at **pl. Kennedy**. Turn your head right and *voilà!*—the **tourist office,** across from the château. To hit the *centre ville,* walk straight past the tourist office onto rue Toussaint, which leads to **place du Ralliement,** the center of town. Go left, and one block down is rue St-Laud, the pedestrian-only zone of shops, *pâtisseries,* and cafés galore. The youth hostel is 20 minutes away by bus from either pl. Kennedy or pl. Ralliement. It's one heck of a walk, so do your best to catch public transport.

Tourist Office: pl. Kennedy (tel. 02 41 23 51 11; fax 02 41 23 51 10), across the street from the château. The staff organizes trips to châteaux, reserves rooms, sells tickets to local events, and changes money for a 20F fee. The rates, posted each day, are fair. Also has a free list of area restaurants. Open Mon.-Sat. 9am-7pm, Sun. 10am-1pm and 3-6pm; Oct.-May Mon.-Sat. 9am-12:30pm and 2-6:30pm.

Money: Along bd. Foch and bd. Bressoneau. From pl. du Ralliement, follow rue d'Alsace and go left on bd. de la Résistance for good rates at **Banque de France,** 13, pl. Mendes-France (tel. 02 41 24 25 00). Open Mon.-Fri. 8:45am-12:15pm and 1:30-3:30pm. Also try **Crédit Commercial de France,** 74, bd. Foch (tel. 02 41 88 86 98), on the corner of bd. du Roi-René. Open Mon.-Fri. 8:30am-5pm.

Trains: rue de la Gare (tel. 08 36 35 35 35). Trains to: Saumur (10 per day, 30min., 54F); Tours (7 per day, 1hr., 82F); Orléans (3 direct per day, 2¼hr., 138F); Nantes (26 per day, 45min., 70F); and Paris-Austerlitz (12 per day, 2¾hr., 229F). **Lockers** 15-20F. Open daily 8am-7:45pm.

Buses: *Gare routière,* pl. de la République (tel. 02 41 88 59 25) To: Saumur (lines 5, 10, and 11; 3 daily, 1 on Sun., 1½hr., 44F) and Rennes (line 20; 2 per day, 3hr., 92F; in winter Mon. and Fri.- Sun. only). Open Mon.-Sat. 6:15am-7:15pm.

Public Transport: Local buses (tel. 02 41 33 64 64) leave from pl. Kennedy or pl. Ralliement and run in all directions from about 6am-8pm, depending on the line. Night buses run to a limited number of places 8pm-midnight. A ride costs 6F.

Taxis: Anjou Taxi (tel. 02 51 87 65 00). 24hr.

Bike Rentals: Anjou VTT Loisir, 2, sq. de la Penthière (*centre de l'horloge;* tel. 02 41 73 83 77). 10-speeds and *VTTs* 50F per ½-day, 80F per day, 150F per weekend. Passport or 1300F deposit. Open Tues.-Sat. 9am-noon and 2:15-7pm, Sun. 2:15-7pm. **Gabillard,** 2, rue J. Perrin (tel. 02 41 88 21 69). *VTTs* 90F per day. Passport or 1000F deposit. Open Tues.-Sat. 9am-12:30pm and 2:15-6:30pm.

English Books: Richer, 6-8, rue Chapponière (tel. 02 41 88 62 79), off pl. St. Croix. Second floor has novels. Offers student discounts. Open 10am-7pm. V, MC.

Laundromat: Laverie du Cygne, pl. de la Visitation. 22F wash, dry 3F per 5min. Open 8am-9pm. **L'averie des Halles,** 15 rue Plantagenêt (tel. 02 41 24 01 83). 22F wash, 25F dry. Open Oct.-May 8am-9pm, June-Sept. 7am-9pm.

Hospital: Centre Hospitalier, 1, av. de l'Hôtel-Dieu (tel. 02 41 35 36 37), across the river and to the right along quai Monge. **Medical emergency** tel. 15.

Police: Gendarmerie, 6bis pl. Freppel (tel. 02 41 88 53 80), or police muncipale, 4, rue des Ursules (tel. 02 41 88 16 16). **Emergency** tel. 17.

Post Office: 1, rue Franklin Roosevelt (tel. 02 41 20 81 81). **Currency exchange.** Poste restante mail should be addressed "Angers-Ralliement," or else it will be carried off to the rue Bamako office, a 30min. walk south of town. Open Mon.-Fri. 9am-6:15pm, Sat. 9am-noon. **Postal code:** 49052.

ACCOMMODATIONS AND CAMPING

Angers becomes crowded in July and August. Though inconvenient, the hostel is huge and usually has room. Many hotels close between noon and 6pm on Sundays.

Auberge de Jeunesse Darwin (HI), 3, rue Darwin (tel. 02 41 72 00 20; fax 02 41 48 51 91). Take bus 8 (direction: Beaucouzé, 20min.) to "CFA." If you miss the last bus at 7:20pm, you can take the night bus 1/S (direction Belle-Baille/Lac de Maine) to

Gaumont from pl. Ralliement until 12:10am; consult the bus maps posted at most bus stops. Green hallways and spartan but comfortable 2- and 3-bed rooms. 320 beds. Kitchen facilities. Members 58F. Breakfast 9F50.

Centre d'Accueil du Lac de Maine, 49, av. du Maine (tel. 02 41 22 32 10; fax 02 41 22 32 11). Take bus 6 to "Accueil Lac de Maine." A lakeside setting and extensive sporting facilities, even a golf course, justify the 20-min. ride. Call ahead to make sure there's space; school groups often book the *centre* in summer. Singles 104F. Doubles 72F per person. Quads 61F per person. Breakfast 18F.

Royal Hôtel, rue d'Iéna (tel. 02 41 88 30 25), off pl. de la Visitation. Family-run hotel almost treats you like one of their own. There's even something here called an elevator that helps weary backpack-laden bones to 40 immaculate, spacious rooms. Firm mattresses. TVs in most rooms. Singles 100-145F, with shower 170-195F. Doubles 130-160F, with shower 190-225F. Breakfast 28F. V, MC, AmEx.

Hôtel des Lices, 25, rue des Lices (tel. 02 41 87 44 10), near the château. 13 clean, insect-free, small rooms with pink coverlets 110-125F, with shower and toilet 160F. Breakfast 22F. Shower 10F. Don't be afraid of the name; it's "lists," as in jousting—which may come in handy to get a room here in summer.

La Coupe d'Or, 5, rue de la Gare (tel. 02 41 88 45 02). Charming owner maintains 18 small, comfy rooms with TV. Singles and doubles without shower 85-140F, with shower 160-240F. Shower 15F. Breakfast 25F. V, MC.

Camping: Camping du Lac de Maine (tel. 02 41 73 05 03; fax 02 41 22 32 11), next to Centre d'Accueil on CD 111, Route de Pruniers. Camp on a sandy lakeside beach. 90F per 3 people, tent, and car; 30F per person. Open March-Nov.

FOOD

Angers is a sweet town to eat in; try the rich chocolates made with *cointreau,* and *quernons,* blue chocolates found only in Angers. Its student population and location away from major tourist stomping grounds bring cheap and international fare, especially on **rue St-Laud. Bd. Foch** displays slightly more expensive, more mainstream options. There is a **covered market** (tel. 02 41 86 01 13) with inexpensive produce and baked goods in the basement of **Les Halles,** at rue Plantagenêt behind the cathedral, down the street from pl. du Ralliement (tel. 02 41 86 01 13; open Tues.-Sat. 7am-8pm, Sun. 7am-1:30pm). The supermarkets are in the suburbs, but if you're hungry enough, the grocery store in the basement of **Galerie Lafayette,** corner of rue d'Alsace and pl. du Ralliement, offers the usual (open Sat. 9am-7pm). **Spar,** pl. de la Visitation (open Mon.-Sat. 8am-9pm, Sun. 9am-1pm; V, MC).

Restaurant des Beaux Arts, at the **Université de Clous,** 35, bd. Roi-René (tel. 02 41 88 47 38), near the tourist office, and the **Université de Belle-Beille,** bd. Lavoisier (tel. 02 41 48 45 76), near the hostel. Cafeteria open to all students with college ID. Wholesome food for an unbelievable price. Salad, *plat,* and dessert for 12F70 ticket. Open only Aug. 30-July 12 11:30am-1:30pm and 6:15-8pm.

La Martinique, 75, rue du Mail (tel. 02 41 87 22 25). Run away to the Caribbean with creole music and pictures of swaying palms. Plus, how many times will you enjoy *la cuisine martiniquaise?* 54F *menu* with green mangoes and *l'antillaise,* a plate of different seafood. Open Mon.-Sat. noon-2pm and 7-10:30pm. V, MC.

Chantegrill, 25, bd. Foch (tel. 02 41 87 00 61). Lively atmosphere, good food. 59F gets you vegetarian all-you-can-eat *buffet fraîcheur* (salads) and the *buffet douceur* (desserts). Otherwise, order the 59F *menu* with leg of lamb or beef carpaccio and the *buffet fraîcheur.* Open Mon.-Thurs. 11:45am-2:30pm and 7-11pm, Fri.-Sun. 11:45am-2:30pm and 7-11:30pm. V, MC.

Restaurant Krishna, 1bis, rue d'Iéna at pl. de la Visitation, carries vegetables (40F), chicken with raisins and coconut (51F), and a 3-course 52F lunch special. Open Tues.-Sun. noon-2:30pm, and 7-10pm. V, MC.

L'Ovibus, 3, rue d'Anjou (tel. 02 41 87 48 90), near pl. de la Visitation. Dimly lit red lamps and black silhouettes of bulls on the walls give this grill a classy feel. 52F *menu* with beef skewers or horse steak (now's your chance), plus an appetizer and dessert. 68F *menu* includes wine. Open Mon. 7-10:30pm, Tues.-Sat. noon-2:30pm and 7-10:30pm. V, MC.

SIGHTS AND ENTERTAINMENT

The awe-inspiring 101m-long **Tapisserie de l'Apocalypse** is considered the largest woven masterpiece in the world. Louis I, Duke of Anjou, ordered the tapestry in Paris in 1373 to show his brother, King Charles V, that he was his equal. Charles may have been unconvinced, but this testimony to the power of sibling rivalry is a technical masterpiece—somehow its makers managed to duplicate its images in reverse on the tapestry's back side, leaving the unfinished threads on the interior. Since it has always hung with its front facing the light, the colors of the rear face retain much of their original vividness. The *tapisserie's* narrative of the Book of Revelations is gripping stuff, too, featuring a seven-headed Satan gobbling down babies and the armies of heaven gathering to do battle. In the end, of course, Good triumphs over Evil, and the City of God descends from above.

The tapestry hangs in Angers' 15th-century **château** (tel. 02 41 87 43 47). The broad stone walls of this feudal fortress stand out as a forbidding anachronism in hectic modern Angers. St. Louis built the fortress and walls from 1228 to 1238, but René the Good, Anjou's last and greatest duke, oversaw the construction of the château itself fifty years later. René not only commanded an empire that included Sicily, Provence, and Lorraine but also found the time to pen several novels and dozens of poems. The castle narrowly escaped destruction during the wars of religion, when Henry III ordered its demolition (fortunately, his subjects had only lowered the towers about one story when he died). The structure boasts 17 towers and a 900-m long, 15-m high curtain wall surrounding the perimeter. Visitors can look down over the wall to see the former moat, which has blossomed into a colorful garden populated by deer. Climb to the top of the northernmost tower for a spectacular view of the city. Tours in French of the spartan royal lodgings leave from the château's chapel every half-hour 10am-noon and 2-5:30pm. Next to the cafeteria, a **contemporary museum** exhibits modern interpretations of the apocalypse (free). For a mere 50F, a **Billet Jumelé** (at the tourist office or individual museums) grants you admission to the château and five of the museums in Angers. (Château open daily June-Sept. 15 9am-7pm; Sept. 16-March 26 9:30am-12:30pm and 2-6pm; Dec.-Feb. 9:30am-12:30am and 2-5:30pm; March 27-May 9am-12:30pm and 2-6:30pm; closed bank holidays. Admission 32F, students 21F.)

Angers' second woven masterpiece hangs just 15 minutes across the Maine river in the **Musée Jean Lurçat,** 4, bd. Arago (tel. 02 41 24 18 45). Housed in a 12th-century hospital, the museum displays the 80m-long *Chant du Monde* (*Song of the World;* 1957-1966), a symbolic, mind-expanding journey through human destiny. Lurçat, inspired by the *Apocalypse* tapestry, abandoned his career as a painter and turned to weaving, eventually producing this *chef-d'oeuvre.* In 10 enormous panels filled with blazing colors, the tapestry explores all of life's joys and sorrows. It may sound like a tall order, but the grand scale and genius of the work leave the visitor stunned. (Artist's commentary available in English. Open daily July-Aug. 9am-6:30pm; Sept.-June Tues.-Sun. 10am-noon and 2-6pm, except bank holidays. Admission 15F.)

The **Galerie David d'Angers,** 37bis, rue Toussaint (tel. 02 41 87 21 03), houses an interesting collection of the 19th-century sculptor's work in a striking 13th-century church. A scale replica of David's masterwork for the Panthéon façade in Paris is on display, as well as many of the 30 statues he designed for city squares. Upstairs, you'll be the center of attention as busts of Gutenberg, Hugo, Goethe, George Washington, and 36 other enduring celebrities stare back at you. The **Musée des Beaux Arts,** rue du Musée (tel. 02 41 88 64 65), adjacent to the Musée David d'Angers, has an impressive collection of medieval icons and paintings by Corot, David, Pisano, Ingres, Degas, and other masters. Founded just after the French Revolution, the museum houses dozens of 18th- and 19th-century portraits. Its first floor displays contemporary works. The 16th-century **Musée Pincé,** 32bis, rue Lenepveu (tel. 02 41 88 94 27), has an eclectic collection of Greek, Roman, Egyptian, and Asiatic artifacts, and some important Japanese prints (all 3 open daily June 12-Sept. 17 9am-6:30pm; Sept. 18-June 11 Tues.-Sun. 10am-noon and 2-6pm; admission to each 10F).

Though the discos are firmly rooted in the suburbs, nightlife in Angers has not suffered much as a result. The cafés along rue St-Laud are always packed with a diverse crowds of coffee-drinkers and people-watchers. At **Le Melbourne,** 5, rue Lenepveu (tel. 02 41 87 50 98), in the *centre ville,* INXS blares as patrons suck down lagers (15-25F) and wine with gusto (open Mon.-Thurs. 8am-11:30pm, Fri.-Sat. 8am-2am; V, MC, AmEx). **Le Kent**, 7 pl. Ste-Croix (tel. 02 41 87 88 55) is *à votre service* with 50 different beers and 70 whiskies (open Mon.-Sat. 9am-2am, Sun. 4-8pm). For all-night dancing, try **Le Newyorkais**, 5 rue Maille (tel. 05 45 87 37 93), the club that never sleeps (open Sun.-Thurs. 11pm-3am, Fri. and Sat. 11pm-4am).

In July, Angers hosts the **Festival d'Anjou.** One of the largest summer theater festivals in France, it attracts renowned French comedic and dramatic troupes to perform in the château. Albert Camus once staged a play in front of a nationwide TV audience here (each show 160F, students 100F; call 02 41 88 14 14 for information).

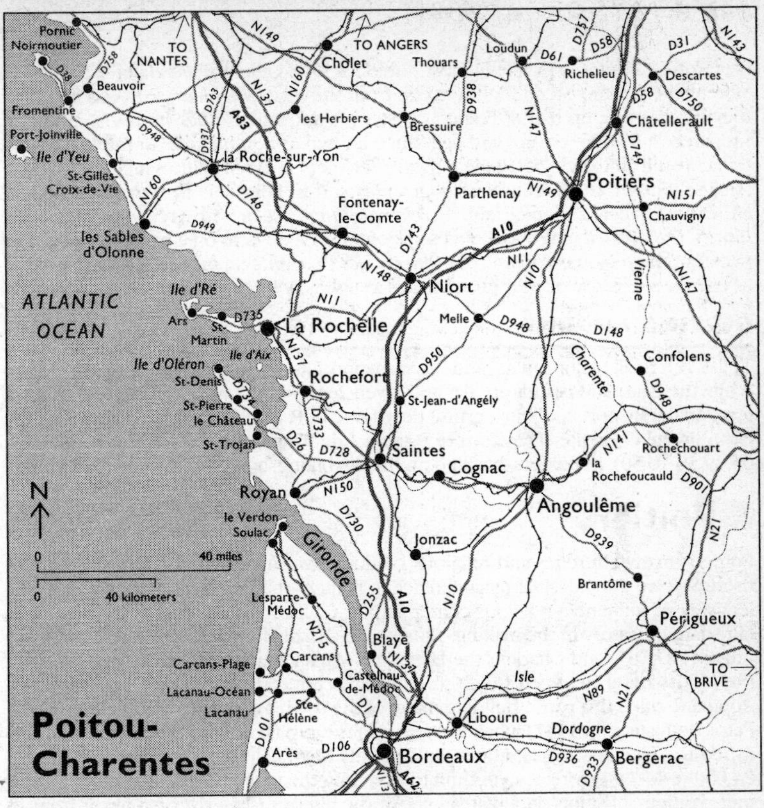

Poitou-Charentes

Though little known outside of France, Poitou-Charentes harbors sun-drenched beaches, sedate canals, craggy cliffs, fertile plains, and a rich history as an influential center of Christianity. The Côte d'Azur may be tops in topless beaches and the Loire Valley may be the king of châteaux, but no other region of France has so impressive a collection of both. Poitou-Charentes is a brilliant collage of pristine natural sights and coastal towns tucked away on the western coast of France.

With the acceptance of Christianity in the 4th century, Poitou-Charentes became entangled in Western history. In 732, Charles "the Hammer" Martel, Duke of the Franks, rebuffed Moorish attempts to claim the region. Beginning in the 11th century, thousands of pilgrims passed through the region *en route* to Santiago de Compostela. Possession of the region in the Middle Ages was tossed to the other side of the Channel with the marriage of Eleanor of Aquitaine and Henry II. Poitou-Charentes remained English during the Hundred Years' War, until Joan of Arc secured it for France. In the 17th century, after the wars of religion, the Protestants of La Rochelle sought English help against Cardinal Richelieu, who besieged the city in spite of the English fleet and relegated it to a century of obscurity. The coastal cities were revived in the 18th century when trade with Canada brought unparalleled wealth. Though coastal towns and islands still live by seafaring, tourism is now a major source of income, and beaches and campgrounds are packed all summer.

Poitou-Charentes is probably most noted for its excellent *fruits de mer* (seafood). Marennes-Oléron oysters, slightly green from the *navicule bleue* seaweed in which they grow, make up half of France's oyster production. *Moules* (mussels) are often prepared in a wine, cream, and egg sauce known as a *mouclade.* In the Marais Poitevin, you'll find rich *fricassée d'anguilles* (eels in a red wine sauce). *Escargots* (snails), known in Charentes as *cagouilles* and in Poitou as *lumas,* are prepared either with a meat-and-spice stuffing *à la saintongeaise* or with a red wine sauce *aux lumas. Cabécou,* a tangy goat cheese, is often served warm on a bed of lettuce. The nectar of the region is *cognac,* but *Pineau des Charentes,* a more affordable mixture of cognac and grape or pear juice, makes a sublimely sweet *apéritif.*

GETTING AROUND

Trains run to all major towns, and bus transport fills in the gaps. Hills rise in the east, while the coast and islands are flat and lovely for biking. You may want to renounce terrestrial transport and join a cruise down one of Poitou-Charentes' main rivers, the Clain or the Charente. The **Comité Régional de Tourisme,** 62, rue Jean Jaurès (tel. 05 49 50 10 50), in Poitiers, has info on hiking, biking, and other modes of trekking.

Poitiers

Poitiers' many churches and religious monuments—including the 4th-century Baptisère St-Jean, the oldest Christian edifice in France—harken back to days when Poitiers was an influential religious center for the Gauls. As such, the town has seen its fair share of history in the making: Clovis won a battle for Christianity over the Visigoths in AD 507, and Charles "the Hammer" Martel almost single-handedly stopped the Moors here. Between the 10th and 15th centuries, the counts of Poitou and Aquitaine ruled this roost, building many of the town's churches and the impressive Palais de Justice. In 1432, when Poitiers was the capital of France, Charles VII established the Université de Poitiers. Its students now account for a third of Poitiers' 84,000 residents, giving it a youthful buzz during the year and leaving it quiet in summer. Poitiers' position on a plateau above the viscous Clain river isolates it from its factories below. As a result, this bustling mini-metropolis retains a small-town atmosphere. If you've had enough of exploring Poitiers' past, fast-forward to **Futuroscope,** a slick theme park quickly becoming one of France's major attractions.

ORIENTATION AND PRACTICAL INFORMATION

Poitiers, a major stop on the Paris-Bordeaux TGV line, fits snugly between train tracks to the west and a semi-circular stretch of the Clain river to the east. The city pulses around the stores, cinemas, and cafés near **pl. Maréchal Leclerc** and **pl. Charles de Gaulle,** three blocks farther north. Buses run from opposite the train station to the central Hôtel de Ville. To get to the **tourist office** from the *gare,* go straight and climb bd. Solférino as it curves uphill to the left. Ascend the long staircase and take rue Arthur Ranc past the post office. At pl. Leclerc, turn left. Take the first left onto rue des Grandes Ecoles; the tourist office will be on your left (10min.).

Tourist Information: Tourist Office, 8, rue des Grandes Ecoles (tel. 05 49 41 21 24; fax 05 49 88 65 84). Free, clearly labeled maps, brochures, lists of hotels, campgrounds, and restaurants. Guided tours (in English upon request, 2-2½hr.) vary daily (July-Sept. 10am and 3pm; 35F, under 25 20F). Info on outdoor activities in the region. Open July-Aug. Mon.-Fri. 9am-7pm, Sat. 10am-7pm, Sun. 9:45am-1pm and 2:45-6pm; Sept.-June Mon.-Sat. 9am-noon and 1:30-6pm. For current info on events, snag the free **Affiche. Service Ville d'Art et d'Histoire,** 1, pl. de la Cathédrale (tel. 05 49 52 54 65), has many of the same brochures.

Money: Banks and 24-hr. **ATMs** are everywhere you look on pl. Maréchal Leclerc.

Trains: bd. du Grand Cerf (tel. 08 36 35 35 35). **Trains** to: Paris (2 per day, 2½hr., 197F); Bordeaux (3 per day, 2hr., 161F); La Rochelle (5 per day, 1¾hr., 105F); Tours (8 per day, 1¼hr., 80F). **TGVs** to: Paris (15 per day, 1½hr., 240-297F); Bordeaux (9 per day, 1¾hr., 168F); La Rochelle (3 per day, 1¼hr., 112F); Tours (13 per day, 1hr., 94F). **Lockers** 30F. **Futuroscope** desk open Mon.-Thurs. and Sat. 8am-8pm, Fri. and Sun. 8am-9pm. SNCF office open Mon. 3:45am-9:45pm, Tues.-Thurs. 5am-9:45pm, Fri. 5am-11:30pm, Sat. 6am-9:45pm, Sun. 6:25am-11:30pm.

Public Transportation: STP buses crisscross the city. Timetables at the tourist office and train station. Buses run 7am-8:30pm. Night buses on 2 *centre ville* lines run until 11:30pm. Few lines operate on Sun. Tickets valid 1hr. 7F50.

Taxis: Radio Taxis, 22, rue Carnot, or in front of the train station (tel. 05 49 88 12 34). 3F per km during the day, 4F35 per km 7pm-7am. 24hr.

Bike Rental: Cyclamen, 49, rue Arsène Orillard (tel. 05 49 88 13 25). 10-speeds 55F per day, 200F per week. Mountain bikes 85F per day, 320F per week. Deposit 500-1000F or passport. Open Tues.-Sat. 8:30am-12:30pm and 3-7pm.

Laundromat: 2bis, rue Carnot. Wash 18F, dry 2F per 4min. Open 7am-8:30pm.

English Books: Librairie de l'Université, 70, rue Gambetta (tel. 05 49 41 02 05), off pl. M. Leclerc. Good selection of imports. Open daily 9am-7:30pm. V, MC.

Youth Information: Centre Information Jeunesse (CIJ), 64, rue Gambetta (tel. 05 46 60 68 68), near pl. Leclerc. Help with jobs, lodgings, hitching, activities, etc. **Budget travel office.** Open Mon.-Fri. 9am-7pm, Sat. 10am-7pm.

Women's Center: Centre d'Information les Droits des Femmes, 53, rue Carnot (tel. 05 49 88 04 41). Open Mon. and Wed. 2-5pm, Tues. and Thurs. 1-6pm.

Crisis Lines: SOS Amitié (tel. 05 49 45 71 71), when you pine for a pal.

Hospital: 15, rue Hôtel Dieu (tel. 05 49 44 44 44). Cross pont Neuf, follow rue de la Pierre Levée 4 blocks, turn right on av. du 11 Novembre and then left on av. J. Coeur. The hospital is on the right.

Medical Assistance: Ambulance tel. 05 49 55 99 66. **Medical emergency** tel. 15.

Police: 38, rue de la Marne (tel. 05 49 60 60 00). **Emergency** tel. 17.

Post Office: rue des Ecossais (tel. 05 49 55 52 35). Poste restante. **Currency exchange.** Open Mon.-Fri. 8:30am-7pm, Sat. 8:30am-noon. **Postal code:** 86000.

ACCOMMODATIONS AND CAMPING

The hostel and campgrounds are far from the city center, but it isn't hard to find a reasonable hotel downtown. Those clustered around the train station are respectable, although clients may receive unsolicited lullabies from the trains chugging through Poitiers' busy station. Call ahead in July and August.

Auberge de Jeunesse (HI), 17, rue de la Jeunesse (tel. 05 49 58 03 05). Take bus 3 from station (direction: Pierre Loti) to "Cap Sud" (Mon.-Sat. every 30min. until 7:50pm, 7F50). Walking, turn right at station and follow bd. du Pont Achard to av. de la Libération. Take right-hand fork to rue B. Pascal. Rue de la Jeunesse is on the right (3km, 35min.). Spotless 3- to 4-bed rooms, showers, and toilets; great mattresses. Swarming school groups. 65F; non-members under 26 72F, over 26 105F. Sheets free. Breakfast 20F. Dinner 50F. Reception Mon.-Sat. 8-10am, noon-2pm, and 7-11pm; Sun. 8-10am and 7-11pm. No curfew, no lockout—go nuts!

Hôtel Jules Ferry, 27, rue Jules Ferry (tel. 05 49 37 80 14; fax 05 49 53 15 02), near Eglise St-Hilaire on a quiet, residential street. From station, turn right along bd. du pont Achard, walk past the Esso station to the second traffic light and climb stairs to the left. At the top, turn right onto rue Jules Ferry. Or, from pl. Leclerc, go down rue Carnot, take a left on rue Cesve and left onto Jules Ferry. Kind anglophone owners; immaculate, cheery, sherbet-colored rooms with phones. Singles and doubles 140F, with shower 160F, with shower and toilet 190F. Shower 15F. Breakfast 25F. Closed Sun. 1-7:30pm. V, MC.

L'Alsace Lorraine, 6, rue du Petit Bonneveau (tel. 05 49 41 25 83), well-situated in *centre ville.* From pl. Leclerc, go down rue Carnot, take the first left at Ibis Hôtel, then the first right. Quiet, spacious rooms; a bit musty. Singles and doubles 125-130F, with shower 180F. Shower 20F. Breakfast 25F. Open Jan. 3-Dec. 24.

Le Printania, 139, bd. du Grand Cerf (tel. 05 49 58 20 15), across from the station. Large and conveniently located. Slightly dim and a bit noisy from trains, but clean. Ask for a room away from the *gare.* Singles and doubles 110-124F, with shower 140F, with bathroom 152F, with TV and bathroom 180F. Breakfast 23-27F.

Camping: Le Porteau, rue de Porteau (tel. 05 49 41 44 88), 2km out of town. Take bus 7 (direction: Centre de Gros; 7F50) and ask to be dropped off *"devant le terrain"* (in front of the field). A lot of grass and clean bathrooms. 11F per person, 12F50 per site, 13F per car. Electricity 8F. Open April-Sept. **Camping St-Benoît,** route de Passelourdin (tel. 05 49 88 48 55), 5km from Poitiers. Take bus 2 (direction: Les Sables) from the station; at "Les Sables," change to bus 10 and go to "St-Benoît." 11F per person, 12F per site, 12F per car. Open April-Sept.

FOOD

Agneau from nearby Montmarillon, *chèvre,* macaroons, and the wines of Haut-Poitou can be found on Poitiers *menus.* The problem is finding a *menu* within reach—most hover around 100-200F. Many hotel bars post adequate 4-course *menus* at 55-60F. Inexpensive pizzerias lie between the cathedral and Notre-Dame-la-Grande on rue de la Cathédrale. There is a **market** at **Les Halles,** on pl. Charles de Gaulle (open Tues., Thurs., and Sat. 7am-1pm). On Saturday, the market expands beyond your wildest dreams. Good ol' **Monoprix supermarket,** rue des Cordeliers, at rue du Marché Notre-Dame fills you up for less (open Mon.-Sat. 9am-7:30pm).

Le Cul de Paille, off pl. Leclerc (tel. 05 49 41 07 35). Locals scribble graffiti on the wall (encouraged by the staff) and chow down on excellent *poitevin* cuisine. Expensive, but worth it. 4-course *menu* 98F. Open daily 9am-10pm. V, MC.

Le Chantegrill (tel. 05 49 01 74 00), pl. Maréchal Leclerc. Classy place offers a meat-and-fish dish with a buffet of veggies and cold plates *à volonté* (all you can eat, baby!) for an unheard-of 60F. Open daily 11:30am-2pm and 7-11pm. V, MC.

Le Poitevin, 76, rue Carnot (tel. 05 49 88 35 04). Regional dishes on an 85F *menu* popular with locals. Open Aug.-July 12 Mon.-Sat. noon-2pm and 7-10pm.

Le Cappuccino, 5, rue de l'Université (tel. 05 49 88 27 39). Generous pizzas (33-46F), pasta (33-48F), and salads (20-40F) make this inexpensive but elegant restaurant a local favorite. Open Tues.-Sat. noon-2pm and 7-11pm. V, MC.

SIGHTS AND ENTERTAINMENT

With so many steeples dotting the skyline, it's no wonder that Poitiers is called *La Ville des Eglises.* The city's impressive places of worship are open from 9am to 6pm unless otherwise noted; wander the city and visit a few. On pl. Charles de Gaulle in the *centre ville,* marvel at the façade of 12th-century **Notre-Dame-la-Grande** and its newly renovated interior. Colorful columns, frescoes, and a Batmobile organ lend an inviting, personal touch, in contrast to the austere Plantagenêt-Romanesque style of most churches of the period. The **Cathédrale St-Pierre,** pl. de la Cathédrale at the end of rue de la Cathédrale, built with a grant from Eleanor of Aquitaine, rises as the leader of a gaggle of sites that represent centuries of human ingenuity. Shrieking gargoyles above the main portal guard the cathedral's towering 18th-century organ and brilliant stained-glass windows. Above the portal, irreverent pigeons hop from heaven to hell and back across the Last Judgment (open daily 8am-7pm).

Glare into the future at the **Espace Mendès France** (tel. 05 49 41 56 25). Next to St-Pierre and a millennium younger, it uses a *son et lumière* to bring expositions to life. Zone out in front of the 12 TV screens spouting movies and MTV. The planetarium projects Poitiers' night sky while the Laserium does wacky things with light (open Tues.-Fri. 10am-7pm, Sat.-Sun. 2-7pm; admission 20F, students 12F; planetarium 32F, students 24F; Laserium 42F, students 32F).

The 4th-century **Batistère St-Jean,** the oldest Christian building in France, squats on rue Jaurès next to St-Pierre. Excavations have uncovered older aqueducts beneath the church. The structure houses friezes and the sarcophagi of early Roman Christians (open daily July-Aug. 10am-12:30pm and 2-6pm; Sept. and April-June same hours but closed Tues.; Nov.-March Wed.-Mon. 2:30-4:30pm; admission 4F).

Next to the baptistery, the **Musée Ste-Croix,** 61, rue St-Simplicien (tel. 05 49 41 07 53), contains relics from Poitiers' Bronze Age and Roman settlements. Thrill to the sight of immense chunks of a wall in a pit. The museum also carries a strong selection of medieval to modern sculpture and 17th- to 20th-century paintings.

Two blocks down the hill from the cathedral, on rue Ste-Radegonde, awaits the 17th-century **Eglise Ste-Radegonde,** with a poster display recounting the traumatic life of its saint. Radegonde was a 6th-century Thuringian princess whose family was slaughtered by the Franks when she was nine years old. Forced to marry Clotaire, king of the Gauls, Radegonde fled and begged a priest to allow her to become a nun. When he wavered, she demanded, "You would fear this man more than you fear God?" The chagrined priest consecrated her; and at her request, the spurned Clotaire built an abbey in Poitiers near the site of this church. Descend into the cool, damp **crypt** below the altar for a glimpse of Radegonde's relics, as well as those of the abbey's first abbess, Agnès. Near pl. Leclerc, the **Musée des Chièvres,** 9, rue Victor Hugo (tel. 05 49 41 42 21), holds Renaissance and 19th-century French and Italian paintings (open Mon. and Wed.-Fri. 10am-noon and 1-5pm, Sat.-Sun. 10am-noon and 2-6pm; admission to both 15F, under 18 free).

Your ticket will also grant you a gander at the mysterious **Hypogée des Dunes,** 101, rue du Père-de-la-Croix (tel. 05 49 01 68 85). Topped by a Gallo-Roman chapel, the 7th-century underground church was discovered in 1878 by a Jesuit priest, Camille de la Croix. Though it now shelters rare Merovingian sculptures, inscriptions on its wall announce that the relics of 72 martyrs are housed in the Hypogée. While the bones of several women and children have surfaced, the reputed relics remain elusive. Take bus 5 (direction: St-Eloi) to "Gendarmerie," or cross the river and follow rue du Pont-Neuf for two blocks. On the left, a narrow pedestrian path (rue de la Pierre Levée) slopes up to the Hypogée (15-min. walk; open April-Sept. Tues.-Fri. 10am-noon and 1-5pm, Sat.-Sun. 10am-noon and 2-6pm; Oct.-March daily 2-6pm).

For some natural splendor, head for **Parc de Blossac,** rue de Blossac, down rue Carnot near the Clain. Fountains bubble and there's even a small animal preserve with peacocks, warthogs, and more. Perfect for a picnic or stroll with your *petit(e) ami(e).* The **Parc Animalier des Bois de Saint-Pierre,** 1km out of town along the Clain, is a leisure paradise with an animal park and fish pond, three pools, and miles of trails (open daily 9am-7pm; animal park and trails open April-Oct. Sat.-Thurs. 10am-7pm, Fri. 1:30-4:30pm; Nov.-March daily 1:30-4:30pm).

Poitiers rocks with an active club and bar scene during the school year, and with festivals all year. The people-magnets of pl. Leclerc and pl. Charles de Gaulle both have late-night cafés year round. One of the best student hangouts *du jour* is **Sherlock's Pub,** just off 17, rue Carnot (tel. 05 49 50 72 18), through the archway across from Parking Carnot. Busts of the pipe-smoking sleuth line the sleek bar (open Aug.-June Mon.-Sat. 3pm-2am). The snug but sturdy **Latex Paradis,** 157, Grand Rue (tel. 05 49 50 73 61), is a delightfully quirky gay hangout (open Tues.-Sat. 5-11pm). The best gay bar in town is **Le Georges Sand,** 25, rue St-Pierre le Puellier (tel. 05 49 55 91 58). Across from Eglise Ste-Radegonde, **La Grand' Goule,** 46, rue du Pigeon Blanc (tel. 05 49 50 41 36), is a mainstay of Poitiers nightlife; *jeunes* jump where their parents twisted (open Tues.-Sat. 11pm-4am; cover 45F with one drink).

In July and August, rock, opera, jazz, and fireworks thunder through town for the **Poitiers l'Eté** festival. Concerts, mostly free, begin around 9pm three to four nights a week. Call the tourist office or the **Maison de la Culture et des Loisirs** (tel. 05 49 41 09 22) for info. Springing into the first two weeks of May, **Le Printemps Musical de Poitiers,** 7, rue des Flageolles (tel. 05 49 41 58 94), is a harmonic convergence of concerts, exhibits, and debates (tickets 30-60F). **Rencontres Musicales de Poitiers,** 79, rue des Frères Voisin (tel. 05 49 58 42 13), features mostly classical works in biweekly concerts late October through late April (tickets 60F, under 26 45F). In early December, the **Festival du Cinéma** features films both artsy and mainstream.

■ Near Poitiers: Futuroscope

Some say that leaving Poitiers without visiting **Futuroscope** (reservations tel. 05 49 49 30 80, general info 05 49 49 30 20; fax 05 49 49 59 38) is like leaving Paris without seeing the Eiffel Tower. It's probably more like leaving Orlando without seeing EPCOT Center. This high-tech playground sports 18 attractions, including **Le Solido,** a 3-D movie that takes you to swim with sea creatures on the ocean floor off the Channel Islands; **Image Studios,** an interactive journey through 100 years of French cinema; and **Le Pavillon de la Vienne,** a humorous 3-D ride through Poitiers and the surrounding countryside on the trail of a man late for his own wedding. Jump on **Le Tapis Magique** and follow a monarch butterfly on its miraculous 3000-miles journey from Canada to Mexico. Streamlined, multilingual, and the cutting edge of information technology, Futuroscope is a sophisticated educational romp for adults and children alike. (Open daily July-Aug. 9am-midnight with free laser show; April-June 9am-7pm, later for weekend-only laser show; Sept.-Nov. 12 9am-6pm, later for weekend laser show; Nov. 13-March 9am-6pm. Admission includes access to all attractions. April-Nov. 11 160F, 2 days 290F; children under 16 125F, 2 days 225F. Nov. 15-March 135F, 260F, 105F, 185F respectively. Some children's rides require an extra 5F per turn.) Futuroscope is in a field 10km north of Poitiers, outside tiny, rapidly expanding **Chasseneuil. Buses** 16 and 17 shuttle from the Bistrot de la Gare, across the street from Poitiers' train station (14 per day, 8am-6:50pm, 30min., 7F50) and from behind the Hôtel de Ville in the *centre ville.* The last bus leaves the park at 7:45pm. Buy tickets from the driver or at the *tabac* inside the Printania Hotel. **Radio Taxis of Poitiers** (tel. 05 49 88 12 34) runs shuttles 15 times daily from the train station (40F per person roundtrip). By **car,** follow A10 (direction: Paris-Châtellerault) and take exit 18. Free parking.

Les Sables d'Olonne

Thousands flock to Les Sables every year to share sun, sweat, and sticky *beignets.* Though a steadily advancing phalanx of high rises and squadrons of sunbathers detract from Les Sables' natural beauty, the beaches are among the finest on the coast. If you're seeking solitude, skip the main beach, plage du Remblai, and head south (to the left as you face the water) to the **plage de Tanchet,** one of the few secrets left. The athletic and adventurous can head northwest to the **Forêt Domaniale d'Olonne,** where huge dunes tumble from dry woodlands to the sea. To get to the center of town from the train station, turn right and walk alongside the station. Turn right onto av. de Gaulle and follow it to pl. de la Liberté. Walk past the park on your right to arrive at small pl. du Poilu de France. From here, rue du Général Leclerc, the first street to the right, leads to the tourist office. From pl. du Poilu de France, you can also take rue de l'Hôtel de Ville on your left to the commercial pedestrian district. To get to the beach and the boardwalk (promenade Clemenceau), make a left off of Hôtel de Ville as you head away from the station.

At the **tourist office,** rue du Maréchal Leclerc (tel. 02 51 32 03 28; fax 02 51 32 84 49), the staff can outfit you with a map and suggest island trips (open June 16-Sept. 14 daily 9am-7pm; Sept. 15-June 15 Mon.-Sat. 9am-12:15pm and 2-6:30pm, Sun. 10am-noon and 3-5:30pm). **Banks** and 24-hour **ATMs** do the nasty on av. du Général de Gaulle. **Banque de France,** 6, av. du Général de Gaulle (tel. 02 51 23 81 00), is once again the best deal in town (open Mon.-Fri. 8:45am-noon and 1:30-3:30pm). Don't expect to find ATMs near the hostel in La Chaume. **Trains** rumble from the station on av. de Gaulle (tel. 08 36 35 35 35) to: La Rochelle (4 per day, 2hr., 100F); Nantes (6 per day, 1½hr., 87F); and Paris (6 TGV per day, 5½hr., 311F); all via La-Roche-sur-Yon. (**Lockers** 20-30F.) To the left of the *gare,* **Sovetours,** rue de la Bauduère (tel. 02 51 95 18 71; open Mon.-Fri. 8:30am-12:30pm and 2:30-6:30pm, Sat. 9-11:30am), sends **buses** to La Rochelle (1 per day, 2hr., 86F) and Nantes (2 per day, 2hr., 111F). **CTA** (tel. 02 40 95 25 75) line 8 goes to: Nantes (2 per day, 3½hr., 115F) via St-Gilles (45min., 37F); Fromentine (2hr., 58F); and Noirmoutier (1½hr., 78F). **Le Cyclotron,** 66, promenade Clémenceau (tel. 02 51 32 64 15), facing the beach, rents 10-speeds (42F per day, 238F per week; deposit 800F) and *VTTs* (75F per day, 338F per week; deposit 1600F). Bikes are due back at 7pm. (Open June-Sept. daily 9am-midnight.) The **hospital** is at 75, av. d'Aquitaine (tel. 02 51 21 85 85). The **post office,** av. Nicot (tel. 02 51 21 82 82), has poste restante (open Mon.-Fri. 8:30am-5:45pm, Sat. 8:30am-noon; **postal code:** 85100).

If you plan way ahead, you can stay at the **Auberge de Jeunesse (HI),** rue du Sémaphore (tel. 02 51 95 76 21; off season 02 40 20 08 94), in neighboring La Chaume. Take bus 1 from pl. de la Liberté (direction: Côte Sauvage, 1 per hr. until 6:30pm, 7F) to "Armandèche," and walk to the left on rue du Sémaphore about 200m. After 6:30pm, take *La Chaumoise,* a shuttle boat that leaves from the quai on the port and runs to La Chaume (every 2min., 6am-midnight, 4F). From the landing point, make a left onto promenade Georges V, then a right on rue de l'Orméau, which becomes rue du Village Neuf. Finally, turn left on rue du Sémaphore and walk about 200m (10-15min. from landing). If you are worried about getting lost, stop by the tourist office and ask for a map. The hostel is small, mellow, and has a fantastic view of the rocky Côte Sauvage. (Kitchen facilities; outdoor bathrooms and showers; 4- and 10-bunk single-sex dorms. 70F, breakfast included; camping 30F per person. Reception 9-11am and 5pm-1am; no lockout; open May-Sept.) The **Hôtel de Départ,** 40, av. de Gaulle (tel. 02 51 32 03 71), has a jovial owner who happily lets nine well-kept rooms and throws in free hall showers. The street noise in the front rooms is sometimes loud (singles and doubles 165F, with shower 195F). There are dozens of **campgrounds** in and around Les Sables—ask the tourist office for a list. The quais and promenades near the **Port de Pêche** overflow with restaurants serving whatever the boats brought in that morning. For lunch, head for the **market** at **Les Halles** (open daily 8am-1pm; Sept. 15-June 15 closed Mon.). The **Super 200 Epicerie,** 8, rue de Patrie, is convenient but expensive (open Mon.-Sat. 8:30am-1pm and 3-8pm, Sun. 9am-1pm). The enormous **Intermarché** more than covers the basics. From the train station, turn right on av. Général de Gaulle, right on rue Nicot, right at the post office, and another right just after the train tracks. The supermarket will be on your left (open Mon.-Sat. 9am-8pm and Sun. 9am-1pm).

The Coastal Islands

NOIRMOUTIER

The fishing boats stationed along the coast of Noirmoutier give a hint of its origins, but its inhabitants have made their fortune through salt farming, and more recently, tourism. In the 16th century, Noirmoutier was the salt capital of France, exporting *le sel* throughout Europe. A Dutch attack in 1674 destroyed part of its stately fortress and most of its salty industry. In this century, the island's 40km of beaches, museums, Mediterranean climate, bike trails through oyster beds, and bridge from the mainland have annually drawn a more peaceful invasion of Dutch, as well as German and French, tourists across the bridge to this former pirate haunt.

Orientation and Practical Information

The island of Noirmoutier, 18km long and 1-2km wide, crunches its main attractions, including the main town of the same name, into its northern half. Buses cruise two to four times daily from Nantes (2½hr., 88F) and Monday to Saturday from Les Sables d'Olonne (2¾hr., change at Fromentine, 85F). Intra-island travel is relatively easy; local buses make the rounds of points of interest about once an hour (7-27F). The **tourist office** in the town of Noirmoitier (tel. 02 51 39 80 71; fax 02 51 39 53 16), route du Pont, has free maps and can help with accommodations. Upon exiting the bus station, turn left and take the first left; walk through the parking lot, along the quai to your right. The office is on the left (open Mon.-Sat. 9:30am-12:30pm and 2-6pm; Sun. 9:30am-12:30pm). The **Crédit Agricole,** pl. de la République (along the quai), has a good rate of **exchange** (open Tues.-Fri. 9:30am-12:30pm and 2-5:15pm, Sat. 9am-12:30pm and 2-4:15pm). On Sundays and Mondays, change money at the **Aquatique** clothing store, pl. de la République (tel. 02 51 39 00 62), for no commission (open Mon.-Sat. 9am-12:30pm and 2:30-7pm, Sun. 10am-12:30pm). This island of diverse delights opens up via **bike.** Rent at **Noirmoutier Souvenirs,** 18, rue de

Rosaire (tel. 02 51 39 28 03), for 35-60F per half-day or 45-80F for the whole day (passport deposit; open daily 9am-7pm; V, MC, AmEx).

Accommodations, Camping and Food

Be sure to reserve a room here before abandoning a cheap berth on the mainland. For a French island resort, lodging in Noirmoutier is vaguely reasonable. **Chez Bébert,** 37, av. Joseph Pineau (tel. 02 51 39 08 97), a 10-minute walk from town, lets clean, simple rooms (open June- Dec. 22; double with toilet 145F, with shower and toilet 250F). The restaurant serves 70F *menus* and doubles as the local senior citizen hang-out. Farther down the street, **La Quichenotte,** 32, av. Joseph Pineau (tel. 02 51 39 11 77), offers airy, spacious rooms with firm mattresses. (Doubles 190-200F, with shower 230-260F. Breakfast 35F. Open Dec. 20-Nov. 11. V, MC.) Two km east of town and sprawled along a beach, the 2-star **La Vendette,** route des Sableaux (tel. 02 51 39 06 24; fax 02 51 35 97 63), has a whopping 600 pitches (2 people and a tent or caravan 80F, slightly cheaper off-season; extra adult 14F, kids 7F; electricity 10F; free hot showers; reserve). Next door **Camping Municipal,** route des Sableaux (tel. 02 51 39 05 56), usually has space (July-Aug. 3 people, car, and tent 61F, drops a bit off-season; electricity 12F; extra adult 14F; shower 4F; V, MC).

Do we have to tell you food is *cher?* Check out **L'Ancrage,** 18, Grande Rue (tel. 02 51 39 09 28). The 65F *"Formule Ancrage"* brings out fresh mussels and an appetizer, and the 85F *menu* includes six oysters, a *plat du jour*, and dessert (open Mon.-Sun. 10am-10:30pm; V, MC). Near the hotels, **Les Chandeliers,** 96, av. Pineau (tel. 02 51 39 54 87), is 15 minutes from the *centre ville.* A charming husband-and-wife team cooks up an excellent 75F dinner *menu* of fresh *crevettes* (shrimp), fish, and apricot pie (open daily noon-2pm and 7-10:30pm; V, MC). Those who'd prefer to give the Gold Card a breather find solace at **Shopi supermarket,** av. Joseph Pineau (open Mon.-Fri. 9am-3pm; V, MC), or **Cours des Halles,** 3, rue de la Prée au Duc (open Mon.-Sat. 8:30am-8pm, Sun. 8:30am-12:30pm and 2-6pm).

Sights

A bike tour of the northern part of the *île* takes about two hours. Heading east from the town of Noirmoutier in the direction "Les Sableaux," you will pass fishermen scouring for mussels and fish in the ocean to your right and **salt marshes** on the left, identifiable by the sparkling white piles in the marshes. Two km east of town is **Les Sableaux,** a marsh where locals and tourists alike bring buckets, roll up their pants, and brave the ankle-deep water to search for shellfish, mussels, and the (very) occasional beached lobster. Two km north of Noirmoutier lies **plage de la Clère,** a great, if not unknown, tanning place overlooking sailing and fishing vessels in the harbor. The way to the fishing village of **L'Herbaudière** features potato farms on the right and salt marshes on the left as far as the eye can see. Thirty **saumiers (salt farmers)** have revitalized a long-dormant industry; several offer tours to the public, explaining (in French) how they collect and isolate pure salt from the ocean. Visit **Michel Gallois,** route de l'Epine (tel. 02 51 39 52 72), 2.5km south of Noirmoutier behind the Super U (open June 15-Sept. 15 Mon.-Sat. 9am-6pm; free), or **Véronique Gendron,** route de Champierreux (tel. 02 51 39 58 67; call around meal times), on the road to La Bosse (open June-Sept. 15 9am-5pm; free). If you don't make it to the salt farms, learn about the exciting life-cycle of table salt at the **Maison du Sel,** rue de l'Ecluse (tel. 02 51 39 08 30; open June 24-Sept. 5 10am-12:30pm and 3:30-7pm; free).

Also between Noirmoutier and Herbaudière is the **Chevrerie** (goat farm), route de l'Herbaudière (tel. 02 51 39 16 19), about 3km west of Noirmoutier. Surrounded by grazing horses, this farm gives interesting insights into how goat cheese is made, and an opportunity to stop baby goats from chewing on your shorts. Sorry, no *chèvre* taste-tests (open May-Sept. 9am-12:45pm and 1:45-7:30pm; admission 12F).

Beaches are everywhere along the coast, but beware—the tourist office labels some pebbly and inhospitable stretches *"plages."* For the best conditions, head for the long expanses of sand along the western and southern coasts. You can go to

plage de l'Epine in **La Bosse** (4km southwest of Noirmoutier) or **plage du Midi in Barbâtre** (10km southeast) by bike trail or by public bus.

The carefree town of Noirmoutier is pleasant, compact, and ideal for strolling. Its well-preserved 12th-century **château,** pl. d'Armes (tel. 02 51 39 10 42), guards the town and the tourist office. Built by Pierre V de la Garnache, it has repelled invading Scandinavians, Normans, and Spanish, none of whom could penetrate its thick stone walls. Frustrated Dutch destroyed the two southern towers in 1674 and disrupted the sacred salt industry for over three centuries. Republicans and Royalists played hot potato with it during the 1789 Revolution. Today, a museum occupies the fortress, with china, ship models, and local landscapes on show. Climb to the top for a sweep of the salt marshes, potato fields, and teensy cars below (open June 15-Sept. 15 10am-7pm; April 10-May 8 10am-6pm; other times Wed.-Mon. 10am-12:30pm and 2:30-6pm; closed Dec.-Jan.; admission 20F, kids 10F). The **Musée de la Construction Navale,** across the quai, features ship-building methods and displays on Noirmoutier's seafaring history (same hours, but closed Mon. rather than Tues.).

ILE D'YEU

Borrowing its name from the Old French word for island (*oya,* modernized to *yeu*), Ile d'Yeu was settled by reclusive monks in the 11th century. They can't have been too reclusive, for word spread quickly—the English used the rocky isle as an offshore base during the Hundred Years' War, and the Spanish later besieged it. After World War II, Maréchal Pétain, leader of Vichy France, was imprisoned in the island's citadel until his death, overlooking the red roofs of **Port-Joinville.** The 5000 inhabitants of the now tranquil island tend fishing boats and their burgeoning aquaculture industry. Ile d'Yeu, 18km off the mainland, avoids the brunt of the coastal tourist attack in the summer. Many adventurous travelers still take the ferry ride over to enjoy its windswept, craggy cliffs, clear turquoise water, and the flat bike paths to the old castle. Needless to say, hotels, restaurants, and transportation are expensive, but those in search of solitude may find Ile d'Yeu to be worth the price.

Orientation and Practical Information

Ile d'Yeu is approximately 10km long and 4km wide. **Port-Joinville,** the ferry port, is on the north side, buffered to the east by golden beaches braving the icy ocean. The windy **Côte Sauvage** (wild coast) wraps around the western and southern parts of the island. The **tourist office** (tel. 02 51 58 32 58) and its maps are one street inland from the quai, on the pedestrian pl. du Marché (open Mon. 9am-noon and 3-6:30pm, Tues.-Sat. 9am-12:30pm and 3-6:30pm). Many ferries cross from the mainland, but sporadic bus connections ensure that only the most determined reach this idyllic isle. **Ferries** leave from Fromentine and St-Gilles-Croix-de-Vie on the coast, and the island of Noirmoutier. The only year-round port, **Fromentine,** is accessible by bus from Nantes and Les Sables d'Olonne (4 per day, 1¾hr., 66F). No buses run between Fromentine and Les Sables on Sundays and holidays. Three or four ferries per day go between Fromentine and Ile d'Yeu (roundtrip 140F, children 85F; V, MC, AmEx). Make reservations and arrive at the *gare maritime* (port) 30 minutes before departure time; call 02 51 49 59 69 for information. **St-Gilles** is accessible by **train** from Nantes (5-8 per day, 1½hr., 69F) or by **CTA buses** (tel. 02 40 46 14 00) from Les Sables d'Olonne (3-4 per day, 45min., 35F). Ask the driver to drop you off at the *embarcadère* (pier). July-August only, **Vedettes Inter-Iles Vendéennes (VIIV**; tel. 02 51 54 15 15; 1hr., roundtrip 160F, students 145F; V, MC) and **Garcie-Ferrande** (tel. 02 51 55 45 42; 1hr., 130F, under 18 90F; V, MC) make two daily roundtrips each to Ile d'Yeu. From **Noirmoutier,** accessible by bus from Les Sables (2-4 per day Mon.-Sat., change at Fromentine, 2¾hr., 85F) and Nantes (3-4 per day, 2½hr., 88F), VIIV ferries make the 45-minute trip to Ile d'Yeu in July and August (3-6 per day, roundtrip 160F, students 145F). Call 02 51 39 00 00 for info and reservations. St-Gilles' **tourist office,** bd. de l'Egalité (tel. 02 51 55 03 66), 500m east of the port, can help you with the details of your trip.

Accommodations and Food

The **Hôtel de l'Escale,** 14, rue de la Croix du Port (tel. 02 51 58 50 28), rents 13 large, clean rooms, most with showers. From the port, turn left at the traffic lights, and the hotel will be on your right. The fun-loving owner runs a hopping bar next door. (Doubles, some with showers, 180F. Quads 280-300F. Breakfast 32F. Reception 8am-2pm and after 6:30pm. July-Aug. reserve or perish. V, MC.) A **municipal campground** (tel. 02 51 58 34 20) is at Pointe de Gilberge, 1km from the port and 50m from the beach (14F per adult, 60F per site, 14F per car).

Markets are only slightly pricier than those on the mainland, but restaurants are expensive. Try the delicious fresh seafood at **La Burette,** 3, rue du Petit Moulin (tel. 02 51 58 31 34), beyond Hôtel de L'Escale. 75F *menu* includes a salad and the catch of the day (seafood dishes 45-78F; open daily noon-2:30pm and 7-11pm; V, MC). **Champion supermarket** is on rue de Calypso, a five- to 10-minute walk from the port. Turn left onto quai Vernier, which becomes rue de Calypso (open Mon.-Sat. 8:45am-12:30pm and 3:30-7:30pm, Fri.-Sat. 3:30-7:45pm, Sat. closes for lunch at 12:45pm; V, MC). A slightly cheaper and fresher option is the **outdoor market,** on quai de la Mairie, Mon.-Sat. 9am-1pm, selling vegetables, fruits, and more.

Sights and Entertainment

It takes four to five hours to cover the island by bike, but a two to three hour ride around the western half hits the highlights. Roads are bumpy, but the **bikes for rent** in Port-Joinville are built for the pebbles. Stores dotting the quai rent *vélos* (25-35F per ½-day, 40-75F per day). Take the rue de la République and head out of town. Don't rely on capricious road names; look for signs pointing to various destinations.

Pedal across the island to the **Côte Sauvage** by winding around the northern coast or by zigzagging inland—a shortcut that includes a close-up of the **Grand Phare,** the 20m-tall lighthouse on the isle's tallest "hill." Once at the coast, roll merrily along to the **Pointe du Châtelet.** One of its tiny bluffs bears a commemorative cross that has withstood the winds since it was installed as a monument to sailors in 1934. Near the cross, 3.5km south of Port-Joinville, crumbles the **Vieux Château.** Hanging precariously on the craggy coast, the château was built by Oliver IV in 1327. Its defenders beat back a Spanish siege in the 16th century, prompting a generous reward from King Henri II. Louis XIV felt France, as a powerful 17th-century empire, did not need this fortress and destroyed it to prevent enemies from using it. Since then, the château has valiantly fended off the relentless waves and harmless tribes of picnickers (open 11am-5pm; obligatory guided tour 10F, free on Mon.).

Port de la Meule, 3km due south of Port-Joinville, shelters a rainbow of bobbing fishing and pleasure boats. 1½km east of Port de la Meule, the soft sand beaches of **L'Anse des Vieilles** are in a cave named, not after old women, but for a local species of fish. **St-Sauveur,** 2km southeast of Port-Joinville, is home to an 18th-century church whose bright stained-glass windows illuminate its dark, musty interior.

The island's mildly spectacular **beaches** sparkle 500m to 5km east of Port-Joinville. From the port, turn left on quai Vernier, which becomes rue de la Plage. Walk 'til you see one you like. **Le Marais Salé** and **Le Petite Conche,** about 3½km away, make for the best bronzing, though you may not want to tackle their icy waters.

For rainy days, Port-Joinville offers two museums. The **Musée Historical,** next to the tourist office, chronicles the island's political history and lifestyles; it includes Pétain memorabilia (tel. 02 51 58 36 88; open July-Aug. daily 10am-noon and 1:45-7pm; admission 12F). Island fishing is represented with a small collection of ship models and photographs in the **Musée de la Pêche,** quai de la Chapelle (tel. 02 51 59 31 00; open June 15-Sept. 15 Mon.-Fri. 10am-noon and 2-5pm; admission 15F).

ILE DE RÉ

Ile de Ré, dubbed *"Ré La Blanche"* for its 50km of white sand beaches and whitewashed houses, is joined by bridge with the mainland and La Rochelle, 5km away. Although its southern half is crammed with tourists, the island contains one of Europe's largest nature preserves, and its northern regions boast less crowded beaches, winding bike paths, pine forests, farmland, and dunes. Nearly 30km long and home to 10 separate towns, Ile de Ré is accessible by car, bus, bike, or ferry. A **drive** across the La Pallice bridge costs a ridiculous 135F in tolls. **Ferries** are also out of the budget question: **Inter-Iles** on the *Vieux Port* in La Rochelle (tel. 02 46 50 51 88) runs ferries twice daily to **Sablanceaux,** at the southern tip of the Ile de Ré near the bridge (1¼hr., 140F, children 100F). Consider heading to the island by bus, bike, or a combination of the two. The comfortable and efficient **Rébus** runs daily from the train station and the *gare routière* in La Rochelle to Sablanceaux (12-15 per day, 25min., 10F), the largest and most visited town, **St-Martin,** in the middle of the island (10 per day, 45min., 24F); and **Les Portes,** at the northern tip near some great beaches (8 per day, 1½hr., 45F). The fit and adventurous can test their muscles and go by **bike**—from La Rochelle, the ride takes less than one hour, and there's no toll across the bridge. Clearly marked paths line the winding route. It's tough pedaling up the 3km bridge, but the descent is work- and care-free.

Every town has a **tourist office,** but St-Martin's has the most complete info: av. Victor-Bouthellier, (tel. 02 46 09 20 06). (Open Mon.-Sat. 10am-noon and 3-5:30pm.) Tourist offices have the free bike path map and guide, *Guide des Itinéraires Cyclables.* The best **currency exchange** rates are at **Crédit Agricole,** 4, quai Foran, on the port, 40F commission (open Tues.-Fri. 9am-12:15pm and 1:30-7pm, Sat. 9am-12:15pm and 1:30-4pm). Once on the island, it is easy to **rent a bike** in any town and pedal along bike paths, coastal sidewalks, and wooded lanes. The biggest and cheapest rental mogul is **Cycland,** whose main office is at 15, rue du Marché, in La Flotte (tel. 02 46 09 65 27). Five branch offices exist, including ones in Sablanceaux, the *gare routière,* and St-Martin, on Impasse rue de Sully (tel. 02 46 09 65 27), (mountain bikes 30F per hour, 60F per ½-day, 75F per day; deposit 1600F, passport, or first-born; open July-Aug. 9am-9pm; V, MC). Dry out damp beach towels at the **Laverie** (laundromat) five doors down from 5, cours Pasteur (open Mon.-Fri. 9am-noon and 2-7pm Sat. 9am-noon and 2-6pm, Sun. 9am-noon). St-Martin's **post office** (tel. 02 46 09 00 16), pl. de la République, has poste restante; **postal code:** 17400.

Ile de Ré is a convenient and satisfying daytrip from La Rochelle, a fact made all the more enticing given that most hotels on the *île* itself start at two stars and 250F. In St-Martin, **Hôtel Le Sully** (tel. 02 46 09 26 94; fax 02 46 09 06 85), rue Jean Jaurès, a block up from the port, offers a relatively reasonable compromise. Blue-tiled steps lead to medium-sized rooms that are clean and noise-free. (Singles with shower 180F. Doubles with shower 200F, with bath 230F. Extra bed 50F. Breakfast 30F; V, MC, AmEx.) In **La Flotte,** 4km east of St-Martin and 9km north of Sablanceaux, stampede to **L'Hippocampe,** 16, rue Château des Mauléons (tel. 02 46 09 60 68), and its small, aging but comfortable rooms. (Singles 99F. Doubles 120F, with shower 153F, with bath 181F. Shower 10F. Breakfast 25F. V, MC.) **Camping Municipal** (tel. 02 46 09 84 10), in Rivedoux near the bridge, costs 59F for one-to-three campers, including site and showers. On the north coast, beachside **La Plage** (tel. 02 46 29 42 62), near St-Clement, lends sites to 2 people and their tent for 58F (open April 1-Oct. 15). Crashing by the surf is illegal but not strictly enforced.

Restaurants are pricey; most towns have pizzerias and *crêperies.* All towns have **morning markets;** St-Martin's is off rue Jean Jaurès, by the port (daily 7:30am-1pm). Or march on to the **Intermarché supermarket** (tel. 02 46 09 42 02), av. Corsaires, off route de La Flotte, between St-Martin and La Flotte (open Mon.-Sat. 9am-12:30pm and 3-7:30pm; July-Aug. also Sun. 8:30am-12:30pm).

Though everybody and his grandmother bikes the southern half of Ile de Ré to St-Martin, crowds thin out as you travel north. Bike trails run through the **Préserve Naturelle de Lileau des Niges,** a wetlands sanctuary 15km north of St-Martin, humming with the song of the rare blue-throated thrush and heron, as well as their more mundane pals, the seagull and the white-crested duck. The marsh bursts with vitality in the summer, but winter's the season to see it: 20,000 birds stop by on their migration from Siberia and Canada to Africa.

On the northwestern tip of the island, 4½km from the marsh, the 1854 **Phare des Baleines (lighthouse)** flashes. The loquacious *gardien* (keeper of the flame) holds

POITOU-CHARENTES

the door as you climb the 262 stairs 57m for a view of the ocean and beaches (open daily June-Sept. 10am-noon and 2-6pm; Oct.-May 10am-noon and 2-5pm; free). Heading back to St-Martin, you'll pass the village of **Ars** *(longa, vita brevis)* and its 17 windmills. St-Martin holds a fortified port built by Vauban and a citadel that serves as a prison. The 15th- to 17th-century Renaissance gallery of the **Hôtel Clerjotte,** av. Victor-Bouthilier, houses the **Musée Ernest Cognacq** (tel. 02 46 09 21 22), filled with ship models and paintings tracing island history (open June 15-Oct. Wed.-Sun. 10am-1pm and 3-6pm; Nov.-June 14 10am-noon and 2-5pm; admission 26F, students 12F).

Climb up the hill from the quai to the imposing 15th-century façade of **Eglise St-Martin.** Built and destroyed no fewer than five times since 1372, Eglise St-Martin's newest renovations contrast sharply with the exterior's time-worn surface (open daily 10am-6:30pm). Three km east of La Flotte, swallows nest and squawk in the remains of the 12th-century **Abbaye des Chateliers,** visible across the flat plain.

If you don't want to submerge yourself in history, cover yourself with sunscreen at the beach. Shake off all inhibitions at the **Plage du Petit Bec** in Les Portes, a clothing-optional beach. If you want to avoid that full-body glow, head to the pine-fringed dunes of **Plage de la Conches des Balaines,** near the lighthouse. Both beaches, at the northern tip of the island, are huge and devoid of the crowd that frequents the beaches on the western coast, like **Sablanceaux** and **Plage du Gros Jarc.**

St-Martin remains alive at night, especially in summer. **Cotton Pub,** (tel. 02 46 09 17 99) and **Boucquingham,** (tel. 02 46 09 01 20), Venelle de la Fosse Bray, are intimate piano bars tucked behind the quai, across from the tourist office. Cotton Pub hosts occasional live jazz concerts (both open Mon.-Thurs. 5pm-2am, Fri.-Sat. 5pm-3am; 60F cover with drink most nights; V, MC). **Le Bastion,** cours Pasteur (tel. 02 46 09 21 92; open Tues.-Sat. 5:30pm-2:30am), across town, is an all-purpose grill, pizzeria, nightclub, and disco prone to wild times and host to once-a-week theme nights in summer—Mexican night (10F tequilas) and cruise night (15F rum punch).

ILE D'OLÉRON

The second-largest French island after Corsica, home to an enormous citadel, and the proud owner of 20km of fine sand beaches and 90km of coastline, Ile d'Oléron is truly an *"île lumineuse."* Romans cultivated what have become some of France's largest and most renowned oyster beds and the current French inhabitants keep pearly traditions alive by coaxing seafood out of calm turquoise waters. As with several other coastal islands, Ile d'Oléron is actually linked to the mainland by a 3km bridge and is perhaps best reached by daily buses which circulate between Saintes or Rochefort-sur-Mer on the mainland and the island town of Le Château. From this convenient island base, local buses make tracks to nearby villages such as St-Pierre, St-Denis, and St-Georges.

In summer, three or four **buses** daily (2 in winter) cross the 3km bridge from Saintes' train station (tel. 05 46 93 21 41; 1½hr., 52F); seven leave from the *gare routière* in Rochefort (tel. 05 46 99 01 36; 1hr., 39F one-way, discounts in summer). Mainland buses all drop off at **Le Château.** To get to the tourist office, turn with your back to the water and head down **av. du Port** following signs to the *"centre ville."* Take a right onto bd. Victor Hugo and head up the hill toward the **tourist office** at pl. de la République (tel. 05 46 47 60 51; fax 05 46 47 73 65), where you will be the grateful recipient of whatever information they do have (open July-Aug. Mon.-Sat. 9am-12:30pm and 2:30-7pm, Sun. 10am-12:30pm; Sept.-June Mon.-Sat. 10am-12:30pm and 2:30-6:30pm). **Crédit Maritime,** near the tourist office on rue Thiers, charges 15F to change traveler's checks (open Tues.-Sat. 8:30am-12:15pm and 1:30-5pm). An island shuttle runs between villages (from Le Château to St-Pierre-d'Oléron, 6-8 per day, 4 on Sun., ½-1hr., 21F; Le Château to Grand Village, by the beaches, 5-6 per day, 2 on Sun., 20min., 10F; Le Château to St-Denis, 3 per day, 1½hr., 31F). **Lacellerie Cycles,** 5, rue du Maréchal Foch (tel. 05 46 47 69 30), just off pl. de la République, helps with routes and rents a variety of **bikes.** (30-50F per ½-day, 40-75F per day; deposit 600F or passport; open Sept.-June Tues.-Sat. 9am-12:30pm and 2-5pm, Sun. 9am-12:30; V.)

Reserve one to three weeks ahead for summer rooms. In Le Château, **Le Mail,** 8, bd. Thiers (tel. 05 46 47 61 40), rents clean, spacious singles with peek-a-boo showers for 170-190F; doubles 180-220F (breakfast 28F; V, MC). At **Le Castel,** 54, rue Alsace-Lorraine (tel. 05 46 47 60 13; fax 05 46 47 77 47), a pleasant manager keeps spotless rooms and a restaurant downstairs with a 60F *menu* (singles and doubles 200F, with shower 250F; breakfast 35F; V, MC). In the relatively bustling center of town, head for the action at **Le Jean-Bart,** pl. de la République (tel. 05 46 47 60 04). Small, simple rooms (150F; V, MC)—get 'em while you can. Downstairs family-run *brasserie* serves up 12-19F sandwiches. Campers can choose from over 50 sites, but some still crash (illegally) on the splendid beaches. In Le Château, try **Les Ramparts,** bd. Philippe Daste (tel. 05 46 47 61 93; fax 05 46 47 73 65; 68F for 1-3 people, 19F per extra person, 19F electricity; open March-Oct). **La Brande,** rue des Huitres (tel. 05 46 47 62 37; fax 05 46 47 71 70), 2.5km west of town, boasts 199 sites, a pool, tennis courts, and a waterslide (75F for two, 20F extra person, 20F electricity; open March 15-Nov.; V, MC). Near Grand-Village and the beaches on the southern coast, the **Camping Municipal des Pins,** allée des Pins (tel. 05 46 47 50 13), offers 300 pitches for 15F each (15F per person, 15F electricity; open Easter-Sept.).

Each town has a Sunday morning **market** (7:30am-1pm). **The Coop,** 3, rue Reytre Frères off pl. République has just enough variety for a picnic. (Open Mon.-Sat. 8:30am-1pm and 4-8pm, Sun. 8:30am-1pm.) For a larger selection, trek to **Super U Supermarché,** 250m out of Le Château, 15, av. d'Antioches, or the **Centre Commercial** in Grand Village (both open July-Aug. Mon.-Sat. 8:30am-8pm, Sun. 9am-12:30pm; Sept.-June Mon.-Sat. 9am-12:30pm and 3-7:30pm, Sun. 9am-12:30pm).

The mighty but crumbling **citadel** in Le Château was built on the ruins of a medieval fortress. In 1621, following a revolt in La Rochelle, skittish Louis XIII ordered it destroyed to prevent its falling to Protestant forces. Indecisive as always, Louis changed his mind and built the current structure in 1630 to protect the coast. Louis XIV and Richelieu were some of its more famous guests; World War I German POWs were some of the more infamous. Allies' bombs destroyed much of the citadel in 1945 to keep German squadrons left on Oléron from regrouping. Ten years ago, the French bureaucracy decided to restore the citadel. Naturally, it remains a shambles, though the ramparts offer a lovely view. Inside, the **Memorial des Soldats de la Nouvelle France** details France's conquests in North America from the early-17th to late-18th centuries. To stir up some excitement, ask the curator about the Louisiana "Purchase"—the one that got away. (Citadel open daily 10am-noon and 3-6pm. Free. Museum open June-Sept. Mon.-Sat. 10am-7pm, Sun. 2-7pm. Admission 15F.) Le Château d'Oleron and St-Pierre have cafés and bars that stay open late. Check the tourist office's bulletin board to see what's shaking in the evenings.

St-Pierre d'Oléron is the island's geographic and administrative center, with a bustling pedestrian sector. This 13th-century town also contains the tomb of French writer and naval officer Pierre Loti (see page 306). The staff of the St-Pierre tourist office, pl. Gambetta (tel 05 46 47 11 39; fax 05 46 47 10 41), knows everything (open July-Aug. Mon.-Sat. 9am-1pm and 2-7:30pm, Sun. 9:30am-1pm; Sept.-June Mon.-Sat. 9:30am-12:30pm and 2-6pm). Its lively port makes **La Cotinière** the most picturesque of the island towns. **Le Grand Village,** 3km southwest of Le Château, is—despite its name—the smallest town, with 586 locals and the island's glitziest, most flamboyantly topless beach. (Tourist office tel. 05 46 47 58 00; fax 05 46 47 42 17). **Plage du Vert Bois,** near Grand Village and separated from the main road by a thick pine forest, feels almost like an island itself. Near the northwestern tip, **St-Denis** invites tourists to climb the 54m lighthouse and peer down at the colorful collage below (open daily 10am-noon and 2-6:30pm; Sept.-June 10am-noon and 2-6pm; free). Call the tourist office for more info at 05 46 47 95 53; fax 05 46 75 91 36. Ten km northwest of the bus drop-off at Le Château, and near the Forêt des Saumonards, the port town of **Boyardville** is one of Oléron's main oyster parks, where locals spend their days collecting the crazy little critters.

La Rochelle

Named after the soft rock on which the earliest settlers built their homes in the 12th century, La Rochelle (pop. 120,000) became Aquitaine's coastal locus of power and profited from its position as a port city vital to France and Britain. In the 17th century, the omnipotent Cardinal Richelieu saw in this bastion of French Protestantism an obstacle to the unification of France and convinced Louis XIII to besiege the town. After many citizens had starved to death, the city finally surrendered.

The city, immortalized by Dumas in *The Three Musketeers,* did not recover its wealth until the 20th century, when vacationers discovered its white sand beaches and refined 14th-century buildings. The towers that protected the city still stand, but even they cannot shield it from the students who attack the town's nightlife during the year and the tourists who invade each summer. They come for a simple reason—La Rochelle is the perfect vacation spot. A stroll along the quai amidst the café-chatter and illuminated towers reveals that the town's sights match its sand and its festivals for entertainment value. La Rochelle's attractions and proximity to the sun-blessed islands should make it a stop on any sun-seeker's itinerary.

ORIENTATION AND PRACTICAL INFORMATION

La Rochelle spreads out from the **vieux port. Quai Duperré** and its many cafés line the port, with the **vieille ville** of pedestrian streets beyond it and the daily markets of the **pl. du Marché** beyond that. To go from the train station to the tourist office, head straight up **av. du Général de Gaulle** to the first square, **pl. de la Motte Rouge.** Make a left onto the quai du Gabut. The tourist office is on the left, in **Quartier du Gabut,** a zone of shops and restaurants (5min.). To reach the center of town directly from the station, take av. du Général de Gaulle through pl. de la Motte Rouge until it turns into **quai Vallin,** which will lead you straight to quai Duperré, with many little streets heading into the *vieille ville* (10min.) and pl. du Marché (15min.).

Tourist Office: pl. de la Petite Sirène, quartier du Gabut (tel. 05 46 41 14 68; fax 05 46 41 99 85). Multilingual staff distributes maps in French (2F, lots of info) and English (1F, rather meager) and brochures about La Rochelle and surrounding islands. Hotel reservations 20F. Open June 16-Sept. 14 Mon.-Sat. 9am-7pm, Sun. 11am-5pm; Sept. 15-June 15 Mon.-Wed. and Fri.-Sat. 10:30am-1:30pm and 4:30-7pm, Sun. 10:30am-12:30pm and 3-5pm. Their free magazine, **Sortir,** says what's hot and what's not. **Currency exchange** (20F fee) June 15-Sept. 15 hypothetically Mon.-Wed. and Fri.-Sat. 10am-1pm and 4-7pm, Sun. 11am-1pm and 3-5pm.

Money: Banks and **ATMs** line sq. Verdun, rue de Palais, rue Chaudrier, and the quais. You guessed it—**Banque de France** has the best rates and no commission on rue Réamar (tel. 05 46 51 48 00), at the intersection of rue Léonce Vieljeux. Open Mon.-Fri. 9am-noon and 1:30-3:30pm.

Trains: bd. Maréchal Joffre (tel. 08 36 35 35 35). To: Poitiers (8-10 per day, 2hr., 105F); Bordeaux (6-8 per day, 2hr., 130F); Niort (13 per day, 1hr., 54F); Nantes (4-5 per day, 2hr., 123F); Paris (3 per day, 5hr., 280F; 7-9 TGVs per day, 3hr., 290-347F plus 36-95F reservation). **Lockers** 15-30F. Info office open 5am-10:30pm.

Buses: Citram buses (tel. 05 46 50 53 57) from pl. de Verdun to Rochefort (3-7 per day, 1hr., 27F) and Angoulême (3 per day, 3½hr., 100F). Buy tickets on board; cash only. For long trips, stick to trains. Open Mon.-Fri. 9am-noon and 2-6pm.

Public Transportation: Pick up a map at the pl. Verdun main office. **Autoplus** (tel. 05 46 34 84 58) runs to campgrounds, hostel, the *centre ville* (buses 10, 19, 21, from the train station, direction: pl. Verdun or Centre Ville), La Pallice near Ile de Ré (bus 1, from *grosse horloge,* direction: La Pallice), and Sablanceaux on Ile de Ré (bus 1, 3-5 per day, ask if the bus is going to Ile de Ré). Fare 7F50.

Taxis: pl. de Verdun (tel. 05 46 41 55 55). 4F per km, 7F per km at night. **Taxis Rochefortais** (tel. 05 46 99 07 64) charge 90F to take 1-4 people to Rochefort.

Bike Rental: Vélos Municipaux Autoplus, off quai Carénage in sq. Meyer or on pl. Verdun near the bus station. La Rochelle's eco-mayor, Crépeau, began this famous free bikes program in the 1970s. Look for the lemon-yellow 10-speeds. Great for

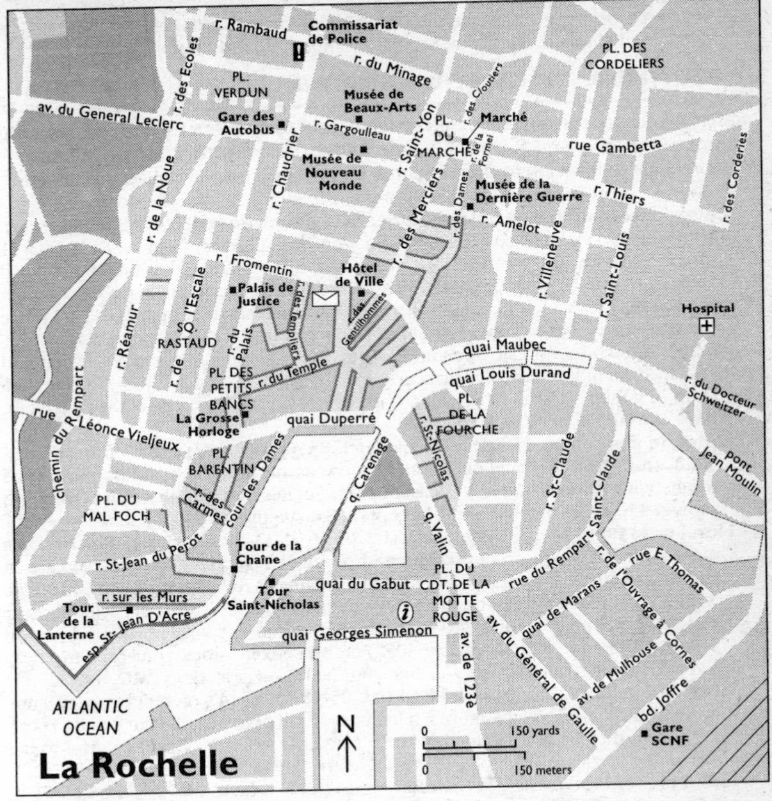

touring town, but a bit too cumbersome to take much further. Free with ID deposit for 2hr., 6F per hr. thereafter. Open May-Sept. 9am-12:30pm and 1:30-7pm. **Loca 2,** 48, rue St-Jean (tel. 05 46 41 84 32), off rue des Carmes by the Tour de la Chaine. Friendly owner gives advice about routes and rents 10-speeds (60F per day), *VTTs* (100F per day), and anything on wheels—even 'blades. 25% off for those under 25. ID deposit. Open daily 9:30am-7pm. V, MC, AmEx.

English Books: Calligrammes, 24, rue Chaudrier (tel. 05 46 41 52 48), near pl. de Verdun. Second floor houses slim pickin's in American fiction and 20th-century literature. Open Tues.-Sun. 9:15am-7:15pm, Mon. 2:15–7:15pm. V, MC.

Youth Center: Centre Départemental d'Information Jeunesse (CDIJ), 14, rue des Gentilshommes (tel. 05 46 41 16 36 or 05 46 41 16 99; fax 05 46 41 50 35). BIJ tickets. *Carte Jeune* 120F. Boards list apartments and jobs. Student *FrancoFolies* tickets 30F. Open Mon.-Fri. 10am-noon and 2-6pm, Sat. 10am-noon.

Laundromat: Vague Bleue, 4bis, quai Louis Durand, across from quai Duperré. One of the attendants is the 'twin' of Stewart Copeland, drummer for the Police. Wash 20F per 7kg, 40F per 16kg, dry 5F per 10min., detergent 2F. Open daily 8am-9pm. Wed. 8am-2pm is "Happy Hour" (wash 15F per 7kg, 30F per 16kg).

Crisis Lines: SOS Amitié, where a friend is just a coin away (tel. 05 46 45 23 23).

Hospital: rue du Docteur Schweitzer (tel. 05 46 45 50 50). From quai Duperré, follow quai Durand away from the towers. Turn left before the viaduct.

Medical Assistance tel. 05 46 27 15 15. **Medical emergency** tel. 15.

Police: 2, pl. de Verdun (tel. 05 46 51 36 36). From quai Duperré, turn right onto rue du Palais and follow it to pl. de Verdun. **Emergency** tel. 17.

Post Office: pl. de l'Hôtel de Ville (tel. 05 46 30 41 30). Poste restante (specify Hôtel de Ville). **Currency exchange.** Telephones. Photocopies 1F. Open Mon.-Fri.

8:30am-6:30pm, Sat. 8:30am-noon. **Main office** on av. Mulhouse, by the train station. Open Mon.-Fri. 8am-7pm, Sat. 8:30am-noon. **Postal code:** 17021.

ACCOMMODATIONS AND CAMPING

Sure, La Rochelle can attract countless numbers of visitors, but can it house them? In summer, even the gargantuan youth hostel fills to capacity from July 1 to August 31. Reservations are *de rigueur.* Hotels gather in the *vieille ville,* around pl. du Marché.

Centre International de Séjour, Auberge de Jeunesse (HI), av. des Minimes (tel. 05 46 44 43 11). Take bus 10 (direction: Port des Minimes) from av. de Colmar, 1 block from station, to "Auberge de Jeunesse" (Mon.-Sat., every 30min. until 7:15pm, 7F50). Or walk past the tourist office and the blue quai du Gabut complex to av. Marillac, which becomes allée des Tamaris and then quai Marillac before intersecting av. des Minimes (30min.). An enormous, hospital-like building with 2-6 beds in each room. Café open until 11pm. 75F. Camping in tents 28F. Sheets and breakfast included. Wheelchair accessible. Lockout 10am-12:30pm. Curfew midnight in winter, 1:30am in summer. Call ahead or write with one night's payment. **Bike rental** 35F per day; ID deposit.

Hôtel de Bordeaux, 45, rue St-Nicolas (tel. 05 46 41 31 22), right off quai Valin, 5min. from station. Excellent location; new owner has 22 sparkling, renovated rooms with phones above a pleasant café. Singles and doubles 120-160F, with shower 170-195F. Breakfast 30F. Reception 8am-9:30pm. V, MC.

Hôtel de la Paix, 14, rue Gargoulleau (tel. 05 46 41 33 44; fax 05 46 50 51 28), on a quiet street between pl. de Verdun and pl. du Marché. French-style staircase in charming 18th-century house leads to high-ceilinged rooms with phones. Lounge with TV. Singles 150F, with shower 160-200F. Doubles 150-160F, with shower 170-220F. 3-5 person suite 250-380F, depending on season. Enormous 5-person suite with terrace 400F. Breakfast 30F. English spoken—tuck your *Let's Go* away and ask why their sign insists you take your hall shower alone. V, MC, AmEx.

Hôtel le Florence, 2, rue Marcel-Paul (tel. 05 46 41 17 24), on quiet street 10min. north of the *centre ville.* A bit of a hike, but gleeful owners will take you in. Locals carouse in the bar downstairs, but there's little noise in the clean, colorful rooms above. Big singles and doubles 130-150F, with shower 170F. Breakfast 25F.

Hôtel Henry IV, 31, rue des Gentilshommes (tel. 05 46 41 25 79; fax 05 46 41 78 64), on pl. de la Caille off rue du Temple in the heart of the *vieille ville.* Spacious, clean rooms with bright, cheery feel. Singles and doubles 155F. Doubles with shower 170-190F. 3-4 person suite with shower 215-235F. Breakfast 28F. V, MC.

Hôtel Printania, 9-11, rue du Brave-Rondeau (tel. 05 46 41 22 86), 2 blocks from pl. du Marché. Ascend the stairs to small rooms. Singles 150F, with shower 180-260F. Doubles with shower 220-260F. Breakfast 28F. Shower 10F. V, MC.

Camping: Camping Municipal du Soleil (tel. 05 46 44 42 53), on av. des Minimes. 2-star site 15min. from center of town; take bus 10. Otherwise, follow directions to the hostel; camping is on the left. 46F for 2 adults, site, and car. 14F per extra adult. Electricity 15F. Open May-Sept. 15. The tourist office has a list of more distant campsites and info on idyllic island camping.

FOOD

The *fruits de mer* are always ripe in La Rochelle, but freshness has its price. Head for the stands of the **covered market** at pl. du Marché for fresh seafood, fruit, vegetables, and a fishy smell (open 365 days a year, 7am-1pm). **Prisunic,** rue de Palais, under the *grosse horloge* and on the left (open Mon.-Sat. 9am-7pm; July 14-Aug. 15 Mon.-Sun. 8:30am-9:30pm; V, MC), sells supermarket standards as do the various **Coops** which have sprung up, most notably at 41, rue Sardinerie (tel. 05 46 41 30 50) and 17, rue Amelot (tel. 05 46 41 07 80). Restaurants congregate in the *vieille ville,* along **rue St-Jean,** and along the quai.

Café de l'Arsenal, 12, rue Villeneuve (tel. 05 46 50 53 75). This cafeteria ain't rife with ambience, but at prices like this, who cares? Big portions begin at 30F. Heaven-sent ice-cream scoops 3F. Open daily 11:30am-2:30pm and 7-9:30pm.

A coté de chez Fred, 30-32, rue St-Nicholas (tel. 05 46 41 65 76). Fred, the *poissonier,* sends his fresh seafood to the kitchen of this restaurant, which is, in the most agreeable of arrangements, next door. Appetizers 34-68F, *plats* 39-118F. Open Mon.-Sat. 12:15-2:30pm and 7:30-10:30pm. V, AmEx.

Chez Armand, corner of rue du Temple and rue des Templiers. Follow the smell of fresh-baked pita bread directly to this "sandwich to go" paradise. Falafels, shawerma, and Tunisian pitas pack enough salad extras to make them meals unto themselves (18F each). Open daily 10am-11pm.

Sri Krishna, 38, rue St-Jean (tel. 05 46 41 56 87). With enough options to please everyone from vegetarians to omnivores, this Indian food mecca is custom-made for anyone tired of seafood. The 89F vegetarian platter is just big enough for two.

Le Soleil Brille Pour Tout Le Monde, 13, rue des Cloutiers (tel. 05 46 41 11 42), deftly assembles sun-ripened salads and daily specials including zucchini stuffed with fish, mushrooms sautéed in lemon butter, eggplant torte, and grilled sausage casserole (36F). Veggies and ruddigores will both depart smiling.

SIGHTS

As if seafood, sun, and surf weren't enough, La Rochelle is also replete with sights and monuments. The 14th-century towers guarding the port helped Renaissance-era La Rochelle thrive as a commercial *entrepôt.* Whenever enemy ships approached, guards linked a chain between the Tour St-Nicolas and the Tour de la Chaîn, barring the harbor. Today, citizens are more concerned about boats leaving the port—sediment and mud have clogged the waters. The **Tour St-Nicolas** (tel. 05 46 41 74 13), on the left as you face the harbor, impresses visitors with formidable fortifications. The climb up passes exhibits about La Rochelle's ongoing melee with the mud. You too may get mired in the maze of narrow staircases that turn you every which way but loose on their way up to the top. The **Tour de la Chaîne** presents a model of the old town in Richelieu's day. (Tour de la Chaîne open daily Easter-Sept. 10am-noon and 2-6pm; Oct.-Easter 2-6pm; admission 20F, children 10F. Tour de la Lanterne and Tour St-Nicolas open June 15-Sept. 15 daily 9:30am-7pm; Sept. 16-Sept. 30 and April-June 14 9:30am-12:30pm and 2-6:30pm; Oct.-March Tues.-Sun. 9:30am-12:30pm and 2-5pm; admission 22F, students 14F.)

Walk along the low rampart running from Tour de la Chaîne to the 58m **Tour de la Lanterne** (tel. 05 46 41 56 04), which, in the 15th century, became France's first lighthouse. The place has a morbid knack for nicknames; it was called the Tour des Prêtres (Priests' Tower) after 13 Huguenots were thrown from the steeple into the water during the wars of religion. In 1822, *quatre sergents* (four sergeants) were kept here before being executed in Paris for crying "Vive la République!" Climb the 162 steps to the top, admiring the often intricate graffiti scrawled on the walls by 19th-century prisoners. At the summit—only 3 inches of stone separates you and a 45m freefall—you can see all the way to Ile d'Oléron on sunny days. (See above for hrs. of Tour de la Lanterne, Tour de la Chaîne, and Tour St-Nicholas.)

From the quai, take bus 10 (direction: Les Minimes) or walk along av. Maillac (35min.) to all 550,000L of the **aquarium,** port des Minimas (tel. 05 46 34 00 00). Soothing songs from whales (and, inexplicably, Enya) whisper as you admire writhing octopi, menacing sharks, sea horses, and a colorful Mediterranean fish, the *merou de Grace Kelly,* in fantastic exhibits. The staff swears you could swim safely amongst the piranhas in its rainforest—*Let's Go* does not recommend swimming with piranhas. (Open daily July-Aug. 9am-11pm; May-June 9am-7pm; Sept.-April 10am-noon and 2-7pm. Admission 42F, students 37F, children 25F. V, MC, AmEx.)

Walking back to the *centre ville* from the aquarium, feel like a kid again at both the wondrous **Musée des Automates** and the retrospective **Musée des Modèles Reduits,** rue du Cerf (tel. 05 46 41 68 08), off av. Marillac. *A la* "It's a Small World," only more inventive and creative, the 300 moving characters include a cheerful clown balancing a ladder on his head. The crown jewel just opened last year: a miniature Montmartre with artists, pharmacists, drunkards, and a lingerie store. A model train loops around the building housing the miniatures of the smaller **Musée des Modèles Reduits** (tel.

05 46 45 31 27), around the corner on rue Desirée. During the *Bataille Navale,* ships maneuver through a tiny sea clouded by cannon smoke. Both are run by a kindly old couple (both open June-Aug. 9:30am-7pm; Sept.-Oct. and March-May 10am-noon and 2-6:30pm; Nov.-Jan. 2-6pm; admission 60F to both; children 30F, or 38F adults, 25F for one museum. V, MC).

Look for the 38m-long ship by the quai marking the **Neptunéa Musée Maritime de la Rochelle,** bassin des Chalutiers (tel. 05 46 28 03 00), near the tourist office. Five decks of exhibits show ship life. Spin the wheel and imagine you're the captain; view the tiny sleeping quarters of the crew and thank God for the *Auberge de Jeunesse.* (Open daily 10am-7pm; admission 40F, students and children 25F.)

Back in the *centre ville,* follow your nose to the one-room **Musée du Flacon à Parfum,** 33, rue du Temple (tel. 05 46 41 32 40; fax 05 46 41 92 40), on the second floor of the Saponaire perfume shop. The first synthetic perfume ever produced is on display, as are a thousand other bottles including a Stalin-era Russian model that must be opened with a can opener. (Obligatory tour. Open Tues.-Sat. 10:30am-7pm; Mon. 2:30-7pm. July-Aug. also Sun. 3-6:30pm. Admission 24F, students 20F).

The pedestrian-only **vieille ville,** dating from the 17th-18th centuries, stretches beyond the whitewashed harbor townhouses. Stroll by the 14th-century **grosse horloge,** but skip the archaeological exhibit inside; a view of the town similar to that from the harbor tower awaits at the top (open July-Sept.15 3-7pm; admission 15F). Stop by the **Palais de Justice** to gawk at the façade or the public hearings (Mon.-Fri. 2pm). The Renaissance façade of the **Hôtel de Ville,** with its prominent statue of its builder, Henry IV, will take your breath away—for free (45-min. French tours of the interior daily July-Aug. 4pm; Oct.-May Sat. and Sun. 3pm; 16F, students 10F).

Near the pl. du Marché stand three good museums (admission 17F for each, students 10F), if you have time. The **Musée des Beaux Arts,** 28, rue Gargolleau (tel. 05 46 41 64 65), houses an impressive collection of paintings, sketches, and tapestries by Delacroix, Rembrandt, Rubens, Titian, and more—look for Paul Signac's depiction of La Rochelle's bustling 18th-century harbor (open Wed.-Mon. 2-5pm, 18F). At 10, rue Fleurian (parallel to rue Gargolleau), the **Musée du Nouveau-Monde** (tel. 05 46 41 46 50) emphasizes the French influence on America's development (open Wed.-Mon. 10:30am-12:30pm and 1:45-6pm, Sun. 1:45-6pm). Between pl. du Marché and cours St-Michel lies the **Musée de la Dernière Guerre** (WWII), 8, rue des Dames (tel. 05 46 41 14 68; open July-Aug. Tues.-Sat. 10am-6pm).

ENTERTAINMENT

The ultra-inviting **La Coursive,** 4, rue St-Jean-du-Perot (tel. 05 46 51 54 00), is a cultural center with info about theater, film, and art festivals (open Mon.-Sat. 1-6:30pm, Sun. 2:30-7pm). La Rochelle's wildly popular festivals attract art-loving, sun-seeking, seafood-slurping mobs like nobody's business. During the first two weeks of July, the city becomes the Cannes of the Atlantic with its **Festival International du Film de la Rochelle** (Admission to all 100 films 450F, 3 films 90F; for tickets, write to 16, rue St-Sabin, 75011 Paris; tel. 01 48 06 16 66; fax 01 48 06 15 40.) Without batting an eyelash, La Rochelle turns right around and holds its **FrancoFolies,** a six-day music festival with francophone performers from all around the world and audiences large enough to move the towers in the port. (Ticket for all concerts 540F; single tickets 50-160F. Call 05 46 50 55 77 or the tourist office.) During the second week of September, hundreds of boats in the Port des Minimes open their immaculate interiors to the public during the **Grand Parois** (for info call 05 46 44 46 39).

Evenings from July to September, **quai Duperré** and **cours des Dames** are closed to cars and open to magicians, mimes, artists, jugglers, and musicians. In the *vieux port,* stop in for a drink and select from 20 imported beers (15-45F) at **MacEwan's,** 7 rue de la Chaîne (tel. 05 46 41 18 94; open daily 6pm-2am). **Cour du Temple,** off rue des Templiers is an alcove inhabited by **Le Mayflower** (tel. 05 46 50 51 39) and **Le Piano Pub** (tel. 05 46 41 03 42). Sample the Mayflower's rum concoction (16F) or toss a serious game of darts while waiting for a Saturday concert at the Piano Pub (both open daily 6pm-3am). The sole gay bar in the *centre ville,* **Le Pastel,** 33, quai

Vallin (tel. 05 46 41 58 81), features art shots of buff males (open Tues.-Sun. 5pm-3am). On rue St-Nicholas, **Le Garibaldi** (tel. 05 46 41 05 49), and **Le Riboulding** (tel. 05 46 41 24 24), face off with music, food, drinks, and live concerts. Le Garibaldi is artsier, while Le Riboulding is a bit mod, but together they offer the perfect atmosphere for a late and lively evening (both open Mon.-Sat. 5pm-3am).

La-Roche-sur-Yon

While not necessarily a destination unto itself, **La-Roche-sur-Yon** (pop. 50,000) is a vital train connection and a potential base for two more exciting areas—the Atlantic coast and the channels of the Marais Poitevin. In an era of growing interest in preservation, La-Roche-sur-Yon has not been shy about "progress," and the result is a thoroughly modern, low-key, and tourist-free city. Potted flowers, boulevards, and parks spring up unexpectedly, making this practical stopover a pleasure as well.

PRACTICAL INFORMATION

La-Roche-sur-Yon has both municipal and departmental tourist offices; you should be able to find all the info you need at either one. To get to the city **tourist office** (tel. 02 51 47 48 49; fax 02 51 47 46 57) from the train station, follow rue Gambetta to the fountain at pl. de la Vendée and take a left onto rue Georges Clemenceau. The office will be on your right just before pl. Napoléon. Bring your magnifying glass to help read the maps. (Open Mon.-Sat. 9am-noon and 2:15-6pm.) 24-hour **ATMs** roll with the homies on rue Georges Clemenceau; **Banque de France,** 54 blvd. Aristide Briand, **exchanges currency.** (Open Mon.-Fri. 9-11:30am and 1:30-3:30pm.) Trains stop for the customary *deux minutes* at the **train station**, blvd. Louis Blanc (tel. 05 40 08 50 50), from Nantes (13 per day, 1hr., 83F); La Rochelle (8 per day, 1hr., 78F); and Les Sables (15 per day, 30min., 37F). Info office open 7am-7:30pm. **Buses** make tracks from the *gare routière,* rue Gaston Ramon (tel. 02 51 62 18 23) to Les Sables and Fontenay le Comte in the Marais Poitevin. Summon local **taxis** with 02 51 62 55 25. In **medical emergencies,** call the **hospital** (tel. 02 51 44 62 15) or dial 15. The **police** camp out at 3 rue Delille (tel. 02 51 45 05 05) but in emergencies, simply dial 17. Across the street from the tourist office, at the **post office**, 8 rue Georges Clemenceau (tel. 02 51 44 22 10) it's business as usual. (Open Mon.-Fri. 8am-7pm, Sat. 8am-noon. Poste restante; photocopies. **Postal code:** 85008.)

ACCOMMODATIONS AND FOOD

Not so pricey as some of its sea-side neighbors, La-Roche-sur-Yon has several unassuming hotels that will put you up without taking you to the cleaners. Don't let the retro look scare you away from **Grand Saint Jean**, 6-7, rue Chazy, (tel. 02 51 37 12 07; fax 02 51 37 11 24). Its well-lit rooms with spacious bathrooms and bouncy beds may be the last bastion of thick shag carpeting. (Doubles 165F, with bath and shower 195F. V.) **Molière** (tel. 02 51 37 08 56), on blvd. Briand at rue Molière, lets basic but clean rooms. (Sings and doubles 115F, with shower 125F. Hall shower 10F.) The tourist office can help with info on nearby campsites.

The **market** in Les Halles (open Tues., Thurs., Sat. 5am-2:30pm, Wed. and Fri. 4-7pm) is a lively social affair, but the folks at the enormous **Intermarché supermarket** (open Mon. 9am-7pm, Tues.-Thurs. 8:30am-7pm, Fri. 8:30am-7:30pm) are more concerned with keeping the checkout line moving. Both are at pl du Marché. **La Pizzeria**, 5, rue Gambetta (tel. 02 51 62 30 95) rolls out some of the biggest pizzas to be had for less than 50F. The garlicky *pizzaoli* (43F) will keep vampires at bay for years! (Open Mon.-Sat. noon-2pm and 7-11pm.)

SIGHTS AND ENTERTAINMENT

Without a church or cathedral for a showcase, La Roche has been left to its own artistic devices. The results are on show at the **Maison Renaissance,** pl. de la Vieille Horloge (tel. 02 51 47 90 86), a rather odd mixture of maps, letters, photographs, architectural models, and gadgets. The oh-so-zealous staff delights in using its VCR. (Open June 13-Aug. Tues.-Sat. 2:15-6:15pm. Admission 15F, students free.)

Student nightlife gathers at **La Table Ronde,** 11, rue Stéphane-Guillemé (tel. 02 51 47 74 69), near Les Halles, where card games and conversation last well into the wee hours. (Open Mon.-Fri. 10am-2am, Sat. 2pm-2am, Sun. 6pm-1am.) Gay nightlife goes art deco at **Almodo Bar,** 19, rue Passage. (Open Mon.-Fri. 6pm-2am, Sat.-Sun. 7pm-2am). From mid-July to mid-August, La Roche transforms itself into the *"Café de l'été"* with free concerts in local bars and at the Jardin de la Marie. Pick up the free *Roche-mag* at the tourist office for details and general goings on.

■ Near La-Roche-sur-Yon: The Marais Poitevin

Serene canals stretching through undisturbed wetlands and forests teeming with plant and animal life have earned this natural reserve to the south of La Roche the nickname *"la Venise Verte"* (the Green Venice). Whether biking along the banks or floating through the canals in the local flat-bottomed *pigouille,* the green poplars, weeping willows, beaver dams, purple irises, and white herons will make you feel as if you've stepped outside of time. Rustic houses peer from beneath the canopy, reminders that a few humans call this Eden home as well. The Marais has changed little since the Middle Ages, when monks dug canals branching off from the Sèvre river in order to enhance agriculture, control floods, and prevent ailments common to the swampy region. The ruins of the 12th-century **Abbaye St-Pierre,** on a sweeping plain in the midst of forest land, are a reminder of the area's origins.

Dozens of tiny villages within its 16,500 hectares, perched on islets protected from potential floods, make convenient bases to explore the canals by foot, bike, or boat. **Coulon,** where you can rent boats or bikes, is situated in an especially beautiful area. To reach Coulon, hop a train from La Roche to Niort and catch one of the **SNCF buses** (line 20) that connect Niort with Coulon (Mon.-Sat. 2-4 per day, 20min., 15F). Daytrips are easiest on Wednesday, Thursday, or Saturday, when buses leave at noon and return 7-8pm. On Monday, Tuesday, and Friday, buses leave only at 7am or in the early evening. Although people do report success hitching in the Marais, a safer alternative is to rent a bike. Ask the **tourist office** in Niort or in Coulon, (tel. 05 49 35 99 29) at pl. de l'Eglise, for suggestions about trails, biking circuits and accommodations in Marais towns or pick up **Le Marais Poiterin à pied** at any tourist office in the Marais. Most villages rent bikes, and Coulon, La Garette, Damvis, Arçais, and Maillezais rent boats. **Rental shops** in Coulon generally charge 30-50F per half-day, 50-80F per day (ID required as deposit) for bikes. **Canoes** cost around 75-100F per half-day. Hotels with no stars begin at 200F in Coulon (needless to say, you should stay in La Roche), but **camping** is at least affordable. In Coulon, try **La Niquière** (tel. 05 49 35 81 19), route de Benêt, complete with tennis courts (tent and two people 63F, additional person 17F).

■ Rochefort-sur-Mer

Belied by its official name, Rochefort-sur-Mer is 15km inland, hugging the banks of the muddy Charente River. Young by French standards, Rochefort was founded in the 17th century when Louis XIV's finance minister, Jean-Baptiste Colbert, sought a sheltered base for the French navy. During the American Revolution, the Marquis de Lafayette left Rochefort on the local frigate *Hermione* to meet George Washington. No longer vigilant against attacking British ships, the *Rochefortiens* nonchalantly keep an eye on visitors sauntering through its beautiful Jardin des Retours. A stepping stone to the Ile d'Oléron, Rochefort is content to let La Rochelle steal the limelight and makes for a relatively untouristed stop along the Atlantic seaboard.

ORIENTATION AND PRACTICAL INFORMATION

Rochefort's two main streets, av. Lafayette and pedestrian-only rue de la République, criss-cross near pl. Colbert, a square of restaurants and cafés that passes as the *centre ville.* To get to the tourist office, head down av. Wilson straight out of the *gare.* Turn right onto av. Pelletan, which curves around in front of a public garden, the cours d'Ablois. Turn left and walk straight through the garden—the glittering glass office will be across the street (10min.). The well-intentioned staff at the **tourist office,** av. Sadi Carnot (tel. 05 46 99 08 60; fax 05 46 99 52 64), gladly surrenders maps and lists of hotels and restaurants, reserves rooms (15F), and organizes daytrips and tours of the city (open daily 9am-8pm; Sept. 16-June 14 Mon.-Sat. 9am-12:30pm and 2-6:30pm). The **train station** sits on av. Wilson (tel. 05 46 82 28 30). Trains to: La Rochelle (8-12 per day, 30min., 30F); Saintes (40min., 42F), and Bordeaux (2½hr., 118F). **Océcars,** at the *gare routière* on pl. de Verdun (tel. 02 46 99 23 65; open Mon.-Fri. 9am-noon and 2-6:30pm, Sat. 9am-noon), runs 7-10 buses per day to La Rochelle (1¼hr., 28F). For a 78F roundtrip or 40F (in July and Aug. only) if you are 25 or under, **Citram** will sweep you away from the *gare* and deposit you at Le Château or Ile d'Oléron (3 buses per day, check schedule). **Bikes** are available in the plaza in front of the tourist office for 6F per ½-day, 12F per day. 250F deposit required. Dial 17 for an **emergency,** 15 for a **medical emergency.** The **post office** (tel. 05 46 99 07 00) is next door at 1, rue du Docteur Peltier. **Currency exchange.** Poste restante. Photocopies. Open Monday-Friday 8am-7pm, Sat. 8am-noon. The **postal code** is 17300.

ACCOMMODATIONS AND FOOD

In summer, you'll need to reserve a couple of weeks ahead to fend off the overflow vacationers from La Rochelle. Behind its bright blue doors, the 50-bed **Auberge de Jeunesse (HI),** 20, rue de la République (tel. 05 46 99 74 62), has excellent kitchen facilities, clean four- to 12-bed rooms, a small garden, no curfew, and lockout 10am-noon. Bring insect repellent (44F; sheets 17F; camping 25F per person; send a 30% deposit if reserving more than a week in advance). In July and August, reception is at the hostel (open 8-10am and 1:30-9pm). The rest of the year, check in at the **Centre Information Jeunesse,** 97, rue de la République (tel. 05 46 82 10 40). From the train station, head straight out onto av. Wilson, which becomes rue Begon; go down one block with the park on your left and turn right at rue Victor Hugo, then take the first left onto rue de la République (15min.; open Mon.-Fri. 9am-noon and 2-6:30pm, Sat. 2:30-5:30pm). Just down from the youth hostel, the **Hôtel Roca Fortis,** 14, rue de la République (tel. 05 46 99 26 32), ensures a peaceful stay with two lovely gardens, almost luxurious rooms, and congenial managers (singles with shower 185F; doubles with shower 220-235F; triples and quads with shower and toilet 325F; breakfast 28F; V, MC). The new **Camping Le Bateau** (tel. 05 46 99 41 00), on rue des Pêcheurs d'Islande, 2km from town on the way to La Rochelle, offers a pool, tennis courts, and hot water next to the river. Bring bug spray! (18F per person, 12F per tent, 8F per car, 16F for electricity.)

The local open air **market** convenes at the intersection of av. Charles de Gaulle and rue Jean Jaurès on Tuesday, Thursday, and Saturday mornings from 7:30am-1pm as it has for three centuries. **Prisunic supermarket** is two blocks up at 46, av. Charles de Gaulle (open Mon.-Sat. 8:30am-7:30pm, and Sun. 9am-noon in July and Aug.). While dining in pl. Colbert may be more scenic, the bargains lie elsewhere. Double your culinary options with a stroll down rue Jean-Jaurès. It is worth considering stopping by Rochefort just to eat at **Chez Nous,** 72, rue Jean-Jaurès (tel. 05 46 99 07 11); from pl. Colbert turn left on rue Cochon Duvivier and take the third right onto Jean-Jaurès. Large local clientele, even larger helpings of *fruits de mer.* Five-course *menus* 58F, 76F, or 98F—after 3 courses you're stuffed (open Mon.-Fri. noon-3pm and 7-11pm, Sat. noon-3pm).

SIGHTS

Rochefort features one of the more eclectic mixes of museums in the region—and that's pretty darn eclectic. Throw medieval, Renaissance, Arabic, and Oriental decor into a blender along with the second day of Woodstock, and you might get **La Maison de Pierre Loti,** 141, rue Pierre Loti (tel. 05 46 99 16 88), former home of Loti (1850-

1923), the writer of *Aziyadé* and *Mon Frère Yves.* Having grown up in a strict household in this stilted town, Pierre felt a need to break out of the mold—and how. His abode includes a mosque on the top floor from which he sang prayers (to the dismay of neighbors), a Turkish smoking room (his study), and a Basque-Gothic banquet hall where Loti threw wild parties. At a Chinese-themed bash, guests wore cheongsams and smoked opium; another bash required them to wear medieval garb and speak in old French. (One-hour obligatory French tours daily except Sun. mornings every 30min. 10-11am and 2-5pm, Wed. also at 6pm; Oct.-Dec.19 and Jan.21-June Wed.-Mon. at 10 and 11am and 2, 3, and 4pm. Admission 40F, students 20F.)

The longest building in France (374m), the **Corderie Royale** (tel. 05 46 87 01 90), near the river, opened in 1670 to build ocean-going ships. It comes complete with masts, ropes, gunpowder, and cannons from the Naval Artillery. The original building, part of Louis XIV's arsenal, burned down in 1944, but has been restored. The structure now houses civil offices and the **Centre International de la Mer,** with a rather uninteresting permanent exhibit that explains the history of rope-making through working machines and pictures. Don't get entangled here (open June-Sept. daily 9am-7pm; Oct.-May 9am-6pm; admission 30F, students 25F).

Surrounding the Corderie, the **Jardin des Retours** (Garden of Returns) is the only garden in France constructed as a cultural project and sustained by the state. It displays foreign flora brought back by sailors from their voyages around the world. Lug your picnic around the labyrinth of hedges near the Corderie, or simply take a sunset stroll through the serene parks lining the opaque Charente river. Next to the Corderie, the **Musée de la Marine,** pl. de la Galissonière (tel. 05 46 99 86 57), houses France's second largest naval collection, with over 30 ship models and figureheads that adorned the bows of ships, including Pandora and her dastardly box (open Nov. 15-Oct. 15 Wed.-Mon. 10am-noon and 2-6pm; admission 29F, students 19F).

The **Musée d'Art et d'Histoire,** 63, av. Charles de Gaulle (tel. 05 46 99 83 99), contains a large model of Rochefort, a collection of Asiatic and Oceanic art, and the requisite 16th- to 20th-century paintings. The most interesting part of the museum is its thousands of sea shells, including huge conches and nautilus shells (open daily 1:30-7pm; Sept.-June Tues.-Sat. 1:30-5:30pm; admission 10F, students 8F).

Saintes

Saintes' three proud cathedral spires and tree-lined streets reveal nothing of the turbulent 2000-year history the town has weathered. Originally founded by the Gauls, it served as capital of Aquitaine under the Romans. Mediolanum, as it was then called, carelessly adopted Christianity in the 3rd century, thereby raising the ire of the Gauls, who burnt the city to the ground. Sacked and plundered by pyromaniacal Gallic tribes between the 3rd and 10th centuries, Saintes didn't miss out on the Black Plague, the Hundred Years' War, or the wars of religion, either.

Through it all, the *Saintais* have stubbornly clung to their religion and their heritage. The Abbaye-aux-Dames and the Eglise St-Eutrope are starting points from which to explore this enchanting town, which has maintained its trademark resilience even in the face of energetic tourist hordes. Bisected by the graceful Charente River and buffered by lush greenery, Saintes rewards visitors' curiosity with a quiet charm even the rampaging Gauls would have appreciated.

ORIENTATION AND PRACTICAL INFORMATION

Saintes lies on the Charente river, along the La Rochelle-Bordeaux railway line, 25km from Cognac. To get to the tourist office, take a sharp left upon leaving the train station and follow **av. de la Marne** until you hit the hopping **av. Gambetta.** Turn right and follow it to the river; the Arc de Triomphe will be on your left. Cross pont Palissy and continue straight on leafy green **cours National;** the tourist office is on your right in a villa set back from the street (15min.). The mellow pedestrian district's hub is **rue Victor Hugo,** three blocks to the left after crossing the bridge.

Tourist Office: 62, cours National (tel. 05 46 74 23 82; fax 05 46 92 17 01). Helpful staff makes reservations, distributes brochures, gives tours (June-Sept. Mon.-Sat. 4 per day, 1½hr., 30F; in English upon request), organizes river cruises (40F, 180F with lunch), and sells walking maps. Open June 15-Sept. 15 Mon.-Sat. 9am-7pm, Sun. 10:15am-7pm; mid-Sept. to mid-June Mon.-Sat. 9am-12:30pm and 2-6pm.

Banks: Banks with **ATMs** sit and spin on cours National. Best rate is at **Banque de France,** 9, cours Lemercier (tel. 05 46 93 40 33; open Mon.-Fri. 9am-noon).

Trains: (tel. 08 36 35 35 35), pl. Pierre Senard. To: La Rochelle (7-8 per day, 1hr., 60F); Bordeaux (7-8 per day, 1½hr., 92F); Cognac (5 per day, 20min., 26F); Angoulême (5 per day, 1hr., 65F); Poitiers (5 per day, 2hr., 150F); Paris (1-2 per day, 5 TGV, 3½hr.-5½hr., 260-350F). **Lockers** 15-20F. Office open Mon.-Sat. 8am-7pm, Sun. 8am-9pm.

Buses: Autobus Aunis et Saintonge, 1, cours Reverseaux (tel. 05 46 97 52 23). To: Royan (3 per day, 1hr., 38F); Le Château on Ile d'Oléron (3 per day, 1¼hr., 57F); and St-Pierre d'Oléron on Ile d'Oléron (1 per day, 2¾hr., 62F). Office open Mon.-Fri. 8am-noon and 2-6:30pm. **Océcars** (tel. 05 46 99 23 65 in Rochefort). To: La Rochelle (1 per day, 2½hr., 52F) and Rochefort (1-2 per day, 1¼hr., 38F). An operator will answer calls Mon.-Fri. 8:30am-noon and 2-7pm.

Taxis: At the *gare* (tel. 05 46 74 24 24). 6F per km, 7F per km at night and Sun.

Bike Rental: Groleau Cycles, 9, cours Reserveaux (tel. 05 46 74 19 03). 55F per day, deposit 1500F. Mountain bikes 80F per day, same deposit. Open Tues.-Sat. 8:30am-12:15pm and 2-7pm. **Jacques Huriaud Cycles,** 36, av. Gambetta (tel. 05 46 92 13 45), near the Abbey. Bikes 40F per day, 270F per week. *VTTs* 60F per day, 270F per week; deposit 1000F. Open Tues.-Sun. 9am-noon and 2-7pm.

Laundromat: Laverie de la Saintonge, 18, quai de la République. 7kg washed for 24F, dried for 5F. Open Mon.-Wed. and Fri.-Sat. 8:30am-7pm, Sun. 10am-7pm.

Medical Assistance: Hospital, pl. du 11 Novembre (tel. 05 46 92 76 76). Turn left onto cours Reserveaux from the tourist office; the hospital is 3 blocks down on the left. **Medical emergency** tel. 15.

Police: rue du Bastion (tel. 05 46 93 52 33). Turn left on cours Reserveaux from the tourist office, then left on rue du Bartion. The station is 1 block down on the right. **Emergency** tel. 17.

Post Office: 8, cours National (tel. 05 46 93 05 84). Poste restante. **Currency exchange.** Open Mon.-Fri. 8:30am-7pm, Sat. 8:30am-noon. **Postal code:** 17100.

ACCOMMODATIONS AND CAMPING

Hotels fill for the early to mid-July festivals; otherwise rooms should be easy to find. Most of the inexpensive lodgings cluster on the train station side of the Charente.

Auberge de Jeunesse (HI), 2, pl. Geoffrey-Martel (tel. 05 46 92 14 92), next to the Abbaye-aux-Dames. From the train station, take a sharp left onto av. de la Marne and then turn right onto av. Gambetta, left onto rue du Pérat, right onto rue St-Pallais. 25m up at pl. St-Pallais, turn left through the archway into the courtyard of the Abbaye. Go straight through, and the hostel will be on your right (15min.). A clean, renovated building that feels like part of the Abbaye itself. Carpeted 4- to 8-bed rooms, comfy mattresses, and stellar connecting bathrooms. Clean kitchen. 66F, breakfast included. Sheets 16F. Camping 27F. Reception 7am-noon and 5-11pm; Oct.-May until 10pm. No lockout or curfew.

Hôtel Voyageurs, 133, av. Gambetta (tel. 05 46 95 09 69). Great terrace. 34 clean, semi-big rooms. Doubles 120F, with shower 170F. 3 people 219F. Breakfast 24F.

Hôtel Parisien, 35, rue Frédéric-Mestreau (tel. 05 46 74 28 92), by the train station. Affable management, clean rooms, and a *jardin* of blooming flowers. Doubles 130F, with shower 170F, with two beds 175F. Triples 160F, with shower 205F. Huge quint with shower 260F. Extra bed 45F. Bungalow for 2 in the garden 160F. Shower 15F. Breakfast 25F. Call several weeks ahead for July-Aug. V, MC.

Hôtel St-Pallais, 1, pl. St-Pallais (tel. 05 46 92 51 03), overlooking the Abbaye-aux-Dames across the square. Clean, spacious rooms with showers. Friendly manager speaks English and tends the sometimes noisy bar downstairs. Singles 100F. Doubles 120F. Triples and quads 180F. Breakfast 24F. V, MC.

Hotel Le Té-Gé-Vé, 45, av. de la Marne (tel. 05 46 93 07 06). It's right by the train station and TGV, *bien sûr.* Above a crowded bar that usually clears out by 11pm. Decent, clean singles with showers. Singles and doubles 100F. Breakfast 28F.

Camping: Camping Au Fil de L'Eau, 6, rue de Courbiac (tel. 05 46 93 08 00). From the train station, follow *auberge* directions to av. Gambetta and turn right onto quai de l'Yser after crossing the bridge (25-30min.). Signs mark the way. Along the banks of the Charente, next to the municipal pool (free for campers) and a mini-golf course (25F). 1km from the *centre ville.* Reception 8am-1pm and 3-9pm; May 15-June and Sept. 9:30am-noon and 4-8pm. 19F per adult, 10F per child, 20F per site including car. Electricity 15F. Open May 15-Sept. 15. V, MC.

FOOD

Saintes is blessed with plenty of mom and pop restaurants and bars with *menus,* especially in the pedestrian district, av. Gambetta, and cours National. Restaurants crowd the pedestrian streets by **rue Victor Hugo;** more expensive places line av. Gambetta. If not for the still-dewy produce, attend one of the Saintes' many boisterous **markets** for the ambiance: Tuesdays and Fridays on cours Reverseaux, Wednesdays and Saturdays by Cathédrale St-Pierre, and Thursdays and Sundays on av. de la Marne and av. Gambetta (all 8am-12:30pm). The huge **E. Leclerc supermarket,** cours de Gaulle (tel. 05 46 92 12 00), is near the hostel. From rue St-Pallais, follow rue du Pont Amilion straight through the rotary; the Brobdingnagian blue building will be on your left (open Mon.-Thurs. and Sat. 9am-7:15pm, Fri. 9am-8:15pm).

Menus in Saintes flaunt the region's inescapable *fruits de mer* (seafood), as well as *escargot* dishes and *mojettes* (white beans cooked in Charenté). Wash it down with *pineau,* a sweeter relative of cognac prepared in the caves around Saintes. Offering few regional specialties, but heaps of traditional stand-bys, the **Cafétéria du Bois-d'Amour,** 7, rue du Bois-d'Amour (tel. 05 46 97 26 54), off cours National in the Galerie Merchandise in the *centre ville,* gives new meaning to "service with a smile." *Plat du jour* with two veggies 29-36F, crêpes 4-11F, beers 7F, cheeses, fruits, and desserts (open daily 11:30am-2:30pm and 7-11pm; V, MC). **Scherazade,** 48, rue St-Eutrope (tel. 05 46 97 20 28), across from the Eglise St-Eutrope. Delicious *labem Mechoui* (lamb chops). Fresh and filling 55F *menu* of hors d'oeuvres (vegetarian version available). 59F *menu* with hummus or falafel served with homemade pita will please you for 1001 nights (open 11:30am-2:30pm and 7pm-midnight; generally closed Sat. July-Aug.; V, MC). **La Romana,** 89, av. Gambetta (tel. 05 46 74 18 11), ladles homemade tomato sauce over pastas, pours it onto pizzas, and practically drowns the satisfying *gratin aubergines* (48F). 59F *menu* includes a choice between such options as pasta stuffed with mushrooms and salmon lasagna. Waitstaff fulfills the all-you-can-eat bread expectation (open noon-2pm and 6-11pm).

SIGHTS AND ENTERTAINMENT

International flags line both sides of the **pont Bérnard Palissy,** which looks out onto most of Saintes' interesting sights, many of which are free and provide a pleasant and educational afternoon of sightseeing. On the left bank of the river rises the Roman **Arc de Triomphe,** more commonly known as the Arc Germanicus. Constructed in AD 18, the impressive stone structure was the entrance to the city for centuries. Along the Arc, the blooming flowers and shaded benches of the **Jardin Public** serenely await picnickers and tired sightseers. Every Sunday in July and August at 3pm, the garden features free performances ranging from demonstrations of traditional *saintonge* folk dancing to flamenco to—grab your Stetson—country music line dancing.

On the esplanade André Malraux, the partially finished puzzle of Roman columns, friezes, and cornices waits at the **Musée Archéologique** (tel. 05 46 74 20 97). Most date from the galling demolition of the town's ramparts in the 4th century (open June-Sept. Tues. 10am-noon and 2-6pm; Oct.-May Tues.-Sun. 2-5pm; free).

Rue Arc de Triomphe (which becomes rue St-Pallais) leads to the **Abbaye-aux-Dames** (tel. 05 46 97 48 48). First built in 1047, the abbey led a quiet life for a while—some Gothic touch-ups here, another gallery there—until plagues, fires, and wars prompted centuries of constant construction and reconstruction. During the Revolutionary anti-religious fervor, the abbey was shut down and turned into a prison. Today, the abbey serves as Saintes' musical and cultural center. Frequent expositions of the work of local artists brighten the pale stone walls of the **Salle Capitulaire,** which was once the daily meeting place for Benedictine nuns; upstairs, a small museum details the history of the abbey with a cartoon-like fresco. The pine-cone bell tower of the church, **Eglise Notre-Dame,** dates from the 12th century, when Eleanor of Aquitaine gave the nuns some friendly architectural pointers during renovations. Abstract contemporary tapestries on the walls depict the six days of the Creation— but you'll need the signs to tell day from night. Consult *l'Abbaye aux Dames: Été* pamphlet at the tourist office for summer concert listings (concerts 35-70F). (Exposition and ramparts open July-Aug. daily 10am-12:30pm and 2-7pm; Sept.-June Thurs.-Fri. and Sun.-Tues. 2-7pm, Wed. and Sat. 10am-12:30pm and 2-7pm. Admission 20F, under 16 free. Guided tours in French 30F; June-Sept. Mon.-Sat. 2 per day. Visiting the church itself is free.)

Cross the flower-lined pedestrian bridge as you head for the **Cathédrale St-Pierre** on rue St-Pierre. Enormous, imposing, and capped by a metal helmet, it's more like a fortress than a house of worship. Saintes never fully rebuilt the cathedral after Protestants destroyed its nave and chapels in 1568. The church's pride and joy is its restored 370-year-old organ (open daily 10am-7pm; free).

From St-Pierre, walk up rue des Jacobins, climb the stairs, and work your way up to cours Reverseaux. Take a left, then turn right on rue St-Eutrope toward **Eglise St-Eutrope,** 15, rue St-Eutrope (tel. 05 46 93 71 12), a split-level Gothic-Romanesque hybrid with a prickly steeple and statues of the apostles lining the back wall of the apse. Once your eyes adjust to the cold and cavernous Romanesque crypt, let them wander left to the white stone that marks the final resting place of the martyred St. Eutrope. These very remains were a stop on the once-important pilgrimage route to Santiago de Compostela in Spain (open daily 9am-7pm; free).

Take rue St-Eutrope away from the *centre ville* and turn right onto rue de Lacurie to get to the **Arènes Gallo-Romaines,** now a crumbled and peaceful amphitheater in a residential neighborhood. Built in AD 40, the structure seated the 20,000 spectators who flocked to see gladiators battle wild animals—as well as each other—to the death. Today, the tunnel entrance and the supporting arches and staircases of this awesome pile of rubble still stand (open daily 9am-8pm; winter 9am-6pm; free).

Historically content to do things at their own pace, the *Santois* extend the same approach to **nightlife.** Downshift and park yourself in a café or pub for an evening of conversation and sunset watching. Along quai de la République, the **Vaudeville** (beer 20F, cocktails 30-50F; open Wed.-Sun. until 2am) and **La Belle Epoque** (beer 15-20F, whiskey 35F; open Wed.-Mon. until 2am) are popular, if somewhat over decorated. **Le Club,** a.k.a. **Tatou,** 5, quai de l'Yser, holds live reggae and world music concerts weekly and is a hangout for the younger set (beers 10-15F; open Mon.-Sat. 8pm-2am). Shoot a rack at the popular **Billard Santais,** 126, av. Gambetta (tel. 05 46 92 17 12), accompanied by 10F beers (open Wed.-Mon. until 2am).

If you've got a car, you can dance up a storm at **Le Santon,** Ste-Vegas (tel. 05 46 93 42 76) route de Royan, where area students go to party. In summer, the adjoining swimming pool provides a respite from steamy body heat (open daily until 2:30-3am, cover 45F). Also in the Complexe Ste-Vegas is the mixed gay-straight bar **Le Spartacus** (tel. 05 46 93 42 76), with a more refined crowd than its neighbor.

In mid-July, the **Jeux Santons,** a two-week celebration of international folk music, soothes Saintes. The Arènes Gallo-Romaines host the opening and closing events. Some events are free; most cost 20-80F (call 05 46 74 47 50, or stop by 43, rue Gautier for info). In July, look also for the classical concerts of the 10-day **Académies Musicales** (tickets 60-240F; call 05 46 97 48 48; fax 05 46 92 58 56 for info).

Cognac

Along the banks of the Charente, which Henry IV labeled the "gentlest and most beautiful river in France," rises the warm, though not quite as beautiful, town of Cognac (pop. 22,000). Trade megaliths Hennessy, Martell, Rémy-Martin, and Otard offer their guests a look inside the distilleries, words of wisdom on the fine art of barrel-making and distillation, and a sampling of sweet liqueur—*gratuit,* as befits their product, a worldwide symbol of hospitality. An ideal daytrip from, or a stop en route between, Saintes or Angoulême, Cognac offers an economic opportunity to partake of this most exclusive of liquors.

ORIENTATION AND PRACTICAL INFORMATION

To get to the **tourist office,** 16, rue du 14 Juillet (tel. 05 45 82 10 71; fax 05 45 82 34 47), follow av. du Maréchal Leclerc out of the *gare* to the first circle and take a right onto rue Elisee Mousnier, following signs to the *centre ville.* Take a right on rue Bayard and cross pl. Bayard onto rue du 14 Juillet (15min.). The staff will find rooms for free and **rents bikes** in July and August (35F per ½-day, 55F per day, 250F per week with passport or 200F deposit; office open Jun. 15-Sept. 15 Mon.-Sat. 9:30am-6:30pm; Sept. 16-June 14 Mon.-Sat. 9:30am-12:30pm and 1:30-6:30pm). **Banks** and **ATMs** line pl. François 1er, at the end of rue du 14 Juillet. Find the **Banque de France** at 39, bd. Denfert-Rochereau (tel. 05 45 82 25 10), for the best rates (open Mon.-Fri. 8:45am-noon and 1:35-4pm). Four to five **trains** (tel. 08 36 35 35 35) chug-chug daily from Angoulême (1hr., 46F), five to six from Saintes (20min., 25F).The **post office,** at 2, pl. Bayard (tel. 05 45 36 31 82), has currency exchange and poste restante (open Mon.-Fri. 8am-6pm, Sat. 8:30am-noon; **postal code:** 16100).

ACCOMMODATIONS, CAMPING, AND FOOD

One-star hotels in Cognac often have room, but call ahead. The centrally located **Hôtel du Cheval Blanc,** 6-8, pl. Boyard (tel. 05 45 82 09 55), rents clean, if worn, rooms with bouncy mattresses. Ask for the quieter rooms facing the back. (Singles 120F. Doubles 125-175F. Free showers. Breakfast 30F. V, MC.) Check the map outside the train station before heading to **Hôtel St-Martin,** 112, av. Paul Firino-Martell (tel. 05 45 35 01 29), that offers decent oldish rooms over a great restaurant. (Singles 120F. Doubles 150F. Shower 15F. Breakfast 25F). Indulge in the generous 60F lunch *menu* (restaurant open noon-2pm and 7-10pm; V, MC). Three-star **Cognac Camping,** bd. de Chatenay (tel. 05 45 32 13 32), on route de St-Sévère, is a 30-minute walk from the *centre ville.* (2 people with site, showers, and electricity, 55F. Wheelchair accessible. Pool. Laundry 20F per 7kg. Open May-Oct.)

Tasting Cognac's famous product doesn't necessarily mean drinking it. Restaurants around **pl. François I** serve local specialties drenched in cognac. You can have your very first sip of V.S.O.P. caliber cognac for 18F at **Cafétéria l'Ara,** 7, pl. François I (tel. 05 45 32 07 51), where 35F cafeteria *menus,* choice of veggies, and institutional desserts are always *en vogue* (open July-Aug. daily 11:30am-2:30pm and 6:30-10pm; Sept.-June closed Tues. evenings). Right in the *centre ville* stands **La Boune Goule,** 42, allée de la Corderie (tel. 05 45 82 06 37). The name comes from a *charentais* expression meaning "good taste"; here, that's an understatement. With the comfort of a 35F all-you-can-eat salad bar and the assurance that "nothing on the menu, except the fries, is frozen," settle down for huge, fresh portions of local cuisine and 30F omelettes (open noon-2:30pm and 7-11:30pm; V, MC). If you're looking for food in warehouse quantities at wholesale prices, avoid the expensive, though admittedly more diverse, **Prisunic** on pl. Francois I (tel. 05 45 82 18 21; open Mon.-Sat. 8:30am-7:30pm), and fly to **LARC,** pl. Boyard, with deals like 10 croissants for 5F (open Mon.-Sat. 9am-12:30pm and 2:30-8pm; V, MC). There is an **indoor market** at pl. d'Armes Tuesday through Sunday (7am-1pm).

SIGHTS AND ENTERTAINMENT

The joy of visiting Cognac lies in making your way from one monolithic brandy bottler to the next, touring warehouses, watching films on the history of each house, and collecting nip bottles. If a nip is not enough, Otard offers its Extra in a blue porcelain bust of François I for 1500F, while Hennessy's silver-gilded flask is a mere 4200F. Allow yourself time to tour. If you want the drink, you'll have to take the tour, and finding one in a language you understand may require quite a wait. Don't forget to figure in the trek from the train station, either, as it can be a hike.

Otard, 127, bd. Denfert-Rochereau (tel. 05 45 82 40 00; fax 05 45 82 75 11), though not the largest of the houses, is the most interesting to visit. It occupies the **Château de Cognac** where the boy who would be King, François I, was born in 1494. This *chais* (aging- and store-house) offers a humorous and at times dramatic tour that includes a glimpse of the cool, damp aging cellars (set to bombastic classical music), a stroll through the Renaissance-style halls, and a description of how cognac is made. The *dégustation* is free, but 10cl nip bottles cost 15F. (Open July-Aug. daily 9:30am-5:30pm; April-June and Sept. 10am-noon and 2-6pm; Oct.-March Mon.-Thurs. 10am-noon and 2-6pm, Fri. 10am-noon and 2-5pm. 10F.)

Hennessy, 1, rue de la Richonne (tel. 05 45 35 72 68), is the largest cognac producer in the world, exporting 99% of its 31 million bottles each year, mainly to the Far East, America, and England. Its tour is less informative but includes a film detailing cognac's history, a short boat ride across the Charente, a look at the **Cooperage** museum that describes the ancient techniques of barrel-making, a stroll past the assembly-line bottling plant, and a 3cl nip bottle (open Mon.-Sat. 9am-6pm; Oct.-May 8:30-11am and 1:45-4:30pm; free). A young international staff leads the tour of the oldest major cognac house, **Martell,** rue de Gate-Bourse (tel. 05 45 36 33 33), founded in 1715. In the courtyard, expert craftsmen are piecing together—using only age-old methods—a *Gabare,* the original cognac runner, which Martell plans to set afloat in the Charente river in the summer of 1997. The complimentary *dégustation* and free nip bottles come from other stock entirely. (Open July-Aug. Mon.-Fri. 9am-5pm, Sat.-Sun. 10am-4:15pm; June and Sept. Mon.-Fri. 9:30-11am and 1:30-5pm; Oct.-May Mon.-Thurs. 9:30-11am and 2-5pm, Fri. 9:30-11am. Free.)

Those who can't get enough of the distillation process can rent a bike or drive 5km out of Cognac on D732 to **Rémy-Martin** (tel. 05 45 35 76 66; fax 05 45 35 77 98). A train carries you from the *caves* to the vines that make the 210,000 barrels of cognac. Aside from the train, it's little different from those in town. (Open daily June15-Sept.15 9:30am-noon and 1:15-6pm; April 15-June 14 and Sept.1-Oct. 15 Mon.-Sat. 9:30am-noon and 1:15-6pm. Admission 20F, under 18 free; includes *dégustation* and a nip bottle.) The tourist office has info on other houses.

The **Musée Municipal du Cognac,** 48, bd. Denfert-Rochereau (tel. 05 45 32 07 25), details the 5000-year history of Cognac, the town, and cognac, the industry. Its gallery has works from the late 19th to early 20th centuries, notably a Rodin and a jarring, Impressionistic *Le Jugement de Paris* (open June-Sept. Wed.-Mon. 10am-noon and 2-6pm; Oct.-May Wed.-Mon. 2-5:30pm; admission 12F, students 6F). If you've had enough Cognac, stumble over for a picnic in the manicured **Jardin de l'Hôtel de Ville** around the museum (open daily 7am-10pm; winter 7am-8pm).

Situated in this fertile river valley, Cognac offers wonderful opportunities for **hiking** (call 05 46 90 16 45 for info) and **canoeing** (tel. 05 45 82 46 24; fax 05 45 83 94 70). In early April, Cognac proudly hosts the **Festival du film Policier,** bringing together 10 cop flicks for jury consideration. Past competitors have included *Presumed Innocent* and *All the President's Men* (tickets to all films 330F, 3 films 110F; call tourist office for info). In late July, the **Blues Passions** concerts showcase American and French blues musicians. For info, visit 9A, pl. Cagouillet (tel. 05 45 32 17 28; fax 05 45 32 66 33; tickets 80F each, under 12 free).

Impress Your Dates

Although Cognac's soils yield only mediocre wine, three centuries ago an inspired wine-maker found that distilling his wines a second time produced a smooth, deliciously sweet drink. Dubbed *vin brulé* (burnt wine) due to the distillation process, the brandy was a quick success across 17th-century Europe. Nowadays, cognac is made by blending the twice-distilled *eaux de vie* (waters of life) and aging the blends for at least two years in oak casks. Each cognac house has a head taster who selects the year's mixture by sampling from thousands of barrels. Before you rush to apply for the job, keep in mind that the apprenticeship lasts up to 20 years and, in many *caves,* the position is a family affair—Hennessy's tasters have heralded from the Fillioux family for seven generations.

The older the cognac, the smoother, sweeter, and more *cher* it becomes. The five designations (in English since the English were the first to trade cognac) are: VS (Very Special, aged 3-5yrs.), VSOP (Very Superior Old Pale, or as the French say, *"Verser Sans Oublier Personne"*—"Pour without forgetting anyone," 8yr.), *Napoléon* (15yrs.), XO (30-35yrs.), and Extra or *Paradis* (over 50yrs.). Unlike wine, which continues to mature after bottling, cognac ages only in the barrel, while it's soaking up the wood's essence. Throw logic to the wind and accept that a cognac made in 1905 and bottled in 1910 is still only five years old today.

Of the 170 million cognac bottles in production, approximately 12 million, will be lost to evaporation as part of the aging process, feeding the black fungus that covers the cognac caves and many houses in town. Locals refer to this vapor as *"la part des Anges"* (the Angels' share). Over 50% of the bottles that do make it out of Cognac are shipped to the Far East, where the city-state of Hong Kong is second only to America in cognac consumption. In Hong Kong, elegant restaurants display shelves of the elaborate bottles, each prominently marked with the name of the tasteful customer whose deep pockets purchased it.

Angoulême

Perched on a natural plateau overlooking the Charente river and its countryside, Angoulême (pop. 46,000) keeps its treasures on its hilltop and relegates the rest of its surroundings to an unparalleled view. The cradle of the French paper industry in the 1600s, the town and its excess supply of writing pads attracted John Calvin to finish his *Institutes of Christian Religion* here in 1534. The revocation of the Edict of Nantes in the 1600s sent the primarily Protestant papermakers packing to Holland. Today, Angoulême has emerged as the capitol of French comic strip production. Countless *Lucky Luke, Tintin,* and *Astérix* volumes roll off the town's presses each day. Fast-paced and always on the make, Angoulême combines fun and adventure with just a hint of dramatic intrigue.

ORIENTATION AND PRACTICAL INFORMATION

Angoulême lies halfway down the TGV line between Bordeaux and Poitiers. The *vieille ville* nestles among ramparts high on a plateau just south of the Charente river and southwest of the train station. It is easy to get lost in the maze of streets, so grab a map from the tourist office branch right outside the train station. To get to the main tourist office at pl. des Halles, follow **av. Gambetta** uphill and to the right to **pl. G. Perrot.** Continue straight up the rampe d'Aguesseau and take a right onto **bd. Pasteur.** The tourist office sits to your immediate left after passing Les Halles.

Tourist Information: Tourist Office, pl. des Halles (tel. 05 45 95 16 84; fax 05 45 95 91 76). Tours (1-1½hr., 20F, students 10F). Open April-Aug. Mon.-Sat. 10am-7pm, Sun. 10am-noon and 2-5pm; Sept.-March Mon.-Fri. 9am-12:30pm and 1:30-6pm, Sat. 10am-noon and 2-5pm. **Kiosk** (tel. 05 45 92 27 57) by the *gare* open Nov.-Feb. Mon.-Fri. 9am-12:30pm and 1:30-6pm, Sat. 10am-noon, and 2-5pm.

Budget Travel: Voyages Wasteels, 49, rue de Génève (tel. 05 45 92 56 89). 20-30% savings on train and plane tix. Open Mon.-Sat. 9am-noon and 2-7pm. V, MC.

Money: Banks and 24-hr. **ATMs** abound in the areas of pl. Marengo and around the Hôtel de Ville. Best rates at **Banque de France,** 4, rue de Château (tel. 05 45 97 00 00), on pl. Hôtel de Ville. Open Mon.-Fri. 8:40am-noon and 1:30-3:30pm.

Trains: pl. de la Gare (tel. 08 36 35 35 35), on the main Paris-Spain rail line. To: Bordeaux (3 per day, 1½hr., 100F); Poitiers (5-6 per day, 1hr., 87F); Saintes via Cognac (4-5 per day, 1hr., 65F). TGVs to: Bordeaux (8-10 per day, 55min., 100F plus 9F reservation); Poitiers (10-12 per day, 45min., 87F plus 7F); Paris (2½hr., 325F); Périgueux (3 per day, 1 on Sun., 2hr., 84F). **Lockers** 30F. Office open Mon.-Sat. 9:30am-noon and 2-7pm.

Buses: Autobus Citram, (tel. 05 45 25 42 60). To: Cognac (7 per day, 1hr., 45F); La Rochelle (1-2 per day, 3½hr., 100F); Bordeaux (1-2 per day, 3hr., 85F). Buses stop at pl. du Champ de Mars. Buy tickets on board. For information, go to the **Cartrans** office, pl. du Champ de Mars (tel. 05 45 95 95 99). Open Tues.-Fri. 9am-noon and 2:15-6:15pm; July-Aug. Tues.-Fri. 2-6pm.

Public Transportation: STGA, 554, route de Bordeaux (tel. 05 45 65 25 00). Kiosk on pl. du Champ de Mars has maps (tel. 05 45 65 25 25; open Mon.-Fri. 1:30-6:30pm, Sat. 1:30-4:30pm). Tickets 7F. Buy a 25F *"ticketourisme"* at the kiosk or the tourist office for a day of unlimited service. Most buses operate Mon.-Sat. 7am-7:30pm. Buses run everywhere, but most sights are in the *centre ville.*

Taxis: Radio Taxis, in front of the train station (tel. 05 45 95 55 55).

Bike Rental: Ets. Pelton, 5, rue des Arceaux (tel. 05 45 95 30 91). 35F per ½-day, 43F per day; 1500F deposit or passport. Mountain bikes 60F per ½-day, 83F per day; 3000F deposit or passport. Sat. afternoon-Tues. counts as 1 day. Open Tues.-Sat. 9:15am-noon and 2-7pm. V, MC.

Laundromat: Lavomatique, 3, rue Ludovic Trarieux, near the Hôtel de Ville.

Youth Center: Centre Information Jeunesse, 6, pl. Bouillard (tel. 05 45 92 86 73), around the corner from the Hôtel de Ville. Friendly staff has info on regional events, helps find jobs, sells cheap concert and theater tickets, and offers general advice. Open July-Aug. Mon.-Sat. 10am-6pm; Sept.-June Tues.-Fri. 10am-noon and 2-6pm, Sat. 10am-noon and 2-5pm.

Hospital: Hôpital de Girac, rue de Bordeaux (tel. 05 45 24 40 40), on the outskirts of town. Closer to town is the private **Clinique St-Joseph,** 51, av. Président Wilson (tel. 05 45 38 67 00). **Medical emergency** tel. 05 45 92 92 92 or 15.

Police: pl. du Champs de Mars (tel. 05 45 39 38 37), next to the post office. Take the first left as you walk up the hill toward the *centre ville.* **Emergency** tel. 17.

Post Office: pl. du Champ de Mars (tel. 05 45 66 66 00; fax 05 45 66 66 17). Poste restante. **Currency exchange.** Photocopies 1F. Open Mon.-Fri. 8am-7pm, Sat. 8am-noon. **Branch office,** pl. Francis Louvel, near the Palais du Justice. Open Mon.-Fri. 8am-6:45pm, Sat. 8am-noon. **Postal code:** 16000.

ACCOMMODATIONS AND CAMPING

Cheap hotels cluster near the intersection of av. Gambetta and the pedestrian district, which leads downhill from the *vieille ville.* The hostel and campground are on Ile de Bourgines, a forested island in the Charente, 2km from the *centre ville.*

Auberge de Jeunesse (HI), (tel. 05 45 92 45 80) on Ile de Bourgines. Exit the station, turn right onto av. Gambetta and right again onto rue Denis Papin, which crosses over the tracks. Continue straight onto Passage Lamaud, a pedestrian shortcut that reaches rue de Paris (5-10min.). Turn right onto rue de Paris and take bus 7 (direction: Le Treuil) to "St-Antoine." Walk, turn left out of the *gare* onto av. de Lattre de Tassigny, take the first left onto bd. du 8 Mai 1945, and at the 3rd traffic light, turn left onto bd. Besson Bey, which goes downhill, to cross a footbridge. A huge swimming pool (13F) will be on your left, in front of the hostel (40min. on foot, 25min. by bus). Gorgeous setting along the Charente. 15 bright 4- to 6-bed rooms in a modern building. TV. Excellent management. 46F. Sheets 16F. Breakfast 18F. Meals 46F. No lockout. No curfew. Call ahead in summer.

Hôtel des Pyrénées, 80, rue St-Roch (tel. 05 45 95 20 45; fax 05 45 92 16 95), around the corner from the post office, off pl. du Champ de Mars. Great management. Noisy rooms on the street. Back rooms have views. 20 rooms, singles and doubles 145F, with shower 200F, with toilet and shower 220F. Extra bed 50F. Breakfast 25F, shower 20F. Phones in all rooms, TV in most. V, MC, AmEx.

Hôtel Le Palma, 4, rampe d'Aguesseau (tel. 05 45 95 22 89; fax 05 45 94 26 66), near the Eglise St-Martial, straight up the hill from the *gare.* Large, brightly decorated rooms above a pricey restaurant. Singles 110F, with shower 150F. Doubles 140F, with shower 180F. Shower 30F. Breakfast 25F. Reception Mon.-Sat. V, MC.

Hôtel les Messageries, 127, av. Gambetta, (tel. 05 45 92 07 62), across from the station. Clean and close. Singles 120F. Doubles with 1 big and 1 small bed 150F. Triples 170F. Hall showers. Breakfast 20F. Reception Thurs.-Tues. Closed Aug.

Hôtel Le Génève, 20, pl. du Palet (tel. 05 45 95 29 06), down rue Génève. Tidy, quiet hotel above a reasonably priced restaurant. Singles 140F. Doubles 160F. All with showers. Breakfast 22F. Reception Mon.-Sat. V, MC, AmEx.

Camping: Camping Municipal, on Ile de Bourgines (tel. 05 45 92 83 22), 3-star camping next to the youth hostel. Reception 7am-noon and 2-10pm. 16F per adult, 8F per child, 27F per site. Showers included. Free access to swimming pool. Open March-Oct.

FOOD

The local specialty, *cagouilles à la charentaise,* snails prepared first with garlic and parsley, then with sausage, smoked ham, and spices, can be found in the restaurants of the *vieille ville* (45-50F). A favorite sweet is the flower-shaped *marguerite* chocolate, named for François I's sister Marguerite de Valois, who exerted considerable influence over Angoulême in the 16th century. Bars, cafés, and *boulangeries* line rue de St-Martial and rue Marengo, but the food becomes funkier, the dishes spicier, and the crowds more interesting as you weave your way into the narrow streets of the quadrant formed by Les Halles, pl. du Palet, Eglise St-André, and the Hôtel de Ville. **Letuffe Chocolatier,** 10, pl. Frédéric Louvel (tel. 05 45 95 00 54), gives free samples and sells them once you're hooked (56F per 250g; open Mon.-Fri. 9am-6pm, Sat.-Sun. 2-6pm; V, MC). The town's freshest produce blooms at **Les Halles,** on pl. des Halles Centrales, two blocks down rue de Gaulle from the Hôtel de Ville (open Mon.-Sat. 7am-1pm). If you get a snack attack, **ATAC** the **supermarket** is at 13, rue Périgueux (open Mon.-Sat. 8:30am-7:15pm, Sun. 9am-12:30pm).

Le Chat Noir, pl. des Halles (tel. 05 45 95 26 27). This black cat is young, energetic, and extra gregarious at night. Salads 30-32F. Sandwiches 11-23F. Bruschetta 27-37F. Open Mon.-Sat. 7am-1am. V, MC.

Au Soleil des Antilles, 19, rue des 3 Notre Dame (tel. 05 45 94 70 15), offers a garlic relish that gives new meaning to the concept of "hot." Savory 45F *menu* includes creole *plat du jour,* rice, 2 veggies, and your choice of wine or *café.* Eat to a live drum beat Fri. and Sat. nights. Open daily noon-2:30pm and 7-11pm.

Restaurant le Saint-André, 14-16, rue des 3 Notre-Dame (tel. 05 45 94 08 22). Relax on the terrace, chat with the people at the next table, and dig in to the savory bargains on the 50F *menu* (appetizer, elaborate main course, cheese, and dessert). Open Tues.-Sat. 11:30am-2:30pm and 6:30-11pm. V, MC.

Le Mektoub, 28, rue des 3 Notre-Dame (tel. 05 45 92 60 96), near Eglise St-André. Good service, friendly folk, and delicious Middle Eastern food. Main dishes 55-89F. Loads o' couscous 55-89F. 50F *plat du jour.* Open Mon.-Sat. noon-2pm and 7pm-midnight, Sun. 7pm-midnight. V, MC.

Maison des Peuples et de la Paix, 6bis, rue Marengo (tel. 05 45 92 48 32), has a cafeteria that extends an open invitation to come enjoy conversation and food from around the globe. The 40F *menu* (posted each week on the front door) has previously included marojam chicken, moussaka, dolmas, couscous, and vegetarian specialties from India and sub-Saharan Africa (includes coffee and dessert). Open Sept. to mid-July Mon.-Fri. noon-1:45pm.

SIGHTS AND ENTERTAINMENT

At the bottom of av. du Président Wilson, you'll find the lovely **Jardin Vert,** where flowers, waterfalls, and baby goats (really) provide respite from the heat above. Descend farther to pl. Dunois and turn right at the contemporary glass building, the **Centre Nationale de la Bande Dessinée et de l'Image (CNBDI),** 121, rue de Bordeaux (tel. 05 45 38 65 65; fax 05 45 38 65 66), which houses the **Musée de la Bande Dessinée.** The exhibits concentrate on the inventors of *B-D* (comics) and more obscure French cartoons from the 19th and 20th centuries, with only two rooms devoted to more well-known figures such as Tintin and Astérix. Come here if you're fascinated by the intricacies of 'toon history (open Tues.-Fri. 10am-7pm, Sat.-Sun. 2-7pm; admission 30F, students 20F). Across the street, the **Atelier-Musée du Papier,** 134, rue de Bordeaux (tel. 05 45 92 34 10), housed in the old paper mill over the Charente that brought renown to Angoulême, presents modern art exhibits involving the postmodern antics of students from Angoulême's Ecole des Beaux-Arts (open Tues.-Sun. 2-6pm; free). Buses 3 and 5 run from pl. du Champ de Mars and pl. de l'Hôtel de Ville to both museums at "Nil-CNBDI" (7F).

The 4th-century ramparts that surround the town provide a spectacular view of the red-roofed houses and green countryside below—on a clear day, you can see Cognac, 30km away. Follow the ramparts far enough from the statue of Sadi Carnot beyond the Hôtel de Ville and you'll reach the splendid 12th-century **Cathédrale St-Pierre** (tel. 05 45 95 20 38). Though the cathedral was restored once in 1634 after Calvinists destroyed it, its present unity and detail is the result of an 1866 renovation by Abadie, the architect who designed the Sacré-Coeur in Paris. Stare back at the 75 perfectly intact characters on the façade narrating the tales of the Ascension and the Last Judgment (open daily 9am-7:30pm).

Behind the cathedral, the **Musée des Beaux-Arts (Musée Municipal),** 1, rue Friedland (tel. 05 45 95 07 69), in a restored 12th-century bishop's palace, displays French paintings galore and an impressive prehistory exhibit, including 50,000-year-old Neanderthal skulls. Don't miss the fabulous collection of African art and pottery (open Mon.-Fri. noon-6pm, Sat.-Sun. 2-6pm; admission 15F, students 5F, under 18 free). In the pl. de Palet in the *centre ville* stands the 12th-century **Eglise St-André,** 6-8, rue Tailleferre, originally a Romanesque church. Redone in Gothic style, it retains its original tower and entrance. Near the church at 34, rue de Génève, lies the disturbing but informative **Musée Charentais de la Résistance et de la Déportation** (tel. 05 45 38 76 87), chronicling Angoulême's experience under Nazi occupation (open Wed.-Sat. 2-6pm; admission 15F, children and students 5F). John Calvin lived on the site of the museum in 1534 and wrote part of the *Institutes of Christian Religion* there. Set in a 16th-century building with walls nearly a meter thick, the nearby **Maison St-Simon,** 15, rue de la Cloche Verte (tel. 05 45 92 87 01), displays avant-garde, often indescribable art (open Tues.-Fri. 10am-noon and 2-5pm, Thurs. 10am-noon and 2-8pm, Sat.-Sun. 2-5pm; free). Pass by the market en route to the tall steeple of the symmetric 19th-century **Eglise St-Martial,** on pl. St-Martial (open 8:30am-7:30pm). Take a right on rue de Montmoreau to reach the small **Musée Archéologique,** 44, rue Montmoreau (tel. 05 45 38 45 17), displaying regional treasures from the Gallo-Roman era to recent centuries: ceramics, arrowheads, and fossils galore (open Wed.-Mon. 2-5pm; free).

As the sun sets, folks hang out in the cafés on **rue Massillon** and **pl. des Halles.** The crowd at **Le Chat Noir** (see **Food**) loiters over drinks until closing. The **Yucutan,** rue Henri IV off rue 3 Fours, tends to be wild during the school year and has concerts in the cool *cave* in the summer (open Sept.-June Tues.-Sat. 6pm-2am; July Wed.-Sat. 6pm-2am). **Le Champagne,** 25, rue d'Aguesseau (tel. 05 45 92 58 09), sits off pl. Marengo. Tuesday and Thursday through Saturday nights are karaoke; Wednesday and Saturday, there's a Brazilian guitarist-singer (open Tues.-Sat. until 2am). Put on your dancing shoes at **Le Piano Rétro Club,** 210, rue St-Roch (tel. 05 45 92 87 11) or **King's Club,** 17, impasse Sauvage (tel. 05 45 95 52 28), off rue du Sauvage; both open Tues.-Sat. 10:30pm-3am, cover 40F including drink (V, MC).

January brings the world-famous **Salon International de la Bande-Dessinée,** 2, pl. de l'Hôtel-de-Ville. Over 200,000 visitors admire four days of brilliant, free comic-strip exhibits in the Hôtel de Ville. Astérix and Obélix are occasionally sighted here (tel. 05 45 97 86 50; fax 05 45 95 99 28). In May, lovers of jazz descend for the **Festival Musiques Métisses,** 6, rue du point-du-Jour (tel. 05 45 95 43 42; fax 05 45 95 63 87). International pianists of all genres twiddle their fingers in nervous anticipation of the two-week **Festival International de Piano, "Piano en Valois,"** in late September and early October. Some concerts are free, but most cost 30-60F; hop over to 4, rue des 3 Notre-Dame (tel. 05 45 94 74 00; fax 05 45 38 13 74) for details.

Limoges

If the thought of porcelain turns you on, Limoges is the place to be. The city's acclaimed *emaux d'art* adorn every other shop window in this industrial center and transportation hub of 150,000, and its museums will fulfill your every ceramic fantasy. Limoges itself holds little allure for tourists other than its dishes, but it serves as a good base for a trip to the nearby ghost-town of Oradour-sur-Glane, a frozen reminder of the Nazi atrocities of the Second World War.

ORIENTATION AND PRACTICAL INFORMATION

To get to the **tourist office,** bd. de Fleurus (tel. 05 55 34 46 87; fax 05 55 34 19 12), from the train station, head straight down av. du Général de Gaulle to pl. Jourdan and cut diagonally across the park to bd. Fleurus. The tourist office is on the left. The staff gives out scads of maps, brochures, and lists of *chambres d'hôtes;* offers two-hour guided theme tours of the city in July and August; and **changes money** with a 20F commission (open Mon.-Sat. 9am-8pm, Sun. 10am-2pm; Sept. 15-June 15 Mon.-Sat. 9am-noon and 2-6:30pm). **Banks** surround pl. Jourdan, while **ATMs** frequent pl. Carnot and pl. de la Motte. **Banque de France's** commission-free counters, on bd. Carnot, have the best exchange rates (open Mon.-Fri. 8:45am-noon and 1:30-3:30pm). The **Centre Régional Information Jeunesse,** 27, bd. de la Corderie (tel. 05 55 45 18 70), has a **budget travel office.** (Open in summer Mon.-Fri. 9am-12:30pm and 1:30-5:30pm, Sat. 1:30-5:30pm; in winter Mon. 2-5:30pm, Tues.-Fri. 9am-12:30pm and 1:30-5:30pm.) With ornate statues adorning its portal, the **train station,** known as the Gare des Bénédictins, was recently named one of the most beautiful in France. Not just a pretty face, the *gare* (tel. 05 55 11 11 80) is also a major transport hub, with shady characters to prove it. **Lockers** 18-33F. **Currency exchange** machine. Trains run to: Paris (12 per day, 3-4hr., 221F); Lyon (1-2 per day, 6hr., 225F); Bordeaux (6 per day, 2½hr., 148F); Toulouse (7 per day, 3½hr., 187F); Poitiers (4-5 per day, 2hr., 103F); and Brive (12 per day, 1hr., 77F). The Limousin region is blanketed by an efficient **bus system;** all 142 pages of the timetable are available at the tourist office or the station on pl. des Charentes (tel. 05 55 77 29 00). The **police,** 2, rue des Vénitiens, can be reached at 05 55 10 31 00 (**emergency** tel. 17); call the **hospital** at 05 55 05 61 23 (**emergency** tel. 15). The **post office** on rue de la Préfecture near pl. Stalingrad (open Mon.-Fri. 8am-7pm, Sat. 8am-noon; **postal code:** 87000) has poste restante and **exchanges moolah.**

ACCOMMODATIONS, CAMPING, AND FOOD

The **Foyer des Jeunes Travailleuses,** 20, rue Encombe Vineuse (tel. 05 55 77 63 97), has clean, simple singles with sinks and desks; a TV room and kitchenette are yours to use (no pots). Walk around the right side of the station, take rue Théodore Bac to pl. Carnot, turn left onto av. Adrien Tarrade, and make the first left onto rue Encombe Vineuse (15min.). (70F, sheets and shower included. Breakfast Mon.-Sat. 15F. Reception 8am-11:30pm.) **Le Relais Lamartine,** 10 rue des Coopérateurs (tel. 05 55 77 53 99) offers up cheerful rooms starting at 95F, with toilet 100F, with shower and toilet 150F. (Hall bath 20F. Extra bed 45F. Breakfast 25F. V, MC.) To reach **Hôtel Arédien,** 37, rue Armand Barbès (tel. 05 55 77 31 72), walk around the right side of the park

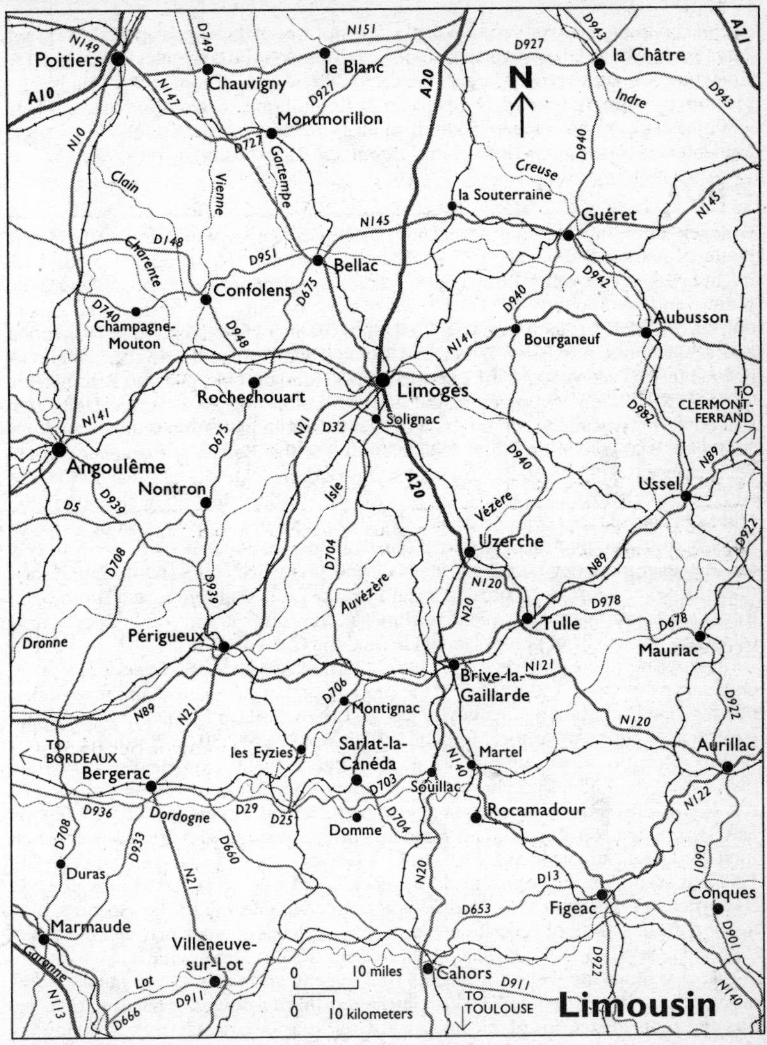

from the *gare,* and turn right on rue Armand Barbès. Small, clean rooms in a quiet area. (Singles 100F, with shower 110-130F. Doubles with shower 150F, with bath 135-175F. Triples 190F. Extra bed 40F. Breakfast 25F. V, MC.) The closest campground is **Camping de la Vallée de l'Aurence** (tel. 05 55 38 49 43), 5km north of Limoges. Take bus 20 Mon.-Sat. (15F per person, 15F per car).

Ethnic eateries abound on rue Charles Michel. Chow down on savory Chinese fare at **Le Pekin,** 13, rue Charles Michel (tel. 05 55 32 92 65). The lunch *menu* with appetizer, main dish, rice, and dessert is 59F (open Thurs.-Tues. noon-1:30pm and 7-11pm; V, MC). For tasty Italian fare, try **Pizzeria Bonell,** 7, rue Montmailler (tel. 05 55 79 42 43). Pizzas 36-42F, *plats* 40-50F. (Open Mon.-Fri. 11:45am-1:45pm and 7-10:30pm, Sat. 7-10:30pm. V, MC.) Head for **Le Paris** microbrewery, at 7, pl. Denis Dussoubs (tel. 05 55 77 48 31), where all of the 50-60F main courses include one of five homebrews. Try the *Blonde, Ambrée, Weisse, Saint-Martial* (Fri. evenings only), or the *Spéciale Brune ("comme en Irlande,"* 15-19F per bottle). Dream of draining one of the immense wooden vats in the back of the dining area (open daily 11am-2am; V, MC). **Les Halles** vegetates off pl. de la Motte on rue des Halles (open Sun.-Fri. 7am-1pm, Sat. 8am-1pm); a larger **market** brightens pl. Carnot Saturday mornings. **Monoprix supermarket** sits on pl. de la République (open Mon.-Sat. 8:30am-7:30pm). The **ATAC supermarket** at pl. des Charents provides similarly prepackaged goodies (open Mon.-Thurs. 9am-7:30pm, Fri.-Sat. 8:30am-7:30pm).

SIGHTS

Limoges' museums worship porcelain. Handle dish-lovers with care at the **Musée National Adrien-Dubouché,** 8bis, pl. Winston Churchill (tel. 05 55 77 45 58); they might crack at the sight of the largest porcelain collection in Europe. Millennia-old pottery and postmodern, UFO-esque tea settings are but a few of the thousands of objects on display. (Open July-Aug. Wed.-Mon. 10am-5:15pm; Sept.-June 10am-noon and 1:30-5:15pm. Admission 20F, ages 18-25 and Sun. 13F, under 18 free; you break it, you buy it.) Each summer the **Exposition de l'Hôtel de Ville,** pl. Louis Betoulle (tel. 05 55 77 29 18), dishes out an exhibit with such offbeat items as a porcelain water-mill powering a porcelain chime, as well as the ho-hum plates and statues (late June-Sept. daily 9am-7pm in the Hôtel de Ville; free). The **Pavillon de la Porcelaine,** route de Toulouse (tel. 05 55 30 21 86), in an industrial zone 3km out of town, has videos and live demonstrations of craftsmanship, as well as a busy sales floor. Next door, the **Musée Haviland** (tel. 05 55 30 21 86) displays an impressive collection of plates by the firm, founded by American David Haviland, that made Limoges a porcelain center. Marvel at pieces by Dalí, Dufy, and Cocteau, and gawk at the stylish settings destined for several American presidents and royalty from Mali to Monaco (both open April-Oct. 8:30am-8pm; Nov.-March Mon.-Sat. 8:30am-6:30pm; free). Take bus 15 (direction: Magré) from pl. des Jacobin behind the Hôtel de Ville (6F).

Get your mind off pottery at the entirely stone **Cathédrale St-Etienne,** pl. St-Etienne, near the tourist office. One of the more impressive cathedrals in the region, it boasts flying buttresses and gargoyles galore, but the brilliantly colored *vitraux* surpass them all (open to visitors Mon.-Sat. 9:30am-6pm, Sun. 2:30-6:30pm).

Next door, the **Musée Municipal de l'Evêché** limits its porcelain to a few fine plates with vivid Biblical scenes and some more interesting Art Deco enamels. The rest of the museum is a mixture of Egyptian artifacts, paintings (including a few by Limoges' native son Renoir), and remnants of the town's Gallo-Roman past (open June Wed.-Mon. and daily Aug.-Sept. 10-11:45am and 2-6pm; Oct.-May Wed.-Mon. 10-11:45am and 2-5pm; free). Next door, the small **Musée de la Résistance et de la Déportation** bears witness to World War II France with Resistance newspapers, photos of partisans and concentration camps, and an Italian fighter plane in the lobby (open June-Sept. 15 10-11:45am and 2-5pm; Sept. 15-May 2-5pm; free).

Take a walk in the well-kept **Jardins de l'Evêché** and the adjacent **Jardin Botanique** next to the museums. The lush **Jardin du Champ-de-Juillet** near the train station is a better place for picnicking or just relaxing: fountains, trees, and flowers abound, and there's not a plate in sight. For a bizarre alternative to the usual assortment of museums and cathedrals, hike up to **La Boucherie,** a district of narrow streets and medieval houses in the *centre ville* where the town's butchers have lived since the 10th century. For a slice of their life, visit the **Maison Traditionelle de la Boucherie,** just beyond the Chapelle St-Aurelien on your right. Friendly young guides lead visitors through a butcher's house, explaining his way of life (open July- Sept. 10am-1pm and 3-7pm; Oct.-June ask tourist office for an appointment; free). One of the traditions La Boucherie has preserved is the festival **Les Petits Ventres,** a mid-October street banquet where residents consume meat of every kind (particularly *abats,* or giblets) in mass quantities. Every seven years, the butchers process into the **Chapelle St-Aurelien,** on rue de la Boucherie, and retrieve the relics of St. Aurelien, their patron saint; they then process through the streets and eat more meat. The next feast is in 2002—start packing your sausages now. In a less sanguinary vein, Limoges hosts contemporary drama in the October **Festival International des Francophones** (office at 11, Avenue Général de Gaulle, tel. 05 55 10 90 10).

■ Near Limoges: Oradour-sur-Glane

On June 10, 1944, Nazi S.S. troops massacred all 642 inhabitants of the farming village **Oradour-sur-Glane** without warning or provocation before setting the whole town ablaze. Perhaps France's most vivid testimony to the Second World War, the town remains in ruins; train wires dangle from slanting poles, and 50-year-old cars rust next to crumbling walls. You can walk freely along the main thoroughfare and peer into the remnants of each home. Signs indicate the name and profession of each person who lived there. Mystery still enshrouds the reason for the Nazis' decision, although one theory maintains that they mistook this town for Oradour-sur-Vayres, an important center of the Resistance. The troops entered at two in the afternoon and ordered all residents into the main square (they also apprehended six unlucky cyclists riding through town). The women and 205 children were herded into the town church where they were burned alive, and the men were corralled into six barns where they were tortured, shot, and set ablaze. At 7pm, when the troops pulled out, six men, a schoolboy playing hooky, and a woman who had jumped out a church window were the sole survivors.

Plaques with heartbreaking messages and pictures mark two glass tombs containing the bones and ashes of the dead. A small museum between the cemetery and town displays bicycles, toys, and watches, all stopped by the heat of the fire at the same moment. (Town open 24hr. Museum open 9am-noon and 2-6pm. Guide answers questions next to the church 9am-noon and 2-6pm. English and French brochures map a walking tour. Free.) After initial hesitation, a new Oradour (pop. 2000) was built next to the martyred village. Four **buses** per day (2 on Sat., none on Sun.) make the trip from the Limoges bus station, pl. des Charentes (40min., 15F50). The hitching along N141, then D9, is reportedly not difficult.

Aquitaine

Winding west from the Massif Central to the Atlantic for thousands of years, the Dordogne, Lot, Vézère, and Isle rivers have slashed through Aquitaine's high, porous limestone *causses* (plateaus), leaving behind towering cliffs and countless caves. These grottoes shelter 20,000-year-old paintings, carvings, and etchings of stampeding bison, frolicking wild horses, and reindeer fleeing hunters' arrows. Emerge from the caves to enjoy the treasures of the spectacular Aquitaine countryside: feudal châteaux, poplar-lined rivers, and valleys carpeted with fields of wheat and sunflowers.

Dubbed the "Capital of Prehistory," Aquitaine was first settled in the mid-Paleolithic era, 150,000 years ago, in the area around Les Eyzies-de-Tayac. The region has turned up more artifacts from the Stone Age—tools, bones, weapons, cave paintings, and etchings—than any other place on earth. The painted caves of Lascaux are the most extensive and best preserved in the world, but floods of tourists caused such drastic deterioration that the caves were closed to the public in 1963; a replica opened 150m away in 1983, appropriately called Lascaux II. Today, the Grotte de Font de Gaume in Les Eyzies-de-Tayac and the Grotte du Pech-Merle, 25km from Cahors, contain extraordinary original cave paintings still accessible to the public.

In 1152, Eleanor of Aquitaine, duchess of nearly half of modern France, married Henry Plantagenêt, less than two months after she ended her marriage with King Louis VII. The union of southwestern France with England began centuries of Anglo-French rivalry. The Dordogne formed a natural barrier between the opposing camps, who erected châteaux as defensive strongholds. *Bastides,* such as Domme, were fortified towns built in the 13th century to unite scattered populations.

After a series of epidemics ravaged crops in the late 19th century, Aquitaine stagnated. Recent restorations have begun to transform the dilapidated stone cottages and farmhouses into second homes for the residents of other French regions. The surging interest in the region has aided the development of tourism resources, as yet untapped by the legions of camera-toters patrolling the rest of the country.

Aquitaine produces rich, dark culinary specialties. World-famous *foie gras,* made of goose *(oie)* or duck *(canard)* livers, is often thinned out into a *mousse* or pâté. The large mushroom known as *cêpe,* as well as the black *truffe* (superior to the Italian white truffle), rooted out by nosy pigs and dogs, are exported to world-famous restaurants, where they can fetch several hundred dollars. More affordable are *confit de canard* and *confit d'oie,* duck or goose cooked in its own fat and accompanied by *pommes sarladaise,* potatoes fried in garlic and the grease from *confit. Pruneaux* (prunes) can be skewered, drowned in *armagnac,* and eaten raw. Although Bordeaux is synonymous with red wine, other local vineyards are gaining recognition. Sweet Bergerac and Monbazillac whites accompany *foie gras* perfectly.

GETTING AROUND

Aquitaine lacks a large transportation hub, discover your favorite hamlet along one of the rivers and explore from there. Bus and train connections in the region are neither frequent nor convenient. Unless you have a car, you may have to bike or hike to the loveliest villages. Many *Grandes Randonnées* pass through remote areas and connect such towns as Les Eyzies, Sarlat, Souillac, and Cahors. Inquire at Dordogne's **Comité Départemental de Tourisme,** 16, rue Wilson (tel. 05 53 53 44 35) in Périgueux, or at any local tourist office for information on canoeing along the Lot, Dordogne, Isle, and Vézère rivers. Hitching is reputedly fairly easy on shorter routes.

Bordeaux

From Barbarian invasions in the 3rd century to the French conquest of Aquitaine in the 15th, Bordeaux has retained an identity as strong as its wines. Eleanor of Aquitaine's marriage to Henry Plantagenêt allied the city with England for three centuries,

until the Battle of Castillon put the town under French rule in 1453. Despite a 300-year Anglo-French political standoff, *bordelais* merchants quietly developed and profited from their aromatic wines. The city has always been, as Henry James wrote, "dedicated to the worship of Bacchus in the most discreet form."

Once as darkened with age as its vintages, Bordeaux (pop. 650,000) has found that its greatest treasure is the city itself; the local government has scrubbed Bordeaux's splendid 18th-century mansions, Gothic cathedrals, and *places.* This restoration, however, is far from over. Scaffolding obscures some monuments, and many disheartening areas have not yet been liberated from their layers of grit and grime.

With a major university, a modest aerospace industry, and a sprinkling of research facilities, Bordeaux has attracted residents from every corner of the globe. Restaurants, nightclubs, art galleries, concerts, and neighborhoods reflect the diversity of the *Bordelais* and endow the city with a relaxed but never dull atmosphere.

ORIENTATION AND PRACTICAL INFORMATION

The scenery along the trek from the train station to the *centre ville* is not Bordeaux's finest (30min.). If you arrive after dusk, consider the bus and taxi options before venturing off along the poorly lit, potentially dangerous **cours de La Marne.** Skip the half-hour hike and walk the 4m to the bus depot in front of the station. Both buses 7 and 8 run to pl. Gambetta every 10 minutes (direction: "Grand Théâtre," less frequently 10-11:30pm, 7F50). Pick up a map at the info booth in the station. If you do walk, head straight down cours de la Marne about 12 blocks until you hit pl. de la Victoire. Take a right onto pedestrian rue Ste-Catherine, cross the wide cours de l'Intendance after about 10 minutes, and the tourist office will be ahead on the right. To get to **pl. Gambetta,** the center of town, take a left on cours de l'Intendance off rue Ste-Catherine, and you'll tumble onto pl. Gambetta after five blocks. Bordeaux is a big city: guard your wallet and yourself, especially at night. This Gargantua takes its Sunday nap seriously; you'll find it's a good time for daytrips.

Tourist Office: 12, cours du 30 Juillet (tel. 05 56 00 66 00; fax 05 56 00 66 01). Large, friendly office. Guided bus tours in French and English of local wineries. (½-day tour leaves 1:30pm; daily May-Oct.; Wed. and Sat. Nov.-Dec.; 150F, students 130F. Full-day tour including lunch May-Oct. Wed. and Sat. 290F, students 250F.) Guided city tours in French and English daily (32F). The free *Bordeaux Tourisme* comes out biweekly. Open Mon.-Sat. 9am-8pm, Sun. 9am-7pm; Nov.-April Mon.-Sat. 9am-7pm, Sun. 9:30am-4:30pm. Also at **train station** (open May 16-Oct. 14 Mon.-Sat. 9am-noon and 12:45-7pm, Sun. 10am-noon and 12:15-6pm; Oct. 15-May 15 Mon.-Sat. 9am-noon and 12:45-6pm).

Budget Travel: Wasteels, 13, pl. de Casablanca (tel. 05 56 91 97 17; fax 05 56 31 91 48), across the street from station, sells BIJ tickets and books charter flights. Open Mon.-Fri. 9am-noon and 2-7pm, Sat. 9am-1pm and 2-6pm. The agency on the ground floor of the **Virgin Megastore,** 15-19, pl. Gambetta (tel. 05 56 51 02 28), handles charters. Open Mon.-Sat. 10am-8pm. Near the tourist office, **Terres d'Ameriques,** 9, pl. Charles Gruet (tel. 05 56 44 68 73; fax 05 56 52 16 05), has cheap air fares. Open Mon.-Fri. 9am-12:30pm and 2-7pm, Sat. 9am-noon.

Consulates: U.K., 353, bd. du Président Wilson (tel. 05 57 22 21 10). Open Mon.-Fri. 9am-12:30pm and 2:30-5pm. In case of emergency, call 05 57 22 01 43.

Money: Thomas Cook (tel. 05 56 91 58 80), at the station. Open in summer Mon.-Sat. 8:10am-7:30pm, Sun. 10am-7pm; shorter hours in winter. **Banks** line cours de l'Intendance, with decent rates and no commission. **ATMs** wait at **Crédit Mutuel,** 61, cours de l'Intendance; on cours Victor Hugo by the *marché;* and a block from the station, at 220, cours de la Marne.

American Express: 14, cours de l'Intendance (tel. 05 56 00 63 33). Open Mon.-Fri. 8:45am-noon and 1:30-6pm. 24-hr. refund assistance (tel. 0 800 90 86 00).

Flights: 11km west of Bordeaux in Mérignac (tel. 05 56 34 50 00). Shuttle bus connects train station and tourist office to airport (every 30min.-1hr. 5:30am-10pm, 40min., 35F). **Air France** (tel. 05 56 00 40 40) flies to London daily, under 25 690F. **Air Inter** (tel. 05 56 13 10 10) flies to Paris.

Trains: Gare St-Jean, rue Charles Domercq (tel. 05 56 92 50 50). City maps available at info desk. To: Paris (10-14 per day, 5-8hr., 290F; TGV 330-380F); Nantes (5-8 per day, 4hr., 217F); Toulouse (10 per day, 2½hr., 159F); Nice (4 per day, 9½hr., 440F); St-Emilion (2 per day, 45min., 42F). **Lockers** 15-30F for 72hr. Open daily 5am-11pm. **Info office** open Mon.-Sat. 9am-7pm.

Buses: Eurolines, rue St-Vincent de Paul (tel. 05 56 92 50 42), goes to Barcelona (1-2 per day, 10½hr., 330F) and other destinations in Spain. **Trans-Gironde** (tel. 05 56 91 31 10) runs south to Arcachon, Biscarosse, and Mimizan. **Bus Hebrard** (tel. 05 56 91 13 10) ventures south into Les Landes thrice daily.

Public Transportation: CGFTE. System crosses the city and suburbs. Tickets 7F50. Maps at the train station and the info offices at 4, rue Georges Bonnac and pl. Jean-Jaurès (tel. 05 57 57 88 88). Open Mon.-Sat. 8am-7:30pm. The *Carte Bordeaux Découverte* allows unlimited city bus use (1-day pass 22F; 3-day pass 52F).

Car Rental: Europcar, 35, rue Charles Domercq (tel. 05 56 31 20 30; fax 05 56 31 26 94), facing the station. Lowest price for weekend (535F), week (1806F). Must be at least 21. Open Mon.-Fri. 7am-11pm, Sat. 8am-8pm, Sun. 3-11pm.

Hitchiking: Stop Voyage, 79, cours de l'Argonne (tel. 05 57 95 91 11). Hooks you up with rides to distant cities or just to the beach. Open Mon.-Sat. 10am-7pm.

Taxis: Aquitaine Taxi Radio (tel. 05 56 86 80 30). A ride to the airport costs 140F.

Bike Rental: At the **tourist office.** 30F per day, 20F per ½-day. Deposit 1000F. V, MC, AmEx. **Cycles Pasteur,** 42, cours Pasteur (tel. 05 56 92 68 20) in the *centre ville.* 70F per day, 150F per weekend, 250F per week. Deposit 1600-3000F (*VTTs* only). Open Mon.-Fri. 10am-12:30pm and 2-7pm.

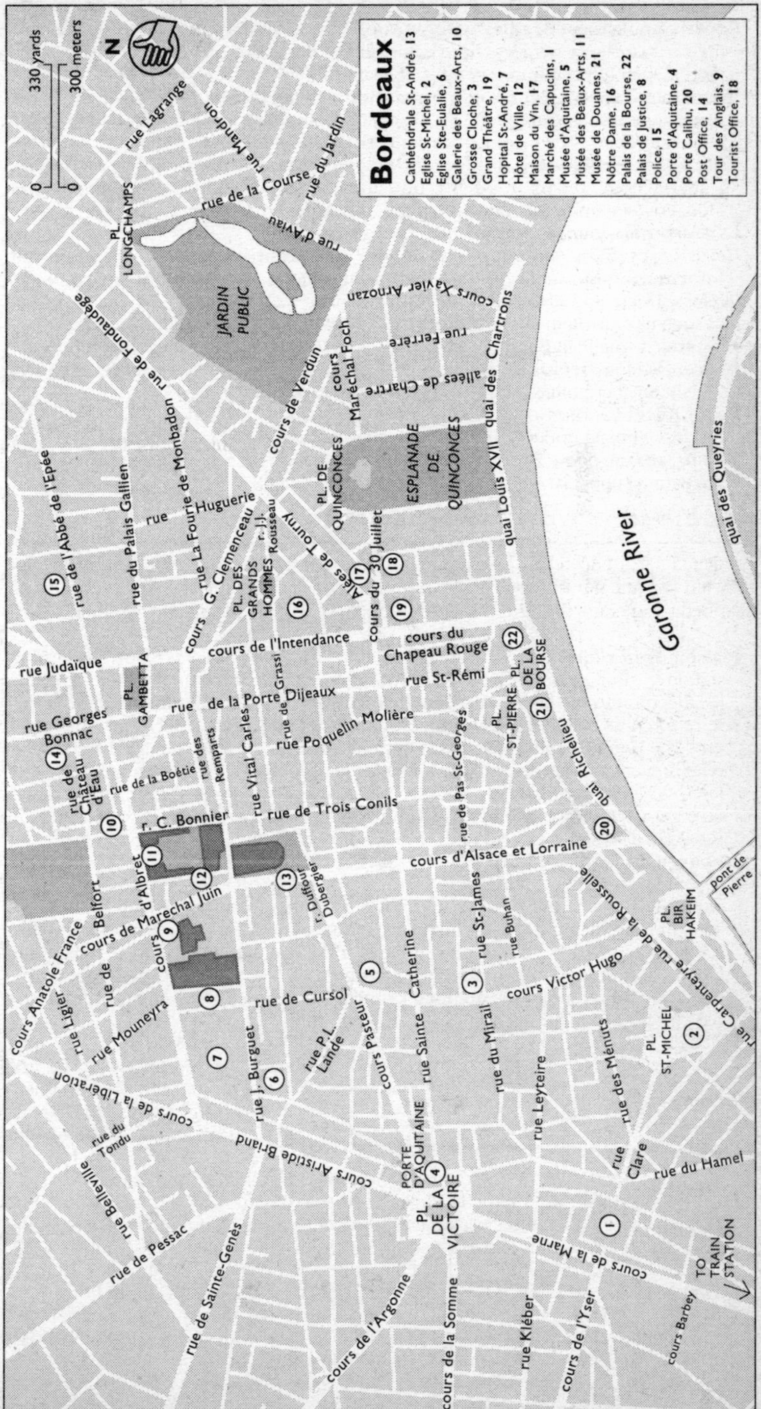
Bordeaux
Cathéthdrale St-André, 13
Eglise St-Michel, 2
Eglise Ste-Eulalie, 6
Galerie des Beaux-Arts, 10
Grosse Cloche, 3
Grand Théâtre, 19
Hopital St-André, 7
Hôtel de Ville, 12
Maison du Vin, 17
Marché des Capucins, 1
Musée d'Aquitaine, 5
Musée des Beaux-Arts, 11
Musée de Douanes, 21
Nôtre Dame, 16
Palais de la Bourse, 22
Palais de Justice, 8
Police, 15
Porte d'Aquitaine, 4
Porte Calihu, 20
Post Office, 14
Tour des Anglais, 9
Tourist Office, 18
N
0 330 yards
0 300 meters
Garonne River
JARDIN PUBLIC
ESPLANADE DE QUINCONCES
PL. LONGCHAMPS
PL. DE QUINCONCES
PL. DES GRANDS HOMMES
PL. GAMBETTA
PL. DE LA BOURSE
PL. ST-PIERRE
PL. BIR HAKEIM
PL. ST-MICHEL
PL. DE LA VICTOIRE
PORTE D'AQUITAINE
rue Lagrange
rue Mandron
rue de la Course
rue du Jardin
rue d'Aviau
rue de Fondaudège
cours Xavier Arnozan
rue Ferrère
allées de Chartre
cours Maréchal Foch
cours de Verdun
quai des Chartrons
quai Louis XVII
quai des Queyries
rue de l'Abbé de l'Epée
rue du Palais Gallien
rue La Fourie de Monbadon
rue Huguerie
cours G. Clemenceau
r. J.J. Rousseau
allées de Tourny
cours du 30 Juillet
cours de l'Intendance
cours du Chapeau Rouge
rue Judaïque
rue St-Rémi
rue de la Porte Dijeaux
rue de Grassi
rue Georges Bonnac
rue Poquelin Molière
rue Vital Carles
rue de Château d'Eau
rue de la Boëtie
rue des Remparts
r. C. Bonnier
rue de Trois Conils
rue de Pas St-Georges
quai Richelieu
cours d'Alsace et Lorraine
pont de Pierre
rue Belfort
cours d'Albret
cours de Marechal Juin
r. Duffour Dubergier
rue St-James
rue Buhan
rue de la Rousselle
rue Carpenteyre
cours Anatole France
rue Ligier
rue de
rue Mouneyra
rue de Cursol
rue Sainte Catherine
cours Victor Hugo
rue du Mirail
rue J. Burguet
rue P.L. Lande
cours Pasteur
rue Leyteire
rue des Menuts
rue Clare
rue du Hamel
cours de la Libération
rue du Tondu
rue Belleville
cours Aristide Briand
rue de Pessac
rue de Sainte-Genès
cours de l'Argonne
cours de la Somme
rue Kléber
cours de l'Yser
cours de la Marne
cours Barbey
TO TRAIN STATION

AQUITAINE

English Bookstore: Bradley's Bookshop, 8, cours d'Albret. Travel guides (including *Let's Go*—in case goats have eaten all but this page), novels, dictionaries, and more. Open Mon. 2-7pm, Tues.-Sat. 9:30am-12:30pm and 2-7pm. V, MC.

Women's Center: Centre d'Information sur les Droits des Femmes, 5, rue Jean-Jacques Rousseau (tel. 05 56 44 30 30). Counseling and job search help. Open Mon. and Thurs. 10am-4pm, Tues. and Fri. by telephone only 2-5pm.

Youth Center: Centre d'Information Jeunesse d'Aquitaine, 5, rue Duffour Dubergier (tel. 05 56 56 00 56). Info about activities and jobs. Open Sept.-May Mon.-Fri. 9am-6pm, Sat. 9am-1pm; June-Aug. Mon.-Fri. 9am-6pm.

Laundromat: cours de Marne, open daily 7am-9pm.

Crisis Lines: SOS Amitié, tel. 05 56 44 22 22. **Centre Accueil Consulation et Information Sexuelle,** pl. de l'Europe (tel. 05 56 39 11 69), for sexual health issues. Doctors available Sept.-July Mon. 2-4pm, Wed. 2-6pm, and 1st and 3rd Sat. of each month 10am-noon. **Phénix** (tel. 05 56 96 49 04) is a suicide hotline.

Hospital: 1, rue Jean Burguet (tel. 05 56 79 56 79). **Medical emergency** tel. 15.

Police: Headquarters at 87, rue de l'Abbé de l'Epée, a.k.a. rue Castéja (tel. 05 56 99 77 77). Smaller police station at train station. **Emergency** tel. 17.

Post Office: 52, rue Georges Bonnac (tel. 05 56 48 87 48), off pl. Gambetta. Poste restante (postal code: 33065). **Currency exchange.** Fax. Open Mon.-Fri. 8am-7pm, Sat. 8am-noon. **Branch office,** pl. St-Project on rue Ste-Catherine, open Mon.-Fri. 8am-6:30pm, Sat. 8am-noon. **Postal code:** 33000.

ACCOMMODATIONS AND CAMPING

Bordeaux's main hostel is close to the station but not the *centre ville.* You may want to avoid the one-star hotels near the station and instead try the sidestreets around pl. Gambetta and cours d'Albret. Reserve a couple of days in advance in summer.

Maison des Étudiantes, 50, rue Ligier (tel. 05 56 96 48 30). Take bus 7 or 8 from station to "Bourse du Travail," and continue on foot in same direction on cours de la Libération to rue Ligier. Walking, follow cours de la Marne through pl. de la Victoire to cours Aristide Briand (which becomes cours de la Libération), turn right onto rue Ligier (30min.). Clean, classy, and closer to the town center than the hostel. Showers and sheets included. Singles and doubles 51F per person, 50F with ISIC. No lockout or curfew. Pot-less, pan-less kitchen. From Oct.-June the newly co-ed *maison* primarily houses monthly residents but may have a few beds free. In July-Aug. it has more space; reserve a day or two ahead. 24-hr. reception.

Auberge de Jeunesse (HI), 22, cours Barbey (tel. 05 56 91 59 51; fax 05 56 92 59 39), 5min. from the station but 30min. from the *centre ville.* Serviced by buses 7 and 8 from the center of town and bus 1 from the quais. Cours de la Marne runs straight from the right end of the train station. Follow it for about 5 blocks and turn left onto cours Barbey. Your new home is at the end of the block. 8- to 10-bed, single-sex dorm rooms and immaculate bathrooms in a worn building. Members 40F. Breakfast 16F. Huge, well-equipped kitchen. Reception 8-10am and 6-11pm. Flexible curfew 11pm. Stringent lockout 10:30am-4pm.

Hôtel la Boétie, 4, rue de la Boétie (tel. 05 56 81 76 68; fax 05 56 81 24 72), on a quiet street off rue Bouffard between pl. Gambetta and the Musée des Beaux-Arts. Check in at Hôtel Bristol, 14ter, pl. Gambetta. Spacious rooms with shower, toilet, TV, and phone. Singles 120F. Doubles 135F, with 2 beds 160F. Triples 180F. Breakfast 20F. Reception 24hr. Same family runs 11 other nearby hotels. At the **Studio Hôtel,** 26, rue Huguerie (tel. 05 56 48 00 14; fax 05 56 81 25 71), 4 hotels house 42 rooms. Singles 98-135F. Doubles 135-160F. V, MC, AmEx (both hotels).

Hôtel d'Amboise, 22, rue de la Vieille Tour (tel. 05 56 81 62 67; fax 05 56 52 92 82); take the first left after walking onto rue de la Porte Dijoux from pl. Gambetta. Attractive, clean rooms above a pedestrian street. One single 120F. Doubles 135F. Triples 180F. Quads 200F. All have TV, toilet, and shower. Same prices 2 blocks away at **Hôtel de Lyon,** 31, rue des Remparts (same tel.). V, MC (both hotels).

Hôtel Saint-Rémi, 34, rue St-Rémi (tel. 05 56 48 55 48). Comfy pink rooms. Singles and doubles 110F, with shower 135-160F. One quad with shower 180F. Breakfast 20F. No hall showers. Reception 7:30am-midnight. V, MC.

Camping: Camping les Gravières, Pont-de-la-Maye in Villeneuve d'Ornon (tel. 05 56 87 00 36). Take bus B (direction: Courrégean) from pl. de la Victoire to its terminus (30min.). By car, leave town on the A62 toward Toulouse and get off at exit 20. 3-star campground in a forest by a river. 150 sites. 19F per person, 11F per child, 19F per tent, 28F per tent and car. Reception 8am-1pm and 3-10pm.

FOOD

Bordeaux, located in the self-proclaimed *Région de Bien Manger et de Bien Vivre* (Region of Fine Eating and Living), takes its food as seriously as its wine. Regional specialties include oysters, *foie gras,* beef braised in wine sauce, and the chocolate-colored (but not chocolate-flavored) cake, *canelé de Bordeaux,* created in 1519.

Affordable, quick restaurants, pizzerias, and *boulangeries* cluster along and just off pedestrian **rue Ste-Catherine** and **pl. Gambetta. Rue St-Rémi,** radiating off pl. de la Bourse, features an eclectic mix of 95F seafood *menus* and family-run Chinese restaurants. Between rue Ste-Catherine and pl. de la Bourse, **pl. du Parlement** and **pl. St-Pierre** provide beautifully preserved 18th-century façades and airy outdoor seating in which to enjoy 70-120F *menus* of local cuisine.

The 19th century ushered in Bordeaux's era of **grands cafés,** each built in its own style, now restored to the original decor. These cafés, listed in the French register of historical monuments, still welcome patrons for a meal or drink and some rest in a bygone era. At the lovely 18th-century **La Belle Epoque,** 2, allées d'Orléans (tel. 05 56 44 75 37), Eric Duffour whips up innovative dishes from local ingredients and serves them with style. A three-course *menu bistro* is 65F. (Open for meals Mon.-Fri. and Sun. noon-3pm and 7-11pm, Sat. 7-11pm; drinks 9am-midnight. V, MC, AmEx.) The tourist office has a small map with a walking tour of historic cafés.

Markets are scattered all over town. The glittering market at **pl. des Grands Hommes** offers regional specialties at upscale prices (Mon.-Sat. 9am-7pm). The **marchés des Capucins,** off cours de la Marne at the end of rue Clare, and on cours Victor Hugo at pl. de la Ferme de Richemont, are much more fun (open Mon.-Sat. 6am-1pm). A **marché biologique** takes place Thursdays from 8am to 1pm at pl. St-Pierre. You may want to pitch a tent by the moving sidewalks in the enormous **Auchan supermarket** (tel. 05 56 99 59 00), near the Maison des Etudiantes at the huge Centre Meriadeck on rue Claude Bonnier (open Mon.-Sat. 8:30am-10pm).

Baud et Millet, 19, rue Huguerie (tel. 05 56 79 05 77), off pl. Tourny. With 900 wines and more than 200 cheeses, this place is *dégustation* heaven. Take a plate and knife, descend into the cool cellar, and take as much as you want from the immense selection of *fromages.* Cheese plus dessert 110F. Go ahead—you're worth it. Or try the tantalizing *salade aux mille fromages* (45F). Some of the finest wines in this galaxy. Open Mon.-Sat. noon-midnight. V, MC, AmEx.

Taj Mahal, 24, rue du Parlement Ste-Catherine (tel. 05 56 51 92 05), a block off rue Ste-Catherine. Make lunch your meal of the day, and slide into a velvet and wood chair for the 70F all-you-can-eat buffet of Indian and Pakistani specialties, some vegetarian. Non-buffet prices from 59F per dish. Sun.-Thurs. there are 95F and 99F 3-course *menus.* Open noon-2:30pm and 7:30-11:30pm. V, MC.

Pizza Jacomo, 19, rue de la Devise (tel. 05 56 51 01 48), off pl. St-Pierre. Packed with locals, this family-run affair offers wood-fire oven pizza (36-40F), rich pasta (from 45F), hearty bread, 12F beers, and tempting 14F desserts. Open Mon. and Wed.-Sat. noon-2pm and 7:30pm-11:30pm, Sun. 7:30pm-midnight. V, MC.

La Boîte à Huîtres, 8, rue de la Vieille Tour (tel. 05 56 81 64 97), off cours de l'Intendance from pl. Gambetta. Jazz complements the oysters (6 for 34F and up) and wine (12F). Tart 28F. Open daily 10am-2pm and 6pm-11pm. V, MC.

Bodega Bodega, 4, rue des Piliers de Tutelles (tel. 05 56 01 24 24). Lively *tapas* bar with lush red curtains, tall wooden stools, and a stuffed bull's head high on the wall. Try the *jamon serrano* (ham, 35F) or *manchego* (goat cheese with cherry jam, 20F). Open Mon.-Sat. noon-3pm and 6pm-2am, Sun. 6pm-2am. V, MC.

SIGHTS AND ENTERTAINMENT

With its many museums and monuments, Bordeaux is about more than world-famous wines. The symmetrical façades and serene fountain of the **pl. de la Bourse** on quai Douane exemplify the 18th-century grandeur of Bordeaux's glory days under Louis XV. Two blocks down the quai towards the city's oldest bridge, the stone **pont de Pierre,** stands the 15th-century **Porte de Cailhau,** pl. de Palais. This *arc de triomphe* commemorates the victory of Charles VIII at Fornoue. On rue St-James, a few blocks away, ticks the spectacular 16th-century **Grosse Cloche,** the belfry of the Hôtel de Ville during the Middle Ages. Two angels roost atop the *horloge,* whose golden hands still tick out the hours with precision.

Nearly 900 years after its consecration by Pope Urban II, **Cathédrale St-André,** pl. Pey-Berland (tel. 05 56 52 68 10), remains the *grande dame* of Bordeaux's Gothic masterpieces. Built between the 11th and 16th centuries but sorely neglected in the ensuing decades, the cathedral underwent extensive renovation throughout the 19th century. The work continues today as workers labor to remove crusty black layers of filth from the façade, which features statues of angels, the apostles, and reliefs of the Last Supper and the Ascension (open daily July-Sept. 7:30-11:30am and 2-6:30pm; Oct.-June closed Sun. afternoons; free organ recital every other Tues. evening mid-May to mid-Sept.). Its bell-tower, the **Tour Pey-Berland,** juts 63m into the sky. Built in the Italian style of a *campanile,* the tower is 15m away from the cathedral. Its masons were concerned that the vibrations of the massive bells might cause the cathedral to collapse. Climb all 229 spiraling steps to the top for the view of your life. (Open daily July-Aug. 10am-7pm; Sept. and April-June 10am-6pm; Oct.-March 10am-5pm. Admission 22F, under 26 14F.)

The **Musée des Beaux-Arts** (tel. 05 56 10 17 18), 20, cours d'Albret near the cathedral, breathes a sigh of relief in its spacious new galleries with canvases by Titian, Delacroix, Renoir, Matisse, and others. Several rooms hold contemporary works (open Wed.-Mon. 10am-12:30pm and 1:30-6pm; admission 20F, students 10F; Wed. free). Across the street, the **Galerie des Beaux-Arts,** pl. du Colonel-Raynal, features rotating exhibits (open Wed.-Mon. 10am-12:30pm and 1:30-6pm, Wed. also 9-11pm; admission varies from free to 40F). The **Musée d'Aquitane,** 20, cours Pasteur (tel. 05 56 01 51 00) is an exceptionally enjoyable historic and ethnographic journey through the region's past from prehistory to the present depicted in classical and folk art. (Open Tues.-Sun. 10am-6pm. English booklet available. Video presentations in French and English. Admission 20F, students 10F; free on Wed.)

Back toward the tourist office on esplanade de Quinconces stands the **Monument aux Girondins,** a column topped with the joyous **Liberty Statue.** Action-packed fountains froth on either side, one a tangle of bodies called **Le Triomphe de la République,** the other a tangle of rearing horses called **Le Triomphe de la Concorde.** A couple of blocks beyond the monument waits the perfect picnic in the **Jardin Public,** the first of its kind in France (open daily 7am-9pm; winter 9am-7pm).

With a magnificent façade, the 18th-century **Opéra de Bordeaux,** pl. de la Comédie (info and reservations tel. 05 56 48 58 54), is worth a visit. You can ogle the interior by attending one of the operas, concerts, or plays performed here; if you have stage fright, the tourist office offers daytime tours (30F, students 25F).

Jump into the 21st century at the **Entrepôt Laine,** 7, rue Ferrère. Two blocks from cours de Maréchal Foch, this colossal gallery contains the far-out **Musée d'Art Contemporain** (tel. 05 56 00 81 50) and the **Arc en Rêve Centre d'Architecture** (tel. 05 56 52 78 36). The grimy, blocky exterior (look for the word *"entrepôt"* over the entrance) is a versatile setting for temporary exhibits of modern painting, sculpture, design and photography, complemented by expositions focusing on specific architects or architectural movements (open Tues.-Sun. noon-7pm, Wed. until 10pm; 30F, students 20F, noon-2pm free). Sip a cappuccino at the rooftop café.

ENTERTAINMENT

During the school year, 60,000 students mob the streets of pl. de la Victoire and pl. Gambetta; the city is calmer in the summer, but far from boring. Closer to the train station, the dance clubs and pubs in **quai Ste-Croix** and **quai de Paludade** are always packed. Even after the clubs kick you out, you can still crow in the dawn, enjoying the drinks and snacks at **pl. Marché des Capucins,** where late-night market workers alternate between guzzling coffee and setting up for morning shoppers. Stick to the more populated and well-lit main streets.

For an overview of nightlife, pick up a free copy of *Clubs and Concerts* at the tourist office, or purchase the bi-weekly magazine *Bordeaux Plus* (2F) at any *tabac.* For in-depth coverage of entertainment options, pick up the annual *Le Petit Fluté* (40F). **The Connemara Irish Pub,** 18, cours d'Albret (tel. 05 56 52 82 57), near pl. Gambetta, fills its tables with friendly locals, its stage with musicians, and its mugs with seven different kinds of beer (open Mon.-Sat. noon-2am, Sun. 6pm-2am; music Tues.-Sun. in summer, Tues., Thurs., and Sat.-Sun. in winter). If *bonjour* is getting old, say *"hola"* to the free tortilla chips at the **Mexican Road Café,** 15-19, pl. Gambetta (tel. 05 56 56 05 56), on the top floor and roof of the Virgin Megastore. *Draguez* French teens until the two-for-one happy hour drinks start flowing (6:30-8:30pm; 25F). Mod bartenders pay as much attention to requests for more chips as models on a catwalk, but the sunset makes the wait worthwhile (open Mon.-Sat. 10am-midnight; Sept.-June daily 10am-midnight; meals noon-2:30pm and 7pm-midnight; V, MC). **Le Plana,** 22, pl. de la Victoire (tel. 05 56 91 73 23), offers musical and alcoholic variety in the heart of the student-swamped *place.* Strike a pose to blasting techno at all-male **Le T-H,** 15, rue Montbazon (tel. 05 56 81 38 16). Young, welcoming crowd (open Tues.-Sat. 8pm-2am). Check out the international films, always in *version originale,* at the **Trianon Jean Vigo cinema** on rue Franklin.

BORDEAUX WINES AND WINERIES

God only made water, but man invented wine.
-Victor Hugo, *Les Contemplations, "La Fête Chez Thérèse."*

The establishment of the Bordeaux wines' reputation has been a collaborative process of 20 centuries, many nations, shameless self-promotion, and all-important geographical conditions. The wines of Bordeaux remained a patchwork of colors and qualities until Louis IX snatched wine capital La Rochelle from the British in 1226. Not to be deprived of his "claret," King Henry II bestowed generous shipping rights on Bordeaux, making it England's cellar. At first the citizens simply shipped out wines produced farther along the Garonne, but the modest riches from this trade encouraged a local planting mania. Soon the wily new winemakers made laws which conveniently banned wines of other regions from entering the city until British trading ships, loaded with Bordeaux wine, had sailed to their winter ports.

Through the 16th and 17th centuries, the newly French city churned out wines designed as sailors' rations. When William of Orange insisted that English ships buy their mass-quantity wines elsewhere, the Bordeaux winemakers turned to producing delicate clarets pleasing to the English aristocracy. In 1666, Bordeaux's Arnaud de Pontac sent his son to London to establish a restaurant, with dishes complementing the family's Haut-Brion. The place packed in the glitterati, including writers Daniel Defoe, Jonathan Swift, and John Locke, who admired the wine so much that he visited the de Pontac vineyards. Their mania crossed the Channel, provoking a mid-18th-century *"fureur de planter"* (passion for planting) among Bordeaux bourgeois.

The vineyards, previously confined to the Médoc regions south of the Gironde, spread to the areas south of the Dordogne, including St-Emilion. As the 19th century approached, the wines had powerful protectors and promoters such as Montesquieu, a local wine-maker, and Thomas Jefferson, who preferred the fine wines of the Château d'Yquem. For the Paris Exhibition of 1855, local officials laid their cards on the table and classified their wines by five categories *(crus)*. Today, the wines of Bordeaux flow into 500 million bottles annually, 65% of them reds.

The area's gravelly, sandy soil and rapid drainage into the Gironde make it an agricultural nightmare but a dream for wine-makers. Mild autumns and winters and long, hot summers are the perfect conditions for grapes. As the September harvest approaches, the region holds its breath in hopes of fair weather. The Médoc wine-makers have a saying, *"Août fait le moût"* ("August makes the must"—the juice).

Red Bordeaux wines break down into three families, each corresponding to grapes from a distinct geographical area: the Médoc and Graves *appellations* from the north and southwest; St-Emilion, Pomerol, and Fronsac from the central Libourne region; and the Bordeaux and Côtes de Bordeaux. The whites, based in southeastern Sauternes, are distinguished as dry or semi-sweet *(liquereux)*.

The best way to start your Bordeaux wine tasting is with a trip to the **Maison du Vin/CIVB,** 1, cours du 30 Juillet (tel. 05 56 00 22 66 or 05 50 00 22 88), across from the tourist office. This regional wine information center lets the Bordeaux wines work their individual charms on your palate, then on your wallet as you head to the vineyards. At the bar in the *Maison,* you can sample (sometimes for free) any of the bottles displayed and chat with a professional *sommelier* whose job it is to evaluate the quality of new wines. For a closer look into the world of wine, show up for a two-hour "Initiation to Wine Tasting" course given in French (twice weekly July-Aug., 60F) and learn the difference between an odor and an *âroma,* explore methods for evaluating wines, and leave confident about basic purchasing. The staff can give you a list of hundreds of local châteaux and tell you about vineyards you may want to visit. Remember that in **grape-lingo,** a château is not a castle, but the headquarters of a vineyard. (Maison du Vin open mid-June to mid-Oct. Mon.-Fri. 8:30am-6pm, Sat. 9am-4pm; mid-Oct. to mid-June Mon.-Thurs. 8:30am-6pm, Fri. 8:30am-5:30pm. Ask the receptionist about a 15-min. video on Bordeaux wines.)

If swishing wines for an hour has tempted your taste buds but not yet wetted your whistle, head to **Vinothèque,** 8, cours du 30 Juillet (tel. 05 56 52 32 05; open Mon.-Sat. 9:15am-7:30pm), or **L'Intendant,** 2, allées de Tourny (tel. 05 56 48 01 29; open Mon.-Sat. 10am-7:30pm, both within 50m of the tourist office). Staffs offer advice and sell wine at prices lower than those at most châteaux (15-19,000F).

A visit to the major châteaux requires a preliminary phone call; the tourist office will help with reservations. The tourist office give **bus tours** of châteaux in the region, with a different itinerary daily (see page 322 for more information).

The region is so densely packed with châteaux that drivers, bikers, and even walkers can easily amble from one to the next along country roads. As always, remember that many of the châteaux are private homes and, though they make and sell wine, they are not in the business of pouring free drinks for stray wanderers. Call ahead, politely ask if they are open to visitors, and approach your meeting not just as a tourist but as a customer, ready to splurge once you find a wine you enjoy.

■ Near Bordeaux: St-Emilion

Planted on the crumbly gravel of the Dordogne Valley just 35km northeast of Bordeaux, St-Emilion has coaxed from its countryside grapes and wines of such excellence that the St-Emilion and St-Emilion Grand Cru appellations are among the best in France. If practice has anything to do with perfection, let it suffice to say that St-Emilion has been cultivating grapes since the Gallo-Roman era. Today, the wine growers of St-Emilion gently crush 12,850 acres of grapes to produce 230,000hl of wine annually, all of which are carefully stored, meticulously rotated, lovingly brushed with egg whites, and attended through the years of maturation.

Make the **tourist office** at pl. des Créneaux (tel. 05 57 24 72 03; fax 05 57 74 47 15), near the church tower, your first stop (open daily 9:30am-12:30pm and 1:45-6:30pm; Nov.-March until 6pm). For a close-up peek into the world of wine-making, consider walking, biking, driving, or taking the tourist office's organized **tours** (all in English and French), each of a particular local château (July-Aug. 2 and 4:15pm; June and 1st week of Sept. 3pm., 51F). Pick up the *Grandes Heures de St-Emilion* for a list of classical music concerts complete with wine tasting hosted by nearby châteaux. The tourist office also **rents bikes** (60F per ½-day, 90F per full day).

Keep in mind that St-Emilion represents only one of the many wine-growing regions in Bordeaux. Consider a trip here an introduction to Bordeaux wine, an opportunity to sample some of the best and to tempt your tastebuds.

The **Maison du Vin de St-Emilion,** pl. Pierre Meyrat (tel. 05 57 55 50 55; fax 05 57 24 65 57), offers a one-hour mini-course similar to that at the Maison du Vin in Bordeaux, but focusing on St-Emilion (mid-July to mid-Sept. at 11am; admission 100F). The Maison also houses a wine shop with wholesale prices and a free grape exhibit.

This humble village gained fame and a name in the 8th century when Emilion, a monk and a hermit, established himself in the hamlet and made it a destination for pilgrims and a place of prayer. Over time, religious orders, monks, and pilgrims wandered in, settled, and left their architectural mark on the growing medieval town. The **Eglise Monolithe** is a tribute to Emilion, who was not only a holy man but a wine connoisseur. Shortly after Emilion's death, the church was painstakingly carved into a cliff face whose caves had been used for religious rites since prehistoric times. A tour of the church passes through ancient catacombs adorned with open sarcophagi and the odd bone or two (9 tours leave daily April-Oct. from tourist office 10am-5:45pm; 8 tours Nov.-March 10am-5pm; admission 33F, students 20F).

Ascend from the depths of the church and climb the steep cobblestone road to the **Clocher de l'Eglise Monolithe,** where a 6F ticket purchased at the white hut outside will give you the chance to climb 198 more rickety wooden steps to the top of the church's bell-tower. The view far surpasses that from the deck of the more crowded **Tour de Ray,** a stone's throw away, which charges the same amount (open daily 10am-noon and 2-6:15pm).

If the wine has left you fuzzy, slip into the secluded garden terrace of **L'Envers du Décor,** rue Clocher (tel. 05 57 74 48 31) for lunch. Slurp cool gazpacho (25F), sip wines by the glass, or savor the *salade jaja* (45F). (Open daily noon-2pm and 7-10pm; Oct.-June closed Sun. evening. V, MC, AmEx.) **Trains** run from Bordeaux to St-Emilion twice daily (30min., 42F). Take a right on the main road from the station and walk the 2km to St-Emilion. **Citram buses** whisk from Bordeaux to St-Emilion, with a change of buses in Libourne (1hr., roundtrip 58F). Check transport schedules carefully, or you'll find yourself wishing on shooting stars in a grape field.

Arcachon

Between the Atlantic Ocean and the pine forests of the Landes Regional Park, Arcachon and nearby **Pyla-sur-Mer** offer beach-combers 80km of pale yellow sands, rising to the skies as Europe's highest sand dune. Arcachon's popularity dates only from the 1850s, when a Parisian banker invested in a rail line from Bordeaux to the coast. Simple and elaborate villas popped up in a vast array of styles as the town gained prestige among vacationing artists (including Toulouse-Lautrec), writers, counts, and duchesses. On Sundays, while Bordeaux sleeps off its weekend wine, Arcachon is up early baking bread, shucking oysters, and swirling exotic ice creams. Unpretentious and sparkling, the town is a sandy pearl in a region of oysters.

ORIENTATION AND PRACTICAL INFORMATION

Arcachon's **tourist office,** pl. Roosevelt (tel. 05 56 83 01 69; fax 05 57 52 22 10), is about three blocks left of the station. A helpful staff distributes maps, festival calendars, brochures, and lists of (expensive) hotels, camping sites, and *chambres d'hôtes* (100-200F). A 24-hour self-serve computer lists hotels, restaurants, and sights when the office is closed. (Open July-Aug. Mon.-Sat. 9am-7pm, Sun. 9am-1pm; Sept. and June Mon.-Sat. 9am-12:30pm and 2-7pm; Oct.-March Mon.-Sat. 9am-12:30pm and 2-6pm; April-May Mon.-Sat. 9am-12:30pm and 2-6pm, Sun. 9am-1pm.) An **annex** is located on the corner of bd. Mestrezat and rue des Pêcheries (open July-Aug. 9am-

7pm). The tourist office runs weekly bus trips in July and August to **St-Emilion** (full day 165F) and **Medoc** (afternoon 120F), including a tour of a wine château and wine tasting. **Crédit Mutuel,** 12, pl. Lucien-de-Gracia has a 24-hour **ATM. Trains** (tel. 05 56 92 50 50) go only to Bordeaux (16-20 per day, 45min., 55F). **Société des Autobus d'Arachon,** 47, bd. Gén. Leclerc, runs buses to Pyla-sur-Mer, LaSalie, and Aiguillon (tel. 05 56 83 07 60; fax 05 56 83 65 46). **Bikes** (50F per day; 800F or passport deposit), *VTTs* (80F per day; 1000F or passport deposit), and scooters (170-250F per day; 4500-8000F or passport deposit) are for rent at **Locabeach,** 326, bd. de la Plage (tel. 05 56 83 39 64; open daily July-Aug. 9am-midnight; Sept. and June 9am-1pm and 2-8pm; Oct.-May open only during school vacations; V, MC). Wash towels at the **Lavarie** on the corner of bd. Général Leclerc and rue Molière (wash 30F per 7kg, dry 2F per 3min.; open 7am-10pm). For **sea and weather conditions,** call 08 36 68 08 33. The **hospital** is on bd. Louis-Lignon (tel. 05 56 54 39 50). The **police** (tel. 05 56 83 33 00) are on pl. Verdun; dial 17 in an **emergency.** The **post office,** 1, pl. Franklin Roosevelt (tel. 05 57 52 53 80), across from the tourist office, has **currency exchange,** and poste restante (open July-Aug. Mon.-Fri. 8:30am-7pm, Sat. 8:30am-noon; Sept.-June Mon.-Fri. 8:30am-6:15pm, Sun. 8:30am-noon; **postal code:** 33120).

ACCOMMODATIONS AND FOOD

Die-hard beach devotees snap up rooms with meals for the whole season. The cheapest rooms start at 200F with *demi-pension* in the summer; in the off-season, meals are optional and the price of a double drops to 135F. A mellow summer hostel, a zillion campgrounds, and the siren song of 100F singles in Bordeaux are your best options. The **Auberge de Jeunesse (HI),** 87, av. de Bordeaux (tel. 05 56 60 64 62), is actually across the bay in Cap-Ferrat, accessible by **ferry** from Arcachon's **Jetée Thiers** (tel. 05 56 54 92 78; morning every hr., afternoon every 30min.; Sept.-June every hr. all day; 30F, roundtrip 45F). After getting off the boat in Cap-Ferrat, walk off the pier straight onto av. de l'Océan and continue along when it becomes rue des Bouvreuils after the roundabout (15min.). Take the next left onto av. de Bordeaux, and the hostel will appear on the right in a few minutes (open July-Aug. only; members 43F; reception 8am-1pm and 6-9pm). The three-star **Camping Club d'Arcachon,** 5, allée de la Galaxie (tel. 05 56 83 24 15; fax 05 57 52 28 51), in Arcachon, has a luxurious pool, *discothèque,* market, bar-restaurant (open 8am-2am), summer concerts, and prices to match. (July-Aug. 1-3 people 110F; June and Sept. 80F; May and Oct. 70F; Nov.-March 65F. V, MC, AmEx.) Choose from five campgrounds in Pyla, including **Camping de la Dune** (tel. 05 56 22 72 17), route de Biscarrosse, a site on the dune flooded with packrats and accessible by bus from Arcachon. (Open May-Sept.; 2 people with car 95F, extra person 22F; prices 10-20F less off-season.)

It would be a crime to leave Arcachon without savoring a few ounces of the 15,000 tons of *huîtres* (oysters) gathered here annually. Beach cafés line av. Gambetta and the shore. Get washed away by **La Marée,** 21, rue de Marechal de Lattre de Tassigny (tel. 05 56 83 24 05), as you enjoy six oysters (35F) or fresh grilled salmon (68F) on its terrace (open daily June-Nov. noon-2:30pm and 7-10:30pm; mid-Feb. to May closed Mon. night-Tues.; V, MC, AmEx). At 7, cours Lamarque de Plaisance, the **Hôtel-Restaurant Le Bayonne** (tel. 05 56 83 33 82) runs a hip *bar à dégustation,* where you can savor six oysters and a glass of white wine for 36F. (Open daily July-Sept. 7:30am-11:30pm; March-June and Oct. closed Mon.; V, MC, AmEx.) The **Leclerc supermarket** stands at 224, bd. de la Plage (tel. 05 56 83 25 21; open Mon.-Sat. 9am-8pm, Sun. 9am-1pm; Sept.-June Mon.-Thurs. 9am-12:30pm and 2:30-7:30pm, Fri.-Sat. 9am-7:30pm; V, MC). A festive **market** on pl. Lucien-de-Gracia overflows with cartfuls of fresh produce and homemade specialties (in summer daily 7am-1pm indoors and out; in winter indoors daily and outdoors on Sat.).

SIGHTS

The area's calm waters, natural parks, islands, and bird sanctuaries attract flocks of tourists. Oysters play a key role in Arcachon's economy, though most of the region's

750 *ostréiculteurs* (oyster-farmers) work from **Gujan-Mestras,** to the west. Daytrips to the Arguin sandbar and other boat tours are run by **UBA** *(Union des Bateliers Arcachonnais)* and depart from the Jetée Thiers pier (tel. 05 56 54 83 01; daily 9am-noon and 2-7pm; June and Sept. 9:30-11:30am and 2:30-6pm).

Arcachon's **Ville d'Hiver,** an arboreal district of turn-of-the-century villas and mansions, lies across the **Parc Mauresque** north of the beach. The neighborhood's curving streets were designed to block ocean winds; this "winter village" is actually 2°C warmer on average than its beachfront counterpart. The villas, whose builders' whimsies strayed from Swiss chalet to clichéd castle, are accessible by guided **tours** leaving from the tourist office (July-Aug. Mon.-Sat. 11am; 20F). The **Parc Ornithologique du Teich** (tel. 05 56 22 80 93), 15km out of town, boasts 260 species of birds in one of France's most important sanctuaries (open daily 10am-8pm; 33F). Summer nights in Arcachon heat up as the beaches cool down with several discos on the beachfront and a casino that looks like a fairy-tale palace.

The ultimate sand experience awaits just a 45-minute bus trip south of Arcachon at **Pyla-sur-Mer.** The gargantuan **Dune du Pyla** is 60 million tons of golden silica sandwiched between the million-acre *forêt landaise* to the east and the Atlantic to the west. Running down the 117m-high dune shin-deep in immaculate sand is just one step short of nirvana. At the bottom, keep running right off the dune into the ocean, or pretend you forgot your bathing suit and mosey a mile down the sand to join the *naturistes* at the **nudist beach.** There are sailboat rentals and a high-priced snack bar on the beach, but don't overindulge; the climb back up the dune is a solid 20-minute sweat. **Buses** leave for Pyla from the Arcachon station (15 per day, last return around 8pm, 45min., 22F roundtrip). Some say that hitching takes half as long. Bring plenty of water and a picnic, or you'll be at the mercy of the snack stands. Ask at the Arcachon tourist office about para-sailing ventures off the dune.

Périgueux

In the first and second centuries, people flocked to Périgueux (then called Vesuna) to shop in its bustling market and delight in the spectacle of gladiators dueling to the death. The market remains—in the form of a Monoprix in the *centre ville*—but the amphitheater has lost its bite and become a lush garden. Modern Périgueux (pop. 33,000) exudes a sleepy charm from the secluded streets and family-run shops of the *vieille ville.* Well-connected to major cities in the region, Périgueux serves as a convenient gateway to the Dordogne Valley and the cave paintings at Les Eyzies.

ORIENTATION AND PRACTICAL INFORMATION

Périgueux's *vieille ville* and tourist office are a 10-minute walk from the train station. Turn right on rue Denis Papin and bear left on rue des Mobiles-de-Coulmiers, which becomes rue du Président Wilson. On your right, you'll pass rue Guillier, which leads to the Roman ruins. The tourist office is two blocks farther. Take a right just after the Monoprix and walk a block down to the office, next to the stone Tour Mataguerre. Rue du Président Wilson leads to the heart of the *vieille ville.*

Tourist Information: Tourist Office, 26, pl. Francheville (tel. 05 53 53 10 63; fax 05 53 09 02 50). Mediocre city map, list of accommodations and restaurants, and brochures galore. French and English guided tours in July and Aug. (Tues.-Fri. 10am and 2:30pm; 22F, students 16F; groups by reservation the rest of the year). Open Mon.-Sat. 9am-6pm, Sun. 10am-5pm; Sept.-June Mon.-Sat. 9am-noon and 2-6pm. **Office Départementale du Tourisme,** 25, rue Wilson (tel. 05 53 35 50 24). Info on Périgord; lists of campgrounds, *gîtes,* and *chambres d'hôtes,* excellent topographic maps (40F). Open Mon.-Fri. 8:30am-noon and 2-6pm.

Money: Banque de France, 1, pl. du Roosevelt (tel. 05 53 03 30 44) has **currency exchange** (open Mon.-Fri. 8:45am-12:15pm and 1:35-3:35pm). Several 24-hr. **ATMs** squat at the intersection of rue Gambetta and cours Michel Montaigne.

Trains: rue Denis Papin (tel. 05 53 09 50 50). To: Paris via Limoges (6 per day, 6-7hr., 263F); Lyon (4 per day, 6½hr., 268F); Bordeaux (10-12 per day, 2½hr., 96F); Toulouse via Brive (7 per day, 4hr., 182F); Limoges (10 per day, 1¼hr., 76F); Les Eyzies (5-6 per day, 30min., 40F). Info office open Sun.-Fri. 4:30am-midnight, Sat. 4:30am-8pm. **Lockers** 15-30F.

Buses: pl. Francheville (tel. 05 53 08 91 06). To: Angoulême (3 per day, 1 Sun., 1½hr., 45F); Brantôme (3 per day, 40min., 24F); Sarlat (2 per day, none on Sun., 1½hr., 43F50); Excideuil (4 per day, 1hr., 33F). Schedules change often. Office open Mon.-Thurs. 8:30-11:30am and 2-5:30pm, Fri. 8:30-11:30am and 2-5pm.

Taxis: Taxi Périgueux, pl. Bugeaud (tel. 05 53 09 09 09). 24hr.

Bike Rental: Au Tour de France, 96, av. du Maréchal Juin (tel. 05 53 53 41 91), near the station. 55F first day, 44F thereafter. *VTTs* 80F first day, 50F thereafter. Passport deposit. Open Mon.-Sat. 8:30am-12:15pm and 2-7:15pm. V, MC, AmEx.

Laundromat: 61, rue Gambetta. Open Mon.-Fri. 8am-10pm and Sat. 7am-8pm.

Youth Center: Centre d'Information Jeunesse (CIJ), 1, av. d'Aquitaine (tel. 05 53 53 52 81). Tons of info. *Carte Jeune* cards 12F. Free Carissimo cards. Helps find long-term student lodgings. Open Mon.-Fri. 9am-noon and 2:30-6:30pm.

Crisis Lines: Aides Aquitaine, 2, rue Victor Basch (tel. 05 53 03 95 77). AIDS info. **SOS Femmes Battue** (tel. 05 53 35 03 03), for female victims of abuse.

Hospital: Centre Hospitalier, 80, av. Georges Pompidou (tel. 05 53 07 70 00). Walk northeast of town from pl. de la Libération to av. Pompidou (8 blocks). **Medical emergency** tel. 05 53 08 81 11 or 15.

Police: rue du 4 Septembre (tel. 05 53 08 10 17), near the post office. From the station, take rue Pepin to rue Maréchal Juin, turn left, continue straight for about 5 blocks, and turn left on rue du 4 Septembre. **Emergency** tel. 17.

Post Office: 1, rue du 4 Septembre (tel. 05 53 53 60 82). Poste restante. **Currency exchange.** Open Mon.-Fri. 8am-7pm, Sat. 8am-noon. **Postal code:** 24000.

ACCOMMODATIONS AND CAMPING

Inexpensive hotels cluster around the train station, on the way into the *vieille ville,* and in the pedestrian area. If the price seems too good to be true, ask to see the room before plunking down your money. The hostel is not marked and can be difficult to find; check the map in front of the station before making the trip.

Foyer des Jeunes Travailleurs Résidence Lakanal (tel. 05 53 53 52 05), off bd. Lakanal. From tourist office, turn left down cours Fénélon and turn right onto bd. Lakanal. When the fire station appears on your left, turn right through the Bridge Club parking lot; go left of the building and through the gate to reach the front of the *foyer.* Very firm mattresses in pleasant 4-bed dorm rooms with sink and shower. 65-75F. Sheets, showers, and breakfast (Mon.-Sat.) included. Mon.-Fri. lunch and dinner (35-40F each). No lockout, no curfew. Open daily 9am-11pm.

Hôtel des Barris, 2, rue Pierre Magne (tel. 05 53 53 04 05). A family-run affair directly across from the cathedral, above an expensive restaurant *gourmand.* Immaculate rooms, free hall showers, friendly management, and a bright breakfast room make the price (singles with toilet 149F; doubles with toilet 169F) seem like a bargain. Ask about student discounts. Reserve. V, MC, AmEx.

Au Bon Coin/Chez Pierrot, 8, rue Chanzy (tel. 05 53 53 43 22), off rue Denis Papin between the station and *centre ville.* Friendly couple manages 10 slightly musty but clean rooms. Singles and doubles 100F. 2 beds 120F. Free hall shower. Breakfast 25F. Reception closed Sun. Reserve 2-3 days in advance. Restaurant downstairs serves simple, filling 50-70F *menus* (wine included). V, MC.

Les Charentes, 16, rue Denis Papin (tel. 05 53 53 37 13), facing the *gare.* Tiny singles and doubles 120-190F. Free showers. Reception 6:30am-11pm. V, MC, AmEx.

Hôtel Regina, 14, rue Denis Papin (tel. 05 53 08 40 44; fax 05 53 54 72 44). A bit pricey, but even the cheapest room comes with a shower, toilet, two beds, and floor-to-ceiling French windows. The amiable staff bends over backwards to help you feel at home. Singles 190F. Doubles 225F. V, MC, AmEx.

Camping: Barnabé-Plage, 80, rue des Bains (tel. 05 53 53 41 45), 1.5km from Périgueux in Boulazac. From cours Montaigne, take bus D (direction: Cité Belaire;

6F; until about 7:30pm) and get off at "rue des Bains." Riverside site packed in July and Aug. Open 9am-midnight. 15F per person, 14F per tent, 9F per car.

FOOD

Charcuteries along rue Limogeanne are palaces of *foie gras* and other delicacies. Budgetarians (and vegetarians) might prefer the produce at the daily morning **market** on pl. du Coderc or the even larger market on pl. de la Cloître near the cathedral (both open mid-Nov. to March Wed. and Sat. 8am-1pm). Not surprisingly, the pricey restaurants lie near pl. St-Louis in the *vieille ville;* the area southwest of the cathedral around pl. Hoche and rue Aubergerie has diverse and more wallet-pleasing options. The shiny **Monoprix,** on pl. de la République in the *centre ville,* is impossible to miss (open Mon.-Sat. 8:30am-8pm). The gardens surrounding any of the Roman ruins are perfect places to spread your picnic blanket.

L'Amandier, 12, rue Eguillerie (tel. 05 53 04 15 51), just off pl. St-Louis. Packed with locals. 53F lunch *menu* and 75F dinner *menu* include chilled cucumber soup, succulent grilled duck, and tasty desserts. Open Mon. and Wed.-Sat. noon-2pm and 7-11pm, Tues. and Sun. noon-2pm. Closed last Sun. of the month. V, MC.

Helliniko, 15, rue des Places (tel. 05 53 09 69 91), in the *vieille ville* off rue Taillefer. With baklava like theirs, it's no wonder locals crowd in every night. 75F *menu* with spinach quiche, filling moussaka, and a choice of Greek desserts. Open Tues.-Sat. noon-2pm and 7-11pm, Mon. 7-10pm. V, MC, AmEx.

L'Aubergerie, 14, rue Aubergerie (tel. 05 53 09 63 88), off rue des Places. Dine on a gorgeous terrace. Self-service cafeteria at lunch, restaurant at dinner. 43-52F lunch *menus.* 65F 4-course *menu* with grilled shrimp and large *plat du jour.* Open daily 11:30am-2pm and 7-10:30pm. V, MC.

SIGHTS AND ENTERTAINMENT

Périgueux is a perfect city for strolling. At the tourist office, pick up walking tour guides (in English on request) of the Renaissance architecture of the *vieille ville* or the Gallo-Roman structures closer to the train tracks. All roads lead to the huge **Cathédrale St-Front.** Built in the shape of a Greek cross around the tomb of St. Front, the cathedral successfully combines Byzantine domes, Romanesque arches, and the stylish turrets of a reformed fortress. A church has stood on this spot since the 6th century, but St-Front's present incarnation came about only in the last century when Abadie (creator of Paris's Sacré-Coeur) all but dismantled the old church to make way for his own house of worship. The exterior, with its 10 spires and five cupolas, contrasts with the inside, which, at first glance, appears to be made of cinder block. Oddly devoid of the ages of grime and dust that mar the interior of other French cathedrals, St-Front has dozens of shimmering *vitraux,* five golden chandeliers, organ chimes built to resemble those of St-Marks' in Venice, and a Baroque altarpiece dedicated to the Assumption (open daily 8am-12:30pm and 2:30-7:30pm; free tours in French upon request; admission to 9th-century cloisters and crypt 10F).

The **Musée du Périgord,** 22, cours Tourny (tel. 05 53 53 16 42), at the corner of rue St-Front, is home to one of France's most important collections of prehistoric artifacts, including fossils from Les Eyzies, 2m-long mammoth tusks, and even an Egyptian mummy whose toes peek out from his crusty coverings. When all those pieces of flint start to look the same, admire Gallo-Roman mosaics, smiling 13th-century samurai masks, or the small gallery (open Sept.-July Wed.-Mon. 10am-noon and 2-6pm; Aug. Wed.-Mon. 10am-noon and 2-6pm; admission 12F, students 6F, under 18 free). The **Musée Militaire,** 32, rue de Farges (tel. 05 53 53 47 36), off rue Taillefer in the *vieille ville,* documents the history of warfare in Périgueux from ancient to modern times through a display of weapons, military attire, and photographs (open daily April-Sept. 10am-noon; Oct.-Dec. 2-6pm; admission 20F).

Crumbling Gallo-Roman structures crop up amid apartments and storefronts across the train tracks on the west side of town. The massive three-quarter cylinder of the **Tour de Vésone** is all that remains of a marble-encased temple that formed the center of the city of Vesuna. Legend has it that the break in the tower was made when St. Front cursed the pagan citizens. A more probable theory claims the Vesunians themselves smashed their tower to procure rocks for a defensive wall. The excavations at the **Villa de Pompeïus** next door have brought to light artifacts now on display in the town museum. Back across the tracks and closer to the train station crumble the ruins of the **Château Barrière,** rue Turenne. Even nearer the *gare,* fountains and shrubbery add cheer to the remains of the first-century Gallo-Roman amphitheater in the **Jardin des Arènes.** The count of Périgord, an English ally, used the 133m-long structure as a stronghold in the Hundred Years' War (Tour de Vésone and gardens open daily April-Sept. 7:30am-9pm; Oct.-March 7:30am-6:30pm).

Up rue de l'Ancien Evêché from the amphitheater, the 12th-century **Eglise St-Etienne-de-la-Cité** was the first Christian edifice in town. The modest Romanesque church has two cupolas (there were four at one point) in addition to nine stained-glass windows decorated with arches and columns in the apse. Twice a month, the recently restored pipes of the 17th-century organ get a chance to toot their own horns in free concerts (check the schedule outside the church). Next to the tourist office is the **Tour Mataguerre,** an amazingly well-preserved tower built by lepers in 1477 and named after an English captain who was kept prisoner in the tower's dungeon for 17 years (visits only through the tourist office).

While the streets may be sleepy at night, the *places* have no intention of calling it an early evening. Expect to find nightlife on pl. St-Salin and pl. St-Louis and frequent concerts on pl. du Marché. Talk into the early morning at the **Café le St-Louis** (tel. 05 53 53 53 90), open until 2am every night. The well-rounded **Café la Rotonde,** 9, cours Montaigne (tel. 05 53 08 30 31), keeps things light and lively every night. **L'Avant Scène,** 3, port de Graule (tel. 05 53 04 47 44), the first right off av. Daumesnil when walking away from the river, offers as many concerts as there are jazz musicians (open 6pm-2am; cover 30F; V, MC). **Gordon Pub,** 12, rue Condé (tel. 05 53 35 03 74), off rue Taillefer, is a friendly English-style pub with equally friendly prices (beer 11F) and a terrace (open Mon.-Fri. 11pm-2am, Sat. 2pm-2am, Sun. 9pm-2am). Across the river, **L'Ande'rois,** 51, rue Aubarède (tel. 05 53 53 01 58), is a gay bar (open nightly) that livens up an otherwise dull neighborhood with dancing Wednesday to Saturday 'til 3am. Dig the crowd at **La Regence,** 16, rue des Chancelier de l'Hôpital (tel. 05 53 53 10 55), in the *centre ville* (open nightly until 2:30-3am).

Périgueux jumps back 500 years most Saturdays in July and August with the **Fêtes du Lys d'Or Périgueux Médiéval.** Parades, jousts, and a mud wrestling match or two add a retro slant to the town's streets. The town quiets down every year for about 10 days in August when it plays host to the **International Mime Festival.** Many of the world's most respected mime companies perform and give free performances and classes; impromptu hecklers' workshops pop up all over town.

Brive-la-Gaillarde

Brive received its nickname, *"la Gaillarde"* (the Bold), when its courageous citizens repelled English forces during the Hundred Years' War. Continuing this tradition of *brio* and gall, Brive (pop. 52,000) became the first town in France to liberate itself from the German occupation in 1944. Since then, it has not given in to the regional tendency to transform its *centre ville* into a medieval playground and has instead sauntered happily into modernity by lining its streets with cafés, restaurants, and clothing store stand-bys. Brive makes a cheap and convenient base for exploration of the treasures of the Périgord and Quercy regions.

ORIENTATION AND PRACTICAL INFORMATION

The **tourist office** (tel. 05 55 24 08 80; fax 05 55 24 58 24) is in a 19th-century lighthouse on pl. du 14 Juillet. Go straight from the *gare* down av. Jean Jaurès to the Cathédrale St-Martin, walk around the church, and go straight on rue Toulzac, which becomes av. de Paris. The office is on the right (open July-Aug. Mon.-Sat. 9am-

12:30pm and 2-7pm, Sun. 10am-1pm; Sept.-June Mon.-Sat. 10am-noon and 2-6pm). For **currency exchange,** try the good ol' **Banque de France,** bd. Général Koenig (tel. 05 55 92 37 00; open Mon.-Fri. 9:30am-noon and 1:45-3pm). There are **ATMs** in front of the train station. The **train station** (tel. 05 55 18 41 16) sends trains to: Rocamadour (3-4 per day, 45min., 40F); Limoges (7-8 per day, 1hr., 74F); Souillac, with a bus to Sarlat (4-5 per day, 30min., 36F); Cahors (8 per day, 1½hr., 75F); Toulouse (5-6 per day, 2½hr., 137F); Bordeaux (2 per day, 3hr., 131F); and Paris (4-6 per day, 4hr., 253F). **Lockers** 15-25F. The **gare routière's** temporary office is at pl. du 14 Juillet (tel. 05 55 24 29 93), next to the tourist office. **Buses** stop at the train station and pl. de Lattre de Tassigny (next to the post office). **STUB** (tel. 05 55 74 20 03) buses run to Sarlat (1 per day, 1½hr., 39F) and smaller towns. **Trans-Périgord** buses (tel. 05 53 09 24 08, in Périgueux) also make a daily run to Sarlat (1½hr., 40F) via Souillac (40min., 25F). Buy tickets on the bus. For a 24-hour **taxi,** call 05 55 24 24 24. Psyched to **bike?** Rent one at **Léon Servanin Cycles,** 7, av. Pierre Sémard (tel. 05 55 88 02 52), 10 minutes from town on the main road to Bordeaux (*VTTs* 80F a day, 300F a week; passport deposit; open Tues.-Sat. 9am-7:30pm; V, MC). Closer to town is **Alain Brissard Cycles,** 40, av. Léon Blum (tel. 05 55 23 04 40), near the train station (*VTTs* 80F per day; open Mon.-Sat. 9am-7:30pm; V, MC). The **Centre Hospitalier** is at bd. Docteur Verlhac (tel. 05 55 92 60 00). In **emergencies**, dial 05 55 23 33 33. The **police** are at 4, bd. Anatole France (tel. 05 55 74 04 36). **Emergency** tel. 17. The **post office,** on pl. Winston Churchill (tel. 05 55 18 33 10), offers poste restante (open Mon.-Fri. 8am-6:45pm, Sat. 8am-noon; **postal code:** 19100).

ACCOMMODATIONS

The **Auberge de Jeunesse (HI),** 56, av. du Maréchal Bugeaud (tel. 05 55 24 34 00), has comfortable three- to four-bed dorms, kitchen facilities, a TV room, and clean, hot showers. Large groups frequent this hostel. From the train station, take av. Jean Jaurès past the St-Sernin church and turn right onto bd. M. Lyautey at the bottom of the hill. Follow as it curves to the left, becoming bd. Jules Ferry, and turn right onto av. Bugeaud after five blocks. The hostel is behind the huge municipal pools. The 108 beds rarely fill up, but it's worth calling ahead in July and August, if only to arrange for free *gare*-to-*auberge* service (members 47F; breakfast 18F; lunch and dinner 47F; reception 8am-11pm; closed 11am-5pm on weekends; no lockout or curfew). Amiable Mme. Benoit lets clean, large rooms in **Le Majestic-Voyageurs,** 67, av. Jean Jaurès (tel. 05 55 24 10 20), across from the *gare* (singles with toilets 60-90F; doubles 100-120F, with shower and toilet 140-160F; free hall shower; breakfast 10-20F; closed Dec. 15-Jan. 15). Smack in the middle of the *centre ville,* **Hôtel Correze,** 3, rue de Correze (tel. 05 55 24 14 07), off rue Toulzac, offers clean, snug singles and homey doubles (both 80F with shower) above a great restaurant (reception Mon.-Sat.; V, MC). Halfway between the *gare* and the *centre ville,* **Hôtel de l'Avenir,** 39, av. Jean Jaurès (tel. 05 55 74 11 84), lets cheery rooms with firm mattresses and serves an inexpensive *plat du jour* (40F; reception Mon.-Sat. 7am-11pm; singles 90F; doubles 110F, with shower 130F, with bath 180-200F; showers 10F; breakfast 25F; closed Dec.; V, MC). The **Camping Municipal des Iles,** bd. Michelet (tel. 05 55 24 34 74), just beyond the youth hostel, sits by the Corrèze river (17F per person, 15F per tent; free showers; reception daily 7am-noon and 2-10pm).

FOOD

Brive's **open-air market** occupies pl. du 14 Juillet on Tuesday, Thursday, and Saturday. Everything from clothes to gerbils hides in the stalls. The food market is dirt cheap, and the shopping is serious—no catering to tourists here. Hang on to your money belt (7:30am-noon). The enormous **Nouvelles Galeries** occupy a block of the *vieille ville,* at the intersection of bd. Général Koenig and av. de Paris. The grocery section is at the back of the store (open Mon.-Sat. 9am-7:30pm; V, MC).

The few cheap restaurants in Brive are concentrated around pl. Anatole Briand and pl. Charles de Gaulle. Try **Viviers Saint-Martin,** 4, rue Traversière (tel. 05 55 24 48

11), on a narrow lane off pl. de Gaulle. The atmosphere is touristy, but the filling, scrumptious 88F or 100F *menus* with *salade de gésiers* (gizzard salad) and *escalope de perche* (perch) will sate you nonetheless (open daily noon-2pm and 7-10pm; Sept. 16-June Thurs.-Tues. noon-2pm and 7-10pm; V, MC). For a more intimate *répas,* try **Restaurant Ruthène,** 2, rue Jean-Maistre (tel. 05 55 23 08 66), on a tiny street off rue Carnot near bd. Général Koenig. The restaurant serves a 50F lunch *menu* with a *plat du jour* and dessert, and a fabulous 65F three-course dinner *menu* with *spécialités au Roquefort,* such as steak dripping with blue cheese. Vegetarians can rejoice in the 50F *salade des Gourmets* (open Mon.-Sat. 11:45am-2:15pm and 6:30-10pm). Near the train station, the friendly, family-run **Restaurant Galata Instanbul,** 36, av. Jean-Jaurès (tel. 05 55 17 96 80), grills meats and serves them, smothered in spicy sauces, on a secluded backyard terrace—all for 38-40F! Entrees 25-30F, sandwiches 22F (open daily 10:30am-2pm and 6pm-midnight).

SIGHTS AND ENTERTAINMENT

The 12th-century **Cathédrale St-Martin,** pl. Charles de Gaulle, is named after the iconoclastic Spaniard who introduced Christianity to Brive in the early 5th century. Its high crossed arches and pale, thin stone columns mark the geographic and cultural center of town. Martin interrupted the feast of Saturnus, loudly proclaiming his faith and smashing idols; the startled worshippers chopped off his head, unknowingly making a martyr of Martin. The crypt under the nave displays sarcophagi unearthed by recent excavations, as well as reliquaries and polychrome statues. The **Musée Labenche,** 26bis, bd. Jules Ferry (tel. 05 55 24 39 39), housed in the beautiful Renaissance Hôtel Labenche, is one of those little-bit-of-everything museums common in small French towns. Don't miss *Les Chasses* (The Hunts), three well-preserved 17th-century tapestries which show the lighter side of hunting—playing cards, getting drunk, and flirting. (Open Wed.-Mon. April-Oct. 10am-6:30pm; Nov.-March 1:30-6pm. Admission 27F, students 13F50, children under 16 8F50.)

Two blocks from the *centre ville* down bd. Jean Jaurès is the **Eglise St-Mernin.** The church, with its dazing blue *vitraux* and clean, simple Romanesque style, was built only a few years ago as a complete reconstruction of the 13th- to 16th-century church that originally stood on the site. From pl. de la République, follow rue Emile Zola to the **Centre National de la Résistance et de la Déportation Edmond Michelet,** 4, rue Champanatier (tel. 05 55 74 06 08; fax 05 55 17 09 44), which honors the Brive native. There isn't a town in France without a street named after Michelet, a leader in the Resistance who endured Dachau for more than a year and later became a minister under de Gaulle. Graphic photos of women and children on their way to the gas chambers, heart-rending last letters to loved ones, and other documents tell the story of the French Resistance movement and the horrors of World War II concentration camps (open Mon.-Sat. 10am-noon and 2-6pm; free).

One week in mid-August, orchestras and choirs from 20 countries converge in Brive to perform free all over the city at 5, 6, and 9pm. During the rest of the year, Brive is pretty slow at night. The **Centre Culturel Communal,** 31, av. Jean-Jaurès (tel. 05 55 74 20 51), has up-to-date info on events (Mon.-Sat. 9am-noon and 2-7pm). Cafés line **av. Paris.** A rowdy, mixed gay-straight crowd alternates between *demis* and *cafés* at **L'Europe,** 21, av. Paris (tel. 05 55 24 19 55), every night until 2am. **La Charette,** 33, av. Ribot (tel. 05 55 87 65 73), over the av. Paris bridge and to the left, bops with techno, disco, and that occasional 80s song that makes you so excited you just can't hide it (cover 60F; women free Thurs. and Fri.; open Tues.-Sat. until 3am). **Le Watson Bar** transforms the otherwise lukewarm rue des Echevins into a hotspot (open Mon.-Sat. 3pm-2am).

■ Near Brive

The fertile **Lot** region southeast of Brive is home to aloof hilltop châteaux, lazy rivers, grazing cows, and tiny hamlets that have never seen a tour bus. That's not to say tourists have ignored this hinterland, but the lack of a big-name attraction has kept many sights relatively crowd free. **Bretenoux** makes a sensible base town for this area and is less than an hour away from Brive by train (4-5 per day, 45min., 39F).

The burnt-red ramparts of **Castelnau-Bretenoux** (tel. 05 65 10 98 00) have kept an eye on the valley below since the 11th century. Castelnau was built atop an enormous pedestal in the shape of a triangle, flanked by three corner towers. In the central *cour d'honneur,* the medieval **Tour Sarrazin** commands a view that extends for miles. English forces surrounded the fortress for many years during the Hundred Years' War but were never able to capture it. Famed 19th-century opera singer Jean Mouliérat gave the interior a more human touch when he restored the château following an 1851 fire. Today, splendid Aubusson and Beauvais tapestries are displayed beside modern operetta scores and 15th-century *vitraux* in the *oratoire.* (Open daily July-Aug. 9am-6:30pm; April-June and Sept. 9am-noon and 2-6pm; Oct.-March 10am-noon and 2-5pm. Admission 27F, students 18F, under 18 10F. Tours in French every 30min., 2 English tours on Thurs. and Fri.; last tour 45min. before closing.)

Castelnau, Montal, and Beaulieu are easily accessible by bike or car from Bretenoux. The train station is 2km from Bretenoux; shuttle buses run from the *gare* to Bretenoux (10min.) and St-Céré (3-4 per day, 15min., 15F; schedule posted outside *gare*). It's probably easier to make the clearly marked 25-minute walk to Bretenoux; from there it's a flat 3km southwest to Castelnau, 8km southwest to St. Céré, and 9km north to Beaulieu. In the Manoir du Fort, the **tourist office** at Bretenoux (tel. 05 65 38 59 53; fax 05 65 39 7214) distributes maps and info about the region (open July-Aug. Mon.-Sat. 9am-12:30pm and 3-7pm, Sun. 10am-12:30pm; June and Sept. 9am-noon and 3-6pm). **Banks** and **ATMs** lurk around the traffic light near the train station. An immense **E. Leclerc supermarket** (tel. 05 65 10 22 00) sits just across from the banks (open Mon.-Thurs. 9am-12:15pm and 2-7:30pm, Fri.-Sat. 9am-7:30pm; V, MC). An **open-air market** with local produce takes place behind the tourist office every Monday and Saturday, 7am-noon. **Camping de Bourgnatelle** (tel. 05 65 38 44 07 or 08 35 33 75 68) is located on a beautiful site straddling the river and overlooking the town (open May-Sept.; in July and Aug. 11F50 per adult, 11F50 per tent, electricity 13F50; V, MC). You can **rent bikes** in Bretenoux from **M. Bladier** (tel. 05 65 38 41 56), on rue d'Orlinde across from the holiday house where Pierre Loti (see page 305) wrote *Prime Jeunesse* and *Roman d'un Enfant* (40F per day; mountain bikes 60F per ½-day, 80F per day, 500F or passport deposit; open Tues.-Sat. 8am-noon and 2-7pm). From St-Céré, it's 2km to the Château de Montal.

In contrast to this weighty medieval fortress, the graceful **Château de Montal** (tel. 05 65 38 13 72), 8km southwest of Bretenoux in **St-Céré,** teases with a stern Renaissance façade but opens to reveal a courtyard and interior bursting with sculpture; even the underside of each step in the grand stairway is masterfully carved. Opulent tapestries, Flemish and Spanish painting, and exquisite furniture adorn this private château (open Aug. daily 2:30-7pm; Sept.-Oct. and Easter-July Sun.-Fri. 9:30am-noon and 2:30-6pm; guided tours in French approximately every 45min; last tour begins 1hr. before closing; admission 20F, students 18F). In St-Céré, you can **rent bikes** at **St-Chaumont,** 45, rue Faidherbe (tel. 05 65 38 03 23; 25F per ½-day, 35F per day; *VTTs* 60F per ½-day, 80F per day; open Tues.-Sat. 9am-noon and 2-7pm).

Ten km north of Bretenoux on route D940, the village of **Beaulieu-sur-Dordogne** stands under the towering steeple of the 13th-century **Abbaye Benedictine St-Pierre.** The portal features an ornate relief of God sitting on his throne, arms spread, while angels and various saints look on (open daily 8am-7:30pm). Down the street along the banks of the river, the 12th-century **Chapelle des Pénitents,** pl. de Monturu (tel. 05 55 91 01 40), now a religious art and history museum, has been beautifully restored in Spanish style, with golden walls and a wooden balcony. The museum features a blue burlap-sack cloak and hood worn by the *pénitents bleus,* an order founded in Beaulieu in the 17th century to help the sick (open daily July-Sept. 15 10:30am-noon and 3-6pm; call the *mairie* at 05 55 91 11 31 for tours off-season; admission 10F). A two-second walk from the river is the **Auberge de Jeunesse (HI),** pl. du Monturu (tel. 05 55 91 13 82), well worn but well kept. Should you wish to make the region more than a daytrip, the hostel makes a perfect base (12- to 14-bed dorms; members 40F; sheets 16F; kitchen facilities; reception open 6-8pm; no lock-out; open April-Sept.). Pitch your tent for pennies along the Dordogne at the **Camping Municipal du Pont** (tel. 05 55 91 00 57; 10F per person, 4F50 per tent, 4F50 per car, electricity 10F; open June 15-Sept. 15; reception 8am-noon and 3-8pm). Many establishments along the river **rent canoes** for 30-40F an hour, 70-80F a day.

Twenty kilometers southeast of Brive, the town of **Collonges-la-Rouge** looks so much like a Disney creation that it is difficult to believe it is real. Round roofs, surprising details, sandstone turrets, and overflowing flower gardens line the narrow streets of this village, easily one of the most beautiful in France. Take a stroll among the tourists crowding the wood-roofed **market** (Mon.-Sat. 7am-1pm) and emerald green vines and trees scattered along **rue Noire,** the gift-shop-lined main street. Despite this beckoning commercialization, Collonges has yet to surrender to its lures. The **Maison de la Sirène** houses a beautiful 18th-century painting of a blond-haired siren clutching a mirror in one hand and a comb in the other, and wondering how to make up for her night on the town (open daily 9:30am-noon and 2-6:30pm). The 12th-century church in the *centre ville* received a facelift during the 16th-century religious wars. Its appearance today confuses both styles; the Gothic steeple rises majestically above the 3m-thick fortressed walls (open daily 9am-7:30pm). Collonges is accessible by bus from Brive (1 per day, 30min., 17F).

Les Eyzies-de-Tayac

Tourists were not the first to discover the verdant hills, solid limestone cliffs, and gentle rivers of the Vézère and Dordogone valleys. In fact, Henry Miller was convinced that the hills "must have been paradise for many thousands of years," a guess that was not far off the mark. The discoveries, mostly within the last century, of 15,000-year old paintings and etchings of bison heads, rhinoceri, elephants, and humans have given people all the more reason to flock to this prehistoric treasure trove. Strict limits on the number of visitors per day at the more popular caves keep crowds from getting out of hand, but there's a down side, too. In summer, be sure to reserve at least two weeks in advance if you want to see more than postcards and ticket stands. Another (less reliable) strategy is to arrive at 9am with abundant optimism and patience and wait for any unclaimed or cancelled reservations.

ORIENTATION AND PRACTICAL INFORMATION

Les Eyzies is linked by train to Agen, Périgueux, and Le Buisson. In July and August, there are also weekly buses from Sarlat and Souillac. From the train station, turn right and walk 1km down the village's only street to reach its center (5min.).

Tourist Office: pl. de la Mairie (tel. 05 53 06 97 05; fax 05 53 06 90 79). Excellent list of caves, **currency exchange,** and tours in summer to sights out of walking distance (call ahead). **Rents bikes** (40F per day, 100F deposit). Info on canoe rentals, horse trails, cycling, and hiking. Open July-Aug. Mon.-Sat. 9am-7pm, Sun. 10am-noon and 2-6pm; March-June and Sept.-Oct. Mon.-Sat. 9am-noon and 2-6pm, Sun. 10am-noon and 2-6pm; Nov.-Feb. Mon.-Fri. 10am-noon and 2-6pm.

Money: Crédit Mutuel, next to the Halle Paysanne, has an **ATM.** Open Tues.-Fri. 9am-12:30pm and 1:30-4:30pm, Sat. 9am-noon.

Trains: (tel. 05 53 06 97 22). To: Périgueux (5 per day, 40min., 40F); Sarlat (2-3 per day, change at Le Buisson, 1hr., 44F); Agen (4 per day, 2hr., 82F); Paris (2 per day, 6-8hr., 273F). Open Mon.-Fri. 6:30am-11pm, Sat.-Sun. 6:30am-10:30pm.

Hospital: (tel. 05 53 31 75 75), in Sarlat.

Police: (tel. 05 53 29 20 17). **Emergency** tel. 17.

Post Office: Near tourist office (tel. 05 53 06 94 11). **Money exchange,** poste restante. Open Mon.-Fri. 9am-noon and 2-5pm, Sat. 9am-noon. **Postal code:** 24620.

TRAVEL GEAR

Let's Go carries a full line of Eagle Creek packs, accessories, and security items.

A. World Journey

Equipped with Eagle Creek Comfort Zone Carry System which includes Hydrofil nylon knit on backpanel and shoulder straps, molded torso adjustments, and spinal and lumbar pads. Parallel internal frame. Easy packing panel load design with internal cinch straps. Lockable zippers. Black, Evergreen, or Blue. The perfect Eurailing pack. $20 off with rail pass. $195

B. Continental Journey

Carry-on sized pack with internal frame suspension. Detachable front pack. Comfort zone padded shoulder straps and hip belt. Leather hand grip. Easy packing panel load design with internal cinch straps. Lockable zippers. Black, Evergreen, or Blue. Perfect for backpacking through Europe. $10 off with rail pass. $150

ACCESSORIES

C. Padded Toiletry Kit

Large padded main compartment to protect contents. Mesh lid pocket with metal hook to hang kit on a towel rod or bathroom hook. Features two separate small outside pockets and detachable mirror. 9" x $4\frac{3}{4}$" x $4\frac{1}{4}$". Black, Evergreen, or Blue. *As seen on cover in Blue.* $20

D. Padded Travel Pouch

Main zipper compartment is padded to protect a compact camera or mini binoculars. Carries as a belt pouch, or use 1" strap to convert into waist or shoulder pack. Front flap is secured by a quick release closure. 6" x 9" x 3". Black, Evergreen, or Blue. *As seen on cover in Evergreen.* $26

E. Departure Pouch

Great for travel or everyday use. Features a multitude of inside pockets to store passport, tickets, and monies. Includes see-thru mesh pocket, pen slots, and gusseted compartment. Can be worn over shoulder, around neck, or cinched around waist. 6" x 12". Black, Evergreen, or Blue. *As seen on cover in Black.* $16

SECURITY ITEMS

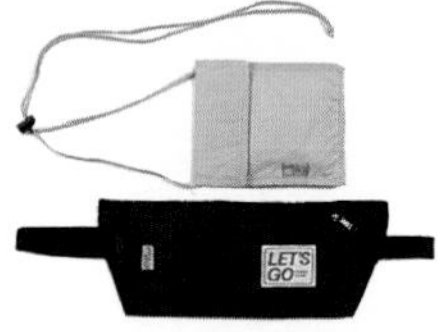

F. Undercover Neckpouch

Ripstop nylon with a soft Cambrelle back. Three pockets. $5\frac{1}{4}$" x $6\frac{1}{2}$". Lifetime guarantee. Black or Tan. $9.95

G. Undercover Waistpouch

Ripstop nylon with a soft Cambrelle back. Two pockets. $4\frac{3}{4}$" x 12" with adjustable waistband. Lifetime guarantee. Black or Tan. $9.95

H. Travel Lock

Great for locking up your Continental or World Journey. Anondized copper two-key lock. $5

CLEARANCE

Call for clearance specials on a limited stock of travel packs, gear, and accessories from the 1996 season.

Prices and availability of products are subject to change.

1-800-5-LETS GO

ORDER FORM

International Student/Teacher Identity Card (ISIC/ITIC) (ages 12 and up) enclose:

1. Proof of student/teacher status (letter from registrar or administrator, proof of tuition payment, or copy of student/faculty ID card. FULL-TIME only.)
2. One picture (1 ½" x 2") signed on the reverse side.
3. Proof of birthdate (copy of passport, birth certificate, or driver's license).

GO25 card (ages 12-25) enclose:

1. Proof of birthdate (copy of passport, birth certificate, or driver's license).
2. One picture (1 ½" x 2") signed on the reverse side.

Last Name | First Name | Date of Birth

Street *We do not ship to P.O. Boxes.*

City | State | Zip Code

Phone (very important!) | Citizenship (Country)

School/College | Date of Travel

Description, Size	Color	Quantity	Unit Price	Total Price
	Total Purchase Price			
	Shipping and Handling (See box at left)			
	MA Residents (Add 5% sales tax on gear & books)			
	TOTAL			

SHIPPING & HANDLING

Eurail pass does not factor into merchandise value

Domestic 2-3 Weeks
- Merchandise value under $30 .... $4
- Merchandise value $30-100 .... $6
- Merchandise value over $100 .... $8

Domestic 2-3 Days
- Merchandise value under $30 .... $14
- Merchandise value $30-100 .... $16
- Merchandise value over $100 .... $18

Domestic Overnight
- Merchandise value under $30 .... $24
- Merchandise value $30-100 .... $26
- Merchandise value over $100 .... $28

All International Shipping $30

From which Let's Go Guide are you ordering? ☐ Europe ☐ USA ☐ Other________

MASTERCARD ☐ **VISA** ☐

Cardholder Name:

Card Number:

Expiration Date:

Make check or money order payable to:

Let's Go Travel

http://hsa.net/travel

67 Mt. Auburn Street • Cambridge, MA 02138 • USA • (617) 495-9649

1-800-5-LETS GO

ACCOMMODATIONS, CAMPING, AND FOOD

Rooms are expensive, and the few cheap ones are booked a month in advance during summer. The inexpensive *gîte d'étape,* nestled against the valley wall 4km from town, is paradise regained. The tourist office has a list of private B&Bs in the surrounding area (140-200F for 1 or 2 people). If you are traveling by bike or car, check for signs along the main roads advertising *fermes* (farms) with camping space (20-45F) and village homes renting rooms (150-300F) during the summer.

Gîte d'Etape: Ferme des Eymaries, route de St-Cirq (tel. 05 53 06 94 73). Cross the tracks at the station, go over the bridge, and turn left at the Elf station. Walk along the road for 2km up and over a hill and turn right 3m before crossing the train tracks. Follow the gravel-dirt road for 1km (40min.). Easily worth the walk. Great owner and dogs. Two 18-bed dorms built into the cliff and a view that will make you want to settle down for good. Kitchen facilities and hot showers. 43F. Breakfast 20F. Call ahead, preferably around meal times. Open April-Oct. 31.

Hôtel des Falaises (tel. 05 53 06 97 35), down the street from tourist office. Simple, clean rooms with a garden or town view. Singles and doubles with shower and toilet 170-190F. Triples with shower and balcony 190-290F. Breakfast 25F. The hotel also manages several newly renovated lodgings between Les Eyzies and Font-de-Gaume at the same rates. V, MC.

Camping La Rivière, on route de Périgueux (tel. 05 53 06 97 14; fax 05 53 35 20 85). From the tourist office, go towards Périgueux on the D47 then cross the bridge and take a left. Snack bar and restaurant, pool, washing machines, canoe rental. 24F per person, 32F per site. Electricity 16F. Also rents rooms: doubles (190F) and quads (250F) with shower and 10% discount weekdays. Breakfast 25F. **Bike rental** 30F per ½-day, 50F per day. Open April 8-Oct. 7 8am-10pm. V, MC.

Most restaurants here require big bucks but dish out exquisite, well-prepared meals. A **market** runs the length of town every Mon. (9am-1pm). Besides that, there is only the **Halle Paysanne des Eyzies,** on route de Sarlat, with cans of expensive *foie gras,* wine, and walnuts (open June 15-Sept. daily 9am-1pm and 2:30-7pm). The rustic wooden setting of **Le Font de Gaume** is perfect to indulge in a 52F veggie and cold-cut buffet (open daily noon-2pm and 7-11:30pm; V, MC, AmEx). **La Grignotière** (tel. 05 53 06 91 67), on the left side of pl. de la Mairie, serves omelettes, salads, meat, and fish, not to mention a simple but filling 50F lunch *menu* on a quiet, shaded terrace. Cheapest *café crème* in town! (Open April-Oct. 15 daily noon-2pm and 7-9:30pm. V, MC.) For something more decadent, turn right at the campground, continue for 2km, and head for **Ferme la Loyotte** (tel. 05 53 06 95 91), which serves a whopping 17-course 130F *menu* with three types of wine, *foie gras, champignons, rillettes de canard*...need we go on? (Open Tues.-Sun. 11:30am-2pm and 7-10pm; March 15-Oct. 30 by reservation only. V, MC.)

SIGHTS

Many folks find themselves in Les Eyzies with a couple of hours to spare as they wait for their scheduled cave tour. The two excellent museums carved into the cliff that looms over the town offer a cheap and educational way to pass the time. The **Musée L'Abri Pataud** (tel. 05 53 06 92 46) sits on the property of a local farmer whose plot consisted of bones, stone tools, and precious little arable land. As it turned out, his farm was built on an *abri* (shelter), where several groups of reindeer hunters lived over a span of 20,000 years. The excavated area exposes layers corresponding to 14 periods of habitation. In the next room, a set of video screens explains prehistory and evolution in rather technical terms. Take a gander at the 18,600-year-old remains of the 16-year-old girl found in a dolmen on the site, then turn around; she's quietly working on an animal skin in front of you. Hers are the most important human remains in Western Europe because she represents a landmark stage between the Neanderthal and Cro-Magnon. The carving of a bison on the ceiling of the museum, visible in a mirror, was discovered accidentally, illuminated by the stray flashlight beam of a technician. (Open July-Sept. 5 10am-7pm; April-June and Sept. 6-Oct. 15 Tues.-Sun. 10am-noon and 2-6pm; Feb. 7-March and Oct. 16-Nov. 15 Tues.-Sun. 2-5pm. Last entry 1hr. before closing. Admission 25F, students 12F.)

The **Musée National de Préhistoire** (tel. 05 53 06 97 03), located in the cliff with the best views of Les Eyzies right beyond its windy terrace, exhibits a collection of weapons, tools, carvings, and bones, including a mammoth skeleton. The collection is currently undergoing a massive expansion project to be completed by the end of 1997. (Open daily July-Aug. 9:30am-7pm; April-June and Sept.-May Wed.-Mon. 9:30am-noon and 2-6pm. Admission 20F, ages 18-25, over 60, and Sun. 13F.)

■ Near Les Eyzies: Cave Paintings

By far the most famous and most remarkable of all the cave paintings in France lie 25km northeast of Les Eyzies, just outside Montignac at Lascaux (see page 347). Ever since the original Lascaux was closed due to significant deterioration, however, the **Grotte du Pech-Merle** (see page 353) and the **Grotte de Font-de-Gaume** (tel. 05 53 06 90 80), 1km outside Les Eyzies on D47, have become the most important authentic caves still open to tourists. As a result, the area around Font-de-Gaume has become a major crossroads of tourist traffic. For a more personal rendezvous with prehistory, dozens of other, less crowded caves wait outside Les Eyzies, Souillac, Sarlat, and Gourdon. The Les Eyzies tourist office runs excursions to the many sights within a 10km radius. Think twice about attempting to reach any of the surrounding sights on bike; the hills are steep, the roads are narrow, and visibility is limited.

Font-de-Gaume contains 15,000-year-old friezes of bison, horses, reindeer, and mammoth. Completed over hundreds of years, these faint but spectacular images show the various artists' advanced technique of using the natural contours of the cave for relief and their desire to capture images of the world around them. Though they discovered the paintings in the 18th century, locals did not realize the artwork's importance until two centuries later, by which time several murals had decayed and been defaced by graffiti. Especially in the farther reaches of the cavern, though, the colors are brilliant enough to see the care and detail that went into the drawings. The highlight is the *vôute* (vault), where 12 bison cover two-thirds of the cave in an almost surreal fashion. Unfortunately, the word has been out for a while; call 05 53 06 90 80 *at least* two weeks in advance to get a ticket in summer. Tours are given in French, English, and German and last an hour. (Open April-Sept. Wed.-Mon. 9am-noon and 2-6pm; March and Oct. Wed.-Mon. 9:30am-noon and 2-5:30pm; Nov.-Feb. Wed.-Mon. 10am-noon and 2-5pm. Admission 32F, ages 18-25 and over 60 21F, ages 7-18 10F, under 7 and artists or art students free. Reservation fee 10F.)

Unlike the Grotte de Font-de-Gaume, whose paintings have been preserved because of its low humidity, the **Grotte des Combarelles,** 2km farther down the road (tel. 05 53 06 97 72), has suffered from a humid atmosphere, and only etchings remain. The more than 600 carvings pale in comparison to Lascaux or Font-de-Gaume but depict a greater variety of species, from donkeys and lions to rhinoceri. Fifty human figures, mostly faces, keep watch from the narrow halls of the cave. Visitors are admitted in intimate groups of six for the 45-minute tour. Because only a dozen tours are given each day, Combarelles is the toughest ticket in town. Reserve far in advance for the summer through the office at the Grotte de Font-de-Gaume. (Open April-Sept. Thurs.-Tues. 9am-noon and 2-6pm; March and Oct. Tues. and Thurs. 9:30am-noon and 2-5:30pm.; Nov.-Feb. Thurs.-Tues. 10am-noon and 2-5pm. Admission 32F, ages 18-25 and over 60 21F, ages 7-18 10F; 10F reservation fee.)

Only 12 figures are visible at the frieze **Abri du Cap-Blanc** (tel. 05 53 59 21 74), 7km northeast of Eyzies on D48, but they are outstandingly preserved. 15,000 years ago, hunters coaxed horses, bison, and reindeer from the thick limestone walls. Undiscovered until this century, the carvings are not as detailed as those in Font-de-Gaume, but the quality of preservation makes up for the lack of intricacy. At the exhibit's centerpiece, a 2m-long herd of animals shuffles along, oblivious to visitors' stares. It's wise to call for tickets at least one week in advance, although if you arrive early in the morning you might be able to snag some tickets for the afternoon. Forty-five-minute tours in French or English (open July-Aug. 9:30am-7pm; April-June and Sept.-Oct. 10am-noon and 2-6pm; admission 28F, children 15F).

15km northwest of Les Eyzies in Rouffignac, **La Grotte aux 100 Mammouths** (tel. 05 53 05 41 71), on the road to Périgueux, houses 250 engravings and paintings. The omnipresent etchings of shaggy mammoths are the most striking, but rhinoceri, horses, and bison also abound. The guided tour (via train) lasts an hour. (Open July-Aug. 9-11:30am and 2-6pm; April 9-June and Sept.-Oct. 10-11:30pm and 2-5pm. Admission 28F, children 10F.)

Not to be outdone by all the cave drawings, nature has crafted some stunning art of her own around Eyzies. The hills are alive with the sound of water in caves drip-dripping to form stalactites and stalagmites that rank well above the average of the usual *grottes.* Most interesting is the **Grotte du Grand Roc** (tel. 05 53 06 92 70), 1.5km northwest of town along the road to Périgueux. The *grotte* lies halfway up the chalk cliffs and commands a blistering view of the valley from its mouth. The cave is filled with millions of stalactites, stalagmites, and *eccentriques*—small calcite accretions that grow neither straight down nor straight up. Found in 1924, this cave shelters thousands of natural phenomena, most notably an *eccentrique* in the shape of an ostrich, an eroded column that resembles Bigfoot's foot, and Mother Nature's version of the Winged Victory of Samothrace. The cave is kept at a constant temperature of 16°C—a welcome break from summer heat. (Open June-Sept. 15 9am-7pm; April-May and Sept. 16-Nov. 11 9:30am-6pm; Feb.-March and Nov. 12-Dec. 10am-5pm. 30-min. guided tour, French only, but many explanatory signs are in English. Admission 35F, children 20F.) Skip the prehistoric habitat next door (tel. and hours same as for Grand Roc), the first prehistoric site unearthed in the area (in 1863). Its treasures now reside in museums elsewhere.

The **Gorge d'Enfer** (tel. 05 53 06 90 60), just upstream from Grand Roc and 2km from Les Eyzies, is full of rushing waterfalls, quiet lagoons, and blooming flora—perfect for that all-important two-hour lunch break (free use of picnic tables and grounds). On-site lies the **Abri du Poisson** (tel. 05 53 06 90 80), a shelter which contains the oldest drawing of a fish in France—a 25,000-year-old, 1m-long salmon. Take a look at the postcard photo and move on—the guided tour is fishy (open April-Sept. Sun.-Fri. 9am-noon and 2-6pm; tour, in French, 14F, students 7F).

Those interested in more recent cave people should head for the **Musée de la Spéléologie,** 91, rue de la Grange-Chancel (tel. 05 53 35 43 77). Located in the Fort de Roc de Tayac, a niche in a cliff high above the Dordogne, it was dug by English soldiers in the Hundred Years' War, who took refuge and turned it into a fortress from which to pester French troops on the river below. The museum documents the region's speleological history with models, documents, and equipment (open July-Aug. 11am-6pm; admission 15F, children under 18 10F, speleologists free).

About 9km northeast of Les Eyzies on route D66, the **Roque St-Christophe** (tel. 05 53 50 70 45) is the most extensive cave dwelling yet to be discovered. Its five floors of terraces stretch over 400m. From 40,000 BC until the Middle Ages, this fascinating sanctuary served as a defensive fort and home to over 3000 people. Embark in some mega-time travel as you visit an 11th-century kitchen, see cavemen fighting an intruding bear, and peer over the 60m high cliff where Protestants sought shelter from a Catholic army in 1580. A 45-minute guided tour (brochures in English) allows you to check out the cave's ovens, monastic remains, and military defenses (visits daily 10am-6pm; Nov. 11-Feb. 11am-5pm, admission 31F, children 16F).

Even in summer, most tourists ignore the opportunities for kayaking and canoeing amidst the Vézère's unspoiled greenery, unusual rock formations, and towering cliffs. Parting the waters of this splendid solitude can prove a welcome break from the cave crush. At the bridge in Les Eyzies, two outfits rent **canoes: Les 3 Drapeaux** (tel. 05 53 06 91 89) and **Fédération Française de Canoe-Kayak** (tel. 05 53 06 92 92; fax 05 53 06 98 45). From June to September, they will let you paddle your way downstream and pick you up for the return journey via van (2hr., canoe 55F, kayak 65F; 4hr., canoe 70F, kayak 80F; all prices per person; open daily 9am-6pm; V, MC).

Sarlat

Thirty-five years ago, Sarlat (pop. 10,700) was a quiet hamlet with little to distinguish it from other towns in the Périgord Noir region. But in 1962 Minister of Culture André Malraux targeted the small town for a massive restoration project, inspired by the *vieille ville*'s architectural unity and minimal modernization (although the desire for increased tourism may have had something to do with it, too). Three years later, the new Sarlat emerged—handsomely restored and surprisingly medieval. Since then, the beige sandstone buildings that crowd the central plaza have provided the setting for the films *Cyrano de Bergerac* and *Manon of the Springs.* Tourists may outnumber locals three to one here in summer, but they have yet to drown out the dancing violinists, acrobats, and artisans who imbue the narrow streets and hidden corners of the *vieille ville* with life. Spend a day in town and then spring into the châteaux and scenery of the Dordogne valley beyond.

ORIENTATION AND PRACTICAL INFORMATION

To get to the center of town from the distant (2km) train station, follow av. de la Gare downhill to the left and turn right at av. Thiers, which becomes av. Général Leclerc. After crossing the small pl. du 14 Juillet, the road becomes **rue de la République,** the thoroughfare bisecting the *vieille ville.* To reach the tourist office, bear right on rue Lakanal, past the church, and left onto rue de la Liberté, which leads to **pl. de la Liberté.** Buses stop at the train station and **pl. Pasteur** in the *centre ville.*

Tourist Office: pl. de la Liberté (tel. 05 53 59 27 67; fax 05 53 59 19 44), in the 16th-century Hôtel de Maleville. A self-serve smorgasbord of excellent brochures, maps, guides, and transport schedules. Accommodations service (10F). **Currency exchange** when banks are closed. Daily tours of town in French June-Sept. (1-2 tours daily in English; 1½hr.; 24F, children 13F). Open June-Sept. Mon.-Sat. 9am-7pm, Sun. 10am-noon and 2-6pm; Oct.-May Mon.-Sat. 9am-noon and 2-7pm.

Money: Banks and 24-hr. **ATMs** samba along rue de la République.

Trains: av. de la Gare (tel. 05 53 59 00 21). Ticket booths open Mon.-Fri. 6am-11pm, Sat.-Sun. 7am-7pm. Sarlat is directly linked to Bordeaux (3-4 per day, 2½hr., 115F), but other destinations require a train change. For Périgueux, catch a train to le Buisson (4 per day, 1hr., 32F). To meet the Paris-Toulouse line, you must take a bus to nearby Souillac and catch the train from there.

Buses: SCETA (tel. 05 55 77 57 65) and **STUB** (tel. 05 55 86 07 07) run buses to: Souillac (4 per day, 35min., 29F); Brive (1 per day, 1½hr., 54F); and Périgueux (1 per day, 1½hr., 57F). Schedules in the *Guide Pratique,* at the tourist office.

Bike Rental: Sarlat Sport Loisirs, Centre Commercial du Pontet (tel. 05 53 59 33 41), under the bridge, past the roundabout to the left of the *gare* as you exit. Owner offers hostelers 15-20% discount. Mountain bikes 90F per day, 500F per week. Open daily 9am-7pm. No deposit. V, MC.

Youth Center: Bureau Information Jeunesse (BIJ), pl. Marc-Busson (tel. 05 53 31 56 36), in the Espace Economie-Emploi. Info on sports, jobs, etc. Open Mon.-Fri. 8am-noon and 1:30-5:30pm.

Laundromat: 74, av. de Selves. Open 6am-10pm.

English Books: Majuscule, 43, rue de la République (tel. 05 53 59 02 54). One whole rack dedicated to novels in English (40-56F). Open Mon.-Sat. 9am-noon and 2-5pm, Sun. 9am-noon; Sept.-June Tues.-Sun. 9am-noon. V, MC, AmEx.

Hospital: Centre Hospitalier, rue Jean Leclaire (tel. 05 53 31 75 75). First right after the hostel, turn right at bottom of the hill, and go left on rue de la Liberté.

Police: pl. de la Grand Rigaudie (tel. 05 53 59 05 17). Take a left off av. Leclerc from the *vieille ville.* **Emergency** tel. 17.

Post Office: pl. du 14 Juillet (tel. 05 53 59 12 81). Poste restante. **Currency exchange.** Open Mon.-Fri. 9am-6pm, Sat. 9am-noon. **Postal code:** 24200.

ACCOMMODATIONS AND CAMPING

Hotels in Sarlat are expensive (200-350F per night). The inexpensive and comfortable youth hostel is not a very carefully guarded secret—children, teenagers, and travelers fill it during July and August. Those blessed with cars can seek out alternative lodgings. Ask for a list of *gîtes* and farms in the surrounding countryside (90-250F) at the tourist office. Dozens of campgrounds surround the town.

Auberge de Jeunesse (HI), 77, av. de Selves (tel. 05 53 59 47 59 or 05 53 30 21 27), 30min. from the station but only a 5-10min. walk from the *vieille ville.* Go straight along rue de la République until it becomes av. Gambetta; follow it for another 100m, then bear left at the fork onto av. de Selves. The hostel will be on your right, behind a green gate. Clean, cozy, and comfortable with great proprietress who gives the hostel a carnival atmosphere. Excellent kitchen. Members 40F. Backyard camping 25F. Sheets 14F. 3 rooms of bunk beds—1 each for women, men, and couples. Free showers. Reception 6-8pm—sometimes earlier, sometimes later. No lockout or curfew. Reserve. Open March 15-Nov.

Hôtel des Récollets, 4, rue Jean Jacques Rousseau (tel. 05 53 59 00 49), off rue de la République. Wonderful, immaculate hotel close to the action but far from the noise. Owner is loaded with helpful hints. Singles and doubles 190F, with shower and toilet 250-2705F. Triples 280-320F. Breakfast 32F. V, MC.

Camping: There are countless campgrounds in the area; those closest to town usually fill up in summer. A good bet is **Le Montant** (tel. 05 53 59 18 50 or 05 53 59 37 73), 2.5km from town on D57. Bar, washing machines, and hot water. 22F50 per person, 27F per tent. Electricity 10F. Open Easter-Sept.

FOOD

Sarlat's epicurean tastes have led to marvelous meals—and high prices. Most regional delicacies—*foie gras, confit de canard,* truffles, and red wine from nearby Bergerac—can be bought directly at farms for much less. One exception is the chocolate-walnut *tarte* (12F) that seems to be the specialty of every *pâtisserie.* The Saturday **market** takes over the entire city (7:30am-12:30pm). Wednesday markets are smaller, but just as fresh (7am-1pm). A gargantuan **Champion supermarket** sits 500m up rue de Selves from the youth hostel (open Mon.-Thurs. 9am-12:30pm and 2:15-7:30pm, Fri.-Sat. 9am-7:30pm).

Restaurant Criquettamus, 5, rue des Armes (tel. 05 53 59 48 10), off the less touristy side of rue de la République. Filling 4-course 70F and 90F *menus* offer delicious regional soups, out-of-this-world *foie gras,* and *confit de canard.* 55F lunch *menu* is of the same quality. Open daily March-Dec. noon-2pm and 7-10pm.

La Tour du Guet, 1, rue Rousset (tel. 05 53 31 10 47), off rue de la République, on a square blissfully free of tourists. The oldest restaurant in Sarlat retains a quiet charm. 70F 4-course *menu* includes soup, a good *plat du jour, foie de canard,* and dessert. Open daily noon-2:15pm and 7-10:30pm. V, MC.

Le Grain de Sel, 5, pl. de la Petite-Rigaudie. Begin a 65F *menu* with a smoked salmon gazpacho and end with a chocolate walnut mousse at this little gem on the edge of the *vieille ville.* Open daily noon-2pm and 7-10pm.

SIGHTS AND ENTERTAINMENT

Malraux's little project in the 60s certainly did the trick: the spotless golden stone buildings of Sarlat's *vieille ville* are the most interesting aspect of the city. Wander through the narrow streets and explore their *foie gras dégustations* (generally free), hidden boutiques, and surprising impromptu street life. Most of the sights—and all of the tourists—are to the right off rue de la République as you enter town from the station. Make your way to the other, hillier side of the road and its relatively deserted, equally picturesque lanes. Follow the herd of map-holders to the **Cathédrale St-Sacerdos,** to the right after leaving the tourist office. The cathedral's low Romanesque arches and pentagonal chancel are worth a visit if only to listen to the Baroque music emanating from its recently restored 18th-century organ. Once or twice a week in July and August, organ concerts fill the grand hall (open daily 7:30am-6:45pm; concert tickets 30-75F). Behind the cathedral is the **Lanterne des Morts,** a 12th-century stone beehive perched on a hill and believed to have been lit for a saint who came this way in 1147. In summer the cathedral's square bursts with painters and craftsmen hawking their wares. To the left as you walk out of the cathedral, the former bishops' residence, the **Ancien Evêché,** puts up art expositions that have included Doisneau photos (open March 2-Nov. 15 11:30am-6pm; admission to ground floor exhibit free, upstairs 15F).

To the right of the cathedral is the **Maison de la Boétie** (tel. 05 53 59 38 59). Built in the 16th century, it now serves as the Chamber of Commerce. The Maison's gable and ornate windows exemplify Italian Renaissance style; its lower common room houses small exhibits by local artists (open daily June-Aug. 10am-5:45pm; free). On the small lane next door, passage de Segogne, artisans display and sell their creations daily in July and August from 10am to 8pm. Through the passage and around the corner from the tourist office in the 16th-century **Hôtel de Maleville,** pl. Lucien de Maleville (tel. 05 53 31 15 38), regional painter Françoise Valenti shows her work each summer. In vibrant watercolors, she depicts scenes from flower markets to beautiful country villas (open July-Sept.; free). Scheduled to open in late 1996 is the **Musée d'Histoire de Sarlat et du Périgord Noir,** in the nearby Hôtel de Plamon.

Go up rue Fénélon to no. 13, **Manoir d'Aillac** (tel. 05 53 59 02 63), a 15th-century abode built by a lawyer who later constructed the *hôtel* where Valenti now displays her work. The museum within shows various antique weapons and costumes and ends with a descent into a cramped hole where 12 unfortunate priests waited out the wars of religion for three months, only to be executed when they finally deemed it safe to leave (open daily May-Sept. 10am-12:30pm and 2-7pm; admission 25F, children 15F). Shift gears at the **Musée d'Automobile,** 17, av. Thiers (tel. 05 53 31 62 81), on the road towards the station. It has corralled over 60 cars, including an 1898 LaCroix 3-wheeler that could hit 75km/h and a sleek red 1929 Voisin, a favorite of Josephine Baker. (Open daily July-Aug. 10am-7pm; Sept.-Oct. 2-6:30pm; April-June 2-6:30pm. Admission 30F, students 20F, kiddies 15F.)

Behind the hostel, the **Musée Aquarium de Sarlat,** 3, rue du Commandant Maratuel (tel. 05 53 59 44 58), is a passable fish bowl featuring 33 species of critters fresh from the Dordogne (open July-Aug. 10am-7pm; April-Nov. 15 10am-noon and 2-6pm; admission 27F, students 22F, children 15F).

Every weekend, street performers and musicians of all stripes converge on pl. de la Liberté, making cafés there crowded and boisterous. The best people-watching is at **Café Gargantua,** rue Tourny (tel. 05 53 31 14 52), near the cathedral. Mellow jazz and young locals keep **Le Bataclau,** 31, rue de la République (tel. 05 53 28 54 34), busy well into the evening. For three weeks in late July and early August, Sarlat hosts the **Festival des Jeux du Théâtre,** a series of plays held in various venues (tickets 40-140F; 15% discount with *carte jeune*). If you'd like more information, contact the Hôtel Plamon (tel. 05 53 31 10 83; fax 05 53 30 25 31).

■ Near Sarlat: The Dordogne Valley

Steep, craggy cliffs and poplar tree thickets overlook the slow-moving turquoise waters of the Dordogne river, which served as a natural boundary between France to the north and British-controlled Aquitaine to the south in the Hundred Years' War. The châteaux, built to keep watch on the enemy, are even more numerous and imposing than the Loire's. Unfortunately, you won't be the first to discover the savage beauty of the Dordogne, but it's still possible to find solitude outside the most prominent towns. *Chambres d'hôtes* offer farmhouse accommodations and convenient access to the historic sites; ask the Sarlat tourist office for info.

The valley lies 15km south of Sarlat; to get there and get around you'll need to rent a car or be prepared for a good bike workout—those hilltops are mighty steep. You can reach châteaux by convenient but expensive excursion buses leaving Sarlat.

Hep! buses (tel. 05 53 28 10 04) leave from pl. Pasteur and visit different châteaux all week long. **CFTA Périgord,** 21, rue de Cahors (tel. 05 53 59 01 48), also runs buses (100-185F) each day. Hitching is reportedly not difficult, although many cars have no room to spare. Arrive at the châteaux before 1pm and beat the crowds.

Many outfits along the Dordogne rent **canoes** and **kayaks. Canoës-Loisirs** (tel. 05 53 28 23 43) and **Périgord Aventure et Loisirs** (tel. 05 53 28 23 82) are near Domme at the Pont de Vitrac. **Canoës-Dordogne** (tel. 05 53 29 58 50) and **Canoë Vacances** (tel. 05 53 28 17 07) are at La Roque-Gageac. **Copeyre** (tel. 05 53 28 95 01) is in Beyrac. Schedules and information available at the tourist office. Prices range from 80F (½-day) to 130F (full day).

CASTELNAUD AND LES MILANDES

Ten kilometers south of Sarlat, the town of **Castelnaud** snoozes in the shadow of its crumbling but mighty château (tel. 05 53 31 30 00). In the 12th and 13th centuries, Castelnaud's *seigneur* engaged in frequent disputes and battles with the *seigneur* of the château of Beynac, 5km down the river. After all, what better way to spice up a dull life than to indulge in some neighborly squabbling? During the Hundred Years' War, the *seigneur* allied himself with the English. The frustrated French bought the castle in 1402 only to lose it six months later. It switched hands thrice more before becoming French for good in 1442. You can tour the castle's ramparts and rooms, admiring the view as you ascend. The château houses the intriguing **Musée de la Guerre de Cent Ans,** which tells the story of sieges during the Hundred Years' War with a number of dazzling visual aids, including one behemoth of a catapult (open daily July-Aug. 9am-8pm; May-June and Sept. 10am-7pm; March-April and Oct.-Nov. 15 Sun.-Fri. 10am-6pm; admission 30F, under 17 15F).

Château Les Milandes (tel. 05 53 29 38 10), 8km from Castelnaud, would have remained just another lonely château were it not for one distinctive owner. Built in 1489 by François de Caumont, whose wife was despondent over Castelnaud's austerity, the château brightened up when African-American singer-dancer Josephine Baker bought it. Raised in the slums of St. Louis and propelled to fame in Paris's Folies Bergère, she fell in love with the Dordogne and created a *village du monde* (village of the world), where she cared for dozens of children from around the world until 1969. The tour through two floors of her homey living space and photos allows access to the lovely garden (open 9am-7pm; Sept.-Nov. and April-May 10am-noon and 2-6pm; Nov.-Feb. 2-6pm; admission 34F, students 30F, under 16 22F). Housed in the **Chapelle des Milandes** next door is an exhibit by the Josephine Baker Association. In July and August it tells the story of the woman Picasso called "the Nefertiti of the present time" (open daily 10:30am-6:30pm; admission 18F, students 12F). Castelnaud and Les Milandes are not accessible by **bus,** but the **bike** rides from Sarlat (10km and 15km, respectively) follow unchallenging riverbanks.

Castlenaud has no tourist office, a few restaurants, and an enormously overpriced grocery store. The only reasonable hotel is just down the road from Les Milandes. The **Hôtel Parc des Milandes** (tel. 05 53 29 52 33) is a scenic (though sometimes noisy) rest spot with a pool, tennis courts, mini-golf, riverside gardens, and a restaurant (singles and doubles with exterior shower 160F; triples 180-220F; breakfast 28F; open June-Aug.; call ahead; V, MC, AmEx). Across the river on the road to Beynac is **La Cabane campsite** (tel. 05 53 29 52 28) and its pool. (15F per person, 14F per pitch; open April-Oct.) Just below Castelnaud, **Périgord Kayak Club** (tel. 05 53 29 40 07) also organizes caving and climbing expeditions in the area.

BEYNAC-ET-CAZENAC

The fortress at **Beynac** (tel. 05 53 29 50 40) sits 150m above the Dordogne in a town of ancient stone houses decorated with wrought-iron balconies and flowered terraces. Beynac has enjoyed a topsy-turvy history with only one thing certain throughout: it was always at odds with Castelnaud, its nearby neighbor. During the Hundred Years' War, Beynac was French, while Castelnaud sided with the English. In the wars of religion, Beynac adhered to Catholicism, but Castelnaud switched to Protestantism. The excellent and obligatory guided tour (45min. in French) takes you behind the 5m-thick walls. The view from the top is (as usual) sensational. (Open daily March-Sept. 9am-noon and 2-6:30pm; Oct.-Nov. 10am-noon and 2-5pm; Dec.-Feb. 2pm-nightfall. Admission 30F, children 15F.) Just below the château, the Gauls never left the **Parc Archéologique de Beynac** (tel. 05 53 29 51 28). Thatch huts with walls of mud, a 5000-year-old dolmen, and even a flock of sheep are scattered through this reproduction of an ancient Gallic village. Feel free to picnic among the artifacts. On the footpath above the park, the **Musée de Beynac** houses a collection of ancient tools, weapons, and agricultural artifacts (park and museum open June 15-Sept. 15 daily 10am-7pm; admission to both 25F, children 12F). Beynac is 4km west of Castelnaud on route D703 and 10km southwest of Sarlat on the hilly D57.

Beynac's **tourist office** (tel. 05 53 29 43 08) occupies a tiny part of a tiny building by the river across from the château. (Open July-Aug. Mon.-Fri. 9am-7pm, Sat. 2:30-6pm, Sun. 10am-noon and 2:30-6pm; June and Sept. daily 10am-noon and 2-5pm).

The cheapest rooms around are at the immaculate **Gîte d'Étape de Beynac** (tel. 05 53 29 40 93 or 05 53 29 50 75), 2km from town toward Castelnaud. In July and August, reserve a week in advance (43F; kitchen facilities). The small, clean rooms at the **Hôtel de la Poste,** on the path to the château (tel. 05 53 29 50 22), have been run by the same family since 1820. (Singles and doubles 160F, with shower 205F. 4-person suite 270F. Showers 10F. Breakfast 28F. Open April-Oct. V, MC.) **Camping Le Capeyrou** (tel. 05 53 29 54 95) is just out of town on the riverbank (21F per person, 28F per site, electricity 12F; open June-Sept.). On the road to Castelnaud, the **Hôtel-Restaurant du Château** (tel. 05 53 29 50 13) serves up scrumptious local dishes with its 5-course *menu* (75F). Open daily noon-2:30pm and 7-9:30pm.

DOMME

Balanced on a hilltop above the Dordogne, Domme is the best-defended of the valley's villages and the one with the best view from the top. Enter the 13th-century *bastide* (fortified town) at the Port de St-Julien and make your way up tiny alleys, past limestone homes, to the top and the main square, pl. de la Liberté. The **tourist office,** on pl. de la Liberté (tel. 05 53 28 37 09; fax 05 53 24 34 62), has lists of homes letting rooms (90-230F) within 4km of Domme. (Open July-Aug. Sun.-Fri. 9:30am-7pm, Sat. 9:30am-12:30pm and 1:30-7pm; April-June and Sept. 9:30am-noon and 2-6pm; March and Oct. 2-6pm; Nov.-Feb. Mon.-Fri. 2-5:30pm.)

A *tour des grottes* (cave tour) descends into a network of caverns of the **Grottes de la Halle**, (tel. 05 53 28 37 09) below the town where inhabitants took refuge during the Hundred Years' War. The tour passes through the Grotte des Rhinocéros, where 60,000 year old bones of guess-what-animal remain partially unearthed. (Open Sun.-Fri. July-Aug. 9:30am-7pm, Sat. 9:30am-12:30pm and 1:30-7pm; April-June and Sept. 9:30am-noon and 2-6pm; March and Oct. 2-6pm; Nov.-Feb. Mon.-Fri. 2-5:30pm. 30-min. French-only tour 25F, students 20F.) From the terrace to the left and down the hill from the post office, gaze at the poplar-lined river gliding past cows and brown-roofed farmhouses. At the other end of the *place,* the **Musée de Périgord** (tel. 05 53 53 16 42) displays costumes and documents of 17th-19th century Périgord, plus such items as the sheet music of a rousing song from the 1920s entitled *"Vive le Divorce"* (open April-Sept. Wed.-Mon. 10am-noon and 2-6pm, Oct.-March Wed.-Mon. 10am-noon and 2-5pm; admission 15F, students 12F, kids 10F).

The **Nouvel Hôtel,** pl. de la Liberté (tel. 05 53 28 38 67; fax 05 53 28 27 13), offers tiny, clean rooms, many of which compensate for their size with gorgeous views (singles and doubles 150-190F, with shower 180-240F; breakfast 30F). Downstairs is an elegant but inexpensive restaurant (tel. 05 53 28 36 81) serving a five-course *menu* (70F) of regional specialties (open daily Easter-Oct. noon-3pm and 5-10pm; V, MC). The campground **Cénac St-Julien** (tel. 05 53 28 31 91) is near the river (15F per person, 20F per pitch; hot showers free; open June-Sept. 15; reception 9:30am-12:30pm and 3-8pm). The river is crowded with canoers, but if you just can't resist, try **Canoë Cénac** (tel. 05 53 28 22 01) by the river near the campground.

Four kilometers downstream from Domme on the D703, the town of **La Roque-Gageac** juts out from the base of a sheer cliff. There's not much to La Roque except its innate charm and stunning setting. Steep, twisting streets hide seemingly untouched medieval-style stone houses which make for a pleasant diversion between Domme and Castelnaud. In case you thought the French couldn't build 'em like they used to, the 15-year-old **Château de la Malartrie** (privately owned) will prove you wrong. For a perfect view of the many châteaux along the Dordogne and *fortifications troglodytiques,* take a **promenade en bâteau.** Every 15 minutes from 10am-6pm, a flat-bottomed boat takes off from the dock beyond the town's big parking lot (1hr. tour, 40F, children 20F; English-speaking guides).

The **Fort Troglodytique Aérien** (tel. 05 53 31 61 94), in a sandy niche of rock high above La Roque, commands a spectacular view of the Dordogne river valley. Its height and position within the rock made it the ideal fortress—it withstood all British assaults during the Hundred Years' War. Climb the narrow metal staircase clinging to the rock to see what remains from the stronghold, dismantled in the 18th century. More interesting are the nooks and crannies of the cave itself, which stretch several meters back into the rock (open July-Aug. daily 10am-7pm; April-June and Sept.-Nov. 11 Sun.-Fri. 10am-6pm; admission 22F, students 16F).

About 20km from Sarlat on D61 hides the peaceful **Manoir d'Eyrignac** (tel. 05 53 28 99 71). This château is surrounded by the largest and lushest garden of the region (open daily 9:30am-7pm; April-May 10am-12:30pm and 2-7pm; Oct.-March 10am-12:30pm and 2pm-dusk; French and English tours 30F, children 12F).

LASCAUX

The most spectacular set of cave paintings yet discovered hides in the caves of **Lascaux**, near the town of **Montignac,** approximately 25km north of Sarlat. Discovered in 1940 by a few teenagers and their dog, Lascaux had to be closed in 1963; the humidity which resulted from millions of tourists' oohs and ahs fostered algae, and micro-stalactites ravaged the paintings that nature had preserved for 17,000 years. Today, only five archaeologists per day, five days a week, are allowed into the original caves. But an abandoned quarry 200m away harbors the 20th century's most elaborate salute to the artistic cave-dwellers—a complete recreation of the original, logically dubbed **Lascaux II** (tel. 05 53 51 95 03), which duplicates every inch of the original cave. Done in the same pigments used 17,000 years ago, the new paintings of 5m-tall bulls, horses, and bison are brighter than their counterparts. While there is the distinct lack of ancient awe and mystery, Lascaux II inspires a sense of wonder all its own. The automatic machine near the **tourist office,** pl. Bertram-de-Born (tel. 05 53 51 82 60), sells tickets. They go fast; get there a few hours early for a tour (45-min. in French or English); the last tour (at 5pm) is usually sold out by noon (open July-Aug. daily 9:30am-7pm; Sept.-Dec. and Feb.-June Tues.-Sun. 10am-noon and 2-5:30pm; admission 50F, children 20F). Follow the signs, cars, and crowds up the hill to the entrance or spend the afternoon in Montinac's *vieille ville.* Spy on the entire yellow-and-red town from the bridge over the Vézère river. The Lascaux twins are about 2km from Montignac.

The train station nearest Montignac is at **Le Lardin,** 10km away. One **bus** for Montignac leaves Brive every evening (1½hr., 30F), and another leaves Périgueux (1½hr., 34F). Two **CFTA** buses run every morning from Sarlat in July and August (Sept.-June 1 per day, ½hr., 20F) and return in early evening. To be guaranteed tickets for Lascaux II, catch the earliest bus; ask for a schedule at Sarlat's tourist office. The trip by bike isn't too steep, with a sharp incline out of Sarlat and smoother road after. Since most visitors return to nearby towns, those with cars are sometimes willing to give lifts to those without. The **Camping Municipal** (tel. 05 53 52 83 95) is just outside town on D65 (9F per person, 9F per site, 10F per car; open April-Oct. 15).

Rocamadour

Built into the face of a cliff above the verdant Alzou Canyon, Rocamadour (pop. 5000) hid its natural beauty until 1166, when the perfectly preserved body of St. Amadour was unearthed near the town's chapel and miracles began to happen. It was reputed that St. Amadour was actually Zacchaeus of the gospel, the tax collector who altered his ways after dining with Jesus. As the story circulated, the town grew into an important pilgrimage site ranking alongside Rome, Jerusalem, and Santiago de Compostela. Today, the sanctity and architectural unity of the **Cité Réligieuse** attract tourists who lend Rocamadour a bit of a carnival atmosphere, especially in summer. Leave the postcard-hawkers below and enter one of the seven chapels to get some idea of what pilgrims experienced upon reaching this holy site.

ORIENTATION AND PRACTICAL INFORMATION

The main **tourist office** (tel. 05 65 33 62 59; fax 05 65 33 74 14) is in the old Hôtel de Ville, on the pedestrian street of the medieval *cité*. It distributes a list of hotels and restaurants, books rooms, sells maps (2F), and operates a **currency exchange** with nefarious rates and 25F commission. For 7F, you can ogle a couple of tapestries by Jean Lurçat (see page 283) in a room upstairs (open daily July-Aug. 10am-8pm; April-June and Sept. 10am-noon and 1-7pm; Oct.-March 2:30-6pm). A smaller office in **l'Hospitalet,** route de Lacave (tel. 05 65 33 62 80), deals primarily with reservations but also sells maps (2F) and gives directions (open daily 10am-8pm; Oct.-May 11am-1pm and 3-7:30pm; Easter-June and Sept.-Oct. Sat.-Sun. and bank holidays 2-8pm). **Trains** run to the Rocamadour-Padirac station (tel. 05 65 33 63 05), 5km from town on route N140. From the station, a flat, winding road leads directly to the top of Rocamadour and l'Hospitalet and takes 45 minutes to walk. Hitching, never safe, is also tough, as most cars are already full. Your best bet is to come by **bus** from Brive (4-5 per day, 45min., 41F). From the south, catch a bus from Sarlat for St-Denis-Près-Martel (Mon.-Sat. 3 per day, 40min. from Souillac, 21F), then a train from St-Denis (3-4 per day, 15min., 18F), or take a direct train from Paris (3-4 per day, 3¾hr., 275F). In July and August, **Voyages Belmont** (tel. 05 65 37 81 15, in Souillac) runs buses from Souillac to Rocamadour on Tuesdays (130F roundtrip). The train station rents **bikes** (45F per ½-day, 55F per day, 1000F deposit), or try **Camping Relais du Campeur** (75F per day; passport deposit). The **police** can be reached at 05 65 33 60 17; in an **emergency,** dial 17. In a **medical emergency,** dial 15. The **post office** (tel. 05 65 33 62 21), with poste restante, is near the main tourist office (open Mon.-Fri. 9am-noon and 2-5pm, Sat. 9am-noon; **postal code:** 46500).

ACCOMMODATIONS AND FOOD

If your wallet has been weighing you down, a night or two in a Rocamadour hotel will work wonders. Reserve at least three or four days ahead in July and August. On the main street, the **Hôtel du Roc** (tel. 05 65 33 62 43; fax 05 65 33 62 11) has emerald-green bedcovers over firm mattresses (singles with shower 160F; doubles with shower 180F; open April-Nov. 3; V, MC, AmEx). Halfway up the Grand Escalier, a lucky few get small but clean 180F doubles with showers at the **Hôtel Ste-Marie** (tel. 05 65 33 63 07; fax 05 65 33 69 08). Expect to pay 20F more for a toilet, and 75F more for a bath and spectacular view—once you've gone this far, it's worth it (open April 15-Oct. 15; V, MC). There's a tasty 59F lunch *menu* in the restaurant downstairs, but for one whole franc less you can have the 58F lunch or dinner *menu* overlooking the terrace of **Le Château de la Carreta** (tel. 05 65 33 62 23). Three-course *menu* (65F) includes rabbit and salad or soup (open daily noon-2:30pm and 7-10pm; V, MC). There are four campsites within 5km of the town. The closest is the **Relais du Campeur** (tel. 05 65 33 63 28; fax 05 65 33 69 60) in l'Hospitalet (reception next to the grocery on route de Lacave, open daily 8am-10pm; 1 site, 2 people 65F; free shower and swimming pool; open Easter-Sept.; V, MC).

Not surprisingly, all restaurants in town cater to tourists. Tiny stores line the town's main street hawking *noix* (almonds), *truffes* (truffles), *foie gras,* and *cabécou* (a local goat cheese milder and nuttier than run-of-the-mill *chèvre*). Several stores at the far end of the pedestrian road offer free *dégustations* of a sweet walnut *digestif,* a specialty of the Quercy region. Most stores also offer other free samples of nutty delights, such as grilled, caramel-coated walnuts and a crumbly hazelnut cake. *Boulangeries* and *épiceries* are pricey, so it is a good idea to bring your own groceries to town. You can't get away from the scenery at picnic spots near the château.

SIGHTS

Millions of pilgrims have crawled on their knees up the **Grand Escalier,** which rises steeply beside the town's main street. Henri II climbed it in 1170 and Louis XI climbed it twice, in 1443 and in 1463. Both were followed by huge crowds as they made their way up step by step. Today some pilgrims still kneel in prayer at each of the steps, but you're much more likely to see tourists kneeling to retrieve film. During the week of September 8, though, the crowds are in full force for the annual *pèlerinage* to Rocamadour, which draws thousands of pilgrims on their way to Lourdes (see page 376). The 12th-century **Cité Réligieuse** at the summit encompasses seven chapels, only two of which can be visited without a guide. The nucleus of the *cité* is the **Chapelle Notre-Dame** (tel. 05 65 33 63 29), a dark, quiet place of prayer with a mosaic floor. The chapel shelters a black ship model, honoring all victims of shipwrecks, a 12th-century Black Madonna wearing a jeweled crown, and a 9th-century bell, said to ring on its own when a miracle is about to occur (open daily July-Aug. 9am-6pm and 6:30-10pm; Sept.-June 9am-6pm; mass in French held daily May-Sept. at 9, 11am and 5pm, Sat. at 9pm as well; Oct.-April 11am). Under Notre-Dame lies the **Crypte St-Amadour,** where the saint's body rested until a Protestant tried to set it ablaze during the wars of religion. Although it wouldn't burn, the body succumbed to the assailant's ax, and the relics are now kept under wraps in the **Musée d'Art Sacrée** (tel. 05 65 33 23 30), which also houses paintings, colorful statues, and other relics. (Open daily June 15-Sept. 15 10am-7pm; April-June 14 and Sept. 16-Nov. 11 10am-noon and 2-6pm. Admission 30F, children 20F.) The small **Basilique St-Sauveur** (tel. 05 65 33 62 61) is home to an evocative gilt wooden altar and pulpit depicting scenes from Christ's life. A guided tour takes visitors to the Crypte St-Amadour, as well as to the Chapelle St-Michel, which has several large frescoes inside (tours in French and English every hour April-Oct. Mon.-Sat. 9am-noon and 2-6pm; free, but a tip would be charitable).

Next to the Cité, climb up the zigzagging **Chemin de Croix,** which depicts each of the 14 stations of the cross in vivid relief—climb it to reach the 14th-century **château.** Built to defend pilgrims, the château is now inhabited by the chaplains of Rocamadour. The view from the **ramparts** isn't so good as the free one from the road (open 8am-8pm; admission 11F, students 8F). Skip the elevator ride (25F)—the pilgrims scaled these heights on their knees.

Check out the unique **Rocher des Aigles** (tel. 05 65 33 65 45), next to the château. A conservation and rehabilitation center, it gives 45-minute shows in which trained birds of prey (eagles, falcons, and hawks) perform stunts and play hopscotch over viewers' legs. The highlight is the graceful bald eagle, who swoops in at over 100 miles an hour to retrieve its lunch from a pool. (Open daily July-Sept. 10am-noon and 2-6pm; shows at 11am and 1, 2:30, 3:30, 4:30, and 5:30pm; April-June Mon.-Fri. 11am, 3 and 4pm; Sat.-Sun. 11am, 3, 4, and 5pm; Oct.-Nov. Mon.-Fri. 3pm, Sat.-Sun. 3 and 4pm. Admission 35F, under 16 20F.)

Near the tourist office in L'Hospitalet stands not only a sight but an event. **La Féerie du Rail** (tel. 05 65 33 71 06), billed as the Euro Mini Land, artisan Robert Masseau spent 31,000 hours over 10 years to create the model world now on display. Built to a scale of 1:87, the model bustles with activity—traffic flows through the streets of a town, boats glide down a river, animals and trapeze artists perform in a circus, and ice skaters twirl across a rink in an incredible audiovisual extravaganza (open daily July 13-Aug. 22 9am-noon and 2-7pm; Aug. 23-Nov. 11 and Palm Sunday-July 12 10am-noon and 2-6pm; admission 31F, children 19F). If Rocamadour in July isn't enough of a zoo for you, strut down the road to the **Forêt des Singes** (tel. 05 65 33 62 72), 2km from l'Hospitalet, where you can hang out with Barbary macaques, monkeys who usually inhabit Morocco's Atlas mountains. You'll have them eating out of your hand—with the help of popcorn supplied by the proprietors (open daily July-Aug. 10am-7pm; April-June and Sept. 10am-noon and 1-6pm; Oct. daily 10am-noon and 1-5pm; Nov. 1-11 Wed., and Sat.-Sun. 10am-noon and 1-5pm; admission 30F, children 20F).

Nine km away, **Les Grottes de Laclave,** route de Souillac (tel. 05 65 37 87 03), showcase the most elaborate stalactites, stalagmites, and *eccentriques* in France. The lengthy tour of the caverns (in French and English, 1¼hr., 1.6km) includes a train ride through numerous well-lit chambers. The *salle des orgues* presents nature's version of Notre-Dame, while in the *salle des mirages* the stalactites on the ceiling are reflected in a pool, creating the amazing illusion of a submerged city. The *salle de merveilles* employs black light to illuminate the fluorescent rocks (open daily 9am-6:30pm; Sept. and March 15-July 14 9am-noon and 2-6pm; Oct. 1-15 9:30am-noon and 2-5:30pm; Oct. 16–Nov. 5 10am-noon and 2-5pm; admission 37F).

Cahors

Resting on an isthmus in the gentle waters of the Lot river and surrounded by densely forested hills, Cahors (pop. 20,000) has briefly glimpsed historic fame. In the 14th century, Cahors resident Jean Duèze became the second Avignon pope, John XXII, founding a university and attracting financiers who made unlikely Cahors the premier banking city in Europe. The papacy returned to Rome, of course, and the banks and university closed, but hope was not lost. Native son Léon-Michel Gambetta (1838-1882), of street, square, and avenue fame, helped to form the Third Republic in 1870 but neglected to choose Cahors as its capital. Another offspring, the area's vineyards, produced wines whose glory might have rivaled that of Bordeaux, if not for a *phylloxéra* epidemic in the late 19th century. Cahors, a World War II Resistance stronghold, also briefly boasted the world's greatest museum when it protected 3200 works of the Louvre from the shelling in Paris.

Cahors remains a pleasant daytrip from Toulouse or a restful stopover for bike tourers—though in mid-July, hundreds of them seem too preoccupied with finishing the Tour de France to appreciate the city's charms. Cahors' participation in the Resistance has been memorialized in one of its museums and the vineyards have returned to producing a high-quality dark red wine, but fame has not come calling recently. Today Cahors' biggest moments are market days, when the city is filled with local produce, flowers, red wine, hospitality, and amiable banter.

ORIENTATION AND PRACTICAL INFORMATION

Cahors' center is a 15-minute walk from the station. Leave the station, cross the street, and head up rue Joachim Murat, which bends to the right and back to the left. In 10 minutes you arrive at (surprise!) **bd. Gambetta,** the city's main thoroughfare. It separates the *vieille ville* from the rest of Cahors. To get to the tourist office, turn right on bd. Gambetta and walk three blocks.

Tourist Office: pl. Mitterrand (tel. 05 65 35 09 56; fax 05 65 23 98 66), near rue Wilson at bd. Gambetta. Offers maps, camping and canoeing info, routes for hiking and biking, and a guide to regional wines. Daily *vieille ville* tours Mon.-Sat. mid-July through Aug. **Voyages Belmon** runs full-day bus excursions to nearby sights daily (Rocamadour, Pech-Merle, Bonaguil, or villages on the Dordogne; 100-210F). Open July-Aug. Mon.-Sat. 10am-12:30pm and 1:30-6:30pm, Sun. 10am-noon; Sept.-June Mon.-Sat. 10am-noon and 2-6pm.

Trains: av. Jean Jaurès (tel. 08 36 35 35 35). To: Paris (7 per day, 5-7hr., 309F); Brive (10 per day, 1½hr., 79F); Souillac (10 per day, 1hr., 57F); Montauban (10 per day, 45min., 54F); Toulouse (9 per day, 1½hr., 86F); and Limoges (6 per day, 2½hr.,

133F). Information booth open Mon.-Sat. 6:20am-9:30pm, Sun. 7:20am-11:20pm. **Lockers** 15-20F. **SNCF buses** from the station serve nearby villages and vineyards. 4 per day to Figeac (1½hr., 60F) and St-Cirq-Lapopie (½hr., 29F).

Money: Banque Populaire, 26, bd. Gambetta (tel. 05 65 23 50 50) has a 24-hr. **ATM.** Bank open Tues.-Sat. 8:30am-12:30pm and 1:30-5:15pm.

Bike Rental: Combes, 117, bd. Gambetta (tel. 05 65 35 06 73). 70F per day, 280F per week. Passport deposit. Open Tues.-Sat. 8:30am-noon and 2-7pm. V, MC, AmEx. Also **Cycles 7,** 417, quai de Regourd (tel. 05 65 22 66 60). Bikes 80F per day, 50F per ½-day. Passport deposit. Open Tues.-Sat. 9am-noon and 2-7pm.

Laundromat: Salon Lavoir, 208, rue Clemenceau. Open daily 7am-9pm.

English Books: Calligramme, 75, rue Joffre (tel. 05 65 35 66 44), a few classics and modern novels. Open Tues.-Sat. 9am-noon and 2-7pm; July-Aug. also Mon. 2-7pm. V, MC, AmEx. **La Maison de la Presse,** 73, bd. Gambetta (tel. 05 65 35 03 93), has a few novels, magazines, and newspapers in English. Open Mon.-Sat. 7:30am-7:15pm, Sun. 9:30am-12:30pm. V, MC.

Youth Center: Bureau Information Jeunesse, 20, rue Frédéric Suisse, next to the hostel (tel. 05 65 22 35 71). Info on study abroad, health, and employment; free condoms. Open Mon.-Thurs. 9am-noon and 2-6:30pm, Fri. closes at 5:30pm. **Direction de la Jeunesse et des Sports,** 66, bd. Gambetta (tel. 05 65 35 49 86).

Crisis Line: Drogue Info tel. 05 65 31 27 46, a local drug hotline.

Hospital: Centre Hospitalier, 335, rue Wilson (tel. 05 65 20 50 50). Turn left off bd. Gambetta from the tourist office. It's 2 blocks past the post office on the left. **Medical emergency** tel. 15.

Police: rue St-Géry (tel. 05 65 35 27 00). **Emergency** tel. 17.

Post Office: 257, rue Wilson (tel. 05 65 35 44 93), between pont Valentré and the tourist office. Poste restante. Photocopies 1F. **Currency exchange.** Open Mon.-Fri. 8am-7pm, Sat. 8am-noon. **Postal code:** 46000.

ACCOMMODATIONS AND CAMPING

The *foyers* and youth hostel in Cahors are well run and in solid shape. A few budget hotels are scattered in corners of the *vieille ville.* Call ahead in summer, particularly around the time of the Tour de France (usually in mid-July).

Foyer des Jeunes Travailleurs Frédéric Suisse (HI), 20, rue Frédéric Suisse (tel. 05 65 35 64 71; fax 05 65 35 95 92). From the train station, bear right onto rue Anatole France and turn left onto rue Frédéric Suisse (10min.). Big on character, this 13th-century building contains a worn stone staircase, iron balustrades, thin mattresses, an exciting assortment of flying insects, TV, and ping-pong. The *foyer* functions as a youth hostel in July and August but accepts travelers year-round. Singles, doubles, and dorms. Members 48F. Sheets 16F. Shower included. Breakfast 18F. Lunch or dinner 48F in cavernous stone-walled dining area. Reception open 24hr.; call ahead if you'll be arriving late. No lockout or curfew.

Foyer de Jeunes en Quercy, 129, rue Fondue Haute (tel. 05 65 35 29 32). From the station go straight on rue Murat, cross bd. Gambetta, and turn left on rue Fondue Haute, a tiny street parallel to and behind bd. Gambetta. Preference to those 16-25. The convent-like *foyer* is in a quiet, central neighborhood. Large, clean singles, doubles, and triples with hardwood floors. TV room, ping-pong, and garden. Kitchen available Sat.-Sun. 68F per person. Shower free. Breakfast 10F, meals 32F; order ahead. Reception Mon.-Fri. 8am-10:30pm. Call ahead if arriving Sat. or Sun.

Hôtel de la Paix, 30, pl. St-Maurice (tel. 05 65 35 03 40), overlooking the covered market in the central *place.* Well-kept, simple rooms and a bar downstairs. Expect morning noise on market days (Wed. and Sat.). Singles 130F. Doubles 150-170F, with bath 170-180F. Shower 10F. Breakfast 30F. Reception Mon.-Sat. only. V, MC.

Hôtel Aux Perdreaux, 137, rue de Portail Alban (tel. 05 65 35 03 50). Clean and quiet rooms. Singles with shower 140F. Doubles with shower 160F, with TV 180F. Triples and quads 200F. Breakfast 20F. Make reservations July-Aug. V, MC.

Camping: Camping Municipal St-Georges (tel. 05 65 35 04 64), offers camping under the stars and an adjacent highway off ramp on the river bank 5min. from the tourist office. Follow bd. Gambetta across pont Louis Philippe. Behind the campground, an alley leads to a path up Mont St-Cyr (10-15min.). 14F per person, 14F per tent. Electricity 15F. Open Easter-Nov. Check the tourist office for listings of other campgrounds in the surrounding areas.

FOOD

Open-air markets liven up pl. Chapou on Wednesdays and Saturdays 8am-noon. Seek out wine-sellers and sample the local reds to pick the perfect bottle for a picnic. On the first and third Saturdays of the month, produce and flowers consume the *vieille ville.* The more modest **covered market** is just off the square (open Tues.-Sat. 7:30am-12:30pm and 3-7pm, Sun. 9am-noon). A **Casino supermarket** broods at pl. Général de Gaulle (open Mon.-Sat. 9am-12:30pm and 3-7:15pm, Sun. 9am-noon; Sept.-June closed Sun. V, MC, AmEx). A smaller Casino sulks at 80, pl. Chapou (tel. 05 65 35 13 17; open Tues.-Sat. 7:30am-12:30pm and 3-7:30pm, Mon. 8:30am-12:30pm and 3-7:30pm, Sun. 8:30am-12:30pm; V, MC). Cafés and *brasseries* line the heavily-trafficked bd. Gambetta. If honking cars don't appeal, plenty of restaurants in quiet nooks of the *vieille ville* serve up local specialties like creamy *foie gras, agneau,* or *omelettes aux truffes,* made with the region's own authentically pig-sniffed truffles. For dessert, try the Cahors *pastis,* a rich apple or prune puff pastry. **L'Orangerie,** 41, rue St. James (tel. 05 65 22 59 06), offers serene vegetarian sensations in a white and pastel room. Menu includes salads, omelettes, tofu dishes, and a 3-course 68F *menu* (open Tues.-Sat. noon-2pm and 7-9pm; summer open until 10pm). At **À La Tentation,** 34, pl. Chapou (tel. 05 65 35 31 44), temptation comes in the form of 79F and 92F regional *menus* that can be eaten outside facing the cathedral (open Tues.-Sun. noon-2pm and 7:30-9:30pm; V, MC).

SIGHTS AND ENTERTAINMENT

The most riveting museum in Cahors is the **Musée de la Résistance, de la Déportation, et de la Libération du Lot,** pl. du Général de Gaulle (tel. 05 65 22 14 25). The museum illustrates Cahors' role as headquarters of the Résistance in southern France with newspaper clippings, transcripts of speeches, and photographs. The horrors of the concentration camps are documented with black and white photos, as are the joys of Cahors' liberation on August 17, 1944. Each room is dedicated to a local resident who lost his or her life in the war (open daily 2-6pm; free).

The **Musée Henri Martin,** 192, rue Emile Zola (tel. 05 65 30 15 13), is under renovation but offers changing exhibits of contemporary art (hours vary).

Like many other churches in Quercy, the 12th-century **Cathédrale St-Etienne,** at pl. Chapou (tel. 05 65 35 27 80), is topped by three domed cupolas of Byzantine inspiration. A long-term restoration project to clean the frescoes on the cupolas and walls of the church recently revealed the shimmering apse. The northern Romanesque portal, formerly the front entrance on the west side, was moved in the 14th century to allow the construction of the fortress-like façade, appropriate to the church's function as a refuge for monks during the wars of religion. The northern wall's beautifully sculpted 1135 **tympanum** depicts Christ's Ascension. To the right of the choir, a door leads to the **cloître,** built around 1500. The cloister overlooks the cathedral domes and is next to the **Chapelle St-Gausbert,** which contains a remarkable fresco of the Last Judgment (cathedral open daily 8am-7pm; Oct.-Easter 8:30am-6pm; groups can go next door to l'Agence des Bâtiments de France and ask for the key to the chapel).

With its six massive stone arches and three towering turrets, the 14th-century **pont Valentré** sprouts out of the Lot river, more a monument than an efficient bridge. Legend holds that its architect, dismayed by delays in construction, bargained with the devil to bring him all the building materials in exchange for his soul. As the work neared completion, the architect told Satan he needed water brought to him in a sieve to finish the bridge. The frustrated devil acknowledged defeat but knocked down the top of the central tower in anger. When a 19th-century architect replaced it, he added a small carving of the devil struggling to pull it down. Although the bridge's turrets seem fantastic and impractical, they helped repel invaders during the

Hundred Years' War and the Siege of Cahors in 1580. You can climb the central 40m-high tower for an obscene 15F (students 10F), but don't bother—the view from the tower doesn't compare to the view of the tower (open July-Aug. 10am-noon and 2:30-6:30pm). Construction of a new bridge will permit the narrow Valentré to be reserved for pedestrians. **Les Bateaux Safaraid,** quai de Pont Valentré (tel. 05 65 30 22 84), depart four times daily April through November and tour the cities perched precariously over the Lot. Included in the 2½-hour boat trip are Laroque de Arcs, Vers, St-Géry, Tour de Faure, Bouziès, and St-Cirq Lapopie (tickets 50-80F).

In the evening, walk a block to the left of the Pont Valentré to **Les Terraces Valentré** (tel. 05 65 35 95 88) to sip sweet drinks by the river and enjoy an excellent view of the extravagant bridge (open May-Aug. 9am-midnight; V, MC).

For three or four days near the end of July, Cahors taps its toes to the likes of The Spit Ball Jones Blues Band as part of the **Festival de Blues.** Tickets (100-200F); for more information call 05 65 35 22 29.

■ Near Cahors: Lot Valley

Long a favorite of bikers and hikers, the secluded Lot Valley has recently opened over 70km of the Lot river near Cahors to boaters. For those who can afford the luxury, this may be the ideal way to visit its medieval villages that cling to cliffs high above the river. The Cahors tourist office has a pamphlet *(Embarquement immédiat)*, and maps with details. **Le Comité Départmental de la Randonnée Pédestre,** B.P. 7 46001 Cahors Cedex (tel. 05 63 35 07 09), honors requests for its publication on hiking trails in the Lot, which is updated three times a year.

About 30km from Cahors off D653 and 7km from the nearest bus stop, the **Grotte du Pech-Merle** (tel. 05 65 31 27 05) remains one of the best-preserved prehistoric caves still open to the public. Discovered by teenagers in 1922, this 3km art gallery of fifteen-meter-high caverns contains 18,000-year-old paintings and engravings of mammoths, bison, and horses, along with a preserved footprint of a 15,000-year-old adolescent. Bring a jacket—it gets chilly 60m underground. Pech-Merle has imposed a daily visitor limit, so arrive early. Tickets are sold from 9:30am-noon and 1:30-5pm. July through August French tours of 30 people leave every half-hour and last an hour. (Open Palm Sunday to Nov. 1 9:30am-6:30pm; admission 44F.) *Gîtes d'étape* and campgrounds line the route to Pech-Merle, and hitching is supposedly easy, though not safe.

Thirty-six km east of Cahors, the exquisite old houses and steep, narrow streets of **St-Cirq-Lapopie** hang over the Lot from a rocky perch, overflowing with flowers and artisans' shops. The brown tile rooftops look just as they did eight centuries ago, thanks to an ordinance forbidding TV antennas. The second stories of many of the half-timbered houses jut out over the first by several feet. The anomaly is a result of the tax structure in the 14th and 15th centuries, when the wily residents paid taxes only on the area of the first floor of their houses.

The view from the ruins of **Château Lapopie,** the highest point in town, extends over the river, cliffs, and broad plains below. Stop by the **tourist office** in the *mairie* (tel. 05 65 31 29 06) for oodles of info on the town and surrounding area (open Easter-Oct. Mon.-Fri. 10am-6pm, Sat.-Sun. 10am-12:30pm and 2:30-6pm; Nov.-Easter Sun. 10am-6pm, call Mon.-Sat.). July through August the office offers walking tours of the village three times per week (20F; Sept.-June call ahead to organize tours for groups of at least 20). The **Musée Rignault** (tel. 05 65 31 23 22) has a small collection livened by yearly temporary exhibits, as well as a wonderful view from its small flower and stone garden (open daily July-Aug. 10am-12:30pm and 2:30-7pm; Sept.-Nov. 11 and Easter-June Wed.-Mon. 10am-12:30pm and 2:30-6pm; 10F). July through August, the **Château de Bernadin de la Vallette's** permanent collection of Surrealist works is an appropriate stop during a visit to the town in which André Breton spent many summers. Four **SNCF buses** a day run past St-Cirq-Lapopie from Cahors' *gare routière* on the way to Figeac (35min., 30F). Ask to be let off at "Tour de Faure, Gare." The town is across the bridge and a beautiful 2km walk up the hill (30min.). Pack your picnic and check the bus schedule before you leave, or you may just find yourself hungry and sleeping under the stars at **Camping la Plage** (tel. 05 65 30 29 51; fax 05 65 30 26 48; 30F per site). The only other reasonable accommodation is the new *gîte d'étape* **La Maison de la Fourdonne** (tel. 05 65 31 21 51; fax 05 65 31 21 48), right in town (50F). The town's sole *épicerie* and one and only *boulangerie* are open July-Aug. daily and Sept.-June Tues.-Sun.

Farther from Cahors in the western corner of the Lot Valley, the beautiful 16th-century **Château de Bonaguil** (tel. 05 53 71 05 22) sits on a hill above a tiny village surrounded by dense forest. Built by the Baron Bérenger de Roquefeuil as a military fortress, the prickly château features seven drawbridges, an impressive system of stone canals which provided running water, and an underground tunnel through which soldiers could wander the château unseen. They needn't have worried—the castle is in the middle of nowhere and was never harmed by direct battle (though it provided a handy target for disgruntled peasants during the Revolution). You can climb the 90 spiraling steps of the château's central **Grosse Tour** for a panoramic view of the countryside. Inside, a museum displays a collection of artifacts discovered around the château. (Admission by guided tour only. Open June-Aug. 10am-12:30pm and 1:30-5:45pm. Tours every hr., English tours 11am and 3pm; Feb.-May and Sept.-Nov. tours at 10:30am and 2:30, 3:30, and 4:30pm. Admission 25F.) Reserve tickets for the castle's concerts and stage productions in August (90-150F; 20% student discount) at **La Maison du Festival** (tel. 05 53 71 17 17) in Fumel. Call the **Fumel tourist office** (tel. 05 53 71 13 70) for any info on the town. From Cahors, take the **SNCF bus** to Fumel (5 per day, 1hr., 42F) and follow D673 for 4.5km and D158 for 3.5km to Bonaguil. Inquire at Cahors' tourist office or train station for bus schedules.

Montauban

Montauban (pop. 55,000) sits quietly on the Tarn river 50km north of Toulouse. The town's 12th-century construction was motivated by the locals' struggle against the wealthy, oppressive abbey at Montauriol ("golden mountain"). Riding a wave of popular discontent, Alphonse Jourdain, the count of Toulouse in 1144, incited the enraged population to sack the abbey and use its bricks to build a town which they named the "white mountain." The village taunted the Catholics again during the wars of religion, when it remained a stubborn Huguenot stronghold. Minutes away from Toulouse, Montauban is a good bet for art-loving daytrippers.

ORIENTATION AND PRACTICAL INFORMATION

To reach Montauban's arcaded central square, **pl. Nationale,** walk down av. Mayenne from the train station and across pont Vieux; continue uphill on Côte de Bonnetiers past the Eglise St-Jacques and turn right on rue Princesse, which runs into pl. Nationale. To reach the tourist office, cross pl. Nationale diagonally to rue Fraîche, which becomes rue Bessières, and turn left onto the narrow rue du Collège. The office is tucked away in the walls of the *ancien collège* on the right (15min.). Bus 3, timed for train arrivals, saves you the walk; get off at bd. Midi-Pyrénées (Mon.-Sat. 7am-7:45pm; 5F). The **tourist office,** 2, rue du Collège, main entrance from pl. Prax-Paris (tel. 05 63 63 60 60; fax 05 63 63 65 12), has free maps. Ask about city tours (July-Aug. twice weekly, 12F). **Montauban Magazine** lists events, and the **Guide de l'Eté Tarn-et-Garonne,** available in September, tells of summer activities and festivals; both are free and in French (open July-Aug. Mon.-Sat. 9am-7pm, Sun. 10am-noon and 3-6pm; Sept.-June Mon.-Sat. 9am-noon and 2-7pm). **Crédit Mutuel,** 8, bd. Midi-Pyrénées (tel. 05 63 03 67 67), has a 24-hour **ATM** and **currency exchange** (open Mon.-Fri. 8:45am-noon and 1:30-5pm, Sat. 8:30am-noon and 1:30-4pm).

Trains roll from the *gare* on rue Salengro (tel. 08 36 35 35 35) to: Paris (7-9 per day, 5½hr., 315F); Toulouse (every hr., 25min., 47F); Bordeaux (9 per day, 2hr., 136F);

Agen (7-9 per day, 1hr., 48F); and Moissac (4-5 per day, 50min., 29F; info office open 8am-7pm). The **bus station** is on pl. Lalaque. **Ste. Moissagaise de Transports** (tel. 05 63 04 92 30) go to Moissac (4 per day, 1hr., 32F). **Jardel** (tel. 05 63 03 18 95) sends buses to Toulouse (6 per day, 1hr., 36F). **SNCF buses** go to Albi (2 per day, 1¼hr., 58F). Call 05 63 63 52 52 for info on **local buses, TM** (Transports Montaubanais). The **hospital** is at 14, rue du Dr. Alibert (tel. 05 63 03 90 00), left onto quai Montmuray after pont Vieux, then right on rue St-Claire. The **police station** is at 30, bd. Alsace-Lorraine (tel. 05 63 21 54 00), right off av. Gambetta from pl. Maréchal Foch; in an **emergency,** dial 17. The **post office** is at 6, bd. Midi-Pyrénées (tel. 05 63 68 84 84; open Mon.-Fri. 8am-7pm, Sat. 8am-noon; **postal code:** 82000).

ACCOMMODATIONS AND FOOD

For better value, stick to hotels closer to pl. Nationale. The **Hôtel du Commerce,** 9, pl. Roosevelt (ask directions to "pl. de la Cathédrale"; tel. 05 63 66 31 32; fax 05 63 03 18 46), has attractive rooms. The top floor has low ceilings. (5 small singles 95-105F. All other rooms have TVs. Doubles 140F, with shower 159-260F. Triples 169F. Quads with shower 230-270F. Shower 10F. Breakfast 30F. V, MC.) The **Hôtel de la Poste,** 17, rue Michelet (tel. 05 63 63 05 95), off pl. Nationale, has well kept rooms. (Singles and doubles 130F, with shower 150F, with shower and toilet 160F. Extra bed 30F. Shower 15F. Breakfast 25F.) Carless campers can make it to **Camping Rural,** 225, route de Corbarieu/D21 (tel. 05 63 63 29 23), south of town. Call ahead to reserve one of the six spots. Buses go to the end of the line, a 1km walk on a marked path from the campground. Directions at the tourist office. (Pitches 15F, plus 10F per person. Pool. Pick-and-pay produce patches. Alliteration free.)

A **market** brightens pl. Nationale Tuesday to Sunday 8am-12:30pm. Many inexpensive restaurants line rues d'Elie and d'Auriol, off pl. Nationale, as well as rue de l'Hôtel de Ville and pl. Maréchal Foch. **Le Contre-Filet,** 4, rue Princesse (tel. 05 63 20 19 75), offers traditional French fare and cheerful décor. The 60F 2-course *menu* includes the house specialty *faux-filet et sauce fameuse* (open daily noon-2pm and 7:30-10:30pm; V, MC, AmEx). Super nachos (34F), tostadas (45F), and cactus (32F) complement the Mexican pottery at **Le Quetzal,** 18, rue des Augustins (tel. 05 63 66 15 34) on the *gare* side of the pont Vieux (open Tues.-Sun. noon-2pm and 7:30-10:30pm; V, MC). Vegetarians can sip organic wines (32F a liter) with the *plat du jour* (40F) at **La Clef des Champs,** 3, rue Armand Cambon (tel. 05 63 66 33 34; open Mon.-Sat. 11:45am-2pm). Between pl. Nationale and the tourist office, **Nouvelles Galeries** sells groceries on its first floor (open Mon.-Sat. 9am-7pm; V, MC).

SIGHTS

The exquisite **Musée Ingres,** 19, rue de l'Hôtel de Ville (tel. 05 63 22 12 92), showcases several thousand works by David's celebrated pupil, Jean-Auguste Dominique Ingres (1780-1867). Extending two floors skyward and three floors underground, this museum is full of surprises. From torture instruments in the basement to vibrant 20th-century pieces, the museum shelters works by countless artists. Don't neglect the ceilings; patterns and architectural oddities lurk above (open July-Aug. daily 9:30am-noon and 2-6pm; Sept.-June Tues.-Sun. 10am-noon and 2-6pm; admission 20F, students free; Sept.-June free Wed. if no temporary exhibit).

Across pl. Bourdelle, the small and once-live **Musée d'Histoire Naturelle Victor Brun,** quai Montmurat (tel. 05 63 22 13 85), is stuffed with specimens of ostriches, penguins, crocodiles, armadillos, fossils, and a tarantula or two (open Tues.-Sat. 10am-noon and 2-6pm, Sun. 2-6pm; admission 12F, 20F during exposition, students free). A **four-museum pass** (25F) includes the **Musée Terroir** and the **Musée Résistance,** as well as the above two museums.

The towering belfry of the **Eglise St-Jacques** boasts holes gouged by Louis XIII's cannons during an unsuccessful 1621 siege of this Protestant lair. Montauban was only conquered after all the neighboring towns had surrendered. The sundial on the wall keeps time precisely enough for locals (open Mon.-Sat. 9am-noon and 2-6pm).

As Protestants fled following the revocation of the Edict of Nantes in 1685, Louis XIV constructed the **Cathédrale,** pl. Roosevelt, whose interior is unusually well lit by clear and amber-colored panes. Four enormous sculptures of Matthew, Mark, Luke, and John keep solemn watch on the grand arches of the nave, the clerestory, and an Ingres painting *Le Voeu de Louis XIII* (open daily 9am-noon and 2-6pm).

Refreshing wandering or picnicking awaits on the gentle slopes of the **Jardin des Plantes,** off the allée du Consul-Dupuy (open summer daily 7am-8pm; winter 7am-7pm). Groups of up to five people can rent an electronic boat to trace a small loop along the river Tarn. Head to the riverbank just below the Musée Ingres (June 15-Sept. 15 daily 10am-6:30pm). Montauban's love of the arts shines in three yearly music festivals. A weekend in mid-April brings the **Festival des Briques et du Rock.** Traditional French songs are prattled at the **Festival "Alors Chante,"** a long weekend in May. The **Jazz Festival** takes place the third week in July. Concert tickets 100-180F, with reduced prices for students (call 05 63 63 60 60 or the tourist office).

Pays Basque (Basque Country)

The Basques hold that their *Euzkadi* (the Basque Country) is one nation, now unjustly divided between France and Spain. Part of the bond is linguistic—many locals speak *euskera*—and part is political. The region has had a turbulent history, plagued by waves of attacking Romans, Visigoths, and Franks. Basque nationalism was born in the 1890s, largely as a reaction against rapid modernization that threatened traditional values. Today, the Basque Country is comprised of four industrialized Spanish and three agricultural French provinces. The French Basques' relative acquiescence to Parisian central authority has been derided by Spanish Basques as complacency. But, in fact, the French Basques covertly supported the aspirations of their more nationalistic brethren across the border (see gray box on page 366).

With the Pyrénées soaring to heights of over 1830m in the south and long stretches of forest and valley stretching across the north, the Pays Basque features some of France's most variegated landscape. Along the coast, beaches of white and gold sand attract droves of sun-seekers. The rip-tides that whip the waters of Biarritz and St-Jean-de-Luz draw Europe's surfing elite. Farther inland, St-Jean-Pied-de-Port's medieval *vieille ville* has preserved its idyllic allure; the nearby Forêt d'Iraty offers some of the region's finest hiking and skiing.

The regional sport *cesta punta,* or jai alai, is the world's fastest ball game. Burly players hurl a hard ball at speeds up to 200km per hour at a wall by means of a *chistera* (basket appendage) laced to the wrist. Try to get to a *fronton* (outdoor arena) or a *trinquet* (indoor arena) to appreciate local players' speed and skill. Tickets to the world cup matches, played all summer in St-Jean-de-Luz, start at 50F.

Folk dances grab center stage during the Basque summer festivals, which are accompanied by boisterous bouts of drinking and the sounds of the *ttun ttun* (snare drum) and *tchirulä* (vertical flute). The festivals overwhelm Basque cities (Bayonne's is particularly famous) and villages in July and August, making it an ordeal to find a hotel room amid the revelry. Every year as the autumn hunting season approaches, Basque mountaineers await the arrival of the migrating ring doves. As the birds are caught in the nets set out for them, celebrations erupt in the villages.

Basque specialties run the gastronomic gamut from Bayonne's cured ham to St-Jean-de-Luz's renowned tuna. The Basque omelette—known as *pipérade*—is served with green peppers, onions, tomatoes, thyme, and salt, and dishes *à la basquaise* contain many of these same ingredients. Local *tapas* are called *pintxos* (or *pinchos*). The rich, cream-filled *gâteau basque* accentuates any meal with a sweet afterthought. Regional *brebis* cheese can be found on all menus. Once a major wine-producing region, the Pays Basque is making a comeback with some vigorous reds, notably Irouléguy. *Izarra* has been distilled at Bayonne's factory since 1904. A sweeter cousin of Chartreuse, this *digestif* comes in two varieties, yellow and green.

GETTING AROUND

Most of the region is poorly served by rail, but Bayonne and Biarritz are fairly easy to reach. With Anglet, they form one big metropolis—STAB buses (7F) tame this urban lion into a pussycat. St-Jean-Pied-de-Port is an easy, beautiful hour's ride through the mountains from Bayonne. Trains run through the area from Bordeaux in the north and Pau in the east. Along the coast from Biarritz to Hendaye, inexpensive buses make up for the scanty rail service. Excursion buses travel to a few towns in the interior, but many find that hitching and cycling are easier ways to head for the hills.

Bayonne

Capital of the Basque province of Labourd, Bayonne (pop. 43,000) has weathered the influences of transient powers. The Romans surrounded the city with ramparts; the English, unconcerned with architectural continuity, erected the enormous Gothic cathedral dominating Bayonne's skyline. The French and Spanish used Bayonne and its region for a game of tug-of-war lasting 200 years. Yet, from its quintessential green and red shutters to the public notices—in six languages—calling for Basque solidarity, it seems that Bayonne's tumultuous past has only strengthened the city's independence and Basque identity. In a region divided by the Nive and Adour rivers and unified by the waters' bounty, Bayonne's fishing boats bring in enough of a catch to keep the town in fresh seafood week after week. Bayonne is content to let the bathing beauties, Biarritz and Angelet, monopolize the summertime crowds while it relishes an historically rare calm in its humble place in the sun.

ORIENTATION AND PRACTICAL INFORMATION

Hemingway once muttered, "Bayonne is a nice town. It is like a very clean Spanish town, and it is on a big river." A bit more explanation may be in order. The merging rivers split Bayonne into three main areas. **St-Esprit,** on the northern side of the Adour, contains the train station and pl. de la République. Pont St-Esprit arches across the Adour to **Petit-Bayonne,** site of Bayonne's museum, inexpensive hotels, lively bars, and restaurants. Five small bridges cross the Nive and connect Petit-Bayonne to **Grand-Bayonne,** on the west bank of the Nive. The oldest part of town, Grand-Bayonne has a buzzing pedestrian zone lined by red-shuttered houses *(arceaux)* over shops and *pâtisseries.* The center of town is manageable on foot, and an excellent bus system makes Angelet and Biarritz a snap to visit.

Tourist Information: Tourist Office, pl. des Basques (tel. 05 59 46 01 46; fax 05 59 59 37 55). From the train station, take the middle fork onto pl. de la République, then veer right over a bridge (pont St-Esprit), and continue through pl. Réduit to the next bridge (pont Mayou). Cross pont Mayou, turn right onto rue Bernède, which soon becomes av. Bonnat, and turn left onto pl. des Basques (15min.). Free city map and help finding rooms. Pick up the *Fêtes en Pays Basque.* Tours of various aspects of the city (in French; July-Sept. 15 Tues., Wed., Fri., and Sat., 30F). Open July-Aug. Mon.-Sat. 9am-7pm, Sun. 10am-1pm; Sept.-June Mon.-Fri. 9am-6:30pm, Sat. 10am-6pm. **Branch** at the train station (tel. 05 59 55 20 45) is open July-Aug. Mon.-Sat. 9am-12:30pm and 2-6pm.

Budget Travel: Pascal Voyages, 8, allées Boufflers (tel. 05 59 25 48 48). BIJ and other student-priced tickets. Open Mon.-Fri. 8:30am-6:30pm, Sat. 9am-noon.

Money: Or et Change, 1, rue Jules Labat (tel. 05 59 25 58 59), in Grand-Bayonne. No commission, good rates. Open daily 10am-7pm. **ATMs** at **Crédit Mutuel,** 5, rue du 49ème Régiment d'Infanterie, and **Crédit Agricole,** pl. de la République.

Trains: pl. de la République (tel. 05 59 55 50 50). To: Paris (7 TGVs per day, 5½hr., 406-456F); St-Jean-Pied-de-Port (5 per day, 1hr., 45F); St-Jean-de-Luz (22 per day, 30min., 24-32F); Bordeaux (9 per day, 1½-2½hr., 130-138F); Toulouse (5 per day, 4hr., 188F); Biarritz (22 per day, 10min., 12-20F). Info office open daily July-Aug. 9am-7:15pm; Sept.-June Mon.-Sat. 9am-noon and 2-6:30pm. **Lockers** 30F for 72hr.

Public Transport: STAB, on pl. du Réduit in Petit-Bayonne (tel. 05 59 59 04 61). Open Mon.-Sat. 8am-noon and 1:30-6pm. Pick up a bus map here or at tourist offices. Lines 1, 2, and 6 to Biarritz; line 4 to Biarritz through Anglet. Every 30-40min. Last bus in any direction around 8pm (7pm on Sun.). Tickets 7F50, *carnet* of 10 65F. Tickets good for 1hr. after validation.

Taxis: Bayonne Radio Taxi (tel. 05 59 59 48 48), 24hr.

Laundromat: Salon Lavoir, pl. Montaut. Open Mon.-Sat. 9am-7pm.

Youth Info: BIJ, rue Pontrique (tel. 05 59 59 35 29). Open Mon.-Sat. 11am-7pm.

Hospital: Rue Jacques Loëb, St-Léon (tel. 05 59 44 35 35). Take bus 3 (direction: Panorama) to "Hôpital." **Medical emergency** tel. 15.

Police: 6, rue de Marhum (tel. 05 59 46 22 22). **Emergency** tel. 17.

Post Office: 11, rue Jules Labat (tel. 05 59 46 32 60), Grand-Bayonne. Poste Restante (postal code: 64181). **Currency exchange.** Open Mon.-Fri. 8am-6pm, Sat. 10am-noon. **Branch office,** bd. Alsace-Lorraine, same hours. **Postal code:** 64100.

ACCOMMODATIONS AND CAMPING

In St-Esprit, decent lodgings dot the train station area. The hotels in Grand-Bayonne are usually more expensive; in Petit-Bayonne browse **rue Pannecau** and **pl. Paul Bert.** Reserve in July and August. The closest hostel is in Anglet (see page 361).

Hôtel Paris-Madrid, pl. de la Gare (tel. 05 59 55 13 98; fax 05 59 55 07 22), to the left of station. Cheerful, personalized rooms. Hip and gracious owners. Singles and doubles 90-120F, with shower 145F, with shower and toilet 165F. Triples and quads with shower and toilet 195-220F. TV room. Shower 5F. Breakfast 22F. Reception July-Sept. 24hr; Oct.-June 6am-12:30am. V, MC.

Hôtel Monte-Carlo, 11, rue Hugues (tel. 05 59 55 02 68), to the right of the station. Clean, bright rooms are a delightful place to shake off the sand. Singles and doubles with shower 120F. Triples and quads with shower 220F. Free showers. Breakfast 24F. Reception open 6am-2am.

Hôtel des Basques, 4, rue des Lisses (tel. 05 59 59 08 02), in Petit-Bayonne. Light and airy rooms overlook pl. Paul Bert. Singles and doubles 110F, with TV, shower, and toilet 150F. Triples 150F. Triples and quads with TV, shower, and toilet 270F. Shower 10F. Breakfast 25F. Reception 24hr. Closed Oct. 15-Nov. 5.

Hôtel des Arceaux, 26, rue Port Neuf (tel. 05 59 59 15 53). The location and the plants filling the hall make up for sloping floors. Singles and doubles 125F, with shower 170-180F, with shower and toilet 200F. Triples with shower 250F. Quads with shower 295F. Shower free. Breakfast 30F. Reception 7:30am-10pm.

Camping: Camping de la Chêneraie (tel. 05 59 55 01 31), on RN117 north of town. Take bus line 1 from the *gare* or tourist office to Leclerc supermarket; the site is 1km away (buses every 12min.). 4-star facility with *everything.* 18F per person, 32F per tent or car, 55F with caravan. Open Easter-Sept. 8am-10pm.

FOOD

The narrow streets of Petit-Bayonne, and to a lesser extent St-Esprit, offer 50-60F *menus* of *jambon de Bayonne* or chicken *à la basquaise,* with peppers and onions. Grand Bayonne, the city's cloth-napkin zone, serves regional specialties in a less budget-oriented atmosphere. The largest **market,** the **Marché Municipal,** on quai Roquebert, attracts vendors from far and wide (Mon.-Thurs. and Sat. 6am-1pm, Fri. 6am-5pm). **Monoprix** squats at 8, rue Orbe (tel. 05 59 59 00 33; open Mon.-Fri. 8:30am-7:30pm, Sat. 8am-7:30pm; V, MC).

Le Bistrot Ste-Cluque, 9, rue Hugues (tel. 05 59 55 82 43). Lost amid flowers, you'll forget you're across from the station. Delicious regional cuisine with fantastic service, huge portions, and an elegant atmosphere. Ever-changing 55F *menu.* Duck 50F, *paella* 55F, big salads 40F. Open daily noon-2pm and 7-11pm. V, MC.

El Mosquito, 12, rue Gosse (tel. 05 59 25 78 05), in Grand-Bayonne. South American food in a cozy den enlivened by sombreros, real puffer-fish lampshades, and wild Cuban jazz. Homemade guacamole and tortillas 30F. Enchiladas 49F. 70F vegetarian or meat *menu* includes Brazilian coffee. Open July 15-Oct. 14 daily 7pm-midnight; Oct. 16-July 14 closed Sun. V, MC, AmEx.

Bodega El Rio, 17, quai Jauréquilberry (tel. 05 59 59 05 46), offers a brief retreat into Spain, complete with frequent live music, occasional dancing, and a huge bull's head mounted on the wall. Fish and meat dishes start at 50F. Open Tues.-Sun. noon-2:30pm and 7-11pm. V, MC.

Chocolat Cazenave, 19, Arceaux Port-Neuf (tel. 05 59 59 03 16), in the arcades. Dessert only. Chocolate at its source: Bayonne introduced it to France. Traditionalist liquid model with whipped cream 25F, sinful cinnamon chocolate with hot buttered toast 36F; ice creams, too. Open Mon.-Sat. 9am-noon and 2-7pm. V, MC.

SIGHTS AND ENTERTAINMENT

With spiny steeples biting into Bayonne's skies, the 13th-century **Cathédrale Ste-Marie** intimidates from afar and impresses from within. The church weathered a brief stint as a cemetery in the 16th century, suffered massive destruction during the Revolution, and has endured sporadic fires. Although the government has doled out extravagant sums to restore and beautify it, Ste-Marie remains grumpy to the bone. Behind the altar, dark oil paintings brood amid sullen recesses and intricate iron chandeliers. Enter the large, graceful cloister at pl. Pasteur (cloister open Mon.-Sat. 9:30am-12:30pm and 2:30-6pm; church open daily 10-11:45am and 3-5:45pm).

The **Château-Vieux de Bayonne,** on nearby av. du 11 Novembre, is a well-kept blond stone block which has housed such notorious villains as the Black Prince and Don Pedro, *le cruel roi de Castille.* During business hours Anglophones run the risk of being inducted by its current tentants, the French Foreign Legion (see page 31). The avenue continues to Bayonne's vast, grassy **fortifications.** Lose yourself in the ageless walls, and try to ignore the multi-level parking lot. Bayonne's graceful **botanical gardens** will keep you out of the city, too (open mid-April to mid-Oct. daily 9:30am-12:30pm and 2-6pm). For sandier delights, the **Metro plage** is calmer than Angelet's sunny circus; take bus M (7F50).

The Rubens room at the **Musée Bonnat,** 5, rue Jacques Laffitte (tel. 05 59 59 08 52), in Petit-Bayonne, is filled with lecherous mythical men. Downstairs, more nude folk abound, painted by Bonnat himself, a celebrated 19th-century *bayonnais* painter who gave his collection to the city and directed the construction of the museum. Highlights include a ghoulish El Greco and Goya's grim, entrancing *La Dernière Communion de San José de Calasanz* (open Wed.-Mon. 10am-noon and 2:30-6pm, Fri. until 8pm; admission 20F, students 10F).

Join die-hard drinkers and their poodles for the tour of the **Izarra Distillery,** 9, quai Bergeret (tel. 05 59 55 07 48), in St-Esprit. The herb-based *izarra* is a pungent Basque liqueur; the green (17-herb) is more potent than the yellow (13-herb) variety. *Izarra* mixes beautifully with the factory's fruit liqueurs, each tastier than the last, and the guides will let you sample them all. Bottles of the fruit liqueurs run 45F, while the yellow and green concoctions cost 100F. (40-min. tours every 30min. July-Aug; throughout the day April-Oct; 15F. Distillery open daily 9-11:30am and 2-6pm; Sept.-Oct. and April-July 14 9-11:30am and 2-4:30pm. Call for tours Nov.-March.)

At 10pm the first Wednesday in August, unrestrained Basque hedonism breaks out as the town immerses itself in the insanely popular **Fête de Bayonne,** five days of concerts, dancing, bullfights, and fireworks. A Red Cross post is set up just for the *fête* to cart off dazed revelers and recharge them for more partying. The **Jazz aux Remparts** festival lures musical immortals for five days in mid-July. Tickets (160-180F per night, 120-140F for students, under 12 20F) are available by calling the Municipal Theater (tel. 05 59 59 07 27; Tues.-Sat. 1-7pm). July 14, 1997, will bring the seventh annual **Marché Médiéval,** a costumed reprise of the past behind the cathedral. October through June, on Thursdays at 4pm, ferocious *pelote à mains nues* matches animate the Trinquet St-André. The orchestra **Harmonie Bayonnaise** stages gentler jazz and traditional Basque music concerts in the pl. de Gaulle gazebo Thursdays at 9:30pm in July and August (free). In August and early September, Bayonne holds several **corridas** (bullfights) in the large Plaza de Toros. Seats (60-470F) sell out fast, but cheap seats in the nose-bleed section should be available on fight days. For ticket information, write or call Bureau des Arènes Municipales, 1, rue Vauban, Bayonne (tel. 05 59 59 25 98). For a wonderful selection of films in *version originale,* head to **L'Atalante,** 7, rue Denis Etcheverry (tel. 05 59 55 76 63), in St-Esprit (35F, 6pm show 30F, students 25F; closed most of July and early Aug.)

Anglet

Staking its claim on five sandy km of Atlantic coast and linked to Bayonne and Biarritz by efficient STAB buses, Anglet (pronounced with a hard "t") has dutifully accepted its fate as a mecca for surf- and sun- worshippers. Daredevil board-riders mob the beaches where the waves are roughest, but relative serenity awaits on the margins. One-dimensional Anglet—home to one of France's wildest hostels—means fun for all, whether you're soaking up rays or shredding some waves.

PRACTICAL INFORMATION

The **tourist office,** 1, av. de Chambre d'Amour, on pl. Leclerc (tel. 05 59 03 77 01; fax 05 59 03 55 91), is exceptionally well equipped to direct ventures in the region and has info on summer surfing contests. If your main goal is sand and surf, don't waste precious sun-time here; the bus maps have all the info you'll need (open July-Sept. 15 Mon.-Sat. 9am-7pm; Sept. 16-June Mon.-Fri. 9am-12:15pm and 1:45-6pm, Sat. 9:45am-1pm). Try the **annex** at the plage de Sable d'Or (tel. 05 59 03 93 43; open July-Aug. and two weeks at Easter daily 9am-7:30pm; April-June and Sept. Sat.-Sun. 9am-7:30pm). **Exchange currency** at decent rates at **BNP,** pl. Leclerc (tel. 05 59 03 89 42; open Tues.-Sat. 8am-noon and 1:45-5pm). Both BNP and nearby **Crédit Agricole** have 24-hour **ATMs.** Schedules and maps of the Biarritz-Anglet-Bayonne **bus system** are available on buses, from tourist offices, or from the **STAB** info booth at pl. de Réduit, Bayonne (tel. 05 59 59 04 61); on rue Louis Barthou in Biarritz (tel. 05 59 24 26 53); or at the hostel (both booths open Mon.-Sat. 8am-noon and 1:30-6pm). Tickets (7F50) are good for one hour. **Tides** are printed in *Calendrier des Marées 1997,* available at the tourist office. Rent **bikes** at **V Tonic,** route des Pontots (tel. 05 59 52 36 48; open Tues.-Sat. 9:30am-12:30pm and 2:30-7:30pm). There's a **laundromat** at plage Chambre d'Amour, 21, av. du Rayon Vert (wash 5kg for 20F; dry 5min. for 2F; open daily 7am-10pm). **Météo France** (tel. 08 36 68 02 64) gives you the weather forecast in French. In the absence of **lifeguards** at night (7pm-10am), call the **fire department** for beach emergencies (tel. 18). In **medical emergencies,** call 15. The **police** are at 5, rue du 8 Mai (tel. 05 59 63 84 64). In an **emergency,** dial 17. The **post office** is inconveniently located near the *mairie* at 7, rue du 8 Mai (tel. 05 59 58 08 40), but offers poste restante, an **ATM,** and photocopies. A smaller branch is at pl. Leclerc, next to the tourist office. **Postal code:** 64600.

ACCOMMODATIONS, CAMPING, AND FOOD

Although there are a few reasonable hotels in Anglet, there's no need to stay anywhere but the **Auberge de Jeunesse (HI),** 19, route des Vignes (tel. 05 59 63 86 49; fax 05 59 63 38 92), 600m directly uphill from plage de Marinella. This well equipped and carefree hostel is home to 140 hormonally spastic, half-naked, tanned youths speaking 30 languages and united only by their affinity for Quicksilver t-shirts—making it the hub of France's surfing subculture. Kitchen facilities are available September to March only. (76F per person. Sheets 23F. Camping 52F. Prices slightly lower Oct.-May. Shower and breakfast included.) Easter to October, you can eat dinner downstairs at the bar (live music; 22-29F for huge servings; happy hour beers 7F), open until 1am. (Reception 8:30am-10pm. No lockout or curfew. Checkout at 10:30am.) They rent surfboards (75F), boogie boards (65F), and wetsuits (50F) 8:30-9:30am. All equipment must be returned by 6:30pm (passport deposit). Hiking, rafting, and rockclimbing excursions 60-120F. Maximum stay three nights when full. Often packed; reservations are accepted only with a deposit. Send a deposit in the mail or pay at the desk to secure a spot. The hostel offers excursions and **surfing lessons.** From the Hôtel de Ville in Biarritz, take bus 4 (every 50min.; direction: Bayonne Sainsontain to "Auberge"). From pl. de la République or pl. de Réduit in Bayonne, take bus 4 (direction: La Barre) to "La Barre," then change to bus 4N (direction: Mairie Biarritz). In summer, bus 4 runs to "Auberge" without the transfer. **Hôtel le Parc,** 57, av. de la Chambre d'Amour, offers 27 simple and clean rooms only 300m from plage des Sables d'Or. (Doubles 145F, with shower 155F. Triples 180F. Quads with shower 205F. Shower 10F. Breakfast 26F. Reception 6:30am-10:30pm. Open March-Oct. V, MC.) Take STAB bus line 7 to "La Chapelle."

Anglet's campgrounds are within walking distance of the beach and boast all sorts of amenities. Shaded, well located **Camping Fontaine Laborde,** 17, allée Fontaine Laborde (tel. 05 59 03 48 16), caters to the young and surfing. Take the 4N, Navettes, or B bus to "Fontaine Laborde," just down the road from the hostel (22F per person, 20F per site, 12F per car; reception all night, unless they fall asleep).

The mini-markets on the beaches will suck you dry with prices triple ordinary rates. For relief, try the food stores on pl. Leclerc, or **Guyenne et Gascogne,** 37, av. de la Chambre d'Amour, for produce and canned goods (open July-Aug. Mon.-Sat. 7:30am-8pm, Sun. 8am-1pm; Sept.-June Mon.-Sat. 7am-1pm and 3-8pm, Sun. 8am-1pm; V, MC). The **Leclerc supermarket,** 43, route du Bois Belin, is a brisk 15-minute walk from the hostel (open Mon.-Sat. 8:30am-8:30pm). Expect pleasant prices from the *crêperies* along Anglet's beaches (crêpes 9-20F, sandwiches 15-25F).

SIGHTS AND ENTERTAINMENT

Anglet's *raison d'être* is its 4km of fine-grained white sand, parcelled out into nine beaches—each with its own name and personality, from the perfect waves of the **plage Les Cavaliers** to the rocky jetty of the **Chambre d'Amour,** where two legendary lovers perished when the tide came in. Swimmers should know that along with the beauty of the crashing tides comes a strong cross-current undertow. When in doubt, go for a swim at one of the seven beaches with a lifeguard on duty (all but Chambre d'Amour and Plage de l'Océan). The **Rainbow Surfshop,** 18-21, av. Chambre d'Amour (tel. 05 59 03 45 37), 10 minutes from the beach, rents a colorful spectrum of tools of the trade: bodyboards (40F per ½-day, 70F per day; 1000F deposit), surfboards (60F per ½-day, 100F per day; 2000F deposit), and wetsuits (30F per ½-day, 50F per day; 1000F deposit). Surf lessons for one or two people cost 170F for the first hour and 150F for each subsequent hour (open daily 9:30am-8pm). There is also a small branch at plage de la Chambre d'Amour (tel. 05 59 03 35 62; open April-Oct. daily 9am-7:30pm). For walking or jogging, the **Fôret du Pignada's** pine needle-covered trails are easy on the knees. Anglet also offers many opportunities for less strenuous participation in surfing—by watching from the sands. Five yearly professional competitions are all fun and free. The **Quicksilver Cup** will be March 22-24 in 1997. Mid-July brings the three-day **France Championship;** for five days at the end of the month the traveling **O'Neill Surf Challenge** takes up residence in Anglet. The **Europe Bodyboard Championship** is three days at the end of August. Three days in mid-September bring the **Europe Surfing Championship.**

Biarritz

Though parts of Biarritz (pop. 29,000) still cling to outmoded pretention, the rest of the city has come back down to earth. Biarritz may never be a budget traveler's dream-come-true, but the city has expanded its offerings—"opened its arms," as Biarritz's motto proclaims—to a wider array of visitors. Budget hotels surface amid the luxury resorts that once hosted Napoleon III and Queen Victoria. A little persistence yields inexpensive restaurants, and the splendid beaches are absolutely free. Though certainly a destination unto itself, Biarritz is also a daytrip *de luxe* from cheaper Bayonne and Anglet.

ORIENTATION AND PRACTICAL INFORMATION

Getting to Biarritz is not so easy as it was in the grand old days when luxury trains glided into the now-deserted station. Today, trains roll as far as **Biarritz-la-Négresse,** 3km away. To get to the *centre ville,* take blue bus 2 (direction: Bayonne via Biarritz; every 20-40min., summer 6:30am-9pm) or green bus 9 (direction: Biarritz HDV; summer 6:30am-7pm). To walk into town from Biarritz-la-Négresse, turn left onto allée du Moura and remain calm as it becomes av. du Président Kennedy. Make a left turn a few km later onto av. du Maréchal Foch, which continues to pl. Clemenceau, Biarritz's main square. Or get off the train in Bayonne and hop a bus to Biarritz (½hr.).

Buses 1 and 2 run from the Bayonne train station to the Biarritz Hôtel de Ville. All buses cost 7F50. From the Hôtel de Ville, the tourist office on pl. d'Ixelles is a brief walk up rue Joseph Petit. To get to pl. de Clemenceau, take av. Edouard VII uphill after getting off the bus.

Tourist Office: Javalquinto, 1, square d'Ixelles (tel. 05 59 22 37 10; fax 05 59 24 97 80), off av. Edouard VII. 4-star office. Staff will track down rooms or campsites. Pick up a free copy of *Biarritzcope*—the *Pariscope* of the *plages*—for monthly events listings. Open daily June-Sept. 8am-8pm; Oct.-May 9am-6:45pm.

Money: Change Plus, 9, rue Mazagran (tel. 05 59 24 82 47). Fair rates, no commission. Open Mon.-Sat. 8am-8pm, Sun. 10am-1pm and 4-7pm; Sept.-June Mon.-Sat. 9:30am-12:30pm and 2-7pm. **ATMs** do the money thing at **Crédit Mutuel,** 4, av. de Verdun, off pl. Clemenceau, and **Banque Populaire,** 10, rue Mazagran.

Flights: Aéroport de Parme, bd. Marcel Dassault (tel. 05 59 43 83 83). Bus 6 from the Hôtel de Ville, to "Parme Aéroport" (every 30min., March-Oct. Mon.-Sat. 7am-7pm, Sun. take bus B). **Air Inter** (tel. 05 59 33 34 35) has 5-7 flights daily to Paris.

Trains: Biarritz-la-Négresse, 3km out of town (tel. 05 59 23 15 69). To: Bayonne (10 per day, 10min., 12F); St-Jean-de-Luz (10 per day, 15min., 15F); Pau (4 per day, 2hr., 85F); Toulouse (4 per day, 4½hr., 193F); Bordeaux (8 per day, 2hr., 143F); and Paris (7 per day, 8hr., 5hr. by TGV, 408-462F). **Storage** 30F per bag, open daily 9am-7:30pm. Also lockers. There is an info office in Biarritz proper at 15, av. Foch (tel. 05 59 24 00 94). Open Mon.-Fri. 9am-noon and 2-6pm.

Buses: ATCRB (tel. 05 59 26 06 99). Buses leave from rue Joseph Petit next to the tourist office. Buy tickets on the bus. To: St-Jean-de-Luz (11 per day, ½hr., 18F); Bidart (11 per day, 15min., 9F); San Sebastián, Spain (2-3 per day, 2½hr., 36F). **Les Cars Basques,** 18, pl. Clemenceau (tel. 05 59 24 21 84), next to Hôtel le Président. Buy tickets at their office. Open daily 9:30am-noon and 1-6pm. Excursions to: La Rhune (Tues. and Fri., 82F); St-Jean-Pied-de-Port and the Pyrénées (Mon., 87F); Pau, Lourdes, and Pyrénées (Wed., 172F). Daytrips to Spain (90-130F).

Public Transportation: STAB serves the Bayonne, Anglet, and Biarritz area. Kiosk with maps and schedules on rue Louis-Barthou. Take av. de Verdun from pl. Clemenceau; rue Louis-Bathou is a quick left turn away. Tickets good for 1hr. 7F50, *carnets* of 10 62F, 52F for students during school year. Main office on bd. de l'Aritxaque in Bayonne (tel. 05 59 52 59 52).

Taxis: Taxi Radio Biarritz (tel. 05 59 23 62 62). 24-hr. service.

Bike Rental: SOBILO, 24, rue Peyroloubil (tel. 05 59 24 94 47). Mountain bikes 90F per day, 500F per week; 1000F deposit or credit card. Scooters 240F per day, 1130F per week; 3000-6000F deposit. The only motorcycle rentals in the Basque country 340-400F per day; 6000F deposit. Lower rates off-season. Open daily 10am-1pm and 3-6pm; Oct.-May Sat.-Sun. only, same hours.

Surfboard Rental: Freedom Surf Shop, 2, av. Reine Victoria (tel. 05 59 24 38 40), a block from Grande Plage. Surfboards 50-60F per ½-day, 80-100F per day; deposit ID. Wetsuits 50F. Lessons 200F for 2½hr. Open Sept.-June Mon.-Sat. 10am-1:30pm and 3-6:30pm and July-Aug. Mon.-Sat 10am-1:30pm and 3-6:30pm and Sun. 11am-12:30pm and 4-7pm.

Laundromat: Le Lavoir, 4, av. Jauleny, by the post office. Open daily 7am-9pm.

Weather Conditions: tel. 08 36 68 02 64 or 08 36 68 08 64 (in French only).

Beach Emergencies: Grande Plage (tel. 05 59 24 92 70). Plage Marabella (tel. 05 59 23 01 20). Plage de la Milady (tel. 05 59 23 63 94).

Hospital: Private clinic in Biarritz, **Polyclinique d'Aguilera,** 21, rue Estagnas (tel. 05 59 22 46 22). **L'Hôpital de Bayonne,** av. Jacques Loëb (tel. 05 59 44 35 35). **AIDS info** (tel. 0 800 36 66 36). **Medical Emergency:** tel. 05 59 63 33 33 or 15.

Police: rue Louis-Barthou (tel. 05 59 24 68 24). **Emergency** tel. 17.

Post Office: 21, rue de la Poste (tel. 05 59 22 41 10). Poste restante. **Currency exchange.** Open Mon.-Fri. 8:30am-7pm, Sat. 8:30am-noon. **Postal code:** 64200.

ACCOMMODATIONS AND CAMPING

Biarritz hotels have more stars than the Milky Way, but fear not—bargains do exist. Write a month ahead for July or August, or enlist the help of the tourist office. Rue du Port-Vieux houses a bunch of budget hotels. All the hotels below are central.

Hôtel Barnetche, 5bis, rue Charles-Floquet (tel. 05 59 24 22 25; fax 05 59 24 98 71). Take rue du Helder from pl. Clemenceau, continue on rue Jean Bart, and walk straight through pl. de la Libération to arrive at rue Floquet. One 12-bed dorm room (90F with no meal obligations) is the best deal in town. Otherwise, try a clean room in the newly decorated hotel. Doubles 220-230F, with shower 270F, with shower and toilet 300F. Triples and quads 110F per person. Free showers. Obligatory breakfast 30F. In Aug., *demi-pension* obligatory (add 85F—the food is good). English spoken. Reception open 7:30am-11pm. Open May-Sept.

Hôtel la Marine, 1, rue des Goelands (tel. 05 59 24 34 09). Brand-spanking-new beds in bright rooms. Singles with shower 150F. Doubles with shower 160F, with shower and toilet 180F. Only 9 rooms. Breakfast 15F. English spoken.

Hôtel Berhouet, 29, rue Gambetta (tel. 05 59 24 63 36). Nice wood furniture. Hot, powerful showers. Singles 110F. Doubles with shower 110F. Shower 20F. Extra bed 40F. Breakfast 20F. Reservations with deposit. Reception 8am-10pm.

Hôtel Palym, 7, rue du Port-Vieux (tel. 05 59 24 16 56). Simple, clean rooms (some with TVs) in a friendly, family-run place with bar and pizzeria. Singles 180F. Doubles 210-30F, with bathroom 280-310F. Triples 270F, with shower and toilet 370F. Breakfast 29F. TV room with English-language channel. Reception 8am-midnight. Prices 10% lower Sept.-June. V, MC.

Hôtel Atlantic, 10, rue du Port-Vieux (tel. 05 59 24 34 08). Clean rooms. Singles and doubles 195F, with bathroom 275F. Triples with bathroom 310F. Prices drop Oct.-March. Showers free. Breakfast 28F. July-Aug. guests are encouraged to take *demi-pension* (2 meals per day; 52F per 2 people). V, MC.

Camping: Biarritz, 28, rue d'Harcet (tel. 05 59 23 00 12). Tranquil and close to Milady beach. In July-Aug. Navette-des-Plages bus stops outside the entrance. Other times, take av. Kennedy from the station and follow signs (30min.). 25F per person, 30F per tent, 9F per car. Reception 8am-9:30pm. Open May 1-Sept. 28.

FOOD

In dining, as with everything in Biarritz, style ranks above substance—and you'll pay for it. Elegant mid-priced eateries line av. de la Marne as it splits from av. Edouard VII. Expect 60-80F *menus* and oceans of chintz floral ruffles. You'll see the sea at the more expensive places on pl. St-Eugenie. The **Marché Municipal** on rue des Halles (open daily 7am-1pm) offers a spate of local produce and an abundance of specialties. Next door is a **Codec supermarket,** 2, rue du Centre (tel. 05 59 24 18 01), just off rue Gambetta, stocked with local wines (open Mon.-Sat. 8:45am-7:45pm, Sun. 8:45am-1pm; Sept.-June closed Sun.; V, MC); **Nouvelles Galeries,** pl. Clemenceau, is also well located (tel. 05 59 24 45 25; open Mon.-Sat. 9am-7:30pm; Sept-June Mon.-Sat. 9am-12:30pm and 2:15-7pm; V, MC). Decadent picnickers can head to **Carte Gourmande,** 9, av. de Verdun (tel. 05 59 24 48 30), and gape at heaping platters of *paella,* couscous, and Basque delights priced by the kilo (open Mon.-Sat. 8am-1pm and 4-8pm, Sun. 8am-1pm; V, MC, AmEx).

Bar Jean, 5, rue des Halles (tel. 05 59 24 80 38). Fight the boisterous crowds at the bar for a taste of self-serve basque *tapas* (5F each); then line up for a ladleful of *sangria* (15F). Open July-Aug. daily 8am-3pm and 7:30pm-midnight; Sept.-June closed Tues. night and Wed. V, MC, AmEx.

Bodega la Muleta, 51bis, rue Gambetta (tel. 05 59 24 02 04). Regional dishes from 40F. On Tues. and Fri. nights July-Aug., you may have to nibble your 5F tapas standing amid swirling skirts and dancing locals. Open July-Aug. daily 7pm-3am; Sept.-June Mon.-Sat. 7pm-2am. V, MC.

Le Chalut, 46, av. Edouard VII (tel. 05 59 22 07 37), offers seafood and shellfish, *paella* (65F), *daurade à l'ail* (69F), a 109F *menu,* and fisherman fixtures. Open Mon.-Sat. noon-2pm and 7-10pm. V, MC, AmEx.

Restaurant Indien, corner of rue Gambetta and rue Victor Million (tel. 05 59 22 27 79), beckons temperamental tastebuds and tight wallets with its 46-50F lunch platters. 3-course 99F *menu.* Open daily noon-2:30pm and 7-11:30pm. V, MC.

La Cafetière, 6, av. de la Marne (tel. 05 59 22 23 52), serves traditional French cuisine in an elegant space—this is no cafeteria. 3-course *menu* 66F; dinner *menu* 82F; fish and meat dishes from 69F. Open July-Aug. daily noon-2:30pm and 7:30-10:30pm; Sept.-June, Tue.-Sat. same hours, Sun. noon-2:30pm. V, MC, AmEx.

SIGHTS AND ENTERTAINMENT

Though dominated by a casino, Biarritz's **Grande Plage** isn't much of a gamble—you're sure to find a dazzling wealth of surfers and bathers here. Just north are the less crowded **plage Miramar,** nestled against the base of the cliffs, and **Pointe St-Martin,** where bare bathers repose on the bare sands. A climb up to the top of the lighthouse is free, and the view is priceless, but don't forget to tip the guide 5-10F (open daily summer 10am-noon and 2-6:30pm; winter holidays 2-5:30pm). Protected from the surf by jagged rock formations, the **Port des Pêcheurs** harbors small craft. **BAB Subaquatique** (tel. 05 59 24 80 40), near the steps to the Plateau de l'Atalaye, organizes scuba excursions (open July-Aug.; 155F, wetsuit included).

Jutting out into the Atlantic from the plateau, the craggy peninsula of the **Rocher de la Vierge** gazes over magical views at sunset. From the Rocher, you can see the coastline north to the lighthouse and south along the **plage des Basques,** located at the foot of stupefying cliffs. Get lost in the endless paths cut into the flower-covered coast only two minutes from the *centre ville,* but check the tide schedule before venturing onto the rocks. At low tide, this beach boasts the cleanest water and the most open sand in Biarritz. Directly below, iron crosses embedded in the half-sunken rocks commemorate sailors lost at sea.

The **Musée de la Mer,** 1, Esplanade du Rocher de la Vierge (tel. 05 59 24 02 59; fax 05 59 24 41 98), is a treat for those who like to watch seals do what they do best—finagle fish. The seals' sashimi hits the water at 10:30am and 5pm. Make fish faces at sea creatures in the museum's 24 aquariums of regional fish. (Open July 1-13 9:30am-8pm; July 14-Aug. 15 9:30am-midnight; Aug. 16-Sept. 30 Mon.-Fri. 9:30am-6pm, Sat.-Sun. 9:30am-7pm; May-June Mon.-Fri. 9:30am-12:30pm, Sat.-Sun. 9:30am-7pm. Admission 45F, students 40F.) A new **Musée du Chocolat,** 4, av. de la Marne (tel. 05 59 24 50 50) has been created out of the private collection of the proprietor of **Henriet,** the fine chocolates store on pl. Clemenceau. His own elaborate chocolate sculptures, the chance to see the sculptor in action, an historical exhibit, and a free *cadeau chocolat,* should be plenty to lure you from the hot streets (20F; 5F more for guided tour; open daily 10am-1pm and 2:30-7pm).

The **Casino Municipal** (tel. 05 59 22 44 66) lords over the Grande Plage. Curse Lady Luck as you blow a month's worth of *baguettes* on the 130 greedy slot machines (open daily 11am-3am), blackjack and roulette tables (open 5pm-3am), and the roulette-like *boules* table (open 9pm-3am). Jeans and sneakers are fine for the ground-floor slot machines; you'll need to look snazzier to get upstairs.

In July and August, *pelote* and Basque dancing hit Parc Mazon Mondays at 9pm. Two *cesta punta* tournaments animate the Fronton Euskal-Jai, Parc des Sports d'Aguiléra (call 05 59 23 91 09 for ticket info). The **Biarritz Masters Jaï-Alaï** occurs during two weeks in mid-July and the **Gant d'Or** Wednesdays and Saturdays at 9:30pm for three weeks mid-August. Take bus 1 from the *centre ville* (direction: Bayonne) to "Chassin" and follow bd. du B.A.B. to the Fronton. Mid-July's **International Folklore Festival** draws dancers, singers, and actors from all over. Ask at the tourist office for the program (tickets free). The traveling **Surf Masters** competition takes over the Grande Plage for five days at the end of August. Throughout September, the festival **Le Temps d'Aimer** includes music, ballet, and art exhibits, all just needing to be loved (tickets 60-200F; some student reductions). Catch some screen time—in

Basquing in Their Own Glow

Linguists cannot pinpoint the origin of the Basques' *euskera.* An agglutinate, non-Indo-European language with similarities to both Caucasian and African tongues, *euskera's* roots suggest that the prehistoric Basques may have migrated from the Caucuses through Africa. Historically referred to by Spaniards as *la lengua del diablo* (the devil's tongue)—though supposedly even he could only muster three words—*euskera* has become a symbol of cultural self-determination. *Euskera* has just half a million speakers, although it is spreading through *ikastolas* (all-Basque schools) and media.

Under Spain's Franco regime, Euskadi eta Askatasuna (ETA; Euskadi and Liberty) began an anti-Madrid terrorist movement that has lasted over 30 years. The radical ETA-affiliated party, Herri Batasuna (the United People), drew loud and significant support, though the party has declined in recent years; ETA's violent tactics are roundly eschewed. Targets are almost exclusively the Spanish military, though explosions of car bombs sometimes include civilian areas. In the summer of 1995, a car bomb claimed by the ETA exploded in front of a post office in Madrid. That July, 3 ETA members in Spain and 14 in France were arrested for hatching a plot to assassinate King Juan Carlos of Spain.

French—at **Cinéma Royale,** 8, av. Foch (tel. 05 59 24 21 72; tickets 43F). Hang out around the **Port des Pêcheurs** until midnight, when the rich and reckless strap on their party boots. The **Brasilia Copacabana,** 24, av. Edouard VII (tel. 05 59 24 65 39), plays good music but doesn't admit backpackers in beach wear (cover 60F).

St-Jean-de-Luz

The mighty sailors of St-Jean-de-Luz claimed Newfoundland well over a century before the history books awarded it to the English. Sheltered in a natural port with the Pyrénées looming above, St-Jean prospered on its lucrative New World whaling rights until France signed them away in 1713. Fortunately, the local seamen's fierce reputation enabled them to make up the lost wealth by pirating and profiteering.

In the long run, however, it was sun, sand, and sardines—not the Jolly Roger—that eventually assured St-Jean's prosperity. English and French vacationers, including the author H.G. Wells, "discovered" the town in the late 19th century, adding to its Basque fishing lure. Separated from Spain by what the Basques consider a largely arbitrary border, St-Jean (pop. 13,000) cultivates its Basque heritage in spite of the trinket shops, multilingual menus, and ubiquitous ice cream stands. Each summer, the town's salty staples become guests of honor (and projectiles) at riotous Basque festivals, including a fish soup bash and the *Nuit de la Sardine.*

ORIENTATION AND PRACTICAL INFORMATION

From the station, turn left onto bd. du Commandant Passicot, then bear right around pl. de Verdun to get to av. de Verdun, which leads to the tourist office on pl. Foch. From pl. Foch, rue de la République runs two blocks to **pl. Louis XIV,** the center of town. The beach is a one-minute walk farther, and **rue Gambetta,** in its pedestrian splendor, takes off to the right.

Tourist Office: pl. Foch (tel. 05 59 26 03 16; fax 05 59 26 21 47). Maps and info on accommodations, events, and excursions. Tours of the town in French July-Aug. twice weekly, during school vacations once weekly. Open July-Aug. Mon.-Sat. 9am-8pm, Sun. 10:30am-1pm and 3-7pm; Sept.-June Mon.-Sat. 9am-12:30pm and 2-6:30pm. Keep up with the festive Basques with a free copy of **Programme des Fêtes,** published in early June. Check out the free book *The Basque Country.*

Money: Change Plus, 32, rue Gambetta (tel. 05 59 51 03 43). July-Aug. there is a second office in the Maison Louis XIV. Fair rates, no commission. Open July-Aug.

Mon.-Sat. 8am-8pm, Sun. 10am-1pm and 4-7pm; Sept.-June Mon.-Sat. 9am-12:30pm and 2-7pm. A 24-hr. **ATM** is at **Crédit Mutuel,** 2, bd. Thiers.

Trains: bd. du Commandant Passicot (tel. 08 36 35 35 35). To: Biarritz (10 per day, 15min., 15F); Bayonne (10 per day, 30min., 24F); Pau (5 per day, 2hr., 95F); Paris (10 per day, 5-10hr., 400-600F). Info office open daily 9:30am-12:50pm and 2:15-6:30pm. **Baggage check:** 30F for 72hr.

Buses: ATCRB, pl. Foch, by the tourist office (tel. 05 59 26 06 99). Buy tix on the bus. To: Biarritz (7-13 per day, 16F); Bayonne (7-13 per day, 20F50); San Sebastián, Spain (2 per day; June-Sept. Mon.-Sat.; Oct.-May Tues., Thurs., and Sat.; 1¼hr.; 23F). Office open Mon.-Fri. 8am-noon and 2-6:30pm; July 14-Aug. 15 also open Sat. 9am-noon. **Pullman Basque,** 33, rue Gambetta (tel. 05 59 26 03 37), runs to Basque villages (June-Sept. Fri., full day, 115F); La Rhune (April-Sept. Tues. and Fri., ½-day, 80F); Pamplona, San Sebastián, and Spanish villages (July-Sept. Fri., full day, 135F). Ticket office open July-Sept. daily 8:30am-12:30pm and 2:30-7:30pm; Oct.-June 9:30am-noon and 2:30-7pm. **Basque Bondissant,** 100, rue Gambetta (tel. 05 59 26 25 87), runs 3 buses daily Mon.-Sat. (Sept.-June Mon.-Fri.) to Col de St-Ignace (roundtrip 17F). Earlier buses connect with trains to La Rhune (see page 369). Leaves opposite the Hôtel de Central; buy tix on board (office open Mon.-Fri. 9am-noon and 2:15-6pm, Sat. 9am-noon).

Bike Rental: Ado Peugeot, 5-7, av. Labrouche (tel. 05 59 26 14 95), 1 block from the *gare.* Bikes 60F per day, 280F per week; deposit 600F. *VTTs* 100F per day, 390F per week; deposit 1200F. Open Mon.-Sat. 8:30am-noon and 2-7pm.

Taxis: At the Gare SNCF (tel. 05 59 26 10 11).

Laundromat: Automatique, 3, rue Chauvin Dragon. Open daily 7am-11pm.

Crisis Lines and Outreach Centers: Souffle de Vie, 7, rue Mlle. Etcheto (tel. 05 59 51 22 18). 24-hr. AIDS shelter and info. **Zubia,** 26, rue Tarnaco (tel. 05 59 47 20 20; Mon.-Sat. 8am-7pm), in nearby Ciboure, helps those with drug problems.

Hospital: av. André Ithurraide (tel. 05 59 51 45 45). **Polyclinique,** av. de Layats (tel. 05 59 51 63 63). 24-hr. **medical emergency** service. Take bd. Victor Hugo away from the tourist office. It will become av. André Ithurralde and then N10 (route de Bayonne). Av. de Layats is on the right. **Ambulance** tel. 15.

Police: av. André Ithurraide (tel. 05 59 26 08 47). On the left, just past the *fronton municipal,* heading away from the tourist office. **Emergency** tel. 17.

Post Office: 44, bd. Victor Hugo (tel. 05 59 51 66 50). **Currency exchange** (*pesetas* only). Poste Restante. Open July-Aug. Mon.-Fri. 9am-6pm, Sat. 9am-noon; Sept.-June Mon.-Fri. 9am-noon and 1:30-5:30pm, Sat. 9am-noon. **Postal code:** 64500.

ACCOMMODATIONS AND CAMPING

Hotels fill up rapidly in summer, and it might be tough to reserve since most budget places save their rooms for regular, long-term guests. Arrive early, especially in August. You may have better luck commuting from Bayonne or Biarritz.

Hôtel Toki-Ona, 10, rue Marion Garay (tel. 05 59 26 11 54), 1 block from station. Immaculate, and usually full—but worth a try. Singles 140F. Doubles 180F. Triples 200F. Breakfast 24F. Shower 8F. Reception 8am-11:30pm. Open April-Sept.

Hôtel Verdun, 13, av. de Verdun (tel. 05 59 26 02 55), across from the *gare.* Clean, pretty rooms and oddly appealing, Brady-era TV lounge. Singles and doubles 165-180F, with shower 180-230F; off-season 130F, with shower 180F. Triple with bath 260F; off-season 170F. Call early to reserve. Free showers. Breakfast 20F. Restaurant below serves 3-course 60F *menu.* Reception open 7:30am-9:30pm. V, MC.

Hôtel Bolivar, 18, rue Sopite (tel. 05 59 26 02 00), off bd. Thiers, on a central but quiet street. Clean, basic rooms without carpets. Singles 185F, with shower 240F. Doubles 195-210F, with shower 240F, with shower and toilet 280F. Triples with bathroom 330F. Quads with bathroom 360F. Free showers available 8am-10pm. Breakfast 30F. Open May-Sept. Reception 7am-10pm. V, MC.

Hôtel Kapa-Gorry, 9, rue Paul Gélos (tel. 05 59 26 04 93), a 10-min. walk from the center of town but only 100m from the beach. From bd. Thiers, walk along the beach. Turn right onto av. Pellot, and follow signs to the hotel. Spacious, well-lit, well-kept rooms. Doubles 180F, with shower 200F. Triples 230F, with shower 260F. Showers 10F. Breakfast 27F. Reception open 8am-11pm. V, MC, AmEx.

Camping: There are 14 sites in St-Jean-de-Luz and 13 more within 13km, most of them 3-star. To walk to most of the campsites, take bd. Victor Hugo, continue along av. André Ithurraide, then veer left onto chemin d'Erromardie (20min.). Or take an ATCRB bus headed to Biarritz or Bayonne, and ask to get off near the *camping,* then walk the extra 800m. **Camping Municipal Chibaou Berria,** chemin de Chibaou (tel. 05 59 26 11 94). 20F per person, 23F per tent and car; electricity 11F; reception 7am-10pm. Take N10 (direction: Bayonne) to chemin de Chibaou and turn left to reach the camping zone. Open June-Sept. 15.

FOOD

St-Jean-de-Luz's Basque and Spanish specialties are the best north of the border. The port's famous seafood is kept on ice outside the expensive restaurants on rue de la République and pl. Louis XIV (*menus* 75-250F). Most are heavy on ambience, or at least on bald and bearded men wheezing Lionel Richie favorites into a harmonica.

Informal **Relais de St-Jacques,** 13, av. de Verdun (tel. 05 59 26 02 55), across from the train station, is less central but less pricey. The *menu* includes soup, *tuna à la basquaise,* and dessert (open July-Aug. daily noon-2pm and 7-9pm; Sept.-June closed Sun.; V, MC). **Margarita,** 4, rue l'Eglise, prepares such one-of-a-kind South American dishes as ostrich with green peppers (78F; open daily July-Aug. 12:15-2:30pm and 7:15-11:15pm; Sept.-June closed Sun.-Mon.; V, MC). **Grillerie de Sardines,** quai de Renon, overlooking the port off rond-point de Lattre de Tassigny (tel. 05 59 51 18 29), is a simple place popular with everyone but sea creatures. Savor omelette-like *tuna pipérade* (54F), grilled tuna (48F), or sardines (38F; open mid-June to mid-Sept. daily 11:30am-2:30pm and 6-10pm; V, MC). **Le Pavillon de Jade,** 7, av. de Verdun (tel. 05 59 26 05 54), across from the station, presents a 70F three-course lunch *menu* and a selection of Vietnamese, Chinese, and Thai dishes (soups 30-40F, main dishes 35-60F, appetizers 25-40F; open daily noon-1:30pm and 7-10:30pm; Sept.-June closed Wed.; V, MC).

Tiny shops huddle on bd. Victor Hugo and on rue Gambetta, between pl. Louis XIV and bd. Thiers. Check out the **market** on pl. des Halles (a handful of merchants open daily 7am-1pm; full force Tues., Fri., and summer Sat. 7am-1pm). Get your Nutella fix at **Codec,** 87, rue Gambetta (tel. 05 59 26 46 46; open Mon.-Sat. 8:30am-12:45pm and 3-7:30pm, Sun. 8:30am-12:30pm), or **8 à Huit,** 46, bd. Victor Hugo (tel. 05 59 26 09 15; open Mon.-Sat. 8:30am-1pm and 3:30-8pm, Sun. 8:30am-1pm).

Chez Dodin, 80, rue Gambetta (tel. 05 59 26 38 04), scoops its own ice cream in its 1960s-style *salon de thé* and taunts cultural purists with its *beret basque* (chocolate mousse shaped like a beret, rolled in chocolate sprinkles, 13F; 11F per scoop; open July-Aug. daily 8:30am-1pm and 2:30-9pm; Sept.-June 8:30am-12:45pm and 2:30-7:30pm; V, MC). **Chez Etchebaster,** at 42, rue Gambetta (tel. 05 59 26 00 80), is known for its cream-filled *gâteaux basques* (open Tues.-Sat. 8am-12:30pm and 3-7:30pm, Sun. 8am-1pm and 4-7pm; V, MC).

SIGHTS

Though young Louis XIV was smitten with the charms of Marie Mancini, he was convinced to iron out border disputes by marrying Maria Teresa of Spain. Lovesick Louis sojourned in St-Jean-de-Luz in 1660, reluctantly awaiting his wedding. Fortunately, the union proved successful; upon the queen's death, the Sun King sighed, *"C'est le premier chagrin qu'elle me cause"* ("This is the first time she has caused me sorrow"). A portal in the **Eglise St-Jean Baptiste,** to the right of the main entry, was ceremoniously sealed for eternity after the royal newlyweds left the church—or so goes the legend. Check out the bilingual prayer books in French and Basque, the glittering display of favorite local saints behind the altar, and the unusual wooden galleries where men traditionally sat while women enjoyed the luxury of nave seating. (Open July-Aug. Mon.-Sat. 8am-noon and 2-7:15pm, Sun. 8am-1pm and 3-7pm; Sept.-June Mon.-Sat. 8am-noon and 2-6:30pm, Sun. 8am-noon and 3-6:30pm.) The **Maison Louis XIV,** pl. Louis XIV (tel. 05 59 26 01 56), is frozen in its glory days as Louis' lair. (Visits only by 30-min. guided tour leaving every 30min.; written explanations in English.

Open June-Sept. Mon.-Sat. 10:30am-noon and 2:30-5:30pm, Sun. 2:30-5:30pm; July-Aug. until 6:30pm. Admission 15F, students 12F.)

Before heading to the beach, take time to walk through the tiny streets overlooking the port, shining with half-timbered, whitewashed houses trimmed in red. In the days before Sherwin-Williams, rumor has it that residents used ox-blood to get the colors just right. Wash your hands of this bloody history anywhere along the stretch of sand that borders the happening **promenade Jacques Thibaud.** Sheltered by protective dikes, St-Jean-de-Luz's beach and harbor provide some of the best conditions for sailing and windsurfing in the Basque region. Farther on, the waves of the **plage d'Erromardi** present the perfect opportunity to hit the surf.

ENTERTAINMENT

Summer rollicks with Basque festivals, concerts, and the championship of *cesta punta* (July-Aug. Tues. and Fri. at 9:15pm, tickets 50-120F at the tourist office). **Toro de Fuego,** with pyrotechnics, dancing, and a man in a bull costume, heats up summer nights in pl. Louis XIV (July-Aug. Wed. at 10:30pm and Sun. at 11:30pm).

The biggest annual festival is the three-day **Fête de St-Jean,** the weekend closest to St-Jean's Day (June 21). At the **Fête du Thon** (the first Sat. in July), the town gathers around the harbor to eat tuna (60F), toss confetti, and pirouette to music. The fun doesn't stop as St-Jean fêtes its favorite little fish with the big **Nuit de la Sardine,** the second Saturday in July at the Campos-Berri, next to the *cesta punta* stadium. It features an orchestra, Basque songs, and, yes, **sardines** (40-60F). The fabulous **Fête du Ttoro,** ffeatures exxciting acctivities innvolving ffish ssoup *(ttoro)*. The *Fête* takes place on the first Saturday in September; the next day, *Luziens* can sheepishly confess to the priests whom they pelted with fish guts hours earlier.

To get in on the fishy fun at sea level, sign up for a four-hour **fishing trip** that leaves from the port (ask at the tourist office). For more water fun, hit **Le Spot,** 16, rue Gambetta (tel. 05 59 26 07 95), for surfing lessons (180F for 2hr., including equipment) or rental equipment (wet suit: ½-day 40F, full day 60F; bodyboard: ½-day 40F, full day 70F; open daily 9:30am-9pm; mid-Sept. to Easter closed Sun.; V, MC). Wiggle out of your wetsuit at the sandy, surfer-filled burger joint in back (heavenly hamburgers 32-45F; open until 10pm; V, MC). **Cinéma Rex,** 74, rue Gambetta (tel. 08 36 68 91 23), offers fun without any sand in your trunks (40F, Mon., Wed., and students 30F; film schedules at the tourist office).

■ Near St-Jean-de-Luz: La Rhune

Ten km southeast of St-Jean-de-Luz, **Col de St-Ignace,** stretching from Ascain to Sare, serves as a gateway to the Basque country's loveliest vantage point. From the departure point on Col de St-Ignace, board the wooden, two-car cog-train which labors at a snail's pace up the mountainside to the 900m summit at **La Rhune.** Each tortuous turn reveals a postcard-perfect display of forests hovering above sloping farmland. Herds of wild Basque ponies *(pottoks)* boldly return your curious stares. The slopes teem with cavalier sheep bounding hell-for-leather down the mountainside. At the peak, chilling air and gusty winds prevail even in summer. La Rhune *(Larun)* is Spanish soil; shop-owners slip in and out of French and Spanish.

Two **trains** depart for La Rhune July through September, daily at 10am and 3pm; additional trains leave every 35 minutes starting at 9am if there are enough people to warrant a departure. May through June and October through November 15, trains leave only on Saturdays, Sundays, and holidays at 10am and 3pm. Purchase tickets (2hr., roundtrip 38F) from the **SHEM** office (tel. 05 59 54 20 26; at the end of the tracks in Col de St-Ignace). In summer, expect a one-hour wait. **Basque Bondissant** (tel. 05 59 26 25 87) runs three buses daily from St-Jean-de-Luz to the departure point at Col de St-Ignace, the last of which is too late in the evening to ascend to La Rhune (roundtrip 19F; see **Buses,** page 367). If you decide to walk back down from La Rhune, take the well-marked path to the left of the tracks down to Ascain, and travel the tricky 3km on D4 back to Col de St-Ignace (1½hr.). Descend cautiously, since loose rocks often make for treacherous footing.

St-Jean-Pied-de-Port

Set against red clay hills, this Pyrenean village (pop. 1600) epitomizes the spicy splendor of the Basque interior. Climb narrow, cobblestoned streets through the *haute ville* to the enchanting, dilapidated fortress, or stroll along the calm Nive for glimpses of the riverbed with its shimmering rocks and acrobatic trout. Through the centuries, this medieval capital of Basse-Navarre has hosted a continual procession of pilgrims. The faithful squeeze through the **Col Roncevaux** (Roncevaux pass) *en route* to Santiago de Compostela, Spain. Though popular with modern tourists, St-Jean beckons the curious to explore a side of the Basque countryside historically trod only by the sandaled feet of pilgrims.

ORIENTATION AND PRACTICAL INFORMATION

From the station, take a right on av. Renaud, following it up the slope until it ends at av. de Gaulle. Turn right to go to the tourist office. There's just one street behind the ramparts—turn left on rue de la Citadelle to get to—gasp—the citadel. Twenty-five km from the village lies the Forêt d'Iraty, a hiker's and cross-country skier's paradise.

Tourist Office: 14, av. de Gaulle (tel. 05 59 37 03 57; fax 05 59 37 34 91), outside the old city walls. Walking and hiking itineraries 10F. Open June to mid-Sept. Mon.-Sat. 9am-12:30pm and 2-7pm, Sun. 10:30am-12:30pm and 3-6pm; mid-Sept. to May Mon.-Fri. 9am-noon and 2-7pm, Sat. 9am-noon and 2-6pm.

Money: Crédit Agricole, 11, rue Ste-Eulalie (tel. 05 59 37 23 11), between pl. Renaud and av. de Gaulle. Open Mon.-Fri. 9am-noon and 2-5pm. 24-hr. **ATM.**

Trains: av. Renaud (tel. 05 59 37 02 00). To Bayonne (7 per day, 1hr., 48F). Station master may let you leave bags for free. Open 6am-12:30pm and 1-7pm.

Bike Rental: Garazi Cycles, 1, pl. St-Laurent (tel. 05 59 37 21 79). Take av. de Gaulle or rue du 11 Novembre and turn left on av. de Jai-Alai. *VTTs* 50F per ½-day, 100F per day, 150F per weekend, 400F per week; passport deposit. Call for bike tours (85F per ½-day, 150F per day). Open Mon.-Sat. 8:30am-noon and 3-6pm.

Medical Assistance: Fondation Luro, Ispoure (tel. 05 59 37 00 55). Take av. de Jai-Alai past the bike rental shop. Cross the bridge into Ispoure, and take an immediate left. The clinic is the 2nd house on the right. For **taxi-ambulance,** call 05 59 37 05 70 or 05 59 37 05 00. **Medical emergency** tel. 15.

Police: on rue d'Ugagne (tel. 05 59 37 00 36). **Emergency** tel. 17.

Post Office: 1, rue de la Poste (tel. 05 59 37 04 80). Poste restante. Open Mon.-Fri. 9am-noon and 2-5pm, Sat. 9am-noon. **Postal code:** 64220.

ACCOMMODATIONS AND CAMPING

St-Jean offers pretty rooms at ugly prices; don't expect anything under 160F. Consider daytripping from Bayonne or stay in the *gîtes;* the tourist office keeps a *gîte* list.

Gîte d'Etape: Off the **GR10** and **GR65** hiking trails. 12 happy bunks await in an 18th-century house just inches from the traffic at 9, route d'Uhart (tel. 05 59 37 12 08). From the tourist office, cross the bridge and take your first right on the opposite bank. The street becomes route d'Uhart after you pass the city walls (5min., follow signs to Bayonne). Hot showers, fridge, kitchen. 45F. The couple that runs the *gîte* has opened up a *chambre d'hôte* (rooms only), supplying doubles that you'll never want to leave for 120F-140F (110F for lone voyagers). Triples 150F. Breakfast 20F. Showers and hiking tips free.

Hôtel Itzalpea, 5, pl. du Trinquet (tel. 05 59 37 03 66; fax 05 59 37 33 18), outside and just opposite the old wall. 9 remodeled, classy rooms. Room 11 enjoys a refreshing mountain view. Singles and doubles with shower, TV, and telephone 200F. Triples and quads 280F. Breakfast 30F. Great restaurant (see below). V, MC.

Hôtel des Remparts, 16, pl. Floquet (tel. 05 59 37 13 79; fax 05 59 37 33 44). Take av. de Gaulle over the Nive and turn right onto the first street. Large, neat rooms with soothing hues. Singles with shower 180-205F. Doubles with shower 200-230F. Triples and quads with shower 265F. Breakfast 30F. Open April-Sept. daily; Oct.-March Mon.-Fri. V, MC.

Camping: Shaded **Camping Municipal** (tel. 05 59 37 11 19) is on the Nive banks. From pl. du Marché, turn onto rue de l'Eglise, following it past the church to the next bridge. Cross the river; the site is on your left on av. du Fronton (13F per person, 8F per tent, 8F per car). **Camping Bidegainia** (tel. 05 59 37 03 75), 1km away on rte. de Bayonne in Uhart-Cize (follow directions to the *gîte* above), is popular with fishers (7F per person, 7F per tent; shower 5F; open March-Oct.; reception 8am-noon and 2-11pm; V). **Europ' Camping** (tel. 05 59 37 12 78), 1.5km from St-Jean on D918 to Bayonne, has a restaurant, pool, and sauna (30F per person, 43F per tent and car; electricity 21F; open Easter-Oct. 8am-10pm).

FOOD

Fresh rainbow trout—served complete with head, eyes, and tail—star in St-Jean's superb show of Basque specialties. **Hôtel Itzalpea's** restaurant assembles a generous four-course 85F *menu* with hearty vegetable *potage,* trout, a choice of meats, and dessert. The 60F *menu* shrinks to three courses of Basque specialties. Trout 40F (open July-Sept. daily noon-2pm and 7:30-9:30pm; Oct.-June Mon.-Wed. noon-2pm, Fri.-Sun. noon-2pm and 7:30-9:30pm; V, MC). The talented staff at **La Vieille Auberge, Chez Dédé,** 3, Porte de France (tel. 05 59 37 16 40), throws together a 50F three-course *menu du chef* of Basques creations and serves it in the cave-like restaurant (open noon-2pm and 7-9pm). The **Restaurant-Bar Chocolainia,** 1, pl. du Trinquet (tel. 05 59 37 01 55), at the entrance of the *haute ville* from the *gare,* serves 10F mugs of warm, sweet sangría that will transform the day into a blur. (3-course *menus* 55-85F; open daily March-Oct. noon-2:30pm and 7-9:30pm; V, MC, AmEx.)

Farmers bring *ardigazna* (tangy, dry sheep's milk cheese) to the Monday **market** on pl. du Marché, a day-long treasure-trove of obscure and delicious concoctions (9am-6pm). Picnic supplies loiter in the *boulangeries* and *boucheries* on **rue d'Espagne.** Cans, cookies, and colas congregate at **Le Relais de Mousquetaires** on rue d'Espagne (tel. 05 59 37 00 47; open Mon.-Sat. 9:30am-12:30pm and 4-7:30pm).

SIGHTS AND ENTERTAINMENT

St-Jean's streets and fairy-tale location create a beautiful location to explore. The ancient *haute ville,* bounded by **Porte d'Espagne** and **Porte St-Jacques,** consists of one narrow street, rue de la Citadelle, bordered by houses made of the region's crimson stone. As you amble up the street, be tempted—in spite of your sophisticated tastes—by the wee little craft shops in the *arceaux.*

The narrow rue de la Citadelle leads from the plastic-trinket feeding-frenzy in the *haute ville* to the remains of St-Jean-Pied-de-Port's **citadel.** Although the interior of this fortress is shut to the public, visitors enjoy unlimited access to the grounds, with guard towers washed in flowered ramparts and a dark, foul-smelling moat. Descend to the *haute ville* on the nearly hidden staircase that runs along the ramparts at the far end of the moat. The staircase leads to the haunches of **Eglise Notre-Dame-du-Bout-du-Pont,** a small distance from pl. du Marché on rue de l'Eglise. Once a fortress, the church betrays its dark past with rocky, low-lit crevices instead of side chapels. Carefully patterned stained glass casts a mist of light over the rest of this simple rock church (open daily 7am-9pm). Stepping out onto the junction of rue de l'Eglise and rue de la Citadelle, take the short walk up to the 13th-century **Prison des Evêques,** 41, rue de la Citadelle. The edifice served first as the medieval headquarters of local bishops and acquired its current name in the 19th century, when it temporarily doubled as a detention chamber. A recorded French narration guides visitors by exhibits of stuffed birds, sheep-shearing tools, and a few broken tombstones. The single gnarled shackle in the dank cellar will send chills up your spine. (Open daily July-Sept. 10am-8pm; Oct. to mid-Nov. and Feb.-May 10:30am-12:30pm and 2-6pm.

Admission 10F.) If you need to see the sun, a pleasant, wooded walk leads from the church along the Nive to the **Pont Romain** (about 2km).

In the summer, *bals* (street dances) and concerts provide free frivolity; Basque choirs and *pelote* matches add local color (June-Sept. Mon. and Fri. 5pm, and Sat. 9pm; 40F; check the tourist office for other times). The soft-hearted, pot-bellied, beret-wearing Basques you've come to know and love get buff for the **Force Basque** competition held the third Sunday in July. Events include the hoisting of 150lb. hay-bales (they've made it into an art) and gritty tug-of-war matches. Admission to the *fronton*—the *pelote arena*—is 40F, but you can watch a match for free from the fence. A four-day weekend around August 15 brings the **Basque Fêtes Traditionelles de Garazi,** with fireworks and singing and dancing in the streets.

Cinéma le Vauban, 4, rue Renaud (tel. 05 59 37 28 47 for listings), has a respectable rotating schedule of current international movies often dubbed into French. On Monday nights at 9:30pm in July and August, gymnasts and clowns turn a bullfight into a cow-tease at a rollicking satire of matadorian ceremony, the **Gala Comic-Taurin,** in the arena, chemin la nasse (45F; info at tourist office).

■ Near St-Jean-Pied-de-Port: The Forêt d'Iraty

Ever since pilgrims trekked across the mountainous trail from Paris to Santiago de Compostela, hiking has been important to the area near St-Jean-Pied-de-Port. Pick up the *Ensemble de Circuits de Randonnées dans et autour de St-Jean-Pied-de-Port* from the St-Jean tourist office (10F, in French). It indicates five marked trails that leave from the office and take one to six hours. Shorter hikes amble through the woods near St-Jean; the longer ones require a bit more planning.

Superb yet easy hiking awaits in the **Forêt d'Iraty,** 25km southeast of St-Jean-Pied-de-Port along the D18, near the Spanish border. The brochure *Bienvenue en Forêt d'Iraty* lists six relatively easy hikes ranging from two to five hours (free at St-Jean's tourist office). The **Chalets d'Iraty** (tel. 05 59 28 51 29; **postal code:** 64560 Larrau), at the base of the French side of the Fôret, has info on hiking, *refuges,* bike rentals, and horseback riding (75F per hour). No public transportation runs to the forest valley, but St-Jean's tourist office offers excursions, as does **Garazi Cycles** (see page 370). On the winding roads, hitching is difficult and dangerous; biking is a muscle-straining venture unless you're in training for the Tour de France.

Gascogne (Gascony)

Ice-capped mountains, plunging slopes of forested greenery, and the **Parc National des Pyrénées** make Gascogne a paradise for lovers of the outdoors. Hiking, mountain climbing, skiing, and mountain biking opportunities face you at every turn, and the national park remains the last refuge of *isards* (mountain antelopes), royal eagles, vultures, and the endangered *ours des Pyrénées* (pint-sized brown bears).

To most, Gascogne also means excellent country cuisine. King Henri IV reminisced about the cuisine of his native Pau even after he had claimed Paris. Gascony still produces the best *foie gras* and goose and duck pâtés in the south. Abundant fresh fish and the *vins de Béarn,* superb rosé wines, complete regional feasts. Local farmers use cow and sheep milk to make various *fromages des Pyrénées,* which range in flavor from mild to sadistically strong. For dessert, try the flaky *croustade* pastry, made with *pruneaux* (prunes) or apples. The region's drink of choice is *armagnac,* a fiery brandy infused with suggestions of the oak casks in which it ages.

The **Grande Randonnée No. 10 (GR10),** passing through the breathtaking Pyrénéan scenery, connects the Atlantic to the Mediterranean. Inexpensive accommodations at convenient intervals facilitate travel through the mountains, but you'll need a good map to find them. Four IGN maps of the *Parc National* (scaled 1:25,000) are available in most bookstores. Although reservations for accommodations are not normally *de rigueur,* consider writing ahead to the offices of the *Parc National* in Cauterets or Gavarnie. This organization, along with the **Club Alpin Français (CAF)** and the **Comité des Sentiers de Grande Randonnée,** oversees a network of *gîtes d'étape* (rural lodgings) along trails. In wilder areas, *refuges* provide adequate shelter. Always equip yourself fully for hikes in the mountains. *Never drink unpurified mountain water.* Remember that weather in Gascogne is extremely unpredictable; be ready for sudden storms and temperature fluctuations.

GETTING AROUND

The best tip for getting around the region is not to consider Gascony a region at all. Though the Gascon towns of Pau, Lourdes, and Cauterets can all be reached from Tarbes, they are well connected to more interesting cities. Toulouse draws the whole region like a whirlpool into its hub train station. Lourdes and Pau are regular stops on the Toulouse-Irun line, permitting easy access to the Pays Basque and to Languedoc-Roussillon. SNCF buses (accepting Eurail) run from Lourdes to Cauterets; check tourist offices for schedules. Using Pau or Lourdes as a base to visit the southern cities may be the most practical way to delve into this sprawling region.

Pau

Fragrant Pau lounges leisurely amid the scents and hues of its floral surroundings, enjoying a panoramic view of the not-so-distant snowy mountain peaks from its elevated bd. des Pyrénées. Pau, whose famed château was the birthplace of Henri IV, formerly served as the capital of the state of Béarn. Annexed to France in 1620, the town receded from the spotlight when the French royalty decided it preferred Biarritz. A much-needed influx of British tourists in the mid-19th century helped Pau to regain its cultural footing. A destination in itself, Pau (pop. 90,000) is a splendid place to relax, socialize, and stock up on necessities for a trek into the mountains.

ORIENTATION AND PRACTICAL INFORMATION

Pau lies 195km west of Toulouse in the foothills of the Pyrénées. Pau's main strips have as many names as Italy has political parties. Fortunately, you can pick up the tourist office's large, indexed map, *Pau-Ville Authentique.* To get to the tourist office and the *centre ville* from the train station, ride the free *funiculaire* across the street, which climbs to **bd. des Pyrénées** every three minutes (Mon.-Sat. 6:45am-12:30pm, 12:55-7:30pm, and 7:55-9:40pm, Sun. 1-9:40pm). If there is a sign with the word *"fermé"* on it, then you too will be climbing the zigzag path outlined in white fences to the top of the hill. At the top, the tourist office is at the other end of tree-lined **pl. Royale.** The *vieille ville* is but a left turn away, down rue Henri IV.

Tourist Information: Tourist Office, pl. Royale (tel. 05 59 27 27 08; fax 05 59 27 03 21), next to the Hôtel de Ville. Gregarious staff. Free hotel reservations. Free copies of *Béarn en Fêtes,* listing summer activities; and *L'été à Pau,* a compilation of the summer's hotels, dance, theater, cinema, music, and sports happenings. *Béarn Pyrénées, Guide des herbergements touristiques en Béarn* lists names and phone numbers for *gîtes d'étape* and campgrounds dotting the area. Office open Mon.-Sat. 9am-6pm, Sun. 9:30am-6pm; Sept.-June Mon.-Sat. 9am-noon and 2-6pm. **Service des Gîtes Ruraux,** 124, bd. Tourasse (tel. 05 59 80 19 13; fax 05 59 30 69 65), in the Cité Administrative, gives advice on mountain lodgings and will make reservations. Open Mon.-Fri. 9am-12:30pm and 2-5pm.

Money: 24-hr. **ATMs** monkey around at 2, rue du Docteur Simian; 23, rue Louis Barthou; and cours Bosquet, across from the post office.

Flights: Aéroport Pau-Pyrénées (tel. 05 59 33 33 00). **Air Inter,** rue Mar. Foch (tel. 05 59 33 34 35), flies March-Oct. to Paris. Call **Voyages L'Etoile** (tel. 05 59 02 45 45) for info on shuttle buses to the airport.

Trains: av. Gaston Lacoste (tel. 08 36 35 35 35), at the hill base by the château. To: Bayonne (7 per day, 1¾hr., 82F); Biarritz (6-7 per day, 2hr., 87F); Bordeaux (9 per day, 2hr., 157F); Lourdes (7 per day, 30min., 39F); Nice (2 per day, 9½hr., 392F); Paris (8 per day, 5hr., 407F); St-Jean-de-Luz (4 per day, 1¾hr., 92F). Info desk open in summer Mon.-Fri. 9am-6:40pm, Sat. 9am-6pm. **Lockers** 15-30F.

Buses: CITRAM—Courriers des Basses Pyrénées, 30, rue Gachet (tel. 05 59 27 22 22). To Agen (1 per day, 3¼hr., 150F). Office open Mon. 2:30-6:15pm, Tues.-Fri. 9:40am-12:15pm and 2:30-6:15pm, Sat. 9:40am-12:15pm. **Société TPR,** 2, pl. Clemenceau (tel. 05 59 82 95 85), across from CITRAM. To: Lourdes (5 per day, 1¼hr., 34F50); Bayonne (2 per day, 2¼hr., 76F); Biarritz (2 per day, 2½hr., 82F).

Public Transportation: STAP, rue Gachet (tel. 05 59 27 69 78), next to the Citram office. Info and maps. Tickets (valid 1hr.) 6F. Open Mon.-Fri. 8:30am-noon and 1:30-6pm. Bus stops are narrow white posts with green tips.

Taxis: (tel. 05 59 02 22 22), 24hr. To the airport from the *centre ville* 100-130F.

Bike Rental: Pedegaye Cyclesport, 23, bd. Charles de Gaulle (tel. 05 59 32 48 74), on the route de Bayonne. *VTTs* 100F per day, 250F per week. Deposit 1000F. V, MC. Open Mon. 2-7pm, Tues.-Sat. 9am-noon and 2-7pm.

Hiking Info: Companie du Sud, 27, rue Mar. Foch (tel. 05 59 27 04 24).

English Books: Librarie Tomet, 3bis, pl. Laborde (tel. 05 59 30 77 33). Open Mon.-Fri. 9am-noon and 2-7pm, Sat. 2-7pm.

Laundromat: Laverie Gambetta, 6, rue Gambetta. Open 7am-10pm.

Youth Center: Bureau Information Jeunesse, Complexe de la République, rue Carnot (tel. 05 59 27 89 49). Open Mon.-Fri. 9am-noon and 2-5pm.

Crisis Lines: SOS Amitié (tel. 05 59 62 02 02), a shoulder to lean on.

Hospital: 4, bd. Hauterive (tel. 05 59 92 48 48). **Medical emergency** tel. 15.

Police: (tel. 05 59 98 22 22), on rue O'Quinn. **Emergency** tel. 17.

Post Office: cours Bosquet (tel. 05 59 98 98 60), at rue Gambetta. **Currency exchange.** Poste restante (postal code: 64089). Photocopies 1F. Open Mon.-Fri. 8am-6:30pm, Sat. 8am-noon. **Postal code:** 64000.

ACCOMMODATIONS AND CAMPING

Auberge de Jeunesse (HI), 30ter, rue Michel Hounau (tel. 05 59 72 61 00; fax 05 59 27 44 60). From the station take bus 7 (direction: Trianon) to "Fossie" (Mon.-Sat. 7:25am-7:10pm, 6F), then backtrack 1 block to rue Père, turn left, and take a right immediately onto rue Michel Hounau. If walking from the *gare,* take the *funiculaire,* cross pl. Royale to rue St-Louis, and turn right on rue Maréchal Joffre. Walk 10min. along this main drag, which becomes rue Maréchal Foch and then cours Bosquet. Bear left onto rue E. Garet at the first fork, turn left on rue Lespy, bearing right onto rue St-François-d'Assise at the next intersection. Walk 2 blocks and turn right at rue Michel Hounau (20min.). A workers' *foyer* that doubles as a hostel. Hotel-style amenities at *auberge* prices. Singles with showers and toilets, cafeteria, and game room. Kitchen. Most rooms are under renovation but should be completed by Feb. '97. Members 66F. Non-members and over 24 98F. Breakfast included, meals 35F. Sheets 15F. Wheelchair accessible. 24-hr. reception.

Hôtel d'Albret, 11, rue Jeanne d'Albret (tel. 05 59 27 81 58). Spacious, quiet rooms and friendly management on a *rue*-ette near château. Singles 85F, with shower 110F. Doubles 90F, with shower and toilet 145F. Triples 125F, with shower and toilet 155F. Shower 10F. Breakfast 18F. Reception 7:30am-10:30pm.

Hôtel le Béarn, 5, rue Maréchal Joffre (tel. 05 59 27 52 50). Centrally located. Singles and doubles with shower 90F. Doubles and triples with shower 130F. Quads with shower 150F. Shower 10F. Breakfast 15F. Reception 6:30am-10:30pm.

Hôtel de la Pomme d'Or, 11, rue Maréchal Foch (tel. 05 59 27 78 48), between post office and pl. Clemenceau. 70s color scheme and dim lighting, but clean and cheap. Ask for a room facing the courtyard. Singles 85F, with shower 105F, with shower and toilet 115F. Doubles 100F, with shower 125F, with shower and toilet 140F. Triples with shower 200F. Shower 10F. Breakfast 20F.

Camping: Camping Municipal de la Plaine des Sports et des Loisirs (tel. 05 59 02 30 49), a 6km trek from the station. Take bus 7 from the station to pl. Clemenceau (direction: Trianon or pl. Clemenceau) and switch to bus 4 (direction: Bocage Palais des Sports), which will take you to the final stop alongside an aquatic stadium with 3 pools (40F per person and tent; open June-Sept.). **Camping du Coy** (tel. 05 59 27 71 38) in Bizanos, is a 20-min. walk east of the train station. (23F per person, 10F per tent; open daily 8am-9pm).

FOOD

The region that brought you tangy *béarnaise* sauce has no paucity (geddit?) of specialties: salmon, pike, *oie* (goose), *canard* (duck), and *assiette béarnaise,* a succulent platter that can include gizzards, duck hearts, and asparagus. Elegant regional restaurants gather in the château area known as the *quartier du hédas.* Inexpensive pizzerias and ethnic eateries can be found on **rue Léon Daran** and adjoining streets. Olympic-sized **Champion** supermarket, in the new **Centre Bosquet** megaplex on rue Bosquet, satisfies shoppers Monday through Saturday from 9am to 7:30pm. The **market** at **Les Halles,** pl. de la République, is a maze of vegetable, meat, and cheese stalls (open Mon.-Sat. 6am-1pm). The **Marché Biologique,** pl. du Foirail, offers organic produce to the health-conscious (Wed. and Sat. 7:30am-12:30pm).

L'Entracte, 2bis, rue St-Louis (tel. 05 59 27 68 31). This *salon du thé* and its outdoor tables are packed at lunch. Generous salads 48F; *plat du jour* 40F; regional meat dishes beginning at 40F. Open Mon.-Sat. 9am-3:30pm and 7-11pm. V, MC.

La Fiancée du Desert, 6, rue Tran (tel. 05 59 27 27 58). Creative mixture of Armenian-Lebanese food. 45F vegetarian *menu,* sandwiches and lamb dishes, and desserts you can smell a block away. Open Tues.-Sat. noon-2:15pm and 5-10:30pm.

Boulangerie Abert, 4, rue du Mal. Joffre (tel. 05 59 80 04 33). Not a restaurant, but some of the finest pastries in town. Sample the melt-in-your-mouth mocha pastry (10F), or choose from 20 flavors of ice cream (single scoop 6F; double scoop 10F). *Salon de thé* in the back. Open Tues.-Sun. 6:30am-7:30pm.

SIGHTS AND ENTERTAINMENT

Formerly the residence of *béarnais* viscounts and Navarrese kings, the 12th-century **Château d'Henri IV** (tel. 05 59 82 38 00) is now a national museum. Pau's pride and joy overlooks the river from the highest point in the town. Glorious Gobelin tapestries, well-preserved royal chambers, elaborately decorated ceilings, and ornate chandeliers grace the castle. French tours of the château leave every 15 minutes and last an hour (open daily 9:30-11:45am and 2-5:15pm; last tour 30min. before closing; English brochure available; admission 28F, ages 18-25 18F, under 18 free). The third-floor **Musée Béarnais** (tel. 05 59 27 07 36) covers the region's cultural development.

Sinister mannequins in native costumes keep visitors looking over their shoulders. Beady-eyed stuffed animals celebrate royal hunting successes. Follow the fascinating evolution of the *beret béarnais* before you exit to the lovely (free) gardens (museum open daily 9:30-11:45am and 2-5:15pm; admission 10F).

Small and well-worn, the **Musée des Beaux-Arts,** rue Mathieu Lalanne (tel. 05 59 27 33 02), features dark and dusty Italian, Spanish, French, Dutch, and Flemish paintings on its ground floor. Climb resolutely to the contemporary art on the second floor (open Wed.-Mon. 10am-noon and 2-6pm; admission 10F, students 5F).

Nightlife ranges from 12F *demi-tasses* to **Le Dakari,** av. de Latre de Tassigny (tel. 05 59 83 91 61), which asks 50F for entrance to its mixed dance-club scene (open Thurs.-Tues. midnight-5am). A worthwhile compromise is **Cinéma le Méliés,** 6, rue Bargoin (tel. 05 59 27 60 52; call 05 59 83 73 33, 24hr., for current listings), which shows some foreign films in *v.o.* (tickets 35F, students 28F; closed Aug.).

Mid-July through mid-August, the annual **Festival de Pau** brings plays, concerts, recitals, ballet performances, and poetry readings to the château courtyard and the Théâtre St-Louis (some free, admission 100-190F, students 60-180F). Pick up a schedule at the tourist office (for reservations, call 05 59 27 27 08). During the first week of August, the **Festival International des Pyrénées** covers the region with 45 folk ballet troups from 25 countries (info and tickets tel. 05 59 39 98 98).

Lourdes

In 1858, young Bernadette Souibirous reported seeing the first of what would total 18 visions of the Virgin Mary in the Massabielle grotto in Lourdes. Over time, "The Lady" instructed Bernadette to repent, drink, and wash in a nearby stream, and to "go and tell the priests to build a chapel here so that people may come in procession." Today, over five million visitors from 100 countries process to Lourdes annually. Toting rosary beads, filling water bottles shaped like the Virgin, and hoping for a miracle, the faithful and the curious flock to the daily Blessing of the Sick.

The original "if you build it, they will come" city, Lourdes (pop. 16,300) is committed to the comforts of its visitors. The service industry cleans 18,000 hotel rooms each day and makes sure that the gardens, streets, lawns, and views are spotless enough to be inspirational in and of themselves. Though the cynical sometimes sojourn at Lourdes planning to revel in the Graceland of the religious world, healing is serious business: thousands of terminally ill people wander, roll, and are carried through Lourdes' streets in search of an unearthly cure. Pilgrimage season runs from about Easter to October. Visit Lourdes in the spring, summer, or early fall, when hiking trails in the Pyrénées offer sanctuary from streets paved with kitschy souvenirs and extraordinary religious rituals.

ORIENTATION AND PRACTICAL INFORMATION

The train station is on the northern edge of town; the *centre ville* is 10 minutes away. To get from the station to the **tourist office,** turn right onto av. de la Gare, bearing left onto av. Maransin at the first intersection. The office, on the right, is in a modern glass complex (5min.). To get to the **grotto** and most other sights, follow av. de la Gare through the intersection, turn left on bd. de la Grotte, and follow it as it snakes right at pl. Jeanne d'Arc. Cross the river Gave to the Esplanade des Processions, the Basilique Pius X, and the grotto (10min.). Lourdes may be the most wheelchair- and visually impaired-accessible town in France.

Tourist Office: pl. Peyramale (tel. 05 62 42 77 40; fax 05 62 94 60 95; e-mail lourdes.edi.fr/lourdes). Despite 5 million visitors each year, the English-speaking staff receives newcomers with aplomb. Good maps and a list of Lourdes' 260 hotels. Board with lists of available rooms outside. Open May-Oct. 15 Mon.-Sat. 9am-7pm, Sun. 10am-6pm; March 15-April daily 9am-12:30pm and 1:30-7pm, Sun. 10am-6pm; Oct. 15-March 14 Mon.-Sat. 9am-noon and 2-6pm. Info booth **Touristes et Pèlerins Isolés** in the arcades to the right of the basilica. Open daily 9am-noon and

2-6pm. All info on religious visits is managed by the Catholic Church-affiliated **Sanctuaire de Notre-Dame de Lourdes** (tel. 05 62 42 78 78), which has a **Forum d'Info** opposite the basilica. The staff speaks 7 languages and is thrilled to help. Open daily 8:30am-noon and 2-6pm; Sept.-June 9am-noon and 2-6pm.

Money: Crédit Mutuel, 3, rue Lafitte, has a 24-hr. **ATM.** Also **BNP,** 9, rue Lafilte.

Trains: Gare SNCF, 33, av. de la Gare (tel. 08 36 35 35 35). To: Pau (7 per day, ½hr., 37F); Bagnères-de-Bigorre via Tarbes (6 per day, 1hr., 40F); Bordeaux (7 per day, 3hr., 165F); Bayonne (5 per day, 2hr., 102F); Toulouse (8 per day, 2½hr., 120F); Paris (5 per day, 7-9hr., 395F). **Lockers** 20F with 72-hr. max.; **luggage storage** 30F. Open daily for info and reservations 8:40am-noon and 1:30-5:40pm.

Buses: *gare routière*, pl. Capdevielle (tel. 05 62 94 31 15), behind the Palais des Congrès. Open Mon.-Fri. 8am-noon and 2-6:45pm, Sat. 8am-noon. **SNCF buses** run from the station to Cauterets (3-6 per day, 50min., 36F). **Tarbes les Pyrénées** runs buses direct to Bagnères-de-Bigorre (3 per day, 1hr.).

Local buses: run from the *gare* to the grotto every 15min. (Easter-Oct. daily 7:45-11:45am and 1:45-6:15pm., 10F).

Taxis: tel. 05 62 94 31 30 for *gare;* Easter-Oct. 05 62 94 31 35 for grotto.

Bike Rental: Cycles Arbes, 51, av. Alexandre Marqui (tel. 05 62 94 05 51), 1km out of town; follow route de Tarbes. *VTTs* 70F per ½-day, 120F per day, 450F per week. Deposit 1500F. Open Tues.-Sat. 9am-noon and 2-7:30pm. V, MC, AmEx.

Youth Center: Forum Lourdes/Bureau Information Jeunesse (tel. 05 62 94 94 00) in the center of pl. de Champ Commun beyond Les Halles. Open Mon.-Fri. 9am-noon and 2-6pm.

Laundromat: Laverie GTI, 10, av. Maransin. Open daily 8:30am-7pm.

Information for people with disabilities: A thorough, religiously inclined guide to the facilities entitled *Guide de Lourdes* (20F) is available from the Association Nationale Pour Integration Handicapés Moteurs, 8, rue Basse (tel. 05 62 94 83 88).

Hospital: Centre Hospitalier, 3, av. Alexandre Marqui (tel. 05 62 42 42 42). At the intersection of av. de la Gare, av. Marqui, and av. Maransin. **Medical emergency:** 2, av. Marqui (tel. 05 62 42 44 36).

Police: 7, rue Baron Duprat (tel. 05 62 42 72 72). The station is 1 block from the tourist office down rue Duprat (on the left). **Emergency** tel. 17.

Post Office: 31, av. Maransin (tel. 05 62 42 72 00). Photocopies. Poste restante. **Automatic currency exchange** takes bills only, not traveler's checks. Open Mon.-Fri. 8:30am-6:30pm, Sat. 8:30am-noon. **Postal code:** 65100.

ACCOMMODATIONS, CAMPING, AND FOOD

Lourdes has more hotels than any French city but Paris, many geared towards fragile pilgrim budgets. The rooms on av. de la Gare are as cheap as any you'll find in town.

L'Auberge de la Jeunesse, Centre des Rencontres "Pax Christi," 4, route de la Forêt (tel. 05 62 94 00 66; fax 05 62 42 94 44; winter tel. 05 59 84 17 08; fax 05 59 30 09 79), a hearty 10-min. walk up the road behind the basilica. Christian organization has 7 single-sex, 12-person dorms for pilgrims and those willing to do dishes. Bed and breakfast 47F, shower included. Lunch or dinner 40F. Sheets 20F. Laundry. No lockout or curfew. Reception 9am-10pm. Open April-Oct. 20.

Hôtel Ste-Monique, 13, rue de la Grotte (tel. 05 62 94 11 93), offers clean, bright orange rooms and spotless bathrooms despite its somewhat dim hallways. Singles 85F. Doubles with shower 145-175F. Triples and quads 220F. Shower 10F. Breakfast 23F. Open Easter-Nov. 5.

Hôtel Paix et Continental, 3, rue de la Paix (tel. 05 62 94 91 31). Walk past the tourist office to pl. du Marcadale; rue de la Paix is across the pl. on the right. Spotless accommodations. Two night min. stay. 2 singles at 70F. Singles and doubles 90F, with shower 150F. Triples and quads 130F, with shower 170F. Shower 15F.

Camping: Camping de la Poste, 26, rue de Langelle (tel. 05 62 94 40 35) has 33 spaces in a convenient location 2min. beyond the post office. 12F per person, 17F per site, hot shower 7F, electricity 15F. If you're under 25 and can warble a fair French rendition of "Jesus Loves Me," you'll be welcome at **Camp des Jeunes, Ferme Milhas,** av. Mgr-Rodhain (tel. 05 62 42 79 95; fax 05 62 42 79 98; tel. 05 62 42 78 38 in winter; ask to be connected to the camp), a 15-min. uphill walk out of town. From the pont Vieux, follow signs to Cité St-Pierre. **Dorm accommodations** in 10-person rooms 26F, singles or doubles 35F; camping in your own tent is 16F. Sleeping bag 26F per night. Showers included. You are strongly encouraged to participate in evening services and community activities with church groups staying at the camp. Ask for directions and reserve at the Service Jeunes booth in the big plaza by the sanctuaries. Closed Christmas week.

The *épiceries* along the processional route will gladly assuage your hunger for uncompassionate—almost sinful—prices. Find relief in **Casino,** 9, pl. Peyramale (tel. 05 62 94 03 87; open July-Sept. Mon.-Sat. 6:30am-12:30pm and 3:30-7:30pm, Sun. 7:30am-12:30pm; Oct.-June closed Mon.) or the bigger **Prisunic supermarket,** 9, pl. du Champ-Commun (tel. 05 62 94 63 44; open Mon.-Sat. 8:30am-7:30pm, Sun. 8am-noon; V, MC), which has a reputation to protect. An impressive congregation of produce, flowers, second-hand clothing, and books gathers daily at the **market** at **Les Halles,** pl. du Champ-Commun (daily 8am-1pm, every other Thurs. until 5pm).

One might think that with 27.86 restaurants per block, Lourdes would have mercy in the form of culinary variety. But in Lourdes, all processions lead straight to *steak-frites* for 45-55F. Inexpensive restaurants and pizzerias multiply like the loaves and fishes. *Menus* from 55-85F stack up along the pilgrim's passage, **rue de la Grotte. La Rose des Sables,** 8, rue des 4 Frères Soulas (tel. 05 62 42 06 82), on the little street beside the tourist office, offers up fantastic couscous (lamb 65F, vegetarian 55F), served in Moroccan-style earthenware (open daily July-Oct. noon-3pm and 7-10pm; Nov.-May closed Mon.; closed June). **Reflect des Îles,** 16, rue Basse (tel. 05 62 94 00 36), on the second floor of Hôtel Chrystal, hides its spicy, abundant, and delicious *reunionists* creations under a bushel of nondescript names such as "vegetable curry" (32F; open Feb.-Nov. daily noon-1:30pm and 7-9pm; V, MC).

SIGHTS

The **Caverne des Apparitions** (better known as *la Grotte*), where Bernadette experienced her visitations, has become the focus of Lourdes' pilgrimage. Try visiting during the lunch hour to avoid lines. Nearby, the spring where Bernadette washed her face is on tap, so you can freshen up or fill your canteen with the transparent treasure. The grotto itself has become a stupendously uninspiring cement creation (no shorts or tank tops; fountain and grotto open daily 5am-midnight).

Two churches were constructed double-decker style above Bernadette's *grotte.* In the **Basilique du Rosaire,** completed in 1889, an enormous Virgin Mary looms like the Wizard of Oz over the huddled masses. The **upper basilique,** consecrated in 1876 with a more traditional interior failed to set a precedent for its younger siblings (both open daily Easter-Nov. 1 6am-7pm; Nov. 2-Easter 8am-6pm).

The stadium-sized echo chamber known as the **Basilique Pius X,** designed as an atomic bomb shelter, garnered an international design prize in 1958, despite looking like a hybrid of the new Paris Opera and the parking garage of the Starship Enterprise. Covering an area of 12,000 square meters, its concrete cavern fits 20,000 souls with room to spare. At 10m intervals, super-electric *gemmail* stain-glass rectangles are appropriately cubist versions of the traditional sunlit model (open daily Easter-Nov. 1 6am-7pm; Nov. 1-Easter 8am-6pm, excluding masses).

The **Procession of the Blessed Sacrament** and the **Blessing of the Sick** are huge ordeals held daily at 4:30pm starting at the *grotte* (or in the Basilica Pius X in bad weather or "great heat"). Fight for bench space or watch from the upper basilica's balcony. As a one-day pilgrim, you can join the procession and march along the esplanade behind rolling ranks of wheelchairs (meet your fellow pilgrims at 8:30am or 2:30pm at the "Crowned Virgin" statue in front of the basilica). A solemn torchlight procession blazes from the *grotte* to the esplanade nightly at 8:45pm. Add to the glow by lighting a long-burning candle for a few francs in the booths by the river Gave. It will be herded by a guard whose job it is to mind the flickering tapers.

The **Musée du Gemmail,** 72, rue de la Grotte (tel. 05 62 94 13 15), more or less successfully converts famous art works to an abstract, multi-layered glass design.

Check out a Mona Lisa with a smile more mysterious than the one in the Louvre (open Easter to mid-Oct. daily 9-11:45am and 2-5:45pm; free). Down the street, the less satisfying **Musée Grevin,** 87, rue de la Grotte (tel. 05 62 94 33 74), offers wax-figure depictions of the lives of Bernadette and Jesus (explanations in English; open daily July-Aug. 9-11:40am, 1:30-6:30pm and 8:30-10pm; April-June and Sept.-Oct. 9-11:40am and 1:30-6:30pm; 33F, students 27F). The **Passeport Visa Lourdes** (130F) provides admission to four museums and two tourist train rides through the town and the surrounding countryside. For **hiking,** the truly experienced can contact **Club Alpin Français,** pl. de la République (tel. 05 62 42 13 67), which leads difficult day-long trips (open Easter-Oct. 9am-noon). The closest group of guides for all levels is in **Argelès-Gazost,** about 15km from Lourdes. Contact the Argelès tourist office (tel. 05 62 97 00 25) between 6pm and 7pm to reach the guides.

For one week beginning Easter weekend, the **Festival International de Musique Sacrée** fills the local holy buildings with Bach and Mozart. Tickets are available through the tourist office (80-160F).

Cauterets

Set in a breathtaking valley on the edge of the **Parc National des Pyrénées Occidentales,** Cauterets is a perfect base for exploring the nearby towns and mountains. In winter, some of the best skiing in the region is just a gondola, chairlift, or T-bar away. Long, white runs drop hundreds of meters down the slopes, while cross-country ski trails delve into the heart of the national park. In summer, green pastures and an extensive network of hiking paths lure international trekkers.

ORIENTATION AND PRACTICAL INFORMATION

Cauterets runs lengthwise along the river Gave and is small enough to walk across in three minutes. From the bus station, turn right and follow av. Leclerc to the tourist office at pl. Foch. Ascend to the mountains on the *téléphérique,* located above the intersection of bd. B. Dulau and rue du Pont Neuf.

Tourist Office: pl. Foch (tel. 05 62 92 50 27; fax 05 62 92 59 12). List of hotels available, but not the best source of info on the outdoors. The *Plan de Ville* is a useful guide to the town. English spoken. Open July-Aug., Christmas, and French winter holidays daily 9am-7pm; Sept.-June 9am-12:30pm and 2-6:30pm.

Hiking Information: Parc National des Pyrénées, Maison du Parc on pl. de la Gare (tel. 05 62 92 52 56; fax 05 62 92 62 23). Regional maps and day-hike maps for sale. Loads of free info on the park and its trails. Includes a small educational **museum** featuring the park's flora, fauna, and activities (10F). Open mid-Dec. to mid-Oct. daily 9:30am-noon and 3:30-7pm; sometimes closed half of May.

Money: Crédit Agricole, 16, rue Belfort (tel. 05 62 92 50 13), has an **ATM.**

Buses: pl. de la Gare (tel. 05 62 92 53 70). **SNCF buses** run to Lourdes (6 per day, 1hr., 35F; tickets at the station). **Lourdes-Les Pyrénées** buses (tel. 05 62 42 22 90) run to Gavarnie via Pierrefitte (2 per day, 55F) and to Luz-St-Sauveur (2-3 per day, 37F); buy tickets on board. Pick up a schedule in any regional tourist office, *gare,* or *gare routière.* Open Mon.-Fri. 9am-7:30pm, Sat.-Sun. 8:30am-7:30pm.

Téléphérique and Ski Information: (tel. 05 62 92 50 27). The *téléphérique* (cable car), 1 block from the station, services Col d'Ilhéou. Summer departures are every 30min. from 9am-12:15pm and 1:45-5:45pm. Winter departures are from 8:45am-5pm (8am-8:30pm during school vacations). Roundtrip 42F. Ski tickets 115F per day, 125F with insurance. Cross-country skiing 20F per afternoon, 30F per day. Better rates on multi-day pass. Ski season is Dec.-April.

Bike and Mountain Equipment: Skilys, route de Pierrefitte (tel. 05 62 92 58 30), on pl. de la Gare. *VTTs* with guide 105-175F per ½-day, 240-350F per day, 1500-2500F deposit; without guide 60F per ½-day, 100F per day. Also rents boots, skis, ski boots, rollerblades, and ice skates. ID deposit. Sells bicycle tire repair kits and tent stakes. Open daily 9am-7pm; winter 8am-7:30pm. V, MC, AmEx.

Weather: Météo-Montagne (tel. 08 36 65 02 65), in French. Forecast for area mountains updated twice daily.
Laundromat: Laverie Automatique, 19, rue Richelieu. Open daily 7am-10pm.
Mountain Rescue Service tel. 05 62 92 75 07, the Gendarmerie.
Medical emergency tel. 05 62 92 40 00.
Police: av. du Docteur Domer (tel. 05 62 92 51 13). **Emergency** tel. 17.
Post Office: 2, rue des Combattants (tel. 05 62 92 53 93). Poste restante. **Currency exchange.** Open Mon.-Fri. 9am-6pm, Sat. 9am-noon; Sept. 15-June Mon.-Fri. 9am-noon and 2-5pm, Sat. 9am-noon. **Postal code:** 65110.

ACCOMMODATIONS AND FOOD

Centre UCJG (Unions Chrétiennes des Jeunes Gens de France) "Cluquet," av. Docteur Domer (tel. 05 62 92 52 95), on the outskirts of town, just past the tennis courts. Sheets, showers, clean kitchen facilities, and a washing machine. **Camp** in your own tent (20F), or in one of their 4 12-bed tents (40F). 6 bungalows for 2-3 people are 55F per person, but reserve well in advance. Open June 15-Sept. 15. In winter, bungalows available if you call ahead.

Gîte d'Etape: Le Pas de l'Ours, 21, rue de la Raillère (tel. 05 62 92 58 07; fax 05 62 92 06 49), a few blocks up the street opposite the tourist office. The *gîte* welcomes hikers, climbers, and skiers. Well-equipped kitchen and 20 clean but crowded co-ed bunks. 65F. Also 3-person hotel rooms at 90F per person. Breakfast 40F. Dinner 80F. Sauna 45F for 1 person, 70F for 2. Clothes laundered 50F; reception 8am-noon and 2-11pm. Open Dec.-April 14 and May 16-Oct. V, MC.

Hôtel-Restaurant Christian, 10, rue Richelieu (tel. 05 62 92 50 04), offers 3-language Bibles and simple but clean rooms. Friendly hosts will guard bags while you hike. Facilities include an elevator, bridge salon, bar, ping-pong table, *pétanque* playing ground, and a garden out back. Singles and doubles 140F, with shower 170F, with shower and toilet 200-226F. Triples with shower 285F. Quads with shower 332F. Breakfast 32F. Open Feb.-Oct. 15. V, MC.

Stop at the covered **Halles market** in the center of town, on av. Général Leclerc, for fresh produce (daily 8:30am-12:30pm and 2:30-7:30pm). An **open-air market** is held Fridays on pl. de la Gare, before the *téléphérique* terminal (July-Aug. 8am-5pm). **Codec supermarket,** av. du Général Leclerc (tel. 05 62 92 50 35), stocks groceries galore (open Mon.-Sat. 8:30am-12:30pm and 4-7:30pm, Sun. 8:30am-12:30pm). On the same street, **Casino,** 18, av. Leclerc (tel. 05 62 92 56 38), has canned goods, produce, and no lunch break (open daily 8am-7:30pm; Nov.-June Mon.-Wed. and Fri.-Sat. 8am-12:30pm and 3:30-7:30pm, Thurs. and Sun. 8am-12:30pm; V, MC). **La Flore,** 11, rue Richelieu (tel. 05 62 92 57 48), concocts delicious 69F, 75F, and 90F three-course *menus* (open June 16-Sept. and Dec.-Easter daily noon-3pm and 7pm-2am; Easter-June 15 and Oct. closed Mon.; V, MC). **Chez Gillou,** 3, rue de la Raillère, bakes *tourtes myrtilles* and *pastis des Pyrenees* (35F) that will send you off with a smile (open daily July-Aug. and Feb.-March 7am-1pm and 3:30-7:30pm; Sept., Dec., and April-June 7:30am-12:30pm and 4-7pm).

SIGHTS

The mountains.

ENTERTAINMENT

Not only have the Pyrénées bestowed their spectacular presence on Cauterets, they have bubbled hot sulfuric waters to the delight of well-heeled guests. The springs have inspired gushings from visitors as exalted as Victor Hugo, George Sand, and Chateaubriand. Believed since Roman times to cure sterility, these *thermes* lure flocks of the faithful to drink, be submerged in, or get hosed down with this wet, smelly cure-all. Cure prices vary, but if you can catch a glimpse of the white-uniformed nurses turning a firehose of sulfuric steam on their lily-skinned charges, you'll be cured of any desire to join the grimacing devotées, free of charge.

The truly lazy and desperate can catch occasional movies at the **Cinéma,** 14, Esplanade des Oeufs (tel. 05 62 92 52 14). The **patinoire** (skating rink) hosts skating nights on an eccentric weekly schedule posted in the window of the tourist office, pl. Clemenceau. The rink itself can be found through the parking lot of the Gare SNCF, pl. de la Gare (admission 32F, children 15F; skate rental 18F). The less athletic can spend the day pursuing the sun as it makes its rounds of the many cafés.

■ Near Cauterets: Pyrénées Mountains

One of France's seven national parks, the **Parc National des Pyrénées** cradles 230 lakes, 400 flower species, the endangered brown bear and lynx, and 200 threatened colonies of marmots in its snowcapped mountains and lush valleys. The park has been the subject of battles among government authorities, environmental activists, and native villages since its boundaries were drawn in 1968. Despite the turmoil, the Pyrénées soothe with sulfur springs, tempt with unattainable peaks, change dramatically with the seasons, and never fail to awe a constant stream of visitors.

Before heading off on any trail, it is important to procure an intelligible map of the area. Experienced hikers can pick up maps at sporting good stores, but anyone in need of advice, suggestions, or clarification should head to the friendly and helpful **Parc National Office,** Maison du Parc (tel. 05 62 92 52 56; fax 05 62 92 62 23), in Cauterets. If you are a more casual hiker, hiking with children, or strapped for time, pick up the office's *Promenades en Montagne* maps (35F) of 15 different trails beginning and ending in Cauterets, all labeled with estimated duration (1hr.-2 days), difficulty, and refuges. These trails have been designed to offer the average person the chance to trade an enjoyable workout for an eyeful of stunning scenery.

Traipsing across the expanse of the Pyrénées, **Grande Randonnée 10 (GR 10)** leads its followers through glorious mountains. Along streams, among pine forests, over craggy rocks and through tiny towns, this well-worn east-west path has introduced hundreds of thousands of hikers to the marvelous powers of the Pyrénées. As far as trails go, the **Haute Randonnée Pyrénées (HRP),** aptly marked by a triangular sign with the head of a *chamois,* is the most challenging mountain experience. Teetering along rocky peaks at the highest elevations, the HRP trails are only for the skilled, well-trained, and well-equipped. Assess your ability and talk with the folks at the Parc National Office before heading up to the thin air. For either level of trail, pick up one of the purple 1:25,000 maps of the *Parc National des Pyrénées* (56F). For the Cauterets region, use the #1647 Vignemale map published by Institut de Géographie Nationale (IGN), at the **Parc National Office** at **La Civette bookstore,** 12, pl. Clemenceau (tel. 05 62 92 53 87; open daily July-Aug. and ski season 8:30am-1pm and 2:30-8pm; otherwise 9:30am-12:30pm and 3:30-7:30pm; V, MC, AmEx).

If gallivanting with mountain goats is too lofty a goal, you can opt for less strenuous ways to enjoy the Parc National. The **Bureau des Guides,** pl. Clemenceau (summer tel. 05 62 92 62 02), in Cauterets, offers beginner to intermediate guided tours and guides for rock-climbing, canyoning, hiking, and skiing (in winter). Medium-difficulty tours cost 70-200F per person, harder ones go for 300-350F per person. Tours leave as early as 6am from the Cauterêts tourist office. Not all trips run daily, so confirm dates (open daily 10am-12:30pm and 3:30-7:30pm).

If you're short on time, consider the four-hour roundtrip journey to the **Pont d'Espagne,** graced by sensational scenery and waterfalls. Follow the chemin Demontzey to the town La Raillère, then take the section of GR10 called "Sentiers des Cascades." If you lose the path, stick to the right bank of the river. Once at the top, many hitch rides back down with the tourists who congregate at the café alongside the bridge. Or take the **télésiège** (ski-lift) from there to an easy path that leads directly to the sky-blue **Lac de Gaube** (*télésiège* June-Oct. daily; 29F roundtrip). A prettier 4-km roundtrip hike begins at the Pont d'Espagne (buses run there from Cauterets) along the Vallée de Marcadau to the Refuge Wallon-Marcadou.

Several **accommodations** options exist for overnight excursions. *Gîtes* in the park average 75F a night and are strategically spaced in towns along the GR10. The Parc

National office in Cauterets will help you plan an itinerary and make *gîte* reservations, as will the Service des Gîtes Ruraux (tel. 05 59 80 19 13) in Pau (see page 374, or page 53 for general information about mountain accommodations). The formal rule of the Parc is that long-term **camping** is not allowed in the wilderness. It is possible, however, to set up a tent at least an hour's walk from the nearest road at dark and break camp at daybreak, provided the site is left as it was found and all garbage is carried out of the Parc. Camping zones also exist near each refuge. You'll have to skip toasting gooey *eigenvalues,* as the lighting of fires is prohibited.

The GR10 breaks its east-west meandering and makes a loop connecting Cauterets with the mountain of Vignemale and the villages of Gavarnie and Luz-St-Sauveur. Circling counter-clockwise from Cauterets to Luz-St-Sauveur, the **Refuges Des Oulettes** (on the IGN map, elevation 2151m; call ahead, tel. 05 62 92 62 97; 67F per night; open June-Sept. and sporadically March-May) is the first shelter choice past the **Lac de Gaube.** Dipping into the **Vallée Lutour,** the **Refuge Estom** (60-70F per night, open all year) rests undisturbed from communication near **Lac d'Estom.**

Tackle the icy expanses of the **Pic du Vignemale** (3298m) and press on to the **Refuge Jan Da Lo** (tel. 05 62 92 40 66), in **Gavarnie** near the halfway mark of the loop to pay the required 48F and to pass out for the night. The grandiose, snow-covered **Cirque de Gavarnie** and its mist-wreathed waterfall are also accessible from Gavarnie. Hordes of tourists heave themselves onto **horses** for the hoist to the Cirque (2hr., odiferous roundtrip from Gavarnie 90F). Gavarnie's **tourist office** (tel. 05 62 92 49 10; fax 05 62 92 41 00) is open daily 9am-noon and 1:30-6:30pm. During the third week in July, the **Festival des Pyrénées** animates the foot of the Cirque de Gavarnie. Nightly performances begin as the sun sets over the mountains; afterwards, torches are distributed to light the way back to the village (tickets 120F, students under 25 100F at tourist offices, bookstores, banks, and hotels in the region).

Should you plan not to continue, you will have to retrace your steps back to Luz-St-Sauveur or take the bus. **Luz-St-Sauveur,** in the Vallée du Toy, is itself an excellent launching pad into the Pyrénées. The **Maison du Parc National et de la Vallée** (tel. 05 62 92 38 38), off Luz's pl. St-Clément, gives precise information (open daily 9am-noon and 2-6pm; off season closed Sat.-Sun.). Lourdes-Les Pyrénées **buses** (tel. 05 62 42 22 90) run to Luz-St-Sauveur from Cauterets (2-3 per day, 37F).

For skiing information in Cauterets, see page 379. **The Bureau des Guides,** pl. Clemenceau (winter tel. 05 62 92 55 06), provides guides and assistance. The tourist office has free *plans des pistes,* maps of downhill and cross-country ski paths with varying levels of difficulty. Many nearby skiing towns are accessible by SNCF buses from Cauterets or Lourdes. **Luz-Ardiden** (tel. 05 62 92 81 60; fax 05 62 92 87 19) offers a day of downhill or cross-country skiing for 100F, students 72F. **Barèges** (tel. 05 62 92 68 19; fax 05 62 92 69 13) and **La Mongie** (tel. 05 62 91 94 15) are the two biggest skiing stations of the Pyrénées; a joint ticket is 140F per day.

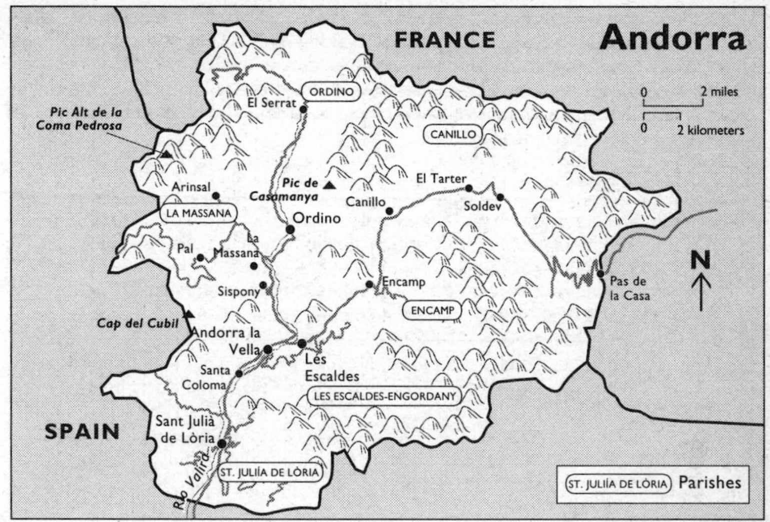

ANDORRA

Perched high in the Pyrénées, Andorra (pop. 65,000, area 468 sq. km) remains one of Europe's most intriguing geographical and political anomalies. Andorra has depended on its two larger neighbors for the tourism and trade that feed its economy—it accepts Spanish pesetas and French francs and has no native currency. While its soaring peaks and pristine wilderness draw many visitors, Andorra's most popular attraction is its low sales tax. A string of duty-free shops has transformed this nation into the mall of Europe. To appreciate Andorra, break away from the outlets and explore beautiful Lilliputian villages cradled by Brobdingnagian mountains.

According to legend, Charlemagne founded Andorra in 784 in gratitude to the area's inhabitants for helping his army against the Moors. In 839, Charles II, Charlemagne's grandson, transferred sovereignty to the Spanish counts of Urgell, who gradually ceded their power over the region to the Church of Urgell. A series of complex marriages delivered partial power to France. Known officially as the *Principat d'Andorra* (Principality of Andorra), Andorra is ruled by two "co-princes"—French President Jacques Chirac and the Bishop of Urgell, Dr. Joan Martí Alanis. A popularly elected "General Council of the Valleys," consisting of 28 members and a Cap de Govern (Prime Minister) elected by the council, serves as the government. Until 1933, only third-generation Andorran men over 25 could vote. In 1990 Andorra created a commission to draft a constitution that was adopted on March 14, 1993, and liberalized the political system, paving the way for political parties.

Andorra's citizenry is trilingual, but Catalan, the official language, is spoken with pride (ask a question in Spanish and the response will come in Catalan). Other manifestations of cultural pride appear in summer when each of the seven parishes holds its own three-day jubilee. These spectacles start in late July and continue through mid-September. The national *festa* is on September 8, in honor of Andorra's patron saint *Nostra Senyora de Meritxell* (Our Lady of Meritxell).

Andorran cuisine closely resembles that of Spanish Catalonia. A pork-lover's paradise, Andorra produces piggy wonders such as *butifarra* (sausage), *bringuera,* and *llonganiça.* These, along with *paella* (rice with saffron, seafood, sausage, and chicken) are local diet staples. *Trinxat,* a mashed potato and cabbage concoction, is more subtly flavored than its ingredients would suggest.

Most Andorran towns are scattered along the principality's three branches of "highways." Additionally, an extensive network of hiking trails and cabins make the country's beauty accessible to those on foot. North of the capital, clear lakes and icy mountain peaks shelter tiny villages. From December to April, many Andorran towns serve as bases for skiing. As major towns are separated by mere kilometers, most of the country is accessible by local buses.

GETTING THERE

Planes and trains defer to cars and buses in Andorra—the country has no airport and no train station. French and Spanish border police require a valid passport or an EU identity card to enter the country. Two highways—one from Spain and one from France—access Andorra. All traffic from France must enter Andorra at the town of **Pas de la Casa;** the gateway town on the Spanish side is **Sant Julià de Lòria.** From France, take the **SNCF train** to l'Hospitalet (on the Toulouse-Ax-les-Thermes-Barcelona line, 4 per day), La Tour de Carol (on the same line, as well as on the **petit train jaune** from Villefranche), or Ax-les-Thermes. **Société Franco-Andorrane de Transports (SFAT),** carrer la Llucuna (tel. 82 13 72), runs from Ax-les-Thermes to Andorra la Vella (3 per day, 2hr., 47F) via l'Hospitalet. **Autos Pujol Huguet,** based in Andorra (tel. 84 10 19), goes to Andorra la Vella from La Tour de Carol (2 per day, 1½hr., about 47F). Most buses stop at **Pl. Guillemó,** known to locals as **Pl. de las Arcades,** off Av. Princep Benlloch at the end of carrer Dr. Negui. **Andor-Inter/Samar buses** (in Toulouse tel. 05 61 58 14 53; in Andorra tel. 82 62 89) run from Toulouse to Andorra (8am, 3½hr., 138F) and leave from pl. de las Arcades. Buses from La Seu drop folks off at the bus stop on Av. Princep Benlloch, 6, off pl. Princep Benlloch. Madrid buses leave from another bus station on carrer **Bonaventura Riberaygua.** To get to the station from pl. Princep Benlloch, follow Av. Meritxell to the other side of the river. Make an immediate right after crossing, an immediate left, then take the fourth right and go straight for four or five blocks (20min.).

GETTING AROUND

Driving in Andorra la Vella is a nightmare. Drivers will find maps useless; it's best to follow signs. There is a free, unpublicized **parking lot** on Prat de la Creu for all cars with foreign registration. Use this centrally located lot and don't bother paying a parking meter; foreign visitors are exempt. From the tourist office, go down the hill to the light. Turn left, go past the multi-story pay lot, and the free lot is on the left.

Efficient **intercity buses** connect villages along the three major highways that meet in Andorra la Vella. The country is navigable in an hour via public transportation; most towns are only 10 minutes away. Bus rides cost about 125ptas, but can be anywhere between 100 and 1525ptas. (Buses do not accept francs.) Bus lines are not indicated by number or color; pay attention to the direction signs posted in bus windows. For more info, contact **Cooperative Interurbana Andorrana,** Av. Princep Benlloch, 15 (tel. 82 04 12). The tourist office's pamphlet is easy to decipher.

Dual French and Spanish administration of the postal system has resulted in separate **post offices,** overseen by France and Spain, within a few blocks of one another. Correspondence forwarded to **Poste Restante** in Andorra la Vella may arrive at either post office; mail marked **Lista de Correos** arrives at the Spanish office. The tourist office recommends the French service (except for Spain-bound mail).

Phone communications in Andorra are handled exclusively by the **STA** network. To use a public pay phone, you must purchase an STA *teletarjeta* (telecard). The cards are available in any post office or kiosk. France Télécom cards do not work in Andorran payphones. Collect calls are not available, and AT&T does not maintain an

As of 1995, all of Andorra's phone numbers, formerly 5 digits, added an 8 in front to make 6 digits. You may still occasionally see 5-digit numbers listed. Just dial 8 before any of these, or you will be subjected to a confusing Catalan recording.

access network with Andorra (despite what the Access Number Guide may say). For **directory assistance** within Andorra, dial 111. Andorra's **telephone code** is 376.

Andorra la Vella

Andorra la Vella (Andorra the Old; pop. 20,000) is a narrow, cluttered road flanked by duty-free shops. Anything but *vella,* the modern city disguises its old quarter well, upstaging it with flashing neon signs. La Vella is not completely misnamed, however, since you will probably sprout some gray hairs waiting to cross the street.

ORIENTATION AND PRACTICAL INFORMATION

The city's main thoroughfare, **Avinguda Meritxell,** rushes through the city beginning at Pl. Princep Benlloch in the heart of the tiny **barri antic** (old quarter). To the left (west) of the *plaça* facing the Eglésia de Sant'Esteve, Av. Meritxell becomes **Av. Princep Benlloch.** Calle Dr. Negüi, the first right (a sharp turn) off Av. Princep Benlloch from the *plaça,* leads to Plaça Guillemó. To get to the tourist office from the **bus stop** on Av. Princep Benlloch, continue east (away from Spain) just past the *plaça* on your left, then take C. Dr. Villanova, which curves down to the right.

Tourist Office: Av. Doctor Villanova (tel. 82 02 14; fax 82 58 23). Many brochures, good map. Open July-Aug. Mon.-Sat. 9am-1pm and 3-7pm; Oct.-June Mon.-Sat. 10am-1pm and 3-7pm, Sun. 10am-1pm. **Info booth** at Av. Meritxell, 33 (tel. 82 71 17). Open Mon.-Sat. 9am-1pm and 4-8pm, Sun. 9am-1pm and 4-7pm.

Money: Banc Internacional, Av. Meritxell, 32 (tel. 82 06 07). **Currency exchange,** no commission. Open Mon.-Fri. 9am-1pm and 3-5pm, Sat. 9am-noon.

American Express: Viatges Relax, Carrer Roc dels Escolls, 12 (tel. 82 20 44), the third right off Av. Meritxell from pl. Princep Benlloch. Open Mon.-Fri. 9am-1pm and 4-7:30pm, Sat. 9:30am-1pm.

Taxis: Stations at pl. Guillemó and at pl. Rebés (tel. 82 69 00 for pick-up).

Car Rental: Avis (tel. 82 00 91), at the bus station on Av. Tarragona, 42. Must be over 19 and have had a drivers license at least 1yr. Prices start at 4900ptas per day, 39ptas per km, or 19,500ptas for 3-day weekend with unlimited mileage.

Weather and Ski Conditions: in French, tel. 84 88 53; in Catalan, tel. 87 10 00.

Hospital: Clinica Nostra Senyora de Meritxell, Av. Fiter I Rossell (tel. 86 80 00). **Red Cross:** tel. 82 52 25

Police: C. Prat de la Creu, 16 (tel. 82 12 22). **Emergency** tel. 110.

Post Offices: French Post Office, Carrer Pere d'Urg, 1 (tel. 82 04 08). Poste restante. Open Mon.-Fri. 8:30am-2:30pm; Oct.-May Mon.-Fri. 9am-7pm, Sat. 9am-noon. **Spanish Post Office,** Carrer Joan Maragall, 10.

ACCOMMODATIONS, CAMPING, AND FOOD

It's as easy to find a place to drop as it is to find a place to shop—pensions abound.

Pensió La Rosa, Antic Carrer Major, 18 (tel. 82 18 10), just south of Av. Princep Benlloch. Immaculate rooms in which blossoms of various species and colors compete for dominance over wallpaper and bed spreads. Exceptional hall bathroom. Singles 1700ptas. Doubles 3000ptas. Breakfast 350ptas.

Hotel Costa, Av. Meritxell, 44 (tel. 82 14 39), above Restaurant Mati. Big rooms, some with views of the city, are bright and well worn. 1300ptas per person.

Camping: Camping Valira (tel. 82 23 84), located behind the **Estadi Comunal d'Andorra la Vella.** Shade, video games, hot showers, and an indoor pool. 500ptas per person, per tent, and per car. Reception open 8am-1pm and 3-9pm. Call ahead—it fills up. 2½km down the road, **Camping Santa Colomba** (tel. 82 88 99) charges 400ptas, but has no video games.

Andorra's restaurants serve mediocre food at mediocre prices. You're better off eating out of the supermarkets in nearby Santa Coloma (you can't miss them) or the **Grans Magatzems Pyrénées,** Av. Meritxell, 10 (open Mon.-Fri. 9:30am-8pm, Sat.

9:30am-9pm, Sun. 9am-7pm). Hunt for restaurants along **Av. Meritxell** and in the streets around **pl. Princep Benlloch. Mex Mex Cantina Mexicana,** at the intersection of carrer Antic Major and carrer del Fossal, offers inexpensive Mexican food. **Restaurant Marti,** Av. Meritxell, 44 (tel. 82 43 44), offers good, cheap victuals.

SIGHTS AND ENTERTAINMENT

Although there is more to Andorra la Vella than shopping, there isn't *much* more. **Casa de la Vall** (House of the Valleys), home to Andorra's tiny parliament, squats at the end of the stone alley winding west from Pl. Princep Benlloch past the church. The 16th-century building, a private home until it was sold to Andorra's General Council in 1702, still has many original fixtures. (Obligatory guided tour of the Casa every hr. Mon.-Fri. 10am-1pm and 3-6pm, Sat. 10am-1pm. Free.) The tourist office sells tickets for Andorra la Vella's annual **Festival Internacional de Música i Dansa,** showcasing an international array of ballet, jazz, and classical concerts. Contact the **Collectiu d'Activitats Culturals,** Av. Princep Benlloch, 30 (tel. 82 02 02). The festival colors the capital on the first Saturday, Sunday, and Monday in August.

Elsewhere in Andorra

Andorra is easily one of the world's loveliest countries. Too few sales zealots shift their eyes from the boutique windows toward the rocky, forested mountains to see what they are missing. Andorra's rural *parròquias* (parishes) are dotted with hamlets, mountain lakes, and some of the best ski slopes in Europe.

THE PARISHES

Many mountain ventures shove off from the *parròquia* of **La Massana** (pop. 5000), directly north of Andorra La Vella—a good 1252m above sea level but easily accessible by bus from the city (every 30min. until 8:30pm, 10min., 100ptas). Ramble through the countryside and visit the town of La Massana's **Eglésia Parròquial de Sant Iscle i Santa Victoria,** a reconstructed Romanesque church with an impressive Baroque altar. A little exploring in La Massana rewards with glimpses of ancestral houses and traditional tobacco farms. The village *fiesta* is held August 15 to 17. The **tourist office** in La Massana (tel. 83 56 93) is in a cabin by the bridge, before the bus stop (open Mon.-Sat. 9am-1pm and 3-7pm, Sun. 9am-1pm and 3-6pm). The **Hotel Rossell,** C. Josep Rossell (tel. 83 50 92; fax 83 81 80), has big, yellow rooms with baths (singles 2500ptas, doubles 4750ptas). **Restaurante Chez Gigi,** in a stone building down an alley off of Av. Sant Antoni, tosses pizzas (700-950ptas). **Camping STA Catarina,** on the outskirts of La Massana on the way to Ordino (tel. 83 50 65), is low on facilities but costs only 350ptas per person and per car (open June 26-Sept. 24). **Establiments Mohis,** on the road to Andorra la Vella across from the exit to Sispony, is a **grocery** (open Mon.-Sat. 8:45am-2pm and 4:30-8pm, Sun. 9am-1pm).

Sispony and the **Alberg Borda Jovell** are a 20- to 30-minute climb from La Massana, Av. Jovell (tel. 83 65 20; fax 83 57 76). To get here from La Massana's bus stop, go back toward Andorra la Vella 75m and turn right at the main intersection. Follow signs south for 1.3km until the *alberg,* a 700-year-old stone house, appears on the left. The renovated, all-wood interior has large bunk-bed-filled rooms with tiny windows and immaculate bathrooms. The friendly owner holds court in the restaurant downstairs and is a good source of info on the area (2100ptas per person including sheets; midnight curfew; V, MC, AmEx).

Santa Coloma, five minutes southwest of Andorra la Vella by bus, features a solitary 12th-century church. The pumice stone bridge of the **Margineda** arches gracefully over the diminutive Gran Valira River in **Sant Juliá de Lorià,** just north of the Spanish border. Neither town, however, is particularly visit-worthy unless your urge to splurge continues unabated—both are mere annexes to the Great Mall of Andorra la Vella. To get a glimpse of what an Andorran village was like before the onslaught of Reebok and Sony, check out **Ordino,** 5km northeast of La Massana. The least populated of Andorra's seven parishes, Ordino is distinguished by its status as former home to the principality's **seignorial mansions** *(pairals)*. Attached to a wall in Ordino's main square is an **iron ring** once used to chain criminals for public exhibition. Ordino's **Rose Festival** takes place on the first Sunday in July.

The colossal **Palau de Gel D'Andorra** (Andorran Ice Palace; tel. 85 15 15), an eclectic recreational facility, dominates the town of **Canillo.** The many marvels of the "palace" include an overflowing swimming pool, ice-skating rink, squash courts, and a cinema, and each is accessible with individual admission tickets. (Palace open daily 11:30am-midnight. Closed Sept. 2-Oct. 6. Each facility has its own hours. 20F for pool, 40F for ice rink, 42F for ½-hr. of squash plus 12F for racquet rental. 17F for gym. Prices and hours subject to change; call before you go.) **Encamp** houses the **Museu Nacional de l'Automòbil** (tel. 84 41 41), 80 antique cars, motorbikes, and bicycles revved up with nowhere to go (open Tues.-Sat. 10am-1pm and 4-7pm, Sun. 10am-1pm; admission 200ptas, seniors and students 100ptas).

TRAILS, GREEN AND WHITE

Andorra lends itself readily to **mountain biking,** with a panoply of trails intended for fat-tire fans. One loop begins and ends in Andorra la Vella, passing through La Comella for a satisfying view of lazy shoppers below (11km). Bikes can be rented in any parish; try **Exploramon** (tel. 86 61 82) in Andorra la Vella. For further information, contact **Federació Andorrana de Ciclisme** (tel. 82 96 92), and check out the tourist office bike route pamphlet. **Club Hipic L'Aldosa** (tel. 83 73 29), in La Massana, has saddle horses and ponies available for excursions.

Those who prefer to hoof it will find myriad **hiking** opportunities in Andorra. The **GR7** trail stretches from Portella Blanca on the French border to Suberri on the Spanish border, hitting an altitude of 2411m at Els Estangs about one-third of the way through. La Massana is home to Andorra's tallest peak, **Pic Alt de la Coma Pedrosa** (2946m). The **GR11** goes through **Arinsal,** northwest of the town on the way to Spain; a network of other trails criss-cross the area. From the tiny **Cortals de Sispony,** 3km west of Sispony, the climb to **Cap del Cubil** (2364m), on the Spanish border, takes an hour and a half. The booklet *Andorra: The Pyrenean Country,* supplied by Andorra's tourist office, provides a complete list of cabin and refuge locations within the principality. Also pick up the booklet *Treks and Walks,* which sketches out 52 possible itineraries, from 15-minute strolls to mammoth hikes.

Andorra's five outstanding **ski** resorts all rent equipment. **Pal** (tel. 83 62 36), 10km from La Massana, is a big one; catch the bus from La Massana at 10am; the return bus leaves at 5pm (250ptas each way). On the French border, **Pas de la Casa** (tel. 82 03 99) provides 27 mechanical lifts, downhill instruction, and night skiing. Cross-country aficionados flock to the slopes of **Soldeu-El Tarter** (tel. 82 11 97), 15km from the French border, between Andorra la Vella and Pas de la Casa. The resort packs an 840m vertical punch and includes 12km of cross-country trails. Other, smaller resorts are **Arinsal** (tel. 83 58 22) and **Ordino-Arcalis** (tel. 83 63 20). Andorra's tourist office publishes the lyrical *Mountains of Snow,* a guide to all its ski resorts. **SKI Andorra** (tel. 86 43 89) can answer miscellaneous questions.

Languedoc-Roussillon

Once upon a time an immense region called Occitania (today Languedoc) stretched from the Rhône to the foothills of the Pyrénées, and from the Catalan coastal region of Roussillon in the southeast to Toulouse in the west. Its people spoke the *langue d'oc* (named for its word for "yes," *"oc"*) as opposed to the *langue d'oïl* spoken in northern France, which evolved into modern French. Independent of France and Spain, the area was lorded over by the Count of Toulouse. In the mid-12th century, when the Cathar religion was introduced by immigrants from Asia, Occitania's nobles and peasants alike were intrigued. Catharism was based on Christian scriptures but professed the existence of two equal antagonistic forces: Good and Evil, as manifested in the transcendent soul versus the material body. Cathars sought transcendence through strict asceticism, and for their pains were called *parfaits.*

The purity of Cathar philosophy was especially appealing to the Occitan people, who were subject to the whims of a tremendously corrupt Catholic Church. Religious sinecures were being handed down almost as inheritances, with few ideological prerequisites (the 12th century witnessed a 19-year-old pope). Disturbed by the loss of Occitan believers—and more importantly, revenues—the Catholic Church launched an inquisition against the "heretics." The Catholic nobility of the north, frustrated by failed Crusades and inspired by possible religious, territorial, and financial rewards, needed little prodding to turn against their rivals in the south. Endorsed by the king, Philippe Auguste, Baron Simon de Montfort set out on the Albigensian Crusade against heretical Occitania, while Pope Innocent III preached doom to all nonbelievers. Cathar communities sought refuge in the châteaux of the nobles sympathetic to their cause, but de Montfort and his troops persistently hunted down Cathar refugees until they fought back by killing Inquisitioners at Avignonet. The Cathars' attack provoked Louis IX to besiege the château at Montségur. The Albigensian Crusade came to a fiery end there on March 16, 1244, when 200 Cathars were burned alive by Catholic troops.

With the region's integration into the French kingdom, the *langue d'oc* faded, and in 1539 the Edict of Villiers-Cotterets made the northern *langue d'oïl* official. Localized manifestations of discontent against Parisian rule were gradually suppressed, and the 1659 Treaty of the Pyrénées legally incorporated Cerdagne and the southern part of Languedoc-Roussillon into French domain. The popularity of thermal spring resorts in the Pyrénées in the early 19th century soothed simmering resentment as prosperity in the region washed over lingering political differences.

While a recent flood of xenophobia has pushed much of France to the right, Languedoc remains faithful to its socialist tradition. Newspapers on the stands today are descendants of the 19th-century journals founded by Jean Jaurès and other local leftist politicians. The *langue d'oc*—commonly referred to as *occitan*—has ceded to standardized French. Students can learn the language at school, however, and count it as a foreign language on the *bac,* the national university qualifying exam. The *occitan* banner, with its yellow and red vertical stripes and a black cross, still flies throughout the region.

One of Languedoc's most popular regional dishes is *cassoulet,* a hearty stew of white beans, sausage, pork, mutton, and goose. In the northwest, cooks perform magical, marvelous wonders with sheep intestines. In Roussillon, try *cargolade* (snails stuffed with bacon) or the many other seafood offerings. The tangy fermented *roquefort* and *St-Nectaire* cheeses complement the assortment of luscious fruits grown in the Garonne Valley. Accompany your meals with a glass of one of the region's full-bodied red wines such as Minervois or Corbières. With dessert or as an *aperitif,* try the sweet white wines of Lunel, Mireval, and St-Jean-de-Minervois.

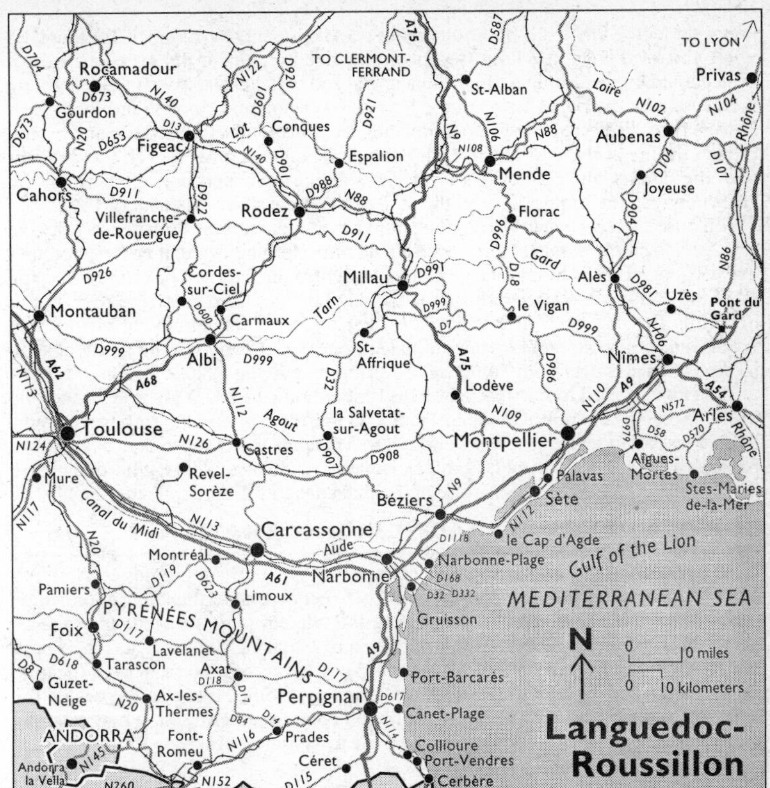

GETTING AROUND

Toulouse may be the hub city of the gods. Frequent train service and cheap accommodations make daytrips a simple pleasure. Unfortunately, its convenience as a hub has led the SNCF to neglect direct connections between surrounding cities. Your first farewell to Toulouse may not be your last, as you constantly double back there to go between towns. **Perpignan** serves as a gateway to the Côte Catalane's sandy expanses, although buses stop running too early for club-goers.

Tourist offices throughout the region distribute itineraries which follow *Les Traces des Cathares* (tracks of the Cathars) and ancient Roman roads. The Canal du Midi (visible in Toulouse and Peripignan) connects the Atlantic to the Mediterranean and also links some towns in the region. Unfortunately, drought has greatly reduced the canal's navigability. The hilly countryside makes **cycling** a bit difficult, but the tiny villages strewn along the way make the effort worthwhile.

Toulouse

Like the signs of the zodiac inlaid in its pl. du Capitole, vibrant Toulouse radiates into eclectic quarters with distinct personalities. From the urban chic of the shopping district to the pizzeria intimacy of rue St-Rome and the moped- and café-swamped rue du Taur, the *"Ville Rose"* cultivates a bouquet of delights for visitors.

Toulouse has a history as colorful as the rose-colored Languedoc brick adorning its edifices. In the 3rd century, "Tolosa" was converted to Christianity though the preachings of St. Sernin. Far from Parisian authority, the city grew to cultural prominence under the 9th- to 13th- century dynasty of the counts Raymond of Toulouse. By wiles and weddings, the counts kept their prized city from the greedy hands of besieger Simon de Montfort, the Plantagenêts, and treacherous vassals while fighting mercilessly for the papal forces in the First and Albigensian Crusades and founding a university to eradicate heresy. No doubt fatigued, Raymond VII ceded his lands to the French throne at the end of the 13th century. The kings proved even less tolerant than the counts, and Toulouse's Protestants died in new and horrible ways in the years between the Inquisition and the St. Bartholomew's Day Massacre of 1572.

Toulouse's streets began to run blue, rather than red, with the 16th-century discovery that a local plant, *pastel*, produced a pale blue clothing dye that Europe couldn't live without. Local industry has only looked brighter since then. Toulouse is the capital of the French aerospace industry, launching satellites from its Ariane rockets and inventing the high-tech Airbus jets and the Concorde. Its high-flying history also recalls the courage of *Little Prince* author Antoine de St-Exupéry, among others, who pioneered mail routes from Toulouse to North Africa in the 1920s.

The city that used to burn its dissidents is now home to 100,000 students and one of the most diverse populations in France. Cosmopolitan enough to have an "anything goes" attitude and just small enough to feel familiar, Toulouse draws locals and passers-by alike into its streets, gardens, squares, and cafés. Those who come here just to change trains are missing one of the most delightful cities in France.

ORIENTATION AND PRACTICAL INFORMATION

Toulouse sprawls on both sides of the Garonne River, but the museums and interesting sights are mostly located within a compact section east of the river, bounded by rue de Metz in the south and bd. Strasbourg and bd. Carnot to the north and east. To reach the tourist office from the station, turn left along the canal and then right onto the broad allée Jean Jaurès. Walk a third of the way around pl. Wilson (bearing right), then take a right onto rue Lafayette. The tourist office is in a small park on the left of the intersection with rue d'Alsace-Lorraine. In July and August, when most students leave, businesses take vacations, and the town quiets down.

Tourist Office: Donjon du Capitôle, rue Lafayette, sq. Charles de Gaulle (tel. 05 61 11 02 22; fax 05 61 22 03 63), in the park behind Capitôle. Though its map will guide you from sight to sight in one piece, the office's free *Toulouse: Hôtels Restaurants* has a much better map of the *centre ville,* and a bus/metro map. Accommodations service. Walking tours of the *vieille ville* in French (July-Sept. 3 per day, 1 Sun.; 45-60F) and bus excursions to nearby sights (April-Nov. 8 per month, 165F). Tours leave daily July-Sept. Office open May-Sept. Mon.-Sat. 9am-7pm, Sun. 9am-1pm and 2-5:30pm; Oct.-April Mon.-Fri. 9am-6pm, Sat. 9am-12:30pm and 2-6pm, Sun. and holidays 10am-12:30pm and 2-5pm. **Currency exchange** open May-Sept. Sat.-Sun. and holidays 11am-1pm and 2-4:30pm. The free *Bataclan* lists regional festivals, or pick up weekly *Flash* (7F) at *tabacs.*

Budget Travel Office: OTU Voyage, 60, rue de Taur (tel. 05 61 12 54 54). Procures cheap flights and train fares for students. Open Mon.-Fri. 9am-7pm. **Nouvelles Frontières,** 2, pl. St-Sernin (tel. 08 36 33 33 33). Specializes in cheap flights for everyone (to Paris, 650F). Open Mon.-Sat. 9am-7pm. V, MC.

Consulates: Canada, 30, bd. de Strasbourg (tel. 05 61 99 30 16). Open Mon.-Fri. 9am-noon. **U.K.,** c/o Lucas Aerospace, Victoria Center, Bâtiment Didier Daurat, 20, chemin de Laporte (tel. 05 61 15 02 02). Open Mon.-Tues. and Thurs.-Fri. 9am-noon and 2-5pm.

Money: Banque de France, 4, rue Deville (tel. 05 61 61 35 35). No commission, good rates. Open Mon.-Fri. 9am-12:20pm and 1:20-3:30pm. **ATMs** are at **Crédit Mutuel,** 29 and 5, allée Jean Jaurès. Also at **Crédit Agricole,** 100, rue Jean Rieux.

American Express Office: 73, rue Alsace-Lorraine (tel. 05 61 21 78 25), in Havas Voyages. Open Mon.-Fri. 9am-1pm and 2-6pm. Sat. 9am-1pm and 2-5pm.

Flights: Aéroport Blagnac (tel. 05 61 42 44 00), 10km northwest of Toulouse. **Air Inter,** 7, rue St-Jerôme (tel. 05 61 30 68 68), flies to Paris 10-13 times per day (one way, 950F; student roundtrip 590F; open Mon.-Fri. 9am-6:30pm, Sat. 9:30am-

Toulouse

Capitole, **11**	Les Jacobins, **6**	Palace d'Assézat, **4**
Cathédrale St-Etienne, **14**	Musée de Vieux Toulouse, **5**	Piscine, **1**
Château d'Eau, **2**	Musée des Augustins, **13**	Post Office, **10**
CROUS, **7**	Notre-Dame la Daurade, **3**	St-Sernin and Musée St-Raymond, **8**
Halle aux Grains, **15**	Notre-Dame du Taur, **9**	Tourist Office, **12**

5:30pm). **Air France,** 2, bd. de Strasbourg (tel. 05 61 10 01 01), goes to London's Heathrow twice daily (1250F roundtrip). **Navettes Aérocar** (tel. 05 61 30 04 89) shuttle from the *gare routière* (by the train station) and allée Jean Jaurès to the airport (every 20min. until 9pm, 30min., 25F).

Trains: Gare Matabiau, bd. Pierre Sémard (tel. 05 61 10 10 00, reservations 05 61 62 85 44). To: Paris (9 per day, 7hr., 342F); Bordeaux (8 per day, 2¼hr., 167F); Lyon (6 per day, 6hr., 298F); Marseille (11 per day, 4½hr., 232F); Perpignan (6 per day, 2½hr., 143F). **Lockers** 15-25F, 72-hr. max. Office open Mon.-Sat. 9am-7:30pm. Tickets also at **Espace Transport,** 7, pl. Esquirol (tel. 05 61 41 70 70; open Mon.-Fri. 8:30am-6pm). **SOS Voyageurs:** (tel. 05 61 62 27 30), helps with any travel problems. Open Mon.-Sat. 7am-6:30pm, Sun. 4:30-9:30pm.

Buses: 4, rue Marengo (tel. 05 61 48 71 84), next to train station. Ask if your Eurail pass applies. Buy tix on bus. To: Foix (45F); Albi (46-49F); Castres (47F); and nearby towns. Station open Mon.-Sat. 7am-7pm, Sun. 8am-noon and 2-7pm.

Public Transportation: SEMVAT (tel. 05 61 41 70 70 or 05 62 11 26 11). Info office on 7, pl. Esquirol (open Mon.-Fri. 8:30am-6:30pm, Sat. 8:30am-noon). Buy tix on buses or ticket booths. Maps available at ticket booths and tourist office.

Taxis: (tel. 05 61 80 36 36). 24hr. Catch 'em at the *gare* and pl. Wilson. 6F30 per km during the day, 9F10 per km at night. A ride to the airport runs 100-130F.

Car Rental: Rent-a-Car, 55, rue de Bayard (tel. 05 61 63 70 26; fax 05 61 63 40 97). Cars 160F per day, 490F per 3-day weekend, or 1100F per week. Open Mon.-Fri. 8:30am-12:30pm and 1:30-7pm, Sat. 8:30am-noon. Call ahead to reserve.

Driver/Rider Service: CRIJ, 17, rue de Metz (tel. 05 61 21 20 20), Open Mon.-Fri. 10am-1pm and 2-6:30pm, Sat. 10am-1pm and 2-6pm.

Bike Rental: Polycycles, 11, route de Bayonne (tel. 05 61 49 11 22; fax 05 61 49 71 34). 120F per day; deposit. Open Mon. 2-7:30pm, Tue.-Sat. 9:30am-7:30pm.

Hitching: For Carcassonne, hitchers take bus 2 to RN113. For Paris, they take bus 10 to terminus. For Auch and Bayonne, hitchers take bus 64 to RN124. For Albi, they take bus 16 or 19. Remember: this is never a good idea.

Laundromat: Laverie St-Sernin, 14, rue Emile Cartailhac. Open daily 7am-10pm. Closer to the hostel, **Laverie Dupuy,** 18, pl. Dupuy. Open daily 7am-9pm.

English Bookstore: The Bookshop, 17, rue Lakanal (tel. 05 61 22 99 92; fax 05 61 21 53 93), down from Les Jacobins. Large selection of novels, some non-fiction, comic books, and *Let's Go.* Trade in used books. Open July-Aug. Tues.-Sat. 10am-noon and 3-7pm; Sept.-June 13 Mon.-Sat. 9:30am-1pm and 2-7pm. V, MC.

Youth Center: Centre d'Information Jeunesse, 17, rue de Metz (tel. 05 61 21 20 20). Info on travel, work, and study. Open Mon.-Sat. 10am-1pm and 2-6:30pm.

Crisis Lines: SOS Amitié: (tel. 05 61 80 80 80). A friend in need is a friend indeed. Open 24hr. **SOS Racisme:** 1, rue Jouxt-Aigues (tel. 05 62 14 61 39). **Service Acceuil Victimes:** 30bis, rue Valade (tel. 05 61 22 29 55). Helps victims of violent crime, mediates disputes. Open Mon.-Fri. 9am-noon, Tues. also 2-5pm.

Hospital: CHR de Rangueil, 1 av. Jean Poulhes (tel. 05 61 32 25 33). **Medical emergency:** 23, bd. de l'Embouchure (tel. 05 61 12 77 77).

Police: Commissariat Central. **Emergency** tel. 17.

Post Office: 9, rue Lafayette (tel. 05 62 15 30 00; fax 05 62 15 31 07), opposite tourist office. Poste restante (postal code: 31049). Photocopies 1F. Telephones. 24-hr. ATM. **Currency exchange.** No charge, good rates; 1.2% commission on traveler's checks. Open Mon.-Fri. 8am-7pm, Sat. 8am-noon. **Postal code:** 31000.

ACCOMMODATIONS AND CAMPING

Inexpensive hotels and their tenants' clients loiter near the train station on bd. Bonrepos, across the canal. Lodging in this unpleasant and unsafe neighborhood, however, is no cheaper than at the many budget hotels scattered in the *centre ville.*

Auberge de Jeunesse (HI), Villa des Rosiers, 125, rue Jean Rieux (tel. 05 61 80 49 93; fax 05 61 20 50 66). Call before making the trek. From station, take bus 22 (direction: Gonin-La Terrasse) to "Leygues." If walking, turn left out of station and follow bd. de la Gare (which undergoes myriad name transformations) for 7 blocks along canal (20min.), then turn left onto rue Jean Rieux and walk for 8 blocks (15min.). Hostel is on your left—well worn and often filled with the pitter-patter of college-age feet. 40F. 50F deposit for key. Turkish toilets. Breakfast 18F. Sheets 16F. Kitchen available. Reception open daily 8-11am and 5-10:45pm. Lockout 10am-5pm. Doors locked at 11pm. Open Jan. 21-Dec. 31. Reserve July-Aug.

Hôtel des Arts, 1bis, rue Cantegril (tel. 05 61 23 36 21; fax 05 61 12 22 37), at rue des Arts near pl. St-Georges. Take metro (direction: Basso Cambo) to "pl. Esquirol." Go down rue du Metz, away from the river; rue des Arts is 3rd street on left. Great location. Spacious, spotless rooms cared for by a kind, hard-working staff. Two singles without windows 80-90F. Singles 105F, with shower 125-140F. Doubles 125-135F, with shower 145-160F. Triples and quads 150F, with shower 170-180F. Breakfast 22F. Shower 15F. Reserve May-June and Sept.-Oct. V, MC.

Hôtel Beauséjour, 4, rue Caffarelli (tel. 05 61 62 77 59), just off allée Jean Jaurès halfway between train station and pl. Wilson. Tall, bright, and cheap rooms with sparkling bathrooms and new beds. TV room. Singles 70F, with shower 135F. Doubles 95-115F, with shower 135-150F. Extra bed 40F. Shower 10F. Breakfast 20F. Call ahead. V, MC, AmEx.

Hôtel du Grand Balcon, 8, rue Romiguières (tel. 05 61 21 48 08), on corner of pl. du Capitole. Great location; good enough for a little prince. St-Exupéry stayed in this grand hotel in 1920; ask proprietor to see the author's room (no. 32) and photos. Large rooms have tiny balconies and lots of light. Singles 110-120F, with shower 150F. Doubles 130F, with shower 150-185F. Triples and quads 150F, with full bathroom 200F. Shower 11F. Breakfast 23F. Closed first 3 weeks of August.

Hôtel de l'Université, 26, rue Emile Cartailhac (tel. 05 61 21 35 69), near pl. St-Sernin. Clean, uncarpeted rooms in a quiet neighborhood. Singles and doubles 105F, with shower 125F. Triples with shower and TV 180F. Shower 10F.

Camping: Pont de Rupé, 21, chemin du Pont de Rupé (tel. 05 61 70 07 35; fax 05 61 70 00 71), at av. des Etats-Unis (N20 north). Take bus 59 (direction: Lespinasse) to "Rupé." Restaurant, bar, and laundry machines (16F wash, 10F dry). 50F one person, 16F additional person). **La Bouriette,** 201, chemin de Tournefeuille (tel. 05 61 49 64 46), 5km outside Toulouse along N124 in St-Martin-du-Touch. Take bus 64 (direction: Colomiers) and ask for St.-Martin-du-Touch. 17F per person, 18-26F per site. Car included. Open year-round. **Les Violettes** (tel. and fax 05 61 81 72 07), on N113, 4km after Castanet, 15km from Toulouse. Take the bus that goes to Carcassonne and ask to get off at the *camping*. Washing machines 20F. 43F for one person and site, 60F for two people and site, 16F50 per additional person. Showers included.

FOOD

Markets take place Tuesday through Sunday mornings at pl. Victor Hugo, pl. des Carmes, and bd. de Strasbourg (6am-1pm). Retreat with your purchases to the Jardin Royal or the Jardin des Plantes. On Wednesdays, the pl. du Capitôle transforms into an open-air department store, and on Saturday mornings it hosts a market of organic produce. Restaurants thrive on the tiny streets on either side of rue St-Rome, but the most economical eateries lie along the rue du Taur on the way to the university. The *brasseries* that crowd pl. Wilson offer 50-80F *menus* and ambience. Lebanese, Chinese, and Mexican restaurants coexist on rue des Filatiers and its less-crowded partner, rue Paradoux. *Boulangeries, épiceries,* and *charcuteries* line rue du Taur and rue Jean Rieux (between the hostel and the canal). Two **supermarkets** face off in the center of town—**Monoprix** at 39, rue Alsace-Lorraine (tel. 05 61 23 39 80; open Mon.-Sat. 8:30am-9pm) and **Casino** near pl. Occitane, at the Centre Commerciale St-Georges (tel. 05 61 22 50 66; open Mon.-Sat. 9am-7:30pm). **CROUS,** 58, rue du Taur (tel. 05 61 12 54 00), provides info on city's university cafeterias and restaurants. Buy meal tickets (13F70) from the office (open Mon.-Fri. 2-4pm) or at the cafeterias (11:30am-1:30pm).

Salade Gasconne, 75, rue du Taur (tel. 05 61 23 90 19). Tastebud-tantalizing regional dishes. Salads 34-49F, but restaurant offers more than just greens. *Foie gras maison* 56F; 3-course *menu* 55F. Open Mon.-Fri. 11:30am-3pm and 7-10:30pm, Sat. 11:30am-3pm. V, MC.

Mille et Une Pâtes, 3, pl. du Peyrou (tel. 05 61 21 80 70), 2 blocks from St-Sernin in a student-studded area. Another location at 1bis, rue Mirepoix, near pl. du Capitôle. Creative, healthy salads (30-42F). *Lasagne au chocolat* 25F. Not quite 1001 versions of pasta, but close to it (39-58F). The take-out prices are cheaper. Open Mon. 11:30am-2pm, Tues.-Sat. 11:30am-2pm and 7:30pm-10pm. (Mirepoix site open Mon.-Sat. 11:30am-2pm and 7-9:30pm.) V, MC.

Le Bar à Pâtes, 8-10, rue Tripière (tel. 05 61 22 16 16), off rue St-Rome. No one knows whether locals pack this place for its whimsical Vespa motif or its pasta. Choose your own pasta and sauce 39F. Bar in basement Sept.-May daily 6pm-2am. Open Mon.-Sat. noon-2pm and 7:15-11:30pm, Sun. 7:15-11:30pm. V, MC.

Les Baguettes, 6bis, impasse Baour-Lorman (tel. 05 61 23 63 80). The 48F and 55F *menus* of Cambodian specialties will add spice to your life and the 60F *menu* offers the thrill of a mystery dessert. Vegetarians can request special dishes. Open Mon.-Sat. noon-2pm and 7-10:30pm.

Le Bol Bu, 8, rue du May (tel. 05 61 21 11 31), off rue St-Rome. This non-smoking *salon de thé* serves organic wholewheat crêpes (12-31F) with traditional and off-the-wall fillings, such as Earl Grey jelly or pears and cinnamon, under its many dangling mobiles. Linger over a pot of one of 80 kinds of tea. Open Mon., Tues., and Sat. noon-7pm; Wed.-Fri. noon-10pm.

Restaurant Cool, 6, rue des Lois (tel. 05 61 21 51 77), the second Middle Eastern take-out place off pl. Capitôle, provides Lebanese hummus (20F), shwarma sandwiches (25F), falafel (17F), and sticky-sweet baklava (10F) for those out after midnight. Open Mon.-Sat. 11am-2am, Sun. 11am-midnight. V, MC, AmEx.

Cacheroutu Diffusion, 37, bd. Carnot (tel. 05 61 23 07 59; fax 05 61 13 78 55), is a kosher *boucherie,* with enough groceries to patch together a meal. Tranquil owner is a good resource for info on upcoming Jewish holidays and cultural events. Open Mon.-Thurs. 8am-1pm and 3-8pm, Fri. and Sun. 8am-1pm. V, MC.

A la Vraie Religieuse, 17, rue du Taur (tel. 05 61 22 65 17). Just when another baguette seems one baguette too many, this *pâtisserie* turns out chocolate puddings (6F, made from last night's leftovers), *gâteau basque* (8F), sweet surprises, and divine delicacies. Open Tues.-Sat. 8am-8pm, Sun. 8am-1:30pm.

SIGHTS

From local artists to canon painters and sculptors, the diversity of Toulouse's artistic offerings makes for an enjoyable afternoon of museum hopping. A 20F pass, available at all museums, allows visits to three museums; 30F broadens the choices to six. The charming map **les Lieux de l'art** marks local museums, galleries, and churches.

Newly restored and only recently open to the public, the **Palace d'Assézat**, rue de Metz near the river, houses the **Foundation Bremberg's** collection of 28 colorful Bonnards, peppered with Dufys, Pissarros, and Gauguins, and filled out with an impressive number and variety of European pieces spanning five centuries. (Daily guided tours in French Tues.-Fri. 3:30pm, Sat.-Sun. 2:30pm and 4pm. Open June-Sept. daily 10am-6pm; Oct.-May 10am-5:30pm. Admission 25F, students 15F, temporary exhibits 15F more.) Continuing along rue de Metz away from the river, the **Musée des Augustins,** 21, rue de Metz (tel. 05 61 22 21 82), off rue Alsace-Lorraine, displays an unsurpassed assemblage of Romanesque and Gothic sculptures. Especially noteworthy are the 15 sniggering gargoyles. (Open June-Sept. Thurs.-Mon. 10am-6pm, Wed. 10am-10pm; Oct.-May Thurs.-Mon. 10am-6pm, Wed. 10am-9pm; admission 12F, students free; more with temporary exhibits.) To learn more about the city's somewhat hectic history, head to the cozy **Musée de Vieux Toulouse,** 7, rue de May (tel. 05 61 13 97 24), off rue St.-Rome. This privately run museum contains several exhibits on local history and popular culture (open June-Sept. Mon-Fri. 3-6pm; Oct.-May open only by appointment: call Fri. afternoon; admission 10F, students 5F). When it reopens in summer or fall of 1997, the **Musée St-Raymond,** pl. St-Sernin (tel. 05 61 22 21 85) will be able to take you *way* back in time. The museum boasts an extraordinary array of archaeological finds dating from prehistory to AD 1000, many uncovered in Toulouse itself. Those who need their fix of antique coins and dead emperors' busts will appreciate this newly renovated space.

An unwavering Catholic stronghold in a region torn by wars of religion, Toulouse shelters some of France's most architecturally distinctive and historically important religious monuments. **Eglise Notre-Dame-du-Taur** (tel. 05 61 21 41 57) was originally known as St-Sernin-du-Taur after Saturninus, the first Toulousian priest, who was martyred in AD 250. Legend has it that disgruntled pagans tied him to the tail of a wild bull that dragged him to his death; the building marks the spot where Saturninus' unfortunate *toro* ride finally ended. The church is a masterpiece of the city's famous ornate brickwork (open daily July-Sept. 9am-6:30pm; Oct.-June 8am-noon and 2-6pm). The martyr's name was shortened over the years to St. Sernin, and his remains now rest in the crypt of the magnificent **Basilique St-Sernin,** the longest Romanesque structure in the world. St. Dominique, the most vigilant of Cathar-hunters, led his inquisition from this church. (Tours leave July-Aug. twice daily, 35F. Church open July-Sept. Mon.-Sat. 9am-6:30pm, Sun. 9am-7:30pm; Oct.-June Mon.-Sat. 8am-noon and 2-6pm, Sun. 9am-12:30pm and 2-7:30pm.) Behind an iron gate, the **crypt** is a treasure trove of ecclesiastical relics gathered since Charlemagne began collecting. (Crypt open Mon.-Sat. 10am-6pm, Sun. 12:30-6pm; Oct.-June Mon.-Sat. 10-11:30am and 2:30-5pm, Sun. 2:30-5pm. Admission to the crypt 10F.) Sunday mornings, a **flea market** surrounds the basilica (9am-1pm).

Yet another relic of the Albigensian Crusade, the 13th-century **Les Jacobins,** rue Lakanal, is an excellent example of the southern Gothic, or *gothique du Midi,* style. Flamboyant decorations are checked by the elegance of the stained glass and serenity of the cloister. Inside, a modest crypt contains the ashes of St. Thomas Aquinas. (Church open July-Aug. Mon.-Sat. 10am-6:30pm, Sun. 2:30-6:30pm; Sept.-June Mon.-Sat. 10am-noon and 2:30-6pm, Sun. 2:30-6pm. Admission to the cloister 10F. Daily guided tours. Weekly summer piano concert tickets 70-130F available at the tourist office.) The **Réfectoire des Jacobins,** 69, rue Pargaminières (tel. 05 01 61 11 39 52), presents regular exhibitions ranging from archaeological artifacts to modern art (open daily June-Sept. 10am-6pm; Oct.-May Wed.-Mon. 10am-5pm; admission 10F).

The **Galerie du Château d'Eau,** pl. Laganne (tel. 05 61 42 61 72), just across from the *centre ville* on the Pont Neuf, is devoted exclusively to photography. Exhibit spaces in the old turret have new displays each month. Don't neglect the catalogues of past exhibits (open Mon.-Wed. 1-7pm; admission 15F, Sun. 10F, students and seniors 10F). The smaller, gallery-like **Centre Municipal de L'Affiche,** 58, allées Charles-de-Fitte (tel. 05 61 59 24 64), just down rue de la République, exhibits clever posters, past and present, produced by local illustrators (open Mon.-Fri. 9am-noon and 2-6pm; free). **L'Espace St-Cyprien,** 56, allées Charles-de-Fitte (tel. 05 61 22 28 64), features avant-garde photography and contemporary art exhibits (open Mon.-Fri. 8:30am-12:30pm and 1:30-7pm; sometimes open Sat. 2-6pm; free). The new **modern art museum,** on the outskirts of town (accessible by subway), is scheduled to be completed in 1998. **La Cité de l'Espace** (tel. 05 62 71 64 80), a park devoted to Toulouse's space programs, will open in spring of 1997.

The fact that Toulouse is built in red brick (hence its nickname, "The Rose City") has more to do with economics than aesthetic preference. Since brick was the most affordable regional building material at the time of the city's growth spurt, it accounts for many of the buildings seen today. The exception is the **stone mansions** of wealthy 15th- and 16th-century dye merchants. An excellent way to view these *hôtel particuliers* is the 2-hr. walking tour (45F), given in French Mon.-Sat. July-Sept. Call the tourist office for info. For greener pastures, head to the **Jardin Royal** and the less formal **Jardin des Plantes,** across the street. They offer plenty of benches and lots of shade. Don't forget the requisite **stroll along the Garonne.** For bicyclists, the **Grand Rond** unfurls into allée Paul Sabatier, which just keeps rolling along to the Canal du Midi.

ENTERTAINMENT

Toulouse has something to please almost any nocturnal whim. The numerous cafés, *glaciers,* and pizzerias flanking **pl. St-Georges** and **pl. du Capitôle** are open late, as are the bars off **rue St-Rome** and **rue des Filatiers.** The weekly **Flash** gives restaurant and bar info and keeps Toulouse up on the ever-changing club scene (7F at *tabacs*). *Flash Eté* (20F) lists summer festivals and events for the entire region. CD-and-book megalith **FNAC** (tel. 05 61 11 01 01), at the intersection of bd. Strasbourg and Carnot, sells tickets to big concerts and has cultural pamphlets and club advertisements (open Mon.-Sat. 9:30am-7:30pm). The **Café des Artistes,** quai de la Daurade (tel. 05 61 12 06 00), with a view of the Garonne river, serves drinks and coffee to a huge yuppie following, and has changing student exhibits at the École des Beaux Arts. (Oct.-May *café-théâtre* in basement, twice monthly; open Mon.-Sat. 8am-2am, Sun. noon-10pm.) **L'Artcor,** 6, rue de Colombette (tel. 05 61 99 61 87), just off bd. Lazare Carnot, is a friendly gay bar and a great place to ask about the discos *du jour* (open Tues.-Sun. from 9pm; winter from 6pm). **Bagdam Café,** 4, rue Delacroix (tel. 05 61 99 03 62), nestled on a nondescript street parallel to bd. Carnot between rue l'Etoile and rue Caraman, is a down-to-earth lesbian bar with a table of resource numbers and pamphlets (open Wed.-Sat. 7:30pm-2am).

Cave Poèsie, 71, rue du Taur (tel. 05 61 42 91 34, reservations 05 61 23 62 00), hosts plays and performances. The full moon is the catalyst for an "open door" night of comedians, poets, photographers, musicians, or whatever the *cave* can dig up. Stop by for a schedule; events begin at 9pm. **Cour de l'Ecole des Beaux Arts,** quai de la Daurade (tel. 05 61 25 66 87), stages classic plays with a modern twist.

July through September, **Musique d'Eté** brings classical concerts, jazz, and ballet to a variety of outdoor settings (75F; tickets sold at concert sites and the tourist office). Tuesdays and Fridays in September, the **Festival International Piano aux Jacobins** tickles Toulouse's ivories (tickets 100-140F, students 60F; tickets available at tourist office). **Cinemas** near pl. Wilson often run major American and English films in *"v.o." (version originale)* with French subtitles. **Utopia Cinemas,** 24, rue Montandy (tel. 05 61 23 66 20), always shows international films in *v.o.* and has a wild decor and some gay-friendly art and information. Arrive on time (33F; closed Aug.). **Cinéma ABC,** 13, rue St-Bernard (B2; tel. 05 61 29 81 00), shows international movies, all *v.o.,* last show around 10pm (42F, 32F on Wed. and for students).

■ South of Toulouse

FOIX

Nestled in the eastern Pyrénées 85km south of Toulouse, Foix (pop. 10,000) still claims kinship with Gaston Phébus, the great 14th-century warrior whose motto Foix claims as its own—*"Toque-y si gauses"* (Touch if you dare). Although Catholic crusaders finally conquered its Cathar stronghold in the 13th century, the château remains in perfect health; it's the invaders who have crumbled to dust. Along with the castle, myriad nearby outdoor activities attract visitors to town. For hiking, kayaking, or spelunking in the Ariège, Foix is an ideal home base.

Orientation and Practical Information

To reach the tourist office, turn right out of the train station and then right onto the main road (N20). Follow the highway to the second bridge, cross it, and follow av. Gabriel Fauré for about three blocks to the office on your right (10min.). The **tourist office,** 45, av. Gabriel Fauré (tel. 05 61 65 12 12; fax 05 61 65 64 63), sends English-speaking guides to the château (open July-Aug. Mon.-Sat. 9am-7pm; Sept.-June Mon.-Fri. 9am-noon and 2-6pm, Sat. 9:30am-12:30pm and 2:30-6:30pm). The **train station,** av. Pierre Sémard (tel. 05 61 02 03 64) is north of town off N20. Trains go from Foix to Toulouse (11 per day, 1hr., 67F); La Tour de Carol (4 per day, 1½hr., 65F); and Ax-les-Thermes (8 per day, 45min., 37F. Info and reservation desk open Mon.-Sat. 7:45am-7:15pm, Sun. 7:45am-9:30pm.) **Société General** has an **ATM** a half-block from the corner of rue Delcassé and rue de la Bistour. **Salt Autocars,** 8, allées Villote (tel. 05 61 65 08 40; fax 05 61 65 58 33), runs to Ax-les-Thermes (6 per day, 28F) and Toulouse (2 per day, 49F). **Intersport La Hutte,** 40-42, rue Delcassé (tel. 05 61 65 00 41), rents **mountain bikes** (70-80F per ½-day, 100F per day, 150F per 2-day weekend). Also offers **ski rental** (cross-country 50F per day, downhill 65F per day; passport deposit; open Mon.-Sat. 9am-noon and 2:15-7pm; V, MC, AmEx). The **hospital** (tel. 05 61 05 40 40) is on av. Gabriel Fauré. Contact the **police** at 05 61 05 43 00. In an **emergency,** call 05 61 65 00 17 or 17. The **post office,** at 4, rue Laffort (tel. 05 61 02 01 02), has **currency exchange** with no commission and reasonable rates; photocopies cost 1F. Foix's **postal code** is 09000; poste restante code: 09008 (open Mon.-Fri. 8am-7pm, Sat. 8am-noon).

Accommodations, Camping, and Food

To appreciate the prehistoric caves and almost shameless beauty of the surrounding countryside, you'll want to stay overnight. The tourist office has a list of *chambres d'hôtes* which go for about 120F (including breakfast). A modern hostel, the **Foyer Léo Lagrange,** 16, rue Peyrevidal (tel. 05 61 65 09 04), provides clean one- to four-bed single-sex rooms and plenty of advice on sightseeing. The energetic owner will even help make travel plans. From the tourist office, head to av. Gabriel Fauré and turn right after the steel "marketplace" structure. (70F. Free showers. Breakfast 15F. Lunch 55F. 24-hr. reception July-Aug.; Sept.-June 8am-9pm. Kitchen available.) The **Hôtel Echauguette,** 1, rue Paul Laffont (tel. 05 61 02 88 88; fax 05 61 65 29 49), just off av. Gabriel Fauré across from the post office, lets quiet, beautifully kept rooms, each with a lamp draped in lace. (Singles and doubles 150-160F, with shower 180F, with toilet and shower 210-280F. Triples and quads 250-290F. Rooms costing more than 200F are reduced 60F Oct.-May. No hall showers. Breakfast 30F. V, MC, AmEx). The elegant **Hôtel Eychenne** is another option, at 11, rue Peyrevidal (tel. 05 61 65 00 04; singles and doubles 120F, with shower 160F. Triples 190F. Triples or quads with bath 250F. Free shower. Breakfast 28F. V, MC). **Camping La Barre** (tel. 05 61 65 11 58), a two-star site 3km up N20 toward Toulouse, sprawls across a large riverside site. Buses to Toulouse stop at the camp (10F per person; tent 8F; car 7F; shower 5F; open April-Oct.).

Foix is an excellent place to sample some *ariégeois* specialties. *Truite à l'ariégeoise* (trout) and *écrevisses* (crayfish), the highlights of the hearty local cuisine, make fantastic (if messy) finger food. Try a cool herbal *hypocras,* named after its supposed inventor, Hippocrates, who should know what's good for you. **Le Petit Creux,** 9, rue Lazéma (tel. 05 61 02 91 43), tosses salads onto safari-animal tablecloths and lists its ever-changing *plats du jour* on giant green apples mounted on the wall. *Menus* 52F (open daily noon-3pm and 7-10:30pm). The staff at **Le Jeu de l'Oie,** 17, rue Lafaurie (tel. 05 61 02 69 39), will ask you to ascend the spiral staircase to the second floor if the first is filled with locals. Menu features goat-cheese salads and grilled fish and meats starting at 50F (open daily noon-2:30pm and 7-10pm). Two doors down, try **La Bodéga,** 7, rue la Faurie (tel. 05 61 02 91 26). Enjoy the turquoise sombrero on the wall, the strains of Spanish music, and yummy *tapas* (30F) or "fiesta" chicken (35F). (Open daily 11:30am-2:30pm and 6:30pm-midnight. V, MC.) On Fridays and alternate Mondays, an **open-air market** sprouts all over Foix, with meat and cheese at the Halle aux Grains, fruits and vegetables at pl. St-Volusien, and clothing along the allées de Villote (food 8am-12:30pm, clothes 8am-4pm).

Sights

One look at the **Château de Foix** (tel. 05 61 65 56 05) and you'll understand why Simon de Montfort failed four times to vanquish the castle (though he easily devastated the town below). Inside this well preserved medieval fort, the **Musée d'Ariège** displays artifacts dating from the Roman empire through the Middle Ages (both open daily July-Aug. 9:30am-6pm; June and Sept. 9:45am-noon and 2-6:30pm; Oct.-May Wed.-Sun. 10:30am-noon and 2-6pm; guided tours almost every hour; admission 25F). The tourist office has a calendar of the château's concerts and storytelling sessions in summer. For the last 10 days of July and the first two weeks of August, a *son et lumière* show enlivens the castle on Fridays and Saturdays.

The **Ariège** boasts some of the most spectacular **caves** in France. An hour-long boat ride takes visitors through the caves on the underground river of **Labouiche** (tel. 05 61 65 04 11), 6km from Foix (open July-Aug. 9:30am-5pm; April-June and Sept. to mid-Nov. 10-11:15am and 2-5pm; 40F, students in the morning 33F). The **Grotte de Niaux** (tel. 05 61 05 88 37; reservations essential), 16km south of Foix, contains 13,000-year-old paintings of leaping herds of bison, deer, and horses. Ask the Foix tourist office about visiting this and other prehistoric caves. **Aurigera,** 2, pl. Lazéma (tel. 05 61 02 87 49), comes to the rescue of those without a car; they will organize trips for individuals or groups to the caves, Montségur, and other local spots of interest.

MONTSÉGUR

High above the plain 35km southeast of Foix along the D9, the now-crumbling **Château de Montségur** was the bustling capital of the Cathar church until 1242, when the Cathars turned the tables on the papal judge in a bloody raid at Avignonet. The massacre prompted Louis IX's Catholic forces to besiege Montségur, which finally fell in 1244. On March 16, two weeks into a truce, more than 200 unrepentant Cathars calmly submitted to death by fire at the castle. Legends surround the events of the night preceding the fire, when the Cathars' bishop entrusted their treasure to four *parfaits* who escaped into the mountains—supposedly with the mythical Holy Grail. A ticket to the château includes entrance to the tiny museum in the village below, which displays castle artifacts, but no carpenter's cup (castle open daily 9am-7pm; it can also be visited at night for free; museum open daily 10am-1pm and 2-7pm, March-Nov.; admission 20F, students 12F). Montségur's **tourist office** (tel. 05 61 03 03 03) is open daily July-Sept. At other times, call the mayor's office for information (tel. 05 61 01 10 27). Without a car, getting to Montségur is far from easy and requires an overnight stay. Two daily **buses** (direction: Lavelanet, 24F) leave Foix from the Centre Culturel Olivier Carol, across the parking lot behind the post office. Ask the driver to drop you off at the turn-off to Montségur, and follow the signs through the town of Villeneuve d'Olmes to **Montferrier** (5km). The **gîte d'étape, La Freychèd** (tel. 05 61 01 10 38; 65F, access to kitchen) welcomes visitors and lets you leave your pack for the additional 5km climb straight up to the hilltop château. There are *gîtes* in Montségur, but Montferrier has a small supermarket, is a one-hour walk down from the château, and lets you climb free of excess baggage. Call ahead. To return to Foix, flag down the bus (check schedules carefully at the Foix tourist office before you leave).

I'll Trade You My '52 Mantle for Your '88 Gerard Longuet

If you're going to be in France for any length of time and need to make a phone call, you'll eventually give up the constant (and futile) search for coin-operated telephones, and invest in a *télécarte.* While making your call, look down at your feet. You'll probably see numerous cigarette butts mixed in with many pieces of plastic wrap similar to the one you just shucked off your own card. But where are the spent cards? Where is the *télécarte* graveyard? The answer is simple but shocking: collectors' albums. That's right: the ads and artwork on the cards turn some designs into valuable commodities. So valuable, in fact, that an entire *télécarte* collection business has developed around the credit-card sized *chef d'oeuvres.* Trading and collecting the cards is as intense and lucrative a hobby as that of collecting baseball cards in the U.S. Stores and markets may have boxes of common and uncommon cards (for 5-10F each), while the rarities reside under protective covering in binders and acrylic cases. The condition of a card, of course, drastically affects its value, while the number of call-enabling *unités* is irrelevant. A 1987-88 carte by Gerard Longuet is one of the gems in the *télécarte* collector's crown. Only 40 exist, and an unblemished one will net you 34,000F. But for the real prize, seek out the November 1988 card "Les Boxeurs," with artwork by Gilles Chagny. There are 100 out there, but only one is signed by the artist. Maybe it's down at your feet right now as you make your call—it's worth checking, because if it *is* there, you've just stumbled across a cool 60,000F.

AX-LES-THERMES (VALLÉES D'AX)

Formerly referred to as the *Pays des Eaux,* **Ax-les-Thermes,** a small resort town (pop. 1400) 40km southeast of Foix and 130km south of Toulouse, owes its appeal partly to the remedial powers of its bubbly sulfuric waters. A steady flow of mostly sedentary visitors partakes of the water's effervescent effects. Ax also makes a good trip for the more active folk interested in hiking or skiing in the hilly hinterland of the *Pyrénées ariégeoises.* The **tourist office,** on pl. du Breilh, has information on local spas and nearby ski areas (open Mon.-Sat. 9am-noon and 2-7pm, Sun. 9am-noon and 2-6pm). To reach the office, turn left out of the train station on av. Delcassé (N20) and follow the street to the pl. du Breilh. Address phone inquiries to the **Vallées d'Ax** tourist office, in Luzenac (tel. 05 61 64 60 60; fax 05 61 64 41 80). **Trains** (tel. 05 61 64 20 72) roll from Ax to Toulouse (5 per day, 1½hr., 90F), La Tour de Carol (4 per day, 1¼hr., 38F), and Foix (5 per day, 40min., 38F). Trains also connect Ax to **L'Hospitalet** (21F), a small town near the Andorran border. Buses await the train's arrival at both La Tour and L'Hospitalet for the final leg of the trip to that mall rat's paradise, **Andorra. Hôpital St-Louis** (tel. 05 61 02 24 02) rests conveniently behind the Bassin. Dial 05 61 64 20 17 for the **police. Currency exchange** clinks at the **post office** on pl. Roussel (tel. 05 61 64 20 48); Ax's **postal code** is 09110 (open Mon.-Fri. 9am-noon and 2-5pm, Sat. 9am-noon). Either stock a picnic in Toulouse or Foix or pack for the trails at Ax's *boulangeries, pâtisseries, épiceries,* and *confisseries,* on rue de l'Horloge (which becomes rue Rigal).

Under the reign of Louis IX in the mid-13th century, the Count of Foix dispatched his leprosy-stricken soldiers to cleanse their feet in the town's 78°C **Bassin des Ledres** (Basin of Misers). Several centuries would pass before the "cures" of Ax gained the sanction of the medical community, as a result of Abraham Sicre's 1758 study on the salubrious properties of Ax's thermal waters. Even today, a gang of *vieillards* still soak their tired tootsies in the *centre ville's bassin.* Try not to think about what's been there, and dunk with them.

Several paths near Ax offer year-round rambles and hikes. The **Grandes Randonnées 10 and 7** (GR10 and GR7) are rather difficult. The easier *sentier Cathar* and *Tour des Vallées d'Ax* accommodate year-round hikers of all levels. A guide based out of the tourist office offers a half-day tour for 55F per person and a full-day tour for 800F per group of up to 12 people. Eight km above Ax, **Bonascre** (tel. 05 61 64 36 36) offers excellent, challenging, and relatively warm skiing with mega-moguls. Cross-country skiing can be found at **Chioula** (tel. 05 61 64 20 00); 10km from Ax, it is also a wonderful mountain-biking spot in summer. Ask at the tourist office for more detailed information about skiing and hiking in the area. They can also help you with info about accommodations if you decide to stay in Ax a while.

Albi

Albi (pop. 50,000) first made a name for itself during the 13th-century Catholic inquisition against Catharism, serving as a Cathar stronghold at a time when calling oneself a Cathar meant burning at the stake. The natives, *Albigeois,* thus lent their name to the word for "heretic" and the famous campaign against Catharism, the "Albigensian Crusades." The foundations of the imposing Cathédrale Ste-Cécile were laid shortly after the crusades, to remind southern France and the remaining *Albigeois* that the Catholic Church had regained definitive authority. Next door the local museum recalls less-belligerent times with an extraordinary assemblage of works by native son Henri de Toulouse-Lautrec. In summer, the city comes alive with exuberant music and theater festivals.

ORIENTATION AND PRACTICAL INFORMATION

Capital of the *département du Tarn,* Albi is an easy daytrip from Toulouse, which lies 76km southwest. To reach the tourist office and the center of town, turn left from the station onto av. Maréchal Joffre. Make another left onto av. Général de Gaulle, and then bear left over pl. Lapeyrouse to the pedestrian *vieille ville*. Rue de Verdusse will lead you toward pl. Ste-Cécile, where signs point to the tourist office (10min.). The hostel is another 10 minutes from the center, in a residential area.

Tourist Information: Tourist Office, pl. Ste-Cécile (tel. 05 63 49 48 80; fax 05 63 49 48 98). Accommodations service (10F in town, 15F elsewhere). *Vieille ville* tours in French June 15-Sept. 15 (25F, students 20F). Generic brochure includes a good map. The free, monthly **Albi Sortir** lists events around the city. **Currency exchange** Sun.-Mon. Open July-Aug. Mon.-Sat. 9am-7:30pm, Sun. 10:30am-1pm and 3:30-6:30pm; Sept.-June Mon.-Sat. 9am-noon and 2-6pm, Sun. 10:30am-12:30pm and 3:30-6:30pm. Pubs, discos, and concerts are listed in **Fiesta,** available at *tabacs* and cafés. The **Comité Départemental de la Randonnée Pédestre** (tel. 05 63 77 32 25) offers outdoors info and advice on the Tarn Valley.

Money: There's an **ATM** at **Crédit Mutuel,** 7, pl. Lapeyrouse (tel. 05 63 54 81 16).

Trains: av. Maréchal Joffre (tel. 08 36 35 35 35). To: Toulouse (15 per day, 1hr., 61F); Castres, backtracking to St-Sulpice (5 per day, 1½hr., 75F); Paris (2 per day, 330F at night with change at Toulouse, 350F direct at 7:44am). Open daily 5:30am-9:30pm. **Lockers** 5F per 24hr.

Buses: Gare routière in the center of pl. Jean Jaurès (tel. 05 63 54 58 61), inside Halte des Autobus newsstand. To Toulouse (7 per day, 1 on Sun., 50F) and Castres (5 per day, 1¼hr., 28F). Open Mon.-Sat. 6am-8pm.

Public Transport: Espace Albibus, rue de l'Hôtel de Ville (tel. 05 63 38 43 43). Ticket 4F50. Buses run roughly 7:30am-7:30pm.

Taxis: Albi Taxi Radio (tel. 05 63 54 36 25 or 05 63 54 85 03). 24hr. At the train station or *gare routière*. 3F per km during the day, 5F per km at night.

Bike Rental: Cycles Andouard, 7, rue Séré-de-Rivières (tel. 05 63 38 44 47). Rents mountain bikes at 80F per ½-day, 100F per day, 500F per week. Deposit 2000F. Open Mon. 2-7pm, Tues.-Sat. 8:30am-noon and 2-7pm. V, MC.

Laundromat: 8, rue Emile Grand. A few blocks from the hostel, off Lices Georges Pompidou. Bring 10F and 2F coins. Open 7am-9pm.

Youth Center: Le Bureau de Jeunesse de l'Albigeois, 19, pl. Ste-Cécile (tel. 05 63 47 19 55), opposite the tourist office. Friendly staff has info on jobs, lodgings, and events. Open Mon.-Tues. and Thurs.-Fri. 1:30-6:30pm, Wed. 10am-6:30pm.

Crisis Lines: Maison des Femmes, 26, rue de Genève (tel. 05 63 49 48 00). Call or visit 24hr. Houses women in trouble. **SOS Amitié** (tel. 05 63 54 20 20), don't jump ship, cuz you've got a friend 2:30pm-10:30am.

Medical Assistance: Centre Hospitalier, rue de la Berchere (tel. 05 63 47 47 47). **Medical emergency** tel. 15.

Police: 23, Lices Georges Pompidou (tel. 05 63 49 22 81). **Emergency** tel. 17.

Post Office: pl. du Vigan (tel. 05 63 48 15 63). Poste restante. Photocopies 1F. 24-hr. **ATM. Currency exchange.** Open Mon.-Fri. 8am-7pm, Sat. 8am-noon. **Postal code:** 81000.

ACCOMMODATIONS AND CAMPING

Tourists pour into Albi in the summer on their pilgrimage to the Toulouse-Lautrec museum. Arrive early or call ahead. For info on *gîtes d'étape* and rural camping, call **ATTER** (tel. 05 63 48 83 01; open Mon.-Fri. 8:30am-12:30pm and 1:30-6pm).

Maison des Jeunes et de la Culture, 13, rue de la République (tel. 05 63 54 20 67; fax 05 63 54 61 55). From the tourist office, take rue Fargues to rue Emile Grand. Take a right on Lices Georges Pompidou and the next left onto rue de la République (10min.). Or take bus 1 (direction: Cantepau) to "République" and walk down rue de la République. Institutional co-ed rooms (and co-ed bathrooms). Thin but well-supported bunks (16 per room). Info on activities. Laundry. 26F. Breakfast 12F. Filling meals 40F. Sheets 15F. Key deposit 20F. Reception Mon.-Fri. 6-11pm, Sat.-Sun. and holidays 8-10pm. No lockout or curfew.

Hôtel La Régence, 27, av. Maréchal Joffre (tel. 05 63 54 01 42), near the station. The owners fill the rooms with antiques. TVs in every room. Singles and doubles 110F, with shower 160-190F. Extra bed 40F. Free showers. Breakfast 25F. V, MC.

Hôtel du Parc, 3, av. du Parc (tel. 05 63 54 12 80; fax 05 63 54 12 80). From the station follow av. Maréchal Joffre as it becomes bd. Carnot. The hotel's on the left across from Parc Rochegude. Exceptionally clean, quiet rooms, all with TV. Bar downstairs. Singles and doubles 160F, with shower 200F, with bath 210-260F. Triples 280-320F. Quads 360F. Free hall shower. Breakfast 29F. V, MC, AmEx.

Camping: Parc de Caussels (tel. 05 63 60 37 06), 2km east of Albi on D999 (route de Millau). Take bus 5 (direction: Piscines) from pl. Jean Jaurès (every hr. until 7pm). Ask driver to stop near the campground, next to **Supermarché Casino.** On foot, leave town on rue de la République and follow the signs (30min.). Pool nearby. 52F per 2 people with car. Hot showers free. Open Easter-Oct.

FOOD

You'll find deals at the large indoor **market** on pl. du Marché (open Tues.-Sun. 8am-12:30pm) or at the **supermarket/cafeteria Casino,** 39, rue Lices Georges Pompidou (open Mon.-Sat. 8:30am-7:30pm; cafeteria open daily 11:30am-9:30pm; entrees 24-47F). A large **market** fills pl. Ste-Cécile on Saturdays from 8am to 12:30pm. A **marché biologique** sells organic products Tuesdays from 5 to 7pm at pl. du Jardin National. *Boulangeries,* cafés, and restaurants surround **pl. du Vigan.** For late-night munchies, head to the grocery **La Glycine,** rue du Dr. Camboulives (tel. 05 63 38 95 64; open Sun.-Thurs. 7pm-2am, Fri.-Sat. 7pm-4am). Students can call 05 63 48 16 92 for info on the **university cafeteria** (meals 12F).

Le Robinson, 142, rue Eurand-Branly (tel. 05 63 46 15 69). Where Lices Georges Pompidou hits the river, a path leads down to this vine-covered paradise. After a meat or fish dish (45-65F) or the 4-course vegetarian *menu* (90F), take a stroll by the pond. Open Wed.-Sun. noon-2pm and 7:30-10pm, Tues. 7:30-10pm. V, MC.

Le Petit Bouchon, 77, rue Croix Verte (tel. 05 63 54 11 75), off Lices Georges Pompidou. Claude serves traditional dishes and conversation, then mixes a secret cocktail that'll leave beer fanatics bellowing for fuzzy navels. 45F, 55F, and 65F *menus.* Open Mon.-Fri. 11:30am-2:30pm and 7-9:30pm, Sat. lunch only. V, MC.

Le Tournesol, 11, rue de l'Ort en Salvy (tel. 05 63 38 38 14), off pl. Vegan. British-French vegetarian couple offers such homemade meatless fare as veggie pâté and meal-size salads (46F), as well as an enticing selection of desserts (13-25F). Open Tues.-Thurs. noon-2pm, Fri.-Sat. noon-2pm and 7:15-9:30pm. V, MC, AmEx.

SIGHTS AND ENTERTAINMENT

Born with a congenital bone disease to an aristocratic family, Henri de Toulouse-Lautrec (1864-1901) led a life of debauchery among the cafés, cabarets, and brothels of Paris. From his fanciful advertisements for the *Moulin Rouge* to his pastels and lithographs, Toulouse-Lautrec depicted life as he saw it, often sparking controversy with his bold interpretations of French society. He died at age 37, leaving behind a lasting homage to nighttime Paris. The collection of works ferreted away by his mother and assembled in the **Musée Toulouse-Lautrec** (tel. 05 63 49 48 70) in the 13th-century Palais de la Berbie is the most complete anywhere—oils, pastels, lithographs, sketches, and drawings, including all 31 of the famous posters of Montmartre nightclubs. Upstairs is a fine collection of contemporary art, including sculpture and painting by Degas, Dufy, Matisse, and Rodin. The balcony off Room 8 provides an excellent view of the surrounding gardens and the river Tarn. (Open June-Sept. daily 9am-noon and 2-6pm; Oct.-March Wed.-Mon. 10am-noon and 2-5pm; April-May 10am-noon and 2-6pm. Admission 20F, students 10F. The tourist office gives guided tours June 15-Sept. 15; 32F, students 22F.)

The artist's family still owns his birthplace, the **Maison Natale de Toulouse-Lautrec** (also called the Hôtel du Bosq), 14, rue Toulouse-Lautrec in *Vieil* Albi; bd. Général Sibille affords a good view of the house. You can visit the 12th-century **Château du Bosc** (tel. 05 65 69 20 83), where he spent childhood vacations, in a forest 45km northeast of Albi (open daily 9am-7pm). Drive up the N88 toward Rodez or take the train to the **Naucelle** station, 4km from the château.

The **Cathédrale Ste-Cécile,** begun in 1282 after papal crusaders vanquished Albi's heretics, doubled as a fortress. Colorful 16th-century frescoes cover the interior. Just below the organ, *The Last Judgment* demonstrates in horrific detail—complete with boiling oil—what will happen to visitors who don't obey the "Silence" signs posted throughout the church. In 1693, the construction of the **chapelle St-Clair** destroyed parts of the fresco. (Church open daily June-Sept. 8:30am-7pm; Oct.-May 8:30-11:45am and 2-5:45pm. Choir admission 3F. The tourist office gives tours June 15-Sept. 15 twice daily; 22F, students 15F. Evening tours of the illuminated church 20F, students 15F. English headphone tours available.) The church's organ bursts into song on Wednesdays at 5pm in July and August (free).

Albi entertains visitors with an abundance of celebrations, all listed in *Albi Sortir* at the tourist office. In the last two weeks of May, **Jazz dans le Tarn** brings high-hats and harmony to the streets. The **Festival Théâtral** takes place in the last week of June and the first week of July (tickets 100F, students 88F). The **Festival de Musique,** a series of concerts, opera, ballet, and guitar recitals, resounds from mid-July through the first week in August (100-120F). The festivities end with a bang as cars burn rubber on the first Sunday in September at the **Albi Grand Prix** (100F).

Nightlife-seekers will have no problem finding fellow coffee-sippers, *glâce*-lickers, and beer-guzzlers along **pl. de l'Archevêché** in front of the cathedral and at Lices Georges Pompidou near pl. du Vigau. Innovative plays run at the **Théâtre du Croix Blanche,** 14, rue de Croix Blanche (tel. 05 63 54 18 63 for schedules). The **Centre Culturel de l'Albigeois** (tel. 05 63 54 11 11), on the felicitously named pl. de l'Amitié Entre les Peuples, off bd. Carnot and opposite **Parc Rochegude,** often shows foreign films in their original languages (Mon.-Sat. at 6 and 8:30pm, Sun. at 3, 6, and 8:30pm). Pick up a schedule at the center (open Tues.-Fri. 2-7pm, Sat. 10am-noon and 2-7pm; 41F, students and seniors 29F).

Albi stands on the western tip of the **Tarn Valley,** an expansive stretch of cliffs, forests, and bucolic villages. The **Gorges du Tarn,** with high limestone cliffs, grottoes, and caves, snake eastward from Albi. The **tourist office,** av. Alfred Merle (tel. 05 65 60 02 42), in **Millau,** 100km east of Albi, has extensive information on car routes, hiking trails, and river rafting through the canyon and will direct you to **Le Rozier,** the best place to begin your descent.

■ Near Albi: Cordes-sur-Ciel

Set on a hilltop 24km north of Albi, Cordes-sur-Ciel served as a sentinel on the Cathar frontier during the 13th-century Albigensian crusades. The walled city has been extensively renovated in recent years, thanks largely to the efforts of artist Yves Brayer, who arrived in 1940. The double-walled, seemingly impregnable *vieille ville,* distinguished by its steeply inclined cobblestone streets, retains its medieval character. The **tourist office** (tel. 05 63 56 00 52; fax 05 63 56 19 52) is on pl. de Halle in Maison Fontpeyrouse (open daily 10:30am-12:30pm and 2:30-6pm). They can help find accommodations or a **campsite** (only a 20-min. walk from Cordes' center). Getting to Cordes can be a logistical nightmare; many choose to hitch there to avoid the hassle. **Trains** go to Vindrac via Tessonnieres (35F), where you can call the minibus service **Barrois** (tel. 05 63 56 14 80) to take you the 4km to Cordes. During the school year (through June), **Cars Becardit** (tel. 05 63 45 03 03) and **Sudcar Rolland** (tel. 05 63 54 11 93) send a couple of **buses** daily to Cordes from Albi (23F). In July and August, Barrois runs **minibuses** twice daily (except Sun.) between Albi and Cordes (23F); these buses also run Tuesday and Saturday throughout the year. Check the schedules of all three services to find even vaguely convenient times. The Cordes **police** can be reached at 05 63 56 00 17.

Eglise St-Michel, with a 19th-century organ from Paris's Notre-Dame, rests at Cordes' summit. The **Musée Yves Brayer** (tel. 05 63 56 00 40) is worth visiting for its fanciful renditions of the town (open Mon.-Wed. 10am-noon and 1-6pm, Thurs.-Fri. 9am-noon and 1:30-6pm, Sat. 9am-noon, Sun. 2-6pm; admission 20F, groups 10F). The **Musée Charles Portal,** with a reconstructed farmhouse interior, features local traditions and archaeology (open July-Aug. daily 11am-noon and 3-6pm; April-June and Sept.-Oct. Mon.-Sat. same hours, Sun. 3-6pm; admission 15F, students 7F). To see amazing sculptures made entirely of sugar—as well as several pieces including a life-size violin and some flowers with accompanying sugared insects—visit the **Musée de l'Art du Sucre,** pl. de la Bride (tel. 05 63 56 02 40). As you leave, you can buy a sugar-sculpted flower (60F) or some of the local specialty candies *truffelines* and *muscalines* (open daily Feb.-Dec. 10am-noon and 2:30-6:30pm; admission 15F, children and groups 10F). **Pâtisserie Mogenaar,** pl. de la Halle (tel. 05 63 56 02 17), sells bags of *croquants,* thin almond cookies that are also a local specialty (starting at 17F), and other nut-based delicacies (open daily 9am-8pm). A food **market** takes place Saturdays 8am-noon at the bottom of the hill. The tourist office leads organized **walks** through the countryside beyond the city walls once a week in July and August. Fire-eaters ply the costumed crowds at the medieval market during Cordes' **Fête du Grand Fauconnier** (a 4-day weekend in mid-July). Partake of hefty fare at one of the Fête's medieval banquets (200F dinner with medieval spectacle; also a pay-per-item option). Costume rentals 50-100F (entrance to each theater piece, concert, or magic show in the streets is 15F; one entrance is free if you're costumed).

Castres

Straddling the brown, garbage-laden Agoût river, Castres muddled through time in a most prosaic fashion until it hit the 11th-century relics jackpot, acquiring St. Vincent's tremendously revered remains. The town became a St-Tropez for pilgrims *en route* to Santiago de Compostela. But alas, the pilgrimage industry isn't what it once was, and Castres (pop. 48,000) has had to change with the times. Relics in short supply, the city has managed to acquire the second-largest collection of Spanish art in France for its **Musée Goya.** In addition, Castres has assembled a prodigious quantity of pamphlets, drawings, and photographs about the life of its native son, Jean Jaurès, whose name graces an avenue in every French town. The daytrip from Toulouse may be a small price for the satisfaction of knowing exactly who Jaurès was.

PRACTICAL INFORMATION

To reach the tourist office from the train station, turn left onto av. Albert 1er and then bear right onto bd. Henri Sizaire. At pl. Alsace-Lorraine, cross the bridge to reach the **tourist office annex** (tel. 05 63 51 20 37), in the parking at bd. Raymond Vittoz (15min.). They provide maps and help with accommodations (open Mon.-Sat. 9am-noon and 2-6pm). For somewhat more extensive help and longer hours, the **tourist office** itself, 3, rue Milhau Ducommun (tel. 05 63 62 63 62; fax 05 63 62 63 60), can be found by turning left onto bd. Raymond Vittoz after crossing the bridge, then taking the first left onto rue Villegoudou, and veering right onto rue Leris. The tourist office is on the left as you continue straight. (20min. from the station. Open July-Aug. Mon.-Sat. 8am-8pm, Sun. 10am-noon and 2-6pm; Sept.-Oct. 15 and April 15-May Mon.-Sat. 8:30am-7pm, Sun. 10am-noon and 2-6pm; Oct. 16-April 15 Mon.-Sat. 8:30am-12:30pm and 1:30-6:30pm, Sun. 10am-noon and 2-6pm.) A 24-hour **ATMs** smile half a block from the station on av. Albert 1er, on the way to the tourist office. **Trains,** av. Albert 1er (tel. 08 36 35 35 35), run to Toulouse (8 per day, 1hr., 70F); Carcassonne via Toulouse (8 per day, 2½hr., 125F); and Albi via St-Sulpice (7 per day, 2hr., 78F). **Lockers** 5F per 24hr. Rent **bikes** at **Tabarly,** 38, pl. Soult (tel. 05 63 35 38 09). Mountain bikes 50F per ½-day, 80F per day; 500F or credit card deposit. (Open Tues.-Sat. 9am-noon and 2-7pm.) The **hospital** is at 20, bd. Maréchal Foch (tel. 05 63 71 63 71). In a **medical emergency** call 05 63 71 15 15 or 15. The **police** are at 2, av. de Gaulle (tel. 05 63 35 40 10). **Emergency** tel. 17. The **post office** (tel. 05 63 71 38 60) is on the corner of allée Alphonse Juin and bd. Henri Sizaire and has poste restante and **currency exchange** with 1.2% commission on traveller's checks (open Mon.-Fri. 8am-7pm, Sat. 8am-noon; **postal code:** 81100).

Local **markets** convene on pl. Jean Jaurès (Tues. and Thurs.-Sat. 7:30am-1pm) and at the **Marché Couvert de l'Albinque,** pl. de l'Albinque (Tues.-Sun. 8:30am-1pm). The **Monoprix,** rue Sabatier at pl. Jean Jaurès, delivers seductively cheap **supermarket** fare (open Mon.-Sat. 8:30am-7:30pm). A few *boulangeries, boucheries,* and *pâtisseries* gather on rues Gambetta and Victor Hugo in the *centre ville.* Restaurants cluster off pl. Jean Jaurès and near rue Villegoudou. For marvelous munchables, head to **Cormary,** 13, rue Victor Hugo (tel. 05 63 59 27 09), sculpting fine chocolates, meringues, marzipan and pastries into ingenious animal shapes (open Mon.-Fri. 6am-1pm and 1:30-7:30pm, Sat. 6am-5:30pm, Sun. 6am-1pm).

SIGHTS AND ENTERTAINMENT

Situated in front of the arabesques and shrubs of the **Jardin de l'Evêché,** the **Musée Goya** (tel. 05 63 71 59 27) houses a terrific sampling of Spanish painting dating back to the 14th century. The museum's treasured Goya collection reigns supreme among the sprinkling of Catalan and Aragonese masters. While the collection includes only three paintings, the oodles of engravings will make any true aficionado cry, "Goya, oh Boya!" (Open June-Aug. Mon.-Sat. 9am-noon and 2-6pm, Sun. 10am-noon and 2-6pm; April-May and Sept. closed Mon.; Oct.-March Tues.-Sat. 9am-noon and 2-5pm, Sun. 10am-noon and 2-5pm. Admission 20F, students 10F; Sept.-June 15F, students 8F. July-Aug. 3-museum ticket 25F, students 15F.)

The **Musée Jaurès,** pl. Pélisson (tel. 05 63 72 01 01), is packed with pamphlets, political cartoons, photographs, and faded newspaper articles that recount Jean Jaurès' spirited rhetoric and life. Jaurès leapt into prominence as leader of the striking glass-workers of Carmaux in 1896 and later joined other socialists, notably Emile Zola, in vehement defense of Captain Alfred Dreyfus, the Jewish officer framed as a traitor by the army (same hours as the Musée Goya; admission 10F, students 5F).

The **Centre d'Art Contemporain,** 35, rue Chambre de l'Edit (tel. 05 63 59 30 20), lodged in an 18th-century *hôtel particulier,* features innovative, up-and-coming artists. (Open July-Aug. daily 10am-noon and 2-6pm; Sept.-June Tues.-Fri. 10am-noon and 2-6pm, Sat.-Mon. 3-6pm. Admission and guided tours 5F; free Sept.-June.)

Those who make it past the unpromising exterior of the **Eglise St-Jacques** at pl. St-Jacques will find themselves surrounded by beautiful wood and graceful oil paintings. The **Eglise de la Platé,** on rue Victor Hugo by rue Chambre de l'Edit, has a series of violet inner domes woven in gold and resting above a marble altarpiece featuring the rococo Notre-Dame de la Platé. From mid-July through the end of August, the **Festival Goya** celebrates Spanish culture with concerts, exhibitions, flamenco and ballet performances, and more. Many events are free; tickets to others (40-160F, reduction for students and groups of 10 or more) are available at the tourist office.

Carcassonne

Carcassonne's fortified Cité has had a rough go of it. Attacked in the first century by Roman invaders (who subsequently gave way to Visigoths and Moors), Europe's largest fortress has come to exemplify stalwart opposition in the face of aggression. When Charlemagne's troops besieged the Cité over a five-year period in the 8th century, legend has it that its widowed Moorish queen rushed to the Moor-held Cité's defense. Dame Carcas fooled the enemy into overestimating the size of her corps, and Charlemagne called off the attack. As the troops retreated, the Grande Dame of Carcas rang *(sonner)* the city's bell to signal her willingness to draw up a treaty—some even say she had a crush on the emperor. Supposedly, the tintinnabulation drew the attention of the king's men, who called to Charlemagne, *"Carcas sonne!"*

To rectify the egregious state into which the ancient fortress had fallen over the years, King Louis-Philippe commissioned the revered architect Viollet-le-Duc in 1844 to restore it. Today, the **Cité de Carcassonne** rises from a precipitous plateau in the Garonne Valley and exudes a protective, maternal air over its modern offspring, the *basse ville.* The Cité's allure is no secret. Even before providing the backdrop for the

1991 movie *Robin Hood: Prince of Thieves,* the Cité attracted droves of tourists and gift shops. By wandering down a narrow side street, you can lose the bustle and imagine the solitude of Dame Carcas' stronghold. At night, the crowds disperse and the fortress, bathed with floodlights and filled with the music of summer concerts, recaptures its elusive charm.

ORIENTATION AND PRACTICAL INFORMATION

The modern *basse ville* (pop. 45,000) lets the Cité steal the show. Hosting offices, shops, hotels, and the train station, the *basse ville* facilitates trips to the Cité. To reach the Cité, catch bus 4, the black line, from the train station or pl. Gambetta (every ½-hr. until 7pm, 5F). Otherwise, it's a pleasant 30-minute hike. To get from the station to the Cité, walk straight down rue Clemenceau, then take the third left onto rue de la Liberté and a right onto bd. Jean Jaurès. At sq. Gambetta, bear left on rue de Pont-Vieux and walk over the bridge. Follow rue Trivalle to rue Gustave Nadaud, which runs along the perimeter of the Cité. The tourist office annex will be on the right as you enter the castle. Street signs can be fickle in Carcassonne, so check all four corners of the intersection.

Tourist Office: 15, bd. Camille Pelletan, sq. Gambetta (tel. 04 68 25 07 04; fax 04 68 47 34 96). Walk straight from the train station over the canal on rue G. Clemenceau. Turn left onto rue de la Liberté and then right onto bd. Jean Jaurès. The office is on the right on sq. Gambetta (10min.). Open July-Aug. Mon.-Sat. 9am-7pm; Sept.-June Mon.-Sat. 9am-12:15pm and 1:45-6:30pm; Oct.-March Mon.-Sat. 9am-noon and 2-6:30pm. **Annex** in the Cité's porte Narbonnaise (tel. 04 68 25 68 81). Open July-Aug. daily 9am-7pm; Sept.-June. daily 9am-1pm and 2-6pm.

Money: Crédit Mutuel, 41, rue de Verdun, offers **currency exchange** and **ATM.** Also a 24-hr. **ATM** at corner of rue Gambetta and rue Aimé Ramond.

Trains: (tel. 04 68 47 50 50), behind Jardin St-Chenier. Carcassonne is a major stop between Toulouse (24 per day, 50min., 73F) and points south and east, such as Montpellier (14 per day, 2hr., 111F); Nîmes (12 per day, 2½hr., 136F); Lyon (2 direct per day, 5½hr., 262F); Marseille (every 2hr., 3hr., 197F); Nice (5 per day, 6hr., 292F); and Narbonne (10 per day, 1hr., 51F). Info office open Mon.-Sat. 9am-noon and 1:30-6:15pm. **Luggage Storage:** 20F for 3 days.

Buses: bd. de Varsovie or near the train station (tel. 04 68 25 12 74). Check posted schedules or ask tourist office. To: Toulouse (3 per day, 2½hr., 52F); Narbonne (2 per day, 1hr., 33F); Foix (1 per day, 3hr., 44F). **Cars Teissier** (tel. 04 68 25 85 45), across from Café Bristol in front of station. Service to Lourdes (45F). Office open Mon.-Sat. 8am-noon and 2-6pm.

Public Transportation: CART, sq. Gambetta (tel. 04 68 47 82 22). Ticket 5F. Mon.-Sat. only. Buses run until 7pm.

Taxis: (tel. 04 68 71 79 63 or 04 68 71 50 50). At the train station or across the canal by Jardin Chenier. 24hr. 7F per km during the day, 10F per km at night.

Laundromat: Laverie Express, 5, sq. Gambetta (tel. 04 68 71 43 76). Wash 20F for 7kg, 40F for 16kg. Dry 6F for 10min. Soap 2F. Open daily 8am-10pm.

Medical Assistance: Centre Hospitalier, route de St-Hilaire (tel. 04 68 24 24 24). **Medical emergency** tel. 15.

Police: 40, bd. Barbès (tel. 04 68 77 49 00). **Emergency** tel. 17.

Post Office: 40, rue Jean Bringer (tel. 04 68 11 71 18). Poste restante (postal code: 11012). **Currency exchange.** Telephones. Photocopies 1F. Open Mon.-Fri. 8am-7pm, Sat. 8am-noon. **Branch office** (tel. 04 68 47 95 45) at the corner of rue de Comte Roger and rue Viollet-le-Duc in the Cité. **Postal code:** 11000.

ACCOMMODATIONS AND CAMPING

Carcassonne's large, comfortable hostel puts you smack dab in the middle of the Cité; your first steps out the door in the morning will be on cobblestones. If the hostel is full, find a hotel in the *basse ville;* those in the Cité are ferociously expensive.

Auberge de Jeunesse (HI), rue de Vicomte Trencavel (tel. 04 68 25 23 16; fax 04 68 71 14 84), in the Cité. Friendly dorms. Terrific manager safeguards valuables. Kitchen available. Sheets 14F. 70F, breakfast included. Members only. Laundry 20F wash, 20F dry. Bar open 6:30pm-1am. Reception open Mon.-Fri. 7am-1am, Sat.-Sun. 7am-noon and 5pm-1am. Lockout 10am-1pm. Curfew 1am, in winter 11pm. Reserve a few days—from April to June, a few weeks—in advance. V, MC.

Hôtel Astoria, at the intersection of rue Montpellier and rue Tourtel (tel. 04 68 25 31 38; fax 04 68 71 34 14), take an immediate left after crossing the bridge in front of the station. Pleasant, virtually spotless rooms. Gracious British-French owners encourage reservations June 15-Sept. 15. Ask for one of the gloriously modern rooms in the annex across the street (cheapest singles 155F, doubles 175-180F). One 95F single. Singles and double 120F, with shower 149F. Showers 10F. Breakfast 25F. Reception 7:30am-11pm. V, MC, AmEx.

Hôtel Bonnafoux, 40, rue de la Liberté (tel. 04 68 25 01 45). From station, follow rue G. Clemenceau and turn at second right, rue de la Liberté. Rooms are plain and bare, some without carpets, but what a price! Singles 80F, with shower 130F. Doubles 105F, with shower 140F. Triples 145F, with shower 190F. Quads 145F, with shower 200F. Student discount of 10F. Showers 18F. Breakfast 20F.

Le Cathare, 53, rue Jean Bringer (tel. 04 68 25 65 92), near post office. Cozy, bright, renovated rooms. Singles and doubles 110F, with shower and TV 150-175F. Triples 175-185F. Showers 15F. Breakfast 26F. Restaurant downstairs posts an ever-changing 58F *menu,* grilled in the dining room fireplace in winter. V, MC.

Camping: Camping de la Cité, route de St-Hilaire (tel. 04 68 25 11 77), across the Aude 2km from the modern town. Currency exchange, pool, tennis courts, grocery store. July-Aug. 75F per site; Sept.-June 50F.

FOOD

Most of the surprisingly inexpensive restaurants in the Cité serve *cassoulet,* a stew of white beans, herbs, and meat (usually lamb or pork)—yes, it's greasy, but don't knock it 'til you try it. On **rue du Plo,** 60F to 70F *menus* abound. Save room for dessert at one of the outdoor *crêperies* on **pl. Marcou.** In the *basse ville,* simple, affordable restaurants line **bd. Omer Sarraut.** Restaurants in the Cité tend to close in winter. For produce, visit the **market** on pl. Carnot (known as marché aux Herbes; Tues., Thurs., and Sat. 7am-1pm), or the **covered market** on pl. d'Eggenfelden, off rue Aimé Ramon (Mon.-Sat. 7am-1pm). Monolithic **Monoprix** graces rue G. Clemenceau at rue de la République (open Mon.-Sat. 8:30am-7pm).

Les Fontaines du Soleil, 32, rue du Plo, in the Cité (tel. 04 68 47 87 06). Breezy patio dining in a beautiful garden court with fountain and evening guitar music. 55F lunch *menu* and dinner *menus* from 69F specialize in fish and, of course, *cassoulet.* Open daily 11:30am-2am; Sept.-June 11:30am-3pm and 6pm-2am. V, MC.

La Riziere, 26, rue G. Brassens (tel. 04 68 47 17 36) in the *basse ville,* whips up vegetarian dishes and other Vietnamese specialties in a fresh, flower-filled interior. Heaping plates start at 45F. Open Tues.-Sun. noon-2pm and 7-11pm. V, MC.

Chez Paulo, 15, rue des Trois Couronnes (tel. 04 68 47 29 60), 2 blocks from pl. Gambetta. This cheery Italian restaurant in the *basse ville* serves up yummy *gnocchi* with gorgonzola sauce (55F), mushroom pizza (45F), and a 3-course 65F *menu.* Open daily 9am-2:30pm and 6:30-11pm. V, MC.

La Rotonde, 13, bd. Omer Sarraut (tel. 04 68 25 02 37), in the *basse ville* across from the station. A late-night *brasserie* and café, with a quick 70F *menu* of veal and pork dishes. Platter of cheese, *plat du jour,* and dessert 47F. An all-you-can-eat *hors d'oeuvres* bar (30F) with vegetables, pâtés. Dessert bar (25F). Open daily 6:30am-2am (sandwiches only 3-6:30pm and after 10:30pm). V, MC, AmEx.

SIGHTS AND ENTERTAINMENT

Occupying a strategic position on the road between Toulouse and the Mediterranean, Carcassonne's original fortifications date back to the Roman Empire in the first century. An early Visigoth fortress here repelled Clovis, King of the Franks, in AD

506, as well as subsequent invaders, but Carcassonne fell with Languedoc during the Albigensian Crusade in 1209. When the Cité passed to the control of the French King Louis IX, he ordered the construction of the second outer wall, copying the double-walled fortress design he had seen in Palestine as a crusader (and—a bit too closely perhaps—as a prisoner). The city lapsed into neglect until Viollet-le-Duc reconceived it in the 19th century. The blue slate roofs he fancied for the towers of the fortress's inner ring are so out of place among the Midi's red-tile roofs that the town has begun to reroof them using local materials.

Originally constructed as a palace in the 12th century, the **Château Comtal** (tel. 04 68 25 01 66) was transformed into a citadel following Carcassonne's submission to royal control in 1226. While entrance to the grounds and outer walls is free, you must pay for a guided tour to be admitted to the château. Included in the visit, the **Cour du Midi** contains the remains of a Gallo-Roman villa, former home to troubadours who entertained their viscounts with song and verse. The **Tour de la Justice's** treacherous staircase leading to nowhere served as a stairway to heaven for the ill-fated heretics who penetrated the fortress and instinctively rushed upstairs; only to be trapped and easily vanquished. Tours in French run continuously (3 daily in English June 15-Sept. 15). All begin inside the château's gates. (Open July-Aug. 9am-7:30pm; Sept. and June 9am-7pm; Oct.-May 9:30am-12:30pm and 2-6pm; tickets sold until 30min. before closing. Admission 28F, ages 18-25 18F.)

Although it feels a bit like an elementary-school haunted house, you'll still be disturbed by a visit to the Cité's torture chamber at the **Exposition Internationale,** 5, rue du Grand Puits (tel. 04 68 71 44 03). Marvel at the objects of persuasion used by the Catholics to show the Cathars the errors of their ways. (Explanations in English. Admission 30F, students 20F; open July-Aug. 9am-11pm; Sept.-June 10am-7pm.) For something cheerier, walk across the street to the **cartoon museum,** newly created by the Exposition's proprietors. It includes original cels from Walt Disney and Tex Avery cartoons (admission approx. 20F).

Those seeking less animated pleasures may wish to proceed to the other end of the Cité and the apse of **Basilique St-Nazaire,** the coolest place in Carcassonne on a sultry summer afternoon. The nave's simple, Romanesque style is enhanced by the lightness of the choir and windows. The tower represents another Viollet blunder—he restored it with crenellations in a Visigothic style that clashes with the charm of the rest of the structure (Oct.-March 9:30am-noon and 2-5:30pm; April-Sept. 9am-noon and 2-7pm). Turned into a fortress after the Black Prince destroyed Carcassonne in 1355, the *basse ville's* **Cathédrale St-Michel,** rue Voltaire (tel. 04 68 25 14 48), still sports fortifications on its southern side, facing bd. Barbès. The church, with its brightly painted interior, exemplifies 14th- and 15th-century *gothique languedocien* (open Mon.-Sat. 7am-noon and 2-7pm; Sun. 9:30am-noon).

During July, the eclectic, month-long **Festival de Carcassonne** graces the Théâtre de la Cité and the Château Comtal with a vibrant program of dance, opera, theater, and concerts (admission 120-270F, under 20 60F). For information, contact Festival de la Cité, Théâtre Municipal, B.P. 236, 11005 Carcassonne (for info tel. 04 68 25 33 13, reservations tel. 04 68 77 71 26). On **Bastille Day,** Carcassonne outdoes other displays of fireworks. Viewed from the *basse ville,* a complex lighting effect makes the Cité look as if it's going up in flames, commemorating the villages burned under Carcassonne's stern mandate when the city's **Tour de l'Inquisition** was the seat of the inquisitorial jury. For two weeks in August, the entire Cité returns to the Middle Ages for the **Cité en Scènes.** People dressed in medieval garb talk to visitors, display their crafts, and pretend nothing has changed in eight centuries. Jousts clang daily. At 9:30pm nightly, a huge multimedia show uses 20th-century technology to bring the 13th century to life. For ticket information, contact Carcassonne Terre d'Histoire, Club Hippique, Chemin de Serres, 11000 Carcassonne (tel. 04 68 47 97 97).

Though its nightlife is limited, Carcassonne manages to create just enough to satisfy insomniacs. Bars and cafés along rue Omer Sarraut and pl. Verdun remain open until midnight. You may have to walk a few dark blocks to reach **Day Break,** 72, rue Aimé Ramon (tel. 04 68 25 52 58), serving good food, local talent, and memories in its small, much-loved space. Live jazz concerts most Friday nights. (Open Mon.-Fri. 10am-3pm and 7pm-midnight; concert nights open until 3am; Sat. 10am-3pm.) Locals dance the night away at **La Bulle,** 115, rue Barbacane (tel. 04 68 72 47 70).

Collioure

Lounging at the very spot where the Pyrénées finally tumble into the Mediterranean, Collioure has seduced unsuspecting visitors for 2000 years. Wearing little more than flowers and brilliant sunlight, this small port captured the fancy of Greeks and Phoenicians long before its sittings with enraptured Fauvists and Surrealists, among them Dalí, Picasso, Dérain, Dufy, and an unknown named Matisse, who baptized the town as an artists' mecca in 1905. An easy daytrip from Perpignan, Collioure casts a spell with its exquisite churches, Vauban château, and enchanting harbor. Throw caution to the wind, stray from your itinerary, and respond to this siren's song.

ORIENTATION AND PRACTICAL INFORMATION

For answers to your queries, head to the **tourist office,** pl. du 18 Juin (tel. 04 68 82 15 47; fax 04 68 82 46 29). The tourist office keeps a list of the area's trails and helps plan hikes (open daily July-Aug. 9am-8pm; Oct.-March Mon.-Fri. 9am-noon and 2-6pm, Sat. 9am-noon; Sept. and April-June daily 9am-noon and 2-6pm). The **train station** (tel. 04 68 82 05 89), at the end of av. Aristide Maillol, sends trains north to Perpignan (26F) and Narbonne (12 per day, 80F), and south to Port Bou in Spain (6 per day, 16F) and Barcelona (5 per day, 67F). Luggage storage is 16F per day. For information on the coastal bus routes, call **Cars Inter 66** (tel. 04 68 35 29 02) or inquire at the tourist office. **Exchange currency** with no commission at **Banque Populaire,** 12, av. de la République (tel. 04 68 82 05 94; open daily 8am-noon and 1:30-5pm). The **police station** is on rue Michelet (tel. 04 68 82 25 63; Sept.-June tel. 04 68 82 00 60). The **post office,** rue de la République (tel. 04 68 82 11 28), has poste restante (open Mon.-Fri. 9am-noon and 2-5pm, Sat. 8:30-11:30am). Collioure's **postal code** is 66190.

ACCOMMODATIONS, CAMPING, AND FOOD

A popular retreat for English, French, German, and Spanish families with money to spend, Collioure fills its picturesque hotels and beaches to the brim during the vacation months of July and August. **Hôtel Triton,** 1, rue Jean Bart (tel. 04 68 82 06 52; fax 04 68 82 11 32), sits on the waterfront and boasts comfortable, modern rooms (doubles with shower 180F, with full bathroom 240-300F; breakfast 32F; reservations recommended July-Sept.; V, MC, AmEx). The legacy of the turn-of-the-century pilgrim painters lives on at the **Hôtel des Templiers,** 12, quai de l'Amirauté (tel. 04 68 98 31 10; fax 04 68 98 01 24). At this restaurant and hotel, Matisse, Picasso, Dalí, and lesser-known artists bartered their work for meals and lodging. Concerned more with local tradition than with making a profit, the proprietors have held on to these works in the face of an increasingly bullish art market. For the price of a drink (try the local *Banyuls,* a sweet *apéritif* at 13F a glass), you can marvel at their canvases, covering every iota of wall space. However, it's only as a guest in the hotel that you will see the other floors' equally packed walls—and live the mixed-up childhood fantasy of sleeping in a museum, with an original work hanging over your bed. (Doubles 290-340F. Triples 420F. Breakfast 35F. V, MC, AmEx.) The proprietors of **Hôtel Les Caranques,** route de Port-Vendres (tel. 04 68 82 06 68; fax 04 68 82 00 92), have carved their little haven out of a hillside with the Mediterranean splashing just below. 250-330F blue and white rooms open onto balconies directly overlooking the water; from the hotel's terrace, walk 10 steps to swim in the sea. Two 200F rooms share a hall shower. (Breakfast 35F. Reserve July-Aug. Closed Oct. 11-May 31.) **Camping Les Amandiers,** 28, rue de la Démocratie (tel. 04 68 81 14 69), is a 20-minute walk north of town (marked on the tourist office map), but only 150m from the beach. Includes hot showers and shaded tent sites (18F per person, 14F per tent; open April-Sept.).

A fantastic **market** on the pl. du Général Leclerc offers inexpensive local fruit, *charcuteries,* clothing, and regional trinkets Wednesday and Sunday 8am-1pm. Reasonably priced *crêperies, boulangeries,* sandwich shops, and cafés crowd **rue St-Vincent** as it nears the port. Beneath an archway topped with a statuette of the Virgin Mary, **El Capilló,** 22, rue St. Vincent (tel. 04 68 82 48 23), serves fresh-from-the-boat seafood and prepares mussels in six different ways, from *moules à la creme* to *moules au safran* (35-43F; open Wed.-Sun. 9am-3pm and 6:30-midnight). For the same 28F you might pay for a pâté sandwich at a *boulangerie,* **Les Vieux Remparts,** av. Boramar (tel. 04 68 82 05 12), will serve it to you while you sit on a beach patio in a padded chair under a parasol. They also dish up expensive *paella* and *bouillabaisse* (open Feb.-Oct. Mon.-Sun. noon-2:30pm and 7-10pm. V, MC). If you've been craving crêpes prepared in a yellow bus parked *inside* a bustling restaurant, then the **Crêperie Bretonne,** 10, quai d'Amirauté (tel. 04 68 82 54 91), is the place to be (open daily June-Oct. noon-midnight; Nov.-March open only during school holidays; April-May open noon-approx. 10pm; V, MC). The **Shopi supermarket,** 16, av. de la République (tel. 04 68 82 26 04), has Collioure's biggest food selection (open Mon.-Sat. 8:30am-12:15pm and 4-7:30pm, Sun. 8:30am-12:15pm), but **L'Express,** pl. Général Leclerc (tel. 04 68 82 12 61), has all the picnic food you need and better hours (open daily 7am-7:30pm; mid-Sept. to mid-June Mon.-Sat. until 7pm).

SIGHTS

Now extending from pl. du 8 Mai 1945 to the port, the 13th-century **Château Royal** (tel. 04 68 82 06 43) was further fortified in 1679 by Louis XIV's strategist Vauban. The public enjoys free access to its grassy ramparts (a picnic heaven) and abandoned concrete tennis court. The palace itself now houses a hodgepodge of permanent exhibits on regional history and changing modern art exhibits, including a permanent exhibit on anchovies. Wander through the labyrinthine tunnels beneath the château and scale the winding stone staircase for a salubrious view of town, sea, and mountains (open daily June-Sept. 10am-5:15pm; Oct.-May 9am-4:15pm; admission 20F, students 10F). The 17th-century **Notre-Dame-des-Anges** rises majestically from the northern tip of the village, but its gilded interior is closed for renovations until April 1998. Those in search of a more natural vantage point can scale the terraces of the **Parc Pams,** located behind the château off route de Porte-Vendres, to its rocky apex high above the sea.

Collioure's main sights, however, are its poetic **beach** and **harbor.** From the rocky promontory of the bay's southern edge to the pebbled expanses of shoreline punctuated by the château and Eglise Notre-Dame-des-Anges, Collioure's little bay shelters bathers in the embrace of its seawalls. A walk onto these stone extensions guarantees a breeze and a wide-angle dose of Mediterranean blue. Soaring over the highest point of the bay's northern shore is a tiny chapel and a crucifix facing out to sea. The *St-Laurent* and the *Ste-Nicole* offer daily ship *promenades en mer* south along the coast to **Port-Vendre** (where they make a brief stop) and on to **Cap Béar.** (Sun.-Mon., Wed., Fri.; 2 per day, 1hr., 45F.) Longer excursions (2hr.; Tues., Thurs., and Sat.) go south along the Côte Catalane to the Spanish border port of Cerbère (80F). Call 04 68 82 00 28 or fax 04 68 98 04 13 for more information. In July and August, a bus also runs from Port-le-Barcarès south to Cerbère, hitting eight beaches (including Collioure's) along the way. Call 04 68 35 43 00 for information.

The **Centre International de Plongé,** 2, rue du Puits-St-Dominique (tel. 04 68 82 07 16; fax 04 68 82 44 74), rents **windsurfers** (50F 1hr., 80F 2hr., 200F 5hr.). The CIP offers training in scuba-diving and windsurfing from April to early November. **Subchandlers Location,** 13, rue de la Tour d'Auvergne (tel. 04 68 82 06 34; fax 04 68 82 44 77), rents equipment to those with a scuba license (60F per ½-day, 90F per day); and surfboards (100F per ½-day, 200F per day; 3000F or ID deposit; open Mon.-Sat. 9am-8pm, Sun. 9am-1pm and 5-8pm; Sept.-June 9am-1pm and 2-7pm).

A walkway built into the bottom of the cliffs leads a few km north to **Argelès** along some refreshingly isolated coastline. The **Randonnée Pedestre Association** organizes more challenging walks and hikes (information at tourist office). **La Sociation Centre**

de Loisirs (tel. 04 68 82 47 55) will even take you **canyoning,** an outdoor activity that combines climbing, rappelling, hiking, and swimming—all to descend a canyon and its waterfall to water level (open daily 7am-10pm).

Céret

Céret (pop. 7500) has been the site of great artistic and botanic blossoming over the years. Renowned for their prized cherry trees that ripen each spring and yield precocious clusters of red fruit, each year the exuberant *Céretons* send the first *cerises* of the season to the President of the Republic. A yearly spring festival brings people from all over the region to Céret's early harvests. Yet it is another flowering that puts Céret on the map of France. Around 1910, some of the least popular artists in France found themselves in Céret. The rural beauty of the town enabled them to create inspired works; their canvases and sculptures are monuments to the rustic simplicity and visual enchantments of Céret. Picasso, Chagall, Manolo, and Herbin discovered a "Cubist Mecca," as Manolo dubbed it, in Céret. They spent several years here, endowing Céret with an impressive collection for its museum, and as sweet a reason as its fine fruit to draw strangers to the town.

PRACTICAL INFORMATION

The **tourist office,** 1, av. Clemenceau (tel. 04 68 87 00 53). From the bus stop on av. George Clemenceau, the tourist office is two blocks up the hill if you're let off outside the town, at the stop "Céret-pont," but it's a 15-minute walk. Follow the signs to the *centre ville.* At the end of rue St-Ferréol, turn left onto bd. Maréchal Joffre, then left again onto av. Clemenceau. Offers friendly service, a map of easy hikes (15F; 6 routes ranging from 2 to 4 hr.), and guided tours of the *vieille villle* (most days in winter around 3pm; 15F). (Open July-Aug. Mon.-Sat. 9am-12:30pm and 3-7pm, Sun. 9am-12:30pm; Sept.-Oct. Mon.-Fri. 10am-noon and 2-5pm, Sat. 10am-noon.) A 24-hr. **ATM** is next door at **Banque Populaire** (open Mon.-Fri. 8am-noon and 1:30-5pm). **Car Inter 66** (tel. 04 68 35 29 02) runs **buses** to Céret from Perpignan (1 per hr., 35min., 31F). The same bus line connects Céret to other towns in the valley. For information on **canyoning** contact Jean Guitard (tel. and fax 04 68 87 31 51). The **police** can be reached at 1, bd. Jean Moulin (tel. 04 68 87 10 15; **emergency** tel. 17). The **post office,** 40, av. Clemenceau (tel. 04 68 87 03 96), is open Mon.-Fri. 9am-noon and 2-5pm, Sat. 9am-noon (**postal code:** 66400).

ACCOMMODATIONS, CAMPING, AND FOOD

Céret makes a good daytrip, but you'll have a few options if you want to sleep where the cherry trees grow. The **Hôtel Vidal,** 4, pl. du 4 Septembre (tel. 04 68 87 00 85), resides in an impressive 1735 house. The hotel's appeal grows with a glimpse of its comfortable rooms, populated by dark wood furniture. (Singles and doubles 125F, with shower 155F, with bath 195F. Extra bed 30% more. Shower 10F. Breakfast 25F. Closed Oct. 15-Nov. 15. V, MC.) The modern, very white **Pyrénées Hôtel,** 7, rue de la République (tel. 04 68 87 11 02), has equally immaculate but simpler rooms. Ask for one with the amazing view of the surrounding foothills. (Singles 130F, with shower 180F. Doubles 160-170F, with shower 200-230F. Triples and quads with bath 280F. Breakfast "of the region" 35F. V, MC.) Céret also has several campsites. A 10-minute walk from the town's center, **Camping Municipal de Nogarede,** av. d'Espagne (tel. 04 68 87 26 72), is a two-star site; a municipal pool is a few blocks away. **Camping Saint-Georges,** route de Maureillas (tel. 04 68 87 03 73; 30min. by foot from the tourist office), has its own pool.

Saturday mornings (9am-12:30pm), a **food market** fills the boulevards between pl. Picasso and pl. de la Liberté. Be sure to pick up some of the fruit that makes Céret almost famous. For a meal, wander over to pl. des Neuf Jets for simple, inexpensive food. An outside table will let you admire the marble "fountain of nine jets," dating from 1313. The lion, symbol of the Spanish kings, was perched above the jets in

1491, when Céret was under Spanish control. When the French got the city back in 1659, they turned the lion's head to face France. A Latin inscription reads: "Come, *Céretons,* the lion is made cock" (the symbol of the French kings). **La Ferme de Céret,** 15, av. Clemenceau (tel 04 68 87 07 91), offers standard French fare amid dark brown wood and bright blue contemporary paintings, or in a back garden (open July-Oct. Tues.-Sun. noon-2pm and 7-9pm; Nov.-June Tues.-Sat. noon-2pm and 7-9pm; Sun. noon-2pm; V, MC). **L'Escapade,** 21, rue St-Ferréol (tel. 04 68 87 40 84) offers a 68F *menu* of simple, elegant food. The 88F Catalan *menu* at L'Escapade includes *escargots à la Catalane.* (Open Tues.-Sun. noon-2pm and 7-10pm. V, MC.)

SIGHTS AND ENTERTAINMENT

As you leave the *centre ville* and enter Céret's outskirts, you will pass over one of three bridges that arch nearby. The 14th-century **Pont du Diable** occupies a special place in locals' hearts. Legend holds that the proliferation of bridges was necessary to foil the Devil's attempts to collapse the first bridge. (See gray box below.)

The seemingly graffiti-bedecked building at 8, bd. Maréchal Joffre is actually the **Musée d'Art Moderne** (tel 04 68 87 27 76), cleverly combining form with function—even the building's name is spray-painted. Inside you will find a room filled with Picasso sketches and pottery, a few Chagalls, a Miró, and many paintings by Pierre Brune, the museum's founder. The second floor offers fascinating and funny contemporary art, including a mirrored piece that makes you its subject and several pieces by Claude Viollet, whose stained-glass windows in the 13th-century **Notre Dame de Sablons** of Aigues-Mortes (see page 434) have scandalized residents there. (Museum open July-Sept. daily 10am-7pm; Oct.-April Wed.-Mon. 10am-6pm; May-June daily 10am-6pm; 35F, students 20F.) To glimpse the remains of the city walls, visit the stone **Porte de France** and the 11th-century brick **Tour d'Espagne,** two very different former entrances to the city; you can even climb up and stand on top of the Tour D'Espagne. However, the best remains of the city's fortifications are alive today: tremendous plane trees, now 200 years old, that were planted to replace the crumbling city walls still mark the boundaries of the *vieille ville.*

The **Maison de l'Archéologie,** next to the Tour d'Espagne (tel. 04 68 87 31 59), opened its doors in the spring of '95. The two exhibition rooms hold local finds, mostly a lot of **clay jars** (open July-Sept. Mon.-Sat. 10am-12:30pm and 2:30-6pm, Sun. 2:30-6pm; call for off-season hours; admission 10F). If you've ever wanted to see **water damage** allowed to run its course in a big French church, Céret provides the perfect opportunity. The **Eglise St-Pierre** is undergoing restorations; take a step inside, noting the marble entrance steps and baptismal font (open Mon.-Sat. 9am-

The Bedeviled Bridges of Céret

The three bridges that arch adjacent to one another in Céret are no quirk of architectural coincidence; there is a diabolical logic behind the bridges that the town of Céret readily acknowledges. When the first bridge was being built in the 14th century, it collapsed into the river below. Efforts to repair the damage were thwarted by a second, more deleterious collapse. The engineer who designed the original bridge reputedly made a Faustian pact with the Devil in order that a third bridge might stand. Vowing to rebuild the bridge overnight, the Devil made the engineer promise that he could claim the first soul to cross the bridge at the cock's crow. Legend has it that in order not to rouse villagers' suspicions of his furtive labors, the Devil played soft Catalan music that night. At dawn, when the bridge had been almost entirely reconstructed, the engineer released a black cat. Surprised in the middle of finishing his bridge work, the Devil chased after his first "soul," leaving one stone unset. Today, this stone remains missing from the bridge. In order to dissuade the devil from carrying away any other souls, the *Céretons* built two bridges adjacent to the unfinished one.

LANGUEDOC-ROUSSILLON

noon and 2-6pm, Sun. 9am-noon). For those in cars, a beautiful panoramic view waits at **Front Fréde** (follow the signs from rue Front-Fréde).

For one weekend late in May, Céret celebrates the **Grand Fête de la Cerise** with two full days of cherry markets, Catalan songs, and the traditional Catalan dance, the *sardane.* The town's *féria* occurs every year on a weekend around July 14. Bullfights in the arena and music in the streets keep everyone up late into the night. The **Festival de la Sardane** is a day of traditional dancing, the third Sunday in August.

Perpignan

Comfortably cradled between the Mediterranean and the Pyrénées, Perpignan bounced between French and Spanish ownership as former capital of the counts of Roussillon and the kings of Majorque and later as the northern capital of the *Catalogne française* (French Catalan). In their centuries-long efforts to annex Roussillon to the state, French kings found themselves repeatedly pitted against a stalwart population of *Perpignannais*—wherein the resistors earned their name of *mangeurs de rats* (rat eaters) from the desperate methods used in their struggle for survival.

These days, the less conflicted citizens of Perpignan (pop. 108,000) peacefully relish their proximity to both the spacious beaches of the Côte Catalane and the splendor of the mountains. From the colors of the cafés to the lyrical accent of their ever-present patrons, Perignan has molded itself into a city where the pace is decidedly relaxed—just fast enough to resemble progress yet slow enough to enjoy the thousand perfumes of its famous flowers.

ORIENTATION AND PRACTICAL INFORMATION

Perpignan's train station, once referred to as "the center of the universe" (like Pai Yang) by a rather off-center Salvador Dalí, provides convenient connections to the Catalan region in Spain, 50km to the south, and the Pyrénées, whose foothills begin rolling 30km west. Most sights, restaurants, cafés, and shops lie inside a triangle formed by the regional tourist office, **pl. de la Victoire** (farther up the canal) and the **Palais des Rois de Majorque.** If you find yourself lost, bus shelters contain an extraordinarily useful map. Take time to appreciate the great effort it must have taken to make Perpignan's streets sound like Sherlock Holmes mysteries: *rue de la Cloche d'Or* (street of the golden clock), *rue de la Lanterne,* and *rue des 15 degrés.*

Tourist Information: The regional tourist office should have all you need to explore the city, making a trek to the inconveniently located city tourist office unnecessary. **Regional Tourist Office,** 7, quai de Lattre de Tassigny (tel. 04 68 34 29 94). From the station, walk straight up av. Général de Gaulle and turn right at pl. Catalogne onto cours Lazare Escarguel. After crossing the canal, turn left onto quai de Barcelone, which becomes quai de Lattre de Tassigny. The office is on the right (15min.). Brochures on hotels, camping, *gîtes d'étape,* restaurants, walks, trains, buses, festivals. City maps. Open June 15-Sept. 15 Mon.-Sat. 9am-9pm, Sun. 9am-1pm; Sept. 16-June 14 Mon.-Sat. 9am-noon and 2-7pm, Sun. 9am-noon. The **city tourist office,** pl. Armand Lanoux (tel. 04 68 66 30 30; fax 04 68 66 30 26), is at the opposite end of town from the train station. From quai de Lattre de Tassigny, continue along the canal to bd. Wilson. Take a right and follow the signs along the Promenade des Platanes to the modern Palais de Congrès (½-hr. walk from train). Staff inundates you with helpful brochures to make up for the long walk, including **L'Agenda,** a guide to events. **Tours** (in French) of the city leave June-Sept. Mon.-Sat. at 3pm (25F). For tours in English, call 04 68 22 25 96. Open June-Sept. Mon.-Sat. 9am-7pm; Oct.-May Mon.-Sat. 8:30am-noon and 2-6:30pm.

Money: Eurochange, 35, av. du Général de Gaulle (tel. 04 68 34 44 34). Good rates and no commission (open Mon.-Sat. 9am-noon and 2-6pm, Sun. 9am-noon); also at 6, rue Grande des Fabriques (tel. 04 68 34 11 01), across from Hôtel Bristol, off pl. Verdun. The change booth across the hall from the tourist office offers similar rates and no commission (open Mon.-Sat. 10am-6pm, Sun. 10am-6pm). 24-hr. **ATMs** are at **Crédit Mutuel,** 3, rue Ed Bartissol, just off pl. Gambetta.

Trains: rue Courteline (tel. 08 36 35 35 35), on av. de Gaulle. To: Narbonne (23 per day, 40min., 53F); Toulouse (15 per day, some change at Narbonne, 3hr., 137F); Paris (4 per day, 6-10hr., 465-510F); Marseille (15 per day, 5hr., 195F); Nice (3 per day, 6hr., 287F); Lyon (40 per day, change at Avignon or Montpellier, 258F). Office open Mon.-Sat. 8am-6:30pm. **Automatic lockers** 30F per 72hr.

Buses: 17, av. Général Leclerc (tel. 04 68 35 29 02), at the *gare routière.* To: Narbonne (1 per day, 1½hr., 57F); Béziers (1 per day, 2¼hr., 87F); airport (4-7 per day, 15min., 32F). **Car Inter 66** (tel. 04 68 35 29 02) runs four buses to all the beaches from Le Barcarès (to the north) to Cerbère (to the south). Schedules at both tourist offices. Car Inter 66 offers a **tourist pass** good for 8 days within the *département* (150F). Office open Mon.-Sat. 8:30am-12:15pm and 2-6:30pm.

Public Transportation: CTP (Compagnie de Transport Public), pl. Gabriel-Péri (tel. 04 68 61 01 13). Tickets 6F50; *carnet* of 10 50F. Bus 1 goes to Canet-Plage every 25min.; board it on bd. Wilson at Promenade des Platanes (last bus 8:30pm, last return 9pm). "La Citadine" is a bus that circulates in the *centre ville;* buses go by every 10min. Mon.-Fri. 1pm-7:30pm. They're free!

Taxis: (tel. 04 68 51 11 84). 24hr. Catch 'em at the train station.

Bike Rental: Cycles Mercier, 1, av. Doumer (tel. 04 68 85 02 71). 80F per day, 400F per week, 800F deposit. Open Mon.-Sat. 9am-12:30pm and 2:30-7:30pm.

Laundromat: Laverie Foch, 23, rue Maréchal Foch. Wash 16F per 4.5kg, 40F per 15kg. Dry 2F per 5min. Open daily 7am-8pm.

Youth Center: Bureau d'Information Jeunesse, 35, quai Vauban (tel. 04 68 34 56 56). Employment listings, accommodations options, and info on local events. Close to hostel. Open Mon.-Fri. 9:30am-12:30pm and 1:30-6pm.

Crisis Lines: SOS Victimes, 11, rue Arago (tel. 04 68 34 92 37); for victims of assault. **Association des Paralysés de France** (for people with disabilities), 6, HLM Emile Roudayre (tel. 04 68 52 10 41; open Mon.-Fri. 9am-noon and 2-6pm).

Hospital: av. du Maréchal Joffre (tel. 04 68 61 66 33). **Emergency** tel. 15.

Police: l'Hôtel de Police, av. de Grande Bretagne, across from the Musée Numismatique Puig (tel. 04 68 35 70 00). **Emergency** tel. 17.

Post Office: quai de Barcelone **Currency exchange** with decent rates. Poste restante (postal code: 66020). Photocopies. Open Mon.-Tues. and Thurs.-Fri. 8am-6pm, Wed. 9am-6pm, Sat. 8am-noon. **Postal code:** 66000.

ACCOMMODATIONS AND CAMPING

Affordable lodgings should be in ample supply in this affable town. Many lie on av. Général de Gaulle, only steps from the station, or in the action-packed *vieille ville.*

Auberge de Jeunesse (HI), La Pépinière, allée de Marc-Pierre (tel. 04 68 34 63 32; fax 04 68 51 16 02). From train station, turn left onto bd. du Conflent. Turn right onto av. de Grande Bretagne, left on rue Claude Marty (rue de la Rivière on some maps), and right onto allée Marc Pierre (10min.). Turkish toilets lurk and hot showers steam in this hostel nestled between the highway and police station. Single-sex, 6- to 8-bed dorm rooms. 49 beds. Small kitchen available 4-11pm. Strictly enforced 11am check-out. Lockout 11am-4pm. No curfew with building key. Members only. 65F, breakfast included. Sheets 18F. Closed Dec. 20-Jan. 20.

Hôtel de l'Avenir, 11, rue de l'Avenir (tel. 04 68 34 20 30; fax 04 68 34 15 63), a 5-min. walk into the Future from the station. Spotless rooms, firm beds, a rooftop terrace, kind, happy owners, and free city maps to boot. One small single 80F, singles 110F, with shower 145F. Doubles 120F, with shower 160F. Triples 190F. Quads 210F. Breakfast 23F. Shower 15F. V, MC, AmEx.

Hôtel Métropole, 3, rue des Cardeurs (tel. 04 68 34 43 34). From cathedral at pl. Gambetta, walk down rue St-Jean and turn left onto rue des Cardeurs. Calm, convenient location in the *vieille ville.* Large rooms with no frills that vary considerably in quality; ask to see a few. Singles and doubles 70-90F, with shower 135F. Additional bed 40F. Breakfast 19F. Reserve in July and Aug.

Express Hôtel, 3, av. de Gaulle (tel. 04 68 34 89 96). The cheapest within reasonable geographic proximity to the *gare.* Filled with pictures of horses snipped from magazines and framed, fading reproductions of Van Goghs and Gauguins. Singles and doubles 70-130F, with shower 110-140F. Triples with shower 170F. Quads 185F, with shower 200F. Extra bed 30F. Shower 15F. Breakfast 20F. V, MC.

Hôtel le Bristol, 5, rue Grande des Fabriques (tel. and fax 04 68 34 32 68), off pl. de Verdun. Soft beds. Sizable rooms and central but quiet location. Singles 125-160F, with shower, toilet, and TV 190F. Doubles 145F, with shower, toilet, and TV 175F. Triples with shower and TV 225F. Shower 15F. Breakfast 25F. Call ahead in July and Aug. V, MC.

La Bonne Auberge, 64, rue Maréchal Foch (tel. 04 68 54 53 78). The new management has kept the prices low on these comfortable rooms. Singles and doubles 100F. Triples 120F. Call to confirm.

Camping: Camping Le Catalan, route de Bompas (tel. 04 68 63 16 92). Take "Bompas" bus from train station (2 per day, 12F). Pools, hot showers. 2 people 74F; Sept.-June 52F. **Camping Le Garrigole,** 2, rue Maurice Levy (tel. 04 68 54 66 10), in town 800m behind the train station. 2 people 62F. Closed Dec.

FOOD

If you've been waiting to try *escargots,* don't crawl an inch farther. Snails are a Catalan specialty; *cargolade* is a serving of your shell-wearing garden friends grilled and smothered with the tasty oil and garlic sauce, *aïoli. Touron,* a sweeter specialty, is nougat available in many flavors. **Pl. de la Loge, pl. Arago,** and **pl. de Verdun** in the *vieille ville* are filled with restaurants that stay lively at night. Pricier options line **quai Vauban** along the canal. Try **av. de Gaulle** in front of the *gare* for cheaper alternatives. An **open-air market** takes place daily at pl. Cassanyes (8am-1pm); another fills pl. de la République (Tues.-Sun. 6am-1pm). Pl. de la République also holds an assortment of fruit stores, *charcuteries, boulangeries,* and the **Marché République** (open Tues.-Sun. 7am-1pm and 4-7:30pm). The requisite **Supermarché Casino,** with its stockpiles of food, is on bd. Félix Mercader (tel. 04 68 34 74 42; open Mon.-Sat. 8:30am-8:30pm). The food section of the **Nouvelles Galeries** at pl. de la Resistance opens its basement doors Monday to Saturday 8:30am to 7pm.

At **Le Perroquet,** 1, av. de Gaulle (tel. 04 68 34 34 36), wolf down the *filet de loup aux câpres* (fish and capers) on the 82F *menu,* or savor other cheap and tasty dishes prepared with Catalan pizzazz. *Menu* at 62F has large selection, including *escargots à la catalane* (open daily 11:30am-2pm and 6:30-10:30pm; Sept.-May closed Wed.; V, MC). **Opera Bouffe,** impasse de la Division (tel. 04 68 34 83 83), serves regional cuisine in an intimate passageway. Owner's pride is "xup-xup," an eccentric combination of seafood and meatballs in tomato sauce. *Menus* at 65F, 85F, and 120F (open Mon.-Sat. noon-2pm and 8-11pm). The cafeteria **Le Palmarium,** on pl. Arago (tel. 04 68 34 51 31), has an outdoor terrace overlooking the canal. Watch TV or admire the interior, featuring a wall-sized photo of old-time Perpignan. *Plats du jour* run 35-50F (open daily 11:30am-2:30pm and 6:30-9:30pm).

SIGHTS AND ENTERTAINMENT

A short walk from the action, Perpignan's **citadelle** keeps watch over the city. Within the citadel lies the 13th-century **Palais des Rois de Majorque** (tel. 04 63 34 48 29); enter from av. Gilbert Brutus. With its immense arcaded courtyard and two curiously superimposed chapels, it is the city's most impressive sight and one of the best examples of medieval military architecture in southern France. The courtyard now serves as a concert hall, sheltering both plays and classical music performances. (Open daily June-Sept. 10am-6pm; Oct.-May 9am-5pm. Ticket sales end 45min. before closing. Admission 20F, students 10F. Tours every hr.) Entrance to the Palais includes entrance to its small *musée* with exhibitions by regional artists.

The **Musée Hyacinthe Rigaud,** 16, rue de l'Ange (tel. 04 68 35 43 40), contains a small but impressive collection of paintings dating from the 13th century by Spanish and Catalan masters; canvases by Rigaud, the court artist to Louis XIV and one of the 17th century's great portraitists; and works by Ingres, Picasso, and Dufy. Check out the top floor's **Collection de Maitre Rey,** a room in which every wall is packed with tiny paintings, each about 8 by 10 inches. A local writer, Rey asked his artist friends, both well known and less so, to paint these works to fill his study. So many diverse works in such proximity makes for mind-boggling minutiae. (Open in summer Wed.-Mon. 10am-noon and 3-7pm; winter Wed.-Mon. 9am-noon and 2-6pm. Admission 25F, students 10F.) A few blocks north, **Le Castillet** is a remarkably well preserved red-brick castle. Built in the late 14th century and redesigned by Louis XI a century later, the structure has served Perpignan as a gate, a prison, and a fortress. It now houses a Catalan museum of popular art. The tower's terrace commands a view of the sea, the Pyrénées, and the Roussillon plains. (Open Wed.-Sun. 9:30am-7pm; winter Wed.-Sun. 9am-6pm. Admission 25F, students 10F.) A paragon of Gothic architecture, the **Cathédrale St-Jean,** pl. Gambetta (tel. 04 68 51 33 72), is partly supported by a macabre pillar depicting John the Baptist's severed head. Inlaid paintings brood alongside gilded altarpieces in the aisles of the church, most likely annoyed that the stained glass hogs all the light (open 9am-noon and 3-7pm).

A **museum passport** valid for one week (40F) allows entrance to four museums including the two mentioned above and the **Musée Numismatique Joseph Puig,** 42, av. de Grande Bretagne (tel. 04 68 34 11 70). Coin-lovers will delight in rare Catalan and Roussillon currencies, as well as other numismatic curiosities (open Tues.-Sat. 9am-noon and 2-6pm; 25F, students 10F).

Annual festivals liven things up several times a year. The **Fête de St-Jean** occurs on June 23, when the sacred fire is brought from the Canigou, a nearby mountain. Dance the *sardana,* munch powdered-sugar cookies called *rouquilles,* and swallow glasses of the sweet *muscat* wine in one gulp. According to popular legend, jumping over a bonfire lit by the *feu* cleanses the spirit. The ritual **Procession de la Sanch** on Good Friday ushers in the Easter holiday with traditional songs and concerts.

Life (especially nightlife) in Perpignan moves along at its usual pace, undaunted by an increasing number of tourists and their sometimes hedonistic desires. The wildest nightlife exists at the clubs lining the beaches at nearby **Canet-Plage** (see below), where young people smoke, drink, and sweat into the summer nights. Be aware, however, that public bus service stops long before the fun starts (8:30pm), and returning to Perpignan will mean taxi time. A "when in Rome..." attitude may be the best approach to evening entertainment in Perpignan. By night, traditional Catalonian dancing in front of Le Castillet makes for a lively café scene around **pl. de Verdun,** especially in summer (Tues., Thurs., and Sat.). Later on, live bands, cheap beer, and a spirited twentysomething crowd at **Le Centre Ville Bar,** on cours Escarvel, animate an otherwise subdued town. Don't be surprised, though, if you find yourself sitting along the canal playing cards at dusk.

■ Near Perpignan

CANET-PLAGE AND THE CÔTE CATALANE

Stretching 50km from Port-le-Barcarès in the north to Cerbère near the Spanish border, the **Côte Catalane** (formerly known as the Côte Vermeille) attracts more French vacationers than any other region except the glitzy Côte d'Azur. One of the most frequented resorts is **Canet-Plage,** a 30-minute bus ride from Perpignan. It's important to pick the right day, however. A cloudy morning in Canet-Plage is like a post-apocalyptic day in Atlantic City. On a sunny day, bodies cram onto the sizzling sands; in the moonlight, the bathers head for the area's oceans of clubs and casinos.

The **tourist office,** pl. de la Méditerranée (tel. 04 68 73 25 20; fax 04 68 73 24 41), doles out brochures, maps, and friendly aid (open July-Aug. daily 9am-8pm; Sept.-June Mon.-Fri. 9am-12:30pm and 2-6:30pm, Sat.-Sun. 9am-12:30pm and 3-6:30pm; Oct.-May Mon.-Fri. 9am-12:30pm and 2-6:30pm, Sat. 9am-12:30pm and 3-6pm, Sun. 10am-noon). **CTP Shuttles** (tel. 04 68 61 01 13) runs buses to **Canet-Plage;** catch them in Perpignan at pl. Catalogne (at the top of Av. Gen. de Gaulle) or at the promenade des Platanes on bd. Wilson (2 per hr., 30min., 13F; last bus from Canet around 9pm, last from Perpignan around 8:30pm, later in July and Aug.). **Bus Interplages** (tel. 04 68 35 67 51) connects the Côte Catalane resorts from Le Barcarès to Cerbère by bus; others worth visiting include **St-Cyprien-Plage, Argelès-sur-Mer,** and **Banyuls-sur-Mer. Collioure** (page 408) may be the best of all (3 buses back and forth per day; 45min.; 29F, roundtrip 53F). In many of these seaside towns, Roussillon's elegant historic architecture merits a visit—if only as a brief interlude between applications of tanning lotion. You can get a **taxi** at av. Méditerranée as it strikes the beach (tel. 04 68 73 14 81 or 04 68 73 08 62; to Perpignan 95-110F). The **police** are at Rés du Casino-pl. Foment de la Sardane (tel. 04 68 73 22 65).

Rent **bicycles** at the two shops a short stroll down av. de la Côte Vermeille. At **Locabike,** no. 144 (tel. 04 68 80 73 43; fax 04 68 73 42 03), a passport can usually go in lieu of the 1000F deposit (40-50F per ½day, 80F per day, 300F per week; open July-Aug. 9am-midnight; April-June and Sept. 9am-noon and 2-6pm). **Sun Bike 66**, 122, av. de la Côte Vermeille, (tel. 04 68 73 88 65), will keep a passport as well as the 800F deposit, and the prices are about the same (40F per 2hr., 60F per ½-day, 80F per day, 300F per week; open daily July-Aug. 9am-10pm; April-May and Sept. 9am-noon and 2-6pm; June 9am-7pm). Both places also rent scooters and mopeds and both take a six-month winter vacation. Off-season, ask the tourist office if **Parking Balcons du Front de Mer** (tel. 04 68 73 08 06), on the corner of av. Côte Vermeille and rue Pecheurs, is renting bikes again at their very reasonable rates.

Those who intend to lose their money at the casinos or on the heavy cover charges at Canet's clubs can make up for it by commuting from Perpignan. But if you're determined to be the first on the beach or the last out of the casino, there are a few inexpensive hotels in town. Prices are generally lower if you're willing to forgo the ocean view. **Hôtel Clair Soleil,** 26, av. de Catalogne (tel. and fax 04 68 80 32 06), lives up to its name with large, bright, pastel orange rooms. (Singles and doubles 170-195F, with shower 205-230F, with bath 265F. Additional bed 40-55F. Shower 15F. Breakfast 25F. V, MC, AmEx.) A tropical mural and colorful patterned fabric enliven the spotless white rooms and halls of **Hôtel Le Méditerranée,** 1, rue Alsace-Lorraine, (tel. 04 68 80 21 85; doubles 190F, with shower 240F. Triples 230F. Quads 270-300F. Free showers. Breakfast 25F. Closed Oct.-April.) At **Hôtel le Marenda,** 73, av. Edouard Herriot (tel. 04 68 73 56 92; fax 04 68 73 00 12), red-carpeted stairs and hallways open into generic hotel-chain quality rooms. (Singles and doubles (including use of hall shower) 190F, with shower 210-250F. Triples 280-340F. Breakfast 28F. V, MC, AmEx.) **Campsites** are plentiful in Canet. The three-star site **Camping Club Mar-Estang** (tel. 04 68 80 35 53; fax 04 68 73 32 94), a 25-minute walk from the tourist office, offers laundry machines (wash 25F, dry 10F), tennis, two pools, a restaurant, a bar, and a supermarket (2 people 58F off season, 98F summer). The two-star **Camping Le Bosquet** (tel. 04 68 80 23 80; fax 04 68 61 06 59) has 25F washing machines and is 300m from the beach (2 people 65F off season, 78F summer; closed Oct.-May).

Tanning does rouse the appetite, and Canet-Plage has plenty of culinary options to tide over your stomach. Along the beachfront, the requisite pizzerias treat you to hot pasta on sizzling days (32-55F). A flea and food **market** sprouts on pl. Foment de la Sardane (Tues.-Sun. 7:30am-12:30pm). Pl. St-Jacques, a 45-minute walk from the beach, hosts a food market Wednesdays and Saturdays (7:30am-noon). The aptly named **Casino grocery store** awaits hunger-stricken high rollers at 12, av. de la Méditerranée (open July-Aug. daily 8am-1pm and 3:30-5pm; Sept.-June Mon.-Sat. 8am-12:30pm and 3:30-7:30pm). *Boulangeries* and *charcuteries* cluster along the same avenue as it strikes the port. Vegetarians can look to **Rajah Mahal,** 23, bd. Tixador (tel. 04 68 80 53 30), a block away from the beach, for reasonably cheap Indian food (breads 12-25F, dishes 30-72F; open daily noon-3pm and 7pm-midnight; V, MC). **Restaurant Taiwan,** 52, av. Côte Vermeille, has a menu populated by 28F dumplings, 45F frogs legs—and a 450F Peking roast duck. A 3-course *menu* is 59F (open April-Oct. daily noon-3pm and 6-11pm; Nov.-March Fri.-Sun. same hours; V, MC). The 64F *menu* at **Le Chianti,** 18, Côte Vermeille (tel. 04 68 80 43 09), offers a salad, dessert, and lasagna, pasta with seafood, or pizza. Look to the 77F *menu* for more interesting seafood options (open daily noon-2pm and 7-11pm; V, MC).

PRADES AND THE CONFLENT

West of Perpignan, perched halfway up the Pyrénées, restful **Prades** (pop. 6000) presides over the mountainous agricultural area called the **Conflent.** Until the beginning of the 20th century, the town reaped the rewards of a lucrative iron-forging industry. Today, Prades' fame is linked instead to the fate of legendary Catalonian cellist Pablo Casals (1876-1973), who spent 23 years in the town as a political exile from Franco's Spain. Following a three-year self-imposed isolation from the musical world (in protest of the world's recognition of Franco's authority), Casals chose **Eglise St-Pierre** (in the central square) as the site of his return concert in 1950. The 1000-year-old **Abbaye de St-Michel de Cuxa,** an easy and beautiful 3km walk from the center of town, hosts the annual **Festival Pablo Casals** from July 26 to August 13. As the keynote event in Prades' cultural calendar, the festival attracts an array of international musicians for three weeks of classical and chamber music concerts and workshops. Tickets (130-160F, 25% student reduction) are available after May 15 from the **Association Pablo Casals,** rue Victor Hugo (tel. 04 68 96 33 07). During the 50 weeks of the year when the festival is not in town, the abbey still merits a visit. Consecrated in 974, it existed peacefully until French Revolutionaries torched and pillaged it. Today Benedictine monks reside in the restored edifice. (Open May-Sept. Mon.-Sat. 9:30am-11:50am and 2-6pm, Sun. 2-5pm; Oct.-April daily 2-5pm. Last admission 45min. before closing. Admission 15F, under 18 8F.)

The **tourist office,** next to the Casals Academy at 4, rue Victor Hugo (tel. 04 68 96 27 58), distributes reams of brochures. Ask for the booklet on **hiking trails** around Prades, which includes directions to the abbey and other day hikes (open Mon.-Sat. 9am-noon and 2-6pm). The tourist office gives free morning tours of the town, including an after-tour *apéritif* and a chat with the super-friendly staff. Located directly above the tourist office and housed in a single room, the **Musée Pablo Casals** displays one of the master's cellos and correspondence between Casals and his buddy, Albert Schweitzer. Also upstairs, the **Musée d'Archéologie** contains prehistoric artifacts discovered in the environs of Prades. (All museums open Mon.-Fri. 9am-noon and 2-6pm, Sat.-Sun. by appointment. Free.) Every Tuesday, an **open-air market** colors the square in front of Eglise St-Pierre (8am-1pm).

Although hotels are few and expensive, **Hostalrich,** 156, av. Général de Gaulle (tel. 04 68 96 05 38), offers 150F singles with shower, and doubles for 160-240F. **Camping Municipal** (tel. 04 68 96 29 83), with a pond, is in a valley five minutes from the tourist office (13F per site, 12F per adult, 10F per car; open April-Sept.).

Trains heads for Prades from the Gare SNCF in Perpignan (7 per day, 50min., 36F). Or explore the beautiful Conflent countryside on two wheels with **mountain bikes** from **Flanent Cycles,** 8, rue Arago (tel. 04 68 96 07 62; open Tues.-Sat. 8am-noon and 2-7pm. 90F per day, 200F for 3 days; 1200F deposit or passport).

VILLEFRANCHE-DE-CONFLENT

Deep in the mountains of the Conflent, beautiful Villefranche-de-Conflent (pop. 260) occupies a prized location in a valley at the base of three mountains at the confluence of the Cady and Têt Rivers. Eleventh-century military ramparts completely enclose the town and its well-preserved 13th- and 14th-century façades. Built into the mountainside high above the town, 17th-century **Fort Liberia** (tel. 04 68 96 34 01) was designed by the military architect Vauban to protect Villefranche after the 1659 Treaty of the Pyrénées established the nearby French-Spanish border. To reach the fortified heights of Liberia, take the **Navette** (20F, students 15F), a bus that departs every 30min. from the Porte de France, or make the 20-minute climb. The subterranean staircase of "1000 steps" (thankfully an overstatement), ascends to the fort and is the only link between the town and Liberia above. (Fort open 10am-6pm. Admission 28F, students 20F.) On June 23, the Catalonian **Fête des Feux de St-Jean** burns brightly in Villefranche. As in Perpignan, torches lit on the nearby Canigou mountain bring the sacred fire back to the village, where locals dance the traditional *sardane,* drink wine, and hop over bonfires as giant puppets look on. Just outside the walls of

Villefranche, a forest of stalagmites sprouts at the **Grotte des Canalettes** (tel. 04 68 96 23 11), discovered in 1951 (open Mon.-Sat. 10am-noon and 2–6:30pm, Sun. 2-6pm; Sept.-June 10am-noon and 2-6:30pm; admission 40F).

The SNCF's **petits trains jaunes** run through the Pyrénées from Villefranche to **Latour-de-Carol** (2½hr., 80F) seven times every day. They connect Latour-de-Carol to Toulouse and Barcelona; buses push on to Andorra. The yellow trains run through the SNCF train station in each town; their schedule is labelled "Villefranche-Perpignan-Latour-de-Carol-Villefranche." All passengers must switch trains at Villefranche. Some cars are open (no walls or roof), allowing their riders to soak in the postcard towns and wildflower fields, as well as raindrops. Many of these villages serve as stopping points along well-marked hiking trails dotted with **gîtes d'étape,** which facilitate longer stays in these mountains. It is a good idea to get started early so as not to be caught unawares by the train schedule. Contact the department tourist office in Perpignan or the **Association Culturelle** (tel. 04 68 96 25 64) in Villefranche for more information. **Hiking** information is available through the **Direction Departemental de la Jeunesse et des Sports** (tel. 04 68 35 50 49). In winter, the fashionable **ski area** at **Font Romeu,** accessible by the *petit train jaune,* is fully equipped with snow machines and ski lifts and offers first-rate skiing. Call the **tourist office** in Font Romeu, av. Brousse (tel. 04 68 30 68 30), for info.

LANGUEDOC-ROUSSILLON

Hotels fill quickly in Villefranche during the summer. **Hôtel Le Terminus,** (tel. 04 68 05 20 24), outside the village next to the train station, rents attractive doubles for 70-80F (doubles with shower 120F; breakfast 20F). The attached restaurant offers 57F and 70F *menus* starring trout. The town hall (tel. 04 68 96 10 78) on pl. de l'Eglise operates **gîtes communaux** but you must stay for a full week—or at least pay the weekly rate (doubles 675F per week; town hall open Mon.-Fri. 9am-noon and 3-6pm). If you succumb completely to the lure of the Pyrénées, ask the conductor of the *petit train jaune* to let you off at **Thuès-les-Bains** (28F from Villefranche, 6 per day, 30min.), where a **gîte-camping à la ferme** called **Mas de Bordes** (tel. 04 68 97 05 00) is perched beside a crumbling stone church in a canyon nook. The Peeters family opens this serene old stone lodge to travelers (50F with kitchen access, camping 20F, option to take inexpensive meals with the family). A natural hotspring bubbles just a few minutes away. The *gîte* is a 3-hr. walk from an entrance to the **GR10,** which stretches from the Atlantic to the Mediterranean. Horseback riding, a nearby lake, skiing in winter, and endless other outdoor activities await in an area too pristine and refreshing to pass up.

The **tourist office,** pl. de l'Eglise (tel. 04 68 96 22 96), can help with lodging and hiking information (open daily in summer 9am-6pm; winter Tues.-Sat. 9am-6pm). The **Association Culturelle,** 38, rue St-Jean (tel. 04 68 96 25 64), has a dedicated staff that offers information on historical hiking tours of the area (open Mon.-Fri. 8:30am-noon and 1:30-5:30pm). During July and August, the *Association* also leads tours of the town (25F). For exhaustive **IGN maps** (65F) and information about hiking locally and throughout the Pyrénées, contact **Editions et Diffusions Randonnées Pyrénéennes,** BP 88, 09200 St-Girons (tel. 04 61 66 71 87). This region is IGN map 10: "Massif du Canignon." IGN maps are also available at *tabacs.*

Narbonne

Faced with memories of their glorious heritage, 47,000 *Narbonnais* are trying to ward off the lingering lethargy that has plagued this sunny city in recent centuries. Founded by a decree of the Roman senate in 118 BC, *Narbo Martius* became Rome's first colony outside of Italy. Back in those good ol' days, Narbonne flourished with its lucrative exportation of farm products. By medieval times, the ascending city had gained the status to install archbishops and viscounts, but its triumph was short-lived. With its fortunes increasingly tied to vineyards, Narbonne was taken aback when grapes from other regions eclipsed its own. Daunted but not squashed, Narbonne has begun active renewal. Surrounding vineyards open their *caves* to tourists, though actual wine-tasting amounts to little more than a dream for those depending on the

SNCF's wheels. Narbonne has created such attractions as the summer theater festival while making the best of its existing assets, including a Gothic cathedral and the popular sands of **Narbonne-Plage** and **Gruisson-Plage.**

PRACTICAL INFORMATION

Narbonne's **tourist office,** pl. Salengro (tel. 04 68 65 15 60; fax 04 68 65 59 12), is a 10-minute walk from the train station. Turn right onto bd. Frédéric Mistral, then turn left onto rue Chennebier, which leads to pl. Salengro. The staff **exchanges currency** for free and offers information on lodging, sights, and activities in the area (open June 16-Sept. 14 Mon.-Sat. 8am-7pm, Sun. 9am-12:30pm; Sept. 15-June 15 Mon.-Sat. 8:30am-noon and 2-6pm). Ask about guided walking tours, in French, of the city, which include entrance to the city's museums (June 15-Sept. 15, 2hr., 30F, students and seniors 20F). **Crédit Mutuel** at pl. de l'Hôtel de Ville (tel. 04 68 90 34 00) has an **ATM** that operates 6am-11pm. The **train station** (tel. 04 67 62 50 50) sends trains to Perpignan (14 per day, 45min., 53F); Carcassonne (15 per day, 30min., 51F), Toulouse (13 per day, 1½hr., 105F); and Montpellier (12 per day, 55min., 75F). Info office open Mon.-Sat. 8am-12:15pm and 1:30-6:15pm. **Luggage storage** is 20F per 24hr. (open Mon.-Sat. 7am-8pm, Sun. noon-8pm). Intercity buses leave from the **gare routière,** near the station, or the terminal on quai Victor Hugo. **Transports Urbains Narbonnais** (tel. 04 68 32 36 43) circulates city buses. The **police** station is on bd. Charles de Gaulle (tel. 04 68 90 38 50). The **post office,** 25, bd. Gambetta (tel. 04 68 65 87 00), has poste restante, **currency exchange** at no commission, and a 24-hr. **ATM** (open Mon.-Fri. 8am-7pm, Sat. 8:30am-noon; **postal code:** 11100).

LANGUEDOC-ROUSSILLON

ACCOMMODATIONS, CAMPING, AND FOOD

Ask at the tourist office if the Foyer des Jeunes Travailleurs has reopened, or if anything similar has replaced it (you might inquire about the Maison des Jeunes de la Culture, tel. 04 68 32 01 00). **Hôtel de la Gare,** 7, av. Pierre Sémard (tel. 04 68 32 10 54), inches from the station, plies 18 rooms with soft, clean carpeting. (Singles and doubles with shower 110F, with shower and toilet 120F. Triples and quads with shower 160F, with shower and toilet 170F. Breakfast 22F.) **Will's Hotel,** 23, av. P. Sémard (tel. 04 68 90 44 50; fax 04 68 32 26 28), is inches from Hôtel de la Gare. Find comfort in the lobby's soft, red-tasselled chairs and the pink butterfly wallpaper. (Singles with toilet or shower 120F. Doubles with shower, toilet, and TV 200-220F. One triple or quad with bath, toilet, and TV 330F. Free showers. Breakfast 27-30F. V, MC, AmEx.) **Hôtel de France,** 6, rue Rossini (tel. 04 68 32 09 75; fax 04 68 65 50 30) is located off bd. du Docteur Ferroul near the pont de la Liberté. Rooms range from attic singles with skylights (110F) to doubles (215F), triples (265F), and quads (315F) with the works. Breakfast 30F; free showers. Reserve July-Aug. (V, MC). Beachside campgrounds abound in the area. **Hôtel de Paris,** 2, rue du Lion d'Or (tel. 04 68 32 08 68), has three cats in evidence and all the pigeons in Narbonne roosting on its roof. (Singles 95F, with shower 145F. Doubles 110F, with shower 145F. Triples and quads with shower 195F and 245F respectively. Free showers; breakfast 25F. V, MC). **Camping des Côtes des Roses** (tel. 04 68 49 83 65) offers tennis, horseback riding, mini-golf, and the Mediterranean (76F per 2 people; open Easter-Sept.). **Camping le Soleil d'Oc** (tel. 04 68 49 86 21) rents tents for 80F per 2 people. Open April-Oct. In summer, about six buses per day head from Narbonne's train station to the grounds.

Inexpensive restaurants cluster off **rue Droite,** branching off to the left of the Palais des Archevêques. Grab a bite from the canal-side vendors lining the **cours de la République,** or pick up picnic items at the **market** on plan (not *place*) St-Paul on Thursday mornings (9am-noon). Along the canal, a *brocante* (flea market) occurs Thursdays and Saturdays (9am-4pm). Also on Saturdays, a market with antiques descends on pl. Voltaire. The **covered market** at **Les Halles,** on the canal on cours Mirabeau is open daily from 6am to 1pm. **Monoprix,** pl. Hôtel de Ville, satisfies all other food needs (open Mon.-Sat. 8:30am-7:30pm). One of the best buys in town is **L'Escargot,** 9, rue Corneille, (tel. 04 68 32 14 70), near Monoprix where André serves many a 53F *menu* to regulars. Try the *escargots maison* (open Tues.-Sat. noon-2:30pm and 7-11pm, Sun. noon-2:30pm). **Le Méditerranée,** 26, rue Felix Aldy (tel. 04 68 32 21 42), may not cure homesickness, but *calamars à l'Americaine* is the house specialty. Pizzas 46-53F, pasta 30-45F, omelettes 22-35F. Lunch *menu* 65F (open Mon.-Sat. noon-2pm and 7-11pm; in winter closes at 10pm; V, MC).

SIGHTS AND ENTERTAINMENT

Narbonne's monuments congregate in the *vieille ville,* and it's easy to make a quick round before heading out to catch a wave. The imposing Gothic structure of the **Cathédrale St-Just et St-Pasteur,** pl. de la Hôtel de Ville (tel. 04 68 32 09 52), is only half as large as its architects intended it to be. Construction began in 1272 but stopped in 1340 during a long, bitter zoning dispute between the archbishops and city hall (the church wanted to dismantle the city's surrounding walls and use them as building material). Although further construction would have given Narbonne France's largest cathedral, the church fortunately lost—the walls saved the city when the English Black Prince attacked in 1355. Scale the 236 steps of the cathedral's **Tour Nord;** at the summit awaits a dizzying 360° view of the *vieille ville's* thatched roofs and the hilly countryside. (Tower 15F; open July-Aug. Mon.-Sun. 9:30am-5:30pm. Cathedral open May-Sept. daily 9-11:50am and 2-5:30pm; Oct.-April closed Sun. afternoon. The cathedral is undergoing restoration that may affect these hours.) A 15th-century Flemish tapestry hangs in **La Salle de Trésor** in the cathedral (open May-Sept. Mon.-Sat. 9:30-11:30am and 2:30-5pm; 10F).

The opulent **Palais des Archevêques,** next to the cathedral, testifies to the wealth of the former archbishops of Narbonne. Within its walls, the **Musée Archéologique** displays a collection of artifacts stretching from hunter-gatherer societies to the relatively recent Gallo-Roman civilization. Across the atrium, the **Musée d'Art et d'Histoire** holds French, Flemish, and Italian 17th-century paintings in the former apartments of the archbishops. An uncovered Roman grain warehouse, **L'Horreum,** rue Rouget de l'Isle, off rue Droite, is Narbonne's only remaining ancient monument and is not yet completely excavated. (All open May-Sept. daily 9:30am-12:15pm and 2-6pm; Oct.-April Tues.-Sun. 10am-noon and 2-5pm). A global ticket (25F, students and seniors 15F) allows entrance to four museums over three days.

Narbonne's **15th Annual Amateur Theater Festival** will take place for one week in late June and early July. For information, call 04 68 32 01 00. Entrance is free. Organ concerts, also free, on summer Sundays at 9pm make wonderful use of the pipe organ in the Cathédrale St-Just. Call 04 68 42 00 87 for info. If time travel sounds appealing, **Le Coche d'Eau du Patrimonie** (tel. 04 68 90 63 98) offers a boat tour in July and August of the Canal de la Robine, an offshoot of the Canal du Midi, that covers 20 centuries of history in a few hours. 33F may not be your ticket to heaven, but it does buy a guided tour of **l'Abbaye de Fontfroide** (tel. 04 68 45 11 08), its enormous rose gardens, and tranquil well-preserved grounds (all 15km away on D613. Tours every 30min.-1hr.). Twice a year, once in May and once in June, the Abbaye hosts classical music concerts.

Nightlife is scarce in Narbonne, but beer-drinkers can order a cold brew (12F) at the bright yellow **Bar le Baroque,** 26, av. Gambetta (tel. 04 68 65 27 39), across from the post office, and watch it travel, via cowboy boots, to their bar stools (open Mon.-Sat. 7:30am-2am).

Béziers

For the past 2000 years, Béziers, a mere 15km from the Mediterranean, has been a city of passage where Celts, Iberians, Phoenicians, Greeks, Romans, Arabs, and Franks have all left their trace. In 1209, when the outlawed Cathars sought refuge in welcoming Béziers, Pope Innocent III's anti-heretical minions sacked the town and slaughtered its inhabitants. Native Paul Riquet revitalized Béziers in the 17th century by building (with a little help from his friends) the 245km **Canal du Midi,** establishing the town as an important passageway for regional trade. Now, the tourists who flock to Béziers' eastern beaches and western vineyards enjoy the canal and its locks. Wine production has sustained this city of 73,000, even through a turn-of-the-century battle with the dreaded *phylloxéra.* Known for its simple table wine, Béziers prides itself on the quality of its vineyards; try the Minervois (24-42F), St-Chinianais (18-50F), or Faugères (18-35F) labels.

PRACTICAL INFORMATION

The **tourist office,** 29, av. St-Saëns (tel. 04 67 76 47 00), can direct you to the local wine producers as well as the nearby beaches. From the train station, climb up rue de la Rotunde to allées Paul Riquet; av. St-Saëns is off the allées on the right. (Open July-Aug. Mon.-Fri. 9am-7pm, Sun. 10am-noon; Sept.-June Mon. 9am-noon and 2-6pm, Tues.-Fri. and Sun. 9am-noon and 2-6:30pm, Sat. 9am-noon and 3-6pm.) There is a 24-hour **ATM** at Banque Courtois, 26, allées Paul Riquet; they also have a **currency exchange** that's open Mon.-Fri. 8:40am-12:45pm and 3:45-5pm. Frequent **trains** (tel. 08 36 35 35 35) connect Béziers to Narbonne (20 per day, 15min., 26F) and Montpellier (28 per day, 40min., 58F). The station's office is open Mon.-Sat. 8am-6pm. **Local bus line** 401 (tel. 04 67 36 73 76) leaves pl. du Général de Gaulle for **Valras beach** (in summer, 11 per day, last return 8pm (Sun. 10pm), 30min., roundtrip 27F). Fifteen km from Béziers, this one-time fishing village has developed into an all-purpose family beach resort complete with water slide and ferris wheel, but a walk down the beach reveals placid expanses of light sand. Buses also stop at the bus and train stations. The **post office,** pl. Gabriel Peri (tel. 04 67 49 86 00), offers poste restante (**postal code:** 34500); open Mon.-Fri. 8am-7pm, Sat. 8am-noon.

ACCOMMODATIONS, CAMPING, AND FOOD

The **Hôtel Angleterre,** 22, pl. Jean Jaurès (tel. 04 67 28 48 42), off the allées Paul Riquet, rents 22 quiet, clean, and cozy rooms with soft carpeting. The posters in the stairwell will make you smile. Reserve July 15-August 15. (Singles 110F. Doubles 140F, with shower 160F. Quads with shower and toilet 280F. Free showers. Breakfast 30F.) Just off av. St-Saëns, the **Alma Unic Hôtel,** 41, rue Guilhemon (tel. 04 67 28 44 31; fax 04 67 28 79 44), has clean, tastefully decorated rooms. Take the red-carpeted stairs all the way to the top to work out in the exercise room or to sunbathe on the terrace. (Singles 120F, with shower 140F. Doubles 130F, with shower 160F. Triples with shower 190F. Quads with shower 240F. Free showers. Breakfast 25F. V, MC, AmEx.) **La Dorade,** 10, rue André Nougaret (tel. 04 67 49 35 39), run by a kind Spanish couple, fills quickly in August. Rue A. Nougaret forms a triangle with av. Georges Clémenceau and av. du Maréchal Foch. (Singles and doubles 120F, with shower 140F. Triples with shower 240F. Quads with shower 240-290F. No hall showers. Breakfast 23-26F.) Their restaurant serves a 55F *menu.* The **Hôtel Le Révèlois,** 60, av. Gambetta (tel. 04 67 49 20 78; fax 04 67 28 92 28), is one block straight ahead from the train station. Reserve in July and August. (Singles and doubles 100F, with shower 140F. Triples with shower 180F. Quads with shower 180F, with bath 200F. Free showers. Breakfast 25F.) Their restaurant's 60F *menu* includes three courses and a drink. Info on **beach camping** at Valras (July-Sept.) is available at the tourist offices in Béziers or Valras (tel. 04 67 32 36 04).

Le Patio, 30, rue Viennet (tel. 04 67 49 14 54), serves pizza, pasta, and fish (35-57F) and the *Palata Exotique,* potatoes served with apples and pineapples (68F with toast and dessert) in a whitewashed dining room with a Mediterranean mural and matador posters. Friday and Saturday evenings, the downstairs grotto houses a lively Spanish bar *à tapas* (open Sun.-Fri. 11:30am-2pm and 7-11:30pm, Sat. 7-11:30pm). Other restaurants with patio dining lead down rue Viennet away from the cathedral. The indoor **market** at Les Halles, allées Paul Riquet, is open Tuesday to Sunday 7am to 1pm. A produce market fills allées Paul Riquet Tuesday through Sunday 8am to noon. The **Monoprix supermarket,** 5, allées Paul Riquet (tel. 04 67 49 31 80), is open Monday to Saturday 8:30am-7pm. Béziers' sweet specialty is the *biterrois,* a pâté of almonds, grapes, and wine in pastry, available at the 13 *pâtisseries* with stickers in their windows from *l'Association des Pâtisseries de Béziers.*

SIGHTS AND ENTERTAINMENT

For those blessed with their own transportation, any of the nearby private vineyards or *caves coopératives,* central outlets for local wines, give tours ending with samples of the St-Chignon, Bourlou, and St-Saturnin wines. **Le Club des Grands Vins des Châteaux du Languedoc** will provide information on *dégustations* of the region's acclaimed *Appellations d'Origine Controlée (A.O.C.):* Minervois, St-Chinian, Faucères, and a spicy red, Cabrières. Contact the club's offices at the Château de Raissac (tel. 04 67 28 15 61), 2km west of Béziers. The cellars of the château itself are open to visitors year-round (Mon.-Sat. 9am-noon and 2:30-7pm).

The **Cathédrale St-Nazaire,** pl. de la Révolution, a Roman church built on the ruins of a pagan temple, was destroyed with the rest of the city in 1209 but rebuilt and expanded in the 14th century. Every day the bells ring out across the canals, countryside, and salmon-colored roofs of the tiny town below. Climb to the top for an unobstructed view of the surroundings, or walk the vine-covered terrace of the *jardin* for a peek at the river and its green banks (open Mon.-Sat. 9am-noon and 2:30-7pm). A balcony, complete with telescope, only 100m from the church provides **yet another magnificent view** of the surroundings.

For a whirlwind tour of the town's three museums, the participating galleries offer a universal pass (15F, students 8F). The **Fabrégat des Beaux-Arts,** pl. de la Révolution (tel. 04 67 28 38 78), and its annex, **Hôtel Fayet,** 9, rue de Capuces (tel. 04 67 49 04 66), house a modest collection of 17th-, 18th-, 19th-, and 20th-century paintings. A few Delacroixes, Géricaults, and Dufys shine through the masses of local work. (Open Tues.-Sat. 9am-noon and 2-6pm, Sun. 2-6pm; Hôtel Fayet closed Sun. Admission 10F, students 5F.) The nearby **Espace Paul Riquet** (tel. 04 67 28 44 18), rue Massol, hosts frequent expositions (open Tues.-Sun. 9am-noon and 2-6pm; Sept.-June closed Sun.). Call the tourist office for dates. The **Musée St-Jacques** (tel. 04 67 49 34 00) displays local relics ranging from prehistoric scratchpads (10-foot rust-red rocks engraved with primitive bows and arrows) to 20th-century railroad ads. A 1913 Renault, driven by *"le plus jeune chauffeur du monde"* ("the youngest driver in the world"—4-year-old Jean Lovign) sits in the corner as a testament to Béziers' child prodigy (open Tues.-Sat. 9am-noon and 2-6pm, Sun. 2-6pm).

For a traditional night out, **Le Café des Arts,** 13, rue de la Coquille (tel. 04 67 28 82 56), starts out mellow and ends up lively. Beers are 10F, cocktails 35F (open Mon.-Sat. 8am-2am). Coffee-lovers will enjoy an early evening at a table outside of **Café Latin,** 13bis, pl. Pierre Sémard (tel. 04 67 28 82 28), across from Les Halles. Or head to **La Rotonde,** 2 av. Wilson (tel. 04 67 76 35 32), at the end of the allées; karaoke at 9:30pm Tuesday through Thursday (open Mon.-Fri. 7:45am-2am, Sat. 10am-2am, Sun. 3pm-2am; Sept.-June closes at 1am).

In mid-August, a local **feria** that has earned Béziers the nickname "the French Seville" fills the evenings with *corridas* and *flamenco* dancing. Tickets for the bullfights are available at the *arènes,* av. Emile Claparède (tel. 04 67 76 13 45), and range from 100 to 450F. **Béziers donne de la voix,** the first two weeks in July, fills Cathédrale Saint Nazaire with classical music. Some concerts are free, others are 100-130F, with discounts for those under 20. For reservations call 04 67 28 40 75.

Sète

Sparsely settled since 1000 BC, Sète sprang to life in 1666 when Louis XIV's finance minister, Colbert, pointed to the "Cap de Cette" as the site for a new port. At the turn of the century, most of the population of the Italian village of Gaet immigrated to Sète to escape the Italian depression, displacing the French town's native population. A hybrid Italian-French culture has emerged in Sète, producing unique cuisine, strange festivals, and an engaging mariner's dialect. Spread along a narrow strip of land cordoning the Bassin Thau from the Mediterranean, the town is now France's largest Mediterranean fishing port, pulling some 14,000 tons of fish from the sea each year. Modern commercial fishing has added industrial machinery to Sète's otherwise postcard-perfect coastline. From the constant drone of the seagulls and the cool breezes to the canals and quais that thread through the city, Sète (pop. 42,000) overflows with the waters of the sea, its economic and cultural lifeblood.

ORIENTATION AND PRACTICAL INFORMATION

Sète's **tourist office,** 60, Grand rue Mario Roustan (tel. 04 67 74 71 71), behind the quai Général Durand, offers tourist-friendly maps (2F), **changes currency** at no commission, and **cashes traveler's checks** at 3% commission. From the station, walk straight onto Pont de Gare, go over the canal and turn right onto quai Vauban. Continue around the corner and cross the first bridge on the right. Go left on the other side and walk down quai Général de Lattre de Tassigny, following the signs (15min.; open July-Aug. daily 9am-8pm; Sept.-June Mon.-Sat. 9am-noon and 2-6pm). A 24-hour **ATM** is located at **Banque Courtois** on the corner of rue Général de Gaulle and rue de 8 mai 1945. The **train station,** quai M. Joffre (tel. 04 67 46 51 03), serves those headed to Montpellier (20min., 28F) and Béziers (approx. 2 per hr., 30min., 42F). The **bus station,** 13, quai de la République (tel. 04 67 74 66 90 for info desk of Montpellier's station), rolls 11 buses daily (3 Sun.) to Montpellier (1hr., 30F) and three to Molière's hometown, Pézenas (1½hr., 38F). Getting anywhere else requires a transfer at one of these towns. **Local buses** (6F) circle the city. Bus 2, most convenient to quai de la Résistance, provides service to both the beaches and to l'Espace Brassens until 7:30pm. **Cycles Estopina,** 4, rue Voltaire (tel. and fax 04 67 74 74 77), specializes in **bike rentals** (2-speeds and *VTTs* 50-60F per ½-day). Be prepared to leave an ID and a 1000-2000F deposit. Fax ahead group requests (open Tues.-Sat. 9am-7:30pm). To reach the **hospital** on bd. C. Blanc (tel. 04 67 46 57 57), take bus 2 to "Hôpital." The **police** can be found at 50, quai de Bosc (tel. 04 67 46 80 22). **Emergency** tel. 17. The **post office,** bd. Danièle Casanova (tel. 04 67 46 64 21), has poste restante (address mail to: 34207 Sète Cedex). (Open Mon.-Fri. 8:30am-12:30pm and 1:30-6pm, Sat. 8:30am-noon; **postal code:** 34200.)

ACCOMMODATIONS, CAMPING, AND FOOD

The **Auberge de Jeunesse (HI), "Villa Salis,"** rue du Général Revest (tel. 04 67 53 46 68; fax 04 67 51 34 01), peers down on the town from the tree-covered sides of Mont St-Clair; follow the directions to the tourist office (see above). At pont de la Civette, turn right onto rue Général de Gaulle and follow the friendly *auberge* signs around the Château d'Eau and up the hill to the coral-colored inn (20min.). 90 beds in four-to-five-bed single-sex rooms. 116F for members includes dinner, breakfast, and the great view. Sheets 16F. Reception daily 8am-11pm; Sept.-mid-May 8am-noon and 6-10pm. No lockout or curfew. At **Hôtel Tramontane,** 5, rue Frédéric-Mistral (tel. 04 67 74 37 92), only 50m off the quai de la Résistance, expect friendly and helpful management, clean rooms and beds, and sparkling bathrooms. (Singles and doubles 125F, with shower and toilet 165-185F. Triples 155-205F. Quads 185-245F. Breakfast 26F. Showers 12F. V, MC.) **Hôtel le Valéry,** 20, rue Denfert-Rochereau (tel. 04 67 74 77 51; fax 04 67 74 58 59), is just minutes from the train station. Spacious staircase and hallways lead to semi-spacious, simple rooms. Singles and doubles 110-130F, with shower 160F. Triples 160F. Quads 170F. Free showers. Breakfast 25F. Reserve July-Aug. V, MC. The 4-star **camping** 10km outside Sète at **Le Castellas** (tel. 04 67 51 63 00) has a pool, bar, supermarket, and wheelchair access (2 person site 85-127F). Open May 15-Sept. 21. A bus goes between Sète's train station and the site twice daily (25min., 13F), and a taxi company has a 30F roundtrip deal for times the bus isn't running. You can also try **L'Europe** (tel. 04 67 78 11 50; fax 04 67 78 48 59), a 4-star site 15km from Sète, offering a pool, a bar, and wheelchair access for 40-130F per couple. (Open May-Sept.)

The restaurants that line **Promenade J.B. Marty** at the end of Grand rue Mario Roustan near the *vieux port* serve the catch of the day grilled, steamed, smoked, boiled, or filleted for 60F and up. Not harborside, but fresh nevertheless, cheaper pizza, pasta, and seafood await in the less touristy eateries on the Gambetta and its offshoots. Eat your pizzas (30-46F) with or without mussels and shrimp at **La Trattoria** 92, Grand rue M. Roustan, (tel. 01 64 74 32 46). They also serve pasta (35-40F) and seafood dishes (80-95F). (Open Tues.-Fri. 11am-2pm and 5pm-midnight, Sat.-Mon. 5pm-midnight. V, MC.) Those who hate the smell, sight, and taste of seafood will appreciate **Restaurant Chandigarh,** 17, rue Paul Valéry (tel. 01 64 46 09 64), and its generous servings of Indian *saghg paneer* (spinach and fresh cheese), rice, and *nan* (bread). Prudent orderers can spend less than 60F (open Tue.-Sun. noon-2pm and 7-11pm; V, MC). Alternatively, head to the **Prisunic supermarket** at 7, quai de la Résistance (tel. 04 67 74 39 38, open Mon.-Sat. 8:30am-8pm, Sun. 9am-noon) or the **daily morning market** at **Les Halles,** just off rue Alsace-Lorraine (open 7am-noon). Vendors on the canal hawk fresh *tielles,* (squid and tomato pizzas), for 11F; but *boulangeries* 50m inland sell them, perhaps less authentic, for as little as 7F.

SIGHTS AND ENTERTAINMENT

On **Mole St-Louis,** a dock built in 1666 at the southern end of town, the **Société Nautique de Sète,** one of France's oldest yacht clubs, lounges. Throughout the summer, many yacht races—including the prestigious **Tour de France à la Voile** at the end of July—set sail from the Mole. The **plage de la Corniche** in the southwest corner of town marks the beginning of 12km of sandy yellow **beaches,** accessible by bus 2 (tickets 6F), or in summer by a beach bus that shuttles between town and beach for 6F. Catch both on the quai de la Resistance at stops marked "La Plage."

Bus 2 also runs to **L'Espace Brassens** (tel. 04 67 53 32 77), which celebrates the popular musician George Brassens, who grew up in Sète, with a retrospective (open daily June-Sept. 10am-noon and 2-6pm; closed Mon. in winter; admission 30F, students 10F). A walk out to the *vieux port* and up the hill along Grand rue Haute leads to the **maritime cemetery** that inspired Paul Valéry's poem *"Cimetière Marin"* (open daily 7am-7pm; Oct.-March 8am-6pm). Valéry, an influential 20th-century poet, was born here in 1871; upon his death in 1945 he was interred in his cherished cemetery. Up the hill, the modern building above the cemetery is the **Musée Paul Valéry** (tel. 04 67 46 20 98), with exhibits on local archaeology, history, Sète's nautical jousts, and Valéry himself (open June-Aug. daily 10am-noon and 2-6pm; Sept.-May Wed.-Mon. 10am-noon and 2-6pm; admission 20F, free Wed.).

If your legs have it in them, climb Chemin de Biscan-Pas from the hostel to the summit of **Mont St-Clair** (183m) for a terrific view of Sète, its canals and docks, and the sea (15min.). The church **Notre Dame de la Salette,** with wall murals from the 1950s, brings fishermen's wives up to this summit on a pilgrimage every September 19. **Amusement park** junkies will revel in the water wonderland of **Le Cap d'Agde,** located 30km from Sète, a developed resort town that includes a water theme park, *discothèques,* a casino, and every resort activity under the sun. Contact their tourist office for more information (tel. 04 67 01 04 04; fax 04 67 26 22 99).

On the final weekend in August (referred to as **La Fête de St. Louis**), Sète holds its animated **tournois de Joutes Nautiques,** in which participants joust from ramps extending from oversized rowboats. Arrive in the morning to secure a spot for the final competition at Monday 2pm—and wear a hat in the intense sun. Most summer Saturday afternoons, the gladiators prepare for the tournament and impress the tourists with exposition battles. On Wednesday or Thursday every week, any novice can go to the Quilles quarter for a jousting lesson. **La Fête de St. Pierre** occurs the first weekend in July. Fishermen spend the preceding week preparing for their festival and taking a break from work. Over the weekend, mornings involve solemn religious rites, while the nights are loud and festive. Sunday morning from 10 to 11am, during the **Benediction au Mer,** fishermen allow the crowds to walk over their decorated boats and they throw chains of flowers into the water in memory of sailors and fishermen lost at sea. Every evening, the popular **La Bodega,** 21, Quai Noel Guignon (tel.

04 67 74 47 50), has live music, from Brazilian to blues to rock. Beers are 19-35F and cocktails are 40-60F (open daily 5:30pm-3am; Oct.-May closed Sun.). **Wembley,** 36, av. Victor Hugo (tel. 04 67 74 67 67), has 120 types of beer, concerts Thursday through Saturday (pop, rock, and country), and karaoke the other nights of the week (open daily 8pm-4am).

Montpellier

Devastated by the Hundred Years' War in the 14th and 15th centuries and by the wine industry's crisis at the turn of this century, Montpellier has reattained a firm economic and cultural footing. This self-proclaimed "Mediterranean Eurocity" does have a certain *je ne sais quoi* and an infectious vitality. An international modern dance festival and numerous theatrical productions keep the town culturally rich and constantly entertaining. Montpellier has also attracted a number of high-tech companies, including IBM, and drawn over 50,000 students to its prestigious university, which lies close enough to the beach to torture students during final exams.

During the day, narrow and surprisingly quiet streets entice visitors into the *vieille ville,* with its elegant 17th- and 18th-century *hôtels particuliers.* Cafés on pl. de la Comédie, fondly known as *l'Oeuf* (the egg), offer expensive coffee and hours of four-star people-watching. Come sundown, the student population casts off its scholarly pose and bursts into nocturnal revelry; the lively bars clustered in pl. Jean-Jaurès are always buzzing.

ORIENTATION AND PRACTICAL INFORMATION

Radiating from the station to the right, **rue Maguelone** leads to Montpellier's modern center, the fountain-filled **pl. de la Comédie.** To find the tourist office upon reaching the *place,* turn right and look for the **three-foot blue cube** marked with an "i." Just before the cube, follow steps on the right downstairs to the tourist office, which is directly below the cube. The huge pl. de la Comédie makes a perfect starting point for forays into the historic center. **Rue de la Loge** leads from the *place* uphill to the center of the *vieille ville,* **pl. Jean-Jaurès.**

Tourist Information: Tourist Office, passage du Tourisme (tel. 04 67 58 67 58; fax 04 67 58 67 59), in Le Triangle. Free maps and hotel reservation service. **Currency exchange** with steep rates. Tours of the city in French (in summer, daily at 3pm; year-round Wed. and Sat. at 3pm; 50F, students 25F). Also tours of the city's historic center (Wed. and Sat. at 3pm; 50F, students and over 60, 25F) and themed tours (3 per month; 55F, students and over 60, 30F). Open June 16-Sept. 14 Mon.-Sat. 9:30am-7:30pm, Sun. 9am-1pm and 3-7pm; Sept. 15-June 15 Mon.-Fri. 9am-1pm and 2-6pm, Sat. 10am-1pm and 2-6pm, Sun. 10am-1pm and 2-5pm. **Branch offices** at the train station (tel. 04 67 92 90 03; open May-Aug. Mon., Thurs.-Fri. 9am-1pm and 3-7pm, Tues. 9am-1pm and 3-6pm), and at Rond Point des Prés d'Arènes (tel. 04 67 22 08 80; open June-mid-Sept. Mon.-Sat. 10am-1pm and 3:30-7pm). Another branch office at 78, av. du Pirée (tel. 04 67 22 06 16; fax 04 67 22 38 10), is open until 8:30pm Sun. in summer. Both the weekly **Sortir à Montpellier** and the monthly **Rendez-Vous** have free listings of cinema, art, and concerts, available at the tourist office. For a complete listing of lodging, entertainment, eating, bars, museums, and sports, see the yearly **Le guide malin de Montpellier** (20F in *tabacs*), or **Le Petit Futé,** (38F).

Budget Travel: Wasteels, 1, rue Cambacares (tel. 04 67 66 20 19) and 6, rue Fbg. de la Saunerie (tel. 04 67 58 74 26), offers good plane, train, and bus prices. Open Mon.-Fri. 9am-12:30pm and 2-6:30pm, Sat. 9am-12:30pm and 2-5:30pm. V, MC.

Money: Banque Courtois, pl. de la Comédie, left of the Opera has a 24-hr. **ATM.**

Trains: pl. Auguste Gilbert (tel. 08 36 35 35 35). **Currency Exchange** (tel. 04 67 58 00 55) at excellent rates, no commission (open Mon.-Sat. 8am-8pm, Sun. 10am-6pm). To: Avignon (20 per day, 1hr., 76F); Marseille (8 per day, 1¾hr., 119F); Nice (5 per day, 5hr., 223F); Toulouse (every 2hr., 2½hr., 154F); Perpignan (10 per day,

1½hr., 110F); Paris (8 TGVs per day, 4½hr., 357-430F). Information office open Mon.-Fri. 8am-7pm, Sat. 9am-6pm. **Automatic lockers** 30F (72hr.).

Buses: rue Jules Ferry (tel. 04 67 92 01 43), on second floor of parking garage next to train station. To: Béziers (every hr., 4 Sun., 1¾hr., 44F); Carnon (10 per day, 5 Sun., 20min., 15F); Nîmes (2 per day, 1¾hr., 42F); Alès (1 per day, 1¾hr., 58F). Info office open Mon.-Fri. 9am-noon and 2-7pm, Sat. 7am-noon and 2-6:30pm.

Public Transportation: SMTU, 27, rue Maguelone (tel. 04 67 22 87 87). Lines 17-29 leave from front of train station (6F50). The free **Petitbus** serves the city center Mon.-Sat. 7:20am-7:30pm; the **Rabelais** (night bus) runs to Agropolis, Hauts de la Paillade, Pas du Loup, and Prés d'Arènes from 9pm-12:30am.

Taxis: TRAM (tel. 04 67 92 04 55) offers 24-hr. service.

English Bookstores: Bookshop, 4, rue de l'Université (tel. 04 67 66 09 08). Large selection includes audio books, video rentals, and *Let's Go.* Open Mon.-Sat. 9:30am-1pm and 2:30-7pm; closed Mon. in August. **Bill's Book Company,** 9, rue du Cheval Vert (tel. 04 67 58 64 42), off the pl. St-Denis. Exciting collection of literary *bijoux,* mostly secondhand paperbacks (9-20F). Bill, the British proprietor, is always up for tea or a chat. Open Tues.-Sat. 10:30am-12:30pm and 2:30-6:30pm.

French-American Center: 4, rue St-Louis (tel. 04 67 92 30 66; fax 04 67 58 9820). All anglophones welcome. Center organizes Franco-American *soirées.* Open Mon.-Fri. 9:30am-noon and 2-6:30pm.

Women's Center: Union Femme Civique et Sociale, 1, rue Embouque d'Or (tel. 04 67 60 57 93). Open Mon. 2:30-5pm and Fri. 9:30-11:30am.

Youth Center: L'Espace Jeunesse, 6, rue Maguelone (tel. 04 67 92 30 50). A welcome and info center for the city's youth. Stop by and ask about theaters, lodging, jobs, and activities. Open Mon.-Fri. noon-6pm.

Laundromat: Lav'Club Miele, 6, rue des Ecoles Laïques. Right near the hostel. Wash 18F per 6kg. Dry 4F for 7½min. Soap 2F. Open daily 7:30am-9pm.

Crisis Lines: SOS Amitié, tel. 04 67 63 00 63, for 24-hr. friendship. **AIDS Information: AIDES Montpellier (SIDA),** 28 bd. Pasteur (tel. 04 67 60 47 07; open Mon.-Fri. 9am-1pm and 2-6pm).

Hospital: St-Eloi, 2, av. B. Sans (tel. 04 67 33 67 33). **Medical emergency** tel. 15.

Police: 13, av. du Prof. Grasset (tel. 04 67 22 78 22). **Emergency** tel. 17.

Post Office: pl. Rondelet (tel. 04 67 34 50 00). From pl. de la Comédie, follow Grande rue Jean Moulin, cross bd. Observatoire onto rue de Fbg. de la Saunerie, and then follow rue Rondelet. Poste restante. **Currency exchange.** Open Mon.-Fri. 8am-7pm, Sat. 8am-noon. **Branch office** at pl. des Martyrs de la Résistance (tel. 04 67 60 03 60). **Postal codes:** 34000 (central), 34026 (branch office).

ACCOMMODATIONS AND CAMPING

The place to be at night in Montpellier is the *vieille ville.* Every listing below (except the Hôtel Fauvettes) is located within it—even the hostel and the Foyer. Search rue Aristide Olivier, rue du Général Campredon (off cours Gambetta and rue A. Michell), and rue A. Broussonnet (off pl. Albert 1er) for other reasonably priced hotels.

Auberge de Jeunesse (HI), 2, impasse de la Petite Corraterie (tel. 04 67 60 32 22; fax 04 67 60 32 30). Take bus 2, 3, 5, 6, 7, 9, or 16 from train station, get off at the Banque Caisse d'Epargne on bd. Louis-Blanc, and walk up rue des Ecoles Laïques. Hostel is on left after 1 block. Or head away from station on rue Maguelone, cross pl. de la Comédie, and continue on rue de la Loge. Turn right onto rue de l'Aiguillière, which becomes rue des Ecoles Laïques (15min.). Impasse de la Petite Corraterie is the last turn on your right. Friendly staff and a modern facility at the edge of the *vieille ville.* 80 beds in 4- to 9-person, single-sex rooms. 3 doubles. Co-ed bathrooms. 63F. Breakfast included. Bar (open 5pm-midnight), microwave, pool table (10F), foosball, and TV. Free luggage storage. Reception open 10am-midnight. Lockout 10am-1pm. Curfew 2am. V, MC.

Foyer des Jeunes Travailleurs, Residence Castellane, 3, rue de la Vieille (tel. 04 67 52 83 11; fax 04 67 60 90 39), an easy-to-miss door in a corner ½block from pl. Jean-Jaurès. For those under 26; sleeping bag required. Clean, modern facilities in a renovated 14th-century mansion a short walk from station. Laundry (wash or dry

10F). 2-day min. stay. Singles 90F. Doubles 80F per person. 6 nights 490F. Breakfast included. Reception daily until 10pm. Rooms available June 15-Sept. 15.

Hôtel Fauvettes, 8, rue Bonnard (tel. 04 67 63 17 60), near Jardin des Plantes. 25-min. walk from station. Take rue de la République until it becomes bd. Prof. Louis Vialleton. Left onto rue de Fbg. St-Jaumes along the Jardin and right onto rue Bonnard. (25min.) Or, take bus 3 to "St-Roch" from the *gare*. Rue Bonnard is left at the light. Charming hotel with garden. Quiet rooms. Singles 95F, with shower 150-170F. Doubles 110F, with shower 150-170F. Triples with shower and toilet 245F. Quads with shower and toilet 265F. Shower 10F. Breakfast 20F. V, MC.

Nova Hôtel, 8, rue Richelieu (tel. 04 67 60 79 85). Entering the pl. de la Comédie from rue Maguelone, the Opera building is on your left; rue Richelieu is a small street directly behind the Opera. Delightful family-run affair. Wide 18th-century staircase leads to renovated rooms of 20th-century hotel chain quality. The hotel has hosted many artists and musicians, including Bruce Springsteen. Singles 119-145F, with shower 159-169F. Doubles 144F, with shower and toilet 189-229F. Triples and quads (two big beds) with shower and toilet 264-299F. Flexible shower charge of 25F. Breakfast 29F. V, MC, AmEx. 10% discount with your *Let's Go.*

Hôtel des Etuves, 24, rue des Etuves (tel. and fax 04 67 60 78 19), off pl. de la Comédie. In the double-mirrored entrance hall, about 30 clones march by your side toward the reception. This personable little hotel is a maze of narrow tile hallways leading to spacious rooms, with TVs. Singles 95F, with shower 105-140F. Doubles with shower 160-185F. Shower free. Breakfast 27F.

Hôtel Majestic, 4, rue du Cheval Blanc (tel. 04 67 66 26 85). Follow rue des Etuves 3 blocks from pl. de la Comédie and turn right. Simple, pink rooms. In rooms not facing the street, keep the shutters closed over the small windows so that the late afternoon sun doesn't turn your room into a sauna. Singles 100F, with shower 150F. Doubles 120F, with shower 150-220F, with bath 240F. Triples 220-300F. Quads 270-300F. Shower 20F. Breakfast 20F.

Camping: Closest is 3km away in **Lattes,** a coastal town. **L'Eden,** route de Palavas (tel. 04 67 15 11 05; fax 04 67 15 11 31), offers 4-star camping with amenities including hot showers, a pool, electricity, and ping-pong. (1 person 50-83F, 2 people 64-124F, 3 people 80-160F, 4 people 96-180F; most expensive in July, this slice of paradise is only open April-Sept.) **L'Oasis** (tel. 04 67 51 11 61), also on route de Palavas, offers 2-person havens for 87F with showers and electricity. Both sites are open April-Oct. To reach either take bus 17 (direction: Palavas) from the train station and get off at the campsites. Bill, the bookstore owner, advises hard-core campers to pick up *Travels with a Donkey* and head for the mountains 20km north of Montpellier in the **Parc National des Cevennes.**

FOOD

Rue des Ecoles Laïques in the old city offers a variety of choices, including Greek, Egyptian, Italian, and Lebanese. Restaurants open late abound in the many *places* of the central *vieille ville.* During the school year, students can be found munching lunch in the eateries on **rue de Fbg. Boutonnet** on the way to the university campus. Contact **CROUS,** 2, rue Monteils (tel. 04 67 41 50 00) or the tourist office for information about the four **university restaurants.** None is located for a tourist's convenience, but one ticket (15F) gets you a full hot meal (lunch and dinner Mon.-Fri., open Sat. on a rotating basis). Morning **markets** are held daily at pl. Cabane and bd. des Archeaux, Tuesday to Sunday at pl. de la Comédie. Inexpensive **groceries** await hungry travelers at **Monoprix** (tel. 04 67 58 27 10), pl. de la Comédie (open Mon.-Sat. 8:30am-8pm). On Sundays, when other grocery stores are closed, **Alimentation/Corbeille de Fruits,** 8, rue des Balances (tel. 04 67 66 36 04), comes to the rescue with doors open daily from 10:30am-9pm.

Tripti-Kulai, 20, rue Jacques Coeur (tel. 04 67 66 30 51). Montpellier's only vegetarian restaurant occupies an uplifting, white space with abstract art on the walls. 50F salad platters; 60F Lotus mega-platter includes homemade veggie paté. Indian drinks and a special Indian dish every Friday. From 2-6pm the *pause tranquille* is

12F for coffee, tea, or juice and a pastry or ice cream. 10% discount for students. Open Mon.-Sat. noon-9pm (no full meals 2-6pm).

La Tomate, 6, rue Four-des-Flammes (tel. 04 67 60 49 38). Known for its wonderful *cuisine française* at amazing prices. *Menus* at 57F, 70F, 90F, and the 112F *gastronomique*. Lunch *menu* 50F. Wood and red-checkered tablecloth atmosphere enhanced by jovial family management. The *soupe des poissons* is *délicieuse*. Reservations recommended Sept-April. Open Tues.-Sat. noon-2pm and 7-10pm.

Pepe Carvalho, 2, rue Cauzit (tel. 04 67 66 10 10), near pl. St-Ravy. Named for the gourmet Catalan detective from the books of Manuel Vásquez Montalbán. Enjoy the lively atmosphere, *tapas* (10F), and drinks (10F with purchase of *tapas*). 50F *menu* includes 5 *tapas* and your choice of beverage. Open daily noon-1am, Sept.-June Mon.-Sat. noon-1am. V, MC, AmEx.

Le Volt Face, 4, rue des Ecoles Laïques (tel. 04 67 52 86 89). Funky wall paintings, inlaid mirrors, and mosaics cover this tiny restaurant. Serving *tapas* (10-30F) in summer and changing themed offerings in winter. 55F 3-course lunch *menu*. 50F *plat du jour*. Open Mon.-Sat. 10am-1am and Sun. 5pm-1am. V.

La Pita Grecque, 6, rue de la Vieille (tel. 04 67 60 51 45), near pl. Jean Jaurès. Simple interior with a few paintings of jazz musicians. Wonderful hummus, falafel, and *kebabs* to stay or to go. Sandwiches 20F, small and large platters 25F and 40F. Open Mon.-Sat. noon-2pm and 6pm-midnight.

SIGHTS AND ENTERTAINMENT

The *vieille ville* is bounded by bd. Pasteur and bd. Louis Blanc to the north, esplanade Charles de Gaulle and bd. Victor Hugo to the east, and bd. Jeu de Paume to the west. The old city's pedestrian streets, bookstores, and the sprawling pl. de la Comédie offer some of the best entertainment in Montpellier, all of it free. Hidden behind grandiose oak doors, the secret courtyards and intricate staircases of *hôtels particuliers*—built in the 17th and 18th centuries by the emerging bourgeoisie—escape the outside bustle. The tourist office distributes a walking guide, and their guided tours of the historic center let you into some of the 100-odd *hôtels*.

Touting itself as *la ville de culture,* Montpellier hosts two impressive collections of pre-Impressionist art. The **Musée Fabre,** 39, bd. Bonne Nouvelle, near the tree-lined esplanade, displays an important and widely heralded collection of works by Courbet, Géricault, Delacroix, and 17th-century Dutch and Flemish painters. The top floor exhibits contemporary and local art (open Tues.-Fri. 9am-5:30pm, Sat.-Sun. 9:30am-5pm; admission 20F, students 10F). The **Collection Xavier-Atger,** 2, rue de l'Ecole de Médecine (tel. 04 67 66 27 77), next to the cathedral inside the Faculté de Médecine, contains drawings and sketches by Fragonard, Watteau, and Caravaggio. Walk through the entrance hall of the *Faculté* to the balcony, turn left, and at the end of the hall take the stairs on the left. Ring bell to enter (open Sept.-July Mon., Wed., and Fri. 1:30-5pm; closed for two weeks around Christmas; free).

In the northwest corner of the old city, the rue Foch, off pl. des Martyrs, leads to the **promenade du Peyrou,** which links the **Arc de Triomphe,** erected in 1691 to honor Louis XIV, to the **Château d'Eau,** the arched terminal of a beautifully preserved aqueduct. Through the arches the imposing statue of king "Ludovico" protects the promenade, a short lane lined with towering magnolias and huge cube-cut trees. The monument has stood guard since 1839, half a century after French Revolutionaries melted down his predecessor to make pots and pans. At night, strategically placed groundlights frame the Sun King with a radiant glow. Bd. Henri IV leads to the **Jardin des Plantes** (tel. 04 67 63 43 22), France's first botanical garden. Designed in 1593 for local botany students to study medicinal herbs, it is now a historical monument. (Free. Open Mon.-Sat. 9am-noon and 2-6pm. At noon a bell rings to announce that the gates are being locked, and if you're still inside, you'll spend the next two hours wilting with the plants in the sun.)

From late June through early July, the **Festival International Montpellier Danse** brings performances, workshops, and films to local stages and screens. (Admission 35-260F; for info call 04 67 60 83 60, for reservations call **Hôtel d'Assas,** tel. 04 67 60 91 91, at 6, rue Vielle Aiguillerie.) The **Festival de Radio France et de Montpellier** sponsors performances of opera, jazz, and classical music during the final weeks of July (admission to concerts 50-150F; for info call 04 67 61 66 81, for tickets call 04 67 02 02 01 or fax 04 67 61 66 82; discounts for those under 25 and seniors). Early summer brings the **Printemps des Comédiens pac Euromedecine** (tel. 04 67 61 04 02), an open-air theater festival in the last two weeks of June and the first week of July. For year-round information on plays and concerts, contact the **Opéra Comédie,** pl. de la Comédie (tel. 04 67 60 19 99; ticket window open Mon. 2-6pm, Tues.-Sat. noon-6pm; tickets 70-180F, 60-150F for under 25 or over 65). The **Corum** (tel. 04 67 61 66 16) houses an opera (call the Opéra Comédie for tickets) and the **Philharmonic Orchestra** of Montpellier (no concerts in summer; 80-140F, discounts for students and seniors).

Cinema Le Diagonal, 18, pl. St-Denis (tel. 04 67 92 91 81), shows new-release films in their original language (32-37F admission). Call the music school **JAM** (Jazz Action Montpellier), 100, rue Ferdinard de Lesseps (tel. 04 67 58 30 30), to see if any jazz artists are scheduled. The *café-théâtre* **L'Antirouille,** 12, rue Anatole France (tel. 04 67 58 75 28), has international music and rock concerts Wednesday-Saturday nights (30-80F; open Mon.-Sat. 8:30pm-1am; Sept.-March Mon.-Sat. 7pm-1am).

Pl. Jean-Jaurès, rue Verdun, and **rue des Ecoles Laïques** remain favorite nightspots. In the summer, once stores have closed, **rue de la Loge** takes on its nighttime identity as a street of vendors, musicians, and stilt-walkers. The back half of a 1955 red Cadillac, complete with tail fins and a Tennessee "Elvis 1" license plate, protrudes precariously from above the entrance to **Rockstore,** 20, rue de Verdun (tel. 04 67 58 70 10), near the station. Bands of varying levels of fame and talent perform thrice weekly to the delight of every teen and 20-something in the south of France. The **disco** upstairs is open until 4am. Go before 11:30pm to avoid the 50F cover (open daily 3pm-4am; disco open at 11pm). For the artsy crowd, **Le Notes en Bulles,** 19, rue des Ecoles Laïques (tel. 04 67 60 38 21), is open Mon.-Sat. 6pm-1am for darts and beer. The name is a play on *noctambule,* a night-wanderer. The bizarre decor includes an astronaut mannequin suspended above the entrance. Happy hour is 6-8pm and on Wednesday, beers are two for one. Gay men throughout the region come to **Martin's Bar,** 5, rue de Girome (tel. 04 67 60 37 15), behind the pl. Marché aux Fleurs—a scene in itself—for drinks before hitting the clubs. Open daily 6:30pm-2am; Sept.-June 20 6pm-1am. The lesbian scene is subtle but friendly at mixed Le Volt Face (see **Food,** page 428).

Nîmes

In 1860, an Austrian immigrant named Lévi-Strauss began importing Nîmes' distinctive heavy fabric to California to make work pants for gold diggers. Produced here since the 17th century, this cloth *de Nîmes* still indicates its origins in its name—denim. But two thousand years before Levi's (rhymes with "lettuce" in France) ever dropped a stitch, togas were all the rage in this city that vies with Arles for the title of *la Rome française.* Nîmes, like Rome, was built with Roman labor on seven hills. The symbol of a crocodile shackled to a palm tree is visible throughout the city, commemorating the Roman emperor Augustus' victory over Antony and Cleopatra in Egypt. Firmly in control of the empire, Augustus sent his victorious soldiers to colonize Nîmes as a Rome away from Rome.

Cleopatra's charms have long since faded, but Nîmes (pop. 132,000) still possesses a remarkably well-preserved Roman arena and temple, as well as remains of the ramparts that once encircled the city. The city is also colored by its proximity to Provence and to Spain. The festivals of the *corridas* (bullfights) at the arena are huge celebrations where southern French and Spanish culture meet. Cafés and *bodegas* are packed all night and *sangría* is poured to the strains of *flamenco* music.

ORIENTATION AND PRACTICAL INFORMATION

Nîmes' restaurants, shops, and museums cluster in the *vieille ville* between bd. Victor Hugo and bd. Admiral Courbet. To get to the tourist office from the *gare,* follow av. Feuchères, veer left around the small park, and scoot clockwise around the arena; go straight on bd. Victor Hugo for five blocks until you reach the Maison Carrée, a Roman temple in the middle of pl. Comédie. Its façade faces rue Auguste.

Tourist Information: Tourist Office, 6, rue Auguste (tel. 04 66 67 29 11; fax 04 66 21 81 04). Free accommodations service. Info on bus and train excursions to Pont du Gard, the Camargue, and nearby towns. Free, detailed map. Festival info. **Currency exchange** at 1% commission. Open July-Aug. Mon.-Fri. 8am-8pm, Sat. 9am-7pm, Sun. 10am-5pm; Sept.-June Mon.-Fri. 8:30am-7pm, Sat. 9am-noon and 2-5pm, Sun. 10am-noon. **Branch office** in the train station (tel. 04 66 84 18 13). Open daily 9:30am-12:30pm and 1:30-3:30pm; Oct.-May Mon.-Fri.9:30am-12:30pm and 2-6pm. **Nîmescope** and **Nîmes Rendez-vous,** both listing events and activities, are free at the tourist offices.

Budget Travel: Nouvelles Frontières, 1, bd. de Prague (tel. 04 66 67 38 94).

Money: Crédit Mutuel, 1, rue Racine (tel. 04 66 21 86 40). 24-hr. **ATM** at the **Crédit du Nord** (tel. 04 66 36 68 68) just behind the Maison Carrée (bank open Mon.-Fri. 8:10-11:55am and 1:10-4:40pm).

Trains: av. Feuchères (tel. 08 36 35 35 35). Nîmes is a stop on the major line between Bordeaux and Marseille. Direct to: Bordeaux (6 per day, 5½hr., 284F); Toulouse (12 per day, 3hr., 177F); Arles (10 per day, 30min., 44F); Montpellier (1 or 2 per hr., 30min., 45F); Paris (7 per day, 4½hr., 350-400F); Orange (14 per day, change at Avignon, 1½hr., 62F); Marseille (10 per day, 1¼hr., 93F). Information office open Mon.-Sat. 8am-6:30pm. Automatic **lockers** 15F for 72hr.

Buses: at the *gare routière,* rue Ste-Félicité (tel. 04 66 29 52 00 for info on intercity lines), behind train station. Timetable posted in the station. Info office open Mon.-Fri. 8am-noon and 2-6pm. **Société des Transports Départementaux du Gard (STDG)** (tel. 04 66 29 27 29). To: Uzès (Mon.-Fri. 10 per day, Sat. 7 per day, Sun. 2 per day, 55min., 29F); Pont du Gard (Mon.-Fri. 9 per day, Sat. 8 per day, Sun. 2 per day, ½hr., 29F); Avignon (Mon.-Fri. 9 per day, Sat. 7 per day, Sun. 2 per day, 1¼hr., 39F). **Cevennes Cars** (tel. 04 66 29 27 29) runs to the same nearby towns.

Public Transportation: Bus de la Ville (tel. 04 66 38 15 40). Tickets good for 1hr. Buses stop running at 7:30pm. Ticket 6F, *carnet* of 5 23F.

Taxis: TRAN office in train station (tel. 04 66 29 40 11). 24-hr. service.

Bike and Moped Rental: Vespa, 6, bd. Alphonse Daudet (tel. 04 66 67 67 46). Bikes 60F per day with 600F deposit. Mopeds 200F per day with 6000F deposit. Open Mon.-Sat. 9am-noon and 2-6:30pm. See also at the hostel.

English Books: 8, rue Dorée (tel. 04 66 21 17 04) in the *vieille ville* is a little anglophone oasis; don't speak French in here. A small collection of novels (popular and classics) and *Let's Go: Europe.* Open Mon.-Sat. 9am-noon and 2-6pm.

Hospital: Gaston Doumergue, 5, rue Hoche, and **Hôpital Carremeau,** rue Professeur Robert Debré, share a helpful switchboard (tel. 04 66 27 41 11). **Medical emergency** tel. 15.

Police: 16, av. Feuchères (tel. 04 66 62 82 82). **Emergency** tel. 17.

Post Office: 1, bd. de Bruxelles (tel. 04 66 76 67 03), across from the park at the end of av. Feuchères. **Currency exchange** at no commission. Poste restante (postal code: 30006). Open Mon.-Sat. 8am-7pm. **Branch office** on 19, bd. Gambetta (tel. 04 66 76 67 90). **Postal codes:** 30000 and 30900, respectively.

ACCOMMODATIONS AND CAMPING

The *vieille ville* is dotted with hotels offering reasonably priced rooms. Reserve ahead during the festival in early June and the biggest summer concerts.

Auberge de Jeunesse (HI), chemin de l'Auberge de la Jeunesse (tel. 04 66 23 25 04; fax 04 66 23 84 27), off chemin de la Cigale, 3.5km from station. Take bus 2 (direction: Alès or Villeverte) to "Stâde, Route d'Alès," then follow the signs up the hill. At night, when buses no longer run, if the hostel minibus is available it will pick you up at the station for free; it will bring you back in the morning for 8F. Walking from station, pass the Maison Carrée (see directions for tourist office) on bd. Victor Hugo and continue straight on bd. A. Daudet. Go left at sq. Antonin onto quai de la Fontaine. Pass the Jardins de la Fontaine and continue straight on av. Roosevelt. Go right onto rte. d'Alès and bear left onto chemin de la Cigale. Follow the signs (45min.). Relaxed hostel set in a botanical park that used to be an olive grove. Bar serves beer, wine, and snacks until 1am. Kitchen, ping-pong, and adult-sized playground. Friendly, hospitable staff. 75 beds in 8- and 13-bed dormitories 64F. A few doubles and singles for 74F. Members only. Camping 44F. Sheets 16F. Free baggage storage. Filling breakfast included. 24-hr. reception April-Sept.; Oct.-March 7:30am-11:30pm. Often filled by school groups April-June; reservations recommended. Mountain **bike rental** 55F per day; in May-Oct. bike to Collias, **kayak** to the Pont du Gard, and then bike back, 140F per day. V, MC.

Hôtel Concorde, 3, rue des Chapeliers (tel. 04 66 67 91 03), off rue Regale. Smack-dab in the *vieille ville.* The talkative proprietors will treat you like family and help plan your daytrips. Singles 110F, with shower 135F. Doubles 115F, with shower 140F. One triple with shower 200F. Showers 21F. Breakfast 25F. Best to reserve in June-Sept.

Hôtel de France, 4, bd. des Arènes (tel. 04 66 67 23 05; fax 04 66 67 76 93). Excellent location with view of the arena. Singles 100-120F. Spacious doubles with shower and toilet 140F. Triples and quads with shower and toilet 180-250F. Shower 15F. Breakfast 20F. V, MC.

Nouvel Hôtel, 6, bd. Admiral Courbet (tel. 04 66 67 62 48). Spotless, very comfortable rooms with TV in the heart of town. Singles and doubles 147F, with shower 185F. Triples with shower 228F. Breakfast 28F. Shower 20F. V, MC, AmEx.

Hôtel du Temple, 1, rue Charles Babut (tel. 04 66 67 54 61; fax 04 66 36 04 36), facing pl. du Château. High-quality, often over-decorated rooms with firm beds and TVs. Singles with shower 150-160F. Doubles (one bed) with shower 150-190F, (two beds) 220F. Triples 230F. Quads 260F. Breakfast 30F. V, MC.

Camping: Domaine de La Bastide (tel. 04 66 38 09 21), on rte. de Générac, 5km south of station. Take bus D (direction: La Bastide) to the *terminus* (buses run until 7:30pm). By car, leave Nîmes heading to Montpellier, then get on rte. de Générac. Three-star site with grocery store, laundry, electricity, and recreational facilities. 33F50 per person, 59F50 per 2 people. Open year-round.

FOOD

Nîmoise cooking is often seasoned with *herbes de Provence* (a mixture of local herbs) and *aïoli* (a thick sauce made with garlic and olive oil). Waiters will advise you to try *la brandade de morue,* dry cod crushed in a mortar with olive oil and served as a turnover, pastry, or soufflé. On the sweet side, *caladons,* honey cookies sprinkled with almonds, are Nîmes' most popular indigenous delight. You might also want to try another local specialty, Perrier water, bottled just 13km away. The greatest concentration of restaurants lies along the pedestrian streets between bd. Victor Hugo and Grand Rue. In the same area the plethora of restaurants around **pl. d'Assas, pl. aux Herbes,** and **pl. du Marché,** with its single palm tree and crocodile fountain, will keep you from going hungry. For those wishing to get a little off the trampled path, cross bd. Victor Hugo and choose a Vietnamese restaurant or bistro along **impasse Porte-de-France** or **rue Bigot.** The terraced herb gardens and ponds on the back slopes of the **Jardins de la Fontaine** make for unforgettable picnicking. Stock up at the **open-air market** on bd. Jean-Jaurès (open Fri. 7am-1pm), or at **Prisunic** (tel. 04 66 21 06 26), on the corner of bd. de la Libération and rue Couronne (open Mon.-Sat. 8:30am-7pm). Luckily for hostel-goers, a large **Marché U,** 19, rue d'Alès (tel. 04 66 64 14 29), is just down the hill from the hostel (open Mon.-Sat. 8am-12:45pm and 3:30-8pm). For a crusty taste of history, **La Maison Villaret,** 13, rue de la Madeleine (tel. 04 66 67 41 79), has been baking bread in its wood-burning ovens since before the Revolution (open Mon.-Sat. 7am-7:30pm).

Le Mansa, 17bis, impasse Porte-de-France (tel. 04 66 21 09 18). The only restaurant in Nîmes to serve up specialty dishes from Senegal. Enjoy dinner—occasionally to the beat of live African drumming—among colorful African fabrics in the skylit interior. Dishes hover around 65F. Open Tues.-Sun. 11am-2pm and 7:30pm-1am.

Les 4 Saisons, 3, rue des Greffes (tel. 04 66 67 21 70). Serving a 55F *menu* that includes salad, *galette,* dessert crêpe, and a ¼-carafe of wine. Specialty crêpes such as the *savoreuse* (mozzarella and smoked salmon) and the *délicieuse* (mushrooms and spinach) earn their names (32-34F). Open Mon.-Sat. noon-2pm and 7-10:30pm. V, MC, AmEx.

Mogador Café, 2, pl. du Marché (tel. 04 66 21 87 90). While contemplating the broken columns of the crocodile fountain, enjoy this café's *tartes* and crêpes (12-29F). Vegetarians emulate Popeye by eating spinach pie (17F). Open daily 8am-10pm; Oct.-March Mon.-Sat. 8am-7pm; April-June 15 daily 8am-7pm. V, MC.

Pizzeria Cerrutti, 25, rue de l'Horloge (tel. 04 66 21 54 88), behind Maison Carrée. Portions will make your wallet smile and your stomach sing. Homemade pasta dishes and pizzas 45F, with wine and coffee 65F. Open daily noon-2:30pm and 7pm-1am. V, MC.

Chapon Fin, 3, rue Château Fadaise (tel. 04 66 67 34 73). Veritable *nîmoise* cuisine—at a price—amid lively decorations including signed photos of toreadors in action and a life-size sculpture of a rooster. Indulge in the 3-course 72F lunch *menu.* Open Mon.-Fri. noon-2pm and 7:30-11pm, Sat. 7:30-11pm. V, MC, AmEx.

SIGHTS

Most museums and monuments are within walking distance of each other between the gardens to the north and the arena to the south. A three-day **pass** (60F, students 30F), which grants entry to all sights, is on sale at the tourist office and the sights.

Nîmes' magnificent **Amphithéâtre Romain** (tel. 04 66 76 72 77), called *les arènes,* is one of the best-preserved Roman monuments in the world. Built in the first century for animal and gladiator combat, it held crowds of 23,000 and eventually a city of 2000 impoverished people during the 18th century. The ancient spirit lives on at *les arènes* with dazzling bullfights in February, late May, early June, and September; otherwise, the amphitheater is used for classical and rock concerts, and, closer to its Roman traditions, an occasional boxing match. (Open summer 9am-6:30pm; winter 9am-noon and 2-5:30pm. Admission 22F, students 16F.)

The **Maison Carrée** (Square House) is actually a long rectangular temple built to harmonious proportions. Dedicated in the first century BC, possibly to Lucius and Caius Caesar, grandsons of Augustus, the temple features fluted Corinthian columns and exquisite decoration. The model for Paris's Eglise Madeleine, among others, the Maison Carée is the most intact of all ancient Greco-Roman temples. Drawings of the building's history and construction hang in its otherwise unimpressive interior (tel. 04 66 36 26 76; open summer daily 9am-noon and 2:30-7pm; winter 9am-12:30pm and 2-6pm; free).

Across the square, the **Carré d'Art** stands gracefully in less enduring aluminum and glass. Nîmes' cultural center houses an extensive **library** (tel. 04 66 76 35 03) and the **Musée d'Art Contemporain** (tel. 04 66 76 35 70), which features a permanent collection of works since 1960 as well as seasonally changing exhibits of 20th-century art. (Library open Tues.-Sat. 11am-6pm. Free. Museum open Tues.-Sun. 10am-6pm. Admission 22F, students 16F.)

The **Musée des Beaux-Arts** (tel. 04 66 67 38 21), rue de la Cité Foule, in a renovated Neoclassical building accented with marble pillars and mosaic floors, contains paintings of the French, Italian, Flemish, and Dutch schools from the 15th to 19th centuries, as well as temporary exhibits. The **Musée du Vieux Nîmes** (tel. 04 66 36 00 64), pl. aux Herbes, next to the cathedral, resides in a 17th-century palace and boasts a remarkable collection of regional arts, furniture, and looms, including a meticulously detailed 18th-century billiards table. (Both open Tues.-Sun. 11am-6pm. Admission 22F, students 16F.)

While away the afternoon amid marble sculptures and cascading waterfalls under the canopy of the **Jardins de la Fontaine,** off pl. Foch to the left along the canals from the Maison Carrée. (Garden open June 15-Sept. 15 7am-11pm; Sept. 16-Oct. 31 and April 1-June 14 8am-9pm; Nov. 1-March 31 8am-7pm.) Walk up the stone staircases on the hillside at the back of the park to the **Tour Magne** (tel. 04 66 67 65 56), built by Augustus in 15 BC and originally part of the ramparts encircling the city. One of the few remnants of that fortification, the frayed tower now gazes over the entire city and the surrounding countryside (open daily 9am-12:30pm and 1-6:30pm; tower admission 10F, students 8F).

ENTERTAINMENT

Major concerts, movies, plays, and operas take place at the *arènes* throughout the year (60-300F). For information or reservations, contact the **Bureau de Location des Arènes,** 1, rue Alexandre Ducros, 30000 Nîmes (tel. 04 66 67 28 02). Open Mon.-Fri. 9am-noon and 2-6pm; ask the tourist office for a list of upcoming events.

In the spirit of the Roman gladiators, Nîmes sponsors three important *corridas* (bullfights). In February, late May, early June, and September, the streets resound with clattering hooves as the bulls are herded to their deaths in the *arènes.* The largest of these festivals is the **Feria de Pentecôte,** held annually around the last week of May and the first week of June. The **courses camarguaises** offer more humane entertainment. The fighters strip the bull of a decoration on his horns and forehead. Ticket prices run 70-350F. Cheap seats are usually available the day of the event.

Nîmes ushers out the longest day of the year with music on every corner; June 21 is the first night of the **Fête de la Musique en France.** Thursday nights from the end of June through early September are the **marchés du soir.** From 7-10pm, local painters, artists, and musicians flock to the city's center to entertain delighted crowds.

Queen's Beer, 1bis, rue Jean Reboul (tel. 04 66 67 81 10), has 45 different kinds of Belgian beer in an impressive international selection (beers 13-20F; open Mon.-Sat. 4pm-1am, Sun. 9pm-1am). The **impasse Porte-de-France** area is home to lots of other active bars. **Lulu Club,** impasse de la Curaterie (tel. 04 66 36 28 20), is a gay dance club occasionally featuring an act filled with flamboyant feather boas and chiffon (30F entrance fee includes 1 drink). At **Cinéma Le Sémaphore,** 25, rue Porte de France (tel. 04 66 67 88 04 and 66 67 83 11), one block over from bd. Victor Hugo, foreign films play in their original languages year-round (32F, 24F for noon shows).

■ Near Nîmes

PONT DU GARD

Built around 19 BC by Augustus' minion, Agrippa, to provide water to the growing city of Nîmes, the Pont du Gard is one of the biggest and best-preserved sections of a former Roman aqueduct. The original covered canal carried water 50km from the Eure springs near Uzès to Nîmes, with only a 17m total fall in altitude, requiring uncanny engineering and masonry skill. Its famous Pont du Gard consists of three levels totaling 52 arches spanning 275m at the water-carrying level. From the 5th to 7th centuries its stone was looted for free building material; it was not until the 18th century that the state restored part of the dilapidated and neglected bridge. Subsequent restorations have returned the Pont du Gard to its original appearance, and a flow of tourists has replaced the 44 million gallons of water it could provide daily. On hot days, bathers enjoy the clear waters of the Gard river, and the adventurous can test their vertigo tolerance by walking on the Pont's breathtaking heights.

The **Société des Transports Départementaux du Gard (STDG)** (tel. 04 66 29 27 29) runs daily buses from the *gare routière* in Nîmes to the Pont du Gard (5 per day, 45min., 30F). Buses leave for the Pont du Gard from Avignon (3 per day, ½hr., 30F). The bus will drop you off and pick you up at the hotel L'Auberge Blanche in what seems to be the middle of nowhere. Follow signs to the parking lot (10min.).

The Pont du Gard's **tourist office** (tel. 04 66 37 00 02), located 200m to the left after crossing the bridge, provides information on campgrounds, hiking, and rock-climbing, as well as a **currency exchange** (open 9am-7pm; Sept.-June 9am-noon and 2-6pm; renovations have closed the office, at least temporarily). The staff will also direct you to **Collias,** 4km away toward Uzès, where **Kayak Vert** (tel. 04 66 22 84 83;

fax 04 66 22 88 78) rents canoes (50F per hr., 145F per day), kayaks (35F per hr., 90F per day), and mountain bikes (80F per ½-day, 110F per day, passport deposit). For 100F, you can paddle 11km downstream from Collias to the Pont du Gard and then shuttle back to Collias (HI cardholders get 15% off the kayak descent). The **Camping le Barralet,** rue des Aires in Collias (tel. 04 66 22 84 52), offers a pool in addition to river bathing. *Epicerie* 200m away. Laundry 20F per wash (no driers). (1 person 33F. 3 people 73F. 2 people with car 63F. 10% discount April-June and Sept. Open April-Sept. V, MC, AmEx.)

AIGUES-MORTES

Despite being populated as much by swamp-bred insects as by humans, Aigues-Mortes has survived since the 13th century. Louis IX had the town built with the express purpose of using it as a port; he launched crusades from there in 1248 and 1270. For one weekend in late August, the **Fête de St. Louis** relives those days with historical pageants, jousting, and a medieval market—book a room early. **Hôtel Carriere,** 18, rue Pasteur (tel. 04 66 53 73 07; fax 04 66 53 84 75), one half-block from pl. St.-Louis, is an inexpensive option. One person with shower and toilet 190F. Doubles 220F. Triples 270F. Call at least 15 days in advance for reservations during the *fête.* The hotel has a restaurant with a 77F *menu* (three courses). Though never attacked, the remarkable fortress **Tour de Constance** (tel. 04 66 53 61 55) remains equipped with the latest in medieval Strategic Defense Initiatives. The tower provides a view of the surrounding countryside and the sea of orange roofs of the *vielle ville,* enclosed within the perfectly preserved city walls. Entrance to the tower allows you to walk the complete circuit of these impressive walls. Huguenots were imprisoned in the tower in the 16th and 17th centuries. A display of mannequins on the second floor includes one unfortunate Protestant woman looking longingly out the window of her dim room; the tableau is based on a painting of the martyrs by Jeanne Lombard (open daily 9:30am-7pm; Sept.-Easter 9:30am-noon and 2-5:30pm; admission 28F, under 26 18F, under 18 15F). The **tourist office,** Porte de la Gardette (tel. 04 66 53 73 00; fax 04 66 53 65 94), is just a half-block from the Tour de Constance (open Mon.-Fri. 9am-8pm, Sat.-Sun. 10am-8pm; Oct.-June 19 9am-noon and 2-6pm). Down the Grand Rue Jean Jaurès from the tourist office, **Notre Dame des Sablons** stands on the corner of pl. St.-Louis with its many restaurants. The bizarre and beautiful modern art stained-glass windows by Bernard Dhonneur and Claude Viallet in this 13th-century church pair splotches of color in every conceivable combination. A note at the entrance begs shocked visitors to understand that these windows are "the *speaking-light* of the multiple colors of the love for God…[they] illuminate today the stones of yesterday."

Horseback riding is available through El Perdido (tel. 04 66 53 78 13), a short walk from the tourist office (80F per hr., 140F per 2hr.). In the second week of October, participants in the **Fête Votive's** "harmless bullfights" try to outwit the bull without hurting him. (See gray box on page 456.) On Wednesdays and Fridays in July and August, a guided tour including both the **Baleine salt works** and the **Listel winery** leaves the tourist office at 1:45pm (48F, under 16 26F; 3½hr.). The **SNCF** runs both trains and buses from Nîmes to Aigues-Mortes from the train station (7 per day, 1hr., 37F). **STDG** also runs buses from Nîmes (5 per day, 1hr., 35F).

UZÈS

Twenty-six km from Nîmes is the small city of Uzès. The **Duché** (tel. 04 66 22 18 96) dominates the center of the *vieille ville.* This complex, begun in the 11th century by the family of the Crussol d'Uzès, who had the enviable exclusive right to mint money in the region, was perpetually renovated for seven centuries. According to local legend, a niece of Charlemagne who inhabited the medieval fortress wrote the first book known to have been written by a woman. The Uzès, descendants of the first duke and duchess of France, still use the fortress as a home. The Duché's **Fenestrelle Tower** overlooks Uzès. The interior features paintings, tapestries, Louis XIII and Louis XIV furniture, and a 15th-century chapel. Admission includes a guided tour in

French, with written English translation. (Open 10am-6:30pm; Oct.-May 10am-noon and 2-6pm; 48F, students 35F.) The **cathedral** sits on pl. de l'Evêché. Burned, rebuilt, and restored many times in its turbulent history, it is now a fascinating mishmash of styles from Romanesque to Renaissance. The cathedral's remarkable 17th-century, 2772-pipe organ has delicately carved shutters. There are organ concerts in October and again in the spring (open daily 9am-6:30pm; free). Across the street, to the cathedral's left, a stone balcony provides a magnificent view of the surrounding countryside. Bulls stampede through the streets and cascades of *pastis* flow freely during the **Fête Votive** in the first week of August. An international music festival, the **Nuits Musicales d'Uzès,** brightens the second half of July. Tickets (70-120F per performance) are at the **tourist office,** av. de la Libération (tel. 04 66 22 68 88; fax 04 66 22 95 19), where you can also pick up a free booklet on Uzès that includes a tourist-friendly map (open July-Sept. Mon.-Fri. 9am-7pm, Sat. 10am-noon and 3-5pm, Sun. 10am-5pm; Oct.-June Mon.-Fri. 9am-noon and 1:30-6pm, Sat.10am-noon). **STD Gard** (tel. 04 66 29 27 29) runs buses to Uzès' tourist office from Nîmes (8 per day, 2 Sun., 55min., 30F) and Avignon (3 per day, 1hr., 37F). Three mid-day buses to the **Pont du Gard** (20min., 18F) make the combination a good daytrip.

Provence: Rhône Valley

Provence's carpets of olive groves and vineyards unroll along hills dusted with lavender, sunflowers, and mimosa, while the fierce winds of the *mistral* carry the scent of the *herbes de Provence:* sage, rosemary, and thyme. The region inspired medieval troubadours and more recently attracted artists such as Cézanne, Picasso, and Cocteau. Van Gogh also ventured to Provence, searching for "another light...a more limpid sky," and spent years struggling to capture the impossibly blue light of the wide *provençal* vistas. Since Roman times, writers have rhapsodized about Provence's fragrant and varied landscape—undulating mountains to the east, flat marshlands in the Camargue, and rocky cliffs in the Vaucluse. Provence's apex is the white limestone peak of Mont Ventoux, which looms about 30km east of Orange. Soon after Petrarch recorded his climb to the summit in 1327, a small chapel at the top began to lure agile pilgrims. Petrarch's lyrical spirit also haunts the Fontaine de Vaucluse, a natural spring 25km east of Avignon.

With their Roman remnants and cobblestone grace, Orange and Arles meet the Rhône as it flows to the Mediterranean. Briefly home to the medieval papacy, Avignon still holds the formidable Palais des Papes. Carouse in Aix-en-Provence or relax in the tranquility of Vaison-la-Romaine in the Vaucluse. Life unfolds along the shaded promenades like an endless game of *pétanque* or a bottomless glass of *pastis.*

Provence is known throughout France for its festivals; in the summer, even the smallest hamlets revel with music, dance, theater, and antique markets. In Avignon, you'll find film, theater, and music (mid-June to mid-Aug.); in Arles, photography (July); in Aix, music (mid-July to Aug.); in Orange, opera (mid-July to early Aug.); and in Vaison-la-Romaine and Carpentras, ballet and classical music (July-early Aug.).

Julius Caesar exalted the virtues of *provençal* wines in his *Commentaries.* The vintners have had two thousand years since then to refine their Châteauneuf-du-Pape, Gigondas, and Côtes du Rhône. Provence's temperate climate yields dozens of varieties of melons, olives, cherries, figs, asparagus, and herbs. Local cuisine features *ratatouille* (a rich blend of eggplant, zucchini, and tomatoes); *bouillabaisse* (a spicy fish stew) served with toasted bread and *rouille* (a saffron-flavored mayonnaise); and soups *au pistou* (made with a fragrant basil-garlic sauce). *Aïoli,* a sauce of olive oil and garlic, goes with hors d'oeuvres, vegetables, and fish soup. Honey gathered in Provence tastes of lavender and citrus flowers.

GETTING AROUND

Rail and bus service between the larger cities in the region is excellent, with direct connections to most of France as well as Italy and Spain. Buses connecting smaller towns are regular but frustratingly infrequent; check bus schedules thoroughly before setting off on a daytrip—make sure the bus on which you plan to return is running on your chosen day and time of year. Many people hitch along the country roads but report long waits for rides out of cities like Aix and Avignon. To see the region, rent a car and take the smallest roads or, better yet, bike or walk.

Orange

In 45 BC, Octavian, the future emperor Augustus, founded the settlement colony of Arausio over the remains of a Celtic market. The Roman homes, arena, baths, and city walls have disappeared, but the immense theater and elaborate triumphal arch are astonishingly well preserved among the 12th-century houses that dot modern Orange (pop. 28,000). Despite its colorful name, this northern *provençal* town hasn't hosted a single citrus grove in its two millennia; "Orange" is a perversion of the Celtic "Arausio." Orange's juice flows from its renowned vineyards, producing the Côtes du Rhône vintage. *Caves* scattered throughout the region produce reds and rosés and offer *dégustations* to those willing to buy. The view from St-Eutrope hill exposes

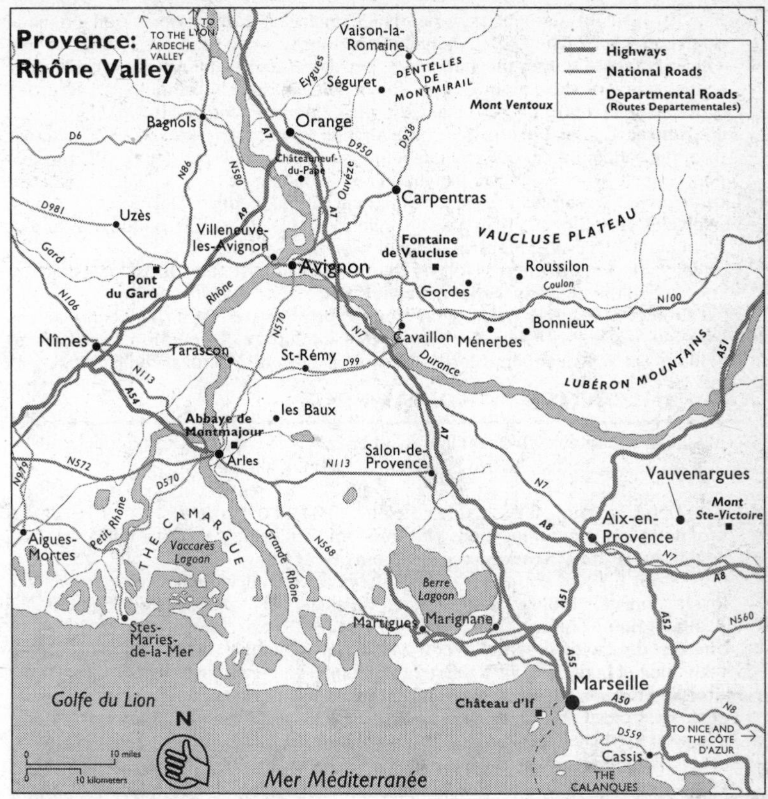

acres of vines and sunflowers in the valleys of the Vaucluse beyond Orange's appropriately hued rooftops.

ORIENTATION AND PRACTICAL INFORMATION

Orange centers around *places* Clemenceau, République, and aux Herbes. To reach the main tourist office from the train station at the eastern edge of town, following the signs to the *centre ville,* walk away from the station along av. Frédéric Mistral, and keep left as it becomes rue de la République; continue through pl. République, go around the building at the far end on its right side, and follow the smaller rue St-Martin straight, which becomes av. Charles de Gaulle. The tourist office will be across cours Aristide Briand and to your right (15min.).

Tourist Office: 5, cours Aristide Briand (tel. 04 90 34 70 88; fax 04 90 34 99 62), near the *autoroute.* Has **currency exchange** with commission built into the so-so rates. Spirited staff will help you in French, English, or German. Open Mon.-Sat. 9am-7pm, Sun. 10am-6pm; Oct.-March Mon.-Fri. 9am-6pm. **Branch office,** across from the Théâtre Antique, is open daily April-Sept. 10am-6pm.

Money: On winter weekends, the only place to change money is the **post office** (Sat. 8:30am-noon). **ATMs** grin at rue de la République and pl. Clémenceau.

Trains: (tel. 08 36 35 35 35), on av. Frédéric Mistral. To: Avignon (21 per day, 20min., 28F); Marseille (7 per day, 1¼hr., 105F); Lyon (11 per day, 2½hr., 131F); Paris (1 per day, 3½hr., 344F). Information desk open daily 5:10am-8:15pm.

Buses: cours Pourtoules (tel. 04 90 34 15 59), across from post office. To: Avignon (Mon.-Sat. about every hr., Sun. 5 per day, 45min., 27F); Vaison-la-Romaine (2-4 per day, 1hr., 24F50); Carpentras (4 per day, 45min., 22F). Office open Mon.-Fri. 8am-noon and 2-5pm. The Châteauneuf-du-Pape tourist office sponsors a 10- to 15-passenger **Navette** during the summer (2 per day, 20min., 25F roundtrip); call their tourist office or the one in Orange for details. During the school year, **Rapides Sud-Est** (tel. 04 90 14 59 00) make the trip (2 per day, 40min., 16F50).

Bike Rental: Cycles Lurion, 48, cours Aristide Briand (tel. 04 90 34 08 77), across from the tourist office. 60F per day. Mountain bikes 100F per day. V, MC or passport deposit. Open Tues.-Sat. 8am-noon and 2-7:30pm.

Laundromat: Lavomatique, 5, rue St-Florent, off bd. Edouard Daladier.

Hospital: Louis Giorgi, chemin de l'Abrian (tel. 04 90 11 22 22), on the outskirts of town out av. H. Fabré. **Medical emergency** 18.

Police: Parc de la Brunette (tel. 04 90 11 33 30), past the tourist office at the entrance to the highway. **Emergency** tel. 17.

Post Office: 679, bd. E. Daladier on cours Pourtoules (tel. 04 90 11 11 00), across from the *gare*. Poste restante. **Currency exchange.** Open Mon.-Fri. 8:30am-6:30pm, Sat. 8:30am-noon. Closed Tues. noon-1:30pm. **Postal code:** 84100.

ACCOMMODATIONS AND CAMPING

Good, cheap rooms are what you'll find at the hotels of Orange. During weekends in late July and early August, however, it's smart to book ahead.

Hôtel Lou Cigaloun, 4, rue Caristie (tel. 04 90 34 10 07; fax 04 90 34 89 76). Beautiful hotel in a central location, with modern furnishings, shower, toilet, and TV. Secure lobby and breakfast room. Rooms typically go for 300-450F, but if the hotel's not full and you ask, the English-speaking staff will give you one of their lovely rooms for 150F, even in summer. Breakfast 35F. Safe parking 30F. V, MC.

Hôtel Le Milan, 22, rue Caristie (tel. 04 90 34 13 31). Spacious, airy, well-furnished, bright rooms with showers over a lively, noisy, though respectable bar. Rooms with one big bed 136F, with toilet 146F. Rooms with two small beds 136F.

Hôtel St-Florent, 4, rue du Mazeau (tel. 04 90 34 18 53; fax 04 90 51 17 25), near pl. aux Herbes. Friendly, helpful owner keeps large rooms with comfortable beds. and well-used bedding. Singles and doubles 120F, with shower 140-180F, with shower and toilet 200-300F. Some have TVs. Extra bed 40F. Breakfast 28F. V, MC.

Hôtel Freau, 3, rue Ancien-Collège (tel. 04 90 34 06 26), centrally located off rue St-Martin. Sweet, grandmotherly owner keeps clean, pleasant rooms with tile floors, some with saggy beds, in her old house. Singles and doubles 100F, with bidet 115F, with shower 145F. Breakfast 25F. Parking 30F. Closed Aug.

Camping: Le Jonquier, rue A. Carrel (tel. 04 90 34 19 83; fax 04 90 34 86 54). From the tourist office, keep going toward the *autoroute;* turn right after the big school onto av. du 18 Juin 1940. Take a left on rue H. Nogueres and after 5min., go right on rue Alexis Carrel; the site will be up on your left. 3-star site with pool, hot showers, and mini-mart. Mini-golf, horseback riding and tennis extra. Reception open 8am-12:30pm and 3-8pm. 28F per person, 30F per tent, car included, electricity 17-20F. Open April 15-Oct. V, MC, AmEx.

FOOD

During the nights of the *Chorégies,* the cafés on pl. aux Herbes and pl. de la République not only raise prices but also keep concert-goers up until 3am. Many restaurants serve *pan bagna,* the traditional salad-filled sandwich of the Midi. Avoid the tourist-priced bars on pl. des Mounets in front of the Roman theater. For good grocery prices near the rue de la République tourist office, take av. Charles de Gaulle to **Intermarché,** the biggest **supermarket** close to town (tel. 04 90 34 32 94; open Mon.-Sat. 8:30am-7:30pm, Fri. open until 8pm). Every Thursday the town erupts into an open air **market,** centering around pl. République and Clémenceau, and cours Aristide Briand, with everything from local produce to handmade jewelry (7am-1pm). Specialty food shops congregate on rue St-Martin between pl. République and cours Aristide Briand, with popular bakeries, a *pâtisserie,* and a fruit stand.

Le Tai, 51, av. de l'Arc de Triomphe (tel. 04 90 34 00 65), near the end of av. Victor Hugo. Young owner serves up tasty Vietnamese, Chinese, and Thai dishes. 3-course *menu* 55F. Open daily noon-2pm and 6:45-11pm. V, MC.

Crep'snack (tel. 04 90 34 70 96), on rue Notre Dame off rue Victor Hugo, next to the cathedral's front door. Slow service on a shady terrace with bubbling fountain. In the winter, their great 55F 3-course *menu,* including drink, is served in a less soothing indoor dining room. Crêpes, pizza, spaghetti, and salads 23-50F. Open Mon.-Sat. 11:30am-3pm and 7-10pm.

La Galette des Princes (tel. 04 90 34 23 53), on montée des Princes d'Orange near the Théâtre Antique end of cours Aristide Briand. 60F 3-course *menu* with such options as quiche or salad and steak, lamb, or pizza. This off-the-beaten-track restaurant has a terrace on a small hill. Open daily noon-2pm and 7-10pm.

Tabac le 2000, pl. aux Herbes (tel. 04 90 34 10 48). Cheap, basic food in a lively atmosphere. 55F 3-course *menu* with such options as steak, fries, and salad. Tomato soup 20F. Open Mon.-Sat. 6:30am-11pm.

SIGHTS AND ENTERTAINMENT

Built around the first century, Orange's striking **Théâtre Antique** (tel. 04 90 51 17 60) is the best-preserved Roman theater in Europe, one of three in the world to have maintained its stage wall (103m wide by 37m tall), now home to hundreds of birds. After the fall of the Roman Empire, this house of pagan entertainment fell into disrepair as peasants set up house in and around its walls. In the mid-19th century, engineers discovered its perfect acoustics and used the remaining front three rows as a model to rebuild the seats to accommodate 9000; the theater reopened in 1869. A 3.5m headless statue, discovered in the orchestra pit and reconstructed in 1931 to resemble the city's founder, Augustus, presides over the scene from above the portal. The theater originally held 10,000 spectators and adjoined a **gymnasium** complete with running tracks, combat platform, sauna, and temple. Free, interesting history lessons disguised as tours in French or English leave daily in July and August; call the tourist office for schedules or to request a tour during other months. (Open April-Sept. daily 9am-6:30pm; Oct.-March 9am-noon and 1:30-5pm; admission 30F, students 25F.) Above the theater the **Colline St-Eutrope** features a panoramic view of the theater and area; free, though acoustically poor, concert seats; and some ruins of the princes of Orange's castle. A ticket to the theater also admits you to the small, uninspiring **Musée Municipal** (tel. 04 90 51 18 24) across the street, which houses stonework unearthed from the theater site, mediocre 17th- and 18th-century artwork from the region, and works by the Welsh artist Sir Frank Brangwyn magnanimously donated in 1939 as a gesture of Anglo-French friendship. As you exit the theater, the ticket window will be on your right, take a left and head up the path; beware of broken glass. (Open April-Sept. Mon.-Sat. 9am-7pm, Sun. 10am-6pm; Oct.-March Mon.-Fri. 9am-noon and 1:30-5:30pm, Sun. 9am-noon and 2-5:30pm.)

Orange's other major monument, the **Arc de Triomphe,** stands on the ancient via Agrippa, which once connected Arles to Lyon. The imposing monument stands in the middle of a highway roundabout, as appropriately placed as the Sistine Chapel would be in Times Square. Eight Corinthian columns adorn this three-arched monument, whose façades depict Roman victories on land and sea over the Gauls. Made of local limestone, the 19m-by-9m arch is believed to have been completed in AD 26 during Emperor Tiberius' rule. During the Middle Ages it was filled in and used to create a defense tower, the **Tour de l'Arc.** In 1721 the additions were removed, and restorations were performed sporadically between 1780 and 1955. It stands today as an elaborate testament to the Romans' healthy self-confidence.

In July, the theater returns to its original function with the **Chorégies,** a series of opera and choral productions. Information is available from the Maison des Chorégies, 18, pl. Sylvain (tel. 04 90 34 15 52 or 04 90 34 24 24), next to the theater. (Open Feb.-June 1 Mon.-Fri. 9am-noon and 2-5pm; June 2-June 30 from Mon.-Sat. 9am-noon and 2-6pm; in July daily 9am-7pm. Tickets run 40-890F, and are often sold out by late June; locals report that there are tickets to be had before the show at bargain prices.

Under 18 and students under 28 can buy obstructed-view seats for as little as 20F, as well as get up to 50% off all other seats.) In August, such "pop masters" as Jerry Lee Lewis and local favorites take the stage in a concert series (tickets 150-800F). For info, call the tourist office or drop by a FNAC ticket outlet.

■ Near Orange

VAISON-LA-ROMAINE

Surrounded by miles of sun-drenched vineyards, Vaison-la-Romaine (pop. 6000) has enjoyed a long history of international tourism. The Romans arrived in 118 BC to build Vaison, which thrived until AD 70. The Christians visited in the 12th century and constructed the château here, which became a country home for the pope from nearby Avignon in the 13th century. Contemporary visitors boost the local economy by arriving in masses to admire the work of their predecessors. Though the town is a manageable daytrip, do as the Romans did and stay a while. Rooms in the town cost a pretty penny, but the youth hostel in nearby Séguret (see page 442) is a fantastic base from which to explore the surrounding area.

To reach the tourist office from the bus station, cross the parking lot of the gas station, and turn right on av. Victor Hugo to pl. Monfort. Continue past the *place* for a block and turn right onto the Grande Rue. Walk two blocks to the tourist office on the right (10min.). The Ouvèze river divides Vaison into the medieval *haute ville* to the south and the sprawling archaeological sites to the north. A tiny *centre ville* scrunches in between the ruins and the river. The **tourist office,** pl. du Chanoine Sautel (tel. 04 90 36 02 11; fax 04 90 28 76 04) boasts a delightful staff who give out maps and historical information. Ask about tours of the sites (in French and English) free with the purchase of the **universal pass** (35F, students under 25 20F, children 10-18F 12F). They offer **currency exchange.** (Open daily July-Aug. 9am-noon and 2-6:45pm; Sept.-June Mon.-Sat. 9am-noon and 2-5:45pm; Nov.-Easter closed Sun.) Get your kicks at the **ATMs** at **Crédit Lyonnais** on Grand Rue; **Societé Générale,** av. Générale de Gaulle; and **Crédit Agricole** on av. Jules Ferry. Get to Vaison by bus from Orange (3 per day, 50min., 24F50) or Avignon (2 per day, 1¼hr., 7F). Call **Voyages Lieutard** for details (tel. 04 90 36 09 90). **Cars Comtadins** (tel. 04 90 67 20 25) services Vaison (Mon.-Sat. 1-2 per day, 45min., 20F50). **Le Bouquiniste,** 57, rue Trogue Pompée (tel. 04 90 36 14 38), has used English books. (Open Mon.-Sat. 9am-noon and 2-7pm.) To explore the area, rent a bike at **Mag 2 Roues,** cours Taulignan (tel. 04 90 28 80 46), near av. Victor Hugo. (*VTTs* 70F per ½-day, 100F per day; passport deposit.) Owner offers tours in the Vaucluse. (Open Mon.-Sat. 8:15am-12:30pm and 2-7:30pm.) The **post office** is at pl. du 11 Novembre (tel. 04 90 36 06 40) and has **currency exchange,** an **ATM,** and poste restante. (Open Mon.-Fri. 8:30am-noon and 2-5pm, Sat. 8:30am-noon; **postal code:** 84110.

Most hotels are pricey; **Hôtel du Théâtre Romain** (tel. 04 90 28 71 98), on pl. de l'Abbé-Jautel near the tourist office, comes closest to inexpensive. The hotel has been undergoing renovations that should be done by the summer of '97. Clean but sometimes stuffy rooms. (Singles or doubles with sink and bidet 155F, with shower 230F, with shower and toilet 260F. Extra bed 70F. Breakfast 35F. V, MC, AmEx.)

In 1483, Pope Sixtus II granted Vaison the right to hold a weekly **market,** a privilege it still exercises every Tuesday. Vendors selling fresh produce, clothes, and pottery fill the town center from 8am-1pm. During the rest of the week, squeeze the melons at the **Super U supermarket,** at the intersection of av. Choralies and av. Victor Hugo (tel. 04 90 10 06 00; open Mon.-Fri. 9am-12:30pm and 2:30-7:30pm, Sat. 9am-7pm). Most restaurants in Vaison have minimum *menus* of 70F. Many of the *caves* in town offer *dégustations* of the local wines. You can taste the Ventoux and the strong reds of Gigondas free if you show an interest in buying. Ask the tourist office for a list of *caves.* **La Pomme,** 3, rue du Port (tel. 04 90 36 38 80), offers light crêpe *menus* (52F and 62F) and *galettes* (17-34F) as well as great ambience and a terrific view of the river. (Open noon-midnight. V, MC.)

Vaison's claim to fame is its Roman ruins. In the **Quartier de Puymin** and the **Quartier de la Villasse,** the ruins of Roman houses, baths, and mosaics stretch over hills carpeted with roses, pines, and cypresses. Although not so large as the one in Orange, the **Roman amphitheater** in the Puymin excavation is still impressive, and it has a beautiful view of the surrounding vineyards. The small **Musée Theo Desplans** boasts the best-preserved sculptures, mosaics, and ceramics from the ruins. The tourist office leads tours of the ruins and museum. (Ruins open daily 9am-noon and 2-6:45pm. Museum open daily 10am-1pm and 2:30-7:30pm. Admission to all 35F, students 20F, ages 12-18 12F.)

Also included with the visit to the monuments is admission to the 12th-century **cloister** near the Quartier de la Villasse. With its pillars and stone perfectly intact, the outer ring has become a gallery for relics from the ancient church. Connected to the cloister, the 11th- to 13th-century **Cathédrale de Notre-Dame** sits precariously on a foundation of recycled Roman columns (both open same hours as ruins).

Across the well preserved **Pont Romain** and up the hill is the medieval **Haute Ville.** Instead of the usual wide-windowed shops, lush and flowery gardens spill over walks and wooden gates. The 12th-century **fortress,** built under Count Raymond V of Toulouse, still fends off invaders. Though the stronghold is locked up for safety reasons, the surrounding cliffs survey the town below, the wine-covered Ouvèze valley, and **Mont Ventoux's** fabled peak (1912m).

From early July to early August, Vaison's impressive **summer festival** brings ballet, opera, drama, and classical music to the Roman theater almost nightly (tickets 120-200F). Near the beginning of August Vaison puts on **Charijazz,** a vocal jazz festival (tickets 60-80F). The second week of November brings **Les Journées Gourmandes,** a celebration of the food of Provence. Call the tourist office for details.

CARPENTRAS

At the foot of Mt. Ventoux, in the fertile plain of the Comtat Venaissin sits Carpentras (pop. 30,000). First settled by the Celts in 500 BC, this market town has been home to a large Jewish population and boasts France's oldest synagogue. Now a flourishing agricultural town, Carpentras will delight Roman ruins aficionados.

The enthusiastic staff at the **tourist office,** 170, allées Jean Jaurès (tel. 04 90 63 00 78 or 04 90 63 57 88; fax 04 90 60 41 02), will ply you with historical information, including the free English booklet *The Road to Jewish Heritage in the South of France.* In the summer these helpful people will send you on free factory tours of local products: *berlingots* (striped, triangular hard candy); *fruits confits* (crystallized fruit), and *appeaux* (bird whistles). Ask about occasional free bus tours of the area, free tastings with an *oenologue* (wine expert), and 25F tours of local monuments (40F for two monuments). **Cars Comtadins,** (tel. 04 90 67 20 25), runs 12 buses per day to Carpentras from Avignon (45min., 19F). From Orange, **Voyages Arnaud,** (tel. 04 90 63 28 40), sends 20 buses per day (45min., 22F). If you desire to stay, **Hotel la Lavande,** bd Alfred Rogier (tel. 04 90 63 13 49), is nearing the end of renovations. Finished rooms have plush new carpets and bedding, comfy mattresses, and a pleasant ambiance, even if hotel reception is somewhat impersonal. (Doubles 145F, with shower 155F, with shower and toilet 165F. Breakfast 30F. Hall showers and parking included. Extra bed 30F. V, MC, AmEx.) Pitch a tent at **Lou Comtadou,** av. Pierre de Coubertin (tel. 04 90 67 03 16), a 10-minute walk from town, direction "St-Didier." (20F per person, 28F per place, including car. V, MC, AmEx.)

The **synagogue** is the oldest official Jewish place of worship in France. Built in 1367, the exterior blends in with the surrounding architecture, but the inside is ornately decorated with over a dozen chandeliers (tel. 04 90 63 39 67; open Mon.-Thurs. 10am-noon and 3-5pm; Fri. closes at 4pm). A few blocks away is the more prominent **Cathédrale Saint Siffrein.** Built from 1405 to 1519, the cathedral flaunts meridional Gothic architecture; strong buttresses frame ogive arches. The cathedral has two entrances: a main walnut wood door and the side **porte Juive** through which converted Jews entered, built of Caromb stone with the peculiar "boule aux rats" carved in the center. The town itself is a site, with varied and interesting architecture, from the Roman arch next to the cathedral to the Italianate, 17th-century **Palais de Justice,** to the covered street of **Passage Boyer.** Each Friday, the town resumes its traditional role and overflows with local goods in an **open air market** (8am-noon). The folks at the tourist office sponsor the **Marché aux Vins** in front of their office, complete with free tastings of wine, fruit, and cheese, as well as a live jazz band (mid-July to Aug.; daily 10:30am-12:30pm). Supplies are available the rest of the week (minus jazz) at the **Intermarché** (from av. Jean Jaurès, walk towards pl. de Verdun, turning right on av. du Mt. Ventoux; turn right again on ch. de la Legue; the supermarket will be down a sidestreet on the right; open Mon.-Sat. 8:45am-7:30pm, Sun. 9am-12:30pm). Take a picnic to the shady park with fountains and waterfalls at the intersection of bd. Alfred Rogier and bd. du Nord.

In the last two weeks of July, ballet, classical music, and opera are performed under the stars at **Estivales** (tickets 120-160F; call the tourist office or FNAC at 04 90 84 35 35). In mid-August, the **Festivals des Saveurs Provençales** (festival of provençal tastes) will allow you to try local products from miles around, as well as listen to stories, songs and comedy.

SÉGURET

Only half an hour from Orange's *gare routière* is the tiny village of Séguret that will steal your heart. A few uncrowded medieval streets make up the town center, but its plum situation on the side of a vineyard-covered hill affords fairy-tale views for miles around. The **Gîte d'Etape Séguret** (tel. 04 90 46 93 31), in a rambling old farmhouse surrounded by vineyards, enjoys unrivalled scenery. Henri, the effusive manager and cook of *cuisine provençale,* has written books on hiking in the region and will direct you to the nearest trail. The pool is so refreshing and the atmosphere so genial you won't mind the sometimes less-than-immaculate dorms and washrooms (75F per night; breakfast included; sheets 16F). Doubles are more of hotel standard (with sink 180F, with toilet and shower 230F). Dinner is worth every franc (80F). As far as buses go, make sure the schedule says "Séguret-Poste" or you'll be walking from a distant *cave.* The town of Sablet is a more common stop, and is a mere 1.5km from the hostel. **Voyages Lieutard** (tel. 04 90 36 09 90) makes the trek between Orange and Séguret-Poste (1 per day each way Mon.-Fri. and Sun., 40min., 21F); between Orange and Sablet (3 per day Mon.-Fri., 1 Sat., and 2 Sun., 35min., 19F); between Vaison-la-Romaine and Séguret-Poste (departs Vaison Mon.-Fri. at 4pm, Sun. 7:10am, 15min., 9F); between Vaison and Sablet (Mon.-Fri. 4 per day, last bus to Sablet at 4pm, Sat. at 11:25am, Sun. at 4:10pm). **Cars Comtadins** (tel. 04 90 67 20 25) goes between Carpentras and Sablet twice per day (Mon.-Sat., last bus to Sablet at 5:30pm; 45min., 18F). From the bus stop in Séguret-Poste, stroll down the hill towards Sablet for one minute. The hostel will be on your right. From Sablet, follow the sign to the Auberge de Jeunesse up towards the hill to Séguret.

For a pleasant two-hour walk, go up the hill from the hostel towards Séguret, until you reach a dirt parking lot. Follow a dirt road for five minutes and you will meet a single lane, paved road popular with cyclists because of its shade and lack of traffic—follow the signs to Vaision (8km, which is not as far as you may think when the road is so pleasant, but take the bus back).

Avignon

Nestled among the vineyards of the Rhône Valley, the walled city of Avignon (pop. 100,000) has danced with cultural and artistic brilliance since it snatched the pope away from Rome some 700 years ago. In 1309, Pope Clement V shifted the papacy to Avignon, in his native France, partly to escape the regional warfare and corruption of feudal Italy and partly to oblige the powerful French king Philippe le Bel. During this "Babylonian Captivity," as it was dubbed by the stunned Romans, seven popes erected and expanded the Palais des Papes, a sprawling Gothic fortress. Innocent VI raised the town's ramparts, which still stand today. In 1377, Gregory XI returned the

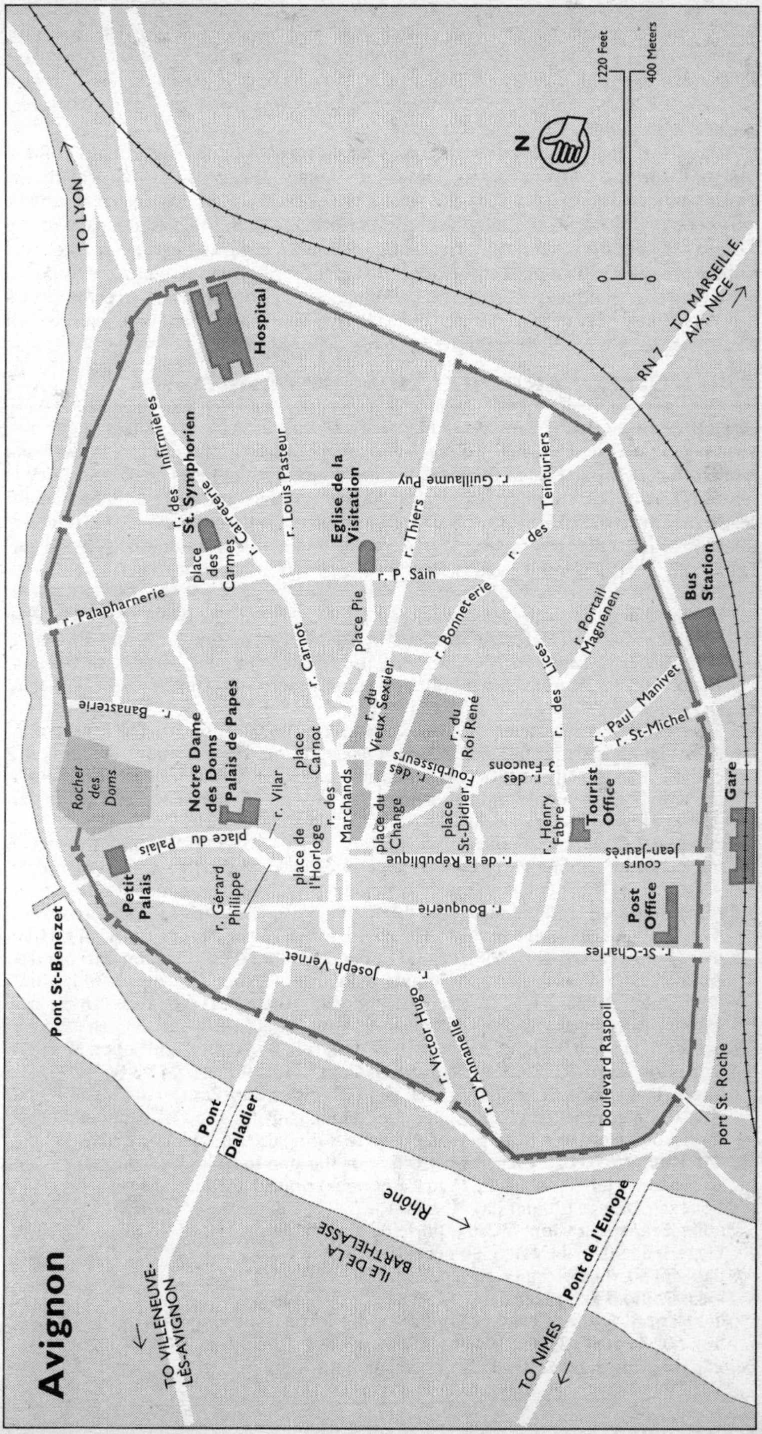

Avignon

TO LYON
TO MARSEILLE, AIX, NICE
RN 7
TO VILLENEUVE-LÈS-AVIGNON
TO NIMES
N
0 1220 Feet
0 400 Meters
Hospital
St. Symphorien
Eglise de la Visitation
Bus Station
Gare
Tourist Office
Post Office
Petit Palais
Notre Dame des Doms
Palais de Papes
Rocher des Doms
Pont St-Benezet
Pont Daladier
Pont de l'Europe
Rhône
ILE DE LA BARTHELASSE
r. des Infirmières
r. Carreterie
r. Louis Pasteur
r. Guillaume Puy
r. Thiers
r. des Teinturiers
r. P. Sain
place des Carmes
place Pie
r. Palapharnerie
r. Bonneterie
r. Portail Magnenen
r. des Lices
r. Carnot
place Carnot
r. Banasterie
r. du Vieux Sextier
r. du Roi René
r. des Fourbisseurs
r. des 3 Faucons
r. Paul Manivet
r. St-Michel
r. Vilar
place du Palais
place de l'Horloge
r. des Marchands
place du Change
place St-Didier
r. Henry Fabre
r. de la République
cours Jean-Jaurès
r. Gérard Philippe
r. Bouquerie
r. St-Charles
r. Joseph Vernet
r. Victor Hugo
r. D'Annanelle
boulevard Raspoil
port St. Roche

RHÔNE VALLEY

papacy to Rome, but he died only a year later. His reform-minded Italian successor infuriated the cardinals into electing an alternate pope, who set up court in the palace at Avignon, beginning the Great Schism and 70 years of rival popes. In the 15th century, the last of the "anti-popes" abandoned Avignon, leaving a legacy of papal aggrandizement—a legion of artists and artisans.

Today, the city is heralded for the famous Festival d'Avignon, a celebration of theater *extraordinaire!* From early July until early August, this friendly town is animated by uninhibited actors who roam the streets with creative methods to advertise their plays; visitors descend to enjoy both the performances and the bacchanalia in the streets. Hotel and restaurant prices soar, accommodations become scarce, and authorities crack down on festival-induced vagrancy. Although Avignon calms down when the bards and players depart, a combination of sights, festivals, street performers, and plenty of students continue to make Avignon an excellent base from which to explore the Rhône Valley and the Vaucluse (see page 449).

ORIENTATION AND PRACTICAL INFORMATION

Avignon's 14th-century ramparts enclose a labyrinthine city of endless alleyways, cramped streets, and squares. To reach the tourist office from the train station, walk straight through porte de la République onto cours Jean Jaurès. The tourist office is about 200m up, on the right. Cours Jean Jaurès becomes rue de la République and leads directly to the pl. de l'Horloge, Avignon's central square. At night, lone travelers should avoid the area around rue Thiers and rue Philonarde. In addition, Avignon harbors many car thieves and pickpockets.

Tourist Office: 41, cours Jean Jaurès (tel. 04 90 82 65 11; fax 04 90 82 95 03). Free brochure lists hotels, restaurants, and museums. Open Mon.-Fri. 9am-1pm and 2-7pm, Sat. 9am-1pm and 2-5pm; during the Festival Mon.-Fri. 10am-7pm, Sat-Sun. 10am-5pm. An **Annex** rests at Pont d'Avignon. Open daily April-Sept. 9am-6:30pm; Oct. and March daily 9am-1pm and 2-5pm; Nov.-Feb. Tues.-Sun. 9am-1pm and 2-5pm. **Bureau du Festival,** 8bis, rue de Mons (tel. 04 90 27 66 50), has festival info. Reservations start in mid-June. The *mairie* sponsors **Point Chalet Acceuil** at 2 entrances to the city (one across from the *gare* the other by Pont Daladier), outfitted with helpful people and info. Open May 15-Sept. 15 Mon.-Tues. and Thurs.-Sat. 9am-6pm, Wed. 2-6pm; during the festival open Sun. 2-6pm.

Money: AOC, 20 and 26, rue Grande Fusterie (tel. 04 90 85 78 40), is off the beaten track, but its commission-free exchange rates make it worth a walk. Open daily 9am-7pm. 24-hr. **ATMs** line rue de la République. **BNP** has an indoor one.

Trains: porte de la République (tel. 08 36 35 35 35). To: Paris (21 per day, 3½hr., 342-426F); Marseille (12 per day, 1hr., 89F); Nice (11 per day, 3½hr., 198F); Montpellier (35 per day, 1hr., 76F); Dijon (11 per day, 4 hr., 238F); Toulouse (6 per day, 3½hr., 198F); Arles (4 per day, 30min., 35F); Lyon (17 per day, 2hr., 146F); Nîmes (28 per day, 30min., 44F); Tarascon (13 per day, 10min., 21F); Orange (18 per day, 15min., 28F). Info desk open daily 9am-6:15pm.

Buses: bd. St-Roch, right of the *gare.* Info desk (tel. 04 90 82 07 35) open Mon.-Fri. 8am-noon and 1:30-6pm, Sat. 9am-noon. **Cars Lieutaud** (tel. 04 90 86 36 75). To Vaison-la-Romaine (3 per day, 1¼hr., 37F). **Rapides Sud-Est** (tel. 04 90 14 59 00) goes to Châteauneuf-du-Pape (2 per day, 30min., 18F50). The Châteauneuf-du-Pape tourist office offers a 10-15 person **Navette** during the summer (2 per day, 20min., 25F roundtrip). Call their tourist office or the one in Avignon for details. **Cars Contadins** (tel. 04 90 67 20 25 in Carpentras) runs to Carpentras (every hr., 19F). To reach Orange (20 per day, 45min.-1hr., 27F), call the *gare routière.*

Public Transportation: TCRA, porte de la République (tel. 04 90 82 68 19) or pl. Pie (tel. 04 90 85 44 93). 6F50 per ride (valid for 1hr.), *carnet* of 10 32F50, weekly pass 46F50, during the Festival 32F50.

Taxis: Radio Taxi, pl. Pie (tel. 04 90 82 20 20). 24-hr. service.

Bike Rental: Cycles Peugeot/Dopieralski, 80, rue Guillaume Puy (tel. 04 90 86 32 49). 60F per day, 240F per week, 1000F deposit. Open Mon.-Fri. 8:30am-noon and 2-7pm; during the Festival also open Sat. 8am-6pm, Sun. 8:30-11:30am. **Véloma-**

nia, 1, rue de l'Amelier (tel. 04 90 82 06 98). *VTTs* 100F per day, 600F per week; passport deposit. Open Mon.-Tues. and Thurs.-Sat. 8am-noon and 2-7pm.

English Bookstore: Shakespeare Bookshop and Tearoom, 155, rue Carreterie (tel. 04 90 27 38 50), down rue Carnot towards the ramparts. Sink into a paperback (from 20F) and a real American brownie (7F) in this haven for homesick anglophones. English cream tea (tea, 3 scones, jam and cream, 25F). Open Tues.-Sat. 9:30am-12:30pm and 2-6:30pm.

Cultural Centers: Centre Franco-Américain de Provence, 10, montée de la Tour, Villeneuve (tel. 04 90 25 93 23; across Pont Daladier, or take bus 10). All nationalities welcome. Cultural exchanges, *au pair* stays, language courses, and the French-American Film Workshop. Open Mon.-Sat. 9am-noon and 2-6pm, by appointment only. **Institute for American Universities,** 5, rue Figuière (tel. 04 90 82 58 50), off rue de la République. Language classes for young Americans. Open Mon-Fri. 9am-1pm and 2-5pm. **Espace Info-Jeunes,** 102, rue Carreterie (tel. 04 90 14 04 05; fax 04 90 27 02 90). Kind staff will help find you housing, info on jobs, careers, study and work abroad. Open Mon.-Fri. 11:30am-6:30pm.

Laundromat: Laverie, 48, rue Carreterie. Open daily 7am-8:30pm.

Crisis Line: AIDS Information Service (toll-free tel. 0 800 36 66 36). 24hr.

Medical Services: Hôpital de la Durance, 305, rue Raoul Follereau (tel. 04 90 80 33 33). **Médécins de Garde** (tel. 04 90 87 75 00 or 04 90 87 76 00) has doctors on call 24hr. **Medical emergency** tel. 15.

Police, bd. St Roch (tel. 04 90 80 51 00), left of train station. **Emergency** tel. 17.

Post Office: cours Président Kennedy (tel. 04 90 27 54 00), inside the walls to the left, across from the station. **Currency exchange.** Photocopiers. Open Mon.-Fri. 8am-7pm, Sat. 8am-noon. **Branch office,** pl. Pie (tel. 04 90 14 70 70). Poste restante: specify Poste Restante-pl. Pie (for pl. Pie) or Poste Restante-Avignon (for main branch). Open Mon.-Fri. 8:30am-12:30pm and 1:30-6:30pm, Sat. 8am-noon. **Postal code:** main office 84000, pl. Pie 84070.

ACCOMMODATIONS AND CAMPING

Avignon's *foyers* usually have room; during the festival, however, even they may be booked. Reasonable hotel rooms must be reserved well in advance. The tourist office has a list of organizations that set up inexpensive accommodations during the festival. Consider staying in Tarascon, Arles, Orange, or Nîmes and commuting by train (21F, 35F, 28F, and 44F respectively). Both Tarascon and Arles have pleasant, typically uncrowded hostels. If you are sleeping outside, buy insect repellent and a can of mace; the Rhône breeds bloodthirsty bugs and knife-toting thugs.

Foyer YMCA/UCJG, 7bis, chemin de la Justice (tel. 04 90 25 46 20; fax 04 90 25 30 64), in Villeneuve, across Pont Daladier. A 30-min. walk from station: cross Pont Daladier, continue straight, and after 200m take a left onto chemin de la Justice; it will be up the hill on your left. Or from the stop in front of the post office (across from the station), take bus 10 (direction: Les Angles-Grand Angles) to stop "Général Leclerc" or 11 (direction: Villeneuve-Grand Terme, 6F50) to "Pont d'Avignon." Clean, modern, small, low-ceilinged 2- to 4-bed dorms. 110F per person includes breakfast, sheets, showers, and access to the pool. 100F per person without breakfast. Doubles, triples, and quads 150F. Breakfast 20F per person. Reception open daily 8:30am-8pm. No curfew or lockout.

The Squash Club, 32, bd. Limbert (tel. 04 90 85 27 78). Walk 30min. along the walls to the right from station, or ride bus 7 (direction: Amandier) from station to "Université." Next to a warehouse in a simple building that acts as a squash club and triathaloners' hangout. Low-ceilinged, single-sex, 16-bed dorms with cramped washroom facilities. During the Festival more spacious coed dorm set up in a squash court. 54F per night. Breakfast 16F. Sheets 16F. Mandatory package deal that includes breakfast and sheets for 70F during Festival. Dinner 45F. Reservations accepted only by mail with deposit. Terrific managers will let you stay for free if you can beat them at squash. Don't count on it, though. Reception open 8-11am and 5:30-11pm. No lockout or curfew. Big **Casino** supermarket nearby.

Foyer Bagatelle, Ile de la Barthelasse (tel. 04 90 86 30 39; fax 04 90 27 16 23). From station, turn left and follow the city wall; cross second bridge (Pont Daladier). Bagatelle is to the right (20min.). Or take bus 10 (direction: Les Angles-Grand Angles) or 11 (direction: Villeneuve-Grand Terme) (6F50) from the post office across from the *gare* to "la Barthellasse." 250-bed institutional *foyer* popular with dreadlocked blonds and a grunge clientele who bond into the wee hours on the terrace. Free showers. Clean 6- to 8-bed dorm room 58F. Sheets 16F. *Demi-pension* 140F. Doubles, triples, and quads 67F per person. Snack bar, cafeteria. No curfew or lockout; keep an eye on valuables. V, MC. *Foyer* is in a **campsite** overlooking the Pont d'Avignon, the ramparts, and the Palais des Papes (July-Aug. 19F80 per person, 8F50 per car, 9F per tent; Sept.-June 17F80 per person, 8F50 per car, 8F50 per tent. Free shower. Reception open 8am-8pm.)

Provence Acceuil, 33, av. Eisenhower (tel. 04 90 85 35 02; fax 04 90 85 21 47) outside porte St-Roche to the southeast of the city. From the *gare* walk left; turn left on av. Eisenhower and walk for another 10min.—hostel will be on your left. Big, international, and clean, though institutional. Stucco-walled, high-ceilinged rooms, all with shower, toilet, sink, sheets, and towels. No dorms. 1 person 110F; 2 people 90F each; 3 75F each. Breakfast 20F. Laundry (wash or dry) 10F. Cafeteria in building has decent enough food *à la carte.*

Hôtel Mignon, 12, rue Joseph Vernet (tel. 04 90 82 17 30; fax 04 90 85 78 46), in a chic area between Palais des Papes and Pont Daladier. Super rooms, soft comforters, great beds, phones, and satellite TVs for those who want their MTV. Singles with shower 150F. Doubles with shower 185F. Doubles with shower and toilet 210F. Triples with shower and toilet 250F. Breakfast in bed 25F. V, MC.

Hôtel du Parc, 18, rue Perdiguier (tel. 04 90 82 71 55; fax 04 90 85 64 86), to the right off cours Jean Jaurès, near the tourist office (3min. from station). A small street, noisy during the Festival. Nicely decorated rooms in subtle tones. Singles 120-130F, with shower 150F, with shower and toilet 175F. Doubles 145-210F depending on amenities and number of beds. Triples 230F. Quads 245F. Hall showers 5F. Breakfast 22F. V, MC.

Hôtel Splendid, 17, rue Perdiguier (tel. 04 90 86 14 46; fax 04 90 85 38 55), across from Hôtel du Parc. Big, well-furnished rooms with comfy beds, TVs, and phones. Singles 140-170F. Doubles 190-220F. Triples 240-250F. Breakfast 25F. Showers 10F per person, but ask nicely and you might not have to pay. V, MC.

Camping Municipal: St-Bénezet (tel. 04 90 82 63 50; fax 04 90 85 22 12), Ile de la Barthélasse, 10min. past Foyer Bagatelle. Hot showers, laundry (15F per 7kg), restaurant, supermarket, and free tennis and volleyball courts. Grassy, shady tent sites. Reception June-Sept. 8am-10pm, April-May 8am-8pm, March and Oct. 8am-6pm. 25F per person, 18F per tent. Open March-Oct. V, MC.

FOOD

The crooked **rue des Teinturiers** hosts a smattering of funky, artsy restaurants. The cafés of **pl. de l'Horloge** are best suited for after-dinner drinks, when clowns, street musicians, and mimes milk crowds for smiles and centimes. **Parc de Rocher des Doms,** overlooking the Rhône, provides scenic picnic spots and has an outdoor café near the pond. Buy provisions in **Les Halles,** the large indoor **market** on pl. Pie (open Tues.-Sun. 7am-1pm), at the less expensive **open-air market** outside the city walls near porte St-Michel (Sat.-Sun. 7am-noon), or at the **Codec supermarkets** on rue de la République (open Mon.-Sat. 8:30am-8pm, Sun. 10am-2pm). If you're too tired to make the hike from the hostels to find something to eat, order in pizza, pasta, couscous, and wine (tel. 04 90 85 09 09).

Woolloomoolloo, 16, rue des Teinturiers (tel. 04 90 85 28 44). Through food, decor, staff, and ambiance, the much-traveled, *très cool* owner brings the world to his funky, mellow restaurant whose Australian Aboriginal name means "young black kangaroo." Main dishes run 55-70F, but a salad, *plat du jour,* and wine or coffee will cost you 58F. Plan to spend an evening here for a long, relaxed dinner. Open Tues.-Sat. noon-2pm and 8pm-midnight.

Le Cloître, pl. du Cloître St-Pierre (tel. 04 90 85 34 63), off rue Carnot near pl. de l'Horloge. Friendly staff and 50-60F carries a salad and a *galette* to your table on the pleasant outdoor terrace. Try the *galette Paysanne* or *crêpe Jeanne.* Open daily noon-2:30pm and 7pm-midnight, closed Sun. in winter. V, MC.

Baguettes d'Or, 41, rue de la Saraillerie (tel. 04 90 86 33 79), or 2, pl. Jerusalem near pl. de l'Horloge (tel. 04 90 86 82 60). A golden opportunity for cheap and filling Vietnamese, Chinese, and Thai food served on a terrace popular with traveling minstrels. 20F Wonton soup. 54F 3-course *menu* includes *nem* (egg rolls). Main dishes 22-40F. Open 11am-3pm and 6pm-midnight. V, MC.

Restaurant le Petit Comptoire, 52, rue des Lices (tel. 04 90 86 10 94). Typical French food for atypical French prices: 63F 3-course and 35F and 55F 2-course *menus* and 32F main dishes. Open Mon.-Sat. noon-2pm and 7pm-midnight, during the Festival open Sun. same hours. V, MC.

Gambrinus, 62, rue Carreterie (tel. 04 90 86 12 32), 200m down the street from porte St-Lazare and the Squash Club. Specializes in *moules;* huge portions of mussels and fries 40F in beer-sign heaven. *Moules marinières* and *à la crème* taste better than *à la bière,* but you be the judge. If you prefer beer in a glass, drafts are 13F. 70F *menu* includes *moules et frites,* ¼-liter of wine, dessert, and coffee. Billiards 10F. Open daily 7am-1:30am. Closed Aug. 10-25 and Jan. 1-15. V, MC.

Cucaracha, 22, rue des Teinturiers (tel. 04 90 85 81 03), down the block from Woolloomoolloo. Spicy Tex-Mex food and decor. Burritos 65F, *plat du jour* and wine 47F, 3-course *menu* 65F. Open Mon.-Sat. noon-2pm and 7-10pm; during the Festival daily noon-3pm and 7pm-2am. V, MC, AmEx.

SIGHTS

The **Palais des Papes** (tel. 04 90 27 50 71) stands in granite Gothic majesty at the highest point in Avignon. Benoît XII, the third of the *avignonnais* popes, ordered its construction in the 14th century. Expanded by his successors, it became a residence for papal legates during the 17th and 18th centuries until the Revolution, when the palace was looted and its contents scattered. It served alternately as a prison and barracks until the city reclaimed it early this century. The self-guided tour of the Palais takes you through the hollow interior. Finish with a climb to the tower for a fairy-tale view. (Open April-July 7 and Oct. daily 9am-7pm; Nov. 2-March 9am-12:45pm and 2-6pm; extended hours—July 7-Aug. 5 until 9pm; Aug. 6-Sept. until 8pm. Admission 34F, students and seniors 26F. Guided tour 43F, students and seniors 35F.) Each year from May to September, the Palais houses an exhibition in the most beautiful rooms. In recent years artists have included Picasso and Rodin; call for details on the 1997 exhibition. (Same hours as the Palais. Admission 35F, students and seniors 28F; with the Palais, 46F and 38F; with Palais and Petit Palais, 60F and 52F. Guided tour of the exhibition 45F and 38F.)

At the end of pl. du Palais, the **Petit Palais** (tel. 04 90 86 44 58), once home to cardinals, holds fine Italian primitive, Gothic, and Renaissance art (open July-Aug. Wed.-Mon. 10:30am-6pm; Sept.-June 9:30-noon and 2-6pm; admission 20F, students 10F; Oct.-March 1 free on Sun.). Next to the Palais sits the 12th-century **Cathédrale Notre-Dame-des Doms,** a Romanesque church with a richly decorated interior. Popes Benoît XII and Jean XXII are entombed within (open daily 10am-7pm).

The newly renovated **Musée Calvet,** 65, rue Joseph Vernet (tel. 04 90 86 33 84), features a potpourri of art, including prehistoric, Egyptian, Greek, Roman, and 16th- through 20th-century works. The 18th-century mansion that houses them is at times more striking than the art itself, combining stark white, high-ceilinged rooms and halls with exceptional natural and artificial lighting (admission 30F, students 15F). Right next door is the smaller, less grand, more peculiar **Musée Requien,** 61, rue Joseph Vernet (tel. 04 90 82 43 51). This museum of natural history has dinosaur skeletons, fossils, stuffed wildlife, and photographs of the surrounding countryside and its non-human inhabitants. (Open Tues.-Sat. 9am-noon and 2-6pm; free.) Avignon's affinity for the world of theater shines through at the **Maison Jean Vilar,** 8, rue de Mons (tel. 04 90 86 59 64), off pl. de l'Horloge. Come here to learn about the history of theater festivals, and *les arts du spectacle* in general. Video and audio recordings of performances, workshops, and lectures are open to the public, as is an elaborate exhibition of international costumes. (Open July daily 10am-1pm and 2:30-6:30pm; Sept.-June Tues.-Fri. 9am-noon and 1:30-5:30pm, Sat. 10am-7pm; closed Aug. Admission 25F, *videothèque* free.)

On a hillside next to the palace, **Le Rocher des Doms,** a beautifully sculpted park, enjoys vistas of Mont Ventoux, the fortifications of Villeneuve-les-Avignon, and 12th-century **Pont St-Bénezet,** the "Pont d'Avignon" immortalized in the French nursery rhyme. Today, the fabled bridge ends disillusioningly halfway across the Rhône, all but four of its original 22 arches worn away by the years. It is said that in 1177 angels instructed a shepherd, who became St. Bénézet, to begin the 11-year task of erecting the bridge. You may want to enjoy the bridge from where you are; it costs 15F (7F students) to walk (or dance) on it (tel. 04 90 85 60 16; open daily 7:30am-9pm). **Pont Daladier** makes it all the way across the river to the campgrounds and offers free views of the broken bridge and the towering Palais des Papes.

ENTERTAINMENT

Rabelais called Avignon *"la ville sonnante"* ("the ringing city") for its clanging church bells. Modern Avignon peals from early July through early August with the riotous **Festival d'Avignon,** when drama, dance, mime, and everything from Gregorian chants to an all-night reading of the *Odyssey* takes over the city (admission varies by activity; some are free). The official festival, also known as the **IN,** is the most prestigious theatrical gathering in Europe and offers at least 12 different venues (festival tickets 50-190F per event; reservations accepted from mid-June). The cheaper and more experimental **Festival OFF** presents over 400 plays, some in English, from mid-July to early August (OFF office, pl. du Palais). Call the tourist office or **Bureau de Festival** for the current phone numbers. You don't need to buy a ticket to get in on the act—fun, free theater overflows into the streets during the day and particularly at night during the Festival. On **Bastille Day,** Avignon ignites fantastic fireworks. For information on Bastille Day festivities or the Festival, contact the Bureau de Festival, 8bis, rue de Mons (tel. 04 90 82 67 08).

Regular performances of opera, drama, and classical music take place in the **Opéra d'Avignon,** pl. de l'Horloge (tel. 04 90 82 23 44). Rue des Teinturiers is lined with theaters that have performances from the early afternoon through the wee hours of the morning, including the **Théâtre du Chien qui Fume** at no. 75 (tel. 04 90 85 25 87). The **Théâtre du Balcon,** 38, rue Guillaume Puy (tel. 04 90 85 00 80), and the **Théâtre du Chene Noir,** 8bis, rue Ste-Catherine (tel. 04 90 86 58 11), are two other busy theaters. The **Utopia Cinéma** (tel. 04 90 82 65 36), on Escalier Ste-Anne behind the Palais des Papes, screens a wide variety of flicks in their original versions (admission 30F, card for 10 showings 240F). The Centre Franco-Américain de Provence (tel. 04 90 25 93 23) sponsors the **French-American Film Workshop** in late June and early July at the Cinéma Vox. The festival showcases feature-length and short films directed by young French and American unknowns, with an occasional attention-grabbing name (admission 30F, pass for 10 showings 250F). The **Maison Jean Vilar,** 8, rue de Mons (tel. 04 90 86 59 64), a theater library, shows free videos; call for a schedule and reservations.

Lively bars color **pl. des Corps Saints** (Holy Bodies). Heavenly bodies or not, be careful whom you get to know—Avignon's prostitutes have taken a liking to this street. Cheap suds and a major sound system draw boisterous Australians and backpackers to the **Koala Bar,** 2, pl. des Corps Saints (tel. 04 90 86 80 87; happy hour Wed. and Fri.-Sat. 9-10pm; beer 6F; otherwise 10F). The *discothèque* **Le Yucatan** (tel. 04 90 27 00 84) heats up summer nights in the *gare routière,* while **Le Blues** piano bar, 25, rue Carnot (tel. 04 90 85 79 71), mellows them out. The nightclub, **L'Esclav',** rue du Limas, swings both ways. Locals abandon the city limits in search of the best and most hedonistic clubs.

■ Near Avignon: Monts de Vaucluse

The Vaucluse, called "the crossroads of Southern Europe" because of its central location between Spain and Italy, is one of France's smallest and loveliest *départements.* Packed within its 2200 square miles in southeastern France are the foothills of the Alps (to the east), the Rhône Valley (to the west), and the Vaucluse mountain range. Thousands of visitors converge on its larger cities for extravagant festivals: Avignon's annual summer festival, Orange's *Chorégies,* and Vaison's tri-annual *Choralies.* In contrast, the region's smaller villages are marked by ancient tractors harvesting grapes at half-pace and men drowsing on shady benches. To learn more about the region, pick up a copy of Laurence Wylie's *A Village in the Vaucluse,* a fascinating study of issues facing traditional French rural communities, based on Wylie's stays in the tiny village of Roussillon. The road to the true Vaucluse is a tiny one leading to a tinier town—you'll know you're on the right track when the dialects slow to a twangy drawl, the roofs begin to change from tile to thatch, and your watch, set to Paris time, just keeps running too fast.

VILLENEUVE-LÈS-AVIGNON

On a hill overlooking *"la ville sonnante"* and its famous palaces sits quiet, complacent Villeneuve-lès-Avignon. Built up around an abbey, a monastery, and a fortress, this small town may be a short walk across the river, but the change of atmosphere makes the calmer streets feel miles away. The **tourist office,** 1, pl. Charles David (tel. 04 90 25 61 33; fax 04 90 25 61 55) will help you find out what's what. (Open daily July-Aug. 8:45am-12:30pm and 2:30-6:30pm; Sept. 1-June, Mon.-Sat. 8:45am-12:30pm and 2-6pm.) **La Chartreuse du Val de Benediction,** av. de Verdun (tel. 04 90 15 24 24), was built by Pope Innocent VI in the 14th century and is one of the largest Cartusian monasteries in France (open daily April-Sept. 9am-6:30pm; Oct.-March 9:30am-5:30pm). Crowning Villeneuve's hill, Mont Andaon, is the **Fort Saint-André** (tel. 04 90 25 45 35). Built by the King of France Jean Le Bon in the 14th century, its fortified walls and double towers were meant to remind the Pope of Avignon that he did not hold a monopoly on power (open daily April-Oct. 9 10am-12:30pm and 2-6pm; Oct. 10-March 10am-noon and 2-7pm). Inside the fortress, the 11th-century Benedictine **Abbaye Saint-André** was the first major construction in the area. Though the original buildings were largely destroyed during the Revolution, the 17th-century remnants remain, sheltering gardens with panoramic views of the Rhône. Down the hill is the **Musée Municipal Pierre de Luxembourg,** rue de la République (tel. 04 90 27 49 66), which features both 14th- and 15th-century religious works and 17th- and 18th-century *provençal* paintings. The most prominent monument visible from Avignon is the Gothic **Tour Phillippe Le Bel** (tel. 04 90 27 49 68), at the intersection of av. Gabriel Péri and Montée de la Tour. Once a dungeon, its only current method of punishment is the climb to the top for a panoramic view of Avignon and the Rhône Valley. (Museum and tower open daily June 15-Sept. 15 10am-12:30pm and 3-7pm; Oct.-March 10am-noon and 2-5:30pm; Sept. 16-June 14 closed Mon.)

CHÂTEAUNEUF-DU-PAPE

Idyllic Châteauneuf-du-Pape (pop. 2065) was not named for its world-famous wines, but rather for the castle built here between 1316 and 1333 for Pope John XXII. Though the château was destroyed by escaping German soldiers in August 1944, one wall remains visible on the outskirts of town. Luckily, the pope's vineyards continue to produce the divine elixir known the world over for its quality and potency: reds from Châteauneuf-du-Pape reach an unbelievable 15% alcohol content. Even the weaker whites can knock revelers under the table.

The **tourist office,** pl. du Portail (tel. 04 90 83 71 08; fax 04 90 83 50 34), in the center of town, provides a long list of *caves* (open July-Aug. Mon.-Sat. 9am-7pm, Sun. 10am-5pm; Sept.-June Mon.-Sat. 9am-12:30pm and 2-6pm). **Les Rapides Sud-Est buses** (tel. 04 90 14 59 00) leave Avignon for Châteauneuf-du-Pape during the school year only (2 per day, 30min., 18F50). In July and August, the local tourist office sponsors a 10-15 passenger **Navette** (2 per day Mon.-Sat., 20min., 25F roundtrip from Orange or Avignon); call the nearest tourist office for details. Hitchers say they feel safe getting rides out of Avignon, even if they have to wait a while.

The **Musée des Vieux Outils de Vignerons,** av. Pierre de Luxembourg (tel. 04 90 83 70 07), a small museum of winemaking in the Père Anselme *cave,* displays the equipment and techniques used in making the famous wine. They offer free tastings, too (open daily June 15-Aug. 9am-7pm; Sept.-June 14 9am-noon and 2-6pm; free). Tasting at the *caves* is free as long as you appear to be a serious buyer; don't disappoint all of them. Small *caves* will give you more personal attention.

GORDES

During World War II, the Germans scorched the many-tiered mountain hamlet of Gordes (pop. 1600), 35km from Avignon. Luckily, many of the village's medieval buildings survived with stony resilience, as has Gordes's sense of jubilee. A fashionable retreat for Avignon festival directors and actors, the village's **Théâtre des Terrasses** welcomes its own music and theater **festival** during the last weekend of July through the first week of August (tel. 04 90 72 05 35; admission 150F, under 22 90F; reserve early). During the rest of the year, the town's most notable attraction is the small Renaissance **château** that serves as an art gallery; contemporary Flemish artist Pol Mara is scheduled for the summer of '97 (open July-Aug. daily 10am-noon and 2-6pm; call the tourist office for winter hours; admission 25F). A 4km walk downhill through lavender fields, the 12th-century **Abbaye du Sénanque** (tel. 04 90 72 05 72) houses a small community of monks and a museum devoted to Saharan studies (open Tues.-Sat. 10am-noon and 2-6pm; admission 20F, students under 25 15F).

Hotels in Gordes are expensive, so consider making the visit a daytrip from Avignon. The **tourist office,** pl. du Château (tel. 04 90 72 02 75; fax the *mairie* at 04 90 72 04 39), has information on camping and lodging in the Vaucluse (open daily 9am-noon and 2-6pm). **Les Express de la Durance** (tel. 04 90 71 03 00 in Cavaillon) runs **buses** from the *gare routière* in Avignon to Gordes via Cavaillon (36F). Schedules make a daytrip unfeasible on certain days; check before you leave. Supplement the quaint bus schedules with **trains** from Avignon to Cavaillon (tel. 08 36 35 35 35; 8 per day, 25min., 31F). A **taxi** (tel. 04 90 72 61 43) from Gordes to Cavaillon will cost about 140F, after 7pm 210F.

ISLE-SUR-LA-SORGUE & FONTAINE DE VAUCLUSE

Made popular by Peter Mayle's sardonic *provençal* portrait in *Hôtel Pastis,* and housing one of the only train stations in the Vaucluse, **l'Isle-sur-la-Sorgue** (pop. 17,000) welcomes tourists to the sunny banks of its landlocked island created by the divisions of the river Sorgue. The **train station,** av. J. Guigue (tel. 08 36 35 35 35), is named *Isle-sur-la-Sorgue-Fontaine-de-Vaucluse* because it serves both towns. Trains roll to Avignon (6-9 per day, 20min., 22F), Cavaillon (6-9 per day, 7min., 12F), and Marseille (4 per day, 1¾hr., 74F). (Station open Mon.-Fri. 9am-noon and 12:30-7:15pm, Sat.-Sun. and holidays 9:15am-noon and 2-6:30pm.) To get from the train station to the **tourist office** in the church on pl. de l'Eglise (tel. 04 90 38 04 78; fax 04 90 38 35 43), take a right out of the station and the first left onto av. de l'Egalité. Walk over the bridge and continue as the road turns into bd. Carnot. Turn right behind the church on pl. de l'Eglise into the welcoming arms of the staff. They'll send you off with maps of the town and a hiking map of the Vaucluse (open June-Sept. Tues.-Sat. 9am-7pm, Sun.-Mon. 9:30am-1pm and 3-7pm; Oct.-May Tues.-Sat. 9am-12:30pm and 2-6pm, Sun. 10am-12:30pm). Stop by the **church** to take in its 17th-century, Italian-influenced interior. The **Hôtel-Dieu** boasts a lavish 18th-century hall and elegant wrought ironwork, plus a lovely garden. **Open-air markets** from 7:30am to 1pm on Thursdays and Sundays provide food and mirth; watch the locals haggle earnestly with the hundreds of antique dealers who flood the area on Saturdays and Sundays. The **Casino supermarket,** 6, rue de la République (tel. 04 90 38 13 31), is a more sedate shopping experience (open Tues.-Sat. 7am-12:30pm and 3:30-7:30pm, Sun. 7am-12:30pm). Once you've stocked up, seen the antiques, and watched the local youth navigate the narrow canals of the Sorgue in anorexic boats, move on to some of the other quiet Vaucluse towns.

Fontaine de Vaucluse (pop. 500) harbors what may be the frigid source waters of the Sorgue, shady picnic spots, hiking paths, and that great forest-fresh smell. The river runs through the tiny town, the water so cold (10-12°C year-round) that you don't need to go for a swim to cool off—just sitting near it can provide relief from the hot summer sun. A short hike reveals the crumbling ruins of a castle with a view of the Sorgue valley and the lofty Mont Ventoux. After glimpsing "Laura," the lovely young wife of an early Marquis de Sade, in an Avignon church on April, 6, 1327, Petrarch spent the next two decades here composing sonnets to her. His famous work *De Vita Solitaria* recounts the time he spent here; the 20m **Colonne,** built in 1804 in the center of town, commemorates his life and work. Don't be annoyed with the swarms of tourists in this tiny town; the surrounding beauty of the Vaucluse offers plenty of fragrant opportunities for short hikes. Get here by **bus** from Isle-sur-la-Sorgue (4-5 per day, 10min., 15F) or directly from Avignon (2-4 per day, 50min., 29F). Call **Voyages Arnauds** (tel. 04 90 82 07 55 in Avignon, tel. 04 90 38 15 58 in Isle-sur-la-Sorgue). The last bus to Avignon leaves at 5:55pm on weekdays, 5:30pm Sundays. From the tree-lined pl. de la Colonne, walk by the riverside on Chemin de la Fontaine to the **tourist office** (tel. 04 90 20 32 22; fax 04 90 20 21 37), where they will ply you with historical info about the area and tell you how to reach the castle ruins and hiking trailheads (open Mon.-Sat. July-Nov. 14 9:30am-7:30pm; Nov. 15-June 10am-6pm). Continue up chemin de la Fontaine to get to **La Source,** a turquoise blue lagoon with near-freezing waters that even Jacques Cousteau couldn't fathom—300m down, he still couldn't get to the bottom of the waters or the mystery of their source. It's best to go in the afternoon when the sun lights up the dark, still water. The riverside is a much more pleasant option any time of day; uncrowded, tree-lined banks and refreshing breezes make it a hard-to-leave haven for weary travelers. To hike to the ruined **Château de Saumane,** formerly owned by the de Sades, return to the Colonne, cross the river, and take the stairs to a path leading to the castle (10min; wear sturdy shoes).

For the night, stay at the rural **Auberge de Jeunesse (HI),** chemin de la Vignasse (tel. 04 90 20 31 65), 1km from town (follow signs from the Colonne) or ask the bus driver to let you off closer to the *auberge.* Wake to a chorus of roosters in this idyllic stone country house with clean, four- to eight-bed dorms. (Members 63F, breakfast included. Sheets 14F. Laundry 20F. Kitchen access. Reception Feb. 15-Nov. 15 8-10am and 5-11pm. Curfew 11:30pm.) The hostel also **rents bikes** for 60F (with a 200F deposit) and can offer suggestions for **hiking** in the Luberon, especially in the nearby national hiking trails, **GR6** and **GR91.**

■ Tarascon

Named for a dragon, the Tarasque, that once terrorized its citizens, Tarascon (pop. 12,000) has truly found the tranquility legend says it once sought so desperately. On the crossroads of Nîmes (25km), Arles (17km), and Avignon (23km), the traffic of the RN570 and D999 outside the *centre ville* is steady, though few stop to explore. The delicious void of tourists allows those who do visit to get a feeling for the true *provençal* lifestyle. Compared to others in the area, the town itself is uninteresting architecturally, save for its château and *église.* Still, it provided the inspiration for Alphonse Daudet's well known children's story, *Tartarin de Tarascon.* Its relaxed atmosphere, clean, uncrowded youth hostel, and inexpensive hotels make it a pleasant and practical base in the heart of Provence.

From the *gare* and bus stop, walk across the courtyard and turn left on cours Aristide Briand; walk two minutes and rue des Halles will be on your right. The **tourist office,** 59, rue des Halles (tel. 04 90 91 03 52; fax 04 90 91 22 96), is eager to help with anything and will offer you a free French brochure, *Tarascon—Une Legende*

Bien Vivante (open Mon.-Sat. 9am-12:30pm and 2-6pm; Jan.-March closed Sat.). The banks along cours Aristide Briand **exchange currency** and cling to **ATMs.** Get to Tarascon by **train** from Arles (7 per day, 10min., 16F) or Avignon (13 per day, 10min., 21F). For **bus** information, call 04 66 29 27 29 to go to Avignon (3 per day, 30min., 22F). Call **CTM** (tel. 04 90 93 74 90) to get to Arles (2 per day, 30min., 16F50). **Station Total,** bd. Jules Ferry (tel. 04 90 91 13 90), rents **mountain bikes** (80F per day, 500F per week) and beach bikes (100F and 600F; credit card or 1000F deposit required). If your clothes have seen one too many wearings, head to the **Washmatic** on cours Aristide Briand (open Mon.-Fri. 8am-7pm, Sat. 8am-noon). The **post office** (tel. 04 90 91 52 00) is to the left of the train station and has poste restante (open Mon.-Tues. and Thurs.-Fri. 8:30am-6:30pm, Wed. 8:30am-12:15pm and 1-6:30pm, Sat. 8:30am-noon; **postal code:** 13150).

The **Auberge de Jeunesse (HI),** 31, bd. Gambetta (tel. 04 90 91 04 08; fax 04 90 91 54 17), is roomy and has comfortable beds in eight- to 12-bed dorms, kitchen facilities, secure bike area, free parking, and a high-ceilinged, *provençal* dining and social room. From the *gare,* turn right and follow the tracks until you reach bd. Victor Hugo; cross the street, and follow the path between the tracks and wall for 20m, turning left on the next major road; walk for five minutes—it will be on your left near a phone booth (15min.) Reservations accepted through the IBN, but this gem of a hostel is rarely full (45F per night; 18F breakfast mandatory first night, optional thereafter; reception open March 2-Dec. 14 7:30-10am and 5:30-11pm; lockout 10am-5:30pm). **Hôtel du Viaduc,** 9, chemin du Viaduc (tel. 04 90 91 16 67), has clean, comfortable rooms that feel more like a home than a hotel. Popular with cyclists, it offers a locked bike area and free parking. (Singles 90F, with shower and toilet 120F. Doubles with shower and toilet 140F. Shower 10F. All-you-can-eat breakfast 20F, under 8 free.) Camp at **Tartarin** (tel. 04 90 91 01 46), behind the castle on bd. du Roy René. The management provides a bar, snack stand, free showers, and lots of shade (20F per person, 18F per tent, 10F per car; open March-Sept.). Shop for groceries at the inexpensive **Monoprix,** bd. Victor Hugo (tel. 04 90 91 04 66; open Mon.-Sat. 8:30am-7pm).

The **Château de Tarascon** (tel. 04 90 91 01 93), built in the early 13th century, was only needed for 200 years until Provence united with the empire of France's Louis XI. Having seen so few years of warfare and been maintained as a prison for centuries, the castle is in fantastic condition. Surrounded by a moat, it boasts a lovely *provençal* garden, an apothecary, an ornate courtyard, graffiti from the Middle Ages, ten stunning tapestries, and frequent art exhibitions. The climb to the roof is well worth it; from here, there is a picture-perfect view of the ruined Château de Beaucaire across the river. Be extremely careful if the *mistral* is blowing, and pay particularly close attention to children: the slits in the floor revealing terrifying drops perfect for small feet (open daily April-Sept. daily 9am-7pm; Oct.-March 9am-noon and 2-5pm; admission 28F, ages 18-25 18F, under 18 15F). Across the street is the **Collegiate Sainte-Marthe.** This church, dedicated to the woman who is credited with taming the wild Tarasque in AD 48, features a potpourri of architectural styles, from Romanesque and Gothic to late Renaissance (open daily 9am-noon and 2-6pm).

Arles

Just south of the Rhône's split into the Grand and Petit branches, Arles (pop. 35,000) is a palette of everything for which Provence is famous. The sturdy arches of its Roman arena have triumphed over the centuries and now preside over summer bullfights, and the amphitheater resumes its original function as a stage for concerts and dance. Arles inspired Vincent Van Gogh, who spent his final years (and an ear) here; many of his most famous paintings are *scènes arlésiennes.* Picasso loved Arles as well and donated a collection of drawings to the city. Arles preserves this artistic heritage with several first-rate museums and an annual international photography festival. The city sports excellent (and affordable) restaurants and spirited summer festivals, both *de rigueur* in Provence. With the wildlife of the Camargue and the beaches of Stes-

Maries-de-la-Mer and Piemanson nearby, daytrips are a delight for those who can tear themselves away from Arles.

ORIENTATION AND PRACTICAL INFORMATION

The most interesting section of town—including the *vieille ville* and most of the Roman remains—lies between the Rhône and bd. des Lices. To make the trek to the tourist office, turn left out of the station and walk to **pl. Lamartine** (a large roundabout with a fountain). Enter the medieval gate and keep left as the road forks. Walk to the small **pl. Voltaire;** turn right just before you leave the square on **rue du 4 Septembre.** Follow the crooked road for five minutes and turn left on **rue de l'Hôtel de Ville.** Follow this road for 10 minutes until you reach the large **bd. des Lices.** The tourist office is straight ahead, across the street.

Tourist Office: (tel. 04 90 18 41 20; fax 04 90 18 41 29), in esplanade Charles de Gaulle at bd. des Lices and across from Jardin d'Eté. Accommodations service 4F. Open April-Sept. Mon.-Sat. 9am-7pm, Sun. 9am-1pm; Oct.-March Mon.-Sat. 9am-1pm and 2-6pm. **Currency exchange. Branch** in *gare* (tel. 04 90 49 36 90) open April-Sept. Mon.-Sat. 9am-1pm and 2-6pm; Oct.-March 9am-1pm and 1:30-5pm.

Money: 24-hr. **ATMs** git down at **BNP,** pl. Lamartine, at the corner of av. Stalingrad near the *gare* and the corner of pl. and rue de la République. **Arène Change,** 22bis, Rond Point des Arènes, has no commission (open daily 10am-7pm).

Trains: av. P. Talabot (tel. 08 36 35 35 35). To: Avignon (10 per day, 20min., 35F); Nîmes (10 per day, 25min., 41F); Montpellier (10 per day, 70min., 74F); Toulouse (7 per day, 3½hr., 199F); Marseille (10 per day, 1hr., 70F); Aix-en-Provence (10 per day, 1¾hr., 92F). **Luggage lockers** 15-20F per 72hr.

Buses: (tel. 04 90 49 38 01). Desk open Mon.-Fri. 6:45am-7:30pm, Sat. 6:45am-noon. **Les Cars de Camargue,** 4, rue Jean-Mathieu (tel. 04 90 96 36 25) run to: Stes-Maries-de-la-Mer (7 per day, 1hr., 35F); Nîmes (4 per day, 50min., 30F). **Cars Ceyte et Fils** or **CTM,** 21, chemin du Temple (tel. 04 90 93 74 90). To: Avignon (5 per day Mon.-Sat., 45min., 38F); Les Baux (4 per day Mon.-Sat., 30min., 27F); Stes-Maries-de-la-Mer (6 per day, 50min., 35F); Tarascon (2 per day, 30min., 17F).

Taxis: tel. 04 90 96 90 03.

Bike Rental: L'Arène du Cycle/Dall'Oppio, 10, rue Portugal (tel. 04 90 96 46 83). 60F per day, 500F deposit. Open Tues.-Fri. 8am-noon and 2-7pm.

Laundromat: Lincoln Laverie, 6, rue de la Cavalerie. Open daily 7am-9pm.

Medical Assistance: Centre Hospitalier J. Imbert, quartier Fourchon (tel. 04 90 49 29 29). **Medical Emergency** tel. 18.

Police: bd. des Lices (tel. 04 90 96 02 04). **Emergency** tel. 17.

Post Office: 5, bd. des Lices (tel. 04 90 18 41 00). Poste restante. **ATM. Currency exchange.** Photocopies 1F. Open Mon.-Fri. 8:30am-7pm, Sat. 8:30am-noon. **Postal code:** 13200.

ACCOMMODATIONS AND CAMPING

Arles teems with inexpensive hotels, especially around rue de l'Hôtel de Ville and pl. Voltaire. Reservations are crucial during the photography festival.

Auberge de Jeunesse (HI), av. Maréchal Foch (tel. 04 90 96 18 25; fax 04 90 96 31 26), 10min. from the town center and 20min. from station. Take bus 8 from pl. Lamartine to "Fournier" (last bus 7pm, 6F). With your back to the tourist office, take bd. des Lices to av. des Alyscamps and follow signs. Near municipal pool and cinema. Clean and modern, with a quiet garden. Personal lockers. **Currency exchange** at no commission. 100 beds in 8-bed dorms. Members 75F for first night, 64F thereafter. Shower and breakfast included. No kitchen. Dinner 45F. Bar open until midnight. Reception 7-10am and 5pm-midnight. Lockout 10am-5pm. Curfew midnight. Reservations only through IBN—call ahead April-June.

Terminus Van Gogh, 5, pl. Lamartine (tel. and fax 04 90 96 12 32), 1 block from station. Faces the foundation of Van Gogh's now-destroyed *maison jaune.* Decorated to match Van Gogh paintings, rooms are bright and pretty, with great, firm beds, and some phone-booth-sized showers. A friendly, comfortable hotel with helpful managers. Doubles 140F, with shower on floor 160F, with shower in room 180F, with shower and toilet 200F. Breakfast 28F. V, MC.

Hôtel Mirador, 3, rue Voltaire (tel. 04 90 96 28 05; fax 04 90 96 59 89). Impeccably modern rooms with great beds, TVs, and phones. Pleasant lobby, lounge, and breakfast area. Family-owned and operated. Singles and doubles with shower 180F, with shower and toilet 210F, with bath and toilet 247F. Extra bed 60F. Breakfast 27F. Parking 40F. V, MC.

Hôtel le Rhône, pl. Voltaire (tel. 04 90 96 43 70; fax 04 90 93 87 03). A cozy hotel with eager owners and an adorable breakfast room (25F). Smallish rooms with clean, modern bathrooms. Pl. Voltaire can be lively at night; ask for a room facing a quiet side street. Rooms with 1 big bed 120-180F, with 2 small beds 160-190F, with 1 big and 1 small 180-200F, depending on amenities. V, MC, AmEx.

Hôtel de France, pl. Lamartine (tel. 04 90 96 01 24; fax 04 90 96 90 87). Large, bright rooms with phones and pretty wooden doors over a busy bar and restaurant. Rooms with one large bed and sink 105F, with shower 150F, with shower and toilet 185-220F. Rooms with 2 beds, shower, and toilet 200F. Rooms for 4 people 350-400F. Prices drop at least 30% in the off season. V, MC.

Hôtel Lamartine, 1, rue Marius-Jouveau (tel. 04 90 96 13 83; fax 04 90 96 08 84), right inside the medieval gate near pl. Lamartine. Simple, clean rooms with dated wallpaper, Turkish toilets and regular toilets in halls. Hotel has an institutional feel. Smoke-free halls. Showers 10F. Singles and doubles with sink 160F, with shower 200F. Quads 240F. 5 or 6 sleep for 360F.

La Gallia Hôtel, 22, rue de l'Hôtel de Ville (tel. 04 90 96 00 63). A pedestrian-zone hotel with character, nestled in a Renaissance home with a small courtyard, over a bar and restaurant. Clean, pleasant rooms. Centrally located, but light sleepers beware—it's very noisy at night. Singles and doubles with sink and shower 120F, with toilet, sink, and shower 140F. Breakfast 27F.

Camping: The closest is **Camping-City,** 67, route de Crau (tel. 04 90 93 08 86), a terrific 2-star site with pool, snack bar, washing machine, and hot showers. Take bus 2 toward "Pont de Crau" from bd. des Lices (7F) and get off at "Greauxeaux." 36F for 1 person, 54F for 2 people, 17F per tent. Open March-Oct.

FOOD

Unique in the pantheon of Provençal cities, the restaurants of Arles feature high quality and low prices. *Arlésien* specialties are seasoned with thyme and rosemary, both of which grow wild in the region. Other regional produce fills the **open-air markets** on bd. Emile Courbes (Wed. 7am-1pm) or on bd. des Lices (Sat. 7am-1pm). For the other days of the week, **Monoprix supermarket** (tel. 04 90 93 62 74) is on pl. Lamartine close to the train station and the city gates (open Mon.-Thurs. and Sat. 8:30am-7:30pm, Fri. 8:30am-8:30pm). **Casino supermarket,** 26, rue Président Wilson (tel. 04 90 96 14 62), is off bd. des Lices towards the center of town (open Mon.-Sat. 8am-12:30pm and 2:30-7:30pm, Sun. 8am-12:30pm). At the cafés on **pl. du Forum,** everyone knows everyone else by midnight, if they didn't at dusk. The cafés on **pl. Voltaire** by the arena are strung merrily with colored lights and animated by rock and jazz music on Wednesday nights in summer.

Le Galoubet, 18, rue du Docteur Fanton (tel. 04 90 96 25 34). Though the decor is simple, the 69F 3-course *menu* is fantastically good, filling, artistically presented, and features such local specialties as *lapin* and *volaille.* The patio becomes lively at night. Open daily noon-2pm and 7-11pm. V, MC, AmEx.

La Mamma, 20, rue de l'Amphithéâtre (tel. 04 90 96 11 60). Don't let the ordinary patio fool you—this place is unique. Delicious pizzas, pastas, and *chaussons* (calzones) 41-62F. 80F 3-course *menu* with a huge portion of tasty lasagna. Relaxing, softly lit environment. Open daily 10am-3pm and 6:30pm-midnight.

Vitamine, 16, rue du Docteur Fanton (tel. 04 90 93 77 36). Small, cheerful restaurant with an amazing array of pasta (32-46F) and 38 different salads (18-48F). Open daily noon-3pm and 7-10pm or midnight, depending on the season.

La Gueule du Loup, 39, rue Arènes (tel. 04 90 96 96 69). Welcoming environment. A truly *provençal* experience. Delicious *magret de canard* (breast of duck) and warm *chèvre* (goat cheese) salad. *Menus* begin at 110F. Open daily noon-1:30pm and 7:30-10:30pm.

SIGHTS AND ENTERTAINMENT

Arles thinks of itself as Rome without the Vespas. The tourist office and major sights offer a 55F **one-day pass** (*forfait,* 35F for students), which allows access to most of the town's monuments and museums.

The elliptical **arènes** (tel. 04 90 96 03 70; admission 15F, students 9F), one of the largest and best-preserved Roman amphitheaters in France (seating approximately 25,000 people), was built by the architect of Nîmes' theater around AD 1. In the 8th century it was converted into a fortified stronghold; three of the four towers still exist. The high wall separating the seating from the combat area protected enthralled spectators from combats between wild beasts; a raised platform gave better views of gladiator battles. Sporadic bullfights staged here from Easter through September are as bloody as anything the Romans watched (tickets 50-450F, children 30F); concerts and plays are more tame. It is only from the arena's upper arches that the construction can be fully appreciated. You may wish to take a closer look at the ancient stones of the tower where two millennia of vandals—including World War II American GIs—have scribbled their initials. Resist any childish impulse to do the same or face the wrath of the local *gendarmes* (open daily 9am-7pm). The nearby **Théâtre Antique** (tel. 04 90 49 36 25) retains the plan, if little of the elevation, of the original Augustan construction. Only two marble columns remain of the original stage wall, eerie guardians of summertime drama. Their fallen companions lie to the side in an ancient pile of carved stone. (Open daily April-Sept. 9am-7pm; Oct.-March 10am-4:30pm; admission 15F, students 9F.) The **Jardin d'Eté,** behind the Théâtre Antique on bd. des Lices is a great place to eavesdrop on concerts. With a variety of shady trees and manicured greenery, it makes an ideal picnic spot. If panoramic vistas and Roman stones still haven't worn you out, the elaborate galleries of the **Cloître St-Trophime** (tel. 04 90 49 33 53; open daily 9am-7pm; admission 15F, students 9F) and the former Roman baths at the **Thermes Constantin** (tel. 04 90 49 35 40; open daily 9am-noon and 2-7pm; admission 15F, students 9F) will do the trick.

The **Espace Van Gogh,** pl. Félix Rey (tel. 04 90 49 39 39), houses an exceptional **Médiathèque.** A community center *à la française,* it features a book and video library, a small theater showing free movies and cartoons, art exhibitions, and a *discothèque.* Creatively designed green steel supports and glass walls are mixed in a surprisingly attractive combination with the walls of a hospital where Van Gogh once stayed. (Open Tues. 12:30-7:30pm, Wed. and Sat. 10am-12:30pm and 2-5pm, Fri. 12:30-6pm.) A 10-minute walk from Arles is the ultra-modern **Musée de l'Arles Antique** (tel. 04 90 19 88 89). With your back to the tourist office, turn left, walk along bd. G. Clemenceau to its end, and follow the signs from there. The blue plastic exterior of this building is a postmodern eyesore, yet the innovative uses of light and space inside show off 90s architecture at its best. Roman tools, statues, mosaics, and other artifacts collected from the area sit alongside many exceptionally detailed models of Roman constructions that show how each was built. (Open daily April-Sept. 9am-8pm; Oct.-March 10am-6pm. Admission 35F, students 25F, children 5F.) Many of the museum's more interesting sarcophagi come from the **Alyscamps** (tel. 04 90 49 36 87), a Roman burial ground later consecrated for Christian use by St. Trophime. Although best seen in the hours of a misty morning, it is also a great spot for a picnic; head down bd. des Lices to its intersection with bd. Emile Combes. Make a right onto av. des Alyscamps; cross the tracks and follow the canal (10min.). Mentioned by Dante in his *Inferno,* this cemetery holds the tombs of 80 generations and once drew pilgrims from all over Europe. The most elaborate sarcophagi have been destroyed or removed, but nothing could mar the tranquility and awe inspired by these ancient avenues (open daily 9am-7pm; admission 15F, students 9F).

Arles' more recent history can be discovered at the **Museon Arlaten,** 29, rue de la République (tel. 04 90 96 08 23), a superb folk museum founded in 1896 by author Frédéric Mistral. In 1906 Mistral used the money he received from his Nobel Prize in literature to buy the striking 16th-century building, which—built around the ruins of a small Roman forum—was a townhouse, convent, and Jesuit college in the 300 years before it became a museum. The history of the region is told through art, antique furniture, clothing, tools, and a life-sized cross-section of a traditional *provençal* house. The attendants wear regional dress, and the signs are in the local dialect. (Open daily year-round 9am-noon, afternoon hours vary: Nov.-March 2-5pm; April-May and Sept. 2-6pm; June 2-6:30-pm; July-Aug. 2-7pm; Sept. 2-5:30pm. Admission 15F, students 10F. No photos.) The **Musée Réattu,** rue du Grand Prieuré (tel. 04 90 49 37 58), once a stronghold of the knights of Malta, now houses a collection of contemporary art, watercolors, and oils of the Camargue by Henri Rousseau and two rooms of canvases by the Neoclassical artist Réattu. The museum takes most pride, however, in the 57 drawings with which Picasso honored the town in 1971. The collection also includes Van Gogh's letters to Gauguin. Upstairs, prominent modern European photographers and artists stage temporary exhibitions (open daily 9am-12:15pm and 2-6:45pm; admission 20F, students 14F).

There are no Van Goghs in the **Fondation Van Gogh,** 26, Rond-Point des Arènes (tel. 04 90 49 38 34), but some of the paintings might fool you. Over 700 artists, poets, and composers have contributed original works to the memory of the Dutchman; the majority are modern interpretations of Van Gogh's own works (open daily in summer 10am-7pm; call for winter hours; admission 30F, students 20F).

During the second week in July, the festival **Rencontres Internationales de la Photographie** is the major development in town. Undiscovered photographers from all over the world court agents by roaming around town with portfolios under their arms. More established photographers present their work in some 15 locations (including parked train cars and a salt warehouse), conduct nightly slide shows (40-80F each, students 30-50F), participate in debates, and offer pricey workshops. When the festival crowd departs, the remarkable exhibits are still left behind. (20-30F per exhibit, students 20-30F; global ticket 140F, free for students with ID—you must get a global pass to get in free.) For more information, visit the tourist office or contact Rencontres, 10, Rond-Point des Arènes (tel. 04 90 96 76 06).

Arles has many colorful local and regional festivals. On May 1, the ancient *Confrèrie des Gardians* (brotherhood of herders of the Camargue's wild horses) parades through town and gathers in the arena for the **Fête des Gardians,** a tame rodeo. On the last weekend in June and the first in July, bonfires blaze in the streets and locals wear traditional costume to the beautiful **Fête d'Arles.** At the end, the city crowns the *Reine d'Arles* (Queen of Arles), a young woman chosen to represent the region's language, customs, and history. Traditional ceremonies, dance performances, and

Toro! Toro! Toro!

In the Camargue and the South of France, there are two major types of bullfights, the Spanish **corrida,** and the *camarguais* **rasateur.** The *corridas* are the gory spectacles of bullfighting lore.The bull in a *corrida* is usually imported from Spain for the pleasure of spectators paying 191-486F (90F general admission) to watch him fall to the *matador's* sword. The home-grown *rasateurs* hurt only the bull's ego and use politically correct free-range bulls raised in the swampy Camargue. The *rasateur,* usually dressed in white, has a brightly colored mitt in one hand and a glove with a razor attached on his other. The bull for his part has multi-colored pom-poms strung between his horns. The *rasateur* uses the mitted hand to distract the bull while attempting to swipe the pom-poms from the bull's head with the other. Tickets to this lively pastime typically run 50-120F (30F general admission). **Toro piscine,** based on Spanish seaside bullfights whose goal was to drive the bull into the sea, has degenerated into a promotional game. Anyone can participate because the bull wears spiffy rubber balls on the tips of his horns. The game ends when the bull—or sometimes the *torero*—is taunted into a small swimming pool.

fireworks occur in the arena at midnight (free). For the bloodthirsty, there are bullfights on the festival's final weekend (admission 50-450F).

■ Near Arles: Les Baux de Provence

"There is nothing terrible and savage belonging to feudal history of which an example may not be found in the annals of Les Baux," wrote 19th-century historian John Addington Symonds. **Les Baux de Provence** (pop. 458, 5000 with tourists), 18km from Arles, is a magnificent site of feudal ruins, a demolished castle, and gracefully restored Renaissance homes. Once home to a regional court drawing the finest troubadours (and a few spectacular debaucheries), the tiny *centre ville* has surrendered to souvenir shops, expensive ice cream stands, and cafés, all supported by over a million tourists annually. The unique and truly spectacular part of the town is less crowded and commercial; the ruins of the **Château des Baux** (tel. 04 90 54 55 56; fax 04 90 54 55 00) are carved out of—and built around—the rocky mountain peak and cover an area five times that of the village below. As you walk through the remains of Les Baux's 13th- and 14th-century citadel and recent archaeological excavations, you'll feel on top of the world, particularly when you pause to contemplate the diabolic view of the **Val d'Enfer** (the Valley of Hell), and the fields below, your view uninterrupted all the way to the Mediterranean. The corroded staircase to the **Tour Sauvasine** (the chateaux's lookout) is more like a ski slope, but pictures of mountains, patchwork vineyards, and olive groves reward those who brave the climb. (Open daily July-Aug. 8:30am-9pm; March-June and Sept.-Oct. 8:30am-7:30pm; Nov. and Feb. 9am-6pm; Dec.-Jan. 9am-5pm. Admission 33F, students 25F, under 17 20F.) One of four museums in town, the **Fondation Louis Jou,** Grande Rue Frédéric Mistral (tel. 04 90 54 34 17), commemorating Les Baux's favorite son, exhibits quality works by the local printmaker, as well as engravings by Durer and Goya (open April-Sept. 11am-7pm; admission 20F, students 10F). Just down the road from the old and new towns is the **Cathédrale d'Images** (tel. 04 90 54 38 65); from the bus stop, continue down the hill and turn right at the crossroads, follow the sign (10min.). Unlike any cathedral in the world, this one is carved out of the stone mountain. Inside 4000m of stone, screens are covered with the most amazing slide show you've ever seen. Created in 1977 by Albert Plecy, the show features photographs and great works of visual art and projects the images onto the walls, accompanied by inspiring music. Shows change seasonally; call to ask what's playing. (Open daily April-Sept. 26 10am-7pm; Sept. 27-Oct. and Dec. 10am-6pm. Closed annually Nov. and mid-Feb. to April. Admission 40F, students 35F, children 25F.)

The **tourist office** in the Hôtel de Ville (tel. 04 90 54 34 39), about halfway up the hill between the parking lot and the Cité Morte, has maps, distributes information on the surrounding region, will help you find budget restaurants, and offers the handy, free French brochure *L'Esprit d'un Lieu—Les Baux de-Provence.* They also have an **ATM** (open Easter-Sept. daily 9am-7pm; Oct.-Easter 9am-12:30pm and 2-6pm). **Buses** to Les Baux run regularly from Arles (Mon.-Sat. 4 per day, 30min., 27F). Contact **CTM,** 21, chemin du Temple (tel. 04 90 93 74 90), for information. The temperature in Les Baux can be lower than that in Arles, particularly when the *mistral* wind blows across the peak. The **post office** has a **currency exchange** with great rates and a small commission. (Open Mon.-Fri. 10am-noon and 2-5pm, Sat. 9-11am.) **Le Mas de la Fontaine** (tel. 04 90 54 34 13) offers seven lovely, clean rooms with comfy beds in a traditional *maison provençale*. At the foot of the village, it exudes quiet with its garden and pool. (Doubles with shower 230F, with shower and toilet 270F, with bath and toilet 290-310F. Triples 370F. Extra bed 60F. Breakfast 30F. Cash only. Open late March to late Oct.) Most backpackers bring picnics to the Cité Morte; it's best to stock up in Arles, but you can buy supplies at the small *épicerie* in the parking lot. Panini stands and *crêperies* abound.

Les Saintes-Maries-de-la-Mer

Local legend has it that in AD 40 a ship carrying Mary Magdalene, Mary Salomé, mother of the Apostles John and James, and Mary Jacobé, Jesus' aunt, among other New Testament folk, washed ashore here. The unwitting missionaries came from Palestine, where they had been put to sea to die a certain death. Today, Les Stes-Maries-de-la-Mer, named for its holy visitors, caters to tourists and sun-worshipers lured by the din of crashing Mediterranean waves. Less flashy than her sister resort towns on the Côte d'Azur, Stes-Maries' tourist-beach culture is only encouraged by *provençal* country ways. Next to and outside of town stretches 100km of the finest, least crowded sand in all of France. You'll know you've reached Stes-Maries when you hear Gypsy Kings cover bands strumming furiously from every seaside restaurant; the place overflows with snack trailers and honky-tonk stores. Seek out its quieter squares and restaurants lulled by *flamenco* rhythms, or take a walk on a stretch of beach that's all your own.

ORIENTATION AND PRACTICAL INFORMATION

There is no train service to Stes-Maries, but buses make the trip from Arles in under an hour. To get to the tourist office from the bus stop, walk down av. de la République (next to pl. Mireille) to the beach. The tourist office is ahead on the left.

Tourist Office: 5, av. Van Gogh (tel. 04 90 97 82 55; fax 04 90 97 71 15), next to the arena. Info on camping and maps. Open daily 9am-8pm.

Money: Change, pl. Jouse d'Arbaud, decent rates, no commission. Open daily 9:30am-12:30pm and 2-7:30pm. **Crédit Agricole** has a 24-hr. **ATM** on pl. Mireille and next to the tourist office.

Buses: Regularly to and from Arles (7 per day, 1hr., 34F50). Buses leave opposite the Station Bar on bd. des Lices in Arles and from the *gare routière*. In Les Stes-Maries, the buses stop just north of pl. Mireille. Call **Les Cars de Camargue,** 4, rue Jean-Mathieu (tel. 04 90 96 36 25), in Arles for more information.

Bike Rental: Le Vélociste, pl. des Remparts (tel. 04 90 97 83 26 or 04 90 97 86 44), next to the church. Friendly folks here will point out great rides. *VTTs* 80F per day. Passport deposit. Open daily 8am-8pm, Sept.-June 9am-7pm.

Medical emergency tel. 18.

Police: (tel. 04 90 97 89 50), av. Van Gogh, by tourist office. **Emergency** tel. 17.

Post Office: 6, av. Gambetta. Poste restante. **ATM.** Open Mon.-Fri. 9am-noon and 2:30-4:30pm, Sat. 8:30-11:30am. **Postal code:** 13460.

RHÔNE VALLEY

ACCOMMODATIONS, CAMPING, AND FOOD

Although sleeping on beaches is illegal, rows of cocooned tourists often adorn the sand at night. Hotels fill quickly in summer, and rooms under 100F are scarce. You can always base yourself in Arles and make the town a daytrip.

Auberge de Jeunesse (HI), hameau de Pioch Badet (tel. 04 90 97 51 72; fax 04 90 97 54 88). Take the bus that runs between Stes-Maries and Arles and to "Pioch Badet" (7 per day; from Stes-Maries, 10min., 11F; from Arles, 40min., 27F). Fills early in summer, so take the 8am bus from Arles. Quiet location with a camp-style ambience and lodgings; creaky bunk beds and some showers that trickle—if you're lucky, but multi-lingual staff and fantastic dinner (48F) make up for it. Members 65F (membership 100F), breakfast included. Sheets 16F. **Bike rental** 60F per day, passport deposit. Midnight curfew, but there's nowhere to go unless you have a car. Reception daily Feb.-Nov. 8:30-10:30am and 5pm-midnight.

Hôtel Méditerranée, 4, bd. Frédéric Mistral (tel. 04 90 97 82 09; fax 04 90 97 76 31), off rue Victor Hugo. Homey, spotless, comfortable rooms with wood-look wallpaper. Doubles 180F, with shower 220F, with shower and toilet 280-300F. Shower 15F. Breakfast 26F. Open Feb. 15-Nov. 15 and Christmas holidays. V, MC.

Camping: La Brise (tel. 04 90 97 84 67), oceanside site 5min. from the center of town. Pool, laundry machines, tennis 200m away. July-Aug. 60F per place and one person, 34F each additional person. Off-season rates vary but drop to 34F per tent and one person and 20F each additional person.

Rice is the Camargue's main crop; you will find it in gelatinous cakes sold at *pâtisseries,* in side dishes at local restaurants, and on the shelves of supermarkets such as the **Petit Casino** on av. Victor Hugo (tel. 04 90 97 90 60; open daily 7:30am-8pm). A **market** fills pl. des Gitanes on Monday and Friday mornings (7am-2:30pm). A band of restaurants lurks away from the waterfront around av. Victor Hugo and serves up French and Spanish specialities such as *paella* (60-70F).

SIGHTS

Local legend recalls that the Marys who landed here were accompanied by their Egyptian servant Sarah, now the patron saint of gypsies. The relics of Sarah were exhumed by King René in 1448, initiating a tradition of pilgrimage by gypsy peoples. The **Pèlerinage des Gitans** unites gypsies from all over Europe annually on May 24 and 25. In traditional costumes, a procession from the church to the sea bears statues of the saints to re-enact the landing of the saints. For *flamenco* aficionados, this is an unequaled opportunity to enjoy the art form. A smaller festival on the weekend following October 22 honors the Marys, with ceremonies similar to Sarah's but without the gypsy gathering.

The relics of the saints glisten from the church's altar during the pilgrimages, but are visible all year in the crypt. The power of the saints has supposedly cured the blind, healed the lame, and halted the mistral winds of 1833. Protruding high above the menagerie of snack bars and tourist-trap stores is the 12th-century **church.** The lofty tower guards a view of the sunset over Stes-Maries, the Mediterranean, and the Camargue (open daily 10am-12:30pm and 1:30-7pm; admission 10F).

During July and August, bullfights and horse shows occur regularly at the modern **arènes** (tickets 70-350F). The second week in July, the **Feria du Cheval** brings horses from around the world for shows, competitions, and rodeos (tickets 70-3500F; call the **Comité des Fêtes** at 04 90 97 85 86 for details).

RHÔNE VALLEY

■ Near Stes-Maries: The Camargue

Between Arles and the Mediterranean coast stretches a wedge-shaped region, bounded by the Grand-Rhône and Petit-Rhône rivers, known as the Camargue. Although in stark visual contrast to the rolling Provençal hills to the north, this vast delta with its tall marsh grasses and bounty of wildlife is music to the eyes. Pink flamingos, black bulls, and the famous white Camargue horses roam freely across this flat expanse of wild marshland, protected by the confines of the natural park. Fields in the northern sections of the marshland supply Provence's tables with *riz de Camargue.* The human inhabitants include *gardians,* rugged herders whose 2000-year tradition makes them the world's first cowboys, and gypsies who have made the area one of their nomadic homes for 500 years.

Aspiring botanists and zoologists should stop at the **Centre d'Information de Ginès** (tel. 04 90 97 86 32) along D570, which distributes information on the region's unusual flora and fauna (open April-Sept. daily 9am-6pm; Oct.-March Sat.-Thurs. 9:30am-5pm). Next door, the **Parc Ornithologique de Pont de Gau** (tel. 04 90 97 82 62), on the bus line from Arles to Stes-Maries-de-la-Mer (stop "Pont du Gau," 7F from Stes-Maries-de-la-Mer), provides pathways through acres of marsh and offers views of marsh birds and grazing bulls. Watch for snakes (non-poisonous), although your greatest foes will be mosquitoes. Rarer local bird species fly through their aviaries (park open daily 9am-sunset; admission 32F).

The best way to see the Camargue is on **horseback.** Organized rides are geared mostly towards beginners and follow somewhat limited routes. Advanced riders are allowed more freedom. Rates are the same from one establishment to another (70F per hr., 180-200F for 3hr., 320-350F per day, meal usually included). **Jeep safaris** are another way to get close to the Camargue's natural beauty (100F for 1½hr., 150F for

2½hr.). The tourist office can direct you to companies offering these tours. The smoothest way to see the Camargue is on a boat. In a business full of tacky boats, Bateau de Promenade (tel. 04 90 97 84 72) has the sexiest, a 17m sea-fishing cruiser (1½-hr. cruise 58F, children 30F). Captained by a local fisherman known as *le pape* (the pope) of the local trade, this boat also offers 2½-hr. sea-fishing expeditions (85F, leaves from Port Gardian in the *centre ville,* with free parking nearby).

Although most of the trails are open only to horseback riders, **bicycle touring** is another way to see much of the area (see **Stes-Maries-de-la-Mer** for more info). Keep in mind that the bike trails may be sandy and difficult to ride on, making mountain bikes a wise choice. Trail maps indicating length, level of difficulty, and danger spots are available from the tourist office in Stes-Maries-de-la-Mer. Bring an ample supply of fresh water—it gets hotter than Hades, and only mosquitoes can find ready ways to quench their thirst. A two-hour pedal will reveal some of the area, but you'll need a whole day if you plan to stop along the miles of wide, deserted white-sand beaches lining the bike trail.

Aix-en-Provence

Blessed with plentiful and affordable restaurants, elegant cafés, and exuberant festivals, Aix (pronounced X) marks the spot for the gastronomic and cultural core of Provence. Even when the city swells with the summer tourist invasion, Aix (pop. 150,000) exudes a *joie de vivre* that is uniquely and endearingly *provençale.* French and international students flood the streets much as they have since the Université d'Aix was founded in 1413. The sand-colored townhouses and iron grillwork flanking the town's streets housed wealthy magistrates from the *Parlement,* the court of justice that operated in Aix between 1487 and the Revolution. Each of Aix's many squares boasts a spectacular foundation; from carved classics like dolphins to modern art's indefinable shapes, the city has been adding fountains since the Plague of 1721, when it rebuilt its water system. The morning flower market on pl. de l'Hôtel de Ville hums to the neighborly tune of gossip, barter, and hurrying footsteps.

Every afternoon at Café Les Deux Garçons, where schoolmates Paul Cézanne and Emile Zola sipped absinthe, animated students and laid-back locals drink less romantic and less lethal *pastis.* From the end of June through early August, Aix bursts into a symphony of revelry as dance, opera, jazz, and classical music festivals take over the city. While Avignon's events are informal, concerts in Aix are sometimes refined and expensive, complete with ushers in tuxedos. Thankfully, the festival assumes a more relaxed air in the streets, with violinists, xylophone players, and ballroom dancers vying for attention and francs along the crooked line of the rues G. de Saporta, M. Foch, and R. Bédarrides. The atmosphere is more bohemian around magisterial **cours Mirabeau,** where guitars blast feedback through cranked amplifiers, open-air painters hawk their watercolors, and Peruvian flutes cut through clinking glasses and peals of laughter rising from the cafés.

ORIENTATION AND PRACTICAL INFORMATION

Shaded under an arched canopy of plantain trees, the cours Mirabeau sweeps through the center of town, linking the splash and spray of the fountain at La Rotonde at the west end with the Catholic college at the east end. The mostly pedestrian *vieille ville* of Aix snuggles inside the *périphérique*—a ring of boulevards including bd. Carnot and Cours Sextius. The tourist office and the central terminus for city buses are on pl. du Général de Gaulle at La Rotonde; to reach them from the train station, go straight onto av. Victor Hugo and bear left at the fork, staying on av. Victor Hugo (5min.) until it feeds into La Rotonde. The tourist office is on the left. From the *gare routière,* facing the small terminal, go left across the parking lot and up the stairs on the right; the tourist office will be on your right, and the stop for bus 12 to the hostel will be on your left after the flower market.

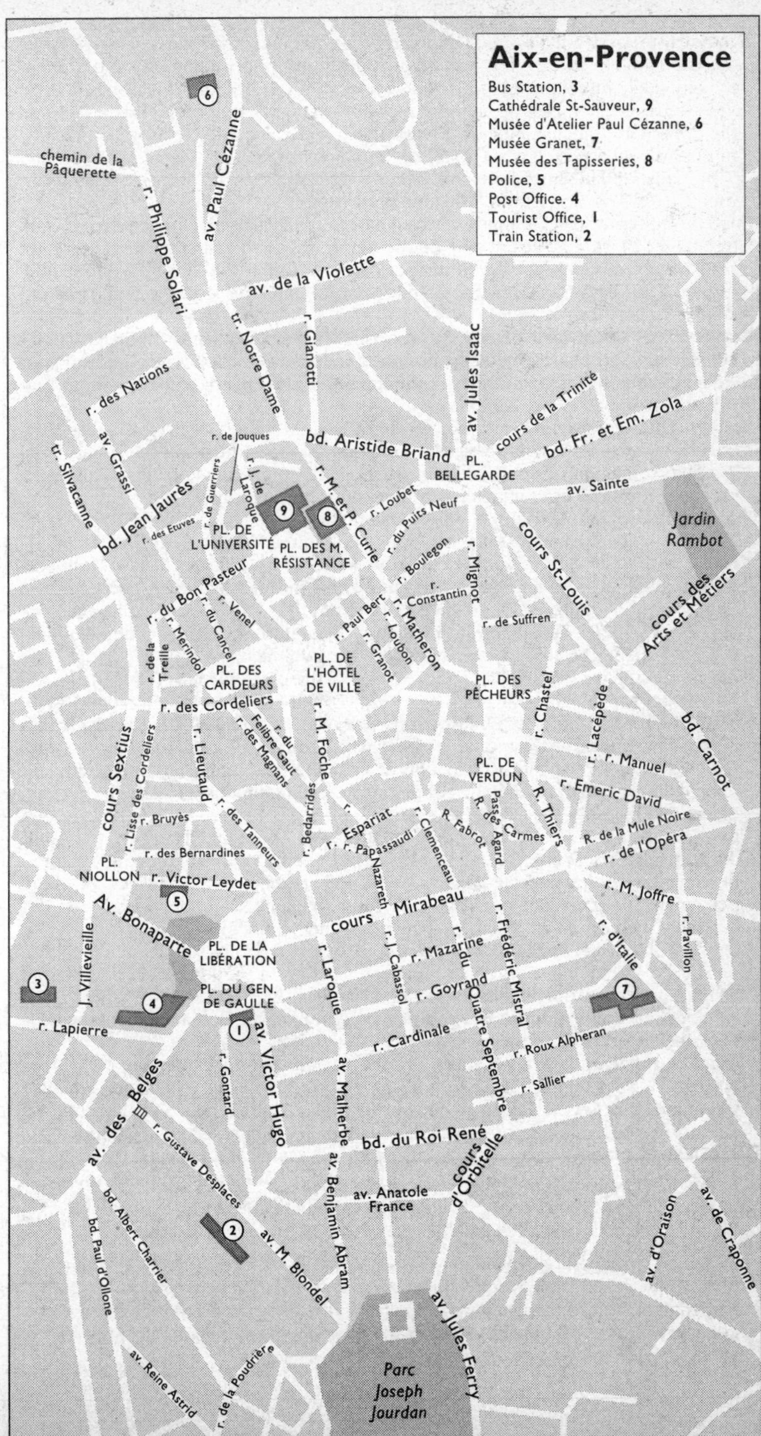

RHÔNE VALLEY

Tourist Information: Tourist Office, 2, pl. du Général de Gaulle (tel. 04 42 16 11 61; fax 04 42 16 11 62). Busy office provides hotel reservations (5F) and tours of the city (daily July-Sept. 9:30am, tours in English Wed.; call for off-season schedule; 45F, students 25F). Pick up the free monthly guide to events, **Le Mois à Aix** and the French and English **Aix La Vivante: a practical guide,** with walking tours, museums, and even recipes. Open July-Aug. Mon.-Sat. 8:30am-10pm; April-May and Sept. daily 8:30am-8pm; June and Oct.-March daily 8:30am-7pm; open Sun. year-round 10am-1pm and 2-6pm, July-Aug. until 10pm.

Festival Information: For music festival info, call the Palais de l'Ancien Archevêché (tel. 04 42 21 14 40). Reserve by phone before July 1 to guarantee a seat, though seats may be available the day of the performance (tel. 04 42 17 34 34). Open mid-June to Sept. daily 9am-1pm and 2-7pm; Sept. to mid-June Mon.-Fri. 9am-1pm and 2-6pm. Tickets start at 100F.

Budget Travel: Council Travel, 12, rue Victor Leydet (tel. 04 42 38 58 82; fax 04 42 38 94 00), off pl. des Augustins. Flights at reduced student prices. Not even your student status will get you through the lines. Open Mon.-Fri. 9:30am-6:30pm, Sat. 9:30am-12:30pm. V, MC, AmEx.

Money: Change Nazareth, 7, rue Nazareth (tel. 04 42 38 28 28), off cours Mirabeau by Monoprix. Good rates, no commission. Open July-Aug. Mon.-Sat. 9am-7pm, Sun. 9am-5pm; Sept.-June Mon.-Sat. 9am-12:30pm and 1:30-7pm. The banks on cours Mirabeau offer menacing commissions but friendly **ATMs.**

American Express: L'Agence, 15, cours Mirabeau (tel. 04 42 26 84 77; fax 04 42 26 79 03). Open daily July-Aug. 9am-9pm; Sept.-June Mon.-Sat. 9am-7pm.

Trains: (tel. 08 36 35 35 35) at the end of av. Victor Hugo, off rue Gustave Desplace. To get about anywhere from Aix, you must pass through Marseille (every hr., last train 9:23pm, 40min., 36F). To Nice (10 per day, 3hr., 161F) and Cannes (12 per day, 2½hr., 152F). Ticket and info window open Mon.-Sat. 9am-5:30pm. No lockers, but you may be able to leave bags with the *gare* manager.

Buses: rue Lapierre (tel. 04 42 27 82 54), behind the post office. **SATAP** (tel. 07 76 67 94) goes to Avignon (4 per day, 1½hr., 70-80F) and Marseille (every 30min. 5:10am-1:10am, 30min., 22F). **Phocéens Cars** (tel. 04 93 39 79 40) goes to Cannes (5 per day, 1¾hr., 120F) and Nice (5 per day, 2¼hr., 128F); ask for their fantastic under-26 student discounts (ISIC or French student ID required). Helpful info desk open daily 6:45am-6pm. Call the *gare routière* for info on buses to Arles (5 per day, 1¾hr., 70F).

Taxis: (tel. 04 42 27 71 11 or 04 42 26 29 30), 24hr. About 50F from *gare* to hostel.

Bike Rental: Troc Vélo, 62, rue Boulegon (tel. 04 42 21 37 40), centrally located between the *mairie* and rue Mignet. *VTTs* 100F per day, 180F for a weekend, 420F per week. 10-speeds 80F per day, 150F for a weekend, 250F per week; passport deposit. Open April-Oct. Tues.-Sat. 9am-noon and 3-7pm; Mon.3-7pm.

English Bookstore: Paradox Bookstore, pl. des 4 Dauphins (tel. 04 42 26 47 99), on rue du 4 Septembre off cours Mirabeau. Section of used books in English and Spanish and a board with jobs. Open Mon.-Sat. 9am-12:30pm and 2-6:30pm.

Laundromat: Lavomatique Bernadines, on corner of rue Bernadines and rue de la Fontaine. Open daily 7am-8pm.

French-American Center: Centre Franco-Américain de Provence, 9, bd. Jean Jaurès (tel. 04 42 23 23 36; fax 04 42 21 40 76). Organizes exchanges, *au pair* stays, and 3- to 4-week language courses in English and French. Social events and excursions too. Services open to all. Open Mon.-Fri. 9am-noon and 2-6:30pm.

American Center: Centre Américain, 409, av. Jean-Paul Coste (tel. 04 42 38 42 38; fax 04 42 38 95 66). Take bus 5 to "Bel-Ormeau," or walk 15 minutes southeast of Aix's *centre ville.* French staff sponsors cultural events, stocks American publications, and arranges French, English, and Spanish lessons, homestays, and study-abroad programs. Open Mon.-Fri. 9am-noon and 2-7pm.

Women's Center: Centre d'Information sur les Droits des Femmes (C.I.D.F.), 24, rue Mignet (tel. 04 42 63 18 92; fax 04 42 21 01 19). Free information and advice on women's issues. Publishes *Information Femmes,* full of info for women (available at the office or *Mairie*). Open Mon.-Tues. and Thurs.-Fri. 9-11:45am and 1:15-3:30pm.

Crisis Lines: SOS Amitié, tel. 04 42 38 20 20; 24-hr. hotline for those in need of a listening ear. **SIDA Info Service,** toll-free tel. 0 800 36 66 36, addresses AIDS-related issues. **SOS Viol,** toll-free tel. 0 800 05 95 95, is a sexual assault hotline.

Medical Emergency: Centre Hospitalier, av. Tamaris (tel. 04 42 33 50 00 or 18), north of La Rotonde. **SOS Médecins:** tel. 04 42 26 24 00. Doctors on call 24hr.

Police: 10, av. de l'Europe (tel. 04 42 93 97 00). **Emergency** tel. 17.

Post Office: 2, rue Lapierre (tel. 04 42 16 01 50), just off La Rotonde. Poste restante. **Currency exchange.** Fax. Open Mon.-Fri. 8:30am-7pm, Sat. 8:30am-noon. The postal **annex** (tel. 04 42 17 10 40), 1, pl. de l'Hôtel de Ville, provides the same services. Open Mon.-Fri. 8am-6:30pm, Sat. 8am-noon; Aug. closed Mon.-Fri. noon-2pm. **Postal codes:** 13100 and 13616-cedex.

ACCOMMODATIONS AND CAMPING

There are few inexpensive hotels near the center, and during the festival they may be booked in advance. Reserve early and hope for cancellations.

Auberge de Jeunesse (HI), 3, av. Marcel Pagnol (tel. 04 42 20 15 99; fax 04 42 59 36 12), quartier du Jas de Bouffan, next to the Fondation Vasarely. Take bus 12 from La Rotonde (every 15-30min. until 8pm, 7F) to "Vasarely." The walk takes about 35min. and is marked by frequent signs. Follow av. de Belges from La Rotonde and turn right on av. de l'Europe. At first rotary after highway overpass, bear left and climb the hill. Hostel is on the left in a private wooded area. Big, clean, and modern, but impersonal and at times unwelcoming. TV room, bar, tennis courts, volleyball net. 9-bed rooms. No sleeping bags. 79F, 68F thereafter; 68F every night if you have your own sheets. Breakfast included. Greasy dinner 35F. No kitchen facilities. Laundry facilities 28F. Curfew midnight. Lockout 10am-5:30pm. Reservations only through HI's IBN. Arrive before noon or after 5:30pm.

Hôtel du Casino, 38, rue Victor Leydet (tel. 04 42 26 06 88; fax 04 42 27 76 58), off cours Mirabeau. Lucky location. Friendly lobby. Clean rooms, fluffy pillows, and outgoing managers who love students. TV lounge. Singles 190-200F. Doubles with toilet 260F, with shower 320F, with shower and toilet 340F. Triples with bath and toilet 380F. Extra bed 60F. Some rooms have beautiful molded ceilings; many have TVs and phones. Free hall showers. Breakfast included. V, MC, AmEx.

Hôtel Vigouroux, 27, rue Cardinale (tel. 04 42 38 26 42), between pl. des Dauphins and Musée Granet. Look carefully—the only sign is a door plaque. Spacious, well-scrubbed, *très* French rooms with high ceilings and hardwood floors, though sometimes stuffy. Polished antique furniture, marble fireplaces. Peaceful but near the action. Singles 150F. Doubles 230-240F. Triples 240-300F. Breakfast 26F.

Hôtel des Arts, 69, bd. Carnot (tel. 04 42 38 11 77; fax 04 42 26 12 57). All of the identical, small, modern rooms have shower, toilet, and phone. Low to the floor, but comfy beds. Ask for a room facing the quieter rue de la Fonderie. Singles 149F. Doubles 175F, with TV 195F. Breakfast 25F. V, MC.

Hôtel Paul, 10, av. Pasteur (tel. 04 42 23 23 89; fax 04 42 63 17 80), past the Cathédrale St-Sauveur. Spacious, simple, and immaculate rooms in a modern hotel. Garden in back; street-side rooms have sound-proofed glass. Make sure yours has a window facing outside. Reserve well ahead if you want one of the two 180F singles with sink, but be forewarned—there is no shower available. Singles and doubles with shower and toilet 180-205F. Triples 250F. Quads (2 adults and 2 kids only) 270F. Breakfast 28F. V, MC.

Camping: Although all the local campgrounds lie outside of town, these 2 are accessible by bus 3 from La Rotonde at the "Trois Sautets" and "Val St-André" stops, respectively. **Arc-en-Ciel** (tel. 04 42 26 14 28), Pont des Trois Sautets, route de Nice, is 2km from the center of town. Pool and hot showers. 30F per person, 28F for place, tent and car included. **Chantecler** (tel. 04 42 26 12 98; fax 04 42 27 33 53), av. St-André, by route de Nice, 3km from the center. Swimming pool, hot showers, telephones, restaurant, and bar. July-Aug. 29F per person, 34F per tent, including car; Aug.-July 28F and 33F respectively.

FOOD

Restaurants in Aix serve specialties seasoned with the garlic *aïoli* sauce and local olives; but the city's culinary reputation rests on its *confiseries* (candy stores). Most almonds used in French cakes and cookies are grown around Aix. The city's *bonbon* is the *calisson d'Aix,* a small iced marzipan and melon treat created in 1473. Other specialties include soft nougat and hard praline candies. Peruse the *pâtisseries* on rue d'Italie or rue Espariat to feed your sweet dreams.

Rue d'Italie's *boulangeries, charcuteries,* and fruit market invite a hearty picnic. For fresher produce, shop at the **open-air market** on pl. de Verdun (Tues., Thurs., and Sat. 7am to 1pm). Hit the **Casino** jackpot at 1, av. de Lattre de Tassigny, near bd. de la République (open Mon.-Sat. 8:30am-8:30pm) and 3, cours d'Orbitelle (tel. 04 42 27 61 43; open Mon.-Sat. 8am-1pm and 4-8pm). **Monoprix** is at 25, cours Mirabeau (tel. 04 42 27 65 03; open Mon.-Sat. 8:30am-8pm). Chinese restaurants line rue Van-Loo, just off cours Sextius. Eat with students at the university **Caféteria Les Gazelles.** Take av. Victor Hugo from La Rotonde to a left on bd. du Roi René, take a right on cours d'Orbitelle, which turns into av. Jules Ferry; Gazelles leaps out on your left (*plat principal* 15F; open Mon.-Sat. 11:45am-1pm and 6:45-8pm).

The streets north of cours Mirabeau are packed with restaurants for all palates and wallets, especially in the eateries of pl. des Cardeurs and pl. Ramus. An espresso at **Café des Deux Garçons** on cours Mirabeau, the former watering hole of Cézanne, costs 9F (12F after 10pm) and buys three hours of sidewalk theater viewing.

Hacienda, 7, rue Mérindol (tel. 04 42 27 00 35), on pl. des Fontêtes off pl. des Cardeurs offers shaded outdoor seating around a fountain. A Spanish name, but French food. 2- and 3-course lunch *menus* for 53F and 62F respectively, including wine. At dinner the 3-course becomes 75F. Tasty *taboulet,* roast beef, and lemon tart make a great meal. Salads 36-48F. Open Mon.-Sat. noon-2pm and 7-10pm.

Autour d'une Tarte, 13, rue Gaston de Saporta (tel. 04 42 96 52 12), off pl. de l'Hôtel de Ville. This tiny place offers quiches galore (20-40F, 12-18F take-out). *Menus* include a quiche, salad, and dessert *tarte* 54-60F. At lunch, quiche, and salad 35F. Delicious pear tarts. Open Mon.-Sat. 8:30am-7:30pm. V, MC.

La Table Provençale, 13, rue Maréchal Joffre (tel. 04 42 38 32 41), at far end of cours Mirabeau. Cozy atmosphere. 65F *menu* with salad, your choice of meat, wine, dessert. Casserole 50F. Open Mon.-Sat. noon-2pm and 7-10:30pm. V, MC.

Chez Nine, 22bis, rue du 11 Novembre (tel. 04 42 38 13 63), off cours Sextius. Caesar-sized pizzas (38-55F) and pastas (38-60F) served in a *cave* by friendly waiters. Pastas in half-portions are still too big. Open Mon.-Sat. 7pm-2am. V, MC.

SIGHTS

Cultured Aix sports several worthwhile museums. All except the Fondation Vasarely can be seen on a 60F pass, available at the tourist office at any one of the museums. The most unusual is the **Chemin de Cézanne,** a walking tour that transforms the city into an open-air exhibit of the life of native son Paul Cézanne (1839-1906). Pick up the tourist office's brochure *In the Footsteps of Paul Cézanne* and follow the bronze markers embedded in the sidewalks. The two-hour walk covers Cézanne's birthplace, the cathedral where he worshipped, and his studio, the **Atelier Paul Cézanne,** 9, av. Paul Cézanne (tel. 04 42 21 06 53), a short walk north of Aix. The studio is unassuming and the walking tour presents Cézanne's life in the context of the history of Aix and its countryside. (Studio open June-Sept. Wed.-Mon. 10-11:50am and 2:30-5:50pm; Oct.-May 10-11:50am and 2-4:50pm. Photography forbidden. Admission 15F; students, children, and seniors 10F).

The **Musée Granet,** pl. St-Jean-Marie-de-Malte (tel. 04 42 38 14 70), contains several Cézannes and a smattering of works by Caravaggio, David, Ingres, and Delacroix, as well as an archaeological section. The collection, mostly by lesser-known Italian, French, and Dutch artists, is illuminated by superb lighting (open Wed.-Mon. 10am-noon and 2-6pm; admission 18F, students 10F).

The stunning contemporary **Fondation Vasarely,** 1, av. Marcel Pagnol (tel. 04 42 20 01 09), Jas de Bouffan, lies outside town, next to the hostel and is a must-see. Take bus 12 (7F) from La Rotonde to "Vasarely." The black and white museum, designed by the artist, houses 42 of wacky Hungarian Victor Vasarely's enormous, experiments with color and shape, known as "mural integrations." The paintings—all in hexagonal rooms—trick viewers into seeing in three dimensions. This modern art can be appreciated for its genius, even by those who dislike the abstract (open daily 10am-1pm and 2-7pm; off-season 10am-noon and 2-7pm; admission 35F, under 23 20F). After this visual tomfoolery, the placid park outside is a welcome relief.

A fine collection of Beauvais tapestries from the 17th and 18th centuries hangs in the **Musée des Tapisseries,** 28, pl. des Martyrs de la Résistance (tel. 04 42 23 09 91), at ancienne pl. de l'Archevêché. Elaborate costumes and photographs from the theater in the courtyard are displayed as well as a striking collection of colorful, contemporary textile pieces, one for every month of the year (open daily 10am-noon and 2-5:45pm; admission 19F, students 15F). **Cathédrale St-Sauveur,** rue Gaston de Saporta, also on the *place,* is a dramatic mélange of additions and carvings from 11th-century Romanesque to late Flamboyant Gothic. The main attraction, the 16th-century carved panels of the main portal, remain in perfect condition. The interior's *Triptych du Buisson Ardent* depicts Aix's Good King René and his queen oddly juxtaposed with the Virgin and Child and the burning bush of Moses. The work is usually shut away, but for a small tip the affable guard may show it to you (church open Wed.-Mon. 8am-noon and 2-6pm). Occasional recitals fill the courtyard with classical and jazz music. Call Festival d'Aix (tel. 04 42 17 34 00) for more info.

The museum at the **Pavillon de Vendôme,** 32, rue Célony (tel. 04 42 21 05 78), houses paintings and furniture from the turn of the 18th century (open Wed.-Mon. in summer 10am-noon and 2-6pm; in winter 10am-noon and 1-5pm; admission 19F, students 15F). In summer the paintings are replaced by photography exhibitions; call to find out what's currently on display. The surrounding **gardens** offer shade, quiet, and the soothing smell of boxwood and roses, plus a goldfish pond, fountain, and shrubs cut in swirling spiral shapes. It's welcome peace in the bustling city. (Gardens free and open the same hours as the Pavillon.)

The **Cité des Livres,** 8-10, rue des Allumettes (tel. 04 42 25 98 88), near the *gare routière,* once one of France's largest match factories, has been renovated into a widely used library, the *Bibliothèque Méjanes,* café, and contemporary art gallery. Guarded by giant replicas of Camus's *L'Etranger* and Antoine de St-Exupéry's *Le Petit Prince,* this bright library stocks current *Newsweeks* plus a collection of British and American literature. Ask the English-speaking staff to show you the way to the **Videothèque d'Art Lyrique,** where you can sit in air-conditioned splendor to view operas and concerts of past Festivals d'Aix for free (tel. 04 42 26 66 75; open Sept.-July Tues.-Sat. noon-6pm). The **Discothèque** features a wide selection of music from around the world on CD for loan (with 95F membership) and also shows documentaries in a small lounge area. Relaxing music and lots of natural light will make you want to get a book and lounge in here. (Library, including Discothèque, open mid-July to mid-Aug. Tues.-Fri. 9am-3:30pm, Sat. 9am-5pm; mid-Aug. to mid-July Tues. and Thurs.-Fri. noon-6pm, Wed. and Sat. 10am-6pm.)

ENTERTAINMENT

Aix's **International Music Festival** (tel. 04 42 17 34 34 or 04 42 21 14 40) is held from mid-July to early August. The program features opera in the **Théâtre de l'Archevêché** (tickets 100-290F), concerts in the **Cathédrale** and **Cloître St-Louis,** 60, bd. Carnot (tickets 120-380F), and recitals by music students at **Cloître St-Sauveur** (tickets 90F). **Aix en Musique** (tel. 04 42 21 69 69), a casual two-week jamboree of big-band jazz and chamber music, begins the second week of June. The tourist office lists concerts; call 04 42 16 11 61 for more info. During the first two weeks of July, Aix holds a **Dance Festival** (tel. 04 42 96 05 01) of ballet, modern, and jazz (tickets 80-150F, students 60-120F). From July 2 to 10, the city puts on an international **Jazz Festival,** which includes one night of jazz salsa and one of big band (tickets 80-200F). The

Comité Officiel des Fêtes on cours Gambetta (tel. 04 42 63 06 75), at the corner of bd. du Roi René, can fill you in on all the festivals. In the spring and winter, student theater and concerts abound at the university. Students and professionals share the **Théâtre Jacques-Prévert,** 24, bd. de la République (tel. 04 42 26 36 50), and the **Théâtre 108,** 37, bd. A. Briand (tel. 04 42 21 06 70).

Aix's students insist on revelry year-round; most clubs open at 11:30pm and don't get going until 2am. Pubs and bars have earlier hours. **Le Scat,** 11, rue Verrerie (tel. 04 42 23 00 23), has both a pub and a terrific club with live music (open Mon.-Sat. 10pm-whenever). **La Chimère,** montée d'Avignon (tel. 04 42 23 36 28), quartier des Plâtrières, outside of town, attracts a sizeable gay crowd to its bar and disco (open Tues.-Sun. 10pm-6am). **Bistro Aixois,** 37, Cours Sextius (tel. 04 42 27 50 10), off la Rotonde, packs students and bands in cramped quarters (daily 10pm-3am). **Le Mistral,** 3, rue F. Mistral (tel. 04 42 38 16 49), plays techno and dance music, but don't show up in shorts, jeans, or sandals (opens Tues.-Sat. at 11:30pm; Tues. women free; Wed.-Thurs. 50F cover, Fri.-Sat. 100F cover). Retro and French music plays nightly at the *boîtes de nuit* **Le Richelme,** 24, rue de la Verrerie (tel. 04 42 23 49 29). **The Jungle Café** features live music every night at 4, bd, Carnot (tel. 04 42 21 47 44). Cafés and bars, some lit by candlelight, line the **Forum des Cardeurs,** behind the Hôtel de Ville. The **Cézanne Cinema,** 21, rue Goyraud (tel. 04 42 26 04 06), rolls eight or 10 films every night, some in English (45F).

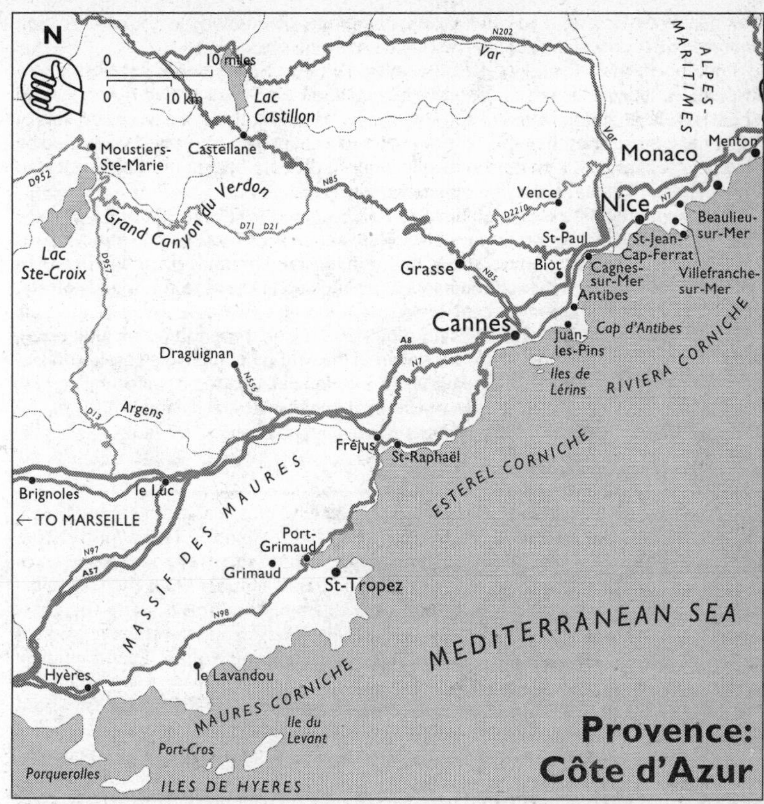

RIVIERA

Provence: Côte d'Azur

A sunny place for shady people.

—Somerset Maugham

Sparkling between Marseille and the Italian border, the sun-drenched beaches and Mediterranean waters of the French Riviera form the backdrop for this fabled playground of the beautiful and wealthy. Its seductive loveliness has almost been its undoing, as developers have turned its charms into profit and its pleasures into big business. Today, the area is a destination for low-budget backpackers and millionaires alike. Many French condemn the coast as a shameless Fort Lauderdale, a mere shadow of its former self, but the Côte remains an uncommon garden of delights bathed in vibrant colors. Pastel villas rim the unique blue hues of the sea, while silvery olive trees shelter roses and mimosas. By day, beaches invite swimming and sunning *au naturel;* by night, clubs and casinos cater to more expensive whims.

The Riviera's resort culture developed in the 18th and 19th centuries, when the English and Russian aristocracy came to its unspoiled fishing villages to cure winter ailments in the sun and sea. Soon, Nice drew a steady crowd of the idle rich whose favored seaside sports included carriage-riding and casino-hopping. In the 1920s, Coco Chanel popularized the *provençal* farmer's healthy tan among her society customers; the parasols went down, the hemlines went up, and a religion of sun worship was born. The Côte became a proletariat playground only after World War II, when new highways and railroads and a government-mandated increase in paid vacation time made the area accessible to the French working class.

Some of the past century's greatest artists came to the Côte for restoration and inspiration. Images linger of F. Scott Fitzgerald and Cole Porter at Cap d'Antibes and of Picasso, Renoir, and Matisse capturing the luminous foothills of Nice. Many towns along the eastern stretch of the Côte lay claim to a chapel, room, or wall decorated by Matisse or Chagall. Superb museum collections in obscure but sunny villages attest to the gratitude of wealthy or talented sun-worshippers.

Nightlife on the Riviera is wild. Revel in Nice's *Carnaval* (Feb. 8-23 in 1997), or see and be on the scene at the Cannes Film Festival and the Monte-Carlo Grand Prix in May. Jazz festivals heat up the summer nights in most towns, and Monaco's Fireworks Festival explodes in August. For a break from the action, head to the islands off the coast of Cannes.

The food is simple and fresh all along the Côte; regional specialities include *bouillabaisse* (hearty fish soup), *soupe au pistou* (a brew of pine nuts, fresh basil, and garlic), *aïoli* (a garlic dip to accompany fresh vegetables), and fresh seafood. Set your feast against the sun-washed hues of the *provençal* wines: reds and whites of the Côte du Rhône or the rosés of the Côte de Provence.

GETTING AROUND

The coast from Marseille to Italy is served by frequent, inexpensive trains and buses. Most attractions lie along the stretch from St-Raphaël to Menton. Trains for the Côte leave Paris' Gare de Lyon hourly in summer; the trip on the TGV to Marseille takes five hours, to Nice seven to eight hours. Available as of summer '96 is the **Carte Isabelle,** a special summer deal (50F) that provides unlimited travel along the coast (good for 1 day only; does not include St-Raphaël). Hitchhiking, never a safe pursuit, is said to be difficult along the coastal highway but less trying on inland country roads. You might want to base yourself in a sedate, less expensive town and make daytrips to the purse-emptying cities and inviting beaches. The Riviera is best visited in early June and in September, when crowds and prices are low and hotel vacancies high. In July and August, all of France tries to squeeze onto the *Côte*'s beaches. Reserve ahead or start looking for a bed in the early morning.

A final note: every woman who has traveled on the Riviera has a story to tell about men in the big beach towns. Unsolicited pick-up techniques range from subtle invitations to more naked displays of interest. Most can be brushed off with a biting *"laissez-moi tranquille!"* (leave me alone) or stony indifference, but don't be shy about enlisting the help of passers-by or the police to fend off Mediterranean Don Juans—it's better to make a scene than be one.

BEACHES

If you're coming just for the sun, try to arrive in early June or in September, when the air and water are warm but the beaches don't look like an open audition for *Baywatch* extras. In summer, optimal swimming tends to be 7-9pm, just before sunset. Bring a beach mat (20F at supermarkets); even the sand beaches are a bit rocky.

Since almost all the towns on the *Côte* lie along one local rail line, just hop off and on to see what you can find. The largest cities have the worst beaches. Marseille has an artificial beach, the Nice beaches are rocky, Cannes' is private, and St-Tropez and Monte-Carlo are remote. Seek out alcoves between towns: Cap Martin (between Monaco and Menton), Cap d'Ail (between Monaco and Nice), and St-Raphaël (between Cannes and St-Tropez). Nearly all beaches are topless; those who like to bare it all will find a wealth of secluded shores. At Héliopolis (one of Europe's largest nudist colonies), on the Ile du Levant, and in the *calanques* between Eze-sur-Mer and Cap d'Ail, *naturistes* will find plenty of company. Do not neglect the less-frequented coastal islands. The Porquerolles and Ile du Levant off Toulon and the Iles de Lérins off Cannes all have fine rock ledges and secluded coves.

Although crashing on the beach is illegal, many travelers sleep where they sun. A number of beaches provide showers, toilets, and even towels for a small fee (10-15F). Those who try to spend the night on the beaches at Nice, Cannes, and Juan-les-Pins may run afoul of more than the law. You could find yourself bedding down next to groups of "respectable"-looking youths whose summer salary is earned in tourists' jewelry, mopeds, and cash. Daytrippers can make use of the lockers available at most train stations—always hide the key or write the code in a safe place. In stations without lockers, you can usually check your bags for 15-30F.

Marseille

France's third largest city, Marseille is like the *bouillabaisse* for which it is famous: steaming hot, pungently spiced, with a little bit of everything mixed in. Though Nice may actually harbor more of the French Mafia these days, Marseille (pop. 1.1 million) still enjoys a reputation for roguishness and danger. As a gateway to Europe, Marseille is the immigration goal of thousands of North and sub-Saharan Africans, creating a thriving stew of cultures as well as ethnic tensions in this center of the growing conservative sentiment in France. In its 2600-year history, Marseille has never taken a political middle ground. In 1792, the *Marseillais'* extreme enthusiasm as they marched to join the Revolution in Paris elevated a rousing march composed in Strasbourg, "To the Army of the Rhine," to the status of a national anthem.

Even without the glamour of the Riviera or the pastoral charm of Provence, the city Dumas called "the meeting place of the entire world" remains strangely alluring, charged throughout with color and commotion. Its daily fish markets, wild nightclubs, nearby beaches, islands, and gardens, with a dash of big-city adventure thrown in, merit a stopover on the way to Nice or Avignon.

ORIENTATION AND PRACTICAL INFORMATION

Making your way down one or two blocks of **La Canebière,** affectionately known to English sailors as the "can o' beer," will encourage you to accept Marseille's seedy reputation as its reality. It seems that all streets in Marseille flow into La Canebière and down to the *vieux port* on the shores of the Mediterranean. To get a broader sense of *le vrai* Marseille, resist this undertow and amble instead down **rue Paradis, rue St-Ferréol, cours Julien,** or the narrow North African **rue des Feuillants.** This is not to say that Marseille doesn't have its share of urban dangers; at night, thieves and pranksters prowl the dusty streets by the train station, roughly bounded by bd. Nedelec, bd. d'Athènes, rue d'Aix, and La Canebière. The areas in front of the opera (near the port) and around rue Curiol (near rue Sénac) are often the meeting grounds for prostitutes and their clients; exercise particular caution here after dark.

Public transportation tames Marseille's urban sprawl. The two **metro** lines (abbreviated M. in text) are clean and simple; the bus system is thorough, if complex—the bus map helps a great deal. To walk to the tourist office exiting the train station, turn left and descend the grand steps. Continue straight down bd. d'Athènes until you arrive at the McDonald's on La Canebière. Take a right on La Canebière and walk all the way to the port. The tourist office is on your left, in front of the Quai des Belges metro entrance (15min.).

Tourist Office: 4, La Canebière (tel. 04 91 13 89 00; fax 04 91 13 89 20). Info on visiting nearby islands, annual festivals, and taxi tours of the city. Free maps and accommodations service. SCNF info and reservations. Bus/metro day pass 20F. Ask for the guide *Le Citadinque.* Open daily July-Sept. 8:30am-8pm; Oct.-June Mon.-Sat. 9am-7pm, Sun. and holidays 10am-5pm. **Annex** at train station (tel. 04 91 50 59 18). Open July-Aug. Mon.-Sat. 10am-2:30pm and 3:30-7pm; Sept.-June Mon.-Fri. 10am-1pm and 1:30-6pm. **TakTik,** a weekly newspaper listing art exhibits, music, dance, theater, art, and film, is free at the tourist office and FNAC in the Centre Bourse, a shopping mall 3 blocks from the *vieux port* on La Canabière. **Marseille Informations,** at the post office, is another free weekly source of times, dates, and places of artsy events. **Atout Marseille** (20F) is published seasonally by the tourist office, with festivals, concerts, expositions, and a map of the town's historical attractions.

Consulates: U.S., 12, bd. Paul Peytral (tel. 04 91 54 92 00). Open Mon.-Fri. 9am-12:30pm and 2-5pm, by appointment. **U.K.,** 24, av. du Prado (tel. 04 91 15 72 10). Open Mon.-Fri. 9am-noon and 2-5pm.

Money: La Bourse, 3, pl. Général de Gaulle (tel. 04 91 13 09 00). Good rates and no commission. Open Mon.-Fri. 8:30am-6:30pm, Sat. 9am-12:30pm and 2-5pm. **Comptoir de Change de Bourse,** 20, La Canebière. Excellent rates and no commission. Open Mon.-Sat. 9am-6pm. **Comptoir de Change Méditerranéen** (tel. 04 91 84 68 88), at the train station. No commission. Open daily 8am-6pm. The first 2 blocks of **rue St-Ferréol** off of La Canebière have 24-hr. **ATMs.**

American Express, 39, La Canebière (tel. 04 91 13 71 21). Currency exchange and travel service. Open Mon.-Fri. 8:30am-6pm, Sat. 9am-noon and 2-5pm.

Flights: Aéroport Marseille-Provence (tel. 04 42 78 21 00). Cheap student flights to Corsica, Paris, and Lyon. Shuttle buses connect airport with Gare St-Charles (every 20min., 5:30am-9:50pm, 42F).

Trains: Gare St-Charles, pl. Victor Hugo, M. Gare St-Charles (tel. 08 36 35 35 35). Reception desk open daily 4am-1am. Info and reservation desk open Mon.-Sat. 9am-8pm. To: Paris (12 TGVs per day, 4¾hr., 400F); Lyon (16 per day, 3½hr., 200F). **SOS Voyageurs** (tel. 04 91 62 12 80), in the station. Cheery volunteer staff will help you get oriented and find lodgings. Open in summer Mon.-Sat. 9am-7pm; in winter Mon.-Sat. 9am-noon and 1-7pm. Baggage **lockers** were closed indefinitely after the summer 1995 Paris bombings; they may have reopened (4:30am-1am, 15-30F).

Buses: Gare des Autocars, pl. Victor Hugo, ½-block from the train station. M. Gare St-Charles (tel. 04 91 08 16 40). Open Mon.-Sat. 7:45am-6:25pm, Sun. 9am-noon and 2-6:25pm. **Car Treize** (tel. 04 91 08 16 40, ask for Car 13) is a blanket organization of Marseille bus companies. Buy tickets on the bus (except to Nice) with exact change. To: Aix-en-Provence (every 12min., 22F, roundtrip 30F if same day and company); Cannes (4 per day, 2¼-3hr., 120F, students 85F); Nice (4 per day, 2¾hr., 130F, students 85F); Avignon (5 per day, 2hr., 86F, roundtrip 128F); Cassis (12-21 per day, 30min.-1hr., 22F); Arles (7 per day, 2-3hr., 82F).

Public Transportation: RTM, 6-8, rue des Fabres (tel. 04 91 91 92 10). Open Mon.-Fri. 8am-6pm. Exact change or tickets (8F, 39F50 for *carnet* of 6; sold at metro and bus stops). Ticket good for 70min. Metro lines 1 and 2 both stop at the train station. Line 1 (blue) goes to the *vieux port* (direction: Timone). Metro runs 5am-9pm. The tourist office distributes the free *RTM Plan-Guide du Réseau.*

Ferries: SNCM, 61, bd. des Dames (tel. 08 36 67 95 00). Information and tickets to Corsica (600F, students 385F), Sardinia, and North Africa. Open Mon.-Fri. 8am-noon and 2-10:30pm, Sat. 8:30am-noon.

Taxis: Taxi Plus (tel. 04 91 03 60 03). **Marseille Taxi** (tel. 04 91 02 20 20). Both 24hr. From station, 80F to Bois-Luzy hostel, about 130F to Bonneveine hostel.

English Books: Librairie Fueri-Lamy, 21, rue Paradis (tel. 04 91 33 57 03). Packed with just enough paperbacks to see you through the next leg of your journey. Open Mon. 1:30-6:45pm, Tues.-Sat. 9am-noon and 1:30-6:45pm. V, MC.

Youth Information: Centre d'Information Jeunesse, 4, rue de la Visitation (tel. 04 91 49 91 55), off bd. Françoise Duparc, north of Palais Longchamp. Info on sports, short-term employment, and activities, including climbing in the *calanques.* Pamphlets for people with disabilities. Open Mon. 1-7pm and Tues.-Fri. 10am-7pm. **CROUS,** 42, rue du 141ème R.I.A. (tel. 04 91 95 90 06), has info on housing, work, and travel for students. Open daily 9am-noon and 2-4:30pm.

Laundromat: Point Laverie, 56, bd. de la Libération. Wash 20F for 7kg. Dry 2F for 6min. Detergent 4F. Open daily 7am-9pm. Another at 8, rue de l'Academie.

Crisis Lines and Outreach Centers: SOS Femmes Violées (tel. 04 91 56 04 10) is a 24-hr. rape crisis hotline. **Office Municipal pour Handicapés et Inadaptés,** 128, av. du Prado (tel. 04 91 81 58 80), an excellent center for people with disabilities. Open Mon.-Fri. 8am-noon and 2-6pm. For transportation service, call 91 11 41 00 a day ahead (8am-noon and 1-6pm); operates daily 6am-midnight.

Marseille

Abbaye St-Victor, 7
Basilique de Notre Dame de la Garde, 8
Bus Station, 2
Cathédrale Nouvelle Major, 1
Musée Cantini, 6
Palais Longchamp/Musée des Beaux-Arts, 4
Tourist Office, 5
Train Station, 3

0 — 500 yards
0 — 500 meters

Late-Night Pharmacy: Pharmacie Brachat Bel, 29, rue Longue des Campucins (tel. 04 91 91 78 92). Open all night, every night.

Hospital: Hôpital Timone, bd. Jean Moulin (tel. 04 91 38 60 00). Take metro line 1 to "Castéllane," then bus 91. Ask the driver to drop you off at the hospital. **Medical Emergency:** For a home visit call 04 91 52 84 85 or 04 91 49 91 91. **Ambulance** tel. 15. **SOS Médecins** (tel. 04 91 52 91 52), doctors on call.

Police: 2, rue du Commissaire Becker (tel. 04 91 39 80 00). Also in the train station on Esplanade St-Charles (same tel.; ask for *poste* 7097). **Emergency** tel. 17.

Post Office: 1, pl. Hôtel des Postes (tel. 04 91 15 47 20). Follow La Canebière towards the sea, turn right onto rue Reine Elisabeth, as it becomes pl. Hôtel des Postes. Minitel. Photocopies 1F. Poste restante and **currency exchange** at this branch only. Open Mon.-Fri. 8am-7pm, Sat. 8am-noon. **Branch office** at 11, rue Honnorat (tel. 04 91 50 89 25), near the station. **Postal code:** 13001.

ACCOMMODATIONS AND CAMPING

Inexpensive hotels abound, especially on rue Breteuil. A herd of one- and two-star hotels ranges on allée L. Gambetta. Resist the cheap accommodations in the North African quarter; the area is dangerous after dark and many hotels are fronts for prostitutes. Both hostels are far from the town center, with efficient, if time-consuming, bus service. They usually have space, even in summer, but call ahead.

Auberge de Jeunesse de Bois-Luzy (HI), allée des Primevères (tel. and fax 04 91 49 06 18). By day, take bus 6 from cours J. Thierry at the top of La Canebière (away from the *port*) or, at night, bus T at 9:10pm, 9:50pm, 10:40pm, 11:30pm, or 12:40am from "La Canebière" to "Marius Richard"; follow signs to the hostel. Or take bus 8 from "La Canebière" by day to "Bois-Luzy"; the hostel will be visible at the top of the hill. If the construction of a new autoroute blocks the path directly up the hill, follow signs to the hostel. This Napoleon III-era château overlooking the city has clean, well-kept rooms, comfy beds, and hot showers. Isolated and sedate, but cheaper and more architecturally engaging than Bonneveine. Plain 3- to 6-person dorms, a few doubles at 50F per person or 65F solo when available. **Campsites** may reopen after autoroute construction is complete (26F, includes shower). Casino supermarket at "Bois-Luzy." 43F. Breakfast 18F. Dinner 43F. Cooking facilities open until 10pm. Laundry 30F to wash and dry 5kg. Luggage storage 5F per 24hr. Reception 7:30-noon and 5-10:30pm. Strict 11pm curfew May-Oct; 10:30pm Nov.-April. Lockout 10:30am-5pm. Call to see if they have space before trekking out here April-June.

RIVIERA

Auberge de Jeunesse Bonneveine (HI), impasse Bonfils, off av. J. Vidal (tel. 04 91 73 21 81; fax 04 91 73 97 23). From station, take metro line 2 to "Rond-Point du Prado." Take bus 44 to pl. Bonnefon (one ticket for metro and bus). Walk up av. J. Vidal. After no. 47, turn into impasse Bonfils. The hostel is on the left. This is the place to stay if you're here for Marseille's public beaches; swimming, surfing, and sunbathing are just 200m away. Low-slung cement-block building with bar, restaurant, pool table, video games, drink and snack machines, travel agency, and 150 beds. 4-5-bed rooms 72F, 4 beds and shower 81F, 2 beds 114F first night, 98F each additional night. Breakfast included. Dinner 48F. Sheets 16F. Laundry 10F per wash. Lockers 10F per 24hr. Reception 7am-11pm. Members only. No lockout. Flexible 1am curfew. Call ahead in summer. Closed in Jan. V, MC.

Hôtel Montgrand, 50, rue Montgrand (tel. 04 91 00 35 20; fax 04 91 33 75 89), off rue Paradis. Great location. Spotless white and blue rooms with soft pillows and firm beds. Singles and doubles (1 bed) 110-130F, with shower 140-175F. Doubles with bathroom 250F. Triples with bathroom 250-310F. Breakfast 25F. V, MC.

Hôtel Gambetta, 49, allée Léon Gambetta (E1; tel. 04 91 62 07 88; fax 04 91 64 81 54), centrally located at the top of La Canebière and near the train station. Clean, well-lit rooms, friendly staff, and a gentle dog lounging in the lobby. Singles 99F, with shower 130F. Doubles with shower, toilet, and TV 200-215F, with bathtub 225F. Shower 15F. Breakfast 25F. V, MC, AmEx.

Hôtel Moderne, 30, rue Breteuil (tel. 04 91 53 29 93). From station walk to the *vieux port* and turn left on quai des Belges. Continue straight on cours J. Ballard, which turns into rue Breteuil. Clean rooms and funky murals. Singles 85F, with shower 100F. Doubles with shower, toilet, and TV 175-200F. Breakfast 25F.

Hôtel Béarn, 63, rue Sylvabelle (D3; tel. 04 91 37 75 83; fax 04 91 81 54 98), between rue Paradis and rue Breteil. Large rooms. Singles with douche 134F, with bath, toilet, and TV 188F. Triples (2 beds) with shower, toilet, and TV 212F. Quads (2 big beds) with shower and TV 262F. Breakfast 20-25F. V, MC, AmEx.

Hôtel Moderne, 11, bd. de la Libération (F1; tel. 04 91 62 28 66). Follow La Canebière away from the port to rue Montsabert de la Libération. 10 rooms, each with a kitsch all its own, are bargains. Singles 74-94F, with shower and TV 134F. Doubles 150F, with shower and TV 158F. Triples with shower 202F. Shower 15F. Breakfast 20F. V, MC. Not to be confused with the other Hôtel Moderne.

FOOD

Marseille is the home of *bouillabaisse,* a fish stew cooked with wine, saffron, and a touch of cayenne pepper. Mussels, eel, lobster, and anything that swims may be thrown in. The restaurant population soars around the *vieux port,* concentrating on **pl. Thiars** and **Honoré d'Estienne d'Orvies,** where one can dine *al fresco* on fresh seafood for as little as 60F or as much as 180F. For a more artsy crowd and cheaper fare, head up to **cours Julien** and take your pick from the bold and eclectic restaurants lining the pedestrian mall. Many of Marseille's superb North African restaurants and markets gather on narrow rue des Feuillants. A few great restaurants open only for lunch are among those listed below. *Marseillais(es)* stock up for their stew at the daily **fish market** (9am-noon) on quai des Belges. Marseille has a **vegetable market** at cours Julien (every morning) and an **open-air market** on rue cours Pierre Puget, beginning at rue Breteuil (Mon.-Sat., starts at 8am). Before you head for the hostels, stock up on the second floor of **BAZE,** on the Canebière across from the AmEx office (open Mon.-Sat. 8:30am-8pm).

L'Ecailler, 10, rue Fortia (D3; tel. 04 91 54 79 39), off quai de Rive Neuve. True *marseillaise* cuisine can be eaten outside in summer or winter (when you'll be enclosed in a warm plastic bubble) at the only one of 4 nearby upscale restaurants offering a 3-course *menu* at 65F. In summer and on weekends, call a day early to avoid a 20-30min. wait. Open daily 11:45am-2:30pm and 7-11:30pm. V, MC.

La Manne, 18, bd. de la Liberté (E1; tel. 04 91 50 97 68). Halfway between the train station and the allée Léon Gambetta, this little restaurant provides friendly service amid a décor of fake flowers and metallic paintings of fishermen and the seaport. The 50F *menu* dinner includes a salad, a main dish *traditionel* or *végétarien,* and a dessert. Open Mon.-Sat. noon-3pm and 7-11pm. V, MC.

Le Sunset Plaza, 24, rue Pavillon (D3; tel. 04 91 33 27 77), off rue St-Ferréol and rue Paradis. Order a falafel to go (25F) or enjoy one of this restaurant's kosher Israeli delicacies at a table surrounded by modern art. Open Sun.-Fri. 11am-3pm.

Sweet Café, 38, rue Sylvabelle (tel. 04 91 57 14 10), between rue de Rome and rue Paradis. This orange and green corner of heaven off rue Paradis offers a quiet and airy respite from the bustling Canebière. Step in for a smoked salmon (32F), vegetarian (25F), or chicken and guacamole (26F) sandwich, or just relax with a *mousse au chocolat orange* (12F). Open Mon.-Fri. 10am-5pm.

Country Life, 14, rue Venture (E3; tel. 04 91 54 16 44; fax 04 91 33 90 29), off rue Paradis. The first floor is a **health food store** complete with bulk foods and expensive skin care products. Open Mon.-Thurs. 9am-6:30pm and Fri. 9am-3pm. On the second floor, a huge skylight and a forest of foliage provide a spacious atmosphere for enjoying the all-you-can-eat vegan 60F *menu* (students 35F), including salad, soup, and several hot entrees. Open Mon.-Fri. 11:30am-2:30pm.

SIGHTS

The shimmering 19th-century **Basilique de Notre Dame de la Garde** balances in splendor on a hill 160m above Marseille. Even in the summer haze of the Marseille skyline, the basilica's gilded Virgin sparkles over the Mediterranean Sea below. To see things from the Virgin's point of view—the harbor islands, the Château d'If, and the surrounding mountains, that is—take bus 60, or follow rue Breteuil from the *vieux port,* turn right on bd. Vauban, and turn right again on rue Fort du Sanctuaire (no shorts or tank tops; open 7am-7:30pm in summer; 7am-5:45pm off-season; free).

The **Abbaye St-Victor** (tel. 04 91 33 25 86), perched on rue Sainte at the end of quai de Rive Neuve (follow the signs from the quai), evokes the ascetic beginnings of Christianity. The eerie 5th-century catacombs and basilica contain an extensive array of both pagan and Christian relics, including the remains of two 3rd-century martyrs. The Abbaye hosts sacred music concerts all year. (Open daily 8am-noon and 2-7pm; 10F to go down to the crypts, open 9am-6:30pm.)

At the elaborate, perhaps excessive, 19th-century **Palais Longchamp,** at the eastern end of bd. Longchamp (M. Cinq Avenues-Longchamp), two *long* stone staircases framing a set of complicated fountains and cascading waterfalls lead to two museums. On the left is the **Musée des Beaux-Arts** (tel. 04 91 62 21 17). Particularly strong in Provençal painting, the museum also exhibits paintings of Marseille's early history, 16th- to 19th-century French painting, and 17th- to 19th-century sculpture. Works by Corbet and Rubens, as well as a case of 36 political satire miniature busts by Daumier, round out the collection (open June-Sept. Tues.-Sun. 11am-6pm, Oct.-May 10am-5pm; admission 10F, students 5F, over 65 free). The **Musée d'Histoire Naturelle** (tel. 04 91 62 30 78), besides the standard natural history fare, has a newly reopened aquarium. You'll only see sea creatures of the region, so forget about sharks and marvel at the bright red starfish instead (open Tues.-Sun. 10am-5pm). Behind the Palais are the shady paths and benches, playground, and pony rides of the former **Jardin Zoologique.**

Haven't had your fill of Roman-Byzantine architecture? The ornate 19th-century **Cathédrale Nouvelle Major** has almost swallowed its smaller, Romanesque predecessor, near the quai de la Tourette (M. Joliette). From the *vieux port,* walk along the quai du Port. As the road turns to the right, the enormous cathedral will appear (open Tues.-Sun. 9am-noon and 2:30-5:30pm).

The **Musée Cantini,** 19, rue Grignan (tel. 04 91 54 77 75), features art from Fauvism to the present in temporary exhibits (open June-Sept. Tues.-Sun. 11am-6pm, Oct.-May 10am-5pm; admission 15F, students 10F, over 65 or under 10 free). The **Musée de la Mode,** Espace Mode Méditerranée, at 11, La Canebière (D2; tel. 04 91 56 59 57), has wacky, contemporary fashion exhibits (open Tues.-Sun. noon-7pm.; admission 15F, students 7F50, over 65 free). The Espace Mode Méditerranée also houses a café, bookstore, and small shop. **MAC,** Galeries Contemporaines des Musées de Marseille, 69, av. d'Haifa (tel. 04 91 25 01 07), features art from the 1960s to today, including works by Pistoletto, César, and Wegman (open Tues.-Sun. 11am-6pm; admission 15F). Behind the Centre Bourse, **Le Jardin des Vestiges** (D2) holds the remains of the original port of Marseille. Limestone blocks stand stacked in the garden like giant Legos. The grassed-over harbor makes a great picnic stop (open Mon.-Sat. noon-7pm; 10F, students 5F, over 65 free). Your ticket to the garden admits you into the mildly interesting **Musée d'Histoire de Marseille** (tel. 04 91 90 42 22), whose rooms survey the city in the ancient, medieval, and Louis XIV eras.

Bus 83 (direction: Rond pont du Prado) from the *vieux port* is your ticket to Marseille's public **beaches.** Catch it on the waterfront side of the street and get off just after it rounds the statue of David (20-30min.). Both **plage du Prado** and **plage de la Corniche** offer wide beaches, clear water, plenty of grass for impromptu soccer games, and scenic views of the grayish-white cliffs surrounding Marseille, though not necessarily ideal sand. **Supermarché Casino,** across from the statue, will serve your every need (open Mon.-Sat. 8:30am-8:30pm).

A short boat-ride away, the **Château d'If** (tel. 04 91 59 02 30) looms ominously on the Ile d'If, one of Marseille's small harbor islands. The château's haunting dungeon, immortalized by Alexandre Dumas in *The Count of Monte Cristo,* imprisoned a number of Huguenots who never made it out alive, and supposedly held the enigmatic man in the iron mask (see gray box below). Its appeal is mainly in the stories surrounding the isle and in the vivid imaginations of its visitors. Although the château was built to defend Marseille from naval intruders, foreign ships have never threat-

The Man in the Iron Mask

Mythologized in Alexandre Dumas Père's novel, *Dix Ans plus tard ou le Vicomte de Bragelonne* (tr. *The Man in the Iron Mask*), the story of this mysterious prisoner remains unsolved. The popular theory, adopted by Dumas and first proposed by Voltaire, is that he was the twin of Louis XIV, imprisoned and forced by his brother to wear the mask to prevent a challenge to the throne. Others claimed that he was the bastard elder brother of the king, or Louis XIV's illegitimate son, imprisoned to prevent a war for the succession. A less romantic, if more credible, theory maintains that the masked prisoner was Eustache Dauger, arrested in July, 1669, for reasons unknown. In prison, Dauger became the valet for former finance minister Nicolas Fouquet. Upon Fouquet's death, Dauger's identity was hidden for fear that he might divulge state secrets. The historical man did not in fact wear an iron mask; his veil was actually black velvet. The only concrete historical information known about the shadowy figure is that he was in the prison Pignerol before 1681, was transferred to different prisons (including the Chateau d'If), and died in the Bastille on Nov. 19, 1703. The name "Marchioly" and "aged about 45" were the only inscriptions on his tombstone.

ened Marseille; the cannons inside the chateau's three stark turrets have only fired in salute. Nearby, bald, barren, and windswept **Ile Frioul** served to quarantine suspected plague victims for two centuries, starting in the 1600s. It was only marginally successful—in 1720 a plague killed half of the city's 80,000 citizens. The ancient hospital is now a public monument. Frequent boats depart from the quai des Belges (M. Quai des Belges) for both the Ile d'If and Ile Frioul. Call the **Groupement des Armateurs Côtiers** (tel. 04 91 55 50 09) for information (20min., roundtrip 45F for each island, 70F for both; open 9am-7pm, Oct.-March 9am-1pm and 2pm-5:30pm; admission 26F, students 17F).

ENTERTAINMENT

Don't let Marseille's seedy reputation scare you from its spicy nightlife. Exercise cosmopolitan caution, and pick up a free magazine to keep up with club openings, theme nights, and concerts (see **Events,** page 469). People-watching and nightlife center around **cours Julien** (E2-3), northeast of the harbor, and **pl. Thiers** (D3) near the *vieux port.* Don't venture alone in the *vieux port* after dark; after 10pm, *everyone* should avoid the North African quarter, cours Belsunce, and bd. d'Athènes.

Trolleybus, 24, quai de Rive Neuve (tel. 04 91 54 30 45), is a mega-club with a room each for techno, rock, and "acid jazz," as well as a gallery of contemporary art (open Thurs.-Sat. 11pm-7am; cover 64F Sat. only). Dress to impress to get in the smaller **Metal Café,** 20, rue Fortia (D3; tel. 04 91 54 03 03), off quai de Rive Neuve (open 11am till morning; no entrance fee but 1 drink required). **Le Club,** no.14, isn't the only club on rue Sénac to blast rock and jazz (open Mon.-Sat. 11pm-2am; cover 30F). Dancing queens love the new **New Can-Can,** 3, rue Sénac (tel. 04 91 48 59 76)—always a weekend party for the city's gay and lesbian community (Thurs. and Sun. 60F, Fri. 70F, Sat. 80F; opens at 11pm; *spectacle* at 2am). **L'Enigme** (D2; tel. 04 91 33 79 20), 22, rue Beauvau, is the only gay place on a street rife with lively bars, parallel to rue Paradis and pl. de Gaulle. **Cours Julien** (E2-3; M. Notre-Dame du Mont-Cours Julien) offers alternative nightlife galore. **L'Espace Julien,** 39, cours Julien (tel. 04 91 24 34 10), hosts a variety of concerts—from African music to pop—at 9pm in a quirky performance space full of wild, 3-D decorations (50-140F). Two blocks away, the **Chocolat Théâtre,** 59, cours Julien (tel. 04 91 42 19 29), stages comic pieces and stand-up at 9pm (70-110F); check out their restaurant (open noon-2pm and 7pm-midnight) and café (9am-2am) for cool drinks on hot nights. Theater buffs can check out the program at the **Théâtre National de Marseille,** quai de Rive Neuve (tel. 04 91 54 70 54; tickets 80-135F; box office open Tues.-Sat. 11am-6pm); and **Théâtre Gymnase,** 4, rue du Théâtre Français (tel. 04 91 24 35 24; tickets 110-160F; box office open Mon.-Sat. 9am-6pm). Unwind with the latest American and French films at **Le**

César, 4, pl. Castallene (E4; tel. 04 91 37 12 80; 40F, students and seniors 35F) and **Cinéma Breteuil,** 120, bd. Notre Dame (tel. 04 91 37 71 36; 38F, students and seniors 30F).

Expect the **International Documentary Film Festival** in June, and festivities surrounding the **Lesbian and Gay Pride March** in the middle of the same month. The **Festival Marseille Méditerranée** and **Festival des Iles** keep Marseille bubbling with music, dance, and theater in July. December brings the **Festival de Musique,** a week-long jubilee of jazz, classical, and pop music at l'Abbaye de Saint-Victoire. Call the tourist office or the **Culture Office** (tel. 04 91 33 33 79) for info on all festivals.

■ Near Marseille

The **Calanques** are inlets of azure water surrounded by walls of jagged rock. Stretching from Marseille to Toulon, their precipices and seas shelter a fragile and rare balance of plants and terrestrial and marine wildlife. Bleached white houses skirt the hills, looking down on the swarms of scuba divers, mountain climbers, cliff divers, and those in search of a *bronzage complet.*

During July and August, the **Société des Excursionnistes Marseillais,** 16, rue de la Rotonde (tel. 04 91 84 75 52), conducts free walking tours of the Calanques twice a week. Their boat trips leave daily in summer from the quai des Belges (roundtrip 100F). You can also take bus 21 (direction: Luminy; 8F) to the end of the line—near the **Morgiou** and **Sormiou.** The first of the chain of inlets, **Callelongue,** lies at the farthest reaches of the Marseille bus lines. Take #19 from the *vieux port* to its final stop in Samena. Then catch #20 and follow the windy coastal roads until its final stop. The bus runs sporadically, but you can kill time exploring hiking trails in the nearby hills. Sometimes line 20 ends prematurely at **Goudes** (the town before Callelongue), which boasts trails leading to peaks, valleys, and secluded inlets.

Twenty-three km from Marseille, the charming resort town of **Cassis** clings to a hillside overlooking the deep greens and blues of the Mediterranean. Immaculate white villas clump around the slopes above Cassis, while the town itself—a network of winding staircases, slender alleyways, and thick gardens—rests beside a devilishly bright port. Unfortunately, this is no undiscovered paradise on the Riviera; tourists abound in Cassis. Swimmers should follow the signs to the **Calanque de Port-Pin,** about 45 minutes east of town. From there, it's about a half-hour hike to **En Vau** and more magnificent calanques. Cassis makes a terrific daytrip, since hotels in town soar beyond the blue of its skies. A reasonable option is the **Auberge de Jeunesse de la Fontasse (HI)** (tel. 04 42 01 02 72), 20km from Marseille off D559. For those on foot, the hostel is a spite-inducing 4km climb from the tourist office (1hr.), but the gorgeous panorama, the proximity to En Vau, and the eco-friendly communal atmosphere may make it worth the pain. Sixty-six beds in 6- to 10-person dormitories, solar energy, and filtered rain water (from taps) only. No showers, but guests sponge-bath at the sinks. Members only. 45F. Light chores required. Kitchen open 5-10pm; stock up at Casino, 1½ blocks down the hill from the bus stop, on the left (Mon.-Sat. 8:30am-12:30pm and 3:30-7:30pm). Flexible reception hours 8-10am and 5-11pm. From Cassis' port, follow signs for the Calanques. When the road ends at two paths, take the (very steep) right path and then watch for subtle, harmonious-with-nature signs printed on rocks. Or, ask for a map to the hostel at the Cassis **tourist office** (tel. 04 42 01 71 17; fax 04 42 01 28 31; open July-Aug. 9am-7:30pm; Sept.-June Mon.-Sat. 9am-1pm and 2-6pm, Sun. 9am-12:30pm). To find **Camping Les Cigales** (tel. 04 42 01 07 34), take av. Agostina to av. Colbert, and then turn right onto av. de la Marne (15-20min.). 60F for 1 person with tent. 90F for 2 people with tent. Cars and campers allowed. Open March 15-November 15. Since the train station is 3km outside of town, it's simplest to take a bus to Cassis. Buses run frequently from Marseille (page 486). One block down the hill from the bus stop, turn right into the Jardin public. The tourist office is on your left as you leave the park.

St-Tropez

The 30m yachts with heartbreaker models dancing on their decks may make you wonder if you belong in this luxurious wonderland. The city was "made" in the 1960s, when Brigitte Bardot and her friends bared all on its beaches, but *St-Trop-d'Aise* (St-Too-Much-Luxury) still shines as a preferred pit-stop for flaunting fabulous wealth and freshly waxed Lamborghinis. It has also become a lively haven for the Côte d'Azur's best-dressed gay community. Although it supports enough exclusive restaurants and boutiques to fatigue even the mightiest of platinum cards, St-Tropez seems to be on intimate terms with everyone. Its manicured streets and hanging flowers create an elegant ambience that welcomes even the humblest of budgets to tan and carouse among the Bold and the Beautiful.

ORIENTATION AND PRACTICAL INFORMATION

The **tourist office,** between av. Général de Gaulle and av. Général Leclerc (tel. 04 94 97 65 53; fax 04 94 97 82 66), is well staffed and stocked with info on sights, buses, boats, and more. It has a free accommodations service (open in summer daily 10am-9pm; in winter 9am-5pm). The **branch office,** on quai Jean Jaurès (tel. 04 94 97 45 21), offers the same services (open daily 9:30am-1:30pm and 3:30-8:30pm). A **Thomas Cook** office is on 10, rue Allard (tel. 04 94 97 88 00; open daily May-Sept. 8:30am-10pm). This is St-Tropez—you'll have no problem finding **ATMs** at any hour. Reaching this self-proclaimed "jewel of the Riviera" requires some extra effort, as the town lies well off the rail line. Boats and buses make the trip from St-Raphaël; the boat is faster, more enjoyable, and not much more expensive than the bus (it's cheaper, in fact, if you have a voucher from the youth hostel in Fréjus). The **Gare Maritime de St-Raphaël** (tel. 04 94 95 17 46), at the *vieux port,* sends four to five boats per day to St-Tropez (50min.; 100F roundtrip, 80F with hostel reduction). You can also catch a ferry from Cannes (Tues., Thurs., and Sat.; leaves 9:30am, returns 6:30pm; 100F; call 04 93 39 11 82). **Sodetrav buses,** at the *gare routière* in St-Raphaël (tel. 04 94 95 24 82), go to and from the St-Tropez *gare routière,* av. Général Leclerc (tel. 04 94 97 88 51), across from the ferry (15 per day, 1½-2¼hr., 46F). Don't expect to hitch near St-Tropez; you'd soil the Porsche's upholstery, *dahling.* Rent your own wheels in other towns or from **Louis Mas,** 3-5, rue Quarenta (tel. 04 94 97 00 60), where **bikes** go for 48F per day (deposit 1000F), mountain bikes for 80F (deposit 2000F), and mopeds for 95-165F (deposit 2500-5000F). (Open daily Easter-Oct. 15 Mon.-Sat. 9am-7:30pm, Sun. 9am-1pm and 5-7:30pm.) The **police** are on rue François Sibilli (tel. 04 94 56 60 30), near the church, and the **hospital** (tel. 04 94 79 47 30) is on av. Foch, off pl. des Lices. The **post office** (tel. 04 94 54 86 65; open Mon.-Fri. 9am-5:30pm, Sat. 9am-noon) is on pl. A. Celli at the *nouveau port.*

ACCOMMODATIONS, CAMPING, AND FOOD

Budget hotels do not exist in St-Tropez, and by mid-June just about everywhere is booked solid. Call ahead or hope for the best at **Les Chimères,** quartier du Pilon (tel. 04 94 97 02 90). It's an airy, comfortable hotel with a garden terrace. (Singles 194-294F. Doubles 294-398F. Includes breakfast. V, MC.). **Camping** is by far the cheapest option, but again, make reservations. The tourist office will tell you which sites have space—few will in July and August. Try four-star **La Croix du Sud** (tel. 04 94 79 80 84; fax 04 94 79 89 21), route des Plages, in Ramatuelle (85F for 1 or 2 people; 120F for 3; open Easter-Sept.), or **Kon Tiki** (tel. 04 94 79 80 17; 113F per car, tent, and 2 people). Both are behind the Pampelonne beach. Camping on the beach is strictly (and actively) prohibited. The closest **hostel** is in Fréjus (see page 480).

The *vieux port* and the narrow streets of the hillside *vieille ville* behind the waterfront are the hubs of St-Tropez's restaurant and café culture. Recline at **Café Senequier,** quai Jean Jaurès, next to the tourist office, and watch the spectacle of yachts, artists, glitz, and gaping tourists. **Au Regalé,** 12, rue du Colonel Guichard (tel. 04 94 97 16 18), next to the Eglise Paroissiale, serves pasta, roast chicken, and *keufte riz* *pilaf* (a Greek specialty) on its 49F *menu* (open daily noon-2:30pm and 7-11pm). If you prefer to create your own ambience, head to the fabulous **grand marché** on pl. des Lices (open daily 5am-2pm) or **Prisunic supermarket,** 7, av. du Général Leclerc (tel. 04 94 97 07 94; open Mon.-Sat. 8am-8pm; in summer also Sun. 9am-1pm and 5-9pm). Great picnic spots lounge along the water only 10 minutes from the *vieux port.* Follow chemin des Graniers to the small, uncrowded **plage des Graniers.** At the beachside **Les Graniers** (tel. 04 94 97 38 50) restaurant and bar, barefoot waitrons serve tables planted in the sand. If you choose to arrive by boat, drop anchor and wait for the restaurant's motorboat to whisk you ashore. Of course, this decadence will cost you; stick to the 14F espresso (open daily 11am-9pm). A small public path continues past the beach, snaking between the shore and villas. Choose a cove and bask *au naturel*—in St-Tropez, tan-lines are a distinct *faux-pas.*

SIGHTS AND ENTERTAINMENT

St-Tropez, unlike Cannes, has a history longer than the shadows cast by its beach umbrellas. In AD 64, Torpes, a Roman noble, defied Nero and refused to renounce his Christian faith. The emperor had the prince beaten, decapitated, and banished to sea, with a dog and a fighting cock to finish him off. A few days later, the three landed in a tiny fishing village whose inhabitants erected a chapel over what remained of poor old Torpes. Every May 16 to18, St-Tropez celebrates the saint's arrival with **Les Bravades,** three intense days of costumed parades bullets flying through the air. The spectacle is comically repeated in summer, with two intense months of strangely dressed foreigners parading the streets and firing cameras at yachts and monuments. St-Tropez's gorgeous *vieille ville,* assortment of stone ruins, and six miles of beaches justify the annual invasion.

To reach the **beaches,** catch a Sodetrav bus (see page 477) on line "St-Tropez-Ramatuelle" (3 per day, Mon.-Sat., 9F) to: **plage Tahiti,** which has the most wealth; **plage des Salins,** the most public space; and **plage de Pampelonne,** the most sand (all 10min.). Great swimming and good rock climbing await at **plage de l'Escalet,** 15km away; buses head there twice daily (25min, 10F).

Although St-Tropez's 16th-century **citadel,** much of which has been renovated with stucco and cement, will offend purists, it offers a helmsman's view of the Gulf, a troop of screaming peacocks, and the **Musée Naval** (tel. 04 94 97 59 43), which displays a small collection of anchors and buoys from the waterfront's less glamorous days. (Both open Wed.-Mon. 10am-6pm (both close at 5pm in winter). Admission 22F, students 11F.) See the sea along footpaths surrounding the citadel. The hillside paths dazzle with wildflowers in red, yellow, white, and violet. For more brilliant colors, the two-story **Musée de l'Annociade,** pl. Grammont (tel. 04 94 97 04 01), exhibits a wild collection of Fauvist and neo-Impressionist paintings (open Wed.-Mon. 10am-noon and 3-7pm; admission 22F, students 11F).

The city shows off that St-Tropez tan at night. Dance 'til dawn with the mixed crowd at **Le Pigeonnier,** 13, rue de la Ponche (tel. 04 94 97 36 85; 80F cover includes first drink, others are 70F a pop; open daily 11pm-dawn). **Chez Maggy,** 7, rue Sybille (tel. 04 94 97 16 12), caters to an anglophone crowd with live music and 25-30F drafts. **L'Atelier,** 3, bd. de l'Aumale (tel. 04 94 97 17 24), offers 40F beers and too-chic atmosphere to a dressed-to-impress crowd (open April-Oct. 9pm-2am).

■ Near St-Tropez: Port Grimaud

Hidden in the rocky coastline and chalky white *calanques* between St-Tropez and St-Raphaël, Port Grimaud tastes of sea-salt and smells of money. In the early 1960s, architect François Spoerry designed his dream world, a luxury complex disguised as a Mediterranean fishing village, where there's a boat on every doorstep. The development sent the sea flowing into canals dug throughout town. Its *faux provençal* **church** boasts stained glass by Hungarian op-artist Victor Vasarely. Boats have replaced cars, which must be left outside the town, and celebrities have replaced natives. But with no roads and no parking lots, the **beaches** remain long and uninterrupted—the most beautiful (and most popular) run along rue Grande.

Hotels are quite expensive, but there are several **campgrounds** just outside town, including the out-of-control, 1400-site **Les Prairies de la Mer** (tel. 04 94 79 09 09) at St-Pons les Mûres, equipped with a mini-market, restaurant, bar, tennis courts, hot showers, and a TV room (103F for 1 or 2 people, extra person 26F, electricity 23F; open April-Oct.; V, MC). Port Grimaud is accessible from St-Tropez by **ferry** in July and August (tel. 04 94 96 51 00; 10 per day, roundtrip 50F). Another ferry (tel. 04 94 95 17 46) cruises from St-Raphaël Saturday at 1:30pm (40min., roundtrip with a free tour of the canals 120F). Port Grimaud is on the St-Raphaël-St-Tropez **bus** line. (From St-Raphaël, 6 per day, 1hr., 36F. From St-Tropez, 4 per day, 20min., 10F.) A bus also stops daily at St-Pons (8F), in the outskirts of Port Grimaud. The **tourist office** is located up the hill in the medieval village of Grimaud proper (in summer there is an **annex** on St-Pons as well). Call 04 94 43 26 98 (or fax 04 94 43 32 40) for more info.

St-Raphaël and Fréjus

Founded by Julius Caesar in 49 BC, Fréjus and its twin city St-Raphaël twinkle with a Riviera brilliance that is more historically interesting and affordable than that of their exclusive neighbors. The towns boast all the wide, sandy beaches, seafood restaurants, and coastal charm of their swanky Côte d'Azur cousins at half the price. Add relatively inexpensive accommodations, Roman amphitheaters, unique museums, and eclectic religious monuments to their prime real estate, and St-Raphaël and Fréjus become the ideal choice for travelers who want to stretch a budget into as much suntime as possible but don't mind heading elsewhere for nocturnal revelry.

ORIENTATION AND PRACTICAL INFORMATION

St-Raphaël is a major stop on the coastal train line. Fréjus, to the west (the towns' centers are 4km apart), is a rapidly developing town dotted with Roman ruins, a Cocteau chapel, a mosque, a pagoda, and a fleet of supermarkets. The sights and the hostel in Fréjus are connected to the restaurants and hotels in St-Raphaël by regular bus service, but be forewarned—buses stop around 7pm.

Tourist Offices: In **St-Raphaël,** across the street from the train station on rue Waldeck Rousseau (tel. 04 94 19 52 52; fax 04 94 83 85 40). It has the scoop on transportation and room availability, as well as free maps. Open July-Aug. daily 8am-7pm; Sept.-June Mon.-Sat. 9am-noon and 2-7pm. **Annex** on the beach (tel. 04 94 82 21 50) open Mon.-Sat. 2-10pm. In **Fréjus,** 325, rue Jean Jaurès (tel. 04 94 17 19 19; fax 04 94 51 0026), next to the fountain in pl. Paul Vernet. Free maps and hotel reservations, piles of brochures, and *more.* Runs tours of the town (in English, 15F). Take bus 6 from St-Raphaël to "pl. Paul Vernet" (6F50). Open July-Aug. Mon.-Fri. 9am-7pm, Sat.-Sun. 9am-noon and 2:30-7pm; Sept. daily 9am-noon and 2-6pm. Office will be moving to av. de Verdun, near the train station, in '97.

Money: No commission at **Cambio Wechsel,** Centre Commercial de la Gare (tel. 04 94 95 67 91; open Mon.-Sat. 9am-12:30pm and 2:30-7pm), to the left of the station. For **ATMs** in St-Raphaël, look around the Monoprix on bd. Félix Martin and Rue Admiral Baux; in Fréjus, try **Caisse d'Epargne,** 206, rue Jean Jaurès, near the tourist office. Both towns' post offices have **ATMs.**

Boats: Les Bateaux de St-Raphaël, at the *vieux port* (tel. 04 94 95 17 46; fax 04 94 83 88 55), cruises to St-Tropez 4-5 times per day in summer (50min., roundtrip 100F). If you are staying at the hostel in Fréjus, ask about ticket reductions.

Trains in St-Raphaël: pl. de la Gare (tel. 08 36 35 35 35). St-Raphaël has connections approximately every 30min. to Cannes (25min., 35F) and Nice (1hr., 58F). The info office (open Mon.-Sat. 8am-7:30pm) has schedules. **Lockers** 15-20F per 72hr. Station open daily 5:30am-11:30pm. **In Fréjus:** rue Martin Bidoure (tel. 04 94 82 16 92). Occasional connections to St-Raphaël (3-4 per day, 8F); Nice (55F); Cannes (32F). Ticket office open daily 8:15am-3:30pm and 4-8:30pm.

Buses: The *gare routière,* in St-Raphaël behind the train station (take the escalator to the walkway over the tracks), is a hub for both local and inter-city travel. **Esterel** (tel. 04 94 53 78 46) runs between St-Raphaël and Fréjus every 30min. from quai 7 (6F50; Mon.-Sat. 7:30am-7pm, Sun. 7am-6pm). **Sodetrav** (tel. 04 94 95 24 82) connects St-Raphaël to St-Tropez (15 per day, 1½hr., 46F). **Forum Cars** (tel. 04 94 95 16 71) makes the scenic trip between St-Raphaël and Cannes with a fantastic view of the *calanques* (8 per day, 70min., 32F50).

Taxis: (tel. 04 94 95 04 25), at the train station.

Police: In St-Raphaël, rue Amiral Baux (tel. 04 94 95 24 24), off the *vieux port.* In Fréjus, av. Einaudi (tel. 04 94 51 90 00). **Emergency** tel. 17.

Post Offices: In **St-Raphaël,** av. Victor Hugo (tel. 04 94 19 52 00), behind the train station. Photocopier, poste restante. **ATM. Postal code:** 83700. Open Mon.-Fri. 8:30am-6:30pm, Sat. 8:30am-noon. In **Fréjus,** av. Aristide Briand (tel. 04 94 17 60 80), just down the hill from the tourist office. Same sorta stuff. **Postal code:** 83600. Open Mon.-Fri. 8:30am-6:30pm, Sat. 8:30am-noon.

ACCOMMODATIONS AND CAMPING

Be sure to book ahead. Most of the inexpensive options are in St-Raphaël, although the youth hostel in Fréjus is a notable exception.

Auberge de Jeunesse de St-Raphaël-Fréjus (HI), chemin du Counillier (tel. 04 94 53 18 75; fax 04 94 53 25 86), 4km from St-Raphaël station. A shuttle bus runs from quai 7 (6F50) of the *gare routière* to the hostel at 6pm; a return shuttle leaves at 8:30am and 6 and 7pm. If you miss the shuttle, take regular buses (every hr. 7:30-11:30am and 2-8pm) and get off at Les Chênes at quai 7. Walk up av. Jean Callies to chemin du Counillier; the hostel is at the top of the unpaved road. 4- to 8- person single-sex rooms, kind managers, restful view of the inland wine valley. 64F. Breakfast included. Hearty dinner 48F. Sheets 16F. Kitchen. Valuables storage. Lockout 10am-6pm. Curfew 11pm. Ask about reductions on bike rentals, tickets for the boat to St-Tropez, and excursions. Rooms for 4-6 people in brand-new *chatelet* with more modern facilities (81F per person).

Centre International du Manoir (tel. 04 94 95 20 58; fax 04 94 83 85 06), in Boulouris. Plush ocean-side site 5km from St-Raphaël. Accessible from the Boulouris train station, 1 stop from St-Raphaël on the line to Cannes. Bus from *gare routière* makes the trip every 30min. until 6:30pm (6F). Comfortable dorms in the annex. Lively bar and a disco. 75-160F in room with 6 beds, 115-220F in room with 2 or 3 beds. Singles 50F more. Breakfast included. Meals 65F. Reception until 8pm.

Hôtel Bellevue, pl. Paul Vernet (tel. 04 94 51 39 04; fax 04 94 51 35 20), in Fréjus, next to rue Reynaude, at the opposite end of the place from the bus stop. Great location in center of town. Pinball machine and foosball. Compact but clean rooms with telephone and TV. Doubles 149F, with shower 230F, with shower and toilet 280F. Breakfast 30F. V, MC.

Hôtel des Pyramides, 77, av. Paul Doumer (tel. 04 94 95 05 95, fax 04 94 19 48 39), in St-Raphaël. Clean, comfy rooms just off the beach, but near train tracks which grumble at night. Singles 130F. Doubles 175-220F. Breakfast 30F. V, MC.

Le Mistral, 80, rue de la Garonne (tel. 04 94 95 38 82). Clean, modest rooms steps from the beach. Lower prices for longer stays and *Let's Go*-ers. Singles 120F-170F. Doubles 150-260F. Triples 210-330F. Quads 240-360F. Breakfast 28F. V, MC.

La Bonne Auberge, 54, rue de la Garonne (tel. 04 94 95 69 72), in St-Raphaël. Close to the train station. Simple rooms sometimes lack basic amenities, but the prices are always nice. Singles 130-170F. Doubles 120-170F, with toilet and shower 200F. Triples 70F per person. Breakfast 25F. Open March-Oct.

Camping: At the youth hostel, in an attractive wooded area. 30F per person with tent. Hot showers free. Also **Royal Camping,** on Camp-Long (tel. 04 94 82 00 20), along bus route to Cannes from St-Raphaël. Perks include hot showers, supermarket, and restaurant. 1-3 people and car 125F. Open mid-March to Oct.

RIVIERA

FOOD

Affordable restaurants center around the *vieux port* and bd. de la Libération in St-Raphaël, and around pl. de la Liberté in Fréjus. If you're planning a picnic, try the **Super Rallye supermarket,** 168, av. André Léotard (tel. 04 94 51 47 30; open Mon.-Sat. 8:30am-8pm, Sun. 8:30am-12:30pm), at the bottom of the hill near the hostel; or try the **Monoprix** on bd. de Félix Martin (tel. 04 94 95 01 69; open Sept.-June daily 8:30am-7:30pm; July 4-Aug. 27 8:30am-8:30pm), off av. Alphonse Karr near the St-Raphaël train station. A **morning market** brings color to pl. Victor Hugo, down the hill from the *gare routière* (Tues.-Sun. 7am-12:30pm). The **Marché Provençal** decorates Fréjus' rue de Fleury and pl. Formige on Wednesday and Saturday mornings.

Le Mistral, 80, rue de la Garonne (tel. 04 94 95 38 82), offers 60F and 75F *menus* with *paella* and couscous (open daily noon-7pm and 6-10pm). **Restaurant La Grillade,** 32, rue Boëtman (tel. 04 94 95 15 16), serves *brochettes d'agneau* (lamb, 65F) and a 78F seafood *menu.* Pizzas run 36-55F (open Mon.-Fri. and Sun. noon-2:30pm and 7-10:30pm, Sat. 7-10:30pm; V, MC). **Le Hanoi II,** 160, rue de la Garonne (tel. 04 94 95 24 51; open daily 6-11pm, closed Thurs. in winter; V, MC, AmEx), specializes in Asian cuisine. Try the *boeuf aux champignons parfumés* (beef and mushrooms, 49F) or the *poulet citronelle gingembre* (chicken with ginger and lemon, 48F).

SIGHTS AND ENTERTAINMENT

Fréjus sports historical monuments from its heyday as an important Roman stronghold. The amphitheater and aqueduct of Forum-Julii, as the town was called in the days of Julius Caesar, are accessible on foot from the *vieille ville.* The distances between sights in the newer parts of town make buses an appealing option.

Fréjus has served as a military base since the Romans set up camp two thousand years ago. Built in the first and second centuries, the city's **Roman amphitheater,** rue Henri Vadon (tel. 04 94 17 05 60), was constructed to entertain rowdy soldiers looking for a home away from Rome. It is free of the elaborate embellishments of the theaters in Nîmes or Orange, which were designed to appeal to more discerning patrician eyes. Recently renovated by the city, the former wrestling ground for gladiators and lions is now the site of bullfights and rock concerts (amphitheater open April-Sept. Wed.-Mon. 9:30am-noon and 2-6:30pm; Oct.-March Wed.-Mon. 9am-noon and 2-4:30pm; free). For info on the events, call the tourist office.

Fréjus displays a remarkably eclectic assemblage of religious architecture from medieval Christian, Buddhist, Muslim, and avant-garde sects. The **Groupe Episcopal de Fréjus,** pl. J. C. Formige (tel. 04 94 51 26 30), off rue de Fleury in the *centre ville,* comprises a 5th-century baptistry, a 12th-century cloister (the wood ceilings are painted with hundreds of miniature beasts and figures depicting the Apocalypse), and an 11th- to 13th-century cathedral (cathedral open daily 9am-noon and 4-6pm; office open Oct.-March Wed.-Mon. 9am-noon and 2-5pm; April-Sept. daily 9am-5pm; tours 22F, students 14F). The **Pagode Hong-Hiên,** 13, rue H. Giraud (tel. 04 94 53 25 29), 10 minutes up av. Jean Callies from the hostel, was built in 1919 to honor Vietnamese soldiers based at Fréjus who died defending France in World War I. The Buddhist temple, built in Tibetan style, still functions as a spiritual center (open daily 9am-noon and 3-6:30pm). The **Mosquée Soudanaise** (or **Mosqueé Missiri de Djenné**), route de Bagnol, serves the area's Muslim community. Modeled after the Grand Mosque in Djenne, Mali, it stands 2km from the *centre ville.* Fréjus' most famous religious edifice is a round chapel designed by film director and *"Prince des Poètes,"* Jean Cocteau. The **Cocteau Chapel,** av. Nicola (tel. 04 94 40 76 30; open April-Sept. Wed.-Mon. 2-6pm; Oct.-March 2-5pm), the artist's last chapel, was built in 1965. Bus 3 from "Les Chênes" in Fréjus runs here every other hour.

The elegant 19th-century **Villa Aurelienne,** av. du Général d' Aimée Calliès (tel. 04 94 53 11 30), on the hill next to the hostel, houses a museum and cultural center. Nearby, a conspicuous remnant of Fréjus' ancient **aqueduct** lines the av. du XVème Corps and disappears underground along the path leading to the hostel. The villa's 20-hectare park hosts photography expositions, a three-day flower extravaganza at the beginning of April known as the **Fête des Plantes,** and a four-day contemporary art exhibit, the **Art Tendence Sud.** An oft-reproduced Greco-Roman double-bust of Hermes, discovered in Fréjus in 1970, has become the town's symbol and normally stares two-facedly at villa visitors, but the Louvre has claimed it for an indefinite period of time. (Villa open in season Tues.-Sun. 2-7pm; off-season Tues.-Sat. 2-6pm.)

Bake in the sun on sandy **plage Fréjus,** a 10-minute walk along the waterfront from the St-Raphaël train station (turn right when you hit the port), or make a splash at Fréjus' water park, **Aquatica,** RN98 (tel. 04 94 53 58 58). It's accessible on the Esterel bus from the *gare routière* in St-Raphaël, just beyond the Casino supermarket. This watery wonderland features eight water slides and the largest wave pool in Europe (open daily July-Aug. 10am-7pm; June and Sept. 10am-6pm; admission 98F).

For free wine tasting, visit the **Château de Cabran** on route de Bagnols in nearby Puget-sur-Argens (tel. 04 94 40 80 32), a vineyard that produces light rosés. The hostel in Fréjus organizes visits (open Mon.-Sat. 10am-noon and 2-7pm).

The first weekend in July is the **Competition Internationale de Jazz New Orleans** in St-Raphaël. Hundreds of musicians face off in the streets and around the port—and it's free (call the tourist office in St-Raphaël for more info).

Cannes

Cannes isn't just the sister city of Beverly Hills, she's her twin. One of the brightest stars on the Riviera, Cannes scintillates with flashy cars, flashy people, and that sandy beach that you—and thousands of other bronzing beauties—have been combing for on the stony Riviera. Even millionaires give their wallets a work-out in Cannes' swank cafés, plush hotels, cozy *coutouriers,* and palm-lined boardwalk.

Lord Brogham, of horse-and-carriage fame, made Cannes fashionable in 1836 when an outbreak of cholera forced him to rest *en route* to Nice. He stopped for a few days in a tiny fishing village just west of the city and decided to stay. Brogham's aristocratic friends came over to keep him company, and the rest is revelry.

Cannes (pop. 78,000) is still a favorite stop for the international jet-set, especially in May, when the **Festival International du Film** brings Hollywood's *crème de la crème* across the seas. Executives sign deals for $50-million flops on cocktail napkins while heartthrobs and starlets stand by, waiting to be taken seriously. Not one of the festival's 350 screenings is open to the public, but the sidewalk circus is absolutely free. On July 4 and 14, you'll have to look up to see the stars at Cannes' annual **Fête Americaine** and **Fête Nationale**—fireworks burst overhead and spirits run high as the whole city takes to the streets. Less reclusive than St-Tropez, Cannes allows even the unshaven budget traveler to tan like the stars without spending a dime. You may be shockingly underdressed, but Giorgio and Calvin will forgive you.

ORIENTATION AND PRACTICAL INFORMATION

Nouveau Cannes, between the station and the sea, with rue d'Antibes running through its center, is the city's shopping hub. Heading right from the station on rue Jean Jaurès leads to the pedestrian district and *vieux* Cannes, also known as **le Suquet,** where cheap eats lurk on rue Meynadier, rue St-Antoine, and rue du Suquet. Eager star-gazers and those seeking the **tourist office** should follow rue des Serbes (across from the station) to **bd. de la Croisette,** Cannes' long and lavish promenade alongside the coast. The tourist office is in the huge Palais des Festivals on the right.

Most of Cannes' daytime activity (and spending) pulses between rue Félix-Faure and the waterfront. Cafés, shops, *grandes dames,* and poodles line this oh-so-chic quarter of town. Stroll down lovely rue Meynadier—one of Cannes' few pedestrian streets—or down the boardwalk along bd. de la Croisette and the beach. Sandy public beaches are sandwiched between parasol-studded private ones, both of which are dotted with docks burdened by multi-million dollar yachts.

Tourist Office, 1, bd. de la Croisette (tel. 04 93 39 24 53; fax 04 92 99 84 23). Loads of info and a free accommodations service. Open July-Aug. daily 9am-8pm; Sept.-

June Mon.-Sat. 9am-6:30pm. Long hours during festivals. **Branch office,** 1, rue Jean-Jaurès (tel. 04 93 99 19 77), in the station, has similar services. Open July 4-Sept. 4 Mon.-Sat. 8:30am-6:30pm; Sept.-June daily 9am-1pm and 2-6pm.

Money: Office Provençal, 17, rue Maréchal-Foch (tel. 04 93 39 34 37), across from the train station **exchanges currency.** Open daily 8am-8pm. **Crédit Agricole,** 83, rue d'Antibes, has a 24-hr. **ATM** jammin' to the groove.

American Express, 8, rue des Belges (tel. 04 93 38 15 87; fax 04 92 98 01 01), off bd. de la Croisette. Open Mon.-Fri. 9am-noon and 2-6pm, Sat. 9am-noon.

AirFrance: 2, pl. du Général de Gaulle (tel. 04 93 39 39 14; fax 04 92 98 91 74). Open Mon.-Fri. 9am-12:15pm and 1:30-5:45pm.

Trains: 1, rue Jean-Jaurès (tel. 08 36 35 35 35). Cannes lies on the major coastal line, with connections approximately every 30min. (6am-midnight) to: St-Raphaël (25min., 32F); Juan-les-Pins (10min., 11F); Antibes (15min., 13F); Nice (35min., 30F); Monaco (50min., 44F); Menton (1hr., 48F). Also hourly trains (6:30am-11:05pm) to Marseille (2hr., 127F). TGV to Paris via Marseille (440F). Info desk open daily 8:30am-5:40pm. Ticket sales 6am-11pm. **Lockers** 20-30F.

Buses: Buz Azur (tel. 04 93 39 18 71). Info and departure from the *gare routière* on pl. de l'Hôtel de Ville. Open Mon.-Sat. 7am-7pm. To: Nice airport (every hr. 6am-7pm, 45min., 70F). Every 20min. to Antibes (30min., 17F) and Nice (1½hr., 28F). Also to St-Raphaël (8 per day, 70min., 32F) and Grasse (every ½hr., 45min., 16F). Buses also leave from the *gare routière* at the train station (tel. 04 93 39 11 39 or 04 93 39 31 37) for Grasse, Fayence, Vallauris, and Valbonne.

Local buses: Tickets 7F; *carnet* of 10 48F50. Weekly pass 52F50.

Taxis: Allô Taxis Cannes (tel. 04 92 99 27 27). Also in front of the train station.

Bike Rental: Holiday Bikes, 16, rue du 14 Juillet (tel. 04 93 94 61 00). Bikes 60-80F per 24hr. Mopeds 120F per 24hr. Scooters from 150F per 24hr. Deposits start at 1000F. Helmet included. Open daily 9am-12:30pm and 3-7pm. V, MC, AmEx.

English Bookstore: Cannes English Bookshop, 11, rue Bivouac-Napoléon (tel. 04 93 99 40 08), 1 block from Palais des Festivals. Mysteries, fiction, and cheap postcards. Open Mon.-Sat. 9:30am-1pm and 2-7pm. V, MC, AmEx.

Youth Center: Cannes Information Jeunesse, 5, quai St-Pierre (tel. 04 93 06 31 31). Info on housing, jobs, and more. Open Mon.-Fri. 9am-12:30pm and 2-6pm.

Laundromat: Lav'Azur, av. Latour-Maubourg. Open daily 7am-9pm.

Crisis Line: SOS Amité (tel. 04 93 26 26 26), for funky French friendship.

Hospitals: Pierre Nouveau, 13, av. des Broussailles (tel. 04 93 69 70 00). **Sunny Bank Anglo-American Hospital,** 133, av. du Petit Juas (tel. 04 93 06 31 06). **Medical emergency** tel. 15 or 04 93 99 12 12. English spoken.

Police: 2 quai St-Pierre (tel. 04 93 47 56 02). **Emergency** tel. 17.

Post Office: 22, rue Bivouac Napoléon (tel. 04 93 06 26 50), off allée de Liberté near Palais des Festivals. Open Mon.-Fri. 8am-7pm, Sat. 8am-noon. **Branch office** at 37, rue Mimont (tel. 04 93 06 27 00). Open Mon.-Fri. 8:30am-noon and 1:30-5pm, Sat. 8am-noon. Both have poste restante. **Postal code:** 06400.

ACCOMMODATIONS AND CAMPING

With the installation of two youth hostels, Cannes has made itself more accessible to the budget traveler. Bargains also lurk near the train station, though the area is less than safe at night. In summer and during the film festival you must definitely book ahead with a deposit. Prices drop dramatically when the summer crowds leave.

Auberge de Jeunesse de Cannes, 36, av. de Vallauris (tel. and fax 04 93 99 26 79). Take the stairs that lead to a passageway under the station. Then follow the signs to the *auberge* (10min.). Brand-spanking-new hostel with terrific English-speaking managers and near-central location. Great atmosphere, cool people, big, comfy beds in 6-bed coed dorms. 80F. Sheets 10F. Laundry: 25F wash, 20F to dry. Kitchens, TV. Office open 8am-noon and 2:30-10:30pm.

Centre d'Hébergement Le Châlit, 27, av. Maréchal Galliéni (tel. 04 93 99 22 11; fax 04 93 39 00 28). Friendly hosts and cozy quarters just 5min. from the train station (same directions as for other hostel, different signs). 31 big beds in 3-8-person rooms. Kitchens, TV. 80F. Sheets 15F. Lockout 11am-5pm. Ask for the door code if you'll be out late (no curfew). Reception 8:30am-9:30pm.

Hôtel Mimont, 39, rue de Mimont (tel. 04 93 39 51 64; fax 04 93 39 51 64), behind train station next to av. de la République. Large, clean rooms, all with telephones, showers, and toilets. Singles 140-180F, doubles 180-200F. V, MC, AmEx.

Hôtel du Nord, 6, rue Jean-Jaurès (tel. 04 93 38 48 79; fax 04 92 99 28 20), across from station. Clean, bright rooms with new bathrooms, TVs, and phones. Owner speaks English and gives advice on exploring the city. Singles and doubles 150-240F. Triples 270-360F. Breakfast 20-30F. Open Dec.-Oct. V, MC.

Hôtel de Bourgogne, 11, rue du 24 Août (tel. 04 93 38 36 73; fax 04 92 99 28 41), on a small street off rue Jean-Jaurès. Central location. Spotless rooms with carpeting and phones, some with TV. TV room. Singles 140-180F. Doubles 160-210F. Triples with shower 250F. Breakfast 25F. V, MC, AmEx.

Hôtel Chanteclair, 12, rue Forville (tel. and fax 04 93 39 68 88), 10min. to the right of the station. Scenic location in the *vieille ville.* Modern rooms with firm beds overlook a courtyard. Owners loan beach mats and sell cheap drinks. Singles 130F (170F in summer), with shower 200F. Doubles 150F (210F in summer), with shower 250F. Triples with shower 330F. Quad with shower 400F. (Prices 50-100F lower off-season.) Breakfast 20F. Reception 'til 7:30pm; call ahead and they'll stay up later for you. No credit cards accepted.

Camping: Le Grand Saule, 24, bd. Jean Moulin (tel. 04 93 90 55 10; fax 04 93 47 24 55), in nearby Ranguin. Take bus 9 from pl. de l'Hôtel de Ville toward Grasse (7F). 3-star site with pool, showers, and laundry. 70F per person, 124F for 2 people and tent. Open April-Oct. V, MC. **Caravaning Bellevue,** 67, av. M. Chevalier (tel. 04 93 47 28 97; fax 04 93 48 66 25). Take the train to Cannes-La Bocca. 211 spaces. 50F per person, tent included. 2 people with tent 80F. Open in summer.

FOOD

Morning markets do the fresh food thing on the *place* between rue Mimont and av. de la République (daily 7am-noon). Other supplies await at **Monoprix supermarket,** 9, rue Maréchal Foch, across from the station (open Mon.-Sat. 8:30am-8:30pm) or **Champion,** 6, rue Meynadier (open Mon.-Sat. 7:45am-7:45pm). The **Casino supermarket,** 55, bd. d'Alsace, has a better selection but higher prices (open daily 8:30am-8pm); and the **cafeteria** upstairs is good for a quick bite (dishes 15-50F; open daily 11am-10pm). The cool shade and breezes filtering through palm-tree-filled **Jardin de la Croisette** render it the perfect picnic spot.

Le Lion d'Or, 45, bd. de la République (tel. 04 93 38 56 57), serves excellent *provençal* cuisine, with super service and an unbeatable three-course 67F *menu.* Try the hearty *soupe de poissons* (open Sun.-Fri. noon-2pm and 7-9:30pm). On a street across from the Champion supermarket, **Restaurant des Artistes,** 5, rue Rouguière (tel. 04 93 39 09 02; open Mon.-Sat. 11:30am-midnight), produces 25F pizzas, 40F *plats,* and the *pièce de résistance*—a 48F *formule des artistes* (main dish and dessert), as well as a 60F (3-course) *menu des artistes.* Right next door, **Les Twins** has all-you-can-eat specials for 50F and a 60F *menu* of pastas and *provençal* fare.

SIGHTS AND ENTERTAINMENT

Blessed with streets and streets of designer boutiques, Cannes has the best window-shopping around. **Rue d'Antibes,** running parallel to the sea, and **bd. de la Croisette,** passing right along the shore, front high-priced displays sporting familiar names—Christian Dior, Hermès, and Gianni Versace. Renounce worldly goods and head west, where the **Castre Cathédrale** and its courtyard stand on the hill on which *vieux* Cannes was built. The tranquil shade of Mediterranean pines and the striking view of Cannes and the Iles de Lérins provide a soothing alternative to the jarring car horns and cement lawns below. Housed in the church, the **Musée de la Castre** (tel. 04 93 38 55 26) exhibits weapons, masks, and instruments from Peru to Timbuktu (open July-Sept. Wed.-Mon. 10am-noon and 3-7pm; Oct. 10am-noon and 2-5pm; April-June 10am-noon and 2-6pm; admission 10F, students free).

Should you tire of indulging in the French national pastime of eyeing passers-by, try a more expensive option—one of Cannes' three casinos. The most accessible, **Le**

Casino Croisette, 1, jetée Albert Edouard (tel. 04 93 38 12 11), next to the Palais des Festivals, has slot machines, blackjack, roulette, and French roulette. (Gambling daily 5pm-4am, open for slots at 10am. No shorts. Ages 18 and over only.) If your luck has soured and you've still got some cash left, take to the clubs (but be prepared to feel under-dressed). **Opéra,** rue Lecerf, is a local favorite that opens at 11:30pm. From 11pm until dawn, dance at **Jane's,** 38, rue des Serbes (tel. 04 92 99 79 59), in the Hôtel Gray d'Albion (cover and first drink 120F, 70F for next drink). **3 Cloches,** 6, rue Vidal (tel. 04 93 68 32 92), is a bar/*discothèque* that caters to the gay community. (70F cover includes first drink. Bar opens at 11pm, disco at midnight.) If you break into a cold sweat over prices at the clubs, enjoy the less expensive and less formal entertainment at the pubs and piano bars within blocks of the waterfront. Try **Kylian's Pub,** 8, rue des Frères Pradignac (tel. 04 93 68 40 00), for drinkin' and dancin' (15F *demi-pressions,* 20F cover; open nightly 9:30pm-2:30am). **Carling's Pub,** 7, rue Clémenceau (tel. 04 93 38 34 06), near the port, has a slightly older, less excited clientele and occasional live music (open daily 7pm-2:30am).

■ Near Cannes

Both **Iles de Lérins** provide a welcome respite from fast-paced Cannes. The smaller island, **St-Honorat,** harbors pine forests and an active monastery, the **Abbaye de Lérins.** Trying to escape the visitors that continually bothered him in his coastal grotto, St. Honorat settled on this secluded isle in the 10th century. The order of monks he founded still works the land, but the saint's attempted getaway has been futile. In high season and on weekends, tourists invade the island's gravel paths and the monastery's gift shop, which sells homemade honey and alcohol. On off-days, however, the islet is an isolated paradise, scattered with ancient chapels and serenaded by a host of chattering birds. On the southeast corner of the island, the original monastery stands broken and deserted, full of rooms to be explored (abbey open daily 9am-6pm; free). The isle's only restaurant serves 20F sandwiches and 15F drinks—bring a picnic. Four times the size of its neighbor, **Ste-Marguerite** hosts twice as many visitors but manages to preserve lusher forests. The island was once home to St. Honorat's sister—you guessed it—Ste. Marguerite. The massive, star-shaped **Fort Vauban** is now a national monument. The beaches on the far shore are cleaner and less rocky than those facing the coast. Seventeen **boats** leave daily between 7:30am and 6pm from the *gare maritime des îles* (tel. 04 93 39 11 82), across from the Cannes tourist office on bd. de la Croisette (St-Honorat 30min., roundtrip 50F; Ste-Marguerite 15min., roundtrip 45F; circuit of both islands 70F).

On a hill 8km from Cannes, **Mougins** hides peaceful streets behind its old fortified walls. Picasso came here in 1924 to find inspiration. The Cannes-Grasse bus stops at Val du Mougins (every 30min., 20min., 8F50); from there it's a pleasant half-hour climb past gracious villas to the *vieille ville.* Once there, you'll probably walk in circles—the town is arranged in concentric rings. Near Mougins' center, the monastery bell tower enjoys a view of the snowy Alps (open July-Aug. daily 2-7pm). The cheapest *menus* in town hover at 150F—a *baguette* might be in order. For more information, call the tourist office (tel. 04 93 75 87 67).

Vallauris, a few km inland and east of Cannes, has long been known as the pottery capital of France. Picasso was entranced by the town's ceramics and worked here shortly after World War II. Meander over to the **Musée National de Picasso,** pl. de la Libération (tel. 04 93 64 16 05), in the 13th-century chapel of a château. It holds the master's *War and Peace* (open Wed.-Mon. 10am-noon and 2-6pm; admission 13F, students 6F50). Many galleries sell mass-produced, low-quality wares, but there are gems to be found. The galleries M. Musarra, Siffre di Sculpteur, and Les 3 Flammes on rue Clemenceau all show original work.

To reach Vallauris, take a bus from Cannes (near the train station or the pl. de l'Hôtel de Ville; every hr. 8am-7:30pm, 40min., 12F) or Antibes (5 per day). Following av. Clemenceau from the *gare routière,* head to the **tourist office,** sq. du 8 Mai 1945

RIVIERA

(tel. 04 93 63 82 58; fax 04 93 63 95 01; open daily 9am-7pm), for info about Vallauris' biannual exhibition of ceramics and modern art from over 30 countries.

Grasse

The air smells better in Grasse, the world's center for perfume manufacturing and home to three of France's largest, oldest, and most distinguished *parfumeries.* This aromatic town was best known for its hide tanning until the end of the 18th century, when its climate was discovered to be ideal for the cultivation of jasmine, rose, lavender, and other floral perfume stand-bys. But Grasse tempts more than just your nose—near the **GR4** hiking trail, the town serves as a springboard for exploration into the Alpes-Maritimes and local prehistoric caves. Whether you spend your time touring the *parfumeries* or the fragrant countryside, Grasse is a treat for the senses.

ORIENTATION AND PRACTICAL INFORMATION

Although Grasse spreads into the valley below, most sights, hotels, and restaurants are concentrated on the southward-facing hillside. The *gare routière,* pl. de la Buanderie (tel. 04 93 36 37 37), welcomes buses daily from Cannes (every 30min., 45min., 19F50) and from Nice (10 per day, 1½hr., 35F). Call **SOMA** (tel. 04 92 93 88 88) or **RCA** (tel. 04 93 55 24 00) for times. No trains stop at Grasse, but across the *place* is an **SNCF info office** to attend to your rail needs (open Mon.-Sat. 8:30am-5:15pm). A summer-only **tourist office annex** on pl. de la Foux (tel. 04 93 36 03 56; fax 04 93 36 86 36), or the **main office** near the Casino on cours Honoré Cresp in the Palais des Congrés, makes hotel reservations, gives out free maps, and advises you on walks and hikes (both offices open daily in summer 9am-7pm, main office in winter Mon.-Sat. 9am-noon and 2-6:30pm). Cash in at **Change du Casino** (tel. 04 93 36 48 48), near the casino on cours H. Cresp (open Tues.-Sat. 9:30am-noon and 2-7pm). **ATMs** roll merrily along at **Crédit Mutuel, Crédit Agricole,** and **Crédit du Nord,** all on bd. du Jeu de Ballon. In a **medical emergency,** dial 04 93 92 55 55. For the **police,** dial 17. There is a **post office** in the parking garage under the bus station (open Mon.-Fri. 8:30am-noon and 2-5pm, Sat. 8:30am-noon).

RIVIERA

ACCOMMODATIONS AND FOOD

If the narrow, walled *traversées* (stairways cut into the hill) and the welcoming aroma of the *parfumeries* induce you to spend the night, Grasse provides several low-cost options, almost all of which offer luxurious vistas of the valley below. **Le Napoléon,** 6, av. Thiers (tel. 04 93 36 05 87), across from the bus station, has clean rooms with renovated bathrooms. (Singles and doubles 140F, with shower 160F. Breakfast 25F. Open Feb.-Dec. 24. V, MC, AmEx.) To get to **Pension Ste-Thérèse,** 39, bd. Y.E. Baudoin (tel. 04 93 36 10 29), climb bd. du Jeu de Ballon behind the tourist office annex and turn right on bd. Baudoin (10min.). This former church perches above central Grasse and savors some of the best views in town. Managed by kind nuns, the hotel boasts quiet rooms surrounding an internal chapel. (Singles 140-230F. Doubles 200-280F. Extra bed 30F. Breakfast 22F. Open Nov. 13-Sept. 30.)

Grasse contains a wealth of restaurants, markets, *boulangeries, fromageries,* and all the other *-ries* in the *vieille ville.* Most of the culinary action centers around the cobblestone **pl. aux Aires**. Also in the vicinity is a **Monoprix** supermarket, rue Paul Goby (open Mon.-Sat. 8:45am–7:30pm). A **market** bustles on pl. aux Herbes every morning from 7am-noon, except Wednesdays, when antique dealers take over.

SIGHTS

The *parfumeries* of **Fragonard, Molinard,** and **Galimard** are Grasse's main attractions. At Fragonard's original 1873 factory, Usine de Fragonard, 20, bd. Fragonard (tel. 04 93 36 44 65), catch a glimpse of perfume design and manufacturing process (open daily 9am-6:30pm; free 15-min. tours every 10min. in English). Nearby Molinard *usine,* 60, bd. Victor Hugo (tel. 04 93 36 01 62), offers similar free tours (open

Mon.-Sat. 9am-7pm, Sun. 9am-noon and 2-6pm). Galimard welcomes tourists at its main facility at 73, route de Cannes (tel. 04 93 09 20 00; free tours daily).

Appropriately, Grasse is the home of the **Musée International de la Parfumerie,** 8, pl. du Cours (tel. 04 93 36 80 20). Don't be discouraged by the dusty Industrial Revolution-era first floor exhibit; on the second floor you will find fascinating artifacts including a 3000-year-old mummy's perfumed hand and foot, whose flesh stayed gruesomely preserved because of the perfuming process. On the fourth floor greenery, sniff the base elements of your favorite perfumes. (Open daily June-Sept. 10am-noon and 1:30-7pm; Oct.-May 10am-noon and 2-5pm. Admission 12F50, students 10F, during special exhibitions 25F, students 20F.)

The enticing essences of Grasse become positively effervescent every May and August during the town's two annual flower festivals. In May, **Exporose** attracts rose growers from around the world for the largest exhibition of its kind. In the first week of August, **La Jasminade** commemorates jasmine, one of the staples of perfume-making, and wafts into Grasse's streets with parades, dancing, and music.

■ Near Grasse: Grand Canyon du Verdon

Plunging views of rock-face cliffs cut by the snow-fed waters of the Verdon river make the **Grand Canyon du Verdon** a sight to see. Seek out the vertiginous views at **Point Sublime** and the **Balcons de la Mescla.** The tourist office in Grasse has info and maps of trails through this gorge. Take the daily bus from here to **Castéllane** run by **VFD** (tel. 04 93 85 24 56, in Nice) which leaves from Grasse's *gare routière* at 8:25am (1½hr., 65F). The **Auberge de Jeunesse (HI)** (tel. 04 92 77 38 72; fax 04 92 77 30 48), 20km from Castéllane at pleasant **La-Palaud-sur-Verdon,** has a friendly manager who can tell you about his favorite hiking trails, including the *Sentier Martel* and the *Sentier L'Aimbut.* The eight-bed rooms are clean and airy, with gorgeous views and kitchen access. (Members 64F, over 26 70F, includes breakfast. Sheets 16F. Lockout 10am-5pm. Reception April-Sept. 8am-noon and 5-9pm.) **Camp** at the hostel for 26F per person. Comfortable, expensive, and tourist-filled lodging is also available at the **Auberge du Point Sublime,** 17km from Castéllane (tel. 04 92 83 60 35; fax 04 92 83 74 31; doubles with shower 220-274F; breakfast 44F; V, MC). For more lodging info, call Castéllane's **tourist office** (tel. 04 92 83 61 14).

■ Antibes

Like St-Raphaël, its *nouveau chic* neighbor to the west, Antibes has become one of the new hot spots on the Riviera. With one of the largest private marinas on the Mediterranean, this beachy town brings floods of yachts and of anglophone sailors who man them. Antibes' beautiful beaches and Picasso museum have actually been drawing crowds for years, but the theater and music festivals and a seaside youth hostel have made it an increasingly popular destination on the budget itinerary. Beat the rush, save a spot on the sand, and unload your pack in town for a few days of music, sun, and relaxation before it's too late. For fantastic nightlife, head to Juan-les-Pins, Antibes' twin sister, 2-3km to the southwest (see page 489).

PRACTICAL INFORMATION

To reach the **tourist office,** 11, pl. de Gaulle (tel. 04 92 90 53 00; fax 04 93 33 85 71), exit the train station, turn right onto av. Robert Soleau, and follow signs for the *Maison du Tourisme.* There you'll find free maps and info on accommodations, camping, and festivals (open July-Aug. Mon.-Sat. 8:30am-7:30pm, Sun. 9am-1pm; Oct.-June Mon.-Sat. 9am-12:30pm and 2-7pm). Another office is at the train station (tel. 04 93 33 77 52; fax 04 92 90 53 01; open Mon.-Fri. 8:30am-6:30pm, Sat. 8:30am-12:30pm). The **Banque National Populaire (BNP)** sits at the corner of av. Robert Soleaud; **Crédit du Nord** is across from the tourist office, at pl. de Gaulle; and **Banque Lyonnaise** faces BNP—all do the **ATM** thing. **Change money** and gawk at old coins at the **Numismatique Change,** 17, bd. Albert 1er (tel. 04 93 34 12 76; open Mon.-Sat. 9am-noon and 2-

7pm). **Trains** leave from the station on av. Robert Soleau (tel. 08 36 35 35 35), near the *centre ville,* to: Cannes (every 30min., 10min., 13F); Marseille (15 per day, 2½hr., 133F); Nice (every 30min., 18min., 21F); and Juan-les-Pins (every 30min., 5min., 7F, last train at 12:25am). **Buses** speed out of the the *gare routière,* on pl. Guynemer (tel. 04 93 34 37 60); from the tourist office, cross pl. de Gaulle and turn left onto bd. Wilson (open Mon.-Sat. 9am-noon and 2-6pm). They truck to: Nice (every 20min. 6:30am-8:05pm, 1¼hr., 24F50); Cannes (every 20min. 7:10am-9:40pm, ½hr., 12F50); Cagnes (every 20min. 6:30am-8:05pm, 1¼hr., 11F50); and Juan-les-Pins (every 20min. 7am-7:40pm; July and Aug. last bus at 12:40am, 10min., 6F50). You can **rent bikes** at **French Riviera Location,** 43, bd. Wilson (tel. 04 93 67 65 67), from 75F per day (deposit 1000F; open Mon.-Sat. 9am-noon and 2-7pm). The **hospital** (tel. 04 92 91 77 77) is on rue de la Fontaine. Dial 17 for the **police.** The **post office** (tel. 04 92 90 61 00), pl. des Martyrs de la Résistance, has poste restante (open Mon.-Fri. 8am-7pm, Sat. 8am-noon; **postal code:** 06600).

ACCOMMODATIONS AND FOOD

The small **Hôtel Jabotte,** 13, av. Max Maurey (tel. 04 93 61 45 89; fax 04 93 61 07 04), and its central courtyard are two minutes from the sea. Follow bd. Albert 1er from pl. de Gaulle to its end; turn right on Mal. Leclerc and follow the beach about ½km. Av. Max Maurey is a right turn off the beach. Marvelously friendly and helpful managers let cottage-like rooms. (Singles 200F. Doubles 250F. Breakfast 35F.) The kindly owner of the **Hôtel National,** 7, pl. Amiral Barnaud (tel. 04 93 34 31 84), will welcome you to her clean, wood-furnished rooms in the *vieille ville.* To get there, take rue du 24 Août from the *gare routière* until you get to pl. Barnaud. Rue Gen. Vandenberg will be on your right; walk down it and turn left on rue Arazy. The hotel, back from the street, will be immediately in front of you. (Singles 140F. Doubles 164F, with shower 250F. Breakfast 26F. Check-out at noon.) If you're up for a hike, you might try the **Relais International de la Jeunesse,** at the intersection of bd. de la Garoupe and av. l'Antiquité (tel. 04 93 61 34 40). It's a 40-minute walk south along the shore from Antibes or Juan-les-Pins. From Juan-les-Pins, walk south on bd. Edouard Baudoin, which becomes bd. du M. Juin, and cross the peninsula on chemin des Ondes. Turn right on bd. Francis Meillard and then left on bd. de la Garoupe. If you're less energetic, take bus 2A from the *gare routière* (every 20min., 6F50; last bus 7:15pm). The hostel is in an old, rambling house with high ceilings and miraculous water pressure. (70F. Reception 1am-11pm. Curfew midnight.)

Vieille Antibes is loaded with *boulangeries,* fruit stands, and restaurants ranging in price from the reasonable to the ridiculous. For a cozy evening, try **Adieu Berthe,** 26, rue Vauban (tel. 04 93 34 78 84), which serves a dazzling array of crêpes starting at 30F (open Wed.-Mon. 7pm-1am). Check out the kitschy **Comic Strip Café,** 4, rue James Close (tel. 04 93 34 91 40), for delicious burgers (33-40F, garnished with fries and slaw) and omelettes—the portions are huge. Colorful cartoons bloom on the walls. The comic book library downstairs has some stuff in English (open daily 11am-10pm). The cheapest deal in town is at the local **market,** every morning from 6:30am-12:30pm on cours Masséna near the Picasso museum. There are also supermarket options: **Codec,** 8, av. Niquet, near pl. de Gaulle (tel. 04 93 34 01 51; open Mon.-Sat. 6am-7:30pm, Sun. 8am-noon); or **Casino** (open Mon.-Sat. 8am-7pm).

SIGHTS

If you've had your share of the sun, retreat to the charming *vieille ville.* Old Antibes, which stretches between bd. Maréchal Foch and the port d'Antibes, is a haven for pricey boutiques and worthwhile museums. Explore one of the numerous artists' *ateliers,* or studios, where they proudly display their work. Once home to celebrated English writer Graham Greene, Surrealist painter Max Ernst, and a host of other writers and artists, Antibes takes great pride in its **Musée Picasso** (tel. 04 92 90 54 20), in the Château Grimaldi on pl. Mariejol. Clinging for dear life to a seaside cliff, this château housed Picasso for a productive six months in 1946. Several small rooms display drawings, ceramics, and a sampling of the canvases he painted here. Picasso's *atelier* on the top floor provides a view of Antibes and the sea and features paintings by his contemporaries de Staël, Hartung, and Mathieu. (Open Tues.-Sun. June 15-Sept. 15 10am-6pm; Sept. 16-Oct. and Dec.-June 14 10am-noon and 2-6pm. Admission 30F, students 15F.) For something completely different, the **Musée Peynet,** pl. Nationale (tel. 04 92 90 54 30), displays over 300 drawings made by local artist Raymond Peynet. (Open daily 10am-noon and 2-6pm. Adults 20F, students 10F.) The **Musée Archéologique** (tel. 04 92 90 54 35), along the waterfront in the Bastion St-Andrée sur les Remparts, digs up archaeological finds from the area and features exhibits on the history of Antipolis, the ancient Greek city on the site (open summer Tues.-Sun. 10am-6pm; rest of the year Tues.-Sun. 10am-noon and 2-6pm; admission 10F, students 5F). The **Cathédrale d'Antibes,** next to the Château Grimaldi, has a 17th-century nave and an altar constructed in 1515. The 16th-century **Fort Carré** stands guard over the waters of the *vieux port.* Continuing along the sea on the scenic ramparts of the *vieille ville,* you'll find some of the Riviera's finest beaches, including plage de la Garoupe, plage de la Salis, and Pointe de l'Ilet.

At night, your best bet for finding some action is a trip to Juan-les-Pins; but if you prefer to nurse a beer in Antibes, hang out with the English-speaking, yacht-sailing crowd at **La Gaffe,** 6, bd. d'Aguillon (tel. 04 93 34 04 06), near the port. Drafts 16F. Across the way, **Le Blue Lady,** rue Lacan, has a more local atmosphere. Both bars open at 6pm and close when customers go back to their boats.

At the end of July, Antibes holds its annual **Eté Musicale** in front of the château. Tickets for this pastiche of jazz, classical music, and opera are available at the Antibes and Juan-les-Pins tourist offices (60-300F). Come the end of July, Antibes sometimes offers a **Festival de Théâtre.** Antibes' **Festival d'Art Lyrique,** during the first two weeks of July, brings world-class opera soloists to the *vieux port.* (For info, call 04 92 90 54 60 or 04 92 90 53 00; tickets 50-150F.)

■ Near Antibes

JUAN-LES-PINS

Like a frat party *à la française,* Juan-les-Pins crams as much fun into the summer nights as possible. Although joined as one—a city known as Antibes-Juan-les-Pins (pop. 70,000)—Antibes and Juan-les-Pins are 3km apart and keep separate train stations, post offices, and tourist offices. They also jive to a different tempo—Juan-les-Pins is younger, hipper, and more hedonistic. Boutiques stay open until midnight, cafés until 2am, and nightclubs close when dancers head back to the beach. The streets are packed with seekers of sea, sun, and sex (not necessarily in that order). The cafés are cheaper and almost as lively as the clubs; even the most miserly traveler can join in the nightly bash. When winter winds blow in, though, the town shuts down like a speak-easy during a police raid.

The English-speaking staff at the **tourist office,** 51, bd. Guillaumont (tel. 04 92 90 53 05), distributes maps, makes hotel reservations, and provides info and reservations for Juan-les-Pins' numerous music festivals. From the station, walk straight for four minutes on av. du Maréchal Joffre and turn right on av. Guy de Maupassant. The office is a two-minute walk on the right, at the intersection of av. Amiral Courbet and av. Gillaumont (open Mon.-Sat. 8:30am-7:30pm, Sun. 10am-1pm). There's also a **branch office** (tel. 04 93 61 73 39) in the train station (open Mon.-Fri. 8:30am-noon and 3-6pm, Sat. 8:30am-noon). The **train station** is on av. l'Esterel, where av. du Maréchal Joffre joins it. Trains leave about every 20 minutes for Nice (22F) and Cannes (11F). To get from Antibes' pl. du Général de Gaulle to Juan-les-Pins by foot, follow bd. Wilson (about 1.5km) and turn left on av. Dautheville.

Juan-les-Pins has little in the way of budget lodgings. If you'd rather not make the post-party trek to Antibes on foot, try the **Hôtel de la Gare,** 6, rue du Printemps (tel. 04 93 61 29 96), which has simple rooms next to the train tracks. (Singles 140F. Dou-

Private or Prudent?

Don't be discouraged by the **"Club Privé"** (Private Club) signs on the doors of many French nightclubs and bars. In all but the most chi-chi, you can walk, or be buzzed, right in. The designation is simply legal protection for owners, allowing them to expel obnoxious guests. Without it, the club would have to wait until the first punch was thrown before escorting rowdy patrons to the door.

bles 160F. Triples 210F. Breakfast 25F.) Although it's illegal, many serious carousers seem to fancy the beach's soft sand as a mattress.

Restaurants in Juan-les-Pins are either classy and expensive or touristy and unappetizing. Assemble your own feast at the **Casino supermarket,** 116, bd. Wilson (tel. 04 93 61 19 04), near the train station (open Mon-Sat. 7:30am-noon and 1-6:30pm). Another **Casino** is close to the beach on av. Amiral Courbet (tel. 04 93 61 00 56), near the tourist office (open Mon.-Sat. 8am-1pm and 3:30-8pm, Sun. 5-8pm).

Five of Juan-les-Pins' six *discothèques* are in the center of town. They all open around 11pm and close around 5am, and their cover charges all hover around 100F (first drink included). Look for posters around town advertising special events at the clubs, including the oh-so-chic *mega-mousse* party, where club-goers dance in a sea of foamy bubbles. Check out the psychedelic **Whiskey à Gogo,** la Pinède (tel. 04 93 61 26 40), and fluorescent **Voom Voom,** 1, bd. de la Pinède (tel. 04 93 61 18 71). **Joy's Discoteque,** av. Dautheville (tel. 04 93 67 78 87), has revues as well as a disco (second drink 50F). The **Soft Club,** av. Guy de Maupassant, often has all-male nights. **Les Pêcheurs,** bd. Edouard Baudoin (tel. 04 93 61 82 58), is a 10-minute walk along the coast from the town center. Mingle with chic locals at **Le Ten's Bar,** 25, av. du Dr. Hochet (tel. 04 93 67 20 67), off av. Guy de Maupassant, away from the beach. Draft beer will set you back 15F. The dress code at all the clubs is simple: look good.

If you have any money left after clubbing, you may want to gamble at the **Eden Casino,** bd. Baudoin (tel. 04 92 93 71 71; open daily 10am-5am; minimum age 18; no shorts or sneakers; free). During the day, take advantage of the uncrowded, sandy beaches. Famous for its antediluvian pine trees, **Pinède,** by av. Gallice, is the site of the annual **Festival International de Jazz (Jazz à Juan),** an outstanding musical program that runs in late July and attracts such greats as Ray Charles and Tracy Chapman (tickets 110-200F, available at tourist offices in Juan-les-Pins and Antibes).

BIOT AND CAGNES

The ancient walled town of **Biot,** one train stop east of Antibes, is known for its fine glassware; many shops are open to the public. Peek into one of France's most prestigious glass-blowing factories, **La Verrerie de Val de Pome** (tel. 04 93 65 03 78; open daily 9:30am-12:30pm and 1:30-7:30pm; free). From the train station, it's a pleasant, well-marked hike along the route de Biot (2km). Along route de Biot, you'll also find **Marineland** (tel. 04 93 33 49 49), an aquarium with one of the best water shows in Europe; it's also home to a waterpark and miniature golf course (open daily from 10am; admission from 88F). Biot has several campgrounds. The best bargain is three-star **Le Logis des la Brague** (tel. 04 93 33 54 72), across from where the train stops. Facilities include hot showers, laundry, and a market (1-2 people 65F; with car or caravan 93-115F; electricity 18F; open May-Sept. 8am-noon and 2-8pm.)

The bustling town of **Cagnes-sur-Mer** is two train stops from Biot. Cagnes' **tourist office** (tel. 04 93 73 66 66; fax 04 93 20 52 63) is at 6, bd. Maréchal Juin. From the station, take a right and then another right under the autoroute. Continue to bd. Maréchal Juin and take a left (open in summer Mon.-Sat. 8:45am-12:30pm and 3-7pm; in winter and spring 8:30am-12:15pm and 2:30-6:30pm). Another branch on the beach is Cros des Cagnes, on av. des Oliviers (tel. 04 93 07 67 08). Filling nine rooms of the house Auguste Renoir occupied from 1908-1919, the **Musée Renoir,** av. des Collettes (tel. 04 93 20 61 07), off av. des Tuilières, contains works from the artist's "Cagnes period" and is surrounded by beautiful gardens of olive and palm trees on a hill overlooking the town (open daily in summer 9am-noon and 2-6pm; in winter

Wed.-Mon. 9am-noon and 2-5pm; admission 25F, students 10F). Cagnes' other attraction is the **Château-Musée des Cagnes,** montée de la Bourgade (tel. 04 93 20 85 57), a 14th-century stronghold built after the Crusades to guard the seaside and its own prisoners (follow the signs from the police station; open in summer Wed.-Mon. 9am-noon and 2:30-7pm; in winter Wed.-Mon. 9am-noon and 2-5pm; admission 25F, students 10F). At the top of its tower, survey the Alps, the coast, and everything in between. Restaurants and cafés ring the *place* beneath the castle.

Nice

Cosmopolitan and chic, sun-drenched and spicy, Nice sparkles as the unofficial capital of the Riviera. A rite of passage for young travelers, Nice holds an energetic nightlife tuned to the tastes of the anglophones who constantly flood the city. Top-notch museums, vibrant art, and bustling beaches make this flowery, palm-lined Riviera town an exciting destination. The city offers excellent local and regional transportation, decent cheap lodgings, and a populace accustomed to tourists. You may also encounter the down-side of big-city life—watch your wallet and yourself.

During the famous annual **Carnaval** (Feb. 8-23 in 1997), native *Niçois* and thousands of temporary inhabitants ring in spring with wild floral revelry, grotesque costumes, and raucous song and dance. Those who can't make it to Nice for Carnaval find plenty of merrymaking in the streets of Vieux Nice any time of the year. Tucked into the southeastern pocket of the city and limited to pedestrians, Vieux Nice's labyrinth of tiny streets teems with flower, antique, and vegetable markets in the mornings. At night, peddlers give way to the boisterous bars, clubs, and restaurants that smaller Riviera towns lack. Be prepared to meet potential traveling companions, to hear more English than French, and to have more fun than you'll remember.

ORIENTATION AND PRACTICAL INFORMATION

The **train station,** Gare Nice-Ville, is in the center of town next to the tourist office on **av. Thiers.** The area around the station is somewhat seedy but packed with cheap restaurants and budget hotels. To the left as you stumble out of the station, **av. Jean-Médecin** runs toward the water to **pl. Masséna** (10min.). Heading right from the train station, you'll run into **bd. Gambetta,** the other main street running directly to the water. Sweeping along the coast, the **promenade des Anglais** (which becomes quai des Etats-Unis) is a people-watching paradise, as are the cafés, boutiques, and overpriced restaurants of the **pedestrian zone** west of pl. Masséna. **Port Lympia,** a warren of alleyways, boulevards, *brasseries,* and *tabacs,* lies on the opposite side of the château, below Vieux Nice.

Unfortunately, Nice's big-city appeal is increasingly coupled with big-city crime. Women should avoid walking alone after sundown, even if they don't mind Mediterranean-style male "friendliness," and everyone should exercise caution at night around the train station and Vieux Nice. Do not ever let your bags or possessions out of sight at any time, anywhere. Seriously: be very careful here.

Tourist Information: Tourist Office, av. Thiers (tel. 04 93 87 07 07; fax 04 93 16 85 16), beside the train station. Books a limited number of rooms after 8am; stake out a place in line early. Crowded, but info on *everything.* Ask for the English pamphlet, *Nice: A Practical Guide,* a bus map and schedule, the English *Museums of Nice,* and a detailed map (essential in Vieux Nice). Open daily June 15-Sept. 15 8am-8pm; Sept. 16-June 14 8am-7pm. **Branch offices** at **1, promenade des Anglais** (tel. 04 93 87 60 60), near the pedestrian zone (open June 15-Sept. 15 Mon.-Sat. 8am-8pm, Sun. 9am-6pm; Sept. 16-June 14 Mon.-Sat. 9am-6pm); **Airport Terminal 1** (tel. 04 93 21 44 11; open daily 8am-10pm); and at **Ferber** (tel. 04 93 83 32 64), on promenade des Anglais near the airport (open Mon.-Sat. 8am-8pm, Sun. 9am-6pm; Sept. 16-June 14 Mon.-Sat. 9am-6pm). To find out what's happening, pick up the monthly **Le Mois à Nice** or weekly **Scènes d'Azur,** with cultural updates and listings of live music (both free at the tourist offices). **Semaine des Spectacles,**

published every Wed., is available at tabacs (8F) and carries entertainment listings for the entire Côte.

Budget Travel Offices: Council Travel, 37bis, rue d'Angleterre (tel. 04 93 82 23 33; fax 04 93 82 25 59), near the train station. Open Mon.-Fri. 9am-7pm, Sat. 9am-4pm. **USIT,** 10, rue de Belgique (tel. 04 93 87 34 96; fax 04 93 87 10 91), near the train station. Open Mon.-Fri. 9:30am-6pm, Sat. 10am-1pm.

Consulates: U.S., 31, rue Maréchal Joffre (tel. 04 93 88 89 55; fax 04 93 87 07 38), can help with a lost passport. Open Mon.-Fri. 9-11:30am and 1:30-4:30pm. **U.K.,** 11, rue Paradis (tel. 04 93 82 32 04). Open Tues.-Thurs. 10am-noon.

Money: Cambio, 17, av. Thiers (tel. 04 93 88 56 80), across from *gare*. No commission. Open daily 7am-midnight. **Banque Populaire de la Côte d'Azur,** 457, promenade des Anglais (tel. 04 93 21 39 50), at airport. Open daily 8am-10pm. 24-hr. **ATMs** at **Crédit Mutuel,** 29, av. Jean Médecin (tel. 04 93 16 31 00).

American Express: 11, promenade des Anglais (tel. 04 93 16 53 53; fax 04 93 16 53 42), at the corner of rue des Congrès. **ATM.** Open daily 9am-9pm.

Airport: Aéroport Nice-Côte d'Azur (tel. 04 93 21 30 30). Take Sunbus 23 (direction: St-Laurent, every 20min., 6am-9pm, 9F) from the train station. The more expensive airport bus (21F; tel. 04 93 56 35 40) runs between the bus station by pl. Masséna and the airport every 20min. Be sure to ask for the Sunbus stop. **Air France,** 10, av. Félix-Faure (tel. 04 93 80 66 11 for info, 04 93 18 89 89 for reservations), near pl. Masséna. To Paris, around 525F. Office open Mon.-Sat. 9am-6pm. Airport open daily 6:15am-10:30pm.

Trains: Gare SNCF Nice-Ville, av. Thiers (tel. 08 36 35 35 35). Information office open Mon.-Sat. 8am-6:30pm, Sun. 8:30-11:15am and 2-6pm. Trains run every 15-45min. (5:05am-12:20am) to Cannes (40min., 37F) and Antibes (25min., 26F); every 10-30min. (6am-12:10am) to Monaco (25min., 22F) and Menton (35min., 28F). In summer, about 11 per day connect with the TGV from Marseille to Paris (7hr., 480F plus 18F reservation fee). Open daily 8am-8pm. **Lockers** 15-30F. **Luggage storage** 30F per day per piece (open daily 7am-10pm). **Gare du Sud,** 4bis, rue Alfred Binet (tel. 04 93 82 10 17), 800m from the Nice-Ville station. Special trains, the *chemins de fer de la Provence,* run through the southern Alps to the thermal baths and hiking at Digne (5 per day, 3¼hr., 105F).

Buses: *Gare routière,* promenade du Paillon (tel. 04 93 85 61 81), between av. Félix-Faure and bd. Jean Jaurès. Buses every 20min. (6:30am-7:30pm) to: Cap d'Ail (45min., 14-16F); Monaco (45min., 17-19F); Menton (1¼hr., 24-26F); Antibes (1hr., 25F); Juan-les-Pins (1hr., 27F); Cannes (1¼hr., 30F); Grasse (1¼hr., 36F).

Public Transportation: Sunbus, 10, av. Félix Faure (tel. 04 93 16 52 10), near pl. Leclerc and pl. Masséna. Long treks to museums and hostels make the 22F day pass, 34F 5-ticket *carnet,* 87F 5-day pass, or 110F 7-day pass well worth it. Buy passes at the agency (open Mon.-Fri. 7am-7pm, Sat. 7am-6pm), the information kiosk at sq. Leclerc (open Mon.-Fri. 6:30am-9:30pm), or on board. Individual tickets cost 8F. Bus 12 goes from train station to pl. Masséna and the beach (every 12min.). Ask at the tourist office for the invaluable bus map *Le Plan Sunbus* and the *Guide Infobus,* which lists schedules and routes.

Ferries: SNCM, quai du Commerce (tel. 04 93 13 66 66; fax 04 93 13 66 81), at the port. Take bus 1 or 2 (direction: Port) from pl. Masséna. To Bastia (4-5hr., one way 252-278F, students 191-209F, ages 4-12 145F, bikes 87F, cars 207-722F) and Ajaccio (6-7hr., same prices). Open Mon.-Fri. 8am-7pm, Sat. 8am-noon.

Taxis: (tel. 04 93 80 70 70). Get a price quote for your destination before you board. 150-200F from the center of town to the airport. Insist that the driver turn on the meter. Many have a 50F night fare minimum.

Car Rental: Ada Location, 24, av. G. Clemenceau (tel. 04 93 82 27 00; fax 04 93 88 87 91). 259F a day with 400km; 549F for the weekend with 800km. Min. age 21 with a year-old license. V, MC, AmEx. **Budget** (tel. 04 93 21 35 81; fax 04 93 21 35 82), across from the *gare.* 375-525F for 2 days with 700km; 675F for 3 days with 1000km; 1820F per week with 2100km. Additional km 1F75. Min. age 25.

Bike and Moped Rental: Nicea Location Rent, 9, av. Thiers (tel. 04 93 82 42 71), near train station. Owners will help with directions. Bikes 120F per day, deposit 2000F or credit card imprint. Also rents mopeds and motorcycles. Open Mon.-Sat. 9am-6pm. V, MC, AmEx. **Cycles Arnaud,** 4, pl. Grimaldi (tel. 04 93 87 88 55), near

Nice

1 Syndicates d'Initiative (Tourist Offices)
2 Post Offices
3 American Express
4 Musée Chagall
5 Musée des Beaux-Arts (Jules Cheret)
6 Université
7 Musée Masséna
8 Hôtel de Ville
9 Opéra
10 Palais de Justice
11 Cáthedrale Ste-Réparate
12 Château
13 Palais Lascaris
14 Cathédrale Russe
15 St-Jacques
16 St-Martin and St-Augustin
17 Gare Routiére
18 Musée d'Art Moderne et Contemporain

A B C D E F G
1 2 3 4

N
Bd. Joseph Garnier
Rue Raiberti
PL. GNL. DE GAULLE
Gare du Sud
Avenue Malausséna
Av. George
Av. de Pessicart
Rue Vernier
Rue Trachel
Rue Mirdago
Rue Marceau
Rue Rouget de Lisle
Av. Biasini
Tunnel Malraux
Av. des Arenes de Cimierz
Voie Malraux
Av. Marechal Lyautey
Bd. de St-Jean-Baptiste
Rt. de Turin
Av. des Diables Bleus
Bd. P. Sola
Av. Paul Arène
Bd. du Parc Impérial
Bd. Gambetta
Bd. Raimbaldi
Av. Emile Buchert
Gare Nice-Ville
Rue Pertinax
Av. Desambrois
Bd. du Tzarewitch
Av. Thiers
Rue Gounod
Rue Auber
Av. Durante
Av. Marechal Foch
Bd. Carabacel
Av. Gallieni
Bd. Gnl. L. Delfino
Rue Barbéria
Av. Georges Clemenceau
Av. d'Etienne d'Orves
Rue Châteauneuf
Rue Giuglia
Rue Berlioz
Rue Rossini
Rue Dévoluy
des Postes
Rue Gioffredo
Av. St-Jean-Baptiste
Bd. Risso
Av. de la République
Rue Auguste
Rue F. Passy
PL. FRANKLIN
Rue Verdi
Bd. Dubouchage
PL. WILSON
Rue Baria
PL. ARSON
Arson
Av. des Baumettes
Bd. Francois Grosso
Jardin d'Alsace-Lorraine
Bd. Victor Hugo
Rue Pastorelli
Av. J. Medicin
Rue de l'Hotel
PL. GARIBALDI
Rue Bonaparte
Av. des Fleurs
Rue Karr
Rue du Maréchal Joffre
Rue Gioffredo
Rue Ségurane
Rue Cassini
Rue Guizhol
PL. MAX BAREL
Rue Bottero
Rue de Rivoli
Rue de Buffa
Rue du Congress
PL. MASSENA
Av. Felix Fauré
Rue
Rue Dante
Rue Meyerbeer
Rue de France
Av. de Verdun
Bd. Jean Jaurés
Cimetiere
Q. Papacino
Av. des Baumettes
Jardin Albert Ie
Quai des États-Unis
Quai Lunel
Bd. de Stalingrad
Av. Xavier Roman
Autoroute Urbaine Sud
Rue de France
Promenade des Anglais
Baie des Anges
0 400 yards
0 400 meters
Q. Rauba-Capeu
PL. GUYNEMER

pedestrian zone. Bikes 100F, 2000F or credit card deposit. Reductions for longer rentals. Open Mon.-Fri. 9am-noon and 2-7pm, Sat. 9am-noon.

English Bookstore: The Cat's Whiskers, 26, rue Lamartine (tel. 04 93 80 02 66). Great selection. Open Mon.-Sat. 9:30am-12:15pm and 2-6:45pm.

Youth Center: Centre d'Information Jeunesse, 19, rue Gioffredo (tel. 04 93 80 93 93; fax 04 93 80 30 33), close to outermost edge of promenade du Paillion. Bulletin board (in French) with student summer jobs. Open Mon.-Fri. 10am-7pm.

Laundromat: Laverie Automatique, rue de Suisse (tel. 04 93 88 78 52), between rue Paganini and rue d'Angleterre. Close to hotels around the station. Wash 6kg for 18F; 15kg for 36F. Dry 5min. for 2F. Open daily 7am-9pm.

All-Night Pharmacy: 7, rue Masséna (tel. 04 93 87 78 94). Open daily 24hr.

Hospital: St-Roch, 5, rue Pierre Devoluy (tel. 04 92 03 33 75). From av. Jean Médecin, turn left on rue Pastorelli, which turns into rue P. Devoluy. **Medical emergency** tel. 18 or 04 93 92 55 55.

Police: (tel. 04 93 17 22 22), at opposite end of bd. Maréchal Foch from bd. Jean Médecin. **Emergency** tel. 17.

Post Office: 23, av. Thiers (tel. 04 93 82 65 00), near the train station. Open Mon.-Fri. 8am-7pm, Sat. 8am-noon. **Branches** at 18, rue Hôtel des Postes, pl. Wilson; 2, rue Clemenceau, off bd. Jean Médecin, pl. Grimaldi on rue de la Buffa, rue Bottero off bd. Gambetta; and at the airport. 24-hr. **ATM.** Poste restante at all branches in Nice—call for specific branch's postal code. **Postal code** (main office): 06000.

ACCOMMODATIONS

To make your début in the world of *niçois* lodgings in style, show up at the av. Thiers tourist office early for help in finding a room or call hotels in advance. Arrive in the city in the morning during the summer, or you'll almost certainly be forced to join the legion of visitors who camp outside the train station, which moonlights as one of the largest and most dangerous bedrooms in France. If you must arrive at night, make sure you have a reservation and directions to the hotel. Women in particular should be careful in the vicinity of the train station at night. Decent, affordable hotels cluster around Notre-Dame, and on rue d'Angleterre, rue de la Suisse, and rue de Russie. This is prime hunting ground for pickpockets—watch out. Nice's hostels and *résidences* (temporary youth hostels in university dorms) are often full.

Relais International de la Jeunesse "Clairvallon," 26, av. Scudéri (tel. 04 93 81 27 63; fax 04 93 53 35 88), in Cimiez, 4km out of town. Take bus 15 to "Scudéri" (direction: Remiez, 20min.) from the train station or pl. Masséna (every 10min.). From the train station, turn left and left again on av. Jean Médecin, then turn right before the overpass on bd. Raimbaldi. Go 6 blocks, and turn right on av. Comboul. Turn left on bd. Carabacel and follow it up the hill as it turns into bd. de Cimiez. Go right before the hospital onto av. de Flirey, and keep trudging uphill until you reach av. Scudéri, then turn left and follow the signs. A large, luxurious hostel in an old villa with a tennis and basketball court and a beautiful, quiet setting. 160 beds in 4- to 10-bunk rooms. Check-in 5pm. Curfew 11pm. Lockout 9:30am-5pm. Bed and breakfast 70F. 3-course dinner 50F.

Auberge de Jeunesse (HI), route Forestière du Mont-Alban (tel. 04 93 89 23 64; fax 04 92 04 03 10), 4km away from it all—but worth the commute. Take bus 14 (direction: Mont Baron to "l'Auberge") from the *gare routière* off bd. Jean Jaurès (Mon.-Fri. every 15min., Sat.-Sun. every 30min.; last bus 7:30pm). Otherwise it's a 50-min. walk: From the train station, turn left and then right on av. Jean Médecin. Follow it down through pl. Masséna and turn left on bd. Jaurès. Go past the concrete Musée d'Art Contemporain and turn right on rue Barla, following the signs up the windy hill. 56 beds in 8- to 10-bed dorms. Usually bubbling with a friendly, bronzed crowd. Reception opens at 5pm. Lockout 10am-5pm. Curfew midnight. 64F, including shower and breakfast. Kitchen facilities.

Résidence Les Collinettes (HI), 3, av. Robert Schumann (tel. 04 93 86 58 48; fax 04 93 37 19 86). Take bus 17 from the train station to "Châteauneuf." Av. Robert Schumann will be up and to the left through the big intersection. Keep walking, pass the restaurant "Les Collinettes" around the curve, and it will be on the left.

Summer hostel set up in a university *résidence:* typical, functional, modern college housing; all singles. Close to bd. des Anglais. Ask for a room overlooking the garden or you'll be lulled to sleep by the whizzing highway. No lockout. 98F, discounts for long stays. Open July 7-Aug. For women arriving in June or September, **CROUS** (tel. 04 93 97 06 64) runs the *résidence* at 66F a night, 3-night max. stay.

Hôtel Baccarat, 39, rue d'Angleterre (tel. 04 93 88 35 73; fax 04 93 16 14 25). Turn left from the train station, walk 50m, and the road is on your right. If all hotels were this nice, your mother would backpack around Europe. Large, clean, beautifully renovated rooms with tasteful lighting, pastel trimmings, and new beds. Friendly, no-nonsense staff create a homey, secure ambience. All rooms and dorms have toilet, sink, and shower. 4- to 5-person dorms 83F. Singles 163F. Double 206F. Prices 10-20F cheaper off-season. Breakfast 15F. V, MC.

Hôtel Les Alizès, 10, rue de Suisse (tel. 04 93 88 85 08), off rue d'Angleterre and next to the pharmacy (look for a sign on the second floor). From the train station, turn left, walk 200m to av. Jean Médecin and turn right. Walk 3min. and the hotel will be on the right, before the cathedral. Friendly, student-loving owners keep 14 comfortable, spotless rooms across from Notre Dame. All rooms with showers, some with toilets. Special *Let's Go* prices. Singles 90F. Doubles 150F. Triples 180F. 60F per extra person. Breakfast free when you show your *Let's Go.* V, MC.

Hôtel Notre Dame, 22, rue de Russie (tel. 04 93 88 70 44; fax 04 93 82 20 38), at the corner of rue d'Italie 1 block west of av. Jean Médecin. Good-sized, clean, quiet rooms with telephones and firm mattresses in a pleasant hotel. Owners also rent out studio apartments with kitchen and bath a few blocks away. Singles 130F. Doubles 160-240F. Triple 300F. Quads 350F. Apartments 350F for 4 people, each additional person 85F. Hotel breakfast 20F. Shower 10F. V, MC.

Hôtel Les Orangiers, 10bis, av. Durante (tel. 04 93 87 51 41; fax 04 93 82 57 82). Walk down the steps by the Thomas Cook agency, cross the street and go down the ramp. The hotel is 50m up on the left. Large, clean, bright 6-bed dorms and rooms, some with balconies, most with showers and fridges. Some singles are a bit small. Exterior of the hotel is peach and green in grand *niçois* style. English-speaking owner offers free beach mat loan and luggage storage. Dorms 85F. Singles 90-95F. Doubles 190-210F. Triples 270-285F. Quads 350-360F. V, MC.

Hôtel des Flanders, 6, rue de Belgique (tel. 04 93 88 78 94; fax 04 93 88 74 90). Large, clean rooms with big bathrooms and well-worn carpets. Friendly owners will negotiate special prices for longer stays. Dorm room for students 90F. Singles 200F. Doubles 220-250F. Triples 340F. Quads 360-400F. Breakfast 25F. V, MC.

Hôtel Lyonnais, 20, rue de Russie (tel. 04 93 88 70 74; fax 04 93 16 25 56). Clean, pleasant rooms with telephones, some with new marble balconies facing the street, some facing a quieter courtyard. Non-smoking halls and stairwells. TV available for 20F per day. Singles 150-220F. Doubles 150-220F. Triples 240-290F. Quads 270-344F. *Let's Go*-ers get a 10% discount off-season. Breakfast 24F. 10-min. shower 15F in summer, 10F the rest of the year. V, MC, AmEx.

Hôtel Belle Meunière, 21, av. Durante (tel. 04 93 88 66 15), near the *gare.* Young anglophones make for a lively atmosphere. The helpfulness and fluent English of the owner's daughter, Marie-Pierre, make visitors right at home. 4- to 5-bed co-ed dorms with well-worn bedding and some lumpy, saggy beds. Dorms with shower (95F) larger than those without (75F). Tepid shower 10F. Doubles 265F. Triples 321F. Quads 400F. Breakfast included. Luggage storage 10F.

Hôtel Meublé Drouot, 24, rue d'Angleterre (tel. 04 93 88 02 03 or 04 93 81 10 39). Clean, dark rooms with firm beds, TVs, and fridges. Singles 101-121F. Doubles 162-182F. For triples and quads, add 81F per person. Some kitchenettes. Free showers and luggage storage.

Hôtel Clair Meublé, 6, rue d'Italie (tel. 04 93 87 87 61; fax 04 93 16 85 28). Renovated rooms with kitchenettes, refrigerators, and snow-white bathrooms. Owner is happy to fetch sleepy clients at station or airport. Singles with showers 140-170F. Doubles 180-210F. Call for reservations.

Hôtel de la Gare, 35, rue d'Angleterre (tel. 04 93 88 75 07). Clean, simple rooms. Get one with a bathroom or you'll be sharing 3 toilets with 21 rooms of 1-3 people. Comfy TV room and free luggage storage. Singles 115-155F. Doubles 180-260F. Breakfast 18F. AmEx.

FOOD

Nice offers a smorgasbord of seafood and North African, Asian, and Italian gastronomic delights, as well as *la cuisine niçoise*—an eclectic mélange of specialties flavored by Nice's familiarity with *provençal* herbs, Mediterranean olive groves, and North African spices. Try the cheap and hearty *socca,* a fresh, thin, soft, olive oil-flavored chickpea bread that sells for about 10F in *vieille ville* restaurants. **Bd. Jean Jaurès,** opposite the fountain, and **cours Saleya,** also in Vieux Nice, are wellsprings of savory *bouillabaisse,* a spectacular seafood soup. *Pissaladière,* a small but tasty onion, olive, and anchovy pizza, is a local favorite. Nice is also the home of the *salade niçoise,* with tuna, potatoes, tomatoes, and a spicy mustard dressing.

The alleys around the *vieux port* hide affordable restaurants and *boulangeries.* Sample the *pain bagnat* (round, crusty bread with tuna, sardines, and crunchy veggies). Vietnamese, Chinese, and Thai restaurants beg for your attention around rue de Suisse near the train station. For generous pizza portions, hit one of the pizzerias on av. Masséna in the pedestrian zone. If you find your stomach and your wallet simultaneously empty, head for one of Nice's university cafeterias, which serve filling meals for about 36F. The convenient **Restaurant Université,** 3, av. Robert Schumann (tel. 04 93 97 10 20), is open September to June daily 11:30am-1:30pm and 6-8pm. The cafeteria at **Montebello,** 96, av. Valrose (tel. 04 93 52 56 59), near the Musée Matisse, is open until mid-August daily 11:30am-1:30pm and 6-8pm.

Cafés and food stands along the beach are expensive, so shop for lunch before you hit the waves. The **fruit, fish, and flower market** at cours Saleya is the best place to pick up fresh local olives, cheeses, and melons (Tues.-Sun. dawn-noon). You'll find everything else at **Prisunic supermarket,** 42, av. Jean Médecin (tel. 04 93 62 38 90; open Mon.-Sat. 8:30am-8:30pm), or **Casino supermarkets,** rue Deudor, behind the Nice Etoile on av. Jean Médecin (tel. 04 93 62 01 50; open Mon.-Sat. 8:30am-8pm), or behind Espace Magnan, on av. Gloria (tel. 04 93 97 60 40). Vieux Nice overflows into the streets and squares at night as diners sample local and ethnic cuisine *en plein air.* Savor the multicultural menus and atmospheres until you find the perfect *plat* to hit the spot. On cours Saleya sits **ParadIce** and the ice cream voted best in all of France by three New Yorkers on a "*glace* tour of Europe." One *boule* goes for 9F, two for 16F, and three for 26F (open 6:30am-2:30am).

Ò Michelangelo, 28, cours Saleya (tel. 04 93 80 05 27). Hearty, satisfying pasta served in a pleasant atmosphere with an appetizing guarantee: you don't like it, you don't eat it, you don't pay for it. *Menu* of salad, pasta, and dessert 70F. Plate with your choice of 3 pastas 59F. White house wine could remove paint. Open Mon.-Fri. noon-2pm and 7-11pm, Sat.-Sun. noon-2:30pm and 7-11:30pm.

Le Faubourg Montmartre, 39, rue Pertinax (tel. 04 93 62 55 03), off av. Jean Médecin. Delicious *niçoise* cuisine at bargain prices. Let the kindly owner know you're a student and *Let's Go*-er and she'll give you the 3-course *menu* for 50F. Try the tender *sole meunière* or the *entrecôte aux poivres* (pepper steak). The *bouillabaisse* is a great value at 110F for 2 people. Open daily 11:30am-3pm and 5:30pm till traffic slows. V, MC, AmEx.

Nissa Socca, 5, rue Ste-Réparate (tel. 04 93 80 18 35), in Vieux Nice, has filling 35F *niçois* dishes and a homey aura. Open Tues.-Sat. noon-2pm and 7-11pm.

Lou Pilha Leva, 10, rue du Collet (tel. 04 93 13 99 08), in Vieux Nice. Cheap and hearty *niçois* food. 30F will take you far: 15F pizzas, desserts, and *tourtes de blettes,* a quiche specialty stuffed with spinach-like filling. 10F *socca* and *pissaladière,* 22F fried calamari. Open daily 7:30am-1am.

Phénom-Penh, 2, rue de la Préfecture (tel. 04 93 85 20 85), off bd. Jean Jaurès near pl. Masséna, has cheap, *à la carte* Chinese and Vietnamese food; *nems* (egg rolls) 4F50 each. Main dishes at 26F. Karaoke Sat. and Sun. 10:30pm till closing. Open daily 11am-midnight.

La Petite Biche, 9, rue d'Alsace-Lorraine (tel. 04 93 87 30 70)—and it's pronounced "beesh," you foul-mouthed thing. *Provençal* specialties and Yankee favorites. *Menus* 40-61F. Open 11:45am-3pm and 6:30-10pm.

Restaurant de Paris, 28, rue d'Angleterre (tel. 04 93 88 99 88), near train station. Generous *menus* at 38F, 48F, and 58F with a wide selection of vegetables, soups, salads, and desserts. Delicious salmon 38F. Open daily 11:30am-3pm and 5:30-11pm; in winter 11:30am-3pm and 6-10:30pm. V, MC.

La Coupole, 4, rue de France in the pedestrian zone (tel. 04 93 87 14 15). Huge 55F 4-course "express *menu*" offered from noon-2:30pm. Good pizza, fresh seafood, and big salads. Open daily noon-1am. V, MC, AmEx.

SIGHTS

Nice's **promenade des Anglais** is a sight unto itself. A cross between a *grand boulevard* and the Malibu boardwalk, the promenade stretches the length of Nice's waterfront and rocky beach. Private beaches crowd the water between bd. Gambetta and the Opéra, but lots of public spaces compensate, especially west of bd. Gambetta. Whatever dreams you've had of Nice's beach, the hard reality is an endless stretch of rocks smoothed by the Mediterranean; bring a beach mat.

The promenade leads east to the **Colline du Château,** a flowery, green hillside park crowned with the remains of an 11th-century cathedral and an artificial waterfall. Jog blithely up more than 400 steps for a view of the rooftops of Nice and the sparkling blue **Baie des Anges** (park open 8am-7:30pm). Return to earth to visit bustling and colorful **Vieux Nice.** Sprawling southeast from bd. Jean Jaurès, this *quartier* is the center of nightlife and a mix of tourist-trap cafés, shops, and *niçois* homes. To experience the old city, stick to the tiniest of the tiny streets.

Nice houses a wealth of art and historical artifacts in its many museums. Venture out of the sun and into their climate-controlled showrooms and you won't regret it. If you plan to visit more than four museums, pick up a **passe-musées** at any museum. A bargain at 120F for adults or 60F for students, this pass allows 15 visits to any of the municipal museums. Unless otherwise noted, **admission** is usually 25F, 15F for students, and free to those under 18 and the handicapped.

The **Musée d'Art Moderne et d'Art Contemporain,** promenade des Arts (tel. 04 93 62 61 62), is at the intersection of av. St-Jean Baptiste and Traverse Garibaldi; take bus 5 (direction: St-Charles) from the station. The museum is part of a large concrete, glass, steel, and marble complex that parallels its contents: bold, new, and strangely elegant. Modernism has never been so friendly or inviting. The museum features over 400 French and American avant-garde pieces from 1960 to the present, including works by Lichtenstein, Warhol, Noland, and Klein, beautifully arranged in the open spaces of the museum's interior. (Open Wed.-Thurs. and Sat.-Mon. 11am-6pm, Fri. 11am-10pm. Admission 27F, students 15F, under 18 free.)

The elegant **Musée National Marc Chagall,** av. du Dr. Ménard (tel. 04 93 81 75 75), is a 15-minute walk north of the station, or take bus 15 (direction: Rimiez and Les Sources, every 20min., 8F) to "Musée Chagall." Making creatively radiant use of glass, space, and light, the museum showcases Chagall's mosaics, sculptures, tapestries, lithographs, engravings, and oils. (Open July-Sept. Wed.-Mon. 10am-6pm; Oct.-June. Wed.-Mon. 10am-5pm. Admission 28F, students and seniors 18F.)

The **Musée Matisse,** 164, av. des Arènes de Cimiez (tel. 04 93 81 08 08), presents the colorful works and personal effects of Henri Matisse, who lived and worked in Nice from 1917 until his death in 1954. The collection, which changes periodically, includes preliminary sketches for his Chapelle du Rosaire in Vence (see page 499) and books illustrated by the artist. (Open April-Sept. Wed.-Mon. 10am-6pm; Oct.-March 10am-5pm. Call for info on lectures, free with admission.)

Housed in the former villa of Ukrainian Princess Kotschoubey, the **Musée des Beaux-Arts,** 33, av. Baumettes (tel. 04 93 44 50 72), highlights the work of Fragonard, Monet, Sisley, Bonnard, and Degas. It also features sculptures by Rodin and Carpeaux. Several warm, playful Chérets adorn the large marble staircase and hall (open Tues.-Sun. 10am-noon and 2-6pm; from the train station, take bus 38 to "Chéret" or 12 to "Grosseo"). The **Musée Masséna,** 65, rue de France and 35, promenade des Anglais (tel. 04 93 88 11 34), at the corner of the promenade des Anglais and rue de Rivoli, is less spectacular than the Musée des Beaux-Arts but still merits a visit. Renoir paintings, watercolors by *niçois* artists Mossa and Costa, and furniture from Italian royal residences fill this once-lavish villa. The gardens would do Gertrude Jeckyl proud. (Open May-Sept. Tues.-Sun. 10am-noon and 2-6pm.)

Nice's aquatic heritage shifts inland from the beach to the city's tiny, one-room aquarium and shell collections at the **Musée International de Malacologie,** 3, cours Saleya (tel. 04 93 85 18 44), in Vieux Nice. (Open May-Sept. Tues.-Sat. 10:30am-1pm and 2-6:30pm; Oct.-April 10:30am-1pm and 2-6pm. Admission 15F, students and seniors 9F.) Other museums include the **Musée Archéologique,** 160, av. des Arènes de Cimiez (tel. 04 93 81 59 57), next to the Musée Matisse, where you can visit the ruins of the Gallo-Roman baths and view excavated coins, jewelry, and sarcophagi (take bus 15, 17, 20, or 22 to "Arènes"). On the other end of the spectrum, the **Musée-Galerie Aléxis et Gustav-Adolf Mossa,** 59, quai des Etats-Unis (tel. 04 93 62 37 11), exhibits the landscapes and symbolist works of the *niçois* father-son team of Alexis (1844-1926) and Gustave-Adolf (1883-1971) Mossa (open Tues.-Sat. 10am-noon and 2-6pm, Sun. 2-6pm; admission 15F, students 9F).

After you've had your fill of Nice's art treasures, take a look at the **Cathédrale Orthodoxe Russe St-Nicolas,** 17, bd. du Tsarévitch (tel. 04 93 96 88 02), left off bd. Gambetta, a five-minute walk east of the train station and a welcome departure from the all-pervasive Gothic and Romanesque. Built in 1912 under the patronage of Tsar Nicholas II, this gorgeous church is a remnant from the days when the Côte d'Azur was a getaway for Russian nobility. Its design borrows from the 17th-century Yaroslav style typified by the Kremlin. (Open 9am-noon and 2:30-6pm, Sept.-May 9:30am-noon and 2:30-5pm; admission 12F.)

Once the spiritual center of another of Nice's religious communities, the **Monastère Cimiez,** pl. du Monastère (tel. 04 93 81 55 41), housed Nice's Franciscan brethren from the 13th century to the 18th and is now a museum. Religious artwork basks under the intricately painted ceiling, and the monks' living quarters are furnished as if the inhabitants had just stepped out to pray. The museum, the monastery's cloister, the lovely and peaceful gardens, and the crowded cemetery in which Matisse is buried are free and open to the public (open Mon.-Sat. 10am-noon and 3-6pm; church open 8:30am-12:30pm and 2:30-6:30pm). Take bus 15 (direction: Rimiez and Les Sources) or 17 (direction: Cimiez) to "Monastère" from the station, or follow the signs and walk from the Musée Matisse.

Nice maintains many beautiful parks and gardens, the most central of which are the **Jardin Albert Ier** and **Espace Masséna** between av. Verdun and bd. Jaurès off the promenade des Anglais and quai des Etats-Unis. The fragrant garden is a quiet refuge with benches, fountains, plenty of shade, and an ornate 18th-century Triton fountain. It also contains the **Théâtre de Verdure,** a small amphitheater that hosts a variety of summer events including jazz concerts and outdoor theater (box office open daily 10:30am-noon and 3:30-6:30pm). Espace Masséna is a large, creative public space with a large fountain and plenty of shady benches, ideal for a picnic.

ENTERTAINMENT

Nice guys do finish last—Nice's party crowd swings long after the folks in St-Tropez and Antibes have called it a night. The bars and nightclubs around rue Masséna and Vieux Nice are constantly frolicking and rollicking with jazz, pizazz, and rock. In Nice especially, what's in quickly becomes what's out, so ask around to find out where the current hip hotspots are. The area around the clubs in Vieux Nice can be dangerous at night and should not be visited alone.

The bar and pub scene is steamy and smoky in the summer, but especially in Vieux Nice; lone female travelers should be wary of fun-lovin' drunkards looking for a good time. The patio at **Chez Wayne,** 15, rue de la Préfecture (tel. 04 93 13 46 99), is *the* place to be for young anglophones on the prowl. Live music every night in the summer and karaoke Sundays. (Pint of beer 28F daytime, 36F at night. Open 2:30pm-midnight.) Right next door is the too-sexy Euro-*Volk* **Master Home** (tel. 04 93 80 33 82) at 11, rue de la Préfecture, where a pint is 28F all the time (open 11am-2:30am). For a more mature European experience, head over to the Dutch pub **De Klomp** 6, rue

Mascoinat (tel. 04 93 92 42 85), for one of their 40 whiskeys (from 35F) or 18 beers on tap (pint 40F) and a variety of live music from salsa to jazz every night. A mixed crowd of nationalities and ages hangs at the British pub **The Hole in the Wall,** 3, rue de l'Abbaye (tel. 04 93 80 40 16). True to its name, this pub is tiny, but it's loads of fun, with mellow live music every night that you won't have to shout over (open daily 8pm-1am). If the Hole is full, **Pub Thor,** 32, cours Saleya (tel. 04 93 62 49 90) will have room for you. The pub is similarly mellow, with live music at 10pm, but you can stand up here while you play pool (1F per min.). Don't come in shorts or sandals (open 11:30am-12:30am). Right next door is **Cyber Café La Douche,** 34, cours Saleya (tel. 04 93 62 40 20), a dark, black-lit bar/club where you can check your e-mail for 25F (30min.) or 45F (1hr.). (Open 4pm-2:30am.) Some of the cheapest beer in town waits at **Pub Pompeii,** 16, rue de l'Abbaye (tel. 04 93 85 04 06). A cramped, smoky pub with live music every night, a young crowd, and 12F sangria. **Bar des Oiseaux** (tel. 04 93 80 27 33), at the intersection of rue de l'Abbaye and rue de St. Vincent, caters to a more artsy, coffee-house crowd. The classy, exotic bar features live theater every night at 8:30pm and jazz once a week (open 11am-3pm and 7pm-2:30am). For the latest info on events pick up **L'Exès,** a free brochure available at the tourist office and some bars.

Nice's **nightclubs** are relentlessly expensive. **Le Studio,** 29, rue Alphonse Karr (tel. 04 93 82 37 66), is free until 1am but charges a 110F cover after that (open Thurs.-Sun. 11pm-6am). Gay clubs include **The Blue Boy,** a disco on rue Spinetta in West Nice, but the liveliest action is in Cannes or Monaco.

To enjoy Nice's nightlife without spending a dime, head down to the promenade des Anglais, where street performers, musicians, and hundreds of people wander the beach and boardwalk till the wee hours of the morning.

The **Théâtre du Cours,** 2, rue Poissonnerie in Vieux Nice, stages traditional dramatic performances Thursday through Saturday at 9pm and Sunday at 7pm (75F). The more experimental **Central Dramatique National,** Promenade des Arts (tel. 04 93 80 52 60), at the corner of av. St-Jean Baptiste and Traverse Garibaldi, offers a show almost every weekend (50-160F). The grand **Théâtre de Nice** on the promenade des Arts (tel. 04 93 80 52 60) hosts concerts and theater performances (50-200F), and the **Nice Opéra,** 4, rue St-François de Paule (tel. 04 93 85 67 31), has an annual performance series of visiting symphony orchestras and soloists (75-250F).

Nice's **La Grande Parade du Jazz** in mid-July at the Parc et Arènes de Cimiez (tel. 04 93 81 07 61), near the Musée Matisse, attracts world-famous European and American jazz musicians to its three stages. Fireworks fan across the city's skies every February as parades roll through the crowds celebrating Nice's **Carnaval.** The **FNAC** (E2) in the Nice Etoile shopping center at 24, av. Jean Médecin, sells tickets for virtually every musical or theatrical event in town.

■ Near Nice

VENCE

The former Roman market town of Vence (pop. 15,000) snoozes in the green hills above Nice. Slightly less touristy and cramped than its neighbor St-Paul, its medieval village provides a refreshing break from the glitz and bustle of nearby Nice. The **cathedral** in its center is unremarkable save for a paintbox-bright mosaic of *Moses in the Bulrushes* by Marc Chagall. Vence is better known for the masterpiece of another artistic maestro— Henri Matisse's **Chapelle du Rosaire** (tel. 04 93 58 03 26). From the bus stop, facing the tourist office, turn left and walk up av. de la Résistance. Take a right on av. Elise and a left on av. des Poilus; at the roundabout go right onto av. de Provence and veer left onto av. Henri Matisse (1.5km). The exterior of the chapel looks like a house, but inside a stark white interior is softened by pale green, blue, and yellow rays of light filtering through the large stained-glass windows. On one of the walls sits Matisse's interpretation of the Christ story in bold black brush strokes.

(Open Tues. and Thurs. 10-11:30am and 2:30-5:30pm; July-Aug. and holidays additional hours Wed. and Fri.-Sat. 5F donation requested.)

A few km from Vence is the **Galerie Beaubourg** (tel. 04 93 24 52 00; fax 04 93 24 52 19), home to the works of such greats as César, Klein, and Warhol. Curious, sometimes elegant contemporary works of art reside in the 19th-century **Château Notre-Dame des Fleurs** and its surrounding gardens (open Mon.-Sat. 11am-7pm; admission 30F, students 15F). To get there from Vence, take the bus from pl. du Grand Jardin (direction: Grasse or Tourette-sur-Loup) and ask the driver to let you off at the gallery (3 buses per day out, 2 per day back, 8F50). Call Tacavl buses (tel. 04 93 42 40 79) for schedules. The **tourist office,** on pl. du Grand Jardin (tel. 04 93 58 03 26; fax 04 93 58 91 81), near the bus stop, shells out free maps and more (open July-Sept. Mon.-Sat. 9am-7pm, Sun. 10:30am-12:30pm; Oct.-June Mon.-Sat. 9am-12:30pm and 2-6:30pm). Get to Vence by **bus** 400 or 410 from Nice's *gare routière* (every 30-40min., 1hr., 21F). Call SAP Buses (tel. 04 93 58 37 60) for info. If you're approaching Vence from Cannes, take the **train** to Cagnes-Sur-Mer (every 20min., 22F) and turn right out of the station onto av. de la Gare. Cross the bridge and go across the street to the stop "sq. du 8 Mai." Catch bus 400 to Vence (20 per day, 12F). The last bus from Vence to Cagnes-sur-Mer and Nice leaves at 6:45pm.

ST-PAUL

St-Paul is a hillside jewel of a town. The impossibly narrow pedestrian streets retain their medieval flavor as they wind through the impeccable town. An art-lover's paradise, St-Paul abounds with attractive, pricey boutiques filled with local paintings, pottery, and handicrafts. Since restaurants in this artists' colony are expensive and the only grocery option is a mini-mart near the town's entrance, you may want to pack a picnic in Nice. The **tourist office** (tel. 04 93 32 86 95; fax 04 93 32 60 27), near the entrance of the village, dispenses free maps and info on galleries and exhibitions (open daily 10am-7pm). **SAP Buses** (tel. 04 93 58 37 60) sends bus 400 to St-Paul from Nice's *gare routière* (19 per day, 55min., 19F50). If you're already in Vence hop on the same bus (7F). To get to St-Paul from Cannes, take the train to Cagnes-sur-Mer (see **Vence** above for more info). From here, take bus 400 (19 per day, 9F50) to St-Paul. The last bus from St-Paul to Cagnes-Sur-Mer and Nice leaves at 6:50pm from the bus stop just outside the entrance to the town.

The pride of St-Paul is the **Fondation Maeght** (tel. 04 93 32 81 63; fax 04 93 32 53 22), 1km from the town center. Get off at the St-Paul bus stop and follow the signs first down then up the steep, winding chemin des Gardettes. Designed by Joseph Sert, the Fondation is part museum and part park, with shrubs and fountains mixed in among works by Miró, Calder, Arp, and Léger. Maeght, an art dealer, was inconsolable after the death of his eldest son. Encouraged by his friends Braque and Miró, Maeght commissioned a small, dark, somber chapel with *vitraux* by Braque and Ubac dedicated to St. Bernard, his son's name saint. The works lean towards abstraction and morbidity; the museum will appeal most to true lovers of modern art. The Fondation's **library** is a treasure-trove of art history and is open to the public. (Call for library hours. Fondation open daily 10am-7pm; Oct.-June 10am-12:30pm and 2:30-6pm. Admission 45F, students 35F. Photography permit 10F.) In early July, the entire city becomes a stage as St-Paul puts on a medieval play in its streets and squares. Call the tourist office for details (80-120F, students and children 60F).

Nice to Monaco

Rocky shores, pebble beaches, and luxurious villas glow along the coast between hectic Nice and high-rolling Monaco. More relaxing than their big-time neighbors, these tiny towns are like freshwater pearls—similar in brilliance, yet gratifyingly unique. Interesting museums, architectural finds, and breathtaking countryside are among the many gifts the coast has to offer. The train offers an exceptional glimpse of the coast up close, while buses maneuvering along the high roads of the *corniches* provide a bird's-eye view of the steep cliffs and crashing sea below. Take one method of transport out and the other back—you won't be disappointed.

VILLEFRANCHE-SUR-MER

The narrow streets and pastel houses of Villefranche-sur-Mer, only two stops from Nice on the local train, enchanted Aldous Huxley, Katherine Mansfield, and a bevy of other writers with their Mediterranean charm. More recently, Tina Turner and Bono have bought homes in Villefranche; one lucky backpacker recently stood too close to The Edge at the local train station. There are no maps to the stars' homes, but trains run from Nice every half-hour from 6:30am to 12:10am (10min., 9F). To reach the **tourist office** (tel. 04 93 01 73 68; fax 04 93 76 63 65) from the train station, exit on quai 2 and turn left. Go down the stairs and turn right, then follow the sea wall until you reach the citadel. Turn right, keeping to the left of the street as it forks into av. Mal. Joffre, and turn left on av. Sadi Carnot; the office will be across the street in the Jardin François Binon (10min.). The staff gives out free maps and suggests excursions to regional villages (open daily July to mid-Sept. 8am-8pm; mid-Sept. to June Mon.-Sat. 8:30am-noon and 2-7pm).

As you stroll from the station along the quai Ponchardier, a sign to the *vieille ville* points the way to **rue Obscure,** the oldest street in Villefranche. Built in the 13th century, this spooky, dungeonesque lane has since been layered with so many homes and shops that the only light comes from lonely iron chandeliers hanging from the street's "ceiling." On quai Courbet stands the pink and yellow 14th-century **Chapelle St-Pierre** (tel. 04 93 76 90 70), decorated from floor to ceiling by former resident and film director Jean Cocteau with boldly executed scenes from the life of St. Peter and the Camargue gypsies and dedicated to the fishermen of the area. (Hours are unpredictable—call to find out about changes and daily closings. Open June 21-Sept. 21 Tues.-Sun. 10am-noon and 4-8:30pm; Sept. 22-Dec. 20 9:30am-noon and 2-6pm; Dec. 21-March 19 9:30am-noon and 2-5pm; March 20-June 20 9:30am-noon and 3-7pm. Admission 12F. No photography.) The mustard-colored 16th-century **Citadelle** is a bit dull. It houses three small museums, the most interesting of which is the **Musée Volti** (tel. 04 93 76 33 27), which creatively displays the lounging, curvaceous female form in works by native Antoniucci Volti, who experimented with bronze, clay, copper, and canvas to create his voluptuous art. The cubism of Henri Goetz and Christine Boumeester taunt the viewer with vivid color and familiar yet abstract images in the **Musée Goetz-Boumeester** (tel. 04 93 76 33 44). Ask yourself: is this a horse or a hairbrush? The **Collection Roux** (tel. 04 93 76 33 33) showcases ceramic figures depicting historical events. (All open July-Aug. Wed.-Mon. 10am-noon and 3-7pm, Sun. 3-7pm; June and Sept. 9am-noon and 3-6pm; Oct.-May 10am-noon and 2-5pm. Free.)

BEAULIEU-SUR-MER AND ST-JEAN-CAP-FERRAT

Beaulieu-sur-Mer lives up to its imaginative name as a pretty place by the sea. The two main beaches are covered with chalky gravel and laced with seaweed. For fun, ask the folks at the **tourist office** (tel. 04 93 01 02 21; fax 04 93 01 44 04), at pl. de la Gare next to the train station, why one of the beaches is called "bay of ants" and another "little Africa." If you don't cause them too much anguish, they will supply you with free town maps (open June 20 to mid-Sept. Mon.-Sat. 9am-12:30pm and 2:30-7pm, Sun. 9am-12:30pm; mid-Sept. to June 19 Mon.-Sat. 9:15am-12:15pm and 2-5:30pm). The office may entice you to visit **Kérylos** (tel. 04 93 01 01 44), a seaside dream villa that archaeologist Theodore Reinach built to emulate the lifestyle of ancient Greeks. Reinach lived his version of an Athenian's life here for twenty years amid detailed frescoes, stunning mosaics, ornate alabaster, and marble embellishments, including an exquisite marble bath, until his death in 1928. This "sea swallow," perched on the Beaulieu cliffs, rewards its visitors with a gratifying Mediterranean vista. (Call for info on 1-hr. English tours and intermittent schedule changes. Open daily July-Aug. 10-7pm; March 15-June and Sept.-Oct. 10:30am-12:30pm and 2-6pm; Dec. 1-March 14 Tues.-Fri. 2-5:30pm, Sat.-Sun. 10:30am-

12:30pm and 2-5:30pm. Admission 35F, students 15F. No photography.) Of more visceral interest to the traveler is the town's large and cheap **Codec supermarket** (tel. 04 93 01 04 61). Facing away from the tourist office, walk along rue G. Clemenceau and turn right on the large bd. Mal. Leclerc; the supermarket will be up the hill on your right (open Mon.-Sat. 8:30am-7:25pm, Sun. 8:30am-1pm).

A calmer, more relaxed version of Beaulieu, the hidden hamlet of **St-Jean-Cap-Ferrat** snuggles inside a tiny, half-clover-shaped peninsula that juts out into the Mediterranean. To get to St-Jean from Nice or Monaco, **Autocars Broch** (tel. 04 93 31 10 52, in Nice) offers the best deal at 9F roundtrip (from Nice, every 30min.-1hr., 6am-6:30pm; from Monaco, every 30min.-1hr., 7:30am-8:30pm). From Beaulieu, walk 25 minutes south along a seaside path full of secluded, rocky beaches and once-beautiful docks and moorings. When you reach the small gravel beach, walk inland to a throng of hotels and restaurants. Get to the tiny **tourist office,** 59, av. Denis Semeria (tel. 04 93 76 08 90; fax 04 93 76 16 67), from the first beach after Beaulieu by taking the road that leads away from the port up to the right on av. Dennis Semeria. The tourist office is on a busy intersection on the left. It has free maps of the region and *St-Jean-Cap-Ferrat à Petits Pas,* free walking tour maps of the peninsula that will help you find your own idyllic beach. (Open July-Aug. Mon.-Sat. 8:30am-12:30pm and 1-5:30pm, Sun. 1-5:30pm; Sept.-June Mon.-Sat. 8:30am-noon and 1-5:30pm, Sun. 1-5:30pm.) Although St-Jean has some one-star hotels, they're not so cheap as those in larger surrounding towns. You could try **La Fregate,** 11, av. D. Séméria (tel. 04 93 76 04 51), with small, clean, pleasant rooms, firm beds, and some nice views. (Singles 225F. Doubles 225-305F. Breakfast 30F. V, MC.) Restaurants line the *nouveau port* and av. Dennis Séméria. You'll find the basics at the **Spar supermarket** on av. Dennis Séméria where it becomes rue Jean Mermoz (open Mon.-Sat. 7:30am-12:30pm and 3:30-7:30pm, Sun. 8am-12:30pm).

A five-minute walk from the tourist office brings you to the **Fondation Ephrussi de Rothschild** (tel. 04 93 01 33 99). The gorgeous Italianate villa houses the superb furniture and art collections of the Baroness de Rothschild. Monet and Fragonard canvases, Gobelins and Beauvais tapestries, Chinese screens and vases, and a stunning tea room all stand within spectacular grounds. Each of the villa's seven gardens stylistically reflects a different part of the world, from Spain to Japan via, *bien sûr,* France. The principal garden is shaped like the prow of a ship with the sea on all sides. The complex is an aesthete's paradise. (Open July-Aug. Mon.-Fri. 10am-7pm, Sat.-Sun. 10am-6pm; March 15-June and Sept.-Nov. 1 daily 10am-6pm; Nov. 2-March 14 Mon.-Fri. 2-6pm, Sat.-Sun. 10am-6pm. Admission 38F, students 25F.) You can also reach the villa directly from Beaulieu. Follow the sea path toward St-Jean, turning right after the three-pronged tree and before the white villa that separates the path from the Mediterranean; from the top of this walled shore access, turn left and follow the road up, turning right at the sign to the Fondation.

St-Jean's pebbled-and-perky beaches attract mostly locals and are thus gloriously uncrowded, earning the area the nickname *Presqu'île des Rêves* (Peninsula of Dreams). Try the **plage Passable** (which is far more than that) or the **plage Paloma,** or walk along the peninsula's 11km of trails to find your spot in the sun. Paloma is past the port on av. Jean Mermoz. To reach Passable, walk to the tourist office and continue down the hill, turning left on Chemin de Passable to the waterfront.

EZE

Three-tiered Eze perches precariously on the *corniches,* a medieval gem in the modern Côte d'Azur. The most colorful of the towns from Nice to Monaco, it is also the most difficult to navigate. **Eze Bord-de-Mer** houses the train station and a stretch of pebble beach popular with windsurfers, kayakers, and sailors. The middle tier sits 429m above sea level—straight up—and holds the heart of the town, **Eze le Village.** The medieval town is here, bearing the marks of its visitors over the centuries, from the Moors to the Piedmontese to the King of Sweden (who found the area so lovely he built a castle here in 1920). The **Sentier Friedrich Nietzsche,** a windy trail where its namesake found inspiration to compose the third part of his epic *Thus Spake Zar-*

athustra, connects the two areas. **Le Col d'Eze,** a more residential area, keeps watch above. During the summer (June 15-Oct. 15), a **Navette mini-bus** connects the three tiers for the ridiculous price of 20F (last one at 6pm). For bus info, call **Autocars Broch** (tel. 04 93 31 10 52) in Nice. From Nice, the bus departs for Eze-sur-Mer from 6am to 6:30pm (every 30min.-1hr., 20min., 12F roundtrip). From Monaco, it leaves from 5:23am to 11:55pm (every 30min.-1hr., 7min., 9F). To get to Eze le Village, try **Rapides Côte d'Azur** (14F50).

Eze le Village offers more than narrow streets and **pretty views**—the **Fragonard Perfumerie** (tel. 04 93 36 44 65), based in Grasse, has its second-largest factory here and offers warehouse prices and free 15-minute tours of the facility (open every day of the year 8:30am-6:30pm). The more intimate **Parfumerie Galimard** (tel. 04 93 41 10 70) also lures in customers with free tours, this time of their museum (open daily March 15-Oct. 8:30am-6:30pm; Nov.-March 14 8:30am-noon and 2-6pm).

Wander under the **Porte des Maures,** which as its name suggests unwittingly served as a gate to admit a surprise attack by the Moors. In the **Jardin Exotique** (tel. 04 93 41 10 30), over 200 species of cacti bristle in challenge—touch at your own risk. The ruins of a 14th-century **fortress** that Louis XIV had destroyed in 1706 crown the path. On a clear day, the view of the sea and mountains takes in distant Corsica (garden open daily July-Aug. 8:30am-8pm; call for winter hours; admission 12F, students 5F). Stop by the newly renovated Baroque **Eglise Paroissial,** shimmering with good old-fashioned Catholic gilt and decorated with a unique combination of Christian and Egyptian symbols. The **tourist office** (tel. 04 93 41 26 00; fax 04 93 41 04 80) can send you off with piles of information, including a map of hiking trails, **Eze Randonnées.** The central office is at pl. de Gaulle in Eze le Village (open daily June to mid.-Oct. 9am-7pm; mid-Oct. to May 10am-1pm and 2-7pm), and there is an annex at the train station (open Mon.-Sat. 9am-1pm and 2-5pm).

CAP D'AIL

Filled with lavish, imposing villas and fences to match, Cap d'Ail (pop. 5000) isn't a place to visit for provincial flavor. Instead, 3km of cliff-framed, foamy seashore, a beachside villa hostel, and numerous airy footpaths make Cap d'Ail a singular place to worship the sun, especially if you want to greet our solar source in the bathing suit you were born in. At **Les Pissarelles,** hundreds of *naturistes* make sure there's always a full moon over the Cap. To join them, or to seek the sun on the more modest **plage Mala,** turn left from the train station and make another left to a stone tunnel with 15 steps down to the rocky inlets and the winding path of the *sentier bord de Mer.* The path will lead you first to Mala and eventually to the nude beach. A more interesting (but more treacherous) path curves along the cliffs around in front of the village; look for steps with a blue railing on the left after the youth hostel.

The **Relais International de la Jeunesse** on bd. de la Mer (tel. 04 93 78 18 58), a light and clean seafront hostel, is currently undergoing renovation. Rooms have 6-12 beds and cost 70F the first night, 60F for each additional night. Men and women are housed separately—the rule is very strictly (even enthusiastically) enforced. (3-night max. stay when busy. Breakfast included, dinner 50F. Beer 8F. Lockout 9:30am-5pm. Free luggage storage. Curfew midnight.) Hostelers who miss the curfew because they took the 30-min. walk along the beach to Monaco sometimes take their chances illegally bedding down on on plage Mala, as few of Cap d'Ail's finest *gendarmes* want to walk down the 152 steps just to oust sleeping backpackers.

Free maps and lists of walking or mountain biking daytrips are available from the kind staff of the **tourist office,** 104, av. de 3 Septembre (tel. 04 93 78 02 33; fax 04 92 10 74 36). These tourism wizards can suggest trips to nearby caves. (Open Mon.-Fri. 9:15am-noon and 2:30-7pm, Sat. 9am-noon and 1-5pm; July-Aug. also open Sun. 9am-noon.) To get there from the train station, walk uphill, keeping left until you are out of the residential area. Turn right at the village, continuing on av. de la Gare. Turn right on rue du 4 Septembre, and the office will be on your right (20min.). The **post office** (tel. 04 93 78 26 04), at the corner of av. du 3 Septembre and av. de Gaulle, has poste restante (address to: 06320 Cap d'Ail; open Mon.-Fri. 9am-noon and 2-5pm, Sat.

9am-noon). To cure the beach munchies, hit the **Casino supermarket** (tel. 04 93 78 36 60), at the corner of av. du 3 Septembre and av. de la Gare (open Mon.-Sat. 8:30am-12:30pm and 3:30-7:30pm). **Trains** run daily from Nice (every 30min.-1hr., 6am-12:10am, 20min., 14F) and Monaco (every 30min.-1hr., 3min., 9F). The **bus** costs less with special roundtrip fares. Call **Autocars Broch** (tel. 04 93 31 10 52) in Nice for more info. Buses leave from Nice (6am-6:30pm, 25min., 14F50) and Monaco (7min., 6F) at least once an hour.

Monaco and Monte-Carlo

Wealth and casual luxury drip from every ornate street lamp and freshly scrubbed sidewalk of sexy, sumptuous Monaco. Here, public escalators and elevators ensure that no one need break a sweat on the chauffeur's day off. A dressy ambiance pervades within the unmarked borders. The sloppily dressed may receive disapproving glances from the city's opulent crowd if the police don't stop them first for violating the public dress code (no swim suits or bare feet away from the beach). Grace Kelly proved that such luxury isn't out of reach by working her way from a blue-collar Philadelphia background to become the fairy-tale Princess Grace in 1956. Before her arrival, Prince Rainier didn't even live in Monaco—it was Grace who insisted they glitz up the palace and invest in beautifying public spaces. Since *Monégasques* (native pop. 5000, with 25,000 hangers-on) pay no income tax, one may wonder how Prince Rainier paid for the prickly Jardin Exotique, ritzy aquarium, and all those hard-working street cleaners. Well, as the Italians say, gambling is a tax on fools—one the Grimaldi princes have levied since 1856. Besides, the country occupies only 1.97 lovely square km of the Côte d'Azur, so the royals didn't have too much to renovate. Monaco makes a lovely daytrip from Nice, but don't look to get any exotic new stamps on your passport. There are no border guards, and the electricity, tap water, military, and money are all French. You can, however, send off postcards emblazoned with the principality's very own stamps.

ORIENTATION AND PRACTICAL INFORMATION

Monaco is 18km east of Nice and 12km west of the French-Italian border. Small enough to be compared to a city, the principality consists of four *quartiers:* Monaco-Ville, Monte-Carlo, La Condamine (which links them), and Fontvieille. When you exit the train station, turn right onto **av. du Port,** then left onto **bd. Albert Ier** overlooking the harbor. Above you on the right sits the *quartier* of **Monaco-Ville** with its *vieille ville,* the Prince's palace, and the museum/mall complex **Fontvieille**. To the left of the port rises the fabled *quartier* of **Monte-Carlo** and its grand casino. To **telephone** a Monaco number from outside, dial the international prefix (00 in France), then 377. To call France from Monaco, dial 00 then 33.

Tourist Office: 2a, bd. des Moulins (tel. 92 16 61 66; fax 92 16 60 00), near the casino. Helpful, English-speaking staff makes free reservations and gives out free maps of the city and the handy English brochure **Tourist Attractions. Annexes** are set up in the train station and in the port June 15-Sept. Main office open Mon.-Sat. 9am-7pm, Sun. 10am-noon.

Money: Compagnie Monégasque de Change, parking des Pêcheurs (tel. 93 25 02 50), next to the Musée de l'Océanographie. Open Mon.-Sat. 9:30am-5:30pm. Closed Nov.-Dec. 25. Also in the **gare,** open Mon.-Sat. 10am-6:30pm.

American Express, 35, bd. Princesse Charlotte (tel. 93 25 74 45; fax 93 25 74 45). Open Mon.-Fri. 9am-noon and 2-6pm, Sat. 9am-noon.

Trains: av. Prince Pierre (tel. 08 36 35 35 35, in France). Direct connections 5:30am-11pm to: Nice (every 30min., 25min., 18F); Antibes (every 30min., 45min., 36F); Cannes (every 30min., 70min., 44F); Menton (every 30min., 10min., 11F). Information desk open Mon.-Fri. 8:05-11:55am and 2-5:35pm. Ticket window open daily 5:30am-8:45pm (automatic machines dispense tickets at other times). **Lockers** 15-30F per 72hr. Open 5am-1am.

Buses: Buses leave from several locations. Buses to Nice (18F50), with stops at Cap d'Ail (6F50), Eze-sur-Mer (10F), Beaulieu-sur-Mer (11F50), and Villefranche-sur-Mer (15F), leave every hr. Mon.-Sat. 6:30am-7pm, Sun. 7:30am-7pm, from pl. du Casino. Buses to Menton (12F) leave from pl. du Casino. For info on buses, call 04 93 85 61 81 in Nice, ask the tourist office, or call **Autocars Broch** (tel. 04 93 31 10 52, in Nice) for cheaper roundtrip day fares (17F to Nice and back).

Public Transportation: Six routes (tel. 93 50 62 41) connect the entire hilly town every 11min., Mon.-Sat. 7am-9pm (Sun. and holidays every 20min. 7:30am-8:45pm). Bus 4 links the train station to the Casino in Monte-Carlo. Tickets 8F50 each, 19F for a *carnet* of 4, 30F for a *carnet* of 8. Buy them on board.

Taxis: tel. 93 50 56 28 or 93 15 01 01. Around 50F from pl. de Casino to the Centre de Jeunesse Princesse Stéphanie, 80-100F to the Relais de Jeunesse in Cap d'Ail.

Bike Rental: Auto-Moto Garage, 7, rue de Millo (tel. 93 50 10 80), near the station. 5-speeds or mountain bikes 80F per day, 485F per week. Credit card deposit. Open Mon.-Fri. 8am-noon and 2-7pm, Sat. 8am-noon.

English Bookstore: Scruples, 9, rue Princesse Caroline (tel. 93 50 43 52). Selection includes *Let's Go: Monaco* (but you're reading it). Open Mon.-Sat. 9:30am-noon and 2:30-7pm. V, MC. **English Radio Station:** 106.3FM. BBC news.

Hospital: Centre Hospitalier Princesse Grace, av. Pasteur (tel. 93 25 99 00 or emergency tel. 93 25 98 69), off bd. Rainier III, which runs along the train tracks. **Medical emergency** tel. 18.

Police: 3, rue Louis Notari (tel. 93 15 30 15). **Emergency** tel. 17.

Post Office: pl. Beaumarchais (tel. 93 50 69 87). Monaco issues its own stamps. For poste restante, specify Palais de la Scala, Monte-Carlo. **Branch office** across from the train station. Both offices open Mon.-Fri. 8am-7pm, Sat. 8am-noon. **Postal code:** MC 98000 Monaco.

ACCOMMODATIONS

Monaco is a glittering and glamorous place to visit, but unless you can secure a spot at the popular Centre de Jeunesse Princesse Stéphanie, you wouldn't want (and probably can't afford) to stay here. 95% of Monaco's hotels are rated two stars or higher, but a couple of "bargains" can be found near the train station or in **Beausoleil,** France, a five-minute walk from Monte-Carlo. Monaco's easy accessibility to the hostels in Antibes, Cap d'Ail, and Nice make it a perfect day (and nightlife) trip. Don't get stuck, though—the last train to Nice leaves at 11:55pm.

Centre de Jeunesse Princesse Stéphanie, 24, av. Prince Pierre (tel. 93 50 83 20; fax 93 25 29 82). From the train station, turn left up the hill and follow the signs 100m to the hostel. Almost as lovely as its namesake, with small 4- and 10-bed dorms, a terrace, and basketball court. Lockers in rooms (30F key deposit). Cooking, eating, smoking, and alcohol forbidden in dorms. In summer, arrive before 9am—reservations accepted only off-season. No lockout. Age limit 26 for non-students, 31 for students with ID. 3-day max. stay in summer, 7 in winter. 70F. Breakfast and sheets free with ID deposit. Laundry 30F. Reception Sept. 16-June, 7am-midnight; July-Sept. 15 7am-1am. Curfew strictly enforced. Check-out 9:30am.

Hôtel Villa Boeri, 29, bd. du Général Leclerc (tel. 04 93 78 38 10; fax 04 93 41 90 95), in Beausoleil. Clean rooms with snazzy bathrooms and satellite TV. Some have balconies overlooking the sea. Singles 195F. Doubles 250-270F. Add 30-80F in July. 35F per extra person. Obligatory breakfast 30F. V, MC, AmEx.

Hôtel Diana, 17, bd. du Général Leclerc (tel. 04 93 78 47 58; fax 04 93 41 88 94), in Beausoleil. Clean, decent accommodations *à la* 70s. One single at 180F, others 220-280F. Doubles 180-340F. Triples 350-375F. Breakfast 35F. V, MC, AmEx.

Hôtel Cosmopolite, 4, rue de la Turbie (tel. 93 30 16 95), very near the train station. Clean, functional rooms with rickety door knobs. Some have psychedelic bedspreads, others are decorated in mustard or mint green. The truly lucky might get a light fixture straight from "The Jetsons." Singles 196-282F. Doubles 220-326F. Triples 332-369F. Quads 380-452F. Breakfast 32F.

FOOD

Monégasque specialties include *barbagiuan,* a crispy fried dough cake, and *stofaci,* a delicious fish casserole cooked with white wine, cognac, tomatoes, and olive oil. Picnickers should stop by the fruit and flower **market** on pl. d'Armes (open daily 6am-1pm) at the end of av. Prince Pierre or the huge **Carrefour** (tel. 92 05 57 00) in Fontvieille's shopping plaza. From the station, turn right and then right again onto rue de la Colle until you reach pl. du Canton, cross the street, and head down the escalator (open Mon.-Sat. 8:30am-10pm).

Most of Monaco's restaurants aren't aimed at budget travelers, but there are a few exceptions, including **Le Calypso** (tel. 93 15 07 77), on Jetée Nord off bd. Louis II, on one of the long arms that stretches into the Port de Monaco. Sitting by the ocean in the shade with the wind blowing, you'll look like you stepped straight out of an *Orangina* commercial. Savor meat, seafood, and salads, especially the lunchtime buffet (42-52F; open 9:30am-12:30am). **Le Périgordin,** 6, rue des Oliviers (tel. 93 30 06 02), is a high-class operation (don't wear shorts) with pedestrian prices during lunch. French specialties grace the 55F lunch *menu* (open Mon.-Fri. 9:30am-2pm and 7:30-10pm, Sat. 7:30-10pm). To satiate that salsa craving, head for **Le Texan,** 4, rue Suffren Reymond (tel. 93 30 34 54) by the station. This Western version of the Hard Rock Café draws celebrities and crowds to its bar every night. The restaurant offers quesadillas (48F), salads (41-67F), fried chicken (75F), and burgers (68-70F). Beer's 14F, 10F during happy hour weekdays from 3:30 to 7:30pm (open 9am-3am).

SIGHTS AND ENTERTAINMENT

The wealth, mystery, and intrigue of Monte-Carlo revolve around the famed **Casino,** where Mata Hari once shot a Russian spy and Richard Burton wooed Liz Taylor with an obscene diamond. Surrounded by gardens overlooking the coast, the 1878 building was designed by Charles Garnier and resembles his Paris opera house. The interior, shining with 19th-century extravagance—red velvet curtains, gilded ceilings, and gold and crystal chandeliers—is worth visiting, even if you're not a gambler. The slot machines open at 10am, while blackjack, craps, and roulette (25F minimum) open at 5pm. These games can also be found at the **Café de Paris,** next to the big casino. Admission here is free, as are the slot machines in the casino itself (opens at 2pm; 21 and over, no shorts, sneakers, sandals, or jeans). Peeking at the *salons privés,* where such French games as *chemin de fer* and *trente et quarante* begin at 3pm, will cost you 50-100F (open at noon). Bring a passport as proof of age. The casino also houses the sumptuous **Atrium du Casino** theater (tel. 92 16 22 99), one-time venue for Diaghilev's Ballet-Russe. You can visit only by attending a ballet or opera performance; tickets cost 150-600F (students 75F).

Even if you've lost your shirt at the casino, you can still admire the royal robes at the **Palais Princier** (tel. 93 25 18 31). Perched on a cliff high above Monte-Carlo, the palace is the sometime home of Prince Rainier and his tabloid-darling family. The Grimaldis have ruled this small but fiercely independent principality since 1297, when things got too hot in Genoa for François Grimaldi and he escaped with a few men-at-arms dressed as monks to capture unsuspecting Monaco. Hence the Grimaldi coat of arms you'll see at the palace: a pair of armed brothers. Things have cooled down since the sordid succession dramas of the 16th century, which ended with a splash when disgruntled *Monagésques* tossed Prince Honoré I into the sea. Ever-vigilant for renegade monks, Monaco performs the **changing of the guard** outside the palace daily at 11:55am, a ritual which, given the size of the principality, recalls a Marx Brothers routine. In their lily-white summer uniforms (they change to black after Labor Day, in accordance with the laws of fashion), the soldiers look about as functional as the palace cannon, strategically positioned to bombard the shopping district. When the flag is down, the prince is away and the doors open to tourists. Take a tour of the small but lavishly decorated palace with its stunning frescoes and marble inlay. Also on display are the hall of mirrors, Princess Grace's stunning official state portrait, Prince Rainier's throne, and—of special interest to American patriots—

the chamber where England's King George III died (open daily June-Sept. 9:30am-6:30pm; Oct. 10am-5pm; admission 30F, students 15F).

Next door is the stately **Cathédrale de Monaco,** 4, rue du Colonel Bellando de Castro (tel. 93 30 88 13). The former princes of Monaco are buried within this white Romanesque-Byzantine church whose ceiling is decorated with saints and palms. Prince Rainier and Grace Kelly were wed here in 1956. The victim of a tragic 1982 car accident, Princess Grace lies in a tomb behind the altar marked simply with her latinized name, "Patritia Gracia." Her younger daughter, Princess Stéphanie, chose a local judge's chambers for her marriage to her former bodyguard two years ago but stopped by the cathedral on her wedding day to place flowers on her mother's grave. A full choir sings mass every Sunday from September to June at 10am (open daily 9am-12:30pm and 1:30-4:30pm; free).

Three naturalist sights must be squeezed into even the most casual daytrip. The tremendous **Musée Océanographique,** av. St-Martin (tel. 93 15 36 00), houses thousands of species of fish and marine animals from every sea on earth. Bolstered by the attentions of former directors—sea-*czar* Jacques Cousteau and energetic, species-discovering marine biologist-cum-prince Albert I—the aquariums are so carefully balanced that they are well on their way to becoming a self-sustaining biosphere. The amazing collection features rare feathered fish, whale skeletons, and other wonderful and strange sea creatures. This museum, built out of 100,000 tons of white stone on the edge of a cliff, is an absolute must-see for anyone interested in marine life. Schedule a good three hours for a full visit. (Open daily July-Aug. 9am-8pm; April-June and Sept. 9am-7pm; Oct. and March 9:30am-7pm; Nov.-Feb. 10am-6pm. Admission 60F, ages 6-18 and students 30F, and worth every centime.) The **Jardin Exotique,** bd. du Jardin Exotique (tel. 93 30 33 65), sticks out in a principality famed for its gardens by virtue of its cactus collection. The garden is privy to exquisite coastal views and dungeon-like grottos with stalagmites and stalactites (open daily May 15-Sept. 15 9am-7pm; Sept. 16-May 14 9am-6pm or nightfall; admission 37F, students 18F). The newest addition to Monaco's fabulous foliage is the **Jardin Japonais,** av. Princesse Grace. Designed by Japanese architect Yasua Beppu, the garden and its cherry trees and tea house may bring you to a zen state, even in the relentless Riviera sun (open daily 9am-sunset; free).

The **Exhibition of H.S.H. the Prince of Monaco's Private Collection of Classic Cars,** les Terraces de Fontvieille (tel. 92 05 28 56), features 105 of the most sexy, stately, and just plain beautiful cars ever made, all part of Prince Rainier's personal collection. It includes the toy race cars of the fun-loving Prince Albert, hackney carriages from the 1880s, and the 1956 Rolls Royce Silver Cloud that carried Prince Rainier and his movie-star bride on their wedding day. Explanatory placards sit on sculptures made with engine parts designed by the Prince himself (open daily Dec.-Oct. 10am-6pm; admission 30F, students 15F). The museum also displays the car that won the first **Grand Prix de Monaco** in 1929. The famed race brings growling, zipping race cars to the principality every year in late May. In fact, the race is so popular that the Moyenne Corniche into Monaco is expanded to accommodate the 100,000 visitors who flood the area for that weekend.

One of the highlights of the summer is the **Fireworks Festival,** an explosive international competition that lights up the sky in late July and early August. If you're around in winter, go to a night of the **Festival International du Cirque,** which features the world's best circuses. A gala on the last night showcases the best acts (Jan. 30-Feb. 6 in 1997). For details about Monaco's events, festivals, and the Grand Prix, call the tourist office or the **Comité des Fêtes** (tel. 93 30 80 04).

In the evening, drop by the famous three-floor blues bar **Stars 'n' Bars,** 6, quai Antoine 1er (tel. 93 50 95 95), which has featured the likes of Prince, Chuck Berry, and the original Blues Brothers Band. They have big screen TVs for major sporting and musical events, billiards, live music every night at 11pm, and a dance floor. The restaurant serves jumbo sandwiches (36-69F) and salads (38-65F) 11am-midnight; the bar is open till 2:30am (beer 14F). You must be 18 for the first-floor sports bar, 21 for the music and dancing above. Arrive before 11pm to avoid long lines.

Menton

With its claim to be the warmest star in the Riviera's galaxy and its large senior citizen population, Menton (pop. 130,000) has become the Fort Lauderdale of France. Finally annexed in 1860, Menton and its former owner, Monaco, had flip-flopped between French and Sardinian control since 1346, leaving vestiges of Italian flavor in the cuisine and local accents. Indeed, Menton marks the last notch on the belt of the French Riviera, making it an ideal mellow layover on your way to Italy.

ORIENTATION AND PRACTICAL INFORMATION

With the train station at your back, walk to the left of the restaurant Le Terminus onto av. de la Gare. After two blocks, turn right onto **av. Boyer,** Menton's main drag, which is bisected by the Jardin Biove. The **tourist office** is on the left at 8, av. Boyer (tel. 04 93 57 57 00; fax 04 93 57 51 00) inside the grandiose **Palais d'Europe.** The staff hands out free maps and make reservations (open late June-early Sept. Mon.-Sat. 8:30am-6:30pm, Sun. 8:30am-12:30pm; early Sept.-late June Mon.-Sat. 8:30am-12:30pm and 1:30-6pm). The **Service du Patrimoine,** 5, rue Ciapetta (tel. 04 92 10 33 66; fax 04 93 28 46 85), gives tours of Menton's historic monuments, art exhibits, and everything else worth seeing in town. Tours in French last an hour and cost 30F. An **ATM** practices reverse peristalsis at the **Societé Général** on av. Boyer, as does the one at **Banque Populaire de la Cote d'Azur,** on av. Felix Faure. To rid yourself of unwanted *lire,* try the 24-hour **currency exchange machine** farther down the street at **Crédit Lyonnais,** 2, av. Boyer (tel. 04 93 28 60 60). To get to and from Menton, hit the **train station** at pl. de la Gare (tel. 04 93 87 30 00), where connections run to major cities in France. Two per hour toddle off to: Nice (35min., 24F); Cannes (80min., 48F); Monte Carlo (10min., 11F); and Cap d'Ail (13F). Also to Ventimiglia (15min., 13F), the first stop in Italy, where you can connect to major Italian cities such as Genoa (7 per day, 4hr., 59F). **Luggage storage** is 30F per day (open 8:30am-noon and 3-7pm), and **lockers** 15-20F per 72 hours (open 7am-10pm). **Buses** depart from the **gare routière** on promenade Maréchal Leclerc (tel. 04 93 28 43 27) and are cheaper than the train if you're making a same-day roundtrip. **Autocars Broch** (tel. 04 93 31 10 52) sends buses every hour on the hour from 7am-8pm to Nice (24F) and Monte-Carlo (10F50); prices are the same for one-way or same-day roundtrip. **Taxis** to the hostel will cost about 35F (tel. 04 93 35 72 37). Call 04 93 92 55 55 in a **medical emergency.** Dial 7 or 04 93 28 66 00 for the **police.** Across from the tourist office is the **post office** at cours George V (tel. 04 93 28 64 84), where **currency exchange** and an **ATM** await (open Mon.-Wed. and Fri. 8am-6:30pm, Thurs. 8am-6pm, Sat. 8am-noon; **postal code:** 06500).

ACCOMMODATIONS, CAMPING, AND FOOD

Hotels fill up quickly here in Menton, and the hostel is a hike from the station. The walk to the **Auberge de Jeunesse (HI),** plateau St-Michel (tel. 04 93 35 93 14; fax 04 93 35 93 07), is grueling. Head straight out of the station, follow rue de la Gare and cross under the train tracks at the bridge. Take the immediate first right onto allée de Namur up the hill, and the second left onto Escaliers des Oranges, and brace yourself for the 300 steps, always following the signs for "Camping St-Michel." Less hardy types may prefer to take bus 6 from the *gare routière,* which departs daily at 8:40 and 11:10am, 2 and 5pm (8F). Otherwise, call the hostel for the minibus (20F per person for 1 or 2 people, 10F per person for 3 or more). The strict management runs a members-only, clean, modern, sex-segregated hostel with free breakfast and a great view. (64F per night. 8-person tents with beds and electricity 55F per person. Dinner 48F. Sheets 12F. Reception open 7-10am and 5-11pm. Lockout 10am-5pm. Curfew 11pm or midnight depending on the season—be sure to ask, you won't be able to get in or out after it. No reservations. Open Feb.-Nov.) The **Hôtel Beauregard,** 10, rue Albert 1er (tel. 04 93 35 74 08), can be found behind and below the train station. Take the steps behind Le Chou Chou *tabac*/bar and turn right on rue Albert 1er. Squeaky-clean rooms (singles and doubles 150-170F, with shower 180-230F; breakfast 28F). If you've had enough stair-climbing, try **Le Terminus,** pl. de la Gare (tel. 04 93 35 77 00; fax 04 92 10 49 81), just opposite the train station, with comfortable, tidy rooms (singles and doubles 155F, with shower 210F; extra bed 40F; free showers; breakfast 27F). Also by the station, **Hôtel de Belgique,** 1, av. de la Gare (tel. 04 93 35 72 66), features exotic knick-knacks in its clean rooms from the owner's far-flung travels (rooms 180-210F, 50F per extra bed; breakfast 25F). Campers find shelter at **Camping Municipal du Plateau St-Michel,** by the hostel on route des Ciappes de Castellar (tel. 04 93 35 81 23). Enjoy hot showers and a view of Menton's bay (17F per person, 17F per site; reception Mon.-Fri. 8am-noon and 2:30-7:30pm, Sat.-Sun. 8am-noon and 5-8pm).

Meet your produce needs at the **Marché Carëi** on av. Sospel at the end of av. Boyer, which serves up fresh fare daily 7am-12:30pm. The **Shopi supermarket,** 35, rue Félix Faure, is open Monday to Saturday 8:30am-12:15pm and 3-7:15pm. For an excellent dinner of local specialties, head to **Le Terminus** (see above). The friendly owner may show you his art collection after he tickles your tastebuds with his 55F *menu,* which may include *Oncle Jean,* pesto-and-rice-filled egg rolls. Otherwise, wander the **plage des Sablettes,** next to the *vieille ville,* with its assortment of stuccoed restaurants and cafés. The pedestrian **rue St-Michel** in the *vieille ville* overflows with shops and restaurants (expect 60-70F *menus*). Look for *boulangeries* on **rue Partouneux,** or join the legions of ice-cream lickers at the **pl. aux Herbes.**

SIGHTS AND ENTERTAINMENT

Menton's prized attraction is the **Musée Jean Cocteau,** quai Napoléon III (tel. 04 93 57 72 30), next to *vieux port* 18 and the *vieille ville* on promenade du Soleil. Though best known for his brilliant work in film and drama, Cocteau was also skilled in the plastic arts. This 17th-century stronghold houses sketches, photographs of Cocteau and Picasso, playfully designed cuff-links, a vase shaped like a woman's face, and a pebbly mosaic of a lizard basking in the sun (open Wed.-Mon. 10am-noon and 2-6pm; free). Cocteau fans should also visit **La Salle des Mariages** in the Hôtel de Ville, an indescribably odd room Cocteau decorated as a Greek temple, replete with leopard rugs and red leather Inquisition-style seats that witness over 500 weddings a year (open Mon.-Fri. 8:30am-12:30pm and 1:30-5pm; admission 5F).

Rising above the municipal market is the bell tower of **Eglise St-Michel,** a 17th-century Baroque church with side chapels decorated by local artists (open 10am-noon and 3-5:15pm). The square in front of the church affords a glorious view of the **plage des Sablettes** below and the Italian coastline beyond.

The original Menton, **Le Monastère Annonciade,** sits calmly on a mountain overlooking the town. The **Chemin de Rosaire,** a path built by a *monégasque* princess to thank God that she hadn't caught the plague, is lined with chapels that lead the way to the monastery. The half-hour walk up the hill may seem tough on your legs, but think of the pilgrims who did it on their knees.

Corse (Corsica)

A story told to Corsican children says that on the sixth day of Creation, God decided to make Corsica. So the Almighty took the turquoise waters of the Mediterranean, the snow-capped splendor of the Alps, and the golden sunshine of the Riviera to create the island the Greeks called *Kallysté* (the most beautiful). Corsica offers a breathtaking and isolated respite for travelers who cannot bear the sight of another museum or the spire of another cathedral. Vineyards, twisting creeks, and sweet-smelling *maquis* (a tangle of lavender, laurel, myrtle, rosemary, thyme and various other herbs) cover the steep, craggy mountains of the interior.

Culturally and historically, Corsica is a blend of French and Italian heritages, but Corsicans prefer to recall their own independent history and will adamantly deny being anything but Corsican. Although all Corsicans speak French, they prefer their own language, an Italian dialect closely related to Tuscan. In the past the French government prohibited Corsicans from speaking the language or even using Corsican place names in an attempt to integrate the island into French society. Corsicans fought back by refusing to pay taxes. Until files were computerized, fiduciary buildings were regularly bombed to destroy income records. More recently, the Corsican language was reinstituted in the public school system, a sign of the island's growing cultural autonomy. Some groups, notably the outlawed Front de Libération National de la Corse, continue attempts to bomb their way to independence. The "nationalist" movement is less a monolith than an uneasy umbrella coalition, encompassing ecological, pro-violence, and anti-violence movements. Most Corsicans deplore the FLNC's extremism and question the sagacity of independence from French government and businesses, which directly provide 70% of Corsica's GNP.

Despite its feisty nationalism, Corsica's only brush with independence was in the 18th century. Prized through the ages, the island has suffered Greek, Roman, Pisan, Genoese, Saracen, and French invasions. Today, 16th-century Genoese *citadelles* dominate the hilly landscape, seeming to survey the Mediterranean for signs of attack. For nearly four centuries, internal clan rivalry prevented unification, leading to a Genoese takeover of the island in 1347. Corsica's contribution to English—*vendetta*—refers to the bloody family feuds that supplanted the Genoan justice system. A series of uprisings in 1729 initiated the Corsican War of Independence, also known as the Forty Years' War. In 1755, the revered Pasquale Paoli proclaimed the island an autonomous republic, created a university, and drafted a new constitution. The retreating Genoese ceded their protectorate to the French, who humiliated Paoli's army at Ponte Nuovo on May 8, 1769. Among the Corsican officers who quickly swore allegiance to France was a certain Charles Bonaparte. On August 15, 1769, his son Napoleon was born in Ajaccio.

Try to visit Corsica in the off season; although tourist services multiply between June 15 and the end of September, ferry prices soar by as much as 50%, and hotel prices can triple. Half the island's million annual tourists (mostly French, Italian, and German) visit in July and August, packing the beaches and hotels in coastal resorts. The summer climaxes in a double-barreled blast of holiday mirth on August 15, as all of France celebrates the **Fête de l'Assomption;** Corsicans observe Napoleon's birthday on the same day. Every town on the island erupts with fireworks in honor of their native son. Still, with a total population of less than 250,000 and the protected haven of the **Parc Naturel Régional** blanketing a quarter of the island, Corsica offers refuge from coastal crowds in its wilderness and the tiny villages of its heartland. Tourists depart by September, leaving the weather at its best and the waters at their warmest. Winter visitors can either stay in slumbering coastal towns or head inland to the snow-capped mountains for downhill and cross-country skiing.

Corsican cuisine is hearty, fresh, pungent, and expensive. Herbs from the *maquis* impart a distinct flavor to local specialties. Along the coast, seafood is excellent; try *calamar* (squid), *langouste* (spiny lobster), *gambas* (prawns), or *moules* (mussels).

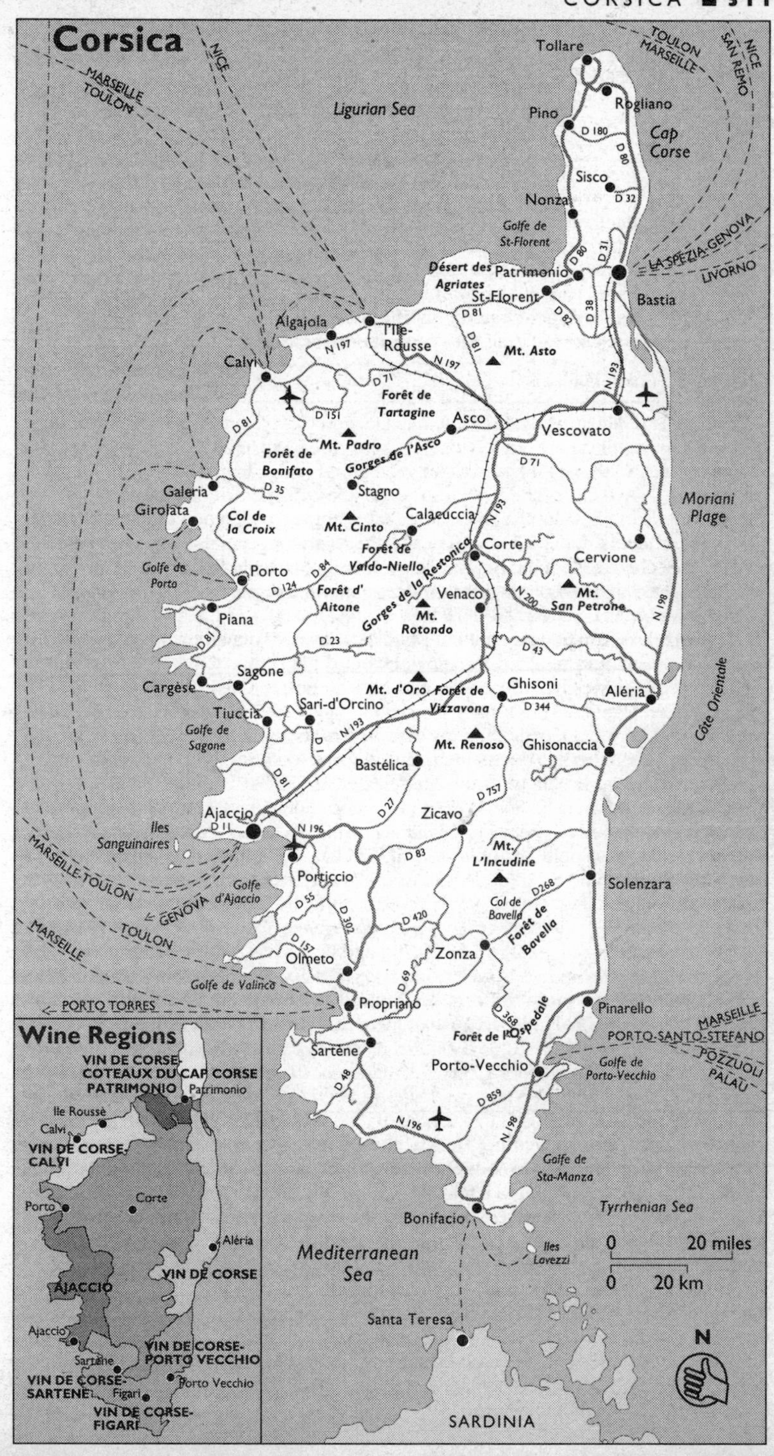
Corsica
Ligurian Sea
Tyrrhenian Sea
Mediterranean Sea
Cap Corse
Tollare
Rogliano
Pino
Sisco
Nonza
Golfe de St-Florent
Désert des Agriates
Patrimonio
St-Florent
Bastia
Algajola
l'Ile-Rousse
Calvi
Mt. Asto
Forêt de Tartagine
Asco
Vescovato
Mt. Padro
Gorges de l'Asco
Forêt de Bonifato
Stagno
Galeria
Girolata
Col de la Croix
Mt. Cinto
Calacuccia
Moriani Plage
Corte
Cervione
Forêt de Valdo-Niello
Gorges de la Restonica
Golfe de Porto
Porto
Forêt d' Aitone
Venaco
Mt. San Petrone
Piana
Mt. Rotondo
Côte Orientale
Sagone
Cargèse
Mt. d'Oro
Forêt de Vizzavona
Ghisoni
Aléria
Tiuccia
Sari-d'Orcino
Golfe de Sagone
Mt. Renoso
Ghisonaccia
Bastélica
Ajaccio
Iles Sanguinaires
Zicavo
Mt. L'Incudine
Porticcio
Golfe d'Ajaccio
Solenzara
Col de Bavella
Forêt de Bavella
Zonza
Olmeto
Golfe de Valinco
Propriano
Pinarello
Sartène
Forêt de l'Ospedale
Porto-Vecchio
Golfe de Porto-Vecchio
Golfe de Sta-Manza
Bonifacio
Iles Lavezzi
Santa Teresa
SARDINIA
NICE
MARSEILLE TOULON
TOULON MARSEILLE
NICE SAN REMO
LA SPEZIA-GENOVA
LIVORNO
MARSEILLE-TOULON
GENOVA
TOULON
MARSEILLE
PORTO TORRES
MARSEILLE
PORTO-SANTO-STEFANO
POZZUOLI
PALAU
0 20 miles
0 20 km
N
Wine Regions
VIN DE CORSE-COTEAUX DU CAP CORSE
PATRIMONIO
Ile Roussè
Calvi
VIN DE CORSE-CALVI
Corte
Porto
Aléria
VIN DE CORSE
AJACCIO
Ajaccio
VIN DE CORSE-PORTO VECCHIO
Sartène
VIN DE CORSE-SARTENE
Porto Vecchio
Figari
VIN DE CORSE-FIGARI

CORSICA

In fall and winter you can order *nacres* (pink-shelled mollusks) and *oursins* (sea urchins). Other delicacies include *pâté de merle* (blackbird pâté), *saucisson* (pork sausage), and *sanglier* (wild boar). Excellent cheeses include *brocciu* and *chèvre,* both white goat cheeses; *niolo* is a sharp, dry goat cheese. Grocery stores stock a variety of honeys, nougats, cakes, jams, and spices, all flavored with the ubiquitous *maquis.* The fragrant, flavorful Corsican wines are as inexpensive as their cousins on the mainland. Tourist offices can provide lists of Corsica's many *caves.*

The **Agence du Tourisme de la Corse,** 17, bd. du Roi Jérôme (tel. 04 95 21 56 56; fax 04 95 51 14 40), in Ajaccio, publishes guides (free at tourist offices) to all of Corsica's hotels, hostels, *gîtes d'étape,* and campsites. There are few inexpensive hotels, and most of them fill early in the morning in July and August. Campgrounds lie close to most cities; a government ban on unofficial camping is strictly enforced. *Gîtes* fill on a first come, first served basis, but latecomers can usually pitch a tent.

GETTING THERE

Air France and **Air Inter** fly to Bastia, Ajaccio, and Calvi from Paris (961F, roundtrip 1375F, discounts of up to 300F); Nice (324-474F, roundtrip 648-945F); Marseille (356-524F, roundtrip 709-1045F); and Lyon (664-1069F, roundtrip 1325-2335F). Flights from Rome to Ajaccio cost 2285F, roundtrip 1580-2544F. Lille to Bastia costs 775-1800F, roundtrip 1550-3600F. Discounted fares apply to everyone under 25 or over 60, and to students under 27, on off-peak "blue flights" (several per week, boxed in blue on the schedule). Phone Air France's offices in Marseille (tel. 04 91 39 36 36) or Paris (tel. 01 45 46 90 00). Air Inter's offices are at the airports in Ajaccio (tel. 04 95 29 45 45) and Bastia (tel. 04 95 31 79 79).

Corsican **ferries** are like incontinent poodles: they're expensive, and they go when you least want them to. The **Société National Maritime Corse Méditerranée (SNCM)** sends ferries from Marseille and Nice to Bastia, Calvi, Ile Rousse, Ajaccio, and Propriano. The passages, many overnight, take 6 to 12 hours. About two boats per day travel between Corsica and the mainland in the off season; a few more go during summer. The schedule fluctuates, so call ahead to confirm times and always arrive well before departure. The trip from Marseille costs 278-310F (under 25 219F); from Nice, 252-278F (191-219F). SNCM does not accept Eurail passes. If you plan to bring a car, it'll cost 207-722F. Prices fluctuate according to day of departure, size of car, and return departure point, if applicable. **SNCM** has offices in Ajaccio, quai L'herminier (tel. 04 95 29 66 88 for info, 04 95 29 66 99 for reservations; fax 04 95 29 66 77); and Bastia, Nouveau Port (tel. 04 95 54 66 88 for info, 04 95 54 66 99 for reservations; fax 04 95 54 66 69). Additional offices include **Agence TRAMAR** in Calvi, quai Landry (tel. 04 95 65 01 38; fax 04 95 65 09 75); and Ile Rousse, av. J. Calizi (tel. 04 95 60 09 56; fax 04 95 60 02 56); as well as **Agence SORBA** in Propriano, quai commandent-L'herminier (tel. 04 95 76 04 36; fax 04 95 76 00 98); and Porto-Vecchio, **Société d'Acconage Porta-Vecchiaise et Inter Sud Voyages,** Port de Commerce (tel. 04 95 70 06 03; fax 04 95 70 33 59). SNCM offices are in Nice, quai du Commerce (tel. 04 93 13 66 99; fax 04 93 13 66 81); Marseille, 61, bd. des Dames (tel. 04 91 56 30 10 for info, 04 91 56 30 30 for reservations; fax 04 91 56 35 86); and Paris, 12, rue Godot-de-Mauroy (tel. 05 49 24 24 24; fax 05 49 24 24 09). **Corsica Ferries** crosses from the Italian ports of Livorno, Genoa, and La Spezia to Bastia (130-190F). Corsica Ferries has offices in Bastia, 5, bd. Chanoine-Leschi (tel.04 95 32 95 95; fax 04 95 32 14 71); in Nice, 3, quai Papacino (tel. 04 93 55 54 04); and Paris, 25, rue de l'Arbre sec (tel. 01 47 03 96 30). Call the Bastia number for reservations. **NAVARMA/Mobylines** sends ferries to Bastia from La Spezia, Livorno, Piombino, and Porto San Stefano on the Italian mainland (150-180F); it also links Bonifacio to Santa Teresa on Sardinia (48-70F). Call the office in Bonifacio, port de Bonifacio (tel. 04 95 73 00 29), for reservations to Sardinia, or the office in Bastia, 4, rue Commandant-Luce-de-Casablanca (tel. 04 95 31 46 29 or 04 95 31 62 47), for others. **Siremar** (tel. 04 95 73 00 96) and **Mobylines** (tel. 04 95 73 00 29) run from Santa Theresa to Bonifacio (July-Sept. 14 per day, April-June 6-8 per day, Oct.-March 2 per day; 58-80F per person (more expensive on weekends), 140-250F per car).

GETTING AROUND

Rumor has it that Machiavelli and the Marquis de Sade collaborated on the design for Corsica's Byzantine transportation system. In this purgatory of high rates, missed connections, and irregular service, the beautiful landscape is a traveler's only solace. **Train** service in Corsica is slow and limited; it doesn't serve all major towns (no rail south of Ajaccio) or accept rail passes. Trains tend to be on time, though. **Bus** companies are based in various cities but are neither cheaper nor more frequent than trains. Call **Eurocorse Voyages** (tel. 04 95 21 06 30) for further info. **Hitchhiking** on the island is possible for patient travelers, often carrying a sign with their destination and willingness to pay for gas, *"Je vous offre l'essence."* Ten liters of gas (about 60F) usually covers 100km on flat roads, but buses are safer and about as cheap.

Renting a **car** liberates groups of three or four. The least expensive models cost 350-530F per day, 1450-1806F per week, but shop around for one with unlimited mileage or you'll be coughing up 2-4F per km (see **Getting Around: By Car,** page 45). Gas stations are scarce, so plan ahead. The police will sometimes help if you run out. **Bicycle** rental can be pricey (about 90-120F per day with 1500F deposit). Puttering **mopeds** *(mobylettes)* or scooters run about 130-200F per day (with a 3000F deposit). Narrow mountain roads and high winds make cycling difficult and risky; drivers should be careful and honk before rounding mountain curves.

Hiking may be the best way to explore the island's mountainous interior. The longest marked route, the **GR20,** is a difficult 160km 13- to 15-day trail that takes hikers across the island from Calenzana (southeast of Calvi) to Conca (northeast of Porto-Vecchio). Do *not* tackle this trail alone, and be prepared for cold, snowy weather, even in early summer. Two other popular routes are the **Mare e Monti,** a seven-day trail from Calenzana to Cargèse, and the easier **Da Mare a Mare,** which crosses the southern part of the island between Porto-Vecchio and Propriano (4-6 days). The **Parc Naturel Régional de la Corse,** 2, rue Major-Lambroschini, Ajaccio (tel. 04 95 51 79 10; fax 04 95 21 88 17), publishes maps, an invaluable guide to *gîtes d'étapes,* and an assortment of other brochures. **Editions Didier et Richard,** 9, Grand-Rue, 38000 Grenoble, makes the best trail maps for the GR20. From January through May, additional trails are available for cross-country skiing. For further information, contact the Parc Naturel Régional. For skiing information, contact the **Comité Régional Corse de Ski,** 34, bd. Paoli, 20200 Bastia (tel. 04 95 32 01 94).

Ajaccio (Aiacciu)

Ajaccio (pop. 60,000), with its beaches, museums, and ties to the mainland, strikes a balance between pleasant beach resort and bustling urban center. Every August 15 the city springs to life to celebrate the birthday of its most famous son, Napoleon Bonaparte, whose name still adorns many of the town's streets, cafés, and hotels. Happy for any excuse to celebrate, locals dance wildly into the night. Join the natives in their revelry—you won't find a cheap place to sleep here, anyway.

ORIENTATION AND PRACTICAL INFORMATION

Ajaccio lies below the middle of Corsica's west coast, 80km north of Bonifacio. **Cours Napoléon,** which runs from pl. de Gaulle past the train station, is the city's main drag. The pedestrian **rue Cardinal Fesch** starts at pl. Maréchal Foch and runs roughly parallel to cours Napoléon. Pl. Foch, pl. de Gaulle, and the citadel (still an active military base) enclose the *vieille ville.* To reach pl. Foch and the tourist office from the ferry dock on quai L'herminier, bear left and walk toward the citadel. From the train station, turn right and walk along the water for about 10 minutes. To reach cours Napoléon, walk through the *place* and up av. du 1er Consul.

Tourist Information: Tourist Office, pl. Maréchal Foch (tel. 04 95 21 40 87 or 04 95 21 53 39; fax 04 95 61 01 19), in the Hôtel de Ville. Free maps and pamphlets. Open daily in summer 8:30am-8:30pm; in winter Mon.-Fri. 8:30am-6pm, Sat.

8:30am-1pm. Get hiking info at **Parc Naturel Régional,** 2, rue Maj Lambroschini (tel. 04 95 51 79 10; fax 04 95 21 88 17). Maps of trails and info on shelters. Open Mon.-Fri. 9am-noon and 2-6pm, closes by 5pm on Friday.

Money: Currency exchange at airport and along cours Napoléon and rue Cardinal Fesch. **Crédit Lyonnais,** 59, cours Napoléon, and **Banque Populaire Provençale et Corse,** pl. Foch, have 24-hr. **ATMs.**

Flights: Aéroport Campo dell'Oro (tel. 04 95 21 13 66), 5km away. Take bus 1 (direction: Ricanto or Aéroport, stop has a red sign) from cours Napoléon (every 20min., 7am-7pm, 20F). To: Nice (4 per day); Marseille (4 per day); Paris (2 per day). For info, call Air Inter (tel. 04 95 23 56 56) or see **Getting There,** page 512.

Trains: rue Jean-Jérôme Levie (tel. 04 95 23 11 03), between cours Napoléon and bd. Sampiero. Bear right from the *gare maritime,* walking away from the *vieille ville* and citadel on quai L'herminier. The station is on the left, past pl. Abbatucci. Open daily 6am-8pm. To: Corte (4 per day, 2hr., 62F); Calvi via Ponte-Leccia (2 per day, 5hr., 134F); Bastia (4 per day, 4hr., 115F). **Luggage storage** 19F.

Buses: *Gare routière,* quai L'herminier (tel. 04 95 21 28 01), part of the *gare maritime.* Info kiosk will help you sift through the assortment of companies, fares, and times; services and companies change seasonally. Open in summer daily 6:30am-8pm; in winter Mon.-Sat. 6:30am-8pm, Sun. 4-8pm. **Eurocorse Voyages** (tel. 04 95 21 06 30) goes via Porto-Vecchio (4 per day, 3hr., 110F) to Bonifacio (4 per day, 3½hr., 110F) and via Corte (2 per day, 1½hr., 60F) to Bastia (2 per day, 3hr., 105F). **Autocars SAIB** (tel. 04 95 22 41 99) runs via Porto (2 per day, 2¾hr., 65F) to Calvi (6hr. with a possible layover in Porto, 130F).

Public Transportation: TCA buses run every 20min. 7am-7pm. Take bus 1 from pl. de Gaulle to the *gare* and airport (20F) or down cours Napoléon (7F50, *carnet* of 10 58F, longer trips cost extra). Bus 5 from av. Dr. Ramaroni stops at Marinella and the beaches on the way to the Iles Sanguinaires (11F50). Schedules and reduced-price *carnets* at **TCA,** Diamant 111, pl. de Gaulle (tel. 04 95 51 43 23).

Ferries: SNCM, quai L'herminier (tel. 04 95 29 66 99 for reservations, 04 95 29 66 88 for info), across from the bus station. Two boats usually leave daily for several mainland cities (see **Getting There,** page 512). Open Mon.-Fri. 8-11:45am and 2-4pm, Sat. 8-11:45am, and whenever the ferries are in.

Taxis: pl. de Gaulle (tel. 04 95 21 00 87). To airport 90F daytime, 110F at night.

Car Rental: Ajaccio Auto Location (tel. 04 95 23 57 10), 350F per day, 1450F per week, unlimited mileage. **Ada Rent-a-Car** (tel. 04 95 23 56 57), 356F per day, 1500F per week, unlimited mileage. **Budget** (tel. 04 95 21 17 18), 390F per day, 1660F per week, unlimited mileage. **Avis** (tel. 04 95 23 92 50), 530F per day, 1530F per week, 300km free per day, 2F per km thereafter. In all cases you must be 23 or older, have had your license for at least 2 years, and leave a deposit.

English Books: Maison de la Presse, 2, pl. Foch (tel. 04 95 21 81 18). Open Mon.-Sat. 8:30am-noon and 2:30-8:30pm, Fri.-Sat. 3pm-midnight.

Hospital: Centre Hospitalier Notre-Dame de la Miséricorde, 27, av. Impératrice Eugénie (tel. 04 95 29 90 90). **Medical emergency** tel. 05 95 29 91 49 or 15.

Police: In the tourist office building (tel. 04 95 29 21 47). **Emergency** tel. 17.

Post Office: 13, cours Napoléon (tel. 04 95 51 84 75). Poste restante. Fax, photocopiers. Open Mon.-Fri. 8am-6:30pm, Sat. 8am-noon. **Postal code:** 20185.

ACCOMMODATIONS AND CAMPING

Ajaccio has many hotels, but brace yourself for prices that exceed those in Paris. Call ahead June-August; rates soar and vacancies plummet. The tourist office can help you find a hotel or recommend short-term apartments.

Hôtel Napoléon, 4, rue Lorenzo Vero (tel. 04 95 51 54 00; fax 04 95 21 80 40). A 3-star hotel with lobby, porters, and official reception on a quiet sidestreet near pl. de Gaulle. Rooms in shades of mustard with A/C, satellite TV, and full bath. Singles 310-370F. Doubles 360-400F. Rooms on the elevator-inaccessible second floor are considerably less expensive (singles 200F; doubles 250F). Breakfast 45F.

Hôtel Kallysté, 51, cours Napoléon (tel. 04 95 51 34 45; fax 04 95 21 79 00). Clean, non-smoking rooms with mini-fridge, TV, A/C, bath, and soundproof windows.

Some have phones. Singles 200-220F. Doubles 235-285F. Triples 330-365F. Quads 430F. Quints 495F. Breakfast 30F. Kitchenette 65F extra. V, MC.

Hôtel le Dauphin, 11, bd. Sampiero (tel. 04 95 21 12 94 or 04 95 51 29 96; fax 04 95 21 88 69), halfway between the train station and *gare maritime.* 16 clean rooms with TV, squishy mattresses, shower, and toilet; some have view of the bay and ferry docks. Lively bar and restaurant downstairs. Hotel entry is unstaffed; single women may feel more comfortable elsewhere. Prices include breakfast; haggle if you don't want it. Singles 202-214F. Doubles 238-274F. Triples 262-292F. V, MC.

Hôtel du Palais, 5, av. Bévérini Vico (tel. 04 95 23 36 42; fax 04 95 23 06 96). Not the best located, most luxurious, or quietest palace, but spacious, clean rooms with showers make up for the lack of an imperial ballroom. Most rooms overlook a busy street, but 2 face a quieter courtyard. Singles 150-210F. Doubles with 1 bed 190-250F, with 2 beds 220-280F. Triples 250-310F. Breakfast 30F. Extra bed 50F.

Camping: Barbicaja (tel. 04 95 52 01 17), 4km away, the closest to town. Take bus 5 from av. Dr. Ramaroni just past pl. de Gaulle to "Barbicaja" (last bus at 7pm). 38F per person, 12F per tent, 12F per car. **U Prunelli** (tel. 04 95 25 19 23), near the bridge of Pisciatello, next to Porticcio, accessible by bus (tel. 04 95 25 40 37; 10F). 35F per person, 12F per tent, 14F per car.

FOOD

The **morning market** on bd. Roi Jérôme and on pl. César Campinchi behind the tourist office offers up all manner of scrumptious comestibles. A smaller market operates near the train station at pl. Abatuzzi on cours Napoléon (open Tues.-Sun. 6am-12:30pm). Try the **rue St-Charles** for a selection of restaurants serving local dishes. Pizzerias and *boulangeries* congregate on **rue Cardinal Fesch** and the pedestrian streets off pl. Foch towards the citadel (pizzas 35-50F). Cheap foods leap into customers' baskets at **Monoprix supermarket,** 31, cours Napoléon (tel. 04 95 21 51 05; open Mon.-Sat. 8:30am-7:15pm). **Caramelys,** 15, roi-de-Rome (tel. 04 95 51 10 66), dishes out the tastiest sweets this side of the Pecos (open daily July-Aug. 10am-noon and 4-10pm; Sept.-June 3-7:30pm; 10F per 100g).

La Calata (tel. 04 95 21 26 77), rue Danielle Casanova, on the quai near the citadel. Dine on the terrace by candlelight under a glorious web of vines *(pergola)* or inside in a cozy booth. Large portions of meat and seafood *paella* (90F). Pizzas 45-48F, pasta 25-50F. Open daily noon-2pm and 7:30-11pm. V, MC, AmEx.

Cafétéria La Serre, 91, cours Napoléon (tel. 04 95 22 41 55), past the train station as you head to the airport. Beautiful greenery, trellises, and fountains. Salads 12-35F, quiche 13F, ½ chicken 32F. Beautiful desserts 12-20F. Open daily in summer 11:30am-3pm and 7-10pm; in winter 11:30am-2:30pm and 7-9:30pm.

Au Bec Fin, 2bis, bd. du roi Jérome (tel. 04 95 21 30 52). Cuisine *à la corse* across from pl. Abatucci. *Menus* from 75F, *plat du jour* 60F. Pasta 60-65F, fish from 35F. Open Mon.-Sat. noon-2:30pm and 7:30-10:30pm.

Chez Paulo, 7, rue Roi-de-Rome (tel. 04 95 51 16 47). 65F *menus* and such Corsican specialties as *sanglier* (wild boar). Pizza (29-35F), pasta (35-140F), and fish (30-95F) served inside and out. Open daily noon-2:30pm and 7pm-5am. V, AmEx.

SIGHTS AND ENTERTAINMENT

If you're a Napoleonophile, you'll find Ajaccio's sights thrilling beyond compare. The **Musée National de la Maison Bonaparte,** on rue St-Charles (tel. 04 95 21 43 89), is modestly tucked away in the *vieille ville* between rue Bonaparte and rue Roi-de-Rome. Napoleon III refurnished the birthplace and childhood home of his uncle. It contains portraits of the Bonaparte family, documents concerning their life in Ajaccio, and family heirlooms. Ironically, the house briefly sheltered Hudson Lowe, Napoleon's jailer on St-Helena. (Open Mon. 2-5:45pm, Tues.-Sat. 9-11:45am and 2-5:45pm, Sun. 9-11:45am. Admission 20F, ages 18-25 13F, under 18 free.)

For variations on the same theme, visit the **Chapelle Impériale,** rue Fesch, the final resting place of most of the Bonaparte family (though Napoleon himself is buried in a modest little Parisian tomb; see page 135). Next door stands the **Palais Fesch,** 50-52, rue Cardinal Fesch (tel. 04 95 21 48 17), the impressive home of Napoleon's uncle. M. Fesch piled up wealth as a merchant during the Revolution. When he renounced his worldly goods for the Church, the new cardinal used the loot to amass a significant collection of 15th- and 16th-century Italian art and made his former residence a museum where Corsican youth could improve their cultural education, donating it to the city in 1839. (Both open Wed.-Mon. 10am-5:30pm; July-Aug. also open Fri. 10am-5:30pm and 9:30pm-midnight.)

The private **Musée du Capitellu,** opposite the citadel at 18, bd. Danielle Casanova (tel. 04 95 21 50 57), abandons the Napoleonic craze to present the history of Ajaccio in paintings, sculptures, and artifacts (open April-Oct. Mon.-Sat. 10am-noon and 2-6pm, Sun. 10am-noon; also nightly July-Aug. 9-11pm). The final member of Ajaccio's museum community is the **Musée à Bandera,** 1, av. Général Levie (tel. 04 95 51 07 34), which contains four rooms of military memorabilia tracing Corsican history from 3000 BC through World War II and (of course) one room dedicated to Napoleon. (Open in summer Mon.-Sat. 10am-noon and 3-7pm; in winter 10am-noon and 2-6pm. Admission 20F, students 10F.)

Southwest of Ajaccio at the mouth of the gulf, the **Iles Sanguinaires** (Bloody Islands) bare their black cliffs to the sea. **Promenades en Mer** (tel. 04 95 51 31 31) runs excursions to the islands daily April through September (120F). Call for reservations. Visible from these boats, the Genoese **Tour de la Parata** can be reached by bus 5 from av. Dr. Ramaroni (every hr. from 7am-7pm, 12F). The bus stops at numerous beaches along the way. The closest beach to the town center is **plage St-François,** beyond the citadel. You can find info on **mountaineering** in the area at **ASPTT Montagne,** 23, bd. Dominique Paoli (tel. 04 95 22 10 55).

On hot summer nights, locals head to nearby Porticcio to the *boîte de nuit* **Le Blue Moon** (tel. 04 95 25 07 70; open nightly in summer, weekends in winter). There's no public transportation after 7pm, but call to ask about the bus the club sends to Ajaccio twice a night. Closer to everything are **Discothèque Le Live** and **Le Cinquième Avenue** (tel. 04 95 52 09 77), both on route des Sanguinaires on the beach side of the citadel. Local women report that these clubs, as well as the lively late-night cafés along quai de la Citadelle, are usually fine for lone women.

Ajaccio often hosts a summer theater or classical music festival. Call the **Service Animation et les Festivités** (tel. 04 95 21 50 90) for more details. August 15 brings the three-day **Fêtes Napoléoniennes** (tel. 04 95 21 50 90), when the entire city celebrates the birth of their municipal obsession. Napoleonic plays, a parade, and special ceremonies culminate in a *pyrosymphonie* (firework display) in the bay.

Porto

Approaching Porto, as you pass through the startling red granite Calanche, the twisted landscape may make you think you've landed on Mars. Descend toward the sapphire waters of the Golfe de Porto to remember you're in the Mediterranean. The curves of the port are gorgeous, but the town's menagerie of modern buildings might induce you to head for its hills. Fortunately, the surrounding countryside with its wealth of natural sights eclipse any memory of the tawdry town. Porto is best used as a base for camping and hiking into the lush natural treasures of the area, including its balmy eucalyptus forest, the Gorges de la Spelunca, and the entrancing Calanche (see **Near Porto,** page 518).

ORIENTATION AND PRACTICAL INFORMATION

Porto is split into the high area, **Haut Porto,** also called **Quartier Vaita,** and the waterside area, **Porto Marina,** where some 15 hotels and restaurants scramble for space. The main road has no name, but it's the only one leading straight to the port. The **tourist office** (tel. 04 95 26 10 55; fax 04 95 26 14 25), a green glass building in front of the marina off the main road, provides information on day hikes, water sports, boat trips, beaches, and accommodations (open Mon.-Sat. 9am-noon and 2:30-

6pm). For info on longer hikes, try the **Parc Naturel Régional de la Corse** (tel. 04 95 21 56 54; open July-Aug. Mon.-Fri. 8:30am-12:30pm and 2-6pm), 10m from the tourist office. To **change money,** try your luck at the **Crédit Agricole** (tel. 04 95 26 14 15), along the main street (open Mon.-Fri. 8:45am-12:15pm and 1:45-5pm), or at a couple of hotels, including **l'Hôtel Idéal,** on the marina.

Autocars SAIB (tel. 04 95 22 41 99 in Ajaccio, 04 95 26 13 70 in Porto) run from Ajaccio (2 per day, 2½hr., 65F) or Calvi (1 per day, 3¼hr., 100F) to Porto. **Autocars Mordiconi** (tel. 04 95 48 00 04, in Corte) go to Porto from Corte in July and August (Mon.-Sat., 100F). **Taxis Ceccaldi Félix** (tel. 04 95 26 12 92) will take you to other villages for a hefty price. **Car, moped,** and **bike rental** from **Porto Location** (tel. 04 95 26 10 13), opposite the supermarkets in high Porto, gives you the option of exploring solo. (Open daily May-Sept., 10am-7:30pm. Cars 390F per day, 1990F per week, 2000F deposit. Mopeds 320F per day, 1700F per week, 4000F deposit. Bikes 90F per day, 500F per week, passport deposit. V, MC.) Emergency numbers include the **pharmacy** (tel. 04 95 26 11 72), **infirmary** (tel. 04 95 26 15 01), **SAMU** (tel. 15), **pompiers** (tel. 18, at Piana), and **police** (tel. 04 95 26 12 78). The **post office** (tel. 04 95 26 10 26), midway between the marina and high Porto, has poste restante. (Open July-Aug. Mon.-Fri. 9am-12:30pm and 1:30-3:30pm, Sat. 8:30-11:30am; Sept.-June Mon.-Fri. 9am-12:30pm and 2-4pm, Sat. 9-11am. **Postal code:** 20150.)

ACCOMMODATIONS, CAMPING, AND FOOD

For a small village, Porto is teeming with hotels; make sure yours doesn't require you to buy meals with your room *(demi-pension)* in the high season, as many places with restaurants do. Mme. Delleaux's **Studios Meublés Romulusa** (tel. 04 95 26 11 58) has the best deal in town: three tidy and well-equipped two-room apartments with kitchen and bathrooms, each 180F for two people or 360F for four. Call well in advance; these rooms go quickly. If you ask very nicely, you might get a discount at the **Restaurant Pizzeria Romulusa** above the apartments. The family atmosphere of **l'Hôtel du Golfe** (tel. 04 95 26 13 33) will welcome you in from the sun (singles 180F, doubles 220F, triples 300F, quads 335F, all with shower and toilet; breakfast 25F). Two **gîtes d'étapes** in nearby **Ota** offer multi-bed rooms. **Les Chasseurs** (tel. 04 95 26 11 37) is 4km inland from Porto on route D124 (60F, kitchen facilities). **Chez Félix** (tel. 04 95 26 12 92) is roughly 6km in on the D124; look for the Marché Félix (50F per night, breakfast 30F). The cheapest way to stay in Porto is to stake a tent at one of the three manicured **campgrounds** in Porto proper. The largest, **Camping Sole e Vista** (tel. 04 95 26 15 71), has showers and a rockin' bar (30F per person, tent 10F, car 10F). **Camping le Porto** (tel. 04 95 26 13 67) is as cozy as camping in your own back yard (27F per person, 10F per tent, 10F per car; hot showers included; reception open 9am-noon and 1-8pm). **Camping Les Oliviers** (tel. 04 95 26 14 49; fax 04 95 26 12 49), on the road to Calvi, has great facilities including free hot showers (36F per person in season, 28F off season, 14F per tent, 14F per car; reception open 8am-8pm).

If it's not a hotel in Porto, it's a restaurant—there are tons of places to eat, but prices vary with the season. If you see a special on *le loup,* don't think Little Red Riding Hood; *loup* is the word for bass here, usually freshly caught by one of Porto's three fishermen. If you happen upon the town when prices are sky high the prepackaged goodies of Ota's **Super Banco** supermarket (tel. 04 95 26 10 92) should help you stay solvent (open daily 8am-8pm).

SIGHTS AND ENTERTAINMENT

Porto's best view stretches beneath Corsica's first **Genoese tower,** built in 1549 by a Genoese governor when he annexed the town. Gasp your way past artists with more enthusiasm for the landscape than talent up the steep pink stone steps any time from 10am to 6pm (until 10pm July-Aug.) for 10F. The crowd thins out after 4pm. Escape the popular and sticky sands of the beach to bask on the sun-heated rocks stretching away from the old tower. The scent of eucalyptus strives mightily to lull you to sleep.

After watching the sun set into the gulf, head for one of Porto's numerous beachside bars, or dance the night away in one of its four *discothèques,* including the 20-year-old **Le FanFan**.

Near Porto: Girolata, Gorges de la Spelunca, and Les Calanche

Natural beauties greater than Porto's sighing eucalyptus beckon from every direction. Head 15km north to the quiet fishing village of **Girolata,** accessible only by sea or foot. Boat excursions let you bask in the glory of the sun and the cliffs on the way (tel. 04 95 26 15 16 for reservations; 2 per day; 170F). Be very, very quiet as you pass the **Réserve Naturelle de Scandola;** no one's allowed on the reserve so that France's last remaining pairs of *balbuzards* (sea or fishing eagles) can spend some quality time together. East of Porto along the D124, the scenery ascends as you pass Ota on your way to a wealth of challenging hikes through the **Gorges de la Spelunca.** Twenty-five km east of Porto, near the hillside town of **Evisa,** the **Forêt d'Aitone** provides a series of waterfalls and a web of trails of varying difficulties, all in the shade of the massive, centuries-old laricio pines. But the most astounding scenery on the entire island may be south of Porto, where the fascinating geological formations of the **Calanche** change mere rocks, as Guy de Maupassant wrote, into a "menagerie of nightmares petrified by the whim of some extravagant god." Eight km from Porto on D81, the **Chalet des Roches Bleues** serves as a bus stop (if you ask the driver) on the Ajaccio-Porto line, and as a starting point for short hikes in the area. The Dog's Head rock, on the sea-hugging side of D81 about 700m from the chalet towards Porto, marks an easy trailhead to the boulder known as the **Château Fort.** Start near the Virgin Mary chapel 400m uphill from the chalet towards Piana for a rewarding vista of the port. Two other steep trails begin closer to the chalet; the one on its Porto side near the bridge is an exquisite semi-torture. Nearby **Piana,** also on the bus line, makes a good base should you decide to heed the siren call of the Calanche.

Calvi

One of Corsica's smaller ferry ports, Calvi (pop. 5000) boasts the charm of a centuries-old city that has also done well in modern times. Unlike her local counterparts, this former Genoese fort has no eyesores of industry, but new and renovated buildings linked by clean, laurel-lined boulevards. From Calvi's fort an inspiring panorama of blues and greens unfolds before the visitor's eyes. With its sandy beaches, warm aquamarine waters, misty mountains, and nearly 2400 hours of sunshine per year (as opposed to Paris's 1700), this city could well be paradise—but surely no benevolent god would charge these prices! Despite the prices, in July and August this small seaside resort attracts tourists *en masse,* ballooning into a veritable United Nations of 25,000 Samsonite-wielding sunseekers.

ORIENTATION AND PRACTICAL INFORMATION

About 120km north of Ajaccio, Calvi is the closest Corsican city to France. Route N197 enters Calvi as av. Christophe Colomb, which begets av. de la République, which turns briefly into bd. Wilson, and finally terminates at the foot of the citadel. The Port de Plaisance hosts a bevy of expensive bars and restaurants at the bay's edge. Note that streets in Calvi rarely have numbers.

Tourist Office: Port de Plaisance (tel. 04 95 65 16 67; fax 04 95 65 14 09). Facing the beach, exit the back of the train station and turn left; follow the signs. Or, take av. de la République towards the citadel, curling right around the taxi stand at pl. de la Porteuse d'Eau. This small, half-hidden yellow building hands out the free, quadrilingual guide *A la découverte de Calvi,* as well as a free map. The knowledgable and *chic* staff won't make hotel reservations, but they do keep abreast of vacancies. Open daily mid-June-Aug. 8:30am-8:30pm; Sept.-mid-June Mon.-Sat. 9am-noon and 2-4pm. Call ahead, as hours tend to fluctuate.

Money: If you must exchange money here, try to stick with one of the banks on bd. Wilson. **Change Wilson** (tel. 04 95 65 37 44) bd. Wilson, changes AmEx traveler's checks at mediocre rates, no commission. Open daily 8am-8pm. From 8pm-8am, the restaurant/bar **Café du Port,** at Caltata Landry, acts as Change Wilson's agent; same rates, no commission. **ATMs** are across from the train station.

Flights: Aéroport de Calvi Ste-Catherine is 7km southeast of town. Unless you have a bike or rent a car, the taxi ride will cost you 60-70F. **Air Inter** (tel. 04 95 65 88 68; flight info 08 36 68 34 24) and **Corse Mediterranée** (tel. 04 95 29 05 00) fly to Paris, Nice, Marseille, Lyon, and Lille. (See **Getting There,** page 512.)

Trains: pl. de la Gare (tel. 04 95 65 00 61), at the end of Corso di la Republica near the Port de Plaisance. To Bastia (2 per day, 3hr., 89F), Corte (2 per day, 2½hr., 75F), Ajaccio (2 per day, 4½hr., 137F), Ile Rousse (Mon.-Sat. 8 per day in season, 4 off-season, 45min., 27F). Open daily 6am-8pm. **Luggage storage** 18F per day.

Buses: Autocar SAIB (tel. 04 95 26 13 70, in Porto) sends one bus daily to Porto (3hr., 100F). **Agence Les Beaux Voyages** (tel. 04 95 65 11 35), on av. Wilson across from the post office, runs buses to Bastia (daily, 2hr., 80F) with connections to Ajaccio. Buy tickets on board; bus stops at pl. Porteuse d'Eau Agence. Open Mon.-Sat. 9am-noon and 2-6pm.

Ferries: Call **Agence TRAMAR** (tel. 04 95 65 01 38) on quai Landry for SNCM tickets and information. Open Mon.-Fri. 8:30am-noon and 2-5:30pm, Sat. 8:30am-noon. Also **Corsica Ferries** (tel. 95 65 43 21; fax 95 65 43 22), on Port du Commerce. Open Mon.-Fri. 9am-noon and 3-7pm.

Taxis: (tel. 04 95 65 03 10), 24hr. Fare to airport 60-70F.

Car Rental: Hertz, 2, rue Maréchal Joffre (tel. 04 95 65 06 64 in Calvi, 04 95 65 02 96 at the airport). 440F per day, 1750F per week. (Open Mon.-Fri. 8am-noon and 2-7pm, Sun. 8am-noon. Airport office open daily 8am-8pm.) **Europcar** (tel. 04 95 65 10 35 in Calvi, 04 95 65 10 19 at airport), av. de la République, down the street from BVJ Corsotel, toward the citadel. 465F per day, 1806F per week. **Avis,** 16 av. de la République (tel. 04 95 65 06 74, airport 04 95 65 06 05). 530F per day, 1980F per week. (Open Mon.-Sat. 8am-noon and 3-7pm; airport location open Sun. 8am-noon.) **Budget** (tel. 04 95 65 09 79; fax 04 95 65 16 17; tel. 04 95 65 23 39 at airport), av. de la République. 450F per day, 1650F per week, unlimited mileage. (Open July-Aug. Mon.-Sat. 7am-11pm; Sept.-June Mon.-Sat. 7am-9pm.)

Bike Rental: Ambrosini, pl. Christophe Colomb (tel. 04 95 65 02 13). 100F per day, 500F per week; passport deposit. Open Mon.-Sat. 8am-noon and 2-6pm.

Medical emergency tel. 18—actually the fire department, but more efficient than the **Emergency Medical Unit,** Route du Stade (tel. 04 95 65 11 22).

Police: (tel. 04 95 65 09 94) av. Marché, in the *mairie.* **Emergency** tel. 17.

Post Office: (tel. 04 95 65 10 40) bd. Wilson, across from the *gare* and 50m to the right. Poste restante. Open Mon.-Fri. 8:30am-5pm, Sat. 8:30am-noon. **Postal code:** 20260.

ACCOMMODATIONS, CAMPING, AND FOOD

Prices for Calvi's hotels change depending on the current flux of tourists. Reserving ahead is wise for the summer months, a must for July. Weekly rentals are often cheaper; ask about these *tarifs dégressifs* at the tourist office. Don't be afraid to bargain with hotel owners in the off season.

Relais International de la Jeunesse U Carabellu (tel. 04 95 65 14 16). Exiting the front of the train station, turn left and walk along av. de la République, turning right at route de Pietra-Maggiore, follow the road signs 4km to the top of the mountain. Large, appealing rooms, some with spectacular views of the bay. Refreshingly quiet. All beds 70F, includes breakfast. Families are given their own room. Single-sex dormitories of 3-5 beds. Clean bathrooms. Sheets 10F. No official campsite, but the friendly staff will let those who ask nicely pitch a tent for free. Open June 1-Sept. 30. Best for those with a car, bike, or strong legs.

BVJ Corsotel, av. de la République (tel. 04 95 65 14 15; fax 04 95 65 33 72). Clean, airy rooms with 2-8 beds, shower, sink. Doubles reserved for couples. Outside on busy av. de la République, traffic races by all day and all night. Be careful not to step out of line or the manager will be quick to let you know it. 100F, 120F with breakfast; dinner 55F. No curfews or lockout. Open late March-Nov. 1.

Hôtel Sole Mare, route de St-François (tel. 04 95 65 09 50; fax 04 95 65 36 64), 300m from the *centre ville* on a residential street. Eager-to-please staff will show you to a quiet, sunny room with balcony, shower, toilet, and fabulous view. Swimming pool. Singles 160-180F, doubles 200-350F, triples 300-400F, quads 350-450F, depending on season. Breakfast 30F. Open April-Oct.

Hôtel Christophe Colomb, pl. Bel Ombra (tel. 04 95 65 06 04; fax 04 95 65 33 20). Clean, agreeable rooms with TV, toilet, and shower at the foot of the Citadel. Doubles 250F, triples 350F, quads 450F in season. Breakfast 35F. Open April-Oct.

Hôtel Belvédère, av. de l'Uruguay (tel. 04 95 65 01 25; fax 04 95 65 33 20). Calvi's only hotel open year-round, the Belvedere features bright halls, small rooms with toilet, shower, and TVs. In a prime location at the corner of bd. Wilson across the street from the citadel. Can be noisy. Doubles 200-350F, triples 250-350F, quads 300-400F, depending on the season. Breakfast 30F.

Casa Vecchia, route de Santore (tel. 04 95 65 09 33 or 04 95 65 17 64; fax 04 95 65 37 93). Cool, quiet, no frills accommodations at decent prices. Singles 150-170F. Doubles with shower 170-190F; with shower and toilet 245-290F; with shower, kitchenette, and toilet 310-360F. Breakfast 26F. Open May-Sept.

Camping: Les Tamaris, route d'Ajaccio (tel. 04 95 65 00 26 or 04 95 65 23 59; fax 04 95 65 35 25). Follow signs from train station. Peaceful, shady camping by a pebble beach. Hot showers included. 25F per person, 10F per tent, 7F per car in season. Terraced restaurant and bar. Open May-Sept. **Paduella,** R.N. 197 (tel. 04 95 65 09 16). This large campsite features hot showers, shady trees, and a short walk (250m) to a sandy beach. 27F per person, 13F per child, 11F per tent, 10F per car. Open May-Oct. **International,** R.N. 197 (tel. 04 95 65 01 75 or 04 95 65 36 11). Scads o' bands play here in summer, attracting a young crowd. Close to beach. 25F per person, 12F per child, 12F per tent, 8F per car. Open April-Oct.

Pickings are slim for cheap food in Calvi; your best bet is to buy the elements for a Corsican feast yourself. The narrow **rue Clemenceau,** limited to pedestrians, boasts the highest concentration of food shops in Calvi and hosts a daily covered market from 7am-1pm. If these hours are too limited for you, you can shop non-stop during the summer at **Supermarché Casino,** av. Christophe Colomb (tel. 04 95 65 21 90; open Mon.-Sat. 8am-8pm, Sun. 8am-1pm). **Food Burger,** a self-proclaimed *"Paninoteca,"* serves tasty grilled *panini* (22-25F) as well as cheeseburgers (12F) and crêpes (8-12F; open April-Sept. daily 9am-midnight; Oct.-March 10am-10pm). The stylish restaurants along the Port de Plaisance may offer tasty food and a great view, but at **La Galère** (tel. 04 95 65 19 54) you'll get local atmosphere and better prices. At the end of rue Clemenceau near the citadel. Pizza and pasta 32-52F; local dishes also available. (Open daily 11:30am-2:30pm and 6-11:30pm.) Otherwise, cheap pizzerias (as cheap as you'll find in Calvi) line av. de la République.

SIGHTS AND ENTERTAINMENT

At the entrance to the **citadel** (tel. 04 95 65 36 74), the inscription *"civitas Calvi semper fidelis"* (the city of Calvi is always faithful) recalls Calvi's loyalty to Genoa during the 16th century. Just beyond the entrance, an information center sells a *Guide of the Fort* (in English, 7F) that includes a map. Jusseveral other Mediterranean towns, Calvi claims to be the birthplace of Christopher Columbus; a small plaque marks the house where he may have been born. Calvi's other famous house tells a more likely story: Napoleon and his family sojourned here in 1793 when fleeing from political opponents in Ajaccio. The powers that be have stuffed the adjacent 16th-century **Cathédrale St-Jean-Baptiste** with as many relics as would fit in one house of worship; wind your way to the top of the citadel to take a peek. The Baroque cathedral holds ecclesiastical works of art, as does the museum in the **Oratoire St-Antoine,** built in 1510. (Cathedral open 9am-noon and 2-7pm daily. Access to the Oratoire by guided tour only; call the tourist office. 45F per person, 15F per person in a group.) Check out the view from **Chapelle de Notre Dame de la Serra.** From there you can see the beautiful pink and cream **Eglise Sainte Marie-Majeure** in the *basse ville* (open 9am-noon and 2-7pm; 45F per person).

If you tire of the wind kicking sand in your face on the 6km stretch of expensive **public beach,** the rocks surrounding the citadel offer a secluded shelter to bask in the sun. Calvi also marks the trail head of the **GR20,** a hiking route which transverses all of Corsica. Ask the tourist office for info on short hikes into the Balagne.

Calvi hosts several festivals, including the **Festival du Jazz** (tel. 04 95 65 16 67) in mid- to late June, when over 200 musicians give impromptu performances. The dramatic re-creation of the crucifixion in the citadel occurs at Easter; called **La Passion du Christ** (tel. 04 95 65 23 57), it attracts religious and secular tourists to its macabre ritual performed to expiate the townspeople's sins for the year. In mid-September, the **Rencontres Polyphoniques** (tel. 04 95 65 23 57) celebrates traditional Corsican singing, and in October the **Festival du Vent** (tel. 04 95 65 16 67) glorifies everything that involves the wind, from wind instruments to windsurfing.

The bars on the **port de Plaisance** glitter brightly in the summer. If the steep prices sober you up, buy your booze at **Balaninu Nobile,** av. Christophe Colomb (tel. 04 95 65 37 10; open April-Sept. daily 8am-noon and 4-8pm, Oct.-March 8am-noon). Locals come from far and wide to **La Camargue** (tel. 04 95 65 08 70), a *discothèque* on the road to Ile Rousse. Things start to get good after midnight; call for the schedule of shuttle buses running from Calvi. For a mellower atmosphere and older crowd, head to the **Tao** piano bar and restaurant (tel. 04 95 65 00 73). Locals are extremely proud of this renowned establishment located in the citadel.

■ Near Calvi: Ile Rousse and the Balagne

In 1758 Pasquale Paoli, leader of independent Corsica, built the town of **Ile Rousse (Isula)** to compete with Calvi, which he resented for its allegiance to Genoa. The coastline between the two rivals presents the most accessible view of Corsica's rugged good looks, luring crowds with its pearl-shaped coves, opalescent waters, and powdery sand. Ile Rousse's **tourist office** is at the foot of pl. Paoli (tel. 04 95 60 04 35; fax 04 95 60 24 74). Exit the station and turn right, following the rte. du port, then bear right at the fork. Walk by the pillared market and across the square. The office can brief you on hotel vacancies as well as camping and hiking; pick up their free pamphlet *Walks and Hikes in the Balagne* (open April-Oct. Mon.-Sat. 9am-1pm and 2:30-7:30pm; Nov.-March 9am-noon). The **trains,** called **Tramways de la Balagne,** travel the coast between Calvi and Ile Rousse (July-Aug. 8 per day, 50 min.; Sept.-June 4 per day). The line is divided into three sections; each costs 9F, a *carnet* of six tickets 44F. Several beaches and campgrounds lie along the route—hop off when you see one that looks particularly enticing, such as the buffeted beach at **Algajola,** popular with windsurfers. SNCM sends **ferries** (191-278F) from Ile Rousse to Nice (2-7 per week). Call **Agence TRAMAR** on av. J. Calizi (tel. 04 95 60 09 56) for more info (open Mon.-Fri. 8:30am-noon and 2-3:30pm, Sat. 8:30am-noon).

Reasonable accommodations exist in Ile Rousse, but calling ahead is crucial. **Hôtel le Grillon,** 10, av. Paul Doumer, off av. Piccioni (tel. 04 95 60 00 49; fax 04 95 60 43 69) has sunny, clean, pleasant rooms with shower toilet, and firm mattresses; some have balconies and TV. (Singles 160-260F, doubles 190-290F, triples 220-320F depending on season. Breakfast 30F. Open March-Oct. V, MC, AmEx.) Since most of the town's other hotels cost more than 300F per night, it might be wise to stay in Calvi and take the train. For camping under olive trees near the beach, try **Les Oliviers** (tel. 04 95 60 19 92 or 04 95 60 25 64), 800m from the town center on the road to Bastia. 25F per person, 13F per tent, 8F per car. Open April-Sept. Or take the train to **Camping Bodri** (tel. 04 95 60 19 70), 1.5km from Ile Rousse on the route toward Calvi. Hot showers, grocery, bar, close to the beach and train tracks (22F per person, 11F per child, 20F per tent, 10F per car; prices halved in Oct.; open May-Oct.).

Picnicking on the beach is allowed as long as you clean up after yourself. The daily **covered market** off pl. Paoli is filled with local fruits and more (daily 7am-1pm). The local **Super U** (tel. 04 95 60 02 46) carries on where the market leaves off (av. Paul Doumer off av. Piccioni; open Mon.-Sat. 8:45am-12:30pm and 3:30-6:30pm). Inexpensive pizza and pasta await the hungry in the snack bars along pl. Paoli, but you'll be rewarded if you move beyond their glitz to **Restaurant des Voyageurs,** rue Graziani (tel. 04 95 60 00 39). Their Corsican *bruschetta* (35-42F), a meal in itself, is worth the trip from Calvi. In the summer, **Le Challenger,** av. Calizi (tel. 04 95 60 20 70), heats up around midnight with dancing, karaoke, and live bands. Under the shady trees of pl. Paoli, **Le Balanino** (tel. 04 95 60 12 90) serves Corsican *menus* for 75F (open Mon.-Sat. 11:30am-2:15pm and 6:30pm-midnight).

To learn about what's under all that azure water, walk 5-10 minutes along the beach toward Bastia to the **Musée Océanographique de l'Ile Rousse** (tel. 04 95 60 27 81). The dark, tomb-like aquarium, with its sea turtles and big fish in small tanks, is accessible only by guided tour (1½hr., 44F adult, 34F child; call for schedule). A number of *caves* operate outlets in Ile Rousse. The tourist office supplies a useful English pamphlet called *Welcome to Corsica—the Golden Vines Island*, as well as others in French. Many vineyards are within a few km of town, but none are accessible by public transport. Visiting hours lengthen during the September harvests.

Both Calvi and Ile Rousse are located in the **Balagne** region of Corsica, dotted with olive trees and pristine mountain villages, many of which are accessible by foot. For the adventurous and healthy, the beach at Lumio is only 15 minutes away by train from Calvi. Here, on the mountain the Romans christened *Ortus Solis* (where the sun rises), the modern village lies meters away from its ancient counterpart Occi, mysteriously abandoned one morning in 1852. Not far off is the **Site archéologique du Monte Ortu** where neolithic artifacts have recently been discovered. Further inland lies **Calenzana,** known as "the garden of the Balagne." The famous **GR20** trail (220km) can be found here, as well as a 17th-century Baroque church named for Ste. Blaise that overlooks the peaceful **Cimetière des Allemands.** Every May 21 local Catholics make a pilgrimage to the **Sanctuaire de Ste-Restitude,** 1.5km out of town, named for the regional patron saint. **Sant Antonino** is to the east toward Ile Rousse. The highest village in the Balagne, it was built on a peak by the Moors in the 9th century, and its narrow streets remain accessible only by foot.

To experience the rich cultural heritage of the Balagne full-force, be sure to head to **Pigna.** The home of a renowned music school, the village plays host to many musical concerts throughout the year, and local craftsmen make traditional Corsican instruments (call 04 95 61 77 31 for concert info). **Autocars Mariani,** bd. Wilson in Calvi (tel. 04 95 65 00 47 or 04 95 65 04 72), can take you over the hills and far away to these sleepy *vieux villages* in a comfy tour bus (tours from 75F; open Mon.-Sat. 9am-noon and 2-7pm). The Calvi and Ile Rousse tourist offices have info on routes for hikers and bikers. To learn about local handicrafts featured in each village, ask for the free booklet *Strada di l'Artigiani.*

Corte (Corti)

Corte's history, character, and mountainous location in Corsica's geographical center distinguish it from its coastal counterparts. Yet, halfway between Ajaccio and Bastia, Corte is in many ways the most Corsican of Corsican towns. Rather than being a relic of Genoese dominance over the island, the town's remarkable citadel, towering 100m over the town, was built by a 15th-century Corsican feudal lord. The city glowers under noticeably more graffiti promoting independence than other Corsican cities. Known as the *"capitale sentimentale de l'île"* (sentimental capital of the island), Corte has an abundance of youth as home to Corsica's only university (2600 of its 6000 residents are students). Thankfully, these impoverished scholars keep prices low in the only city on the island that approaches reasonableness for budget travelers. Despite an overabundance of blockish buildings in the lower town, the old city's stone stairways, unexpected fountains, and wild roses lend grace to the upper reaches of this mountain refuge.

ORIENTATION AND PRACTICAL INFORMATION

To reach the *centre ville* from the train station, turn right on D14 (alias av. Jean Nicoli), cross two bridges, and follow the road until it ends at **cours Paoli.** To reach the **citadel,** turn left onto cours Paoli until you reach **pl. Paoli,** the place to be if you're a pizzeria. Struggle up the steep **rue Scoliscia** until you faint at the citadel's gates. Corte is easily accessible by foot, though it helps if you're going downhill.

Tourist Information: Commission Municipale du Tourisme (tel. 04 95 46 26 70). Helpful info on activities around Corte, as well as a reservation service. At the top of ruelle de la Fontaine off pl. Paoli. Useful bus schedule. Open July-mid-Sept. Mon.-Sat. 9am-8pm; mid-Sept.-June Mon.-Sat. 8am-noon and 3-7pm, Sun. 9am-noon. The **Parc Naturel Régional** office (tel. 04 95 46 04 88), at the citadel, has hiking information and advice for excursions. Open late June-Sept. 9am-1pm and 4-7pm.

Travel Agencies: Cyrnéa, 9, av. Xavier Luciani (tel. 04 95 46 24 62; fax 04 95 46 11 22), has info on and sells tickets for flights, trains, and ferries. Open Mon.-Fri. 9am-noon and 3-7pm, Sat. 9am-noon.

Money: ATMs lurk at **Crédit Agricole** and **Société Général,** both on cours Paoli.

Trains: (tel. 04 95 46 00 97), at the rotary where av. Jean Nicoli and N193 meet. To: Bastia (2-4 per day, 1¾hr., 55F); Calvi via Ponte-Leccia (2 per day, 2½hr., 75F); and Ajaccio (4 per day, 2½hr., 63F). **Luggage storage** 19F per bag per day. Open daily April-Sept. 7:45am-6:30pm; Oct.-March 7:45am-noon and 2-6:30pm.

Buses: Eurocorse Voyages (tel. 04 95 31 03 79). Call to find out pickup locations; there's no actual office in Corte. To: Bastia (2 per day, 1¼hr., 55F) and Ajaccio (2 per day, 2hr., 60F). **Autocars Mordiconi** (tel. 04 95 48 00 04), runs to Porto (July-Sept. 15 only, 1 per day, 3½hr., 100F). Call for alternate off-season schedule.

Taxis: Taxi Salviani (tel. 04 94 46 04 88), at the train station.

Car Rental: Europcar, 28 cours Paoli (tel. 04 95 46 02 79). 580F per day, 1890F per week. 2F per km above 200km. Open Mon.-Fri. 8:30am-noon and 2-6pm.

Moped Rental: Scoot'Air, pl. Paoli (tel. 04 95 46 01 85). 1-person mopeds 150F per day, 800F per week; 2-person mopeds 200F per day, 1000F per week. Passport deposit. Open Mon.-Fri. 8:30am-noon and 2:30-7pm.

Youth Center: Bureau Information Jeunesse de Corte (BIJC), rampe Ste-Croix (tel. 04 95 61 03 26). Open Mon.-Fri. 8:30am-noon and 2-6pm.

Hospital: Hôpital de Corte, allée du 9 Septembre (tel. 04 95 45 05 00). Across from Ecomarché. **Medical emergency** tel. 15.

Police: (tel. 04 95 46 00 17). **Emergency** tel. 17.

Post Office: 3, av. du Baron Mariani (tel. 04 95 46 08 20). Poste restante. Open Mon.-Fri. 8am-noon and 2-5pm, Sat. 8am-noon. **Postal code:** 20250.

ACCOMMODATIONS AND CAMPING

Students take off in the summer, leaving plenty of affordable university housing behind. Corte also sports champion camping facilities. Always call ahead, though.

CROUS, 7, av. Jean Nicoli (tel. 04 95 45 21 00; fax 04 95 61 01 57). Students with ID can stay in university housing July-Sept. for 60F per night, 593F per month. Reserve as far ahead as possible. Office open Mon.-Fri. 9am-noon and 2-3:30pm.

Gîte d'Etape: U Tavignanu, Chemin de Balari (tel. 04 95 46 16 85). A 20-min. hike from the train station. Take a left and bear right when the road forks, following first allée du 9 Septembre and then the signs. Beds in a farmhouse in a lovely, shaded area. Swim in the bubbling creek or take a walk amid the shaded, moss-covered stones. 80F includes breakfast. Camping 20F per person, 10F per tent.

Hôtel-Residence Porette (H-R), 6, allée du 9 Septembre (tel. 04 95 61 01 21). Bear left from the station until you reach the stadium. Follow its curve for 100m. Clean, dorm-like rooms. Bath and toilets down the hall. Quieter rooms face the courtyard. Full of university students. Weight room (free), sauna (29F), laundry service, restaurant, and pool. Singles 135F. Doubles 145-195F. Triples 175-279F. Quads 299F.

Breakfast 24F. Offers guided tours in the National Forest and discounts on car rentals and train tickets. Reception open daily in summer 7am-10:30pm; in winter 7am-2pm and 4-10:30pm. AmEx

Hôtel du Nord, 22, cours Paoli (tel. 04 95 46 00 68). Conveniently situated on the main drag, these clean, spacious rooms are a real bargain for groups. Doubles 190-290F. Triples 270-310F. Quad 340F. 6-person room 400F. V, MC.

Hôtel de la Poste, 2, pl. du Padoue (tel. 04 95 46 01 37), off cours Paoli and near (you guessed it) the post office. 12 spartan rooms in a quiet, old-fashioned building. Doubles 165-200F. Triples 210-240F.

Camping: U Sognu (tel. 04 95 46 09 07), on the route de la Restonica, is the closest campground. From pl. Paoli, turn right on av. Xavier Luciani and then turn right. From the train station, follow the directions to the *gîte d'étape* above, watching for signs indicating an earlier turn-off. A 5-min. walk brings you to the campground's clean, if weathered, facilities and their dashing owner. 28F per person, 14F per child, 16F per tent. Hot showers included. Snack bar. Also offers horseback riding beginning at 60F per hour. Open March-Oct.

FOOD

Exotic Fast Food, in pl. Paoli, is a godsend. Ignore any images the name might conjure, and go for their hot, large *panini* sandwiches served on to-die-for bread (18-25F). To attract the university crowd, the establishment has named its sandwiches after great European intellectual figures—Pasteur, Freud, Marie, and Pierre (Curie, of course; open 9am-midnight). When local students crave a more complete meal and a touch of home, they head to **Restaurant Le Bips,** cours Paoli (tel. 04 95 46 06 26). Brigitte, the owner, presents chic French and Corsican food in this stone-arched dining room and terrace and offers special prices for students. Official prices are 50-120F for fish and 65-150F for meat; tell her *Let's Go* sent you. (Open Sun.-Fri. 8am-3:30pm and 6pm-1am.) Afterward, grab a drink at the **Brasserie le Bips** (open daily 7am-2 or 3am). Finally, there are two supermarkets in Corte: **Eurospar,** av. Xavier Luciani (tel. 04 95 46 08 59; open daily 7:30am-12:30 pm and 3-7:30pm), and the huge, American-style **Casino** (tel. 04 95 46 24 25; open Mon.-Sat. 9am-noon and 3-5pm), next to the H-R on allée du 9 Septembre.

SIGHTS AND ENTERTAINMENT

The *vieille ville* of Corte, with its steep, inaccessible topography and stone **citadel** (tel. 04 95 46 24 20) peering over the Tavignano and Restonica valleys, has always been a bastion of fierce Corsican patriotism. Today, less tempestuous battles are fought against the elements as the town renovates the overgrown 15th-century edifice. Occasionally, the site exhibits contemporary Corsican art, in preparation for a museum scheduled to open in 1997. (Open daily June-Sept. 9am-8pm. Admission 15F, 10F per person in a group.)

Mommy Dearest

As you wander the citadel amid grass sprinkled with wildflowers, imagine it in 1746, filled with desperate Genoese soldiers defending the thick stone ramparts against a Corsican attempt to reclaim the city. The coarse band of attackers followed Jean-Pierre Gaffori, a local physician later to become leader of the free Corsican nation, up the mountainside to besiege the city. As the Corsicans reached the top, the Genoese soldiers played their trump card: they held Gaffori's young son by the ankle from the citadel's *nid d'aigle,* or eagle's nest, lookout. The bewildered Corsicans stopped dead, not daring to fire their cannons and risk hurting their leader's child. Suddenly, a woman leaped in front of the Corsican patriots, crying "Fire! Fire!" She was Faustine Gaffori, wife of their general and mother of the dangling child. "Don't think of my son!" she shouted, "Think of the homeland!" Reinvigorated, the Corsicans continued their assault and conquered the citadel, where they found the boy safe and sound.

After the students leave for the summer, nightlife in Corte becomes, well, subdued. Ask the tourist office about the **folk music festival** in July. **Hiking** (call 04 95 21 56 54 for maps and trail information and 04 95 51 79 10 for weather conditions in the mountains), **biking,** and **horseback riding** (tel. 04 95 46 24 55; 90F per hour, 200F per ½-day, 400F per full day) are all options. When you've had enough physical exertion, sit in a café on **cours Paoli** and absorb the town's laid-back *esprit.*

■ Near Corte: Gorges de la Restonica

Southwest of Corte the tiny D623 stretches 16km through the Gorges de la Restonica, one of Corsica's loveliest and least-populated areas, many parts of which you can visit in less than a day. Biking here is best left to Tour de France veterans, but swimming is possible, if chilly, in the surrounding lakes and rivers. Breathtaking views from the pristine peaks will make you feel like you've conquered the world. Follow the D623 in the direction of the river to the trail, marked in orange, that leads to the **Lac de Melo** (1hr.) This snow-fed beauty lies at 1711m, near the foot of **Mont Rotondo** (2622m), and is ringed by peaks including Corsica's highest—**Mont Cinto** (2700m). You can continue to **Lac de Capitellu** (1930m) and join the red-and-white-marked **GR20,** the challenging trail that winds its way across the entire breadth of Corsica (best attempted in mid-June to Oct.). In winter, cross-country ski trails replace many of the summer hiking paths. Be prepared for cold, even snowy weather as late as June. For info and itinerary help, see the **Parc Naturel Régional** office in Corte (see **Tourist Information,** page 523). Get their pamphlet *Vallée de la Restonica* to plan your daytrip. Or write to Parc Naturel Régional de Corse (see page 513). Topographic maps, essential for all longer hikes, are available from local bookstores, as is an English guide called *Landscapes of Corsica* (95F).

■ Bastia

The builders of Bastia (pop. 45,000) must have thought paving was the answer to their problems. Half the city is under construction, and the other half looks as if it should be. An American bombardment in 1943 destroyed 80% of Bastia, leaving the residents no choice but to rebuild *en masse.* The result is a city littered with square, graceless buildings. Most of Old Bastia looks as if it was once beautiful, but almost without exception that time has passed. Things could be worse, though; pl. St-Nicolas gleams against the night, and the crowds that fill the *vieux port* lend the city much-needed color and life. If you came to Corsica for its natural beauty, you should probably limit your time in Bastia and use it as a base for the villages of Cap Corse.

ORIENTATION AND PRACTICAL INFORMATION

From the *gare,* turn right onto av. Maréchal Sebastiani toward the immense, paved pl. St-Nicolas and the tourist office. The commercial bd. Charles de Gaulle; bd. Paoli, Bastia's shopping center; and rue César Campinchi, with its many *pâtisseries* and cafés, run perpendicular to av. Sebastiani and lead west to the old port and town.

Tourist Office: pl. St-Nicolas (tel. 04 95 31 00 89 or 04 95 31 81 34; fax 04 95 55 96 00). Info on Bastia, Cap Corse, hotels, camping, and transport. Helpful staff makes reservations free. Open daily April-Oct. 8am-8pm; Nov.-March 8am-7pm.

Money: Banks lurk on bd. de Gaulle and rue Campli. **Banque de France,** 2, cours Pierangeli (tel. 04 95 32 82 00), is at the end of pl. St-Nicolas. Open Mon.-Fri. 8:15am-12:10pm and 1:30-3:30pm. **Crédit Mutuel,** 21, César Campinchi (tel. 04 95 31 73 19), has an **ATM;** also at **Crédit Lyonnais** (tel. 04 95 54 93 00), nearby.

Flights: Bastia-Poretta (airport tel. 04 95 54 54 54), 23km away. A bus (tel. 04 95 31 06 65) timed for flights leaves from pl. de la Gare, by the *préfecture* (½hr., 35F). To: Marseille (4 per day, 50min., 353-521F); Nice (4 per day, 40min., 321-471F); Paris (2-3 per day, 1½hr., 891-961F). **Air Inter** and **Air France** coexist at 6, av. Emile Sari (tel. 04 95 31 79 79). Open Mon.-Fri. 8:30am-noon and 2-5pm.

CORSICA

Trains: pl. de la Gare (tel. 04 95 32 80 61), off av. Maréchal Sebastiani. To: Calvi (2 per day, 3hr., 89F); Corte (4 per day, Sun. 2 per day, 1½hr., 55F); Ajaccio (4 per day, Sun. 2 per day, 3hr., 118F). **Luggage storage** 19F per bag per day.

Buses: Rapides Bleus, 1, av. Maréchal Sebastiani (tel. 04 95 31 03 79). Open Mon.-Fri. 8:15am-noon and 2-6:30pm, Sat. 9am-noon. To Ajaccio (2 per day, 3hr., 105F) and Porto-Vecchio along the Côte Orientale (1-2 per day, 2¼hr., 110F).

Ferries: SNCM, Nouveau Port (tel. 04 95 54 66 66). Open Mon.-Fri. 8-11:45am and 2-5:30pm. Turn left from av. Maréchal Sebastiani just past pl. St-Nicolas. (See **Getting There** on page 512.) **Corsica Ferries,** 5bis, rue Chanoine Leschi (tel. 04 95 32 95 95), float to Livorno and La Spezia (4-5hr., 150F) and Genova (6-8hr., 190F) in Italy. Ferries dock at the quai de Fangs, next to pl. St-Nicolas.

Taxis: Radio Taxis Bastiais (tel. 04 95 34 07 00), airport 180F. **Les Taxi Bleus** (tel. 04 95 32 70 70), airport 190F weekdays, 250F nights and weekends. 24hr.

Car Rental: ADA Location, 35, rue César Campinchi (tel. 04 95 31 09 02; fax 04 95 31 17 43), or at the airport (tel. 04 95 54 55 44). 356F per day, 1790F per week, unlimited mileage. Open Mon.-Sat. 8am-noon and 2-7pm.

Youth Center: Centre Information Jeunesse, 3, bd. Auguste Gaudin (tel. 04 95 32 12 13). Info on jobs, excursions, and travel. Open July-Aug. Mon.-Fri. 8am-6pm; Sept.-June Mon.-Fri. 8am-noon and 2-6pm.

Crisis Lines: Corsida (tel. 04 95 32 77 77), an AIDS hotline.

Hospital: Centre Hospitalier Général (CHG), rue Impériale (tel. 04 95 55 11 11). **Medical emergency:** tel. 15.

Police: cartier Montésoro (tel. 04 95 54 50 22). **Emergency** tel. 17.

Post Office: av. Maréchal Sebastiani (tel. 04 95 32 80 70). Poste restante. **ATM.** Open Mon.-Fri. 8am-7pm, Sat. 8am-noon. **Postal code:** 20200.

ACCOMMODATIONS AND CAMPING

Bastia's hotels are often cheaper, better furnished, and more spacious than those in Corsica's resort towns. Vacancies are also more common, but it is always prudent to call ahead. Check for off-season discounts.

Hôtel Central, 3, rue Miot (tel. 04 95 31 71 12; fax 04 95 31 82 40). Centrally located with many beautifully renovated rooms (even unrenovated rooms are clean and bright). All have showers and noise-reducing windows. Some have balconies, TVs. Singles 170-230F. Doubles 200-250F. Triples 250-300F. Quads 350F.

Hôtel Athena, 2 rue Miot (tel. 04 95 31 07 83; fax 04 95 31 26 41). Clean, almost luxurious rooms with A/C; some are a little small. Hotel has a formal feel to it. Singles 180F. Doubles 250F. Triples 350F. Quads 400F.

Studios Meublés San Carlu, 10, bd. Auguste Gaudin (tel. 04 95 31 70 65). Newly refurbished studio apartments look out onto 20th-century laundry hanging from 13th-century buildings in the *vieille ville.* Kitchenettes and full bathrooms. Best for those staying in Bastia for more than a night. 200F per night for 2 people.

Hôtel de l'Univers, 3, av. Maréchal Sebastiani (tel. 04 95 31 03 38), just down from the train station. A bit noisy, but good location. Phones in all rooms. Singles 150-250F. Doubles 170-300F. Triples 200-350F. Quads 220-350F. Breakfast 30F.

Camping: Les Orangiers, Quartier Licciola-Miomo (tel. 04 95 33 24 09 or 04 95 33 23 65). 22F per person, 12F per tent. Open May-Sept. **J.J. Casanova,** route du Tennis-Miomo (tel. 04 95 33 91 42). 24F per person, 12F per tent. Open May-Oct. **Camping San Damiano** (tel. 04 95 33 68 02), on route de la Lagune de Pinette, 7km south of Bastia. 29F per person, 10F per tent. Open April-Oct. Camping also exists to the north in Miomo (buses leave every ½hr. Mon.-Fri., every hr. Sat., 6:30am-7pm). Buses run south to Biguglia 11:30am and 6pm Mon.-Sat.

FOOD AND ENTERTAINMENT

Restaurants encircle the *vieux port,* many with terraces from which you can watch the boats sail by. **Chez Mémé,** quai de la Libération (tel. 04 95 31 44 12) provides a 5-course Corsican meal for 80F. (Open daily 9am-1pm and 6pm-1:30am. V, MC, AmEx.) **Bd. Général de Gaulle** on pl. Nicolas is full of outdoor cafés and inexpensive restaurants. The winding wooden staircase and brick walls of **Le Dépot,** 22, rue César

Campinchi (tel. 04 95 32 80 70) lend a rustic atmosphere to fire-cooked pizza (28-50F), *plats du jour* (70-98F), and pasta (42-68F). *Menus* begin at 68F. (Open daily noon-2pm and 7-11pm.) The **market** on pl. de l'Hôtel de Ville is open Tuesday-Sunday from 6am-1pm; the best selection of goods is on weekends. A **Cali supermarket** offers its wares at 18, rue César Campinchi (open Mon.-Sat. 7:30am-1pm and 6-9pm, Sun. 7:30am-1pm). From Tuesday-Sunday at 11pm, locals head to **U Fanale** on pl. Galetta (tel. 04 95 32 68 38); the club features retro music as well as tunes by modern Corsican groups and those ever-wacky *Québécois.*

SIGHTS

Eglise St-Jean Baptiste, an 18th-century church on pl. de l'Hôtel de Ville, is enough to make an atheist think twice with its immense proportions, gilded domes, and sky-high *trompe l'œil.* The simple **Jardins Romieu,** located beside the citadel, provide a calming blanket of shade and birdsong in this paved city. The beautiful 15th-century **Palais des Gouverneurs Génois,** overlooking the port, houses the **Musée d'Ethnographie** which in turn houses geological specimens, archaeological artifacts, and displays on traditional Corsican life. Those with a penchant for the morbid can visit the cells of condemned resistance fighters. (Open Mon.-Fri. 9am-noon and 2-4pm, Sat.-Sun. 10am-noon and 2-4pm; admission 15F.) Climb the steps in the far left corner of the museum courtyard until you reach the shady garden above, then follow the steps to the clock tower for an unrivalled view of the coast. Nearby is the ornately gilded, Baroque **Oratoire Sainte-Croix,** with an intricate mosaic at its entrance.

■ Near Bastia: Cap Corse

This mini-peninsula thrusting into the Mediterranean Sea is a necklace of tiny former fishing villages connected by a narrow road of perilous curves and breathtaking views. Mountains rise a kilometer above the sleepy and rocky shores. The 18 villages of Cap Corse have largely resisted the lures of overdevelopment, making the 140km route from Bastia to St-Florentine an exquisite natural respite. Life is less hectic and more enjoyable here; the air is fresher, the water is bluer, and the greenery is greener. The best way to view its sheltered coves and tree-covered mountains is undoubtedly by some private means of transport (see **Car Rental** on page 526). An express driving tour of the entire Cap will take at least half a day. Be alert and cautious, as one wrong move can result in an uncomfortably close view of the mountains or sea. It is best to drive on a weekend, when traffic on the winding D80 thins out. If you have a fear of off-road travel, it might be best to start the trip from the St-Florentine area (the west side of the peninsula), where your vehicle hugs the mountain-side rather than the sparkling cerulean sea below. To start from Bastia on the west side, take bd. Paoli, then bd. Auguste Gaudin past the citadel onto D81 (direction: St-Florentine). For the daredevil east-to-west route, simply drive through pl. St-Nicolas and turn left at the second rotary, following signs to the Cap.

Transports Michele (tel. 04 95 35 61 08, in Ersa), at the top of the peninsula, offers full-day tours of the Cap which depart Bastia on Sundays from 1, rue de Nouveau Port at 9am, stop at villages along the way, lunch at the glorious blue slate beach at Albo, and return to Bastia at 5pm (July-late Sept. only; 80F). From Calvi, **Autocars Mariani** (tel. 04 95 65 05 32) runs similar excursions to the Cap, leaving at 7am and returning at 7:30pm on Fridays (June-Sept.; 145F). The cheapest way to see Cap Corse is to take a **public bus** from pl. St-Nicolas in Bastia. (Buses Mon.-Fri. every ½hr. 6:30am-noon and 1:30-7pm, Sat. 6:30am then every hr. 8am-noon and 2-7pm, Sun. every hr. 8am-noon and 2-7pm. Fewer Sept.-May.) They'll only take you as far as Sisco (30min. away), but you'll get a taste of the Cap at a bargain price (11F). Ask nicely and the driver will drop you off wherever you feel the urge to explore.

Erbalunga (25min. from Bastia) is the largest of the villages accessible by public bus. The village's ocean breezes will cool you off and calm you down. *Crêperies* and sandwich shops loiter by the marina. On the weekends, **Pizz'anto** (tel. 04 95 33 92 70) offers a small selection of pizza (35-45F), salads (35F), and desserts (5-35F) served ten feet from the azure waters of the Mediterranean. Walk three minutes from the bus stop toward Sisco to find this secluded get-away. For a larger meal, **La Petite Auberge** (tel. 04 95 33 20 18) offers pizza (45-55F), pasta (45-60F), and meat and fish dishes from 60-80F. (Open daily 7am-3pm and 5:30pm until the restaurant empties. V, MC.) Or you can picnic, stopping for supplies at **à 2 pas** (tel. 04 95 33 24 24), a supermarket by the bus stop. (Open 8:30am-12:15pm and 4-7:45pm.)

Up above Erbalunga's pleasing, weather-beaten buildings lies the ever-peaceful **Monastère des Benedictines du St-Sacrement.** Built in 1862, it now houses eight nuns and one priest. A girls' school operated here from 1899 to 1963; the buildings have now been turned into a reception center. From the bus stop, walk two minutes and take a left on the little road after La Petite Auberge. When you reach the arch with the cross on top, follow the signs to the *église.* The divine shade of the monastery's walls is ample compensation for the hike. The large, neo-Roman church features groined vaulting and a breathtaking silence. The entrance is the far door on the right. (Mass Mon.-Sat. 9am, Sun. and holidays 9:30am.)

The famous sanctuary in **Lavasine,** just south of Erbalunga, draws pilgrims every September 8. The curved, pebble beach of **Miomo,** about 10 minutes from Bastia, draws people in search of more secular pleasures. Unfortunately, the only sand on the Cap does its thing at **Pietra Carbona,** well out of the path of the public bus.

If you do have a car, be sure not to miss **Rogliano;** its precarious perch on the mountain defies gravity, and its ruins of a Genoese castle, Château de San Colombano, and large 16th-century church, San Agnello, seem to defy time. Rogliano's beachside sister town, **Macinaggio,** 40km from Bastia, is one of the few port towns where you can find supplies and services—including gas, a supermarket, and a **tourist office** (tel. 95 35 40 34). In the port of **Centuri,** on the other side of the peninsula, boats bring in their daily haul of lobsters, mussels, and fish, ensuring that the seafood in its restaurants is always fresh.

For updates on Cap-related tourism, contact the **Communaute-du Commune du Cap Corse,** Maison du Cap Corse, 20200 Ville di Pietra Bugno (tel. 04 95 31 02 32).

Les Alpes (The Alps)

Commercialized resorts and undisturbed hamlets may entertain or enchant visitors, but natural architecture is the Alps' real attraction. The curves of the Chartreuse Valley grow to rugged crags in the Vercors range and crescendo into Europe's highest peak, Mont Blanc. Magnificent but hardly unspoiled, the Alps basked in international attention when the region hosted the 1992 Winter Olympics. The spotlight prompted a reevaluation of government wilderness policies and a renewed commitment to the preservation of some of the world's most beautiful and delicate scenery.

The Alps are shared by two provinces, Savoie and Dauphiné. The lower one, Dauphiné, includes the Chartreuse Valley, the Vercors regional park, the smaller Ecrins national park in the east, and the Belledonne and Oisans mountains. The university center of Grenoble has been the region's cultural and intellectual capital since the 14th century, when Louis XI designated the town a permanent parliamentary seat.

Savoie, which includes the peaks of Haute Savoie, the Olympic resorts in the expansive Tarentaise valley, and the awesome Vanoise national park, bears the name of the oldest royal house in Europe. Around 1034, the region became the possession of Humbert aux Blanches Mains, founder of the House of Savoie and a vassal of the German emperor. Humbert settled at Chambéry and began extracting exorbitant tolls from neighboring kings who wanted to march through the pass. By the 14th century, this powerful kingdom included Nice, the Jura, Piedmonte, and Geneva, a choice expanse that attracted the military attention of generations of French monarchs. In 1860, weary from centuries of invasion, *Savoyards* voted by a landslide to become French, and the region was incorporated into the Republic.

Once you get to the Alps, head in the most logical direction—up. After the spring thaw, flowery meadows, icy mountain lakes, and staggering panoramic views reward experienced and amateur hikers alike. Most towns have sports shops renting footwear and tourist offices providing free trail guides. Trails are clearly marked, but serious climbers should invest in a *Topo-Guide* (hiking map). Talk with local hiking information offices for advice on trail and weather conditions and itineraries.

Make any skiing arrangements a couple of months in advance. Grenoble, Chamonix, and Val d'Isère serve as excellent bases. The least packed and cheapest months are January, March, and April; most resorts close in October and November, between hiking and skiing seasons. **FUAJ,** the French Youth Hostel Federation, offers week-long skiing and sports packages. For more info, contact local FUAJ offices, youth hostels, or the office at 27, rue Pajol, 75018 Paris (tel. 01 46 07 00 01).

Food here takes a Swiss twist, perfect for cold winter nights. Regional specialties include *fondue savoyarde*—bread dipped into a heavenly blend of three alpine cheeses, white wine, and kirsch. Other cheesy dishes include *raclette* (strong Swiss cheese melted and served with boiled potatoes, pickled onions, and gherkins) and *gratin dauphinois* (potatoes sliced thin and baked in a cream and cheese sauce). *Savoyards* and *dauphinois* also cure excellent ham and salami and net trout from the icy mountain streams, which end up in a buttery preparation called *truite meunière.* The renowned alpine cheeses are mild and creamy: try *tomme,* the oldest of Savoie cheeses, *St-Marcellin* (half goat's milk), *beaufort,* and *reblochon.* Fine regional wines include the whites of Apremont, Marignan, and Chignin, and the rich reds produced in Montmélian and St-Jean-de-la-Porte. If there's room left for dessert, try the *roseaux d'Annecy* (liqueur-filled chocolates), *St-Genux* (a *brioche* topped with pink praline), or the *gâteau de Savoie* (a light sponge cake). *Eaux de vie* (waters of life), strong liqueurs distilled from fruits, are popular here, especially when made from local *framboises* (raspberries).

GETTING AROUND

TGV **trains** will whisk you from Paris to Aix-les-Bains or Annecy at the gateway to the serious mountains; from there it's either slow trains, special mountain trains, or more often, torturously slow **buses.** Always allow much longer than you think it should take to go anywhere. The farther into the mountains you want to get, the harder it is to get there, both in terms of travel time and frequency. Service is at least twice as frequent, especially on buses, during the high season (Dec.-April). **Biking** through the Alps is, needless to say, an option only for the serious cyclist. **Hiking** options range from simple strolls through mountain meadows to some of the most difficult climbing in the world. *Always* check with local hiking bureaus before starting *any* hike; even in summer you can encounter snowstorms and avalanches.

Grenoble

With 40,000 students, Grenoble is one of France's largest university centers. On your way to the city, you'll understand why so many choose to study here. Like Lyon, its larger neighbor, Grenoble has grown up around two rivers, the Isère and the Drac. But this ancient Roman capital of Dauphiné is also nestled at the convergence of four mountain chains, each lined with snow-capped peaks and sapphire-blue lakes. Grenoble hosts the eccentric cafés, dusty bookshops, shaggy radicals, and serious politics you'll find in any university town, but it also boasts majestic surroundings cherished by hikers, skiers, bikers, and café loungers alike. Stendhal, the city's most famous bookworm, grumbled that "at the end of every street, there is a mountain." The author hated the city, and the wry *Grenoblois* thanked him for his bile by erecting one of their many museums in his honor.

In the 1960s, the election of a municipal Socialist government encouraged an immigration of liberals and non-native French, including a significant North African community, that gives Grenoble a cosmopolitan feel. Local industry has moved beyond its traditional glove-making to include atom-smashing, hydro-electricity, and nuclear power. Moreover, Grenoble is a convenient and economical base for jaunts to nearby mountains as well as an intriguing city in itself, with a pedestrian *vieille ville* dating from medieval days, trendy shops, dozens of colorful festivals, and ubiquitous students. Whether you're here to hike the hills or puff cigarettes in a café, Grenoble will impress you with its floating peaks and soaring discussions.

ORIENTATION AND PRACTICAL INFORMATION

To get to the tourist office and center of town from the train station, turn right onto pl. de la Gare and take the third left onto av. Alsace Lorraine, following the tram tracks. Continue along the tracks on rue Félix Poulat and rue Blanchard. The tourist office complex will be on your left, just before the tracks fork (10min.). Tram line A (direction: Grand' Place) runs to "Maison du Tourisme." The center of a visitor's universe, the complex holds a bank, bus office, SNCF counter, and post office.

Tourist Information: Tourist Office, 14, rue de la République (tel. 04 76 42 41 41; fax 04 76 51 28 69). Good map, hotel info, train and bus schedules, and reservation service. **Currency exchange.** Ask about guided tours of the old city July-Aug. Open June-Sept. Mon.-Sat. 9am-12:30pm and 1:30-7pm, Sun. 10am-noon; Oct.-May closes at 6pm Mon.-Sat. Pick up a free copy of **Grenoble Magazine,** published annually in English, with info on museums, points of interest, and feature articles. **Échappée Belle** lists museums and sights in the region. If you're staying a while, consider buying the **Guide DAHU** (15F)—a French *Let's Go: Grenoble* written annually by local students, it lists *restos,* bars, discos, and sights.

Hiking Information: CIMES (Centre Informations Montagnes et Sentiers) will be upstairs from the tourist office in '97 (tel. 04 76 42 45 90; fax 04 76 15 23 91). Organizes hiking trips and sells detailed guides of alpine hiking, mountaineering, and cross-country skiing trails. A plethora of free, informative brochures. Open Mon.-Fri. 9am-noon and 2-6pm, Sat. 10am-noon and 2-6pm. **Club Alpin Français,** 32, av. Félix-Viallet (tel. 04 76 87 03 73). Advice on all mountain activities. Map library. Organizes hiking, rock- and ice-climbing, and parachuting trips. Open Mon. 2-7pm, Tues.-Wed. 10am-7pm, Thurs.-Fri. 10am-8pm, Sat. 9am-noon.

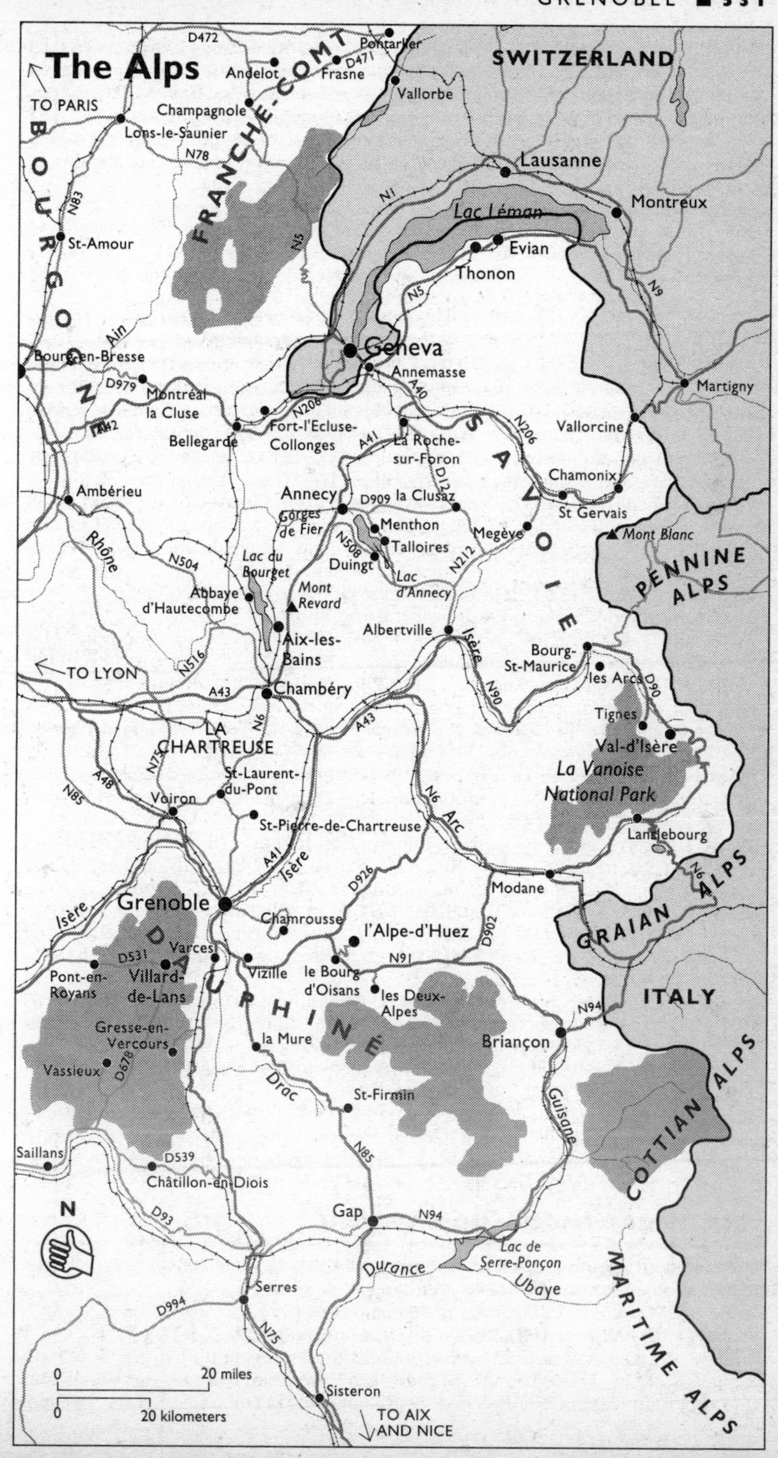
The Alps
TO PARIS
SWITZERLAND
FRANCHE-COMT
BOURGOGNE
Pontarlier
Andelot
Frasne
Vallorbe
Champagnole
Lons-le-Saunier
Lausanne
Lac Léman
Montreux
St-Amour
Evian
Thonon
Geneva
Bourg-en-Bresse
Montréal la Cluse
Annemasse
Martigny
Bellegarde
Fort-l'Ecluse-Collonges
La Roche-sur-Foron
Vallorcine
SAVOIE
Chamonix
Ambérieu
Annecy
la Clusaz
St Gervais
Gorges de Fier
Menthon
Talloires
Mont Blanc
Rhône
Duingt
Megève
Lac du Bourget
Lac d'Annecy
PENNINE ALPS
Abbaye d'Hautecombe
Mont Revard
Aix-les-Bains
Albertville
Bourg-St-Maurice
TO LYON
Chambéry
les Arcs
LA CHARTREUSE
Tignes
Val-d'Isère
La Vanoise National Park
St-Laurent-du-Pont
Voiron
St-Pierre-de-Chartreuse
Lanslebourg
Arc
Isère
Modane
Grenoble
Chamrousse
l'Alpe-d'Huez
GRAIAN ALPS
Varces
Villard-de-Lans
Vizille
Pont-en-Royans
le Bourg d'Oisans
les Deux-Alpes
DAUPHINÉ
ITALY
Gresse-en-Vercours
la Mure
Briançon
Vassieux
Drac
St-Firmin
Guisane
COTTIAN ALPS
Saillans
Châtillon-en-Diois
N
Gap
Lac de Serre-Ponçon
Durance
Ubaye
MARITIME ALPS
Serres
0
20 miles
20 kilometers
Sisteron
TO AIX AND NICE
D472
D471
N78
N83
N5
N1
N9
Ain
D979
N206
A40
A41
D12
D909
N508
N212
N504
N516
A43
N90
D90
N6
N75
A48
N85
D926
D902
N91
N94
D531
D678
D539
D93
D994

Budget Travel: Jeunes Sans Frontière-Wasteels, 50, av. Alsace-Lorraine (tel. 04 76 47 34 54), and 20, av. Félix-Viallet (tel. 04 76 46 36 39). BIJ tickets, cheap excursion packages. Both offices open Mon.-Fri. 9am-7pm, Sat. 9am-6pm. V, MC.

Money: Comptoir Grenoblois de Change, 5, rue Philis de la Charce (tel. 04 76 51 33 76), near the tourist office. Exchanges currency Tues.-Sat. 9am-noon and 2-6pm. There are several **Crédit Mutuel** 24-hr. **ATMs.** Look for one outside the Casino supermarket near the hostel. Also in the train station.

Flights: Aéroport de Grenoble St-Geoirs, St-Etienne de St-Geoirs (tel. 04 76 65 40 55). Buses leave 1¼hr. before each flight from the *gare routière* (30F). Flights to other French cities only. **Air Inter,** 42, cours Jean Jaurès (tel. 04 76 85 69 70). Open Mon.-Fri. 9am-noon and 2-6pm. **Air France,** pl. Victor Hugo (tel. 04 76 87 63 41). Open Mon.-Fri. 8:30am-noon and 1:30-6pm, Sat. 8:45am-12:15pm.

Trains: Gare Europole, pl. de la Gare (tel. 08 36 35 35 35). To: Chambéry (15 per day, 30min., 55F); Annecy (9 per day, 2hr., 86F); Marseille (14 per day, 2½hr., 197F); Lyon (16 per day, 1½hr., 93F); Paris (11 per day, 4hr., 335F); Nice (8 per day, 6½hr., 286F). Office open daily 8:30am-7:45pm. **Lockers** 20-30F per 72hr.

Buses: Gare routière, left from train station. Summer excursions as well as service to ski resorts and area towns. **VFD** (tel. 04 76 47 77 77) is the largest. Buses to: Geneva (1 per day, 2¾hr., 143F, students 115F); Nice (1 per day, 9hr., 293F, students 235F); and Chamonix (1 per day, 3hr., 152F). Office open 6:45am-7pm.

Public Transportation: Transports Agglomeration Grenobloise (TAG). Desk in the tourist office open Sun.-Fri. 8:30am-6:30pm, Sat. 9am-6pm. Ticket 7F50, *carnet* of 10 51F. 2 tram lines run roughly every 10min. 5am-midnight; buses run 6am-9pm. Each TAG stop posts a complete transit (and city) map.

Taxis: tel. 04 76 54 42 54. 24hr. A ride to the far-out airport costs (gulp) 325F.

Bike Rental and Climbing Equipment: Borel Sport, 42, rue Alsace-Lorraine (tel. 04 76 46 47 46). Bicycles 50F per day, deposit 1000F or a credit card imprint. Also rents mountain climbing equipment. Shoes 35F per day. Ski equipment 65-110F per day. Open Mon.-Sat. 9am-noon and 2-7pm; May-Nov. closed Mon. V, MC.

Laundromat: Lavomatique, 14, rue Thiers, near the train station.

English Bookstore: Just Books, 1, rue de la Paix (tel. 04 76 44 78 81). Pricey paperbacks, big used books section. Open Tues.-Sat. 9am-noon and 2-7pm.

Women's Center: Centre d'Information Féminine, 9, rue Raoul Blanchard (tel. 04 76 54 08 19). Free advice and pamphlets. Open Mon., Wed., and Fri. 1-5pm. Special session Thurs. 2-4pm for foreign women.

Youth Center: Centre Régional d'Information Jeunesse, 8, rue Voltaire (tel. 04 76 54 70 38), near the tourist office. Info on housing, jobs, study, and events. BIJ tickets. Open Mon. and Fri. 1-6pm, Tues.-Thurs. 10am-6pm, Sat. 2-6pm.

Snowfall Information Service: tel. 04 76 51 19 29. **Weather:** tel. 01 39 65 80 80.

Crisis Lines: SOS Amitié (tel. 04 76 87 22 22), friendship line. **AIDES,** 16, rue Chanrion (tel. 04 76 63 82 44), AIDS outreach. **Alcooliques Anonymes** (tel. 04 76 87 74 00), for alcohol problems.

Hospital: Centre Hospitalier Régional de Grenoble, La Tronche (tel. 04 76 76 75 75). Take bus 31 (direction: Malpertuis) or 602 (direction: Lumbin/Crolles/St-Nazaire) to "La Tronche/Hôpital." **Medical emergency** tel. 04 76 42 42 42 or 15.

Police: 36, bd. Maréchal Leclerc (tel. 04 76 60 40 40). Take bus 31 (direction: Malpertuis) to "Hôtel de Police." **Emergency** tel. 17.

Post Office: 17, rue Beyle–Stendhal (tel. 04 76 43 53 11). Poste restante. Open Mon.-Fri. 8am-6:45pm, Sat. 8am-noon. **Branch office** at 12, rue de la République, next to tourist office. Photocopies. Both have **currency exchange.** Open Mon. 8am-6pm, Tues.-Fri. 8am-6:30pm, Sat. 8am-noon. **Postal code:** 38000.

ACCOMMODATIONS AND CAMPING

Plenty of budget hotels are scattered throughout the pedestrian zone. For rentals, see the tourist office's board *Locations Meubles.*

Auberge de Jeunesse (HI), 18, av. du Grésivaudan (tel. 04 76 09 33 52; fax 04 76 09 38 99), about 4km from Grenoble in Echirolles. From the *gare,* follow tram tracks down av. Alsace-Lorraine to cours Jean Jaurès; turn right and bus stop is 25m to your right. Take bus 8 (direction: Pont Rouge) to "La Quinzaine." From "La Quin-

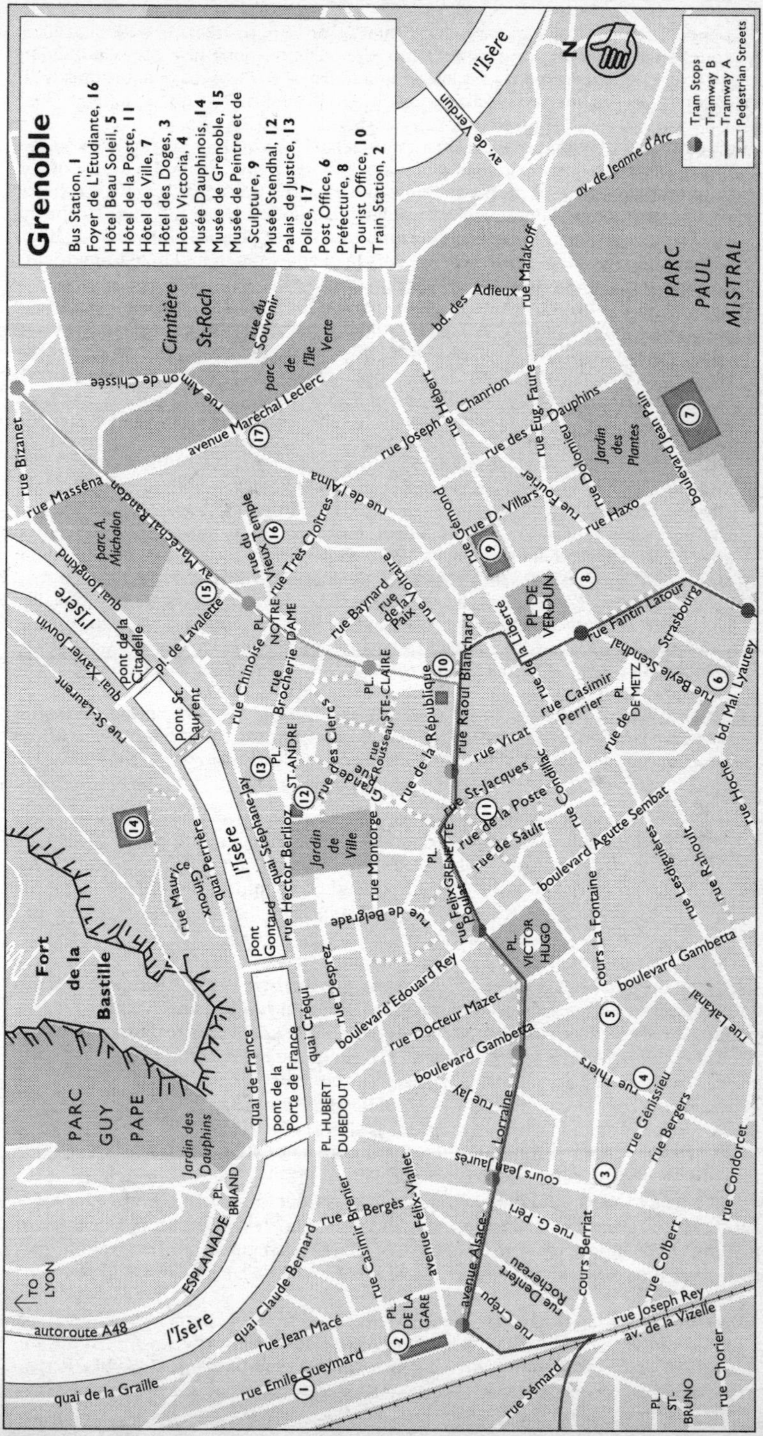

Grenoble
Bus Station, 1
Foyer de L'Etudiante, 16
Hôtel Beau Soleil, 5
Hôtel de la Poste, 11
Hôtel de Ville, 7
Hôtel des Doges, 3
Hôtel Victoria, 4
Musée Dauphinois, 14
Musée de Grenoble, 15
Musée de Peintre et de Sculpture, 9
Musée Stendhal, 12
Palais de Justice, 13
Police, 17
Post Office, 6
Préfecture, 8
Tourist Office, 10
Train Station, 2
Tram Stops
Tramway B
Tramway A
Pedestrian Streets
N
TO LYON
Fort de la Bastille
PARC GUY PAPE
Jardin des Dauphins
Cimitière St-Roch
PARC PAUL MISTRAL
Jardin des Plantes
Jardin de Ville
parc A. Michalon
parc de l'Ile Verte
l'Isère
PL. HUBERT DUBEDOUT
PL. DE LA GARE
PL. VICTOR HUGO
PL. DE VERDUN
PL. GRENETTE
PL. ST-ANDRE
PL. STE-CLAIRE
PL. NOTRE DAME
PL. ST-BRUNO
PL. BRIAND
ESPLANADE
autoroute A48
pont de la Porte de France
pont Gontard
pont St. Laurent
pont de la Citadelle
boulevard Gambetta
boulevard Edouard Rey
boulevard Agutte Sembat
cours Jean Jaurès
cours Berriat
cours La Fontaine
avenue Alsace-Lorraine
avenue Félix-Viallet
avenue Maréchal Leclerc
av. de Jeanne d'Arc
av. de Verdun
quai Créqui
quai de France
quai Stéphane-Jay
quai Perrière
quai Xavier Jouvin
quai Jongkind
quai Claude Bernard
quai de la Graille
rue de la République
rue Raoul Blanchard
rue Félix Poulat
rue de Belgrade
rue Montorge
rue Hector Berlioz
rue St-Laurent
rue Chinoise
rue Brocherie
rue des Clercs
rue Très Cloîtres
rue du Vieux Temple
rue de Strasbourg
rue Haxo
rue Lesdiguières
rue Condorcet
rue Joseph Rey
av. de la Vizelle
rue Sémard
rue Chorier
rue Emile Gueymard
rue Jean Macé
rue Casimir Brenier
rue Bergès
rue Docteur Mazet
rue Thiers
rue Génissieu
rue Bergers
rue Colbert
rue Lakanal
rue Hoche
bd. Mal. Lyautey
rue Beyle Stendhal
rue Fantin Latour
rue Casimir Perrier
rue de la Liberté
rue Vicat
rue St-Jacques
rue de la Poste
rue de Sault
rue Condillac
rue Joseph Hébert
rue Chanrion
bd. des Adieux
rue Malakoff
rue des Eug. Faure
rue des Dauphins
rue Dolomieu
rue Fourier
rue D. Villars
rue Génénond
rue de l'Alma
rue Voltaire
rue de la Paix
rue Baynard
rue Masséna
rue Bizanet
rue Aimon de Chissée
rue du Souvenir
av. Maréchal Randon
pl. de Lavalette
boulevard Jean Pain
rue Mauric Gignoux

zaine," the hostel is 1 block behind the Casino supermarket. If walking, follow cours Jean Jaurès and turn right just before Casino (1 long hr.). Modern building with garden, bar, game room, kitchen, laundry, and TV. 4- to 6-bed rooms. 67F. Sheets 17F. Shower and breakfast free. Open Mon.-Sat. 7:30am-11pm, Sun. 7:30-10:30am and 5:30-11pm. No phone reservations. V, MC, AmEx.

Le Foyer de l'Etudiante, 4, rue Ste-Ursule (tel. 04 76 42 00 84; fax 04 76 44 36 85), near pl. Notre-Dame, on a quiet street close to the center. From the tourist office, follow pl. Ste-Claire to pl. Notre-Dame and take rue du Vieux Temple on the far right. Dorm rooms, some with lofts; full of friendly students. Kitchen, TV, piano, and laundry facilities. Singles 90F. Doubles 65F per person. Shower and sheets included. 2-night min. preferred. Accepts men and women mid-June to mid-Sept.; women only for month-long stays the rest of the year.

Hôtel de la Poste, 25, rue de la Poste (tel. 04 76 46 67 25), in the bosom of the pedestrian zone. Friendly managers, petunias, and a little dog welcome you to aging but spacious rooms, all with new beds. Singles 90F, with shower 150F. Doubles 160F, with shower 200F. Triples 190F. Quads 200F. Hearty breakfast (eggs, bacon, the lot) 30F. Continental breakfast 25F. 24-hr. reception. V, MC.

Hôtel Beau Soleil, 9, rue des Bons Enfants (tel. 04 76 46 29 40; fax 04 76 46 58 58), off bd. Gambetta near pl. Victor Hugo. Bright, well-kept rooms with peach accents. Singles from 130F, with shower 155F. Doubles from 140F, with shower 170F. Shower 16F. Breakfast 22F. Reception 7am-10pm. V, MC.

Hôtel de Doges, 29, cours Jean Jaurès (tel. 04 76 46 13 19; fax 04 76 47 67 95), at the intersection of cours Berriat. Clean, pastel rooms with phones on a central street. Staff speaks English. Singles 100F, with shower 160F. Doubles 120F, with shower 160F. Breakfast 22F. Shower 15F. Reception 7am-1am. V, MC, AmEx.

Hôtel Victoria, 17, rue Thiers (tel. 04 76 46 06 36), 5min. from the train station. Elegant lobby and large, immaculate rooms, some with TV. Singles 120F, with shower 155F. Doubles 130F, with shower 180-210F. Triples with shower and toilet 250F. Quads with shower and toilet 280F. No hall shower. Breakfast 28F. Reception 7am-11:30pm. V, MC, AmEx.

Camping: Les 3 Pucelles, in Seyssins (tel. 04 76 96 45 73), just on the southwest corner of Grenoble, near the hostel. The closest campsite to town and the only one open all year. 60 sites. 30F per person and tent. Call ahead in the summer.

FOOD

Grenoble boasts many affordable restaurants with a refreshing variety of specialties. Regional restaurants cater to locals at **pl. de Gordes,** between pl. St-André and the Jardin de Ville. Local baked goods are chock-full of walnuts—the nuts so local the French call them *noix de Grenoble.* They conspire with marzipan and chocolate in a sweet local treat, also called *noix de Grenoble*.

There is a smattering of East Asian restaurants between pl. Notre Dame and the river, and they virtually own **rue Condorcet.** Inexpensive North African restaurants and *pâtisseries* congregate around **rue Chenoise** and **rue St-Laurent,** between the pedestrian area and river (*menus* around 50-55F). Cafés and restaurants cluster around **pl. Notre-Dame** and **pl. St-André,** both in the heart of the *vieille ville.* Dozens of lively, cheap pizzerias flip pies across the river on **quai Perrière** below the *téléphérique.* Locals recommend **Chez Rofolo** and **Pompeii.**

With so many students, cafeteria cuisine is almost a local specialty. For info on **University Restaurants** open during the school year, call **CROUS** at 04 76 57 44 00 to find out what's open and when. Buy a meal ticket (13F) while waiting in line.

Still haven't found something? **Prisunic,** across from the tourist office (open Mon.-Sat. 8:30am-7:30pm), or **Casino,** near the youth hostel (open Mon.-Sat. 8:30am-8:30pm), will supply your *al fresco* feasts. **Markets** are another good option; they spring up Tues.-Sun. on pl. St-André, pl. St-Bruno, pl. Ste-Claire, and pl. aux Herbes.

Le Valgo, 2, rue St. Hughes (tel. 04 76 51 38 85), at pl. Notre-Dame. Friendly service, a cozy interior, and excellent food make this a local favorite for *spécialités des Hautes-Alpes.* Hearty mountain meat pies, turnovers, and *ravioles* (38-68F). Perfect portions (some with large green salad). *Menus* start at 65F. Open Tues.-Wed. lunch, Thurs.-Sat. lunch and dinner. V, MC.

Brasserie Bavaroise, 2, rue Vicat (tel. 04 76 51 76 55), near the tourist office. Delicious meals in an unpretentious setting full of locals. Quaint wooden decor in the upstairs dining room. 60F lunch *menu* and lots of seafood (62-80F). Open Mon.-Sat. noon-2pm and 7pm-1am. Closed Aug. 1-15.

Moitié Toi Moitié Moi, 7, rue Très-Cloîtres (tel. 04 76 15 22 99), dishes up food from the Cameroons in portions you could split with a friend. Meat dishes (39-50F) come with soup, *gingembre* (great homemade gingerbeer), African sweet *frites* or rice, and a *digestif.* Salads (30-35F). Open lunch and dinner. Closed Sun.

Mamma di Roma, 10, pl. Edmond-Arnaud (tel. 04 76 54 37 49), at rue Très-Cloîtres, is locally recommended for Italian fare. Try one of the many reasonably priced pastas or meats. Tasty (if timid) portions of *tagliatelles* with the "Mamma di Roma" sauce are 41F. Also has a 58F lunch *menu.* Open daily, lunch and dinner, except Saturday lunch and Sundays.

Le Tonneau de Diogène, 6, pl. Notre-Dame (tel. 04 76 42 38 40). Simple, tasty food served at outdoor tables. Breakfast with fresh O.J. and eggs (35F), salads (15-36F), and a variety of omelettes (18-25F). 38F student *menu.* Open Mon.-Fri. 7am-1am, Sat. 9:30am-1am, Sun. 11:30am-1am.

Un Rayon de Soleil, 1, rue Condorcet (tel. 04 76 43 19 19), is a *crêperie* offering a 42F *menu* including salad, cider, and 2 crêpes. Open daily noon-2pm and 7pm-midnight. Sometimes closed for lunch in summer.

SIGHTS

Grenoble's intellectual populace supports enough fine museums for a city twice its size. The *Guide DAHU* and the tourist office have complete lists of Grenoble's museums, most of which are closed on Tuesdays. Start with the **Musée Dauphinois,** 30, rue Maurice Gignoux (tel. 04 76 85 19 00), toward the bottom of the Bastille hill on the north bank of the Isère. A far cry from the standard yawn-inducing French regional museum displaying wax dummies and folk art, this one boasts constantly updated futuristic exhibits. The latest, *"La Grande Histoire du Ski"* (The Great History of Skiing), is appropriate to the area, recounting the sport from its earliest days to the present high-tech pursuit. Relive the great debate over whether female skiers should be permitted to wear pants, and finish off the tour by learning about local Roman history and mountain peoples (open May-Oct. Wed.-Mon. 10am-7pm; Nov.-April 10am-6pm; admission 15F, students 10F).

Across the river sits the semi-cylindrical **Musée de Grenoble,** 5, pl. de Lavalette (tel. 04 76 63 44 44). Before moving on to the contemporary art that occupies about half of the museum, be sure to take a peek at the paintings in the *dauphinois* rooms. Some look like actual photographs of the region's natural splendors (open Thurs.-Mon. 11am-7pm, Wed. 11am-10pm; admission 25F, students 15F).

The recently renovated **Musée de la Résistance et de la Déportation,** 14, rue Hébert (tel. 04 76 42 38 53), has fewer artifacts and less documentation than similar museums in France but makes up for it with dramatic multimedia displays (open Wed.-Mon. 9am-noon and 2-6pm; admission 15F, students 10F).

A former warehouse at 155, cours Berriat, built by Gustave Eiffel, houses **MAGASIN** (Centre National d'Art Contemporain; tel. 04 76 21 95 84), an exhibition center for fabulous displays of contemporary art. From the train station, take an immediate right then a right again under the tracks onto cours Berriat; walk straight for about 15 minutes. Or take tram A (direction: Fontaine La Poya) to "Berriat" (open Tues.-Sun. noon-7pm; admission 15F, students 10F). The **Musée Stendhal,** 1, rue Hector Berlioz (tel. 04 76 54 44 14), next to the Jardin de Ville, investigates Grenoble's most reluctant citizen, 19th-century author Stendhal (open Wed.-Sun. 2-6pm; free).

Students and recent immigrants now occupy most of the 18th-century houses on the river bank, Grenoble's most attractive neighborhood. The Victorian **Pont St-Laurent,** an early suspension bridge, takes the place of a former Gallo-Roman bridge. Overlooking the manicured **Jardin de Ville,** the elaborate Renaissance **Palais de Justice** has a set of intricately carved ceilings. Organized palace visits depart from pl. St-

André at 10am on the first Saturday of each month (30F)—you have to sneak a look the rest of the time. The bubble cable cars that pop out of the city every three minutes have become an icon of Grenoble, but the actual ride is not that spectacular. The **Téléphérique Grenoble Bastille** (tel. 04 76 44 33 65) leaves from quai Stéphane-Jay and rises 263m to the Bastille fortress. You can climb even higher on the well-marked trails that leave from the cable car station. Beware—they're not easy. (Open Nov.-March Tues.-Sun. 10am-6pm, Mon. 11am-6pm; April-June 15 and Sept. 16-Oct. Tues.-Sat. 9am-midnight, Mon. 11am-7:30pm, Sun. 9am-7:30pm; June 16-30 and Sept. 1-15 Tues.-Sun. 9am-midnight, Mon. 11am-midnight; July.-Aug. Tues.-Sun. 9am-12:30am, Mon. 11am-12:30am. Roundtrip 33F, 21F one way. Students 17F, 12F one way.) From the top, descend through the **Jardin des Dauphins** and **Parc Guy Pape.** (Open, weather permitting, June-Aug. 9am-7:30pm; Sept.-Oct. and April-May 9am-7pm; Nov.-Feb. 9am-4pm; March 9am-5:30pm.)

ENTERTAINMENT

Hot nightspots in Grenoble come and go quickly; try to talk to local students and take a peek in the *Guide DAHU.* Bars include **Le Saxo,** 5, pl. Agier (tel. 04 76 51 06 01; open daily 7pm-2am), and **The London Pub,** 13 rue Brocherie (tel. 04 76 44 41 90; open Mon.-Sat. 3pm-1am, Sun. 6pm-1am). Both are less expensive than clubs, where covers run 50-100F and drinks nearly as much. One disco that won't break the bank is **Le Club des Étudiantes,** 50, rue St-Laurent (tel. 04 76 42 00 68), but you'll need a student card to get in. A popular gay club is **Le Boys,** 124, cours Berriat (tel. 04 76 21 81 20; open daily at 11pm).

The **Maison de la Culture**—so hip its calls itself Le CARGO—imports national and international performers to its three world-class theater and dance spaces (tel. 04 76 25 05 45; 4, rue Paul Claudel; tram stop "Maison de la Culture"). The tourist office carries schedules for Le CARGO and other local theaters; ask about student discounts. Grenoble's annual offerings include February ice car racing, a mid-August outdoor Feast of the Assumption, and the spectacular July 14 fireworks over its Bastille. The **Festival du Court Métrage** (short films) takes place in early July and features films both indoors and outside in pl. St-André (for info contact the Cinémathèque, 4, rue Hector Berlioz, tel. 04 76 54 43 51). The **European Theatre Festival,** with shows ranging from free-100F, hams it up in July (call the Bureau du Festival 10am-11pm at 04 76 44 60 92 for further info). Keep on top of the active festival scene with the tourist office's free *Festivals, Spectacles, and Manifestations.*

■ Near Grenoble

Four mountainous regions surround Grenoble, but they aren't the only source of daytrips in the area; Dauphiné is proud of its *"Huit Merveilles"* (eight wonders), which include elaborate natural caves. The tourist office carries information on excursions to towns such as **Pont-en-Royans** and other natural beauties. A short bus ride from Olympic slopes, Grenoble is an ideal skiing base. Rent equipment in town to avoid high prices at the resorts. The biggest ski areas lie in the **Oisans** to the east. The **Alpe d'Huez** boasts an enormous 2250m vertical drop and sunny south-facing slopes. The 220km of trails are serviced by 81 lifts and cover all difficulty levels, but lift tickets are a bit pricey: 165-200F per day, 960F per week (tourist office tel. 04 76 80 35 41; fax 04 76 80 69 54; ski area tel. 04 76 80 30 30). **Les Deux Alpes** offers the added bonus of a slopeside youth hostel. Its lift system includes two gondolas to whisk you up the 2000m vertical. Lift tickets are 178F per day and 1012F per week. Les Deux Alpes claims the biggest skiable glacier in Europe and has limited summer skiing (tourist office tel. 04 76 79 22 00; fax 04 76 79 22 00; ski area tel. 04 76 79 75 00; youth hostel tel. 04 76 79 22 80; fax 04 76 79 26 15).

The **Belledonne** region, northeast of Grenoble, lacks the towering heights of the Oisans but compensates with lower prices. **Chamrousse** is its biggest and most popular ski area. It offers a lively atmosphere (with a youth hostel), but the skiing pales in comparison to the Oisans. Nonetheless, if conditions are right there's plenty of good

The Postman's Dream House

The village of Hauterives is an unlikely place for a palace; but sometimes the most extraordinary things happen to the most ordinary places and people. On an April day in 1879, the local postman tripped over an oddly shaped rock as he was making his 32km of daily rounds. Absentmindedly, he shoved it in his pocket and drifted off into a daydream, building castles in the sky around the pebble he had pocketed. Well, one pebble led to another, and soon Ferdinand Cheval was taking a wheelbarrow into the fields every evening to collect piles of odd little rocks. The neighbors may have thought him a bit eccentric, but that was only the beginning. Over the next 32 years, the postman shaped his stones into a fantasy palace just outside the village. Rock by rock, it grew into an unbelievably detailed world of grimacing giants, frozen palms, unearthly minarets, and swirling staircases. When the postman finally laid down his trowel, the *"Palais Idéal"* (Ideal Palace) was almost 80m long and over two stories high.

The palace, an indescribable mix of Middle Eastern architecture with Western elements and hallucinatory images, has become a national monument. In the spirit of its free-form construction, you can climb all over the castle and explore for yourself the caves and crevices, mottos and mysteries sculpted by two hands and the postman's unshakable faith. An unparalleled example of folk architecture, the palace is without a doubt the funkiest thing in all of Gaul (tel. 04 75 68 81 19; open April-Sept. 9am-7pm; Sept. 16-Nov. and Feb.-April 14 9:30am-5:30pm; Dec.-Jan. 10am-4:30pm; admission 22F, under 16 15F).

Driving from Grenoble, take A48 north; at Voreppe switch to A49 toward Romans. At Romans, take D538 straight north to Hauterives (about 1hr.; from Lyon, head south on A7 and change to D538 at Vienne). During school vacations, **La Regie Drôme** (tel. 04 75 02 30 42) sends a mid-morning bus from Romans to Hauterives and an early evening bus back (24F50; 40min., call for schedules). You can take the train from Grenoble to Romans (10 per day, 1hr., 61F). Hauterives' **tourist office** can help (pl. de Janauer; tel. 04 75 68 86 82; open April-Oct. daily 9:30am-noon and 1:30-6pm; Nov.-March closed Sun.).

skiing at great value, especially for beginners. Lift tickets are 125F per day, 700F per week (tourist office tel. 04 76 89 92 65; fax 04 76 89 98 06; youth hostel tel. 04 76 89 91 31; fax 04 76 89 96 66). Only half an hour from Grenoble, the resort also makes an ideal daytrip in the summer. Chamrousse maintains four **mountain bike** routes of varying difficulty and has a 230-km network of **hiking** trails.

The neighborly slopes and tiny prices of the **Vercors,** south of Grenoble, are popular among locals. In traditional villages with small ski resorts, such as **Gresse-en-Vercors** (tourist office tel. 04 76 72 38 31), vertical drops hover at 1000m, and the drive from Grenoble can take 25 minutes. Rock-bottom prices (tickets about 60F per day, 300F per week) make the area a stress-free option for beginners, or anyone looking to escape the hassles of major resorts. Teeming with ibex, mountain goats, and country villages, the Vercors and its regional park, have plenty of great **hikes.** Contact **CIMES** (see page 530) for maps and details.

North of Grenoble rise the lush green slopes of the **Chartreuse** mountain range, which boasts its own handful of ski areas. The most interesting thing here is not the snow, but the *liqueur.* In 1605, the monks of the **Monastère de la Grande Chartreuse** tried to manufacture the elixir of long life; they came up with the celebrated yellow-green *Chartreuse* (around 70F in town). Only three monks know the 130-ingredient recipe. You cannot visit the monastery (the monks live in silence and seclusion), but there's a great view of it from **St-Pierre-de-Chartreuse,** about 1km from the main road. The **Musée de la Correrie** (tel. 04 76 88 60 45), in St-Pierre-de-Chartreuse, details the monks' daily routine with spooky hooded models (museum open May-Sept. 9:30am-noon and 2-6:30pm; April and Oct. 10am-6pm; admission 12F). The St-Pierre **tourist office** (tel. 04 76 88 62 08) has more information. From Grenoble, buses run to **Voiron,** from which it's a short trek to St-Pierre-de-Chartreuse

(5 per day, 45min., 18F). While in Voiron, take a free tour of the **Caves de la Grande Chartreuse,** 10, bd. Edgar Kofler (tel. 04 76 05 81 77). The 40-minute tour ends with a tasting (open daily July-Aug. 8am-6:30pm; Sept.-Oct. and Easter-June 8:30-11:30am and 2-6:30pm; Nov.-Easter Mon.-Fri. 8:30-11:30am and 2-5:30pm).

Chamonix

In other Alpine towns the peaks provide harmless backdrops, but in Chamonix daggers of mammoth glaciers seem to reach down and menace the village. **Mont Blanc,** Europe's highest peak (4807m), reigns just to the east. Squeezed in between the mountainous walls of **Le Brévent** (2525m) and **L'Aiguille du Midi** (3842m), Chamonix has exploited its natural surroundings since 19th-century gentlemen-climbers scaled the peaks in sweaters. The town hosted the first modern Winter Olympics in 1924, and many of its streets bear the names of climbers and guides.

Two foreign countries lie within skiing distance of Chamonix, filling its hostel and ski dorms with climbers and skiers swapping tall tales in many languages. Chamonix's slopes are among the toughest in the world and its mountains the most challenging to scale. Some 62 lifts and *téléphériques* (cable cars) defeat gravity to take you to hiking trails that wag their way up the mountain to icy lakes, creeping glaciers, and treacherous snow-covered ridges. If you're more of a spectator, Chamonix's inexpensive dorms provide eye-opening views and excellent opportunities to retreat to the land of perpetual snow and soaring heights.

ORIENTATION AND PRACTICAL INFORMATION

The center of town is the intersection of av. Michel Croz, rue du Docteur Paccard, and rue Joseph Vallot, each named for a past conqueror of Mont Blanc's summit. From the station, follow av. Michel Croz through town, turn left onto rue du Dr. Paccard, and take the first right to the pl. de l'Eglise and the tourist office (5min.).

Tourist Office: pl. du Triangle de l'Amitié (tel. 04 50 53 00 24; fax 04 50 53 58 90). Efficient, modern center with lists of hotels and dorms and a map of campgrounds. Hotel reservations (tel. 04 50 53 23 33) require a 30% deposit for reservations of 2 or more nights. Sells the hiking map *Carte des Sentiers d'Eté* (25F) and *Chamonix Magazine* (3F). Lists area's 62 *téléphériques* with hours, phone numbers, and prices. User-friendly computer (French and English) gives numbers and **weather conditions. Currency exchange** with good rates. Open daily July-Aug. and winter vacation-weeks 8:30am-7:30pm; Sept.-June 9am-noon and 2-6pm.

Hiking Information: Maison de la Montagne, pl. de l'Eglise, next to the church. The **Office de Haute Montagne** (tel. 04 50 53 22 08) is a good place to start planning your hike. The knowledgeable staff will help you to plan your adventures, and you can purchase detailed maps (54-69F). (Open in summer daily 8am-1pm and 1:30-7pm; off-season closed Sat.-Sun.) Next door is the **Ecole du Ski.** Downstairs, the **Compagnie des Guides** (tel. 04 50 53 00 88) organizes skiing and climbing lessons and leads guided summer hikes and winter ski trips. Register the day before 5-7pm (prices vary). **Club Alpin Français,** 136, av. Michel-Croz (tel. 04 50 53 16 03), has information on mountain *refuges* and road conditions. Register with guides the day before hikes 6-7:30pm. Bulletin board matches drivers, riders, and hiking partners. (Open July-Aug. Mon.-Sat. 9:30am-12:30pm and 3-7pm; Sept.-June Mon.-Tues. and Thurs.-Fri. 3-7pm, Sat. 9am-noon.)

Money: There's a 24-hr. **ATM** in train station and a **BNP** on rue Dr. Paccard.

Trains: av. de la Gare (tel. 04 50 53 00 44). Chamonix is served by a special train running from St-Gervais to Martigny; other destinations require a change of train. To: Paris (1 per day, 8hr., 400F); Lyon (5 per day, 4hr., 179F); Annecy (6 per day, 2½hr., 102F); Grenoble (5 per day, 5-6hr., 160F). Info office open daily 9:05am-noon and 2-6:30pm. **Lockers** 10F. **Storage** in the office 30F per bag per day.

Buses: Société Alpes Transports, at the train station (tel. 04 50 53 01 15). To: Annecy (2 per day, 2¾hr., 89F); Grenoble (1 per day, 3½hr., 152F); Geneva (2 per day, 2hr., 188F to airport); Courmayeur, Italy (8 per day, 40min., 50F).

Public Transportation: Chamonix Bus, pl. de l'Eglise (tel. 04 50 53 05 55). 1 line goes up and down the valley from Les Chavands at 1 end to Le Tour/Col des Montet/Lognan at the other. Tickets 7F, *carnet* of 6 38F, *carnet* of 10 59F.
Taxis: tel. 04 50 53 13 94.
Bike Rental: Chamonix Mountain Bike, 132, rue des Moulins (tel. 04 50 53 54 78). Bike with helmet, lock, and maps 70F per ½-day, 95F per day, 450F per 6-day week. ID deposit. Open daily 9am-7pm. V, MC, AmEx.
Ski Rental: There are dozens of ski rental places in town. If you don't want new, state-of-the-art equipment, don't pay more than 80F per day, 350F per week. For reasonable rates, try **Chamonix Mountain Bikes** (above). Skis 39-100F per day, 200-500F per week. Snowboards 95F per day, with boots 140F, 595F per week, boots included. Passport deposit or credit card imprint.
Hiking Equipment: Sanglard Sports, 31, rue Michel Croz (tel. 04 50 53 24 70), in the town center. Staff speaks English. Hiking boots 45F per day, 270F per week. Open 9am-7:30pm; Sept.-June 9am-12:30pm and 2:30-7:30pm. V, MC, AmEx.
English Books: Librairie Jean Landru, 74, rue Vallot (tel. 04 50 53 14 41). Paperback best-sellers. Open 8:30am-12:15pm and 2:30-7:30pm; July-Aug. 8am-7:30pm.
Laundromat: Lav'matic, 40, impasse Primevère. Open daily 8am-8pm.
Weather Conditions: At Maison de la Montagne, tourist office, Club Alpin Français, or in the window of Pharmacie Mont Blanc at intersection of av. Croz and rue Vallot. Call 08 36 68 02 74 for a recording (in French) of weather and road conditions; English version July-Aug. 04 50 53 17 11. For a French recording of snow and avalanche conditions, call 08 36 68 10 20.
Mountain Rescue: PGHM Secours en Montagne, 69, route de la Mollard (tel. 04 50 53 16 89). Register any ambitious hiking itinerary here. Open daily 8am-noon and 2-7pm; 24hr. for emergencies.
Medical Services: Centre Hospitalier, 509, route des Pélerins (tel. 04 50 53 84 00). **Ambulances Sterna** (tel. 04 50 53 46 20). **Medical emergency** tel. 15.
Police: 48, rue Hôtel de Ville (tel. 04 50 55 99 58). **Emergency** tel. 17.
Post Office: pl. Jacques-Balmat (tel. 04 50 53 15 90), next to the bridge over the Arve. **Currency exchange.** Poste restante. Open Mon.-Fri. 8:30am-12:15pm and 2-6:15pm, Sat. 8:30am-noon. **Postal code:** 74400.

ACCOMMODATIONS AND CAMPING

Mountain chalets with dorm accommodations combine affordability with astounding settings but close off-season (Oct.-Nov. and May). Hotels and many dormitories require reservations (preferably 6 weeks in advance) for the hectic school vacations (Dec. and Feb.). The crowds return in July and early August. But the hardest time to get a room is early February, when a car race (no, not skiing) takes over the city. The tourist office has a list of mountain *refuges* and hotels nearby.

Auberge de Jeunesse (HI), 127, montée Jacques Balmat (tel. 04 50 53 14 52; fax 04 50 55 92 34), in Les Pélerins, at the foot of the Glacier de Bossons. Take the bus from pl. de l'Eglise (direction: Les Houches) to "Pélerins Ecole" (7F), and follow the signs uphill to the hostel. By train, get off at "Les Pélerins" and follow the signs. You can also walk down route des Pélerins (30min.). One of those places you see in HI brochures; a glacier looks close enough to touch from your window. Vibrant, international crowd. 74F. Singles 125F. Doubles 89F per person, 97F with shower. Sheets 17F. Breakfast free. Other meals 50F. Free bike loan for guests staying 1 week. Wheelchair access. Vegetarian meals on request. Reception 8am-noon and 5-8pm and 9-10pm; drop bags off anytime. No curfew. Winter ski packages (meals, skis, passes, housing) run 970-3150F per week. V, MC.
Le Chamoniard Volant, 45, route de la Frasse (tel. 04 50 53 14 09; fax 04 50 53 23 25), 15min. from town center, 1 block before La Tapia. From train station, turn right, go under bridge, and take a right across the tracks, a left on chemin des Cristalliers, and a right on route de la Frasse. A melting pot of outdoor enthusiasts. Log-cabin decor. Kitchen facilities. Dorms (4-8 beds per room) 60F. 5F reduction for *Let's Go* users. Sheets 20F. Breakfast 25F. Shower included. Reception open 10am-10pm. *Fondue Savoyard* or *Tartiflette* dinner 66F.

Gîte d'Etape La Tapia, 152, route de la Frasse (tel. 04 50 53 18 19; fax 04 50 53 67 01). From the *gare,* turn right, go under the bridge, and take a right across the tracks, a left on chemin des Cristalliers, and a right on route de la Frasse. It's 1 block after Le Chamoniard (15min.). Friendly, English-speaking staff. Unbeatable views from immaculate rooms. Kitchen. 4- to 5-bunk dorms 70F. Breakfast 25F. Fondue or *raclette* dinner 75F. Reception 9am-noon and 5:30-9pm.

Gîte le Vagabond, 365, av. Ravanel-le-Rouge (tel. 04 50 53 15 43; fax 04 50 53 68 21). A sparkling-new *gîte* near the center of town. Kitchen and laundry facilities. Hip bar and restaurant downstairs run by the friendly staff. Vegetarian or meat *plats du jour* 38F. English breakfast 40F. Dorm rooms 65F (plus 50F deposit for keys). Sheets 6F. Showers 5F. Reception noon-2pm and 4pm-1am. V, MC.

Gîtes d'Etape: Chalet Ski Station, 6, route des Moussoux (tel. 04 50 53 20 25), near *télécabine de Planpraz.* Straight up the hill from the tourist office. No kitchen, but space for cooking if you have a camp stove. 60F for 4- to 9-bunk dorm. Shower 5F. Sheets 30F. Reception open Dec. 20-May 10 and June 25-Sept. 20 9am-11pm. Check-out 11am. Reduced rates on *téléphérique.*

Les Grands Charmoz, 468, chemin de Cristalliers (tel. 04 50 53 45 57). Rooms have great views. U.S. headquarters in Chamonix—the town's July 4th celebration is held in the backyard. From the station, turn right, go under bridge, take a right across the tracks, and turn left onto chemin des Cristalliers (10min.). 4-bed dorm 72F per person, doubles 184F. Kitchen facilities. Showers and sheets included. Reserve ahead and confirm the day before your arrival.

Camping: The tourist office distributes info on campgrounds. Several lie near the foot of the Aiguille du Midi *téléphérique.* **L'Ile des Barrats,** route des Pélerins (tel. 04 50 53 51 44), is one of the nicest. From the *téléphérique,* turn left, walk through a main intersection, continue for 5min., then look to your right (26F per person, 20F per tent, 12F per car, 16F for electricity; reception open May-June and Sept. 9am-noon and 4-7pm; July-Aug. 8am-noon and 2-8pm). **Les Rosières,** 121, clos des Rosières (tel. 04 50 53 10 42), off route de Praz, is the closest on the other side of Chamonix and often has space (open Dec. 15-Oct. 15). Follow rue Vallot for 2km or take a bus to "Les Nants" (24F per person, 11F per tent, 11F per car; reception 8am-9pm). *It is illegal to pitch tents in the Bois du Bouchet.*

FOOD AND ENTERTAINMENT

Stick to the basics in Chamonix—anything but fondue will probably break the bank. The well-stocked **Supermarché Payot Pertin,** 117, rue Joseph Vallot, is the cheapest place for groceries (open Mon.-Fri. 8:15am-12:30pm and 2:30-7:30pm, Sat. 8:15am-7:30pm, Sun. 8:30am-12:15pm). **Markets** take place Saturday mornings at pl. du Mont Blanc and Tuesday mornings in Chamonix Sud, near the foot of the Aiguille du Midi *téléphérique.* Indulge in a little *après-ski* tale-telling at **The Jekyll,** 71, route des Pélerins (tel. 04 50 55 99 70). Straight out of Dublin, the place is run (and overrun) by friendly foreigners. Drink your Guinness (29F) with fabulous food. "American size" portions of Irish favorites, pastas, and salads (29-49F), not to mention great home-made chips. (Open daily 4pm-2am, earlier in bad weather.) If Irish isn't your style, get crazy the Australian way at **Wild Wallabies,** rue de la Tour (tel. 04 50 53 01 31), right next to the Casino. Specialties include excellent BBQ (platters 55F per person), gourmet pizzas, and Aussie brews. (Open daily 11am-2am.) You'll find pastas (45F) fresh over the Italian border at **La Spiga d'Oro,** 80, rue Ravanal-le-Ronge (tel. 04 50 53 06 49; V, MC). **La Cantina,** 37, impasse des Rhododendrons (tel. 04 50 53 64 20), is a rowdy Mexican restaurant with 60F *plats.* Its basement bar features live music. **Le Sabot,** 254, rue Paccard (tel. 04 50 55 99 23), in Galerie Blanc Neige, serves a good selection of pasta (40-45F), *galettes* (15-50F), and salads (18-45F) on a spectacular terrace or in a cozy dining room. (Open daily noon-2pm and 6-10:30pm; Christmas, July-Aug. and Feb.-March open noon-midnight. V, MC.)

Chamonix has three discos. **Le Refuge,** 269, rue Paccard (tel. 04 50 53 00 94), is closest to town and fills up *late* (open daily 10:30pm-dawn; cover 60F, women free Thurs.). Every July and August, the **Semaines Musicales du Mont-Blanc** bring chamber music and jazz groups to Chamonix (tickets 80-120F, reserve at tourist office).

SKIING AND HIKING

Though Chamonix is incomparable, it's not unconquerable. If you've come to climb up these mountains or to ski down them, you're in for a challenge, and certain precautions are in order (for general info, see **Skiing,** page 56). If you're in Chamonix for only a few days, buy daily tickets at individual areas—one ski area is more than enough for a day. If you plan to ski for four or more days, consider a **Skipass Mont Blanc,** available at the Chamonix tourist office. The pass is valid on all lifts in the valley and also good at Courmayeur-Val Veny in Italy. A weekly pass runs about 1000F.

Chamonix has many opportunities for **glacier skiing.** The vast expanses provide breathtaking views, but glaciers are not snow fields. Stay within sight of the trail markers on a glacier or you may ski down a *crevasse.* If you ski off-trail in Chamonix, check your route with the ski patrol and/or the Office de Haut Montagne. Off-*piste* in the Grands Montets and Vallée Blanche is mostly glaciers; beware of *crevasses.*

Beginners may enjoy the festive, busy atmosphere of Chamonix but will find cheaper lift tickets and almost as much fun at lower mountains in the Vercors and Alps (see page 536). **Glacier du Mont Blanc** (tel. 04 50 53 12 39) is a popular area for beginners. It's not that big (400m vertical), but it's near the huge **Glacier des Bossons** and has night skiing (Wed.-Thurs.; 1-day pass 75F). **Balme,** on the southern tip of the valley, is the best bet for intermediates. Excellent views on sun-drenched slopes make it a delightful spot for cruising runs (tel. 04 50 54 00 58; 1-day lift pass 114F). **Le Brevent** (tel. 04 50 53 13 18), a famous proving ground for experts, has expanded skiing for beginners and intermediates. The panoramas of **Mont Blanc** are spectacular, but the skiing is not worth the prices for beginners, though advanced intermediates and experts will find plenty of terrain (1-day lift pass 122F). The classic run for crazy people is the **Vallée Blanche,** a 20-km trail over a glacier from the summit of Aiguille du Midi back down to Chamonix (144F for the *téléphérique*). The run is ungroomed, unmarked, and has no ski patrol. Check conditions before you go, don't ski alone, and bring means to call for aid. Reserve a spot on the *téléphérique* in high season (tel. 04 50 53 40 00).

Chamonix slows down briefly in May and June, but in summer the town is abuzz again with sports enthusiasts. The **Téléphérique de l'Aiguille du Midi** (tel. 04 50 53 30 80, 24-hr. reservations 04 50 53 40 00) runs all year. Those with acrophobia (fear of heights) or argentophobia (fear of shelling out big bucks) might avoid the pricey and often frightening ride, which ascends above towering forests and rocky, snow-covered cliffs to the needlepoint peak at the top. Among the brave and well-to-do, however, few are disappointed by the ride. Go early, as clouds and crowds usually gather by mid-morning. The prices rise the farther you go. The first stop, **Plan de l'Aiguille** (60F, roundtrip 76F), just isn't worth it. (It's less than half the price of the next stop, **l'Aiguille du Midi,** but for spectacular views you should go to the top.) At the summit, the panorama is magnificent, but the experience of being at 3842m is equally worthwhile. Bring warm clothes and take it easy up top: the air is thin (1½-hr. roundtrip 170F; additional 13F to go to summit for a slightly better view). If you've gone that far you might as well pay the extra 86F for the roundtrip to and from Helbronnes. Four-person gondolas take you into the heart of the glacial beast and let you rest in Italy for great views of three countries, the Matterhorn, and Mont Blanc as well as the opportunity for the once in a lifetime picnic on the glacier. The *téléphérique* descends the other side of the mountain into Italy at La Palud, near the resort town of **Courmayeur (tourist office** tel. (00) 391 65 84 20 64). Bring a passport and cash. Unlike France, Italy doesn't accept credit cards for the cable car. Go all the way to your final destination, then stop to look around on the way back while you're waiting for a car. Consider hiking back down to Chamonix from Plan de l'Aiguille (2hr.). (*Téléphérique* open daily 7am-5pm; Sept.-June 8am-5pm.)

There are several *téléphériques* open year-round. A board on pl. de l'Eglise lists the lifts currently open. Chamonix has hundreds of kilometers of **hiking trails** with routes ranging from forests to glaciers. A web of trails wraps around the town, each marked by lines painted on trees indicating degree of difficulty. The 25F map, available at the tourist office, is a good bet. Climbers should buy the IGN topographic map, available at the Office de Haute Montagne and local bookstores. If you're experienced, you can ascend **Mont Blanc,** a two- or three-day hike. Whatever you do, don't go alone. Even in August, you can be caught in a vicious blizzard; in 1996 the top had more snow in summer than at the height of winter. The Maison de la Montagne, Compagnie des Guides, and CAF (see page 538) all have crucial information.

One of the more arresting phenomena in Chamonix is the **Mer de Glace** (tel. 04 50 53 12 54), a glacier that slides 30m per year. Special trains run from a small station next to the main train station (daily May-Sept. 8am-6pm; 48F, roundtrip 63F), but you might prefer the two-hour hike. Accessible via *téléphérique* (12F, one-way up 9F) or a short hike, the nearby tourist-laden **Grotte de Glace** is a kitschy cave in which the ice has been carved into various imaginative shapes (admission 15F). Consider taking the train then hiking back. It's downhill, and just as you run out of breath, the **Luge d'Eté** (21F), a concrete chute, whisks you to the bottom. You can also ride the luge without the hike (tel. 04 50 53 08 97; open daily July-Aug. 10am-7:30pm; Sept. and June 10am-noon and 1:30-6pm; Oct.-Nov. Sat.-Sun. 1:30-6pm).

There are numerous sports shops around town that rent bikes and lead parachuting, canoeing, and river rafting excursions. For the thrill-seeking athlete, the **Ecole Parapente de Chamonix,** 79, rue Whymper (tel. 04 50 53 50 14), offers an initiation into the high-flying art of paragliding for a mere 500F (package available May-Aug.). **Sportif Chamonix** also has an ice rink, 18-hole golf course, and tennis club.

Annecy

You may forget Annecy is a real town when you walk through the *centre ville.* With narrow cobblestone streets, winding canals, a turreted castle, and overstuffed flower boxes—all bordering the purest lake in Europe—Annecy feels more like a fiberglass Disneyland fabrication than a modern city with a metropolitan population of 120,000. Nonetheless, relentlessly photogenic Annecy draws visitors into its beauty. This capital of Haute Savoie consistently claimed the title in the National Flower City contest until its continued success forced it to withdraw permanently from the competition. Though Annecy has traded its petals for tourists, the visitors can't spoil the magic of the lake and mountains.

ORIENTATION AND PRACTICAL INFORMATION

Most activity centers around the lake, southeast of the train station. The canal runs east to west through the old town, leaving the elevated château on one side and the main shopping area, closer to the *centre ville,* on the other. To reach the tourist office from the train station, take the underground passage from the station to rue Vaugelas, turn left, and follow rue Vaugelas for four blocks. The tourist office is straight ahead in the large, modern Bonlieu shopping mall.

Tourist Office: 1, rue Jean Jaurès (tel. 04 50 45 00 33 or 04 50 45 56 66; fax 04 50 51 87 20), at pl. de la Libération. Detailed maps, info on hiking, hotels, campgrounds, rural lodgings, excursions, and climbing. Ask for the helpful *Guide Pratique d'Annecy,* or the *Sentiers Forestiers* for hikes. 2-hr. tours (32F) Mon.-Sat. at 10am and 3pm in summer. **Topo guides** for the area are 57F. Open daily July-Aug. 9am-6:30pm; Sept.-June Mon.-Sat. 9am-noon and 1:45-6:30pm, Sun. 3-6pm.

Money: Several **currency exchanges** can be found in the *vieille ville* (watch out for high commissions). The 24-hr. change machine outside the tourist office has good rates. There is an **ATM** in the departure area of the train station and another on the corner of rue Jean Jaurès and rue Sommeiller.

Trains: pl. de la Gare (tel. 08 36 35 35 35). To: Grenoble (9 per day, 2hr., 86F); Aix-les-Bains (10 per day, 30min., 37F); Chambéry (13 per day, 1hr., 48F); Chamonix (7 per day, 2¼hr., 102F); Lyon (9 per day, 2hr., 110F); Paris (10 per day, 4hr., 404F); Nice (2 per day, 8hr., 352F). Info office open Mon.-Sat. 8:40am-7:15pm, Sun. 9:10am-7:15pm. **Lockers** 15-30F per 72hr.

Buses: Adjacent to the train station. **Voyages Frossard** (tel. 04 50 45 73 90) runs to Geneva (6 per day, 1hr., 48F) and Lyon (2 per day, 3 hr., 90F).

Public Transportation: SIBRA (tel. 04 50 51 70 33). Tickets 7F, *carnet* of 8 38F. Schedule at booth in Bonlieu, near the tourist office. Open Mon.-Sat. 9am-7pm. Extensive service, but only minibuses run on Sun. (including 91 to the hostel).

Taxis: Stand at the train station (tel. 04 50 45 05 67).

Bike Rental: Annecy Sports Passion, 3, av. de Parmelan (tel. 04 50 51 46 28). Rents *VTCs* (70F per ½-day, 100F per day, 110F per weekend) and skis (85-120F per day, boots and poles included). Passport or credit card imprint deposit. Open Tues.-Sat. 8:30am-noon and 2-7pm. V, MC.

Laundromat: Lav'Presse, 13, rue Revon. Open Sun.-Fri. 8am-7pm, Sat. 8am-5pm.

Women's Center: Centre d'Information Féminine, 4, Passage de la Cathédrale (tel. 04 50 45 61 25). English spoken. Open Tues.-Wed. and Fri. 9am-noon, Mon. and Thurs. 9am-noon and 2-5pm. **BIJ** office in Bonlieu (tel. 04 50 33 87 40).

Crisis Lines: SOS Amitié (tel. 04 50 27 70 70). **AIDES,** 5 av. de Chevêne (tel. 04 50 52 74 85 or toll-free 0 800 36 66 36), a local AIDS info number.

Hospital: 1, av. des Trésun (tel. 04 50 88 33 33). From the tourist office, follow quai Chappuis toward the lake past the Hôtel de Ville and into pl. Bois. Bear left onto rue des Marquisats, continue for 1 long block along the lake and take a right onto av. de Trésun immediately after you pass the Hôtel de Police. **Medical emergency** tel. 04 50 51 21 21 or 15. For an on-call **doctor,** dial 04 50 52 81 81.

Police: 15, rue des Marquisats (tel. 04 50 52 32 00). Follow directions to the hospital up to rue des Marquisats. **Emergency** tel. 17.

Post Office: 4, rue des Glières (tel. 04 50 33 67 00), off rue de la Poste, down the street from the train station. **Currency exchange.** Poste restante (postal code: 74011). Open Mon.-Fri. 8am-7pm, Sat. 8am-noon. **Postal code:** 74000.

ACCOMMODATIONS AND CAMPING

Annecy's prices confirm its popularity. The few budget hotels are in the neighborhood behind the station. Reservations are recommended, especially in high season.

Auberge de Jeunesse "La Grande Jeanne" (HI), route de Semnoz (tel. 04 50 45 33 19; fax 04 50 52 77 52). Minibus 91 (direction: Semnoz) leaves from the train station, but only runs in summer (7F, last bus 7pm). At other times, take bus 1 (direction: Marquisats) from the train station to "Hôpital." Follow D41, which changes names several times (follow the frequent signs pointing to Semnoz). After a 15min. uphill hike, the hostel will be on your right. Walking from the tourist office, head along the canal on quai Chappuis. After a bridge, it will change to rue des Marquisats. Turn right on av. de Trésun and follow the directions above (45min.). A gorgeous new chalet in the woods near trails. Rooms with 3-5 beds, each with a shower. Bar, game room, kitchen, TV room, and friendly staff and clientele. Leave your laundry at the desk and it will be washed, dried, and folded by morning (40F). 69F, breakfast free. Sheets 16F. Meals 48F. Reception 7:30am-11pm (10pm in winter). No lockout or curfew; ask for a key if you'll be out late.

Hôtel Savoyard, 41, av. de Cran (tel. 04 50 57 08 08), in a residential area behind station. Enthusiastic managers define hospitality. Great, large, rustic singles and doubles 100F, with bathroom 180F. Breakfast 20F.

Hôtel Plaisance, 17, rue de Narvik (tel. 04 50 57 30 42). Bright, large rooms in good condition. TV room, pretty dining room. Charming owner is used to young, foreign clientele. Singles 130F. Doubles 140F, with shower 180F. Triples 235F. Quads 285F. Shower 12F. Breakfast 25F. V, MC.

Hôtel Rive du Lac, 6, rue des Marquisats (tel. 04 50 51 32 85; fax 04 50 45 77 40). The most expensive rooms have spectacular balcony views of mountains towering over the lake. Simple rooms are big and bright, and the price is right. Singles and doubles from 136F. Triples 184F. Quads 205F. Shower 10F per 6min. Breakfast 24F. Restaurant downstairs serves a 66F *menu.* V, MC.

Camping: 8, route de Semnoz (tel. 04 50 45 48 30; fax 04 50 45 55 56). Close to town and *busy.* Adjacent food store sells basics at reasonable prices. 26F per person, 33F per tent and car, 23F per small tent, 20F for electricity. Reception open April-Aug. 8am-10pm. Ring buzzer off-season (open Dec. 15-Oct. 15). V, MC. Dozens of campgrounds border the lake in the town of **Albigny,** reachable by Voyages Crolard buses or by following av. d'Albigny from the tourist office (1.5km).

FOOD

Whether you choose a restaurant on the canal or a lakeside picnic, the surroundings will be as enjoyable as the food, if not more so. Fill your picnic basket with the soft local *reblochon* cheese at the **markets** on Tuesday, Friday, and Sunday mornings around **pl. Ste-Claire,** and Saturday morning on **bd. Taine.** Many small grocery stores line av. de Parmelan. There is also a **Prisunic supermarket** that fills the better part of pl. de Notre-Dame (open Mon.-Sat. 8:30am-7:30pm).

Quoi de n'Oeuf, 19, fbg. Ste-Claire (tel. 04 50 45 75 42). Eggheads jump at the all-you-can-eat *tartiflette,* salad, and dessert offer. Open daily noon-2pm and 7-10pm.

Restaurant Le Phénix Imperial, 8, rue Poquier (tel. 04 50 45 48 57), a tiny covered alleyway off rue Vaugelas. Specializes in Vietnamese cuisine. Most dishes 20-50F. *Potage Phénix,* with bamboo shoots, mushrooms, and shrimp 26F. Desserts include banana ice cream with Grand Marnier and caramel (25F). Vegetarian dishes, too (20-25F). Open Mon.-Sat. 11:30am-3pm and 7-11:30pm. V, MC.

Taverne le Freti, 12, rue Ste-Claire (tel. 04 50 51 29 52). A find for those fond of flambéed *fromage. Raclette* 61-67F. *Fondue savoyarde* (58F) and other varieties 52-97F. Salads 20-37F. Open Tues.-Sun. 7-11:30pm.

Taverne Grecque, 15, fbg. Ste-Claire (tel. 04 50 45 50 26). Good atmosphere and great gyros (takeout sandwich 25F). Also has 55F lunch *menu* with *feuilles de vigne* (rolled grape leaves). Open lunch and dinner. V, MC, AmEx.

Au Bord du Thiou, 4, pl. St-François-de-Sales (tel. 04 50 45 54 09). On the canal near the Palais de l'Ile. Great choice for salads (18-38F), crêpes (16-42F), and ice cream. The *crêpe Rock* includes Roquefort cheese, nuts, raisins, and cognac (30F). Open daily noon-2pm and 5pm-midnight. Closed end of June to early July.

SIGHTS AND ENTERTAINMENT

A stroll through the *vieille ville* may cost you several rolls of film and a hundred sighs; all of Annecy is one big, beautiful sight. Cross the street from the tourist office to walk through the **Champ de Mars,** a grass field dotted with *boules* players, sunbathers, and picnickers. At the mouth of the Canal du Vassé, which runs along the Champ de Mars, is the **Pont des Amours** (Lovers' Bridge), one of a few that merits its cheesy name. The **Jardin de l'Europe,** a web of paths surrounding manicured hedges, fountains, and statues, lies on the other side of the bridge. The *jardin* sticks out like a thumb into the water, bordered by canals and the Lac d'Annecy. Escape on a **pedal boat** from **Bateaux Dupraz** on quai Napoleon (tel. 04 50 51 52 15). Some boats come with a slide so you can take a dip in the lake (35-52F per 30min., 60-77F per hour; slides 10F extra; tours of the lake 52-55F; V, MC).

Follow the swans along the canal du Thiou and past the Baroque locks to the formidable **Palais de l'Isle** (tel. 04 50 33 83 62). This 12th-century fortress was originally the mansion of the de l'Isle family. The skinny building forming an island in the middle of the canal was converted into a prison in the 1400s and is now an uninteresting museum devoted to Annecy's history. Save yourself the 20F; it's more impressive from the outside. The pedestrian passages of quai Perrière, rue de l'Isle, and rue Ste-Claire to the south of Palais de l'Isle are Annecy at its most charming. On market mornings (Tues., Fri., and Sun.), rue Ste-Claire becomes crowded with vendors hawking cheese and fresh vegetables in pyramids of Kodak-quality perfection.

After a stroll through the bustling streets, you may opt for a swim in the cold, crystalline lake. **Plage des Marquisats,** south of the city down rue des Marquisats, is free but crowded. It's 18F to swim at glamorous **Parc Public de l'Impérial** (tel. 04 50 28 11 82), an aquatic wonderland (20-min. up av. d'Albigny) with waterslides, sailing, tennis, swim lessons, and a casino (open daily May-Sept. 10am-7:30pm).

Towering over Annecy is its 12th-century **château,** a short, huffing-and-puffing climb from the *vieille ville.* Once a stronghold of the counts of Geneva, the castle and its imposing parapets now house unexciting archaeological and artistic exhibits (tel. 04 50 33 87 30). Temporary shows are often well mounted, however, and the **Observatoire Regional des Lacs Alpins,** in the rear of the castle, has interesting displays on lake ecosystems as well as a cool subterranean aquarium. If the exhibits don't impress you, the view will. (Open daily July-Aug. 10am-6pm; Sept.-June Wed.-Mon. 10am-noon and 2-6pm. Admission 30F, students 10F.)

Although it may be hard to tear yourself away from the city's cosmetic charms, a hike or bike ride through its Alpine forests will prove that Annecy is a natural beauty, too. A dozen breathtaking **hikes** begin on the **Semnoz,** a limestone mountain south of the city. The trailhead is practically in the backyard of the hostel. If you're staying in town, take bus 91 (summer only) to "Tillier." The *Office National des Forêts* distributes a color map, *Sentiers Forestiers,* with several routes (free at the tourist office or hostel). Long-haulers may consider the **Grand Randonée 96 (GR96),** which circles the lake on a trail marked with yellow and red lines. There's an exquisite, scenic *piste cyclable* (bike route) hugging the lakeshore. The **Bureau de la Montagne** (tel. 04 50 45 00 33) covers all mountaineering activities, including hikes (70F per ½-day, 110F per day), rock-climbing, ice-climbing, and canyoning excursions (desk in the tourist office open daily 5:30-6:30pm; sign up the night before). For information on sports options in the area, from mini-golf to windsurfing, call **Annecy Sport Information** (tel. 04 50 33 88 31; Mon.-Fri. 3-7pm; next to the tourist office). The *Guide Pratique* has pages of info on outdoor recreation.

After a hard day shooting the rapids or conquering the slopes, relax at the bars lining the canal in the *vieille ville;* if you're still feeling antsy, head to **Discothèque l'Esprit,** 37, av. Chavoire (tel. 04 50 23 33 43), a lakeside local favorite. Follow the lakeshore north on av. d'Albigny through its name changes (30min.). Dance, music, drama, or cinema is usually up at the **Théâtre d'Annecy** (tel. 04 50 33 44 11) in the Bonlieu Mall across from the tourist office (about 95F, students 40F).

Fête fetishists can pick up schedules at the **Comité des Fêtes** kiosk across from the tourist office. A small jazz festival heats up the middle two weekends of July (60-100F). The grandaddy of them all is the **Fête du Lac,** enlivening the first Saturday in August with fireworks and water shows (35-260F). Each year the floats on the lake take on wacky themes; "Monsters and Legends," "Adventures in the Far West," and "Beyond the Planet Earth" have been featured in the past.

■ Near Annecy

Ten km west of Annecy, waterfalls roar over the cliffs of the glacier-carved **Gorges du Fier** (open daily June 15-Sept. 15 9am-7pm, March 15-June 14 and Sept. 16-Oct. 15 9am-noon and 2-6pm; admission 23F; 40min. walk; call 04 50 46 23 07 for info). The **Château de Montrottier** (tel. 04 50 46 23 02) is five minutes up from the entrance to the gorges. The castle contains centuries-old Asian costumes, armor, and pottery (open Easter-Oct. 15 daily 9am-noon and 2-6pm; obligatory tour 25F, students 20F). The **Voyages Crolard** (tel. 04 50 45 09 12) excursion bus includes admission to the Gorges and the château (Mon. 2:45pm from the *gare routière,* 100F; return at 7pm). Alternatively, take the train to **Lovagny** and then walk 800m to the gorges (1-2 per day stop at Lovagny at odd hours, 10min., 12F); or take bus A to the end of the line at Poisy and walk 4km southwest to Lovagny and the château.

The smaller villages on the Lac d'Annecy make for excellent daytrips; ask at the tourist office for suggestions. All are within 20km of Annecy and accessible by bus (call Voyages Crolard; 2-3 per day in high seasons, 50-75F). Driving, take D909 along the east shore, which intersects with N508 at Doussard, to return to Annecy along the west lake shore. Nine km southeast of Annecy along the lake, descendants of the Menthon family still own their 13th- to 18th-century ancestral home at **Menthon-St-Bernard.** An earlier version of the château was the 10th-century birthplace of St. Bernard, who built the two hospices nearby. **Talloires,** 13km from Annecy, makes a good starting point for the one-hour hike to the waterfalls at **La Cascade d'Angon** and to the beautiful gardens of the **Ermitage de St-Germain** (also 1hr.). Ask the tourist office in Annecy or Talloires (tel. 04 50 60 70 64; fax 04 50 60 76 59) about boat rides from Annecy to Talloires. **Doussard,** south of the lake and surrounded by nature preserves, is known as "the source of the lake" because its rivers fill Lac d'Annecy (tourist office tel. 04 50 44 60 24; fax 04 50 44 45 96). **Duingt** (*mairie* tel. 04 50 68 67 07; fax 04 50 77 03 17), midway along the west side of the lake, intimidates Talloires across the water with its looming 11th-century château (closed to the public). Nearby **St-Jorioz** has particularly spectacular views of the mountains (tourist office tel. 04 50 68 61 82; fax 04 50 68 96 11).

In winter, hotel prices drop and skiers pour in. The nearest resort is **La Clusaz,** 32km away (accessible by bus) with 130km of downhill skiing and 56 lifts. Contact the **tourist office** in La Clusaz (tel. 04 50 32 65 00; fax 04 50 32 65 01) at Boîte Postale 7, 74220 La Clusaz for info. There is a well-equipped **youth hostel** outside La Clusaz (tel. 04 50 02 41 73; fax 04 50 02 65 85) on route du Col de la Croix Fry.

Aix-les-Bains

With its deep thermal springs and towering peaks, Aix-les-Bains (pop. 25,000) is a city of contrasts. The upper part of town is dominated by the **Thermes Nationaux,** a therapeutic hot spring whose healing properties were first recognized in Roman times. Up by the baths an old, monied, and mostly French crowd passes its languid days in search of the fountain of youth. But they have only to descend to the lower part of town to find an endless well of agelessness—the athletic, international windsurfers and sunbathers who gather by the beach. The lively lower section of Aix borders France's largest natural lake, the Lac du Bourget. Aix-les-Bains is united by two conditions. No matter where you walk in town, you will be struck by its natural beauty, and no matter where you turn, you will encounter droves of tourists.

ORIENTATION AND PRACTICAL INFORMATION

Aix's center is just east of the train station; the lake is a 25-minute walk in the opposite direction. To get to the tourist office from the station, cross bd. Wilson and head down av. Charles de Gaulle, cross pl. J. Moulin, and walk along the edge of the park for one block. The tourist office is to the left, opposite the *Thermes Nationaux*.

Tourist Office: pl. Maurice Mollard (tel. 04 79 35 05 92; fax 04 79 88 88 01). The building has served as everything from a Roman temple to a medieval fortress. Detailed map, hotel and restaurant info, as well as the brochure *Aix Poche.* City tours. Ask for **Le Fil de la Semaine,** a weekly listing of concerts, special events, and guided tours, or *Guide des Plaisirs.* Open Mon.-Sat. 8:45am-noon and 2-7:30pm, Sun. 9:30am-12:30pm; Oct.-April closed Sun. **Lakeside annex** at Grand Port, pl. Herriot (tel. 04 79 34 15 80) open June-Sept. daily 10am-noon and 2-6pm.

Money: Banks with **currency exchange** cluster around pl. Carnot. There's an **ATM** in the station at **Crédit Mutuel** as well as at **BNP** across from the Casino.

Trains: pl. de la Gare (tel. 04 79 85 50 50, reservations 04 79 62 40 60). To: Paris (20 per day, 3½hr., 332F); Lyon (18 per day, 1½hr., 87F); Annecy (10 per day, 30min., 37F). Office open Mon.-Sat. 8:30am-noon and 2-6:30pm. **Lockers** 15-30F.

Public Transportation: STDA, 7F50 per ride. Info kiosk on the edge of Parc de Verdure (tel. 04 79 88 80 60), or get free route maps at the tourist office.

Laundromat: Lav Plus, 26, av. Grand Port. Open daily 7am-9pm.

Hospital: 49, av. Grand Port (tel. 04 79 88 61 61). Fromthe tourist office, take a sharp left onto av. du Temple de Diane, then a right into pl. Carnot, which will turn into rue de Genève, then av. Grand Port. **Aixoises Ambulances,** 3, rue Isalène (tel. 04 79 88 33 13). **Medical emergency** tel. 15.

Police: 2bis, av. Victoria (tel. 04 79 35 00 25). **Emergency** tel. 17.

Post Office: av. Victoria (tel. 04 79 35 15 10), at av. Marie de Solms. Poste restante (postal code: 73109). Photocopies 1F. **Currency exchange.** Open Mon.-Fri. 8am-7pm, Sat. 8am-noon. **Postal code:** 73100.

ACCOMMODATIONS, CAMPING, AND FOOD

To accommodate its varied visitors, this health resort has dozens of cheap hotels. Try bd. Wilson, by the train station, or av. du Tresserve, three blocks right of the station.

Auberge de Jeunesse (HI), promenade de Sierroz (tel. 04 79 88 32 88; fax 04 79 61 14 05). Take bus 2 left of station (direction: Plage d'Aix) to "Camping," and walk 3min. along the stream away from the lake. By foot, from the station, turn left onto bd. Wilson. After 2 blocks, go under tracks via the pedestrian underpass and onto av. du Petit-Port to the roundabout Carrefour Lamartine. Continue to pl. Labor, then turn left onto chemin du Pêcheur. After 1 block, this joins bd. Garibaldi; follow it through an S-turn to promenade de Sierroz, turn left, and walk 1 long block along the stream (35min; not so confusing as it sounds). Modern and packed with groups; individuals should reserve a week ahead. Spotless 3- to 6-bed dorms with skylights. Young, hip, laid-back staff. 51F. Sheets 19F. Dinner 49F, breakfast 19F. Reception 7-10am and 6-10pm. Lockout 10am-6pm. No curfew.

Notre Dame des Eaux, 6, bd. des Côte (tel. 04 79 61 13 87; fax 04 79 34 06 96). Small, comfortable rooms in a tranquil setting. Reserve 3 to 4 *months* in advance—it's very popular with elderly spa-goers. Singles 110F, with shower 180F. Doubles 160F, with shower 200F. Reception open 24hr. V, MC, AmEx.

Hôtel Angleterre, 22, av. Victoria (tel. 04 79 35 05 33) and, just down the street, **Hôtel Floréal,** 16, av. Victoria (tel. 04 79 35 03 59). From station, walk up av. Charles de Gaulle, turn left onto av. Marie de Solms, then right onto av. Victoria (3min.). One owner runs these 2 places with identical small but spotless rooms in a great location. Singles 95F. Doubles 110-120F, with shower 180F. Shower 10F. Breakfast 25F. You can check into either place at the Angleterre 24hr. if you call ahead. Floréal check-in open only 6:30am-10pm. V, MC.

Hôtel Windsor, 17, rue Davat (tel. 04 79 88 49 25; fax 04 79 35 38 78), in the *centre ville,* has firm beds in clean rooms. Singles 145F, with shower 190F. Doubles 210F, with shower 230F. Breakfast 32F. Reception 6:30am-10pm. V, MC, AmEx.

Camping: Camping Municipal Sierroz (tel. 04 79 61 21 43), conveniently across from the lake, 2km from the station, down the street from the hostel. Showers, grocery store, and volleyball. 17F per person, 29F per tent, 18F per car, electricity 14F; Oct.-May prices slightly lower. 2F tax per person. Reception 8am-6:30pm. Always packed; reservations required July-Aug. Open March 15-Nov. 15. V, MC.

There's a **Prisunic supermarket** at 17, rue de Genève (open Mon.-Sat. 8:30am-12:30pm and 2-7:30pm). There are also **markets** on pl. Clemenceau Wednesday and Saturday mornings. Grand Port is dotted with inexpensive eateries offering pleasant lake views and serving fillets of the lake's scaly ex-residents. **Restaurant Skiff Pub,** Grand Port (tel. 04 79 63 41 00), has pasta (38-48F; open daily 7am-1:30am; V, MC). Up in the center of town, try **Tassili,** 12, av. Grand Port (tel. 04 79 88 03 85), where you can eat a dozen different kinds of couscous (50-115F; open Tues.-Sun. noon-3pm and 7pm-midnight). Meet hordes of young ice cream aficionados at the incredible *glâcerie* **Sibérienne,** 42, bd. Pierpont Morgan (tel. 04 79 61 09 83), near the lake. Specialties (28-40F) are served in ostentatious glasses with gaudy trimmings—paper umbrellas and beyond. A banana split is 35F (order take-out cones inside—4F for 1 scoop, 8F for 2, 12F for 3; open in season daily 3pm-1:30am).

SIGHTS AND ENTERTAINMENT

Unlike the rest of inland France, water—not wine—is the lifeblood of Aix. Its **Thermes Nationaux** (tel. 04 79 35 38 50), across from the tourist office, are far more sophisticated than their Roman predecessors. The *thermes* offer mud baths, underwater massage, and pool therapy. The full cure can only be taken by French citizens armed with a doctor's prescription, but visitors can still partake of an array of water massages and treatments (25-110F)—ask for information for *cures libres.* A first-class dip in the thermal *piscine* will cost you 50F for one hour between 6am-noon. If you don't want to get your feet wet, take a tour of the modern baths followed by a descent to see the remains of the ancient Roman ones (Tues.-Sat. 3pm, 20F; tours leave from opposite tourist office). Only 30 people are permitted on each tour, so buy your tickets by 2:30pm. Outside, visit the grottoes and the sinus-clearing sulphur springs. The **Musée Faure,** bd. des Côtes (tel. 04 76 61 06 57), atop a hill overlooking the town, diverts spirits sodden by bath water with works by Sisley, Pissarro and Degas. On the top floor, there's a room of beautiful Rodin sculptures. (Open Mon. and Wed.-Fri. 9:30am-noon and 1:30-6pm, Sat.-Sun. 9:30am-noon and 2-6:45pm. Admission 20F, students 10F, children under 15 free.)

Aix's more lively watery tourist draw is the crystal-clear **Lac du Bourget.** Any stop on bus 2 (direction: Plage d'Aix) between Grand Port and the end of the line is near the lake. When you're through marveling at the mountains rising from the water, take a swim at one of Aix's beaches, like the **plage Municipale** and the **plage de Mémars** at opposite ends of the developed rocky coast (both free). Keep in mind that this is Alpine lake swimming—the scenery is breathtaking and the water is, too. The **Centre Nautique,** pl. Daniel-Rops (tel. 04 79 61 48 80), offers a heated pool on its private beach (25F, under 18 18F). Winter visitors will find an indoor pool (same prices; both open daily 9:30am-7:30pm). You can rent boats at many locations along the shore. In Grand Port, **Nautis-Aix** rents sailboats and motorboats (tel. 04 79 88 24 34; 170-450F per hour; open daily 11am-7pm). The **Club Nautique de Voile d'Aix-Les-Bains** (tel. 04 79 34 10 74) gives sailing lessons (170F per hour).

One reason to stay in Aix-les-Bains is a morning excursion to the **Abbaye d'Hautecombe** (tel. 04 79 54 26 12). Gregorian chants emanate from mass at this Benedictine abbey, restored in the 19th century and sheltering the tombs of the princes of Savoie (open Mon. and Wed.-Sat. 10-11:30am and 2-5pm, Sun. 10:30am-noon and 2-5pm; free, donations appreciated). The boat to the abbey from Aix's Grand Port gives views of the abbey rising dramatically from the water's edge (5 per day, 2½hr., 50F; 1-2 per day Sept.-June). A trip to Sunday mass leaves at 8:30am (tel. 04 79 35 05 92 for info). Other excursions cover the history and ecology of the lake (50-190F).

The village of **Le Revard,** a 20-minute bus ride from Aix, is surrounded by an extensive network of trails for hiking and cross-country skiing. A popular cross-country ski area is **La Feclaz** (tel. 04 79 25 80 49). For transportation info, call **Ailleurs avec Guillermin** (tel. 04 79 34 02 22). Other bus companies run tours also. Contact the **Syndicat d'Initiative du Revard** (tel. 04 79 54 00 83) for more details.

Aix hosts (mostly free) summer concerts in the **Théâtre de Verdure** (tel. 04 79 88 09 99). Larger concerts take place at the Palais du Congrès and the Esplanade du Lac. For a weekend at the end of August, Aix mounts a **Fête des Fleurs** (Flower Festival), with fireworks, floral floats, and proverbial good, clean fun. In July, Aix presents a three-opera **Estivades d'Opérette** (tel. 04 79 88 09 99; tickets 50-360F).

The *curistes* have the run of the *discothèques* in the *centre ville;* the young escape to clubs on the outskirts of the city. Students frequent **Pub 31,** 31, rue Casino (tel. 04 79 88 15 75), and **Brasserie de la Poste,** av. Victoria (tel. 04 79 35 00 65). Hostelers and lakeside dwellers can join the young crowds at **Welsh Pub,** 2, bd. Robert Barrier (tel. 04 79 63 42 05), in Grand Port.

Chambéry

The ancient capital of Savoie, Chambéry retains its Italian- and French-influenced culture unbeknownst to the flocks of tourists that pass through its train station on their way to the high Alps. In 1232, the savvy dukes of Savoie settled in a magnificent château in this crucial gateway town. Because all traffic through the Alps passed beneath their windows, the dukes' control of Chambéry brought them enormous influence and wealth. Today the château is run by a no-less-fearsome French bureaucracy, and its towers dominate the covered arcades and wide boulevards of the pedestrian *vieille ville.* The city's charms were best sung by Jean-Jacques Rousseau in his *Confessions.* Chambéry may not prove so exciting for you as for him, but that shouldn't deter you from packing up your skis and staying a day or two.

ORIENTATION AND PRACTICAL INFORMATION

Chambéry is 10 minutes by train from Aix-Les Bains and an hour from Grenoble. The *centre ville* lies south of the train station, with the château and *vieille ville* in the southwest corner. To reach the tourist office from the station, walk left on rue Sommeiller one long block and cross pl. du Centenaire to bd. de la Colonne (5min.).

Tourist Office: 24, bd. de la Colonne (tel. 04 79 33 42 47; fax 04 79 85 71 39). Wheelchair access from 19, av. des Ducs de Savoie. English-speaking, brochure-wielding staff. Open June-Sept. Mon.-Sat. 9am-12:30pm and 1:30-6:30pm, Sun. 10am-12:30pm; Oct.-May Mon.-Sat. 9am-noon and 1:30-6pm. In the same building is the **Association Départementale de Tourisme de la Savoie** (tel. 04 79 85 12 45). Information including hotels, campgrounds, and ski resorts (same hours).

Hiking Information: Club Alpin Français, 70, rue Croix d'Or (tel. 04 79 33 05 52). Advice on hiking and skiing. Open Tues.-Fri. 5:30-7:30pm, Sat. 10am-noon.

Money: ATMs at **Crédit Agricole** in the station or **Crédit Mutuel,** 10, rue Veyrat.

Trains: pl. de la Gare (tel. 08 36 35 35 35; reservations 04 79 62 46 60). To: Lyon (10 per day, 1½hr., 83F); Grenoble (15 per day, 30min., 55F); Annecy (13 per day, 1hr., 48F); Geneva (7 per day, 2hr., 80F); Paris (24 indirect per day, 4hr., 370F). Info office open Mon.-Fri. 8:30am-12:20pm and 1:30-6:50pm, Sat. 8:30am-5:50pm. **Lockers** 15-30F per 72hr.

Buses: Several companies run from the **gare routière,** pl. de la Gare (tel. 04 79 69 11 88), across from the station. A good, if slow, option for visiting Alpine villages. To Annecy (8 per day, 1hr., 43F) and Grenoble (6 per day, 1hr., 48F).

Public Transportation: STAC, bd. de la Colonne (tel. 04 79 69 61 12). Runs 7:30am-7pm. Kiosk at bd. de la Colonne, stop "Eléphants" open Mon.-Fri. 7:15am-7:15pm, Sat. 7:20am-12:20pm and 2:20-5:40pm. Ticket 6F50, *carnet* of 10 35F30, student *carnet* 25F40.

Taxi: Allo Taxi, tel. 04 79 69 11 12, 24hr.

Bike Rental: Cycles Peugeot, 20, rue Jean-Pierre Veyrat (tel. 04 79 62 36 72), adjacent to the château. Mountain bikes 70F per ½-day, 100F per day, 250F per weekend (Sat.-Mon.). ID *plus* 2800F deposit. Open Tues.-Sat. 9am-noon and 2-7pm. Opens at 8am in summer. V, MC, AmEx.

Laundromat: 1, rue Doppet. Open daily 7:30am-8pm.

Youth Information Center: Centre d'Information et de Documentation Jeunesse (CIDJ), 4, pl. de la Gare (tel. 04 79 62 66 87). Info on sports, hostels, and *foyers.* Bulletin board posts rides, jobs, baby-sitting, and housing information. BIJ/Transalpino tickets. Open Mon. and Wed. 9am-12:30pm and 1:30-6pm, Tues. and Fri. 9am-6pm, Thurs. 10am-12:30pm and 1:30-7pm, Sat. 10am-noon.

Women's Center: Maison des Associations, sq. R. Marcon (tel. 04 79 33 95 50).

Hospital: Centre Hospitalier, pl. François-Chiron (tel. 04 79 96 50 50). From the tourist office, turn right on bd. de la Colonne, then left at the Musée des Beaux-Arts onto rue Veyrot. Bear right at the château; the hospital is on the left. **Medical emergency** tel. 15.

Police: 585, av. de la Boisse (tel. 04 79 62 84 00). To get there, take a right from the train station onto av. de la Boisse and walk 3 blocks. **Emergency** tel. 17.

Post Office: sq. Paul Vidal (tel. 04 79 96 69 15). Poste restante. **Currency exchange.** Photocopies. Open Mon.-Fri. 8am-7pm, Sat. 8am-noon. **Postal code:** 73000.

ACCOMMODATIONS AND CAMPING

There are several budget options in the center of town, but if none of these work out look for a bed around the Hôtel de Ville.

Hôtel le Mauriennais, 2, rue Ste-Barbe (tel. 04 79 69 42 78; fax 04 79 69 46 86), near the château. Most rooms have been newly renovated; comfortable and clean, considering the cost. Singles 80F. Doubles 110F. Triples 160F. Quads 160F. Hall showers 12F, students free. Breakfast 22F.

Hôtel du Château, 37, rue Jean-Pierre Veyrat (tel. 04 79 69 48 78), next to the château, of course. Large, simple rooms in a great part of town. The only genial, family-run hotel/bar/**tattoo parlor** in all of France. Singles 85F. Doubles 120F. Triples 160F. Quads 180F. Shower 14F. Breakfast 22F. Reception 6:30am-9pm.

Hôtel des Voyageurs, 3, rue Doppet (tel. 04 79 33 57 00), offers simple rooms in a central location. Singles 130F, with shower 150F. Doubles 160F, with shower 190F. Quads 180F, with shower 240F. Breakfast 25F. Reception 7am-9:30pm.

Camping La Nivolet, 3km away in Bassens. (tel. 04 79 85 47 79). 15F per person, 7F per car, 15F per tent. Reception May-Sept. 9am-noon and 2-8pm.

FOOD

Budget meals are easy to find in the *vieille ville.* If you want to mingle with locals over great food with friendly service, head to **La Poterne,** 3, pl. Maché (tel. 04 79 96 23 70), at the entrance to the château, with *menus* at 67F (lunch only), 91F, and higher and *fondue savoyarde* at 75F (open Mon. noon-2pm, Tues.-Sat. noon-2pm and 7:30-10pm; V, MC). Delectable fish (50-70F) and meat (55-110F) dishes are waiting to be discovered at Hollywood-themed **Le Clap,** 4, rue Ste-Barbe (tel. 04 79 96 27 08), where each item on the menu is named after a movie. Stage lighting illuminates the ceiling and movie posters cover the walls. Improve your French by translating desserts like *"La Guerre des Etoiles"* (Star Wars) while sitting on a director's chair (open Mon.-Fri. noon-2pm and 7pm-midnight, Sat. noon-2pm; closed first week of Aug.; V, MC). **La Bodega,** 18, rue Jean-Pierre Veyrat (tel. 04 79 96 10 65), has *après-ski* panache. Gorge on pasta (39-50F), pizza (38-58F), or a 45F *plat du jour. Menus* 60-68F. (Open Aug. 22-July Mon.-Sat. noon-3pm and 7pm-midnight. V, MC.) **Les Halles,** pl. de Genève, is the town's Saturday-morning **market.** A **Prisunic** lurks on the corner of rue de Boigne and pl. du 8 Mai (open Mon.-Sat. 8:15am-7pm).

SIGHTS AND ENTERTAINMENT

For six centuries, Savoie's power emanated from the 13th-century **Château des Ducs de Savoie.** Its last prominent master was Vittorio Emanuele II, the first king of unified Italy. Enter through the intimidating 15th-century Porte de l'Eglise St-Dominique. Partially destroyed by an 18th-century fire, the **Ste-Chapelle** was rebuilt and (in the 19th century) repainted in a *trompe l'oeil* style. Invasions by French kings eventually convinced the dukes to transfer the capital, and Jesus' alleged burial cloth (kept in the chapel in the 16th century), to Turin, Italy, where the shroud remains. (Obligatory 1hr. tour July-Aug. daily 2:30, 3:30, 4:30 and 5:30pm; May-June and Sept. daily 2:30pm; April and Oct. Sat.-Sun. 2:30 and 4pm; Nov.-March Sat.-Sun. 2:30pm. 25F; Nov.-March 35F including tour of the *vieille ville.*)

The **Fontaine des Eléphants**—the best-known monument in Chambéry—was erected in 1838 to honor the Comte de Boigne. The elephants stand in the traditional form of the Savoie cross, spouting occasional showers of water under the weight of DeBoigne himself. North of the aquatic stampede in pl. du Palais de Justice is the **Musée des Beaux-Arts** (tel. 04 79 33 75 03), home to France's second-largest collection of Italian paintings. Italian masterworks by Titian, Tintoretto, and Lorenzo Lutto hang by French works by Watteau and Fragonard, and a smaller Dutch collection. The **Musée Savoisien** (tel. 04 79 33 44 48), south of the pachyderms on bd. du Théâtre in an old Franciscan convent, contains an archaeological collection, including pottery and jewelry, exhibits on Chambéry's history, and fragments of the 13th-century mural of Cruet. (Museums open Wed.-Mon. 10am-noon and 2-6pm; admission to each 20F, students 10F.)

Stroll through *vieux* Chambéry past the Italian-influenced *hôtels particuliers* on **rue Croix-d'Or** and **pl. St-Léger,** as well as the arcades of **rue de Boigne.** The tourist office has a list of the most interesting mansions. The tourist office offers a guided, 1½-hour tour of the *vieille ville* during the summer; evening tours include a *dégustation* at a 16th-century *cave* (tours daily 4 and 9pm; 30F). The **Jardins du Verney** across from the *gare* delight picnickers with shaded benches and graceful fountains. Across town, the Château de Boigne (not open to the public) is surrounded by the **Parc des Loisirs de Buisson Rond** and its 6000-plant rose garden.

Two km out of town stands the **Musée des Charmettes** (tel. 04 79 33 39 44). In this house, Jean-Jacques Rousseau put his political theorizing on hold from 1736-1742 to live in semi-debauchery with the older and wiser Mme. de Warens. The episode was the source of his famous *Confessions.* The museum displays Rousseau memorabilia; the vine-covered garden looks out onto Chambéry and the mountains. Getting there is half the fun—but not nearly so much fun as Rousseau had. From pl. de la République, follow rue de la République, which becomes rue Jean-Jacques Rousseau and eventually chemin des Charmettes. From there, it's a 15-minute walk along a bubbling brook by mountain meadows. It's also all uphill; the museum appears just after you run out of breath (open April-Sept. Wed.-Mon. 10am-noon and 2-6pm; Oct.-March Wed.-Mon. 10am-noon and 2-4pm; admission 20F). In summer, actors in period dress put on a show loosely based on Rousseau's stay at the cottage (80F; 2hr.; 9pm in July and 8:30pm in Aug.).

Val d'Isère

Val d'Isère may be named for the river that flows through the small village, but it makes its livelihood from the peaks above. The tiny hamlet's sole purpose is to worship the mountains, the snow, and native son Jean-Claude Killy. Killy is a legend here, and not only because he won the gold in all the men's downhill events in the 1968 Grenoble Olympics. Killy is the dynamo who brought Olympic events to Val d'Isère in 1992, just after he helped turn its main street into a tourist-laden strip of expensive hotels, restaurants, and ski boutiques. His eponymous **Espace Killy,** an immense network of trails and lifts connecting Val d'Isère to neighboring **Tignes,** covers well over 10,000 hectares. With an average annual snowfall of 10m, Val d'Isère is not modest about its powdered slopes. But in summer, snow and prices melt. Mountain bikers and climbers fill the hotels that stay open, and skiers retreat to the **Glaciers du Pissaillas** where slushy white stuff persists until mid-August.

ORIENTATION AND PRACTICAL INFORMATION

There are no trains to Val d'Isère, and getting there takes time and money. Upon seeing the glitz that has already found its way into the once-pristine valley, you'll be glad the trains have stayed away. The nearest station is in Bourg-St-Maurice, 30km north; a bus leaves for Val d'Isère (3 per day, 65F). Take the bus to **Les Boisses** (55F) if you are going to the hostel. In summer, the last bus is at 6:15pm. Bus and train service is more frequent in winter. There are no street names in Val d'Isère. The tourist office is about 100m from the bus stop on the left.

Tourist Office: Boîte Postale 228 (tel. 04 79 06 06 60; fax 04 79 06 04 56). Free maps, brochures, and accommodations service. Open June 25-Aug. and Dec. to mid-May 8:30am-7:30pm; Sept.-Nov. and mid-May to June 24 9am-noon and 2-7pm. **Annex** at the entrance to Val d'Isère, a small shack on the right as you make your way up to town from La Daille (tel. 04 79 06 19 67). Open daily in summer 10am-noon and 4-6pm; weekends only in winter.

Money: A 24-hr. **ATM** stands at **Crédit Agricole,** 10m below the tourist office.

Buses: Autocars Martin (tel. 04 79 06 00 42 for reservations), 100m down main street from tourist office. Main office at pl. de la Gare (tel. 04 79 07 04 49), in Bourg-St-Maurice. Open June-Nov. Mon.-Tues. and Thurs.-Fri. 9:30am-noon and 3:30-7pm, Sat. 7-11:45am and 2:45-7pm, Sun. 9am-noon and 2:45-7pm; Dec.-May Mon.-Fri. 9am-noon and 2-7pm, Sat. 6:45am-1pm and 2-8:30pm, Sun. 7:45am-noon and 2-7pm. In winter, buses to Geneva airport (3 per day, Sat.-Sun. 5 per day, 4hr., 270F). Buses to and from Les Boisses and the youth hostel (5 per day, summer 2 per day, 10min., 18F). **SNCF** info and reservation desk (tel. 04 79 06 03 55), in the same building, open Tues.-Sat. 9:30am-noon and 2:30-7pm.

Taxis: tel. 04 79 06 19 92.

Hitchhiking: Infrequent buses, no trains, and sympathetic locals make hitching a popular mode of transport (for the imprudent). Those going from the hostel to Val d'Isère cross the dam and wait by the highway. No one hitches after dark.

Bike and Ski Rental: Jean Sports (tel.04 79 06 04 44), 100m up from tourist office. *VTTs* 90-120F per day. Skis 30-50F per day in summer; 140F in winter. Passport deposit. Open daily 8:30am-7:30pm. Closed April-June 24 and Sept.-Oct.

Laundromat: La Grande Lessive, 200m below tourist office, left at the rotary. Open daily 7:30am-10pm.

Weather, Ski, and Road Info: Call tourist office or listen to Radio Val (tel. 04 79 06 18 66; 96FM). **Ski lifts,** tel. 04 79 06 00 35. **Ski Patrol,** tel. 04 79 06 02 10.

Hospital: In Bourg St-Maurice (tel. 04 79 41 79 79). **Medical emergency** tel. 04 79 06 19 92 or 15.

Police: tel. 04 79 06 10 96. **Emergency** tel. 17.

Post Office: (tel. 04 79 06 06 99), across from the tourist office. Poste restante. Fax. **Currency exchange.** Open in summer Mon.-Fri. 9am-noon and 2-5pm, Sat. 9am-noon; in winter Mon.-Fri. 8:30am-7:30pm, Sat. 8:30am-noon. **Postal code:** 73150.

ACCOMMODATIONS, CAMPING, AND FOOD

Finding rooms in summer is tricky, finding them in winter is tougher, and off-season it's well-nigh impossible—things aren't full, they're closed. Call **Val Hôtel** (tel. 04 79 06 18 90; fax 04 79 06 11 88) or **Val Location** (tel. 04 79 06 06 60; fax 04 79 41 95 59) for centralized reservations. For youth hostel info, see page 553.

Le Relais du Ski (tel. 04 79 06 02 06; fax 04 79 41 10 64), past the tourist office on the left and one of the better deals in town. Small singles 160F. Doubles 190F. Triples 250F. Quads 290F. In winter 230F, 300F, 370F, and 390F respectively. Breakfast 35F. Hearty restaurant. *Plat du jour* 48F. Fish or meat 70-90F. V, MC.

Hôtel le Savoie (tel. 04 79 06 24 87; fax 04 79 06 29 09), 300m below tourist office on right. Really comfortable beds. Some rooms are huge with bath. First arrival gets first pick. All rooms are 140F per person, breakfast included. Superb restaurant downstairs, and right next to the most popular pizzeria in town. The catch is that it's only open June-Oct. Reception 8am-noon and 3-10pm. V, MC.

Hôtel Bivouac (tel. and fax 04 79 06 05 48), past the tourist office on the right. Follow the arrow and bear right on the 2nd road. The sign is hidden around the left side of the chalet. Gorgeous singles from 165F. Doubles from 240F. Triples from 315F. Quads 440F. In winter 270F, 300F, 420F, and 480F respectively. Breakfast and showers included.

Refuges: The cheapest beds in town are at the 2 *refuges.* In the winter, they're packed with off-*piste* skiers who attach *peaux de phoques* (po d'#@!%—seal skins) to their skis for uphill traction. For **Le Prarion** (tel. 04 79 06 06 02), take the shuttle to "La Bailleta." From there, it's a well-marked 1¾-hr. hike along the valley. **Le Fond Des Fours** (tel. 04 79 06 16 90) is a 2-hr. hike from "Le Manchet" shuttle stop. In the winter, you'll need to walk all the way (3hr.). Both are staffed Nov.-May 15 and June 15-Sept. 15. At other times there's wood, gas, utensils, and covers. 68F, breakfast 35F. Meals 80F. Reserve 48hr. ahead and get directions.

Camping: Camping les Richardes (tel. 04 79 06 26 60), 500m up from tourist office. Plain campground in a **Beautiful Setting** with few trailers. Crowded in Aug. Reception 9am-noon and 5-8pm. 12F per person, 8F per tent, 7F50 per car. Electricity 11F50. Showers 6F. Open June 15-Sept.

Perhaps someday Jean-Claude Killy will bring affordable dining to Val d'Isère as Prometheus descended with fire to primitive man. Until he does, stick to the supermarkets. Pack for the *pistes* at **Marché U,** 100m below the tourist office (open daily 8:30am-1pm and 3:30-7:30pm) and **Sherpa,** 200m above the office (open Mon.-Sat. 7am-10pm in season). The pizzeria **La Perdrix Blanche** (tel. 04 79 06 12 05), serves a 55F *menu* and pizza from 42F, including a vegetarian special (48F). They also have pasta (48F) and crêpes (15-45F). The **Bar-Restaurant L'Olympique,** 200m up and across the street from the tourist office, has a hearty 85F *menu* and a *fondue savoyarde* with green salad (78F) in a relaxed atmosphere. Next door, **Danny's Tandoori** (tel. 04 79 06 08 37) serves up food and drinks on a spectacular terrace.

SKIING AND HIKING

Over 100 lifts and *téléphériques* give access to 300km of trails; you can ski for a week without repeating a run. Lift tickets are 148F per half-day, 213F per day (cheaper over longer periods). They're valid on the entire Espace Killy, including Val d'Isère and Tignes. Excellent high-altitude beginner runs descend from the **Marmottes** and **Borsat Express** in the valley between Val d'Isère and Tignes. There's plenty of challenge in the expanses of off-*piste* skiing in the **Gorges de Malpasset** or the **Pisaillas glacier.** Find out about weather conditions and let the ski patrol know your itinerary. *Never* ski off-*piste* alone. Pisaillas is skiable July to mid-August; the snow softens after 11am (lifts open at 7:30am; 102F per ½-day, 127F per day).

Hikers should buy the detailed *Val d'Isère—Balades et Sentiers* and a hiking map (50F for both) in English at the tourist office. Its 40 routes spanning 100km include popular descents from the **Rocher de Bellevarde** or **Tête du Solaise.** *Téléphériques* whisk you up the peaks. Spectacular vistas unfold on the way down. (*Téléphérique* to Solaise runs from 9am. Last ascent 4:50pm, last descent 4:55pm. Bellevarde cable car starts at 9:30am. Last ascent 4:30pm, last descent 4:40pm. Both *téléphériques* are 55F, roundtrip 65F. You can bring a mountain bike on board for free.)

Mountain Guides (tel. 04 79 06 06 60) has ice climbing (440F per day) and rock climbing (440F per day) schools, and canyoning trips for 400F. Their desk in the tourist office opens at 6pm and closes with the office. The hostel arranges week-long **outdoor packages** of skiing, hiking, biking, and watersports (1590-4380F). The hostel also organizes paragliding excursions and horseback riding, biking, and rock-climbing trips. Trips are led by experts from the area, and prices are the lowest around. For more info, ask for the *Passeport Loisirs Tignes.*

■ Near Val d'Isère: Tignes

Tignes is as much a ski haven as Val d'Isère, but it tops its neighbor when it comes to summertime fun. The town's lake is a giant playground teeming with tourists and their small children, and high-rise hotels are more prominent than peaks. Come winter, the former Olympic Village lies sedate under snow and the elements rule again. If summer snowboarding, sailing, or screaming aren't your cup of tea, escape to the hills for secluded hiking and some of the freshest mountain air you'll ever find.

Tignes' **tourist office** (tel. 04 79 40 04 40; fax 04 79 06 45 44) has plenty of info on the town. The enormous **ski lift system** (tel. 04 79 06 34 66) offers half-day passes for 145F and full-day passes for 209F. **Buses** to Tignes leave from Val d'Isère (2 per day, 35min., 35F) and Bourg-St-Maurice (5 per day, 1hr., 67F).

At the junction of the routes to Val d'Isère and Tignes, the **Auberge de Jeunesse "les Clarines" (HI)** (tel. 04 79 06 35 07, reservations 04 79 41 03 36) benefits from its proximity to the two tacky ski towns as well as its relative seclusion. A pleasant mountain trail toward the hostel begins at La Daille, the foot of Val d'Isère. Follow the river down to the lake, and bear left along the shores until you ford a cascading creek. Ascend to your left, up the hill where the trail joins the road. Uphill to the left is Tignes le Lac; to the right is Les Boisses and the hostel (1½hr.). Otherwise, take the "Tignes/Val Claret" bus from Bourg-St-Maurice (57F) or Val d'Isère (18F) to "Les Boisses." Spotless dorm rooms, some with bath and shower, await at this friendly *auberge,* as do a TV room, bar, and info on outdoor activities. 118F per person—a steal in the Val—gets you breakfast, dinner, and a bed. Reception 5-10pm, but you can drop off bags any time. Ask for the door code if you're going to be out past 10pm. Reserve in September for December or February, or six weeks ahead for January, March, or April. Just up the road a network of trails (marked by yellow signs) will lead you into the **Poue de la Vanoise,** where fabulous views of the mountains (including Mont Blanc on some days), glaciers, mountain goats, and sheep await. The *chemin* to the **Refuge du Martin** affords excellent views of **Le Geant,** a spectacular, monstrous mural painted on the massive hydroelectric dam near the hostel.

Lyon and the Auvergne

France's visitors crowd Paris to the north and descend to Provence and the Riviera in the south. Wine lovers linger in Bordeaux or Beaune and outdoor enthusiasts scale and ski the Alps or Pyrénées. Few, however, penetrate the country's interior. The lucky adventurer who does will find rugged beauty and lively cities—as elsewhere in France—without mobs of tourists to inflate prices or trample scenery.

The Auvergne is a bizarre and breathtaking landscape. Giant lava needles, extinct volcanic craters, and verdant pine forests rise out of the Massif Centrale. The hills no longer spew forth molten lava, but release icy, crystalline springs. The mineral waters of Vichy, Le Mont Dore, and Volvic attract both *curistes* and bottling plants. The cathedrals and churches of the Auvergne are hewn from its jet-black volcanic stone, giving them an austere, solemn appearance. Like the landscape, life here can be harsh. The unemployment and poverty that hampers the Auvergne is manifest in the industrial city of Clermont-Ferrand, masked by rural beauty in the countryside.

During the Middle Ages, pilgrims trod the foothills of the Auvergne en route to Spain, while popes, troubadours, and Bourbon kings added color to the intricate social tapestry. Pope Urban II chose Clermont-Ferrand as the launching pad for the First Crusade in 1095. During the Hundred Years' War, this region was held initially by the dukes of Berry and in ensuing years by the *dauphin,* Charles VII. Residing in his capital at Bourges, he took advantage of its proximity to northern France to recapture the area from the English.

To the east, Lyon, the second-largest city in France, caps the Rhône Valley as the antithesis of the Auvergne. While insular *auvergnat* farmers are miles from train tracks and highways, the Rhône has served as one of France's most important trade arteries for two millennia. Roman ships sailed from the Mediterranean to Lyon; today, TGVs glide along the same route. While people from the Auvergne practice traditional folk arts, citizens of Lyon choose from performances in Roman theaters or Tony Garnier's exquisite modern opera house.

World War II further isolated the interior from the Rhône Valley. Vichy, with its empty hotels designed for spa-goers, became headquarters for the collaborationist French government headed by Maréchal Philippe Pétain. The vast majority of locals supported the government; Lyon, however, was the center of the French Resistance. Many *Lyonnais* died in valiant efforts to sabotage Nazi schemes.

Despite their divergent cultures and histories, both *Auvergnats* and *Lyonnais* love to eat. The farm kitchens of the Auvergne simmer with stewing pork, cabbage, hens, veal, turnips, and potatoes. *Auvergnat* food is hearty and rich; try *potée* (pork stew) or *tripoux* (tasty sheep's feet stuffed with sheep's stomach). The sauces are, fortunately, often strong and laced with earthy red wines. Apricots from local orchards grace the dessert tray in tarts and jams. Finish your Auvergnat feasts with the acclaimed *cantal* cheese. Locals call it *"fourme,"* a term from which the French have derived *fromage,* a revered national institution.

Lyon, with its world-renowned chefs and *haute cuisine,* is a far cry from the country kitchens of the Auvergne. Mouthwatering poultry and beef dishes garnished with specialties of the surrounding regions—truffles, pistachios, and cream—attest to the advantages of Lyon's central location. Don't miss *andouillettes* (pork sausages) or *quenelles* (fish dumplings). Complement your once-in-a-lifetime *lyonnais* meal with the famous Beaujolais vintages. France's first vineyards, the Côtes du Rhône have nurtured grapes since the Greeks took a fancy to the region.

GETTING AROUND

Trains run to Lyon, major cities, and a few small villages along the way; more remote areas are served only by private bus companies with schedules timed for workers and local students rather than tourists. The Auvergne's steep, winding roads are

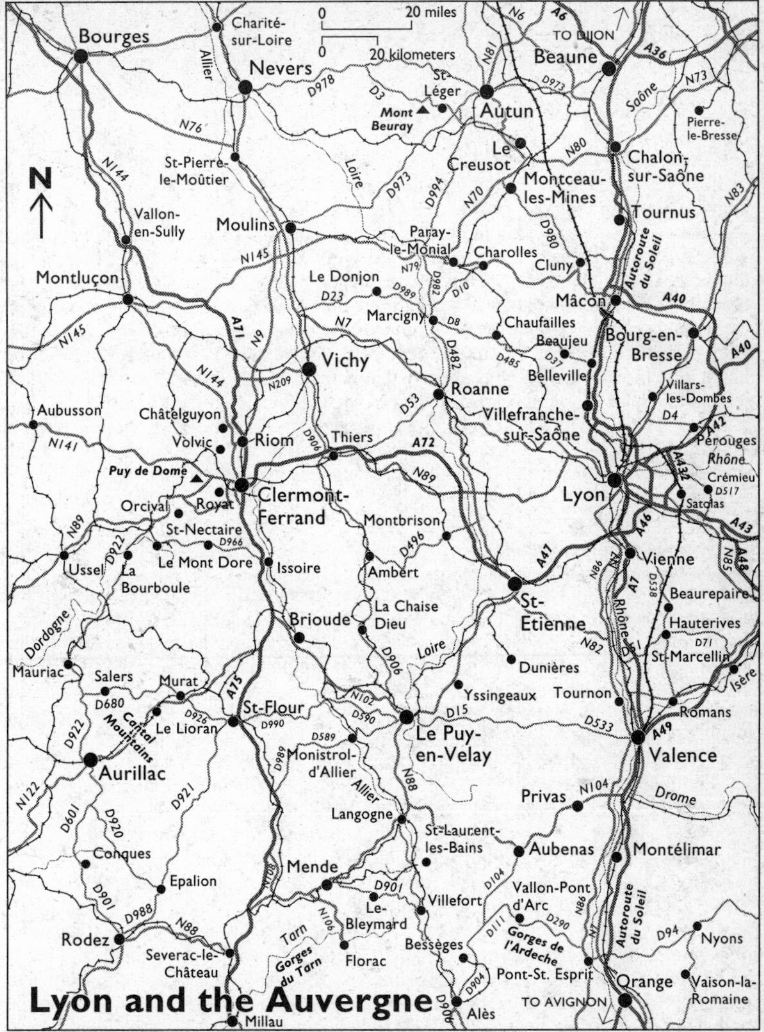

made for the *Tour de France,* not a leisurely pedal. The locals tend to be friendly, which bodes well for those who like to hitch—a practice which is never wise.

Lyon

France's second-largest city is second in little else. With industrial and culinary *savoir faire,* Lyon (pop. 1.5 million) has established itself as a cultural and economic alternative to the capital. Despite its historical reputation for bourgeois *froideur,* Lyon is friendlier and more relaxed than Paris, with a few centuries more history.

Situated at the convergence of the Rhône and Saône rivers, Lyon has benefited from its position as a hub since Julius Caesar used "Lugdunum" as a military base to conquer Gaul. Caesar Augustus ordered roads connecting this provincial capital of Gaul to Italy and the Atlantic, permanently establishing Lyon's status as a major cross-

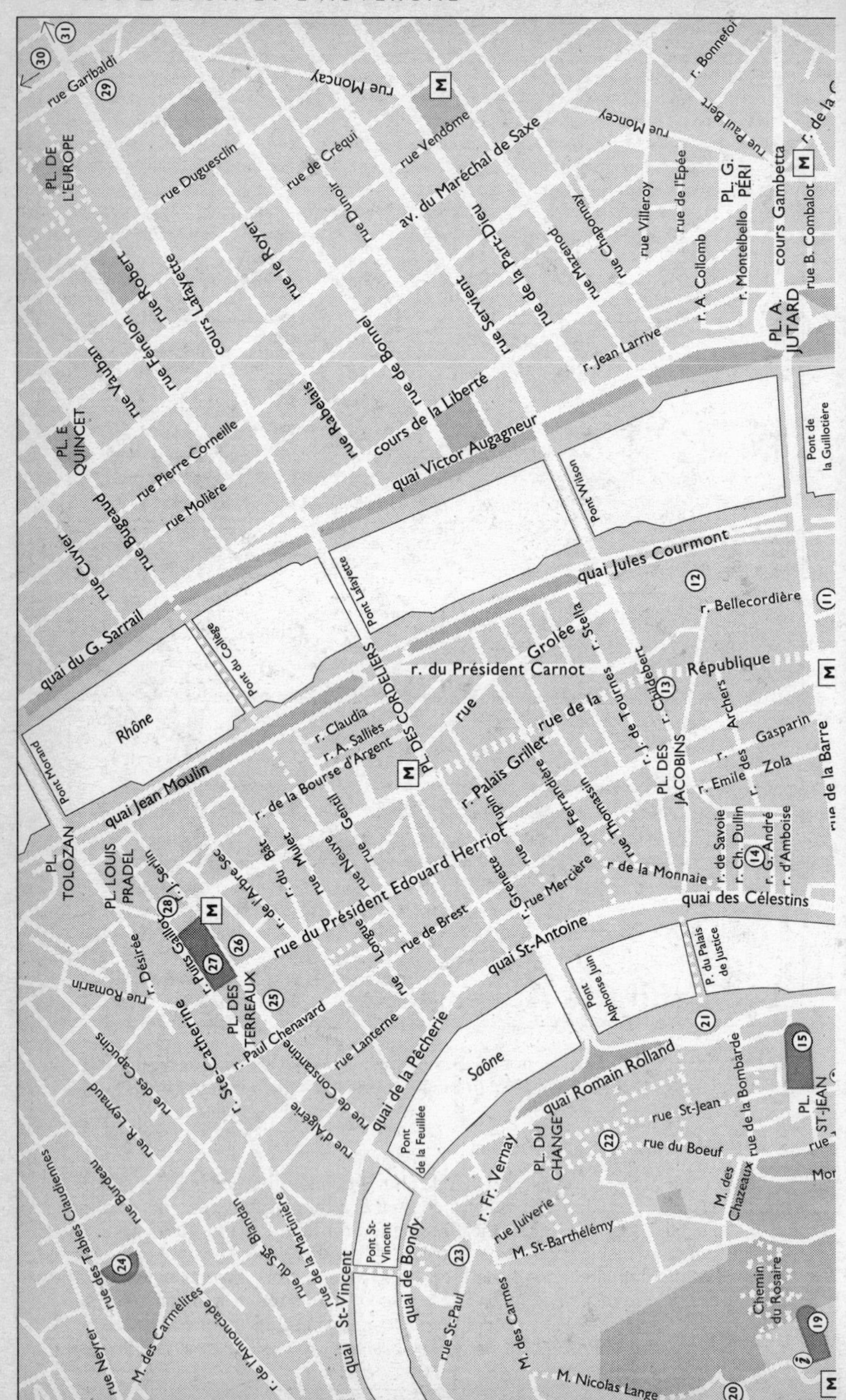
rue Garibaldi
PL. DE L'EUROPE
rue Moncey
rue Duguesclin
rue de Créqui
rue Vendôme
av. du Maréchal de Saxe
rue Moncey
r. Bonnefoi
rue Paul Bert
r. de la
PL. G. PÉRI
cours Gambetta
rue B. Combalot
r. Montelbello
r. A. Collomb
rue de l'Epée
rue Villeroy
rue Chaponnay
rue Mazenod
rue de la Part-Dieu
rue Servient
rue Dunoir
rue le Royer
cours Lafayette
rue Robert
rue Fénelon
rue Vauban
PL. A. JUTARD
r. Jean Larrive
rue de Bonnel
rue Rabelais
cours de la Liberté
quai Victor Augagneur
PL. E QUINCET
rue Pierre Corneille
rue Molière
rue Bugeaud
rue Cuvier
quai du G. Sarrail
Pont de la Guillotière
Pont Wilson
Pont Lafayette
Pont du Collège
Pont Morand
Rhône
quai Jules Courmont
r. Bellecordière
r. Stella
Grolée
r. du Président Carnot
République
rue
rue de la
r. Childebert
PL. DES CORDELIERS
r. Claudia
r. A. Salliès
r. de la Bourse
d'Argent
quai Jean Moulin
r. Palais Grillet
r. J. de Tournes
PL. DES JACOBINS
Archers
Gasparin
r. Emile
Zola
rue de la Barre
PL. TOLOZAN
PL. LOUIS PRADEL
r. J. Serlin
r. de l'Arbre Sec
r. du Bât
rue Mulet
rue Neuve
Gentil
rue Tupin
rue Ferrandière
rue Thomassin
r. de Savoie
r. Ch. Dullin
r. G. André
r. d'Amboise
r. de la Monnaie
quai des Célestins
rue du Président Edouard Herriot
rue Grenette
rue Mercière
rue de Brest
rue Longue
rue Désirée
r. Puits Gaillot
PL. DES TERREAUX
rue Romarin
quai St-Antoine
Pont Alphonse Juin
P. du Palais de Justice
r. Ste-Catherine
r. Paul Chenavard
rue Lanterne
rue
rue de Constantine
rue d'Algérie
quai de la Pêcherie
Saône
quai Romain Rolland
rue St-Jean
rue du Boeuf
rue de la Bombarde
PL. ST-JEAN
rue
Mon
rue des Capucins
rue R. Leynaud
rue Burdeau
rue des Tables Claudiennes
Pont de la Feuillée
PL. DU CHANGE
r. Fr. Vernay
rue Juiverie
M. St-Barthélémy
M. des Chazeaux
Chemin du Rosaire
rue du Sgt. Blandan
rue de la Martinière
rue Neyret
M. des Carmélites
r. de l'Annonciade
quai St-Vincent
Pont St-Vincent
quai de Bondy
rue St-Paul
M. des Carmes
M. Nicolas Lange
M
30
31
29
28
27
26
25
24
23
22
21
20
19
15
14
13
12
11

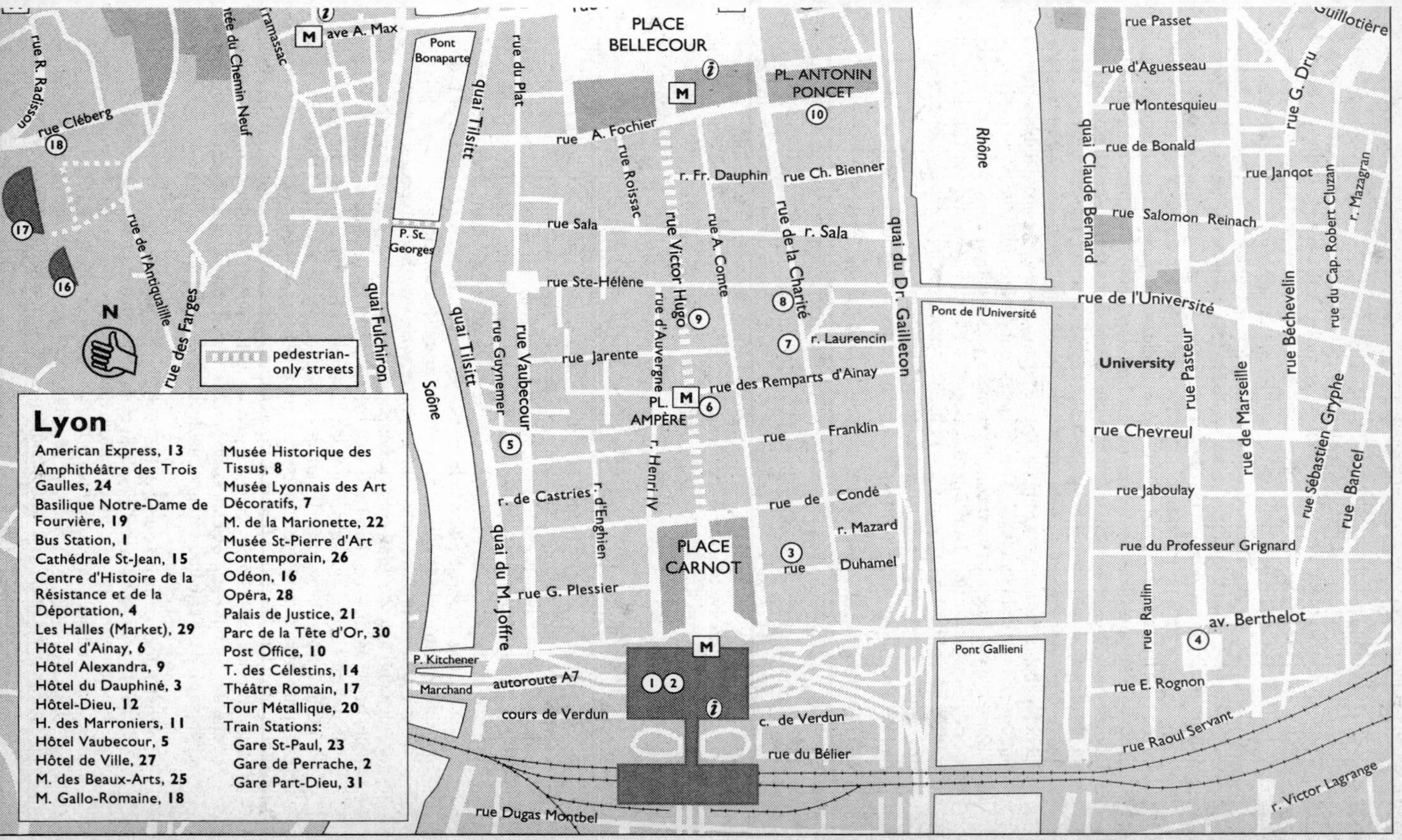
Lyon
American Express, 13
Amphithéâtre des Trois Gaulles, 24
Basilique Notre-Dame de Fourvière, 19
Bus Station, 1
Cathédrale St-Jean, 15
Centre d'Histoire de la Résistance et de la Déportation, 4
Les Halles (Market), 29
Hôtel d'Ainay, 6
Hôtel Alexandra, 9
Hôtel du Dauphiné, 3
Hôtel-Dieu, 12
H. des Marroniers, 11
Hôtel Vaubecour, 5
Hôtel de Ville, 27
M. des Beaux-Arts, 25
M. Gallo-Romaine, 18
Musée Historique des Tissus, 8
Musée Lyonnais des Art Décoratifs, 7
M. de la Marionette, 22
Musée St-Pierre d'Art Contemporain, 26
Odéon, 16
Opéra, 28
Palais de Justice, 21
Parc de la Tête d'Or, 30
Post Office, 10
T. des Célestins, 14
Théâtre Romain, 17
Tour Métallique, 20
Train Stations:
Gare St-Paul, 23
Gare de Perrache, 2
Gare Part-Dieu, 31
pedestrian-only streets
N
PLACE BELLECOUR
PL. ANTONIN PONCET
PLACE CARNOT
PL. AMPÈRE
Rhône
Saône
quai Claude Bernard
quai du Dr. Gailleton
quai Tilsitt
quai du M. Joffre
quai Fulchiron
Pont de l'Université
Pont Gallieni
Pont Bonaparte
P. St. Georges
P. Kitchener
rue de l'Université
University
rue Victor Hugo
rue de la Charité
rue A. Comte
rue d'Auvergne
rue Vaubecour
rue Guynemer
rue du Plat
rue Roissac
rue A. Fochier
rue Sala
r. Sala
rue Ste-Hélène
rue Jarente
rue des Remparts d'Ainay
r. Henri IV
r. d'Enghien
r. de Castries
rue G. Plessier
rue Franklin
rue de Condé
r. Mazard
rue Duhamel
r. Laurencin
r. Fr. Dauphin
rue Ch. Bienner
cours de Verdun
c. de Verdun
rue du Bélier
autoroute A7
Marchand
rue Dugas Montbel
r. Victor Lagrange
rue Raoul Servant
rue E. Rognon
rue Raulin
av. Berthelot
rue du Professeur Grignard
rue Jaboulay
rue Chevreul
rue Pasteur
rue de Marseille
rue Béchevelin
rue Sébastien Gryphe
rue Bancel
rue du Cap. Robert Cluzan
r. Mazagran
rue G. Dru
rue Janqot
rue Salomon Reinach
rue de Bonald
rue Montesquieu
rue d'Aguesseau
rue Passet
Guillotière
ave A. Max
Tramassac
montée du Chemin Neuf
rue des Farges
rue de l'Antiquaille
rue Cléberg
rue R. Radisson

roads and cultural capital. Despite the town's position as a trade and religious center during the Middle Ages, it was not until the Renaissance that Lyon truly gained prominence. After the invention of moveable type in the 15th century, the city assumed the role of press to Europe. Tiny silkworms imported from China in the 16th century aided Lyon's rise to European power, making it a center of the French Renaissance and reinforcing its reputation as a financial center. The glory of the *lyonnais* Renaissance shows itself in the ornate façades and elegant courtyards of 16th-century townhouses lining the crooked streets of Vieux Lyon.

Lyon's local marionette, Guignol, has parodied political figures here since 1808, but he isn't the only *Lyonnais* to have resisted the status quo. Lyon's citizens refused the post-Revolution Terrorists' demands in the 1790s, prompting a siege and the massacre of thousands by Robespierre's minions. Local silkworkers rioted for better conditions during the Industrial Revolution of the 19th century. The city also served as the center of the French Resistance to the World War II Nazi occupation and the French collaborationist government. The Germans, however, managed to destroy all but one of Lyon's ancient bridges on their way out of town in 1944.

This home of cinema's inventors, the Lumières, is also the culinary light of France. World-renowned chefs Paul Bocuse, Georges Blanc, and Jean-Paul Lacombe all learned to boil water in Lyon's kitchens. The modern city has the comforts of a metropolis: skyscrapers and sidewalk cafés, nifty transport systems and flowering parks, concert halls and *discothèques.* Lyon is a must-see—and a must-taste.

ORIENTATION AND PRACTICAL INFORMATION

The Saône and Rhône rivers converge in Lyon, cradling the city in a huge "Y." East of the Rhône lies most of the city's population, the Part-Dieu train station, and its modern commercial complex. The **presqu'île** (peninsula) inside the giant "Y" is the *centre ville* with the Perrache train station, **pl. Bellecour,** the main tourist office, and the Terreaux neighborhood. The **Fourvière** hill and its basilica to the west overlook the city as **Vieux Lyon** unfolds below to the Saône riverbank. Orient yourself by Fourvière and its Tour Metallique, a mini Eiffel Tower, to the west, and the Tour du Crédit Lyonnais, a reddish-brown crayon towering over Part-Dieu to the east.

Lyon is divided into nine *arrondissements* whose mishmash order ensures their irrelevance, even to natives. The first, second, and fourth lie in the crook of the *presqu'île.* The second includes the Perrache train station and pl. Bellecour. The Terreaux neighborhood is in the first *arrondissement.* Vieux Lyon and Fourvière both lie in the fifth. Part-Dieu is in the third, and the sixth is to the north. To the south and southeast of the third lie the seventh and eighth respectively. Most trains from Paris stop at both the **Gare de Perrache** and the **Gare de la Part-Dieu.** Perrache is more central and has a **tourist office** to help you get started. Both are connected to Lyon's ultra-quiet metro, which whisks passengers throughout the city.

To get to the **tourist pavilion** from Perrache, walk straight onto pedestrian rue Victor Hugo and follow it until it ends at expansive pl. Bellecour. The tourist office is on the right (15min.). From Part-Dieu, exit the station by the fountains and take a right. Walk right for three blocks and turn left onto cours Lafayette. Cross the Rhône (on pont Lafayette) and continue straight as the street changes to pl. des Cordeliers. Turn left on rue de la République and follow it to pl. Bellecour (30min.). Or ride the metro (line A from Part-Dieu, line B then A from Perrache) to the "Bellecour" stop. Lyon is a reasonably safe city. Solitary travelers should feel comfortable almost anywhere during the day, but at night be especially careful. Watch out for pickpockets inside Perrache, at pl. des Terreaux, and in pl. Bellecour's crowds.

Tourist Information: Tourist Office Pavilion, at pl. Bellecour, 2ème (tel. 04 72 77 69 69; fax. 04 78 42 04 32). M. Bellecour. Unparalleled efficiency with a smorgasbord of information. Superb map. Brochures and info on accommodations. Guides to Lyon's unique *traboules, bouchons,* and *hôtels particuliers.* Ask about the "key to the city" (90F), which allows admission to 7 museums. Open mid-June to mid-Sept. Mon.-Fri. 9am-7pm, Sat. 9am-6pm; mid-Sept. to mid-June Mon.-Fri. 9am-6pm,

Sat. 9am-5pm. If you're arriving at the **Perrache station,** pick up a map in the **annex** in the Centre d'Echanges (open Mon.-Fri. 9am-1pm and 2-6pm, Sat. 9am-5pm). The small **office** near the cathedral, av. Adolphe Max, 5*ème*, on **pl. St-Jean,** is the only one open on Sunday (open mid-June to mid-Sept. Mon.-Fri. 9am-7pm, Sat. 9am-6pm, Sun. 10am-6pm; mid-Sept. to mid-June Mon.-Fri. 9am-1pm and 2-6pm, Sat. 9am-5pm, Sun. 10am-5pm). But wait—there's more! Another office is at **Villeurbanne,** 3, av. Aristide Briand (tel. 04 78 68 13 20), just outside the city limits. M. Gratte-Ciel (open Mon.-Fri. 9am-6pm, Sat. 9am-5pm). Ask at the tourist office for **Lyon Poche,** a free weekly guide listing movies, theater, concerts, exhibitions, food, TV, and nightlife. If that's not available, get your hands on a copy of the tourist office's own **Spectacles/Evénements.** If you're in town in Sept., pick up a free copy of the ubiquitous **Le Petit Paumé,** published by students, listing restaurants, nightlife, etc., or borrow one where you're staying.

Budget Travel: Wasteels (tel. 04 78 37 80 17), in Perrache's Galerie Marchande. BIJ tickets. Long lines. Open Mon.-Fri. 9am-7pm, Sat. 9am-6pm. V, MC.

Consulates: Canada, 74, rue de Bonnel, 3*ème* (tel. 04 72 61 15 25), 1 block towards the river from Part-Dieu. Open Mon.-Fri. 10am-noon. **U.K.,** 24, rue Childebert, 2*ème* (tel. 04 72 77 81 70). M. Bellecour. From pl. Bellecour and the tourist office, follow rue de la République to the first cross-street. Open Mon.-Fri. 9am-12:30pm and 2-5:30pm. **Ireland,** 4, rue Jean Desparmet, 8*ème* (tel. 04 78 76 44 85). Open Mon.-Thurs. 8:30-11:30am and 2-4pm, Fri. 8:30-11:30am.

Money: Currency exchange at **AOC,** in the tourist offices on pl. Bellecour and Perrache, or at **Thomas Cook** (tel. 04 72 33 48 55), in the Part-Dieu train station. Open 24hr. Also in Perrache (tel. 04 78 38 38 84; open Mon.-Sat. 7:15am-7:15pm, Sun. 8:30am-noon and 1-7:15pm). At last count, Lyon had 584 24-hr. **ATMs.** If you have trouble finding one, try **Crédit Mutuel** at 15, pl. Bellecour, 2*ème*.

American Express: 6, rue Childebert, 2*ème* (tel. 04 78 37 40 69). Open May-Sept. Mon.-Fri. 9am-noon and 2-6:15pm, Sat. 9am-noon; Oct.-April Mon.-Fri. 9am-noon and 2-6:15pm. **Exchange** closes at 5:30pm.

Flights: Aéroport Lyon-Satolas (tel. 04 72 22 72 21). Flights within France and to cities in Europe, North Africa, and the Middle East. The **TGV,** which now stops at the airport, is cheaper and more convenient than the 50 daily flights to Paris. **Satobuses** (45min., 46F) shuttle to Perrache via Part-Dieu (every 20 or 30min.; last shuttle 9pm daily). **Air France,** 10, quai Jules Courmont, 2*ème* (tel. 04 72 56 22 22). **Air Inter,** 100, rue Garibaldi, 6*ème* (tel. 04 72 11 56 56). Both open Mon.-Fri. 9am-6pm, Sat. 9am-5pm.

Trains: Lyon has two major stations, Part-Dieu and Perrache. TGVs to Paris stop at both. Check the schedule posters at either station to find out about other destinations. If confused, ask the information desk or SOS Voyageurs to help you. Lyon's stations are communities unto themselves, with malls, food stands, and thieves. **Perrache** (tel. 04 72 40 11 64), between the Saône and Rhône rivers, is more central. **SOS Voyageurs** (tel. 04 78 37 03 31) provides wheelchairs, baby-changing facilities, and sick beds. Staff will meet you at the platform and help you find a connection if you call ahead (open Mon.-Fri. 8am-8pm). **Le Mail** (tel. 04 78 42 24 28) offers similar services 24hr., a place to leave bags, and even beds for the desperate. SNCF information and reservation desk open Mon.-Sat. 8am-7:30pm. Station closes midnight-5am. **Part-Dieu** (tel. 04 72 40 34 66), is in the business district on the east bank of the Rhône. Sympathetic **SOS Voyageurs** staff (tel. 04 72 34 12 16) helps Mon.-Sat. 8am-10pm, Sun. 9am-10pm. SNCF info desk open Mon.-Fri. 9am-7pm, Sat. 9am-6:30pm. To: Paris (33 per day, most TGV, 2-5hr., 262F); Grenoble (15 per day, 1¼hr., 92F); Dijon (17 per day, 2hr., 130F); Strasbourg (9 per day, 6hr., 246F); Geneva (8 per day, 2hr., 112F); Marseille (13 per day, 3hr., 197F); Nice (20 per day, 6hr., 288F); Venice (4 per day, 10hr., 283F); Rome (4 per day, 11hr., 346F). **Lockers** at both stations 15-30F for 72hr.

Buses: On the bottom floor of the Perrache train station. Open Mon.-Sat. 7:30am-6:30pm; Sept.-June Mon.-Sat. 6:30am-5pm. Service to Vienne, Annecy, and Grenoble. Companies include **Philibert** (tel. 04 78 98 56 00), **CDL** (tel. 04 78 70 21 01), and **Cars Faure** (tel. 04 78 96 11 44). There's also an **international bus terminal** across the hall from the domestic bus terminal. **Eurolines** (tel. 04 72 41 09 09) throughout Europe. **Iberbus** (tel. 04 72 41 72 27) goes to Spain.

Public Transportation: TCL (tel. 04 78 71 80 80). Info offices at both train stations and major metro stops. Map **(Plan de Poche)** available from tourist office or any TCL branch. Swiss-like efficiency. Ticket for 1hr. in 1 direction, connections included. 7F80 per ticket, *carnet* of 10 66F50, students 55F. *Ticket Liberté* (23F50), good for one day's unlimited travel on all services, sold at tourist and TCL offices but not in stations. **Metro** operates 5am-midnight. **Funiculaires** (hill trolleys) operate until 8pm and go from pl. St-Jean to the top of Fourvière and to St-Just. **Buses** (tel. 04 78 71 70 00) run 5am-9pm; a few lines run until midnight.

Taxis: Taxi Radio de Lyon (tel. 04 72 10 86 86). 24hr. Airport service: from Perrache 200F, from Part-Dieu 180F; add 80F between 7pm and 7am.

Hitchhiking: Some say that the *autoroute* ramps to Paris are hard places to find a ride. Taking bus 2, 5, 19, 21, 22, or 31 and standing past Port Mouton at the intersection with N6 is reputedly easier. Those heading to Grenoble take bus 39 to the rotary at bd. Mermoz Pinel. This is a big city; big-city weirdos abound.

English Bookstore: Eton, 1, rue du Plat, 2ème (tel. 04 78 92 92 36), one street west of pl. Bellecour toward the Saône. Good selection, decent prices. Flash *Let's Go* for a 5% discount. Open Mon. 2-7pm, Tues.-Sat. 10am-12:30pm and 1:30-7pm.

Youth Centers: CROUS, 59, rue de la Madeleine, 7ème (tel. 04 72 80 13 00 or toll free 0 800 03 25 58). Info on university housing and cafeterias. Open Mon.-Fri. 10am-4pm. **Hostelling International,** 5, pl. Bellecour, 2ème (tel. 04 78 42 21 88), sells student ID cards (60F) and membership cards to those who can prove one year of French residence (100F, under 26 70F). Open Mon.-Fri. 10am-noon and 2-6pm, Sat. 10am-2pm. **Bureau d'Informations de Jeunesse (BIJ),** 9, quai des Célestins (tel. 04 72 77 00 66), lists jobs, *au pair* opportunities, and sports. Open Mon. noon-7pm, Tues.-Fri. 10am-7pm, Sat. (Sept.-June only) 10am-5pm.

Women's Center: Centre d'Information Féminine, 18, pl. Tolozan, 1er (tel. 04 78 39 32 25). Open Mon.-Fri. 9am-1pm and 1:30-5pm.

Laundromat: Lavadou, 19, rue Ste-Hélène, around pl. Ampère. Open 7:30am-8:30pm. **Lav 123,** 123, rue Jean Jaurès. Open 7am-8pm.

Help Centers: CISL (tel. 04 78 01 23 45), for foreign visitors. **SOS Amitié** (tel. 04 78 29 88 88). **SOS Racisme** (tel. 04 78 39 24 44; Mon.-Fri. 6:30-8:30pm). **AIDS Lyon Rhône-Alps,** 21, pl. Tolozan, 3ème (tel. 04 78 28 61 32).

Medical Services: All hospitals have English-speaking doctors on call. **Hôpital Edouard Herriot,** 5, pl. Arsonval (tel. 04 72 11 73 00). M. Grange Blanche. Best equipped for serious emergencies, but far from center of town. For non-emergencies, go to **Hôpital Hôtel-Dieu,** 1, pl. de l'Hôpital, 2ème (tel. 04 72 41 30 00), near quai du Rhône. Call **SOS Médecins,** 10, pl. Dumas de Loire (tel. 04 78 83 51 51) for home visits 24hr. **Medical emergency** tel. 15 or 04 78 33 15 15.

Police: 47, rue de la Charité (tel. 04 78 42 26 56). **Emergency** tel. 17.

Post Office: pl. Antonin Poncet (tel. 04 72 40 65 22), next to pl. Bellecour. Photocopier, **currency exchange,** and poste restante (postal code: 69002). Open Mon.-Fri. 8am-7pm, Sat. 8am-noon. **Telegraph** services Mon.-Sat. 8am-midnight, Sun. 8am-2pm. **Postal codes:** 69000-69009; main post office and *centre ville* are 69002. Last digit indicates *arrondissement.*

ACCOMMODATIONS AND CAMPING

France's second financial center, Lyon fills its central hotels Monday to Thursday nights with businesspeople who are gone by the weekend. Even if the hotels near Perrache are full, cheap accommodations should be available near pl. des Terreaux. Students looking for university housing should call CROUS (see above).

Auberge de Jeunesse (HI), 51, rue Roger Salengro, Vénissieux (tel. 04 78 76 39 23). Take bus 35 to "George Lévy" from pl. Bellecour (direction: St-Priest; last bus at 9pm). Alternatively, take either bus 48 express or 36 (direction: Minguettes) from Part-Dieu or bus 32 (direction: Etats-Unis-Vivani) from Perrache to "Etats-Unis-Vivani." Continue walking on bd. des Etats-Unis in the direction of the bus. The sidewalk will turn into a footpath after a Peugeot dealership. Keep following it as it turns to the right and parallels the autoroute. Friendly HI stickers will assure you that you are getting closer to the hostel (on the right). If walking from Perrache, turn right outside the station and cross Pont Galliéni to av. Berthelot. Make a right on bd. des Etats-Unis, and follow the directions above. From Part-Dieu, make a left on bd. Marius and continue as it becomes rue des Tchéslovaques. Turn left on av. Berthelot, make a right on bd. des Etats-Unis, and follow walking directions above (1½hr.). Friendly, modern hostel makes up for the hike with comfortable 4- to 8-bunk dorms, kitchen, bar, TV, and international crowd. Bag storage. 48F. Sheets 16F. Laundry 30F. Breakfast 17F. Reception 7:30am-noon and 5pm-12:30am. Reservations accepted. Grape-picking jobs listed in Sept.

Centre International de Séjour, 46, rue du Commandant Pegoud, 8ème (tel. 04 78 01 23 45 or 04 78 76 14 22; fax 04 78 77 96 95), near the youth hostel. From Perrache, take bus 53 to "Etats-Unis-Beauvisage" (direction: St-Priest, last bus 11:30pm). From Part-Dieu, take bus 36 (direction: Minguettes, last bus 11:15pm). Mostly student groups. TV rooms. Small, modern rooms with shower and comfortable sitting rooms in hall. Singles 130F in high season, 123F in low season (July-Aug., Christmas week, and all Fri. and Sat. nights). Doubles 104F per person, low season 93F. Triples 88F per person, low season 84F. Quads 82F per person, low season 78F. Breakfast included. Self-service meals from 32F. 24-hr. reception. Checkout by 9am. Reserve at least 3 weeks in advance; groups get priority. V, MC.

Résidence Benjamin Delessert, 145, av. Jean Jaurès, 7ème (tel. 04 78 61 41 41; fax 04 78 61 40 24). From Perrache, take any bus that goes to "Jean Macé," walk under train tracks, and look left after 2½ blocks. From Part-Dieu, take metro to "Jean Macé." Small, bright, clean dorm rooms with phones; TV room. Laundry service. 70F, with shower 75F. Mid-Sept. to mid-June 90F, with shower 95F. Reserve 2 weeks ahead in summer, 6 months ahead during school year. 24-hr. reception.

Hôtel Vaubecour, 28, rue Vaubecour, 2ème (tel. 04 78 37 44 91; fax 04 78 42 90 17). M. Ampère-Victor Hugo. Near Perrache. Spacious, elegant, old-world rooms (many fireplaces) enhanced by old-world prices. Friendly, English-speaking staff and plenty of *Let's Go*-ers. Singles from 110F, with shower 140F. Doubles from 130F, with shower 160F, with 2 beds 186F. Shower 15F. Breakfast 25F. V, MC.

Hôtel d'Ainay, 14, rue des Remparts d'Ainay, 2ème (tel. 04 78 42 43 42). M. Ampère-Victor Hugo (right by the station). The sparkling hallways and rooms may be devoid of germs, but character has been scrubbed away by the Lysol. Cheap, sunny, comfortable rooms with very firm beds. Anglophone staff. Singles from 130F, with shower from 198F. Doubles 165F, with shower 208F. Breakfast 24F. Reception Sun.-Thurs. 6:30am-10pm, Fri.-Sat. 7am-11:30pm. V, MC.

Hôtel Alexandra, 49, rue Victor Hugo, 2ème (tel. 04 78 37 75 79; fax 04 72 40 84 34). Large, old hotel in ideal location. Small, elegant rooms with TV, phone. Singles 150F (no TV), with shower 190F, with shower and toilet 240F. Doubles 173F, with shower 210F, with shower and toilet 262F. Triples with shower 269F. Quads with shower 300F. Breakfast 25F. 24-hr. reception. V, MC, AmEx.

Hôtel du Dauphiné, 3, rue Duhamel, 2ème (tel. 04 78 37 24 19; fax 04 78 92 81 52). Near Perrache. Clean and comfortable rooms vary in size, all have showers. The pricier rooms are huge. Singles from 155F. Doubles from 205F. Triples from 280F. Quads 300F. Breakfast 25F. 24-hr. reception. V, MC.

Hôtel des Marronniers, 5, rue des Marronniers, 2ème (tel. 04 78 37 04 82), on pl. Bellecour across the street from the post office. High ceilings and fresh flowers grace clean rooms around a quiet courtyard. English-speaking staff. Singles 110F, with shower 140F. Doubles 140F, with shower 170F. Triples 180F. Quads 200F. Breakfast 22F. Wake-up calls. Reception 24hr.

Camping: Dardilly (tel. 04 78 35 64 55). From the Hôtel de Ville, take bus 19 (direction: Ecully-Dardilly) to "Parc d'Affaires." Hot showers, swimming pool, grocery store, bar, TV, and restaurant. 53F per tent and car. V, MC.

FOOD

The galaxy of *Michelin* stars adorning Lyon's restaurants confirms what the *Lyonnais* know and proudly declare—this is the gastronomic capital of Western civilization. Nonetheless, a typical *lyonnais* delicacy consists of a flagrantly unacceptable cow part prepared in a subtle, creamy sauce. Since organs such as brain, stomach, and intestines are in high demand nowhere else, you might think their world-wide surplus would send prices plummeting. But attach the description *"Specialité Lyon-*

naise," and suddenly 200F seems reasonable. *Lyonnais* food is as bizarre as it is elegant and as creative as it is delicious. Luckily, the tradition is a part of the city's fabric; you can sample *haute cuisine* even in (relatively) inexpensive restaurants.

Local *bouchons* are descendants of inns where travelers would stop to dine and to have tired horses *bouchonné* (rubbed down) with straw. These cozy restaurants serve authentic local cuisine and are often moderately priced. They cluster in the Terreaux district and along rue Mercière in the second *arrondissement.* Nearly every *bouchon* serves a version of *andouillettes,* sausage made of (what else) cow intestines. Savor *St-Marcellin,* a gooey, pungent cheese from the nearby Alps. As for the wine, there's a local saying that three rivers flow through Lyon: the Saône, the Rhône, and the Beaujolais. Your bottle will have traveled all of 40km from its *cave.*

Finish off dinner with *Torte Tatin,* an upside-down rendition of apple pie *à la mode. Lyonnais* are also proud of their *cocons,* chocolates wrapped in marzipan, which honor the city's cocooned silk worms. Chocolate lovers swoon at Lyon's grandest *pâtisserie,* the famous **Bernachon,** 42, cours Franklin Roosevelt, 6ème (tel. 04 78 24 37 98). The showcases sparkle with heavenly pastries and ambrosial *Palets d'Or,* recognized as the best chocolates in France—and not only because they're made with gold dust. (Open June 15-Sept. 15 Tues.-Sat. 8am-7pm, Sun. 8am-1pm; Sept. 16-June 14 Tues.-Sat. 8am-7pm, Sun. 8am-5pm. V, MC, AmEx.)

Markets abound all over town. The largest are at **quai St-Antoine** and on **bd. de la Croix Rousse** on the Rhône (both Tues.-Sun. 7:30am-12:30pm). A more elegant (though slightly more expensive) alternative is the covered **Les Halles,** 102, cours Lafayette, 3ème (open Tues.-Sat. 7:30am-noon and 3-7pm, Sun. 7:30am-noon). Paul Bocuse, the Elvis Presley of chefs, gets his ingredients here, but mere mortals are welcome as well. At **Sibilia et ses filles,** the gastronomic royalty buy *andouillettes* and other meats; **Renée and Renée Richard** supplies their cheeses.

The **Prisunic supermarket,** rue de la République, at pl. des Cordeliers, 2ème (open Mon.-Sat. 8:30am-7:30pm); **Monoprix,** rue Grenette at rue de Brest, 2ème (open Mon.-Sat. 8:45am-7pm); and **Maréchal Centre,** rue de la Platière at rue Lanterne, 1er (open Mon.-Sat. 8:30am-12:30pm and 3-8:30pm), all offer large selections of the usual culinary suspects. Still, all these neighborhood markets pale before the awesome size and puny prices of the **Carrefour Supermarché,** whose 78 check-out aisles loom across the highway from the youth hostel. You could also try **Ed,** the discount supermarket, also located near the hostel.

Lyon's most famous food is at **Paul Bocuse's** (tel. 04 72 42 90 90), 9km out of town; meals cost approximately the equivalent of Andorra's GNP. You need not sell your body organs to eager *lyonnais* chefs to enjoy Bocusian cuisine, however. The master has two places in Lyon with scrumptious food at more reasonable prices.

Le Nord, 18, rue Neuve, 2ème (tel. 04 78 28 24 54). Dark green and red interior gives this *brasserie* a British feel, but the food is Bocusian *lyonnais.* Favorites such as *quenelles* (fish dumplings) and *andouillettes* in a mustard sauce are 72-98F. Reserve 3 days ahead. Open daily noon-2pm and 7-11:30pm. V, MC, AmEx.

Le Sud, 11, pl. Antonin Poncet, 2ème (tel. 04 72 77 80 00), right off pl. Bellecour. One of Bocuse's "bargains." Opened in the summer of '95, the place has received immediate accolades and crowds. The colorful yellow and blue dining room adds Mediterranean ambience to Provençal and Italian cuisine. Pizzas and pastas with exotic ingredients 54-85F. 78F *plat du jour* and 120F *menu.* Reserve 2 days in advance. Open noon-2pm and 7-11:30pm. V, MC, AmEx.

Rue St-Jean is also a good place for authentic food; *menus* tend to start around 75F. Other *Let's Go* picks for *langue à la Lyonnais* include:

Chez Mounier, 3, rue des Marrioniers, 2ème (tel. 04 78 37 79 26). This tiny place with local clientele satisfies both tummies and weary wallets with generous portions of traditional specialties on its 4-course 59, 83, and 93F *menus*—a steal in Lyon. Just around the corner from Le Sud. Open daily noon-2pm and 7pm-late.

Chabert et Fils, 11, rue des Marroniers, 2ème (tel. 04 78 37 01 94). You can feel the history in this *bouchon*. Familiar favorites include *museau de boeuf* (snout of cattle, doncha know) on the 97F *menu*. Open daily noon-2pm and 7-11pm. V, MC.

La Mère Vittet, 26, cours de Verdun, 2ème (tel. 04 78 37 20 17), near Perrache. Advertising for *les insomniaques,* this gourmet restaurant serves authentic *lyonnais* cuisine 'round the clock, 364 days a year. *Menus* start at 100F, and there are delicious options *à la carte* for around 50-60F.

If *lyonnaise* cuisine doesn't tempt you, or if its cavalier attitude towards price appalls your wallet, try the cheaper ethnic restaurants that congregate on the wide streets off **rue de la République** (2ème). The **Consistoire Israélite** (tel. 04 78 37 13 43) can direct you to seven local **kosher** restaurants.

Chez Carlo, 22, rue du Palais Grillet, 2ème (tel. 04 78 42 05 79), near Garioud. Locals say this is the best pasta and pizza in Lyon (42-46F). Extensive dessert list (30F). Open Tues.-Sat. noon-2pm and 7-11pm, Sun. noon-2pm. V, MC.

Le Confort Impérial, 10, rue Confort, 2ème (tel. 04 78 42 41 88), between rue de la République and pl. des Jacobins. Winner of the *"Baguettes d'Or"* for gourmet Chinese cookery. The mayor of Lyon, the Chinese ambassador, and the former emperor of Vietnam have all raised a chopstick here. 3-course lunch *menu* 52F; dinner *menus* begin at 68F. Interesting *à la carte* options around 40F (10 veggie dishes). Open Tues.-Sun. noon-2:30pm and 7-10:30pm. V, MC, AmEx.

Le Patisson, 17, rue Port de Temple, 2ème. A small, simple vegetarian joint off quai des Célestins. *Menus* 61F and 68F. *Plat du jour* 49F. Open Mon.-Thurs. 11:30am-2pm and 7-9:30pm, Fri. 11:30am-2pm. V, MC, AmEx.

L'Etoile de l'Orient, 31, rue des Remparts d'Ainay, 2ème (tel. 04 72 41 07 87). M. Ampère-Victor Hugo. Regulars pack this star for North African food and decor straight out of "Casablanca." Couscous 50-100F. 120F *menu.* Specials—*chackchouka* and *melloukia*—50-55F. Open Thurs.-Tues. noon-2pm and 7-11pm.

University Restaurants: Résidence André Allix, 2, rue des Soeurs Bauvier, 5ème (tel. 04 78 25 47 13); **Résidence Jean Mermoz,** 29, rue Prof. J. Nicolas, 8ème (tel. 04 78 74 41 64); **Résidence la Madeleine,** 4, rue Sauveur, 7ème (tel. 04 78 72 80 62); **Caféteria Université Lyon 2,** 16, quai C. Bernard, 7ème (tel. 04 72 73 07 02); **Résidence Jussieu,** 3, av. A. Einstein, Villeurbanne (tel. 04 78 93 34 21); and **Puvis de Chavanne,** 29, rue Marguerite, Villeurbanne (tel. 04 78 89 62 02). The last two are open in the summer; contact CROUS (see above) for times and prices.

SIGHTS

Fourvière and Roman Lyon

The two rivers slicing through the foothills of the Alps create a spectacular setting for Lyon. Admire the landscape from atop **Fourvière Hill,** the nucleus of Roman Lyon. It harbors the city's most impressive ruins. Later, the Fourvière attracted Lyon's religious communities, including a cluster of monasteries in the 17th century. The 19th-century basilica stands guard over the city, but it's quite a walk from Vieux Lyon. If you're homesick for your Stairmaster, you can dive into the network of staircases and ramps leading up the hill. Along the way, there's a series of parks, a striking modern fountain on the Montée du Chemin Neuf and, on Montée St-Barthélémy, a zig-zagging shortcut through the romantic **Chemin de la Rosaire**—when it's open. Most prefer to take the *funiculaire* from the head of av. Max in Vieux Lyon, off pl. St-Jean, to the top of the hill (direction: Fourvière). Once there, admire the view on the **Esplanade Fourvière,** where a model of the cityscape points out local landmarks. On a clear day, scan for Mont Blanc, about 200km east. Behind the Esplanade is the **Basilique Notre-Dame de Fourvière.** Lyon's archbishop vowed to build a church if the Prussians did not attack the city during the Franco-Prussian War. Lyon was spared, and the bargaining bishop was obliged to follow through. This basilica was not built in a period where simplicity denoted elegance and wealth. If the towers flanking the ornate façade don't tell you that, one step inside will. Multicolored mosaics on the walls and ceilings, gilded pillars and statues, and elaborate carvings adorn every square inch of the interior.

If you walk down the hill making a left as you exit the church, you'll see signs for the **Musée Gallo-Romain,** 17, rue Cléberg, 5*ème* (tel. 04 72 38 81 90). The museum holds a huge collection of mosaics, jugs, helmets, swords, statues, jewelry, and a well-preserved bronze tablet inscribed with a speech by Lyon's native son, the emperor Claudius (open Wed.-Sun. 9:30am-noon and 2-6pm; admission 20F, students 10F). Just next door, the most spectacular reminder of Lyon's Roman history was discovered as modern developers dug into the hill to build apartment buildings. The **Théâtre Romain** still functions as a venue for all types of shows (call 04 78 95 95 95 for show info; tickets and info at FNAC on rue de la République). Performances are also staged next to the theater in the **Odéon,** a small auditorium meant for the Gallo-Roman elite. The theaters' immense boulders and honey-comb ruins make intriguing jungle-gyms and picnic spots. The setting sun behind Fourvière puts on its own show, casting a rosy glow over the city's red-tile roofs.

Vieux Lyon

Nestled up against the Saône at the bottom of the Fourvière hill, the narrow cobblestone streets of **Vieux Lyon** wind between lively cafés and magnificent medieval and Renaissance townhouses. The **hôtels particuliers,** with delicate carvings over their doorways, shaded courtyards, and ornate turrets, are the product of the great wealth Lyon gained as the center of Europe's silk and publishing industries from the 15th to 19th centuries. These regal residences around rue St-Jean, rue du Boeuf, and rue Juiverie have housed Lyon's elite for 400 years—and still do. The tourist office provides an ever-changing list of the houses open to your prying eyes.

The most distinguishing feature of Vieux Lyon's townhouses is their **traboules,** long tunnels leading from the street through a maze of courtyards, often with vaulted ceilings and little statuary niches. Originally constructed to transport silk safely from looms to storage rooms around the city, the *traboules* were invaluable information and escape routes for the local Resistance in World War II. French Nazi collaborators from other regions did not have the *Lyonnais'* familiarity with the *traboules.* If the door is open, peek into a *traboule,* or get a list of addresses from the tourist office. No. 16, rue du Boeuf, leads to a rosy stucco courtyard with a winding five-story pink stucco tower known as the **Tour des Avocats.**

The 12th-century **Cathédrale St-Jean,** at the southern end of Vieux Lyon, towers over pl. St-Jean. The soaring columns lining its nave look too fragile to have withstood eight centuries of the *Lyonnais'* revolutionary rampages. Henri IV met and married Marie de Médicis here in 1600. Every hour statuettes pop out of the 14th-century **astronomical clock** by the choir, bang on their bells, and retire for another nap. Sit and watch beams of sunlight in the brilliant stained glass. (Cathedral open Mon.-Fri. 7:30am-noon and 2-7:30pm, Sat.-Sun. 2-5pm; free 15-min. tours daily June 20-Aug. 15 10-11:30am and 2-5:30pm. Hours will be modified in 1997.)

Down rue St-Jean, take a left at the pl. du Change to the **Hôtel de Gadagne,** pl. du Petit College, 5*ème* (M. Vieux Lyon; tel. 04 78 42 03 61), and its relatively minor museums. The **Musée de la Marionette** exhibits puppets from around the world, including models of Guignol, the famed *lyonnais* cynic, and his inebriated friend, Gnaffron. In the same building, the **Musée Historique de Lyon** displays relics of Lyon's 2000-year past—including Roman artifacts and the beds where Napoleon and Joséphine once slumbered (both open Wed.-Mon. 10:45am-6pm; admission to either or both 20F, students 10F). The **Palais de la Miniature,** 2, rue Juiverie (tel. 04 72 00 24 77), devotes itself to microscopic art and extraordinarily complex origami. See the world's smallest bear perched atop a pearl visible with a magnifying glass (open 10am-noon and 2-7pm; admission 25F, students 20F).

Le Presqu'île and les Terreaux

Monumental squares, statues, and fountains are the trademarks of the **presqu'île,** the lively area between the Rhône and the Saône. Its heart is **pl. Bellecour,** a barren expanse of Martian-red gravel fringed with shops and flower stalls. Lemot's equestrian statue of a young and fit Louis XIV dominates the square. From there, walk east along pedestrian **rue de la République;** the McDonald's, movie theaters, FNAC, and rushing crowds establish the street as the urban aorta of Lyon. It runs through pl. de la République and terminates at pl. Louis Pradel in the 1er, at the tip of the **Terreaux district.** Once a marshy wasteland, the area was filled with soil centuries ago, creating dry terraces *(terreaux)* and establishing the neighborhood as *the* place to be for chic *Lyonnais.* The **Opéra,** pl. Louis Pradel, looks like an indoor hockey arena perched atop a building. Across the square, the spectacular Renaissance **Hôtel de Ville** cools its elaborate front façade by the waters of the pl. des Terreaux. After dark, lights transform its newly constructed fountains and cascades into illuminated rivers on the white stone plaza. In summer, Bartholi's fountain of frenzied horses stamping and spraying fills with hot, daring children who play in the cool, *evil* water. Sidewalk cafés, bars, and clubs keep this area hopping late at night.

The **Musée des Beaux-Arts** (tel. 04 72 10 17 40) is across pl. des Terreaux at no. 20. The museum's particular strengths include a small but distinguished collection of French painting, works by Spanish and Dutch masters, a wing devoted to the Italian Renaissance, and a beautiful sculpture garden. In the Impressionist collection, look for the Rodin miniatures and Monet's famous view of Charing Cross. The collection spans the ages from Egyptian hieroglyphs to paintings from the 60s (open Wed.-Sun. 10:30am-6pm; admission 20F, students 10F). A few blocks north of the museum, on rue Burdeau, 1er, an unfortunate band of Christians met their demise at the Roman **Amphithéâtre des Trois Gaulles** in AD 177.

La Croix-Rousse and the Silk Industry

Lyon is proud of its historical dominance of European silk manufacture. Originating in the 15th century, Lyon's silk industry operated 28,000 looms by the 18th, mainly in the Croix-Rousse district on a hill in the 1er. The 1801 invention of the power-loom by *Lyonnais* Joseph Jacquard intensified the sweatshop conditions endured by the *canuts* (silk workers). The workers' rebellion came to a head in the 1834 riot, in which hundreds of workers were killed. Mass silk manufacturing is based elsewhere today, and Lyon's few silk workers are employed at delicate handiwork, reconstructing and replicating rare patterns for museum and château displays.

La Maison des Canuts, 10-12, rue d'Ivry, 4ème (tel. 04 78 28 62 04), demonstrates the weaving techniques of the *canuts lyonnais* (open Mon.-Fri. 8:30am-noon and 2-6:30pm, Sat. 9am-noon and 2-6pm; free). The Maison's shop sells silk made by its own *canuts.* A scarf runs 125F, but you can take home a silkworm cocoon for a few francs. An extraordinary collection of silk and embroidery hangs back in the 2ème at the **Musée Historique des Tissus,** 34, rue de la Charité. (tel. 04 78 37 15 05. Open Tues.-Sun. 10am-5:30pm. Maps in French and English. Tour in French Tues. and Sun. at 3pm, 45F, students 24F. Admission 26F, students 13F; Wed. free.) Weave through its affiliated **Musée Lyonnais des Arts Decoratifs,** down the street at 30, rue de la Charité, 2ème (tel. 04 78 37 15 05), which displays furniture, porcelain, silver, and tapestries from the 17th and 18th centuries (open Tues.-Sun. 10am-noon and 2-5:30pm; free with ticket from Musée des Tissus).

Finish your visit to Croix-Rousse by admiring the **Mur des Canuts,** at the corner of bd. des Canuts and rue Denfert-Rochereau, a giant fresco painted on the side of a building in 1987. The subject is the life of the silk workers in the 18th and 19th centuries. Its creators have graced Lyon with dozens of other giant paintings, including an interesting one nearby, at quai St-Vincent and rue de la Martinière, 1er, entitled **Fresque des Lyonnais.** The piece depicts 30 famous people from Lyon, ranging from the emperor Claudius to Paul Bocuse.

East of the Rhône and Modern Lyon

Lyon's newest train station and monstrous space-age mall form the core of the ultra-modern **Part-Dieu district.** Many see the whole place as an eyesore and Part-Dieu's greatest virtue as its shops—perhaps the only ones in France open between noon and 2pm. Locals call the commercial **Tour du Crédit Lyonnais,** on the other side of the mall, *Le Crayon* for its unwitting resemblance to a giant pencil on end. Next to it, the shell-shaped **Auditorium Maurice Ravel** hosts major cultural events.

The **Centre d'Histoire de la Résistance et de la Déportation,** 14, av. Bertholet, 7ème (tel. 04 78 72 23 11 or 04 72 73 33 54), has assembled documents, photos, and films of the Lyon-based Resistance. The museum is in a building in which Nazis tortured detainees during the Occupation and is one of the few museums of its kind in France completely accessible to English speakers (open Wed.-Sun. 9am-5:30pm; admission 20F, students 10F). Nearby, more of Lyon's wall paintings make up the open-air **Musée Urbain Tony Garnier,** 4, rue des Serpolières, 8ème (tel. 04 78 75 16 75), off of bd. des Etats-Unis. Architect Tony Garnier designed the surrounding buildings, and the murals are interpretations of his work (open Tues.-Sat. 2-6pm; guided tours of the museum Sat. at 2 and 4pm, 25F; free). The **Musée Africain,** 150, cours Gambetta, has three floors depicting the daily life, social customs, and religions of West Africa (open Wed.-Sun. 2-6pm; admission 10F, students 5F).

Film buffs will want to see the **Institut Lumière,** 25, rue du Premier-Film, 8ème (tel. 04 78 78 18 95; M. Monplaisir/Lumière), a museum that examines the lives of the *lyonnais* brothers who invented the first film projector (open Tues.-Sun. 2-7pm; admission 25F, students 20F). During the summer, free films are screened every Tuesday outside the institute. Recent arrivals who can't wait to get a museum under their belts can take in the contemporary **Espace Lyonnais d'Art Contemporain (ELAC),** on the top floor of the Perrache train station (tel. 04 78 42 27 39; hours and prices vary). A more extensive collection of modern art is at the **Musée d'Art Contemporain** (tel. 04 78 30 50 66), in the futuristic *Cité International de Lyon* on quai Charles de Gaulle, 6ème (M. Masséna). The Cité is a super-modern complex with offices, shops, theaters, and—don't jaywalk—Interpol's world headquarters.

Right next to the *Cité* is the massive **Parc de la Tête d'Or,** so called because legend has it that a golden sculpture of the head of Jesus is buried within. It's a good place to escape the bustle of the city. The park sprawls over 259 acres, and you can rent paddle boats to explore its artificial lake, complete with artificial island. Very real lions, elephants, and a thousand other animals fill the **zoo;** two giant greenhouses encase the **botanical garden;** and the **rose gardens** are breathtakingly beautiful in the summer (park open daily April-Sept. 6am-11pm; Oct.-March 6am-9pm).

ENTERTAINMENT

Lyon's major theater is the **Théâtre des Célestins,** 4, rue Charles Dullin, 2ème (tel. 04 78 42 17 67). Tickets run 70-200F; those under 23 can get discount subscriptions. The **Opéra,** pl. de la Comédie, 1er (tel. 04 72 00 45 45), has pricey tickets (95-290F), but 70F standing-room only "seats" go on sale the evening of the show. The 1997 program includes Puccini's *La Bohème,* Verdi's *Don Carlos,* and if you hurry, you may still be able to snag tickets for *Pavarotti on Ice!*

In the summer, Lyon bursts with festivals and special events nearly every week. Pick up the free **Spectacle/Evénements** guide at the tourist office. Highlights include the **Fête de la Musique,** in early June, when performers take over the city streets, and the **Bastille Day** celebration on July 14. Fireworks over the Saône light the sky, and discos and pubs stay open all night. The acclaimed **Orchestre National de Lyon** has a full season (tel. 04 78 95 95 95). The **Théâtre National Populaire** is at 8, pl. Lazare-Goujon, in the suburb of Villeurbanne (tel. 04 78 03 30 40). Call the **Maison de la Danse** (tel. 04 72 78 18 18) for info on dance in Lyon.

From the beginning of September through mid-October, Lyon hits its cultural peak with two annually alternating festivals. Even-numbered years erupt with the **Biennale de la Danse Lyon,** which draws modern dance performers from around the world (tickets 40-240F per performance; reserve at the Maison de Lyon, pl. Bellecour, 2ème; tel. 04 72 41 00 00). The **Biennale d'Art Contemporain** (tel. 04 72 40 26 26) is slated for 1997 in the magnificent **Halle Tony Garnier,** 20, pl. Antonin Perrin, 7ème. The celebration combines a major modern art exhibit with workshops on music and cinema. The **Festival de Musique du Vieux Lyon** brings artists from around the world to perform in the churches of Lyon's old town. (Mid-Nov. to mid-Dec. Tickets 90-230F. For info, contact the Festival at 5, pl. du Petit Collège, 5ème; tel. 04 78 42 39 04; fax 04 78 42 39 28.) Every December 8, Lyon places candles in its windows and ascends with tapers to the basilica for the **Fête de Lumières.** The celebration (which becomes a city-wide block party) honors the Virgin Mary on the Feast of the Immaculate Conception for protecting Lyon from the Black Plague. July 1 starts the two-week **Festival du Jazz à Vienne,** welcoming jazz masters to Vienne, a medieval town south of Lyon, accessible by bus or train. For festival info, call 04 74 85 00 05 or Vienne's tourist office (tel. 04 74 85 12 62; 11, cours Brillier).

Lyon, the birthplace of cinema, is a superb place to see silver screen classics. The **Cinéma Opéra,** 6, rue J. Serlin (tel. 04 78 28 80 08), and **Le Cinéma,** 18, impasse St-Polycarpe (tel. 04 78 39 09 72), specialize in black-and-white oldies, all *v.o.* (original language; 30-40F). You'll find avant-garde films and classics at the **CNP Terreaux Cinéma,** 40, rue Président Edouard Herriot, 1er (tel. 04 78 27 26 25). Mass modern thrills fill the cinemas on rue de la République.

Students pass their nights at Lyon's *"Pubs Anglais."* Exercise your British accent at **Albion,** 12, rue Ste-Catherine, 1er (tel. 04 78 28 33 00). 26F pints of Guinness before 9pm (open Mon.-Thurs. 5pm-2am, Fri.-Sat. 5pm-3am, Sun. 5pm-1am).

No one has to beat the bushes for **nightclubs** in Lyon. There's a whole row of them off the Saône, on quai Romain Rolland, quai de Bondy, and quai Pierre Scize in Vieux Lyon (5ème). The city's best clubs shake, rattle, and roll to U.S. themes. Shake your funnybone at **B-52,** 67, rue des Rancy, 3ème (tel. 04 72 61 13 61). The decor is 1950s American, but the music isn't all in English and the clientele is almost completely local (open Fri.-Sat. 10pm-4am, call for other days; 60F cover includes first drink). Rattle the rafters at **Road 66,** 8, pl. des Terreaux, 1er (tel. 04 78 27 37 42)—just off Route 66. 15F beers, billiards, James Dean, a dance floor, and an airplane named "heavenly body" pack this crowded joint in the *centre ville* (open 2pm-4am). Roll into the world of techno at **L'Empire,** 30, bd. Eugène Deruelle, 3ème (tel. 04 78 69 08 55), a sleek *discothèque* near the Part-Dieu complex (open 10:30pm-4am, Thurs.-Fri. 'til 5am, Sat. 'til 6am; cover changes daily).

The tourist office's city guide lists entertainment catering to Lyon's active gay community. A mixed gay and lesbian crowd gathers for a drink at **Le Verre à Soi,** 25, rue des Capucins, 1er (tel. 04 78 28 92 22). Drinks are half-price from 5 to 10pm (open Sun.-Fri. 3pm-2am, Sat. 7pm-3am). **Le Broadway,** 9, rue Terraille, 1er (tel. 04 78 39 50 54), is a nearby bar that caters to men (open Wed.-Mon. 6pm-*late*). **Le Mylord,** 112, quai Pierre Scize, 5ème (tel. 04 78 28 96 69), is dance oriented (open Mon.-Sat. 10:30pm-6am; cover 60F with 1 drink, Sun. free).

Bourges

Bourges (pop. 76,000) is proud of its location at the *coeur* (heart) of France, the geographical center of the legendary *hexagone.* Although inhabited for nearly 2500 years, Bourges did not gain prominence until 1433, when Charles VII's corrupt finance minister, Jacques Coeur, chose it as the site for his collection of châteaux. Clinging tenuously to their territories during the Hundred Years' War, Charles and his successor, Louis XI, held court at Bourges. The British, a bit presumptuously as it turned out, sniggered at Louis XI, "King of Bourges."

Time has not spoiled the town; within a few blocks of the station you can wander through a medieval fairy-tale village of twisting cobblestone streets, half-timbered houses, and Gothic turrets. If you ever find your way out, one of the grandest cathedrals in France awaits. The slow but steady pace of change here is also apparent in Bourges' relatively sedate nightlife. Still, the several excellent museums and the town's endlessly twisting streets should keep your pulse racing.

ORIENTATION AND PRACTICAL INFORMATION

While its narrow streets delight camera-toters, they are frustrating to anyone with a specific destination. Head straight (well, crooked) for the tourist office and its crucial map. To get there from the train station, follow av. H. Laudier and its continuation, av. Jean Jaurès, into the *vieille ville*. From there, bear left onto rue du Commerce, then right two blocks later onto rue Moyenne, which will take you to the office (15min.). Or catch bus 1 (direction: Val d'Auron, 6F) to "Victor Hugo."

Tourist Office: 21, rue Victor Hugo (tel. 02 48 24 75 33; fax 02 48 65 11 87), facing rue Moyenne near the cathedral. Excellent free maps and info. 1½-hr. walking tours (in French) leave daily July-Sept. at 3pm (30F, students 20F); night tours July-Aug. Fri.-Sat. 8:30pm (40F, students 30F). Open July-Sept. Mon.-Sat. 9am-7pm, Sun. 10am–7pm; Oct.-June Mon.-Sat. 9am-6pm, Sun. 10am-12:30pm.

Money: 24-hr. **ATMs** litter rue Moyenne. **Banque Populaire** and **Crédit Lyonnais** are at the corner of rue Moyenne and rue Jacques Coeur.

Trains: pl. Général Leclerc (tel. 02 47 20 50 50 for info, 02 48 70 10 52 for reservations). Many trains transfer at Vierzon. To: Paris (13 per day, 2½hr., 147F); Tours (21 per day, 1½hr., 106F); Lyon (6 per day, 4hr., 183F); Clermont-Ferrand (7 per day, 3hr., 137F); Nevers (7 per day, 1hr., 59F). **Bag check** 10F. Info office open Mon.-Sat. 9am-6:30pm. Tickets sold daily 6am-9:15pm.

Buses: Run from the *gare routière*, rue Pré Doulet (tel. 02 48 24 36 42), and stop at the train station. The *Réseau Vert* bus timetable is free at the tourist office.

Public Transportation: CTB (tel. 02 48 50 82 82). Reliable service with good coverage. Train station has schedules. Tickets 6F, *carnet* of 10 50F.

Taxis: Radio-Taxis de Bourges (tel. 02 48 24 50 00).

Bike Rental: Cycl'one, 28, rue Jean Jaurès (tel. 02 48 24 85 64). 70F per ½-day, 90F per day, 350F per week. Passport or credit card deposit. Open Mon.-Tues. 2:30-7:30pm, Wed.-Sat. 9:30am-12:30pm and 2:30-7:30pm. V, MC.

Youth Center: B.I.J., Halle/St. Bonnet, bd. de la République (tel. 02 48 65 39 97).

Laundromat: Lavomatiques, 117, rue Edouard Valliant; also 15, bd. Juranville. Wash 7kg for 23F. Dry 4F per 10min. Soap 5F. Open 7am-8pm; Sun. 8am-8pm.

Crisis Lines: SOS Amitié (tel. 02 38 62 22 22); friendship all day, all night. **SOS Femmes Victimes de Violence** (tel. 02 48 21 05 34); 24-hr. line for women who are victims of violent crime. **Actif SIDA** (tel. 02 48 24 70 70); AIDS info.

Hospital: route de Nevers (tel. 02 48 48 48 48). **Medical emergency** tel. 15.

Police: 6, av. de St-Armand (tel. 02 48 55 85 00). **Emergency** tel. 17.

Post Office: 29, rue Moyenne (tel. 02 48 68 82 82)—one of the most poetic *postes* in France. **Currency exchange.** Photocopies. Poste restante (postal code: 18012 Bourges Cedex). Open Mon.-Fri. 8am-7pm, Sat. 8am-noon. **Postal code:** 18000.

ACCOMMODATIONS AND CAMPING

Bourges' cheaper hotels are outside of the *centre ville*. Unoccupied beds may be hard to find during major festivals and in the height of summer.

Auberge de Jeunesse (HI), 22, rue Henri Sellier (tel. 02 48 24 58 09), 10min. from the center of town. From the station, take av. H. Laudier onto av. Jean Jaurès to pl. Planchat. Follow rue des Arènes, which becomes rue Fernault and then rue René Ménard, before making a sharp left onto rue Henri Sellier. The hostel is set back from the street, behind the Salle Germinal (25min.). Or take bus 1 (direction: Val d'Auron) to "Conde." Walk along pl. Malraux, turn left on rue Vieille Castel and take it to the end. Turn right onto rue du Château d'Eau, right onto rue Charles Cochet, and right again onto rue Henri Sellier. A fine hostel with a bar, snack bar, laundry facilities (25F), good kitchen facilities, and clean 3-8 bunk rooms, some with private showers. 63F, 45F without breakfast. Sheets 17F. Reception Mon.-Fri. 8am-noon and 2-11pm, Sat.-Sun. 8am-noon and 5-10pm. Doors locked at 11pm and noon-2pm, but a code allows entry for residents.

Centre International de Séjour, "La Charmille," 17, rue Félix-Chédin (tel. 02 48 70 25 59; fax 02 48 69 01 21). Cross the footbridge over the tracks at the station and head up rue Félix-Chédin (5min.). This lively youth center—half hostel, half *foyer*—is the **skateboard mecca of Europe,** with bowls, ramps, and half-pipes to prove it. In summer, many of the world's best skaters offer classes. 88F per person for 4-bed rooms. Breakfast, sheets, TV room, and skateboard facilities included. Lunch or dinner 52F. Laundry facilities, TV room. V, MC.

Hôtel de l'Etape, 4, rue Casanova (tel. 02 48 70 59 47; fax 02 48 24 57 93), off rue Juranville on a quiet street close to downtown. By far the best hotel deal in town. Incredibly spacious and clean rooms with phone. Singles and doubles 95F, with shower 120F. Enormous quads 220F. TV 20F. Breakfast 22-24F. Extra bed 30F. Ask for the key if you'll be out after 11pm. Reception 7am-11pm. V, MC.

Au Rendez-vous des Amis, 6, av. Dormoy (tel. 02 48 70 81 80). Head left out the station and right onto av. Dormoy. Not the best location, and squishy beds, but a cheap place to sleep. Singles and doubles 85F, with shower 130F. Breakfast 22F.

Hôtel St-Jean, 23, av. Dormoy (tel. 02 48 24 13 48; fax 02 48 24 79 98). Well-furnished rooms with phone, TV. Single with shower 125F. Double with toilet 140F, with shower 180F. Triple 260F. Shower 30F. Breakfast 27F. Closed Feb. V, MC.

Camping Municipal, 26, bd. de l'Industrie (tel. 02 48 20 16 85). Follow directions to the first hostel but continue on rue Henri Sellier away from the *centre ville* and turn right on bd. de l'Industrie. 16F per person, 17F per tent and car, 24F per caravan. Reception June-Aug. 7am-10pm; March 15-May and Sept.-Oct. 15 8am-noon and 3-8pm; Oct. 16-Nov. 15 8:30am-noon and 2:30-6pm.

FOOD

The cobblestone streets off rue d'Auron, rue Bourbonnoux, rue Corsarlon, and rue Mirabeau form a network of pedestrian walkways lined with shops, cafés, and restaurants. Look for bargains on such specialties as *poulet en barbouille* (chicken roasted in an aromatic red wine) and *oeufs en meurette* (eggs in red wine). Many a *Let's Go* reader has walked away happy from **Le St-Alban,** 32, rue Moyenne (tel. 02 48 65 89 75), near the cathedral (regional *plats du jour* about 40F). Bourges has a number of **produce markets,** the largest of which fills pl. de la Nation on Saturday mornings. Another notable one rocks pl. des Marronniers on Thursdays until 1pm, while there is a smaller permanent market Tuesday through Sunday at pl. St-Bonnet (open 7:30am-1pm and 3-7:30pm, closed Sun. afternoon). There is a mammoth **E. Leclerc supermarket** on rue Prado off bd. Juraville (open Mon.-Fri. 9:15am-7:20pm, Sat. 8:30am-7:20pm). The central **Nouvelles Galeries,** rue Moyenne at rue du Docteur Témoin, stashes a **supermarket** in its basement (open Mon.-Sat. 9am-7pm).

D'Antan Sancerrois, 50, rue Bourbonnoux (tel. 02 48 65 96 26). *L'amour du vin* carried to new heights: *carte* that changes every 2 months includes dishes cooked in wine. Delicious *veau au vin* (veal in wine sauce) 62F; *oeufs en meurette* 36F. Open Tues. 7-10:30pm, Wed.-Sun. noon-2pm and 7-10:30pm. V, MC, AmEx.

Le Phénicien, 13, rue Edouard Vaillant in pl. Gordaine (tel. 02 48 65 01 37). Delicious Middle Eastern delights with pita for a pittance and falafel for 5F50. Servings 16-18F or scrumptious *menu* with 4 appetizers and meat dish 40F (lunch only), with dessert and coffee 50F. Open Mon.-Sat. 11am-11pm.

La Main à la Pat, 108, rue Bourbonnoux (tel. 02 48 24 23 59), behind the cathedral. Chattering locals dig into pizzas baked over a wood fire (32-55F) under exposed beams. Eponymous salad has chicken and avocado (35F). Other salads 32-52F. Open Mon. 7pm-midnight, Tues.-Sat. noon-2pm and 7pm-midnight.

Le Brownie, pl. Gordaine (tel. 02 48 24 04 70), in a half-timbered house on a central square. U.S. license plates adorn this small, trendy burger joint. *Menus* 55F, 70F, and 110F. Boffo burgers such as "Madison," with green pepper sauce, served with fries and salad (40-45F). Open Mon.-Sat. 11:30am-2pm and 7-11pm. V, MC.

SIGHTS AND ENTERTAINMENT

One of France's most magnificent cathedrals, the **Cathédrale St-Etienne** (tel. 02 48 24 07 93) is notable for its well-preserved 13th-century façade representing the Last Judgment. The intricate stonework shows everything from the grimaces of gleeful demons stewing the damned to the angelic smiles of souls bound for the domes of the eternal Jerusalem. Restored, brilliantly clean *vitraux* light the interior. Prominent organists tickle the ivories and pipes of the cathedral's organ during summer concerts; if you're lucky, you'll walk in on a practice session. (Tourist office has schedule. Concerts every Tues. July-Aug.; 75F, students 50F. Cathedral open daily June-Sept. 8:30am-8pm; Oct.-May 8:30am-6pm.) The crypt and tower of the cathedral are included in the *billet jumelé* (45F), which also gets you into the Palais Jacques Cœur. Otherwise, take a trip to the crypt and climb the tower for 27F (students 18F). The crypt tour focuses on the cathedral's metamorphosis from Gallo-Romanesque David to Gothic Goliath and displays sculptures removed from the North tower due to pollution damage (tours hourly; the tourist office has info).

The **Palais Jacques-Coeur** (tel. 02 48 24 06 87) isn't exactly a testimony to the conniving financier's own egotistical motto: *A vaillants Coeurs, rien d'impossible* ("To bold Hearts nothing is impossible"), but it's impressive nonetheless. The obligatory tour winds past late medieval reception halls, bedrooms, and Mr. Heart's personal steam room. In 45 minutes you'll see more of the palace than Jacques ever did; he was imprisoned in 1451, years before its completion. (1 tour per hr., in French; first at 9:15am; Sept.-June no tours noon-2pm; July-Aug. last tour 6:10pm; April-June and Sept. last tour at 5:10pm; Oct.-March last tour at 4:10pm. English brochure at the front desk. Admission 27F, ages 18-24 18F.)

The **Musée du Berry,** rue des Arènes (tel. 02 48 57 81 15), gathers prehistoric, Gallo-Roman, and medieval artifacts in an elegant 16th-century *hôtel.* A 15th-century merchant built the luxurious **Hôtel Lallemant,** 6, rue Bourbonnoux (tel. 02 48 57 81 17), which houses furniture, tapestries, and other decorative works from the 16th to 18th centuries. Inside the **Musée Estève,** 13, rue Edouard-Branly (tel. 02 48 24 75 38), the vibrant colors of local hero Maurice Estève's work contrast with the white stone carvings of the museum's home, built in 1489. (All 3 museums free. Museums open 10am-noon and 2-6pm; Berry and Estève closed Tues., Lallemant closed Mon., and all 3 closed Sun. mornings.)

Although bars and cafés pepper the *vieille ville,* nightlife centers north and west of the cathedral. **Les Jardins de César,** 10, pl. Mirepied (tel. 02 48 65 95 85), on the corner of rue du Commerce and av. Jean Jaurès, is a sleek underground club whose crowded dance floor glitters with mirrors and colored lights (open Tues.-Sun. 10pm-4am; cover of around 60F gets you a drink). Next door, the more relaxed **Pub Birdland** ("Bourges' London Pub"), 4, av. J. Jaurès (tel. 02 48 70 66 77), is conducive to drinking. Sample a meter of beer (10 glasses, 150F) or the gargantuan *pyramid*—6 liters—for 380F. (Open Mon.-Sat. 4pm-2am, Sun. 9pm-2am.)

Over 200,000 ears perk up to the **Festival Printemps de Bourges** (in April). Most tickets are 50-180F, but informal folk, jazz, classical, and rock concerts are free (contact the Association Printemps de Bourges, rue Henri Sellier; tel. 02 48 24 30 50). The city gets a little wilder for the **Festival International des Groupes de Musique Experimentale de Bourges** (early June; contact GMEB at 02 48 20 41 87). The **Fête de Jacques-Coeur,** with traditional music and dance, brings light-hearted fun to the last two weeks in June through Bastille Day. From July 14 'til August, amble over to **Un Eté à Bourges,** a conflagration of classical and rock concerts and theater (tickets 50-90F, some events free; pick up a schedule at the tourist office).

■ Near Bourges: Route Jacques-Coeur

Jacques may have left his *coeur* in Bourges, but his ego spilled far into the surrounding countryside. The Route Jacques-Coeur is a string of 17 châteaux (plus one 12th-century abbey thrown in for good measure), many once owned by Jacques, that stretches from La Buissière in the north to Culan in the south. Less ostentatious than the Loire châteaux, the castles provide a respite from long lines, tour groups, and architectural monotony. Make sure to get a stamp at each visit—see four and the fifth is free. The châteaux are less than 90km from Bourges, but you'll need a car or bike to reach them. At best, buses run once daily and return to Bourges the next morning.

For info on transport and bus excursions, contact the tourist office in Bourges, in St-Amand-Montrond (tel. 02 48 96 16 86), or Bourges' **Comité Départmental de Tourisme du Cher,** 5, rue Sérancourt (tel. 02 48 67 00 18).

All 17 châteaux are sure to please, but **La Verrerie** (tel. 02 48 58 06 91), a 15th-century Renaissance castle on a lake in the middle of the Ivoy forest (45km north of Bourges), is the most popular. For something a bit closer to home, the bike ride to **Maupas** and **Menetou-Salon** makes a perfect daytrip (about 50km roundtrip). The **Château de Maupas** (tel. 02 48 64 41 71) is open Palm Sunday to October 1 (open Mon.-Sat. 2-7pm, Sun. 10am-noon). **Menetou-Salon** (tel. 02 48 64 80 54) is the closest, just 20km north of Bourges. Jacques bought the estate in 1448, but his bout with Charles and the architecturally devastating Revolution (AD 1789) left the castle in ruins until the 19th century, when the Prince of Arenburg, inspired by the Jacques Coeur Palace at Bourges, decided to finish its construction. Though the current prince resides in New York City and only visits his château-cum-hunting camp a mere four times per year, personal touches make Menetou a treat. Most impressive is his collection of autos, ranging from the Range Rover that roved the range from Alaska to Tierra del Fuego in the 1980s to a snazzy Hispano-Suiza paraded by the Prince when he returns. The prince's personal art collection ranges from Rodin to a 70s self-portrait that makes him look less like French royalty and more like a Disco King. But the estate isn't all about sex, cars, and rock and roll. You'll also visit the chapel last used when the present prince was baptized 35 years ago. To get there from Bourges, take D940 north to D11 and follow the signs to Menetou-Salon. The mandatory tour lasts about an hour and ends with a *dégustation* of the Menetou vintages. (Open Easter-Sept. Wed.-Mon. 10am-noon and 2-6pm; last tour around 5:15pm. Admission 50F, students 20F, under 15 free. Cameras prohibited.)

Le Puy-en-Velay

In stark, surreal contrast to the gentle green hills around them, jutting crags of volcanic rock pierce the sky at Le Puy-en-Velay. Fifteen centuries ago, traveling bishops decided this was the place to worship the Virgin Mary. Today, an assortment of statues and chapels balancing atop these rocky pinnacles attests to their builders' determination to conquer nature with human will. In the shadow of these natural skyscrapers is an intriguing Romanesque and Byzantine cathedral, itself dwarfing the red-tiled homes crowding steep cobblestone streets.

Le Puy (pop. 21,000) doesn't survive on heavenly worship alone; it is the historical center of the French lace industry, and souvenir shops are loaded to the teeth with *dentelle* to prove it. Make the trip to Le Puy, though, and you'll be just as awestruck as the bishops were 1500 years before you. The spectacular natural surroundings and centuries of human additions call out for exploration.

ORIENTATION AND PRACTICAL INFORMATION

At the confluence of the Borne and Loire rivers and surrounded by the fertile slopes of extinct volcanoes, Le Puy is 132km southeast of Clermont-Ferrand and 134km southwest of Lyon. Although manufacturing TGV parts is a major component of Le Puy's economy, the city is far from the major train routes and tough to reach. Most trains arriving from southern France or Clermont-Ferrand require a change at Brioude, while trains from Lyon or Paris require a change at St-Etienne (Châteaucreux). From the station, walk left along av. Charles Dupuy and turn left onto bd. Maréchal Fayolle. After five minutes you will reach two adjacent squares, pl. Michelet and pl. de Breuil. The tourist office and most hotels are here and on nearby bd. St-Louis; the cathedral and *vieille ville* are uphill to the right.

Tourist Office: pl. du Breuil (tel. 04 71 09 38 41; fax 04 71 05 22 62). Hiking info and city tours in French (July-Aug. daily at 10am and 4pm, 2hr., 30F). Good map with hotels and restaurants marked in French. Spunky office just took over city bus service. Open July-Aug. Mon.-Sat. 8:30am-7:30pm, Sun. 10am-noon; May-June and

Sept. 8:30am-noon and 1:45-6:30pm; Oct.-April Mon.-Sat. 8:30am-noon and 2-6:30pm. **Annex** at 23, rue des Tables, off av. de la Cathédrale. Open July-Aug. Mon.-Sat. 10am-12:30pm and 1:45-6pm.

Trains: pl. Maréchal Leclerc (tel. 08 36 35 35 35). To: Lyon (8 per day, 2½hr., 107F); St-Etienne (Châteaucreux; 8 per day, 1¼hr., 73F); Clermont-Ferrand (7 per day, 2½hr., 170F). **Lockers** 15-30F. Info Mon.-Sat. 9am-noon and 1:30-6pm.

Buses: (tel. 04 71 09 25 60), next to the train station. Useful free *Horaire Hiver* has times for all transportation in the area. To St-Etienne (9 per day, 2¼hr., 39F) and Clermont-Ferrand (1 per day, 3hr., 64F). Open Mon.-Fri. 7:30am-12:30pm and 2-7pm; Sat. 7:30am-12:30pm. Buy tickets on bus.

Taxis: Radio-Taxis, pl. du Breuil (tel. 04 71 05 42 43). 24hr. 10F plus 7F per km.

Laundromat: Lavoself, 12, rue Chèvrerie, at rue Boucherie Basse off pl. Michelet. Wash 14F per 5kg. Dry 8F per 20min. Open Mon.-Sat. 7:30am-noon and 1-8pm.

Medical Assistance: Centre Hospitalier Emile Roux, bd. Dr. Chantemesse (tel. 04 71 04 32 10). **Clinique Bon Secours,** 67bis, av. Maréchal Foch (tel. 04 71 09 87 00). **Medical emergency** tel. 15 or 04 71 02 02 02.

Police: rue de la Passerelle (tel. 04 71 04 04 22). **Emergency** tel. 17.

Post Office: 8, av. de la Dentelle (tel. 04 71 07 02 05), at Charles Dupuy. Poste restante. **Currency exchange.** Open Mon.-Fri. 8am-7pm, Sat. 8am-noon. **Branch office,** 49, bd. St-Louis (tel. 04 71 09 43 89). **Postal code:** 43000.

ACCOMMODATIONS AND CAMPING

In the summer, call to reserve a room if you plan to arrive late in the day.

Centre Pierre Cardinal (HI), 9, Jules Vallés (tel. 04 71 05 52 40; fax 04 71 05 61 24). From the train station, head left down av. Dupuy. Cross the square at the end of the street and turn left on rue Chèverie. Make a right on rue Général LaFayette. After the zigzag, hook a left. The hostel will be on your right, in a beautiful building (once a Revolutionary barracks) overlooking the city (15min.). Friendly management keeps an excellent kitchen, cool cellar-like TV room, 4-bed rooms and an 18-bed dorm. 37F. Sheets 19F. Breakfast 10F. Reception daily April-Sept. 8am-11:30pm; Oct.-March Mon.-Fri. 2-11:30pm. Only groups with reservations can stay Sat. or Sun. during low season. If no one is in the office, use the phone at the entrance to call the *accueil* (dial 9). Curfew 11:30pm.

Maison St-François, rue St-Mayol (tel. 04 71 05 98 86; fax 04 71 05 98 87). At the top of rue des Tables, make a left onto rue Bec de Lièvre. Go right, up rue Gasmanent, through the portal, around a bend, and rue St-Mayol will be on your left. Practically in the *cathédrale,* this *gîte* opened in '96 with 19 beds in a newly renovated building. No reservations. Kitchen, living rooms, and TV rooms. Friendly staff. Call ahead to see if you should make the trek. 50F. Hall showers. Meals 50F.

Hôtel le Régional, 36, bd. Maréchal Fayolle (tel. 04 71 09 37 74), near pl. Michelet on the noisy corner of av. Dupuy. Wonderfully well-kept rooms with phone. Lively bar downstairs. Singles and doubles 110F, with shower 150F and up. Triples 190F. Quads 280F. Shower 15F. Breakfast 26F. Reception 6am-11pm. V, MC.

Hôtel ETAP, 25, av. Charles Dupuy (tel. 04 71 02 46 22; fax 04 71 02 14 28). Singles 180F. Doubles and triples 200F. All rooms have TV, bath, 3 beds. 24F all-you-can-eat breakfast buffet. Reception 6:30-11am and 5-10pm. V, MC, AmEx.

Camping: Camping Municipal Bouthezard, chemin de Bouthezard (tel. 04 71 09 55 09), in the northwest corner of town. Walk up bd. St-Louis, continue on bd. Carnot, turn right at the dead end onto av. d'Aiguille, and look to your left (10-15min.). Or, take bus 6 (direction: Mondon) from pl. Michelet (1 per hr., 10min., 5F). 13F per person, 13F per site, 9F per car. 43F for 2 people, site, and car. Electricity 16F. Reception 8am-9pm. Open daily Easter-Oct. 15 7am-10pm.

FOOD

Look for inexpensive restaurants on the sidestreets off **pl. du Breuil.** There is a **Casino supermarket** on the corner of av. de la Dentelle and rue P. Farigoule with a cafeteria above it (supermarket open Mon.-Sat. 8:30am-8pm; cafeteria open daily 11am-10pm; meals 26-50F). Saturday morning in **pl. du Plot** is a festival of local cheeses, sausages, and fruits (6am-12:30pm). In 1860, M. Rumillet Charnetier created *vervaine,* an alcoholic brew of local herbs and honey which warms the belly with a sweet mint flavor. This algae-green *digestif* goes for 65-149F per bottle, but **Pagès,** the distillery, gives free tastes as it sells its product on the pl. Cadelade (tel. 04 71 05 25 84). Speaking of things green, Le Puy has recently been recognized for its lentils. *La lentille verte du Puy* is one of the world's best.

Le Village Gaulois, 4, pl. Cadelade (tel. 04 71 02 05 32). Wooden beams span the ceiling, eclectic Viking items cover the stone walls, and reggae fills the air—quite a stimulating atmosphere for *auvergnate* cuisine. Fondues 58-80F. *Plats* 40F. Open daily noon-3pm and 6pm-1am. V, MC.

Le Tajine, 16, rue Chènebouterie (tel. 04 71 02 07 19). Classy Moroccan restaurant in a medieval building with a courtyard. Sample couscous (65-70F) and *tajines* (55-65F). Friendly owner will make specialties such as *pastilla* (70-88F) on request. Homemade bread. Open Tues.-Sun. 10am-4pm and 5pm-midnight.

Café Le Palais, 27, pl. du Breuil (tel. 04 71 09 01 81). Stylish café with 43F *plats du jour.* Salads 20-48F. Open Mon.-Sat. noon-2pm; drinks and ice cream 'til 1am. Open Sun. mid-July to mid-Aug. V, MC, AmEx.

Pomme d'Api, 17, rue Vibert (tel. 04 71 02 42 00). A popular *crêperie* in the middle of town stuffs *galettes* with almost anything. Try one with goat cheese and hazelnuts (26F), or such specialty *galettes* as the *Indienne* with chicken, potatoes, onions, and curry (36F). Open Tues.-Sat. noon-2pm and 7-9pm.

SIGHTS AND ENTERTAINMENT

Towering over the lower city, the **Cité Episcopal** has attracted pilgrims and tourists for over a thousand years. Established as the seat of a local bishopric in the 5th century, the religious complex quickly ran out of room on its treacherous spot atop a volcanic rock. The **Cathédrale Notre-Dame** (tel. 04 71 05 98 74), the centerpiece of the *cité,* rests half on rock and half on pillars anchored to the hillside. From the lower town, you can reach the cathedral via any road leading up, but the most dramatic ascent is via the stone steps of the **rue des Tables,** which rises straight towards the exquisite façade. A striking aspect is its black and white stripes and geometric designs—a result of Moorish and Spanish influences. The domes are Byzantine, a Middle Eastern innovation adopted after the Crusades. At the altar a copy of Le Puy's mysterious **Vièrge Noir** (Black Virgin) smiles enigmatically. The 12th-century Virgin's dark skin stumps many a theologian, but that may be the least of her worries. When she was burnt by Revolutionaries in 1789, locals discovered that this pilgrim-lure wasn't the Virgin at all, but a statue of the pagan goddess Isis. The wooden replacement is still paraded reverently through the streets on August 14, the evening before Assumption Day—quite apt in this case (cathedral open daily 8am-7pm; Oct.-Easter 8am-5pm).

If you plan on visiting Le Puy's other attractions, consider buying a **billet jumelé** (33F), which admits you to all the sights in the *Cité Episcopal,* as well as the Musée Crozatier, Chapelle St-Michel, and Rocher Corneille. The 12th-century **cloister** (tel. 04 71 05 45 52) is the most remarkable of the sights surrounding the cathedral. Its black, white, and peach stone arcades reflect an Islamic influence, brought back to Le Puy by pilgrims to Santiago de Compostela in Spain. Beneath flame-red tiling and black volcanic rock lurks an intricate frieze of grinning faces and mythical beasts. Amid the Byzantine arches of the **salle,** an amazingly vivid and well-preserved 13th-century fresco depicts the Crucifixion (hit the light switch around the corner as you enter on the left for a better view). Your ticket also gets you into the gilded **Chapelle des Reliques,** which houses the celebrated Renaissance mural **Les Arts Libéraux.** It is thought to be unfinished—of the seven liberal arts, only Grammar, Logic, Rhetoric, and Music are represented. The same ticket allows a look at the **Trésor d'Art Religieux** (tel. 04 71 05 45 52), containing walnut statues, jeweled capes, and paintings. (All open July-Sept. 9:30am-6:30pm; April-June 9:30am-12:30pm and 2-6pm; Oct.-March 9:30am-noon and 2-4:30pm. Admission 22F, students 14F.)

Just at the edge of the *vieille ville,* you can climb the **Rocher Corneille,** the eroded core of an ancient volcano. The summit looks out over a sensational countryside of jagged crags interrupting the otherwise serene terrain of green hills and red-roofed houses. Insatiable thrill-seekers can climb the cramped 23m statue of Notre-Dame de France for a view from the various hatches throughout the Lady's body; her halo has been sealed from the public for security reasons. On the walkway at the base of the statue, a pile of cannons is military booty from Sebastopol; 213 of them were melted in 1860 to cast the statue. (Open daily May-Sept. 9am-7pm; Oct.-March 15 10am-5pm; March 16-April 9am-6pm. Admission 10F50, students 5F50.)

Nearby, the 10th-century **Chapelle St-Michel d'Aiguilhe** (tel. 04 71 09 50 03) crowns a narrow, 80m spike of volcanic rock. The rustic stained glass of this primitive edifice sheds little light on a fading 12th-century fresco and 10th-century woodcut crucifix discovered during excavations on the peak. Many begin the 1500km **Chemins de St-Jacques** pilgrimage here. (Open June 15-Sept. 15 9am-7pm; June 1-14 9am-noon and 2-7pm; Sept. 16-Nov. 12 9:30am-noon and 2-5:30pm; Dec. 21-Jan. 3 and Feb. 11-March 15 2-4pm; March 16-31 10am-noon and 2-5pm; April-May 10am-noon and 2-6pm; closed Jan. 4-Feb. 10. Admission 10F, children under 14 5F.)

At a less taxing altitude, the **Musée Crozatier** (tel. 04 71 09 38 90) can be reached by strolling through the **Jardin Henri Vinay** (which tucks away picnic spots and a tiny zoo). The elegant museum's three floors boast medieval carvings from the cathedral and cloisters; an assortment of archeological, mineral, and animal specimens from the area; pleasant paintings; and temporary exhibits. The second floor, devoted to local art and traditions, includes a display of Le Puy's needlework from the 16th through 20th centuries. At first glance, the glass cases of black lace resemble the storefront of a naughty lingerie shop. (Open May-Sept. Wed.-Mon. 10am-noon and 2-6pm; Oct.-April Mon. and Wed.-Sat. 10am-noon and 2-4pm, Sun. 2-4pm. Admission 12F, students 6F, free Oct.-April and Sun. afternoons.)

Though Le Puy's lacework began as a cottage industry, by the 16th century almost every woman in the region was employed at its creation. The Revolution's attack on bourgeois culture reduced demand for lace, and mechanical production at the turn of the century dealt another painful blow to the lacemakers' art. The **Centre d'Enseignement de la Dentelle,** 2, rue Duguesclin (tel. 04 71 02 01 68), was founded in 1976 to safeguard the techniques of an art in decline and to encourage its resurgence. The small museum exhibits lace from around the world, including some unusual contemporary work (open Mon.-Fri. 9-11:30am and 2-5:30pm).

Saturday is market day in Le Puy, and practically every square in town puts on its own show. From 6am to 12:30pm, farmers bring fruits, vegetables, cheeses, breads, jams, and honey. The one in pl. du Plot throws in a few live chickens, rabbits, and puppies. The adjacent **pl. du Clauzel** hosts an **antique market** (7:30am-1pm). Bargaining for the wares—World War II medals, pipe paraphernalia, and old silverware—is *de rigueur.* At **pl. du Breuil** the biggest spread of all includes new and used clothing, hardware, toiletries, and footwear.

In the third week of September, Le Puy goes Renaissance for the week-long **Fête du Roi de l'Oiseau** (tel 04 71 09 38 41), derived from the title bestowed annually on the town's champion *tireur* (archer) of the *papagaï* (parrot, in old French). Locals dress in costume, jugglers and minstrels ramble the streets, and food and drink in the *vieille ville* can be bought only with currency minted for the festival. A tunnel system carved centuries ago into the rock below the *vieille ville* is opened up and turned into one great party hall, with beer and wine flowing freely. (60F admission to nightly 9pm shows—more if you're not in costume; rentals available.)

Clermont-Ferrand

The Auvergne's capital has, well, a little trouble attracting tourists. The city (pop. 140,000) is an important rail hub and boasts the museums and theaters you expect in a regional capital, but its reputation is less than spotless. As headquarters of the Michelin tire empire and home to many smoke-spitting factories, Clermont is regarded by its neighbors as a soot-covered industrial landfill. This vision may be a bit dire: the buildings in downtown Clermont are black not from soot, but because they're made of volcanic stone. This lava rock, used to build the city's ominous cathedral, gives the *vieille ville* a unique look and surrounds Clermont with some of France's most spectacular natural wonders.

Clermont became an industrial giant quite by accident. A Mme. Daubrée, niece of the Scottish scientist Macintosh (whose experiments with rubber and benzene led to the invention of a jolly good rainproof coat), made some rubber balls to keep her children busy. The balls caught on, and in 1886 her relatives the Michelins used the rubber to make bicycle tires, kicking off the town's major industry. For most of this century, Clermont was Michelin. The economy revolved around tires, but recent financial trouble has resulted in cutbacks that have sent unemployment soaring.

You may tire quickly of Clermont, but if you're passing through, consider spending the night. Accommodations are right by the station, and a walk through the historical areas of town is a welcome change of pace for the imaginative tourist.

ORIENTATION AND PRACTICAL INFORMATION

Take bus 2, 4, or 14 (7F) from the station to lively **pl. de Jaude.** Bounded on either end by statues of local hero Général Desaix and the valiant Vercingetorix, the *place* is an expansive, tree-lined esplanade with cafés, a theater, and the modern **Centre Jaude,** a vast, slightly upscale shopping center. If you'd rather make the 20-minute walk, go left from the station onto av. de l'Union Soviétique, left again onto bd. Fleury, and take a quick right onto av. Carnot. The street bends to the left and turns into rue Maréchal Joffre for two blocks, then curves back right, turning into rue Maréchal Juin and then bd. Desaix before it dumps you onto pl. de Jaude. Get a map at the tourist office in the train station before you go.

Tourist Office: 69, bd. François Mitterrand (tel. 04 73 93 30 20). From pl. de Jaude, head down rue Gonod, which becomes bd. Charles de Gaulle, and bear left onto bd. Gergovia. Buses 2 and 4 go this way (get off at "Salins/Gare Routière"). Excellent map and bus timetables. Open June-Sept. Mon.-Sat. 8:30am-7pm, Sun. 9am-noon and 2-6pm; Oct.-May Mon.-Fri. 8:45am-6:30pm, Sat. 9am-noon and 2-6pm. **Branches** at the **train station** (tel. 04 73 91 87 89; open June-Sept. Mon.-Sat. 9:15-11:30am and 12:15-5pm; Oct.-May Mon.-Fri. 9:15-11:30am and 12:15-5pm) and **pl. de Jaude** (tel. 04 73 93 24 44; open July-Aug. Mon.-Sat. 8:30am-7pm, Sun. 9am-noon and 2-6pm; Sept. and June Mon.-Sat. 9am-noon and 2-6pm).

Budget Travel: Wasteels, 69, bd. Trudaine (tel. 04 73 91 07 00), sells BIJ tickets at the end of long lines. Open Mon.-Sat. 9am-noon and 2-7pm, Sat. closes at 6pm.

Trains: av. de l'Union Soviétique (tel. 08 36 35 35 35). To: Paris (7 per day, 3hr., 230F); Lyon (14 per day, 3hr., 145F); Bordeaux (5 per day, 6hr., 260F); Le Puy (5 per day, 2½hr., 106F). **Lockers** 15-30F per 72hr. (inaccessible 10:30pm-5:30am). Info office open Mon.-Sat. 8am-7:30pm; ticket window daily 5:30am-7:30pm. In the station, **SOS Voyageurs** (tel. 04 73 30 12 79) helps travelers.

Buses: *Gare routière,* 69, bd. F. Mitterrand (tel. 04 73 93 13 61). Behind the main tourist office. Buses throughout the Massif Central, including Le Puy (2 per day, 3¼hr., 63F). Office open Mon.-Sat. 8:30am-6:30pm. **Luggage storage** 5F per day.

Public Transportation: 15-17, bd. Robert Schumann (tel. 04 73 26 44 90). Buses blanket the city. Ticket 7F, day passes 22F. Service runs 5:30am-11pm.

Taxis: Taxi Radio (tel. 04 73 19 53 53). Open 24hr.

English Books: Book'in, 38, av. des Etats-Unis (tel. 04 73 36 40 06), has a tiny selection of mostly used books (classics and lurid novels) in the back. Open Mon. 2-7pm, Tues.-Sun. 10am-noon and 2-7pm, Fri.-Sat. 10am-7pm.

Youth Centers: Espace Info Jeunes, 5, av. St-Genès (tel. 04 73 92 30 50). Open Mon.-Fri. 10am-6pm, Sat. 10am-1pm and 2-6pm. The **Fédération International des Auberges des Jeunesse** office, 14, rue du Port (tel. 04 73 91 48 56; fax 04 73 92 82 44), has info on youth hostels and international travel and sells BIJ tickets. Open Mon. and Sat. 11am-7pm, Tues.-Fri. 10am-7pm.

Laundromat: Laverie Automatique, pl. Renoux. Wash 5kg for 16F. Detergent 2F. Dry 2F per 5min. Open 7am-8pm. Also at 62, av. Charras.

Crisis Line: SOS Amitié (tel. 04 73 37 37 37), 24-hr. friendship line.

Hospital: Hôpital Gabriel-Montpied, 30, pl. Henri Dunant (04 73 62 57 00). **SOS Médecins:** 2, bd. Côte-Bladin (tel. 04 73 92 12 12). **Medical emergency** tel. 15.

Police: 2, rue Pélissier (tel. 04 73 98 42 42). **Emergency** tel. 17.

Post Office: 1, rue Louis Renon (tel. 04 73 30 63 00). **Branch office** at pl. Galliard (tel. 04 73 31 70 00). Both have poste restante (specify main branch's postal code: 63033 Cedex 1) and **currency exchange.** Both open Mon.-Fri. 8am-7pm, Sat. 8am-noon. **Postal code:** 63000 for the main office, 63100 for the branch.

ACCOMMODATIONS AND CAMPING

Plenty of decent, inexpensive hotels cluster conveniently near the train station. Finding a cheap room in the center of town can be more challenging. Use the tourist office's *Guide Practique* to find other *foyer* accommodations.

Auberge de Jeunesse "Cheval Blanc" (HI), 55, av. de l'Union Soviétique (tel. 04 73 92 26 39; fax 04 73 92 99 96). Across the street and to the right of the train station. The "international" atmosphere created by the worldly clientele, the Kuwaiti proprietor, and the cream-colored stucco and red-tile arched façade is only enhanced by the Turkish toilets. Bunks for 2-8 people. Kitchen facilities. Members preferred. 58F, breakfast included. Sheets 16F. Lockout 9:30am-5pm. Curfew 10:30pm. Open March-Oct. Reception 7-9:30am and 5-11pm.

Foyer St-Jean/Auberge de Jeunesse (HI), 17, rue Gauthier de Béauzat (tel. 04 73 31 57 00; fax 04 73 31 59 99), off pl. Gaillard. From the station, take bus 2 or 4 to "Gaillard." Modern complex holds well-furnished rooms (some with private bathrooms), a bar, tennis courts, and laundry facilities. Great location near the *vieille ville.* Singles, doubles, or triples 80F per person, non-members 90F. Sheets and breakfast included. Meals 40F. Often full; call ahead. Reception open 9am-7pm.

Hôtel Parisiene, 78 av. Charras (tel. 04 73 92 54 32). 7 rooms, singles 75-100F, doubles 85-100F, with shower 115F. 2 beds, 2 people, 120F. Call ahead.

Hôtel d'Aigueperse, 4, rue Aigueperse (tel. 04 73 91 30 62), near the station off av. Albert et Elizabeth. Spacious, flowery rooms, some in disrepair. Affable proprietor. Still more Turkish toilets. Singles 88F. Doubles 98F, with shower 124F, with 2 beds 196F. Shower 10F. Breakfast 17F50. 24-hr. reception.

Camping: Le Chancet, av. Jean-Baptiste Marrou (tel. 04 73 61 30 73). From the station, take bus 4 to "Préguille." 3-star campground has volleyball, game room, and laundry facilities. Package prices. 2 people, 1 vehicle, 1 tent, 51F. 1 person, 1 tent, 31F, with vehicle 38F. Electricity 17F.

FOOD

The area around **rue St-Dominique,** off av. des Etats-Unis, has dozens of ethnic eateries, while the narrow streets behind the cathedral (especially **rue des Chaussetiers**) specialize in local cuisine. The **Nouvelle Galleries** on the east side of pl. Jaude shelters an inexpensive **supermarket** (open Mon.-Sat. 8:30am-7pm). For local fruits, veggies, and cheeses head to the **Marché St-Pierre,** off pl. Gaillard, a huge **covered market** with hundreds of *auvergnat* specialities (Mon.-Sat. 6am-7pm).

Au Bon Pinard/Mme. Griffet, 7, rue des Petits Gras (tel. 04 73 36 40 95). On the second floor of a plain-looking building in the *vieille ville.* Every day Mme. Griffet sends her husband to the markets to buy fresh ingredients then cooks up a 58F lunch *menu* renowned throughout the city for quantity and quality. *Auvergnat* specialties change according to what M. Griffet brings back. Open noon-2pm.

Maiko, 65, rue du Port (tel. 04 73 90 79 15). An origami version of the Puy-de-Dome greets customers in this charming Japanese restaurant. Tempura 40F. Lunch *menu* with miso soup, salad, and grilled fish 50F. Dinner *menus* start at 70F. Open Mon.-Sat. noon-2pm and 7:30-10:30pm.

Le Relais Pascal, 15, rue Pascal (tel. 04 73 92 21 04). Dozens of *auvergnat* dishes and a selection of over 100 wines. 85F *menu* includes *assiette auvergnate* (local meats), *tripaux* (tripe!), cheese, and dessert. 55F lunch *menu* changes daily. Call at least 2 days in advance to order *Coq au vin* or *potage auvergnac.* Also holds occasional *dégustations.* Open Tues.-Sat. 8:30am-10pm.

1513, 3, rue des Chaussetiers (tel. 04 73 92 37 46). Travel back in time and dine in the enchanting garden or the candlelit cavern, both built in 1513. 55F lunch *menu* features crêpes and wine or cider. Open 11:30am-1:30am. V, MC, AmEx.

SIGHTS

Some believe that Clermont-Ferrand occupies the site of ancient Gergovia, where Vercingetorix defeated Julius Caesar. Although the site of the ancient **oppidum** of Gergovia lies not far from Clermont-Ferrand, an intellectual battle still rages as to whether the great battle actually took place on ground now occupied by the city.

Clermont-Ferrand was once two separate cities, Clermont and Montferrand, intense economic and political rivals in the 16th century who merged in 1630, signaling Clermont's victory. Montferrand, a 40-minute walk away, is often forgotten; many locals simply call their city Clermont. The *vieille ville* of Clermont, called the **Ville Noire** (Black City), is one of the most fascinating old town districts in France. The buildings are made of black volvic stone, or hardened lava rock. Contrasting with the bright red roofs, the dark streets and houses in Vieux Clermont are wonderful for strolling. Follow rue du Port to the Romanesque 12th-century **Basilique de Notre-Dame-du-Port.** On sunny afternoons, simple stained glass windows project a rainbow onto the church's somber stones (open 8am-7pm). Built between 1248 and 1287, the Gothic **Cathédrale Notre-Dame de l'Assomption,** pl. de la Victoire, commands attention with its majestic black volcanic stone. The strength of this lava-based material allowed the architects to elongate the graceful spires to a height of 100m. The cathedral is spectacular when viewed from a distance, its black spikes piercing a sea of red tile roofs. Up close it looks like a nocturnal predator. The three rose windows and the 13th-century *vitraux* in the chapels behind the altar are magnificent. A free guided tour of the windows (in French) is given several times a week from mid-June to mid-September (schedules at tourist office or inside cathedral; open Mon.-Fri. 8am-noon and 2-6pm, Sat. 9:30am-noon and 3-7pm).

Clermont-Ferrand has four museums—three in Clermont and one in Montferrand. For 21F you can buy a ticket that will get you into any two of them. The **Musée Bargoin,** 45, rue Ballainvilliers (tel. 04 73 91 37 31), is undoubtedly the most interesting. Devoted to prehistoric and Gallo-Roman archaeology, the museum displays artifacts recovered from the Temple of Mercury on the Puy de Dôme, as well as Pompeiian wall paintings (some adorned with Roman graffiti), 2000-year-old hair braids, mummified infants, and wooden votive offerings (open Tues.-Sun. 10am-6pm; admission 22F, students 12F). In the same building (included in admission price), the **Musée du Tapis d'Art** lays out a beautiful collection of Persian rugs (open Tues.-Sun. 10am-6pm). One block away, the **Musée Lecoq,** 15, rue Bardoux (tel. 04 73 91 93 78), is devoted to the botany, zoology, mineralogy, and geology of the Auvergne (open Tues.-Sat. 10am-noon and 2-5pm, Sun. 2-5pm. Same rates as Musée Bargoin). The **Musée du Ranquet,** 34, rue des Gras (tel. 04 73 37 38 63), records the last two centuries of Clermont-Ferrand's existence but may have you bouncing off the walls (admission 12F; same hours as Musée Bargoin). Take a break from the museums in the nearby **Jardin Lecoq,** with winding shady paths, a flower garden, an artificial lake, and a couple of *phoques*—seals, that is—for good measure.

The medieval houses of **Vieux Montferrand** are 40 minutes away up av. de la République, but buses 17 (direction: Blanzat or Cébazat) or 10M (direction: Aulnat) will whisk you there quickly from the *gare.* Like Clermont, Montferrand is dominated by a (less magnificent) volcanic stone church. **Notre-Dame-de-Prospérité** stands on the site of the long-demolished château of the *auvergnat* counts. For a more secular sight, take a look at the full moon on the 15th-century carvings on the **Maison de l'Apothicaire,** on the corner of rue de Cordeliers and rue de la Rodade. Having served as everything from nunnery to police headquarters, the 18th-century convent on rue du Seminaire now acts as the region's **Musée des Beaux-Arts,** (tel. 04 73 23 08 49).

This old dog has learned its new trick remarkably well. The modern structure in traditional stone leads you through 14 centuries, encompassing relics, sculpted capitals, and a wide range of surprisingly impressive works from the last 500 years (open Tues.-Sun. 10am-6pm; admission 22F, students 12F).

ENTERTAINMENT

Clermont's students complain that the city's nightlife is sluggish, but they struggle valiantly to start it up at a few popular nightspots. Foos while you booze at **Le Clown,** 65bis, rue Anatole France (tel. 04 73 92 17 75), a small, friendly bar behind the train station (beer 10-14F; open Mon. 6pm-1am, Tues.-Thurs. and Sun. 8am-1am, Fri.-Sat. 8am-2am). **Le Palais de la Bière,** 3, rue de la Michodière (tel. 04 73 37 15 51), on the corner of pl. Galliard and av. des Etats-Unis, has less ambience but more room, with exotic beers and *brasserie* fare to boot (open Mon.-Fri. noon-2pm and 7pm-1am, Fri. until 2am, Sat.-Sun. 8pm-2am). **Club l'Arlequin,** 2, rue d'Etoile (tel. 04 73 37 33 88), off av. des Etats-Unis, strives to be an exclusive club in an inclusive city (drinks 30-40F; open Tues.-Sun. midnight-4am; cover and first drink Sun. and Tues.-Thurs. 50F, Fri.-Sat. 60F; no sneakers). If Arlequin won't take you, the sports bar **Blue Sport Café** down the street most certainly will. If an exclusively male atmosphere is your style, **L'Exclusif,** 14, rue des Petits Gras, has plenty, with drag shows every Thursday (cover 50F, drinks 40F; open Mon.-Tues. and Thurs.-Sun.).

The first week in February, filmmakers from all over Europe gather for Clermont-Ferrand's annual **Festival International du Court Métrage** (International Festival of Short Films), considered the "Cannes du Court" (tickets 26-40F per night). For info, contact Sauve Qui Peut le Court Métrage, 26, rue des Jacobins, 63000 Clermont-Ferrand (tel. 04 73 91 65 73; fax 04 73 92 11 93).

■ Near Clermont-Ferrand: Puy de Dôme

Clermont-Ferrand's greatest attraction is its proximity to an extinct volcanic hinterland filled with crystal-clear lakes and pristine mountain villages. Although difficult to reach without wheels of some sort, the **Parc Naturel Régional des Volcans d'Auvergne** (Auvergne Volcano Natural Park; tel. 04 73 62 21 45 or 04 73 65 64 00), west of Clermont-Ferrand, rewards hikers, bikers, and skiers with France's longest stretches of unspoiled and strictly protected terrain. France's largest regional natural park was founded in 1967 to save the local scenery from industrial development and to preserve cottage industry and agriculture. Historical monuments in the park, including medieval castles built from volcanic stone and churches in the local Romanesque style, have been restored. A booklet available at the Clermont-Ferrand tourist office marks and catalogues hiking paths. The protected area includes three main sections—the **Monts Dore,** the **Monts du Cantal,** and the **Monts Dômes**—the last of which is the best place to explore the many extinct volcanoes.

From the top of the massive, flat-topped **Puy de Dôme** (1465m), you can see across the Chaîne des Puys, encompassing an eighth of France. If you scale the Dôme in the fall (especially November) you may behold the wondrous *mer de nuages* (sea of clouds): a blanket of clouds obscures the plains below, and only isolated mountain peaks protrude into the clear blue sky. In 1989, to celebrate the bicentennial of the ideals of the 1789 revolution, Puy de Dôme was renamed Mount Fraternité. For a month, beams of laser light and the signal "Fraternité" shone from the summit to the delight of the excited masses below. Today, even on hazy days, the mountain remains impressive for the beauty of its terrain, the ruins of a Roman temple on the summit, and the paragliders whisking by its steep sides.

Although the Puy de Dôme lies only 12km from Clermont-Ferrand, reaching it takes planning. Occasional excursion buses make the ascent for steep prices (69F); contact the tourist office. Otherwise, head out of town on av. du Puy de Dôme and follow the signs for about 8km to the base of the mountain. Head up the road until you're halfway around the mountain, and then follow the *sentier des muletiers,* a Roman footpath that leads to the top in about 40 minutes. Get a good weather forecast for the day, as conditions change rapidly—hailstorms on the summit are not uncommon, even in June. Hitching from the town to the base of the Dôme is reportedly easy, though never completely safe. In summer, drivers must leave their cars at the base and take a bus (18F roundtrip); otherwise, the toll is 12F. At the peak, the **Centre d'Acceuil de Puy de Dôme** (tel. 04 73 62 21 45) has informative displays and leads free guided tours of the summit every 45 minutes (open July-Aug. 9am-8pm; June and Sept. 9am-7pm; April 20-May 10am-6pm).

The **Comité Départemental de Tourisme du Puy de Dôme,** 26, rue St-Esprit (tel. 04 73 42 21 23 in Clermont-Ferrand), has reams of pamphlets on the area. The office also sells its colorful *Puy-de-Dôme* guide (50F) with historical and cultural info on the area's towns (open Mon.-Thurs. 8:30am-12:15pm and 1:45-5:30pm, Fri. 8:30am-12:15pm and 1:45-5pm). **Chamina Sylva,** 24, av. Edouard Michelin (tel. 04 73 90 94 82 or 04 73 92 81 44), also in Clermont, sells maps and suggests hiking and climbing excursions (open Mon.-Fri. 9am-1pm and 2-6pm). The tourist office will also provide you with mountains of info on how to access the Puy de Dôme.

Riom

Declared the capital of the Auvergne in 1256, Riom thrived as an economic crossroads and political center until Louis XIV decided he preferred Clermont. The king's whim was to become the town's blessing. The only thing Riom rises above today is a valley of patchwork countryside, but its ancient wealth, apparent in its *hôtels particuliers* (mansions), still graces the town, untainted by heavy industry and passed over by enemy bombs. It's difficult to fill an action-packed day in Riom. Try instead to spend a leisurely afternoon in the town's museums, churches, and fountain-filled streets paved black with volcanic stone and lined with ancient red-tiled homes.

PRACTICAL INFORMATION

Despite its small size, Riom sees lots of **train** traffic from the busy Paris-Clermont-Ferrand line. Dozens of dailies connect Riom with Clermont-Ferrand (10min., 17F) and Vichy (25min., 40F). The station (tel. 04 73 30 18 95) info desk is open 6am-7:30pm, Sunday 10am-9pm. **Lockers** are 20F. To reach the *vieille ville* and tourist office from the station, head straight out on av. Virlogeux, bear right along the side of the park, and cross bd. Desaix. Continue straight onto rue du Marthuret and turn right onto rue du Commerce just after Eglise Notre-Dame-du-Mathuret (10min.). The **tourist office,** 16, rue du Commerce (tel. 04 73 38 59 45; fax 04 73 38 25 15), distributes a free town map and has a free reservations service (open June-Sept. daily 9am-6:30pm; Oct.-May Wed.-Mon. 9am-noon and 2-6:30pm). There is a 24-hour **ATM** at **BNP,** next to the Musée Mandet on rue de l'Hôtel de Ville. The *gare routière* in Clermont-Ferrand (tel. 04 73 63 28 22) is the closest bus station. In a **medical emergency,** dial 15 or 04 73 27 33 33. The **Centre Hospitalier "Guy Thomas"** (tel. 04 73 63 28 28) is located at 79, bd. Clémentel. The **police** are at 20, av. Virlogeux (tel. 73 33 43 63; **emergency** tel. 17 or 04 73 38 24 20). The **post office,** 25, rue Croisier (tel. 04 73 33 73 73), has a decent **currency exchange, ATM,** and poste restante (open Mon.-Fri. 8am-7pm, Sat. 8am-noon; **postal code:** 63200).

ACCOMMODATIONS, CAMPING, AND FOOD

Expensive hotels and the 10-minute train ride to Clermont-Ferrand make Riom a good daytrip. One option, the **Grand Hotel Desaix,** 1, pl. des Martyrs de la Résistance (tel. 04 73 38 20 36), offers clean, comfortable rooms, some with a fireplace. (Singles 95F, with shower 120-140F. Doubles with shower and toilet 150F. Triples with shower and toilet 180F. Quads with shower and toilet 200F. Extra bed 20F. Breakfast 20F. 24-hr. reception. V, MC, AmEx.) Its dining room handles the problem of affordable dining with a 49F *menu du jour.* Four km from Riom on route de la Piscine, rough it in style at **Clos de Balanede** (tel. 04 73 86 02 47), **campsites** with the whole kit and kaboodle—grocery store, snack bar, tennis courts, pool, and laundry. (19F per person, 15F per site, 7F per vehicle. Electricity 12F. Reception June-Sept. 9am-noon and 2-6pm; April 10-May and Oct. 1-7 8am-10pm.)

Your best cut-rate culinary choices are a picnic in the park or a pizza on rue Croisier. Get your baguette, tomato, and cheese at the **Economia supermarket** on 16, rue de l'Hôtel de Ville (open Tues.-Sun. 7am-12:30pm and 2:30-6:30pm). For a much wider selection of baguettes, tomatoes, and cheeses, head to the mammoth **Stoc supermarket.** Make a left out of the station and go under the tracks. Look to your right—*le voilà!* (Open Mon.-Sat. 9am-7:30pm, Sun. 9am-noon.) If you fear capitalistic monoliths, seek refuge at the **market** Wednesday and Saturday mornings on pl. de la Fédération. **Le Banmé,** 52, rue Gomot (tel. 04 73 38 42 36), has Vietnamese delights on their 45F lunch *menu* (open Mon. 7-11pm, Tues.-Sun. noon-2pm and 7-11pm). Just down the block, **Le Pescajoux,** 49, rue Gomot (tel. 04 73 63 03 67), has a 50F *menu* with crêpes, *kir,* and *café* (open daily noon-2pm and 7-10pm; V, MC).

SIGHTS AND ENTERTAINMENT

The austere **Eglise Notre-Dame-du-Marthuret,** 44, rue du Commerce, shelters the moving 14th-century **Vierge à l'Oiseau,** recognized as one of the Middle Ages' most beautiful statues. Long believed to be one of the Auvergne's enigmatic *Vièrges Noires,* the figure was revealed to be a fully painted Virgin and child after a good scrubbing in 1991 removed a layer of soot. Across town stands the **Ste-Chapelle,** the only remaining vestige of the **Palais de Justice,** built in the 14th century by Jean de Berry. The Duke brought prestige to Riom, although he wasn't popular with the locals. In this chapel, de Berry, then 60, married an *auvergnate* girl 48 years his junior. The obligatory guided tour includes the opportunity to sit in the intricate 19th-century choir stalls used by clergy, nobility, and judges (July-Aug. daily every 30min. 2:30-5pm; Sept.-May by appointment only; admission 15F, students 10F). You can get into the Ste-Chapelle, clock tower, and both museums plus get a guided tour of the city by buying the **city passport** for 45F (students 25F).

Riom's two museums are well worth visiting. The handsomely renovated **Musée Mandet,** 4, rue de l'Hôtel de Ville (tel. 04 73 38 18 53), housed in adjacent 16th- and 18th-century *hôtels particuliers,* preserves a delightful collection of Gallo-Roman bronzes, pottery, and jewelry, early French and Flemish paintings and sculpture, and a battalion of swords and armor. The **Musée Régionale Folklorique d'Auvergne,** 10bis, rue Delille (tel. 04 73 38 17 31), shelters an interesting collection of local crafts, costumes, and musical instruments. (Open Wed.-Mon. June-Sept. 10am-noon and 2:30-6pm; Oct.-May 10am-noon and 2-5:30pm. Admission 18F, students 10F; both museums 25F; free Wed. English pamphlet available.)

After the museums, stroll down the streets of the *vieille ville* by the Renaissance mansions. One of the most impressive, the **Maison des Consuls,** rue de l'Hôtel de Ville, sports five arcades, a row of busts of women and Roman emperors glaring down from above the first-story windows, and a variety of shops. The nearby **Hôtel Guimoneau,** 12, rue de l'Horloge, hides a beautiful 16th-century courtyard and an ornately sculpted stairway. It's a private home, but don't be shy—peek inside the courtyard. Busts of Monsieur and Madame Guimoneau smile approvingly on your nosiness from above. An adjoining wall displays carvings representing Strength, Justice, dear Prudence, and Temperance. Across the street, the **Tour de l'Horloge** lords over a dazzling panorama of red Riom rooftops melting into the greenery of the Monts Dômes nearby. In 1646, during a great hurricane, the bell tower fell into a neighboring courtyard. The house's owner was so pleased with the new addition that he refused to return it and had to be brought to court (open May-Sept. Tues. and Sat.-Sun. 2-6:30pm, Wed.-Fri. 10am-noon and 2-6:30pm; admission 5F).

Harkening back to days of old, artisans strut their stuff in a parade in early June when Riom thanks its amiable saint for saving the village in the **Fête de la Ste-Amable.** Every year in June (sometimes spilling over into July), ivory-tweakers traipse to the week-long festival **Piano à Riom** (tel. 04 73 38 97 78; tickets 50-150F, under 25 35-50% discount). The **Festival de Jazz** (tel. 04 73 38 01 13) bops into town early in

September (tickets around 60F). The markets and music on rue de l'Horloge also provide potential for entertainment.

Vichy

A summer day in downtown Vichy is not much different now from a hundred years ago. In the morning wealthy Parisians emerge from their hotel rooms to sip from the famous springs *(sources)* that supposedly restore youth (or at least the digestive system). At noon they lunch at posh cafés, then spend the afternoon hours strolling through Vichy's manicured parks. By evening they're dressed for the opera or for informal concerts in the gardens. With this abundance of understated elegance, you'll think you've slipped back into a bygone era, a Gatsby-esque world of wealth and pleasant lethargy.

The haze of this past grandeur is intentional. Vichy moors itself in the days when its history recorded little other than the comings and goings of Napoleon III because more recent events are too painful to recall. From 1940 through 1944, sedate Vichy was the capital of France. Forced by the occupying German forces to leave Paris, the French government set up shop in this central spa town, with its emptied hotels and extensive rail connections.

In the famed opera house, the Parliament convened on July 9 and 10, 1940 to decide the fate of the Third Republic: 569 of the 649 members voted to abolish it and elected Maréchal Phillipe Pétain to lead the new state. Although under constant pressure from Hitler and the Germans' northern French government, the Vichy regime was independent of Berlin. Nationwide approval of Pétain's policies buttressed Germany's position in France until the Allies' victory in 1944 (see page 66).

Vichy is the constant reminder of the country's darkest days this century. The city itself chooses to ignore the episode. There is not a single monument, museum, or plaque acknowledging Vichy's role in World War II. Stroll through the town today and you'll be seduced by its flowery gardens and quiet elegance—the beauty of Vichy's Belle Epoque.

ORIENTATION AND PRACTICAL INFORMATION

Vichy's **tourist office,** 19, rue du Parc (tel. 04 70 98 71 94), as well as the most popular *sources,* lie in the **Parc des Sources,** about 10 minutes from the train station. Leaving the station, walk straight on rue de Paris; at the fork take a left onto rue Georges Clemenceau and then a quick right onto the pedestrian rue Sornin. The tourist office is straight ahead across the park, in the former Hôtel du Parc that housed the nucleus of the Pétain leadership. It distributes a good, free map and a list of Vichy's countless hotels and restaurants and will help find rooms for no charge. In addition, it gives out a comprehensive booklet of suggested walking and car tours in Vichy and the region. The only way to see Pétain's Vichy is to take a French guided tour from the office. Significant buildings of the World War II era are not marked, so you won't notice anything walking around by yourself (tours leave June-Sept. Tues. at 3pm; July-Aug. additional tour Thurs. at 3pm; 25F). Find out about operas, concerts, discos, and special events in town with the free **Vichy Quinzaine.** The office's **currency exchange** has poor rates and operates on weekends only (office open July-Aug. Mon.-Sat. 9am-7:30pm, Sun. 9:30am-12:30pm and 3-7pm; Sept.-June Mon.-Sat. 9am-noon and 2-6pm). There are 24-hour **ATMs** in the train station, on rue de Paris, and luckily or not, in the casino.

The **train station,** pl. de la Gare (tel. 04 70 97 21 00), is on the busy Clermont-Ferrand-Paris line. Trains to: Clermont-Ferrand (24 per day, 30min., 47F); Riom (24 per day, 25min., 39F); and Paris (6 per day, 3hr., 203F). Info office open Monday to Saturday 9am-6:20pm, Sunday 9am-noon and 2-6:20pm. **Lockers** cost 15-30F per 72 hours, but there's no access 10pm-6am. **Buses** for the surrounding region leave from the *gare routière* (next to the train station; office open Mon.-Fri. 8am-noon and 2-6pm). **Public buses** (5F) run to such distant places as the campground, but Vichy is generally walkable. The buses don't go to the Centre Omnisports. Pick up a schedule at the tourist office. **Rent bikes** at **Chalet des Suppliques,** Parc Napoleon III, av. Aristide Briand at the bridge (tel. 04 70 97 04 78). City bikes 50F per ½-day, 65F per day, 110F per weekend. Mountain bikes 70F, 90F, and 160F. ID, cash, or credit card deposit required. In a **medical emergency,** dial 15. The **Centre Hospitalier** (tel. 04 70 97 33 33) is on bd. Denière. The **police** are at 35, av. Victoria (tel. 04 70 98 60 03; **emergency** tel. 17). The **post office,** pl. Charles de Gaulle (tel. 04 70 30 10 75), has poste restante, an **ATM,** and **currency exchange** with competitive rates (open Mon.-Fri. 8am-7pm, Sat. 8am-noon; **postal code:** 03200).

ACCOMMODATIONS, CAMPING, AND FOOD

In keeping with Vichy's mission to pamper, even its two **hostels** are *de luxe.* The **Villa Claudius Petit,** 76, av. des Célestins (tel. 04 70 98 43 39), offers ultra-modern singles for 75F. Each room has a great bed, bathroom, refrigerator, stove, and sink. There's a TV room, laundry facilities, and a pleasant outdoor atrium. Sheets are included and breakfast costs 10F (reception Mon.-Fri. 9am-noon and 2-6pm, Sat.-Sun. 3-9pm). The same folks run the **Villa d'Europe,** 33, rue de Paris (tel. 04 70 97 41 49). Singles are 68F and include similar amenities but have a communal kitchen (reception Thurs. 4-7pm and Sat.-Sun. 3-9pm; other times calls transferred to Villa Claudius; breakfast 5-10F). The cheapest place in town is the **Centre International de Sejour,** B.P. 2617 (tel. 04 70 59 51 00; fax 04 70 32 27 09), in the Omnisports complex (see below). It's a 45-minute walk from town, but it's only 45F (singles 58F). For the sluggish, the Centre has a TV room, laundry facilities, and two- to four-bed rooms (all rooms have private showers; sheets included; breakfast 19F; other meals 51F; reception open daily 8am-6am).

Hôtel d'Iena, 56, bd. John Kennedy (tel. 04 70 32 01 20), has small, comfy rooms right by the Parc d'Allier. Flash (the dog) and the friendly staff will help you forget why hotel chains were ever invented. (Singles 105F, with shower 130F. Doubles with shower and toilet 160F. Triples 180F. Quads 210F. Showers 10F. Breakfast 23F. V, MC.) **Hôtel du Rhône** lies between the train station and the *thermes* at 8, rue de Paris (tel. 04 70 97 73 00; fax 04 70 97 48 25), offering delightful doubles and triples with comfy beds. Rooms with TV and shower are 150F; deluxe rooms with full bath are 220F (extra bed 40F; breakfast buffet 35F, breakfast 15-25F). The restaurant downstairs offers regional specialties for 39-80F (open Easter-Oct.; V, MC, AmEx).

The **Camping Municipal,** 61, rue du Stade (tel. 04 70 32 30 11), is the nearest of several campgrounds along the river (13F50 per person, 3F70 per tent, 3F20 per car; electricity 12F50; open April-Oct.; reception 7am-10pm). Take bus 4 (direction: Chantemerle) from the train station (2 per hr., 6:30am-7:45pm, 6F) and get off after the bridge; cross the street and head straight toward the "Le Bellerive" sign atop the high-rise apartment. Continue along the lamp-lined pavement onto rue du Stade. The tourist office has a list of campgrounds, many farther away with better views.

Restaurants in Vichy are usually expensive; most are connected to hotels. Bars and pubs abound on **rue de Paris,** and legend has it that mysterious golden arches have been spotted along this street. If you venture into a restaurant, stick to basics. The pizzas and pastas (37-52F) are super at **L'Alligator,** 1, quai d'Allier (tel. 04 70 98 30 47), in the park. The pleasant riverside eatery also offers ice cream and liqueur concoctions (36F). There's dancing to an accordion band every Sunday after 5pm (open April 16-Sept. daily 10am-1am, meals served noon-2pm and 7-10pm; V, MC). Take a break from tasting Vichy's waters to try the tasty *tartines* at another *source*—**Barau vins,** 10, rue du Casino (tel. 04 70 59 85 68). The *Gaspard* has *jambon cru* nestled under layers of St-Nectare (30F). They also have salads and desserts (20F). (Open Tues.-Sat. noon-2pm and 7pm-1am. AmEx.) Right next to Hôtel d'Iena, **Les Parcs et l'Apéro,** 58, bd. John Kennedy (tel. 04 70 32 57 91), serves up French favorites on its 55F, 75F (vegetarian), 85F (4-course), and 115F *menus.* Pastas go for 32-48F. Compose your own summer salad special from their varied list of ingredients for 38F (open July-Sept. 14 daily noon-2pm and 7-10pm; Sept. 15-June Tues.-Sat. noon-2pm and 7-10pm, Sun. noon-2pm). To break bread in Vichy's superb parks, head to **Prisu-**

nic, av. Clemenceau and rue Ravy-Bretent (open Mon.-Sat. 8:30am-7:30pm, Sun. 9:30am-12:30pm and 3-7pm). A large **covered market** springs forth Tuesday through Sunday mornings in pl. Léger at the intersection of rue Jean Jaurès and bd. Gambetta (surely an historic meeting); regional farmers have their day in the sun on Saturdays.

SIGHTS AND ENTERTAINMENT

Take a sip of Vichy's nectar, and you'll wonder how the town ever made it big—the water is disgusting. The heart of the action for the ailing is the glass and white wrought-iron **Halle des Sources** (tel. 04 70 97 39 59) at the edge of the Parc des Sources where most of the *curistes* go each morning to take a dose of lukewarm, carbonate-charged water. Anyone can drink from the *sources* for 9F (plus 1F for a cup; open daily 6:15am-8:30pm). If you go, take small swigs—it looks like plain water, but it's powerful stuff. Start with the cold springs. *Célestins* is easiest to digest but tastes like Alka-Seltzer. *Parc* will give you the runs, and *Lucas* smells like rotten eggs. Still thirsty? The hot springs are even more vile. *Chomel* is the most popular because there aren't (many) side-effects. *Grand Grille* is the strongest—don't drink it unless you want to spend the next day cooling your heels on porcelain. Wait out your stomach cramps in the beautiful **Parc des Sources.** Surrounded by a wrought-iron gallery, ornate lampposts, and the opera house, it's Vichy elegance at its height.

The *sources* bubble free of charge at the **Sources des Célestins** on bd. Kennedy, a cold spring, and in the rotunda of the **Source d'Hôpital** (behind the casino), where you can slurp from a genuinely nauseating hot spring—give thanks to the *Let's Go* researcher who tested this for you, and stay away.

A wide array of flora and fauna romp within the verdant confines of the English-style gardens in the elegant riverside **Parcs de l'Allier,** commissioned by Napoleon III. For those who already have their health, Vichy's ultimate recreational facility lies across the river and a brisk 20- to 25-minute walk along the promenade to the right of pont de Bellerive. The sprawling **Centre Omnisports** (tel. 04 70 59 51 00) offers sailing, wind-surfing, archery, canoeing, kayaking, rafting, tennis, swimming, and mountain biking (open daily 9am-noon and 2-6pm). Do it all by buying the **Pass'sport** (100F per day, 50F per ½-day, and 500F per week). Waterskiing and rowing cost extra. Get your Pass'sport at the tourist office or at the reception in the Centre Omnisports (info office open daily 8:30am-noon and 2-5pm; bring a photo ID).

Cheap (possibly) thrills are at the **Grand Casino** in the Parc des Sources. Some of the slot machines accept 1F bets (open daily noon-4am). For more refined entertainment, attend an organ concert in the **Eglise St-Louis,** rue Clemenceau (tickets 80F, students 60F). Six operas ring during the summer in the beautiful **Opera House** at 1, rue du Casino. The ticket office for both opera and organ concerts (tel. 04 70 30 50 30 for reservations and info) is on the side of the opera house, on rue du Parc (tickets 110-190F, under 25 80-160F).

■ Le Mont Dore

Le Mont Dore wedges itself among a sleepy chain of volcanoes in the heart of the Massif Central. The mountains cannot approach the majesty of the Alps or the Pyrénées, but the odd rock phenomena, craggy peaks and ridges, and deep craters connect with an unexpected, unique grace. Elephants, rhinoceri, and tigers once roamed bamboo forests in the region, and their fossils remain encrusted in volcanic rock. The lava cooled, millions of years flowed by, and in the 18th century a spa community sprung up around Le Mont Dore. Pine trees and lush meadows now cover the slopes, populated with *curistes* who seek relief from asthma and rheumatism in the warm waters that seep up through cracks in the lava. In the winter, skiers flock to **Puy de Sancy** (1886m) on the southern tip of town, the highest peak in the Auvergne. When the snow melts the *pistes* give way to trails, and hikers have their chance at this rugged, bizarre, and beautiful region.

PRACTICAL INFORMATION

From the train station, head up av. Michel Bertrand and follow the signs to the **tourist office,** av. de la Libération (tel. 04 73 65 20 21; fax 04 73 65 05 71), which distributes free maps and organizes hikes and bike circuits (50F). It **exchanges currency** without commission on weekends, when banks are closed (open July-Aug. Mon.-Sat. 9am-12:30pm and 2-6:30pm, Sun. 10am-noon and 4-6:30pm; May-June and Sept. closes at 6pm on Sun.; Oct.-April closed Sun.). The town's lonely 24-hour **ATM** is at **Crédit Agricole,** on the corner of rue Meynadier and rue du Capitaine Chazotte at pl. de Gaulle. Expect long lines. The **train station** (tel. 04 73 65 00 02) is at pl. de la Gare (info desk open daily 6am-12:30pm and 2-9:30pm). Trains to Clermont-Ferrand (5 per day, 1½hr., 62F) and Paris (2 per day, 5hr., 261F). Rent **bikes** at **Bessac Sports,** rue de Maréchal Juin (tel. 04 73 65 02 25) for 50-70F per ½-day or 100F per day. You can leave your passport in lieu of a 500F deposit (open 9am-noon and 2-7pm; V, MC). Rent **skis** at Bessac for 45F per day; or at **Techniciens du Sport,** 17, pl. Charles de Gaulle (tel. 04 73 65 06 79), 50-115F per day, 310-720F per week. In a **medical emergency,** dial 15 or call **Centre Médico Thermal,** 2, rue du Cap-Chazotte (tel. 04 73 65 33 33). The **police station** (tel. 04 73 65 01 70; **emergency** tel. 17) is on av. Michel Bertrand. The **post office,** pl. Charles de Gaulle (tel. 04 73 65 02 04), offers **currency exchange** and poste restante (open Mon.-Fri. 8am-6pm, Sat. 8am-noon; Sept.-June 8:30am-12:30pm and 2-6pm; **postal code:** 63240).

ACCOMMODATIONS AND CAMPING

The town is crowded in winter and summer but has many pleasant and inexpensive one-star hotels. To get to the **Auberge de Jeunesse "Le Grand Volcan" (HI),** route du Sancy (tel. 04 73 65 03 53; fax 04 73 65 26 39), from the station, climb av. Guyot-Dessaigne, which becomes av. des Belges. Continue on D983 (which changes names several times) 3km into the countryside (1hr.). When you see ski lifts, the hostel will be on your right. Buses leave for the hostel from opposite the train station (1 per hr., 9am-6pm; summer 2-6pm; 10F, 15F roundtrip). Ask to be dropped off at the *auberge de jeunesse,* a slope-side chalet. The fantastic hostel has one- to six-bed rooms, a mini-TV bar, and a mini-game room. Half-outdoor kitchen facilities and washing machine are at your disposal (soap 10F). Less than 1km from its source, the Dordogne river (in miniature, of course) flows through the back yard (50F, sheets included; breakfast 18F; meals 47F; no lockout or curfew).

The **Hôtel du Centre,** 8, rue Jean Moulin (tel. 04 73 65 01 77), above the lively Café de Paris, rents good, simple rooms overlooking the center of town at great prices. Weekends feature accordion and jazz performances downstairs. (Singles 75F. Doubles 80F. Triples 90F. Breakfast 25F. Open Dec. 15-Nov. 15. Reception 8am-8pm.) **Hôtel Helvetia,** 5, rue de la Saigne (tel. 04 73 65 01 67), is cozy and clean and keeps a family restaurant downstairs (singles and doubles with phone, some with lofts, 130F, with shower 160-180F; extra bed 30F; shower free; breakfast 25F). Stuffed bighorn sheep greet you at rustic **Les Mouflons,** 56, rue Clemenceau (tel. 04 73 65 02 90), at the southern end of town. The rooms are comfortable and colorful. (Singles and doubles 120F, with shower and toilet 170F. Extra bed 50F. Breakfast 25F. Reception 7am-10pm. Open Dec. 20-Oct. 20. V, MC.) There are four **campgrounds** in and around Le Mont Dore. The most convenient is **Les Crouzets,** av. des Crouzets (tel. 04 73 65 21 60), across from the train station. (Office open Mon.-Fri. 9am-noon and 2-6pm, Sat.-Sun. 9-10:15am and 4:30-5:45pm. Okay to set up first and pay later. Laundry facilities. Free hot showers. 12F per person, 11F per site, car included.) One km behind the station is **L'Esquiladou,** route des Cascades (tel. 04 73 65 23 74; 14F per person, 13F per tent; open May 15-Sept.).

FOOD

It's difficult to find a restaurant in Le Mont Dore that isn't hitched to a hotel. Such *pensions* serve non-guests but usually give discounts to their guests. Most *menus* in town begin at 65F, and a good meal will run 70-90F. The **Auberge des Skieurs,** 7, rue Montloisier (tel. 04 73 65 05 59), makes up for its tiny dining room with huge helpings of local delights. The hearty few whose hunger would outlast the three-course 70F meal can go for the 90F four-courser. The place fills up quickly, so call ahead (open daily noon-2pm and 7-9pm; V, MC). Despite the incessant buzz of its overhead insect zapper, everything's fine at **A Tout Va Bien,** rue Marie Thérèse (tel. 04 73 65 05 14), on the corner of av. Général Leclerc, covered with Astérix cartoon paraphernalia. In addition to a 61F *menu* of regional dishes, their *fondue gauloise* (73F) and *fondue auvergnate* (93F) allow you to stone-cook your own meat (open noon-2pm and 7-9pm). At **Le Bouguat,** 23, av. Georges Clemenceau (tel. 04 73 65 28 19), you'll feel like you're dining in an upscale, spacious farmhouse (79-129F *menus;* open Mon. 4:30-9:30pm, Tues.-Sun. noon-1:30pm and 7-9:30pm). **Le Tremplin,** 3, av. Foch (tel. 04 73 65 25 90), has wood oven pizza for 38-54F (evenings only in summer). The cheapest and most scenic meals are mountaintop picnics. Get supplies at the **Economia supermarket** on rue du Cap. Chazzotte (open Mon.-Sat. 8am-12:30pm and 3-7:30pm, Sun. 8am-12:30pm; V, MC). There's a modest **covered market** on pl. de la République (8am-noon and 2-7pm), which loses its inhibitions on Fridays and goes topless (8am-4pm).

SIGHTS AND ENTERTAINMENT

There's not a whole lot to do in the town, but you can introduce yourself to the *curiste* tradition at the **Etablissement Thermal** on pl. du Panthéon (tel. 04 73 65 05 10). Five of the springs used today were first channeled by the Romans, who found that the sources did wonders for their horses' sinuses. Around 1810, the present-day center was built as a "hospital." The curious can visit *les thermes* only during guided tours given several times daily in French (10F). Visitors are invited to sample the miraculous juice from the glass-enclosed pool as it burps with sulfur and ferric gases. Rub a bit on your hands—it's an excellent moisturizer. The visit ends with a dose of the *thermes'* celebrated *Douche Nasale Gaseuse.* A tiny blast of carbonated gas and helium evacuates those sinuses like no sneeze ever could (tour hours vary).

Down the hill on av. Michel-Bertrand, the **Musée Joseph Forêt** (tel. 04 73 65 20 21) honors the celebrated art editor, a Mont Dore native who left much of his collection to the town in 1985. For his grand finale, Forêt recruited seven painters and seven writers to collaborate in the publication of the largest book in the world. **Le Livre de L'Apocalypse,** weighing a quarter-ton, includes works by Dalí and Cocteau. A facsimile of the work (the original had to be sold in bits to pay for its production) sits in the back (hours and dates vary, so call ahead; admission 15F, students 10F). The **Tannerie Discothèque,** rue Perpere, takes the chill away from 11pm on. If you break your legs on the mountain, you can play your day away at the **casino.**

HIKES AND BIKES

Trails through these volcanic mountains cover dense forests, crystal-clear waterfalls and cascades, and bizarre, moon-like rock outcroppings. Scaling these mountains is relatively easy (the summit of Puy de Sancy is a doable day hike), but as always, if you plan on taking an extended hike, go over your route with the tourist office. Leave an itinerary for any multi-day route with the police at the base of Puy de Sancy (tel. 04 73 65 04 06). All hikers should equip themselves with maps. The tourist office sells pocket-sized *Sancy Haute Dordogne* (38F), with hiking, car, and bike circuits; topographical information; and meticulous maps of Le Mont Dore's surroundings. You may want to invest in their *Massif du Sancy et Artense* guide (78F), which elaborates 38 *randonnées* (hikes) originating from all areas of Le Sancy; the IGN map (57F) is a must for any serious trek (see page 54 for general hiking info).

A great intermediate hike begins at the base of the **Puy de Sancy,** near the youth hostel. Ascend the mountain via the Sancy trail, clearly labelled with yellow markers. You'll pass the source of the Dourdogne river along the way. Snow patches into July are not uncommon at the summit. A less scenic but less challenging way to get to the top is the *téléphérique* (every 15-20min., 9am-6pm; 30F, 35F roundtrip). You'll be king of the mountain as the Massif Central unfolds for your delight. East of Puy de Sancy, wildflowers carpet the cloistered **Vallée de Chaudefour.** Many endangered plant species exist here, so tread lightly. On clear days the Alps are visible to the east. At the peak, follow the **Grande Randonnée 30 (GR30),** marked with parallel red and white lines. If you see crossing red and white stripes, you've either been drinking too much or you've left the trail—turn around. The GR30 follows a narrow ridge and goes by rugged coves and craters of the once-furious, fire-spewing peaks, as well as vast pastures full of sheep, horses, and cows. Somewhere along the ridge, stop for a picnic and gaze at the grazing locals. When you get to the **Salon du Capucin,** a towering mass of rocks overlooking town, you can descend back into Le Mont Dore on foot or (about halfway down the trail) via an old funicular that will huff and puff in your place (10-11:40am and 2-6pm; one-way 18F, roundtrip 23F).

Volcanic lakes like **Lac Servière** (20km northeast of Le Mont Dore) fill in the craters of the Mont Dore region and are suitable for windsurfing, sailing, fishing, and (when warm enough) swimming. **Lac d'Aydat,** farther to the northeast, welcomes swimmers and offers pedal-boats and other water amusements. **Lac Chambon,** 20km east of Le Mont Dore (via D996E), offers the same and lies near **Murol,** where actors pretend it's the 13th century and fill a restored château-fortress with some repartée in Old French (tel. 04 73 88 67 11; call for seasonal hours: July-Aug. shows every 45min. daily 10am-6pm, no shows Wed. and Sun. mornings; admission 40F).

The tourist office books excursions, run by **Maisonneuve** (tel. 04 73 65 20 21), of the region's lakes, volcanoes, châteaux, and cheese and honey farms (reserve at tourist office). But the best excursions are unplanned explorations. With or without a map, you can follow the criss-crossing *chemins* surrounding Le Mont Dore through the area's hills and valleys and high up to pastures in the sky. Find your way over—or around—**Puy Gras** to **Lac de Guerey** (7km north). From there, it's just a few paces to a picnic above the valley framed by the massive rocks of **Tuilière** and **Sanadoire.** The circuit takes five hours on foot, six if you take time out for lunch.

For a quick thrill, the 30-minute hike from the southern end of town leads to the **Grande Cascade,** where the adventurous can stand under projecting rocks behind falling water—the rocks near the base of the waterfall are extremely slippery.

Many of the cross-country ski trails, or *chemins,* around Le Mont Dore are suitable for **mountain bikes.** The **downhill ski slopes** on the north face of the Puy de Sancy often get lots of snow. Skiing here cannot approach the conditions and challenge of the Alps, but rentals and lift tickets are much cheaper (see page 584 for info).

Bourgogne (Burgundy)

The greatness of Burgundy's wines overshadows everything else in this geographically and historically rich region. Burgundy was once the home of a fearsome duchy that extended its influence as far north as Amsterdam and of a powerful monastic order that controlled monasteries from Italy to England. The dukes and the abbots left palaces and churches strewn across the Burgundian hills. Today, these buildings shelter museums, pilgrims, and hordes of tourists who come seeking the famous fruit of the Burgundian vines.

Battleground of many a first-century Gallic border war, Burgundy was a major player in the Roman conquest—Autun was founded as a Roman capital. In the 5th century, the Burgondes, a relatively refined tribe of barbarians from the Baltic, settled on the plains of the Saône and modestly named the region after themselves.

Burgundy reached its ecclesiastical peak with the spread of its 12th-century religious orders. From their immense base in Cluny, the Benedictines ruled thousands of monasteries throughout Europe. Cluniac filial abbeys and churches dot the region today in Paray-le-Monial, Auxerre, Nevers, La Charité-sur-Loire, and Vézelay.

There was a time when the dukes of Burgundy were more powerful than the kings of France. This famous lineage (1364-1477) began with Philippe le Hardi (the Strong), whose marriage to Marguerite de Flandres brought a wealth of artists from the north to their capital at Dijon. Their son, Jean sans Peur (the Fearless), was unfortunately also *sans* good looks, but made up for it with bravery, wit, and intelligence. The state reached its maximum size and power under Jean's son, Philippe le Bon (the Good), who expanded his territories to include most of Holland, Belgium, Luxembourg, Flanders, Artois, Picardie, and the region bound by the Loire and the Jura. The last of the dukes, Charles le Téméraire (the Bold), was an arrogant, ambitious fellow who kept Burgundy permanently in battle. After a particularly bloody siege of the town of Nancy, his body was found in a frozen pond, half-eaten by wolves, and a delighted Louis XI took the opportunity to annex Burgundy to France.

In order to appreciate this region fully, you must eat, drink, and be merry. With just a few French phrases, you can taste your way to connoisseurship of the finest Burgundian vintages. Whether you like your grape juice *fruité* (fruity), *moelleux* (mellow), *vif* (lively), or *velouté* (velvety), Burgundy is sure to please. Head for the châteaux to sample whites such as the dry Pouilly-sur-Loire from Nièvre and Chablis from L'Yonne, as well as full-bodied reds including Vougeot, Gevrey-Chambertin, Nuits-St-George, and Corton from the Côte d'Or, and Givry from Saône-et-Loire. Signs advertising *dégustations* at local *caves* flank Burgundy's vineyards.

And what's a good wine without an equally distinctive meal to accompany it? Start off with a *kir* (white wine and *crème de cassis,* a black currant liqueur) and *gougères* (puffed pastry filled with cabbage or cheese). Move on to *jambon persillé* (a gelatin mold of ham and parsley) or a few *helix pomatia* (*escargots,* or snails, to gardeners) in butter and garlic. For the *plat de résistance,* indulge in traditional *coq au vin* (chicken in wine sauce) or *boeuf bourguignon.* Don't forget Dijon *moutarde* (mustard made with white wine instead of vinegar). Also search out *epoisses* or *brillat savarin* cheeses, and look for such sweet specialties as *pain d'épices* (gingerbread) or pastries using cherries and black currants.

Burgundy is known for its Roman ruins, its magnificent Romanesque churches, and its regal châteaux standing guard over precious vineyards. The most compelling feature of Burgundy, however, is the land itself: green and gold, slipping over gently-sloped hills, transversed by lazy, curling streams and dark, dense forests.

In the fall, Burgundy presents an unforgettable opportunity to participate in festivals related to the *vendange* (grape harvest), which feature costumes, parades, and lots of wine drinking. For an up-close-and-personal view of the *vendange,* consider participating. Usually beginning in September and lasting through October, grape-picking means long hours and back-breaking work. You won't get rich, but you can make some cash—salaries are fixed by the French agricultural administration. For more information, write l'Agence Locale pour l'Emploi, 6, bd. St-Jacques BP 115, 21203 Beaune Cedex (tel. 03 80 24 60 00). Some work camps and *vendanges* are reserved just for students—contact Emplois Temporaires Etudiants, Annexe Administrative de CROUS, 6b, rue Recteur Bouchard, 21000 Dijon (tel. 03 80 39 69 32).

GETTING AROUND

With Dijon as its main transportation hub, Burgundy is crisscrossed by SNCF lines. Smaller towns without train stations are usually served by bus; expect bus prices to match those of train fares. **TRANSCO** offers extensive bus service, but only in the Côte d'Or (tel. 03 80 42 11 00). Hikers and cyclists will find the gently sloping lands well suited to their ventures. Parts of the Morvan and some small towns and isolated châteaux can only be reached by bike, car, thumb, or foot.

Semur-en-Auxois

Though legend attributes Semur-en-Auxois' founding to Hercules, the earliest written record of the town (pop. 5100) is from 606. In that year, monks of the Abbaye de Flavigny signed their charter in a village they called *Sene Muros*—the "old walls." Today, the *vieille ville's* towers and ramparts crown an unspoiled provincial town of cobblestones and archways overlooking a bend in the Armençon river. Venture under the Sauvigny Gate (built in 1417) and the arch that bears the city's motto in old French: *Les Semurois se plaisent fort en l'acointance des Estrangers* (The people of Semur take great pleasure in welcoming strangers). The quote is commonly attributed to 16th-century monk Sébastian Münster; happily, it is still true today.

PRACTICAL INFORMATION

Semur's **tourist office,** pl. Gaveau (tel. 03 80 97 05 96), where rue de la Liberté meets the gates of the *vieille ville,* has bus schedules, free maps, and a list of hotels and restaurants (open July-Aug. Mon.-Sat. 8:30am-noon and 2-6:30pm, Sun. 10am-noon and 3-6pm; Sept.-June closed Sun.). **SNCF information and reservation office** is in the tourist office (open Tues.-Fri. 9am-noon and 2-6pm, Sat. 9am-noon and 2-5pm). **TRANSCO** (tel. 03 80 42 11 00) runs **buses** through the Côte d'Or, connecting Semur with: Dijon (3 per day, Sun. 1 per day, 1½hr., 54F); Avallon (4 per day, Sun. 1 per day, 1hr., 38F); and Montbard (3 per day, Sun. 2 per day, 21min., 13F). Trains only stop 18km away in Montbard. Rent a **bike** at **Maison Familiale Rurale,** 10, rue du Couvent (tel. 03 80 97 07 08; ask for M. Mathieu; 45F per ½-day, 75F per day, 15F per evening) or from **Robert Bonvalot,** 10, rue de l'Ancienne Comédie (tel. 03 80 97 01 91; 35F per ½-day, 60F per day; open Tues.-Sun. 9am-noon and 2-7pm). **Banks** lie just outside the *vieille ville;* **Crédit Mutuel,** at 6, rue de la Liberté, and **Crédit Agricole,** at 34, rue de la Liberté, have 24-hour **ATMs.** Most businesses in Semur are closed Mondays. The **hospital** is on av. Pasteur (tel. 03 80 89 64 64). Call 15 in **medical emergencies.** For help, call the **police** at 03 80 97 11 17. In case of **emergency** dial 17. Semur's **post office** has **currency exchange** and poste restante and is located on pl. de l'Ancienne Comédie (tel. 03 80 97 00 86; open Mon.-Fri. 8am-noon and 1:30-5:30pm, Sat. 8am-noon; **postal code:** 21140).

ACCOMMODATIONS, CAMPING, AND FOOD

Your best bet for cheap sleep in Semur is the **Carrefour Rencontres Accueil Communication (CRAC),** 10, rue du Couvent (tel. 03 80 97 03 81). Terrific owners keep a wonderful place in an old convent with a sunny courtyard, a library of books about the region, and a homey breakfast room. (*Let's Go*-ers and HI members 60F per person. Otherwise, singles are 85F, with shower 100F. 2-bed doubles 130F, with shower 150F. Triples 170F, with shower 190F. Free hall shower. Breakfast 25-35F.) Delicious home-cooked lunches and dinners are 60F and include salad, *plat,* cheese, and dessert. The **Foyer des Jeunes Travailleurs (HI),** 1, rue du Champ de Foire (tel. 03 80

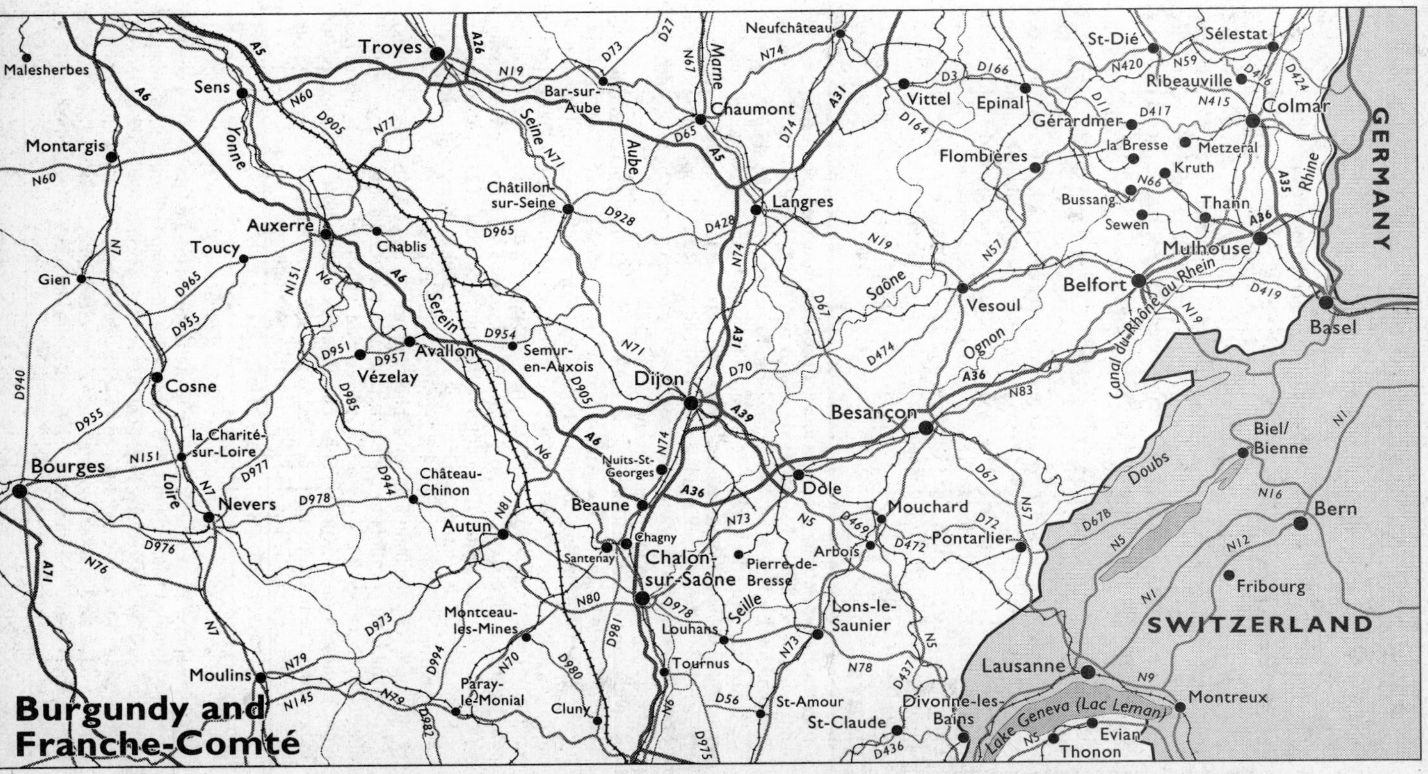
Burgundy and Franche-Comté
GERMANY
SWITZERLAND
Malesherbes
Troyes
Sens
Montargis
Auxerre
Toucy
Gien
Chablis
Avallon
Vézelay
Semur-en-Auxois
Cosne
la Charité-sur-Loire
Bourges
Nevers
Château-Chinon
Autun
Moulins
Paray-le-Monial
Montceau-les-Mines
Cluny
Bar-sur-Aube
Chaumont
Châtillon-sur-Seine
Langres
Neufchâteau
Dijon
Nuits-St-Georges
Beaune
Chagny
Santenay
Chalon-sur-Saône
Louhans
Tournus
St-Amour
St-Claude
Divonne-les-Bains
Lons-le-Saunier
Pierre-de-Bresse
Dole
Mouchard
Arbois
Pontarlier
Besançon
Vesoul
Vittel
Epinal
Flombières
Gérardmer
la Bresse
Bussang
Sewen
Kruth
Metzeral
Thann
Mulhouse
Belfort
St-Dié
Ribeauville
Sélestat
Colmar
Basel
Biel/Bienne
Bern
Fribourg
Lausanne
Montreux
Evian
Thonon
Lake Geneva (Lac Leman)
Rhine
Canal du Rhône au Rhin
Doubs
Ognon
Saône
Seille
Marne
Aube
Seine
Serein
Yonne
Loire
A5
A6
A26
A31
A35
A36
A39
A71
N1
N5
N6
N7
N9
N12
N16
N19
N57
N59
N60
N66
N67
N70
N71
N73
N74
N77
N78
N79
N80
N81
N83
N145
N151
N415
N420
D3
D11
D27
D56
D65
D67
D70
D72
D73
D74
D164
D166
D416
D417
D419
D424
D428
D436
D437
D469
D472
D474
D678
D905
D928
D940
D944
D951
D954
D955
D957
D965
D973
D975
D976
D977
D978
D980
D981
D982
D985
D994

BURGUNDY

97 10 22; fax 03 80 97 36 97), off rue de la Liberté, has comfortable institutional singles with a TV room, kitchen facilities, phone, and cafeteria (meals 40F) downstairs (50F, non-members 70F; breakfast 8F; sheets 15F; reception Mon.-Sat. 11am-2pm and 5-9pm, Sun. 5-9pm). The **Hôtel des Gourmets,** 4, rue Varenne (tel. 03 80 97 09 41), offers large rooms out of a Laura Ashley catalogue in the heart of the *vieille ville.* (Singles and doubles 120-150F, with shower 180-200F. Triples and quads 180-190F. 6-person room 300F. Extra bed 25F. No hall showers. Breakfast 35F. Reception 8am-10pm; closed Mon. evening and Tues. Open Jan.-Nov. 14. V, MC, AmEx.) **Camping Municipal du Lac de Pont** (tel. 03 80 97 01 26) stakes its claim 3km south of Semur on a scenic lake. Laundry service, mini-mart (13F per person, 9F per site, 6F per car, electricity 11F; reception 9am-noon and 4-8pm; open May-Sept.). It also **rents mountain bikes** (25F per hr., 50F per ½-day, 75F per day).

When hunger strikes, **Le Sagittaire,** 15, rue de la Liberté (tel. 03 80 97 23 91), hits the bull's-eye with friendly service and inexpensive, tasty dishes (pizza 29-43F, huge salads 32-42F, 3-course weekday lunch *menu* 53F, dinner *menu* 83F; open Tues.-Sun. noon-2:30pm and 7:30-10:30pm). You're always welcome at **Chez Madame Fanfan,** 15, rue Buffon (tel. 03 80 97 28 97), to try excellent local specialties (including *coq au vin*) served on a terrace (59F daily lunch *menu du jour;* open daily noon-midnight; V, MC). For groceries, stop at the small **Casino supermarket** at 32, pl. Notre Dame (open Tues.-Sun. 8:30am-12:30pm and 2:30-7:30pm), or head a few blocks down rue de la Liberté to the **Intermarché** on av. du Général Maziller (open Mon.-Thurs. 9am-12:15pm and 2:30-7:15pm, Fri. 9am-7:45pm, Sat. 9am-7:15pm).

SIGHTS

Down rue Buffon, leering gargoyles menace the town from their perches on the 15th-century façade of **Eglise Notre-Dame** and its two square towers. The 13th-century tympanum on the **Porte des Bleds** faces rue Notre-Dame. On the skinny left pillar, sculpted snails slime their way to St. Thomas' feet—smug in the knowledge that they are pet symbols of the Burgundians. Escape the *escargots* in the Chapel of the Butchers, donated by the butcher's guild in the 15th century. (Church open 9am-noon and 2-6pm; closes at 5pm in winter. Cookie-cutter free tours given by bionic French high school students July-Aug.; English pamphlet available.)

Leaving the church, head straight on rue Fevret to rue du Rempart and the huge **Tour de l'Orle d'Or,** the dungeon of Semur's dismantled château. Don't expect a torture chamber—the building now houses an assortment of regional inventions, including a 19th-century bicycle (open July-Aug. daily 10am-6pm; 30min. tour in French or English; admission 12F). The building housing the **Musée Municipal,** rue Jean-Jacques Collenot (tel. 03 80 97 24 25), off pl. de l'Ancienne Comédie, was a Dominican convent in the 17th century. The museum boasts 12,000 specimens of minerals and fossils, statues and carvings from the Middle Ages, and painting and sculpture from the 17th to the 19th centuries—including three Corot canvases and plaster models by Augustin Dumont (check with tourist office for times and prices).

The stroll from pont Joly to pont Pinard, around the bend of the Armançon River, affords lovely views of the town. The *vieille ville* is illuminated from 10pm to midnight nightly from mid-June to September. Semur is surrounded by some of Burgundy's most beautiful countryside. The tourist office's *Promenades* lists walks. Just 3km south of Semur, the **Lac de Pont** is ideal for swimming and picnics.

Dijon

Dijon's prospects looked bleak in 1513, as 30,000 Swiss gripped the city in a vise-like siege. Negotiations faltered until, in a stroke of Burgundian brilliance, the *Dijonnais* sent wine casks across enemy lines. The foes, with inebriation-induced generosity, acquiesced and retreated from the town. After their *coup de vin,* the dukes of Burgundy commanded as much power as any European monarch. Today, Dijon is more famous for its wine-based mustards. Its enviable location at the tip of the Côte d'Or,

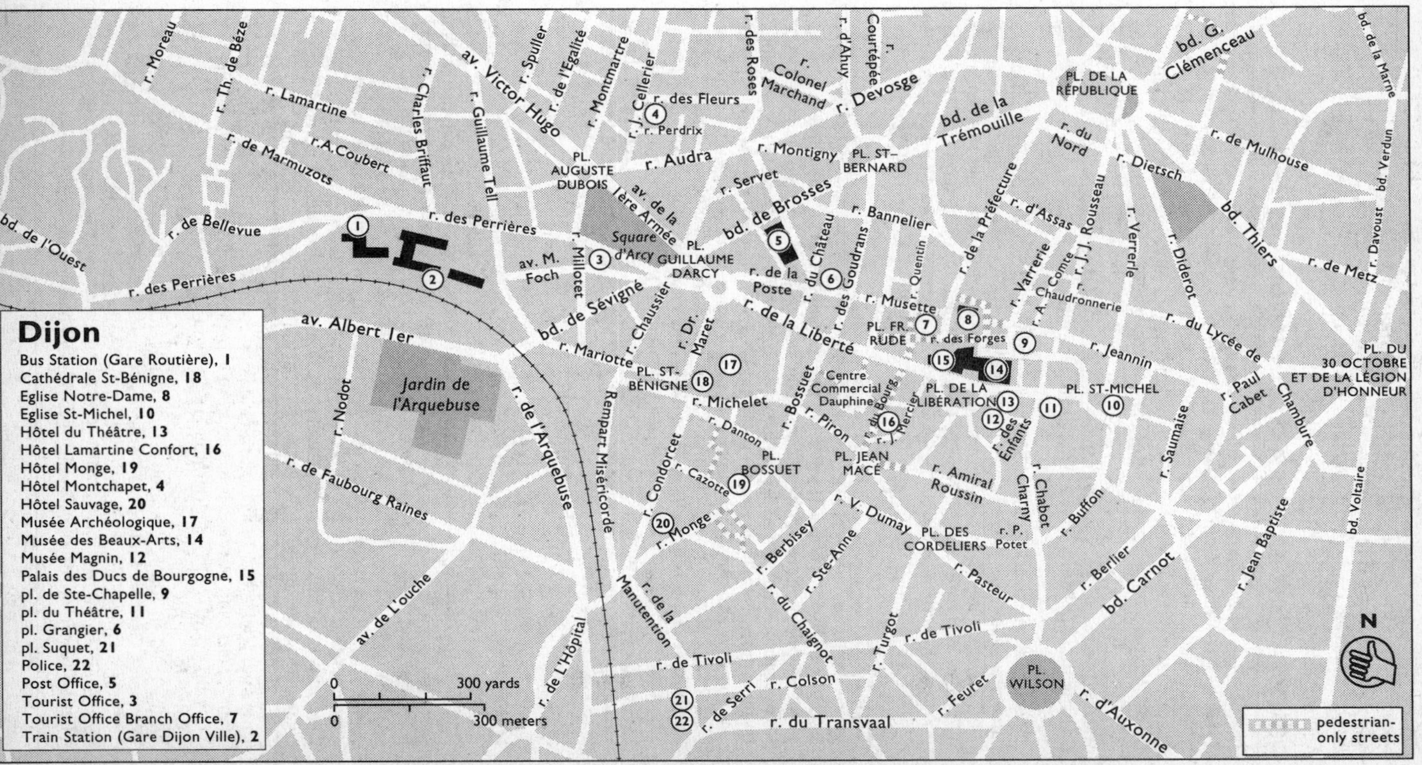
Dijon
Bus Station (Gare Routière), 1
Cathédrale St-Bénigne, 18
Eglise Notre-Dame, 8
Eglise St-Michel, 10
Hôtel du Théâtre, 13
Hôtel Lamartine Confort, 16
Hôtel Monge, 19
Hôtel Montchapet, 4
Hôtel Sauvage, 20
Musée Archéologique, 17
Musée des Beaux-Arts, 14
Musée Magnin, 12
Palais des Ducs de Bourgogne, 15
pl. de Ste-Chapelle, 9
pl. du Théâtre, 11
pl. Grangier, 6
pl. Suquet, 21
Police, 22
Post Office, 5
Tourist Office, 3
Tourist Office Branch Office, 7
Train Station (Gare Dijon Ville), 2
pedestrian-only streets
N
0
300 yards
0
300 meters
PL. DE LA RÉPUBLIQUE
bd. G. Clémenceau
bd. de la Trémouille
r. Devosge
PL. ST-BERNARD
PL. AUGUSTE DUBOIS
r. Audra
av. Victor Hugo
PL. GUILLAUME DARCY
Square d'Arcy
av. de la 1ère Armée
bd. de Brosses
bd. de Sévigné
r. de la Liberté
av. Albert 1er
Jardin de l'Arquebuse
r. de l'Arquebuse
Rempart Miséricorde
PL. ST-BÉNIGNE
PL. FR. RUDE
PL. DE LA LIBÉRATION
PL. ST-MICHEL
PL. JEAN MACÉ
PL. BOSSUET
PL. DES CORDELIERS
PL. WILSON
PL. DU 30 OCTOBRE ET DE LA LÉGION D'HONNEUR
Centre Commercial Dauphine
bd. Thiers
bd. Carnot
r. des Perrières
r. de Bellevue
bd. de l'Ouest
r. Chabot Charny
r. d'Auxonne
r. du Transvaal
r. de Tivoli
r. de Metz
r. Verrerie
r. Diderot
r. Jeannin
r. Musette
r. des Forges
r. des Godrans
r. Bannelier
r. de la Préfecture
r. Pasteur
r. Berbisey
r. Monge
r. Condorcet
r. Michelet
r. Mariotte
r. Chaussier
r. Dr. Maret
r. de la Poste
r. du Château
av. M. Foch
r. Millotet
r. Guillaume Tell
r. Charles Briffaut
r. de Marmuzots
r. Lamartine
r. Th. de Bèze
r. Moreau
r. Nodot
r. de Faubourg Raines
av. de L'ouche
r. de L'Hôpital
r. de la Manutention
r. du Chaignot
r. Ste-Anne
r. V. Dumay
r. Amiral Roussin
r. Buffon
r. Berlier
r. Jean Baptiste
bd. Voltaire
r. Saumaise
r. Paul Cabet
r. Chambure
r. du Lycée de
r. de Mulhouse
r. Dietsch
r. du Nord
r. d'Assas
r. J.J. Rousseau
r. Montigny
r. Servet
r. des Roses
r. d'Ahuy
r. Courtépée
r. Colonel Marchand
r. des Fleurs
r. Perdrix
r. J. Cellerier
r. Montmartre
r. de l'Egalité
r. Spuller
r. Turgot
r. Feuret
r. Colson
r. de Serri
r. Cazotte
r. Danton
r. Piron
r. Bossuet
r. Quentin
r. Chaudronnerie
r. A. Comte
r. des Enfants
r. P. Potet
r. du Bourg
r. J. Mercier
bd. de la Marne
bd. Verdun
r. Davoust

one of the world's finest wine regions, draws many tourists and locals to its *vieille ville.* Boasting myriad museums, festivals, and sidewalk cafés, and bursting with a lively international student population, the *Dijonnais* are almost as spicy as their mustard. So, should you visit Dijon? But of course.

ORIENTATION AND PRACTICAL INFORMATION

Despite its size, Dijon is easy to explore. Its main east-west axis, pedestrian **rue de la Liberté,** runs roughly from **pl. Darcy,** with the tourist office, to **pl. St-Michel.** From the train station, follow av. Maréchal Foch straight to pl. Darcy (5min.). The *vieille ville* and most of Dijon's sights are on the small streets radiating north and south from rue de la Liberté. The **pl. de la République,** northeast of pl. Darcy, is the central roundabout for roads leading out of the city. Beware of the free but notoriously useless map proffered by the tourist office—it only covers the city center, or a version of it. Thank them politely and reach for the free bus map instead.

Tourist Information: Tourist Office, pl. Darcy (tel. 03 80 49 11 44). Hotel and restaurant list and maps. Free *Divio 1997* is a huge book of useful info. Accommodations service 15F. **Currency exchange.** Open daily 9am-9pm; Oct 16-April 30 9am-7pm. **Branch office** at 34, rue des Forges (same tel.), open May-Oct.15 Mon.-Sat. 9am-noon and 1-6pm; Oct.16-April Mon.-Fri 9am-noon and 1-6pm. For info on things artistic and cultural, ask for **Culture,** free at the tourist office.

Money: There are 24-hr. **ATMs** on rue de la Liberté.

Trains: cours de la Gare (tel. 08 36 35 35 35), at the end of av. Maréchal Foch. To: Paris by TGV (every other hr., 1¾hr., 230F); Lyon (10 per day, 2hr., 132F); Strasbourg (4 per day, 4hr., 201F); Nice (6 per day, 8hr., 372F). 24-hr station and ticket officer. Reservations and info office open Mon.-Fri. 9am-7pm, Sat. 9am-6pm. **SOS Voyageurs** (tel. 03 80 43 16 34) helps confused travelers Mon.-Sat. 8:30am-6pm.

Buses: av. Maréchal Foch (tel. 03 80 42 11 00), connected to train station, to the left as you exit. **TRANSCO** ticket and info office open Mon.-Fri. 7:30am-6:30pm, Sat. 7:30am-12:30pm. At other times, go to the *chef du Gare's* office near the bus *quai* or buy tickets on the bus. Buses roll 10 times per day along a scenic route to Beaune (1hr., 36F80), Nuits St-George (40min., 23F), and other towns.

Public Transportation: STRD (tel. 03 80 30 60 90), groovy concrete booth on pl. Grangier. Covers greater Dijon Mon.-Sat. 6:30am-7:15pm. Map at the tourist office. Tickets 5F20, available on bus. Five-trip pass 23F, 12-trip pass 40F, 1-day pass 15F40, 1-week pass 42F30. Buses run from 6am until about 12:30am, though evening buses are limited.

Taxis: Taxi Radio Dijon, (tel. 03 80 41 41 12).

Hitchhiking: Those thumbing to Paris via Sens take av. Albert 1er. South-bounders sometimes take av. Jean Jaurès (N74 for Chalon). Rides often posted at CIJB.

Car Rental: Avis, 5, av. Maréchal Foch (tel. 03 80 43 60 76). 575F per day, 300km included; 1980F per week, with 2000km. Open Mon.-Sat. 8am-noon and 2-7pm.

Bike and Car Rental: Travel Bike Location, 28, bd. de la Marne (tel. 03 80 72 31 00, fax 03 80 73 38 40), off pl. Bouhey, one block from pl. de la République. 90F per day, 390F per week. Also rents cars, minivans, and a wide array of scooters and motorcycles. Passport deposit is preferred, but negotiable. V, MC, AmEx.

English Books: Librairie de l'Université, 17, rue de la Liberté (tel. 03 80 44 95 44). Paperbacks on 2nd floor. Open Mon. 10:15am-7pm, Tues.-Sat. 9:15am-7pm.

Youth Information: Centre d'Information Jeunesse de Bourgogne (CIJB), 18, rue Audra (tel. 80 44 18 44). Info on lodgings, French classes, events, grape-picking jobs, sports, and travel. Sells youth hostel ID cards and discount train tickets (*billets* BIJ, WASTEELS). Open Mon-Fri. 9:30am-6pm; closes at 5pm in summer. **CROUS,** 3, rue du Docteur Maret (tel. 03 80 40 40 40 for cafeteria and general info, 03 80 40 40 23 for housing info). Open Mon.-Fri. 9am-noon and 1:30-5pm.

Women's Center: Solidarité Femmes, 4, rue Choncelier de l'Hôpital (tel. 03 80 67 17 89). A clearinghouse for information; confidential referral service.

Laundromat: 36, rue Guillaume Tell, balances above the train station. Wash 20F. Dry 2F per 4min., 5F per 12 min. Soap 5F. Open daily 6am-9pm.

Crisis Lines: SOS Amitié (tel. 03 80 67 15 15). **Alcooliques Anonymes** (tel. 03 80 30 27 00).

Medical Assistance: Centre Hospitalier Regional de Dijon, 3, rue Faubourg Raines (tel. 03 80 29 30 31). **SOS Médecins** (tel. 03 80 73 55 55, weekends and holidays 03 80 41 28 28) has doctors on-call. **Medical emergency** tel. 03 80 41 12 12, or dial 15.

Police: 2, pl. Suquet (tel. 03 80 44 55 00). **Emergency** tel. 17.

Post Office: pl. Grangier (tel. 03 80 50 62 19), near pl. Darcy. Poste restante (postal code: 21031). Photocopies. **ATM.** Open Mon.-Fri. 8am-7pm, Sat. 8am-noon. **Postal code:** 21000.

ACCOMMODATIONS AND CAMPING

In summer, reasonably priced hotels fill quickly. Reserve or use the tourist office's accommodations service. The *foyers* are a 45-minute walk from the station. Call **CROUS** (above) in advance if you'd like university housing (about 70F per night).

Foyer International d'Etudiants, 6, rue Maréchal Leclerc (tel. 03 80 71 70 00; fax 03 80 71 60 48). Take bus 4 (direction: St-Apollinaire) to "Parc des Sports." From av. Paul Doumer, turn right onto rue du Stade, then take the first left. International is this *foyer's* middle name. You'll hear English, Japanese, German, and Spanish—but not much French. TV rooms, tennis court, laundry, kitchen. Renovated cafeteria. Huge singles with big desks 70F. 24-hr. reception.

Auberge de Jeunesse (HI), Centre de Rencontres Internationales, 1, av. Champollion (tel. 03 80 72 95 20; fax 03 80 70 00 61), 4km from station. Take bus 5 from "Bar Bleu" on pl. Grangier (direction: Epirey), and get off at end of line (Epirey c.r.i.)—you'll be in front of the concrete megahostel. International is this place's last name—TVs in the lobby add to the airport-concourse ambiance. Lots of noise and lots of fun, with a bar/disco, language courses in summer, TV and game rooms, laundry facilities. 6- to 8-bed dorms 69F, 64F with an HI card. Singles with shower 130F, with shower and toilet 144F. Breakfast, sheets, showers included. Self-serve lunch and dinners 30-50F. Reservations strongly advised June-Sept. 24-hr reception. No keys before 5pm, but no lockout.

Hôtel Montchapet, 26-28, rue Jacques Cellerier (tel. 03 80 55 33 31). In quiet neighborhood 10min. from the station, north of av. Première Armée Française off pl. Darcy. Proprietors are the fairy-tale grandparents you always imagined. They let spotless rooms with air-conditioning and firm beds, many with TV. Lots of students. Singles 140F, with shower 180F. Doubles 210F, with shower 220F. Triples 320F. Quads 360F. Extra bed 40F. Shower 20F. Breakfast 32F. V, MC, AmEx.

Hôtel Monge, 20, rue Monge (tel. 03 80 30 55 41; fax 03 80 30 63 87). Set back from the street, with a courtyard. Clean and cozy rooms. Huge, modern bathrooms. Singles 120F, with shower 160F. Doubles 130F, with shower 170F. Two beds with shower and toilet 260F. Shower 10F. TV 10F. Breakfast 25F. Students get a 5% discount. V, MC, AmEx.

Hôtel Lamartine Confort, 12, rue Jules Mercier (tel. 03 80 30 37 47; fax 03 80 41 84 84), on an alley off rue de la Liberté. Beds are a bit saggy. Singles 160F, with bath 210F. Doubles 170F, with bath 220F. Triples with shower and toilet 250F. Extra bed 50F. TV 30F. Breakfast 25F. Reception closes at 10pm. V, MC, AmEx.

Hôtel du Sauvage, 64, rue Monge (tel. 03 80 41 31 21; fax 03 80 42 06 07), near Eglise St-Jean below rue Bossuet off rue de la Liberté. Rugged, wood-beamed building on a quiet courtyard. Most rooms have showers. Singles 170F, with toilet 200F. Doubles add 20F. Parking garage 35F. TV 20F. Breakfast 30F. V, MC.

Camping: Camping Municipal du Lac, 3, bd. Kir (tel. 03 80 43 54 72). Exit the back of the station and turn left on av. Albert 1er. After 1km, turn left on bd. Kir, then follow the signs. Or take bus 12 (direction: Fontaine d'Ouche) to "Hôpital des Chartreux." While it's near a busy street, this lakeside campground is quiet. 14F per person, 12F per tent, 8F per car. Electricity 16F. Open April-Oct. 15.

FOOD

Dijon's reputation for cuisine, dating from Gallo-Roman times, has inflated restaurant prices. *Charcuteries* provide a chance to sample *dijonnais* specialties; take *jambon persillé* (ham pâté with parsley), *tarte bourguignonne* (pie with meat and mushrooms in cream sauce), or quiche *aux champignons* (with mushrooms) to the **Jardin de l'Arquebuse** for a picnic behind the train station. *Dijonnais* chefs doctor their delicacies with heavy doses of local vinegars, wines, and mustards. Try **rue Bebisey** and **rue Monge** for a wide variety of restaurants.

University cafeterias stay open all summer; **R.U. Maret,** 3, rue Docteur-Maret (tel. 03 80 66 39 85), has an all-you-can-eat dinner for 12F with student ID (open Mon.-Fri. 11:30am-1:30pm and 6:30-8pm, Sat.-Sun. 11:40am-1:15pm and 6:40-7:45pm). There is a large **supermarket** in the basement of the **Galeries Lafayette,** 41, rue de la Liberté (open Mon.-Sat. 9am-7:15pm), and a well-stocked **Prisunic** at 11, rue Piron, off pl. Jean Macé (open Mon.-Sat. 8:30am-8pm). The pedestrian area from pl. F. Rude north to rue Bannelier explodes into a colorful **market** on Tuesday, Friday, and Saturday mornings (6am-noon). **Les Halles,** a huge covered market near rue Odobert on Quentin south of Bannelier, keeps the same hours.

La Vie Saine, 27-29, rue Musette (tel. 03 80 30 15 10), off pl. Grangier. Enjoy the sumptuous salad bar (quiches, vegetarian tarts) and dessert bar afterwards (tarts, chocolate mousse, custard, fruit). All you can eat 55F. Open Mon.-Sat. noon-2pm. V, MC, AmEx.

La Riviera, 52, rue Berbisey (tel. 03 80 49 82 26), has a filling lunch and dinner *menu* for 65F—a rarity in Dijon—that includes an Italian salad, a creamy *volaille* dish, regional *fromage,* and dessert (try the *glace* made with Burgundy's own cassis berries). V, MC.

L'Auberge de Pekin, 11, rue de la Prévoté (tel. 03 80 30 25 87), near the cathedral. Plenty of Thai, Chinese, and Vietnamese choices in the 20-40F range. Five-course lunch *menus* 50F or 68F. Open daily 11:45am-2:30pm and 7-11pm. Closed Mon. Take Out. V, MC, AmEx.

Pick-Up Café, 9, rue Mably (tel. 03 80 30 61 44). Decorated with American street signs and beer logos, it looks like the *Cheers* set dubbed into French. Salads 10-38F. Sandwiches 13-18F. 30 beers, 18 whiskeys. Open daily 8am-2am. V, MC.

SIGHTS

In their 100-year heyday (1364-1477), the wealthy dukes of Burgundy were fearless (Jean sans Peur), good (Philippe le Bon), and bold (Philippe le Hardi and Charles le Téméraire). These leaders built the colossal **Palais des Ducs de Bourgogne** on the pl. de la Libération at the center of the *vieille ville.* The plans for the palace's semi-circular design were drawn up by Jules Hardouin-Mansart, architect of Versailles, and were executed by his apprentices much later in 1686-1701. Most of the buildings currently house administrative offices, but the elegant **Musée des Beaux-Arts,** pl. de la Ste-Chapelle (tel. 80 74 52 70), occupies the palace's east wing. Its European works from the 14th to 20th centuries include impressive but esoteric collections of Tuscan primitives, Renaissance art, and Flemish and Burgundian masters. Don't get so absorbed in the exhibits that you forget to look out at the beautiful courtyard. The palace's famous **Salle des Gardes** is dominated by the huge sarcophagi of Philippe le Hardi, Jean sans Peur, and his wife Margaret. Thirty-nine delicately detailed mourners keep vigil at Philippe's tomb. The walk up the small (hidden) winding staircase offers a good view of the *salle* from the balcony. Save time for the memorable 19th- and 20th-century French drawings, paintings, and sculptures and Victor Hugo's small canvases (open Wed.-Mon. 10am-6pm; admission 18F, free to students and on Sundays; contemporary wing closed noon-1:30pm; a 20F **museum pass** admits you to all Dijon museums). In the courtyard, the **Tour Philippe Bon** was built by the good duke in the 15th century. From it, he enjoyed an altogether different view of the city, the surrounding valleys, and the foothills of the Jura (11 ascents Wed.-Mon. 9am-5:30pm Eas-

It's a Hoot!

Even though pigeons play on the eves outside **l'Eglise Notre Dame,** nobody seems to notice their picturesque perch. Uncharacteristically aesthetically pleasing, these fowl *still* get the cold shoulder from those down below. Passers-by are busy rubbing away for good luck—not a magic lamp, not a rabbit's foot, but the wise one himself, Mr. Owl. Outside by the church's left wall, look closely as passers-by stop to polish the symbol of the city, a shiny little worn-down lump that used to be an owl. This vehemently observed, centuries-old tradition has transformed the owl into a hardly identifiable piece of rock—everybody's doin' it. So, when in Dijon, do as the *Dijonnais* do—rub the lump.

ter (March 30, 1997) through the 3rd Sun. of Nov. (the 16th); at other times, 3 on Wed. 1:30-3:30pm; admission 15F, students 8F).

The façade of the Burgundian Gothic **Eglise Notre Dame,** pl. Notre Dame (tel. 03 80 74 35 76) is a morass of gargoyles set in devilishly pensive expressions. Its technicolor *vitraux* shed little light on the somber interior. To the right of the choir sits the 11th-century statue of the **Vierge Noire** (Black Virgin), a deep polychrome. The colorful tapestry to her right celebrates Dijon's liberations from the bellicose Swiss and from German occupation in 1944. Outside, the **Horloge à Jacquemart,** commissioned by Philippe le Hardi in 1382 after his victory over the Flemish, ticks above the church's tower. In 1610, the lonely male statue who sounded the hour was given a spouse, later, a son to strike the half-hour, and finally, in 1881, a daughter daintily to announce the quarter-hour.

Visiting the **Eglise St-Michel** on pl. St-Michel (tel. 03 80 63 17 84) can be a dramatic experience. Enter through the central portal to vivid and cheery stained-glass windows. Be respectful of worshipers as you make your way toward the altar, and, as a Bach fugue rings in your ears, turn around to the darkest, most foreboding organ in Dijon (call to see if the guided tours halted by renovations have resumed).

Across from pl. de la Libération, the **Musée Magnin,** 4, rue des Bons Enfants (tel. 03 80 67 11 10), houses an extensive collection of paintings in the elegant 17th-century **Hôtel Lantin.** Though most of the artists are obscure, the mansion is worth a visit. With period furnishings, rich wallpapers, and works clustered in intimate groups, you'll feel as if you've been invited to the home of an ardent art collector for a private showing (open June-Sept. Tues.-Sun. 10am-6pm; Oct.-May Tues.-Sun. 10am-noon and 2-6pm; admission 15F, students 10F).

The elegant 93m apse and spire in the austere **Cathédrale St-Bénigne,** on pl. St-Bénigne (tel. 03 80 30 14 90), memorialize the 2nd-century missionary whose martyred remains were unearthed near Dijon in the 6th century. Different from others in Dijon, the abbey covers an unusual (and spooky) circular crypt dating from AD 1007 (crypt open Easter-Oct. daily 9am-5pm; admission 5F). Go inside the church for a peek out the beautiful *chaire en bois* pulpit.

Next door, the **Musée Archéologique,** 5, rue Docteur Maret (tel. 03 80 30 88 54), unearths the history of the Côte d'Or. Housed in the former cloisters of St-Bénigne's Benedictine abbey, the collection includes Gallo-Roman sculpture, medieval statuary, household items, and weapons (open Oct-May Wed.-Mon. 9am-noon and 2-6pm.; June-Sept. 9:30am-6pm; admission 12F, free to students and on Sundays).

For a retreat from Dijon's countless churches and monuments, take a walk around the **Jardin de l'Arquebuse,** 1, av Albert 1er (tel. 03 80 76 72 83). Stop to identify each of 3500 species in the meticulously laid out botanical garden, or simply stroll among the weeping willows and reflecting pools of the arboretum (park open daily 7:30am-8pm; Oct.-Feb. 7:30am-5:30pm; March-June 7:30am-7pm).

No trip to Dijon is complete without a stop at **Grey Poupon,** 32, rue de la Liberté, *moutarde au vin* makers since 1777 (array of decorated pots on sale—12-600F).

ENTERTAINMENT

In June, Dijon's **Eté Musical** hosts many of the world's best symphony orchestras and chamber groups. From mid-June to mid-August, **Estivade** brings dance, music, and theater to the streets. Dijon devotes a week in the first half of September to the **Fête de la Vigne** (tel. 03 80 30 37 95), a well-attended celebration of the grape. Opera, classical music, and operettas are performed mid-October through late April at the **Théâtre de Dijon,** pl. du Théâtre (tel. 03 80 67 20 21), a beautiful 18th-century opera house (tickets 110-240F, 50F for students within 30min. of curtain). Investigate the shows (both classic and contemporary) at **Nouveau Théâtre de Bourgogne,** located at Théâtre du Parvis St-Jean, rue Danton (tel. 03 80 30 12 12).

International students are the *raison d'être* of **Atmosphère**, the **Club International d'Etudiants,** 7, rue Audra (tel. 03 80 30 52 03 or 03 80 30 66 03), a combination bar, pool hall, nightclub, and *discothèque* (open daily 3pm-3am; free). Across the street, **Le Kilkenny,** 1, rue Auguste Perdrix (tel. 03 80 30 02 48), is an authentic Irish pub with arched stone ceilings, 34F pints of Guinness, music from the Emerald Isle, and a not-quite-authentic large, loud, drunken clientele (open Mon.-Sat. 6pm-3am, Sun 7pm-3am). Not to be missed is **Le Brighton,** 33, rue Auguste Comte (tel. 03 80 73 59 32), a British pub on street level with a Mexican disco in the basement (open daily 3pm-3am). **Le Cintra,** on 13, av. Foch (tel. 03 80 43 65 89) and **Hunky Dory,** next door at 5, av. Foch (tel. 80 43 40 07), are both a bit quieter, with karaoke and a thirty-esque crowd. Dijon's painfully hip gather on **rue Berbisey. Cappuccino,** 132, rue Berbisey (tel. 03 80 41 06 35), is almost as fun and *chic* as its clientele (open 3pm-1am, Sat. 3pm-2am). Up the street at number 47, **L'Univers'** (tel. 03 80 30 98 29) infinitely expanding crowds often spill onto the sidewalk (open 11:30am-1am, 'til 2am on weekends).

Beaune

Ah, Beaune—the wine! the food! the *tourists!* The only French you may hear here is the name of a vineyard, but the town has the irresistibly Gallic spirit and charm. A common bond unites locals and Beaune's flocks of visitors: their deep love of Burgundy, in its liquid form. Surrounded by the famous **Côte de Beaune** vineyards, the town is packed with wineries offering free *dégustations.* Beneath Beaune's streets a labyrinth of *caves* (wine cellars) protects the bottles from the tipsy throngs above. Sampling your way into a stupor, however, is ill advised—there's too much else to see. Until the 14th century, Beaune was the official residence of the dukes of Burgundy, who later moved to Dijon. As you wander the cobblestone streets of the enchanting *vieille ville* and admire their lavish **Hôtel-Dieu,** you may wonder how the nobles managed to tear themselves away. Surrounded by 15th-century ramparts, Beaune has enough free drink and unusual architecture to delight even the richest of dukes and most world-weary of tourists.

ORIENTATION AND PRACTICAL INFORMATION

Almost everything there is to see lies within the circular ramparts that enclose Beaune's *vieille ville.* To get to the center of town from the train station, head straight on av. du 8 Septembre, which becomes rue du Château. Turn left onto rempart St-Jean, following it up and down the stairs as it crosses rue d'Alsace and mutates into rempart Madeleine. The fourth right is rue de l'Hôtel-Dieu, which leads to the Hôtel-Dieu and the tourist office (15min.). The streets of the *centre ville* run in concentric rings around Basilique Notre-Dame; without a map, you may end up literally walking in circles (especially after a few *dégustations*).

Tourist Office: rue de l'Hôtel-Dieu (tel. 03 80 26 21 30; fax 03 80 26 21 39). Free maps and brochures. Hotel reservations 15F. Lists of *caves* offering tours. Guided tours of *vieille ville* with headset 35F (French or English; 300F deposit). Tours July-

Aug., in French. **Currency exchange** when banks are closed. Open Mon.-Sat. 9am-8pm, Sun. 9am-6pm; June 15-Sept. 15 also Sun. 9am-7pm.

Money: Crédit Lyonnais on pl. Monge and **Banque Populaire** on pl. de la Halle (across the street from the tourist office) both have 24-hr. **ATMs.**

Trains: av. du 8 Septembre (tel. 08 36 35 35 35). To Chalon-sur-Saône (6 per day, 25min., 29F); Lyon (6 per day, 1½hr., 110F); Dijon (15 per day, 25min., 37F); TGV to Paris (2 per day, 2hr., 230F). **Lockers** 15F. Ticket window open Mon. 5:30am-8:30pm, Tues.-Sun. 6:15am-8:30pm.

Buses: TRANSCO (tel. 03 80 42 11 00 in Dijon). To Chalon-sur-Saône (2 per day, 45min., 36F80); Dijon (10 per day, 1hr., 36F); Autun (1 per day, 42F). Stops at wineries along the Côte d'Or, but the complexities of getting back may sober you up quickly. Schedule available at the tourist office. Buses depart from several locations; ask which is most convenient for you.

Car Rental: Avis, 5bis, bd. Jules Ferry (tel. 03 80 24 96 46). 403F per day, 200km included; 2014F per week, with 2100km. Open Mon.-Sat. 8am-noon and 2-6pm.

Bike Rental: Bourgogne Randonnées, 7, av. du 8 Septembre (tel. 03 80 22 06 03), near the train station. Bikes 20F per hr., 90F per day, 170F for 2 days, 380F per week. Passport deposit. Open daily 9am-noon and 1:30-7pm.V, MC.

Laundromat: Blanc-matic, next to the supermarket off pl. Madeleine. Wash 20F. Dry 60F per 5kg. Soap 5F. Open daily 7:30am-7pm.

Hospital: Centre Hospitalier, av. Guigone de Salins (tel. 03 80 24 44 44). **Medical emergency** tel. 15. **Ambulance** tel. 03 80 24 64 00.

Police: av. du Général de Gaulle (tel. 03 80 22 16 16). **Emergency** tel. 17.

Post Office: bd. St-Jacques (tel. 03 80 26 29 50), *poste*-modern building with red steel girders outside. Poste restante. **Currency exchange.** Photocopies 1F. Open Mon.-Fri. 8am-7pm, Sat. 8am-noon. **Postal code:** 21200.

BURGUNDY

ACCOMMODATIONS AND CAMPING

Beaune welcomes hordes between April and November—especially on weekends. Make reservations far in advance. For cheaper accommodations, base yourself in Dijon or Chalon-sur-Saône, a 20-minute train ride away. In Beaune, the hotels around pl. Madeleine tend to be a bit less expensive than those in *centre ville.* A **Villages** hotel (see page 51) is 30 minutes out on rue Burgalat (tel. 03 80 24 14 50).

Hôtel Rousseau, 11, pl. Madeleine (tel. 03 80 22 13 59). From the station, head left on rue des Lyonnais until it turns into rue Celer, then turn right onto rue Faubourg Madeleine. Hotel is in the far right-hand corner. Beautiful wooden beds in clean rooms that open onto a secluded courtyard. Proprietors keep a large garden and cages of white doves out back. Strict 11:30pm curfew. Singles from 125F. Doubles from 170F, with shower 300F. Shower 20F. Breakfast included.

Hôtel le Foch, 24, bd. Foch (tel. 03 80 24 05 65; fax 03 80 24 75 59). Take av. de la République from the tourist office and turn right on bd. Foch. Simple, carpeted rooms with TVs. One suite with a sitting room and futon couch costs the same as a regular double. Singles and doubles 160F, with shower 200F. Extra bed 40F. Breakfast 28F. Free garage parking. Reception open 7am-9pm.V, MC.

Camping: Les Cent-Vignes, 10, rue Dubois (tel. 03 80 22 03 91), 500m from the town center off rue du Fbg. St-Nicolas. Head north on rue Lorraine from pl. Monge. Full by mid-afternoon in summer. 15F per person, children 7F50, 22F per tent or car, electricity 19F. Hot showers included. Restaurant and grocery store. Reception 8am-12:30pm and 1:30-10pm. Open March 15-Oct. 31. V, MC. About 7km away in Mersault, **La Grappe d'Or** (tel. 03 80 21 22 48; fax 03 85 87 06 14) has a pool, tennis courts, and bike rental. 17F50 per person, 23F per tent, 12F50 per car. 130 sites. Reservations recommended. Open April-Oct.

FOOD

The areas around **pl. Madeleine** and **pl. Carnot** boast restaurants with reasonable *menus.* For grocery shopping, you'll find all you need at the **Casino supermarket,** 28, rue du Fbg. Madeleine (open Mon.-Sat. 8:30am-7:30pm). Or hit the large **market** on pl. Carnot on Saturday mornings. If you want to break away from the restaurant scene, check out the amazing *charcuterie* at 4, rue Monge (tel. 03 80 22 23 04). **Roger Batteault's** shop is jam-packed with food customers.

Les Tontons, 22, rue du Fbg. Madeleine (tel. 03 80 24 19 64). Snazzy ambiance enhances traditional French and Burgundian favorites. *Menus* from 65F served within the stone walls of this lively joint. Open Mon.-Sat. noon-2pm and 7-10:30pm, although the bar is open later. Luke Skywalker would be proud. V, MC.

Café l'Hallebarde, 24, rue d'Alsace (tel. 03 80 22 07 68). An informal place with great lunch deals served with wine or beer. 60F for the *plat du jour,* wine, and a dessert. Or skip the dessert and pay 52F. Serves a wide variety of regional specialties. Open Tues.-Sat. for lunch and dinner, Sun. for lunch. V, MC.

L'Auberge Bourguignonne, 4, pl. Madeleine (tel. 03 80 22 23 53). Waiters in white await in this warm, traditional restaurant with an attractive stone façade. *Menus* at 79F and 89F. The cheese tray looks like the whole *fromage* section in Carrefour. Open noon-2pm and 7-9:30pm. Closed Mon. Oct.-April. V, MC.

Véry Table, 16, rue Louis Véry (tel. 03 80 24 62 44). Laid-back pizza place with pies (47-50F) and salads (40F). Rolling Rock and Lone Star beers available for the homesick. Open noon-10:30pm. V, MC.

SIGHTS AND ENTERTAINMENT

In 1443, Nicolas Rolin, chancellor to the duke of Burgundy, built the **Hôtel-Dieu** to hasten the city's recovery from recent ravages of war, poverty, and famine. His gift marked the beginning of 500 years of growth that resulted in the wine-wealthy tourist mecca that is now Beaune. The hospital, which continued to treat patients until 1971, has become the town's biggest non-potable tourist attraction. Its fascinating facilities are best taken in before your sobriety is spent on *dégustations.* Although reserved for the poor, the hospital managed to give its patients royal treatment through Rolin's bequest of 58 hectares of the area's finest vineyards. Every November, its vintages are still sold in one of the world's most famous charity auctions. In the **pharmacy,** jars of ingredients look like they could lurk in a well-stocked witch's chamber. Leave time to enjoy the Hôtel's greatest treasure, the 15th-century **Polyptych of the Last Judgment** by Roger von der Weyden, also commissioned by the magnanimous Rolin (open daily 9am-6:30pm; Nov. 22-March 23 9am-12:30pm and 2-7:30pm; admission 29F, students 22F).

Of course, wine is the fuel that keeps the hospice going, and a trip to Beaune mandates a descent into one of its many *caves.* The tourist office has info on *dégustations.* Wherever you are, ask questions about the wine-making process and the life of a *vigneron,* swirl the wine around in your glass, stick your nose in, inhale deeply, and admire the liquid's color in the light. Consider buying a bottle if you like it—most are less expensive here than anywhere else. Amateur wine-tasters learn how to pass as *connaisseurs* at the **Ambassade du Vin,** 8, rue Monge (tel. 03 80 21 53 72). Daily tasting workshops introduce oenology and its basic vocabulary (French and English classes at 10:30am and 5:30pm; 90F per person).

The largest of the cellars belongs to **Patriarche Père et Fils,** at 5-7, rue du Collège. An audio-guided visit leads you into the *caves* down a staircase descending from the altar of an 18th-century chapel; there are thousands of bottles to worship below (open daily 9:30-11:30am and 2-5:30pm; 40F plus a 10F deposit for the *tastevin,* the wine-tasting cup; all proceeds go to charity). The **Marché aux Vins,** rue Nicolas-Rolin (tel. 03 80 22 27 69), housed in a 15th-century church, funnels in a stream of tourists from the nearby tourist office and Hôtel-Dieu. For 50F, you can descend into a candle-lit *cave* and follow a trail of 20 wine kegs, each with a different Burgundian vintage for your sampling delight. Don't drink your limit too quickly—the best *(les grands crus)* always come near the end. Relish the Corton, the Côte de Beaune's sole *grand cru* (open June-Aug. Mon.-Thurs. 9:30am-noon and 2-7pm, Fri.-Sun. 9:30am-7pm; Sept.-May daily 9:30am-noon and 2-6:30pm). Other *caves* may be too specialized for an introduction; a few welcome mainly German tourists with clinking *Geldbörses.* Stumble up from the *caves* and dock your liver in the beautiful **Parc de la Bouzaise** (open daily April-Oct. 9am-9pm; Nov.-March 10am-6pm) beyond the city ramparts or at **pl. des Lions** just within.

The **Musée du Vin** lures oenophiles inside the **Hôtel des Ducs de Bourgogne,** rue d'Enfer (tel. 03 80 22 08 19), off pl. Général Leclerc. This former mansion of the Dukes of Burgundy dates from the 15th and 16th centuries. You can poke your head inside the wine cellar for free (to the left of the entrance). Take a look at the antique presses and vats, reminiscent of oversized Lincoln Log constructions. The painstakingly detailed museum takes you past bar graphs, pie and temperature charts, and topographical maps. Rush on to the exhibits tracing the evolution of the shapes of wine bottles, wine glasses, carafes, and *tastevins.* Vaguely sacrilegious paintings show Beaune's patron saint, the Virgin Mary, cradling a grape-clutching baby Jesus (open daily 9:30am-6pm, ticket booth closes at 5:30pm; admission 25F, students 15F; English pamphlet available for 3F). Your ticket to the wine museum also admits you to the **Musée des Beaux-Arts** and the **Musée Etienne-Jules Marey** (tel. 03 80 24 56 98), both on rue de l'Hôtel de Ville off rue de Lorraine. The former has a mediocre collection of Gallo-Roman funerary monuments and a small cache of paintings by 15th- and 16th-century Dutch and Flemish artists, as well as a sizeable group by Beaune's own Impressionist, Felix Ziem (open April-Nov. daily 2-6pm).

■ The Côte d'Or: The Wine Route

Whereas Beaune cautiously guards its bottled treasure in dark *caves* beneath the city, the carefree acres of rolling green vineyards to the north and south expose their glorious fruits to the Burgundian elements. The Côte d'Or—a 60-km strip of land between Dijon and Santenay, 20km south of Beaune—has nurtured wine grapes since around 400 BC. Traces of limestone in the soil, the precisely correct lay of the land, and ideal measures of rain and sun make the Côte the perfect place to cultivate grapes, and among the most valuable real estate in the world.

The Côte d'Or south of Dijon is divided into two wine producing regions: the **Côte de Nuits,** which extends down to the village of Corgoloin, and the **Côte de Beaune,** which goes south from there to Santenay. The wines from the Côte de Nuits are almost all red, and the great ones are made with the *Pinot Noir,* a purple-skinned, white-juiced wonder of a grape. The *Chardonnay* and *Pinot Blanc* grapes are responsible for the great white wines of the Côte de Beaune. These wines are known for their delicacy, whether smooth and dry or rich and fruity.

In vino veritas. In wine is truth, and the truth is that a trip through the Côte d'Or has the potential to break the budget traveler. If you're not planning to buy a 500F bottle of Chambertin, you can enjoy the Côte without having to indenture yourself as a grape-picker. Its ancient châteaux surrounded by an endless carpet of vines are worth seeing for themselves; the wine only sweetens the journey.

Most of the Côte d'Or wines may be sampled at one of Beaune's *caves de dégustations,* so seek out locations on the Côte that offer something more than the free sip or two that you could get in the city. Ten km south of Dijon, the **Château de Gevrey-Chambertin** (tel. 03 80 34 36 13), at the top of the Chambertin vineyards, is the home of the most celebrated wine in all of Burgundy. The tour, hosted by the gracious and justifiably proud English-speaking proprietor, takes you through her 10th-century château, built to protect the wine and the villagers (in that order). Louis XIV's doctor, who knew his wine perhaps better than his medicine, prescribed the Chambertin for his corpulent patient. (The wine was also a favorite of Napoleon, who is not a favorite of the *châtelaine.*) You'll see a millennium of history, including a 10th-century guard tower and an Impressionist painting by the owner's grandfather. The tour ends with a taste of her prized vintages, which she sells for 90-200F per bottle. (Open daily 10am-noon and 2-6pm; Nov.-March Mon.-Sat. 10am-noon and 2-5pm and Sun. 11am-noon and 2-5pm; 30-min. tour 20F.)

"Jamais en vain. Toujours en vin," is the motto of the **Château du Clos de Vougeot** (tel. 03 80 62 86 09), about 16km south of Dijon. Built in 1551, it stands sentinel in a vast vineyard, its size more impressive than its architecture. What really catches

the imagination, though, are the activities of the owners of the château, the *Confrérie des Chevaliers du Tastevin* (Brotherhood of the Knights of the *Tastevin*). The Brotherhood was founded in 1934 to promote the sale of Burgundian *crus* during a miserable slump in sales brought on by Prohibition and the Depression. Now 12,000 strong, the brothers still hold chapter meetings at the château. The tour, available in English on audio cassette, brings you past four massive wine presses, each capable of crushing four tons of grapes. You'll also see the wine hall, where the knights perform initiation rituals based on those described in the works of Molière and Rabelais. The Brothers may have their fun here, but there's no wine tasting or buying at the château. (Open April-Sept. Sun.-Fri. 9am-6:30pm, Sat. 9am-5pm; Oct.-March Sun.-Fri. 9-11:30am and 2-5:30pm, Sat. 9-11:30am and 2-5pm; closes at nightfall during the winter. Admission 16F, students 12F.)

About 15km southwest of Beaune, the **Château de Rochepot** (tel. 03 80 21 71 37), springs straight out of a fairy tale with its pointed turrets, glazed slate roof, and wooden drawbridge—though what you see today is a scrupulous 19th-century renovation of a 13th-century original. The 45-minute tour includes a peek at the Guard Room, the ingenious kitchens, the dining room, the old chapel, and the "Chinese" room (open Wed.-Mon. 10-11:30am and 2:30-5:30pm; admission 26F).

The **Route des Grands Crus,** the road slipping through the region, is mostly flat and lacks heavy traffic, making it just as ideal for **biking** as it is for viniculture (bike route maps available from the Beaune or Dijon tourist offices). Thanks to the SNCF, biking from Dijon to Beaune and returning with your bike on the train is doable in one day. Unfortunately, **trains** stop only in Beaune, Nuits-St-Georges, and Dijon. The reasonable distances between villages make **hiking** an option as well, especially if you time it right to catch a bus back. **TRANSCO buses** (tel. 03 80 42 11 00) stop throughout the Côte, but service is infrequent. If you don't want to walk, you may wait hours for a bus to come. **Bacchus Wine Tours** runs four daily guided minibus tours in English from Beaune (170-190F; info at the tourist office). Expect to pay about 500F per day for a **rental car** in Beaune or Dijon. This becomes more affordable when shared by several wine lovers and one tolerant, teetotaling *chauffeur.*

Tournus

Tournus, a sleepy little town of 7000, is less captivating than its Burgundian sisters. Now and then the twisted streets of the *vieille ville* are appealing, but the buildings they pass are uniformly gray and forgettable. The Abbaye St-Philibert, dating back to Roman times, is the main draw for tourists, although others may be lured by Tournus' magnificent location on the banks of the Saône river.

ORIENTATION AND PRACTICAL INFORMATION

From the train station, walk right on av. Gambetta, then left on rue Docteur Privey to get to the **tourist office** on pl. Carnot (tel. 03 85 51 13 10; fax 03 85 32 18 21). The friendly and knowledgeable staff hands out maps, lists of hotels and restaurants, and piles of brochures. Hotel reservations 15F (open daily 9am-noon and 2-7pm). It's hard to find **currency exchange** when banks are closed (neither the tourist office nor the post office changes money); plan ahead if you are considering a weekend trip. There is a 24-hr. **ATM** at **Société General** on rue de la République next to the tourist office. The easiest way to reach Tournus is to catch a **train** to Chalon-sur-Saône (on the Dijon-Lyon line), then take a train or bus from there. **Buses** are cheapest; the **gare routière** (tel. 03 85 48 79 04) is in front of the Chalon train station (info office open Mon.-Fri. 8:35am-noon and 2:15-6:15pm). For info on bus schedules, contact the Autocar Information Line, 6, quai de Verdun (tel. 03 85 51 01 69). The office has schedules, but as Tournus is served by many different bus companies, you will have to call each one directly to get prices. **Secam/Maisonneuve** (tel. 03 85 34 99 00) has a Chalon-Tournus bus line (#10, 7 per day, 30min., 22F). Two other bus companies are **Carione Val de Saone** (tel. 03 85 93 10 90) and **Autocars Lux Voyages** (tel. 03 85

48 37 92). **Trains** leave from the station on av. Gambetta (tel. 03 85 51 07 30) to Dijon (4 per day, 1½hr., 72F); Chalon-sur-Saône (8 per day, 15min., 25F); Mâcon (8 per day, 25min., 32F); Lyon (6 per day, 1½hr., 79F); and Paris (1 per day, 225F plus 20F TGV reservation). In case of **medical emergency,** dial 15. The **police station** is on route de St-Gengoux (tel. 03 85 51 12 34). In **emergencies,** dial 17. The **post office** (tel. 03 85 51 09 55) is on rue du Puits des Sept Fontaines (open Mon.-Fri. 8am-noon and 1:30-5:30pm, Sat. 8am-noon; **postal code:** 71700).

ACCOMMODATIONS, CAMPING, AND FOOD

The weary *Let's Go*-er's hosts-with-the-most in Tournus are **Les Poètes Disparus: Gîte de France** (tel. 03 85 40 26 09; fax 03 85 40 20 10). About 12km outside Tournus near Simandre, the *gîte* has two rooms (1-3 people per room) available for travelers under 30. 90F per person; includes breakfast, common bathroom, garden, pond, swimming pool, sauna, and bikes, all in *Les Poètes'* private home. Make a "last minute" reservation no more than five days in advance. Minivan will pick you up in Tournus in the evening (V, MC, AmEx). Reserve one of the four charming rooms above **Le Voleur du Temps** restaurant, 32, rue du Docteur Privey (tel. 03 85 51 71 93). From the station, go right on av. Gambetta and take the third left onto rue du Docteur Privey. African and European art decorates each room. (Singles 110F. Doubles 130F. Hall toilet and shower. Breakfast 25F.) Downstairs, the restaurant specializes in African dishes from the Ivory Coast and Senegal. Some local dishes are also on the menu. Dine in a room bedecked with ebony African masks or in a tranquil courtyard surrounded by ivy-covered walls (open daily noon-2pm and 2-9:30pm; V, MC, AmEx). The **Hôtel-Gras,** 2, rue Fénélon (tel. 03 85 51 07 25), is centrally located, and the rooms are large, clean, and bright—but old. (Singles 95F, with shower 148F. Doubles 145F, two beds with shower 230F. Breakfast 25F. Reception Mon.-Sat. 10am-midnight.) The restaurant downstairs serves *quenelles au brochet* (fish dumplings drenched in a creamy sauce) on its 65F and 105F *menus* (V, MC). Tournus' new campground, **Camping Municipal,** rue des Canes (tel. 03 85 51 16 58), is located right on the river. From the station, go left on av. Gambetta. You should see signs pointing you down the first street on your right. Take a left at the bottom of the hill and continue past the swimming pool *(piscine).* (10F per person, 10F per tent, 10F per car, 10F for electricity. Open April-Sept.)

The local **market** (Sat. 8am-1pm on pl. Carnot) stretches from one end of town to the other. To stock up at **Stoc supermarket,** go right on quai Midi (on the river) and then right again on rue Rougelet (open Mon.-Thurs. 8:30am-12:30pm and 2:30-7:15pm, Fri.-Sat. 8:30am-7:15pm). If you can stand the French Muzak at **Croq' Chaud,** 5, rue de la République (tel. 03 85 51 03 47), outside pl. Carnot, you can munch hearty portions at casual prices. The 50F *menu* includes salad, steak, fries, and dessert (open Mon.-Sat. noon-2pm and 7-10pm; V, MC, AmEx).

SIGHTS

The foundations of the **Abbaye St-Philibert** extend to AD 177 when St. Valenan tried to introduce Christianity to Tournus. He was martyred for his troubles on a hillside over the Saône. A sanctuary built near his tomb was later converted into an abbey bearing his name. In the 9th century, along came a band of monks fleeing the Norsemen in Noirmoutier, carrying with them the relics of their hometown saint, St. Philibert. Apparently, Philibert was a bigger pilgrim-pleaser than Valenan, and eventually the name of the abbey was changed accordingly. With its crenelated parapets and lofty spire, the building has the authority of a castle or military structure. Indeed, the church has played a dual role throughout the ages, protecting the town from pesky Norsemen, Hungarians, and other unwanted guests. Inside, you'll see everything through rose-colored glass—accentuated by the salmon-colored stone used on the pillars and arches. The remains of St. Philibert repose in the axial chapel at the far end of the abbey. Be sure to pay the 1F to light the crypt that lies beneath the church (stairway on the left at the far end of abbey). The Romanesque abbey is accessible from av. Gambetta by rue Albert-Thibaudat or from the *centre ville* by rue Jean-Jacques Rousseau off rue Docteur Prive.

Tournus' **Hôtel Dieu** is scheduled to open its doors to the public in the spring of '97. Near the Abbaye St-Philibert, the hospital once treated poor *paysans* and the military. It houses an array of attractions similar to other *Hôtels Dieu* in Burgundy.

There is not much to do in Tournus once evening falls, but you might try **Le Caveau,** 20, quai de Verdun (tel. 03 85 32 55 88), a piano bar/pub on the Saône with bean-bag seating (open at 4pm).

Paray-le-Monial

In mid-June France celebrates **la fête de Dieu** (the festival of God), and all activity focuses on the tiny town of Paray-le-Monial. It was here, in 1673, that Sister Marguerite-Marie Alacoque had her revelation of the *Sacré-Coeur* (Sacred Heart). The message was from Jesus Christ himself—"Here is the heart that adored humanity"—and its spiritual impact has spread far beyond the banks of the lazy Bourbince. The visions were carried to the Vatican by the 19th century, which spread the message of *Sacré-Coeur* through the Catholic world and dedicated France to its worship. The country's most important Sacré-Coeur basilicas are the wedding cake on Paris' Montmartre hill and the former Clunaic church here. Thus, Paray has established itself as a religious center second in France only to Lourdes. Pilgrims outnumber tourists in this tiny town, and the hymns flowing from its myriad chapels increase the serenity of this already tranquil setting.

ORIENTATION AND PRACTICAL INFORMATION

From the train station it's a short walk to the center of town and the tourist office, but it can be tricky—especially if you follow the signs. Exit left out of the station and make a right on av. de la Gare. Cross the canal bridge and veer right on av. Charles de Gaulle. At the end of the street, make a left on rue des Deux Ponts. At this point you will see a sign pointing to the *Office de Tourisme.* Do not let it tempt you; it points to a distant parking lot. Continue straight until you cross the bridge over the Bourbince (while admiring the view of the basilica), then turn right on av. Jean Paul II (renamed for the Pope's 1986 visit). When the road forks, you'll be in front of the **tourist office** and smack dab in the center of town (15 min.). The office will equip you with a free map. (Open daily July-Aug. 9am-7pm; May-June and Sept.-Oct. 9am-noon and 1:30-6:30pm; Nov.-April Tues.-Sat. 9am-noon and 1:30-5:30pm.) There is a 24-hr. **ATM** at **Crédit Agricole** on pl. Champ de Foire. **Trains** (tel. 03 85 81 13 25) in and out of Paray are infrequent. They take you to Paris (6 per day, 214F), Chagny (2 per day, 63F), and Lyon (2 per day, 96F). You can ride **SNCF buses** to local hubs Roannes (5 per day, 38F) and Le Creusot with its TGV terminal (4 per day, 40F). Cluny is 1½ hours away by bus (50F). The **hospital** is at 15, rue Pasteur (tel. 03 85 88 60 60). For an **ambulance,** call 03 85 88 83 36. The **police** are at 13, bd. Henri de Régnier (tel. 03 85 81 11 05). In an **emergency,** dial 17. The **post office** is on pl. de la Poste (open Mon.-Sat. 9am-noon and 2-6:30pm; **postal code:** 71600).

ACCOMMODATIONS AND CAMPING

Righteous Paray draws pilgrims year-round, although rooms are easy to find outside of summer. Comfortable, cheap rooms abound in the **Christian Foyers** near the basilica. The **Foyer du Sacré-Coeur,** 14, rue de la Visitation (tel. 03 85 81 11 01; fax 03 85 81 26 83), is a charming, quiet place in the center of town. Rooms are tastefully decorated, some with crucifixes hovering protectively over the bed. Pilgrims predominate, but pagans and tourists are welcome. (Singles from 95F. Doubles from 150F, with bath or shower from 180F. Breakfast 20F, lunch 60F, dinner 55F. Reception 8am-9pm.) The **Hôtel du Nord,** 1, av. de la Gare (tel. 03 85 81 05 12; fax 03 85 81 58 93) has simple, clean rooms, although they smell a bit musty. There's a comfortable sitting room with a TV. (Singles 135F. Doubles 145F, with bath, toilet, and TV 230F.

Showers 15F. Breakfast 25F. Reception 6:30am-11pm; V, MC.) There is a **Foyer des Jeunes Travailleurs** in Paray, but it's quite a hike from the town center (rue Michel Anguier; tel. 03 85 81 07 44; fax 03 85 81 28 16). Take a left out of the train station, then turn right on av. de la Gare. Cross the bridge and veer left on rue du 8 Mai. Before you cross the second bridge, turn left onto rue Pierre Lathuilière and follow until the end; make a right on route du Gué-Léger. When that ends, turn right and then make your first left on av. Chalon-sur-Saône. Make a right on rue Verdun, then a left on rue Michel Anguier. The *foyer* will be on your left (40min.). Clean, large singles and doubles with toilet, shower, and a mini-fridge 125F, with kitchen 175F. Laundry facilities, TV and game rooms. Breakfast 21F, lunch and dinner 42F. On your way to this *foyer,* you'll pass **Camping de Mambré,** route du Gué Leger (tel. 03 85 88 89 20), on the right. Bustling campsite with a pool and laundry. (Bungalows 200F, 300F in high season. 34F per tent, 14F per person; July-Aug. 36F per tent, 17F per person. 24-hr. reception. Open April-Oct.)

FOOD

A strip of cheap eateries squats on rue Victor Hugo off pl. Guignault, but a prettier place for lunch is the south side of the Bourbince, with views of the basilica. There's a huge **E. LeClerc supermarket** on rue Pierre Lathulière along the southern bank of the Bourbince (open Mon.-Thurs. 9am-12:30pm and 2:30-7:15pm, Fri.-Sat. 9am-7:15pm). **La Tarterie,** 9, rue Victor Hugo (tel. 03 85 81 21 66) is *the* place to go if you like tarts. 42F and 53F *menus* offer salad and dessert tarts. If you prefer your tart *à la carte,* choose from eight varieties filled with anything from salmon to asparagus for 19F each. They also serve pasta (open daily 10am-7pm; July 14-Aug. 15 10am-1am; V, MC, AmEx). There's a market Fridays 'til 1pm behind the Hôtel de Ville.

SIGHTS

Its towering spire visible throughout town, the **Basilique du Sacré-Coeur** is Paray's *raison d'être.* Although Paray didn't emerge as a religious center until the mid-1800s, when devotion to the Sacred Heart began to catch on in mainstream Catholicism, the basilica dates from the 11th century. It was built by order of St. Hugues, Abbot of nearby Cluny, and exhibits a simplified Cluniac-Romanesque style. Some of the abstract sculpted motifs appear in Middle Eastern art and may have been inspired by Hugues' travels in Moorish Spain. A spectacular view of the exterior is to be had from across the Bourbince, where the two belfries and portal cast reflections that seem to plunge into the calm river. From the steps of the reliquary, you can see the *chève,* or apse of the church, with its three chapels radiating like tentacles from the massive structure. Inside, the simple gray stone walls, devoid of embellishment, draw your attention and thoughts upward.

Rue de la Visitation (the street packed with visiting nuns and pilgrims) leads from the basilica to the other religious sights. The **Parc des Chapelains** behind the church is a peaceful spot for quiet reflection (unless a massive pilgrimage service is underway). In the park there's a diorama depicting Ste. Marguerite-Marie's life (tel. 03 85 88 85 80; open daily April-Oct. 9am-6pm). *La Chambre des Souvenirs* (relic chamber) is also behind the basilica. Ste. Marguerite-Marie's baptismal certificate, personal letters, and other effects are preserved behind glass. There's even a reconstruction of her bed next to a life-sized wax model of the kneeling saint. Continue along rue de la Visitation to the **Monastère de la Visitation,** sometimes referred to by directional signs as *la Chapelle des Aparitions.* This is the site where Jesus is said to have revealed himself to Marguerite-Marie. The small chapel lit by an indigo glow from the stained glass seems an apt place to encounter an apparition. At the end of rue de la Visitation, make a left to get back to the *centre ville.* On **pl. Guignault,** the sand-colored façade of the 16th-century **Hôtel de Ville** is adorned with portraits of French royalty. The **Tour St-Nicholas,** also from the 16th century, stands guard over pl. Guignault. Once the belfry of the long-gone St-Nicholas church, it's now just a pretty face with a beautiful staircase adorning its façade.

Cluny

At the height of its religious power, the town of Cluny was inhabited by about 5000 people. Today its once enormous abbey stands half demolished and Cluny's importance is in the memory of its former greatness; there are no more *Clunysois* today than there were in 1049. Lying between rolling green mountains in the Grosne river valley, Cluny makes a beautiful (if modest) base for biking and hiking through this region soaked in history.

ORIENTATION AND PRACTICAL INFORMATION

Cluny's **tourist office** is in the Tour des Fromages at 6, rue Mercière (tel. 03 85 59 05 34; fax 03 85 59 06 95) in the *centre ville.* Pick up their helpful map as well as the *Practical Guide* to Cluny. Accommodations service 15F. (Open daily 10am-12:30pm and 2:30-7pm.) A 24-hour **ATM** relinquishes its loot at **Crédit Agricole** on rue Lamartine. The only way to reach Cluny is by car, bike, or **bus.** You can catch a bus from Chalon-sur-Saône or Mâcon (3 per day, 1hr., about 25F). There is also service from Paray-le-Monial (1 per day, 50F). The **SNCF** bus/train combo from Tournus is 48F. For **bike rental** info call 03 85 59 08 34 or 03 85 50 00 77. For **ambulance** and **taxi,** call 03 85 59 04 87. The police are at rue Porte de Paris (tel. 03 85 59 06 32). In **emergencies,** dial 17. For **medical emergencies,** dial 15. The **post office** (tel. 03 85 59 07 98) is located off Chemin du Prado near the pont de la Levée (open Mon.-Fri. 8am-noon and 2-6pm, Sat. 8am-noon; **postal code:** 71250).

ACCOMMODATIONS, CAMPING, AND FOOD

The best deal for families and groups is **Cluny Séjour,** rue Porte de Paris (tel. 03 85 59 08 83; fax 03 85 59 26 27), right behind the bus stop. (74F per person per night includes breakfast and hall shower. Singles 111F. Reception opens at 5pm.) Another solid deal is the **Hôtel du Commerce,** 8, pl. du Commerce (tel. 03 85 59 03 09; singles from 100F, doubles from 150F, both 195F with shower; extra bed 40F; breakfast 27F; closed daily noon-3pm;V, MC). The restaurant **Candy,** 38, rue du Merle (tel. 03 85 59 29 63), is well worth a try. *Menus* start at 39F. 70F garners five copious courses including *boeuf bourguignon.* Open daily for lunch and dinner (V, MC, AmEx). Locals recommend **Les Marronniers,** 20, av. Général de Gaulle, for regional specialties on their three- (50F) or four-course (60F) *menus*. There is **camping** at **St-Vital,** rue de Griottons (tel. 03 85 59 08 34; fax 03 85 59 16 34), across the pont de la Levée near the municipal pool. (15F per person, 7F50 for children under 7. 8F50 per tent. 8F50 per car. Electricity 10F. Open May15-Oct. 1. Reservations recommended.) The **Maximarché supermarket** on av. Charles de Gaulle is open Monday to Sunday. There is a **local market** every Saturday morning near the abbey, and a string of *charcuteries* stretches next to the tourist office on rue Mercière.

SIGHTS

Most attractions in Cluny are somehow connected to the abbey. Begin your tour with a great view from atop the **Tour des Fromages** (located at the tourist office; admission 6F, students 4F; 120 steps). Next, walk along rue d'Avril for a peek at the well-preserved **Maisons Romanes.** This path leads straight into the **Portes d'Honneur;** framed within are the spires of the abbey. The **Musée d'Art et d'Archeologie** (tel. 03 85 59 23 97), on the left through the Porte d'Honneur, houses a repetitive collection of archaeological elements from the abbey. Your ticket to the museum admits you to all the abbey-related sights (tickets are 32F, students 21F).

Overall, the **Abbaye** itself has been the center of attention for hundreds of years. At the height of its power in the 11th and 12th centuries, it controlled well over 1000 dependent monasteries and 10,000 monks in an ecclesiastical empire that stretched into Asia. Until the construction of St. Peter's Basilica in Rome, its church was the largest in all of Christendom, and the abbot's power rivaled the pope's. But the bigger they are, the harder they fall, and Cluny was no exception. During the Revolution and the years that followed, the structure was looted, sold, and used as a quarry. By 1823, all that remained is what you see today. Now the structure is home to **Ecole Nationale Supérieure d'Arts et Métiers** and the central cloister sits alone, surrounded by student housing. Still, the roughly one-half of the original abbey that still survives gives an idea of the power and wealth that was once invested in these walls. Follow the *sens de la visite* signs through the remains of the great transept and into the beautiful garden filled with enormous roses. (Hours vary, but approximate 10am-noon and 2-6pm daily. Check with the tourist office before visiting.)

■ Near Cluny: Château de Cormatin

Just north of the former religious capital of Cluny lies a modern-day mecca for young faithfuls, Taizé. From there it's just a stone's throw to the **Château de Cormatin** (tel. 03 85 50 16 55). Built in the 17th century, Cormatin is the largest château from Dijon to Lyon open to the public. Within its walls lurk beautiful furniture, tapestries, and all the flair of the French Renaissance, protected by a murky moat and gorgeous gardens. The tour (in French) is signalled by a bell outside the château every half-hour and brings you through the castle's interior (English pamphlet available). Note the psychedelic wine bottles that line the great staircase. The most elaborate chamber is the gilded *"studiolo."* When the guide closes the outside shutters, the paintings come to life in the dimness. Outside lies the tortuous **Labyrinth Garden.** Other areas of the *jardin* let puzzle-addled brains rest. Cormatin is accessible from Cluny by bike or bus (14F). (Open daily May-Sept. 10am-noon and 2-6:30pm,Oct.-April 10am-noon and 2-5:30pm. Admission 33F, students 23F, children 17F.)

■ Autun

Autun's history is that of rivalries that weren't. Around 15 BC, the emperor Augustus founded Augustodunum—later shortened to Autun—to create a "sister and rival of Rome." It worked for a while, but the place lacked staying power, and invading barbarian tribes nearly finished off the city. The only proof of Autun's former status is an enduring collection of impressive ruins. In the 12th century, the city's bishop tried to jump-start Autun by building a church to house the relics of St. Lazarus. His Romanesque edifice was popular with pilgrims, but fire took care of the belfry and invading tribes known as "renovators" finished off Lazarus' tomb, leaving the vaguely Gothic edifice visible today. In the 15th century, *Autunois* Nicolas Rolin helped to make the town a center of economic activity, but it was nearby Beaune he endowed with an exquisite hospital that continues to draw crowds. Though Autun (pop. 20,000) is off the beaten path, the big dreamers who have pulled for the town through the ages left their imprint. With its serpentine streets, historically impressive edifices, and age-old ruins, Autun continues to inspire high hopes.

ORIENTATION AND PRACTICAL INFORMATION

The main street, **av. Charles de Gaulle,** connects the train station to the central pl. du Champ de Mars, a parking lot surrounded by important-looking buildings. To get to the more picturesque part of town, head uphill to the *haute ville.* Rue St-Saulge and rue aux Cordiers both run from pl. du Champ de Mars into rue Chauchien, which changes name twice before reaching the cathedral in the *vieille ville.*

The **tourist office,** av. Charles de Gaulle (tel. 03 85 86 30 00 or 03 85 52 20 34; fax 03 85 86 10 17), is off pl. Champ de Mars. They have a handy free map with a list of restaurants and hotels (open April-Sept. Mon.-Sat. 9am-noon and 2-7pm; Oct.-March Mon.-Fri. 9am-noon and 2-6pm, Sat. 9am-noon). There's an **annex** at 5, pl. du Terreau (tel. 03 85 52 56 03), next to the cathedral (open June-Sept. Mon.-Sat. 9am-7pm). Autun's **train station** is at pl. de la Gare on av. de la République (office open Mon.-Sat. 8:30am-7:30pm). Not many trains come through, but you can get to Paris (4 per day, 5hr., 211F) and Lyon (2 per day, 166F). **SNCF buses** (tel. 08 36 35 35 35) run to Châlon-sur-Saône (4 per day, 2hr. 54F), and **TRANSCO buses** (tel. 03 80 42 11 00) jog to Dijon daily at 5pm (2½hr., 77F). For a **taxi** call 03 85 52 05 06. **Crédit Mutuel,** pl. Champ de Mars, has a 24-hour **ATM,** and there is a **BNP** beside the tourist office. The **hospital** is at 9, bd. Fr. Latouche (tel. 03 85 86 65 66; fax 03 85 56 65 09). The **police** (tel. 03 85 52 14 22) are at 29, av. Charles de Gaulle. In an **emergency,** dial 17. You can **exchange currency** at the **post office** on rue Pernette (tel. 03 85 52 20 93; open Mon.-Fri. 8:30am-6:30pm, Sat. 8:30am-noon; **postal code:** 71400).

ACCOMMODATIONS, CAMPING, AND FOOD

There are cheap hotels near the train station; places nearer the *centre ville* tend to be pricier. Make reservations in advance during the summer. **Hôtel de France,** 18, av. de la République (tel. 03 85 52 14 00; fax 03 85 86 14 52), has many rooms with TV and phone. (Singles from 100F. Doubles from 115F, with shower from 155F. Breakfast 23F. Closed Sun. 'til 5:30pm.) **Hôtel les Arcades,** 22, av. de la République (tel. 03 85 52 30 03; fax 03 85 86 39 09), boasts rooms with huge bathrooms and comfy beds. (Singles 120F, with shower 150F. Doubles 130F, with shower 250F. Buffet breakfast 30F.) Stake your claim at **Camping Municipal de la Porte d'Arroux** (tel. 03 85 52 10 82), an easy 20-minute walk from town. From the train station, turn left on av. de la République, left on rue de Paris, and go under the Porte d'Arroux. Cross the bridge and veer right on route de Saulien; the campground is on your left. There is a restaurant and a grocery store nearby. (13F per person, 12F per tent, 8F per car. Open April-Oct. In July and Aug., extra 14F fee for campground security.)

For *gaulloise* cuisine, try **Auberge de la Bourgogne,** 39-40, pl. du Champ de Mars (tel. 03 85 52 20 96). Choose zee leetle *escargots* or *grenouilles* (frog legs 60F). Four varieties of trout (around 55F); *menus* start at 55F. The four-course, 75F *menu* has savory *coq au vin* (open Tues.-Sun. noon-2pm and 7-10pm; V, MC, AmEx). Roman-themed restaurants—pizzerias and pasta joints—line the cobblestone streets of the *haute ville*. **Relais des Hauts-Quartiers,** 2, rue des Bancs (tel. 03 85 86 10 73), has sunflower-colored, Mediterranean dining rooms and about a dozen pizza (35-45F) and pasta (40F) options (open Wed.-Mon. noon-2pm and 7:15-10pm; V, MC). If you're looking for more authentic Roman ambiance, Autun's 2000-year-old ruins are prime picnicking territory. Prepare for your invasion at **Atac,** at the corner of av. Charles de Gaulle and rue Renault (open Mon.-Sat. 8:30am-12:15pm and 2-7pm).

SIGHTS

At the top of the *haute ville,* the **Cathédrale St-Lazare** rises above the Morvan countryside. In the course of 900 years of clerical quarrels, one group objected to the marvelous **tympanum** above the church doors and covered it in plaster, unwittingly protecting the masterpiece from the ravages of the Revolution. Jesus presides over the Last Judgment while Satan tinkers with the weighing of the souls, and the apostles look on as the chosen move to an eternal Jerusalem. The artist's name, Gislebertus, is visible below Jesus' feet. In the dimly lit nave, intricately carved capitals illustrate Biblical scenes, but the best rocks await in the *salle capitulaire* above the sacristy. Some of the figures leering out from the 800-year-old carvings resemble slightly satanic muppets. If the belfry's renovators have finished their work, you can climb over 200 steps for views of Autun's rooftops and *la campagne.*

There isn't much left in Autun from the Roman period, considering that the city was the largest in Gaul, with a circus, theater, and amphitheater. The sights still standing are all outside the ancient city walls in accordance with Roman custom. Arm yourself with a map (free at the tourist office) if you plan to roam the ruins. Standing behind the train station, across the river Arroux, is the huge brick **Temple de Janus.** The temple, once 24m high and 16m wide, was dedicated in the first century to an unknown Roman deity. It wasn't Janus, a panel erected by the city sharply insists, although a shady cult maintained the Janus myth for centuries. To reach it, walk along the rue de Paris until you pass under one of the city's two remaining Roman gates, the **Porte d'Arroux.** With two large arches for vehicles and two smaller ones for pedestrians, this gate led to Agrippa's Way, the trade route between Lyon and Boulogne.

Cross the river, then take the footpath leading to the left. After you pass the temple, the path returns to town via rue Fbg. St-André. The other gate, the **Porte St-André,** is at the intersection of rue de la Croix Blanche and rue de Gaillon. It is flanked by a guard house, now a small chapel.

The **Théâtre Romaine,** accessible by av. du Dragons off pl. de Charmasse, could once seat 12,000 enthralled spectators. It now entertains plebeian picnickers most of the year. Occasionally, however, the theater roars to life when 600 locals re-enact the early days of Augustodunum, bringing Caesar, the Roman legions, chariot races, and games to life in a *son et lumière.* The spectacle takes place during the first three weekends of August (tickets at the tourist office; ask them for info). From the hillock at the rear of the amphitheater, you can see the bizarre 30m-high jumble of bricks 1km away known as the **Pierre de Couhard.** For a better look, follow the signs from the cathedral, but be warned—it's uphill all the way. The purpose of this stone heap remained unknown until excavations unearthed a 1900-year-old plaque cursing anyone who dared disturb the eternal slumber of the man buried inside.

All of Autun's attempts at greatness come together in the **Musée Rolin,** at 3, rue des Bancs (tel. 03 85 52 09 76), next to the cathedral. The diverse collection, housed in the 15th-century mansion of Burgundian chancellor Nicolas Rolin, includes beautiful Gallo-Roman mosaics, a Roman helmet of bronze and gold shaped like a leafy human face, Gislebertus' poignant sculpture of Eve at the Fall, the noseless man of Nazareth, and elegant armoires and beaux-arts tableaux from all over France. (Open April-Sept. Wed.-Mon. 9:30am-noon and 1:30-6pm; Oct. Wed.-Sat. 10am-noon and 2-5pm, Sun. 10am-noon and 2:30-5pm; Nov.-March Wed.-Sat. 10am-noon and 2-4pm, Sun. 2:30-5pm. Admission 17F, students 8F50.)

Nevers

Canals, forests, fields, and the Loire and Nièvre rivers all converge on Nevers. Although this small city (pop. 50,000) on the western edge of Burgundy was the setting for Marguerite Duras' novel and screenplay *Hiroshima Mon Amour,* its real claim to fame is as the final resting place of Ste. Bernadette de Lourdes. Bernadette Soubirous, the young girl who reported conversing with the Virgin Mary in Lourdes (see page 376), came to Nevers in July of 1866 to enter the Couvent St-Gildard. Miraculously she's still there, preserved in the convent's chapel. Beyond the bustle of a modern industrial city, Nevers sequesters carefully tended parks, modest squares, and a long tradition of excruciatingly detailed ceramics. If at first you aren't impressed by this reticent city, remember Duras' admonition, "Saying that Nevers is a tiny town is an error of both the heart and the spirit."

ORIENTATION AND PRACTICAL INFORMATION

From the train station, head four blocks up av. Général de Gaulle to Nevers' main squeeze, pl. Carnot. The **tourist office** (tel. 03 86 68 46 00; fax 03 86 68 45 98) is in the Palais Ducal, diagonally across the square from av. de Gaulle. The office offers free accommodations service, tours (mid-June to mid-Sept. Sun.-Fri. 5pm; 25F, students 15F), and the usual plethora of info (open July-Aug. Mon.-Sat. 9am-7pm, Sun. 10am-7pm; Sept.-June Mon.-Sat. 9am-noon and 2-6pm). There are **ATMs** on pl. Carnot. **Trains** pass through Nevers to: Dijon (4 per day, 2½hr., 144F); Lyon (1 direct per day, 3½hr., 166F); Paris (12 per day, 2hr., 161F); Bourges (2 per day, 1hr., 59F); and Clermont-Ferrand (6 per day, 1½hr., 116F). Ticket and info windows (tel. 08 36 35 35 35) are open daily 5:45am-9:10pm. Just to the left of the station as you exit is the *gare routière* (tel. 03 86 57 16 39), with limited **bus service.** If a medieval rampart jumps when you weren't expecting it, go to the **Centre Hospitalier,** 1, av. Colbert (tel. 03 86 68 30 30, **medical emergency** 15), or the **police,** 6bis, av. Marceau (tel. 03 86 60 53 00). In case of **emergency,** dial 17. The **post office,** 25bis, av. Pierre Bérégovoy (tel. 03 86 21 50 21), has poste restante (postal code 58000) and **currency exchange** (open Mon.-Fri. 8am-6:30pm, Sat. 8am-noon; **postal code:** 58019).

ACCOMMODATIONS AND CAMPING

The tourist office has a list of hotels and restaurants in the area. Rooms near the station and *centre ville* start around 115-130F, but there are some cheaper (85-100F) options on rue Fbg. de Mouësse, about a 25-minute walk from the station. There is a **Foyer des Jeunes Travailleurs** right by the cathedral. They cater to long-term residents—call to see if they can take you. (Residence Clair Joie, 2, rue Cloître St-Cyr; tel. 03 86 59 86 00; 100F per person, sheets and breakfast included.) Several blocks to the left of the train station at 5bis, rue St-Gildard, **Hôtel Beauséjour** (tel. 03 86 61 20 84; fax 03 86 59 15 37), across from the convent, boasts clean and pleasant rooms with phones and TVs. (Singles and doubles 115-130F, with shower 150-205F. Shower 20F. Extra bed 40F. Breakfast 25F. Reception 24hr. V, MC.) Closer to the station, **Le Thermidor,** 14, rue Claude Tillier (tel. 03 86 57 15 47), has large, plain rooms. (Singles 130F. Doubles 140F. Triples 210F. Quads 260F. With shower 150F, 160F, 280F, and 300F respectively. Breakfast 25F. Reception 7am-10pm. Closed at the beginning of Aug. and Sun. in winter. V, MC.) The classy two-star **Hôtel Villa du Parc,** 16ter, rue de Lourdes (tel. 03 86 61 09 48; fax 03 86 57 85 17), is conveniently located across the park from pl. Carnot. (Singles and doubles 130F, with shower 155F. No hall showers. Extra bed 50F. Breakfast 28F. Free parking. Reception 7am-10:30pm. V, MC, AmEx.) The award for the most scenic site in town goes to the **Camping Municipal** (tel. 03 86 37 56 52), which surveys the *vieille ville* across the Loire. From the cathedral, follow rue de la Cathédrale to the river, cross the bridge, and turn left (10F per person, 10F per tent, 8F per car; reception 8am-8pm).

FOOD

Nevers' *vieille ville* is studded with pricey *brasseries,* but there are inexpensive spots in all directions from pl. Carnot. **Rue du 14 Juillet,** between pl. Carnot and the cathedral, boasts a bevy of inexpensive ethnic restaurants. Try such Moroccan delights as couscous (65-95F) at **L'Alhambra,** 55, rue du 14 Juillet (tel. 03 86 59 35 06; open Tues.-Sun. noon-2:30pm and 7-10:30pm). Up the street, **Restaurant Asie,** 29, rue du 14 Juillet (tel. 03 86 59 12 77), has a 49F lunch *menu* and a four-course evening feast for 79F. Munch on Chinese and Vietnamese specialties and finish your repast with lichee nuts and banana ice cream in coconut milk. *A la carte* dishes go for 25-50F (open Mon. 7-10:30pm, Tues.-Sun. noon-2:30pm and 7-10:30pm; V, MC). **La Grignote,** 7bis, rue Ferdinand Gambon (tel. 03 86 36 24 99), welcomes wanderers with its delicious seafood specialties (quiche 32F, fish 58-90F, scrumptious desserts 26-35F; open Tues.-Wed. noon-2:30pm, Thurs.-Sat. noon-2:30pm and 7:30-10:30pm). The self-service restaurant at the **foyer** is pleasant and open to the public. Meals go for around 45F. The baguette-hunk-of-cheese-and-an-apple crowd finds inner peace at **Stoc supermarket,** 12, av. Général de Gaulle, half a block from pl. Carnot (open Mon.-Fri. 9am-7:30pm, Sat. 8:30am-7:30pm, Sun. 9am-noon). A **market** does its thing in Marché Carnot (entrances on rue Général de Gaulle and rue St-Didier; open Mon.-Fri. 7am-12:30pm and 3-7pm, Sat. 7am-7pm).

SIGHTS

The **Cathédrale St-Cyr et Ste-Juliette** (tel. 03 89 59 06 74) was rebuilt five times between 502 and 1945; all the ages are at work here. Unfortunately, the builders never got it quite right—if you stand in the center and gaze at the ceiling, you can see that the nave is crooked. Since the church is also a bit vertically challenged, you can get a close look at its leering gargoyles. The original stained glass of the Gothic apse in the east was destroyed by bombing during World War II; the apse now showcases modern stained glass created by five artists between 1977 and 1983. Each window features one dominant color; as the sun moves across the sky, they bathe the walls of the apse in deep shades of green, orange, violet, and red (open June-Sept. Tues.-Sat. 10am-noon and 2-7pm). Opposite the cathedral, fairy-tale turrets cap the **Palais Ducal** (tel. 03 86 68 46 00). Its exhibits are tenuously connected to Nevers: an aquarium of local fish; a racecar to commemorate the *Nevers Magny Cours* (a racetrack that erupts in the last week in June for the Grand Prix de France); and an automated, if not animated, duke who holds forth on the city's history (open daily May-Sept. 9am-7pm; Oct.-April 9am-noon and 2-6pm; free). On pl. Charte, to the east of the cathedral, the simplicity of the 11th-century **Eglise St-Etienne** obscures the fact that poor Duke William of Nevers spent so much money on its construction that he couldn't afford to join his fellow knights on the First Crusade.

Across from pl. Carnot, the **parc Salagro** covers the center of town. At the edge of the park, the **Couvent St-Gildard,** on the corner of rue Jeanne d'Arc and rue St-Gildard (tel. 03 86 57 79 99), houses the Congregation of the Sisters of Nevers and Ste. Bernadette herself. The convent is a strange combination of tourist thrills and religious devotion; pilgrims from all over the world come to pray here. A small museum in the convent gives a thorough overview of Bernadette's life and displays many artifacts, including copies of letters describing her visions. Thanks to a spectacular waxing, the star of the show reposes peacefully in a glass case in the chapel, seemingly oblivious to the furor she created in her native Lourdes. The friendly nuns will be happy to answer questions and serve as tour guides (museum and chapel open daily April-Sept. 7am-7:30pm; Oct.-March 7am-noon and 2-7pm; free).

The tourist office can provide you with the brochure *Cheminements Piétons,* which details several walks through the city. A walk among the gardens lining the **Promenade des Remparts,** from the Loire to av. Général de Gaulle, follows the crumbled remains of 12th-century Nevers. Also along the Promenade is the **Musée Municipal Frédéric Blandin** (tel. 03 86 23 92 89). Installed in the 13th-century Abbaye Notre-Dame, it houses a collection of the ceramics for which Nevers is famous as well as paintings and temporary exhibits (open May-Sept. Wed.-Mon. 10am-6:30pm; Oct.-April 10am-noon and 2-5:30pm; admission 10F, students 5F).

■ Near Nevers: La Charité-sur-Loire

Twenty-three km north of Nevers (by frequent **trains,** 25min., 27F), the red roofs, church spire, and ramparts of La Charité-sur-Loire make the tiny town on the banks of the Loire an ideal daytrip. Founded in the 8th century and appropriated by Cluniac monks, La Charité grew in power and wealth until it was known as "the eldest daughter" of Cluny, with 400 dependent monasteries throughout Europe. Unfortunately, the stronghold that Joan of Arc was unable to conquer in 1429 was virtually annihilated by a 1559 fire and the wars of religion. The helpful **tourist office,** pl. Ste-Croix (tel. 03 86 70 15 06), gives excellent guided tours of the church and surrounding city (July-Aug. Mon.-Sat. 10am-noon and 3-6pm, Sun. 3-6pm), has informative brochures on regional sites, and will help you find a place to stay (open daily July-Aug. 10am-2pm and 2-6pm; April-June and Sept. 10am-noon and 3-4pm). Call the *mairie* (tel. 03 86 70 16 12) for info in the off season.

Second only to Cluny in its power and size, the **Eglise Notre Dame** is La Charité's *raison d'être.* The tourist office has a detailed binder in English to guide you through the massive structure. A three-tiered transept and blood-red *vitraux* line the interior, now half the size of the original. At the far end of the apse, La Charité herself is depicted in the glass. On the south wall by the exit, check out the 12th-century **Tympanium of the Transfiguration** with its odd statuettes and 3-D border. Though it may not look like much, behind the church lies the surviving portion of the original **Eglise St-Laurent.** Discovered in 1975, this *chantier de fouilles archéologique* (excavation site) is the find of the century for La Charité. From the ruins, you can get a good look at the apse, a 12th-century chapel, and the **Bell Tower of Bertrange.** After passing the cloister and cellars, the tour will lead you toward the tiny yet fascinating **Musée Adam** (tel. 03 86 70 34 83), where the prized artifacts from the excavation now reside. There is a room devoted to regional handicrafts, as well as one room of decorative arts, carefully selected to include only those works produced by France's most renowned artists. The most impressive part of the museum, however, is its collection of dramatic sculptures and statues by Pina, Rodin's Italian student. Remarkably, one of the pieces is made entirely of wax. (Open April-June and Sept. Wed.-Mon. 2:30-6pm; July-Aug. 10am-noon and 2:30-6pm. Admission 20F, students and seniors 10F.) Upon entering the museum, a walk along the now-grassy Roman ramparts will give you a great view of the town and the Loire. For another look, cross the Pont de Pierre to the **Faubourg,** where you can picnic in the church's reflection. If you feel the urge to get out of town, the **Forêt des Bertranges,** just 5km from town, has over 10,000 hectares of woods, trails, and fountains. To get there, go east on RN151 past the cemetery on your right.

Avallon

The *vieille ville* of Avallon (pop. 10,000) peeks above medieval walls high on a granite mountain. The town's impressive ramparts, designed by the prolific military architect Sébastien "The Fortifier" Vauban, serve as a great point to survey the entire Yonne region. However, nothing can arrest the inevitable onslaught of yawns that an extended visit to too-tranquil Avallon can muster. No longer a military target, the town makes an excellent base from which to attack the nearby forest of the Morvan.

ORIENTATION AND PRACTICAL INFORMATION

The **tourist office,** 4, rue Bocquillot (tel. 03 86 34 14 19), is next to the Eglise St-Lazare, a 15-minute walk from the train station. Head straight on av. du Président Doumer and make a right onto rue Carnot. At the large intersection turn left onto rue de Paris, which passes a large parking lot, becomes the pedestrian street Grand Rue Aristide Briand, passes through the Tour de l'Horloge, and lands you at the office. The staff offers a free map and accommodations service, as well as **currency exchange.** (Open July-Aug. daily 9:30am-7:30pm; Sept. 9:30am-12:30pm and 1:30-6:30pm; Oct.-Easter Tues.-Sat. 9:30am-12:30pm and 1:30-6:30pm; Easter-June daily 9:30am-12:30pm and 2:30-6:30pm.) On Mondays in winter, call the *mairie,* 37-39, Grande Rue A. Briand (tel. 03 86 34 13 50; open Mon.-Fri. 8:30am-12:30pm and 1-5pm). **Trains** (tel. 03 86 34 01 01) run to Laroche-Migennes, which connects to Paris (7 per day, 3hr., 145F) and Dijon (3 per day, 3hr., 90F); direct trains run to Autun (3 per day, 2hr., 69F) and Auxerre (5 per day, 1hr., 48F). (Station open Mon.-Sat. 5:40am-9pm, Sun. 6:50am-9pm.) The staff at the tourist office also has schedules for **TRANSCO buses** (tel. 03 80 42 11 00) that roll from the train station to Dijon (3 per day, 2½hr., 88F) with a stop in Semur-en-Auxois (45min., 40F). **SNCF buses** leave from the **gare** for Vézelay (2 per day, 30min.). For **car rental,** try **Europcar,** 28, rue de Lyon (tel. 03 86 34 39 36). Economy cars (390F per day) include 200km mileage and insurance (open Mon.-Fri. 8am-noon and 2-6pm). **Bikes** are available from **Touvelo** on rue de Paris (tel. 03 86 34 28 11; 100F per day; open daily 8am-noon and 2-6:30pm). **Centre Hospitalier,** Avallon's **hospital,** is at 1, rue de l'Hôpital (tel. 03 86 34 66 00). **Medical emergency** tel. 15. **Police,** 2, av. Victor Hugo (tel. 03 86 34 17 17). **Emergency** tel. 17. **Post office,** 9, rue des Odebert (tel. 03 86 34 91 08; open Mon.-Fri. 8am-noon and 2-6:30pm, Sat. 8am-noon; **postal code:** 89200).

ACCOMMODATIONS AND FOOD

The **Foyer des Jeunes Travailleurs,** 10, av. de Victor Hugo (tel. 03 86 34 01 88; fax 03 86 34 10 95), is 20 minutes from the train station and 15 minutes from the *vieille ville.* From the station, walk straight ahead on av. du Président Doumer, turn right onto rue Carnot, which becomes route de Paris after the intersection, then go left onto av. de Pepinster at the next major intersection. Stay on Pepinster when it becomes av. du Morvan and, finally, go left onto av. Victor Hugo. Singles in the modern high-rise are large and simple (78F first night, 73F thereafter; breakfast 16F; meals 46F). Nearer to the station lies the **Hôtel au Cheval Blanc,** 55, rue Lyon (tel. 03 86 34 55 07), with bright and spacious rooms, all with showers (doubles and singles 150F, with toilet 210F; triples and quads 210F; breakfast 24F). Downstairs, a rustic restaurant offers an excellent three-course *menu* at 52F (reception 7am-3pm and 5-midnight; V, MC, AmEx). Around the corner from the post office at 4, rue de l'Hôpital, stands **Au Bon Accueil** (tel. 03 86 34 09 33), which rents large rooms with TV and phone (singles 145F; doubles 195F; rooms for 3-5 people 235F). The popular restaurant downstairs has 52-152F *menus* with lots of options and the best fries this side of France—possibly the most affordable meals in town (reception 7am-11pm, closed Sun. night; V, MC). **Camping Municipal de Sous-Roche** (tel. 03 86 34 10 39) lies 2km away; walk straight from the train station onto av. du President Doumier, right on rue Carnot, then straight through the big intersection. Head straight along route de Lourmes and then veer left on rue de Sous Roche. Climb to the riverside campground (17F per person, 12F per site, 12F per tent or car; open March 15-Oct. 15; reception 8am-noon and 4-10pm).

At the top of town, try **La Tour,** 84, Grand Rue A. Briand (tel. 03 86 34 24 84), for delicious Italian food in a warm atmosphere. Big salads go for 20-30F, pizzas 28-38F, and pastas 38-50F (open daily 11:30am-2:30pm and 7:15-10:15pm; V, MC, AmEx). The tiny **Casino supermarket** does its thing on rue de Paris, a block or two past the intersection with rue Carnot toward town (open Tues.-Sat. 8:15am-12:30pm and 3-7pm, Sun. 8:45am-noon). For that megastore experience, you can trek to the more distant **Casino** at the corner of rue de la Marland and av. de Pepinster, off route de Paris (open daily 9am-7:30pm). A **market** grabs pl. Vauban on Saturday morning; a smaller one takes place Thursday mornings in the parking lot by the post office.

BURGUNDY

SIGHTS

A walk along the narrow paths of the western and southern ramparts yields an excellent view of the dense forests, verdant pastures, and crumbling châteaux of the Vallée du Cousin. The tourist office can give you a detailed map of an 8km walk that covers the area's highlights and will point out its numerous biking circuits.

Two prominent remnants of days gone by stand side-by-side at the southern end of the *vieille ville.* A 15th-century slate watchtower, the **Tour de l'Horloge,** straddles Grande Rue A. Briand and keeps the *Avallonais* on schedule. Down the street, the **Eglise Collégiale St-Lazare** gained its present name in AD 1000 when Henry LeGrand, Duke of Burgundy, donated a part of St. Lazare's skull to the church. Two ornate Romanesque doorways consisting of a series of recessed arches, depict cherubim, the Zodiac, and the Elders of the Apocalypse carrying instruments. The crypt below dates from the 4th century (open daily 8:45am-7pm; winter until 6pm).

The **Musée du Costume,** 6, rue Belgrand, off Grande Rue A. Briand (tel. 03 86 34 19 95), has far more flair. Eight rooms of the prince of Condé's 17th-century house bustle with bustles and *bijoux* each summer as mannequins don period dress for the annual exhibition (open mid-April to Oct. daily 10:30am-12:30pm and 1:30-5:30pm; admission 20F, students 12F). Behind the tourist office, the **Musée de l'Avallonais** (tel. 03 86 34 03 19) contains an interesting but poorly presented collection of artifacts, statues, and jewelry from Gallo-Roman times to the Middle Ages, as well as contemporary religious art. Many exhibits look like junior high science-fair fare (open May 15-Sept. 15 Wed.-Mon. 2-6pm; admission 15F, students 8F).

Vézelay

Perched high on a hill 15km from Avallon, the village of Vézelay (pop. 580) smiles on the valley below, watching over the surrounding fertile pastures and dense forests. The houses in town, covered with red tile roofs and wild roses, seem lost in time. Considered one of the most beautiful villages in France, Vézelay lives up to its tremendous reputation. Yet most people don't come to Vézelay to admire the crumbling ramparts or soaring views—pilgrims and tourists alike flock to the 12th-century Basilique de la Madeleine and its crypt, which shelters Mary Magdalene's relics. The host is at its thickest on July 22, the official day of homage to *la Madeleine.*

ORIENTATION AND PRACTICAL INFORMATION

Vézelay's **tourist office,** rue St-Pierre (tel. 03 86 33 23 69; fax 03 86 33 34 00), just down the street from the church, offers free maps, has an accommodations service (10F), and **exchanges currency** (open June 15-Oct. daily 10am-1pm and 2-6pm; Nov.-June 14 Fri.-Tues. 10am-1pm and 2-6pm). There is no train station in Vézelay; **trains** run from Paris through Auxerre to nearby Sermicelles (7 per day, 30min., 38F); a **bus** shuttles passengers to Vézelay (Mon.-Fri. 2 per day, 1 on Sat.). Call the train station at Sermicelles (tel. 03 86 33 41 78) for schedules and prices. The **SNCF** also runs buses from Avallon to Vézelay (1-2 per day, 20min., 21F). If you're feeling lucky, spin the roulette wheel of public transport with **Cars de la Madeleine** (tel. 03 86 33 35 95) which goes from Avallon to Vézelay twice a week from Avallon's Café de l'Europe, returning in the late afternoon. Schedules vary according to driver's whim; for current times, call the Vézelay tourist office or Cars de la Madeleine (16F each way). **Bicycles** are available from **Garage Gauche,** route d'Avallon, on your right at the foot of the *ville.* Mountain bikes are 60F per half-day, 120F per day (open daily 9am-1pm and 2-7pm). Many report that **hitchhiking** in the area is easy; we say it's never safe. Dial 15 in a **medical emergency,** and 17 for the **police.** The **post office,** on rue St-Etienne (tel. 03 86 33 26 35), has an **ATM** and poste restante (open Mon.-Fri. 9:45am-noon and 2:15-6pm, Sat. 8:45-11:45am; **postal code:** 89450).

ACCOMMODATIONS AND FOOD

Plenty of expensive restaurants and hotels in Vézelay stand ready to relieve poor pilgrims of their worldly goods. Thank heavens for the few charitable options. Next to the tourist office, the Sisters of the **Centre Ste-Madeleine,** rue St-Pierre (tel. 03 86 33 22 14), provide beds, showers, and kitchen facilities—bring your own sheets or sleeping bag. Rooms are rustic and adorned with wooden crosses. (40F per person in 20-bed dorm, 50F in 2- to 7-person rooms, singles 85-100F, 1F tax per person. You must buy a 15F "Association St-Pierre" membership at the Centre. No smoking. Reception 8am-8pm, with a 6-6:45pm break for mass). On a peaceful, rural site 700m from town, the simple but comfy **Auberge de Jeunesse (HI),** route de l'Etang (tel. 03 86 33 24 18 or 03 86 33 25 57), offers more pagan accommodations in six-person rooms. Follow the signs to the *gendarmerie* from the base of the hill to the left. Go past the police station; the hostel is 400m down the road on your left (45F per bed; kitchen; reception 8:30-10am and 5:30-8pm; lockout 10am-5:30pm; open June-Sept.). Drink in the view with your morning coffee from the **campground** behind the hostel (15F per person, 5F per tent). For a bit more comfort and privacy, the friendly **Hôtel de la Terrasse** (tel. 03 86 33 25 50), in front of the basilica at pl. de la Madeleine, offers large, attractive rooms in a great location. (Singles and doubles 130-190F, with shower 220-250F. Triples or quads 250-300F, with shower 350F. Breakfast 30F. Reception daily 8am-8pm; closed Tues. and Wed. morning Sept.-June.) Run by the Fraternité Monastique de Jérusalem, the **Maison Pax-Christi,** rue des Ecoles (tel. 03 86 33 35 98), provides inexpensive beds just below the basilica. Closed for renovations in 1994, it should return in July of '97.

You won't have to shell out much for good food at **Crêperie L'Auberge de la Coquille**, 81, rue St-Pierre (tel. 03 86 33 35 57). Enjoy *galettes,* crêpes, and salads (14-45F) in a sunny courtyard or rural dining room (weekday *menus* 45F and 65F; open daily in summer 11:45am-11:30pm; in winter 11:45am-10:30pm). Take a gamble at **Casino supermarket,** near the bottom of rue St-Etienne (open daily 8:30am-7:30pm; Oct.-June closes from 12:30-3:30pm, Wed. and Sun. closes at 12:30pm).

SIGHTS

In the 11th and 12th centuries, Christians flooded Vézelay to venerate the remains of **St. Mary Magdelene.** As it goes with millennia-old bones, however, the authenticity of the relics was thrown into doubt in the 13th century when another set was discovered at St-Maximin in Provence, near where Ste. Marie had landed in AD 40 (see page 458). Today, the relics at Vézelay remain officially sanctified by the Catholic Church; many still journey to commune with them in the crypt of the **Basilique Ste-Madeleine.** The basilica itself is a graceful mix of Romanesque and Gothic elements, restored from 1840 to 1859 by Viollet-le-Duc. The 12 columns of the colonnade represent the apostles; the lone square pillar represents Judas and imperfection. Carved in 1140, the **tympanum** above the narthex's main portal portrays a risen Christ welcoming worshipers to the inner nave of the church. To appreciate the extraordinary interior carvings, take an informative, though somewhat preachy, tour given by a Christian guild of volunteers "welcoming visitors so that they discover the Christian meaning of the monument beyond its architecture and iconography" (available in English; July-Aug. daily 10am-noon and 2-5pm, by appointment the rest of the year; tel. 03 86 33 35 98). The church suggests a 30F offering in thanks for its guide; those who prefer poverty to damnation may want to pay it (open July-Aug. 7am-6pm; Sept.-June sunrise-sunset; basilica illuminated July-Aug. Tues. and Fri. 9-10:30pm). In summer a small **museum** above the chapter room displays sculptures removed from the church and chronicles the 19th-century restoration work (open July-Sept. Wed.-Mon. 10am-noon and 3-7pm; admission 10F). To take in the surrounding countryside, follow the signs pointing behind the church past the ruins of the 12th-century abbey to the *terrasse.*

BURGUNDY

■ Near Avallon and Vézelay: The Morvan

Both Avallon and Vézelay make an excellent starting ground for a foray into the **Parc Naturel Régional du Morvan,** with its densely wooded forests, clear lakes and streams, fields of clover and wild flowers, and druidic ruins. The Celts named the region "Morvan" (Black Mountain), a term that suits this granite-sloped landscape. Though the government named it one of 23 regional parks, its bourgeois Burgundian neighbors are fond of noting that "nothing good comes from the Morvan, neither good people nor a good wine." As for the wine, they certainly know what they're talking about—the Morvan's rocky slopes refuse to yield a single shriveled *raisin.* Rather, the park is a haven for hiking, biking, canoeing, and spelunking.

Les Car Charles (tel. 03 86 84 61 67) runs buses Tuesday, Thursday, and Saturday between Avallon and Dun Les Places (45F), about 5km from **St-Brisson,** in the heart of the region. The tourist office at Avallon is an excellent source of information on the Morvan. They provide pamphlets and advice about hiking, mountain biking, *gîtes d'étape,* and *chambres d'hôtes* in the area. Another resource is the **Maison du Parc Naturel Régional du Morvan,** 58230 St-Brisson (tel. 03 86 78 79 00; fax 03 86 78 74 22), the park's official visitors' center. They provide information about transportation throughout the region. The Maison sports a small room for expositions, fish-breeding ponds, a deer enclosure, an arboretum trail with information about local trees, a micro-garden, and even a Resistance museum (open daily June-Sept. 10:15am-6pm; Oct.-May Mon.-Fri. 8:45am-noon and 1:35-5:30pm; museum open 10:15am-6pm; in winter by appointment only; admission 20F, students 10F). **Morvan Sports Nature,** in Dun Les Places (tel. 03 86 84 63 22), organizes white-water rafting, cave, and high adventure course excursions (190F).

■ Auxerre

In 418, St. Germain converted Auxerre to Christianity. The Abbaye St-Germain was to be the most prestigious Catholic institution of its day. With the Revolution, Auxerre fell from grace and became thirsty Paris's prime supplier of Chablis and Burgundies. Divine retribution came in the form of a 19th-century *phylloxera* crisis and technological advances; the invention of the iron horse made the town obsolete as a transportation hub. Since then, Auxerre (pop. 41,000) has returned to its more pious ways and nowadays tends to the temperamental frescoes of its churches. The haze of its bacchanalian past still lurks in the fairy tale spires of its Tour d'Horloge, the narrow, half-timbered charm of the quartier de la Marine, and the ample shelf space devoted to the region's wines at the local Monoprix.

ORIENTATION AND PRACTICAL INFORMATION

From the train station make a bee-line for the tourist office by veering left and crossing onto rue Jules Ferry. Turn right onto av. Gambetta, and ford the river on pont Bert. The tourist office is on the right, three blocks down quai de la République.

Tourist Office: 1-2, quai de la République (tel. 03 86 52 06 19; fax 03 86 51 23 27), below the cathedral, on the banks of the Yonne. Map, lists of hotels and campgrounds. **Currency exchange** when banks are closed. Accommodations service 15F. Evening walking tours include tastings of wine, cheese, and chocolates (25-30F). Open mid-June to mid-Sept. Mon.-Sat. 9am-1pm and 2-7pm, Sun. 9:30am-1pm and 3-6:30pm; mid-Sept. to mid-June Mon.-Sat. 9am-12:30pm and 2-6:30pm.

Money: Banks hover protectively around **Crédit Agricole** and other **ATMs** at the corner of pl. des Cordeliers and pl. Charles LePère.

Trains: Gare Auxerre-St-Gervais, rue Paul Doumer (tel. 08 36 35 35 35), east of the Yonne. Mostly indirect to: Paris (13 per day, 2hr., 118F); Lyon (8 per day, 4½hr., 211F); Dijon (8 per day, 2-4hr., 122F); Avallon (9 per day, 1hr., 48F); Autun (3 per day, 3hr., 101F). **Luggage storage** hides from you in the *gare* restaurant, 4-15F.

Buses: *Gare routière,* a real headache to get to, on rue des Migraines (tel. 03 86 46 90 66). From the tourist office, walk north on quai de la République, which becomes quai de la Matine. Turn left on bd. de la Chainette. Rue des Migraines is directly across the roundabout. **Les Rapides de Bourgogne** (tel. 03 86 46 90 90) serves Troyes (1 per day, 83F).

Public Transportation: Le Bus (tel. 03 86 46 90 90), faultless service to Auxerre and its suburbs. Line 1 circles the *centre ville*, passing both the train and bus station every 30min. Schedule and map at the tourist office. One-way ticket 6F20.

Taxis: Taxis Auxerre (tel. 03 86 48 25 32).

Bike Rental: SARL Oskwarek, 22, rue de Preuilly (tel. 03 86 52 71 19). 100F per day, 150F weekend, 350F per week. Passport deposit.

Youth Center: Bureau d'Information Jeunesse de l'Yonne (BIJY), 70, rue du Pont (tel. 03 86 51 68 75). Info on youth activities and concerns. Free guide to regional events. Open Mon.-Fri. 8am-noon and 2-6pm.

Hospital: Hôpital Général, 2, bd. de Verdun (tel. 03 86 48 48 48). **Medical emergency** tel. 03 86 46 45 67.

Police: 32, bd. Vaulabelle (tel. 03 86 40 85 00), rue Lacune de Ste. Pallaye (tel. 03 86 52 86 93). **Emergency** tel. 17.

Post Office: pl. Charles-Surugue (tel. 03 86 48 57 21), in the town center. **Currency Exchange.** Poste restante (postal code: 89011). Open Mon.-Fri. 8am-7pm, Sat. 8am-12:15pm. **Postal code:** 89000.

ACCOMMODATIONS, CAMPING, AND FOOD

Foyer des Jeunes Travailleuses (HI), 16, bd. Vaulabelle (tel. 03 86 52 45 38). Follow the signs from the train station to the *centre ville,* cross the pont Bert, and turn left on quai de la République; the first right is rue Vaulabelle. In an inconspicuous apartment building to the left, back from the street just past a Total gas station. Simple, clean, pleasant singles. 76F, breakfast free. Meals 36-41F.

Foyer des Jeunes Travailleurs, 16, av. de la Résistance (tel. 03 86 46 95 11; fax 03 86 46 89 70). Facing the tracks, turn right and walk to the end of the platform. Cross the foot bridge and continue straight onto av. de la Résistance. The *foyer* is the high-rise on your right (5min.). Dim rooms and delicate shower ecosystems. Singles 76F. Doubles 130F. Breakfast included. Reception daily 8am-9pm.

Hôtel St-Martin, 9, rue Germain-Bénard (tel. 03 86 52 04 16), off bd. Vauldille. Small but attractive rooms with cheerful floral wallpaper. Singles 100F. Doubles 110F. Triples 170F. Quad 250F. Shower 10F. Breakfast 20F. Closed Sun. and Aug.

Hôtel l'Ecu, 5, rue Joubert (tel. 03 86 52 09 96). Little luxury in this 300-year-old house with downstairs bar, but the price is right. Singles 85F. Doubles from 100F. Triples from 125F. Shower 10F. Closed Sun. and Aug. Reception 8am-11pm.

Hôtel de la Renomée, 27, rue d'Egleny (tel. 03 86 52 03 53; fax 03 86 51 47 83), in the *vieille ville.* Plain, spacious rooms. Some overlook a courtyard, others over a busy street. Singles 100F, with shower and TV 115F. Doubles 115F, with shower and TV 165F. Breakfast 23F. Restaurant downstairs has *menus* from 51F. Private parking. Closed Sun. and last 3 weeks in Aug. Reception 7am-10pm. V, MC.

Camping: (tel. 03 86 52 11 15), 8, route de Vaux, south of town on D163. Shady 3-star grounds along the Yonne, with TV and laundry facilities. 12F per site, 14F per person and car. Open April-Sept. Reception April 7am-8pm, May-Sept. 7am-10pm.

At **Le Trou Poinchy,** 34-36, bd. Vaulabelle (tel. 03 86 52 04 48), the food is exquisite and the prices excellent. Try the bistro (main courses 45-55F, tasty 75F *menu*), the cool restaurant (98F and 115F *menus*), or hang out on the terrace (open daily noon-2:30pm and 7:30-10:30pm; closed Sun. night and Wed. Nov.-March; V, MC, AmEx). For curry in a hurry, fly to **Nirmala Tandoori,** 43, rue Toubert, opposite the Théâtre Municipal (tel. 03 86 52 46 98), and sink into their 3-course express 45F lunch *menu* of chicken curry or chicken tandoori, onion bhaja, and basmati rice. Dinner *menus* from 59F. (Open Mon.-Sat. 11:30am-2pm and 6:30-10:30pm. V, MC.) **La Crêpe 'rimbambelle,** 10, rue Fécauderie (tel. 03 86 51 37 10), serves extravagant and elegant crêpes and *galettes* from 12F. Filling salads 30F. (Open daily 11:30am-2pm and 7-11pm. V, MC, AmEx.) **Monoprix supermarket,** 10, pl. Charles Surugue, will keep you in Nutella through a month of Sundays; the cafeteria attracts lunching locals (dishes 21-37F; open Mon.-Sat. 8:30am-7:30pm; open until 8am Fri.). A **market** engulfs pl. de l'Arquebuse Tuesday mornings and Fridays until 6pm; schlepp to the market on pl. Degas in the outskirts for Sunday morning goat-cheese cravings.

SIGHTS AND ENTERTAINMENT

The 13th–century **Cathédrale St-Etienne** spans a high hill along the Yonne, turning its embellished face to the *vieille ville.* The Gothic interior is the fourth successor to the original 5th-century Roman edifice. Joan of Arc shines brilliantly in a *vitrail* to your left as you enter the church. Peer at the ochre fresco *Christ on Horseback* in the serene 11th-century **crypt;** it's worth risking the crick in your neck to gaze at the simple, almost primitive rendition. Currently undergoing restoration, the small **treasury** guards enamel-work, relics, illuminated manuscripts, and the 5th-century tunic of St. Germain—in need of a good pressing by now (open Mon.-Sat. 9am-noon and 2-6pm, Sun. 2-6pm; admission 8F to crypt, 10F to crypt and treasury).

The **Abbaye St-Germain,** at 2, pl. St-Germain, attracted medieval pilgrims seeking to honor St. Germain and medieval scholars seeking the wisdom of its ecclesiastic college. The guided tour (in French) descends through a series of chapels, the lowest of which was built directly on the rock to anchor the abbey in place. Its 9th-century frescoes, depicting the stoning of St. Etienne, are the oldest in France. Their deterioration has been caused not only by the centuries, but also by camera flashes (now prohibited) and the chemicals in human breath (try to hold yours). (Tour every ½-hr. Open April-Oct. Wed.-Mon. 10am-6:30pm; Nov.-March 10am-noon and 2-5:30pm. Admission to museum, chapel, and guided tour of crypt 20F, free for students. For information call 03 86 51 09 74.) Access to the church and crypt is through the excellent **Musée St-Germain,** whose informative and user-friendly explanations clarify pre-historic, proto-historic, and Gallo-Roman items (open July-Aug. Wed.-Mon. 9am-12:30pm and 2-6:30pm; Sept.-June 9am-noon and 2-6pm).

Towards pl. de l'Hôtel de Ville, the **Tour de l'Horloge,** a two-faced 15th-century clock tower in gold and terra cotta, serves as a *porte* to the pedestrian zone and the *vieille ville.* The **Musée Leblanc-Duvernoy,** 9bis, rue d'Egleny (tel. 03 86 52 44 63), in swank quarters between rue Gaillard and rue de l'Egalité, contains elegant 18th-century Beauvais tapestries, as well as life-changing painting and pottery (open Wed.-Mon. 2-6pm; admission with St-Germain ticket). Duck into the Neoclassical 17th-century **Chappelle des Visitandines,** which shelters 72 expressive polychrome wooden sculptures by local artist François Brochet. The pieces, made between 1948 and 1981, were donated by the artist (open July-Aug. Wed.-Sun. 2-6pm; free).

Franche-Comté

"Free country" is on the alert. The valleys of the Doubs—blessed with a sprinkling of manmade canals in towns like Dole and Besançon—are in danger of subversion by "Le Grand Canal." Yet to be approved or implemented, the proposed waterway would join the Rhine and Rhône rivers, subsuming whatever lies in its path, including the verdant beauty of the Doubs. It may, however, have to drown a few boys of Besançon along the way; loosely translated, the province's name means "free country," a testament to its 700 years of struggle to maintain political independence. These isolationist tendencies are being challenged by a recent campaign to draw tourists to the area. Playing the very card that has kept the tour buses away—its relative seclusion, its lack of big cities, and its preponderance of villages with lots of charm and no Holiday Inns—Franche-Comté is beginning to lure tourists.

Franche-Comté has always attracted considerable attention. Inhabited by the Celts in 58 BC, Franche-Comté came under German rule in 1032 but was ceded to Philippe le Bel of France in 1295. In 1447, the Habsburgs annexed the region, only to lose it to Spain in 1556. Finally, in 1604, the French seized control of the war-torn area once and for all; Louis XIV annexed Franche-Comté and dispatched Vauban to fortify the area. Rising over the plains of the French heartland and nestled against Switzerland and Alsace, the region has been ideal for military strategists. Only a few decades ago, the Comté switched flags again, forming part of Nazi-occupied France.

Today, the Jura mountains in the region are used for more peaceful pursuits. The rolling, green summits make excellent destinations for summer hikes. Blanketed in snow in the winter, the Jura is home to some of France's finest cross-country skiing, including the **Grand Traversée de Jura**, a 400km network of cross-country trails that spans the entire region. Besançon, Dole, and Pontarlier are all known for their lush, wooded environs and remote, seemingly endless forests.

Although natural beauty is the region's biggest appeal, Franche-Comté is not all wilderness; the region gained world renown and prosperity when Daniel Jean-Richard, a Genevan artisan, established a small watchmaking shop in the Jura. Before long, Jean-Richard's success enticed other Genevan watchmakers, frustrated with the fierce competition in Switzerland, to move to the Jura and establish their own shops. When Frédéric Japy developed a way to mechanize the production of watches, the price of local timepieces dropped through the floor, forcing Geneva to cater to the upper end of the market and establishing Franche-Comté as the leader in watchmaking for the budget timekeeper. By the 1830s, the region had surpassed Paris as the watch capital of the world, a distinction Besançon maintains today.

The area from Arbois down to Lons-le-Saumier is the region's wine route, producing respectable *appellations* with a decidedly fruity flair. *Vin jaune,* or yellow wine, is unique to the region. Aged for six years in oak casks, the prized *comtois* nectar develops a hazelnut flavor, a yellowish tinge, and an astronomical price. The area around Fougerolles is know for its *eau-de-vie* (spirits flavored with cherry, raspberry, pear, and plum), and Pontarlier has its own licorice-flavored *anis apéritif.* The regional cheese is the sharp *comté;* 600 liters of milk go into 50kg of this firm, nutty *fromage*. Look also for creamy *morbier* with its telltale blue-black streak, and sweet *emmental.* The tables of Franche-Comté are laden with bountiful smoked ham, hard sausage, farm-fresh chicken, and river trout. Traditional dishes are often prepared with a cream-based sauce or graced by the celebrated *vin jaune.*

Forgotten for many years by tourists and industry alike, Franche-Comté is beginning to burst into the spotlight and attract high-tech companies by recalling its history of science and innovation. As the area's most famous scientist, Louis Pasteur, boldly claimed, "My greatest discovery is my region." The deluge of visitors spawned by the new tourism campaign may enable others to make great discoveries in Franche-Comté.

GETTING AROUND

Franche-Comté's proximity to Switzerland, Germany, and the Alps makes it a convenient stop on many itineraries. Trains run frequently between the larger cities in the region but cross many hills and mountains. Besançon is the regional transportation hub, sending daily trains to just about anywhere you want to go in Franche-Comté. Service is slow at times; expect delays. **Monts Jura** buses provide decent service to smaller towns (some of which are not reachable by train) and excursions into the mountains. As elsewhere in France, hitchhiking is rarely easy here.

Dole

As you munch your cereal in the morning, give thanks to this idyllic corner of Franche-Comté; Louis Pasteur, *homme savant* and the world's most celebrated milkman, was born here in 1882. Since his methods of pasteurization have altered what we eat and how we see living things, the *Dolois* conclude that their man (and hence their town) changed the world. Although pasteurization is nothing to sneeze at, the discovery of germs is not all Dole (pop. 28,000) has to offer. Its beautiful canals, winding pedestrian passageways, flower-laden gardens, and tranquil atmosphere provide escapes from the bustling student populations of Besançon and Dijon and the foggy stupor of wine-tasting in Beaune. Settle for a day along the banks with (germ-free) cheese and crisp baguette, or cycle through the anything-but-sterile surrounding countryside and ponder the meaning of microscopic life.

ORIENTATION AND PRACTICAL INFORMATION

Dole's center is **pl. Grévy,** a few blocks north of the river. Exiting the train station, turn left on av. Aristide Briand. Turn left again on bd. Wilson, following the signs to the **Office de Tourisme.** Turn right on av. de la Paix and follow to the end. The tourist office is on your right in pl. Grévy (10min).

Tourist Information: Tourist Office, 6, pl. Grévy (tel. 03 84 72 11 22). Friendly staff, small office. Free map and hotel list. Guided tours of the city in French (25F, students 20F). Open July-Aug. Mon.-Fri. 6:30am-noon and 1:30-6:30pm, Sat. 9am-noon and 2-6pm, Sun. 10am-noon; Sept.-June Mon. 2-6pm, Tues.-Fri. 8:30am-noon and 2-6pm, Sat. 9am-noon. In the same building, **Jura Vert** (tel. 84 82 33 01) carries info on the Jura mountains. Pick up a copy of **Passeport Intersites** for discounts on sites throughout the Jura.

Money: 24-hr. **ATM** at **Banque Populaire,** pl. Grévy (tel. 03 84 82 07 23).

Trains: pl. de la Gare (tel. 03 84 79 72 09). To: Dijon (23 per day, ½hr., 44F); Besançon (19 per day, ½hr., 42F); Strasbourg (10 per day, 3½hr., 181F); Belfort (5 per day, 1½hr., 107F); Pontarlier (4 per day, 1hr., 74F); Paris TGV (6 per day, 2½hr., 250F).

Buses: Monts Jura, 17, av. Aristide Briand (tel. 03 84 82 00 03; fax 03 84 82 46 88). Excursions to towns in the Juras and beyond. Office open Mon.-Thurs. 8am-noon and 2-6pm, Fri. 8am-noon and 2-5pm, Sat. 8am-noon.

Public Transportation: Dolebus, 17, av. Aristide Briand (tel. 03 84 82 22 32). Tickets 4F50, *carnet* of 10, 35F. Office open Mon.-Fri. 9am-noon and 2-5pm.

Taxis: 7F per kilometer. Outside the train station, but the town is quite walkable.

Bike Rental: Moto CMS, rue du Gouvernement, just off pl. Grévy (tel. 03 84 72 23 62). 100F per day, 180F per weekend. Deposit varies by model, up to 2500F (yikes!) or passport. Open Mon. 3-7pm, Tues.-Sat. 9am-noon and 2-7pm. V, MC, AmEx.

Hospital: Centre Hospitalier Louis Pasteur, av. L. Jouhaux (tel. 03 84 79 80 80). **SAMU** tel. 15. **Medical emergency** tel. 03 84 82 36 36. **Ambulance,** 44, rue des Arènes (tel. 03 84 82 66 33).

Police: Local Police, 1, rue du 21 Janvier (tel. 03 84 79 63 10). **National Police,** 44, av. Jacques Duhamel (tel. 03 84 79 00 77). **Emergency** tel. 17.

Post Office: 5, av. Aristide Briand (tel. 03 84 79 42 41). Poste restante and **currency exchange.** Open Mon.-Fri. 8am-6:30pm, Sat. 8am-noon. **Postal code:** 39100.

ACCOMMODATIONS AND CAMPING

Comfortable student foyers welcome budget travelers throughout the year, and Dole's several reasonably priced hotels usually have space.

Auberge de Jeunesse le St-Jean (HI), pl. Jean XXIII (tel. 84 82 36 74; fax 84 79 17 69). Turn right out of the station and then left onto rue Jantet. Follow it to the end and make a right on bd. Wilson. Turn left onto av. Pompidou at the second big intersection, then take the next right onto rue Général Lachiche. Where the street makes a sharp left, walk straight into the hostel's gravel parking lot (15min.). Spacious and clean dorm-like rooms 64F; sheets and shower free. Laundry. Breakfast 18F. Lunch or dinner 39F. Reception Mon. and Thurs. 8:30-11:30 am and 1:30-6pm, Tues. and Wed. 8:30-11:30am and 1:30-7pm, Fri. 8:30-11:30am and 1:30-4pm, Sat.-Sun. 6-7pm. Call ahead.

Foyer L'Accueil Dolois, 8, rue Charles Sauria (tel. 03 84 82 15 21; fax 03 84 82 25 81), is in a beautiful former convent in the center of town. From the station, head left, then straight ahead on av. Aristide Briand until the pavement turns to brick. Turn right onto rue Raguet-Lépine; the foyer is at the end of the street. Caters mostly to locals. Preference given to those under 25. Showers and toilets on each floor. Ping-pong, TV rooms, computer room, kitchen, and laundry facilities. Reception 9am-midnight. 80F per person; breakfast and sheets included. No lockout. Midnight curfew. Often full during the school year. Its **Restaurant-Associative** serves 5-course lunches (noon-3:30pm) and dinners beginning at 7:15pm. 36F for guests, 40-45F for others.

Hôtel Moderne, 32, av. Aristide Briand (tel. 03 84 72 27 04), is the cheapest of three pleasant, inexpensive hotels across from the train station. Functional singles (two can crowd in) 80F, with bath 120F. No hall showers. Larger rooms with bath 180F. The baths live up to the hotel's name. Bar downstairs. Reception 5am-11pm. V, MC, AmEx.

Camping: Camping du Pasquier (tel. 03 84 72 02 61), right on the canal. From the *gare,* walk straight ahead on rue Aristide Briand, left on rue de la Sous-Préfecture, to pl. Grévy. Follow the signs from there (20min.). Hot showers. 2 people, car, and tent, 60F. 2 people and tent, 43-50F. Open March 15-Oct.15 daily 7am-10pm. Reception 8am-noon and 3-10pm. Bungalows for long stays. Call ahead.

FOOD

Dole's canal no longer defends the Holy Roman Empire from France but does make the perfect backdrop for a picnic. **Rue de Besançon** is rife with quality *charcuteries, épiceries,* and a **Casino supermarket** (open Mon.-Sat. 7:30am-12:30pm and 3-5:30pm, Sun. 8:15am-12:15pm; closed Wed. afternoon). You'll find a larger selection and lower prices at the **Intermarché supermarket** on the corner of av. L. Johaux and av. Georges Pompidou (open Mon.-Thurs. 8:45am-12:15pm and 2:30-7pm, Fri. 8:45am-12:15pm and 2:30-7:15pm, Sat. 8:45am-7pm). Check out the **Marché de la Ville,** near the **Basilique** (every Tues., Thurs., and Sat. 8am-noon).

La Bucherie, 14, rue de la Sous-Préfecture (tel. 03 84 82 27 61), serves excellent pizza (35-53F) in an underground restaurant with fresh roses on every table. 60F *menu.* Try the unusual and delicious *Franc-Comtoise pizza du chef* with artichokes, *escargots,* and bacon (45F). Salads 20-46F. Open Tues.-Sat. noon-2pm and 7-10pm, Sun. noon-2pm.

Taj Mahal, 73, rue Pasteur (tel. 03 84 72 01 57), provides tasty alternatives to regional specialties. Their lunch *menu* includes choices of tandoori meats, curries (with rice), and dessert. Savor lamb *kebab* (26F). The vegetarian curry, *legumes korma* (20F), is the best deal in the house. Open daily 11:30am-1:30pm and 6:30-10pm. V, MC, AmEx.

Chez Coco, 34, rue des Vieilles Boucheries (tel. 03 84 79 10 78), at the bottom of a stairway off rue de Arenes. *Menus* of regional cuisine at 55F, 65F, and 80F. *A la carte* 40F. Open June-Aug. daily 11:30am-10pm, Sept.-May Mon.-Sat. noon-5pm.

La Demi-Lune, 39, rue Pasteur (tel. 03 84 72 82 82), adjacent to Pasteur's birthplace. Cheerful dining room and a terrace overlooking the canal. 55F *menu* includes *entrée, plat,* ¼ wine, and *café. Galettes* (12-75F) with local specialties—*jurasienne* items feature the ubiquitous *comté* cheese. Open noon–midnight.

SIGHTS

Visiting Dole without stopping at the **Maison Natale de Louis Pasteur** would be like climbing the Eiffel Tower without bothering to look at the view. The house, 43, rue Pasteur (tel. 03 84 72 20 61), has been converted into a museum honoring the man, his work, and his family. Pasteur was not only a model child, a budding genius, a teacher at the Sorbonne, and an outspoken humanitarian, but also a gifted artist before he devoted his life to micro-organisms. A visit takes 45 minutes, with an English translation of the French legends available on request. The collection of Pasteur memorabilia ranges from the personal (baby bonnet, last will and testament) to the technical (microscopes, test tubes, spinal cord of a rabid rabbit). Don't let this museum slip pasteurize. (Open July-Aug. Wed.-Sat. 10am-6pm, Sun. 2-5pm; Nov.-Mar. Wed.-Mon. (except Sun. mornings) 10 am-noon and 2-5pm. Sept.-Oct. and April-June Wed.-Sat. 10am-noon and 2-6pm, Sun. 2-5pm. Admission 20F, students 10F, disabled and children under 12 free.)

An arch to the right of the house leads to the **Canal des Tanneurs,** where Pasteur's father cured hides. Continue along the canal to your right to see the willow-lined estuaries and picture-perfect stone bridges, Dole's most endearing attractions. You can explore an extensive network of **underground locks** and waterways. From Pasteur's house, go left on rue Pasteur, pass rue de Prelot, and walk thirty steps or so. Turn around. On your right, you should see a "hidden" stairway called **Passage Raynaud III,** an (occasionally locked) entrance to the underground canals.

Stepping out of the house, you will soon discover that Dole's most interesting sights lie not under the microscope but rather along the network of canals, paths, and gardens in the southern part of the *vieille ville.* Friendly *Dolois* often invite strangers to join the endless games of *boules* in the **cours St-Marius,** across from the pl. Jules Grévy. A path leads to a man-made set of canals, grottoes, and waterfalls. On hot days, some of the locals throw caution to the wind and jump in to cool off. For more secluded walks, stick to the river Doubs and its canals.

The 73m spire of the 16th-century **Basilique Notre-Dame** is easily visible from all points in Dole. The church is the largest in Franche-Comté. Be sure to take a glance inside at the magnificent organ looming in the back of the cathedral. Events in its free concert series are listed at the tourist office.

A couple of blocks away, the **Musée Municipal,** 85, rue des Arènes (tel. 84 72 27 72), contains works by Vouet, Le Brun, Courbet, and others, as well as an archaeological section with Celtic, Gallo-Roman, and Merovingian displays (open Tues.-Sun. 10am-noon and 2-6pm; free).

Pontarlier and the Jura

Eight hundred and forty meters in the sky sits the quiet town of Pontarlier, a good base from which to reach even greater heights in the **Haut-Jura mountains.** Pontarlier's hotels fill with both outdoor-adventure-seekers and businesspeople seeking profit through international trade in this town only 12km from Switzerland. From the tourist's point of view, its premier attraction is its natural setting, although Pontarlier and its main street are delightful even without the nearby mountains. Much older than the Alps, the Jura have become rounder and smoother with age. Covered with alternating dense pine forests and sunny meadows, the mountains are criss-crossed with countless trails for hiking, mountain biking, and skiing.

ORIENTATION AND PRACTICAL INFORMATION

To reach the **tourist office,** 14bis, rue de la Gare (tel. 03 81 46 48 33; fax 03 81 46 83 32), exit the station, cross through the rotary, and bear left on rue de la Gare. Go one block. The tourist office will equip you with reams of info on hiking, skiing, and other outdoor sports. Ask for the free regional guide, *Le Doubs: C'est Tonique.* A full-color topographical map of the region's hiking and biking trails is 57F (open Mon.-Sat. 9am-noon and 2-6pm, Sun. 10am-noon and 3-6pm). There are several **ATMs** in town, including one at **Banque Populaire,** across the street from the tourist office. Others can be found on rue de la République at **Crédit Lyonnais** and **Caisse D'Epargne.** The **train station** (tel. 03 81 46 56 99) is on pl. de Villingen-Schweningen—*jurasien* for "pl. de la Gare." Trains go to Dole (3 per day, 1hr., 74F), Dijon (2 per day, 1½hr., 101F), and Paris (1 TGV per day, 3hr., 300F). Pontarlier is easily reached from Besançon; **Monts Jura buses** (tel. 03 81 39 19 54 in Pontarlier or 03 81 83 06 11 in Besançon) run between the two towns (6 per day, 55min., 48F). The **hospital** is at 2, Flog St-Etienne (tel. 03 81 38 54 54). The **police** are at 10, rue Michaud (tel. 03 81 38 51 10), dial 17 for **emergencies.** The **post office** is across the street at 17, rue de la Gare (tel. 03 81 39 00 67; open Mon.-Fri. 8am-6:30pm, Sat. 8am-noon; **postal code:** 25300). If renovations are still in progress, you will find **La Poste** at 58, rue de la République.

ACCOMMODATIONS, CAMPING, AND FOOD

The hostel, **l'Auberge de Pontarlier (HI),** is quiet in summer yet clean and comfortable. From the tourist office, go left on rue Marpaud. The hostel is on your left after 100m, at 2, rue Jouffroy (tel. 03 81 39 06 57; fax 03 81 39 24 34; 46F; sheets 16F; breakfast 18F; extra 25F per room for doubles). **Hôtel de France,** 8, rue de la Gare (tel. 03 81 39 05 20), is another solid deal, offering sunny, airy rooms and cozy beds (singles 100F, with shower 130F; doubles 150F, with shower 180F; triples 200F, with shower 250F; quad with shower 300F). There is also a brand-new **campground** on rue du Tolombief (tel. 03 81 46 23 33; fax 03 81 46 83 32). Ask at the tourist office for directions. 34-75F per night. They also have *chalets* (2 people per day 200F, additional person 20F; 6-person capacity; weekly 2100F, monthly 7500F; off-season prices are lower).

Stock up for a picnic at the **Supermarché Casino** on rue de la République, near the Porte St-Pierre, or go through its back entrance on rue de Demparts, across the street from the youth hostel. **Les Rives du Doubs,** 2, rue de la République (tel. 81 46 20 27), has a wonderful riverside terrace. Dip into a *fondue comtoise* (48F for two people), made with the good ol' sharp *comté* cheese. The proprietor recommends the *tartiflette au Mont d'Or* (55F). Whether you are in search of ambiance or a take-out menu, **Pizzeria Gambetta,** 15, rue Gambetta (tel. 81 46 67 17), is Pontarlier's answer. Their wood oven pumps out pizzas of over 20 varieties (35-43F) with toppings ranging from the more traditional to eggs, tuna, potatoes, or mustard. Design your own for 48F. They also serve regional grilled meat dishes and ice cream. Don't worry, if to-go (*à émporter*) is your style but pizza is not your taste, the friendly staff will make any of their dishes for the road.

SIGHTS

Nature is Pontarlier's greatest attraction, and many tourists use the town as a base for numerous outdoor activities. In winter, Pontarlier's big sport is *ski du fond,* or **cross-country skiing.** There are over 60km of *pistes* for cross-country skiing right around the city. Eight trails on two slopes, *Le Larmont* and *Le Malmaison,* cover every difficulty level. A daily pass costs around 30F, 20F for kids 10-16. **Sport et Neige,** 4, rue de la République (tel. 03 81 39 04 69) rents equipment for 45F per day, 245F per week, children 40F and 210F, respectively. (Open in winter 9am-noon and 2-6pm; V, MC.) The two large alpine ski resorts in the Jura are **Metabief Mont d'Or** (tel. 03 81 49 13 81) and **Les Rousses** (tel. 03 84 60 02 55), both accessible by bus from Pontarlier. **Le Larmont** (tel. 03 81 46 55 20) is the alpine ski area nearest to Pontarlier. Even the biggest Jura ski resorts are half the price of their counterparts in the Alps. Expect good deals not only on lift tickets, but also on food, lodging, and equipment rentals. There is a reason for the cool, lower prices—the Jura are much colder than the Alps. Dress in layers so that you don't lose feeling in crucial outer digits. The snow is also unpredictable; brown spots and large patches of ice on the slopes are not unknown. For **ski conditions,** call **Allo-Neige, Massif de Jura** (tel. 03 81 53 55 88).

In the summer, skiing gives way to **hiking** and **mountain biking.** There are two *VTT* (mountain bike) departure points in Portarlier, to the north and south of town. Rent a bike at **Cycles Pernet,** 23, rue de la République (tel. 03 81 46 48 00), for 80F per day (passport deposit; open Tues.-Sat. 9am-noon and 2-7pm; MC, V, AmEx). If you like to hike, the **Grande Randonnée 5 (GR5),** an international 262km trail, runs through Pontarlier. For the less ambitious, smaller trails, some paved, circulate around Pontarlier. The tourist office's map (10F) marks the trails and six departure points around town—one near the train station at pl. St-Claude.

Besançon

Everyone in Besançon can walk to the forest within a half-hour. As small children, the *Bisontins* are sent to *"Une Petite Ecole dans la Forêt,"* a little school in the forest, to teach them the benefits of maintaining France's greenest city. This emphasis on trees doesn't mean Besançon (pop. 120,000) is just a quiet, shady village. Home to a major university and an international language center, (the **Centre de Linguistique Appliquée**), Besançon teems with intellectual excitement. The population is young, hip, and always on the move, rushing through the shopping district by day and piling into cafés, bars, and sweaty *discothèques* by night. When the *Bisontins* tire of this routine, they escape to the nearby alpine ski slopes. The city's hopping center predates the arrival of students, however, and the ancient ruins are there to prove it. Originally settled by Gauls, Besançon has been ruled at various times by Germany, Burgundy, and Spain. Over the past two centuries, Besançon has established itself as France's watch-making capital, ensuring the prosperity of this "green thumb" along the Doubs river.

ORIENTATION AND PRACTICAL INFORMATION

Besançon's *vieille ville, citadelle,* and cultural centers all lie within a thumb-shaped turn of the Doubs. Heading downhill will bring you downtown. To reach the tourist office from the station, walk left on av. de la Paix, which passes in front of the station. Turn right onto av. du Maréchal Foch; it curves to the left to go along the river. Pass pont Denfert-Rochereau and continue to pl. de la Première Armée Française. The tourist office is in the park to your right, and the *vieille ville* is across the pont de la République (10min.).

Tourist Information: Tourist Office, 2, pl. de la 1ère Armée Française (tel. 03 81 80 92 55; fax 03 81 80 58 30; minitel 3615 Bisontel). Lists of hotels and restaurants, info on excursions and festivals. Accommodations service 10F (free for Besançon hotels). Offers guided tours for individuals and groups. **Currency exchange** when banks are closed (tel. 03 81 88 31 95). Open April 1-Sept. 30 Mon. 10am-7pm, Tues.-Sat. 9am-7pm; Oct. 1-March 31 Mon. 10am-6pm, Tues.-Sat. 9am-6pm; open Sun. June 15-Sept. 15 10am-noon and 3-5pm, Sept. 16-June 14 10am-noon. **Besançon Informations,** 2, rue Megevand (tel. 03 81 83 08 24). Info on sports, wheelchair facilities, health care, lodging, festivals. Open Sept.-June Mon.-Fri. 8am-noon and 1:30-6pm, Sat. 9am-noon; July-Aug. Mon.-Fri. 8am-noon and 1:30-5:30pm. Pick up the aptly named pamphlet **Culture Info.**

Money: There are **ATMs** *everywhere.*

Trains: av. de la Paix (tel. 03 81 53 58 22). To: Paris-Gare de Lyon via Dole and Dijon (7 per day, 2½hr., 225F); Lyon (6 per day, 2½hr., 240F); Belfort (10 per day, 1hr.,

77F); Strasbourg (10 per day, 3hr., 156F); and Dijon (9 per day, 1¼hr., 73F). Info office open Mon.-Sat. 8:30am-6:15pm.

Buses: Monts Jura, 9, rue Proudhon (tel. 03 81 83 06 11), across pont de la République. To Pontarlier (6 per day, 1hr., 48F). Office open Mon.-Thurs. 7:30am-6:15pm, Fri. 7:30am-6:45pm, Sat. 7:30am-12:45pm and 2:30-5:30pm.

Public Transportation: CTB, info, pl. du 8 Septembre (tel. 03 81 48 12 12). Open Mon.-Sat. 9am-7pm. Tickets 6F, *carnet* of 10, 49F; valid 1hr. Buy on bus.

Taxis: (tel. 03 81 88 80 80). 24-hr. service. Minimum charge 11F50.

Mountain Bike Rental: Cycles Pardon, 31, rue d'Arènes (tel. 03 81 81 08 79). 100F per day, 60F per ½-day. 3000F deposit. Open Mon. 2:30-6pm, Tues.-Sat. 9am-noon and 2-7pm. V, MC, AmEx.

Laundromat: Several in town. **Blanc-Matic,** 54, rue Bersot, near the bus station. Open 7am-8pm. There is another Blanc-Matic near the hostel.

English Books: Camponovo, 50, Grande Rue (tel. 03 81 65 07 70; fax 03 81 81 53 19). Open 9am-12:30pm and 1:30-7pm. Closed Mon. mornings in summer.

Youth Information: Centre Information Jeunesse (CIJ), 27, rue de la République (tel. 03 81 21 16 16). Info, BIJ/WASTEELS tickets, ride board. Open Mon. 1:30-6pm, Tues.-Fri. 10am-noon and 1:30-6pm, Sat. 1:30-6pm. Closed Sat. July-Aug. V, MC.

Hiking Information: Club Alpin Français, 14, rue Luc Breton (tel. 03 81 81 02 77), in the *vieille ville.* Sponsors organized hikes and outdoor activities. Information about mountain biking, climbing, and skiing in the area. Open Tues.-Fri. 5-7pm, during ski season also open Sat. 9:30-11:30am.

Crisis Lines: SOS Amitié (tel. 03 81 88 12 12). **Collectif Homosexuel de Franche-Comté** (tel. 03 81 83 58 05), a gay hotline for regional services, events, and advice. **Centre d'Information et Consultation Sexualité** (tel. 03 81 83 34 73), for general sexual concerns. **Alcooliques Anonyme** (tel. 03 81 88 64 63). **Solidarité Femmes,** rue Charles Nodier (tel. 03 81 81 03 90), is a center for battered women.

Hospital: Centre Hospitalier Universitaire, pl. St-Jacques (tel. 03 81 66 81 66).

Medical Assistance: tel. 15.

Police: av. de la Gare d'Eau (tel. 03 81 21 11 22). **Emergency** tel. 17.

Post Office: 23, rue Proudhon (tel. 03 81 65 55 82), off rue de la République. **Currency exchange.** Open Mon.-Fri. 8am-7pm, Sat. 8am-noon. **Postal code:** 25019. **Main office** at 4, rue Demangel (tel. 03 81 53 81 12), in the new town. Has poste restante (specify postal code 25031 Besançon-Cedex). **Postal code:** 25000.

ACCOMMODATIONS AND CAMPING

Hotels in Besançon are generally affordable and rarely full. **CROUS** (tel. 03 81 48 46 46; fax 03 81 53 15 81) arranges housing in summer in ordinary dorm singles (100F, 70F with student ID). Call as far in advance as possible.

Foyer Mixte de Jeunes Travailleurs (HI), 48, rue des Cras (tel. 03 81 88 43 11; fax 03 81 80 77 97). Turn left from the station on av. de la Paix, which turns into rue de Belfort. After 10min., turn left on rue Marie-Louise, which turns into rue des Cras. Hostel is uphill on the right (40min.). Ask locals for "Foyer Les Oiseaux." Spare yourself the walk and take bus 7 from pl. Flore off rue de Belfort on av. Carnot (direction: Orchamps, 3 per hr.). Get off at the "Oiseaux" stop. Large, bright rooms with private bathrooms. TV room, game room. Singles 90F, 80F the second night. Doubles 80F per person, 70F the second night. Showers, sheets, and breakfast included. Lunch or dinner 36F. Reception 9am-7pm. Often full, so call ahead.

Foyer de la Cassotte (FJT), 18, rue de la Cassotte (tel. 03 81 80 90 01; fax 03 81 80 94 03). From the train station, head left on rue Belfort, go through pl. Flore, continue on av. Carnot, and turn left on rue de la Cassotte. Women only (men and women July 1-Aug. 31). Quiet courtyard has rosebushes and benches. Laundry and ironing facilities. Comfortable singles 80F. Shower and breakfast included. Meals 32-35F. Sheets 20F. Doors and reception closed 3-5am. Call ahead.

Centre International de Séjour, 19, rue Martin-du-Gard (tel. 03 81 50 07 54; fax 03 81 53 11 79). Take bus 8 from the "Foch" stop, near the station (direction: Campus) to "Intermarché." To get to "Foch" from the station, follow av. de la Paix as it curves downhill to the left. Take the first right onto av. Foch; the stop is on the left side. Restaurant, TV room. Reception 7am-1am. Singles 94F, with shower and toilet 152F. Doubles with 2 beds 60F per person, with shower and toilet 90F. Triples or quads 51F per person, shower included. Breakfast 18F50. Meals 56F.

Hôtel Florel, 6, rue de la Viotte (tel. 03 81 80 41 08; fax 03 81 50 44 40), 1min. to left of station. Comfortable, spotless, carpeted rooms; some on the top floor have wood-beamed ceilings. Singles and doubles with TV 135-155F, with shower 175-195F. Doubles with 2 beds and shower 230F. Triples 170F, with bath 250F. Breakfast 25F. Shower 20F. Parking in back. V, MC.

Hôtel du Levant, 9, rue des Boucheries (tel. 03 81 81 07 88), on pl. de la Révolution. Feels cramped, although well located. Singles 100F, with shower 130F. Doubles 140F, with shower 160F. Breakfast 20F. Restaurant downstairs has *menus* from 57F and *plats* from 32F. V, MC.

Hôtel Granvelle, 13, rue du Général Lecourbe (tel. 03 81 81 33 92; fax 03 81 81 31 77). Located at the foot of a stairway leading to the citadel. Immaculate courtyard rooms. All rooms have shower, TV, and phone. Singles 185F. Doubles with toilet 240F. Triples with toilet 290F. Quads 340F. Breakfast 30F. V, MC, AmEx.

Camping: Camping de la Plage (tel. 03 81 88 04 26), route de Belfort in Chalezeule northeast of the city. Take bus 1 (direction: Palente) to the end. A shuttle takes you to the *plage*. A four-star municipal campground, with access to a nearby pool. 11F50 per person, 9F50 per car or tent. Open May 15-Oct. 1.

FOOD

An eclectic group of restaurants along **rue des Boucheries** and **rue Claude-Pouillet** caters to Besançon's cosmopolitan student population. Pl. de la Révolution stages an **outdoor market** (Tues. and Fri. 6am-12:30pm, Sat. 6am-7pm). Buy groceries at **Monoprix,** 12, Grande Rue (open Mon.-Sat. 8:30am-8pm). Sharp *comté* cheese is abundant in Besançon; among the famous Arbois wines is the expensive *vin jaune,* which goes well with *comté*. Many *charcuteries* along **rue des Granges** sell *jambon de Haut Doubs,* a regional smoked ham.

La Boîte à Sandwiches, 21, rue du Lycée (tel. 03 81 81 63 23), off rue de la République. Over 50 sandwiches with witty names and such exotic ingredients as crab, hearts of palm, grapefruit, and bananas (11-25F). Every possible salad concoction (15-35F). Fantastic breads. Eat-in or take out. Open Mon.-Fri. 11:30am-2:30pm and 6:30pm-late, Sat. noon-2:30pm.

Au Petit Polonais, 81, rue des Granges (tel. 03 81 81 23 67). The swell vinyl booths give the lie to the fact that this is the oldest continually functioning restaurant in town. Generous *menus* (55-120F) with regional specialties that taste as good as they look. Open Mon.-Fri. 11:30am-2pm and 7-10pm, Sat. lunch only.

Restaurant Au Feu Vert, 11, rue des Boucheries (tel. 03 81 82 17 20). This small restaurant on pl. de la Révolution provides an informal and inexpensive way to enjoy regional specialties. *Menus* start at 48F, weekdays only. *Plats* 18-54F. Lunch service starts at 11:30am, dinner at 6:30pm. V, MC, AmEx.

SIGHTS

The Citadel, Besançon's greatest attraction, literally rises above the rest. Built in 1647 by Louis XIV's military architect, Vauban, the fortress sits atop the site of an ancient Gallo-Roman acropolis—the knuckle above Besançon, pressing and offering some of the best views of the *vieille ville* and its surroundings. The series of buildings within the 20m-thick walls of the citadel houses a variety of museums, an aquarium, and a zoo. (All facilities open summer Wed.-Mon. 9:15am-6:15pm, winter Wed.-Mon. 4:45am-4:45pm. Admission including museums, 40F, *tarif reduit* 30F, groups 30F per person, students 20F. Call 03 81 65 07 44 for info). To reach the citadel, follow the steep Grande Rue, which turns into rue de la Convention. Turn right on rue du Chapitre, left onto rue des Fusillés de la Résistance, and keep heading uphill. At the foot of the citadel stands the **Porte Noire** (Black Gate), a stern Roman triumphal arch, likely constructed during the reign of Marcus Aurelius in the 2nd century. Perfectly framed between the columns is the ornate 18th-century **Cathédrale St-Jean,** (tel. 03 81 83 34 62). Its interior mixes architectural styles from the 12th to the 18th century. Look for the beautiful *Rose de St-Jean* (a circular altar of white marble, possibly dating from the 11th century). Fra Bartoloméo's newly renovated *La Vierge aux Saints,* a rich masterpiece from the Italian Renaissance, may be back in 1997. (Church open Wed.-Mon 9 am-7pm; free). Flocks of butterflies are impaled on the walls of the **Musée d'Histoire Naturelle** (tel. 03 81 65 07 42). The mammals, birds, and fish that fell to the taxidermist's tools are interesting enough, but the overpowering smell of formaldehyde may send you gasping for fresh air. Follow the friendly peacock up the hill. Lions and llamas lounge in the sun, monkeys chatter, and bison roll their eyes and swish their tails in languid boredom at the out-of-place **zoo** (tel. 03 81 65 07 42). The **Aquarium** houses species of fish indigenous to the region. Creep up to its second-floor **Insectarium,** where enormous beetles, giant tarantulas, and hundreds of thousands of roaches, ants, termites, and crickets crawl in glass cases to the delighted screams of onlooking children.

In the center of the citadel, the **Musée de la Résistance et de la Déportation** (tel. 03 81 65 07 55; no children under 10) warns the visitor, "Not to bear witness would be to betray their memory." This vivid and disturbing commemoration of the Holocaust—the only one of its kind in Europe—uses letters and photographs to chronicle the Nazi rise to power and the German occupation of France. Special emphasis is given to the military role of Franche-Comté in World War II. Ask a guard to open the exposition room on the third floor, which contains a collection of sculptures and drawings by two local men who were deported to Nazi concentration camps, only one of whom survived. The citadel is also home to a meteorological museum and a radio station. On your way out, stop by the **Musée Comtois** (tel. 03 81 65 07 51), with folk art and crafts from Franche-Comté. From this museum's base you can climb to the top of the tower that surveys the region's capital. Walk along the ramparts for a great view of the Doubs and the valley below.

Behind the church sits the locally crafted **Horloge Astronomique,** the sum of 30,000 parts. Assembled in the 19th century, this clock runs 70 dials that give 122 different indices. Dials indicating the century and the seconds are all powered by the same pendulum. Every hour, Jesus leaps from his tomb as Hope blesses Faith and Charity. You must pay for the guided tour to visit the clock (tours Wed.-Mon. at 9:50, 10:50, and 11:50am, 2:50, 3:50, 4:50, and 5:50pm; Oct.-April 1 tours Thurs.-Mon. only; closed Jan.; admission 14F, ages 12-17 7F).

The ground floor of the **Musée des Beaux-Arts,** pl. de la Révolution (tel. 03 81 82 39 89), houses Egyptian mummies, amulets, and statuettes. The exceptional painting collection includes more than 6,000 works by Tintoretto, David, Ingres, Géricault, Van Dyck, Rubens, Titian, Constable, Courbet, Matisse, Picasso, Renoir, and other masters. Sexuality is a popular theme here; don't miss Lucas Cranach's 16th-century image of a nubile young *Lucrèce* about to do herself in with an oversized dagger. (Open Wed.-Mon. 9:30-noon and 2-6pm; admission 21F, students free; to take photos (without flash) buy a 6F badge at the front desk.)

Les Vedettes Bisontines (tel. 03 81 68 13 25) runs daily *bâteau-mouche* cruises on the Doubs and inside the citadel canals from pont de la République, near the tourist office (April-Oct. 2-4 per day; 1¼hr., 45F). For the same price, **Les Bâteaux Mouches "Le Pont Battant"** (tel. 03 81 68 05 34) cross the bridge; they operate cruises with commentary from July to September (2 per day). For both, days and tours vary, so call ahead (especially to reserve for group tours).

A walk along the promenades of the Doubs is a great way to take in the elegant beauty of Besançon's old buildings. Promenade Micaud and Promenade Helvétie, near pont de la République on the same bank as the tourist office, are great places to picnic, play, or enjoy the Doubs. Notice the 19th-century **synagogue** on quai de Strasbourg, with its onion-dome turrets and Moorish architecture.

ENTERTAINMENT

The students of Besançon pack bars and *discothèques* until early morning. The king of Besançon's dance clubs is **Le Queen** (tel. 03 81 61 17 49), about 1km from the tourist office at 8, av. de Chardonnet. The street is not well lit—go in a group. A large dance floor with London Underground decor is surrounded by plush couches, two bars, and many drunken *Bisontins* (50F cover includes one drink, or two non-alcoholic; open Wed.-Sat. 10pm-4am). In the *vieille ville,* cool down that Saturday night fever at **Sypssi,** pl. Granvelle (tel. 03 81 83 51 32). The BeeGees would feel right at home on its three dance floors, complete with disco balls, plush red carpet, and floor lights (you and your leisure suit can enter for 50F, includes one drink; open Tues.-Sun. 10:30pm-4am). For a complete listing of *discothèques*, ask at the tourist office. The **Building Café** at 26, rue Proudhon is a popular bar, but watch out for flying darts as you enter. Sip a beer to the sound of cracking billiard cues while recreating your favorite *Pulp Fiction* moment in a Cadillac-turned-table-for-four. An alternative late night outlet is the **Casino du Parc** (tel. 03 81 80 27 27), on rue de la Mouillère across the street from the tourist office. A smoky room houses rows of video poker and slot machines, some with 2F minimums and plenty of opportunities to bet big (open Sun.-Thurs. 11am-3am, Fri.-Sat. 11am-4am; admission free).

The tourist office publishes several comprehensive lists of events. In July and August, the city sponsors **Festiv'été,** with theater, music, dance, expositions and a film festival (many events are free; call the tourist office for info). **Jazz en Franche-Comté** brings a flurry of free concerts in June and July (tickets range from 40-150F and some events are free; contact C.I.J. at 03 81 21 16 16 for info). The **Festival International de Musique** erupts during the first two weeks of September with classical concerts every night (tickets 50-350F depending on locale; 20% discount for students; tel. 03 81 83 08 14). Also, the hostel sponsors an array of events (ASEP-FJT les Oiseaux) each month. Pick up a schedule at the FJT or at the Tourist office.

■ Near Besançon

BELFORT

With craggy ramparts and a fortified château looming protectively over the *vieille ville,* Belfort (pop. 53,000) has long claimed the best views in Franche-Comté. A respectable set of museums, a lively pedestrian zone, and a strategic location on the ever-so-Savoureuse river near the Swiss and German borders make Belfort a worthwhile stopover. Belfort became a key defensive city in 1675, when France enlarged and strengthened the fortress after acquiring the town from Austria in the Treaty of Westphalia. The result of military master Vauban's work is an impressive château and a set of sturdy ramparts built to accommodate 10,000 troops. The **Château de Belfort,** built in the 12th century and also modified by Vauban, now houses Belfort's **Musée d'Art et d'Histoire** (tel. 03 84 54 25 50), where military memorabilia meets modern art (open daily May-Sept. 10am-7pm; Oct.-April 10am-noon and 2-5pm, closed Tues.; admission 11F, students free). For the best view of the city, the Jura mountains, and the Savoureuse, take time to explore the labyrinth of gravel paths that lead along the mossy ramparts, over grassy knolls, to the towers. Adventurous types may want to attempt the *Promenade des Hauts du Belfort,* a loop that takes you around the entire fortification (the tourist office has info). Every summer, music fans from all over Europe groove together at **Les Eurockéennes,** a three-day festival modeled on Woodstock. It draws 100,000 in early July to hear upcoming acts at the Malsaucy outdoor concert arena, 6km from Belfort. Past headliners have included everyone from Lou Reed and Patti Smith to Ministry, Beck, and the Pixies' Frank Black (3-day tickets about 400F; 1-day passes available). Ask for details at Belfort's **tourist office,** at pl. de la Commune (tel. 03 84 28 12 23), in the pedestrian zone (open Mon.-Sat. 9:30am-6:30pm, Sun. 10am-7pm). Belfort's **train station,** on av. Wilson (tel. 08 36 35 35 35), runs trains to Strasbourg (10 per day, 2hr., 130F); Dijon (15 per day,

2hr., 136F); and Besançon (10 per day, 1hr., 76F). The town's cheapest bed is at the **Foyer des Jeunes Travailleurs,** 6, rue de Madrid (tel. 03 84 21 39 16; 60F, non-members 70F). From May to September, pitch your home away from home in the **Camping Municipal,** promenade d'Essert (tel. 03 84 21 03 30) on av. Leclerc near the *foyer* (7F per person, 6F per tent, 4F per car).

CAVES OF THE JURA

The prehistoric glaciers and subterranean springs of Franche-Comté began carving out intricate underground grottoes long before anyone had ever heard of Romanesque or Gothic. Tourist offices in Besançon, Arbois, Pontarlier, and other *comtois* towns will have info on all the caves. The **Club Alpin Français** in Besançon, 14, rue Luc Breton (tel. 03 81 81 02 77), carries information on spelunking expeditions (open Tues.-Fri. 5-7pm). The closest cave (15km from Besançon), **Grotte d'Osselle** (tel. 03 81 63 62 09) is home to 3000 bear skeletons (open June-Aug. 9am-7pm; Sept. 9am-noon and 2-6pm; Oct. Mon.-Fri. 2:30-5pm, Sat.-Sun. 9am-noon and 2-6pm; April-May 9am-noon and 2-6pm; admission 29F, students 24F, children 17F). To cool off, head 525m underground to the **Grotte de la Glacière** (tel. 03 81 60 44 26), a subterranean safe-deposit box for a sparkling collection of minerals and crystals (open July-Aug. daily 9am-7pm; March-June and Sept.-Nov. 9am-noon and 2-5pm; admission 28F, students 25F). Both are easily accessible by car on N83 or D30. Near Arbois, the **Grottes des Planches** (tel. 03 84 66 07 93) has bizarre mineral deposits that are constantly changing shape and color. Cave-dwellers made the *grottes* their home in 3000 BC (open April-Sept. daily 9:30am-6pm). Catching a ride with someone who's heading to the Grottes des Planches from Arbois is said to be easy. If you're not feeling lucky, try the walk. It takes less than an hour if you follow the signs from pl. de la Liberté in Arbois, and the flat road leads through a green valley and picturesque country towns.

Alsace-Lorraine

Alsace and Lorraine have been the political pawns of France and Germany since the 3rd and 4th centuries, when barbarian tribes first swept westward through these regions. Things haven't let up ever since; they were ravaged most recently after the Franco-Prussian War of 1870-1871 and during both World Wars. The result is a mixture of French and Germanic influences with an often fervent loyalty to France. Having jointly endured almost two millennia of shifting political fortunes, Alsace and Lorraine maintain a fascinating blend of local *patois* (lingo), cuisine, architecture, and customs. Culture in the region is a hearty hybrid of the best of both the French and German cultures that transcends national sovereignty.

While many associate Alsace with Lorraine, natives of one region may be dismayed to be confused with their counterparts in the other. In Alsace's Vosges, wooded hills slope down to sunlit valleys and deep blue lakes, where hiking, camping, and cross-country skiing flourish in an unspoiled setting. Hundreds of kilometers of trails dotted with *fermes auberges* (overnight refuges) are marked on maps and guides available from tourist offices. The well-preserved cities of Alsace offer geranium-draped half-timbered Bavarian houses flanking their many waterways. Strasbourg, a stone's throw across the Rhine from Germany, was the birthplace of both Gutenberg's printing press and *La Marseillaise,* a Rhine Army hymn that became the French national anthem after Revolutionaries from Marseille enthusiastically adopted it for their march to Paris. Although Strasbourg has retained its patriotic fervor, today it is also an international center, home to both the European Parliament and the Council of Europe. The villages and vineyards of Alsace's Route du Vin align themselves along a narrow corridor running 140km from Marlenheim to Thann. One of the world's finest whites, dry Riesling is the king of the local wines, while sharper Gewurtztraminer is quite fragrant. Cheese and wine often come together in the *caves* offering *dégustations* along the Route du Vin.

Although many Alsatians are proudly, loyally French, Alsace did spend much of the last century under German rule. The region's German influence is apparent in its architecture, the local Alsatian dialect (often mistaken for German), and cuisine that pairs *baguettes* with sauerkraut and sausage. Among traditional dishes are *tarte à l'oignon, choucroute garnie* (sauerkraut cooked in white wine sauce and topped with sausages and ham), *coq au Riesling* (chicken in a white wine sauce), and *baeckaoffe* (a casserole of marinated beef, pork, lamb, and potatoes). *Tarte flambée,* another popular specialty, is a bacon tart traditionally cooked in a wood stove. Alsatian cheeses include Germanic *münster* and Swiss *emmenthal.*

West of Alsace, Lorraine unfolds among similar hills and wheat fields, but its cities are serenely elegant in their Renaissance and Baroque architecture. This alternately wooded and industrial region derives its name from the Frankish Emperor Lothair, who received the so-called "Middle Kingdom" between France and Germany when the 843 Treaty of Verdun split Charlemagne's empire. It was annexed to France in 1766, at the death of the duke of Lorraine in a Lunéville fireplace. Devastated by two World Wars, Lorraine has rebuilt its cathedrals and cultural centers. Nancy pulsates around its splendidly gilded pl. Stanislas. Tiny Bar-le-Duc, former capital of the powerful duchy of Bar, was one of the few towns to avoid the World Wars' destruction. Fortified Metz was a thriving city when Paris was just a fishing village, and boasts one of the oldest churches in France. Verdun stands in chilling contrast to Metz: reduced to rubble in World War I, the site of one of the most horrible battles in history is marked by military cemeteries and somber crypts.

What Lorraine's culinary specialties lack in delicacy, they make up in heartiness: the bread is heavier than French breads, and potatoes or cabbage normally complement meals. Bacon, butter, and cream are key ingredients in artery-hardening dishes such as *quiche lorraine,* the region's claim to gastronomic fame. In original versions of this much-maligned peasant dish, a hollowed-out loaf of stale bread was filled with egg custard and a few bits of meat. The hearty pâtés of Lorraine often contain marinated veal and beef. Desserts include *madeleines* (lemony tea cakes in the shape of a shell called a *ramequin*) from Commercy, *macarons* from Nancy, and *dragées* from Verdun. The fantastically rich chocolate-cherry *gâteau Forêt Noire* (Black Forest cake) is a specialty borrowed from Bavaria.

GETTING AROUND

Metz, Nancy, and Strasbourg are major train hubs with frequent service to all areas of France as well as other countries. Between smaller towns, notably Verdun and the Route du Vin, buses are more practical. Within Lorraine and especially Alsace, biking is a good option, although both regions are too hilly for the casual rider. Keep in mind that the Vosges, the small mountain range dividing the two, will seem a lot larger when you're huffing and puffing your way up. Renting a car or bike and taking a tour bus excursion are practical ways to see the battlefields at Verdun and many of the villages on the Route du Vin. Hitchers take advantage of the heavy industrial traffic, especially in Lorraine.

Strasbourg

"Willkommen, bienvenue, welcome." Balancing a few kilometers from the Franco-German border, cosmopolitan Strasbourg seems to belong to both cultures. Covered bridges, half-timbered houses, flower boxes, and breweries reflect Germanic influence, while wide boulevards, spacious squares, a Gothic cathedral, and ancient vineyards have a distinctly French flavor. German is heard on the streets as often as French, and as many *winstubs* line the squares as *pâtisseries*. Equitable Strasbourg (pop. 260,000) also hosts European Union offices, including the European Parliament, the Council of Europe, and the European Commission for the Rights of Man.

When the king of France annexed Strasbourg in 1681, the townspeople demanded a charter as a free city. Since then, despite its cultural high-wire act, the city has had a soft spot for *les grenouilles*. Strasbourg refused to shift its allegiance in 1870, when a two-month siege changed the street signs into German until the city was returned to France at the end of World War I. Even the German occupation of 1940-1944 couldn't shake the citizens' loyalty to France. This independence and energy is perpetuated in part by Strasbourg's large student population. Founded in 1566, the Université de Strasbourg enrolls over 35,000 French and foreign students. At night, they drop their books and pack the clubs and squares.

ORIENTATION AND PRACTICAL INFORMATION

The *vieille ville* is virtually an island in the center of the city, bounded on all sides by a large canal. From the station, go straight down rue du Maire-Kuss, cross the bridge (pont Kuss), and continue on Grand' Rue, which becomes rue Gutenberg and then rue Hallebardes. Turn right on rue du Dôme to find yourself on the cathedral steps. If you turn right after crossing the bridge from the station, you arrive in **La Petite France,** a neighborhood of old Alsatian houses, narrow canals, and restaurants.

Tourist Information: Tourist Office, 17, pl. de la Cathédrale (tel. 03 88 52 28 28; fax 03 88 52 28 29), next to the cathedral, *natürlich*. **Branches** at pl. de la Gare (tel. 03 88 32 51 49) and pont de l'Europe (tel. 03 88 61 39 23). Eye-straining map 3F. Big ol' map 28F. Walking tour map 20F, in English. Festival info, free list of hotels and restaurants. Different tour of town every Sat. at 2:30pm (38F, students 19F; in French). For **current events,** pick up the seasonal **Shows and Events** guide, or the monthly **Strasbourg Actualités** (covering parliament sessions, market days, concerts, and bands), both free. Offices open June-Sept. Mon.-Sat. 8:30am-7pm and Sun. 9am-6pm; Oct.-May daily 9am-6pm. **Departmental Tourist Office,** 9, rue du Dôme (tel. 03 88 15 45 88 or 03 88 15 45 80; fax 03 88 75 67 64), offers info on the Route du Vin between Strasbourg and Colmar.

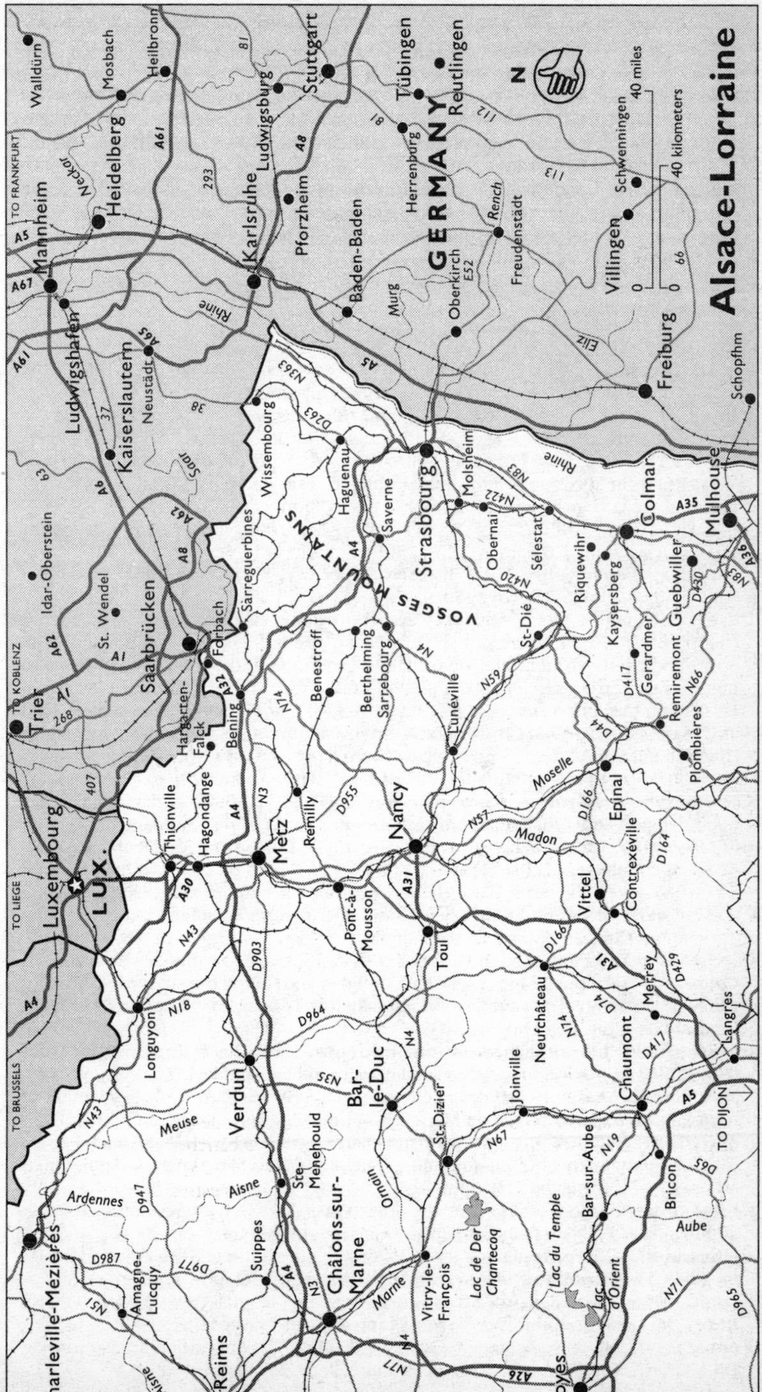
Alsace-Lorraine
GERMANY
LUX.
VOSGES MOUNTAINS
N
0 40 miles
0 40 kilometers
TO FRANKFURT
TO KOBLENZ
TO LIEGE
TO BRUSSELS
TO DIJON
Walldürn
Mosbach
Heilbronn
Mannheim
Heidelberg
Karlsruhe
Ludwigsburg
Stuttgart
Pforzheim
Baden-Baden
Tübingen
Reutlingen
Herrenburg
Oberkirch
Freudenstädt
Villingen
Schwenningen
Freiburg
Schopfhm
Ludwigshafen
Kaiserslautern
Neustädt
Idar-Oberstein
St. Wendel
Saarbrücken
Forbach
Trier
Luxembourg
Thionville
Hagondange
Hargarten-Falck
Bening
Sarreguerbines
Wissembourg
Haguenau
Saverne
Strasbourg
Molsheim
Obernai
Sélestat
Colmar
Mulhouse
Riquewihr
Kaysersberg
Guebwiller
Gerardmer
Remiremont
Plombières
Epinal
St-Dié
Lunéville
Benestroff
Berthelming
Sarrebourg
Metz
Remilly
Nancy
Pont-à-Mousson
Toul
Vittel
Contrexéville
Neufchâteau
Merrey
Langres
Chaumont
Joinville
Bricon
Bar-sur-Aube
Longuyon
Verdun
Bar-le-Duc
St-Dizier
Ste-Menehould
Charleville-Mézières
Amagne-Lucquy
Suippes
Châlons-sur-Marne
Vitry-le-François
Reims
Troyes
Lac de Der Chantecoq
Lac du Temple
Lac d'Orient
Ardennes
Meuse
Aisne
Marne
Ornain
Aube
Moselle
Madon
Rhine
Neckar
Murg
Rench
Elz
Saar
A1
A4
A5
A6
A8
A26
A30
A31
A32
A35
A36
A61
A62
A65
A67
E52
N3
N4
N18
N19
N35
N43
N51
N57
N59
N66
N67
N71
N74
N77
N83
N363
N420
N422
D65
D74
D164
D166
D263
D417
D429
D430
D903
D947
D955
D964
D965
D966
D977
D987
E11
37
38
63
81
268
293
407

Budget Travel: Havas Voyages, 23, rue de la Haute-Montée (tel. 03 88 32 99 77; fax 03 88 23 55 56). Great vacation packages and plane prices. Open Mon.-Fri. 9am-noon and 1:30-6:30pm, Sat. 9am-noon and 2-5pm.

Consulates: U.S., 15, av. d'Alsace (tel. 03 88 35 31 04, cultural services 03 88 35 38 20, visa info 03 88 35 30 51), next to pont John F. Kennedy. Open Mon.-Fri. 9:30am-noon and 2-5pm. **Canada,** rue du Ried (tel. 03 88 96 65 02), in La Wantzenau. Open Mon.-Fri. 11am-noon.

Money: Change Cathédrale, 7, pl. du Marché-aux-Cochons-de-Lait (tel. 03 88 23 26 46), behind the cathedral. **Currency exchange** at mediocre rates. Open 9:30am-6pm. **Caisse d'Epargne** has branches and **ATMs** all over town, including 24, pl. des Halles; 14, pl. de la Cathédrale; and 9, pl. de la Gare. **ATMs** are also at 25, rue du Vieux-Marché-aux-Vins, a block from pl. Kléber in the *centre ville,* and near La Petite France, at 41 rue Finkwiller, off rue du Bain-aux-Plantes.

American Express: 31, pl. Kléber (tel. 03 88 75 78 75). Mail service, currency exchange, travel agency, the usual. Open Mon.-Fri. 8:45am-noon and 1:30-6pm.

Flights: Strasbourg-Entzheim (tel. 03 88 64 67 67; fax 03 88 68 82 12), 15km from Strasbourg. **Air France,** 15, rue des Francs-Bourgeois (tel. 03 88 21 86 00); **Air Inter,** pl. Brant (tel. 03 88 61 49 12), and other carriers send frequent flights to Paris (students 250-350F), Lyon, and London. Shuttle buses (tel. 03 88 64 67 67) run from pl. de la Gare at rue du Maire-Kuss; from 37, rue du Vieux-Marché-aux-Vins; and from 2bis, rue de Molsheim (Mon.-Fri. every 30min., 37F).

Trains: pl. de la Gare (tel. 03 88 22 50 50, reservations 03 88 32 07 51). To: Metz (7 per day, 1½hr., 110F); Nancy (15 per day, 1½hr., 106F); Paris (16 per day, 4hr., 263F); Luxembourg (6 per day, 2hr., 150F); Frankfurt (15 per day, 3hr., 215F); Zurich (12 via Basel, 2½hr., 220F); Brussels (6 per day, 5hr., 286F). Info office open daily 7:30am-9pm. **SOS Voyageurs,** pl. Gare (tel. 03 88 32 12 59.

Buses: Compagnie des Transports Strasbourgeois (CTS). Offices at pl. Kléber (tel. 03 88 77 70 70; open Mon.-Fri. 7:30am-6:30pm, Sat. 9am-12:30pm and 1:30-5pm) and the Gare Centrale (open daily 10am-noon and 1:15-6:15pm). Bus and new futuristic tram service. Schedules and maps free at offices. Buy one-way tickets (7F) on bus. Buy a *carnet* of 5 (29F) or 10 (58F), or a 1-day unlimited pass (19F) at CTS offices or *tabacs.* City service is extensive, but buses go to only a few larger towns along the Route du Vin, such as Obernai (11 per day, 1hr., 20F).

Taxis: pl. de la République (tel. 03 88 36 13 13). 24hr. About 120F to airport.

Car Rental: Avis Train & Auto, pl. Gare (tel 03 88 32 30 44). 1-day rental 575F, 600km. Open Mon.-Fri. 7am-11pm, Sat. 8am-noon and 2-6pm, Sun. 4-8pm.

Bike Rental: Vélocation at 3 locations: Ste-Aurélie Gare, 1, bd. de Metz (tel. 03 88 52 01 01); Etoile, pl. de l'Etoile (tel. 03 88 44 35 63); and pl. du Château (tel. 03 88 21 06 38). Bikes 20F per ½-day, 30F per day. Tandems 40F per day. Deposit 1000F and passport. Metz and Etoile open Mon.-Fri. 6am-8pm, Sat. 8am-7pm, Sun. 9am-7pm. Pl. du Chateau open daily 9am-7pm.

Hitchhiking: Those hitching to Paris take bus 2, 12, or 22 to route des Romains. To Colmar they take bus 3, 13, or 23 to bd. de Lyon and follow the signs for Colmar to the highway ramp. The Germany-bound take bus 1, 14, 21, or 24 to Etoile and get on route de Rhin. You know the risks.

English Books: Librairie Internationale Kléber, 1, rue des Francs-Bourgeois (tel. 03 88 75 53 36). Pricey best-sellers and classics in English. Open Tues.-Sat. 9:15am-7pm. **La Librocase,** 2, quai des Pêcheurs (tel. 03 88 25 50 31). Small selection of used English paperbacks. Open Mon.-Fri. 2-7pm; Sept.-June 9am-7pm.

Youth Center: CROUS, 1, quai du Maire-Dietrich (tel. 03 88 21 28 00; fax 03 88 36 77 79). Meal vouchers (19F) sold Mon. 9am-noon, Tues.-Fri. 11:30am-1pm. Open Mon.-Fri. 9-11:30am and 1:30-6pm.

Laundromat: 2, rue Deserte, near the *gare.* Wash 16F. Dry 2F per 7min., 10F per 20min. Soap 2F. Open daily 8am-8pm. Also at 9, rue Gloxin.

Crisis Lines: SOS Femmes, tel. 03 88 24 06 06; rape hotline. **SOS Amitié,** tel. 03 88 22 33 33. **Alcooliques Anonyme,** tel. 03 88 32 79 36; local AA chapter.

Hospital: Hospices Civils de Strasbourg, 1, pl. de l'Hôpital (tel. 03 88 16 17 18), across the canal from the *vieille ville.* **Medical emergency** tel. 15.

Police: 11, rue de la Nuée-Bleue (tel. 03 88 32 99 08). From cathedral, take rue du Dôme north, which runs into rue de la Nuée-Bleue. **Emergency** tel. 17.

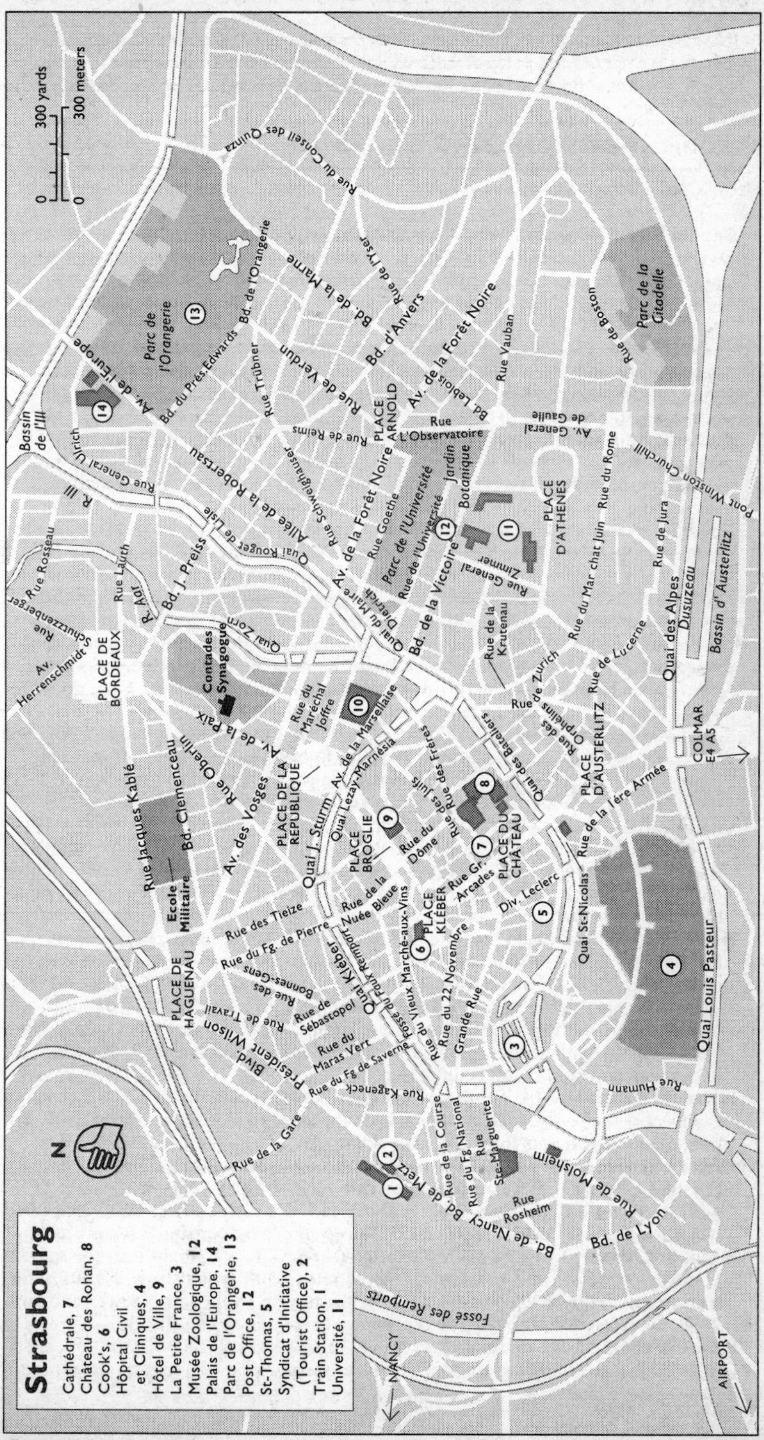

Strasbourg
Cathédrale, 7
Château des Rohan, 8
Cook's, 6
Hôpital Civil
et Cliniques, 4
Hôtel de Ville, 9
La Petite France, 3
Musée Zoologique, 12
Palais de l'Europe, 14
Parc de l'Orangerie, 13
Post Office, 12
St-Thomas, 5
Syndicat d'Initiative
(Tourist Office), 2
Train Station, 1
Université, 11
N
0 300 yards
0 300 meters
NANCY
AIRPORT
COLMAR
E4 A5
Parc de l'Orangerie
Parc de la Citadelle
Parc de l'Université
Jardin Botanique
Bassin de l'Ill
Bassin d'Austerlitz
PLACE DE BORDEAUX
PLACE DE HAGUENAU
PLACE DE LA REPUBLIQUE
PLACE BROGLIE
PLACE KLÉBER
PLACE DU CHÂTEAU
PLACE D'AUSTERLITZ
PLACE D'ATHENES
PLACE ARNOLD
Ecole Militaire
Contades
Synagogue
Av. de l'Europe
Bd. de la Marne
Bd. d'Anvers
Av. de la Forêt Noire
Rue de Verdun
Allée de la Robertsau
Bd. J. Preiss
Av. de la Paix
Av. des Vosges
Rue Oberlin
Bd. Clemenceau
Rue Jacques Kablé
Blvd. Président Wilson
Rue de la Gare
Bd. de Metz
Bd. de Nancy
Bd. de Lyon
Rue de Molsheim
Fossé des Remparts
Quai Louis Pasteur
Quai St-Nicolas
Quai des Alpes
Rue de la 1ère Armée
Div. Leclerc
Grande Rue
Rue du 22 Novembre
Quai Kléber
Quai J. Sturm
Bd. de la Victoire
Rue de Zurich
Rue du Mar chal Juin
Rue de Rome
Rue de Jura
Rue de Lucerne
Pont Winston Churchill
Av. General de Gaulle
Rue Vauban
Rue de Boston
Rue du Conseil des Quinze
Rue Humann
Rue Kageneck
Rue du Fg de Saverne
Rue du Maras Vert
Rue de Sébastopol
Rue des Bonnes-Gens
Rue de Travail
Rue du Fg. de Pierre
Rue des Tieize
Rue de la Nuée Bleue
Rue du Dôme
Rue des Frères
Rue des Juifs
Rue Gr. Arcades
Rue du Vieux Marché-aux-Vins
Rue de la Course
Rue du Fg National
Rue Ste-Marguerite
Rue Rosheim
Quai des Bateliers
Rue des Orphelins
Rue de la Krutenau
Rue General Zimmer
Rue de l'Université
Rue Goethe
Rue Schweighauser
Quai Rouget de Lisle
Quai Zorn
Rue Lauth
Rue Rosseau
Rue Schutzzenberger
Av. Herrenschmidt
Rue General Ulrich
Rue Trübner
Bd. du Prés. Edwards
Bd. de l'Orangerie
Rue de Reims
Rue de l'Yser
Bd. Leblois
Rue L'Observatoire
Quai du Maire Dietrich
Rue du Maréchal Joffre
Av. de la Marseillaise
Quai Lezay-Marnésia

Post Office: Main office at 5, av. de la Marseillaise (tel. 03 88 52 31 00). Branches at 5, pl. du Château and 1, pl. de la Gare. All have **currency exchange,** photocopies, and long lines. Poste restante at main office (postal code: 67074). **Postal code:** 67000. Main office open Mon.-Fri. 8am-7pm, Sat. 8am-noon.

ACCOMMODATIONS AND CAMPING

Strasbourg is *sehr à la mode:* everyone stays here. Make reservations or arrive early.

Centre International d'Accueil de Strasbourg (CIARUS), 7, rue Finkmatt (tel. 03 88 32 12 12; fax 03 88 23 17 37). From the station, take rue du Maire-Kuss to the canal, turn left, and follow quais St-Jean, Kléber, and Finkmatt. Take a left onto rue Finkmatt; the hostel is on the left (15min.). YMCA-affiliated. Sparkling facilities, central location. International clientele makes CIARUS social. 12-bunk rooms 75F (May 15-Sept. 15 only). 6- to 8-bunk rooms 86F. 4-bunk rooms 98F. Singles 177F. Baggage storage. Breakfast included. Lunch or dinner 48F. No lockout. Curfew 1am; call ahead if you'll be late. Wheelchair access. Reception 6:30am-1am. For reservations call 03 88 22 16 05 Mon.-Fri. 9am-noon and 2-7pm. V, MC.

Auberge de Jeunesse René Cassin (HI), 9, rue de l'Auberge de Jeunesse (tel. 03 88 30 26 46; fax 03 88 30 35 16), 2km from station. To get to bus stop from station, go up rue du Maire-Kuss, cross canal, and take 2nd left onto rue du Marché-aux-Vins. Take bus 3 (direction: Holtzheim-Entzheim Ouest) or bus 23 (direction: Illkirch) to "Auberge de Jeunesse" (every 30min., 15min., 7F). To trek, take a right from station onto bd. de Metz and follow it as it becomes bd. Nancy and bd. de Lyon. Turn right onto rue de Molsheim and go through underpass. Follow rte. de Schirmeck 1km to rue de l'Auberge de Jeunesse. Friendly staff. 6-bed dorms 68F. 2- to 4-bed rooms 97F. Singles 147F. Sheets 16F. Camping 41F per person. Breakfast and shower free. Meals 47F. Curfew 1am. No lockout. No phone reservations. Reception 7am-11:30am and 2pm-midnight. Closed Jan.-Feb. 10. Members only.

Auberge de Jeunesse, Centre International de Rencontres du Parc du Rhin, on rue des Cavaliers on the Rhine (tel. 03 88 45 54 20; fax 03 88 45 54 21). 7km from station. From the station, take tram to Homme de Fer, change to bus #2 (direction Pont du Rhin), alight at Pont du Rhin (30min). Turn right behind the tourist office onto rue des Cavaliers. Sparkling rooms with toilet and shower. Near the Rhine and a modern water-park (discount at the hostel). Volleyball and basketball courts. Karaoke bar. Rates per person July-Aug. and Nov.-Feb: singles 182F. Doubles 136F. Triples and quads 96F. Rates per person Sept.-Oct. and March-May: singles 153F. Doubles 116F. Triples and quads 84F. Breakfast included. Lunch or dinner 54F. Lunch packet 30F. No lockout. Curfew 1am, but later check-in possible. Phone reservations accepted. V, MC.

Hôtel Patricia, 1a, rue du Puits (tel. 03 88 32 14 60; fax 03 88 32 19 08), in the *vieille ville* by Eglise St-Thomas. From the station, take rue du Maire-Kuss across bridge, then right on Grand' Rue. Turn right on rue de la Division Leclerc and right again onto rue des Servuriers. Take your first left onto rue des Puits (10min.). 16th-century home with spacious, comfortable rooms. Singles from 135F. Doubles from 160F. Rooms with shower 200-240F. Triple 290F. Breakfast 25F. Shower 12F. Reception 8am-8pm. V, MC, AmEx.

Hôtel de Bruxelles, 13, rue Kuhn (tel 03 88 32 45 31; fax 03 88 32 06 22). Large rooms near the *centre ville.* Singles and doubles from 145F, with shower 240F. Triples, quads, and quints from 230F. Breakfast 25F. 24-hr. reception. V, MC.

Hôtel Michelet, 48, rue du Vieux Marché-aux-Poissons (tel. 03 88 32 47 38). Friendly family keeps clean rooms by cathedral. Singles 125F, with toilet 145F, with shower 170F. Doubles 135F, with toilet 170F, with shower 200F. Extra bed 30F. Breakfast in bed 15F. Shower 12F. Reception 7am-noon and 2-8pm. V, MC.

Hôtel le Colmar, 1, rue du Maire-Kuss (tel. 03 88 32 16 89). Right near the station. Friendly owners; tidy, spartan rooms. Singles 130F, with shower 160F, with shower and bath 215F. Doubles 150F, with shower 180F, with shower and bath 230F. Breakfast 20F. Shower 15F. Reception 7am-9pm, or call ahead.

Hôtel Weber, 22, bd. de Nancy (tel. 03 88 32 36 47; fax 03 88 32 19 08). From station, turn right onto bd. de Metz, which becomes bd. de Nancy. Large, plain rooms. Singles from 120F, with shower 190F. Doubles from 120F, with shower 190F. Shower 12F. Breakfast 25F. 24-hr. reception. V, MC, AmEx.

Hôtel le Grillon, 2, rue Thiergarten (tel. 03 88 32 71 88; fax 03 88 32 22 01), 1 block from the station on your way to the *centre ville.* Take the first left off rue du Maire Kuss. Bright, clean rooms; hardwood floors. Singles from 160F, with shower 220F. Doubles from 200F, with shower 250F. Triples 320F. Quads 390F. Quints 460F. Extra bed 70F. Free showers. Breakfast 25F. 24-hr. reception. V, MC.

Camping: La Montagne Verte, 2, rue Robert Ferrer (tel. 03 88 30 25 46). Take the tram to Homme de Fer. Change to bus 3 (direction: Holtzheim-Entzheim Ouest) or 23 (direction: Illkirch) to "Nid de Cigogne." Continue on foot down rte. de Schirmeck then turn right onto rue de Schnolkeloch. Perks include showers, tennis courts, and a bar. 23F per site, 18F per person, 9F per child. Tent and car included. Reception 8am-noon and 2-8pm. Gates close at 10pm. Open March-Oct.

FOOD

Restaurants around the cathedral and La Petite France are predictably expensive, but here you'll also find small *winstubs*—informal places traditionally affiliated with individual wineries. *Winstubs* invariably have Alsatian timber exteriors and interiors with red-and-white checkered tablecloths. *Strasbourgeois* restaurants are known for their delicious *choucroute garnie,* sauerkraut spiced and served with meats.

No fewer than 19 **markets** come to Strasbourg every week, most running from 7am to 1pm. Those most accessible from the *centre ville* include the Saturday morning produce market on pl. du Marché-aux-Poissons and the Wednesday and Friday markets on pl. Broglie (until 6pm) and quai Turckheim. Of the several supermarkets scattered around the *vieille ville,* **ATAC Supermarket,** 47, rue des Grandes Arcades (tel. 03 88 32 51 53), off pl. Kléber, grabs highest honors for its eminently fresh produce and great prices on staple items (open Mon.-Sat. 8:30am-8pm).

At the enormous, triple-decker *winstub* **Au Pont St-Martin,** 13-15, rue des Moulins (tel. 03 88 32 45 13), you'll peer at canal locks over huge servings of seafood, salads, and *choucroute* (Mon.-Fri. 3-course, 56F lunch *menu, à la carte* 40-98F; open noon-11pm. V, MC). Students like the lively **Pizzeria Aldo,** 8, rue du Faisan (tel. 03 88 36 00 49), near pl. St-Etienne. Design your own huge pizza (46F), salad (42F), or dessert (33F), with countless combinations for the same price (open daily noon-2pm and 6:30pm-1:30am; V, MC, AmEx). At **Bistro de la Gare,** 18, rue du Vieux Marché aux Grains (tel. 03 88 32 18 34), feast on *carpaccio de boeuf* or try one of their generous 58 or 72F *menus* (open 11:30am-3pm and 6:30pm-midnight; V, MC, AmEx). Near the cathedral, try **Au Gutenberg,** 8, pl. Gutenberg (tel. 03 88 32 82 48), for hearty local fare—sauerkraut, salads, and a large menu *à la carte* 39-84F (open daily 8am-1am; V, MC, AmEx). Pickled cabbage coming out of your ears? Escape to **La Case de l'Ile Bourbon,** 34, Grand Rue (tel. 03 88 32 60 23), for real French-Caribbean and French-African food. Rices, skewered meats, and fish go for 48-77F *à la carte* (open Sat. 11:45am-2pm, daily 11:45am-2pm, 7-11pm; V, MC).

SIGHTS

Constructed from the 11th century to the 15th, the ornate, Gothic **Cathédrale de Strasbourg** (tel. 03 88 24 43 34) thrusts its heaven-tickling tower 142m into the sky. It was the tallest monument in Christendom until the last century. Inside the south transept of the cathedral, the massive **Horloge Astronomique** demonstrates the wizardry of 16th-century Swiss clockmakers. Each day at 12:30pm, the apostles troop out of the face while a cock crows to greet St. Peter. Get there at least a half-hour early in July and August (tickets go on sale at 11:50am at the south entrance to the cathedral; commentary in French and German at 12:10pm; admission 5F). In front of the clock, the cathedral's central **Pilier des Anges** (Angels' Pillar), decorated by an anonymous 13th-century master from Chartres, depicts the Last Judgment and its seraphic jury. The same artist also crafted the statues flanking the south portal that portray the church and the synagogue as two women. Climb the **tower** to follow in the footsteps of the young Goethe, who scaled its 330 steps regularly as a cure for his acrophobia.

(Tower open 8:30am-7pm. Admission 12F, students 11F. *Son et lumière* April-Oct. daily at 9:15pm in French; at 8:15pm in German. Admission 29F, students 16F. Cathedral open Mon.-Sat. 7-11:40am and 12:45-7pm, Sun. 12:45-6pm. Guided tours in French 15F; Mon.-Fri. at 10:30am and 2:30 and 3:30pm, Sat. 10:30am and 2:30pm, Sun. 2:30 and 3:30pm.)

Strasbourg's **museums** (tel. 03 88 52 50 00) manifest unheard-of solidarity. They cluster near the cathedral and (with exceptions noted below) are open Mon.-Sat. 10am-noon and 1:30-6pm, Sun. 10am-5pm; admission to each 20F, students 10F.

The **Château des Rohan,** 2, pl. du Château, a magnificent 18th-century building commissioned by the first Cardinal de Rohan-Soubise, houses a trio of small museums. Most impressive is the **Musée des Arts Décoratifs,** which features opulent furnishings that preserve its original splendor. Upstairs, the **Musée des Beaux-Arts** stocks a solid collection from the 14th to 19th centuries, including works by Giotto, Botticelli, Raphael, Rubens, El Greco, Van Dyck, and Goya. The **Musée Archéologique** presents the history of Alsace from 100,000 BC to AD 800—enough pots to satiate the most tireless connoisseur (3 museums 40F, students 20F).

The superb **Musée d'Art Moderne,** 5, pl. du Château, shows Modernist and Impressionist works by Gauguin, Picasso, Klimt, Chagall, Klee, Rodin, and *strasbourgeois* Arp (guided tours 40F, closed Tues.). The 14th- to 16th-century mansion opposite the cathedral, **Maison de l'Oeuvre Notre-Dame** (tel. 03 88 32 48 95 or 88 32 06 39), is more interesting for its façade than for its collection of sculpture and stained glass (closed Mon.). Just across the pont du Corbeau, the **Musée Alsacien,** 23, quai St-Nicolas (tel. 03 88 35 55 36), showcases folk art (closed Tues.).

La Petite France, the old tanners' district, preens in the southwest corner of the *centre ville.* Its slender Alsatian houses, with steep roofs and carved wooden façades, overlook narrow canals and locks. Postcards were probably invented here. Swans glide beneath the shadow of the 13th-century towers on **pont du Couverts,** which links several small islands. On the north side of town, **pl. de la République,** next to the imperial Palais du Rhin, is a magnificent example of 19th-century urban design. Just north of the *place,* on rue Auguste Lamet, the **Jardin du Contades,** designed for military competitions, is now a peaceful strolling ground.

Strasbourg's largest and most spectacular park is **l'Orangerie.** Locals routinely escape to its shaded walks, peaceful fountains, and wide lawns, designed by Le Nôtre in 1692 after he cut his teeth on Vaux-le-Vicomte and Versailles. Waterways with man-made ponds and waterfalls can be explored by rowboat (30F per ½-hr.). The park also cages a small **zoo** (free). There are free **concerts** summer evenings at 8:30pm at the Pavillion Josephine. Take bus 23, 30, or 72 to "l'Orangerie."

Built of Vosges sandstone and oxidized aluminum, the **Palais de l'Europe,** seat of the Council of Europe and the European Parliament, lies at the northwest edge of the Orangerie on av. de l'Europe. During sessions (one week per month), you may register at the desk to sit in the visitors' gallery, where headsets translate debates into several languages. (Bring your passport. Guided 1-hr. visits by advance request only. Call 03 88 41 20 29 several days ahead. When not in session, individual visits can be arranged by calling 03 87 17 20 07.)

Get a taste of Strasbourg's German side at the **Kronenburg Brewery,** 68, route d'Oberhausbergen (tel. 03 88 27 41 59), which features a free guided tour, a look at different stages of brewing, a film, and a (limited, alas) tasting session. (Visits by appointment only, available in English, Mon.-Fri. 9-10am and 2-3pm, also 11am and 4pm during the summer.) **Heineken,** 4-10, rue St-Charles, Schiltgheim (tel. 03 88 62 90 80), also offers free tours of its brewery in English, French, and German (by appointment only; call 03 88 19 58 00 to schedule, Mon.-Fri. at 2 and 3pm).

Goethe, Napoleon, and Metternich graduated from the **Université de Strasbourg.** Follow bd. de la Victoire or rue de Zurich out to its new quarters at the esplanade. The faculties are in the Palais de l'Université area, which extends across bd. de la Victoire to the botanical gardens by rue Goethe and rue de l'Université (open March-Sept. Mon.-Fri. 8-11:45am and 2-5pm, Sun. 8-11:45am; Oct.-Feb. closed Sun.).

ENTERTAINMENT

Laze away summer afternoons and evenings on **pl. de la Cathédrale,** where musicians, mimes, comedians, caricaturists, and acrobats perform. Wet 'n' wild **water-jousting** competitions take place Tuesday and Thursday evenings on the Ill River outside the Palais des Rohan (July-Aug. 8:30pm). If your yen for aquabatics has not been sated, fountains dance to lights and music while a tightrope walker traverses the two towers of **Vauban's Ponts Converts** (July-Aug. daily 10:30pm). **Circuits en Bateau** boats leave every half-hour from the quai below pl. du Château (behind the cathedral). Cruises March-Oct. last 1¼hr. (39F, children 19F50).

In the courtyard of the **Château des Rohan,** folk dancers demonstrate their craft June-August (Sun. 10:30am and various evenings 8:30pm). June brings the **Festival International de Musique,** which has featured Jessye Norman and the London Philharmonic. At the beginning of July, the **Festival de Jazz** brings such luminaries as 1995 headliners Ray Charles and Fats Domino. For info on either festival, contact Wolf Musique, 24, rue de la Mésange (tel. 03 88 32 43 10). **Musica** (tickets tel. 03 88 21 02 02; admin. 03 88 21 02 21; fax 03 88 21 02 88), a contemporary music festival from mid-September to early October, consists of concerts, operas, films, and music played underwater in the public pool. From October through June, the **Orchestre Philharmonique de Strasbourg** (tel. 03 88 15 09 09 for tickets, 03 88 15 09 00 for info), performs at the Palais de la Musique et des Congrès, behind pl. de Bordeaux. The **Théâtre National de Strasbourg** stages productions at 7, pl. de la République (tel. 03 88 35 44 52; tickets 70-120F, students 50-85F). The **Opéra du Rhin** features opera and ballet in the 19th-century hall at 19, pl. Broglie (tel. 03 88 75 48 01; tickets 60-230F). The **Festival Européen du Cinéma d'Art et d'Essai,** 32, rue du Vieux-Marché-aux-Vins (tel. 03 88 75 06 95), unreels each November and December.

Nightlife in Strasbourg picks up from September to May, when the students are in town. Bars and pubs lie in the cathedral's shadow on rue des Frères, its sibling rue des Soeurs, and rue de la Croix. Most close around 2am on weeknights, later on weekends. **Café Brant,** 11, rue Goethe, at quai du Marlene, er, Maire-Dietrich, across from the university, packs students chomping sandwiches (14F) or gulping beers (12F) at its sidestreet tables (open 9am-8:30pm). Let your inner yuppie see and be seen at perennially hip **Les Aviateurs,** 12, rue des Soeurs (whiskey 35-50F, beer 18-45F, Dom Perignon 800F; open Tues.-Sun. 8pm-3am; V, MC). For live jazz in a livelier spot with no cover and plenty of students, try **Gayot Piano Jazz Bar,** 18, rue des Frères (tel. 03 88 36 31 88; open daily 10:30am-2am; live bands Wed.-Sat.; V, MC). Heavenly *a capella* challenges gritty rock in the smoky, bohemian **Café des Anges,** 5, rue Ste-Catherine (tel. 03 88 37 12 67; opens weeknights 9:30pm, Fri.-Sat. 10pm; cover charge varies). **Le Rock's Academy,** 56, rue Jeu des Enfants (tel. 03 88 32 21 43), off pl. Homme de Fer, is a popular disco.

■ La Route du Vin

Alsace's vineyards align themselves along a 140km spine stretching roughly from Strasbourg to Mulhouse, known as the Route du Vin (wine route). The area's beauty and *bouquets* make it a popular tourist destination. During the grape harvest in September and early October, the tiny villages tucked along the Route du Vin host bacchanalian *fêtes.* Residents don traditional Alsatian red capes and black hoods, wine and beer flow, and *choucroute* is doled out amid dancing and cavorting.

Alsace's grapes were first fermented long before the Romans savored them but gained recognition in the 16th century, when the nearby Rhine was opened for shipping. Most growers in this strip of Alsace, which is never more than 4km wide from Marlenheim to Thann, have tiny vineyards and a second job. Nevertheless, they produce satisfying, fragrant whites, and a few fruity reds and rosés. Alsatian wines are required to be bottled within the two *départements* of the region within the year of their harvest. When buying, remember that none but the most expensive vintages hit their peak until they are two to five years old and have matured in their distinctive green, fluted bottles. Unlike any other region in France, Alsace names its wines for the grapes, except for the mixed Edelzwicker. Sylvaner is light and fruity, popular and often reasonably priced; dry Riesling turns up its hearty nose at the less prestigious; Guwürztraminer can develop a sweet floral aroma; Pinot Noir accounts for the 6% of Alsace's non-white wine production; and Crémant, the Alsatian bubbly, provides a satisfying and cheap alternative to champagne.

Hitchhiking is said to be slow, and bus service from Strasbourg, Sélestat, and Colmar to the smaller towns is infrequent or non-existent. **Car rental** is practical, if expensive, from Strasbourg (see page 630) and Colmar (see page 639). **Biking** is a popular alternative, especially from Colmar (see page 639), but the gentle yet persistent hills may challenge novices. **Trains** serve several larger towns, such as Sélestat.

Look for vine wreaths outside establishments where *vin nouveau* is available. The best source of information on regional *caves* is the **Centre d'Information du Vin d'Alsace,** 12, av. de la Foire aux Vins (tel. 03 89 20 16 20; fax 03 89 20 16 30), at the Maison du Vin d'Alsace in Colmar. Your best bet for info on the towns of the Route du Vin or other regional advice is the **departmental tourist office** in Strasbourg (see page 628). A few local bus companies organize **tours** of the Route du Vin. The Strasbourg tourist office (tel. 03 88 52 28 28) has info. **Astra** (tel. 03 88 21 59 70) runs daily bus tours for 95-150F per person.

The Route comprises over 100 villages, each more beautiful than the next. Regard our limited list as a small *dégustation* of what's out there. At the foot of the Vosges, **Molsheim** is the largest wine town and quite popular with tourists. The town hall, the **Metzig,** retains its tower, clock, and moondial from the 16th century, along with two angels who emerge from their hiding places to strike the hours. A Gothic church looms over the town, a remnant of the once-powerful Jesuit university which set up shop here. For more information on Molsheim, contact the **tourist office** at 17, pl. de l'Hôtel de Ville (tel. 03 88 38 11 61; open Mon.-Fri. 8am-noon and 2-6pm, Sat. 10am-noon and 2-4pm; in summer also Sat. 9am-noon and 2-6pm, Sun. 10am-noon and 2-4pm). The office organizes free visits to the vineyards and *caves* and a free *dégustation* (July-Aug. Mon. and Thurs. at 10am). Near the Metzig, the small **Musée Régional** displays wine equipment and other curiosities (open Mon.-Fri. 2-6pm; free). **Trains** run from Strasbourg (every 30min., 15min., 19F).

Kintzheim, near Sélestat, has a **tourist office,** pl. de la Fontaine (tel. 03 88 82 09 90), open in summer daily 10am-noon and 2-6pm. An aviary of predatory birds soars just overhead at the ruined **Château de Kintzheim** (tel. 03 88 92 84 33; open April-Sept. from 2pm; Oct.-Nov. 11 Wed. and Sat.-Sun. only; call ahead for visits; admission 45F, students 30F). At **La Montagne des Singes** (tel. 03 88 92 11 09), 200 Moroccan macaques hang out in 20 hectares of Vosgian forest (open April-Oct. daily 10am-noon and 1-6pm, Nov.-March 10am-noon and 1-5pm; admission, including popcorn for the primates, 40F, children 25F). Ascend 757m to the peak of a nearby mountain, where tourists photograph the view from the **Château du Haut Koenigsbourg** (tel. 03 88 82 50 60). Constructed in the 12th century but destroyed in a nasty brush with the Swedes during the Thirty Years' War, it was occupied and rebuilt by Emperor Wilhelm II of Germany in the late 19th century. The château now offers a reconstruction of life in the late Middle Ages. (Open daily June-Sept. 9am-6pm; March and Oct. 9am-noon and 1-5pm; April-May 9am-noon and 1-6pm; Nov.-Feb. 9am-noon and 1-4pm. Admission 36F, students 22F, children 15F.) The closest **train station** to Kintzheim is Sélestat, 3km of hilly terrain away (see page 637). **STAHV buses** (tel. 03 89 41 40 27) run from Colmar (12 per day, 20min., 9F60).

In 1753, Voltaire insisted that the vineyards of **Riquewihr** be used as collateral on a loan he made to its Duke. The Duke's word was as good as his wine, and Voltaire never got his hands on the precious vines. The 16th-century walled village lures thousands in summer, and prices for food and lodging soar. Built in 1291, the **Musée du Dolder,** rue du Général de Gaulle, in the Tour du Dolder, has a collection of 15th-century firearms (open daily April-Oct. 9:30am-noon and 1:30-6:30pm; admission 10F). The beautiful **Tour des Voleurs** (Thieves' Tower) contains a blood-curdling torture chamber stocked with devices that would titillate the Marquis de Sade (open daily April-Oct. 9:30am-noon and 1:30-6:30pm; admission 10F). The **tourist office,** 2, rue de la 1ère Armée (tel. 03 89 47 80 80; open daily July-Aug. 10am-12:30pm and 1:30-6:30pm; March-June and Sept.-Nov. 10am-12:30pm and 1:30-6pm), has a list of rooms in private houses. The **Camping Intercommunal** (tel. 03 89 47 90 08), 1km from the town center, has showers and a bakery (20F per person, 10F per child, 25F per site; open April-Oct.; reception 8:30am-7:30pm).

A few km south of Riquewihr at the entrance to the Weiss valley, the ancient, flower-filled village of **Kaysersberg** attracts its fair share of visitors. The 13th-century fortress is just a ruin, but graceful, half-timbered 15th-century houses cluster around the fortified bridge. Among them is the birthplace of Nobel Prize-winning Dr. Albert Schweitzer, now a museum. The 13th-century **Eglise Ste-Croix** is home to Jean Bogartz's outstanding altar piece, completed in 1518. Set off a medieval courtyard at 62, rue du Général de Gaulle, the town's **musée** displays some polychrome statues and a prized 14th-century sculpture of the Virgin (open July-Aug. 10am-noon and 2-6pm; June and Sept.-Oct. Sat.-Sun. 10am-noon and 2-6pm; admission 10F, students 5F). On rue du Général de Gaulle, you'll find the **tourist office** (tel. 03 89 78 22 78; open May-Aug. Mon.-Fri. 8am-noon and 1-6pm, Sat. 9am-noon and 2-6pm, Sun. 10am-noon and 2-4pm; Sept.-April Mon.-Fri. 8am-noon and 1-5pm). The **municipal campground,** out of town on rue des Acacias (tel. 03 89 47 14 47), offers swimming, tennis, golf, and ruins by the river (18F per adult, 9F per child, 13F per site; open April-Sept.). Take the **bus to** Kaysersberg from Colmar (12 per day, 30min., 11F40).

Sélestat

Halfway between Colmar and Strasbourg, Sélestat is often overlooked by tourists on their way between the two larger cities. As a result Sélestat (pop. 15,600) has avoided acquiring the Disneyland looniness of some of the Route du Vin's more frequented towns. An imperial city of the German Empire from AD 1217, and a center of humanism in the 15th century, Sélestat has painstakingly preserved its rich cultural heritage. Its central location makes it an ideal base from which to explore the heartland of Alsace. But few who stop here can resist the half-timbered charm and jolly old spirit of the town which, in 1521, was the birthplace of the Christmas tree.

ORIENTATION AND PRACTICAL INFORMATION

The **tourist office,** 10, bd. Général Leclerc (tel. 03 88 58 87 20; fax 03 88 92 88 63), in the Commanderie St-Jean, is at the north end of the *centre ville.* To get there from the station, go straight on av. de la Gare, through pl. Général de Gaulle, to av. de la Liberté. Turn left onto bd. du Maréchal Foch, which veers right and becomes bd. Général Leclerc after pl. Schaal. The office is a few blocks down on your right. Free list of hotels and restaurants; small map. Detailed map 10F. Free hotel reservations; fair **currency exchange.** (Open May-Sept. Mon.-Fri. 9am-12:30pm and 1:30-7pm, Sat. 9am-noon and 2-5pm, Sun. 10am-noon and 2-4pm; Oct.-April Mon.-Fri. 8am-noon and 2-6pm, Sat. 10am-noon and 2-4pm.) **Crédit Mutuel** at 6, pl. d'Armes (tel. 03 88 92 20 85; open Tues.-Fri. 8am-noon and 1:30-5:15pm, Sat. 8am-noon and 1:30-4pm) has a 24-hour **ATM.** The **train station** at pl. de la Gare (ticket tel. 03 88 92 91 65, info tel. 03 36 35 35 35) runs trains to Paris (5 per day, 6½hr., 281F) and Lyon (6 per day, 5½hr., 233F); and often to Strasbourg (20min., 43F) and Colmar (10min., 23F). **Bike rental** is at **Sport 2000,** 3, pl. d'Armes (tel. 03 88 92 05 43; 60F per ½-day, 90F per day; open Mon. 2-7pm, Tues.-Fri. 9am-noon and 2-7pm, Sat. 9am-noon and 2-6pm). The **hospital** is at 23, av. Pasteur (tel. 03 88 57 55 55). In case of **medical emergency,** dial 15. The **police** are at bd. du Général Leclerc (tel. 03 88 58 84 22); dial 17 in **emergencies.** The **post office** is on rue de la Poste (tel. 03 88 58 80 14; open Mon.-Fri. 8am-noon and 1:30-6pm, Sat. 8am-noon). Sélestat's **postal code** is 67600.

ACCOMMODATIONS AND CAMPING

Until the new hostel opens in 1997, there will be only a few budget hotels in Sélestat. If the July and August crowds shut you out, you can always hop back on the train to

Strasbourg. In a residential area on the eastern edge of town, the **Hôtel de l'Ill,** 13, rue des Baterliers (tel. 03 88 92 91 09), off bd. des Thiers, has warmly decorated, quiet rooms. (Singles 120F. Doubles 180F, with shower 220F. Triples 300F. Breakfast 28F. Showers 25F. Reception daily 7am-11pm. V, MC, AmEx.) **Hôtel Au Relais d'Alsace,** 2, rue du 4ème Zouaves (tel. 03 88 92 24 34), is between the train station and the *vieille ville.* Walk straight from the station on av. de la Gare, past pl. du Général de Gaulle, onto av. de la Liberté, which becomes rue du 4ème Zouaves. Big and comfy singles and triples don't have showers, but hall showers are free. (Singles 150F. Doubles 160F, with toilet and shower 230F. Triples 190F. Breakfast 28F. V, MC.) Across the street, **Hôtel Au Lion d'Or,** 4, rue du 4ème Zouaves (tel. 03 88 92 06 13), is an economical option. (Singles or doubles 180F. Triples 210F. Breakfast 28F. Free hall showers. Reception 9am-midnight; V, MC, AmEx.) **Camping Les Cigognes** (tel. 03 88 92 03 98) is outside the old ramparts on the south edge of the *vieille ville.* Public tennis courts and parks nearby (13F per person, 12F per site, electricity 6F).

FOOD

Sélestat brings good tidings for cheap food. If the world is your picnic, head to **Intermarché supermarket** at pl. de la Victoire (tel. 03 88 92 06 14; open Mon. 2:30-7pm, Tues.-Fri. 8:30am-noon and 2:30-7pm, Sat. 8:30am-12:30pm and 2:30-5:30pm). Every Tuesday morning, an **open air market** fills the town center with cabbage and other necessities. For the cheapest Italian favorites this side of your own kitchen, join the locals at **Halte Pizzas,** 14, rue d'Iena (tel. 03 88 82 91 91). Pasta dishes from 11F, huge pizzas from 27F (open Mon. and Wed. 11am-2pm and 5-11:30pm, Fri.-Sat. 11am-2pm and 5-11pm, Sun. 5-11:30pm). At **Le Snack Pitchoun,** rue Ste-Barbe, eat dirt-cheap home cookin' in clean, cave-like surroundings: salads 7-35F, sausage platters 13-15F, cheeseburger and fries 18F. For a little more, the **Winstub au Bon Pichet,** 10, pl. du Marché-aux-Choux (tel. 03 88 82 96 95), boils up Alsatian favorites. Large salads with *foie gras,* duck, pâté, or smoked salmon 45F. Meat and fish dishes 60-75F, *menu* 60F. (Open Tues.-Sun. 11am-2pm and 6-10pm. V, MC.)

SIGHTS AND ENTERTAINMENT

According to local legend, Sélestat was founded by Sletto, a giant. His **massive thigh bone** is only one of the treasures of the extraordinary **Bibliothèque Humaniste,** 1, rue de la Bibliothèque (tel. 03 88 92 03 24). In the 15th century, Sélestat drew humanist scholars, including Erasmus, from all over the region; its library was founded in 1452. Upon his death in 1547, Beatus Rhenasus donated his own collection to the library. Among the *bibliothèque's* impressive and exquisitely embellished documents is the first reference to "America," a well-preserved Merovingian lectionary from 630, Erasmus' letters to his friend Beatus, Charlemagne's 9th-century regulations, and the thigh bone of a certain prehistoric woolly mammoth who now goes by the name "Sletto." (Open Mon.-Fri. 9am-noon and 2-6pm, Sat. 9am-noon; July and Aug. also open Sat.-Sun. 2-7pm. Admission 11F, kids 6F.)

Surrounded by ivy-covered homes, the church of **Ste-Foy** rises above the *vieille ville* and the pl. Marché-aux-Poissons. Constructed by Benedictine monks between 1152 and 1190, Ste-Foy is one of the most beautiful Romanesque churches in the region. Its symmetrical front towers date from the late 19th century, but the central octagonal tower is original. **St-Georges** stands defiantly across the square, built by the townspeople from the 13th to 15th centuries out of resentment for the monastery's ill-wielded power. The church is essentially Gothic, with 14th- and 15th-century frescoes adorning its transept and well-wrought 19th-century glass.

The rapid decline of humanism, coupled with religious and political disorder, made the 16th and 17th centuries a dark period in Sélestat's history. The **tour des sorcières,** in front of pl. Maréchal de Lattre de Tassigny, is the 13th-century tower in which the Catholic church imprisoned over 100 "witches" between 1629 and 1642. The visitor to Sélestat should not miss the modern art work by Sarkis, **La Rêve** ("The Dream"), constructed on remnants of the old ramparts across town. Cryptic, poetic phrases such as "the butterfly bats its wing" and "because I have always loved you" cover the crumbling walls. Every other year the town hosts a contemporary art exhibition cleverly named **Sélast'Art** (mid-Sept. to mid-Oct.). Painting of a different kind is showcased in the annual, highly colorful Easter "egg-zhibition" (around Easter). Sélestat's major festival is its **Corso Fleuri,** or flower festival, the second Sunday in August, with impressive floats made of fresh local flowers. A program of cultural events can be picked up at the tourist office.

Located at the heart of Alsace, Sélestat is surrounded by a number of scenic villages and châteaux. Most notable is the **Château du Haut-Koenigsbourg,** about 8km from town along D159 (see page 636). Hiking trails abound in **La Forêt d'Ill,** 2km from Sélestat. Half-timbered homes in **Ebermunster,** about 3km from town, cluster around one of France's finest German Baroque churches. Sélestat is a relaxed base from which to taste the bounty of the Route du Vin (see page 635).

Colmar

Surrounded by vineyards and the craggy Vosges Mountains, Colmar derives its name from the *colombes* (doves) Charlemagne kept at his estate along the Lauch river. While the town (pop. 65,000) is extensive, most of the museums and churches lie within a small radius along the cobblestone streets of the pedestrian zone and the scenic 15th- and 16th-century alleys of its Petite Venise. Housed in the city's former Dominican monastery and church are two superlative works of Renaissance religious art—Grünewald's *Issenheim Altarpiece* and Schongauer's *Virgin in the Rose Bower*—which themselves justify a visit. Unfortunately, the word is out: Colmar's streets are flooded with tour buses and packs of Germans stricken with *wanderlust.* Avoid the weekenders, or make Colmar a daytrip from Strasbourg or Sélestat.

ORIENTATION AND PRACTICAL INFORMATION

Colmar lies 75km south of Strasbourg along the Route du Vin. To get to the tourist office from the station, take the first left as you walk out the main exit onto rue de la Gare and follow it as it becomes rue de Lattre de Tassigny and rue Roesselmann. Turn right onto rue des Unterlinden; the tourist office will be on your left (10min.).

Tourist Office: 4, rue des Unterlinden (tel. 03 89 20 68 92). Professional staff hands out hotel and restaurant listings, daytrip and Route du Vin info, and a good city map. Hotel reservations with first night's deposit. City tours July-Aug. (in French and German; Tues., Thurs., and Sat.; 20F, students 10F). **Currency exchange** (cash only). Open July-Aug. Mon.-Sat. 9am-7pm, Sun. 9:30am-4pm; Sept.-June Mon.-Sat. 9am-6pm and Sun. 10am-4pm.

Money: Several 24-hr. **ATMs** cluster at the entrance of the rue des Prêtres, around **Crédit Mutuel.** There's a **Banque de France** across from the station, and a **BNP** at 6, av. de la République (tel. 03 89 20 73 99).

Trains: pl. de la Gare (tel. 08 36 35 35 35). To: Paris (10 per day, about 6hr., 296F); Lyon (4 per day, 4½hr., 229F); and Basel (17 per day, 1hr., 62F). Many to: Sélestat (20min., 23F); Strasbourg (30min., 56F); and Mulhouse (30min., 40F). **Lockers.** Office open Mon.-Fri. 6:30am-8pm, Sat. 8:30am-6:30pm, Sun. noon-7:30pm.

Buses: pl. de la Gare, to the right as you exit the train station. Numerous companies run to Kaysersberg (20 per day, 30min., 11F); Riquewihr (6 per day, 30min., 13F); Ribeauville (6 per day, 30min., 13F), and many other small towns on the Route du Vin. The tourist office's *Actualités de Colmar* lists schedules.

Public Transportation: Allo Trace, rue Unterlinden (tel. 03 89 20 80 80), next door to the tourist office. Tickets (4F90), *carnet* of 10 40F50. Buses run 6am-8pm.

Taxis: pl. de la Gare (tel. 03 89 41 40 19 or 03 89 80 71 71). 24hr.

Car Rental: Europ'Car, pl. Rapp (tel. 03 89 24 11 80), rents economy cars for 398F per weekend with 200km mileage. Open Mon.-Sat. 8am-noon and 2-6pm.

Bike Rental: Cycles Meyer, 6, rue du Pont Rouge (tel 03 89 79 12 47), across from the tourist office. 70F per day, 130F per 2 days, 160F per 3 days, 280F per week. Open Mon.-Sat. 8am-noon and 2-6:30pm.

Hospital: Hôpital Pasteur, 39, av. de la Liberté (tel. 03 89 80 40 00). From station, take underpass to rue du Tir, turn right, then left on av. de la Liberté. **Ambulance** or **medical emergency** tel. 15.

Police: 6, rue du Chasseur (tel. 03 89 41 43 05). **Emergency** tel. 17.

Post Office: 36-38, av. de la République, (tel. 03 89 41 19 19 or 03 89 24 62 71), across from the Champ-de-Mars. **Currency exchange.** Poste Restante. Photocopies 1F. Open Mon.-Fri. 8am-6:30pm, Sat. 8am-noon. **Postal code:** 68000.

ACCOMMODATIONS AND CAMPING

Try to stay in a hostel; hotels are expensive and usually booked in summer.

Maison des Jeunes (Centre International de Séjour), 17, rue Camille-Schlumberger (tel. 03 89 41 26 87), in a nice neighborhood. Walk straight out of the *gare* onto av. Raymond Poincaré and take 3rd right (10min.). TV room. Sat.-Sun. groups only. 47F. Sheets 16F. No breakfast for individuals. Reception Mon.-Sat. 7am-noon and 2-11pm, Sun. 8am-noon and 5-11pm. Curfew 11pm.

Auberge de Jeunesse (HI), 2, rue Pasteur (tel. 03 89 80 57 39). Take bus 4 (direction: Logelbach) to "Pont Rouge." To walk, take the underground passage in the station and exit to the right onto rue du Tir. Follow it as it merges with av. Général de Gaulle. Turn left onto rue du Florimont halfway across the bridge over the railroad tracks. Take a right on rue du Pont Rouge; continue through the intersection on the rte. d'Ingersheim to rue Pasteur. (20min.). Clean, bright rooms. Members only. 66F in 7-bunk rooms, 86F in 2- to 4-bunk rooms. Breakfast and showers free. Sheets 20F. Lockout 9am-5pm. Curfew midnight, 11pm in winter.

La Chaumière, 74, av. de la République (tel. 03 89 41 08 99). Exit the *gare,* walk straight one block and turn left on av. de la République (2min.). Comfortable rooms with shower face a quiet courtyard. Rooms without shower face a noisy street. Downstairs bar and the owner are exceptionally friendly. Free hall shower. Singles 170F, with shower 220F. Doubles 180F, with shower 240F. Triples 245F. Breakfast 28F. Reception daily 7am-11pm, July-Aug. closed Sun. 1-3pm. V, MC.

Hôtel Primo 99, 5, rue des Ancêtres (tel. 03 89 24 22 24; fax 03 89 24 55 96), centrally located. Flamingo-pink exterior belongs in Miami Beach, but rooms are tasteful, modern, and spotless. Singles 139F, with shower and toilet 219F. Doubles 199F, with shower and toilet 279F. Free TV and hall shower. Breakfast 33F. Extra bed 50F. Wheelchair access. Reception 24hr. V, MC.

Camping: Camping de l'Ill, route de Neuf-Brisach (tel. 03 89 41 15 94), about 3km from town. Take bus 1 (direction: Horbourg-Wihr) to "Plage d'Ill." Along the river. Fills quickly in summer. Immaculate bathrooms, store, and restaurant (90F *menu,* 60F dishes). 14F per person, 16F per tent and car. Open Feb.-Nov.

FOOD

There are a large number of reasonably priced restaurants to choose from, including the old standby, **Monoprix supermarket,** across from the tourist office (open Mon.-Fri. 8:30am-8:30pm, Sat. 8am-7:30pm). **Markets** are set up Saturday mornings on pl. St-Joseph and Thursday mornings on pl. de l'Ancienne Douane. Canal-side cafés capitalize on the scenery in La Petite Venise and the Quartier des Tanneurs. Cheap sandwich shops can be found on rue Vauban.

Settle in the cobblestone courtyard of **Le Streusel,** 4, passage de l'Ancienne Douane (tel. 03 89 24 98 02), for specialties including tarts, fish, and meats. Menu changes daily. *A la carte* 45-60F; mouth-watering *myrtille* pie (open Tues.-Sat. 8am-6:30pm, Sun. 9am-6:30pm; V, MC). **L'Amandine,** 1, pl. de la Cathédrale (tel. 03 89 23 66 82), has great prices despite its ideal location across from the cathedral. Regional specialties, mongo salads, pasta dishes, *choucroute,* pâtés, and quiches 28-74F; 60F *menu.* **Pizzeria Le Midi,** rue Vauban (tel. 03 89 41 07 43), has excellent local and Italian food. Pizzas 35-40F; pasta 38-48F; local specialties 55-80F (open daily 10am-midnight. V, MC). **La Pergola,** 24, rue des Marchands, on a terrace, offers 50F pizzas and four generous *menus* of regional fare (69-99F) in a perfect location (open daily noon-2:30pm and 6:30-10pm. V, MC, AmEx).

SIGHTS AND ENTERTAINMENT

At first glance, one might mistake Colmar for a giant gingerbread village. The city's restored Alsatian houses epitomize the regional architecture and local penchant for adorning plaster with various pastel hues. For the finest specimens, visit the **Quartier des Tanneurs,** then follow rue des Tanneurs over a small canal to the area called **La Petite Venise.** Carved wooden doors line the canals, and geraniums preen in window boxes above cobblestone streets. A few blocks away, across the street from the tourist office, is the impressive **Musée Unterlinden,** pl. Unterlinden (tel. 03 89 20 15 50). The 13th-century Dominican cloister contains a spectacular collection of Northern Renaissance art and a fountain at its center. The museum's crown jewel is Mathias Grünewald's *Issenheim Altarpiece* (1516), an ambitious polyptych (multi-paneled painting) juxtaposing realistic scenes of Christ's crucifixion with more fantastical Biblical depictions. Two rooms feature 20th-century art, including a Monet, a Picasso, and eerie works by Fauvist Georges Rouault (open April-Oct. daily 9am-6pm; Nov.-March Wed.-Mon. 9am-noon and 2-5pm; admission 30F, students 20F).

Colmar became an important religious center in the 13th century, when Dominican and Franciscan monks established themselves. Today the **Eglise des Dominicains,** illuminated by 14th-century stained-glass windows, shelters a 1770 Silberman organ and Martin Schongauer's intricate 1473 *Virgin in the Rose Bower* (displayed mid-March to Dec. 10am-1pm and 3-6pm; admission 8F, students 5F). Polychrome roofs, amber-colored stone, and the pealing bells of the "cathedral," actually the **Collégiale St-Martin,** pl. de la Cathédrale, dominate Colmar's center. Built between 1250 and 1315, the church tucks away several impressive woodcarvings.

Two blocks away, the **Musée Bartholdi,** 30, rue des Marchands (tel. 03 89 41 90 60), houses the works and art collection of one Frédéric Auguste Bartholdi (1834-1904), best known for sculpting a 47m statue of his mother entitled *Liberty Enlightening the World*—though Americans insist on calling it the *Statue of Liberty.* Whisper sweet nothings into Liberty's ear in one of the upstairs rooms. The museum also has a one-room exhibit on Jewish life in Alsace from Roman times to today (open March-Dec. Wed.-Mon. 10am-noon and 2-6pm; admission 20F, students 10F). The tourist office has a map marking six monuments by Bartholdi and one *to* him.

Colmar, at the tip of the Route du Vin, boasts a number of *viticulteurs.* It is worth your while to buy a bottle from a local *cave.* A warm welcome, a great selection of local wines, and a 400-year legacy await at **Robert Karcher et Fils,** 11, rue de l'Ours (tel. 03 89 41 14 42), in the *vieille ville* (white wines 25-37F a bottle, reds 33-40F, liqueurs 95-135F; open daily 8am-noon and 2-7pm; V, MC).

The 10-day **Alsatian Wine Festival** in early August is the region's largest wine fair. **Eglise St-Pierre** stages Thursday night concerts August to early September (45F, under 21 25F; the tourist office has a schedule). The Collégiale St-Martin's organists pipe at the **Heures Musicales** (every Tues. June-Sept. at 8:30pm; for info call the tourist office; tickets 50F, students 40F). In the first half of July, the **Festival International de Colmar** features world-class musicians (concerts 80-100F, students 40-50F). In early September, the anticipated **Journée Choucroute** (Sauerkraut Day), means feasting, dancing, and everyone's favorite cabbage sensation.

Nancy

Nancy dates from the 11th century, when Gérard d'Alsace, founder of the duchy of Lorraine, built a castle between two marshes of the Meurthe river. During the Middle Ages, Nancy remained a small feudal village whose cottages huddled behind the protective walls of their overlord's castle. In 1588, the enlightened Duke Charles III built Nancy's "new town," with its straight streets and perfectly squared corners. But Nancy owes its architectural fame to Stanislas Lecsyznski (1677-1766), dethroned king of Poland and father-in-law to Louis XV. Named Duke of Lorraine, Stanislas set about joining Old and New Nancy with his flamboyant pl. Stanislas, designing it down to the last gilded brass gate and intricate façade. In keeping with its tradition of architectural juxtapositions, bustling Nancy (pop. 100,000) merges industrial areas and concrete high-rises with art nouveau architecture, Baroque squares, and a medieval *vieille ville.* The cultural heart of Lorraine, Nancy boasts a resident symphony, ballet and opera companies, and plenty of museums. The city's 30,000 students fuel a local passion for jazz kindled by the live bands at many bars and restaurants and Nancy's many festivals.

ORIENTATION AND PRACTICAL INFORMATION

The town center is **pl. Stanislas.** As you exit the station to the left, take a right at the Hôtel Altéa on rue Raymond-Poincaré, which turns into rue Stanislas, and opens onto pl. Stanislas and the tourist office. Be careful around the train station at night.

Tourist Information: Tourist Office, 14, pl. Stanislas (tel. 03 83 35 22 41; fax 03 83 37 63 07), to the right of the triumphal arch. Many brochures, lists of hotels and restaurants. Free map is adequate; detailed map 23F. **Exchanges currency** when banks are closed. Hotel reservations 15F. 30min. tours of the city June-Sept. 36F. Call in advance for an English tour, or take a headphone tour any time (36F, 300F deposit). Open Mon.-Sat. 9am-7pm, Sun. 10am-noon and 2-5pm; Oct.-May closed Sun. afternoon. Pick up the free monthly **Spectacles à Nancy,** or the weekly **Les Rendez-Vous Nanciens** for movies and nightlife.

Budget Travel: Wasteels, 1bis, pl. Thiers (tel. 03 83 35 42 29). Specializes in student passes and discount rates. Open Mon.-Fri. 8:30am-6:30pm, Sat. 9am-6pm.

Money: 24-hr. **ATM,** 31, rue Gustave Simon, just behind pl. Stanislas. At night, the **Société Générale ATM,** 44, rue St-Dizier, is on a busier street.

Airport: Flights to Paris, Lyon, Toulouse, Marseille, and Nice. Shuttles to the airport from the train station (5 per day, 1hr., 40F). For info, call 03 83 21 56 90.

Trains: pl. Thiers (tel. 03 83 56 50 50 for info, 03 83 37 60 60 for tickets). To: Strasbourg (every 30min., 1hr., 106F); Metz (hourly, 40min., 49F); Bar-le-Duc, (11 per day, 1hr., 78F); Paris (hourly, 3hr., 201F); Saverne (6 per day, 50min., 80F). Office open Mon.-Fri. 9am-7:30pm, Sat. 9am-6:30pm, Sun. 6:30am-8:30pm.

Buses: Rapides de Lorraine, pl. Colonel Driant (tel. 03 83 32 34 20), departs across the street in pl. Monseigneur Ruch. To: Verdun (5 per day, 3hr., 87F); Lunéville (7 per day, 1hr., 28F); Vittel (1 per day, 2hr., 64F). Office open Mon.-Fri. 7:45am-noon and 2-6:15pm, Sat. 8:30am-noon. **Transcars: Les Courriers Mosellans,** pl. Colonel-Driant (tel. 03 83 32 23 58), serves local towns.

Public Transportation: Agence Bus, 3, rue Dr. Schmitt (tel. 03 83 35 54 54). Open Mon.-Sat. 7:30am-7pm. Tourist office gives free schedules and maps. Buy tickets from the driver, at the *gare,* at the info office on pl. de la Cathédrale, or at automatic distributors. Tickets 7F, *carnet* of 10 44F. Buses run 5:30am-8pm.

Taxis: 1, rue Crampel (tel. 03 83 37 65 37). 10F initial fee; 6F per km, 11F at night.

Car Rental: The creatively named **Rent-A-Car,** 96, rue Stanislas (tel. 03 83 37 97 97; fax 03 83 37 44 73). 199F per day, unlimited mileage. 999F per week.

Bike Rental: Michenan, 91, av. des 4 Eglises (tel. 03 83 17 59 53), near pl. Stanislas. Wide selection. 90F for the 1st day, 50F each additional day. 300F per week. Open Tues.-Sat. 9am-noon and 2-6:45pm.

Laundromat: Self Lav-o-matic, 107, rue Gabriel Mouilleron. Wash 15F for 5kg, 30F for 10-12kg. Dry 5F per 15min. Open daily 8am-9pm.

English Books: Le Hall du Livre, 38, rue St-Dizier (tel. 03 83 35 53 01); selection of magazines, classics, and best-sellers. Open Mon.-Sat. 9am-8pm, Sun. 11am-7pm.

Hospital: CHU Nancy, 29, av. de Lattre de Tassigny (tel. 03 83 85 85 85). Take bus 1 (direction: Jarville Sion) to "Hôpital Centrale." **Medical emergency** tel. 15.

Police: Commissariat Central, 38, bd. Lobau (tel. 03 83 17 27 37). Take bus 29 (direction: Tomblaine/Ste-Marguerite) to "Loritz." **Emergency** tel. 17.

Post Office: 8, rue Pierre-Fourier (tel. 03 83 39 27 10), behind the Hôtel de Ville and pl. Stanislas. Poste restante (postal code: 54039). **Currency exchange.** Photocopiers. Open Mon.-Fri. 8am-7pm, Sat. 8am-noon. **Postal code:** 54000.

ACCOMMODATIONS AND CAMPING

Look for budget hotels around **rue Jeanne d'Arc** (at least a 15-min. walk from **pl. Stanislas**) behind the station. To get to rue Jeanne d'Arc from the *gare*, take a right out the door and another right over the bridge on **av. Foch.** It's the second cross street. Call **CROUS,** 75, rue de Laxar (tel. 03 83 91 88 00), for lodgings.

Centre d'Accueil de Remicourt, 149, rue de Vandoeuvre (tel. 03 83 27 73 67), in Villiers-les-Nancy, 4km southwest of town in the Château de Remicourt. Take bus 26 (direction: Villiers Clairlieu) from the station to "St-Fiacre" (2 per hr., last bus at 8pm). Just downhill from the bus stop, turn right onto rue de Vandoeuvre and walk uphill for 3min. Look for the signs. For those who can't get enough of châteaux, here's a chance to stay in one. Clean, modern 2- and 4-bed rooms within the ancient walls. TV, game room. Showers, sheets, and breakfast included. No curfew or lockout. 4-bed rooms 65F. 2-bed rooms 85F. Non-members 70F and 90F. Reception open 5:30-10pm (if you need to check in earlier, call ahead and ask nicely). Phone reservations accepted Mon.-Sat. 8:30am-10pm.

Hôtel Pasteur, 47, rue Pasteur (tel. 03 83 40 29 85). From rue Jeanne d'Arc, turn right onto rue de Mon-Désert and left onto rue Graffigny to rue Pasteur. Rooms with floral wallpaper on a quiet street in an upscale neighborhood. Singles 100F, with shower 110F. Doubles 100F, with shower 120F. Extra bed 25F. Breakfast in bed 23F. Reception 7:30am-10:30pm. V, MC, AmEx.

Hôtel Le Jean Jaurès, 14, bd. Jean-Jaurès (tel. 03 83 27 74 14; fax 03 83 90 20 94), on a continuation of rue Patton and rue Kennedy. Elegant hotel has beautiful, bright rooms with ornate period piece furniture. Some overlook a private garden, some a busy street (through sound-proofed glass). Singles 125-210F. Doubles 140-230F. Breakfast 25F. Reception 7am-midnight. V, MC, AmEx.

Grand Hôtel de la Poste, 56, pl. Mgr. Ruch (tel. 03 83 32 11 52; fax 03 83 37 58 74). Great location. Plain but clean, airy rooms in a former Episcopalian *palais* built in 1780. Psychedelic-striped, velvet paper in the halls. Singles 125F, with toilet 145F. Doubles 145F, with toilet 165F. Breakfast 22F. 24-hr. reception. V, MC.

Hôtel de l'Academie, 7, rue des Michottes (tel. 03 83 35 52 31; fax 03 83 32 55 78). Pleasant rooms grouped around a small atrium. Big beds. Located between the *gare* and pl. Stanislas. Singles with shower 95-112F. Doubles with shower 122-135F. Extra bed 30F. Breakfast 20F. Reception Mon-Sat. 8am-11pm. V, MC.

Camping: Camping de Brabrois, av. Paul Muller (tel. 03 83 27 18 28), near the Centre d'Accueil. Take bus line 26 or 46 (direction: Villiers Clairlieu) to "Camping." Beautiful site overlooking the town; access to woodland trails. Telephones, showers, grocery store (open 7am-1pm and 4-9pm). 15F50 per person, 7F per tent, 6F50 per car. Electricity 10F50. Reception open April-Oct. 7am-10pm.

FOOD

Nanciens and tourists alike pack the cafés in and around pl. Stanislas from noon until well after midnight. The area around **rue des Maréchaux** and **Grande-Rue** is full of restaurants, most with *menus* at 60F or less. Grande-Rue also provides everything necessary for a picnic in the nearby parc de la Pépinière. The hungry will find happiness in the large **Prisunic supermarket,** on the other side of pl. Stanislas on rue St-Georges behind the post office. The huge **Match** on rue Joffre is also open late (open Mon.-Sat. 7am-midnight). Don't forget the **market** located in pl. Henri Mengin, near the Eglise St-Sébastien (open Tues.-Sat. 9am-noon and 2-5pm).

Aux Délices du Palais, 69, Grande-Rue (tel. 03 83 30 44 19) near the Palais Ducal. Eat large fresh sandwiches or quiche (20-30F) and meditate on psychedelic murals and plastic kitsch. Open 9am-11pm.

Mère Grand, 1, pl. Lafayette. Cuisine served near the fountain. 4-course *menu* 55F, *plats* 40-80F. Open Wed.-Mon. noon-2pm and 4:30-11pm. V, MC, AmEx.

La Gavotte, 49, Grande-Rue (tel. 03 83 37 65 64). Serves such traditional cuisine as crêpes with gruyère. Entrees 31-37F. Open Tues.-Sun. noon-2pm and 7-10pm.

La Mitonne, 2, rue St-Michel, near St-Epvre (tel. 03 83 32 06 15). Enjoy fondues (54-65F) amid wooden beams and stone walls. Meat, fish, and vegetarian dishes 60-70F. Open Mon. dinner only Tues.-Fri. noon-2pm and 7:30pm-midnight.

SIGHTS AND ENTERTAINMENT

Designed by 18th-century architect Emmanuel Héré, the baroque **pl. Stanislas** provides a setting for the balustrades, gilt-tipped wrought iron railings, and fountains of the 17th-century Hôtel de Ville. Nancy's **Musée des Beaux-Arts,** 3, pl. Stanislas (tel. 03 83 85 30 72), shelters an impressive collection of 17th-century paintings and a decent selection of modern works by Matisse, Modigliani, and Dufy (open Mon. noon-6pm, Wed.-Sun. 10:30am-6pm; admission 25F, students free Wed.; Thurs.-Mon. 20F). From pl. Stanislas, pass through the impressive, if ostentatious, five-arch **Arc de Triomphe** to reach **pl. de la Carrière,** which contains a slightly more understated assemblage of Baroque architecture and wrought-iron ornaments.

Just to the north of pl. de la Carrière is one of Nancy's most impressive spaces, the enormous **Parc de la Pépinière.** Peacocks preen in its free **zoo,** while tourists and *Nanciens* pose in the outdoor café. Portals of pink roses lead into the deliciously aromatic **rose garden,** a collection of gaudy specimens from around the world. If you're feeling under par, putt your cares away in the well-maintained **mini-golf course** (18F, evenings 22F). (Park open June-Aug. 6:30am-11:30pm; May and Sept. 6:30am-10pm; March-April and Oct.-Dec. 6:30am-9pm; Dec.-Feb 6:30am-8pm.)

The **Musée Historique Lorrain** (tel. 03 83 32 18 74), housed in the **Palais Ducal** at 64, Grande-Rue, contains assorted paintings, sculpture, and tapestries from the palace, and René II's standard, reputedly the oldest extant French flag (open May-Sept. 14 Wed.-Mon. 10am-6pm; Sept. 15-April Wed.-Mon. 10am-noon and 2-7pm; admission 25F, students 20F). Just off Grande-Rue at pl. St-Epvre is the **Basilique St-Epvre.** Built from 1864-1871, it is an impressive neo-Gothic church with 2500 square meters of stained glass created by international artists (open daily 2:30-6pm).

Many of Nancy's minor museums are outside the *centre ville.* The **Musée de l'Ecole de Nancy,** 36, rue du Sergent-Blandan (tel. 03 83 40 14 86), opposite the train station, illustrates Nancy's contribution to the turn-of-the-century Art Nouveau movement with carved-wood paneling and glasswork, notably that of Emile Gallé, the artist of the Paris Metro signs (open April-Sept. Wed.-Mon. 10am-noon and 2-6pm; Oct.-March Wed.-Mon. 10am-noon and 2-5pm; admission 20F, students 15F). To get to the museum, take bus 25 (direction: Vandoeuvre Est) to "Nancy Thermal."

Other museums beyond the town center feature lions and tigers and bears—**Musée de Zoologie et Aquarium Tropical,** 34, rue Ste-Catherine (tel. 03 83 32 99 97; near pl. Stanislas; open daily 10am-noon and 2-6pm; admission 30F, students 10F)—phones—**Musée du Téléphone (Maison de la Communication),** 11, rue Maurice Barrès (tel. 03 83 34 85 89; open July-Sept. 15 Wed.-Fri. 10am-noon and 2-6pm, Sat.-Sun. 2-6pm; admission 15F, students 10F)—and ores—**Musée de l'Histoire de Fer,** av. du Général de Gaulle, Jarville (tel. 03 83 15 27 70; open Wed.-Mon. 10am-noon and 2-6pm; in winter til 5pm; admission 15F, students 8F). Oh, my.

In mid-October, **Jazz-Pulsations** beats from dusk to dawn in the Parc de la Pépinière. Call the tourist office for info. For year-round sax, the tunnels of **Le Blue Note,** 3, rue des Michottes (tel. 03 83 30 31 18), echo with live jazz and rock (cocktails 35-45F; open Mon.-Thurs. 6pm-4am, Fri.-Sat. 6pm-5am). Even in summer, students pound the packed dance floor of **Les Caves du Roi,** 9, pl. Stanislas (tel. 03 83 35 24 14; open Tues.-Sat. 11pm-4am; 25F cover charge, Fri. 30F, Sat. 35F). **La Luna,** 27, rue de la Visitation (tel. 03 83 36 51 40) means fun for gay Nancy. **Cameo,** 16, rue de la Commanderie (tel. 03 83 40 35 68), screens English films, series, and retrospectives in *v.o.* for appreciative students (tickets 38F, students 29F).

From Nancy, it's a short train ride (4 per day, 1½hr., 64F) to **Vittel,** where France's famous mineral water is bottled. Fashionable resorts have monopolized many of the town's hot springs, but the public still enjoys access to the large **Parc des Thermes** (tel. 03 29 08 76 54) and its water sports. The forest surrounding Vittel invites a pleasant sojourn. The **tourist office,** 136, av. Baloumie (tel. 03 29 08 08 88; fax 03 29 08 37

Twingo!

The cost of a French license, including obligatory driving lessons, is 5000F. Combine this with the expense of the ever-*essence*-ial gasoline (about 5F per liter), and little moolah is left over for the actual automobile. The French have compensated with chic, economy-sized, and inexpensive cars which put American road-hogging, gas-guzzling behemoths to shame. The Renault **Clio,** Fiat **Panda,** and Citroen **Campus** are common autos you'll see on the road in a rainbow of colors from banana yellow to neon green. Automobile manufacturers make unlikely alliances. Swatch and Mercedes joined up to produce the **Smart,** a jaunty city car built in France that resembles a brainy, aerodynamic beetle. Only in ever-fashionable France would United Colors of Benetton and Renault collaborate to design the infinitely cute and popular **Twingo.** A fun punch-buggy-esque game to play when you're on the road is "Twingo." Every time you see a Twingo, shout, "Twingo!" *Let's Go* does not recommend sudden outbursts of Twingo. Twingo. Heh heh. Twingo!

99), will equip you with a list of budget accommodations and trail maps (open May-Sept. Mon.-Sat. 10am-noon and 2-6pm, Sun. 2-6pm; Oct.-April Mon.-Fri. 9am-noon and 2-6pm). **Buses Rapides de Lorraine** (tel. 03 83 32 34 20) runs once daily in the evenings (2hr., 64F) from Nancy's pl. colonel Driant to Vittel.

■ Near Nancy: Lunéville

Lunéville's 15 minutes of fame came and went in the early 18th century when Duke Léopold of Lorraine fled from French-occupied Nancy to this negligible town (pop. 24,000). Here he and Duchess Elizabeth-Charlotte relished peeled grapes at an elegant court, the **Château de Lunéville,** often compared to a mini Versailles. It later became the residence of Duke of Lorraine (and former King of Poland) Stanislas. He reveled in its pristine flower gardens, artificial lakes, shaded walkways, Greco-Roman statues, and fountains until he perished in the flames of his own fireplace. Dignified black and white swans floating on the canal by the gardens are reminders of the former elegance of this stately mansion, now in need of renovations and largely off-limits to tourists. The château houses the **Musée Municipal** (tel. 03 83 76 23 57), where you'll find an Egyptian mummy among unexceptional military exhibits. The museum also contains Lunéville *faïencerie,* enameled ceramics renowned since the 18th century for their floral patterns and *chinoiseries*—interpretations of Asian designs (open Wed.-Mon. 10am-noon and 2-6pm, Oct.-March Wed.-Mon. 10am-noon and 2-5pm; admission 10F, students 5F, under 18 free).

Lunéville is on N4, 30km east of Nancy and 70km southeast of Metz. To reach the tourist office and the château from the station, walk straight down rue Carnot, through pl. Léopold and take an immediate left onto rue Banaudon. Two blocks later, turn right onto rue de la République. The château is three blocks down, on the right (10min.). The **tourist office,** pl. de la 2ème D.C. (tel. 03 83 74 06 55; fax 03 83 73 57 95), is at the tip of the left wing of the château (open daily 9am-noon and 2-6pm). An **ATM** gets fat on the corner of rue Banaudon and pl. Leonard. **Trains** roll from 2, pl. Pierre Sémard (tel. 08 36 35 35 35) to Paris (12 per day, 3½hr., 216F), Strasbourg (1 per day, 1¼hr., 87F); and Nancy (13 per day, ½hr., 32F).

Pack a picnic and head for the château gardens. Provisions can be bought around pl. Léopold in the heart of the *vieille ville.* The town's **market** struts its stuff on pl. Léopold (Tues. Thurs. and Sat. mornings.) **Prisunic,** pl. Léopold (open Mon.-Sat. 8:30am-7:30pm) will also fill your basket. Most of Lunéville's restaurants cluster by the château; rue de Lorraine is lined with *salons de thé* and *brasseries.*

Saverne

In the 3rd-century Roman travel guide *Itinerarium Antonin,* the author recommends *Tabernis* (now Saverne) as a "good place to rest." Today, Saverne (pop. 11,000), with its sleepy canals, picture-book square, and sculpted Vosges scenery, remains a soothing place to stay. In 870, the Treaty of Mersen officially attached Saverne to the German Empire, where it remained for more than seven centuries. The Germanic influence is still evident in the town, from its half-timbered houses to its cascading flowerboxes and regional specialties, *tarte flambée* and sauerkraut. Saverne's position on a narrow pass through the Vosges mountains has made it a town long contested by kings and armies—from English crusaders in the 12th century to Germans during World War II. Now that the smoke has cleared, it seems that the Romans were right: Saverne is a peaceful and beautiful base for exploring surrounding castles, towns, and forests.

ORIENTATION AND PRACTICAL INFORMATION

To get to the **tourist office** from the train station, turn right onto rue de la Gare, cross the Zorn river, and take a left onto Saverne's main street, **Grand Rue.** Turn left again to enter pl. Général de Gaulle. The office (tel. 03 88 91 80 47; fax 03 88 71 02 90) is at the entrance to the Château des Rohan. It gives away a fair map and list of hotels, restaurants, and campgrounds, and has a variety of inexpensive or free hiking and biking trail maps (open June-Sept. Mon.-Fri. 9am-noon and 2-6pm, Sat.-Sun. 10am-noon and 3-6pm; Oct.-May Mon.-Fri. 10am-noon and 2-4pm, Sat. 10am-noon and 2-5pm). For **hiking information,** see the Club Vosgien (page 647). **Crédit Mutuel,** 8, rue de la Gare (tel. 03 88 01 83 00), has **currency exchange** and an **ATM** (open Mon.-Tues. and Thurs. 8:30am-noon and 2-6pm, Wed. 8:30am-noon and 3-6pm, Fri. 8:30am-noon and 2-7pm). There's another **ATM** at pl. de Gaulle in Sogenal. **Trains** (tel. 03 88 91 33 66) and **buses** leave from pl. de la Gare. Trains to: Paris (8 per day, 4hr., 241F); Strasbourg (up to 24 per day, 40min., 41F); Nancy (8 per day, 1hr., 80F); and Metz (5 per day, 1hr., 85F). Ticket office open Mon.-Fri. 4:45am-8:30pm, Sat. 7am-7pm, Sun. 10:45am-8:30pm. **Lockers** 5F. For a **taxi,** call 03 88 91 23 44. **Europ'Car,** 16, rue St-Nicolas (tel. 03 88 71 55 53), is the town's only **car rental** outfit (580F per day with 300km). **Rent bikes** at **Cycles OHL** (tel. 03 88 91 17 13), pl. St-Nicolas (75F per ½-day, 95F per day). **Hôpital Ste-Catherine** is at 19, Côte de Saverne (tel. 03 88 71 67 67); in a **medical emergency,** dial 15. **Police** are at 29, rue St-Nicolas (tel. 03 88 91 19 12); dial 17 in an **emergency.** The **post office,** 2, pl. de la Gare (tel. 03 88 71 56 40), also faxes and photocopies (open Mon.-Fri. 8am-noon and 1:30-6:30pm, Sat. 8am-noon; **postal code:** 67700).

ACCOMMODATIONS, CAMPING, AND FOOD

Why stay in a pricey Saverne hotel when you can stay in a castle? The **Auberge de Jeunesse** (tel. 03 88 91 14 84; fax 03 88 71 15 97) occupies the fourth floor of the Château des Rohan, right in the center of town. Spacious, 6-bunk rooms have great views (63F including breakfast; 83F in single or double; free showers; lockout 10am-5pm; curfew 10pm). If you're looking to stay out late, the **Hôtel de la Marne,** 5, rue Griffon (tel. 03 88 91 19 18; fax 03 88 91 01 24), has a great location and the best prices in town. (Singles 105-120F, with shower 140F. Doubles 160-170F, with shower 190F. Triples 240F. Breakfast 35F. 24-hr. reception. V, MC.) The pleasant **Hôtel National,** 2, Grand Rue (tel. 03 88 91 14 54, fax 03 88 71 19 50), keeps spotless, tastefully decorated modern rooms in a central location with an elevator. (Singles 130F. Doubles 180F. Triples with shower and TV 310F. Quads with shower and TV 360F. Buffet breakfast 33F. 24-hr. reception. Wheelchair accessible. V, MC.) If slumbering under the stars is more your thing, head for **Camping de Saverne** (tel. 03 88 91 35 65), rue du Père Libermann, a three-star campground near tennis courts and trails to the Vosges. It features showers, a grocery store, and lots of roses (13F per person, 7F per tent, 12F with car; electricity 10F; open April-Sept. 7am-10pm).

S'zawermer Stuebel, 4, rue des Frères (tel. 03 88 71 29 95), is an adorable Italian restaurant in a converted wine cellar with vaulted ceilings. Pizzas 30-45F, pasta 34-38F, two-course *menus* 48 and 69F (open daily 11:30am-2:30pm and 6:30-10pm; V, MC). Eat *tarte flambée* (40-50F) under hanging pots and pans at **Karpfel,** pl. Général de Gaulle. Red-checked tablecloths and a view of the château are *compris* (open daily noon-2pm and 6:30-11pm). **Restaurant de la Marne,** 5, rue de Griffon (tel. 03 88 91 19 18), has a colorful terrace by the canal. Quiche and salad 35F (open daily 11am-10pm; V, MC). **Moller-Oberling,** 66-68, Grand Rue (tel. 03 88 91 13 30), is a *salon de thé* offering quiche, *tarte flambée,* and gourmet pizza (20-35F; open Mon.-Fri. 7am-7pm, Sat. 7am-6pm, Sun. 8am-12:30pm and 2-6pm; V, MC). There is a giant **Match Est supermarket** at 8, rue Ste-Marie (tel. 03 88 91 23 63), a 10-minute walk from the town center (open Mon.-Thurs. 9am-noon and 2-7:30pm, Fri. 8:30am-8pm, Sat. 8:30am-6pm). Look out for the **market,** pl. de Gaulle, Thursday mornings.

SIGHTS

Saverne, which calls itself "the city of the rose," delights in the 20,000 blossoms in over a thousand varieties that line the paths of its **Rosarie** (tel. 03 88 71 83 33). Swing-sets cater to the young and the regressive alike. West of the town center, follow Grand Rue and bear left along the Zorn to the garden. (Open daily May 1-Sept. 30 10am-7pm. Admission 15F, students 10F. Wheelchair accessible.)

Saverne's **Château des Rohan** (tel. 03 88 91 06 28) has been rebuilt many times since its founding in the 12th century. Napoleon was its most recent benefactor; in 1852, he had the château rebuilt to serve as a residence for the widows of rich civil dignitaries. Used as barracks in the First and Second World Wars, the château now houses school rooms, the youth hostel, and an uninspiring archaeological museum (open June-Sept. Wed.-Mon. 2-6pm; admission 8F, students 4F). Pick up the tourist office's free guide for a pleasant walking tour of the nearby *vieille ville.*

Saverne's greatest asset, however, is its endless web of forested **hiking trails** and **bike trails** through the farmlands. Saverne is an ideal base for exploring the Vosges mountains. Even if you are not up for a long hike, try the 45-minute jaunt through shaded woods to the lovely 12th-century castle **Le Haut Bar.** The château offers extraordinary views of the countryside (follow the rue du Haut Bar/D171 southwest; maps at the tourist office). Near the château is the **Tour du Télégraphe Chappe** (tel. 03 88 52 98 99), a mechanical contraption which, on clear days, sent visual messages to a tower atop Strasbourg's cathedral. During the Franco-Prussian War a line of such towers sent messages all the way from Paris to Strasbourg. (Open July-Aug. Wed.-Mon. noon-6pm. 5F, 3F children.) The **Club Vosgien** offers free one- to four-hour hiking tours in the area, leaving from the Ecluse du Canal in the *centre ville.* Call 03 88 91 18 77 for schedules. Or, do it yourself; trails are in good shape and clearly marked. Bikers can pick up the free brochure *Cyclo Tourisme* from the tourist office, with a map and suggested routes.

Metz

Settled by the Romans, Metz was converted to Christianity in the 2nd century by St. Clement. Legend has it that the town agreed to follow the pilgrim's religion if he could slay *Le Graouilly,* a fierce, fire-breathing fiend with a nasty habit of gobbling up unwitting citizens. Clement, confident of his divine purpose, tossed his coat at the menacing beast, blinding and ultimately killing the wicked creature. Metz's myriad other conversions were not so easily settled. The city was recognized as French by the Treaty of Westphalia in 1648 but became German after the Treaty of Frankfurt in 1871. In 1918, Metz was wrenched from German hands by Maréchal Pétain's forces, though Pétain's World War II government would be much more accommodating to the Germans who annexed the city.

When the tanks rolled out of Metz after World War I, city administrators decided to preserve the denuded tracts of land in the town center as parks. Modern Metz reflects its history of mixed Franco-German parentage—and still boasts 49 square meters of green park for each of its 130,000 residents. Metz has over 21km of walking trails, sculptured gardens, sinuous canals, and golden cobblestone streets. Nonetheless, refreshingly few tourists visit this attractive town. Metz offers a superb Gothic cathedral, bustling shopping district, spirited festivals, and enough locals lingering over three-hour lunches to ensure that no one mistakes it for Germany.

ORIENTATION AND PRACTICAL INFORMATION

The cathedral dominates the skyline of the **pl. d'Armes** in Metz's *vieille ville;* the **tourist office** is just across the *place* in the Hôtel de Ville. To get there from the station, turn right and follow the contour of the gardens, making a left onto rue Haute-Seille. At pl. des Paraiges, bear left onto rue Fournirue and follow it to the cathedral and the tourist office. You can also take bus 11 from the pl. Charles de Gaulle (direction: St-Eloy) directly to pl. d'Armes. Metz is a big city; use cosmopolitan caution.

Tourist Information: Tourist Office, pl. d'Armes (tel. 03 87 55 53 78 or 03 87 55 53 76; fax 03 87 36 59 43). Free small city map or bus system map. More helpful map 6F. Hotel and restaurant list, accommodations service 15F. Poor rates at the cash-only **currency exchange.** City tours daily (3pm, 2hr., 50F; call at least 1 day ahead for an English tour; audio-guide rentals in English or French 45F). Open July-Aug. Mon.-Sat. 9am-9pm, Sun. 10am-1pm and 2-5pm; Sept.-Oct. and April-June Mon.-Sat. 9am-7pm, Sun. 10am-1pm and 3-7pm; Nov.-March Mon.-Sat. 9am-7pm, Sun. 10am-1pm. Pick up events info in their monthly **Spectacles à Metz.**

Budget Travel: Agence Wasteels, 3, rue d'Austrasie (tel. 03 87 66 65 33). Student rates and passes. Open Mon.-Fri. 9am-noon and 2-7pm, Sat. until 6pm.

Money: An **ATM** networks with passers-by at 1, av. Robert Schumann, the northeast corner of pl. de la République.

Trains: pl. du Général de Gaulle (tel. 03 87 63 50 50 for info, 03 87 50 60 60 for reservations). To: Paris (11 per day, 3hr., 200F); Strasbourg (9 per day, 1½hr., 110F); Luxembourg (16 per day, 1½hr., 60F); Nancy (17 per day, 1hr., 50F); Lyon (7 per day, 5hr., 255F); Nice (5 per day, 12hr., 460F). Fewer trains Sun. and in winter. Open Mon.-Fri. 8:30am-7:30pm, Sat. 8:30am-6pm. **Lockers** 15-30F.

Buses: Les Rapides de Lorraine, 2, rue Nonnetiers (tel. 03 87 75 26 62), across the tracks from the train station. To: Verdun (7 per day, 1hr., 65F); Nancy (9 per day, 2hr., 55F); and to tiny towns in the region. Station open Mon.-Tues. and Thurs.- Fri. 6:15am-1pm and 1:30-7:15pm, Wed. 6:15am-7:15pm, Sat. 6:15am-1:15pm and 2-6:30pm. Tix window open Mon.-Fri. 7:25am-noon and 2-5:30pm.

Public Transportation: TCRM, 1, av. Robert Schumann (tel. 03 87 76 31 11). Ticket 5F, *carnet* of 6 20F. Maps at tourist office; buses pass pl. de la République.

Taxis: (tel. 03 87 56 91 92), at train station. 10F initial fee; 6F per km, 10F at night.

Car Rental: Avis, at the train station (tel. 03 87 50 60 30).

Hitchhiking: The only legal place from which to hitch a ride in *any* direction is just west of the train station under the ramp of av. Joffre, before *autoroute* entrances.

Bike Rental: Majchzak, 71, rue Allemands (tel. 03 87 74 13 14). Bikes 50F per day; *VTTs* 80F per day. Open Mon. 2-7pm, Tues.-Sat. 8am-noon and 2-7pm.

Laundromat: 7, rue de la Fontaine. Wash 15F. Dry 5F per 12min. Soap 10F. Higher fees for large loads. Change machine. Open daily 7am-7pm.

Hospital: Hôpital Notre-Dame-de-Bon-Secours, 1, pl. Phillipe de Vignuelles (tel. 03 87 55 31 31). Stop "Bon secours" on bus line 2 (direction: Montigny-St-Privat), line 13 (direction: Montigny), or line 16 (direction: Marly). **Medical emergency** tel. 15 or 03 87 62 27 111.

Police: 6, rue Belle Isle (tel. 03 87 37 91 11). Stop "Pontiffroy" on bus line 3 (direction: Metz-Nord) or line 11 (direction: St-Eloy). **Emergency** tel. 17

Post Office: 1, pl. du Général de Gaulle (tel. 03 87 56 73 00). Poste restante. Fax and photocopies. **Currency exchange** at good rates. Open Mon.-Fri. 8am-7pm and Sat. 8am-noon. **Postal code:** 57000.

ACCOMMODATIONS AND CAMPING

Foyer Carrefour (HI), 6, rue Marchant (tel. 03 87 75 07 26; fax 03 87 36 71 44). From station, turn right onto rue Vauban, which becomes av. Jean XXIII, and left onto rue Haute-Seille. At pl. des Paraiges turn left onto rue Fournirue. Take a right onto rue Taison which becomes rue Marchant (15min.). Or take bus 3 (direction: Metz-Nord), or 11 (direction: St-Eloy) to "St-Georges." Superb facilities, central location. 3-4 bed dorms 66F per person. Singles and doubles 76F. Sheets 19F for more than one night 24F. Showers and breakfast included. Dinner 30F members, 35F non-members. Overflow housing in lovely, modern annex a block away. No curfew or lockout. Members only. Fills quickly, especially on weekends. V, MC.

Auberge de Jeunesse (HI), 1, allée de Metz Plage (tel. 03 87 30 44 02; fax 03 87 33 19 80), on far side of town from station. Take bus 3 (direction: Metz-Nord) or 11 (direction: St-Eloy; last bus 8:50pm) from the station to "Pontiffroy." Excellent hostel with super perks: valuables and bike storage, games, TV. Loans bikes to guests. Give them your laundry and they'll return it clean in the morning (35F). *C'est la vie!* 6-bed dorms 64F per person. Singles and doubles 74F per person. Showers and breakfast included. Hearty dinner 48F. Sheets 16F. No curfew. Lockout 10am-5pm. Reception 7-10am and 5-10pm. Members only.

Hôtel Métropole, 5, pl. du Général de Gaulle (tel. 03 87 66 26 22; fax 03 87 66 29 91). Luxurious hotel boasts spotlessly clean, newly renovated rooms across from the *gare.* Singles 210-240F. Doubles with bath and toilet 240-270F. Buffet breakfast with fruits, breads, cereals, yogurt 28F. 24-hr. reception. V, MC, AmEx.

Hôtel Moderne, 1, rue Lafayette (tel. 03 87 66 57 33; fax 03 87 55 98 59), by pl. Général de Gaulle. Simple and clean. Singles 120F, with shower 160F. Doubles from 138F, with shower 160F. Extra bed 50F. Breakfast 26F. V, MC, AmEx.

Hôtel Bristol, 7, rue Lafayette (tel. 03 87 66 74 22; fax 03 87 50 67 89), near Hôtel Moderne. Large, basic rooms. Singles from 110F, with shower 160F. Doubles from 130F, with shower 170F. Breakfast 26F. 24-hr. reception. V, MC, AmEx.

Camping: Metz-Plage (tel. 03 87 32 05 58, during winter 03 87 32 42 49). Enter behind the hospital on rue Belle Isle. Shaded spot by Moselle river and the hostel. Phones, showers, electricity, snack shop, fishing, and indoor pool. Wheelchair accessible. 21F for 1 person and tent, 15F per extra person, 14F per car. Max. stay 28 days. No reservations. Reception May 2-Sept. 7am-8:30pm.

FOOD

Food shops cluster near the *auberge de jeunesse* on rue du Pont des Morts and toward the station on rue Coisin. The **Centre St-Jacques** (a mall off pl. St-Jacques) tucks away a number of specialty stores and cheap eateries on its three levels, as well as a **SUMA supermarket** (open Mon.-Sat. 8:30am-7:30pm). **Markets** spread over the streets near pl. St-Jacques on Tuesday, Thursday, and Saturday mornings.

Surprisingly reasonable restaurants gather on the prime people-watching turf of **rue des Clercs,** including the *crêperie* **St-Malo,** 14, rue des Clercs (tel. 03 87 74 56 85), which serves *galettes* crammed with ham and gruyère, salads, and crêpes smothered with ice cream (10-30F; open Mon.-Sat. 11:45am-11pm; V, MC). Munch North African cuisine next to the cathedral at **La Baraka,** 25, pl. de Chambre (tel. 03 87 36 33 92), where the staff will serve you mounds of vegetarian couscous (45F), or with lamb (65F). (Open Thurs.-Tues. noon-2pm and 7pm-midnight.) Or try **Le Beverly,** 2, pl. St-Jacques (tel. 03 87 37 35 33). Great big salads 30-50F, *plats* 15-80F; also serves quiches and pastas (open 7-2am; V, MC). Pizzerias line rue Dupont-des-Loges. Among them, **La Storia,** 10, rue Dupont-des-Loges (tel. 03 87 36 06 40), serves up pizzas from 30F and pasta from 38F. (Open daily noon-2pm and 7-11pm.)

SIGHTS AND ENTERTAINMENT

Only the naves of St-Pierre in Beauvais and Notre-Dame in Amiens soar higher than that of the **Cathédrale St-Etienne,** pl. d'Armes, (tel. 03 87 75 54 61) erected between the 13th and 16th centuries. When Metz authorities sought to build a church large enough to impress Rome, they took into account the existing cathedral and joined the two together. (The pillars of the older sections are simpler in design than those of the new.) Its 6500 square meters of sensational stained-glass windows have caused some to call St-Etienne the "Lantern to God." Perhaps most spectacular are the modern windows; several in the western transept are by Chagall. Tours of the cathedral (including its *crypte* and unimpressive *trésor*), and nearby churches are given in French daily May-September (15-40F; info office open May-Sept. Mon.-Sat. 9am-7pm, Sun. noon-7pm; Oct.-April Mon.-Sat. 9am-noon and 2-5:30pm, Sun. 2-5:30pm). Call the tourist office to arrange an English tour (45F). The mustard stone used for the cathedral's exterior, *pierre de jaumont,* is reserved for the restoration of churches and public buildings; the uniformity of Metz's recent constructions is the result of clever paint jobs.

A block away, the city's treasures gather at the **Musée d'Art et d'Histoire,** 2, rue du Haut-Poirier (tel. 03 87 75 10 18). The most impressive part of the collection is the comprehensive archaeology and history exhibit, tracing in astonishing detail Metz's rise from an important Roman post to an independent city-state. Upstairs are interiors of entire medieval and Renaissance homes. The plain rooms of the art wing house works by Corot, Zurbarán, and others. During its expansion in 1935, the museum found that it had been built on the site of the old **Roman baths.** An exhibit exposes the meticulous methods Romans used to assess their water quality—visitors can wander onto the aqueducts of the Roman sewer system. (Open daily 10am-noon and 2-6pm; admission 20F, students 10F; free Wed. and Sun. mornings.)

Down the rue des Clercs from pl. d'Armes is the **esplanade,** a formal garden overlooking the Moselle Valley. Picnickers wishing to dine among elegant flower beds and graceful fountains should arrive early; the best benches go quickly. The tourist office's *Promenades et Jardins* maps the gardens and trails of Metz's endless parks.

Back toward the *centre ville* from the southeast corner of the esplanade, stairs lead to the **Basilique St-Pierre-aux-Nonnais,** whose simple white brick interior hides an illustrious past. Built by the Romans in the 5th century as part of a monumental set of baths, it has since been extensively rebuilt but is thought to be the oldest church in France. Today, St-Pierre serves a secular function as the local cultural center, the **Arsenal.** Exhibitions are held here periodically; the tourist office has schedules. Next door stands the octagonal **Chapelle des Templiers.** One of the only remaining structures of the powerful and mysterious Knights of the Temple, the 13th-century chapel resembles a witch's hat and is modeled after Charlemagne's Aix-la-Chapelle in Germany (open Tues.-Sun. 2-6:30pm).

To the northwest of St-Etienne is the 18th-century **pl. de la Comédie,** built on a former swamp. The *place* served a less-than-comedic function during the Revolution, when the guillotine was its main attraction. Its centerpiece is the 1751 theater, where today, opera, ballet, dance, and drama (classical and modern) flourish at the **Opéra-Théâtre** (tel. 03 87 55 51 71). For information and schedules, pick up the free semi-annual brochure *Metz en Scène* at the tourist office. For tickets, call the **Bureau de Location** (tel. 03 87 75 40 50; open Mon.-Fri. 9am-12:30pm and 4-6pm).

Metz has won an award for being France's most artfully lit city by night. A free map of Metz by night can be picked up at the tourist office. Be sure to stop by the cathedral to see the glowing stained-glass windows. In summer, a free **son et lumière** is held at dusk on the pond at the foot of the esplanade, complete with Vegas-style colored lights, fountains, and assorted tunes by Wagner, *Les Beatles,* and Elvis (July-Sept. Fri.-Sun. and holidays). Students pack the bars and cafés at **pl. St-Jacques,** the central gathering point at night. Grind the night away at **Le Club Tiffany,** 24, rue Coëtlosquet (tel. 03 87 75 23 32), just outside the pl. de la République (open Wed.-Fri. and Sun.-Mon. 10pm-5am, Sat. 10pm-5:30am; cover 60F with a drink). The **Caveau de Trinitaires** (tel. 03 87 75 04 96), just down the street from the Foyer Carrefour hostel, hosts jazz and rock concerts. There is also a gay club, **Le Club,** 20, rue Ours (tel. 03 87 36 55 76), down rue Winston Churchill out of pl. de la République (open 10pm-5am; cover and a drink 60F).

Verdun

Verdun and its war memorials testify to the horror of the battles France and Germany fought in the area 80 years ago during World War I. Each side lost almost 400,000 soldiers in the Battle of Verdun, which raged from February to October of 1916. Moving reminders of the destruction surround the city: the 15,000 marble crosses in the National Cemetery, the Trench of Bayonets, where most of the French 137th Regiment perished, and Verdun's chosen symbol, a dove floating above two hands clasped in peace. Some wounds have healed; the battlefields that were once soaked with the blood of Verdun's thousands of casualties are now carpeted with grain. Others wounds go deeper—Verdun left a permanent scar on the French psyche. Because of their system of troop rotations, almost three-quarters of the French Army experienced what some have called the worst battle in history.

Despite the long shadow cast by wartime devastation, Verdun (pop. 30,000) has painstakingly rebuilt itself into an attractive city popular with the French and foreigners alike. Much of Verdun is modern and commercial, built to blend with the remnants of the original town. The restored twin peaks of the cathedral recall a less tumultuous past, and the frequent fishing boats and rowers cruising up and down the Meuse add a tranquil note to the pedestrian district. Still, the most compelling reason to visit Verdun is its series of unforgettable war monuments.

ORIENTATION AND PRACTICAL INFORMATION

To get to the tourist office from the bus station, turn left onto rue Frères Boulhaut and continue until you reach the Port Chaossee. Turn left again and cross the bridge onto pl. de la Nation; the tourist office will be on your right. To reach the bus station from the *gare,* just walk straight ahead on ave. Garibaldi. The **tourist office,** pl. de la Nation (tel. 03 29 86 14 18; fax 03 29 84 22 42), offers helpful information on the memorials, hotels, and restaurants. Their free map is not very useful, but they sell an excellent one for 2F50. The office also offers a daily four-hour bus tour of major battlefields and monuments around the city (tours in French and English depart daily May to mid-Sept. 2pm, 145F). (Office open Mon.-Sat. mid-June-Aug. 8am-8pm; Sept. 1-8 8:30am-7pm; Sept. 9-Nov. 9am-noon and 2pm-6pm; Dec. 9am-noon and 2pm-5pm; Jan.-Feb. 9:30am-noon and 2:30-5pm; March-April 9am-noon and 2-6pm; May to mid-June 8:30am-7pm.) A 24-hour **ATM** yawns off the quai de Londres, next to the **Banque Populaire. Trains** from Verdun's station (tel. 08 36 35 35 35), built by Eiffel, at pl. Maurice Genovoix, run infrequently to Metz (4 direct per day, 1½hr., 74F). (Ticket booth open Mon. 4:45am-6:50pm, Tues.-Fri. 5:45am-6:50pm, Sat. 9:45am-noon and 2:30-7pm, and Sun. 2:15-7:30pm.) A better option is the extensive **bus** service on the other end of av. Garibaldi at the **Gare Routière,** pl. Vauban (tel. 03 29 86 02 71), which runs to Metz (4 per day, 2hr., 66F); Clermont (9 per day, 1hr., 37F); Bar-le-Duc (3 per day, 1hr., 54F); and Nancy (8 per day, 2½hr., 87F). Sunday service is restricted (station open Mon.-Fri. 9am-noon and 2-6pm). **Rent cars** at the **Grand Garage de la Meuse,** 6, av. Colonel Driant (tel. 03 29 86 44 05), just down the street from the train station (180F per day plus 1F50 per km; open Mon.-Sat. 8am-noon and 1:45-5:45pm). For **bike rental,** try **Flavenot Damien,** 1, Rond-Point des Etats-Unis (tel. 03 29 86 12 43), by the *gare* (50F per ½-day; 100F per day, 150F per weekend; passport deposit; open Mon. 2-7pm, Tues.-Sat. 9am-12:30pm). The **hospital** is at 2, rue d'Anthouard (tel. 03 29 83 84 85). The **police** (tel. 17) are at pl. du Gouvernement. The **post office,** av. de la Victoire, is across the river from the tourist office (tel. 03 29 83 45 58; open Mon-Fri. 8am-7pm, Sat. 8am-noon). Poste restante (address mail to: 55107 Verdun, B.P. 729). **Postal code:** 55100.

ACCOMMODATIONS, CAMPING, AND FOOD

The luxurious **Auberge de Jeunesse** du "Centre Mondial de la Paix," pl. Monseigneur Ginisty (tel. 03 29 86 28 28; fax 03 29 86 28 82), is the best deal in town. From the train station, cross to rue Louis Maury. When you reach the square continue up on rue de la Belle Vierge. The hostel is at the end of the cathedral. Wide, well-lit hallways decorated with stained glass give way to large four-bed rooms. One dormitory-style room with nine beds. (67F, breakfast included. 16F sheets. Handicapped accessible. Members only. Closed January. Reception daily 8-10am and 5-11pm.) Reasonably priced hotels cluster on **av. Garibaldi.** The centrally located **Hôtel de la Porte Chaussée,** 67, quai de Londres (tel. 03 29 86 00 78), opens its own *porte* to reveal spacious, clean rooms. (Singles and doubles from 100F, with shower from 180F. Triples 200F. Quads 220F. Showers 15F. Breakfast 25F. Reception 8am-noon and 4pm-midnight. V, MC.) The **Hôtel le Franc Comtois,** 9, av. Garibaldi (tel. 03 29 86 05 46), lets small, clean rooms with squishy beds. (Singles 105-150F. Doubles 105-220F. Breakfast 22F. Reception 7:30am-12:30am. V, MC.) There is a crowded three-star **camping** site 1km from town at **Les Breuils**, allée des Breuils (tel. 03 29 86 15 31 or 03 29 86 75 76), past the Citadelle Souterraine on av. du Cinquième R.A.P. Turn right on av. Général Boichut, then take the first left and you'll find the showers, bar, grocery store, and pool (19F per person, 15F per car; open April-Oct. 7am-10pm).

Cheap eateries can be found on the quai de Londres. For hearty if not heart-healthy regional dishes, step up to **La Table d'Alsace,** 31, rue Royeurs (tel. 03 29 86 58 36). 60F *menu* includes generous main course of chicken, veal, or fish; side dish; and dessert. Tortes and quiches 30-45F (open daily 11:45am-2:30pm and 6:45-10pm). For great ambience, try the **Pub Rive Gauche,** 25-27 quai de Londres (tel. 03 29 86 25 86), which serves by the riverside when the weather is warm (open daily noon-2pm and 6-10pm; V, MC, AmEx). Light fare can be found at **F. Stadelmann,** 16, rue Chaussée (tel. 03 29 86 04 10), a *pâtisserie* and *salon de thé* serving large salads (38F50-48F50), quiche (14F), and scrumptious strawberry tarts (14F). (Open daily 7am-7:30pm; closed Mon. afternoon.) If you want to splurge, **Le Forum,** 35, rue des Gros Degrés (tel. 03 29 86 20 14), offers traditional dishes with lunch menu at 60F and a dinner menu from 85-140F in an intimate, cave-like setting. (Open daily Mon.-Tues. and Thurs.-Sat. noon-2pm and 7pm-11pm, Wed. and Sun. noon-2pm.) Stock up on groceries at the **supermarket Match** in front of the train station on Rond-Point des Etats-Unis (open Mon.-Sat. 9am-12:15pm and 2:30-7:15pm). Verdun's main **market** is Friday morning (7:30am-12:30pm) on the homonymically harmonious rue de Rû. Other markets grace the *marché couvert,* off rue Victor Hugo (Tues. and Fri. 7:30am-12:30pm), and the quai de Londres (Wed.-Fri. 7am-6pm).

SIGHTS

In front of the Porte Châtel drawbridge on pl. St-Paul, Rodin's powerful bronze **Victory** suffers the agony of a triumph gained in bloody battle. The drawbridge itself dates from the 12th century, when ramparts protected Verdun from northern invaders. Built in 1350, **Porte Chaussée,** on the quai de Londres, served as a prison and a guard tower before ultimately providing passage into the city for troops during the Great War. Armed with courage and a good flashlight, any enterprising visitor can peer into the pitch-black basement dungeons of the Porte. Toward the *haute ville* rises the more traditionally styled **Monument à la Victoire,** a flight of 72 granite steps surmounted by a resolute warrior figure and cannons aimed at the German front (open daily 9am-noon and 2-6pm).

Behind the monument at the top of the hill, the **Musée de la Princerie** (tel. 03 29 86 10 62) is an elegant Renaissance building whose galleries are built around a cloister. The museum holds an intriguing 12th-century ivory comb engraved with scenes of the Resurrection and an apparition of Mary Magdalene, as well as centuries-old local earthenware, arms, and armor. The tile floor and stone walls keep the museum cool, even in the heat of summer. Check out the tower's lengthy spiral staircase, leading absolutely nowhere (open April-Oct. Wed.-Mon. 9:30am-noon and 2-6pm; adults 10F, children free). A few blocks away, the beautiful **Cathédrale Notre-Dame** crowns Verdun's *haute ville.* Although partially destroyed by shelling, its reconstructed Romanesque interior now boasts a fine collection of stained glass (open daily 9am-noon and 2-6pm). The **public garden** at Parc Municipal Japiot (tel. 03 29 84 14 57) provides a relaxing respite along the shady, grass-covered banks of the Meuse (open mid-April-Sept. 8:30am-8pm; Oct. to mid-April 9am-5pm). The local art gallery, **Espace Terre ou Art** (tel. 03 29 83 72 85), is on rue Dame Zabée. From pl. Maréchal Foch, follow rue Beaurepaine as it turns into rue Poincaré, then turn left onto rue Dame Zabée (open daily 3-8pm; Nov.-March 3-6pm).

The massive cement and stone **Citadelle Souterraine** (down the rue de Rû, 10min. out of town), constructed on the site of the ancient Abbaye de St-Vanne, sheltered 10,000 soldiers on their way to the front. The 4km of underground galleries were equipped with everything to support an army, including nine huge ovens that could cook 29,000 rations of bread in 24 hours. Today, a small, very chilly section of the tunnels can be seen on a tour in rollercoaster-like cars. Prepare to see World War I as if played out by French actors-turned-holograms. (Tours 30min., in French and dubiously dubbed English; admission 30F, under 16 15F; call the tourist office for times. Citadelle open daily April-June 9am-7pm; Sept. 9am-1pm and 2-6pm; Oct. to mid-Dec. 9am-noon and 2-5pm; mid-Dec. to mid-Feb. 2-4pm; mid-Feb. to March 9:30am-12:30pm and 2-4:30pm. Admission 17F, students 13F.)

Farther out and accessible only by tour bus, car, or bicycle are **Fort Vaux** and **Fort Douaumont.** Crucial territories due to their strategic views of the surrounding countryside, both these forts were sites of devastating combat. On February 25, 1916, Fort Douaumont fell to the Germans almost without a shot after a breakdown in communications left it guarded by 57 reserve officers. Douaumont was recaptured in October by the Moroccan colonial infantry at the cost of thousands of lives. Fort Vaux was lost in June, after several days of hand-to-hand combat in which the Germans held the superstructure while the French defended the underground caverns. The unbearable tunnels were filled with gas, smoke, and wounded soldiers. Empty cisterns forced the eventual evacuation and surrender of the fort. (For tours or information, call the tourist office; fort open daily April-Aug. 9am-6:30pm; mid-Sept. to Dec. 9:30am-noon and 1-5:30pm; Jan.-mid-Feb. 11am-3pm; mid-Feb-March 10am-noon and 2-4:30pm.) Along the road to Douaumont, the stark, concrete **Mémorial-Musée de Fleury** (tel. 03 29 84 35 34) is a private memorial erected by ex-servicemen in honor of their friends who died in combat. It is built on the site of what was once Fleury, a small village of 400 inhabitants who grew cereals and worked in the forests. The site of bitter fighting, Fleury changed hands 16 times and, like eight other villages in the area, was completely wiped off the map. The museum attempts to convey battlefield conditions with reconstructed trenches and disquieting photographs of the anguished faces of the soldiers (open daily March 23-Sept. 9am-6pm; Oct. 9am-noon and 2-6pm; Nov.-mid-Dec. 9am-noon and 2-5:30pm; Jan. 23-March 22 9am-noon and 2-6pm). Near the fort, the artillery shell-shaped **Ossuaire de Douaumont** contains the remains of 130,000 unidentified French and German soldiers whose bodies were removed by volunteers of the Society of Friends (Quakers) from the battlefield (open daily April-June 9am-6:30pm; Sept. 9am-noon and 2-6pm; Oct. and March 9am-noon and 2-5:30pm; Nov. 9am-noon and 2-5pm). The nearby **Tranchée des Baïonnettes** marks the trench where an entire company of infantry perished, very likely buried alive in an unmarked mass grave.

Champagne

Brothers, brothers, come quickly! I am drinking stars!

—Dom Perignon

Grapevines have existed in Champagne since the Tertiary Period, but the Romans were the first to undertake systematic wine production. Though the natural effervescence of champagne enchanted everyone who tasted it, the key to consistent production remained a mystery. Not until the 17th century did a few individuals, among them Dom Perignon, hit upon the idea of tying down the cork to bottle the sparkling bubbles. From that moment on, the wine's popularity expanded. Even Voltaire rhapsodized that "the sparkling froth of this fresh wine is the brilliant image of our French people."

The name "champagne" is selfishly guarded by the region's vintners. According to French law, the name can only be applied to wines made from grapes of the region and produced according to the rigorous and time-honored *méthode champenoise,* which involves the blending of three different varieties of grape, two stages of fermentation, and frequent realignment of bottles by *remueurs* (highly trained bottle turners) to facilitate removal of sediment. If they are scrupulously faithful to the procedure, foreign impostors may use the word "champagne" with its place of origin ("California champagne," for example) on their bottles. Sparkling wines made by a different process are called *"mousseux" or "crémant,"* which refers to a less effervescent variety. You can see the *méthode* in action at the region's numerous wine cellars *(caves).* Originally carved by Roman chalk miners, the fascinating *caves* smell of penicillin mold, which thrives in the cool, damp air. Some *caves* have operated as wineries since Roman times. Epernay may have the most kilometers of tunnels, but the most impressive of Champagne's 640km of *crayères* (chalk quarries turned *caves*) lie beneath Reims. As each producer will remind you, it's the region's unique combination of altitude, climate, chalky soil, and cellars carved from limestone that makes champagne production possible.

John Maynard Keynes once remarked that his major regret in life was not having consumed enough champagne. Make up for lost time and ensure this does not happen to you. Many champagne houses in both Epernay and Reims offer free samples of the "wine of kings and king of wines" to polish off their tours. You can also enjoy regional gastronomical specialties (essentially, anything cooked *in* champagne) such as *volaille au champagne* (poultry) or *civet d'oie* (goose stew). Buying by the bottle can be expensive, even if you purchase directly from a *cave.* Impersonal supermarkets may have the best deals.

There is more to Champagne than champagne. French civilization is deeply rooted in its chalky soil. In 451, at the mysterious Champs Cataluniques, Romans, Visigoths, and Franks turned back the pillaging forces of Attila the Hun. At Reims in 496, the newly Christian Clovis received the first French royal coronation, inaugurating the city's symbolic association with the French monarchy. Every king from Henri I to Charles X (except Henri IV and Louis XVIII) was crowned here. Charles VII helped turn back the tides of the Hundred Years' War by receiving the *sacré* at the cathedral in 1429, at the insistence of Joan of Arc. Thousands died here during the wars of religion, the Franco-Prussian War, and in World Wars I and II.

GETTING AROUND

Champagne is a great place for excursions into the countryside by car, bike, or foot. Drivers should follow any of the lovely *routes de champagne* through the Montagne de Reims, the Val de Marne, or the Côtes des Blancs. Tourist offices distribute road maps; ask for the free pamphlet *The Champagne Road.* Wander off to the small villages and lakes dotting the region south and west of Epernay or check out Champagne's two national parks, ideal for hiking. The tourist office in Troyes has

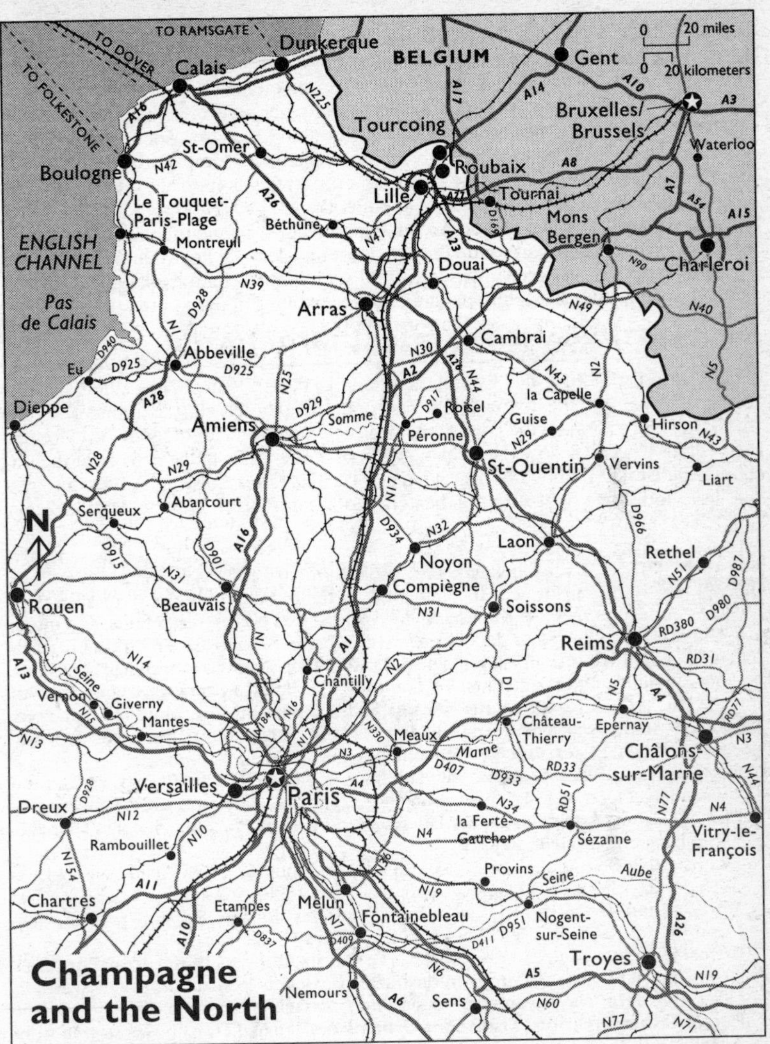

information on the Forêt d'Orient, while the office in Reims sells a booklet of trails through the Parc Naturel de la Montagne de Reims (15F). The Forêt de Verzy, a curious forest of twisted, umbrella-shaped dwarf beeches *(tortillards),* and the vast Forêt de Germaine are also worth visiting. Trains connect Reims to the rest of France, but you will have to rely on capricious buses to reach the smaller villages.

Reims

Since the Frankish king Clovis was baptized here in AD 496, Reims has been significant in the lives of French leaders. Joan of Arc's mission was to deliver the indecisive Charles VII to Reims; his coronation here gave the French a figurehead to rally around. With Joan's help, Charles managed to defeat "Les Goddams" (the nickname the French gave the English because of their penchant for the expression). In 1814, the city had the somewhat dubious honor of being the site of Napoleon's last victory, causing General Marmont to declare Reims "the last smile of Fortune." Fortune frowned on another would-be conqueror of Europe on May 8, 1945, when the Germans surrendered in the small schoolroom Eisenhower used as his headquarters.

Although Reims has been around for two thousand years, prosperity and growth didn't have much effect until the 19th century, when the champagne started flowing prodigiously from the city's many *caves.* As a result, Reims (pop. 185,000) was built according to the 19th-century idea of a model French city. Enormous squares, long, broad, tree-lined avenues, and an overall expansiveness mimic the wide, sun-soaked fields and vineyards that surround the city. Most travelers put Reims on their maps for its fabulous *caves* and are surprised to find such architectural masterpieces as the Cathédrale de Notre-Dame and Basilique St-Remi waiting above.

ORIENTATION AND PRACTICAL INFORMATION

Trains from Paris's Gare de l'Est roll the scenic 154km to Reims. The cathedral is the center of town, and the town's sights, restaurants, and hotels cluster around it. To get from the train station on the edge of the *centre ville* to the heart of town, head for the cathedral's towers. Follow the right-hand curve of the traffic circle in front of the station to pl. Drouet d'Erlon (actually a street). Turn left after Eglise St-Jacques onto rue de Vesle and take a right after the theater onto rue du Tresor. The tourist office is on the left (15min.).

Tourist Office: 2, rue Guillaume de Machault (tel. 03 26 77 45 25; fax 03 26 77 45 27), on sq. du Trésor near the cathedral, in the old charterhouse. Free map with sites and *caves* marked; the *Guide du Touriste* lists hotels, restaurants, and more. **Currency exchange** at decent rates when banks are closed. Free hotel reservations. Recorded tour in eight languages (30F). Free guide to wheelchair-accessible hotels, sights, and restaurants. To find out about **local events,** pick up a copy of the weekly **Les Rendez-vous Remois.** Office open July-Aug. Mon.-Sat. 9am-8pm, Sun. 9:30am-7pm; Easter-June and Sept. Mon.-Sat. 9am-7:30pm, Sun. 9:30am-6:30pm; Oct.-Easter Mon.-Sat. 9am-6:30pm, Sun. 9:30am-5:30pm.

Budget Travel: Wasteels, 22, rue Libergier (tel. 03 26 85 79 79). ISIC cards, train discounts. Open Mon.-Fri. 9am-noon and 2-7pm, Sat. 9am-noon and 2-6pm.

Money: Crédit Agricole, 25, rue Libergier, and **Crédit Mutuel,** 35, cours Jean Baptiste Langlet, both have **ATMs.**

Trains: bd. Joffre (info tel. 08 36 35 35 35; reservations tel. 03 26 78 60 60). To: Paris (18 per day, 1½hr., 113F); Metz (8 per day, 3hr., 152F); Strasbourg (7 per day, 4hr., 218F); Laon (9 per day, 1hr., 48F). Info desk open Mon.-Fri. 8:30am-7pm, Sat. 9am-6pm. Ticket sales daily 5:45am-8:30pm. **Lockers** 15-20F.

Buses: A variety of local companies serve the small towns of the area. **Euralines** runs buses to various European destinations; tickets available through Wasteels (see above) or **Via Voyages,** 11, rue Condorcet (tel. 03 26 47 91 19).

Public Transportation: Transport Urbains de Reims (TUR) buses stop in front of the train station. Information office at 6, rue Chanzy (tel. 03 26 88 25 38), open Mon.-Sat. 8:30am-12:30pm and 2-6pm. 5F per ticket, 32F per *carnet* of 10.

Taxis: Call 03 26 47 05 05 or 03 26 02 15 02. 24hr.

Car Rental: Avis (tel. 03 26 47 10 08; fax 03 26 40 11 79), at the station, cours de la Gare. Economy car around 535F for 2 days with 600km included.

Hitchhiking: Those headed to Paris follow N31 via Soissons; they take bus B or 2 (direction: Tinquieux). Hitchers who are heading to Luxembourg often try N380; they take bus B (direction: Point de Witry) and get off at the terminus.

Bike Rental: Cycl'o Vert, at the tourist office (tel. 03 26 97 97 77). ½-day 35F. Full day 100F, 2 days 150F (open Fri.-Sun. 9am-6pm).

English Bookstore: Bookshop, 21, rue Élus (tel. 03 26 84 99 81; fax 03 26 50 83 08), has an extensive selection of English books and some videos. Open Mon. 2-7pm, Tues.-Fri. 10am-noon and 2-7pm, Sat. 9:30am-noon and 2-6pm.

Youth Center: Centre Information Jeunesse, 41, rue Talleyrand (tel. 03 26 47 46 70; fax 03 26 88 16 71). BIJ tickets, activities. Open daily Mon.-Fri. 1-6pm.

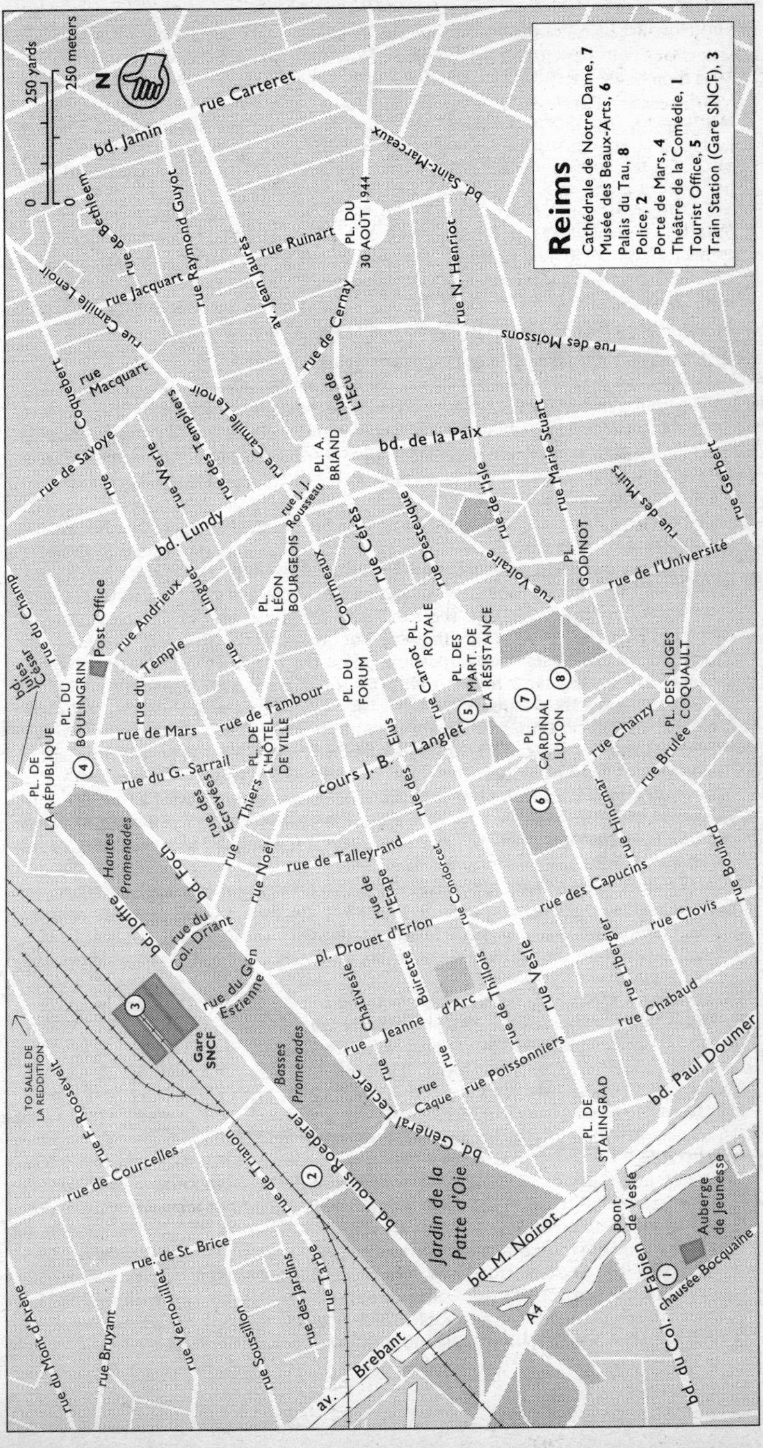

Reims
Cathédrale de Notre Dame, 7
Musée des Beaux-Arts, 6
Palais du Tau, 8
Police, 2
Porte de Mars, 4
Théâtre de la Comédie, 1
Tourist Office, 5
Train Station (Gare SNCF), 3
0 250 yards
0 250 meters
N
bd. Jamin
rue Carteret
bd. Saint-Marceaux
PL. DU 30 AOÛT 1944
rue Ruinart
av. Jean Jaurès
rue de Cernay
rue N. Henriot
rue des Moissons
rue de Bethleem
rue Jacquart
rue Raymond Guyot
rue Camille Lenoir
rue Macquart
rue Coquebert
rue de Savoye
rue Werlé
rue des Templiers
rue de L'Ecu
PL. A. BRIAND
bd. de la Paix
rue de l'Isle
rue Marie Stuart
rue des Murs
rue Gerbert
bd. Lundy
rue J. J. Rousseau
PL. LÉON BOURGEOIS
rue Courmeaux
rue Cérès
rue Desteuque
rue Voltaire
PL. GODINOT
rue de l'Université
rue Andrieux
rue Linguet
Post Office
PL. DU BOULINGRIN
bd. Jules César
rue du Champ
rue du Temple
rue de Mars
rue de Tambour
PL. DU FORUM
rue Carnot
PL. ROYALE
PL. DES MART. DE LA RÉSISTANCE
PL. CARDINAL LUÇON
PL. DES LOGES COQUAULT
rue Chanzy
rue Brulée
PL. DE LA RÉPUBLIQUE
rue du G. Sarrail
PL. DE L'HÔTEL DE VILLE
cours J. B. Langlet
rue des Elus
rue Thiers
rue des Ecrevées
Hautes Promenades
bd. Foch
rue Noël
rue de Talleyrand
rue de l'Etape
rue Condorcet
rue Hincmar
rue des Capucins
rue Boulard
bd. Joffre
rue du Col. Driant
rue du Gén Estienne
pl. Drouet d'Erlon
rue Chativesle
rue Buirette
rue de Thillois
rue Vesle
rue Libergier
rue Clovis
rue Chabaud
Gare SNCF
TO SALLE DE LA REDDITION
rue Jeanne d'Arc
rue Caque
rue Poissonniers
Basses Promenades
PL. DE STALINGRAD
bd. Paul Doumer
rue F. Roosevelt
rue de Courcelles
rue de Trianon
bd. Louis Roederer
bd. Général Leclerc
Jardin de la Patte d'Oie
pont de Vesle
Auberge de Jeunesse
chaussée Bocquaine
bd. du Col. Fabien
bd. M. Noirot
A4
rue. de St. Brice
rue Vernouillet
rue des Jardins
rue Tarbe
rue du Mont d'Arène
rue Bruyant
rue Soussillon
av. Brebant

CHAMPAGNE

Laundromat: Laverie de Vesle, 129, rue de Vesle (tel. 03 26 50 09 12). Wash 20F per 7kg, 40F per 16kg. Dry 2F per 5min. Detergent 2F. Open daily 7am-11pm.

Crisis Lines: SOS Amitié (tel. 03 26 05 12 12); suicide prevention. **SOS Femmes** (tel. 03 26 40 13 45); moral support and contraception or abortion info.

Hospital: 45, rue Alexis Carrel (tel. 03 26 78 78 78). **Ambulance** at 29, rue Cognacq-Jay (tel. 03 26 06 10 46). **Medical emergency** tel. 15 or 03 26 06 07 08.

Police: 40, bd. Louis Roederer (tel. 03 26 61 44 00). From the station turn right onto bd. Roederer and walk 2 blocks; it's on the right. **Emergency** tel. 17.

Post Office: rue Olivier-Métra (tel. 03 26 50 58 22), at pl. de Boulingrin, near the Porte de Mars. Open Mon.-Fri. 8am-7pm, Sat. 8am-noon. The **branch office,** 1, rue Cérès (tel. 03 26 40 42 14), on pl. Royale, is closer to the *centre ville* and has good rates for **currency exchange.** Open Mon.-Fri. 8:30am-6pm, Sat. 8:30am-noon. Both have poste restante (specify "51084 Reims-Cérès" for branch office, "51084 Reims-Boulingrin" for main office). **Postal code:** 51100.

ACCOMMODATIONS AND CAMPING

Reims is popular; reserve a few days in advance, especially at the hostel. Inexpensive hotels cluster near rue de Thillois, pl. Drouet d'Erlon, and in the area above the cathedral and near the *mairie.* The tourist office has information on Reims' numerous *foyers,* which start at about 60F and may accept travelers for a couple of nights.

Centre International de Séjour/Auberge de Jeunesse (HI), chaussée Bocquaine (tel. 03 26 40 52 60; fax 03 26 47 35 70), next to La Comédie-Espace André Malraux. Continue straight away from the train station through the park (1 block), following the right-hand side of the traffic circle, then turn right onto bd. Général Leclerc. Follow bd. Leclerc to the canal and cross the first bridge you come to (pont de Vesle, on your left). Chaussée Bocquaine is the first left; the hostel is about a block down, set back from the road on the left (10-15min.). Attractive singles and doubles in a large building with TV, snack machines, phones, and kitchen facilities. Singles 82F. Doubles 65F per person. Sheets and showers included. Breakfast 10F. Reception daily 7am-midnight.

Hôtel d'Alsace, 6, rue Général Sarrail (tel. 03 26 47 44 08; fax 03 26 47 44 52), near the *mairie*. Stained glass in the halls and large, flowered rooms, some recently renovated, all with TV and telephone. Relaxed bar downstairs. Singles 115-120F, with shower 155-170F. Doubles 130F, with shower 165-180F. Triples 160F, with shower 205-220F. Showers 12F, free if you stay a few nights. Breakfast 25F. 24-hr. reception. V, MC.

Hôtel Thillois, 17, rue de Thillois (tel. 03 26 40 65 65). An immaculate, charming hotel with bright rooms and a central location. Proprietress understands English. TV and telephone in every room. Singles 120F, with shower 140F. Doubles 140F, with shower 160F. No hallway shower. Breakfast 28F. Reception daily 7am-10pm. V, MC, AmEx.

Hôtel Jeanne d'Arc, 26, rue Jeanne d'Arc (tel. 03 26 40 29 62). Great prices and location. Plain, clean rooms. Hall showers. Singles 85-110F. Doubles 95-130F. Triples 120-140F. Quads 130-150F. Reception daily 8am-11:30pm. V, MC.

Au Bon Accueil, 31, rue Thillois (tel. 03 26 88 55 74). Take a right off pl. d'Erlon. Large, bright rooms with comfy beds. Singles 80F, with shower 110F. Doubles 100F, with shower 160F. Triples 160F, with shower 180F. Quads 220F, with shower 260F. Shower 10F. Breakfast 25F. 24-hr. reception. V, MC.

Hôtel Azur, 9, rue des Ecrevées, near the *mairie* at pl. de l'Hôtel de Ville (tel. 03 26 47 43 39; fax 03 26 88 57 19). Elegant rooms with TV and phone. Singles 165-250F. Doubles 180-280F. Triples 320-340F. Quads 410F. Reception Mon.-Sat. 7am-10pm, Sun. 8am-noon and 6-10pm. V, MC.

Camping: Camping-Airotel de Champagne, av. Hoche, route de Châlons (tel. 03 26 85 41 22; fax 03 26 82 07 33), 9km from downtown. Take bus F (direction: Farman or Z.I. Pompelle) to stop "Parc des Expositions." 3-star site with 4-day max. stay. Showers included. 22F per adult, 10F per child, 19F per site, 5F per car. Electricity 19F. Grocery store and restaurant on site. Open Easter-Sept.

FOOD

Fast-food joints, cafés, and bars abound on **pl. Drouet d'Erlon.** Along its sidestreets, a few small restaurants serve diverse and reasonably priced *menus.* The two-story behemoth **Monoprix supermarket** is a sure crowd-pleaser, housed in a graceful 19th-century building on the corner of rue de Vesle and rue de Talleyrand, one block from the cathedral (open Mon.-Sat. 8:30am-9pm). Reims has one or two **open-air markets** (daily 6am-1pm). For the locations, call 03 26 77 78 79 or pick up a brochure from the tourist office.

La Forêt Noire, 2, bd. Jules César, on pl. de la République (tel. 03 26 47 63 95). Small, family-run place serves traditional Alsatian specialties—huge *flamme küeche* (30-40F) and *baeckeoffe,* a hearty pot-roast-like dish (74F). Lunch *menu* 64F, others from 98F. Open Mon.-Sat. noon-2:30pm and 7-10pm. V, MC.

Les Brisants, 13, rue de Chativesle (tel. 03 26 40 60 41), two blocks from the station, right off pl. Drouet d'Erlon. Will it be the pastel dining room or the sun-filled courtyard? 77F and 127F *menus,* lots of grilled meats, *galettes,* and crêpes. Open Mon.-Sat. noon-2:30pm and 7-11pm. V, MC, AmEx.

Taj Mahal Indian Restaurant, 151, rue Vesle (tel. 03 26 40 03 50). Large vegetable grills and curries 40-45F. Also chicken, fish, lamb Tandoori. Lively and very popular. Open daily noon-2:30pm and 7:30-11pm. V, MC.

L'Os et l'Arête, 15, rue du Colonel Fabien (tel. 03 26 04 63 12), near the youth hostel. 48F (weekdays only), 78F, 125F, and 160F *menus* of regional specialties, or brick oven pizza for 30-56F. Open Tues.-Fri. and Sun. noon-2pm and 7-10:30pm, Sat. 7-10:30pm. V, MC.

La Station Sandwich, 11, pl. Drouet d'Erlon (tel. 03 26 88 17 14). Fast food *au français.* Large, high-quality sandwiches on fresh French bread 11-21F. Mini sandwiches 6-10F. Centrally located. Open daily 10am-1am.

DRINK

Four hundred kilometers of *crayères* (Roman chalk quarries) wind underground through the countryside around Reims. Today, they shelter bottles emblazoned with the great names of Champagne—Pommery, Piper-Heidsieck, Mumm, Taittinger. Some of the smaller *caves* were built in former chapels; others contain illuminated shrines to St. Jean, the patron saint of *cavistes.* This religious tradition is consistent with the origins of the wine's success. Dom Perignon, who spent 50 years of his life perfecting the *méthode champenoise,* was the blind cellarer of the Abbey of Hautvillers, near Epernay. The tourist office has maps listing the *caves* that are open to the public. Many houses give tours by appointment only; call ahead.

The tours below are all offered in French and English; call to ask about other languages. Tours range from subtle to obvious ploys to get you to buy some of the bubbly. As the houses themselves will no doubt point out, buying champagne at the house is the cheapest way to get it—if you really *need* a bottle of Cordon Rouge. If you missed the free taste that caps off Mumm's tour, order a *coupe de champagne* in any bar (about 25-30F). The even smaller *coupette de champagne* (15-20F) will at least tease you with a bit of bubbly. For more reasonably priced champagne, ask the advice of the local wineshops near the cathedral and look for occasional sales on local brands—or check the prices at **Monoprix.** Good bottles start at 70F.

Pommery, 5, pl. du Général Gouraud (tel. 03 26 61 62 55; fax 03 26 61 63 98), resides in a magnificent group of 19th-century English-style buildings, and its tours live up to the elegant expectations generated by the exterior. Mme. Pommery, who took over her late husband's champagne business, became one of France's foremost vintners. Today, Pommery houses over 29 million bottles of champagne. Mme. Pommery introduced art into the workplace, lining the *cave* walls with exquisite carvings by Gustave Navlet (tours daily by appointment only 11am-5pm; Nov.-March Mon.-Fri. only; admission 30F, children free). **Taittinger,** 9, pl. St-Nicaise (tel. 03 26 85 84 33), in a former abbey complete with crypt, has some of the oldest and creepiest *caves;* its tour is a fabulous history lesson beginning with a home-brewed movie (open Mon.-

Fri. 9:30am-noon and 2-4:30pm, Sat.-Sun. 9-11am and 2-5pm; Dec.-Feb. Mon.-Fri. only, 28F). **Mumm,** 34, rue du Champ de Mars (tel. 03 26 49 59 70), makes up for an inane movie with an interesting tour and a glass of Cordon Rouge at the end. If you're lucky, you may get to see the *riddler* at work—you'll understand once you take the tour (open daily 9-11am and 2-5pm; Nov.-Feb. Mon.-Fri. only; tours 20F). **Piper-Heidsieck,** 51, bd. Henry Vasnier (tel. 03 26 84 43 44), offers an appallingly cheesy tour on an amusement park-style electric train. Unlike Disney, you get champagne at the end (open daily 9-11:45am and 1:30-6:15pm; March-April and Oct.-Nov. daily 9-11:45am and 2-5:15pm; Dec.-Feb. Thurs.-Mon. 9-11:45am and 2-5:15pm; 35F). **Veuve Clicquot-Ponsardin,** 1, pl. des Droits-de-l'Homme (tel. 03 26 40 25 42), leads mediocre tours but screens a fine film about Madame Clicquot, one of the *grande dames* of champagne history (visits by appointment only April-Oct. Mon.-Sat.; free tasting included).

SIGHTS

The main sights of Reims are scattered throughout the *centre ville* and are easily toured on foot. The **Cathédrale de Notre-Dame** presided over a long line of royal coronations, beginning with the baptism of Clovis in 496. The coronation of Charles VII, at the tail of the Hundred Years' War, may be the most famous. The present cathedral, the third to occupy the site, is built with blocks of golden limestone quarried in the Champagne *caves.* Inside, elaborately detailed figurines of saints and apostles stare down disconcertingly. The west façade contains a spectacular rose window, its deep blues made from lapis lazuli. Mortar fire during World War I shattered many of the building's other original windows, but all have been replaced. Perhaps the most spectacular is a sea-blue set by Marc Chagall integrating elements from Genesis to the baptism of Clovis. Most of the stained-glass windows are in the eastern portion of the cathedral; visit in the morning for the best view (open Mon.-Sat. 7:30am-7:30pm, Sun. 8:30am-7:30pm). In July and August, daily tours in French depart from the tourist office at 10:30am, 2:30, and 4:15pm (35F, students 15F). For tours in English, consult the tourist office. If you're up for a climb, take the tour of the upper parts of the cathedral that departs from inside the church to the right of the main entrance. (June 15-Sept. 15 every 30min. 10-11:30am and 2-5:30pm. 19F, ages 12-17 10F, under 12 free. Tours in French only.)

Just left as you exit the cathedral stands the former archbishop's palace, the **Palais du Tau,** pl. du Cardinal Luçon (tel. 03 26 47 81 79; fax 03 26 47 85 65), so named because the original floor plan resembled a "T." Rooms that once housed each king's first banquet now display exquisite tapestries, statuary from the cathedral (including a Goliath-sized Goliath), and Charles X's gold and velvet coronation vestments. The cathedral's dazzling treasure includes Charlemagne's 9th-century talisman and the 12th-century chalice from which 20 kings took communion. (Open daily July-Aug. 9:30am-12:30pm and 2-6pm; March 16-June and Sept.-Nov. 14 daily 9:30am-12:30pm and 2-6pm; Nov. 15-March 15 Mon.-Fri. 10am-noon and 2-5pm, Sat.-Sun. 10am-noon and 2-6pm. Admission 26F, students 17F, under 17 7F.)

South of the cathedral stands the less visited but equally interesting **Basilique St-Remi,** a Gothic renovation of a Carolingian Romanesque church believed to contain the tombs of many of France's earliest kings. Behind the altar lies the tomb of St. Remi himself, whose baptism of Clovis brought Catholicism to the French people. In 1996-97, Reims will celebrate the 1500th anniversary of the baptism with archaeological excavations and exhibitions. The interior of the basilica is 122m long but only 28m wide, giving it the appearance of a huge, dark vault (open Mon.-Wed., Fri., and Sun. 8am-7pm or dusk, whichever comes first; Thurs. and Sat. 7am-7pm or dusk). Adjacent to the church is the **Abbaye St-Remi,** 53, rue Simon (tel. 03 26 85 23 36), which shelters an extensive collection of religious art, military uniforms, and artifacts from the Merovingian and Carolingian eras (open Mon.-Fri. 2-6:30pm, Sat.-Sun. 2-7pm; admission 10F, under 16 free).

Built in the 18th century as an abbey, the graceful **Musée des Beaux-Arts,** 8, rue Chanzy (tel. 03 26 47 28 44), houses a mélange of paintings and tapestries, including a noteworthy display of ceramics and two rooms of Impressionist canvases (open Wed.-Mon. 10am-noon and 2-6pm; admission 10F, students free).

The **Salle de Reddition,** 12, rue Franklin Roosevelt (tel. 03 26 47 84 19), is the simple schoolroom where the Germans surrendered to the Allies on May 8, 1945. It displays the actual maps used by the Allies for planning battle strategies, period newspapers, photos, and an excellent film. (Open April-Oct. Wed.-Mon. 10am-noon and 2-6pm. Nov.-March open only by appointment with the Musée des Beaux Arts. Admission 10F, students free.)

Perhaps the most majestic of Reims' many large squares is the **pl. Royale,** where a Cartellier statue of Louis XV smirks at all the tourists. To the west, just on the edge of the modern pl. de la République, loom the ruins of the third-century **Porte de Mars.** This massive triumphal Roman arch, the largest in the Empire, was one of four erected in honor of Augustus two centuries after his death.

ENTERTAINMENT

Throughout July and August, Reims hosts the fantastic **Flâneries Musicales d'Eté,** with free classical concerts. Pick up a brochure at the tourist office. For more free fun, head to the cathedral every Saturday night in July and August for **Cathédrale de Lumière,** an impressive spectacle illuminating the cathedral and nearby buildings and culminating in a light show on the cathedral façade (1hr., 11pm in July, 10pm in Aug.; ask at the tourist office for more info).

Reims is understandably proud of its **Comédie de Reims,** chaussée Bocquaine (tel. 03 26 48 49 00; fax 03 26 88 76 95), which presents a wide variety of plays (tickets around 110F, students 70F). **Cinéma Gaumont,** 72, pl. Drouet d'Erlon (tel. 03 26 47 54 54) and **Opéra Cinémas,** rue Théodore Dubois (tel. 03 26 47 29 36), show mostly American movies (*v.o.;* tickets 30-50F).

A university town, Reims has more jazz clubs, wine bars, and discos than the average reveler could navigate in a month of Saturdays. The pedestrian streets around **pl. Drouet d'Erlon** are lively local hangouts. Cafés line the avenue. For the music connoisseur, the jazz club and café **Le Croque-Notes,** 24, rue Ernest Renan (tel. 03 26 88 41 28), hosts a different concert every night (open Mon.-Sat. 6pm-3am). Drink your meter of beer (from 90F) at the *très populaire* **Au Bureau,** 40, pl. d'Erlon (tel. 03 26 40 33 06). Choose between the pub setting inside or café seating outdoors (open daily 10am-3am). Get stuck at **The Glue Pot,** 49, pl. d'Erlon (tel. 03 26 47 36 46), with beers from 12-21F (prices rise at night). The only thing Flemish about **Au Lion du Belfroi,** pl. d'Erlon (tel. 03 26 47 48 17) is its name. Swill beer under the head of the hippo or elephant in this café-turned-safari (beer 12-27F). Shake your booty French style at **Le Boss,** 17, rue Lesage, to *le techno.* When you're tired, shoot billiards next door. (Club open Wed.-Sat. 10:30pm-5am. Wed.-Thurs. 20F, Fri. 40F, Sat. 60F. Billiards daily noon-4am.)

Epernay

If Reims is the jewel of champagne country, Epernay is its 24-carat setting, solidly upholding the region's fame and wealth with the countless bottles of bubbly it turns out each year. The world's most distinguished champagne producers have put their labels on the palatial mansions along av. de Chamagne. But the edifices are merely a taste of the real wealth contained below; Moët & Chandon, Perrier-Jouet, Mercier, and De Castellane, among others bury their 700 million bottles of treasure stored in miles of subterranean tunnels. Each year, Epernay's visitors eagerly guzzle more than 30,000 bottles—roughly one for every local citizen.

Situated at the juncture of the grape-growing regions of Montagne de Reims, the Côte de Blancs, and the Marne Valley, Epernay sparkles above-ground with the opulence granted by its liquid gold. The town hall, public gardens, and museums are grand 19th-century symbols—all bequeathed to the town by former champagne merchants. It may all seem a little too effervescent, but relax and let festive Epernay go to your head. Tour a *cave,* raise a glass, and sip a few stars.

ORIENTATION AND PRACTICAL INFORMATION

To get to **pl. de la République,** the town's center, from the train station, walk straight ahead through pl. Mendès France (you'll pass a fountain) and one block up rue Gambetta. From pl. de la République, turn left onto av. de Champagne to reach the tourist office and the myriad *caves* (5min.).

Tourist Office: 7, av. de Champagne (tel. 03 26 53 33 00; fax 03 26 51 95 22). Excellent free maps and info on Epernay's *caves,* plus suggestions for 3 different *routes champenoises.* List of hotels and restaurants; accommodations service (25F). The *Guide Touristique* tells all, from the town's history to its architecture. The tourist office publishes a free paper called **Le Magazine des Manifestations Epernay,** which lists local events and festivities. **Currency exchange.** Open mid-April to mid-Oct. Mon.-Sat. 9:30am-12:30pm and 1:30-7pm, Sun. and holidays 11am-4pm; mid-Oct. to mid-April Mon.-Sat. 9:30am-12:30pm and 1:30-5:30pm.

Trains: cour de la Gare (tel. 08 36 35 35 35). To: Paris (12 per day, 1¼hr., 102F); Reims (15 per day, 20min., 31F); and Strasbourg (2 per day, 4hr., 211F). Station open 6am-8pm. Info office open Mon.-Sat. 9am-noon and 2-6pm. **Lockers** 30F.

Buses: Gare routière, rue Rousseau, off pl. Notre-Dame. **SDTM TransChampagne** (tel. 03 26 65 17 07) offers service to Bergères (Mon.-Sat. 2 per day, 40min., 31F) and itty-bitty villages along the way. Info telephone answered Mon.-Fri. 9:30am-noon and 2-5pm.

Public Transportation: Sparnabus, 30, pl. des Arcades (tel. 03 26 55 55 50), runs the relatively infrequent local bus service. One way ticket 6F, 41F for 10.

Taxis: Prevost Taxi, (tel. 03 26 54 91 51).

Bike Rental: The only place in the area is **Cycl'o Vert,** 34, rue Carnot (tel. 03 26 97 97 77), in Verzy, 20km from Epernay—but for 15F extra, they'll bring the bike to you. 70F per ½-day, 110F per day, 170F per weekend. Also offers guided tours of the area and info on hiking and biking trails. Open daily 9am-noon and 2-7pm; Oct.-June Sat.-Sun. 9am-noon and 2-7pm, weekdays by request only.

Car Rental: Avis Rental Cars, Gare d'Epernay (tel. 03 26 51 54 40). From 535F per weekend, 600km included.

Laundromat: 18, av. Jean Jaurès. Wash 22F per 7kg, 50F per 15kg. Dry 2F per 5min. Detergent 2F. Open daily 7am-8pm.

Hospital: Hôpital Auban-Moët, 137, rue de l'Hôpital (tel. 03 26 58 70 70). **Medical emergency** tel. 15.

Police: 7, rue Jean Chandon Moët (tel. 03 26 54 11 17), 1 block from pl. de la République down rue Fleuricourt. **Emergency** tel. 17.

Post Office: pl. Hughes Plomb (tel. 03 26 53 31 68). Poste restante. Photocopies 1F. **ATMs.** Mediocre rates for **currency exchange.** Open Mon.-Fri. 8am-7pm, Sat. 8am-noon. **Postal code:** 51200.

ACCOMMODATIONS AND CAMPING

Epernay is not a great place for the budget traveler to stay; there is no hostel and the few budget rooms in town fill quickly. In July and August, call at least one week in advance or try Reims. Travelers ages 18-25 should head straight for the **Foyer des Jeunes Travailleurs,** 8, rue de Reims, just two blocks from the tourist office (tel. 03 26 51 62 51; fax 03 26 54 15 60), which offers singles, doubles, and triples in huge rooms for 75F per person, breakfast included, in a complex with TV, game room, laundry facilities, kitchen, and cafeteria (reception Mon.-Fri. 9am-8pm, Sat. 10am-2pm). A bright spot in the dismal accommodations scene is the comfortable **Hôtel St-Pierre,** 1, rue Jeanne d'Arc (tel. 03 26 54 40 80), with elegant rooms a few blocks from pl. de la République. (Singles 108F. Doubles 120F, with shower 143-195F. Breakfast 27F. Reception Mon.-Sat. 24-hr., closed Sun. 12-5pm. Closed two weeks in Aug. V, MC.) **Le Chapon Fin,** just across from the station at 2, pl. Mendès France (tel. 03 26 55 40 03; fax 03 26 54 94 17), provides plain but clean singles and doubles from 120F, with shower 140-180F. (Triple with shower 180F. Breakfast 20F; restaurant downstairs. Reception 7:30am-3pm and 5:30-11pm.) A **campground** resides about 4km from the station, at allée de Cumières (tel. 03 26 55 32 14; 13F per person, 17F per tent and car; shower included; open April-mid-Sept.).

FOOD

Restaurants in Epernay are either expensive or inconveniently located. For something light, try any of the cafés between the train station and the pl. de la République. Food shops abound in the area around **pl. Hughes Plomb.** There's a **Prisunic supermarket** at the corner of rue St-Thibault and rue J. Pierrot (open Mon-Fri. 8:30am-12:30pm and 2-7pm, Sat. 8:30am-7pm). On Wednesday and Saturday mornings Epernay has **markets** in the Halle St-Thibault on pl. des Arcades. The *foyer* at 8, rue Reims (tel. 03 26 51 62 51), houses the **MJC caféteria,** where a complete meal costs 43F (open Mon.-Fri. 11:30am-1:30pm and 6:45-8pm, Sat. 11:30am-1:30pm).

Intimate and classy, **La Cave a Champagne,** 16, rue Gambetta (tel. 03 26 55 50 70), serves a 69F dinner *menu,* with a wide selection of appetizers, main dishes, and desserts (open Wed.-Mon. noon-2pm and 7:30-10:30pm; V, MC). Across the river, at 20, rue Jean Moulin, you'll find **L'Kénavo** (tel. 03 26 51 00 25), where you can enjoy specialties from all regions of France on a patio (*galettes* 40-59F, fondue 71F for 2 people; open Tues.-Sun. noon-2pm and 7:30-11pm). Have a hamburger (15F) or *croque monsieur* (13F) at **American Frites,** 2, rue Gambetta (tel. 03 26 51 67 46), along with salads (13-25F) and the eponymous *frites* (11-15F). (Open Mon.-Thurs. 11:30am-3pm and 5:30-10:30pm; open Fri.-Sat. 11:30am-3pm and 5:30-11pm.)

SIGHTS AND ENTERTAINMENT

One of the richest streets in the world, the sweeping **av. de Champagne** is distinguished by its mansions, gardens, and monumental champagne firms. The best known is **Moët & Chandon,** 20, av. de Champagne (tel. 03 26 51 20 00), producers of the king of wines, *Dom Perignon.* Moët's tours are led by lively guides in English, French, or German, and end with a tasting. Napoleon, a buddy of Jean-Rémy Moët, usually picked up a few thousand bottles on his way to the front. Unfortunately for the emperor, Epernay is not on the way to Belgium; tour guides like to joke that the lack of Moët's bubbly caused the French fiasco at Waterloo (open Mon.-Sat. 9:30-11:30am and 2-4:30pm; March-Nov. closed Sat.; admission 20F).

A 10-minute walk away, **Mercier,** 70, av. de Champagne (tel. 03 26 51 22 22), is located in the middle of a vineyard. Mercier's tour takes place on an electric train. Check out the penicillin growing on the walls of the *caves.* Long before it had been discovered by scientists, penicillin was sought out by *cave* workers who recognized its extraordinary healing powers. The audiovisual program that starts the tour is a blend of MTV, *Life* magazine, and *Star Wars*—just bide your time 'til the tasting (open Mon.-Sat. 9:30-11:30am and 2-4:30pm, Sun. and holidays 9:30-11:30am and 2-5:30pm; Dec.-Feb. closed Tues.-Wed; admission 20F).

The famed Parisian restaurant, Maxim's, orders from **De Castellane,** 57, rue de Verdun (tel. 03 26 55 15 33), housed in a monstrous building across the street—look for the tower. The tour includes the large museum, the tower, and the *caves,* and ends with a glass of their pride and joy (open daily 10am-noon and 2-6pm; tours in English, French, or German; 20F). For an extra 15F, your tour also includes the **Jardin des Papillons,** 63bis, av. de Champagne (tel. 03 26 55 15 33), where butterflies indigenous to the Andes and the Appalachians flit freely in the large tropical greenhouse (open May-Sept. daily 10am-noon and 2-6pm; admission 22F). Tour one of the new kids on the block at the 20-year-old **Vranken,** 42, rue de Champagne (tel. 03 26 53 33 20), amid flashing slide shows and melodramatic music. (Open May-Oct. Mon.-Fri. 9:30-11:30am and 2-5:30pm, Sat.-Sun. 10:30am-2pm.)

Those without wheels can tour the city and surrounding countryside on **Bacchus,** a saucy little tram that leaves across the street from the tourist office. You'll get a bumpy but entertaining ride through Epernay and up into the hillside for a look at the vineyards and a great view of the city (tel. 03 26 55 55 50; fax 03 26 59 58 79 in French and English; 7 per day; 30F).

Along with Epernay's preoccupation with dark, moldy caves, **nightlife** of a more conventional sort ferments here. **Le Tap-Too,** 5, rue des Près Dimanche (tel. 03 26 51 56 10), is a former warehouse now housing four clubs in one; eet eez veree cool and you can tap, too (open daily 10pm-4am; cover on Fri. 60F, includes one drink; Sat. 40F before 11pm, 80F after, including drink). The super-trendy café, **Le Progres,** 5, pl. de la République, is *the* place for drinks or coffee (open Mon.-Thurs. 6am-midnight, Fri.-Sat. 6am-1am).

At the heart of *la Route Touristique du Champagne,* Epernay is an excellent base for exploring the surrounding countryside. The "Champagne route" is a set of **hikes** through the vineyards, châteaux, and mountains of the region. The tourist office can provide the free brochure *Balades Champenoises,* which maps out treks and provides regional practical information in French. Once you have selected a hike, detailed maps of the area can be purchased at the tourist office; or for more specific information, contact **Amis de la Nature,** 1, square Léo Delibes (tel. 03 26 54 90 43).

■ Troyes

In the later Middle Ages, Troyes' fairs made it the hub of European commerce and the undisputed capital of Champagne. Increased champagne production in the north forced Troyes into obscurity and a fire in 1524 destroyed the city for the third time in a millennium. After the fire, the town's artists and architects applied their skills to making new churches, gabled houses, tiny streets, and narrow passages.

Modern Troyes (pop. 65,000) bears little resemblance to its grape-crazy northern neighbors. It has no *caves,* and the downtown area's nickname—*"bouchon de champagne"* (champagne cork)—stems from the shape of its streets, not the success of its industry. Still, the charming city welcomes travelers with an array of museums, elegant Renaissance homes, an effervescent Gothic cathedral, and cobblestone pedestrian streets. Troyes is a mere 25km from France's great lakes in the Forêt d'Orient, and swimming, sailing, and other water sports abound.

ORIENTATION AND PRACTICAL INFORMATION

Troyes' train station is just three blocks from the *vieille ville* where the town's shops, restaurants, and hotels gather. From the station, the tourist office is one block farther on your right. To get to the *vieille ville,* cross over bd. Carnot and continue straight onto rue Général de Gaulle. The pedestrian district occupies the side streets on the right, just after Eglise Ste-Madeleine.

Tourist Office: 16, bd. Carnot (tel. 03 25 73 00 36; fax 03 25 73 06 81). Free detailed city map. Reservations service 15F. Bus schedules and calendar of local events. For info on cultural events, pick up the free brochures *Sorties* and *Ville en Musiques.* From July to early Sept., guided tours of the city leave daily at 3pm (English tours, for large groups only, 35F). Open Mon.-Sat. 9am-12:30pm and 2-6:30pm. An **annex** (tel. 03 25 73 36 88), with a **currency exchange,** is across from Église St-Jean in the pedestrian area (open Sun. 10am-noon and 2-5pm).

Money: Société Generale, 11, pl. Maréchal Foch (tel. 03 25 43 57 00). **Currency exchange.** Open Mon.-Fri. 8:30am-12:30pm and 1:30-5:30pm. 24-hr. **ATM.**

Trains: av. Maréchal Joffre (tel. 08 36 35 35 35). Few destinations are directly linked to Troyes. Most involve a trip to Paris-Est (12 per day, 1½hr., 113F). The main eastern line serves Mulhouse (4 per day, 3hr., 189F). Info office open Mon.-Sat. 8:30-11:45am and 2-7pm. Open Mon.-Sat. 4:45am-9pm, Sun. 6am-10:15pm.

Buses: Go left as you exit the *gare.* **SDTM TransChampagne,** 86, rue de Fagnières (tel. 03 26 65 17 07), goes to Reims (4 per day, 2hr., 101-106F). **Courriers de L'Aube,** 15, rue Gustave Michel (tel. 03 25 71 28 40), serves Chaumont (97F) and Sens (72F). Open Mon.-Fri. 9:30am-12:30pm and 3:30-6:30pm. **Les Rapides de Bourgogne** (tel. 03 86 46 90 90) hop to Auxerre (1 per day, 2½hr., 83F).

Public Transportation: Bus L'Autoville, office in front of market (tel. 03 25 70 49 10). Extensive and frequent service. Ticket 6F50, 3 for 15F, *carnet* of 7 31F.

Taxis: Taxis Troyens (tel. 03 25 78 30 30) in the circle outside the station. 24hr.

Car Rental: Avis, cour de la Gare (tel. 03 25 73 02 40). Economy cars 535F. Open Mon.-Fri. 8am-12:30pm and 1:30-7pm, Sat. 8:30am-noon and 2-7pm.

Bike Rental: Les Loisirs du Lac (tel. 03 25 80 29 31), rue des Mazées.

Laundromat: Laverie Automatique, 9, rue Clemenceau.

English Books: Les Passeurs de Textes, 5, rue Emile Zola. Zola and friends in translation, of course. Open Mon. 2:30-7pm, Tues.-Thurs. 9:30am-12:30pm and 2:30-7pm, Fri.-Sat. 9:30am-7pm.

Youth Center: Bureau Information Jeunesse, 30, rue Claude Huez (tel. 03 25 73 69 09), sells discount tram and plane tickets and has info on activities, health, housing, and more. Open during school year Mon.-Fri. 9am-noon and 2-6pm.

Hospital: 101, av. A. France (tel. 03 25 49 49 49). **Medical emergency** tel. 15.

Police: tel. 03 25 43 51 00. **Emergency** tel. 17.

Post Office: 2, pl. Général Patton (tel. 03 25 73 09 69). One block to the right as you exit the train station. Poste restante (mail to: "10013 Troyes-Voltaire"). Photocopies, faxes. Open Mon.-Fri. 8am-6:30pm, Sat. 8am-noon. **Postal code:** 10000.

ACCOMMODATIONS AND CAMPING

Auberge de Jeunesse (HI), 2, rue Jules Ferry (tel. 03 25 82 00 65), 7km from Troyes in Rosières. Take bus 6 (direction: Chartreux) from the tourist office to the final stop (last bus 10pm). From there, take bus 24 to the hostel (4-5 per day), or walk 2.2km down a country road. Dorm-style rooms house 4-6 people. Kitchen facilities. Reception 8am-10pm. 50F on first night, 47F thereafter. Sheet rental 15F. Breakfast 20F. Camping 30F per person. It's a hassle if you lack wheels.

Les Comtes de Champagne, 54-56, rue de la Monnaie (tel. 03 25 73 11 70; fax 03 25 73 06 02). This superb 2-star hotel with a leafy courtyard patio is housed in a beautifully restored 12th-century building that was once the mint for the counts of Champagne. Singles from 120F, with shower from 160F. Doubles from 120F, with shower from 180F. Triples 300F. Free hall shower. Phones in rooms. Breakfast 27F, 32F in room. Extra bed 40F. Garage 25F. Reception 7am-11pm. V, MC.

Hôtel Butat, 50, rue Turenne (tel. 03 25 73 77 39), off rue Emile Zola, in a quiet district. Forget that you're budget traveling until you see the low bill. Big, beautiful rooms, all with TV and phone. Reception 7am-noon and 1:30-10pm. Closed Sun. afternoon. Singles from 120F, with shower 170F. Doubles from 140F, with shower 195F. Triples 270F. Breakfast 25F, 30F in room. V, MC, AmEx.

Hôtel Ambassy, 49, rue Raymond Poincaré (tel. 03 25 73 12 03). Friendly owner offers clean, calm rooms in a central location. TV room, happenin' bar/restaurant downstairs. Singles and doubles 120F. Triples 150F. Free hallway showers. Breakfast 30F. Reception 7am-3am. V, MC.

Hôtel du Théâtre, 35-37, rue Lebocey (tel. 03 25 73 18 47). Walk straight out of the *gare,* cross bd. Carnot and take a left after the statue onto rue Paul Debois, then right onto rue Argence until it veers slightly right and turns into rue Lebocey. Large, plain rooms, all with shower. If you're lucky, you'll get one with a day-glo orange bedspread. Singles 150F. Doubles 170F. Triples 205F. Extra bed 50F. Breakfast 22F. Reception daily 7am-midnight. V, MC, AmEx.

Camping: Camping Municipal (tel. 03 25 81 02 64), on N60, 2km from town. Take bus 1 (direction: Pont St-Marie). A 3-star site with showers, toilets, TV, phones and laundry. 25F per person, 25F per tent or car. Open April-Oct. 15.

FOOD

The **quartier St-Jean** has many inviting restaurants. Reasonably priced international eateries line **rue de la Cité** near the cathedral. **Les Halles,** a covered market near the Hôtel de Ville, shelters both farmers and produce from the Aube region (open Mon.-Thurs. 8am-12:45pm and 3:30-7pm, Fri.-Sat. 7am-7pm, Sun. 8:45am-12:45pm). Try the creamy *fromage de Troyes* or the *andouillette de Troyes,* a tasty sausage. You can also buy groceries at the **Prisunic supermarket,** 78, rue Emile Zola (open Mon.-Sat. 8:30am-8pm), or the **Coopérative Hermès,** 39, rue Général Saussier, off rue

Emile Zola (tel. 03 25 73 39 17), a natural foods grocery (open Mon. 2:30-7pm, Tues.-Sat. 8:30am-12:30pm and 2:30-7pm). Take your picnic to the fountains and flowers near the river of **pl. de la Libération,** at the end of rue Emile Zola.

La Paninotoca, 27, rue Paillot de Montabert (tel. 03 25 73 91 34), serves fresh panini (Italian sandwiches), hot or cold, in a friendly spot. Best of all, *c'est pas cher!* Sandwiches 16-27F. Open Mon.-Sat. noon-3pm and 7pm-midnight. V, MC.

Restaurant Italien Pizzéria, 28, rue Paillot de Montabert (tel. 03 25 73 92 44), serves pizza from 33F and salad from 36F to a young crowd. Open Mon.-Sat. noon-2pm and 7:30-11pm. Closed Mon. lunch. Open until midnight Fri.-Sat.

Grill St-Jean, 19-23, rue Champeaux (tel. 03 25 73 52 26), attracts locals and travelers alike with its specialty—*andouillettes.* 66F *menu* includes salad, pizza or pasta, and dessert. Open daily 11:30am-4pm and 6:30pm-midnight. V, MC, AmEx.

Au Jardin Gourmand, 31, rue Paillot de Montabert (tel. 03 25 73 36 13), tucked away on a narrow cobblestone street, offers salads, fish, steaks, and *andouillettes* for 20-75F. Open Mon.-Sat. noon-2pm and 7:30-10pm. V, MC.

Restaurant Au Bon Bec, 82, rue Urbain IV (tel. 03 25 73 09 53), in the heart of the *vieille ville.* 45F lunch *menu* of quiche, salad, pastries, and coffee. More substantial 65F dinner *menu. A la carte* 30-60F. Open Mon.-Tues. and Thurs.-Sat. noon-3pm and 7-10:30pm, Wed. noon-3pm. V, MC.

SIGHTS AND ENTERTAINMENT

Perhaps the best way to explore Troyes is to wander through the streets around the Musée de l'Histoire de Troyes. In contrast to the commercial Quartier St-Jean, this residential area exemplifies Troyes' commitment to the preservation of its past in its beautifully restored 16th-century *hôtels particuliers* and narrow wood-framed passageways. The balance of the *bouchon de champagne* boasts eight museums and nine churches dating from the 12th to the 17th centuries.

The **Cathédrale St-Pierre et St-Paul** is a 13th- to 17th-century Gothic masterpiece, with Flamboyant detailing on the façade, 112 stained-glass windows, and one of the longest naves in France. The only thing that mars St-Paul's perfection is its tower, unfinished since 1545. The treasury houses the jewels of the counts of Champagne as well as manuscripts, statues and religious relics dating from the 9th century to the present (open daily 9am-1pm and 2-7pm).

Built in 1150, the **Eglise Ste-Madeleine** is the oldest in Troyes. Particularly impressive is its stone *jubé,* a structure erected to separate the nave from the chancel. One of seven in France, this *jubé* is crafted with lace-like intricacy. The **Basilique St-Urbain,** illuminated by 13th-century stained-glass windows, was founded by Pope Urban IV, a Troyes native, in 1261. Its lofty, simple interior was constructed in less than three decades, which accounts for the remarkable unity of style. The **Eglise St-Jean au Marché** witnessed the marriage of Catherine of France to Henry V of England in 1420. The groom's signature on the Treaty of Troyes in 1420 opened the door to an English invasion—a misfortune only rectified on July 9, 1429, when Joan of Arc liberated the town from the English. Note the 15th-century fresco of the Last Judgment in the chancel. (All 3 churches open July-Aug. daily 10:30am-7pm; Sept. 1-15 10:30am-5pm; Sept. 16-June 30 10am-noon and 2-4pm.) Troyes couples history and theater in **Le Chemin des Bâtisseurs de Cathédrales,** a free *son et lumière* focusing on the churches of Ste-Madeleine, St-Urbain, St-Jean, and St-Pantaléon (late June-Aug. Thurs.-Sat. at 10:30pm, check times with tourist office).

If you plan to visit several of Troyes' museums, buy a pass (60F, students 10F) that will allow you to visit all but the Maison de l'Outil. Most elegant is the **Musée de l'Art Moderne,** pl. St-Pierre (tel. 03 25 76 26 80), in the 17th-century Episcopal Palace next to the cathedral. Knitwear king Pierre Levy donated more than 4000 works by such artists as Braque, Cezanne, Degas, Gauguin, Matisse, Picasso, Seurat, and Rodin. The museum also contains African arts and an attractive sculpture garden (open Wed.-Mon. 11am-6pm; admission 30F, students and children 5F; free Wed.).

On the other side of the cathedral is the **Musée des Beaux-Arts,** 21, rue Chretien-de-Troyes (tel. 03 25 42 33 33), housed in the old Abbaye St-Loup. The museum displays an array of archaeological finds (including an Egyptian mummy), taxidermic specimens, Merovingian weaponry, Gallo-Roman statuettes, medieval sculpture, and a large but obscure collection of 15th- to 19th-century paintings. A locked glass door on the second floor affords a peek into one of the largest and oldest libraries in France. Some 85,000 volumes—many of them 1300 years old—line the shelves. The scope of the collection is partly due to French Revolutionaries, who confiscated books from nearby abbeys and monasteries (museum open Wed.-Mon. 10am-noon and 2-6pm; admission 30F, students and children 5F; free Wed.).

Two museums in the older downtown impress more with their architecture than with their collections. The **Musée Historique de Troyes et de la Champagne,** rue de Vauluisant (tel. 03 25 42 33 33, ext. 36 92), is located in the 16th-century Hôtel de Vauluisant, an imposing gray stone mansion with a tall tower and wide courtyard. Peruse the religious articles, documents, and Renaissance *troyen* sculpture and painting. In the same building is France's only **Musée de la Bonneterie,** a hilarious assortment of the gloves, hats, and hosiery for which Troyes is famous. Upstairs is a collection of stockings embroidered with everything from peacocks to dominos; downstairs, trace the industry's evolution to modern machines (both open Wed.-Mon. 10am-noon and 2-6pm; admission 30F, students and children 5F; free Wed.).

The **Maison de l'Outil et de la Pensée Ouvrière,** 7, rue de la Trinité (tel. 03 25 73 28 26), is a marvelously restored 16th-century half-timbered *hôtel* with plentiful wood carvings. Inside it resembles a giant tool shed, with axes and hammers, hoes and horseshoes. Pick up a folder (in English or French) if you want to learn the French term for weed-whacker (open daily 9am-noon and 2-6pm; admission 30F, students 20F). The **Pharmacie Musée** (tel. 03 25 80 98 97), in the 19th-century Hôtel Dieu on quai des Comtes de Champagne, houses apothecaries' utensils and other items (open Wed.-Mon. 10am-noon and 2-6pm; admission 20F, students 5F).

Troyes is a short distance from over 12,500 acres of freshwater lakes. The **Lakes of the Forêt d'Orient** offer watersports, hikes, and biking for nature enthusiasts. **Lake Orient** specializes in sailing and windsurfing, **Lake Temple** is reserved for fishing and birdwatching, and **Lake Armance** is reserved for speedboats and water-skiing. There are also a number of horseback riding centers and trails. The **Comité Départmental du Tourisme de l'Aube,** 34, quai Danpierre (tel. 03 25 42 50 91; fax 03 25 42 50 88), provides free brochures and info on hotels and restaurants in the area. The tourist office has seasonal bus schedules from Troyes to the Great Lakes.

Movie theaters, pool halls, and shops crowd rue Emile Zola. The **City Jazz Cabaret,** 5, rue de la République (tel. 03 25 73 71 60), has live jazz Wednesdays (open until 5am). A mellow, yuppie crowd hits **Le Tricasse** (tel. 03 25 73 14 80), at the corner of rue Paillot de Montabert and rue Charbonnet, with its live music and classy wood interior (open Mon.-Sat. 4pm-3am). For the gregarious pub group, hang at **Bar Montabert,** 24, rue Paillot de Montabert (tel. 03 25 73 58 04), for a bit o' the cheaper bubbly—i.e., beer. (Open Mon.-Thurs. 6pm-3am and Fri.-Sat. 6pm-4am.)

The North

Even after five decades of peace, the memory of two World Wars is never far from the inhabitants of northern France. The world's battlefronts have moved across the region four times in this century alone. Nearly every town bears scars from merciless bombing in World War II, and German-built concrete observation towers still peer over the land. Regiments of tombstones stand as reminders of the massacres at Arras in Flanders, Cambrai in Artois, and the Somme river in Picardie.

The North remains the final frontier of tourist-free France. Although thousands traveling to and from Britain pass through Calais, Boulogne, and Dunkerque every day, surprisingly few take the time to explore the ancient towns between the ports and Paris. This is perhaps fortunate, as it has left the countryside unspoiled by commercial traffic and the natives welcoming to travelers. The people of the Pas-de-Calais and Picardie regions proclaim themselves France's friendliest *départements.* After a few days of Northern hospitality, you'll be inclined to agree. Chalk cliffs loom over the beaches along the rugged coast, and cultivation gives way to cows and sheep grazing near collapsed bunkers and coils of rusty barbed wire. Once a possession of Flanders, the region still shows its Flemish architectural influence. In Picardie, tranquil seas of wheat extend in all directions, broken by the occasional clump of trees or wooden windmill. Certainly, the North's industrial history has changed many towns into soot heaps to be avoided if at all possible. But as you flee the ferry ports, don't overlook the hidden treasures: the jewel-like cathedrals of Amiens and Laon, the intriguing Flemish culture of Lille and Arras, and the historic rural charm of small towns like Montreuil-sur-Mer, whose imposing ramparts smile upon an undulating green valley.

Sample the local specialties: *moules* (mussels swathed in an astounding variety of sauces) and beer along the coast and in Flanders; and in Picardie, *pâté de canard* (duck pâté), *flamiche aux poireaux* (a creamy quiche-like tart with leeks), and *ficelle Picarde* (a cheese, ham, and mushroom crêpe).

THE NORTH

GETTING AROUND

A logical base for a visit to the North is **Lille,** the capital of the Nord/Pas-de-Calais region and a major transportation hub. Getting to smaller towns often involves changing trains in **Amiens.** Ferries usually dock in **Calais,** where no one wants to linger. The **Channel Tunnel** connects France to Britain at Calais and provides a viable alternative to ferries and airplanes (for more Chunnel info, see **Getting to France** on page 42 or **Deep-Sea Tunnels** on page 673). The countryside is flat enough to allow bicycling, but towns are far apart. Consult the main tourist offices in Lille and Amiens, the **Comité Régional de Tourisme du Nord/Pas-de-Calais,** 6, pl. Mendes, 59000 Lille (tel. 03 20 14 57 57; fax 03 20 14 57 58), or the **Comité Régional de Tourisme de Picardie,** BP 2616, 80026 Amiens (tel. 03 22 91 10 15; fax 03 22 97 92 96), for info about transportation and touring routes.

Boulogne

Legend has it that in AD 636, a boat carrying only a statue of the Virgin Mary washed up on the beach of Boulogne, which subsequently became a great pilgrimage site. Today Boulogne (pop. 50,000) is a mecca for none but a stopover for many, ushering thousands of passengers through its ferry terminal daily. If your stay lasts longer than you'd like, explore the areas away from the industrial port. Despite the relentless passage of tourists and time, Boulogne has preserved its local character and avoided acquiring Calais' British flavor.

ORIENTATION AND PRACTICAL INFORMATION

Leaving the train station, check the large map at the front doors. To reach central **pl. Frédéric Sauvage** from the Gare Boulogne-Ville, go left on bd. Voltaire until you reach the canal, then turn right and follow bd. Diderot past the Pont de l'Entente Cordial (the first bridge you'll see on your left). The **post office** will be on your right and the **tourist office** one block farther, on your left. **Pont Marquet,** the bridge adjacent to the tourist office, leads to the **ferry booking offices.** The tree-lined ramparts are always shady, but at night they become more so—in the negative sense.

Tourist Office: pl. Frédéric Sauvage (tel. 03 21 31 68 38; fax 03 21 33 81 09). Free accommodations service, ferry brochures, and map. More extensive map 2F. Open June-Sept. Mon.-Sat. 9am-7pm, Sun. 10am-6pm; Oct.-May Mon.-Sat. 9am-7pm, Sun. 10am-12:30pm and 1:30-5pm. Free **calendar of events.**

Money: Banque de France, 1, pl. de l'Angleterre (tel. 03 21 99 59 50), across from the post office, **exchanges currency** Mon.-Fri. 8:30-noon and 1:30-3:30pm. 24-hr. **ATMs** are at **Crédit Agricole,** 26, rue National, **Crédit du Nord,** 37, rue Faidherbe, and **Caisse d'Epargne,** on the corner of rues St-Nicholas and des Pipots.

Trains: Gare Boulogne-Ville, bd. Voltaire (tel. 08 36 35 35 35). To: Paris (8 per day, 3hr., 157F); Lille (8 per day, 2½hr., 102F); and Calais (12 per day, ½hr., 40F). **Lockers** 5-10F. Information office open Mon.-Sat. 9:15am-noon and 2-6:45pm.

Ferries: Hoverspeed (tel. 0 800 90 17 77). Car Ferry to Folkestone every 3hr. from 10:30am-9pm, with one early (7:30am) and one late (12:15am) trip added Fri.-Mon. 240F roundtrip. Bicycles 40F. Call for discounts, exact times, and prices.

Public Transportation: Buses going all directions pull into the train station and the bus depot at pl. de France regularly. Buy tickets on the bus (4-6F). For more info call **Espace Bus,** 14, rue de la Lampe (tel. 03 21 83 51 51).

Taxis: at the train station or **Radio Taxi Boulogne** (tel. 03 21 91 25 00).

Bike Rental: Cycles Berquez, 20, pl. de France (tel. 03 21 31 34 41). ½-day 50F, full day 80F. 1000F or passport deposit. Open 9am-noon and 2-7pm.

Laundromat: 62, rue de Lille. Wash 16F per 10kg. Dry 2F per 5min.

Helplines: SOS Amitié (tel. 03 21 71 01 71). **SOS Solitude** (tel. 03 21 32 99 00).

Hospital: Hôpital Duchenne, allée Jacques Monad (tel. 03 21 99 33 33). From pl. Frédéric Sauvage, follow rue de la Lampe away from the canal to rue Victor Hugo (which becomes rue Nationale). Take a right and continue under train tracks, across rue de Brequerecque, onto rue Ed. Branly, and finally onto rue de l'Hôpital. **Medical emergency** tel. 03 21 90 33 15.

Police: 9, rue Percochel (tel. 03 21 83 12 34). Follow bd. Danou out of pl. Frédéric Sauvage for one block, then turn left onto rue Percochel. **Emergency** tel. 17.

Post Office: pl. Frédéric Sauvage (tel. 03 21 99 09 09). Poste restante (postal code: 62321). Open Mon.-Fri. 8:30am-6:30pm, Sat. 8:30am-noon. **Postal code:** 62200.

ACCOMMODATIONS AND FOOD

There are many hotel rooms in the 120-200F range, especially clustered near the ferry terminal. During the peak season, weekends, and when there's something special going on, these rooms fill up quickly; call ahead or show up early.

Auberge de Jeunesse (HI), 1, place de Lisle (tel. 03 21 80 14 50; fax 03 21 80 45 62), across from the *Gare-Ville.* The best in hostel accommodations. Three terrific beds per well-decorated non-smoking room. Shower and toilet in each room. Dining hall, kitchen, pool table, bar with TV/VCR and karaoke. 83F includes breakfast. Members only. Reception 7:30am-1am. Curfew 1am. In July and Aug., reserve a week in advance in writing or by phone with V or MC. Handicapped accessible. Come to Boulogne because you missed your train…stay for the hostel.

Hôtel Hamiot, 1, rue Faidherbe (tel. 03 21 31 45 06). Across the street from the tourist office and facing the canal. Tidy, simple accommodations. Singles and doubles 120-210F. Extra bed 50F. Breakfast 28F. Small pets 30F. V, MC.

Hôtel le Mirador, 2-4, rue de la Lampe (tel. 03 21 31 38 08; fax 03 21 83 21 79), off bd. Danou. Faces the canal and pl. d'Angleterre. Large, airy rooms. Singles 130-190F. Doubles 130-220F. Triples 260F. Extra bed 45F. Hall shower 25F. V, MC.

Hôtel Au Sleeping, 18, bd. Daunou (tel. 03 21 80 62 79). Near the train station. Housing project exterior, pleasant rooms, telephones. The charm is in the prices. Singles and doubles 100-200F. Triples 140-200F. Reception 7am-9pm. V, MC.

Food shops abound, especially in the area around the tourist office. A **P.G. Supermarché,** 54, rue Daunou (which begins at the north end of pl. d'Angleterre in the Centre Liane), shakes its booty about 500m from the tourist office (open Mon.-Sat. 9am-8pm). Next to the supermarket is a **Maraset Cafeteria,** where a steak and veggies go for 28F (open Sun.-Fri. 11:30am-9pm, Sat. 11:30am-10pm). An excellent **market** is held every Wednesday and Saturday 7:30am-12:30pm on pl. Dalton. Charming restaurants cluster on **rue de Lille** in the *vieille ville.* Not-so-charming but cheap food is to be found on the waterfront around **pl. Gambetta. Le Volcano,** 4, rue de Faidherbe (tel. 03 21 32 30 61), has pizza (starts at 27F), salads (20-30F), mussels and fries (35F), and a *menu* for 68F or 90F (open daily noon-midnight). Soak in the atmosphere of the *vieille ville* at **Joly-Desenclos,** 44, rue de Lille (tel. 03 21 80 50 52). Quiches 27F, salads from 12F, omelettes 25F, crêpes from 8F (open daily 7:30am-8pm). Escape the fish and ferries in the bars and cafés lining **pl. Dalton.**

SIGHTS

Boulogne's *vieille ville* stands atop the hill where the Romans settled to watch their domain. The 13th-century wall surrounds a labyrinth of bewitchingly crooked streets. Walk on the ramparts for terrific views of the harbor, town, and countryside.

The massive **Château-Musée** (tel. 03 21 10 02 20, 03 21 80 56 78 for a tour in French or English), rue de Bernet, dominates the eastern corner of the ramparts. Built around 1230, it houses an art collection of astounding size, scope, and beauty which includes Greek vases, local earthenware pottery, and last but not least, Napoleon's second-oldest hat. (May 15-Sept. 14 open Mon.-Sat. 9:30am-12:30pm and 1:30-6:15pm, Sun. 9:30am-12:30pm and 2:30pm-6:15pm; Sept. 15-May 14 Mon.-Sat. 10am-12:30pm and 2-5pm, Sun. 10am-12:30pm and 2:30-5:30pm. Admission 20F, students 13F.) Inside the walls, on pl. Godefroy de Boillon, the 13th-century **beffroi** (belfry) of the Hôtel de Ville sends acrophobes into a swoon with its dizzying view of the port and claustrophobes into a panic with its narrow and treacherous staircase (open Mon.-Fri. 8am-6pm, Sat. 8am-noon; free).

Just down rue de Lille is the 19th-century **Basilique de Notre-Dame,** which sits above the labyrinthine **crypts** of a 12th-century edifice. One of the 14 chambers contains the remnants of a 3rd-century Roman temple; another exhibits relics and religious objects. (Crypt and treasury open Tues.-Sun. 2-5pm. Admission 10F. Church open Mon.-Sat. 8am-noon and 2-7pm, Sun 8:30am-12:30pm and 2:30-7pm.)

When the residents of Boulogne aren't catching fish or eating them, they're admiring them at the high-tech **Nausicaa,** bd. Ste-Beuve (tel. 03 21 30 99 99), which feeds its visitors a fascinating multilingual flow of information at each aquarium exhibit. A favorite of quivering schools of children, Nausicaa can be crowded and claustropho-

THE NORTH

Take a Hike!

You've had one mussel and one ferry too many. Don't panic! The coast between Calais and Boulogne is 30km of the most beautiful scenery this side of the *Manche.* From Boulogne, the dunes turn to creamy-colored cliffs. Trails line the coast past deserted bunkers, gently rolling fields, and tourist-free beaches. Route D940 runs through several charming coastal towns including Audresselles, Wimereux, and Ambletense (where you'll find a Napoleonic fort). So pack a picnic and head for the cliffs. **Bus** service runs Monday to Saturday—call Cariane (tel. 03 21 34 74 90) for info—and the road is a reasonable bike ride.

bic; arrive late in the day. (Open May 15-Sept. 14 daily 10am-8pm; Sept. 15-May 14 Mon.-Fri. 10am-6pm, Sat.-Sun. 10am-7pm. Closed two weeks in Jan. 50F, students 44F.) Next to Nausicaa is the **beach,** where you can rent windsurfers (60F per hr., 600F per week), catamarans (300F per 2 hr., 700F per week), and **char à voiles,** high-tech soap box racers with sails (tel. and fax 03 21 83 25 48).

In the evening check out the bars and brasseries at pl. Dalton, in particular the cozy **Pub "J.F. Kennedy,"** 20, rue du Doyen (tel. 03 21 83 97 05), serving mounds o' *moules* (42F) and beer (15F). Open 9am-2am, food noon-11pm.

Montreuil-sur-Mer

When Victor Hugo visited Montreuil-sur-Mer in 1837, he quipped that "Montreuil-on-the-sea" would have been better named "Montreuil-on-the-field." Not a drop of sea water has been seen since the 10th century in this, one of France's earliest ports. Fortunately for Montreuil, when the fickle sea retreated she left a rich countryside fed by the Canche river. Montreuil and its surroundings are an idyllic location for tranquil walks, hikes, and picnics. Although the town could not keep its ocean, it did preserve its history. Its cobblestone streets, painted cottages, Gothic edifices, and crumbling castle are a testament to a thousand years of struggle and graceful endurance. The town that inspired parts of *Les Misérables* shines unpretentiously as a tourist-free break from Boulogne and the port towns.

ORIENTATION AND PRACTICAL INFORMATION

To reach the **tourist office,** 6 pl. de la Poisonnerié (tel. 03 21 06 04 27), in the heart of the citadel on pl. Darnetal, climb the stairs across from the *gare* and turn right on av. du 11 Novembre. Pass under the door of the citadel veering left onto the cavée St-Firnan. Turn left again onto rue du Mont Hulin and continue past the church to pl. Gambetta. Walk through Gambetta and turn right into the square. The charming staff won't make reservations but will distribute a free map and brochures galore (open Tues.-Sat. 10am-12:30pm and 2-6:30pm). There are several **banks** and **ATMs** about, such as **BNP** (tel. 03 21 06 03 98), pl. Darnetal (open Tues.-Sat. 8:30am-noon and 1:30-5pm) and **Crédit du Nord,** pl. de Gaulle. Montreuil's **train station** (tel. 03 21 06 05 09) lies just outside the walls of the citadel in the *ville-basse.* Trains dash to Boulogne (6 per day, ½hr., 37F); Arras (8 per day, 1½hr., 69F); Calais (4 per day, 1hr., 65F); and Lille (7 per day, 2hr., 90F). The ticket office is open Mon.-Fri. 5am-7:45pm, Sat. 5:45am-7:45pm, and Sun. 7:30am-7:45pm. Because of its narrow medieval streets, Montreuil must be tackled on foot. To get into the countryside, rent **bicycles** from **Oxygène,** 11, pl. de Gaulle (tel. 03 21 86 14 25). One hour 25F, ½-day 50F, full day 80F, one week 400F (open Tues.-Sat. 9am-12:30pm and 2-7:30pm, Sun.-Mon. 2-7:30pm). There is a **hospital** (tel. 03 21 89 45 45) at 2, rue des Juifs. **Medical emergency** tel. 15; for **police,** dial 17. The **post office** (tel. 03 21 06 04 50), pl. Gambetta, is open Tues.-Fri. 9am-noon and 2:30-5:30pm, Sat. 8:30-11:30am.

ACCOMMODATIONS, CAMPING, AND FOOD

The **Auberge de Jeunesse (HI), "La Hulotte"** (tel. 03 21 06 10 83), in the citadel on rue Carnot, is in a castle built between the 10th and 14th centuries. Closed on Tuesdays. Access to kitchen (and to the citadel ramparts after hours). 40F per person. **L'Ecu du France,** 5 Porte de France (tel. 03 21 06 01 89) offers a vine-covered courtyard, terrific views, and clean, bright rooms (singles and doubles 150-180F; breakfast 25F). Across the way is **Au Pigeon Blanc,** pl. de Gaulle (tel. 03 21 06 04 95). Pink wallpaper, leopard skin bedcovers—kitsch, but clean and conveniently located (singles and doubles 150-275F; breakfast 25F; extra bed 50F). There's a beautiful **campground** in the *ville-basse,* 744, route d'Etaples (tel. 03 21 06 07 28). By the banks of the river; pool, restaurant, and tennis nearby (36F with car, 22F without).

La Paloma (tel. 03 21 86 36 75), pl. de Gaulle, whips up salads (15-40F), pasta (38F), and omelettes (30F) with Italian flair (open daily 9:30am-10pm; V, MC). Right next door you'll find **Le Caveau** (tel. 03 21 06 05 21), pl. de Gaulle, serving pizza from 38F, 10F beers, and a 49F *menu* (open Mon.-Sat. 10:30am-11pm). **Le Renouveau** (tel. 03 21 06 04 23), 26, rue d'Hérambault, offers pepper steak and *frites* for 62F and Belgian waffles (10F) along with foosball, a pool table, and a jukebox stuck on country and French techno. *C'est cool!* (Open Mon.-Sat. 7:30am-8pm.) Picnic fare bides its time at **Supermarket Cedico** (tel. 03 21 06 04 69), pl. de Gaulle (open Tues.-Fri. 8:45am-12:30pm and 2-7:15pm, Sat. 8:45am-7pm, and Sun. 9am-noon).

SIGHTS AND ENTERTAINMENT

Walking atop the 3km-long **ramparts** surrounding Montreuil is like walking on the firmament. Green rivers below slip through thick fields of wildflowers. Stop along the way to visit the **citadel,** a castle that served as the entrance to and defense of the town for six centuries before Vauban reinforced it. Montreuil has seen military action from the Norman invasion through World War I (citadel open Wed.-Mon. 9am-noon and 2-6pm; adults 10F, children 6F). Tumbledown timber cottages line the **rues Pittoresques;** most notable are the **rue du Clape en Bas** and the **Cavée St-Firmin.** Walking down them, you can recapture the Montreuil of Hugo's time. The author set scenes of *Les Misérables* here after visiting during an economic slump. On these streets, fictionally speaking, the convict Jean Valjean became a factory-owner and mayor, and Fantine breathed her last. They did so more tangibly for Richard Boleslawski's cameras, which shot the 1935 film version of Hugo's novel here. The **Chapel de l'Hôtel Dieu** and the **St-Salure Abbey** are intricately carved Gothic churches dating from the 13th century.

August 15th brings the **Day of the Street Painters.** The small-but-mighty **Malins Plaisirs,** is an exuberant celebration of theater, opera, and dance starting the third week of August. The tourist office publishes an annual calendar of events.

Calais

When Calais, England's last French possession, finally fell to the French Duke of Guise in 1558, Queen Mary lamented bitterly, saying that when she died, the name "Calais" would be found engraved on her heart. Today, Calais (pop. 80,000) does not carve itself on anyone's heart, though 16 million voyagers pass through this convenient port annually on their way to fairer lands. The commercial center, while gaudy, is carefully laid out, and Calais has pleasant parks and an attractive sea coast. As you wait for your ship to come in, the **Musée des Beaux Arts** and the flamboyant **Hôtel de Ville** with Rodin's *Burghers of Calais* outside will carve away the minutes.

ORIENTATION AND PRACTICAL INFORMATION

The Calais-Ville **train station** (in the town center) offers connections to most major French cities. Free **buses** connect the hoverport, ferry terminal, and train station every 30 minutes in the daytime. A gliding **hovercraft** is the fastest way across the Channel and costs just a bit more than ferries (35min. by hovercraft, 1½hr. by ferry).

The town's shopping and restaurant district lies on one main drag which goes through five names: bd. Pasteur, bd. Jacquard, bd. Clemenceau, rue Royale, and rue de la Mer. Avoid the area around the ferry terminals and harbor at night.

Tourist Information: Tourist Office, 12, bd. Clemenceau (tel. 03 21 96 62 40; fax 03 21 96 01 92), 1 block from the *gare* (turn left, cross bridge, on your right in the middle of the block). Free reservations, map. Better map 16F. **Currency exchange.** Open Mon.-Sat. 9am-7pm. **Le Nord-Littaral** is the city's newspaper.

Money: Exchange rates are disheartening everywhere, so you might as well change money at the ferry or hovercraft terminals (both 24hr.), the post office, or the banks lining the main drag. **Crédit Lyonnais,** bd. Jacquard, has an **ATM.**

Trains: Gare Calais-Ville, bd. Jacquard (tel. 08 36 35 35 35). To: Paris (8 per day, 3hr., 177F; 1 TGV per day, 1¾hr., 220F); Lille (14 per day, 1½hr., 81F); Boulogne (20 per day, 30min., 39F); Dunkerque (3 per day, 1hr., 43F); Etaples/Le Toquet (15 per day, 45min., 59F). Info office open Mon.-Fri. 9:30am-6:30pm, Sat. 9am-5:30pm. Ticket office open daily 4:30am-8pm. **Lockers** 30F per day.

Buses: 10, rue d'Amsterdam (tel. 03 21 34 74 40; fax 03 21 97 73 33). Office open Mon.-Fri. 8am-noon and 2-6pm. To Dunkerque (10 per day, 2hr., 25F50) and Boulogne (2 per day, 1hr., 24F).

Ferries: Hoverspeed, Hoverport (tel. 0 800 90 17 77; fax 03 21 46 14 56). To Dover (every hr. on the hr., 1½hr., one-way or 5-day return 240F, with Interail pass 172F, open return 470F). **SeaFrance,** Car Ferry Terminal (tel. 03 21 46 80 00). To Dover (every ½hr., 1½hr., one-way or 5-day return 230F, students 200F; open return 440F, students 400F). Office at 2, pl. d'Armes (tel. 03 21 34 55 00), in the shadow of the Tour du Guet. Open Mon.-Thurs. 9:30am-12:30pm and 1:30-6pm, Fri. closes at 5:50pm. **P&O Ferries,** Car Ferry Terminal. To Dover (every 45min., 1¼hr., one-way or 5-day return 220F, open return 440F). Office at 41, pl. d'Armes (tel. 03 21 46 04 40). Open Mon.-Fri. 8:30am-6pm, Sat. 8:30am-noon. Bikes free, but riders must board with the cars. Call for specific times and prices.

Deep-Sea Tunnels: Two types of train link Britain and France via the Channel Tunnel, or *Tunnel sous la Manche:* the "Eurostar" passenger trains and "Le Shuttle," a private company that moves those with cars or motorcycles under the waves. For Eurostar info and reservations, call 08 36 35 35 39. Le Shuttle leaves from **Gare TGV Frethun** (take bus 7 from Gare Calais-Ville), 550F-1030F for a car, 320F-600F for a motorcycle. 7am-11pm, 3 TGVs per hour; 11pm-7am, 1 TGV every 75min. Call 03 21 00 61 00 for reservations and schedule. Also see page 42.

Public Transportation: STCE, 16, rue Caillette (tel. 03 21 36 45 65). Bus 3 (direction: Blériot/Plage) from the train station is your ticket to ride to the beach, with its youth hostel and campgrounds (4F50-6F50).

Taxi: Taxis Radio Calais (TRC) (tel. 03 21 97 13 14) gives friendly, 24-hr. service.

Car Rental: pl. d'Armes. **Budget** (tel. 03 21 96 42 20), open Mon.-Fri. 8am-noon and 2-6:30pm; Sat. 8am-noon and 2-6pm. **Avis** (tel. 03 21 34 66 50), open Mon.-Sat. 8am-12:30pm and 2-7pm. **Hertz** (tel. 0 800 05 33 11), open Mon.-Sat. 8am-noon and 2-7:30pm.

Laundromat: Lavorama, pl. d'Armes near Match supermarket. Wash 7kg for 16F. Dry 8min. for 2F. Detergent 2F. Open daily 7am-9pm.

Helpline: SOS Amitié (tel. 03 21 71 07 71), when you need a (French) friend.

Hospital: L'Hôpital du Calais, 11, quai du Commerce (tel. 03 21 46 33 33). **Medical emergency** tel. 15.

Police: pl. de Lorraine (tel. 03 21 97 53 17). **Emergency** tel. 17.

Post Office: pl. d'Alsace. Photocopies. Poste restante. Open Mon.-Fri. 8:30am-6pm, Sat. 8:30-11.30am. **Postal code:** 62100.

ACCOMMODATIONS, CAMPING, AND FOOD

Many travelers in Calais must stay the night, and hotels take advantage of their captive audience. You can stay in hostel heaven at the huge **Centre Européen de Séjour,** but budget hotels are few and fill up quickly in summer.

Centre Européen de Séjour/Auberge de Jeunesse (HI), av. Maréchal Delattre de Tassigny (tel. 03 21 34 70 20; fax 03 21 96 87 80), 1 block from the beach. From the train station, turn left and follow the main drag through its chameleonic name changes past place d'Armes; cross the bridge and take your first left onto bd. Général de Gaulle. Walk past the funny-looking white sports center and take the first right onto rue Alice Marie (looks like a parking lot); the wonderful white hostel is the third building on your left. Or take bus 3 from the station (4F50, every 20min., 8am-8pm). 162 beds in 84 spiffy rooms. Pairs of rooms share an adjoining bathroom. Pool table, TV, bar, cafeteria. 77F per night with breakfast. Non-members pay 10F extra and can stay only one night. Sheets 16F. First-rate cafeteria open Mon.-Sat. 7-9am, noon-1pm, and 5-8pm. No dinner served on Sat. **Bicycle rental** 60F per day and passport deposit. 24-hr. reception.

Hôtel le Littoral, 71, rue Aristide Briand (tel. 03 21 34 47 28). Friendly management and comfortable rooms near station. Singles 100-140F, with shower 160F. Doubles 140-160F, with shower 170F. Triples 170F, with shower 190F. Quads 200F. Hall shower 15F. Breakfast 25F. Reception noon-10pm. V, MC.

Hôtel Victoria, 8, rue du Commandant Bonningue (tel. 03 21 34 38 32). A short taxi ride from ferries or the *gare.* Blossoms with cheerful, pretty rooms in floral decor, each with its own TV and telephone. Singles 147-197F. Doubles 164-224F. Triples 231-281F. Quads 258-303F. Extra bed 48F. Breakfast 28F. V, MC, AmEx.

Camping: Camping Municipal, 26, av. Raymond Poincaré (tel. 03 21 97 89 79), off rue Royale. Packs 'em in like sardines, but makes up for crowding with a great location 1 block from the beach, near the hostel. 27F per person, 44F for two. Showers free. Reception open Mon.-Sat. 8am-noon and 2-5pm, Sun. 8am-noon.

Calais caters to that strange breed looking for boring food at middling prices in multilingual tourist traps. Rebel and make for the **market** at pl. Crèvecoeur (Thurs. and Sat. mornings) or pl. d'Armes (Wed. and Sat. mornings). Otherwise, look for a *boulangerie* on bd. Gambetta, bd. Jacquard, and rue des Thermes or supermarket—**Match,** pl. d'Armes (open Mon-Fri. 9am-12:30pm and 2:30-7:30pm, Sat. 9am-7:30pm), or **Prisunic,** 17, bd. Jacquard (open Mon.-Sat. 8:30am-7:30pm, Sun. 9am-7pm). If you feel like a cooked meal, any of the restaurants along **rue Royale** and **bd. Jacquard** will do. The hostel and campsite's cafeterias are filling and inexpensive.

SIGHTS

Rodin's moving sculpture, **The Burghers of Calais,** stands in the garden of the **Hôtel de Ville** (tel. 03 21 46 62 00), telling a story from the Hundred Years War. In 1347, six of the town's most respected citizens surrendered the keys to the city and offered themselves for hanging to England's King Edward III in exchange for the lives of the starving townspeople. Thanks to an eleventh-hour intervention by Edward's French wife Philippine, the Burghers kept their lives. (Hôtel de Ville open Mon.-Fri. 8am-noon and 1:30-5:30pm.) Another casting of the statue graces the courtyard of Paris's **Musée Rodin** (see page 135).

Directly across from the town hall, in Parc St-Pierre, a camouflaged bunker served as the German navy's principal telephone exchange from 1941 to 1944. The building now houses the **War Museum** (tel. 03 21 34 21 57), an uninspiring collection of military artillery and uniforms (open Wed.-Mon. 10am-6pm). The nicest part of Calais is its **beach;** follow rue Royale through its name changes to bd. Jacquard until the road ends. Walk west along the shore, away from Calais' unattractive harbor.

Le Musée des Beaux-Arts et de la Dentelle, (tel. 03 21 46 63 17), rue Richelieu, near the tourist office and *gare,* houses a collection of lace, as well as older Flemish and Dutch paintings and some modern pieces by Picasso, Dubuffet, and Alechinsky (open Wed.-Mon. 10am-noon, 2-5:30pm; 15F admission, 10F student, free Wed.).

The place to be in Calais at night is the **rue Royale** along the main drag. Disco off your sea legs at the popular **555,** 63, rue Royale (tel. 03 21 34 36 75). (Open Tues.-Sun. 10:30pm-4am, Sun. "*matinee*" 3-7pm. Tues.-Fri., Sun. 50F with drink, Sat. 70F with drink, Sun. "*matinee*" 35F without drink.)

Dunkerque

Despite its position as France's third largest sea port, Dunkerque (pop. 74,000) feels more residential than commercial. Unlike other port cities, Dunkerque absorbs its voyagers without sinking under their weight. Dunkerque survived Flemish, Burgundian, Spanish, and English rule before becoming definitively French in 1662. Its Flemish past is evident in the architecture of the *vieille ville,* but the scars of the German invasion and the Allied defense of the town are fresher. Dunkerque's darkest hour came in June, 1940, when battleships, yachts, rowboats, and anything else British that could float gathered here to evacuate the last defenders of France escaping the advancing German army. Over eighty percent of Dunkerque was razed during the war, but the *Dunkerquois* have rebuilt a bustling and prosperous city. The beaches of its suburb **Malo-les-Bains** make a great summer escape.

ORIENTATION AND PRACTICAL INFORMATION

Dunkerque lies on N1, 40km from Calais and 20km from the Belgian border. To reach the tourist office from the station, go straight ahead through pl. de la Gare to rue du Chemin de Fer and follow the main drag, **bd. Alexandre III,** which becomes rue Clemenceau when it veers to the left at pl. Jean Bart. After a block on rue Clemenceau, take a left onto rue Ronarch. The office is on the corner in the belfry.

Tourist Information: Tourist Office, rue Amiral Ronarch (tel. 03 28 66 79 21 or 03 28 26 27 28; fax 03 28 26 27 80), on the ground floor of the belfry. Excellent maps. Hotel reservations. **Currency exchange.** Open Mon.-Fri. 9am-12:30pm and 1:30-6:30pm, Sat. 9am-6:30pm. **Branch office** at the beach, 48, digue de Mer (tel. 03 28 26 28 88). Open daily 9am-noon and 1-7pm, April-Sept. only. Ask for **Dunkerque Magazine,** a monthly with info on local events.

Money: Crédit Agricole, 15, rue Amiral Ronarch, across the street from the tourist office, has a 24-hr. **ATM.**

Trains: pl. de la Gare (tel. 08 36 35 35 35). To: Paris (15 TGVs per day, 1½-2hr., 239F); Arras (21 per day, 1½hr., 86F); Lille (21 per day, 1-1½hr., 70F); Calais (7 per day, 1hr., 42F); Boulogne (6 per day, 1½hr., 68F). Ticket window open daily 5am-8pm; info office open daily 6:30am-6:30pm. **Lockers** 15-30F.

Ferries: Sally (tel. 03 28 26 70 70; fax 03 28 21 45 94), entrance to ticket office on rue des Fusilliers Marins. Three-minute walk from the train station. Walk out onto ave. Guynemer, turn left onto rue de Lille. At the fork in the road, turn right onto rue de Fusiliers. To Ramsgate (5 per day, 2½hr., one-way 70-90F, adult and child 60-80F, roundtrip adult 90-110F and child 70-90F). Car rates depend on the number of passengers, season, and time of day. 440-1060F one-way with one adult. Call ahead for prices and reservations. Student discount 25% weekdays, 10% weekends. Office open daily 9am-6pm. Ferry terminal open daily 7am-midnight.

Public Transportation: (tel. 03 28 59 00 78); extensive system; free maps at the tourist office, electronic information system at train station. Buses run every 10-20min. from 6am-9pm. Tickets 8F, *carnet* of 10 44F.

Taxis: (tel. 03 28 66 73 00), at the train station and pl. Jean Bart. Dunkerque center to Malo-les-Bains about 50F in the evening.

Car Rental: Avis, 9, rue Belle Vue (tel. 03 28 66 67 95). **Hertz,** 8 av. Guynemer (tel. 03 28 59 25 13). Be sure to call ahead.

Bike Rental: Loca Plage, 40, av. du Casino (tel. 03 28 63 66 06). 120F per day. 100F or passport deposit. Open daily 9am-8pm.

Laundromat: Superlav, 78, rue Faidherbe, 2 blocks from hostel. Wash 5kg for 16F, 7kg for 20F. Dry 2F per 4min. Open 8am-7pm.

Bookstore: Maxi-Livres, 25, pl. Jean Bart (tel. 03 28 65 06 63). A section of anglo-bargains. Open Mon. 2-7:30pm, Tues.-Sat. 9:30am-noon and 2-7:30pm.

Helplines: SOS Amitié (tel. 03 20 55 77 77). A friend in need is a 24-hr. friend.

Hospital: Hôpital de Dunkerque, 130, av. Louis Herbeaux (tel. 03 28 29 59 00). From the station, follow rue Chemin de Fer onto bd. Alexandre III. Turn left onto rue Clemenceau, then right on rue du Leughenaer, then right again onto av. Louis Herbeaux. **Medical emergency** tel. 15.

Police: quai des Hollandais (tel. 03 28 64 51 09). Follow rue Clemenceau to the pl. du Minck and turn left onto quai de Hollandais. **Emergency** tel. 17.

Post Office: 20, rue du Président Poincaré (tel. 03 28 65 91 65), on pl. de Gaulle. Photocopies 1F. Poste restante. **ATM. Currency exchange** with good rates. Open Mon.-Fri. 8:30am-6:30pm, Sat. 8:30am-noon. **Postal code:** 59140.

ACCOMMODATIONS AND CAMPING

Dunkerque is filled with reasonably priced hotels. Though finding a room should not be a problem, reservations are always a good idea, especially in July and August.

Auberge de Jeunesse (HI), pl. Paul-Asseman (tel. 03 28 63 36 34; fax 03 28 69 52 57), on the beach. From station, take bus 3 (until 9pm) to "Piscine." Turn left and walk past pool and rink. Barrack-like hostel will be on your right, with official hostel doberman in front. Walking, exit the train station onto av. Guynemar. Turn left onto rue de Bergues, which becomes rue des Fusiliers Marins. Follow the shore, passing a three-masted ship on your left, as it becomes quai Hollandais and you reach pl. du Minck. Cross left to rue du Leughenaer and follow it to pl. de la Victoire; turn left onto av. des Bains. Cross the Bains bridge and turn left onto allée Fenelon; pl. Asseman is ahead on the right. The doberman's still there. (30min.) Single-sex, army-bunker 8-bed rooms, cramped but clean. Co-ed bathrooms. Members only. Curfew 11pm, none July-Aug. 44F. Sheets 16F. Breakfast 18F. Meal 42F

Hôtel Eole, 77-79, digue de Mer (tel. 03 28 69 13 64; fax 03 28 69 52 57), on the beach in Malo-les-Bains. Tacky wallpaper doesn't detract from astounding sea views or friendly service. Singles 150-220F. Doubles 180-250F. Restaurant downstairs. Reserve well in advance. 24-hr. reception. V, MC.

Hôtel le Lion d'Or, 2, rue de Chemin de Fer (tel. 03 28 66 08 24). Attentive management keeps clean, simple rooms near the station. Rooms are cheerful and warm. Singles 90F. Doubles 110-120F. Breakfast 22F. Reception 24hr. V, MC.

Hôtel du Tigre, 8, rue Clemenceau (tel. and fax 03 28 66 75 17). Pleasant, simple rooms. Singles 90F, with shower, phone, and TV 170F. Doubles 120F, with shower and TV 220F. Extra bed 50F. Breakfast 33F. No hall showers. 24-hr. reception. V, MC.

Camping: Dunkerque Camping Municipal, bd. de l'Europe (tel. 03 28 69 26 68). Take bus 3 (every 20min., 6am-9pm) to "Malo CES Camping" or follow av. des Bains east for 4km. Really rough it with free shower, TV, and pool. 50F per adult, 37F50 per child, tent 10F, car and caravan 11F. Electricity 18F. Reception 7am-8pm July-Aug.; Sept.-June open 7am-6pm.

FOOD

Reasonably priced restaurants abound in Dunkerque, especially along the beach and near the center of town. *Moules* (mussels) in various wine sauces are a local specialty. Try the Flemish *potje vlesch*, a *dunkerquois* dish made with rabbit, chicken, and lamb in aspic, served cold. Vegetarians and picnic fiends will find the giant **Uniprix,** pl. République, sympathetic to their plight. (Open Mon.-Sat. 8:30am-8pm.) There is also a **market** (Wed. and Sat. 9am-4pm) at pl. Général de Gaulle.

Le Roi de la Moule, 129, Dique de la Mer (tel. 03 28 69 25 37). Fresh fish and mussels served in tasteful family-run restaurant. Seafood specialties 60-80F. Open Thurs.-Tues. noon-2pm and 7-10pm. V, MC.

Tête d'Ail, 26, rue Terquem (tel. 03 28 66 22 03), near the Musée des Beaux-Arts. Intimate, decorated in teal and florals. Traditional French seafood dishes, many in garlic *(ail)* sauces. The 80F 3-course *menu* is daunting, as is the 47F lunch *menu.* Open March-Oct. Mon.-Fri. noon-1:30pm and 7pm-2am, Sat. 7:30pm-2am, Sun. noon-1:30pm. V, MC.

Restaurant La Fondue, 37, rue de Bourgogne (tel. 03 28 63 23 90). Elegant, charming restaurant serves large fondues for two (63-89F). Open Mon.-Fri. noon-3:30pm and at 7:30-10pm, Sat. 7:30-10pm. V, MC.

SIGHTS AND ENTERTAINMENT

Though not extraordinarily beautiful, the beach area of **Malo-les-Bains** is a focal point of *dunkerquois* activity on sunny days in summer. Cafés and bars line the **digue de Allieés** and the **digue de Mer.** Jet skis and windsurfing equipment can be rented on the beach. A few blocks away, Dunkerque's tiny aquarium, the **Musée Aquarophile,** 45, av. du Casino (tel. 03 28 59 19 18), hides 1000 exotic fish amid the greenery of the **Jardin Malo.** (Open Wed.-Mon. 10am-noon and 2-6pm. Admission 12F, students 6F, Sun. free. On rainy days, call ahead to make sure it's open.)

Directly opposite the tourist office on rue Clemenceau, the 15th-century **Eglise St-Eloi** shelters Flemish paintings inside its impressive Gothic walls. The church is the final resting place of Jean Bart (1650-1702), the famous pirate who became admiral of the Royal Navy under Louis XIV. The church's 500-year-old **belfry,** across the street, houses 48 bells. Most impressive among these is the enormous seven-ton "Jean Bart" bell (the townsfolk have a fondness for naming anything and everything after this favorite son). In the summer, the belfry's viewing deck surveys the city. (Open July-Aug. Tues.-Sun., elevators hourly 9:30am-5:30pm; admission 12F, children 8F. Closed in inclement weather.)

One pass (adult 20F, student 10F) gains you admission to Dunkerque's two art museums (both open Wed.-Mon. 10am-noon and 2-6pm). The **Musée des Beaux-Arts** (tel. 03 28 66 21 57), near the theater on pl. du Général de Gaulle, houses a collection of 16th- to 18th-century paintings by French and Flemish artists, many from the Dunkerque area. The ground floor presents a large collection of model ships chronicling advances in naval technology through the centuries. Across the bridge from the youth hostel, eccentrically manicured paths enclose wacky modern sculptures in the garden of the **Musée d'Art Contemporain,** rue des Bains (tel. 03 28 59 21 65). Unless you're a serious fan of modern art, you may be less thrilled by the zany sculptures and paintings inside the building, a postmodern castle shaped like a paper sailor's hat (museum open Wed.-Mon. 10am-noon and 2-5:30pm; garden open daily 9:30am-8pm in summer; until 6:30 in spring and fall and 5:30 in winter).

To learn more about this port city's historic sea trade, visit the **Musée Portuaire,** 9, quai de la Citadelle (tel. 03 28 63 33 29), housed in a 19th-century tobacco factory, one of the few buildings not destroyed during World War II (open July-Aug. Wed.-Mon. 10am-6pm; Sept.-June 10am-noon and 2-6pm).

The **Maison des Jeunes et de la Culture Terre Neuve,** 43, rue du docteur Louis Lemaire (tel. 03 28 66 47 89), offers a bit of everything—an art gallery, a jazz club three nights each month (except from July-Sept.), and a nightly cinema, **Studio 43,** that runs the gamut from cult to cute. Adults 30F, students 25F. (Office open Mon. 2-7pm, Tues.-Sat. 9am-noon and 2-7pm.) *Discothèques* pop up all over, especially on or near the beach. The red rocket of **NASA,** 67, digue de Mer, is a launchpad for reggae on the beach from 10pm 'til dawn, while your techno-disco dance music can be found at local favorite the **Kennedy Club,** on the edge of digue de Mer near the hostel. For do-it-yourselfers, **Amazonia,** on quai Freycinet, has popular karaoke.

Lille

Founded in the 11th century as a transit station for boats passing down the Deûle River, Lille (pop. 170,000) is no longer an island but remains an international hub just across from Brussels. In 1363, Flanders presented the town to Burgundy as dowry when Margaret of Flanders married Philip the Bold. Though it has been part of France for close to seven centuries, Charles de Gaulle's hometown has retained much of its Flemish flavor, evident in its older architecture and in the inhabitants' consumption of mussels and beer. Lille feels virtually tourist free, though it easily beats out the gaudy ports as the most inviting city in the region. A huge number of students (¼ of Lille's population) fosters a bustling and varied nightlife. Whether shopping and strolling on the festive rue Bethune or downing a beer in the intimate *vieille ville,* you can enjoy big city charms with none of the big city hassle.

ORIENTATION AND PRACTICAL INFORMATION

Lille is easy to get around, but be sure to get a map before tackling the *vieille ville,* a maze of narrow streets running from the tourist office north to the cathedral. The newer part of town, with its wide boulevards and 19th-century architecture, culminates in the **Wazemmes market.** Lille has a large shopping district; look for the super-*chic* (and super-*cher*) shops behind the **Opéra,** off pl. du Théâtre. Cheaper goods lie in the area around the tourist office, around **rue de Béthune.** The areas around the train station and the Marché de Wazemmes may be dangerous at night.

Tourist Office: pl. Rihour (tel. 03 20 30 81 00; fax 03 20 30 82 24). M. Rihour. From the *gare,* head straight down rue Faidherbe for 2 blocks and turn left through pl. du Théâtre and pl. de Gaulle. Beyond pl. de Gaulle, you'll see a huge marble monument and behind it the 15th-century castle housing the tourist office. Free maps.

Better map with walking tours 2F. Free accommodations service. **Currency exchange.** Open Mon.-Sat. 9am-7pm, Sun 10am-noon and 2-5pm.

Budget Travel: Wasteels, 25, pl. des Reignaux (tel. 03 20 06 24 24). Student rates for rail and air travel. Open Mon.-Sat. 9am-7pm.

Money: A **Crédit Agricole ATM** sits on rue Gambetta across from the Prisunic. There is also a **Banque Populaire ATM** and an automatic bill-changer (European currencies only) on rue de Béthune, across from Aux Moules.

Flights: Aéroport de Lille-Lesquin (tel. 03 20 49 68 68). Shuttles (30F) depart from *gare* every 2-3hr. Tourist office has bus schedules. Daily flights to Paris.

Trains: pl. de Gare (tel. 08 36 35 35 35). M. Gare Lille Flandres. To: Paris (21 TGV per day, 1hr., 216-340F); Arras (15 per day, 40min., 51F); Calais (10 per day, 1hr., 81F); Brussels (19 per day, 1½hr., 100F). **Currency exchange. Lockers** 15-30F.

Public Transportation: Central **bus** terminal next to the train station. **Metro and Tramway** serve the town and periphery Mon.-Sat. 5:12am-12:12am, Sun. 6:24am-6:26pm. Info at the tourist office or the office on pl. des Buisses (tel. 03 20 98 50 50). Open Mon.-Fri. 7:30am-6pm. Tickets 7F70, *carnet* of 10 60F.

Taxis: Taxi Union (tel. 03 20 06 06 06). Call the tourist office for 1-hr. taxi tours of Lille in French or English (160F).

Car Rental: Avis in the train station (tel. 03 20 06 35 35 or 03 20 06 40 32; fax 03 20 74 15 10). Economy cars at 1980F per week.

Bike Rental: Peugeot Cycles, 64, rue Leon Gambetta (tel. 03 20 54 83 39). 50F per day, 1000F deposit. Open Mon. 2-7pm, Tues.-Sat. 9am-noon and 2-7pm.

English Books: Le Furet du Nord, 11, pl. du Général de Gaulle (tel. 03 20 78 43 13). Fair selection: classics, mysteries, science fiction, and, stranger than fiction, *Let's Go*. 5% discount with student ID. Open Mon.-Sat. 9:30am-7:30pm.

Youth Center: Centre Régional d'Information de la Jeunesse, 2, rue Nicolas Leblanc (tel. 03 20 57 86 04), at pl. de la République next to the post office. Matches riders with drivers, posts job listings and notices about local events and concerts. Open Mon. 1-6pm, Tues.-Fri. 10am-6pm, Sat. 10am-12:30pm.

Gay and Lesbian Concerns: Write to **Andromède,** BP 1016, 59011 Lille Cedex, or contact **SOS Solitude Gaie** (tel. 03 20 04 24 17). **Les Flamands Roses,** ½, rue Denis du Péage, M. Fives (tel. 03 20 47 62 65), has info on activities. **La Café des Femmes,** 19, rue du Cirque, welcomes Lille's lesbian community Wed. nights.

Laundromat: Lavotec, 137, rue Solferino (tel. 03 20 77 14 45), M. Republic. Wash 4-6 kg for 14F; dryer 4F for 5min. cycle. Open 6am-9pm.

Crisis Line: SOS Voyageurs (tel. 03 20 31 62 12), in the train station, helps travelers. Volunteer staff is usually there in the morning and afternoon.

Hospital: Cité Hospitalière, 2, av. Oscar Lambret (tel. 03 20 44 59 62), M. CHR-Oscar Lambret. **Medical emergency** tel. 15.

Police: 16, bd. du Maréchal Vaillant (tel. 03 20 62 47 47), a few blocks from M. Mairie de Lille. **Emergency** tel. 17.

Post Office: 7, pl. de la République (tel. 03 20 54 70 13). M. République. **Currency exchange** at average rates. Photocopies 1F. Poste restante (postal code: 59001). Open Mon.-Fri. 8am-6:30pm, Sat. 8am-noon. **Postal code:** 59000.

ACCOMMODATIONS

Pleasant hotels in Lille are not cheap. The **Hôtel Formule 1** (tel. 03 20 33 46 00) offers its chain charms in nearby Mons-en-Baroeul (see page 51). Ask about summer university housing at **CROUS,** or, if you're staying a month or more, the **Fédération des Etudiants,** 125, rue Meurein (tel. 03 20 30 60 26).

CROUS, 70, rue de Cambrai (tel. 03 20 88 66 00, foreign students tel. 03 20 88 66 33), offers university singles for students in the distant **Résidence Hélène Boucher** (tel. 03 20 43 43 77) and **Résidence Bachelard** (tel. 03 20 43 48 71), easily accessible by metro (M. Cité Scientific). 39F per night. 669F per month. Sheets 12F. Call Résidence office directly for lodging. Office open 9am-noon and 1:30-3pm. CROUS office open Mon.-Fri. 9am-noon and 1:30-4:30pm. 3-day advance notice required, but call as far ahead as possible.

Hôtel Saint-Nicolas: 11, rue Nicolas Leblanc (tel. 03 20 57 37 26). M. République. Every room is different in this hotel tucked away behind the Musée des Beaux-Arts.

Some rooms are gigantic. Singles 110F. Doubles 140F. 55F per additional person. Breakfast 20F. Hall shower 15F. Reception closes Sun. noon-8pm.

Hôtel Faidherbe, 42, pl. de la Gare (tel. 03 20 06 27 93; fax 03 20 55 95 38). M. Gare Lille Flandres. Clean, family-run establishment near the station. Singles 130F, with shower 150F, with shower and toilet 170F. Doubles 150F, with shower 180F. Triples 220-260F. Quads 220F. Shower 20F. Breakfast 23F. Wheelchair accessible. *Let's Go* readers get a 10% discount. 24-hr. reception. V, MC.

Hôtel des Voyageurs, 110, pl. de la Gare (tel. 03 20 06 43 14). Dark rooms are a bit musty, but near the *gare* and inexpensive. Singles 130F, with shower 150F. Doubles 150F, with shower 170F. Breakfast 15F. Reception 6am-1am. V, MC.

Camping: Les Ramiers, 1, chemin des Ramiers (tel. 03 20 23 13 42), in Bondues. Take the tramway from the *gare* to Tourcoing center; take bus 23 (direction: Bondues Eglise) to "Bondues centre," then take rue Césair Loridan 1km. 13F50 per site, 9F per person, 4F per car. Showers, electricity, volleyball. Open April-Nov.

FOOD

Inexpensive restaurants and cafés pepper the fashionable pedestrian area around **rue de Béthune,** a neighborhood also filled with *pâtisseries, boulangeries,* pizzerias, and ice cream stands. Lille is known for fish, *maroilles* cheese, *genièvre* (juniper berry liqueur), and especially mussels. **Rue Léon Gambetta** is a paradise for picnic-seekers, culminating in the enormous **Marché de Wazemmes** on pl. de la Nouvelle Aventure. Wazemmes has both an indoor market (Mon.-Thurs. 7am-1pm, Fri.-Sat. 7am-8pm, Sun. 7am-3pm) and a large outdoor market (Sun., Tues., and Thurs. mornings). Eura-Lille, the big, black shopping center next to the train station, has an enormous **Carrefour** with everything from Tintin towels to *camembert* (open daily 9am-10pm). **Prisunic supermarket** is at 125, rue Léon Gambetta (open Mon.-Sat. 8:30am-8pm), and **Shopi** is at 86, rue des Stations (open Mon. 3-7:30pm, Tues.-Sat. 9am-12:30pm and 2-7:30pm). Thanks to Lille's substantial student population, the cafés in the pedestrian section jangle through the early morning hours.

Aux Moules, 34, rue de Béthune (tel. 03 20 57 12 46). Popular hangout loved by locals for its specialty—mussels, mussels, and more mussels! (51-61F) Annually accumulates the city's (world's?) largest pile of mussel shells during the first weekend in September, when Lille empties its attics and garages for the **braderie,** a city-wide yard sale. Open daily noon-midnight. V, MC, AmEx.

Les Brasseurs, 22, pl. de la Gare (tel. 03 20 06 46 25). A Lille pub institution, renowned for Welsh rarebit (43F) and beer galore. Try a glass each of 3 different beers for 22F, 4 beers for 26F. Open daily 11am-midnight.

La Crêperie de Beaurepaire, 1, rue St-Etienne (tel. 03 20 54 60 54), 2 blocks from pl. de Gaulle. Sit in the cobblestone courtyard or join the students indoors under the beautiful vaulted ceilings. *Galettes* 11-97F, crêpes 11-33F. Open Mon.-Sat. 11:45am-2pm and 7-11pm. The pleasing food, ambience, and prices have also traveled to **Beaurepaire II,** 6, pl. du Lion d'Or (tel. 03 20 74 20 36).

Le Mahajarah, 4, rue du Sec Arembault (tel. 03 20 57 67 77), near pedestrian center. Indian restaurant specializing in tantalizing vegetarian plates 39-49F. Plenty of lamb and chicken, too. Open Mon.-Sat. noon-2pm and 7-10:30pm. V, MC.

SIGHTS AND ENTERTAINMENT

One of France's finest museums, Lille's **Musée des Beaux-Arts** (tel. 03 20 57 01 84) allegedly resides in a majestic 19th-century building on pl. de la République. Until restorations are complete—supposedly by April 1997—you'll have to settle for admiring it from the outside. Console yourself a few blocks away with the impressive Gothic **Eglise Sacré-Coeur,** rue Nationale (open daily 8am-7pm).

The **Vieille Bourse** (Old Stock Exchange), on pl. du Général de Gaulle between rue des Sept Acaches and rue Manneliers, is a triumph of the Flemish Renaissance. Its four buildings border a courtyard that once served as France's only stock exchange. It has since switched over to less cutthroat trades—today's court houses flower and book markets. Nearby stand two other masterpieces: the **Chamber of Commerce**

and Industry (tel. 03 20 63 77 77) and its tower on pl. du Théâtre, and the 14th-century **Eglise St-Maurice** (tel. 03 20 06 07 21; M. Rihour; open Mon. noon-6:30pm, Tues.-Sat. 8:30am-6:30pm, Sun. 9:45am-1pm and 5-7:30pm).

North of pl. du Théâtre stands the **Cathédrale de Notre-Dame-de-la-Treille,** pl. Notre-Dame-de-la-Treille (tel. 03 20 31 57 98), an unfinished neo-Gothic church begun in the 19th century (open daily 2-5:30pm). Despite the unappealing brick of the west façade, the church contains some fine chapels, interesting choir masonry, and, if you can catch it, the **Musée Diocésain d'Art Réligieux,** in the crypt (open Sat. 4-5pm, 1st Sun. of each month 11am-noon; free).

The **Musée de l'Hospice Comtesse,** 32, rue de la Monnaie (tel. 03 20 49 50 90), was founded in 1237 and used as a hospital in the 1400s. Now it displays antique furniture and art but is most noted for the 17th-century tilework on its walls. There is also an exhibit on musical instruments with violins of all shapes and sizes and a clarinet in the shape of a snake. Some 16th- and 17th-century Flemish and Danish paintings from the Musée des Beaux-Arts are here temporarily (open Wed.-Mon. 10am-12:30pm and 2-6pm; admission 10F, Wed. and Sat. afternoons free).

The Musée d'Art Moderne, 1, allée du Musée (tel. 03 20 05 42 46), in the Parc Urbain, houses a surprisingly important collection of Cubist and postmodern art, including works by Braque, Picasso, Léger, Miro, and Modigliani. Take Bus 10 or 41 to "Parc Urbain-Musée" (open Wed.-Mon. 10am-6pm; adults 25F, students 15F).

Charles de Gaulle's birthplace at 9, rue Princesse (tel. 20 31 93 03), has a vast collection of photographs and newspaper clippings as well as his car and the dress in which the leader of the Resistance and two-time French president was baptized (open Wed.-Sun. 10am-noon and 2-5pm; admission 8F).

The **citadelle** on the city's north side is yet another fortress resculpted in the 17th century to Vauban's specifications. To enter this active army base, sign up at the tourist office for a tour in French (April-Oct. Sun. 3-4pm and 4:30-5:30pm; 35F). Otherwise, settle for a view from the **Jardin Vauban** across the street. The **Paris Gate,** on pl. Vollant, once opened onto the Roman road connecting Lille to Paris.

Students head into town to party, mostly in two distinct areas. Around **les Halles Centrales,** pubs line the **rue Sulferino** and **rue Masséna. L'Irlandais,** 160-162, rue Sulferino (tel. 03 20 57 04 74), is known for its big beers, big heart, and big crowds (open 4pm-2am). When you've lost your inhibitions and pitch, **L'Equator,** next door at 148, rue Sulferino (tel. 03 20 42 05 70), offers karaoke after 9pm. College bars and pubs line rue Masséna 3-55. For billiards, soccer, and 10F beer, head to **Gino Billiard** (tel. 03 20 54 45 55; open noon-2am). Try the meter of beer next door at **Magnum** (tel. 03 20 05 86 16)—10 glasses in a row (100F; open noon-2am).

Get in touch with your inner sophisticate in the *vieille ville,* where clubs and intimate, coffee-house-esque bars line the streets. Stumble down numbers 10-51 rue Jean-Jacques Rousseau until 2am, from the vodkas of **Le Kremlin** (tel. 03 20 51 85 79) to **La Piroge** (tel. 03 20 31 70 82). **L'Angle-Saxo,** 36, rue d'Angleterre (tel. 03 20 06 15 06), is a jazz bar with a lounge and fiery drinks (around 45F; open 9pm-2am). **L'Illustration,** 18, rue Royale (tel. 03 20 12 00 90), serves up martinis (15F) by candlelight to a stylish, eclectic crowd (open Mon.-Sat. 3pm-4am). The disco-bar **Le Vagabond,** 22, pl. Louise de Bettignies (tel. 03 20 31 89 91), welcomes Lille's gay and lesbian community and anyone else looking to dance or chat with the amiable *patronne* (open 9pm-4am; 25F cover charge). Also on pl. Louise de Bettignies are **Le Caveau de la Treille** (tel. 03 20 31 00 51; open Tues.-Sat. 9:30pm-4am) and **L' Imaginaire** (tel. 03 20 78 13 81; open 10pm-2am), both offering live music.

■ Near Lille: Douai

The crowning moment of Douai's glory was in 1479 when the city, a bastion of Flemish power, repelled an attack by the French Louis XI. During the Anglican Reformation in the 16th century, English Roman Catholics sought refuge in the town. While enjoying Flemish hospitality, they translated the first English version of the Bible. All good things must come to an end, though, and in 1667 Douai fell and has been

French ever since. Despite damage inflicted by the World Wars, Douai (pop. 44,500) remains a lively, if not beautiful, town that sports a comprehensive art gallery, the largest church in the Pas-de-Calais, and a 14th-century Flemish belfry. The town makes an interesting daytrip from Lille or Arras, especially between July 7 and 10, when the *Fêtes de Gayant* seize the streets.

From the *gare* cross to av. du Maréchal Leclerc and turn left. Follow the curve, then turn right onto rue Valenciennes. The **tourist office,** 70, pl. d'Armes (tel. 03 27 88 26 79; fax 03 27 99 38 78), is on the left in the gray stone building. (Open Mon.-Sat. 9am-noon and 2-6pm; July-Aug. also open Sun. 9am-noon and 2-6pm.) **Banks** line rue de Paris and rue de Bellani. **Trains** run to Arras (20 per day, 25min., 25F) and Lille (20 per day, 20min., 33F). (Ticket booth open Mon.-Fri. 6am-8:15pm, Sat. 6am-7:30pm. Info office open Mon.-Fri. 9am-7pm, Sat. 9am-6pm.) **Buses** (tel. 03 27 99 19 93) leave from the *gare* to all points in the city. The **hospital** (tel. 03 27 99 62 62) is at 329, rue Canteleu. In case of **medical emergency,** dial 15. For the **police,** dial 17. The **post office,** 81, pl. Charles de Gaulle, is open Mon.-Fri. 8am-6:30pm and Sat. 8am-noon (**postal code:** 59500).

The best thing about Douai is its **beffroi** (belfry) and **Hôtel de Ville.** The *beffroi* dates from the 19th century and miraculously survived the shelling during both World Wars. 54m tall, it houses the largest carillon in France with 62 bells, the largest of which weighs over five metric tons. The parts of the Hôtel de Ville not destroyed by the wars date from the 15th to 18th centuries. On the tour you'll see the marriage room where all *Douiasians* tie the knot, the Gothic Chamber, where the lion of Flanders juts out of the wall to light your way, and the bells themselves (which you'll be able to hear up close). A great view through wire awaits those who climb the *beffroi* (tours in French only, Mon.-Sat. hourly 2-5pm; Sun. 10-11am and 3-5pm; July-Aug. daily 10-11am and 2-5pm). The **Musée de la Chartreuse,** 130, rue des Chartreux (tel. 03 27 87 17 82), has a little something for everyone. The building is a mix of 15th- and 17th-century Flemish design, 17th-century Italian Renaissance, and 18th- and 19th-century Classical French; it seems as if a group of châteaux from different eras have been glued together with a Romanesque chapel and placed on a pretty lawn. Inside you'll find a mix that focuses primarily on 15th- and 16th-century Italian and Flemish masters but includes works by David, Corot, and Monet (open Wed.-Mon. 10am-noon and 2-5pm, Sun. 10am-noon and 3-6pm; admission 12F, children 6F). The **Collegiale St-Pierre** is the largest church in the Pas-de-Calais and, like the Musée de la Chartreuse, features a mix of styles from the 17th and 18th centuries. Inside is a gigantic organ originally from St. Petersburg and an elaborate chapel dedicated to the Virgin Mary (open Mon.-Fri. 10am-noon and 2-5pm).

Arras

Though historians say the name "Arras" derives from the hanging tapestries produced here in the 16th century, locals maintain that the name honors a band of rats that stalked the unfortunate city in the Middle Ages, enabling the king of France to conquer the town. Every year on Whit Sunday, the **Fête des Rats** pays homage to the rodents. In 1758, Arras avenged itself on the conquering monarchy as the birthplace of Robespierre, who masterminded the guillotining of Louis XVI. In modern times, Arras crumbled during the atrocities of the World Wars. During the First, thousands gave their lives in bitter trench warfare in the nearby countryside; two decades later, the Germans shot hundreds of Resistance fighters here. By 1945, only 15% of the city was left standing. Painstakingly restored, Arras (pop. 46,000) has regained a distinctively stern appearance honed over centuries of hardship.

ORIENTATION AND PRACTICAL INFORMATION

To get to the **tourist office** and **pl. des Héros** from the train station, walk straight across pl. Foch past the fountain and onto rue Gambetta. Turn right onto rue Ronville (opposite the post office), then turn left onto rue de la Housse, by the church of St-

Jean Baptiste. The tourist office is across the square, inside the Hôtel de Ville (5min.). **Grande Place** is to the right, on the other side of the pl. des Héros.

Tourist Office: pl. des Héros (tel. 03 21 51 26 95), on the ground floor of the Hôtel de Ville. Friendly staff provides good maps and the usual *très* informative brochures. Free accommodations service. Guided tours in French and English. Open Mon.-Sat. 10am-noon and 2-6pm, Sun. 10am-noon and 3-5pm. **Branch Office** in front of the train station open April to mid-Oct. Mon.-Fri. 8-10am and 1-5:30pm.

Money: Crédit Agricole, 9, Grande Place (tel. 03 21 50 41 80), has a 24-hr. **ATM** (bank open Tues.-Fri. 9am-12:30pm and 2-6pm, Sat. 8:15am-12:45pm and 2-4pm), as does the **Crédit Mutuel** (tel. 03 21 71 32 32) behind the Hôtel de Ville (bank open Tues.-Fri. 8:30am-noon and 1:30-5pm, Sat. 2-4pm).

Trains: pl. Maréchal Foch (tel. 08 36 35 35 35). To: Paris (17 TGVs per day, 50min., 172F); Lille (30 per day, 40min., 51F); Dunkerque (20 per day, 1hr., 86F); Amiens (15 per day, 1hr., 60F); Lyon (2 TGVs per day, 3hr., 409F). Info Mon.-Sat. 8am-7:30pm. Tickets Mon.-Sat. 5:40am-8:45pm, Sun. 8:15am-9:30pm. **Lockers** 14-30F.

Buses: Buses from Arras to Vimy leave from the **Gare Routière** (tel. 03 21 51 34 64). From the train station, turn left onto rue du Dr. Brassart. After crossing the bridge turn right, and the station will be just ahead of you. Buses run about 7 times daily, 7am-7pm. One way tickets 8F30.

Taxis: At the station, or call **Arras Taxi** (tel. 03 21 23 69 69). To Vimy, 80F. Otherwise, 11F initial fee, plus 3F per km during day or 6F per km at night.

Car Rental: Avis, 6 rue Gambetta (tel. 03 21 51 69 03), across from the train station. 2 days with up to 600km 635F. Other agencies cluster near the station.

Bicycle Rental: Ringo, rue St-Aubert (tel. 03 21 51 12 86). 65F per day, no deposit. Open Tues.-Sat. 8:30am-noon and 2pm-6pm. Also at the hostel (below).

Laundromat: Superlav, pl. Ipswich, 2 blocks from the tourist office. Wash 19F per 5kg, 34F per 10kg. Dry 4F per 8min. Detergent 3F. Open daily 7am-8pm.

Hospital: 57, av. Winston Churchill (tel. 03 21 24 40 00). Take bus B, C, D, H, HI, M, Z, or ZI to "l'Hôpital." **Medical emergency** tel. 15.

Police: 18, bd. de la Liberté (tel. 03 21 24 50 17). **Emergency** tel. 17.

Post Office: 17, rue Gambetta (tel. 03 21 22 94 94), 1 block from the train station. **Currency exchange** with good rates. Photocopies 1F. Poste restante. Open Mon.-Fri. 8am-6:30pm, Sat. 8am-noon. **Postal Code:** 62000.

ACCOMMODATIONS, CAMPING, AND FOOD

Arras has precious few budget hotels. Reserving space during high season at the youth hostel, located in the center of town, is wise.

Auberge de Jeunesse (HI), 59, Grande Place (tel. 03 21 22 70 02; fax 03 21 07 46 15). In a Flemish townhouse. Pleasant dorm rooms with shower and kitchen. 54 beds. Lounge with TV/VCR. 45F. Blankets 22F. Breakfast 18F. **Bike rental** 60F per day (deposit 1200F or passport). Curfew 11pm, lockout 10am-5pm. Closed Dec.-Jan. Reception 7:30-10am and 5-11pm.

Ostel des Trois Luppars, 47, Grande Place (tel. 03 21 07 41 41; fax 03 21 24 24 80). Immaculate, spacious rooms with modern decor in a 15th-century building that was the only one in the square to survive both World Wars. Telephones, showers, baths, and TV. *Let's Go* readers use the sauna for free. You get all you pay for: singles from 220F, doubles 240F. 24-hr. reception. V, MC, AmEx.

Hôtel du Beffroi, 28, pl. de la Vacquerie (tel. 03 21 23 13 78), behind the Hôtel de Ville. Perfectly located. Painstaking *patrons* provide rooms with phones and pretty pictures. TV room with free tea and coffee. Singles 150-170F. Doubles 170-180F. Breakfast 30F. Reception open 7am-9pm. V, MC, AmEx.

Hôtel Le Passe Temps, pl. du Maréchal Foch (tel. 03 21 71 58 38), to the right of the station. Simple, clean rooms. Singles 130F, with shower and TV 195F. Doubles 150F, with shower 180F, with bath and TV 240F. Extra bed 25F. Breakfast 27F. Closed first 3 weeks of Aug. Reception 7am-1am, closed Sun. 1-5pm. V, MC.

Camping: 138, rue du Temple (tel. 03 21 71 55 06), at av. Fernand Lobbedez. From station, turn left onto rue du Dr. Brassart, then left on av. du Maréchal Leclerc.

Cross the bridge and continue 5 blocks to campground (10min.). 13F per person, 7F50 per tent, 7F50 per car. Free hot showers, electricity 14F. Open April-Sept.

Inexpensive cafés skirt **pl. des Héros** and the pedestrian area; more elegant restaurants dress the **Grande Place.** Try *Les Best Ribs in Town* (56F) at **Le Saint-Germain,** 14, Grand Place (tel. 03 21 51 45 45), followed by *crème brûlée* (29F) and a free gumball (open daily noon-1am; V, MC, AmEx). Seek out Middle Eastern fast food around the block at friendly **Le Chawama,** 3, rue des Trois Visages (tel. 03 21 50 06 67; open Mon.-Sat. 10:30am-11pm, Sun. 4-11pm; *kebab* plates 20-28F). **Le Palerme,** 50, Grande Place (tel. 03 21 58 53 84), lets you eat your pizza and pasta (30-50F) in either a café or an old cellar complete with vaulted ceilings. If you're feeling extravagant, treat your tummy to a gourmet 80F or 150F *menu* in the classy and classic **Restaurant aux Grandes Arcades,** 12, Grande Place (tel. 03 21 23 30 89; open 7am-10pm). The pedestrian shopping area between the post office and the Hôtel de Ville bustles with *boulangeries* and other specialty shops—plus a huge **Monoprix supermarket** on rue Gambetta across from the post office (open Mon.-Sat. 8:30am-7:30pm). The pl. des Héros and adjoining squares erupt into vibrant color during Arras' boisterous **open-air market** (Wed. and Sat. 8am-1pm).

SIGHTS AND ENTERTAINMENT

Arras is centered around two great squares, both surrounded by rows of nearly identical houses. **Grande Place's** homogeneity is disturbed by a lone Gothic housefront (the Ostel des Trois Luppars; see **Accommodations** above), dating from 1460. A total of 345 columns support the first floors of the 15th-century Flemish townhouses. Although barbed wire sliced the square down the middle during World War I when the French and Germans occupied opposite sides, it shows few battle scars. A block away, boutiques, bars, and cafés line the equally beautiful **pl. des Héros.**

The **Hôtel de Ville,** with its 75m belfry topped by the gold lion of Arras, has reigned over pl. des Héros since the 15th century. The building is a faithful copy of the original, which was destroyed in 1914. You can peep into the Municipal Chamber, the reception room, and the marriage chamber, where all marriages officially take place (a church wedding is not sufficient). You can survey the town from the **belfry.** (Admission 14F, students 8F. Admission to the belfry, *les Boves* (see gray box below), and a film in English and French 30F50, students 20F.)

A few blocks behind the Hôtel de Ville lies the appropriately gigantic 18th-century **Abbaye St-Vaast.** The abbey's 19th-century church combines a striking Neo-classical style with a traditional Gothic floor plan. The plain white walls and massive columns shelter an amazing pipe organ (open Mon.-Sat. 3-6:30pm; closes at 5pm in winter). Also inside, the **Musée des Beaux-Arts** (tel. 03 21 71 26 43) displays a collection of medieval sculpture and tapestry, including fascinating funeral monuments. Look for the gruesome skeletal sculpture of Guillaume le Franchois with worm-infested entrails, exquisite 18th- and 19th-century French and Dutch porcelain, and 19th-century paintings, especially by members of the school of Arras, including Corot, Dutilleux, Desavary, and Dourlens. (Open Mon. and Wed.-Sat. 10am-noon and 2-6pm, Sun. 10am-noon and 3-6pm; Oct.-March closes at 5pm. Admission 14F, students 7F; with special exhibitions, 18F and 9F respectively.)

For a small town, Arras has a fast pulse. The **Couleur Café,** 35, pl. des Héros (tel. 03 21 71 08 70) is crowded into the wee hours. **La Taverne de l'Ecu,** 18, rue Wacquez Glasson (tel. 03 21 51 42 05), offers a beer-filled, rustic atmosphere. **The Golden Age,** just between pl. des Héros and Grande Place on rue de la Taillerie, is a jazz club popular with the local British and Canadian contingent. Arras is at its most cosmopolitan at the **Noroit,** 6, rue des Capuchins (tel. 03 21 71 30 12), which plays international art films and hosts concerts and plays several times a month.

Arras' Subterranean World

Les Boves, a fantastic labyrinth of subterranean tunnels, was originally created for the extraction of chalk in the 10th century. After 200 years of mining, the city abandoned the passages until the 17th century when overpopulation pushed the city's poor underground. In the 18th century, the mysterious, macabre caves became *de rigueur* for aristocratic masquerades and were redeemed as forbidden Christian chapels during the Revolution. Finally, Les Boves served as a home for 11,500 British soldiers during World War I. In the four years that they lived here, the British set up a tramway, kitchen, and hospital underground. Although you will not find many people willing to discuss it, Les Boves also served as a Nazi stronghold against the American army in WWII. The tunnels stretch into the neighboring villages and distant battlefields. The Arras tunnels can be visited only in tours organized by the tourist office (see price list under the Hôtel de Ville; tours leave roughly every 45min. 10am-noon and 2-6pm).

■ Near Arras: World War I Battlefields

Over 20 war cemeteries and countless unmarked graves dot the green countryside around Arras that hosted heavy fighting during the First World War. Five or six **trains** go daily from Arras to Vimy (15F), but the cheaper bus lets you off closer to the memorial. Seven daily **buses** run between Arras' Gare Routière and Vimy (8F one way, 20min.). Look for the bus-stand marked **Lille-Lens-Arras.** From the Vimy bus or train station, be prepared to walk a good 2-3km to reach the memorial. Head in the direction of Arras along **N25,** and after 1km you will see the entrance to Vimy on the right-hand side of the highway. It's another 2km from the entrance to the memorial itself. If you (and your strong thighs) choose to rent a **bike,** be aware that the ride from Arras to the memorials entails a lot of highway navigation. The more hurried may want to save time and energy by renting a car or cab at the train station (see bike, car, and cab info on page 682).

The **Vimy Memorial** (tel. 03 21 48 72 29), 10km northeast of Arras along the N25, honors the 66,655 Canadians killed in World War I. Despite the pastoral setting, electric fences and signposts warning visitors that undetonated mines lie off the marked trails heighten the immediacy of the area's history. Grass-covered craters immortalize soldiers' tragically misplaced footsteps. Well-informed, energetic Canadian student volunteers give tours of the dark trenches and tunnels. For Canada, the battle at Vimy ridge is a source of great national pride and pain. 3598 Canadians were killed and 7004 wounded at this crucial victory. The 11,285 peaceful trees in the park represent the number of Canadian soldiers whose final resting place is unknown (open 10am-5pm; tours of tunnels April-Nov. 15; free).

Farther west along D49, the cemetery at **Neuville-St-Vaast** holds the graves of 44,000 German soldiers. Each cross represents four fallen soldiers. The **Musée La Targette** (tel. 03 21 59 17 76), in front of the Monument au Flambeau, commemorates the World Wars with a display of over 3500 painstakingly collected documents, uniforms, and objects made by soldiers (open 9am-8pm; admission 20F).

North of Neuville on D937 is the French cemetery, basilica, and museum of **Notre-Dame-de-Lorette.** The bodies of 22,970 unknown and 19,000 listed soldiers from World War I rest here. The museum's first floor displays letters and photos sent by families. (Open daily June-Sept. 8am-7pm; Oct.-Nov. and March 8am-5pm; Dec.-Feb. 9am-4:30pm; April-May 8am-6pm. Museum open daily March-Nov. 9am-8pm; Dec.-Feb. Sat.-Sun. 9am-7pm. Admission to museum 20F.) **Buses** run from Arras to La Targette/Neuville-St-Vaast and Souchez/Notre-Dame-de-Lorette (3-4 per day, 10F). Notre-Dame-de-Lorette is ¼km from the bus station via shortcuts to the left. Don't walk along the highway; just ask locals for the path if you're confused.

Amiens

The pinnacle of Amiens' glory may have been in 1533, when the spire was finally placed atop its achingly beautiful cathedral. Today the cathedral remains one of Europe's greatest examples of Gothic architecture. Apart from that, Amiens (pop. 160,000) is not especially alluring; nondescript buildings, treeless avenues, and disappointing concrete plazas cover the capital of the Picardie region. Fortunately the town can boast of the Quartier St-Leu, a twisting maze of streets and canals, and of the tranquil *hortillonages,* former marshlands cultivated since Caesar set up a winter camp here in 12 BC. Although you shouldn't go 20,000 leagues out of your way to get here, Jules Verne's home city merits a stop on your itinerary.

ORIENTATION AND PRACTICAL INFORMATION

The train station lies at the eastern edge of town within walking distance of the *centre ville.* To get to the main tourist office, take rue Noyon, which begins directly across the street from the station. Rue Noyon turns into rue des Trois Cailloux after four blocks. Turn right at pl. Gambetta. The tourist office is on the corner of rue Dusevel and rue des Crignons. To get to Amiens' center from the station, walk straight on rue Noyon and rue des Trois Cailloux into pl. de l'Hôtel de Ville. Be careful at night in the area around the Cirque, on the southern edge of town.

Tourist Information: Tourist Office, 12, rue du Chapeau de Violettes (tel. 03 22 91 79 28; fax 03 22 92 50 58), near Eglise St-Germain. Friendly staff offers ample brochures, including a guide to the city's many festivals. Free map. Makes reservations and runs tours. Open Easter-Sept. daily 9am-12:30pm and 1:30-7pm; Oct.-Easter Mon.-Sat. 9am-12:30pm and 1:30-6pm, Sun. 11am-4pm. Early in 1997 the office will move to 6bis, rue Dusevel (tel. 03 22 71 60 50; fax 03 22 71 60 51).

Money: The **Crédit Agricole** has an **ATM** at the train station. Banks line rue Noyon, including **BNP** and **Credit Lyonnais.**

Trains: Gare du Nord, pl. Alphonse Fiquet (tel. 03 22 92 50 50). To: Paris (24 per day, 1hr., 95F); Lille (10 per day, 1½hr., 94F); Rouen (5 per day, 1½hr., 92F); Calais (12 per day, 2hr., 113F); Boulogne (15 per day, 1½hr., 90F); Le Toquet (4 per day, 1hr., 73F); Montreuil (via Etaples; 4 per day, 1hr., 82F). Ticket office open 5am-10pm. Info office open Mon.-Sat. 8am-6:30pm. **Lockers** 30F per day.

Public Transportation: SEMTA (tel. 03 22 91 40 00). Buy tickets on the bus or at the office at pl. Alphonse Fiquet, left as you exit the *gare* (open Mon.-Sat. 7:00am-6:30pm). 6F per ride, *carnet* of 10 39F. All buses stop at pl. Alphonse Fiquet, 6am-9pm. One line operates 9pm-midnight; grab a schedule at the office.

Taxis: (tel. 03 22 91 30 03). 11F plus 3-4F per km.

Car Rental: Avis, 64, rue des Jacobins (tel. 22 92 30 00). One day 585F, one week 1980F. Open Mon.-Fri 8am-noon and 2-7pm, Sat. 9am-noon and 4-6pm.

Bike Rental: Amiens Cycles, 4, route de Paris (tel. 22 95 03 39). 100F per day, 1000F or passport deposit. Open Tues.-Sat. 9:30am-7:30pm.

Laundromat: Laverie des Majots, 15, rue des Majots. Open daily 7am-9pm.

English Books: The huge **Librairie Martelle,** 3, rue des Vergeaux (tel. 03 22 92 03 76), stocks English-language paperbacks from the trashy to the canonical. Open Mon. 1:30-7pm, Tues.-Sat. 9am-12:30pm and 1:30-7pm.

Helpline: Service Accueil Urgence (tel. 03 22 91 26 26). All purpose, 24hr.

Hospital: Hôpital Nord, pl. Victor Pauchet (tel. 03 22 66 80 00). Take bus 10 (direction: College César Frank) to "Hôpital Nord"; bus 11 makes the return trip. **Hôpital Sud,** av. Laennec (tel. 03 22 45 60 00). Take lines 2 or 6 (direction: Hôpital Sud) to the end. **Medical emergency** tel. 15.

Police: 1, rue Marché-Lanselles (tel. 03 22 71 53 00 or 03 22 43 73 02). **Emergency** tel. 17.

Post Office: 7, rue des Vergeaux. Poste restante (postal code: 80050). Fax, photocopiers. Open Mon.-Fri. 8am-7pm, Sat. 8am-noon. **Postal code:** 80000.

ACCOMMODATIONS

CROUS, 25, rue St-Leu (tel. 03 22 71 24 00), rents singles in university housing. Most dorms are a few km out of town, but the price is unbeatable. Singles 56F. Reserve in writing, or in the summer have the tourist office call as soon as you arrive to make your reservation. Also does long-term stays (900F per month).

Hôtel Victor Hugo, 2, rue l'Oratoire (tel. 03 22 91 57 91). Well-located, elegant, immaculate rooms with TV and phone. Singles 135-195F. Doubles 135-250F. Extra bed 50F. Hall shower 10F. Breakfast 27F. Pets 10F extra. V, MC.

Hôtel Puvis de Chavannes, 6, rue Puvis de Chavannes (tel. 03 22 91 82 96). Bright, attractive rooms complete with nifty art prints and telephones. Friendly proprietress and a well-behaved dog, Thaïs. Singles and doubles 125-185F. Hall shower 10F. Pets 10F extra. Breakfast 27F. V, MC.

Hôtel de la Paix, 8, rue de la République (tel. 03 22 91 39 21; fax 03 22 92 02 65). A stone's throw from everything. Simple, peaceful rooms with TV, phone, and tropical bedspreads. The pristine hall showers are free. Doubles 185-275F. Triples 330F. Extra bed 80F. Breakfast 29F.

Les Touristes, 22, pl. Notre-Dame (tel. 03 22 92 50 99). Large rooms across from cathedral. If you get bored with the fantastic view, check out the wallpaper. Singles 130-150F. Doubles 150-170F. Breakfast 25F. Call ahead for reception.

FOOD

Picardie's regional specialties, *pâté de canard* (duck pâté), *tuiles amiénoises* (chocolate macaroons), and *ficelles picarde* (thin crêpes stuffed with mushrooms, ham, and cream) abound in Amiens' restaurants and cafés. *Confisier* and *chocolatier* **Jean Trogneaux,** 1, rue Delambre (tel. 03 22 91 58 27), perpetuates the delicious legacy of the *macaron d'Amiens* (almond macaroon), a treat found in the city since the 16th century. Bring a serious appetite to **Le Mongeoire,** 3, rue des Sergents (tel. 03 22 91 11 28), if you're going to dig into their 56F and 64F *menus* (offering generous combinations of crêpes and *galettes*) or order crêpes *à la carte,* starting at 10F. (Open Tues. and Thurs.- Fri. 11:30am-2:30pm and 5-11pm, Wed. and Sat. 11:30am-2:30pm and 4-11:30pm.) **Le T'chiot Zinc,** 18, rue de Noyon (tel. 03 22 91 43 79), offers delicious and plentiful French and *picard* dishes (89F *menu,* entrees from 27F) and turns into a busy hang-out spot at night (open Mon.-Sat. noon-2:30pm and 4:30pm-10:30pm). There's food and much more in the shops around the Hôtel de Ville, at **Shopi supermarket,** 20, pl. Hôtel de Ville (open Mon. 10am-12:30pm and 2-7:30pm, Tues.-Thurs. 9am-12:30pm and 2-7:30pm, Fri.-Sat. 9am-1pm and 2-7:30pm), or at the vast **Match supermarket,** in the mall to the right of the station (open Mon.-Sat. 9am-10:30pm). Amiens' main **market** is on Saturday on pl. des Halles, from daybreak to dusk, with a less bustling one Thursday mornings. **CROUS,** 25, rue St-Leu (tel. 03 22 71 24 00), offers institutional food at its *restaurant universitaire.* 13F with a student ID, 27F for everyone else. Call for times.

SIGHTS AND ENTERTAINMENT

When the burghers of Amiens decided to rebuild their **Cathédrale de Notre-Dame** in 1220 they sought to make it even grander than those in Paris and Laon. Just 60 years after construction began, the highest nave in France (42m) was completed. The impressive cathedral is twice the size of Notre Dame in Paris. The astoundingly complex west façade, with 4000 figures acting out episodes from the Old and New Testaments, was a lesson for pilgrims at a time when few were literate. The cathedral's interior is just as impressive, with a labyrinth of tilework at the center of the nave created for meditating worshipers wishing to simulate a mini-pilgrimage by crawling to their goal. Look behind the choir at the Weeping Angel, a small crying angel that became famous when the Allies drove Germany out of Amiens in WWI and Allied soldiers mailed thousands of postcards of the angel to celebrate their victory. The stained glass isn't quite equal to that at Chartres or Paris, but you'll be too awestruck to care. (Open April-Sept. Mon.-Sat. 8:30am-7pm, Sun. 8:30am-12:30pm and 2:30-

7pm; Oct.-March Mon.-Sat. 8:30am-noon and 2-5pm.) The cathedral's **treasury** displays sacred valuables from across the centuries (the treasury was closed temporarily in '96; check to see if it's opened again).

The **Quartier St-Leu,** just north of the Somme River, is the oldest section of Amiens. Built along a system of waterways and canals, its narrow winding streets and numerous galleries have a classic flavor that evokes a kinder, gentler Parisian Latin Quarter. Nearby are the *hortillonnages,* market gardens spread over the inlets created when the Romans built canals through the marshland. Paths wander among the canals, which still supply Amiens with produce and flowers. Barge tours are also available (10:30am and 3:30pm from the Embarcaderie d'Amont; call 22 09 62 17).

Jules Verne (1828-1905) spent most of his life in Amiens and wrote his fantastical novels here. Today his home is a small but appropriately quirky museum, complete with holographic models of the Nautilus and a dummy of Verne himself. The museum also houses the friendly but rather dull **Centre de Documentation Jules Verne,** 2, rue Charles Dubois (tel. 03 22 45 37 84), featuring scads of documents by and about the author (museum open Tues.-Sat. 9:30am-noon and 2-6pm; admission 15F, children under 6 5F). Verne lies 0.00046 leagues under the surface of the earth in an impressive tomb in the **Cimitière de la Madeleine,** about a 20-minute walk from the center of town. Take line S (direction: Etouvie) and hop off at "Cimitière."

The **Picardy Museum,** 48, rue de la République (tel. 03 22 91 36 44), houses a small but distinguished collection of French paintings, sculpture from the Middle Ages to the 19th century, and an exhibit on Roman Amiens in a surprisingly gaudy Second Empire building (open Tues.-Sun. 10am-12:30pm and 2-6pm; admission 20F, under 17 or student 10F; tour 37F). Its sister museum, the **Musée de l'Hôtel de Berny** (tel. 03 22 91 36 44) is a 17th-century mansion housing original furniture, tapestries, and an exhibit on locks (open summer Thurs.-Sun. 1-6pm, winter Sun. 10am-12:30pm and 2-6pm; admission 10F, under 18 free).

At night, the gas-lit and cobblestoned **pl. du Don** and the **quai Beln** in the Quartier St-Leu teem with energetic French students. The **Riverside Café,** pl. du Don (tel. 03 22 92 50 30), draws the biggest crowd. Modeled on a 50s American bar, the place is definitely local. Loud rock rolls inside, and tables invite cozy discussion outside (beer 13-52F; open daily 4pm-2am, closed Sun. in winter). **Au Sixième Siecle** (tel. 03 22 80 94 75), across the canal on rue Motte, is a little quirkier. The six-room café in a 16th-century river house is open daily 4pm-1am.

■ Near Amiens: Compiègne

Tranquil Compiègne (pop. 50,000) has tripped through 1200 years of diplomatic notoriety without being much affected by it. The town first gained prominence in the 8th century, welcoming Frankish and Byzantine officials to the banks of the Oise. The English captured Joan of Arc here in 1430 during a siege in yet another round of the Hundred Years' War. The armistice ending World War I was signed in a forest clearing about 6km away on November 11, 1918; in 1940 Adolf Hitler forced the French to surrender at the same spot. Beech trees, landscaped grounds, and the 17th-century château make today's Compiègne a picturesque town with a few skeletons hidden in the *armoire.* Under the German occupation, Compiègne served as one of France's largest detention centers for Jews on their way to concentration camps—a journey that ended in death for more than half the voyagers. This dark period in the town's history is carefully neglected by most tour guides, and visitors can enjoy Compiègne's château, three unusual museums, and web of hiking trails in peaceful ignorance.

First stop at the **tourist office** (tel. 03 44 40 01 00; fax 03 44 40 23 28) in the Hôtel de Ville for a free and useful map, one-hour walking tour of the city, and all sorts of delightful information. To reach the office from the train station, walk across the parking lot, take a right along the canal, and take the next left across the bridge onto rue Solférino. Continue up this street and the Hôtel de Ville appears soon enough on the left. (Open Easter-Oct. Mon.-Sat. 9am-12:15pm and 1:45-6:15pm, Sun. 9:30am-

12:30pm and 2:30-5pm; closed Sun. Nov.-Easter, Dec. 25, and Jan. 1.) Compiègne is easily accessible by **train** from Paris (Gare du Nord) and Amiens.

The main attraction of the town is the **Musée National du Château de Compiègne** (tel. 03 44 38 47 00; fax 03 44 38 47 01). Fond of the original château's rustic appeal, Louis XIV quipped, "I am lodged as king at Versailles, as gentleman at Fountainbleau, as peasant at Compiègne." Louis XV found this "quaintness" less beguiling, and in 1751 he began building the large palace whose profile you see today. In the 19th century, Compiègne served as second home to Napoleon Bonaparte and later to Napoleon III. The château's interior bears the mark of his ostentatious tastes, an often conscientiously opulent ensemble of nude nymphs and tapestried chairs. Compiègne also harbors a *trompe l'oeil* bag of tricks—secret doors, baffling paintings with every appearance of carved marble, and other curiosities. Also part of the museum complex is the **Musée de la Voiture,** featuring 18th-, 19th-, and early 20th-century coaches and omnibuses including those used by Napoleons I and II. (Château accessible only by guided tour in French, every 15min. April-Sept. Wed.-Mon. 9:15am-6:15pm, last tour 5:30pm; Oct.-March 9:15am-4:30pm, last tour 3:45pm.)

No visit to the palace is complete without a tour of the **grounds** designed at Napoleon's request in 1811. Meandering walkways, shady trees, natural-looking flower beds, and a 5km long *grande pelouse* (great lawn) make this the perfect place for a stroll or a picnic. Just beyond this vast expanse of manicured grass lies the untamed Forest of Compiègne, a more adventurous setting for a bike ride or hike. Check with the tourist office for details about the hunting season.

Six km into the forest is the **Clairiève de l'Armistice (Armistice Clearing)** (tel. 03 44 85 14 18). It was here in 1918 that the Supreme Commander of the Allies, Maréchal Foch, brought his railway carriage for the signing of the Armistice in November and left it as a monument to the French Victory. On June 20, 1940, that same carriage was taken by Hitler as a trophy of the French capitulation. Destroyed by allied bombing, it was replaced by a replica and a small **museum** (open May-Sept. Wed.-Mon. 9am-noon and 2-6:15pm; Oct.-April 9am-noon and 2-5pm).

A highlight of the tourist office's walking tour is the **Musée Divenal** (tel. 03 44 20 26 04), with strong collections of Greek vases, regional archaeology, Renaissance *objets d'art,* and an Egyptian collection featuring the mummy of a child. (Open March-Oct. Tues.-Sat. 9am-noon and 2-6pm, Sun. 2-6pm; Nov.-Feb. Tues.-Sat. 9am-noon and 2-5pm, Sun. 2-5pm. Closed Jan. 1, May 1, July 14, Nov. 1, and Dec. 25). The route also passes the **Tour Jeanne D'Arc (Tour Beauregard),** a striking ruin commemorating Joan's time as a prisoner in Compiègne, and the **Parc de Sougeons,** from which unfolds an arresting view of the Oise River. The **Eglise St. Jacques** holds an impressive stained glass of Joan taking communion on May 23, 1430 (the day she was captured). Another attractive church in Compiègne is the **Eglise St-Antoine,** a 16th-century marvel with a gorgeous rose window.

Laon

In the days of the Carolingian empire, between the 8th and 10th centuries, residence in this cloistered town was a privilege reserved for kings. Today any visitor is welcome to share the warmth of Laon (pop. 26,000) as it soars unexpectedly from the flat, surrounding farmlands. In its *haute ville,* quiet, faded stone houses and steep cobblestone streets weave around a magnificent cathedral and 12th- and 13th- century buildings. You may be inspired to exclaim, as Victor Hugo did, that *"à Laon, tout est beau"* (in Laon, everything is beautiful).

ORIENTATION AND PRACTICAL INFORMATION

For those not excited by the prospect of a climb, the best way to get to the tourist office from the *gare* is by **POMA,** a roller-coaster-like car which runs every 2½ minutes from the station to the *haute ville* (Mon.-Sat. 7am-8pm, Sun. 2:30-6pm; Sept.-June no service Sun.; tickets 6F, roundtrip 8F, *carnet* of 10 49F). Your other option is to head up the *steep* staircase across from the station. The **tourist office** is located just to the right of the cathedral; direct yourself towards its towering spires. From the POMA station, cross the parking lot and turn left onto pl. Général Leclerc. The office, pl. du Parvis (tel. 03 23 20 28 62; fax 03 23 20 68 11), occupies the **Hôtel-Dieu,** an impressive Gothic structure that served as France's first hospital in the 12th century. Friendly staff offers a free map and lists of hotels and restaurants. **Currency exchange** at less friendly rates. (Open daily July-Aug. 9am-7pm; Sept.-June Mon.-Sat. 9am-12:30pm and 2-6:30pm, Sun. 11am-1pm and 2-5pm.) Direct **trains** run from Laon's station on pl. de la Gare (tel. 03 23 67 50 50) to: Paris (15 per day, 1½hr., 103F); Reims (14 per day, 1hr., 48F); Amiens (5 per day, 2hrs., 84F). **Lockers** 10-30F. (Ticket office open Mon.-Fri. 5:15am-9pm, Sat. 6:15am-8:30pm.) In case of emergency, dial 17 for **police** (non-emergency tel. 03 23 79 23 82), 15 for **medical emergency,** or contact the **hospital,** rue Marcellin Berthelot (tel. 03 23 24 33 33), right next to the Eglise St-Martin. There is a **post office** (tel. 03 23 21 55 78 or 03 23 27 12 00) next to the station on pl. de la Gare, with **currency exchange,** an **ATM,** and poste restante (open Mon.-Fri. 8am-7pm, Sat. 8am-noon; **postal code:** 02000).

ACCOMMODATIONS, CAMPING, AND FOOD

The best deal in town is the **Maison des Jeunes,** 20, rue du Cloître (tel. 03 23 20 27 64), down the street from the cathedral. Orange hallways lead to simple but spacious, sky-blue singles and doubles for 65F per person. (Showers and sheets included. Breakfast 6F50, lunch and dinner 33-37F. Call ahead for reception.) For a little extra, you can have a more comfortable room and an enormous bathroom at **Les Chevaliers,** 3-5, rue Sérurier (tel. 03 23 23 43 78; fax 03 23 23 40 71). (Singles 120F, with toilet 150-170F, with shower 190F, with bath and toilet 230-250F. Doubles 140F, with toilet 180-200F, with shower, bath, and toilet 260-280F. Triples with shower 250F, with bath and toilet 280-300F. Quads with shower 280F. Extra bed 30F. Free newspaper. Breakfast included; cozy café downstairs with garden terrace. Reception 6-11am and 2:30-8:30pm. V, MC.) Several hotels open their doors near the train station, including **Hôtel Welcome,** 2, av. Carnot (tel. 03 23 23 06 11), which supplies spacious, modern rooms. (Singles 100F, with shower 120F. Doubles 120F, with shower 150F. Triples with shower 150F. Shower 15F. Breakfast 25F. Reception *closed* daily noon-2pm and Sun. afternoon. V, MC.) In nearby **Chéret** (5km southeast of Laon), a generous couple shares their antique farmhouse, **Le Clos** (tel. 03 23 24 80 64), its roses, fountains, and sheep with weary travelers. Every room is different; meals are fresh from the garden and *cave* (singles 180-220F; doubles 200-250F; includes showers and mouth-watering breakfast). Campers can head for **La Chênaie,** allée de la Chênaie (tel. 03 23 20 25 56; 13F50 per person, 8F per site, 8F per car; showers included; open April-Oct.).

If you crave local fare, look for menus featuring *tarte aux poireaux* (leek pie) and anything made with the locally produced *maroilles* cheese or *genièvre* liqueur. **La Dolce Vita,** 13, rue de Change (tel. 03 23 20 69 60), proffers steak (50F), fish, enormous portions of homemade pasta (from 41F), and pizza made with *maroilles* (32F). Stained-glass windows and a wood-burning stove add to the warm atmosphere (open Mon.-Thurs. noon-1:30pm and 7-10pm; Fri.-Sat. noon-1:30pm and 7-10:30pm; V, MC). Go further afield with the delicious and enormous North African dishes (65-88F; 60F *menu*) of **L'Aziza,** 11, rue de la Herse (tel. 03 23 20 14 44), one block from the cathedral (open Tues.-Sun. noon-2:30pm and 6-10:30pm; V, MC). Crêpe fanatics should head over to the family-run **La Crêperie,** 23, rue St-Jean (tel. 03 23 23 05 53), for a plethora of pancake *plats* (10-48F; open Mon.-Sat. 10am-1am). Cheaper fare can be found a the **Maison des Jeunes restaurant** (see **Accommodations** above). A series of food shops ply their trade on **rue de la Herse. Point Coop,** 11, rue de Bourg (tel. 03 23 23 05 84), is a small, inexpensive **grocery store** (open Mon. 2:30-7:30pm, Tues.-Sat. 6:30am-12:30pm and 2:30-7pm, Sun. 9am-noon).

SIGHTS AND ENTERTAINMENT

A maze of narrow, twisting alleys and medieval walls surrounds Laon's magnificent five-towered Gothic cathedral. The *haute ville* is a 10-minute walk up a dauntingly steep staircase; it's easier to hop on the POMA cars. Capital of France under the Carolingian kings and birthplace of Roland, the folk hero and nephew of Charlemagne, Laon started construction of the **Cathédrale de Notre-Dame** in 1150 and completed the masterpiece a mere 50 years later. To learn all its ins and outs, you must join the guided tours (in French; English booklet 3F) that leave from the tourist office (tours July-Aug. Sun.-Fri. 3pm, Sat. 6pm; Sept.-Nov. and April-June Sat., Sun., and holidays 3pm; 35F, students 20F). Take a good look at the western façade, which tells the story of the Last Judgment in explicit detail. Each tower displays the carved head of an ox, in memory of the two oxen that miraculously appeared to bring building materials to the workers on the top of the hill. (Open daily 8am-7pm.)

Two blocks from Notre-Dame on rue Georges Ermant are the **Musée de Laon** (tel. 03 23 20 19 87), with a distinguished collection of Greek vases, and the 13th-century **Chapelle des Templiers.** Note the carved 14th-century "skeleton" of Guillaume de Harcigny, physician to Charles VI, and the two statues of prophets that once supported the cathedral façade. Many of their fellows around the chapel bear the scars of the French Revolution—they, too, were beheaded. (Both open April-Sept. Wed.-Mon. 10am-noon and 2-6pm; Oct.-March Wed.-Mon. 10am-noon and 2-5pm. Museum 11F, students 6F. Chapel free.)

A walk along the **ramparts** will treat you to beautiful views of the surrounding countryside. On your way, you'll see the 14th-century **Port d'Ardon,** the fortified **Porte de Soissons,** and the tranquil **Abbaye and Eglise St-Martin.**

The **Maison des Arts,** pl. Aubry (tel. 03 23 20 28 48) houses painting and photography exhibits as well as a theater space (open Tues.-Sat. noon-7pm, Sun. 3-7pm). Laon hosts a number of festivals throughout the year, and is particularly well known for its **Festival de Musique,** from late September through mid-October. In the summer, the city hosts free concerts Sundays 5pm at various historical monuments.

Appendices

FESTIVALS AND HOLIDAYS

In summer almost every town celebrates a local *fête* **(festival)** that may include carnivals, markets, and folk dancing. For info write for the brochure *Festive France,* available from any branch of the **French Government Tourist Office** (see page 1). *Let's Go* lists festivals in the Entertainment section of each town. Try to be somewhere special for **Bastille Day** on July 14, the national holiday that commemorates the fall of the Bastille and the Revolution of 1789. Expect pandemonic celebrations in large cities. During the **Fête de la Musique,** on June 21, musicians rule the streets.

Banks, museums, and other public buildings close on the following **public holidays:** January 1, Easter Monday (March 31 in 1997), May 1 (Labor Day), May 8 (Victory in Europe Day), Ascension Day (the 40th day after Easter, a Thursday—also May 8 in 1997, as it happens), Whit Monday (the seventh Monday after Easter, May 19 in 1997), July 14 (Bastille Day), August 15 (Assumption Day), November 1 (All Saints' Day), November 11 (Armistice Day), and December 25 (Christmas). When a holiday falls on a Tuesday or Thursday, the French often also take off the Monday or Friday, a practice known as *faire le pont* (to make a bridge). Note that banks close at noon on the day of, or the nearest working day before, a public holiday.

CLIMATE CHART

Average maximum and minimum daily temperatures are given in degrees Celsius, followed by the average rainfall in centimeters.

	January	April	July	October
Ajaccio	13/4; *7.5*	19/9; *5.5*	29/18; *7.0*	22/13; *9.5*
Bordeaux	9/1.6; *6.8*	17/7; *6.5*	27/14; *5.0*	19/8; *9.5*
Brest	8.4/4.4; *8.8*	13/7; *6.3*	21/13; *5.0*	16/9; *9.0*
Cherbourg	8.3/4.4; *8.3*	12/6; *5.0*	19/14; *4.8*	15/10; *11.5*
Lille	6/0.5; *5.0*	14/4; *7.0*	24/13; *7.0*	15/7; *7.5*
Lyon	5/-1.1; *5.3*	16/6; *7.0*	27/14; *7.0*	16/7; *7.8*
Marseille	12/3.3; *5.0*	15/5; *1.5*	26/14; *1.5*	24/13; *9.3*
Paris	6/0; *4.3*	16/5; *5.3*	24/13; *5.3*	15/6; *5.5*
Strasbourg	4/0; *6.5*	15/5; *8.5*	26/14; *8.5*	14/6; *6.8*
Toulouse	8/2; *6.3*	17/7; *3.8*	28/15; *3.8*	19/9; *5.5*

TIME ZONES

France is one hour ahead of Greenwich Mean Time (Britain and Ireland), six hours ahead of New York and Toronto, and nine hours ahead of California and Vancouver. France is one hour behind most of South Africa, including Johannesburg, seven hours behind Perth, and nine hours behind Sydney. French time falls one hour back in the Fall and springs one hour forward in the Spring for daylight saving's time; both switches occur about a week before similar changes in U.S. time.

WEIGHTS, MEASURES, AND TEMPERATURES

1 millimeter (mm) = 0.04 inch	1 inch = 25mm
1 meter (m) = 1.09 yards	1 yard = 0.92m
1 kilometer (km) = 0.62 mile	1 mile = 1.61km
1 gram (g) = 0.04 ounce	1 ounce = 25g
1 kilogram (kg) = 2.2 pounds (lb)	1 pound = 0.55kg
1 liter = 1.06 quarts	1 quart = 0.94 liter

To convert from °C to °F, multiply by 1.8 and add 32.
To convert from °F to °C, subtract 32 and multiply by 0.55.

°C	35	30	25	20	15	10	5	0	-5	-10
°F	95	86	75	68	59	50	41	32	23	14

Glossary

Here you will find a compilation of some of the French terms *Let's Go* uses, along with their pronunciations. The gender of the noun is either indicated in parentheses (f. or m.) or by the article (feminine, *la*; masculine, *le*). The pronunciation we suggest does not include the article (*l'*, *la*, *le*, or *les*). To include this article, simply add the sounds "l" for "l'," "luh" for *"le,"* "lah" for *"la,"* and "lay" for *"les"* before the word or phrase. Eu and eue (pronounced the same) have a pronunciation in between the English "ew" and "uh"; in this guide we have used "uh" to indicate this sound. The sound indicated by "zh" is pronounced like the "s" in "pleasure."

l'abbaye (f.)	abbey	ah-BAY
l'allée (f.)	lane, avenue	ah-LAY
l'abri (m.)	shelter	ah-BREE
l'aller-retour (m.)	round-trip	ah-LAY ruh-TOOR
l'arc (m.)	arch	AHRK
les arènes (f.)	arena	ah-REHN
l'auberge (f.)	inn, tavern	oh-BEHRZH
la banlieue	suburbs	bahn-LEUH
la basse ville	lower town	bahs VEEL
la bastide	walled town	bahs-TEED
le beffroi	belfry	behf-WAH
la bibliothèque	library	bihb-lee-oh-TECK
le billet	ticket	bee -YAY
le bois	forest	BWAH
la boulangerie	bakery	boo-LAHN-zhuh-REE
le cap	cape, foreland	KAHP
la cathédrale	cathedral	kah-tay-DRAHL
la cave	cellar	KAHV
le centre ville	center of town	SAHN-truh VEEL
la chambre	room	SHAHM-bruh
la chambre d'hôte	rural bed and breakfast	SHAHM-bruh DOHT
la chapelle	chapel	shah-PEHL
la charcuterie	butcher shop	shahr-kyu-TREE
le château	castle; in wine regions, a vineyard or producer	shah-TOH
le cimetière	cemetery	see-meh-TYAYR
la cité	walled city	see-TAY
le cloître	cloister	KLWAH-truh
la côte	coast	KOHT
le couvent	convent	koo-VON
la croisière	cruise	krwah-ZYAYR
le cru	vineyard, vintage	KRU
la dégustation	tasting	day-GOOS-tah-SYOHN
le donjon	keep (of a castle)	dohn-ZHON
la douane	customs	DWAHN
l'école (f.)	school	ay-KOHL
l'église (f.)	church	ay-GLEEZ
le faubourg (or fbg.)	quarter	foh-BOOR

APPENDICES

la fête	celebration, festival	FEHT
la ferme	farm	FEHRM
la foire	fair	FWAHR
la fontaine	fountain	fohn-TEHN
la forêt	forest	foh-RAY
la gare	(train) station	GAHR
la gare routière	bus station	GAHR root-YAYR
le gîte rural	rural bed and breakfast	ZHEET roo-RAHL
la haute ville	upper town	OHT VEEL
l'horloge (f.)	clock	ohr-LOHZH
hors-saison	off-season	ohr SAY-sohn
l'hôtel (particulier) (m.)	town house	oh-TEL (pahr-tee-cool-YAY)
l'hôtel de ville (m.)	town hall	oh-TEHL duh VEEL
l'hôtel-Dieu	hospital (archaic)	oh-TEHL DYOO
l'île (f.)	island	EEL
la mairie	town hall	meh-REE
le marché	market	mahr-SHAY
la montagne	mountain	mohn-TAHN
le mur	wall	MYUR
le palais	palace	pah-LAY
le parc	park	PAHRK
la place	square	PLAHS
la plage	beach	PLAHZH
le pont	bridge	POHN
le quartier	section (of town)	kahr-TYAY
la randonnée	hike	rahn-duh-NAY
la rue	street	RU
le salon	drawing or living room	sah-LOHN
le sentier	path, lane	sehn-TYAY
le téléphérique	cable car	tay-lay-fay-REECK
les thermes (m.)	hot springs	TEHRM
la tour	tower	TOOR
la vallée	valley	vah-LAY
la vendange	grape harvest	vahn-DANZH
la vieille ville	old town	VYAY VEEL
les vitraux (m.)	stained glass	vee-TROW

HELPFUL PHRASES

please	*s'il vous plaît*	seel voo PLAY
thank you	*merci*	mehr-SEE
hello	*bonjour*	bohn-ZHOOR
good evening	*bonsoir*	bohn-SWAHR
How are you?	*Comment allez-vous?*	KOH-mehn TAH-lay VOO
I am well.	*Je vais bien.*	ZHUH VAY BYEHN
good-bye	*au revoir*	OH ruh-VWAHR
Excuse me.	*Excusez-moi.*	ehks-KOO-ZAY MWAH
Help!	*Au secour!*	OH suh-COOR
He (she) is drunk.	*Il (elle) est ivre.*	eel (ehl) AY EEVRWH
Leave me alone.	*Laissez moi tranquille.*	LAY-say mwah trahn-KEEL
I am hurt/ill.	*J'ai mal.*	zhay MAHL
Do you speak English?	*Parlez-vous anglais?*	PAHR-lay VOO zahn-GLAY
I don't understand.	*Je ne comprends pas.*	ZHUH NUH kohm-PRAHN pah

How much	*combien*	kohm-BYEHN
I'm sorry.	*Je suis désolé.*	ZHUH SWEE day-soh-LAY
who	*qui*	KEE
what?	*Comment?*	koh-MOH
how	*comment*	koh-MOH
why	*pourquoi*	poor-KWAH
when	*quand*	KAHN
What is it?	*Qu'est-ce que c'est?*	KEHS-kuh SAY
I would like	*Je voudrais*	ZHUH voo-DRAY
I need	*J'ai besoin de*	ZHAY buhz-WAN DUH
I want	*Je veux*	ZHUH VUH
I don't want	*Je ne veux pas*	ZHUH NUH VUH PAH
to rent	*louer*	loo-AY
The bill, please.	*L'addition, s'il vous plaît.*	lah-dees-YOHN, seel voo PLAY
Where is/are	*Où est/sont*	OO AY/SOHN
the bathroom	*les toilettes.*	twa-LET
the police	*la police*	po-LEES
the hospital	*l'hôpital*	O-pital
to the right	*à droite*	ah DWAHT
to the left	*à gauche*	ah GOHSH
up	*en haut*	ahn OH
down	*en bas*	ahn BAH
straight ahead	*tout droit*	TOO DRWAH
a room	*une chambre*	oon SHAHM-bruh
double room	*une chambre pour deux*	oon SHAHM-bruh POOR DEUH
single room	*une chambre simple*	oon SHAHM-bruh SAYM-pluh
with	*avec*	ah-VECK
without	*sans*	SAHN
a shower	*une douche*	oon DOOSH
breakfast	*le petit déjeuner*	puh-TEE day-jhuh-NAY
lunch	*le déjeuner*	day-jhuh-NAY
dinner	*le dîner*	dee-NAY
shower included	*douche comprise*	DOOSH kohm-PREEZ
included	*compris*	kohm-PREE

NUMBERS

one	*un*	**twenty**	*vingt*
two	*deux*	**thirty**	*trente*
three	*trois*	**forty**	*quarante*
four	*quatre*	**fifty**	*cinquante*
five	*cinq*	**sixty**	*soixante*
six	*six*	**seventy**	*soixante-dix*
seven	*sept*	**eighty**	*quatre-vingt*
eight	*huit*	**ninety**	*quatre-vingt-dix*
nine	*neuf*	**one hundred**	*cent*
ten	*dix*		

MENU READER

l'agneau (m.)	lamb
le beurre	butter
bien cuit	well done
la bière	beer
le bifteck	steak
le blanc de volaille	breast of chicken
le boeuf	beef
les boissons (f.)	drinks
la brioche	pastry-like bread
le canard	duck
les cervelles (f.)	brain [sic]
le champignon	mushroom
chaud	hot
la chèvre	goat (cheese)
choix	choice
le citron	lemon
le côte	rib or chop
le crème Chantilly	whipped cream
le crème fraîche	fresh heavy cream
le croque-monsieur	toasted, open-faced ham and cheese sandwich
les crudités (f.)	raw vegetables, usually in dressing
l'échalote (f.)	shallot
l'entrée (f.)	first course (appetizer)
l'escargot (m.)	snail
le faux-filet	tenderloin steak
le flan	custard
le foie gras	liver of a goose
forestière	with mushrooms
frais	fresh
la fraise	strawberry
les frites (f.)	French fries
le fromage	cheese
le gâteau	cake
la glace	ice cream
la grenouille	frog (legs)
l'haricot vert (m.)	green bean
le jambon	ham
le lait	milk
le lapin	rabbit
le légume	vegetable
le magret de canard	breast of duck
maison	home-made
la moutarde	mustard
la moule	mussel
nature	plain
l'oeuf (m.)	egg
l'oignon (m.)	onion
le pain	bread
les pâtes (f.)	pasta
la pâtisserie	pastry; pastry shop
le plat	main course
le poisson	fish
la pomme	apple
la pomme de terre	potato
le potage	soup
le poulet	chicken
la salade verte	green salad
le saucisson	large dried sausage
le saumon	salmon
le steak tartare	raw meat topped with a raw egg
la tarte tatin	caramelized upside-down apple pie
le thé	tea
la viande	meat
la vichyssoise	cold cream soup with leeks and potatoes
le vin	wine

Index

INDEX

D

INDEX

INDEX

★Let's Go 1997 Reader Questionnaire ★

Please fill this out and return it to us at **Let's Go, St. Martin's Press,** 175 5th Ave. NY, NY 10010

Name: ____________________ **What book did you use?** ______________

Address: ____

City: ______________________ **State:** ______ **Zip Code:** __________

How old are you? under 19 19-24 25-34 35-44 45-54 55 or over

Are you (circle one) in high school in college in grad school employed retired between jobs

Have you used Let's Go before? yes no

Would you use Let's Go again? yes no

How did you first hear about Let's Go? friend store clerk CNN bookstore display advertisement/promotion review other

Why did you choose Let's Go (circle up to two)? annual updating reputation budget focus price writing style other: ______________________

Which other guides have you used, if any? Frommer's $-a-day Fodor's Rough Guides Lonely Planet Berkeley Rick Steves other: ______________________

Is Let's Go the best guidebook? yes no

If not, which do you prefer? ______________________

Which part of Let's Go do you feel needs most to be improved, if any (circle up to two)? packaging/cover practical information accommodations food cultural introduction sights practical introduction ("Essentials") directions entertainment gay/lesbian information maps other: ______________________

How would you like to see these things improved?

____

____

How long was your trip? one week two weeks three weeks one month two months or more

Have you traveled extensively before? yes no

Do you buy a separate map when you visit a foreign city? yes no

Have you seen the Let's Go Map Guides? yes no

Have you used a Let's Go Map Guide? yes no

If you have, would you recommend them to others? yes no

Did you use the internet to plan your trip? yes no

Would you buy a Let's Go phrasebook adventure/trekking guide gay/lesbian guide

Which of the following destinations do you hope to visit in the next three to five years (circle one)? Australia China South America Russia other: ______________________

Where did you buy your guidebook? internet chain bookstore independent bookstore college bookstore travel store other: ______________________

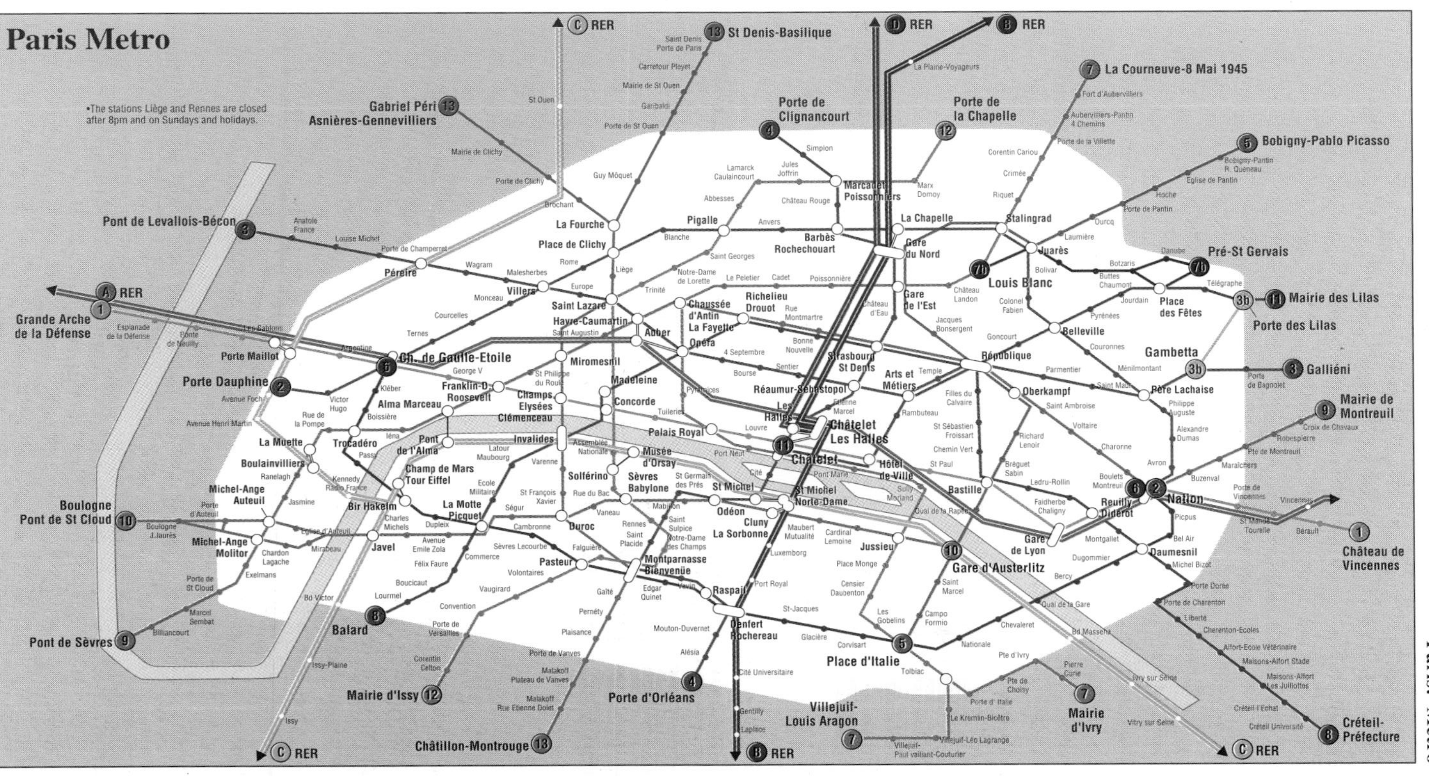
Paris Metro
•The stations Liège and Rennes are closed after 8pm and on Sundays and holidays.
C RER
St Denis-Basilique
D RER
B RER
La Courneuve-8 Mai 1945
Gabriel Péri
Asnières-Gennevilliers
Porte de Clignancourt
Porte de la Chapelle
Bobigny-Pablo Picasso
Pont de Levallois-Bécon
Pré-St Gervais
A RER
Grande Arche de la Défense
Mairie des Lilas
Porte des Lilas
Gallieni
Mairie de Montreuil
Porte Dauphine
Boulogne Pont de St Cloud
Château de Vincennes
Pont de Sèvres
Balard
Mairie d'Issy
Porte d'Orléans
Châtillon-Montrouge
Villejuif-Louis Aragon
Mairie d'Ivry
Créteil-Préfecture
Place d'Italie
Gare d'Austerlitz
Gare de Lyon
Nation
Bastille
République
Châtelet
Les Halles
Gare du Nord
Gare de l'Est
Ch. de Gaulle-Etoile
Saint Lazare
Montparnasse Bienvenüe
Invalides
Opéra

Paris: Overview and Arrondissements

1 Cimetière de Montmartre
2 Sacré Coeur Basilica
3 Parc La Villette
4 Parc des Buttes Chaumont
5 Jardins du Trocadero
6 Palais Chaillot
7 Cimetière de Passy
8 American Embassy
9 British Embassy
10 Petit Palais
11 Grand Palais
12 Arc de Triomphe
13 Madeleine
14 Gare St-Lazare
15 Parc Monceau
16 Palais de la Découverte
17 Opéra Garnier
18 Galeries Lafayette
19 Printemps
20 Gare du Nord
21 Gare de l'Est
22 Opéra Bastille
23 Palais Omnisports de Bercy
24 Ministère des Finances
25 Gare de Lyon
26 Parc de Montsouris
27 Cité Universitaire
28 Cimetière Montparnasse
29 Gare Montparnasse

30 Bureau des Objets Trouvés (Lost and Found)
31 Louvre
32 Palais Royale
33 Forum des Halles
34 Musée de l'Orangerie
35 Central Post Office
36 Bourse
37 Bibliothèque Nationale
38 Ecole des Arts et Métiers
39 Archives Nationales
40 Musée Carnavalet
41 Musée Picasso
42 Centre George Pompidou
43 place des Vosges
44 Musée Victor Hugo
45 Notre Dame
46 Mémorial de la Déportation
47 Université de Paris (Sorbonne)

48 Ecole Normal Supérieure
49 Musée de Cluny
50 Museum Nationale d'Histoire Naturelle
51 Panthéon
52 Eglise St-Etienne du Mont
53 La Mosquée
54 Jardin des Plantes
55 Jardins du Luxembourg
56 Eglise St-Sulpice
57 Théâtre Nationale de l'Odéon
58 Eiffel Tower
59 Champs de Mars

60 Ecole Militaire
61 UNESCO
62 Hôtel des Invalides
63 Assemblée Nationale
64 Musée d'Orsay
65 Cimetière de l'Est du Pere Lachaise

LG/Par95-Arrond4c.30 9-13-94

18e
19e
10e
2e
3e
11e
20e
4e
5e
12e
13e
N
bd. Ney
bd. Macdonald
Canal de l'Ourcq
av. Corentin Cariou
bd. Sérurier
av. Jean Lolive
rue de la Chapelle
bd. Ornano
Championnet
rue Duhesme
rue des Poissonniers
r. l'Evangile
rue d'Aubervilliers
rue Archereau
rue de l'Ourcq
rue Riquet
rue Marx Dormoy
rue de Flandre
rue de Crimée
Bassin de la Villette
av. Jean Jaurès
bd. Indochine
bd. d'Algérie
rue Custine
rue de Clignancourt
bd. Barbès
bd. de Rochechouart
bd. de la Chapelle
PL. DE STALINGRAD
r. Armand Carel
r. David d'Angiers
rue Manin
av. Trudaine
RER
av. Secrétan
PL. DU COLONEL FABIEN
Canal St-Martin
rue La Fayette
Châteaudun
rue du Fg. Poissonnière
r. Paradis
r. d'Hauteville
bd. de Strasbourg
bd. de Magenta
r. Château d'Eau
bd. de la Villette
du Temple
rue des Pyrénées
bd. Mortier
PL. GAMBETTA
bd. Montmartre
Poissonnière
St-Denis
blvd. St-Martin
rue du Faubourg
av. Parmentier
rue St-Maur
bd. de Belleville
av. Gambetta
rue Montmartre
rue Réaumur
PL. DE LA RÉPUBLIQUE
rue de Turbigo
rue Oberkampf
la République
r. Etienne Marcel
rue du Louvre
rue St-Honoré
Halles
rue de Rivoli
bd. de Sébastopol
rue St-Martin
rue Beaubourg
rue du Temple
rue des Archives
rue Vieille du Temple
bd. Beaumarchais
bd. R. Lenoir
rue du Chemin Vert
bd. Voltaire
rue de la Roquette
bd. de Ménilmontant
Pont Neuf
rue de Charonne
av. Philippe Auguste
bd. de Charonne
bd. Davout
quai St-Michel
Ile de la Cité
rue St-Antoine
Ile St-Louis
bd. Henri IV
rue du Faubourg St-Antoine
rue de Montreuil
NATION
quai de la Tournelle
PL. MAUBERT
r. des Écoles
quai St-Bernard
rue de Lyon
rue Ledru Rollin
PL. DE LA NATION
Cours de Vincennes
LUXEMBOURG
PL. DE LA CONTRE-SCARPE
rue Monge
Pont de Sully
bd. Diderot
bd. Picpus
av. du Dr. Arnold Netter
rue d'Ulm
rue Mouffetard
r. G. St-Hilaire
rue Buffon
rue Censier
Seine
av. Daumesnil
rue de Picpus
rue Guy Lussac
r. C. Bernard
GARE D'AUSTERLITZ
Pont de Bercy
bd. de Bercy
PL. FÉLIX ÉBOUÉ
Mi. Bizot
bd. Soult
bd. de Port Royal
bd. St-Marcel
av. des Gobelins
bd. de l'Hôpital
rue de Bercy
quai de Bercy
rue de Charenton
av. du Gén.
Parc Zoologique
bd. Arago
PL. D'ALESIA
rue de la Gare
rue Jeanne d'Arc
rue du Chevaleret
Pont de Tolbiac
bd. Poniatowski
St-Jacques
bd. A. Blanqui
av. de Choisy
rue de Tolbiac
Pont National
Bois de Vincennes
Alésia
rue de Tolbiac
rue National
BD. MASSÉNA
rue de Paris
av. d'Ivry
rue Regnault
bd. de Masséna
av. d'Italie
bd. Kellerman
CITÉ UNIVERSITAIRE
0
1 mile
0
1 km

Paris: 1er and 2e

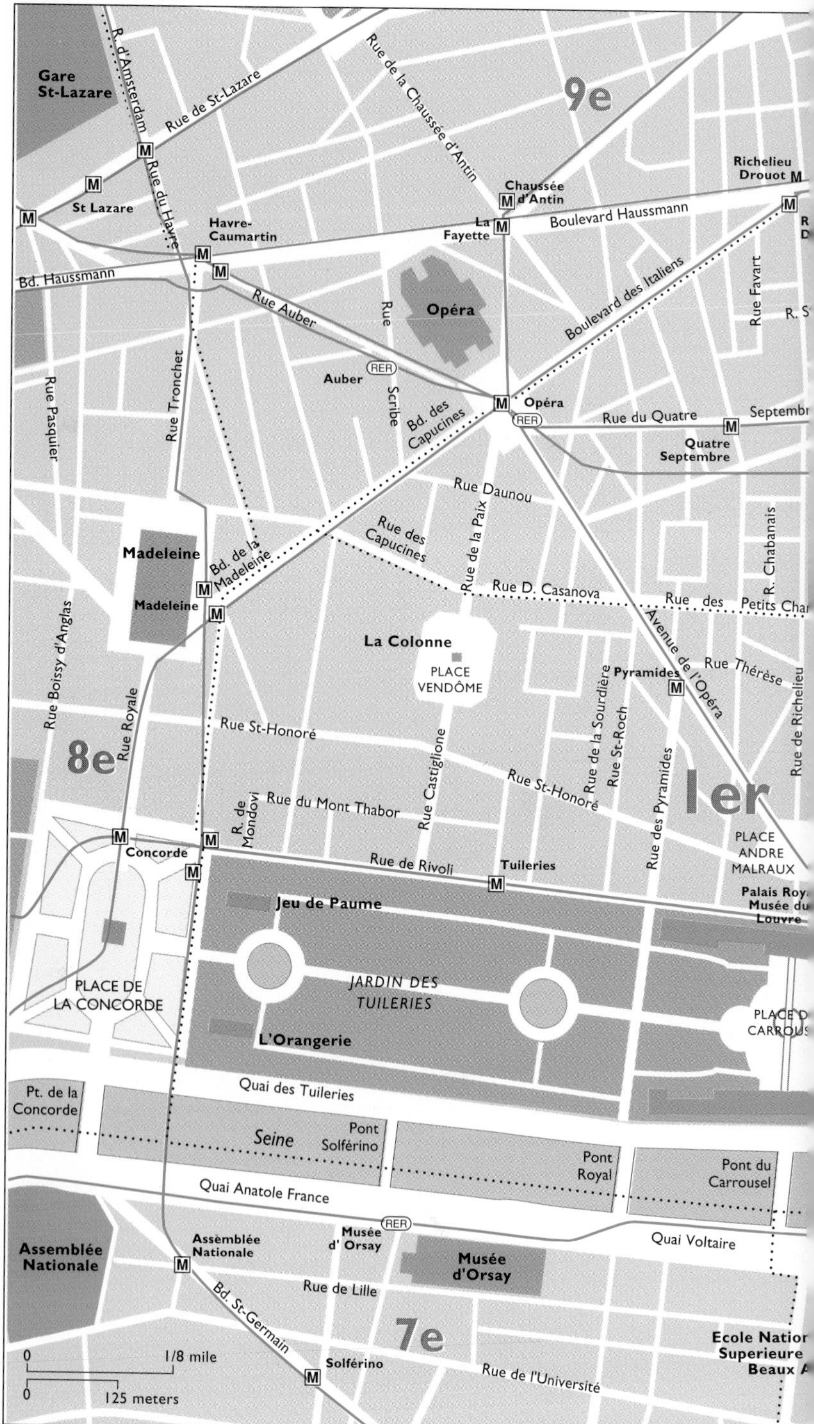

Gare St-Lazare
R. d'Amsterdam
Rue de St-Lazare
Rue de la Chaussée d'Antin
9e
Richelieu Drouot
St Lazare
Rue du Havre
Chaussée d'Antin
Havre-Caumartin
La Fayette
Boulevard Haussmann
Bd. Haussmann
Rue Auber
Rue Scribe
Opéra
Boulevard des Italiens
Rue Favart
R. S
Auber
RER
Rue Pasquier
Rue Tronchet
Bd. des Capucines
Opéra
Rue du Quatre Septembre
Quatre Septembre
Rue Daunou
Rue des Capucines
Rue de la Paix
R. Chabanais
Madeleine
Bd. de la Madeleine
Madeleine
Rue D. Casanova
Rue des Petits Champs
La Colonne
PLACE VENDÔME
Avenue de l'Opéra
Pyramides
Rue Thérèse
Rue Boissy d'Anglas
Rue Royale
Rue St-Honoré
Rue de la Sourdière
Rue St-Roch
Rue Castiglione
Rue de Richelieu
8e
Rue St-Honoré
Rue des Pyramides
1er
R. de Mondovi
Rue du Mont Thabor
Concorde
Rue de Rivoli
Tuileries
PLACE ANDRE MALRAUX
Palais Royal Musée du Louvre
Jeu de Paume
PLACE DE LA CONCORDE
JARDIN DES TUILERIES
PLACE DU CARROUSEL
L'Orangerie
Quai des Tuileries
Pt. de la Concorde
Seine
Pont Solférino
Pont Royal
Pont du Carrousel
Quai Anatole France
Quai Voltaire
Assemblée Nationale
Assemblée Nationale
Musée d' Orsay
Musée d'Orsay
Rue de Lille
Bd. St-Germain
7e
Ecole Nationale Superieure Beaux Arts
0 1/8 mile
0 125 meters
Solférino
Rue de l'Université

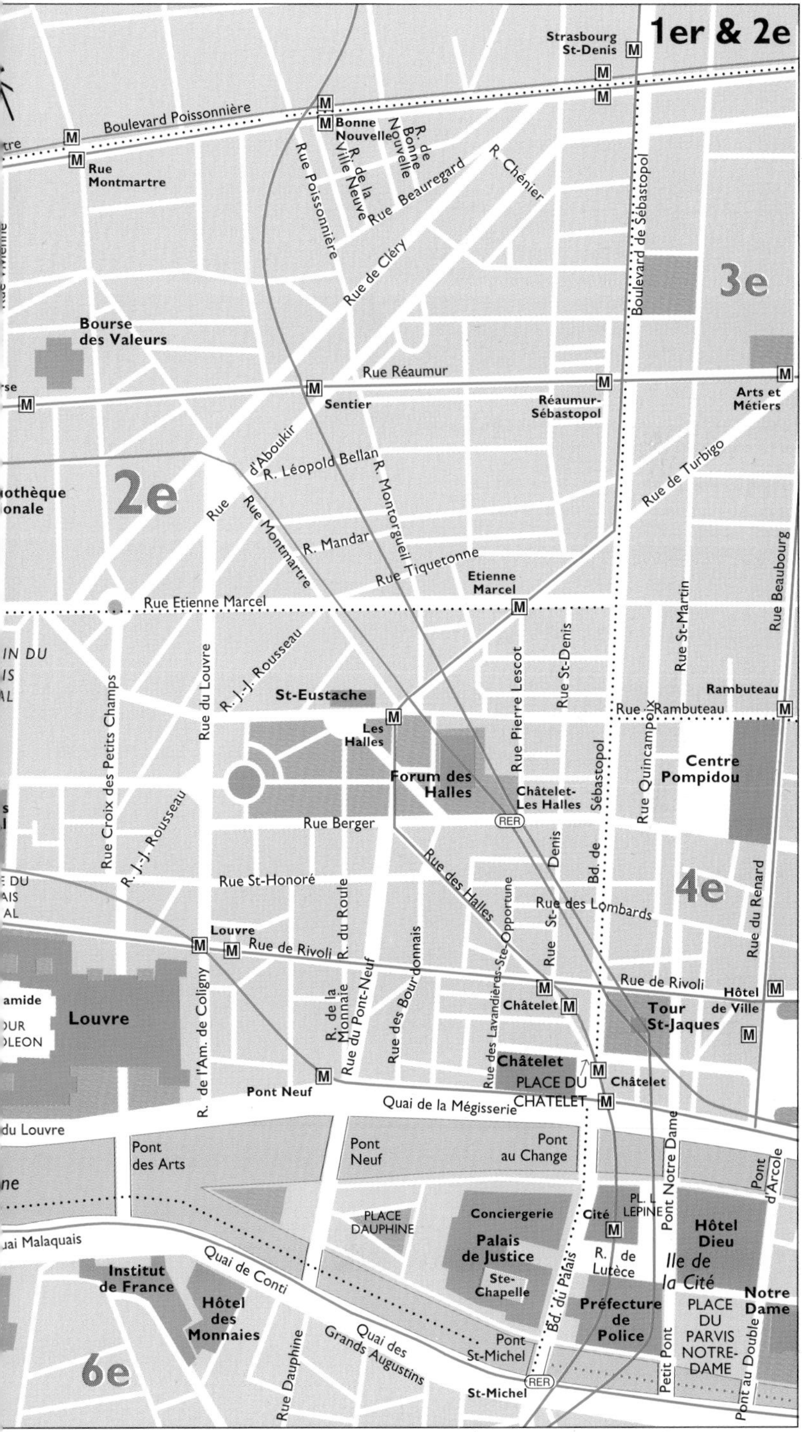

1er & 2e

Strasbourg St-Denis
Boulevard Poissonnière
Bonne Nouvelle
Rue Montmartre
R. de Bonne Nouvelle
R. de la Ville Neuve
Rue Poissonnière
Rue Beauregard
R. Chénier
Rue de Cléry
Boulevard de Sébastopol
3e
Bourse des Valeurs
Rue Réaumur
Sentier
Réaumur-Sébastopol
Arts et Métiers
2e
R. Léopold Bellan
Rue d'Aboukir
R. Montorgueil
Rue de Turbigo
Rue Montmartre
R. Mandar
Rue Tiquetonne
Etienne Marcel
Rue Etienne Marcel
R. J.-J. Rousseau
Rue du Louvre
St-Eustache
Rue Croix des Petits Champs
Rue Pierre Lescot
Rue St-Denis
Rue St-Martin
Rue Beaubourg
Rambuteau
Rue Rambuteau
Les Halles
Forum des Halles
Châtelet-Les Halles
Sébastopol
Rue Quincampoix
Centre Pompidou
RER
Rue Berger
R. J.-J. Rousseau
Rue des Halles
Bd. de
St-Denis
4e
Rue du Renard
Rue St-Honoré
Rue des Lombards
R. du Roule
Louvre
Rue de Rivoli
Rue Ste-Opportune
Rue des Lavandières
Rue de Rivoli
Hôtel de Ville
Louvre
R. de l'Am. de Coligny
R. de la Monnaie
Rue du Pont-Neuf
Rue des Bourdonnais
Châtelet
Tour St-Jaques
Châtelet
PLACE DU CHATELET
Châtelet
Pont Neuf
Quai de la Mégisserie
du Louvre
Pont des Arts
Pont Neuf
Pont au Change
Pont Notre Dame
Pont d'Arcole
PLACE DAUPHINE
Conciergerie
Cité
PL. L LEPINE
Hôtel Dieu
Quai Malaquais
Palais de Justice
R. de Lutèce
Ile de la Cité
Institut de France
Quai de Conti
Ste-Chapelle
Bd. du Palais
Préfecture de Police
PLACE DU PARVIS NOTRE-DAME
Notre Dame
Hôtel des Monnaies
Quai des Grands Augustins
Pont St-Michel
Petit Pont
Pont au Double
6e
Rue Dauphine
RER
St-Michel

Paris: 5e and 6e

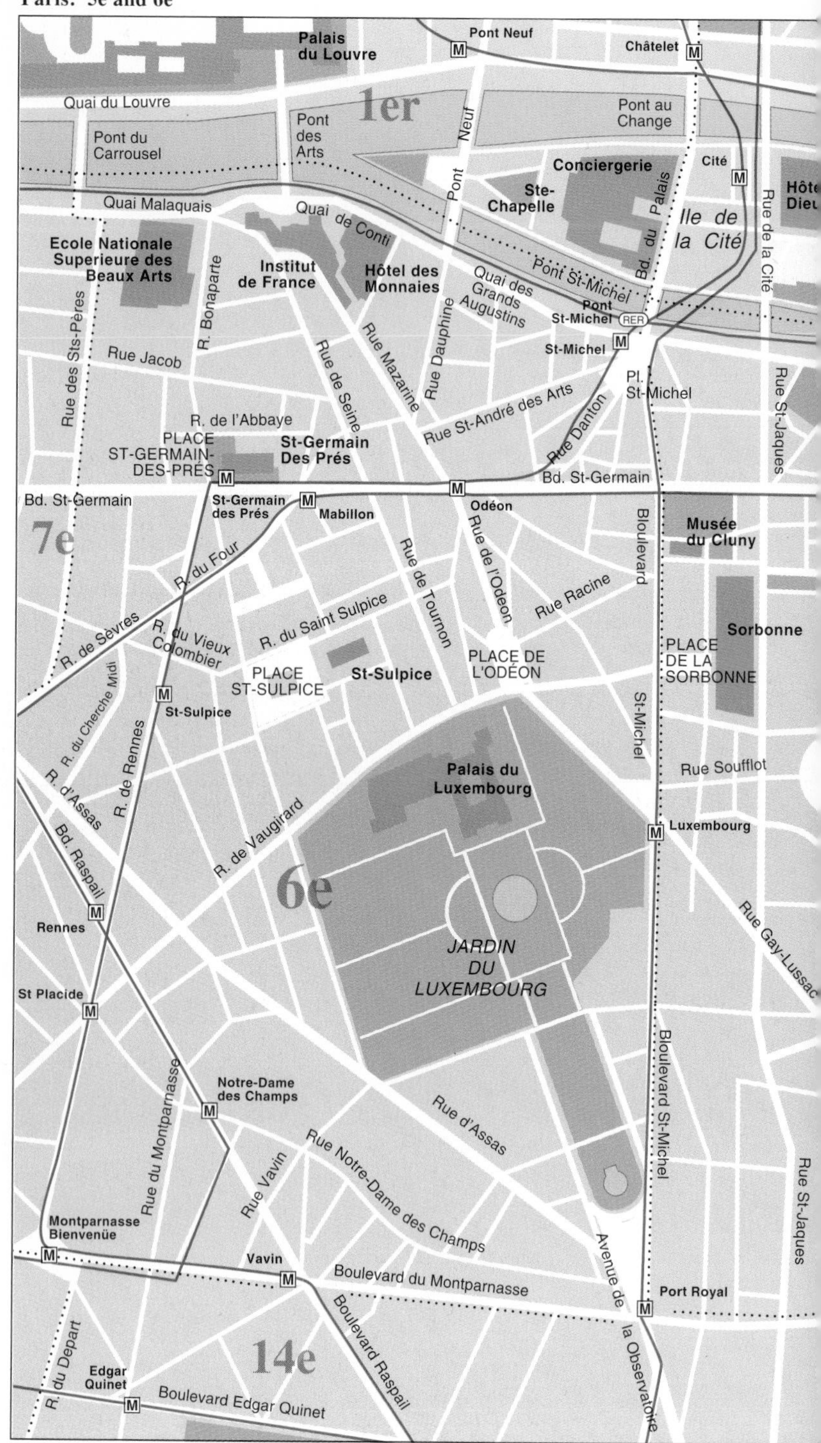

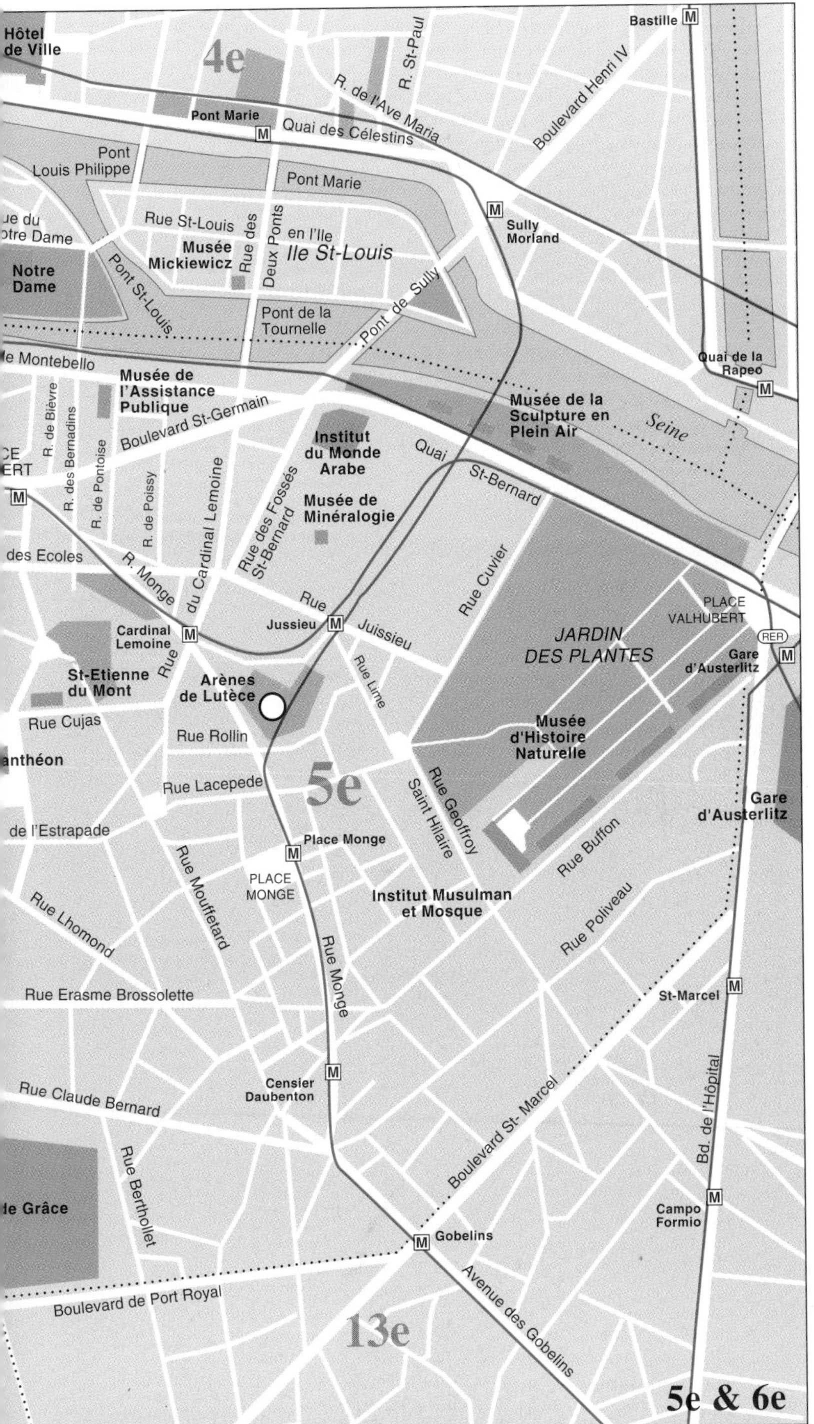

Hôtel de Ville
4e
R. St-Paul
Bastille
R. de l'Ave Maria
Boulevard Henri IV
Pont Marie
Quai des Célestins
Pont Louis Philippe
Pont Marie
Sully Morland
Rue St-Louis
Rue des Deux Ponts
en l'Ile
Ile St-Louis
Musée Mickiewicz
Notre Dame
Pont St-Louis
Pont de Sully
Pont de la Tournelle
Quai de la Rapeo
Musée de l'Assistance Publique
Musée de la Sculpture en Plein Air
Seine
R. de Bièvre
R. des Bernadins
R. de Pontoise
R. de Poissy
Boulevard St-Germain
Institut du Monde Arabe
Quai St-Bernard
Rue du Cardinal Lemoine
Rue des Fossés St-Bernard
Musée de Minéralogie
des Ecoles
R. Monge
Rue Cuvier
Rue Jussieu
Jussieu
PLACE VALHUBERT
Cardinal Lemoine
JARDIN DES PLANTES
RER
Gare d'Austerlitz
St-Etienne du Mont
Arènes de Lutèce
Rue Lime
Rue Cujas
Rue Rollin
Musée d'Histoire Naturelle
Panthéon
Rue Lacepede
5e
Rue Geoffroy Saint Hilaire
Gare d'Austerlitz
de l'Estrapade
Place Monge
Rue Buffon
PLACE MONGE
Rue Mouffetard
Institut Musulman et Mosque
Rue Lhomond
Rue Poliveau
Rue Monge
Rue Erasme Brossolette
St-Marcel
Censier Daubenton
Rue Claude Bernard
Boulevard St-Marcel
Bd. de l'Hôpital
Rue Berthollet
de Grâce
Campo Formio
Gobelins
Boulevard de Port Royal
Avenue des Gobelins
13e
5e & 6e

Paris: RER

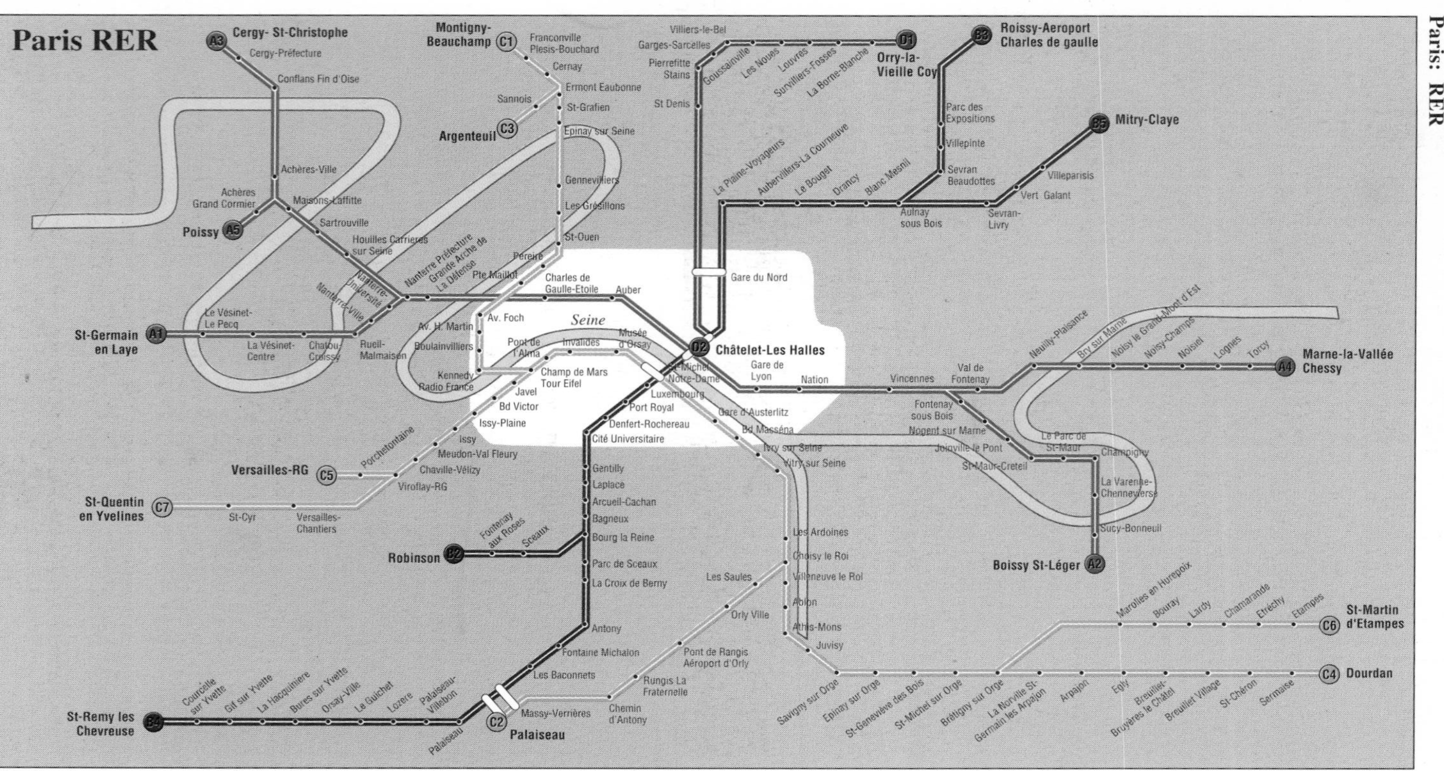

Paris RER
Cergy- St-Christophe
Cergy-Préfecture
Conflans Fin d'Oise
Achères-Ville
Achères Grand Cormier
Maisons-Laffitte
Sartrouville
Houilles Carrières sur Seine
Poissy
St-Germain en Laye
Le Vésinet-Le Pecq
La Vésinet-Centre
Chatou-Croissy
Rueil-Malmaison
Nanterre-Ville
Nanterre-Université
Nanterre Préfecture Grande Arche de La Défense
Montigny-Beauchamp
Franconville Plesis-Bouchard
Cernay
Ermont Eaubonne
Sannois
St-Grafien
Argenteuil
Epinay sur Seine
Gennevilliers
Les Grésillons
St-Ouen
Pereire
Pte Maillot
Av. Foch
Av. H. Martin
Boulainvilliers
Kennedy Radio France
Charles de Gaulle-Etoile
Auber
Seine
Pont de l'Alma
Invalides
Musée d'Orsay
Champ de Mars Tour Eiffel
Javel
Bd Victor
Issy-Plaine
Issy
Meudon-Val Fleury
Chaville-Vélizy
Viroflay-RG
Porchefontaine
Versailles-RG
St-Quentin en Yvelines
St-Cyr
Versailles-Chantiers
Villiers-le-Bel
Garges-Sarcelles
Pierrefitte Stains
St Denis
Goussainville
Les Noues
Louvres
Survilliers-Fosses
La Borne-Blanche
Orry-la-Vieille Coy
Roissy-Aeroport Charles de gaulle
Parc des Expositions
Villepinte
Sevran Beaudottes
Mitry-Claye
Villeparisis
Vert Galant
Sevran-Livry
Aulnay sous Bois
La Plaine-Voyageurs
Aubervilliers-La Courneuve
Le Bouget
Drancy
Blanc Mesnil
Gare du Nord
Châtelet-Les Halles
Gare de Lyon
Nation
St-Michel Notre-Dame
Luxembourg
Port Royal
Denfert-Rochereau
Cité Universitaire
Gare d'Austerlitz
Bd Masséna
Ivry sur Seine
Vitry sur Seine
Vincennes
Val de Fontenay
Neuilly-Plaisance
Bry sur Marne
Noisy le Grand-Mont d'Est
Noisy-Champs
Noisiel
Lognes
Torcy
Marne-la-Vallée Chessy
Fontenay sous Bois
Nogent sur Marne
Joinville le Pont
St-Maur-Creteil
Le Parc de St-Maur
Champigny
La Varenne-Chennevierse
Sucy-Bonneuil
Boissy St-Léger
Gentilly
Laplace
Arcueil-Cachan
Bagneux
Bourg la Reine
Fontenay aux Roses
Sceaux
Robinson
Parc de Sceaux
La Croix de Berny
Antony
Fontaine Michalon
Les Baconnets
Massy-Verrières
Palaiseau
Palaiseau-Villebon
Lozère
Le Guichet
Orsay-Ville
Bures sur Yvette
La Hacquinière
Gif sur Yvette
Courcelle sur Yvette
St-Remy les Chevreuse
Les Ardoines
Choisy le Roi
Villeneuve le Roi
Les Saules
Orly Ville
Ablon
Athis-Mons
Juvisy
Pont de Rangis Aéroport d'Orly
Rungis La Fraternelle
Chemin d'Antony
Savigny sur Orge
Epinay sur Orge
St-Geneviève des Bois
St-Michel sur Orge
Brétigny sur Orge
La Norville St-Germain les Arpajon
Arpajon
Egly
Breuillet-Bruyères le Châtel
Breuillet Village
St-Chéron
Sermaise
Dourdan
Marolles en Hurepoix
Bouray
Lardy
Chamarande
Etréchy
Etampes
St-Martin d'Etampes